Principles of Cri

Principles of Criminal Law

Third Edition

A P Simester

W J Brookbanks

NOTICE OF DISCLAIMER: This publication is intended to provide accurate and adequate information pertaining to the subject matters contained herein within the limitations of the size of this publication. Nevertheless it has been written, edited, and published and is made available to all persons and entities strictly on the basis that its authors, editors, and publishers fully exclude any liability by any or all of them in any way to any person or entity for damages in respect of or arising out of any reliance, in part or full, by such person or entity or by any other person or entity, upon any of the contents of this publication for any purpose.

PUBLISHED BY:
Brookers Ltd
Level 1, Guardian Trust House
15 Willeston St
Wellington

© (text) the authors 2007

© (edition and format) Brookers Ltd 2007

Second edition published by Brookers Ltd, 2002

First edition published by Brookers Ltd, 1998

ALL RIGHTS RESERVED: Excluding the sample policies, no part of this publication shall be adapted, modified, reproduced, copied, or transmitted in any form or by any means including written, electronic, mechanical, reprographic, photocopying, or recording means.

Furthermore, excluding the sample policies, this publication shall not be stored in whole, part, adapted, or modified form, in or for any retrieval system of any nature without the written permission of the copyright owner.

Applications for authorisation of a reserved right of the copyright owner shall be made in writing to the publisher.

WARNING: The doing of any unauthorised act in relation to a copyright work may result in both a civil claim for damages and criminal prosecution.

ISBN 978-0-86472-585-1

Publishing editor: Nicholas Gibb

Cover design by Base Two, Wellington, New Zealand
Typeset by Brookers XBook Processor
Printed by Printlink, Wellington, New Zealand

To Gerry

Preface

In preparing this third edition, we have responded to a number of significant developments. Not least of these was the enactment of a new regime of property offences, replacing Part 10 of the Crimes Act 1961, which necessitated the rewriting of chapters 19 and 20. Substantial legislative reforms have also been made to the sexual offences. Changes in the common law concerning duress and necessity, which are now recognised by courts overseas to be separate defences, have led to a restructuring of chapter 13. Additionally, we have taken the opportunity to introduce a new chapter on the principles of criminalisation; which, although not often taught in law schools, seem to us to be an important part of the criminal law.

Notwithstanding these changes, the aim of the book remains the same. We have set out, once again, to explain the doctrines and rules of criminal law with regard both to the general part and to the specific offences taught in university syllabuses. In this, as ever, we are indebted to the team at Brookers for considerable and patient assistance.

Perhaps the most important events, however, have been outside Parliament and the courtrooms. Since publication of the second edition, the criminal law has seen the loss of two of its leading academics, each of whom had a considerable influence on New Zealand's law. That exercised by Professor Sir John Smith was indirect: as England's foremost academic, Sir John played a key role in shaping the modern law of crimes, ushering the common law toward a more rational and intelligible structure.

The influence exercised by Professor Gerald Orchard was more immediate. New Zealand's leading criminal lawyer, Gerry guided generations of students, colleagues, practitioners, judges and, of course, co-authors. He did so with a brilliantly incisive mind and a wonderful sense of humour. We miss him, and our nation is the poorer for his passing.

APS

WJB

AUTHORS

A P Simester
>BCom LLB (Auck) DPhil (Oxon)
>Professor of Legal Philosophy, University of Nottingham
>Professor-elect of Law, National University of Singapore

W J Brookbanks
>LLM BD (Melb)
>Barrister and Solicitor of the High Court of New Zealand
>Professor of Law, University of Auckland

SELECT BIBLIOGRAPHY

Books listed in this bibliography are refered to in the text as set out below in the first column. Bibliographical details are given in the second column.

Adams	Robertson (ed), *Adams on Criminal Law*, Wellington, Brookers, 1992.
Adams (2nd ed)	Adams, *Criminal Law and Practice in New Zealand* (2nd ed), Wellington, Sweet & Maxwell (NZ) Ltd, 1971.
Ashworth, *Principles*	Ashworth, *Principles of Criminal Law* (2nd ed), Oxford, Clarendon Press, 1995.
Garrow and Turkington	Turkington, *Garrow and Turkington's Criminal Law in New Zealand*, Wellington, Butterworths, 1992.
Hart and Honoré	Hart and Honoré, *Causation in the Law* (2nd ed), Oxford, Clarendon Press, 1985.
Smith and Hogan	Smith and Hogan, *Criminal Law* (8th ed), London, Butterworths, 1996.
Williams, *CLGP*	Williams, *Criminal Law: The General Part* (2nd ed), London, Butterworths, 1961.
Williams, *TBCL*	Williams, *Textbook of Criminal Law* (2nd ed), London, Stevens, 1983.

Contents

Chapter 1	Definition and Application	1
Chapter 2	Interpretation, Proof, and the Rule of Law	23
Chapter 3	The Actus Reus	41
Chapter 4	Mens Rea	91
Chapter 5	Strict and Absolute Liability	133
Chapter 6	Secondary Participation	159
Chapter 7	Vicarious and Corporate Liability	197
Chapter 8	The Inchoate Offences	217
Chapter 9	Infancy	277
Chapter 10	Insanity	287
Chapter 11	Intoxication	331
Chapter 12	Compulsion	357
Chapter 13	Duress of Circumstances, Necessity, and Impossibility	391
Chapter 14	Mistake	429
Chapter 15	Self-Defence and Defence of Property	457
Chapter 16	Culpable Homicide	497
Chapter 17	Non-fatal Offences of Violence	561
Chapter 18	Sexual Offences	605
Chapter 19	Theft and Receiving	661
Chapter 20	Deception	699
Chapter 21	The Moral Limits of Criminalisation	719
Table of Statutes and Regulations		739
Table of Cases		747
Subject Index		775

Chapter 1

DEFINITION AND APPLICATION

1.1	Introduction	1
1.2	A search for definition	1
1.2.1	The harmful nature of the prohibited event	2
1.2.2	Punishment	3
1.2.3	Convictions	4
1.3	Ambit	5
1.3.1	Criminalisation ex ante	6
1.3.2	Ex post: censure	7
(1)	*The need for mens rea*	8
(2)	*Theories of culpability*	9
(3)	*Regulatory offences*	10
(4)	*Allowing defences*	11
(5)	*Accountability*	12
1.3.3	Ex post: sanction	15
(1)	*Restorative justice: the Sentencing Act 2002*	17
1.4	Structure of a criminal offence	19
1.4.1	Defences: a separate element	20

1.1 Introduction

The aim of this chapter is to introduce some of the theory that surrounds the criminal law: to explain why the criminal law matters and to highlight the issues it raises. First, the chapter considers the defining features of the criminal law, those which distinguish it from other varieties of law. Secondly, the ambit of criminal law is investigated — when is it apt to declare someone a criminal? The discussion in this chapter will lead on, in chapter 2, to discussion of the Rule of Law principles that constrain the enactment and interpretation of the criminal law; and later, in chapter 21, to consideration of what sorts of actions properly attract criminal prohibitions.

1.2 A search for definition

Like other types of law, the criminal law is a means by which the State participates in the ordering of its citizens' lives. Yet throughout the world, every society with a formal legal system distinguishes between criminal and civil law.[1] This raises a question about the scope of the criminal law: what marks a law out as criminal rather than civil?

---

1 Robinson, "The criminal-civil distinction and the utility of desert" (1996) 76 Boston ULR 201, 201, 202.

One way of approaching that question is to look for a definition of the criminal law. Broadly speaking, a crime is an event that is prohibited by law, one which can be followed by prosecution in a criminal proceeding and, thereafter, by punishment:[2]

> "A crime must be defined by reference to the *legal* consequences of the act. We must distinguish, primarily, not between crimes and civil wrongs but between criminal and civil proceedings. A crime then becomes an act that is capable of being followed by criminal proceedings, having one of the types of outcome (punishment etc) known to follow these proceedings."

Criminal law, in turn, is the variety of law that prohibits such crimes.

But to define criminal law only in these procedural terms fails to shed any light on a more fundamental problem: why does the distinction between criminal and other law matter? It is true that criminal prosecutions follow a different legal procedure from their civil counterparts. But if that is the sole difference, and there is no underlying reason for separating the two, drawing the distinction would be pointless.[3] We need to identify the distinguishing features that also justify treating crimes as a separate body of law.

1.2.1 The harmful nature of the prohibited event

One suggestion might be that the harm proscribed by criminal law is greater in degree than in the civil law, or is somehow public rather than private in nature. For example, across most if not all cultures, the criminal law contains provisions proscribing serious forms of violence and dishonesty. However, while it is true that prevention of harm is central to the criminal law, the distinctiveness of criminal wrongs cannot be captured by reference simply to the moral gravity of the wrongdoing and the importance of the interest being violated. For one thing, most harms are both public and private. The major oil spillage in Sydney harbour that gave rise to the *Wagon Mound* tort cases affected more than one person,[4] while by contrast an ordinary assault typically involves a single victim. Similarly, consider the situation where D Ltd has placed a large contract for the supply of raw materials with V Ltd. D is aware that without the contract V would be forced to close with the loss of hundreds of jobs. If, despite this, D breaks the contract in order to obtain supplies from a cheaper overseas source, it commits no offence. It seems, therefore, that the events prohibited by criminal laws are not inherently distinguishable from those regulated by other sorts of law. Indeed, the same act can sometimes lead to both criminal and civil liability. If D takes V's car without V's consent, for example, he may be prosecuted for theft. He can also be sued in tort for conversion.

That having been said, there is intuitive appeal in the idea that criminal wrongs are typically more serious than their civil counterparts; sufficiently serious that, whether or not they also give rise to civil causes of action, the State feels constrained to step in and regulate them directly. This can be seen in the rule that a victim who forgives his attacker may discontinue his civil suit for damages, but cannot stop the prosecution of that attacker. Criminal offences are not

---

2   Williams, "The Definition of Crime" (1955) Current Legal Problems 107, 123.
3   Moreover there would be a problem explaining why the distinction is maintained in those countries that do not observe the procedural safeguards normally found in criminal law. See Robinson, "The criminal-civil distinction and the utility of desert" (1996) 76 Boston ULR 201, 203.
4   *Overseas Tankship (UK) Ltd v Morts Dock & Engineering Co Ltd (The Wagon Mound)* [1961] AC 388; [1961] 1 All ER 404 (PC); *Overseas Tankship (UK) Ltd v Miller Steamship Co Pty* [1967] 1 AC 617; [1966] 2 All ER 709 (PC). Cf public nuisance cases: *Halsey v Esso Petroleum Co Ltd* [1961] 2 All ER 145; [1961] 1 WLR 683.

merely a private matter. The public as a whole has an interest in their prevention and prosecution. Thus, according to Allen, behaviour is criminalised "because it consists in wrongdoing which directly and in a serious degree threatens the security or well-being of society, and because it is not safe to leave it redressable only by compensation of the party injured".[5] Allen's remark is a useful pointer to why assaults are crimes while breaches of contract are not. Assault involves an interference with fundamental rights of the victim, rights which the State is perceived to have a duty to protect. By contrast, individuals are normally able to protect themselves against breach of contract, and can satisfactorily undo any damage suffered with the aid of the civil law.

Another possible basis for differentiating civil from criminal law is that criminal acts are intrinsically morally wrong. (Such acts are sometimes called mala in se.) To some extent this is true of the more serious, stigmatic offences — assault, murder, and so forth.[6] But much of the modern criminal law involves prohibitions which are only wrong because they are illegal (mala prohibita). There is no intrinsic moral difference, for instance, between driving at 100 km/h on the highway and driving at 105 km/h; but the latter is an offence. And conversely, lying may be immoral, but it is not per se a criminal act.

So there are limits to the extent to which we can safely elaborate on our initial definition by reference to the things that criminal law prohibits. In part, this reflects the fact that criminal law presents political problems as well as legal and academic ones. In chapter 21, we shall discuss some of the reasons why the State criminalises certain harms rather than others. However, it should always be borne in mind that, in practice, criminal laws are characteristically deployed to control behaviour and events because there is a public — and political — interest in doing so.

1.2.2 Punishment

A second element of the preliminary definition given in 1.2 was punishment. Perhaps the main distinction between criminal and civil law is that the criminal law licenses punishment as opposed to compensation? The latter, it might be said, is the province of the civil law.[7]

Punishment is an important facet of the criminal process. Indeed, it is an indispensable feature of criminal offences. Parliament does not say: "Do not assault other people, *please.*" That would not be a law at all. Rather, the law declares: "Do not assault other people, *or else* …". Of course, civil laws also specify sanctions. However, as Posner points out, the nature of the civil sanction differs from that found in criminal law. A defendant who is convicted of a crime will normally be imprisoned or fined. By contrast, someone who loses a civil action faces perhaps an injunction, an order for specific performance, or a requirement to pay damages.

Posner argues that this difference reflects a crucial distinction between the functions of criminal and civil laws. In his opinion, the criminal law exists to impose punishments such as imprisonment in situations where tortious remedies are an insufficient deterrent.[8] But Posner's

---

5   *Legal Duties and Other Essays in Jurisprudence*, Oxford, Clarendon Press, 1931, 233-234. Cf Coffee: "Characteristically, tort law prices, while criminal law prohibits." On this view, the criminal law should be invoked when the "price" of an action, that the defendant would have to pay in tortious damages, is insufficiently prohibitive. Coffee, "Does 'unlawful' mean 'criminal'?: Reflections on the disappearing tort/crime distinction in American law" (1991) 71 Boston ULR 193, 194.
6   Cf Gross, *A Theory of Criminal Justice*, New York, Oxford University Press, 1979, 13.
7   Moore, *Law and Psychiatry: Rethinking the Relationship*, Cambridge, Cambridge University Press, 1984, 81.

explanation is doubtful. Both criminal and tortious remedies can operate as deterrents. Each is likely to be regarded as unwelcome by a defendant, and indeed civil damages awards often far exceed criminal fines in magnitude.

On the other hand, it is instructive to consider the reasons *apart from deterrence* which underlie the imposition of sanctions in these cases. In particular, whether or not they have deterrent effects, civil remedies are not normally regarded as punitive. Punishment involves more than simply imposing something unwelcome upon a defendant. A *punitive* sanction imposes hardship *because the recipient deserves it*. Damages in a contract dispute, for instance, are a sanction; but ordinarily they are imposed without censure. It is not necessary to show that a defendant is at fault when he breaches his contractual obligations.

Punishment, by contrast, is imposed with censure as an integral aspect. It responds to the fact that the defendant has done something wrong.[9] Indeed, the level of sentence is one way in which a court signals the wrongfulness of the defendant's actions.[10] Of course, there are also fault-based actions in the law of tort. Nonetheless, damages for tort losses are normally compensatory, not punitive, and are understood as such. That is why one may usually insure against contractual or tortious damages, but not against criminal fines.[11]

Punishment, then, is one function of the criminal law. But punishment is not what is unique about crime. Indeed, punishment is not even a specifically legal phenomenon, let alone specifically the province of criminal law. We do not require a criminal conviction before punishing children or for a footballing foul, and it is sometimes possible to obtain exemplary damages in civil cases. One may even be fined or imprisoned for a civil contempt of court. Conversely, neither is a conviction always accompanied by sanctions. Sometimes offenders are discharged without receiving any sentence for their wrongdoing. This suggests that while punishment is *an* important characteristic of the criminal law, it is not the defining marque.

1.2.3 Convictions

In addition to prohibition and punishment, a third aspect of the criminal process is the conviction itself — the type of judgment that the court makes. Convictions are the most distinctive aspect of criminal law. In particular, while it also licenses the imposition of sanctions, a criminal conviction (at least for stigmatic offences) is regarded as a penalty *in its own right*, both by legal officials, such as judges, and by the public.[12] This is because it has the effect of labelling the accused as a criminal.[13] A conviction makes a public, condemnatory statement about the defendant: that she is blameworthy for doing the prohibited action. It is,

---

8   Posner, "An economic theory of the criminal law" (1985) 85 Col LR 1193.
9   For discussion, see von Hirsch, *Censure and Sanctions*, New York, Oxford University Press, 1993.
10 Cf R v Martineau [1990] 2 SCR 633; (1990) 79 CR (3d) 129 (SCC), 645; 138 (Lamer CJ): it is a "fundamental principle of a morally based system of law that those causing harm intentionally be punished more severely than those causing harm unintentionally".
11 *Askey v Golden Wine Co Ltd* [1948] 2 All ER 35; (1948) 64 TLR 379; cf *Clunis v Camden and Islington Health Authority* [1998] QB 978; [1998] 3 All ER 180 (CA).
12 Otherwise, there would be no reason to distinguish a "discharge without conviction" from a "conviction and discharge", as is done in ss 106 and 108 Sentencing Act 2002.
13 "Non-conviction of the blameless should be an informing principle of the substantive criminal law. A conviction for a stigmatic offence is a sanction in its own right and parsimony in the distribution of sanctions should be fostered." Sullivan, "Making excuses" in Simester and Smith (eds), *Harm and Culpability*, Oxford, Clarendon Press, 1996, 131, 152.

literally, a pronouncement that she is "guilty". By contrast, civil judgments seem merely to pin the salient breach on a defendant, without necessarily saying anything about her moral culpability. Thus, as we have noted, a plaintiff can sue for breach of contract without having to show fault by the defendant. The adverse civil verdict is made for the plaintiff's benefit and entails no formal public censure; the adverse criminal verdict is a pronouncement made on behalf of society, and is a form of community condemnation.

This facet is not mentioned in the definition of criminal law that we proposed earlier. Rather, it is something that accompanies the procedural differences. Thus the essential distinction between criminal and civil law lies not so much in the operation as in the social significance of the criminal law — in the way criminal laws and convictions are understood. The criminal law has a communicative function which the civil law does not, and its judgments against the accused have a symbolic significance that civil judgments lack. They are a form of condemnation: a declaration that the accused did wrong. Public recognition of this fact can be seen in the relevance of the criminal law to applications for a visa, or for admission to practise as a lawyer, in which applicants are required to disclose any previous convictions. Or consider the difference between publicly denouncing someone as a "convicted criminal" and calling her a "tortfeasor".[14] The law exists in society, not in the abstract. Correspondingly, the law's labelling of a defendant as "criminal" imports all the resonance and social meaning of that term.

1.3 Ambit

Three salient functions of criminal law emerge from the discussion so far. The first might be called *criminalisation*: the law sets out for citizens those things which must not be done.[15] The second thing the law does is *convict* persons who are proved to have transgressed its prohibitions. Finally, it may *punish* those whom it convicts; and, more generally, the criminal law poses the threat of punishment to reinforce its function of criminalisation.

The criminal law, then, is a powerful and condemnatory response by the State. It is also a bluntly coercive system, directed at controlling the behaviour of citizens. To criminalise an action is to declare that it should not be done and, typically, to deploy sanctions as supplementary reasons not to do it. In a sense, criminal law is the means by which the State bullies citizens into complying with its programme for society.

When should the criminal law be invoked? No one, including the State, should coerce others without good reason. The manipulation of people's conduct calls for justification, especially when it is accompanied by censorious and punitive treatment of those who do not comply. Unless there are compelling reasons, the criminal law should not be deployed by Parliament.

Nonetheless, sometimes the use of the criminal law *is* justified. Imagine the following scenario:

> One fine September morning, Jim is discovered dead in his home. His skull has been crushed by a blow inflicted with a heavy object. The police are called. Upon further investigation, they establish that he was murdered by his daughter, Alice, who killed him in order to receive her inheritance under his will.

---

14   The former is certainly defamatory. Cf *Carver v Pierce* (1648) Sty 66; 82 ER 534, an action for slander based on the words, "Thou art a thief, for thou hast stollen my dung".
15   Or allowed to subsist: see 3.2.2.

Intuitively, most of us would regard this as a classic example of criminal wrongdoing. The reasons are twofold. First, what Alice has done is precisely the sort of activity that the State should prohibit. Murder is both harmful and wrong, and people ought to be protected against it. Secondly, Alice is clearly blameworthy, and deserving of censure for her actions. Thus she is precisely the sort of person who should receive the condemnation of a criminal conviction, as well as the punishment that a conviction exposes her to.

Alice's behaviour is a central case for the application of criminal law. It involves deliberate, culpable infliction of the sort of serious harm that the criminal law is meant to prevent. However, not every case is as clear as this. Suppose the following alternatives:

> Case 1: Jim is discovered dead in his home. This time, the police establish that he died instantly after being struck by a vase. The vase was accidentally dislodged from the bookshelf by Barbara.
>
> Case 2: During an argument, Clare insults Jim. Jim is deeply hurt by Clare's words.

It is much less obvious that the criminal law should intervene in these situations. In case 1, Barbara has caused Jim's death, but there is no suggestion that she is at fault. Given this, it is inappropriate — indeed, wrong — to apply to her the sanctions of public condemnation and punishment. In case 2, Clare has wronged Jim, and deserves censure. But not by the criminal law. Unlike murder, this is not the sort of behaviour that ordinarily should be prohibited by the Draconian technique of criminalisation.

In questioning when the application of criminal law is legitimate, guidance may be had from the functions identified earlier. There are two dimensions to the operation of criminal law: ex ante and ex post. Ex ante, the law marks out actions that are prohibited, and warns citizens not to do those actions lest they be punished. Ex post, it censures (convicts) and punishes (sentences) persons who transgress its prohibitions. In the following pages, we investigate these two roles separately, and discuss some of the issues affecting when they should be invoked.

1.3.1 Criminalisation ex ante

Why should some behaviour be criminalised, while other behaviour is permitted? The answer to that question is complex and somewhat fragmented. Prima facie, a Legislature has the power to proscribe almost any sort of conduct,[16] and in New Zealand there has been little attention directed toward the question of whether it is right or wrong to criminalise a particular event or action. Earlier, we pointed out that there is no obvious distinction between actions which are criminal and those which generate civil liability (1.2.1). When the Legislature marks some action as criminal, however, it condemns it and rules it out as an acceptable option for citizens. A responsible Legislature ought to take such drastic measures only if there are compelling reasons so to do.

---

16 Except perhaps in extreme cases: "Some common law rights presumably lie so deep that even Parliament could not override them." *Taylor v NZ Poultry Board* [1984] 1 NZLR 394, 398 (Cooke J). See also Mann, "Britain's Bill of Rights" (1978) 94 LQR 512; *Snyder v Massachusetts* 291 US 97 (1934), 105. Rishworth, "Affirming the fundamental values of the nation" in Huscroft and Rishworth (eds), *Rights and Freedoms: The New Zealand Bill of Rights Act 1990 and the Human Rights Act 1993*, Wellington, Brooker's Ltd, 1995, ch 3. The question of substantive limits on the powers of Parliament is not specific to criminal law, and will not be pursued here.

There are a number of reasons to oppose the overuse of criminal law, but the most important of them is concern for individual autonomy. The need for tolerance, which underpins any liberal society, is grounded in autonomy. Prohibiting whatever is "wrongful" is likely to intrude much too far upon the liberties of citizens. This is not only to say that, in a liberal society, freedom of choice is to be fostered. It is also to claim that if the law is to respect the right of citizens to control their own lives, it should not deprive them of that control without good reason.

The criminal law stands in the way of free choice. It coerces people by threatening them with criminal liability unless they submit to its commands. Consequently, it circumscribes the individual's capacity to live her own life, in a manner that she herself dictates. By restricting the ways in which a person may shape her life, the law has the potential to prevent her from pursuing the goals and aspirations which matter to her. Indirectly, the criminal law imposes the legislature's view of how society should behave upon its citizens.

Even though it is right, indeed necessary, to have criminal prohibitions, the fact that they restrict autonomy means we should be careful of overextending the reach of the criminal law, and of damaging the right of self-determination. When a person's choices are not voluntary, but instead decided by laws, the life she lives is not entirely her own.[17] Of course, if one considers each crime separately, a criminal prohibition is unlikely to interfere with someone's freedom in any substantial, pervasive, or long-term sense. Outlawing arson still leaves us with a wide range of alternative activities, most of which are law-abiding. But the point about autonomy is more general than that. The effect of criminalisation must be assessed cumulatively, not in isolation. There are already thousands of things the State forbids. Autonomy requires us to have good reason before extending the reach of the criminal law.

None of this is to say that people ought to be allowed to disregard the interests of others, or that there is anything wrong with most of the criminal prohibitions we presently have. But it is a ground for the criminal law to beware of interfering more than the necessary minimum — a prima facie reason against the use of criminal sanctions. Bearing this in mind, once we have discussed various specific offences we will return to this issue in chapter 21 and ask, what *should* the legislature prohibit through the criminal law? What sorts of considerations should a responsible legislator take into account when deciding whether to create a criminal offence?

1.3.2 Ex post: censure

Our search for definition fastened on the pronouncement of guilt through conviction as the distinguishing mark of criminal law. This pronouncement connotes fault on the part of the criminal. When the court finds an accused guilty of committing a crime, and purports to punish her through sentencing, there is a public implication that she is blameworthy. Of course, there are offences of a minor character (for example related to parking infringements) where this element of reproof may be relatively trivial — such offences are often characterised as not being "truly" criminal in nature. Paradigmatically, though, censure is inherent in criminal convictions.

---

17   Raz, *The Morality of Freedom*, Oxford, Clarendon Press, 1986, 382.

(1) The need for mens rea

An institution which condemns and punishes people must take care to do so accurately. Being just matters. In particular, if a person is not to blame when something goes wrong, the censure of the criminal law is not appropriate — and if it is inflicted on her, the public will tend to think that is because she *is* to blame. When the law labels a defendant as "criminal", it simply cannot avoid this implication. Consequently, it should not convict those for whom that implication is unjustified.

The grounds for wanting to avoid mislabelling defendants are twofold. First, it is unfair and unjust to stigmatise someone as a criminal when they do not deserve condemnation. Secondly, if the criminal law is seen regularly to make mistakes, it will lose its moral credibility. This, Robinson points out, will diminish its effectiveness as a tool of social control:[18]

> "The criminal law can also be more directly effective in increasing compliance with its commands. If it earns a reputation as a reliable statement of what the community perceives as condemnable and not condemnable, people are more likely to defer to its commands as morally authoritative ... A distribution of liability that the community perceives as doing justice enhances the criminal law's moral credibility; a distribution of liability that deviates from community perceptions of justice undermines it."

For these reasons, the criminal law ought not to convict people unless they are culpable for doing a prohibited action.[19] Therefore, in so far as possible, criminal offences should be structured so that there can be no conviction without fault. This is achieved by including within every criminal offence some element that reflects culpability.

Suppose the following example:

> Pam has killed Alex. Pam is a doctor, and Alex was one of her patients. Pam gave him a painkiller, to which he had an allergic reaction and died. Causing another's death is generally regarded as a very undesirable thing, and the police investigate. Pam's actions satisfy the definition of "homicide" within s 158 Crimes Act: the killing of a human being by another, directly or indirectly, by any means whatsoever. Pam, the police conclude, has committed homicide.

On these facts alone, is Pam therefore bad, or blameworthy? Should we convict her of murder? The answer is no. Alex may have been the one patient in a million who was unknowably allergic to the painkiller and died as a consequence. It is important not to kill people, but it does not follow from the fact that killing is undesirable, and normally prohibited, that someone should automatically be convicted or punished for causing another's death. In the criminal law, this principle is expressed by the maxim, actus non facit reum nisi mens sit rea: an act does not make a man guilty unless his mind is (also) guilty. There must be mens rea — a guilty mind. The action must be done intentionally or recklessly, or wilfully or knowingly, or negligently, or with some other mental state as a result of which we can say that the defendant is culpable.

---

18   Robinson, "The criminal-civil distinction and the utility of desert" (1996) 76 Boston ULR 201, 212, 213. Robinson's point is made about criminalisation, but applies in this context also.

19   For an interesting debate which touches on this proposition, see Reiman and van den Haag, "On the common saying that it is better that ten guilty persons escape than that one innocent suffer: Pro and con" in Paul, Miller Jr, and Paul (eds), *Crime, Culpability, and Remedy*, Oxford, Basil Blackwell, 1990, 226.

In Kenny's words, "no external conduct, however serious or even fatal its consequences may have been, is ever punished unless it is produced by some form of mens rea".[20]

(2) *Theories of culpability*

The argument for having a mens rea element in criminal offences assumes that proof of mens rea establishes culpability. However, to what extent this is true is debated by criminal theorists.[21] Academics commonly argue over two accounts of when we may legitimately blame someone for her actions, which can only be sketched here. The first, which is reflected in the law regarding serious crimes, is sometimes called a "subjective" analysis: that culpability depends on morally defective *choices*. We blame someone for choosing to do a wrong action — for instance, for choosing to set fire to the house. Conversely, fault is not made out unless someone *deliberately* does something bad.

The upshot of this approach is that the actus non facit reum nisi mens sit rea maxim transforms into a requirement that we should not convict without advertence. As will be seen in chapter 4 on mens rea, in New Zealand this would include such mental states as intention and recklessness. If Pam gave Alex the painkiller in order to kill him, we can blame her for causing his death because she intended to do so. Conversely, on the subjective account, it is perfectly reasonable for Pam to dose Alex if she is unaware that the medicine will kill him. Failing to take account of the risk of death is not something for which she can be blamed.

The alternative account is "objective". It grounds fault in *conduct* rather than choices, arguing that an action attracts blame if it inflicts harm when a reasonable person would not have acted that way. Under the objective analysis, awareness of wrongdoing is not essential. If homicide is undesirable, then Pam has a reason not to do it whether or not she foresees the risk. Homicide does not become acceptable just because it is done inadvertently. Since it involves harm, not only does Pam have a moral (and, in this case, legal) duty not to do it, but she also has a duty to *take care* so that she does not do it inadvertently either. On this account, Pam may legitimately be convicted of a crime if she is unreasonably careless.

The objective view works best when explaining why someone may be blamed for negligence, and in giving substance to the idea of the "reasonable person". The "reasonable person" is archetypally a person of decent character. Thus if the defendant has failed to behave like a

---

20 Kenny, *Outlines of Criminal Law* (2nd ed), Cambridge, The University Press, 1904, 39. This proposition is subject to qualification in respect of strict liability. See 1.3.2(3), and chapter 5. Note that the present claim is only that mens rea is *necessary* for culpability. Unfortunately, liability for an offence of mens rea is sometimes incurred notwithstanding the absence of moral fault: *Yip Chiu-Cheung v R* [1995] 1 AC 111; [1994] 2 All ER 924 (PC), following dicta in *R v Kingston* [1995] 2 AC 355; [1994] 3 All ER 353 (HL), 364-366; 359-361; and *Gordon v Schubert* [1956] NZLR 431. However, these cases are somewhat unusual: where mens rea is present but moral fault is absent, this is usually recognised by the availability of defences. See 1.3.2(4); Fletcher, *Rethinking Criminal Law*, Boston, Little Brown & Co, 1978, 511f, 799f.

21 See, for example, Hampton, "Mens rea" in Paul, Miller Jr, and Paul (eds), *Crime, Culpability, and Remedy*, Oxford, Basil Blackwell, 1990, 1 (also in (1990) 7 *Social Philosophy and Policy* 1); Moore, "Choice, character, and excuse" in Paul, Miller Jr, and Paul (eds), *Crime, Culpability, and Remedy*, Oxford, Basil Blackwell, 1990, 29; Bayles, "Character, purpose and criminal responsibility" (1982) 1 Law & Phil 5; Arenella, "Character, choice, and moral agency" in Paul, Miller Jr, and Paul (eds), *Crime, Culpability, and Remedy*, Oxford, Basil Blackwell, 1990, 59; Duff, "Choice, character and criminal liability" (1993) 12 Law & Phil 345; Hart, "Negligence, mens rea, and criminal responsibility" in *Punishment and Responsibility: Essays in the Philosophy of Law*, Oxford, Clarendon Press, 1968, 136; Sullivan, "Making excuses" in Simester and Smith (eds), *Harm and Culpability*, Oxford, Clarendon Press, 1996, 131.

reasonable person, we may infer culpability, since her conduct has fallen short of reflecting that decent character.

These subjective and objective approaches are extreme alternatives, and middle ground is available. In New Zealand, inadvertent negligence *is* normally thought to be a standard of fault, but foresight of wrongdoing generally involves *greater* culpability. As we shall see in chapter 4, New Zealand has for the most part adopted a subjectivist stance, particularly over the interpretation of "recklessness", which is the minimum fault requirement for many stigmatic criminal offences. Suppose that David causes a fire in his house and is charged with reckless arson. In many jurisdictions, including New Zealand, recklessness requires some degree of actual foresight. So for David to be guilty he must have actually foreseen the risk of setting fire to the house when he did the act that caused it. Were he merely negligent (or even grossly so), he would have to be acquitted. In these jurisdictions, the subjectivist holds sway. On the other hand, the law in England regarding this offence was for a considerable period objective:[22] David could be convicted of reckless arson even though he did not notice the risk, at least if the risk was an obvious one.

If fault is a prerequisite of criminal liability then it is easy to see why recklessness or other foresight-based mental states are so often required before a defendant can be convicted for his actions. Much more difficult are statutes that define an action to be an offence when it is done negligently. Indeed, subjectivists often argue that people should never be convicted for negligence.[23] We disagree, and it seems to us that one may fairly be blamed for an unreasonable failure to take care; though no doubt the criminalisation of such cases ought to be sparing. But whether one adopts a subjective or objective stance, and whatever one's views regarding the culpability of negligence, one thing is clear. Without at least some form of fault, a defendant should not be convicted of a crime. This proposition is reflected in New Zealand's criminal law where, in the absence of advertence to the harm (or, in some cases, of negligence), a defendant must be acquitted of any serious criminal offence.

(3) *Regulatory offences*

What, then, of strict liability? There are many crimes for which the prosecution need not prove any element of fault before the defendant may be convicted. In these offences, the defendant's liability is said to be "strict", and the actus non fit reum maxim is said not to apply. For example, under the Resource Management Act 1991 a defendant may be convicted for discharging contaminants into water if the prosecution shows merely that contaminants were discharged.[24] There is no need to prove that the defendant's involvement was a culpable one.

We deal with strict liability offences more fully in chapter 5. For now, two observations may be made. The first is that, as we shall see, the courts have moved to make "strict" liability in effect a standard of fault — where culpability on the part of the defendant is presumed, but may be rebutted. If D can prove that the harm was not at all his fault, he will be acquitted. Thus the essential difference between offences of strict liability and those of negligence is the

---

22 *MPC v Caldwell* [1982] AC 341, also reported as *R v Caldwell* [1981] 1 All ER 961 (HL). The decision in *Caldwell* was eventually reversed by *R v G and another* [2003] UKHL 50; [2004] 1 AC 1034, which restored English law to a subjective test.
23 See 4.6.4.
24 Section 15. See *Hastings CC v Simons* [1984] 2 NZLR 502 (CA), concerning the predecessor s 34(1)(b) Water and Soil Conservation Act 1967.

burden of proof. Arguably, for some minor offences it may be appropriate for that burden to rest upon the defendant rather than the prosecution.

The fact that such offences may be minor raises a second point. Strict liability offences tend not to involve the same level of public censure as serious crimes. A parking offence, for example, comprises an altogether different order of wrongdoing from murder. This is not to deny that traffic offences and their like are part of the criminal law, although perhaps they should not be.[25] But most people in ordinary life distinguish minor, regulatory-type offences from "true" crimes, and the element of public condemnation is and should be conveyed only by a conviction of the latter type. The difference in social significance is illustrated by the question we mentioned earlier, commonly found in visa and employment applications, about an applicant's criminal record. It is not a request that is intended to elicit disclosure of minor infractions such as parking infringements.

(4)   *Allowing defences*

The medical homicide example (1.3.2(1)), in which Pam kills Alex, illustrates one way in which the defendant may be absolved of fault when a prohibited consequence occurs. Her answer is that, although she killed Alex, it was an accident. She neither intended his death, nor was she negligent in bringing it about: she lacked mens rea. Sometimes, however, a person may not be culpable even though she harms another person deliberately. For example:

> Anne is a police officer in the Armed Offenders Squad. She is standing outside a bank when a robbery occurs. John, who is one of the robbers, comes out of the bank and runs toward her, pointing a gun. In order to protect herself, Anne shoots and injures John.

Prima facie, this is a crime. Anne cannot claim that she shot John by accident. Nevertheless, Anne is not to blame. Her action, we would say, is *justified*, and she does not deserve to be convicted of any crime.

In order to deal with this sort of case, the law recognises a number of general defences, under which the defendant may acknowledge that he did an otherwise prohibited act and yet escape conviction. Examples of these justificatory defences are self-defence, prevention of crime, and defence of property. In effect such defences allege that, although D's conduct was harmful and normally unlawful, his conduct was nevertheless appropriate in the circumstances.[26] They claim that the defendant's conduct was the right (or an acceptable) thing to do, and so was not deserving of censure. As such, justifications are generalised: they involve judgments about the situation which apply to all the participants; so, for example, John is not entitled to resist Anne's justified use of force.

---

[25] According to Robinson, "Serious deterrent sanctions can and ought to be imposed [for regulatory violations] but they can as easily and effectively be imposed under an administrative system distinct from criminal law that carries a noncriminal label, such as 'violation'". "The criminal-civil distinction and the utility of desert" (1996) 76 Boston ULR 201, 214. Cf Mann's proposal for a separate system of justice to deal with such minor crimes, in "Punitive civil sanctions: The middle ground between criminal and civil law" (1992) 101 Yale LJ 1795.

[26] Indeed one may say of such cases that no prohibited harm occurred. Thus Smith remarks, "Where the defendant's conduct can fairly be described as coming within the terms of the proscribed activity, an offence has, prima facie, been committed: liability will ensue unless he advances some explanation of his conduct which shows that it was justified, in which case there is no actus reus". "On actus reus and mens rea" in Glazebrook (ed), *Reshaping the Criminal Law: Essays in Honour of Glanville Williams*, London, Stevens & Sons, 1978, 95, 97.

There are other predicaments where inflicting harm can be defensible on a more restricted basis. In these cases a person may choose to do something wrong, ie unjustified, but we may nevertheless think her insufficiently blameworthy to warrant the censure of the criminal law. For example:

> Susan is arrested after taking part in the bombing of a Government building. She had driven the car in which the bombers, a gang of terrorists, had made their escape. After her arrest, it is discovered that she did so only because the terrorists had burst into her house and threatened to kill her otherwise.

In this type of case, Susan's conduct may not be justified, and other people would be entitled to try to stop her. Nevertheless her culpability is lessened by the fact that she was coerced. Thus she has an *excuse*. The rationale for allowing excusatory defences is that advanced by Hart: "unless a man has the capacity and a fair opportunity or chance to alter his behaviour to the law its penalties ought not to be applied to him."[27] Susan's wrongdoing was deliberate, but understandable. By admitting compulsion as a defence,[28] the criminal law acknowledges that Susan did not have a genuine and fair opportunity to choose not to break the law. We may have no reason to praise her. But she does not warrant the penalties of the criminal law, because she is below the threshold of blameworthiness that is appropriate to criminal liability.

(5) *Accountability*

So far in 1.3, we have argued that the criminal law should convict only people who are culpable when a prohibited event occurs, and that events should be prohibited only when they are sufficiently harmful to override considerations such as the need to protect the autonomy of citizens. There is, however, a further requirement to be met before the criminal law will convict someone of a crime: accountability. Recall the example with which we began this discussion:

> One fine September morning, Jim is discovered dead in his home. His skull has been crushed by a blow inflicted with a heavy object. The police are called. Upon investigation, they establish that he was murdered by his daughter, Alice, who killed him in order to receive her inheritance under his will.

This, as we said earlier, is a plain case. But it is not just the fact that Alice is culpable which licenses her conviction. Culpability, by itself, is insufficient. Suppose that Jim's brother, David, had suspected Alice might try to murder Jim and had done nothing to warn him? David may be blameworthy, but ought we to prosecute him? Certainly not for homicide, at any rate. The difference between David and Alice is that only Alice is legally accountable, or *responsible*, for Jim's death. Only Alice has performed an action that caused Jim's death. Because he is not legally responsible, there is simply no point in prosecuting David, however much we may disapprove of his conduct.[29]

Although a great range of differing conduct can be subjected to criminal sanction, the process of finding guilt and pronouncing a conviction entails certain limits on the boundaries of criminalisation. The finding of guilt on which the conviction is based assumes a degree of accountability for something done or omitted to be done. Unless one subscribes to some

---

27 Hart, *Punishment and Responsibility: Essays in the Philosophy of Law*, Oxford, Clarendon Press, 1968, 158, 181.
28 Cf s 24; see also ch 12.
29 Or, as Lord Esher MR put it, "A man is entitled to be as negligent as he pleases towards the whole world if he owes no duty to them". *Le Lievre v Gould* [1893] 1 QB 491 (CA), 497.

extreme version of Calvinism or other doctrine of the damned, guilt is not a state of being, a natural property. Guilt can be generated only in respect of something additional to what the defendant *is*; something for which he is accountable. Otherwise, the "presumption of innocence" is meaningless. Consider, for example, a nation-state where the Government is following a policy of expelling all citizens who are not members of the dominant ethnic group. Acting through civil law process, such a State could pass legislation confiscating the property of minority citizens and impose various forms of disability in terms of profession, marriage etc, in ways all too familiar. But it would be incoherent for the State to make it a crime simply to be a member of a minority racial grouping; there would be nothing on which the conviction could be based.

The constraint may be ineffective in practice. Where the political environment is so extreme that a State is willing to create an offence simply of being a member of less favoured groups, it is quite likely the judges of that State would be unreceptive to the argument sketched here. But in countries with a judiciary prepared to judge in good faith, the need for accountability — for something additional to one's state of being — should properly limit the scope of criminalisation. This should have been required in the notorious English case of *R v Larsonneur*,[30] a case castigated by Jerome Hall as the "acme of strict injustice!"[31] On what can be ascertained from the available law reports, D, in circumstances wholly beyond her control, was brought from the country then known as Eire into police custody in the United Kingdom. Once there, she was charged with being an alien (she was French) who was in the United Kingdom without permission to land. With an excessively literal interpretation of the legislation in question, the Divisional Court upheld the trial conviction. Lord Hewart ruled that the circumstances of her entry and continuing confinement were "perfectly immaterial". It was enough, said the Court, that she was present in the United Kingdom without permission. In substance then, she was convicted solely for being French. But that, in our submission, is not enough.

Even at the level of principle, the argument from incoherence is narrow. It would be perfectly coherent, however unconscionable, for the nation-state described above to make it a crime for members of a minority group to give birth to children. Neither does the argument rule out what are known as *status*, or *situational*, offences, such as being an illegal immigrant. If it can be shown that there were acts or omissions for which D is responsible and by which D could have avoided the proscribed status, then the accountability requirement is satisfied. Translated into criminal law doctrine, this condition is embodied in a requirement of voluntariness, which is discussed in 3.4. Where one's status is involuntary, it cannot legitimately be a criminal offence simply to be what one *is*. The criminal law is concerned with the acts, omissions, and, on occasion, acquired status of human beings. It takes human beings as its starting point and then asks what they are accountable for.

In addition to the requirement of voluntariness, the need for accountability can raise other difficult issues. Suppose a further variation on the death of Jim:

> Case 3: Jim is discovered dead in his home. The police establish that he died after being struck by a vase which fell accidentally from the bookshelf. However, his daughter, Edith,

---

30   *R v Larsonneur* (1933) 24 Cr App R 74; 149 LT 542 (CCA). The case is discussed further at 3.2.2(1).
31   *General Principles of Criminal Law* (2nd ed), Indianapolis, Bobbs-Merrill, 1960, 329, n 14.

had observed the scene and deliberately failed to summon an ambulance in time to save him.

This is very similar to Alice's case, except for one aspect: our complaint here is not about what Edith did but about what she *failed* or *omitted* to do. Another way of expressing the difference might be to say that, unlike Alice, Edith did not *cause* Jim's death.[32] Either way, however, because of that distinction, criminal liability does not necessarily follow.

The issues of omission and causation will be discussed in more detail in chapter 3, but it is important to note that these, too, are crucial matters affecting the range and intrusiveness of the criminal law. Prohibiting an omission is not like prohibiting an action. When the law prevents Ian from (say) punching Bob, it leaves him with plenty of options and rules out only one. Ian is free to choose what to do or not do instead. By contrast, when the law proscribes an omission, it tells him exactly what to do. If Jim is dying, Edith *must* rescue him — she is not free to choose what to do or not do instead. One option is *required*, and all the other options are ruled out. Thus liability for omissions is much more likely to impinge upon individual autonomy and freedom of action.

In a liberal community, the right to autonomy is fundamental.[33] If the law is to acknowledge and respect individuals as independent members of society, then it must judge them according to their own actions, and not those of others. The process of shaping and controlling a person's life should be left to that person, and would be undermined were citizens constantly forced to assume responsibility for events they do not bring about.[34] For this reason, it is a guiding principle of the law that defendants are liable according to what *they* do, not what others do and they might prevent; correspondingly, they should be left free to live their own lives and pursue their own goals without having legal duties to act or intervene constantly thrust upon them, unanticipated, unpredictable, and unwanted, because of the actions of others. This is why there is no general duty to prevent crime.[35] It is also why principles of accountability are so important.[36]

Implicit in this reasoning, however, is that omissions are special not because they deny culpability, but because of the implications of their proscription for individual freedom. Thus they are not ruled out *tout court*. In practice, a criminal law duty to intervene is imposed, if at all, only when the defendant has a special connection to the harm — for example, when the defendant is the victim's parent.[37] But even that need not be true. Sometimes an altruistic reason for a stranger to get involved may justify the extension of responsibility. Suppose that Ian, a passer-by, sees a child drowning in a paddling pool. He can rescue the child at no risk

---

32 Cf Moore, *Act and Crime: The Theory of Action and its Implications for Criminal Law*, Oxford, Clarendon Press, 1993, 267-278. But the law may disagree: see 3.3.4(1).
33 See 1.3.1.
34 Thus *Hart and Honoré*, lxxx-lxxxi: "respect for ourselves and others as distinct persons would be much weakened, if not dissolved, if we could not think of ourselves as separate authors of the changes we make in the world." For further discussion, see 3.2.1.
35 Cf *R v Coney* (1882) 8 QBD 534, 557, 558; *R v Clarkson* [1971] 3 All ER 344; [1971] 1 WLR 1402 (Can CMAC), 347; 1405-1406.
36 There is a pragmatic side to accountability. If a swimmer drowns, the law cannot afford to prosecute every person on the beach. More generally, the State could not possibly contemplate prosecuting everyone who might have prevented it each time a prohibited harm occurs. So the general principle against liability for omissions has a realistic air about it as well as a philosophical justification.
37 See 3.2.1(2).

to himself. In this situation, for Ian not to intervene would be monstrous. Although New Zealand criminal law does not at the moment criminalise such cases, it might justifiably do so, depending on such factors as the seriousness of the impending harm and the degrees of risk and inconvenience involved in averting it. In many other jurisdictions, it is a crime not to rescue someone in peril when doing so involves no personal danger.[38]

Similarly, the criminal law need not always require D's behaviour to *cause* a specified consequence. For example, the law of secondary liability recognises the responsibility of those who do not themselves perpetrate a crime, but are nevertheless parties to its commission.[39] Suppose, for example, that David plans to kill Tony. Knowing this, Rebecca lends David her gun. Rebecca is a participant in Tony's murder, and his death may be attributed to her as a secondary party. The point here is that Rebecca does not cause Tony's death.[40] (David would have killed him anyway, using someone else's gun.) But she is not like a mere bystander, who can claim that David's action has nothing to do with her; that it is none of her business. Instead, she has involved herself in the murder, and *made* it her business. Thus, although it is David who kills Tony, Rebecca shares in the responsibility for his death.

Like liability for omissions, secondary liability involves an extension of the criminal law beyond the core cases of wrongdoing. As such, it involves a greater intrusion on people's freedom of action: not only may D not strike V, he may not do anything to help someone else strike V either, a much greater limitation upon what he is left free to do. This raises difficult questions of policy: if Rebecca is a shopkeeper, should she refuse to sell matches to David if she suspects or believes he has an illicit purpose? Secondary liability has the potential to force individuals to police the actions of others, and squarely raises issues of autonomy once more.[41] It is a hard question how far such extensions of responsibility should go, since, like vicarious liability,[42] they can have the effect of imposing liability largely on the basis of the defendant's status rather than his behaviour. Yet, once again, accountability is not ruled out tout court.

1.3.3 Ex post: sanction

Although punishment is not a constitutive element of the criminal conviction and lies outside the scope of this text, one cannot overlook its salience in the criminal process. If we were to dismantle punishment and its forbidding infrastructure, much of the raison d'être of the criminal law would go with it. Despite its importance, however, the question why we punish remains a matter of perennial and irresolvable dispute and has given rise to a vast and

---

38 See Ashworth, "The Scope of Criminal Liability for Omissions" (1989) 105 LQR 424.
39 See ch 6.
40 See, for example, *Hart and Honoré*, 51ff, 363ff; Smith, "Aid, abet, counsel, or procure" in Glazebrook (ed), *Reshaping the Criminal Law: Essays in Honour of Glanville Williams*, London, Stevens & Sons, 1978, 120, 131-134.
41 Particularly in cases of complicit liability for omissions, which may arise when the secondary party has some form of control over the wrongdoer. See, for example, *Du Cros v Lambourne* [1907] 1 KB 40, in which the passenger in a car was convicted of being a party to dangerous driving, on the basis that he owned the car and failed to exercise his right of control over the driver's actions.
42 The doctrine of vicarious liability provides a second route with which a causal requirement may be bypassed. However, vicarious liability is normally to be avoided in criminal law, since it arises out of a more general relationship between the defendant and the actual perpetrator of a wrong, and so is not specific to the wrongful action; consequently the defendant risks being convicted of a crime for which he is not morally responsible. As a rule, "*Qui peccat per alium peccat per se* is not a maxim of criminal law". *Tesco Supermarkets Ltd v Nattrass* [1972] AC 153; [1971] 2 All ER 127 (HL), 199; 155 (Lord Diplock). See further 6.1.

challenging literature.[43] In the following paragraphs, we can only sketch the major competing punishment theories, as any attempt to enter the debate would not do it justice.

The common starting point is to conceive of punishment as something which is problematic, something which must be justified. One should always be sure that the legal verdict which licenses punishment is well founded, a restraint with implications for criminal procedure and evidence. If we can be sure of the facts for the instant case, one group of theorists, commonly known as retributivists, would then ask whether punishment is *deserved*.[44] Desert is a function of the moral quality of the conduct; if it is bad (ie wrongful and culpable), a measure of hard treatment may be dispensed, the measure dependent on how bad that conduct is.[45] Once the grounds of desert are present, punishment ceases to be problematic. Indeed, it becomes something that ought to be imposed, something that will restore the moral balance which the malefactor has disturbed. A consistent retributivist will confine punishment to immoral conduct and will typically (though not necessarily) find immorality in the state of mind and disposition of the person to be punished rather than the consequences of her actions.[46] Consistent retributivism would entail a criminal law more scrupulous about finding fault sufficient to allow just punishment.

Retributivism is contrasted with utilitarianism, a species of consequentialism which asserts that punishment is justified only if the welfare of society is advanced. For a utilitarian, the pain of the person to be punished is a disutility, a diminution in the quantum of general welfare. Accordingly, pain should be inflicted only if it entails net gains in welfare across society: the institution of state punishment must produce overall beneficent effects. The particular beneficent effect that utilitarians most commonly claim for punishment is general deterrence, ie that without hard treatment of offenders there would be more offending and less welfare overall. As the term "consequentialism" implies, the moral character of a defendant's action is determined primarily by its results. A death remains a death whether it ensues from a brutal killing or a blameless accident. Many attempts have been made to demonstrate that blame and desert matter to utilitarianism,[47] but the relationship is, at best, a contingent one.[48] There is no reason, internal to utilitarianism, why a legal system should differentiate deliberate killings from accidental deaths. If it could be demonstrated that an unvarying penalty of life imprisonment for anyone who causes death in whatever circumstances would radically diminish the number of untimely deaths, then a utilitarian has reason to endorse that practice, and the only permissible objections to such indiscriminate hard treatment must be made in terms of its cost to net social utility. Indeed, consequentialism need not imply a system of criminal law. Other forms of deterrence may be more efficient tools for social control.

Consequentialism and retributivism are incompatible theories. Some theorists, most notably H L A Hart, have argued for a composite theory of criminal responsibility and punishment,

---

43 For excellent introductions to questions of punishment and sentence see Duff and Garland (eds), *A Reader on Punishment*, Oxford, Oxford University Press, 1994 and von Hirsch and Ashworth (eds), *Principled Sentencing: Readings on Theory and Policy* (2nd ed), Oxford, Hart Publishing, 1998.
44 A classic account is von Hirsch, *Doing Justice: The Choice of Punishments*, New York, Hill and Wang, 1976.
45 On evaluating the gravity of wrongdoing see von Hirsch, *Censure and Sanctions*, New York, Oxford University Press, 1993, ch 4.
46 A stimulating example is Ashworth, "Taking the Consequences" in Shute, Gardner and Horder (eds), *Action and Value in Criminal Law*, Oxford, Clarendon, 1993, 107.
47 Hart, *Punishment and Responsibility: Essays in the Philosophy of Law*, Oxford, Clarendon Press, 1968, chs 1, 7.
48 See Wootton, *Crime and the Criminal Law* (2nd ed), London, Stevens, 1981.

expressed in terms of a distinction between the "general justifying aim" of the criminal law on the one hand and the principles of criminal responsibility and just punishment on the other. For Hart, the general purpose of the criminal law was consequentialist: to deter anti-social conduct. However, this goal is properly inhibited by reference to issues of blame and proportion when adjudicating guilt and passing sentence. The inhibition is necessary to ensure fairness and to maximise autonomy. Although Hart argued for his composite theory with incomparable elegance, the predominating if not the exclusive element within it would appear to be retributivism. To be sure, utilitarianism is given the task of determining which conduct will be punished. Yet retributivism would generate many of the same primary norms and it is retributivism which resolves who will be punished and how much punishment will be meted.[49]

(1)   *Restorative justice: the Sentencing Act 2002*

On 30 June 2002, the Sentencing Act 2002 and the Parole Act 2002 came into force, together replacing the Criminal Justice Act 1985. They represent the first major reform of New Zealand's sentencing laws since 1985. Although both statutes represent a comprehensive reform of sentencing and parole laws, they do not constitute an exhaustive code on sentencing in New Zealand. The legislation operates in conjunction with other relevant statutes which affect, or are affected by, the sentencing process; including the Criminal Procedure (Mentally Impaired Persons) Act 2003 and the Intellectual Disability (Compulsory Care and Rehabilitation) Act 2003, aspects of which are considered further in chapter 10, together with the Victims' Rights Act 2002.

The Sentencing Act and the Parole Act effect major changes to sentencing practice in New Zealand, one of which is to introduce restorative justice as a new sentencing rationale.

(a)   Sentencing purposes, principles, and reasons

The Sentencing Act, for the first time, sets out the purposes and principles for which a court may sentence or otherwise deal with an offender. One of the objectives of the legislation was to increase transparency and consistency of sentencing decisions and to provide more guidance in matching the type and severity of sentences to the seriousness of the offending and the culpability of the offender.[50] In order to achieve this goal, s 7 defines the purposes of sentencing, while s 8 outlines the principles intended to guide the courts when sentencing or otherwise dealing with offenders. Section 9 defines aggravating and mitigating factors which courts must take into account in sentencing. Judges expressly address these statutory guidelines when deciding on an appropriate penalty.[51] The list of functional justifications (purposes) for punishment in s 7 includes accountability of offenders, provision for victims' interests, reparation, denunciation, protection, and rehabilitiation; and is exhaustive.[52] These purposes are familiar ones, traditionally taken into account by the courts in determining appropriate sentences — thus s 7 contributes to clarity and transparency, rather than reform.[53]

---

49   See the critique of Hart's "mixed theory" by Galligan, "The Return to Retribution in Penal Theory" in Tapper (ed), *Crime, Proof and Punishment*, London, Butterworths, 1981, 144.
50   See *The Sentencing Act 2002: Monitoring the First Year*, Wellington: Ministry of Justice, 2004, para 8.
51   Cf *R v Topia* 8/6/06, Potter J, HC Whangarei S05-029-1272, para 13; *R v Ho* 12/4/05, Winkelmann J, HC Auckland CRI-2005-092-567, paras 10 and 11.
52   Hall, *Sentencing Law and Practice*, Wellington, LexisNexis, 2004, 294.
53   *R v Iona* 27/3/03, CA416/02, para 23.

Concomitantly, the legislation now requires judges to give reasons for sentencing decisions. While the Act allows judicial discretion in determining the level of particularity with which reasons may be given, sentencing decisions have been successfully challenged for failure to give sufficient reasons,[54] something that usually results in the appellate court's considering the matter afresh.

Section 8, which defines the principles of sentencing, establishes a list of mandatory conditions that must be taken into account in every sentencing decision. As with s 7, these principles are not new to the courts, and do not reflect any particular order of priority. The weight attached to each principle is determined by the purpose of the sentencing decision and the individual facts of each case.[55] Although they mandate taking into account information of the effect of offending on victims, the views of victims have not "been elevated to some new height".[56] Courts are also mandated to impose the least restrictive outcome that is appropriate in the circumstances. This requirement is given force by the hierarchy of penalties listed in ss 11-17 of the Act, which range from discharge to imprisonment. A substantial body of case law now supports each of the principles listed and should be consulted in determining the scope of the obligation defined.

(b)   Restorative justice

Restorative justice now commands a central place in the sentencing scheme in New Zealand. Following the success of the restorative model in youth justice, restorative justice has now been incorporated into the wider criminal justice system. In addition to specific provisions in the Sentencing Act (below), restorative justice is also provided for in s 7 Parole Act 2002, in relation to the decision-making powers of the Parole Board. In effect, the express incorporation of restorative justice principles into the Sentencing Act has also given a more expansive role to reparation as a principle of punishment. While the concept is not defined in the Act, it is broadly understood to involve community-based processes, offering an inclusive way of reconciling offenders and crime victims through facilitated meetings. As such, it has three broad purposes:[57]

"(i)   to take into account the interests of victims of crime and provide for those interests to be met in criminal justice processes;

"(ii)   to hold offenders directly accountable to their immediate victims and to the wider community associated with both the victim and the offender and the community at large;

"(iii)   to take into account the interests of the community by addressing the issues and problems which gave rise to the offending and by taking measures to prevent re-offending."

While restorative justice (RJ) has gained considerable ground within contemporary criminal justice and penal practice, attempts to re-define the nature of crime and the purposes of its punishment should be approached with caution. Cornwell has identified three potential disadvantages to RJ's aim of seeking the reconciliation of offenders and their victims:[58]

---

54   See *Jensen v Police* 2/5/03, Nicholson J, HC Auckland A39/03; *R v Boyd* 24/6/03, CA89/03.
55   *Adams on Criminal Law — Sentencing*, Wellington, Brookers, 2007, SA8.01.
56   *R v Iona* 27/3/03, CA416/02, para 23.
57   Sentencing Bill, Explanatory Note; Hall, *Sentencing Law and Practice*, Wellington, LexisNexis, 2004, 58-59.

"(i)   RJ is based on a 'hybrid collation' of human rights theories, which accords both perpetrators and victims at least notional if not substantive 'rights' as a matter of principle within the criminal punishment process.

"(ii)   RJ is driven by a 'reductivist' agenda that seeks to make less use of custodial sanctions, not primarily because these may be unnecessary or socially undesirable, but more because of a desire to distance the model from considerations of retribution and desert. For this reason the model veers towards a 'neo-revisionist' model of criminal justice based on the idea or reintegration via reparation and reconciliation, but without a clear underpinning punishment philosophy.

"(iii)   RJ depends on an apparent presumption that the offender will opt for the potential sentencing advantages to be gained from compliance with a reparative model of punishment, but without much clarity about the outcomes justifiably following in circumstances of non-compliance or refusal to participate."

However, despite these potential concerns, RJ is now effectively adopted into the mainstream of New Zealand criminal justice, and has been considered by the courts in numerous decisions at all levels of the hierarchy. Significant provisions facilitating a RJ approach can be found throughout the Sentencing Act. The principal provision is s 10, under which the fact that the offender has made any offer, agreement, response, etc, to make amends is to be considered when imposing sentence. Section 25 empowers the Court to adjourn the proceedings to enable restorative justice processes to occur and any agreement reached to be fulfilled. Section 26 enables the Court to obtain a pre-sentence report including information regarding any move made in terms of s 10, or the outcome of any RJ process that has occurred. Finally, s 111 provides that where an offender has been ordered to come up for sentence if called upon, failure to perform in terms of the matters specified in s 10 may justify the recall and re-sentence of an offender. Conversely, the successful outcome of a RJ conference may contribute to a significant reduction in the sentence imposed.

1.4   Structure of a criminal offence

The discussion in this chapter has practical implications for criminal offences. We have characterised the criminal law as a system of prohibition and censure. Correspondingly, the main elements of crimes are twofold: harm and fault. The first of these is primarily an external element:[59] an event or conduct which causes the harm that the law is designed to prevent. For example, the external element in murder is the killing of one human being by another.[60] This external element is known as the *actus reus* of the offence. It sets out the physical thing that must happen before the criminal law can be invoked, and will be discussed in detail in chapter 3.

Generally, the actus reus is not enough by itself to constitute an offence. In 1.3.2(1) we discussed the example of Pam, a doctor, who killed Alex by injecting him with a painkiller to

---

58   Cornwell, *Criminal Punishment and Restorative Justice*, Winchester, Waterside Press, 2006, 35.
59   Although it may not be entirely external. Sometimes actions acquire a harmful or criminal character only when done with a particular mental state. For illustrative discussion of this point, see Horder, "Crimes of ulterior intent" in Simester and Smith (eds), *Harm and Culpability*, Oxford, Clarendon Press, 1996, 153; see also 4.4.
60   Section 160.

which he was allergic. Pam has done the actus reus of a murder. But if Alex's allergy was unknowable, then Pam is not to blame, and should not be convicted. Alex's death is simply a tragic accident. The need for fault in an offence gives us the second element, which is known as *mens rea*. This is what might be termed the "mental" element — the guilty mind, such as the intention, knowledge, or recklessness, of the defendant with respect to the actus reus. Mens rea is the subject of chapter 4.

Like the actus reus, the mens rea varies for each offence. In some crimes, intention or recklessness will be required before D can be convicted, while in others negligence or some other fault element may suffice. An example will help to illustrate. Suppose that Tom has been charged with an offence against s 205(1)(b) Crimes Act 1961. He recently married Jill, who he believed was a widower. Jill's first husband, Sam, had been lost at sea some years ago. However, it later turns out that Sam had not drowned, as everyone thought, and was still alive at the time of Tom's wedding. Hence Jill was already married, and her marriage to Tom was bigamous. Section 205(1)(b) provides as follows:

"(1)   Bigamy is ...

• • • •

"(b)   The act of a person who goes through a form of marriage in New Zealand with any other person whom he or she knows to be married or in a civil union ..."

In this crime, the actus reus is going through a form of marriage in New Zealand with a person who is married or in a civil union. The mens rea of the crime is knowledge, ie believing (correctly) that the other party to the ceremony is already married or in a civil union. On the facts given, Tom will not be guilty of bigamy as he lacks the mens rea required for an offence against s 205(1)(b).

Sometimes the mens rea can be present without the actus reus. Imagine this time that Tom believes Jill is married, but that (unknown to either of them) Jill's previous husband had suddenly died on the day before the wedding. In this case Jill is no longer married to Sam, and Tom does not commit bigamy because the actus reus is missing.[61]

1.4.1   Defences: a separate element

The examples above illustrate that both specified parts of the offence, the actus reus and the mens rea, must be proved before there is any question of D's being guilty of a crime. Even if both parts are proved, however, there might still be a defence available, and so we have a third basic element of every crime: the absence of a valid defence.

Suppose, for example, that Tom had indeed known Jill was married, but had been forced to go through the ceremony because Jill's father had "asked" him to do so, while wielding a shotgun suggestively. Tom has performed the actus reus of s 205(1)(b), with the required mens rea. So we can say that he has committed a *prima facie offence*. Despite this, he will not be convicted since he has a further defence of duress or compulsion.

The word "defence" can sometimes be misleading, because it tends to be used by lawyers to describe any reason why the defendant should be acquitted. Thus if the defendant has an alibi, he will rely on this for his defence. More precisely, however, an alibi is not a defence but rather

---

61   Cf *R v Deller* (1952) 36 Cr App R 184 (CCA).

a denial that there was a prima facie offence at all. If the alibi is accepted, it means that the defendant did not do the actus reus. Similarly, automatism is not so much a defence as a denial of responsibility for the actus reus. Duress and self-defence, by contrast, deny neither actus reus nor mens rea, but rather seek to defend the commission of a prima facie offence by reference to events not contemplated in the actus reus.[62]

Normally, defences are dealt with in a separate section of the Crimes Act, and are not expressly set out as part of each offence. Similarly, they are treated in separate chapters of this text. This is because defences are normally of general application to all crimes, unless expressly or impliedly excluded by the statute which creates a particular crime. Indeed many defences are not referred to at all in the Crimes Act, and are merely incorporated by s 20, which preserves the common law defences without their needing to be restated. The fact that defences make up a third element was accepted by Lord Wilberforce in *DPP for Northern Ireland v Lynch*. Duress, he stated:[63]

> "is something which is superimposed upon the other ingredients which by themselves would make up an offence, ie, upon act and intention. 'Coactus volui' sums up the combination: the victim completes the act and knows that he is doing so; but the addition of the element of duress prevents the law from treating what he has done as a crime."

In case it is helpful, we represent this relationship by the following diagram:

The offence of bigamy

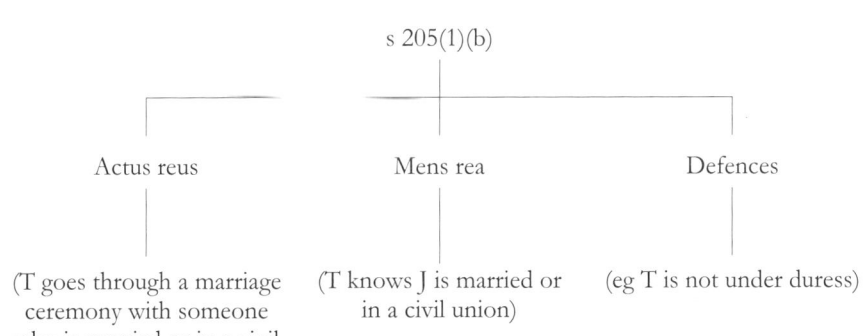

---

62 Cf Smith, "On actus reus and mens rea" in Glazebrook (ed), *Reshaping the Criminal Law: Essays in Honour of Glanville Williams*, London, Stevens & Sons, 1978, 95, 97ff; Simester, "Mistakes in defence" (1992) 12 OJLS 295, 295, 296.
63 *Northern Ireland v Lynch* [1975] AC 653; [1975] 1 All ER 913 (HL), 679-680; 926.

Chapter 2

INTERPRETATION, PROOF, AND THE RULE OF LAW

2.1	**The Rule of Law**	23
2.1.1	No conviction without criminalisation	24
2.1.2	Retrospective crimes	24
2.1.3	Fair warning	26
(1)	*Use of evaluative concepts*	28
2.1.4	Fair labelling	29
2.2	**Statutory interpretation**	30
2.2.1	Ordinary meaning	31
2.2.2	Legislative background	32
2.2.3	Strict construction	32
2.2.4	Summary	34
2.3	**The burden of proving actus reus and mens rea**	34
2.3.1	Exceptions	36
(1)	*Explicit overriding by legislation*	36
(2)	*Insanity*	37
(3)	*Strict liability*	37
(4)	*Where the statute is silent as to mens rea*	37
2.3.2	No presumption of intention	38

2.1 The Rule of Law

It is temptingly easy for a government to misuse the criminal legal system as a convenient means of social ordering. The criminal law, in seeking to secure benefits to society at large, can be a major threat of *in*security for any individual charged with the commission of a crime. Indeed, in some respects the criminal justice system constitutes New Zealand's most potent peace-time threat to the civil rights of those citizens suspected of and prosecuted for crimes. Accordingly society, while endeavouring to control and reduce criminal conduct, must be sensitive to the rights and legitimate expectations of those charged with crime.

Central to the protection of those rights and expectations is the Rule of Law, which demands that those under the State's control should be dealt with by fixed and knowable law, and not according to the discretion of State (including judicial) officials. As such, the Rule of Law embodies a cluster of legal values, including certainty, clarity, and prospectivity, which have at their heart not merely the constitutional premise that Government should operate under the law, but also the ideal that citizens should be able successfully to live within the law, by deriving guidance from the law itself.[1] This, in turn, requires that the criminal law must be an organised, ascertainable system of legal rules — and not ad hoc responses to the conduct of individuals.

The Rule of Law exists, first and foremost, at the level of principle. It comprises values to which the law should aspire and to which legislators and judges should pay heed when enacting and interpreting law. It is not a legally mandatory doctrine in its own right, save in so far as it operates as an informing principle of statutory interpretation.[2] In this chapter, we consider some of the main principles associated with the Rule of Law and their significance for the criminal law.

2.1.1 No conviction without criminalisation

The first limiting principle is inherent in the definition of criminal law offered at the beginning of chapter 1: that a crime involves, among other things, an event prohibited by law.[3] This implies that nobody should be convicted of a criminal offence unless what was done is, in law, a crime. Nullum crimen sine lege, the maxim goes: no crime without law.[4] In New Zealand, this requirement is codified by s 9 Crimes Act 1961, the effect of which is to exclude criminal liability unless an offence has been committed against a New Zealand statute.[5]

Suppose, for example, that Jane is a visitor from another country where adultery is a criminal offence. While in New Zealand she has an affair with a married man. Even though she believes she is committing a crime, she cannot be convicted of any offence, since adultery is not illegal under New Zealand's criminal law. A case that illustrates this principle is *R v Deller*.[6] The defendant sold a car, stating as he did so that it was free of encumbrances. In fact, he thought the car was encumbered, because he had earlier mortgaged it to a finance company. Deller was charged with obtaining the proceeds of the car sale under false pretences. As it happened, however, the earlier mortgage was apparently invalid, and hence the car *was* unencumbered. By chance, his pretence was not false. He could not be convicted since he had broken no law.[7]

2.1.2 Retrospective crimes

A corollary of the nullum crimen principle is that there should be no retrospective criminalisation, whereby citizens might be convicted on the basis of conduct that was not, *when they did it*, an offence. In such cases, it is not enough that relevant law is to hand at the

---

1 See Raz, *The Authority of Law: Essays on Law and Morality*, Oxford, Clarendon Press, 1979, ch 11; Colvin, "Criminal Law and the Rule of Law" in Fitzgerald (ed), *Crime, Justice and Codification: Essays in Commemoration of Jacques Fortin*, Toronto, Carswell, 1986, 125.
2 See, for example, *Nicholson v Dept of Social Welfare* [1999] 3 NZLR 50 (CA), 58, where the Court of Appeal referred to the "vice of creating practical uncertainty as to when the offence is complete" in preferring an alternative construction of s 127 Social Security Act 1964. According to Lord Steyn, "in the absence of express words or a truly necessary implication, Parliament must be presumed to legislate on the assumption that the principle of legality will supplement the text": *B (a minor) v DPP* [2000] 2 AC 428; [2000] 1 All ER 833 (HL), 470; 845.
3 See 1.2.
4 Sometimes called the principle of *legality*, especially in the United States. See Hall, *General Principles of Criminal Law* (2nd ed), Indianapolis, Bobbs-Merrill, 1960, 27f.
5 The section is subject to exceptions for contempt and courts martial.
6 *R v Deller* (1952) 36 Cr App R 184 (CCA).
7 At least, at that time. Under modern law, it appears that Deller could now be convicted of an attempt. See chapter 7.

time of the trial. It would still be true that at the time of D's conduct he committed no applicable crime. Remedying the legal deficiency by passing a retrospective law, which deemed the offence into existence at the time of its commission, would be to contradict rather than uphold the Rule of Law. Particularly given the dramatic implications of criminal penalties for the lives of individuals, criminal liability is not the sort of nasty surprise that should be sprung on citizens ex post facto.

In England, the evolutionary nature of the common law has resulted in a less than scrupulous observance of this constraint. In *R v R*, for example, the House of Lords abolished an exemption in the common law crime of rape, which had meant that a husband could not be convicted of raping his wife.[8] While that change is to be welcomed as a matter of social and legal policy, the retrospective rather than de futuro manner in which it was achieved is more controversial, since it led to R's being convicted for conduct that was apparently not a criminal rape when done. An even more extreme case is that of *Shaw v DPP*.[9] Shaw was charged with conspiring to corrupt public morals — an offence that had not existed until he was indicted for it. His indictment was upheld by the House of Lords. *Whether or not* the defendant's actions were covered by an existing law, the courts were said to have residual power to criminalise his conduct.[10]

As it happens, the recognition of common law offences is disallowed in New Zealand by s 9 Crimes Act 1961, which limits criminal proceedings to only those offences created by a New Zealand statute. Nonetheless, a result such as that in *Shaw* could still be achieved by retrospective legislation. Such devices, it is submitted, are inappropriate in the criminal law.

It is important to optimise the transparency and predictability of the criminal law by stating its rules clearly in advance. Failure to do so undermines the entire operation of the law, as a system of rules designed to guide society's behaviour, when the rules are unknown. When interpreting criminal statutes, the common law supplies a presumption against retrospective crimes. That presumption is buttressed by s 7 Interpretation Act 1999, which provides generally that enactments do not have retrospective effect. Although the express terms of a legislative enactment may override the presumption, it provides a signal protection against that possibility. Moreover, were Parliament expressly to override that presumption, it would also be in clear contravention of s 10A Crimes Act 1961 and s 26(1) New Zealand Bill of Rights Act 1990, which provide that no criminal enactment shall have a retrospective effect. As things stand, both as a matter of statutory interpretation and under the terms of the New Zealand Bill of Rights Act 1990, courts are required to accept Parliament's will. Nonetheless, the

---

8   *R v R* [1992] 1 AC 599; [1991] 4 All ER 481 (HL). Technically, the House of Lords did not abolish the exemption but rather purported to recognise that, by the time of the defendant's actions, the historical immunity for spouses was no longer part of the law. (Cf the decision by the European Court of Human Rights in *SW v UK* (1996) 21 EHRR 363.) Given acknowledgement of the exemption in quite recent cases such as *R v Steele* (1976) 65 Cr App R 22, and *R v Sharples* [1990] Crim LR 198, this otherwise vital distinction smacks of sophistry. From D's (and most lawyers') point of view, the immunity *was* effectively abolished by their Lordships.

9   *Shaw v DPP* [1962] AC 220; [1961] 2 All ER 446 (HL).

10 *Shaw* is objectionable on a second count: it criminalises *immoral* activity. See below, 21.3. The House of Lords has since disavowed further extensions of the common law to enforce morality: *Knuller (Publishing, Printing and Promotions) Ltd v DPP* [1973] AC 435; [1972] 3 WLR 143 (HL). See Goodhart, "The *Shaw* case: The law and public morals" (1961) 77 LQR 560; Note (1962) 75(2) Harv LR 1652; Smith, "Judicial law making in the criminal law" (1984) 100 LQR 46.

existence of ss 10A and 26(1) should at least ensure that courts will, in the absence of the clearest language, be loath to infer that a newly created crime, or a statutory increase in penalty,[11] is to be given retrospective effect.[12] In addition, ss 10A and 26(1) may act as a warning sign: any finding that they are overridden involves public acknowledgement that a part of the criminal law transgresses the Rule of Law and contravenes the defendant's basic human rights.

2.1.3 Fair warning

Apart from its constitutional implications, the most important reason for requiring criminal offences to be created prospectively is that failure to do so undermines predictability in the law. In *Shaw v DPP* (above), the enterprising Mr Shaw had been assured by his lawyer that his proposed publication, the *Ladies' Directory*, passed muster in legal terms. Yet the House of Lords found that he, with others, had conspired to corrupt public morality. If even competent legal advice cannot predict the unlawfulness of a defendant's conduct, his attempt to live within the law is a farce.

However, it is important to notice that, in *Shaw*, predictability was threatened not merely because the offence was created retrospectively. Suppose, as some have argued, that the House of Lords resurrected rather than invented this species of conspiracy, and that the principle against retroactivity was not breached. Either way, the nebulous terms of the offence leave to speculation what kinds of thing one must not conspire to do.[13]

This shows that non-retroactive legislation is not the only standard set by the Rule of Law, and that the need for predictability has more general implications. The criminal law is not there solely to tell police and judges what to do after someone offends, but also to tell *citizens* what not to do in advance. As such, it is not enough for there to be a law in place before people can commit a crime. They should also be told about it. That is the reason why non-publication or unavailability of a statutory instrument may be a defence, if a person commits a crime under that instrument while unaware of its existence.[14] There must be an opportunity for defendants to know the law before they are convicted of breaking it:[15]

> "Respect for law, which is the most cogent force in prompting orderly conduct in a civilised community, is weakened, if men are punished for acts which according to the general consensus of opinion they were justified in believing to be morally right *and in accordance with law*."

---

11   In the context of penalties, see also s 6 Sentencing Act 2002 (previously s 4(2) Criminal Justice Act 1985, which has since been repealed), which prohibits a court imposing any sentence that it could not have imposed at the time the relevant offence was committed.

12   Cf *R v King* [1995] 3 NZLR 409; (1995) 13 CRNZ 289; *Hedges v Waitakere CC* 21/5/92, Barker J, HC Auckland AP114/92; *Dept of Labour v Latailakepa* [1982] 1 NZLR 632 (CA). Note that s 10A applies "notwithstanding any other enactment", so is subject to implied repeal only by *later* statutes.

13   Similarly, even if the view of the European Court (2.1.2; especially above n 8) that *R v R* involved no retrospective criminalisation were accepted, the decision remains problematic because of its element of surprise.

14   *Grant v Borg* [1982] 2 All ER 257; [1982] 1 WLR 638 (HL); *Burns v Nowell* (1880) 5 QBD 444 (CA); *Lim Chin Aik v R* [1963] AC 160; [1963] 1 All ER 223 (PC); *Golden-Brown v Hunt* (1972) 19 Fed LR 438; *R v Catholique* (1980) 104 DLR (3d) 161.

15   *State v O'Neil* (1910) 126 NW 454, 456 (emphasis added). See Brett, "Mistake of law as a criminal defence" (1966) 5 MULR 179, 204.

The Rule of Law mandates that people should be governed "by rules which are fixed, knowable, and certain".[16] This requires both that the rule be stated in advance, and also that it be stated clearly. Clarity is essential if citizens are to have *fair warning* that by their prospective actions they are in danger of incurring a criminal sanction.[17] If individuals understand the law, they will be able properly to decide what to do in light of the guidance that the law is meant to provide. Only then can the law act as the deterrent it is intended to be. And only then do citizens have a fair opportunity to steer themselves clear of criminal liability.

Once again, however, fair warning is a Rule of Law aspiration that is not always achieved in practice. Before the decision in *R v R* (see 2.1.2), it was widely assumed that, at common law, a cohabiting husband was immune from the charge of raping his wife. Nonetheless, the House of Lords found the immunity to be ungrounded in law. To what extent can New Zealand anticipate greater judicial restraint in light of the New Zealand Bill of Rights Act 1990? There is overseas authority for interpreting s 26(1) in such a way that it protects fair warning. In *Kokkinakis v Greece*, the European Court spoke of the principle that:[18]

> "[T]he criminal law must not be extensively construed to an accused's detriment, for instance by analogy; it follows from this that an offence must be clearly defined in law. This condition is satisfied where the individual can know from the wording of the relevant provision and, if need be, with the assistance of the courts' interpretation of it, what acts and omissions will make him liable."

The passage makes it clear that statutory interpretation — the legitimate principles of which are considered below — can be reviewed under the terms of a provision such as s 26(1). However, it remains uncertain how far such powers of review are being exercised, or what factors are being taken into account when doing so. If conduct has been engaged in on the reasonable assumption that it was lawful, that should count as a factor to be considered by a court. But it may be that the kind of conduct at issue should properly influence a court. Hence, if the objection is one of fair warning rather than a constitutional one of retrospective criminalisation, a decision like *R v R* is defensible, perhaps, on the footing that R's conduct did constitute a crime when done by anyone else and that the reasons for criminalisation apply just as forcefully to a husband as to anyone else. It should have made no difference had R received an assurance from a lawyer, immediately before making his wife submit to intercourse by drawing a knife, that in legal terms he would not be committing rape. That is not, of course, to say that courts may craft new law in order to catch husbands who treat wives in that fashion.

---

16 Ashworth, *Principles*, 70, and see ch 3.5 generally; Raz, *The Authority of Law: Essays on Law and Morality*, Oxford, Clarendon Press, 1979, 214, 215.

17 Cf *Papachristou v City of Jacksonville* (1972) 405 US 156; 31 L Ed 2d 110, 162; 115 (vagrancy ordinance void for vagueness). Fair warning is also relevant to inadvertence-based liability, for example, for negligence. It is one reason why criminal liability for serious crimes should normally be confined to reckless or intentional wrongdoing. This is because if there were widespread exposure to State interference for inadvertent wrongdoing, then it would be much harder for citizens to plan and get on with their lives, without fearing the unforeseen disruption that facing criminal charges entails. See, for example, Hart, "Punishment and the elimination of responsibility" in *Punishment and Responsibility: Essays in the Philosophy of Law*, Oxford, Clarendon Press, 1968, 158, 181, 182. However, this argument is not insuperable. To the extent that the Rule of Law interdicts unpredictable interference by the State, liability for negligence is reasonably predictable. Moreover, unless negligence liability were no deterrent, the argument prima facie deprives victims of protection from similarly unlooked-for intrusions by other citizens.

18 *Kokkinakis v Greece* (1994) 17 EHRR 397, 423. Cf *G v Federal Republic of Germany* (1989) 60 DR 256, 262. The passage quoted is apropos of art 7, the corresponding article of the European Convention on Human Rights.

It is merely to say that in considering what the current law is, the fact that the defendant thought it was different does not count for much if what the defendant did breached in the most fundamental way his wife's right to bodily integrity. By contrast, if the owner of a factory has done his best to comply with health and safety law and has received professional assurance that he has done enough, this should be recognised when determining whether he has provided a safe system of work that takes "all practicable steps to ensure the safety of employees".[19]

It is for Parliament to make law and, although judicial interpretation of law may properly be purposive, the text of statutes cannot always be stretched to cover the conduct in question. The Rule of Law requires a system of legal ordering, not ad hoc responses to the conduct of individuals; as such, it is particularly important in the criminal law to identify where the law and judges' jurisdiction run out. We have seen that, in the past, common law judges have been prepared to go beyond that point in order to criminalise conduct they disapproved of even in cases where the policy arguments for criminalisation were not clear-cut. That is contrary to adjudication under law, and it is to be hoped that s 26(1) will enhance the case against such judicial activism.

(1) *Use of evaluative concepts*

A legal system, then, should seek to provide as much guidance and predictability as it can. However, realism is required when deciding what degree of certainty is attainable in particular laws. Explicitness is necessarily compromised in offences that involve vague and open-ended concepts such as "unreasonable", "excessive",[20] and "fraudulent". Similarly, if we drive a car we know, or should know, that we must drive with "due care and attention". The phrase sets a standard for a myriad of driving contexts and inevitably must leave an ultimate assessment to the court, which will find the phrase of no more than open-ended guidance. What degree of error or inattention will turn us into criminals cannot be stated with exactitude. If the criminal law is to involve itself with standards of safety, which surely it must, it cannot give a rigid specification of the circumstances under which criminal liability will follow.

At the same time, both Legislature and judiciary should be cautious about the deployment and interpretation of such expressions. Consider, for example, the imposition of negligence-based criminal liability, through offences which are typically couched in terms of the "unreasonableness" of the defendant's behaviour. The touchstone, be it "unreasonable" or "negligent", is not susceptible of accurate or formal definition. What is "reasonable"? Nowhere does the law say, and to some extent the individual must judge the law's standard for herself, and risk the court's disagreeing with her. Such gambles ought to be minimised,[21] and where possible these discretionary terms should be replaced by more concrete definitions of what counts as illegal, and what as legitimate.

This reservation should not be overstated, and it cannot be claimed that such terms deprive individuals of advance warning altogether. The defendant's judgment is not purely a guess:

---

19   Section 6 Health and Safety in Employment Act 1992.
20   Cf s 62 Crimes Act 1961.
21   "[A] statute which either forbids or requires the doing of an act in terms so vague that men of common intelligence must necessarily guess at its meaning and differ as to its application, violates the first essential of due process of law." *Connally v General Construction Co* (1926) 269 US 385, 391. Cf Rawls, *A Theory of Justice*, Massachusetts, Belknap Press of Harvard University Press, 1971, 239: "if the precept of no crime without a law is violated, say by statutes, being vague and imprecise, what we are at liberty to do is likewise vague and imprecise."

words such as "reasonable" are not meaningless.[22] We understand them, and know how to apply the implicit judgments they import. The use of broad evaluative terms such as "negligent" and "fraudulent" may well provide an acceptable level of guidance where there is a high degree of social consensus about appropriate behaviour in the area of activity under regulation. One may assume that degree of necessary consensus, for instance, in matters of road safety; accordingly a requirement to drive with due care and attention may tell us all we really need to know.

Moreover, evaluative standards are useful. Terms like "reasonable" and "dangerous" give the law flexibility to deal with cases that a legislator might not foresee. It is too much to expect a statute to list every mode of negligent homicide, and meaningful terms like "unreasonable" save us from being straightjacketed by a rigid specification of the circumstances under which criminal liability will or will not follow. Indeed, without such flexibility, the law would be unfair and incomplete. There will always be matters which require regulation, but where a degree of imprecision is inevitable. Over many years, for example, courts have sought a legal definition of when an act was sufficiently close to the commission of a crime to constitute an attempt to commit that crime. Various tests were tried; all were unsatisfactory. Nowadays it is generally enough to ask whether an act was more than merely preparatory, ie a step in the commission of the crime itself.[23]

Nonetheless, evaluative terms *are* imprecise, and for that reason, at least in serious crimes, they should normally be used only sparingly and for clear cases of wrongdoing. This is one justification of the common law's requirement that negligence be "gross" before one may be guilty of manslaughter:[24] it is not merely that D's culpability is greater, but also that we can be more sure D is culpable.[25] Sometimes, the imprecision is such that these terms ought not to be used at all. It is doubtful whether there is a sufficient degree of consensus about the acceptable contents of literature, plays, and film to render the standards "indecent" and "obscene", employed in indecency laws, a sufficient guide to producers and publishers of artefacts in those fields.[26] If a government wishes to maintain a regulatory presence there, it is better that it regulates by description, expressly identifying those things which are not to be written, photographed, or filmed: hence the use of a classification system under the Films, Videos, and Publications Classification Act 1993.

2.1.4 Fair labelling

We have seen that the ex ante guidance the law is meant to provide requires it to be clearly stated. However, there is another reason for expecting clarity in criminal offences. When a crime occurs, justice must not only be done, it must also be *seen* to be done. The law needs precision in order to identify exactly what offence the wrongdoer has committed. If he is publicly convicted of "murder", D should *be* a murderer and not a parking offender. At the same time, neither would it be satisfactory for the law simply to label all convicted offenders unspecifically as "criminals", for that would equate the convictions of rapists with pickpockets. The criminal law speaks to society as well as wrongdoers when it convicts them, and it should

---

22 Lucas, "The philosophy of the reasonable man" (1963) 13 Phil Qtrly 97.
23 See chapter 8.
24 See chapter 16.
25 An interesting discussion is Horder, "Gross negligence and criminal culpability" (1997) 47 U Toronto LJ 495.
26 Cf s 124 Crimes Act 1961 and the Films, Videos, and Publications Classification Act 1993.

communicate its judgment with precision by accurately naming the crime of which they are convicted. This requirement is known as the principle of fair labelling.[27]

The need for fair labelling is one reason why we should not combine the separate offences of murder and manslaughter into a single crime of culpable homicide, as was proposed in the Crimes Bill 1989. In the eyes of society, these are two different types of wrongdoing, and the communicative function of the law would be impaired were the law to blur that difference. Sir Robin Cooke (as he then was) recognised this when he criticised the Crimes Bill proposal:[28]

> "The issue is social and moral as much as legal ... it should remain open to a jury, having heard the evidence, to condemn a crime as so heinous as to cry out for the name of murder."

Underlying this objection is the point that different offences criminalise *actions* which have differing social significance, and not just *outcomes*. So, for example, it would be a mistake to assimilate vandalism with negligent damage to property. Even though the harm to property is the same, vandalism expresses a certain sort of contempt for society and the victim that negligent damage does not. If the criminal law were not to distinguish between the two, a conviction would be potentially misleading.

The law must make clear what sort of criminal each offender is — what the conviction is *for*. It should communicate this to the defendant, so that he may know exactly what he has done wrong and why he is being punished, in order that his punishment appears meaningful to him, not just an arbitrary harsh treatment. In addition, the law should communicate the crime to the public, so that they too may understand the nature of his transgression. The public record matters. While an employer may have few qualms about hiring a convicted fraudster as an orderly in a children's hospital, it would be an entirely different matter to contemplate employing someone who has been in jail for paedophilia.

2.2 Statutory interpretation

In the previous section, we noted that the Rule of Law should not be cast as a demand for unattainable measures of predictability and certainty. A degree of imprecision is inherent in the enterprise of legal ordering. Statutes are necessarily expressed in general terms, and must be interpreted and applied to particular cases. The agent of this process is the court.[29]

In practice, the judicial task is more substantial than it need be. While legislators cannot be expected to foresee every variant case that might arise when they create an offence, the standard of drafting in this country is such that offences frequently omit to specify quite obvious matters, such as what (if any) mental element an offence requires, on whom a burden of persuasion may lay, and whether omissions as well as acts are within the conduct proscribed. Moreover,

---

27 Cf Ashworth, "The elasticity of mens rea" in Tapper (ed), *Crime, Proof and Punishment: Essays in Memory of Sir Rupert Cross*, London, Butterworths, 1981, 45, 53-56; Williams, "Convictions and fair labelling" [1983] 42 CLJ 85.
28 "The Crimes Bill 1989: A judge's response" [1989] NZLJ 235, 239.
29 For general discussion, see Ashworth, "Interpreting criminal statutes: A crisis of legality?" (1991) 107 LQR 419; Hall, "Strict or liberal construction of penal statutes" (1935) 48 Harv LR 748; MacCormick and Summers (eds), *Interpreting Statutes: A Comparative Study*, Aldershot, Dartmouth, 1991; Jeffries, "Legality, vagueness, and the construction of penal statutes" (1985) 71 Va LR 189; Kremnitzer, "Interpretation in criminal law" (1986) 21 Israel LR 358.

some fundamental aspects of the criminal law, such as causation, are untouched by statute. Consequently, the role of judges is pivotal and powerful.

One way of observing the rights and expectations of citizens under the Rule of Law is for judges to show a proper restraint when interpreting the rules of the criminal law. In the civil law — say, a case involving the law of restitution — a judgment may earn praise for the way it reconceptualises the grounds of restitution, thereby vindicating new restitutionary claims. Similar creativity in the criminal law is generally to be avoided, since the scope for condemnation and punishment is thereby enlarged:[30]

> "[By contrast with] standard civil cases, when the ruling assumption is that one of the parties has a right to win, ... [t]he accused in a criminal case has a right to a decision in his favour if he is innocent, but the state has no parallel right to a conviction if he is guilty. The court may therefore find in favour of the accused, in some hard case testing rules of evidence, for example, on an argument of policy that does not suppose that the accused has any right to be acquitted."

In 2.1.3, we noted the remark by the European Court of Human Rights that "the criminal law must not be extensively construed to an accused's detriment, for instance by analogy".[31] This need for restraint means that interpreting a criminal statute should involve determining its meaning in a non-expansive way. Hence, the approach to interpretation of a criminal statute differs slightly from the proper approach to statutory interpretation in the civil law. It is not possible in a text of this nature to provide more than a brief overview of the relevant principles, and what follows is necessarily incomplete. When questions about the meaning of an offence arise, there are three steps for a court to take.

2.2.1 Ordinary meaning

In the first instance, the interpretation of a criminal statute will not differ in technique from the interpretation of a civil statute. Modern statutory interpretation, both civil and criminal, should first take the form of ascertaining the *ordinary meaning in context*.[32] The reference to context is particularly important. It is a feature of language that meaning is not merely lexical, but also depends on the surrounding words and the purpose of the writer. For example, s 240 creates an offence, among other things, of inducing, by deception, another person to endorse certain documents. On one meaning, to "endorse" something is to express approval of it. But it is quite clear, both from the lexical context (a document "capable of being used to derive a pecuniary advantage") and from the purpose of the offence (to criminalise obtaining by deception), that the intended meaning is to assign by writing.

Even the best-drafted statute can require interpretive decisions by the court. If grammatical context as well as lexical meaning is addressed, one meaning will usually emerge as clearly the best suited to effect the purposes of the statute or the relevant part of it. Where it does so, there can be no objection, even in the case of a criminal statute, to an interpretative choice that goes against the defendant. When one interpretation of a statutory provision is distinctly preferable to any competing interpretation, there is nothing particular about the interpretation

---

30 Dworkin, "Hard cases" in *Taking Rights Seriously*, London, Duckworth, 1978, 81, 100.
31 *Kokkinakis v Greece* (1994) 17 EHRR 397, 423.
32 Cf Burrows, *Statute Law in New Zealand* (3rd ed), Wellington, LexisNexis, 2003, ch 10; Evans, *Statutory Interpretation: Problems of Communication*, Auckland, Oxford University Press, 1988, 19-22, 59f; Bell and Engle, *Cross on Statutory Interpretation* (3rd ed), London, Butterworths, 1995, 31-33, 48.

of criminal statutes: the "ordinary meaning in context" prevails. The technique outlined here is endorsed by s 5 Interpretation Act 1999, which applies to both civil and criminal statutes and requires courts to ascertain the meaning of a statutory provision from its text and in the light of its purpose.[33]

2.2.2 Legislative background

Sometimes the meaning cannot be determined within the four corners of the statute itself. In such cases, the courts have the power to investigate the legislative background of an Act in order to ascertain the intention of Parliament.[34] Unfortunately, whether or not the legislative history is consulted depends upon the inclination of judges. In the notorious case of *MPC v Caldwell*,[35] to which we return in chapter 4, Lord Diplock conceded that there was an issue of interpretation in respect of the meaning to be given to the culpability term, "reckless". He resolved the issue by recourse to "ordinary" English, which informed him that the term comprehended not only defendants who perceived the likely consequences of their conduct, but also defendants who failed to give thought to the obvious consequences of that conduct. He signally failed to consider a Law Commission report which stated, unequivocally, that only defendants who actually perceived the consequences of their conduct were to be found reckless in cases of criminal damage.

2.2.3 Strict construction

Finally, if, after examining the statutory context, there is still some uncertainty about which interpretation is preferable, then the court should give the benefit of that uncertainty to the accused. This is a presumption of strict construction. It is justified by the requirement to give fair warning, which implies that ambiguity in offences should not be understood so as to create unpredictable offences; statutes should not require citizens to guess at their meaning, and so should be construed against imposing liability on a defendant who reasonably thought she was within the terms of the law. The principle of strict interpretation, confined to criminal and taxation statutes, may be expressed as follows:[36]

> "if a penal provision is reasonably capable of two interpretations, that interpretation which is most favourable to the accused must be adopted."

This is not to say that *any* measure of doubt over the meaning of a statute should be construed in the defendant's favour. The strict construction principle is a default rule, one to rely on if the meaning of the statute cannot be ascertained by other standard techniques. In the past, the principle of strict construction has been read as entailing that the benefit of *any* favourable interpretation which passes a minimal threshold of plausibility must always be given to the

---

33 Arguably, the section is an even stronger endorsement of the approach stated here than was its predecessor, s 5(j) Acts Interpretation Act 1924, according to which every Act shall be deemed remedial and receive a "fair, large, and liberal construction and interpretation" so as best to achieve its object according to its true intent, meaning, and spirit. The new s 5 is more tightly expressed.

34 *Marac Life Assurance Ltd v CIR* [1986] 1 NZLR 694 (CA); *NZ Maori Council v A-G* [1987] 1 NZLR 641 (CA); *Pepper (Inspector of Taxes) v Hart* [1993] AC 593; [1993] 1 All ER 42 (HL). In terms of the Rule of Law, consulting such sources as *Hansard* is unobjectionable provided the source is adequately made available to the public so that potential defendants have fair warning of its import. See Evans, *Statutory Interpretation: Problems of Communication*, Auckland, Oxford University Press, 1988, 289.

35 *MPC v Caldwell* [1982] AC 341, also reported as *R v Caldwell* [1981] 1 All ER 961 (HL).

36 Per Lord Reid in *Sweet v Parsley* [1970] AC 132; [1969] 1 All ER 347 (HL), 149; 350. Cited by the Court of Appeal in *Millar v MOT* [1986] 1 NZLR 660; (1986) 2 CRNZ 216 (CA), 668; 224.

(i) The prosecution has the burden of bringing evidence which prima facie proves all actus reus and mens rea elements of the offence *beyond reasonable doubt*.

(ii) Once the prosecution has done so, it is then open to the defendant either to raise a reasonable doubt about the evidence the prosecution has brought or to point to some further evidence which raises a doubt as to whether the prosecution's evidence is sufficient to prove both actus reus[45] and mens rea beyond reasonable doubt.

(iii) Alternatively, if the prosecution proves both actus reus and mens rea, the defendant has an *evidentiary burden* to raise any evidence which suggests the possible availability of a defence (for example, that the actus reus was done in self-defence).[46] If he does so, or if the evidence introduced by the prosecution does so,[47] the prosecution assumes the burden of proving beyond reasonable doubt that the relevant defence is not available in this case.[48] This rule applies to statutory as well as common law defences,[49] unless the legislature provides otherwise (below, 2.3.1(1)).

The defendant does *not* have to prove that he is innocent. The jury may think that he is untrustworthy, and be unconvinced by his story. But if it thinks there is a reasonable possibility that he is not guilty of the crime charged, he must be acquitted. As the Privy Council put it, in *Don Jayasena v R*: "the only burden laid upon the accused in this respect is to collect from the evidence enough material to make it possible for a reasonable jury to acquit."[50] In practical terms, the effect of the *Woolmington* approach is that a defendant need not collaborate in his own conviction; however strong the grounds of suspicion against him he need not give any account of himself or in any other way assist the prosecution make its case. As such, the presumption of innocence is an essential counterpart to the defendant's right not to incriminate himself.

The crux is the standard: "beyond reasonable doubt." It means the jury must acquit if there is a realistic or genuine doubt about the defendant's guilt, although not if the doubt is only vague or fanciful.[51] Such a high standard is needed for the State to be sufficiently sure that it is

---

45 This includes claims of involuntariness or automatism: *R v Burr* [1969] NZLR 736 (CA), 748; *Police v Bannin* [1991] 2 NZLR 237, also reported as *B v Police* (1991) 7 CRNZ 55, 241, 242; 58, 59; *Millar v MOT* [1986] 1 NZLR 660; (1986) 2 CRNZ 216 (CA), 667, 668; 224, 225; *Bratty v A-G for Northern Ireland* [1963] AC 386; [1961] 3 All ER 523 (HL), 406, 407, 413, 414; 523, 530, 531, 534-536. See 3.4.4.

46 *R v Matoka* [1987] 1 NZLR 340 (CA), 344; *R v Nepia* [1983] NZLR 754 (CA). The evidentiary burden to introduce defences differs from the option to refute evidence of actus reus or mens rea in step (ii). The latter is sometimes called a *tactical burden* on the defendant. The difference is that, where there is an evidential burden on D to suggest (for example) a defence, its absence will be *presumed* by the court unless D discharges that burden. By contrast, a tactical burden involves no presumption. Thus, D may choose not to respond to the prosecution's evidence of actus reus and mens rea and simply hope that the jury is not convinced by it.

47 Thus the defence must be considered even if the defendant has not raised it himself — or, indeed, disclaims it. See *R v Tavete* [1988] 1 NZLR 428; (1987) 2 CRNZ 579 (CA).

48 *R v Kahu* [1947] NZLR 368 (CA); *R v Kerr* [1976] 1 NZLR 335 (CA), 340.

49 *R v Rangi* [1992] 1 NZLR 385 (CA); *Bay of Plenty Regional Council v Bay Milk Products* [1996] 3 NZLR 120; cf s 25(c) New Zealand Bill of Rights Act 1990; *R v Phillips* [1991] 3 NZLR 175 (CA). (The position in England appears to be different, in that the defendant now bears the onus of proving any *statutory* defence to the balance of probabilities, in both summary proceedings and trials on indictment: *R v Hunt* [1987] AC 352; [1987] 1 All ER 1 (HL).)

50 *Don Jayasena v R* [1970] AC 618, 623.

51 *R v Harbour* [1995] 1 NZLR 440; (1995) 12 CRNZ 317 (CA), 448; 324; *R v S* 20/12/91, CA273/91.

imposing criminal liability accurately. It is not enough that the defendant "very likely", or even "probably" did the crime, otherwise there would be too many cases of error and consequent miscarriages of justice. The possibility of error is all the greater when it is also remembered that the State typically has far greater resources with which to conduct a prosecution than the defendant has with which to defend himself. In addition, the high standard of proof acts as a constraint upon the decision to prosecute. Without the presumption of innocence, those who make that decision would have an immense and potentially oppressive power to disrupt citizens' lives.[52]

2.3.1 Exceptions

(1) *Explicit overriding by legislation*

It is not uncommon for a statute to modify the normal burden of proof, especially in respect of particular elements within an offence. An example of this is the crime of sexual conduct with a person aged under 16, contrary to s 134 Crimes Act 1961. Section 134A provides a defence "if the person charged proves" that he or she reasonably believed, and had taken reasonable steps to establish, that the victim was aged at least 16; and that the victim consented. In this case, once the prosecution has proved the elements of an offence under s 134, the defendant has a legal (and not merely evidential) burden to prove that the conditions of the defence exist. In such cases, the defendant must prove to the civil standard, of balance of probabilities.[53]

An important and more general statutory modification to the normal burden is found in s 67(8) Summary Proceedings Act 1957, which places on the accused *when in summary proceedings* the burden of proving any statutory defence, again to the balance of probabilities.[54]

This is not a textbook on evidence. However, it is submitted that for the reasons given in the last section, and especially in light of s 25(c) New Zealand Bill of Rights Act 1990, statutory exceptions of these sorts are generally to be deplored.[55] Effectively, they reverse the presumption of innocence and replace it with a presumption of criminality, whereby the defendant is to be convicted of a crime unless she exculpates herself. As such, they expose the defendant to conviction for a crime without the prosecution being required, at any stage, to lead evidence which proves her guilt beyond reasonable doubt. There *are* occasions when it may be apt to require the defendant, who may have more information about salient events than the prosecutor, to suggest reasons why she should not be convicted.[56] But rather like the tort doctrine of res ipsa loquitur, this is a device to be sparingly used and only if the prosecution has established a prima facie case. Moreover, even then the desired result can usually be achieved by imposing on the defendant an *evidential* burden to introduce defences without requiring her to discharge the full legal burden of persuading the court that she is innocent.

There may sometimes be scope for the courts, as a matter of statutory interpretation, to read reverse-burden provisions as imposing only an evidential burden. In *Grey v Police*,[57] Hammond J

---

52   As Ashworth points out: *Principles*, ch 3.5(m).
53   *R v Phillips* [1991] 3 NZLR 175 (CA); *R v Hansen* (2005) 22 CRNZ 83 (CA). See also Orchard, "The golden thread: somewhat frayed" (1988) 6 Otago LR 615.
54   *Niven v MOT* (1988) 4 CRNZ 16 (HC).
55   See, for example, Roberts, "Taking the burden of proof seriously" [1995] Crim LR 783; Jeffries and Stephan, "Defenses, presumptions and burden of proof in the criminal law" (1979) 88 Yale LJ 1325.
56   See the discussion of (and reservations about) strict liability, at 5.1.1(3)(b), 5.2.3(2)(a), (b).

relied on s 25(c) New Zealand Bill of Rights Act 1990 to read down s 67(8) Summary Proceedings Act 1957. As we noted above, the reverse burden of proving statutory defences that is imposed on defendants in summary proceedings is generally thought to be on the balance of probabilities. However, his Honour concluded that, at least in the context of s 29 Summary Offences Act 1981 (which creates the offence of being found in a building "without reasonable excuse"), the accused bore only an evidential burden of raising the statutory defence. This approach finds support in the English courts, which have asserted that it always is a question of statutory interpretation whether a particular reverse-burden provision imposes an evidentiary or balance-of-probability onus on the accused; a question that depends in part on the seriousness of the offence and the purpose of the legislation.[58] In New Zealand, however, the conclusion reached in *Grey v Police* has not been matched in other cases.[59]

(2)   *Insanity*

A second exception is the defence of insanity. In line with the common law,[60] the Crimes Act 1961 makes a statutory presumption of sanity in s 23(1). Once again, the defendant must prove this defence on the balance of probabilities[61] — an incongruous anomaly given that the defendant bears only an evidential burden in respect of other general defences and that the consequence of proving insanity may be incarceration.[62] Note, however, that the need for a defendant to show insanity arises only if the prosecution can prove the actus reus and mens rea[63] beyond reasonable doubt in the normal way. Insanity is discussed in detail in chapter 9.

(3)   *Strict liability*

A most important exception is considered in chapter 5. In offences of strict liability, the defendant carries the burden of proving a defence of absence of fault, once again to the balance of probabilities.

(4)   *Where the statute is silent as to mens rea*

There is one situation where mens rea is required but the prosecution does not bear the initial burden of proving it beyond reasonable doubt. As we shall see in the discussion of strict liability (chapter 5), frequently the statute creating an offence specifies only the actus reus elements of that offence and neglects to mention the need for mens rea. In such instances the courts must determine whether the offence is one of strict liability or, alternatively, one in which mens rea is unexpressed but in fact required (sometimes called an "implied mens rea offence"). In the latter case, the burden of proof can best be summarised as follows:

---

57   *Grey v Police* 31/10/01, HC Hamilton AP65/01.
58   *Sheldrake v DPP* [2004] UKHL 43, [2004] 3 WLR 976; cf *R v DPP ex p Kibelene* [1999] 3 WLR 972 (HL).
59   Cf *R v Phillips* [1991] 3 NZLR 175 (CA). Neither has *Grey v Police* been followed even in the context of s 67(8) Summary Proceedings Act 1957: *Francis v Police* 1/5/03, Heath J, HC Auckland AP194/02.
60   Cf the M'Naghten rules, *M'Naghten's Case* (1843) 10 Cl & Fin 200; 8 ER 718; [1843-60] All ER Rep 229 (HL), 210; 722; 233; *Woolmington v DPP* [1935] AC 462; [1935] All ER 1 (HL), 475; 5.
61   *R v Roulston* [1976] 2 NZLR 644 (CA); *R v Cottle* [1958] NZLR 999 (CA), 1014, 1022. The same is true regarding unfitness to plead.
62   For excellent discussion, see Jones, "Insanity, automatism, and the burden of proof on the accused" (1995) 111 LQR 475.
63   Or at least if, following proof of the actus reus, mens rea can be inferred upon presumption of the defendant's sanity.

(a) Where the statute states expressly that something is an element of the offence, then the prosecution must prove that and every other specified element beyond reasonable doubt, in accordance with step (i) (2.3). In particular, the prosecution must actively prove any specifed mental elements, and those mental elements may not be presumed.[64]

(b) However, if mens rea is not specified in the statute but is instead an implied requirement, step (i) applies only to the actus reus. The mens rea will be presumed, once the prosecution has proved the actus reus, unless there is evidence suggesting that mens rea was lacking. In the absence of such evidence, the defendant has an *evidential* onus to point to evidence that suggests why there might be a reasonable doubt as to whether the mens rea element was present. The onus on the defendant is no more than evidential; once it is discharged, the prosecution must prove mens rea beyond reasonable doubt.

In *R v Strawbridge*,[65] the Court of Appeal recognised that the latter rule applies for crimes of implied mens rea. We shall return to its discussion in 5.2.2(2), once we have considered strict and absolute liability offences.

2.3.2 No presumption of intention

Proving mens rea is often difficult. It is impossible to look directly into the minds of defendants in order to know whether they had mens rea at the time of the offence. Usually, if the defendant does not confess to having it, the prosecution will be put to proving the relevant state of mind through supporting evidence, for example of the defendant's actions before, during, and after the actus reus occurred. Suppose that D is found to have shot V. If there is evidence that D planned the shooting in advance, this may be admissible to support the allegation that D's actions were intentional. The same is true if it is shown that D took careful aim at V's heart before pulling the trigger. In this case, proof by the prosecution that the prohibited harm (ie V's death) was a natural consequence of D's actions will support the inference that D intended it. Similarly, proof that the defendant foresaw the outcome (for example, because D knew the gun was loaded) may also help to support such a conclusion. Inferences of this variety depend on a recognition that there is no reasonable interpretation of the evidence other than that the defendant had mens rea.

But such inferences are a matter of evidence only. They are neither irrebuttable nor substantive rules of criminal law. In New Zealand, intention is a purely subjective concept, and any inference made from the evidence is *not* a presumption. For instance, it may be undermined by the fact that when D pointed the gun at V, she was too intoxicated to recognise the obvious consequence.[66] Where the prosecution is obliged to prove mens rea, it must do so beyond reasonable doubt. Supporting evidence (for example of foresight) is simply a part of what the

---

64 *R v Strawbridge* [1970] NZLR 909 (CA), 915.
65 *R v Strawbridge* [1970] NZLR 909 (CA), 915. See 5.2.2(2).
66 *R v Kamipeli* [1975] 2 NZLR 610 (CA), 617. Contrast the English case *DPP v Smith* [1961] AC 290, also reported as *R v Smith* [1960] 3 All ER 161 (HL), which held that (i) if the reasonable person would have foreseen that outcome, then the defendant must be taken to have done so; and (ii) if the defendant foresaw it, then he intended it. *Smith* was later reversed in the United Kingdom by legislation, and the Privy Council treated it as wrongly decided in *Frankland and Moore v R* [1987] AC 576; [1987] 2 WLR 1251 (PC).

prosecution may show in order to convince the court that, in light of all the evidence, it may safely conclude beyond reasonable doubt that D had the required mens rea.[67]

---

[67] Cf R v Noel [1960] NZLR 212 (CA), 215, 216.

Chapter 3

THE ACTUS REUS

3.1	Introduction	42
3.2	The behaviour element	43
3.2.1	Behaviour and omissions	43
(1)	*Why omissions are special*	44
(2)	*Exceptions*	45
(3)	*Statutory restrictions: offences that cannot be committed by omission*	49
(4)	*Omissions and consequences: causation*	51
(5)	*Distinguishing acts from omissions*	51
3.2.2	Crimes with no (explicit) behaviour element	52
(1)	*Crimes involving states of affairs*	53
(2)	*Crimes of possession*	55
3.3	Consequences: the need for causation	56
3.3.1	Rule of thumb	57
3.3.2	Causation in law	58
(1)	*Significant cause*	59
(2)	*Causal salience*	59
(3)	*Multiple causes*	60
3.3.3	Intervening causes	61
(1)	*Natural events*	61
(2)	*Other persons*	62
(3)	*The victim*	73
(4)	*Summary of approach to intervening causes*	74
3.3.4	Omissions	75
(1)	*As causes*	75
(2)	*As interventions*	76
(3)	*Two case studies*	78
3.4	The requirement of voluntariness	79
3.4.1	Involuntary behaviour	81
(1)	*Loss of physical control*	81
(2)	*Impaired consciousness*	81
(3)	*Imperfect deliberative capacity?*	84
(4)	*Insane automatism*	85
3.4.2	Omissions, states of affairs, and possession	85
(1)	*States of affairs*	86
(2)	*Possession*	87

(3)   *Distinction between impossibility and ignorance of duty*..........88
3.4.3   Involuntariness: responsibility by antecedent fault..........88
(1)   *Involuntariness and antecedent fault in strict liability offences*..........89
3.4.4   Evidential issues..........90

3.1 Introduction

In chapter 1 we discussed some of the reasons why a person cannot and should not be guilty of a crime unless both (i) he has caused or is otherwise responsible for the external event prohibited by law — the actus reus — and (ii) he had a specified mental state (falling within the requirements of the particular crime) with respect to that external event — the mens rea. If D kills P, she may have brought about the actus reus of murder, but it does not follow that she has committed any offence. When the doctor gives a painkiller to her patient, who turns out to be unknowably allergic to it, she may kill that patient: but it is an accident, and no criminal liability will follow. The mens rea is missing. Conversely, if she administers the drug intending it to kill him, and he dies of an unrelated heart attack, she does not murder him.[1] The actus reus is missing. In the next two chapters, we investigate the orthodox general principles of criminal law regarding these two elements. It is convenient to begin here with the actus reus.

The actus reus of a crime is that part of the definition which does not refer to the defendant's mental state. It can usefully be divided into three types of ingredient: behaviour, consequences, and circumstances. Often the circumstances or consequences surrounding something the defendant does are relevant to her wrongdoing, and so the offence does not just turn on D's behaviour. It is an essential part of our concept of murder, for instance, that someone dies. Thus the victim's death — a consequence — is a constitutive part of the actus reus of murder in the Crimes Act 1961. Such offences are sometimes called "result crimes"[2] because they cannot be committed unless the defendant's actions cause the specified result or consequence actually to occur.

An example of a crime requiring *circumstances* is bigamy, which involves D's going through a marriage ceremony (the behaviour) while being married to someone else (the circumstance). It is important to realise that since specification of the actus reus of each offence differs, and is a matter for the Legislature to decide,[3] there is no requirement that all three types of ingredient be present in the actus reus of each offence. Hence the actus reus of murder — ie the killing of one person by another — requires that there be (i) some (unspecified) behaviour on the part of the defendant with (ii) the consequence that another person dies. By contrast, the actus reus of rape is made out if there is (i) behaviour (sexual intercourse) by the defendant with the victim, in (ii) circumstances where the victim does not consent to it. No consequence is necessary.

---

1   *R v White* [1910] 2 KB 124; [1908-10] All ER Rep 340 (CCA).
2   The term is from Gordon, *The Criminal Law of Scotland* (2nd ed), Edinburgh, Green for the Scottish Universities Law Institute, 1978, 63.
3   Bearing in mind the sorts of constraints mentioned in the previous chapters, for example constraints of ordinary language (2.2) and political morality (1.3.1).

3.2 The behaviour element

Normally, the actus reus doctrine requires an action of some sort; something *done* by the defendant. This is not always obvious. It might sometimes appear as though result crimes such as murder could be specified solely by reference to the consequence, and without the actus reus containing any behavioural element. Thus it is the outcome which is emphasised in Kenny's definition of actus reus: "such result of human conduct as the law seeks to prevent."[4] And consider, for instance, the crime of murder. Surely it is the result, death, which is central to that crime? V's death is the harmful result that, as Kenny puts it, the law seeks to prevent. Without that death, murder is not and cannot be committed. The relevant harm has not occurred.

But the view that it is only the consequence or result that matters is not quite right. The law is not concerned with deaths *per se*, but rather with deaths that other people bring about: "a dead man with a knife in his back is not the actus reus of a murder. It is putting the knife in the back thereby causing the death that is the actus reus."[5] Correspondingly, s 158 Crimes Act 1961 defines homicide not as "the death of a human being", but as "the killing of a human being by another". The result *is* important: it helps to mark out what type of wrongdoing the law is concerned with. Indeed, it is the nature of the result, rather than of the behaviour which causes it, that gives homicide its special moral and social significance. Murder is murder whether done by knife or poison, and this is why the behaviour element of the actus reus is unspecific. But it exists all the same.

On the other hand, it is possible for an actus reus to consist *only* of behaviour. This is especially true of inchoate crimes, such as incitement and attempt, where there is no requirement that the incitement be effective or that the attempt be successful.[6] Crimes of this type are sometimes termed "conduct crimes", since the actus reus requires proof only of specified conduct by the defendant and does not specify any particular circumstances or consequences.

3.2.1 Behaviour and omissions

Where behaviour is an element of the actus reus, standard legal doctrine stipulates that the behaviour requirement is a requirement of positive action by the defendant. Except occasionally, an omission will not do. Thus it is a crime for D deliberately to drown P, but no crime for D gleefully to stand on the beach and watch while his enemy, P, is caught in the tide and drowns nearby.[7]

This standard doctrine in fact comprises two rules. First, behaviour specified in an actus reus can prima facie be satisfied only by a positive act on the part of the defendant, and not by the defendant's omission. Secondly, there are certain exceptions to the first, prima facie rule. These exceptions usually arise when the defendant has a *duty* to intervene and prevent the prohibited harm from occurring, whereupon his failure to do so counts as an omission satisfying the

---

4   Turner, *Kenny's Outlines of Criminal Law* (19th ed), Cambridge, Cambridge University Press, 1966, 17.
5   Smith and Hogan, 31.
6   Ch 8.
7   Cf Stephen, *A Digest of the Criminal Law (Indictable Offences) (4th ed)*, London, Macmillan & Co, 1887, art 213. Other writing includes Glazebrook, "Criminal omissions: The duty requirement in offences against the person" (1960) 76 LQR 386; Hughes, "Criminal Omissions" (1958) 67 Yale LJ 590; Ashworth, "The Scope of Criminal Liability for Omissions" (1989) 105 LQR 424.

behavioural element of that actus reus. The first rule is general in nature: the exceptions, and the duties upon which they are based, are specific and confined.

In the above approach the criminal law resembles the civil law, which is generally averse to imposing liability for omissions,[8] and is willing to do so only in special cases where the reasons in favour are strong enough to override that aversion. The distinction between misfeasance and non-feasance is, as Fleming has said, "deeply rooted in the common law".[9] Civil law duties to intervene depend on, for example, the defendant's having created the risk[10] or in some other way having assumed responsibility for it.[11] Similarly, an omission to reject a contractual offer cannot constitute its acceptance.[12] Silence is no representation in the tort of deceit;[13] neither is it per se a misrepresentation when negotiating a contract.[14]

(1)   *Why omissions are special*

One might, of course, accept that the law often does distinguish between acts and omissions, but still ask why that distinction *should* make any practical difference to criminal liability. There are various reasons. One is based on considerations of autonomy. We value living in a society where citizens are respected as individuals — where they are free to live their own lives and pursue their own priorities without having their choices determined by legal duties to act or intervene. The prohibition of omissions is far more intrusive upon individuals' autonomy and freedom than is the prohibition of acts, which is why the systematic imposition of (criminal or civil) liability for failures to act is to be resisted.[15]

This is not to suggest that there should never be liability for omissions. Those writers who advocate a criminal law duty of easy rescue, for example, have at least an arguable case.[16] Rather, the present argument is that liability for omissions should be exceptional and not as widespread as liability for actions. At any moment in time, the number of positive actions we are doing is

---

8   Per Lord Keith in *Yuen Kun Yeu v A-G of Hong Kong* [1988] AC 175, 192, there is no liability in negligence "on the part of one who sees another about to walk over a cliff with his head in the air, and forbears to shout a warning". Cf *Hill v Chief Constable of West Yorkshire* [1989] AC 53; [1987] 1 All ER 1173; *Curran v Northern Ireland Co-ownership Housing Assn Ltd* [1987] AC 718; [1987] 2 All ER 13; *Quinn v Hill* [1957] ALR 1127, [1957] VR 439, 1133; 446; *East Suffolk Rivers Catchment Board v Kent* [1941] AC 74; [1940] 4 All ER 527; *Gautret v Egerton* (1867) LR 2 CP 371, 375. According to Salmond and Heuston, *The Law of Torts* (20th ed), London, Sweet & Maxwell, 1992, 224, "in the absence of some existing duty the general principle is that there is no liability for a mere omission to act".
9   Fleming, *The Law of Torts* (8th ed), Sydney, Law Book Co, 1992, 146.
10 *Johnson v Rea Ltd* [1962] 1 QB 373; [1961] 1 WLR 1400; *Racine v CNR* [1923] 2 DLR 572.
11 For example *Horsley v MacLaren* (1971) 22 DLR (3d) 545; [1972] SCR 441.
12 *Felthouse v Bindley* (1862) 11 CB (NS) 869; 142 ER 1037; cf *Allied Marine Transport Ltd v Vale do Rio Doce Navegacao SA, The Leonidas* [1985] 2 All ER 796 (CA).
13 *Peek v Gurney* (1873) LR 6 HL 377; [1861-73] All ER Rep 116, 392, 403; 124, 128; *Arkwright v Newbold* (1881) 17 Ch D 301, 318; *Lietzke (Installations) Pty Ltd v EMJ Morgan Pty Ltd* (1973) 5 SASR 88.
14 *Fox v Mackreth* (1788) 2 Cox Eq Cas 320, 321; *Keates v Earl of Cadogan* (1851) 10 CB 591; 138 ER 234; *Bell v Lever Bros Ltd* [1932] AC 161; [1931] All ER Rep 1, 227, 33.
15 See, very generally, Simester, "Why omissions are special" (1995) 1 Legal Theory 311; also the earlier discussion in 1.3.2(2), 1.3.2(5). There is philosophical controversy whether the act-omission distinction, of and by itself, is morally significant. Nonetheless, it is worth observing that acts usually manifest a greater level of hostility than do omissions, and we tend to feel very differently about killers than about non-savers. Omissions are often incidental to the defendant's practical deliberations — they disclose a different and lesser fault, of limited imagination or empathy, rather than malice.
16 See, eg, Ashworth, "The Scope of Criminal Liability for Omissions" (1989) 105 LQR 424; Hughes, "Criminal Omissions" (1958) 67 Yale LJ 590.

very small. But the number of things we are failing to do is enormous. This is because there are very few ways in which one can do an action, whereas the number of ways in which one can fail to do something is much greater. For example, while D is not saving the drowning swimmer she may be walking, reading a book, swimming herself, playing cricket, etc. But she cannot do any of these things while she *is* saving the swimmer. The burden the law imposes when it prohibits a person from doing something is therefore lighter and less intrusive than when it orders that person to act. Enforced forbearance involves the sacrifice of fewer options, and is more likely to leave the defendant with a chance of conforming to law without significant derangement. "Compare being banished to Liechtenstein with being banished from Liechtenstein."[17] Or, in a more apposite example, compare being prohibited from drowning the other swimmers when sunbathing at a beach to being required to save (or, indeed, drown) them. Wholesale liability for omissions would force us constantly to interrupt our own actions and plans in order to prevent outcomes that are brought about by others: to become, in effect, our brothers' keepers. It would be incompatible with New Zealand's political nature as a liberal State.

A second consideration is that if prohibited omissions involve the sacrifice of more options, then they are also likely to require a greater sacrifice of our own interests. If D buys a piece of furniture for his home, why is he not held responsible for the lives that money would save in, say, Ethiopia? One factor is our widespread acceptance that people are to some extent entitled to prefer their own interests, and the interests of those near to them, above the interests of others. A mother who gives her own child pocket money warrants no reproof when she does not do the same for the child next door. Of course, such a view may be no more than a moral mistake. But if so, it is an inescapable feature of our society, and the law must bow to its almost universal acceptance. Moreover, given that individuals exist in different and specific situations, they are typically better placed to assess and contribute to their own lives, and to the lives of those they know, than to the lives of strangers. These points help to explain examples where someone does not save starving children in foreign countries: they limit the extent to which the needs of strangers take precedence over and mandate the sacrifice of our own plans and interests. We cannot do everything, and it would be absurd to expect us to try. When making decisions, we are entitled to acknowledge that our own lives, and the lives of people we are close to, are important to us. So, even apart from questions of autonomy, the law's adoption of the act-omission doctrine can be justified as a simple and workable means by which the law can recognise the priority individuals are entitled to accord the content of their own lives.

(2)   *Exceptions*

(a)   Specific statutory offences

Many statutes now contain offences which expressly impose liability for an omission. Often these are offences which can *only* be committed by omission, such as failing to provide a breath specimen, or failing to file a return to the Inland Revenue Department or the Companies Office. Such offences involve specific reference to a behavioural element on the part of the defendant. A second variety of statutory crime which can be done, indirectly, by omission is

---

17   Bennett, "Morality and consequences" in McMurrin (ed), *The Tanner Lectures on Human Values*, vol 2, Salt Lake City, University of Utah Press, 1981, 45, 78; cf Bennett, *The Act Itself*, Oxford, Clarendon Press, 1995, 93. A similar principle applies in the context of false imprisonment: *Bird v Jones* (1845) 7 QB 742; 115 ER 668.

that where the actus reus names no behavioural element at all, and requires only proof of certain events or circumstances.[18] (We discuss this type of offence in 3.2.2.) Characteristically, offences of this latter sort are an indirect imposition of liability for D's omission to prevent the specified event or outcome occurring. Of course, in these cases liability will also lie for bringing the outcome about by a positive act. But no such act is *required*.

In the context of homicide, the Crimes Act 1961 has enacted certain specific categories of liability for omission. Because they overlap with the duties existing at common law, these will be noted where relevant in the discussion below.[19]

(b)   Duties imposed on persons in a special relationship to the victim

Sometimes, even without a specific offence, the law holds that considerations such as autonomy and self-interest are outweighed. This occurs when the defendant is found to be under a more general legal duty, such as the duty of parents to their children. A stranger can stand by and watch a child starve or drown. But that child's parent cannot.

The law does not normally require us to be guardians of the interests of others. But parents already *are* the guardians of their children, and are responsible for their welfare. The law does no more than reflect that by imposing a legal duty upon parents to intervene on behalf of their children. In the context of homicide, these particular duties are expressly reflected in the Crimes Act 1961. Section 152, for example, sets out a duty of parents to provide the necessaries of life to their children.[20] It must be remarked, however, that the duties of parents are more wide-ranging than this. A parent's failure to effect an easy rescue of her child would count as the actus reus of murder even though it is scarcely a failure to supply "necessaries". And more generally, a parent who willingly permits another to assault his child (when he can prevent this happening) is himself guilty of an assault.[21]

So a parent has a duty to rescue his child from harm. But is this so if the child is 30? Where the child is no longer dependent on her parents, a special relationship still exists between them, but it no longer involves the same commitment to responsibility for the child's welfare.[22] The latter is surely the more important feature. Thus, it is submitted, parents do not ordinarily owe legal duties to their adult children.[23] Neither do children owe such duties to their parents. This is not to deny that people have moral obligations to their relatives. But it is quite a different matter to hold them criminally liable for failing to discharge those obligations.

The view that, rather than the closeness of their emotional or other relationship, it is D's responsibility for V's welfare that is the decisive feature is reflected in s 151. This section places a duty to provide the necessaries of life on the shoulders of those with "charge" of anyone "unable ... to provide himself with the necessaries of life". The same view ties in also with

---

18 For example, the offence in *Finau v Dept of Labour* [1984] 2 NZLR 396 (CA).
19 To the extent that these statutory provisions do not exhaust the scope of corresponding common law duties, the common law duties will continue also to apply: *R v Lunt* [2004] 1 NZLR 498, (2003) 20 CRNZ 681 (CA). The provisions appear to be capable of applying to other offences. See, for example, 17.5.
20 Cf ss 151 and 154; also, at common law, *R v Gibbins and Proctor* (1918) 13 Cr App R 134 (CCA).
21 Cf *R v Emery* (1993) 14 Cr App R (S) 394; *R v Russell* [1933] ALR 76; [1933] VLR 59. See also the discussion of *R v Brough* 27/2/97, CA507/96 and *R v Witika* [1993] 2 NZLR 424; (1992) 9 CRNZ 272 (CA) at 6.4.3.
22 Cf s 152, the application of which terminates when the child reaches the age of 16 years; also *R v Ridley* (1811) 2 Camp 650, 652.
23 *R v Smith* (1826) 2 C & P 449; 172 ER 203; *R v Shepherd* (1862) 9 Cox CC 123; contra *R v Chattaway* (1922) 17 Cr App R 7.

the case law regarding legal duties owed toward someone who is in the defendant's care. In *R v Stone and Dobinson*,[24] S and his mistress D (both somewhat backward) were held to have assumed responsibility for the care of S's sister, who died from a combination of anorexia nervosa and their incompetent neglect. *Both* were convicted of manslaughter, irrespective of the fact that only S was related to V.[25]

It would seem that a marriage or similar relationship contains, by its nature, a mutual obligation to protect one's spouse or partner. In *R v Russell*, R's wife had drowned herself and their sons while R was present. R was convicted of the manslaughter of not only the sons but also the wife.[26] Presumably that responsibility would not extend to a mere sexual relationship.[27]

(c)   Duties imposed on persons assuming a particular responsibility

The cases discussed so far have been concerned with duties arising from a wide-ranging and unspecific responsibility for another's welfare. Such duties tend to be general in nature, with the result that the criminal law treats omissions like actions for most purposes. A more complex relationship is that between the doctor and her patient.[28] This duty is a confined one — a doctor on her way home may drive past the scene of an accident without attracting criminal liability for doing so. The duty applies only to the patients in her care. In such cases, injury resulting from the doctor's failure to provide proper care is regarded by the criminal law just as if it were brought about by an act of improper treatment.

Even to her patients, however, the doctor's duty is not all-encompassing. She may not kill by positive act, but it appears that she may withdraw care, with judicial approval, from a patient in a persistent vegetative state.[29] The duty is not to keep the patient alive, but to make reasonable efforts to do so, consonant with proper medical practice,[30] and only insofar as doing so is in the patient's best interests.[31]

---

24   *R v Stone and Dobinson* [1977] QB 354; [1977] 2 All ER 341 (CA). Arguably, the court's finding of an assumed responsibility was doubtful on the facts; see Ashworth, "The Scope of Criminal Liability for Omissions" (1989) 105 LQR 424, 443. The case is also unsatisfactory on questions of causation (did the neglect make any difference?) and of gross negligence (given the couple's intellectual limitations; see 4.6.2).
25   Cf *R v West London Coroner, ex p Gray* [1988] QB 467; [1987] 2 All ER 129; *R v Conde* (1867) 10 Cox CC 547; *R v MacDonald* [1904] St R Qd 151; *R v Foster* (1906) 26 NZLR 1254 (CA); *R v Instan* [1893] 1 QB 450; *R v Marriott* (1838) 8 C & P 425; 173 ER 559; *R v Nicholls* (1874) 13 Cox CC 75; *R v Bubb* (1850) 4 Cox CC 455. See Williams, "Criminal omissions - The conventional view" (1991) 107 LQR 86, 90. A valuable and wide-ranging discussion may be found in *R v Taktak* (1988) 14 NSWLR 226; 34 A Crim R 334.
26   *R v Russell* [1933] ALR 76; [1933] VLR 59 (McArthur J dissenting).
27   Cf *People v Beardsley* 113 NW 1128 (1907); discussed by Hughes, "Criminal Omissions" (1958) 67 Yale LJ,590 624. Or, nowadays, to an estranged spouse: contra *R v Plummer* (1844) 1 Car & K 600; 174 ER 954. In *R v Smith* [1979] Crim LR 251 (CA) the Court of Appeal assumed that the institution of marriage did not of itself generate a duty of care between spouses. See France, "The law of omissions - Proposals for reform" (1992) 7 Otago LR 625.
28   Cf s 155. For another example of role-based responsibility, see *R v Curtis* (1885) 15 Cox CC 746 (duty of a local authority officer to provide medical assistance to a destitute person).
29   *Auckland Area Health Board v A-G* [1993] 1 NZLR 235; (1992) 8 CRNZ 634; *Airedale NHS Trust v Bland* [1993] AC 789; [1993] 1 All ER 821 (HL). See also the case note by Finnis, "Bland: Crossing the Rubicon?" (1993) 109 LQR 329.
30   Cf *TBCL*, 236.

Another source of specific criminal law duties is civil law obligations. The classic case is *R v Pittwood*.[32] D had been employed by a railway company to keep the gate at a level crossing. He went to lunch forgetting to close the gate. A haycart subsequently entered the crossing and was struck by a train. D was convicted of manslaughter. It is not clear whether D's duty depended on his having been hired to discharge a duty to the public that was owed by his employers,[33] or was grounded on the fact that he was hired to protect other people and that they were likely to be injured by his dereliction. The latter seems to have been the rationale adopted by Wright J.[34] Either way, however, cases such as *Pittwood* will now usually fall within the scope of s 157, which establishes a legal duty whenever D "undertakes" to do an act the omission of which may be dangerous to life.

(d)   The continuing act doctrine

Sometimes a defendant brings about an actus reus without mens rea but then, while the harmful consequences continue, intentionally omits to remedy or discontinue them. In such cases the "continuing act" doctrine may be applied, and liability imposed without the need to find a legal duty owed by the defendant.[35] In *Fagan v MPC*,[36] F accidentally drove onto a policeman's foot. When apprised of his action, he refused to move the car. He was convicted of assault on the basis that his refusal to remove the vehicle amounted to a continuation of the original (positive) act of battery[37] and was not a mere omission. Hence it could satisfy the actus reus requirement.

A similar case is *R v Kaitamaki*.[38] D had sexual intercourse with V without her consent. D's evidence was that he became aware V was not consenting only after penetration had occurred. However, he did not then withdraw from intercourse. The trial judge directed the jury that "if, having realised she is not willing, he continues with the act of intercourse, it then becomes rape". On appeal, the Privy Council affirmed the correctness of the direction.[39]

(e)   Duties imposed on persons with a special relationship to the harm

In *R v Miller*,[40] a vagrant set fire to his mattress with a cigarette while sleeping. He awoke to find the mattress smouldering. Without taking any steps to extinguish the fire, he simply moved to the next room and went to sleep. The house itself caught fire, and he was charged with

---

31 *Airedale NHS Trust v Bland* [1993] AC 789; [1993] 1 All ER 821 (HL), 868, 869; 869, 870 (Lord Goff). See also the difficult cases involving the degree of care owed by doctors to handicapped neonates: *Arthur* (1981) 12 BMLR 1; *Re B (1981)* [1990] 3 All ER 927; *Re F (Mental Patient: Sterilisation)* [1990] 2 AC 1 (HL).

32 *R v Pittwood* (1902) 19 TLR 37. See also *R v Hughes* (1857) Dears & B 248; 169 ER 996; approved in *R v Roberts* [1942] 1 All ER 187 (CCA), 192; *Kelly v R* [1923] VLR 704 (SC Vic), 708 (reversed on a different ground in (1923) 32 CLR 509 (HCA)).

33 Cf *R v Smith* (1869) 11 Cox CC 210, where a watchman who deserted his post was held not liable for manslaughter because his employer had no duty to provide a watchman. The decision is criticised by Turner in *Kenny's Outlines of Criminal Law* (17th ed), Cambridge, Cambridge University Press, 1958, 169.

34 "the man was paid to keep the gate shut and protect the public ... A man might incur criminal liability from a duty arising out of contract": *R v Pittwood* (1902) 19 TLR 37, 38.

35 Cf, in contract, the law governing a representation which later becomes false but where the change of circumstances is not disclosed: *With v O'Flanagan* [1936] Ch 575; [1936] 1 All ER 727 (CA) ("continuing representation").

36 *Fagan v MPC* [1969] 1 QB 439; [1968] 3 All ER 442.

37 Which had not itself been an assault because F lacked mens rea at that time.

38 *R v Kaitamaki* [1984] 1 NZLR 385, also reported as *Kaitamaki v R* (1984) 1 CRNZ 211; [1985] AC 147 (PC), 386; 212; 151. See also *R v Cooper and Schaub* [1994] Crim LR 531.

39 Note that this doctrine involves continuing an earlier *act*. There is no parallel common-law doctrine of continuing omission: cf *Nicholson v Dept of Social Welfare* [1999] 3 NZLR 50 (CA).

arson. Although the English Court of Appeal upheld his conviction on the basis of a continuing act, the House of Lords took an alternative approach. It acknowledged that the arson had been committed by M's knowing omission to deal with the fire, and held that this omission could satisfy the actus reus requirement because M's unintentional starting of the fire *created* a legal duty. The duty is "to take measures that lie within one's power to counteract a danger that one has oneself created".[41] The relevant sorts of "danger" are those which threaten an interest protected by the criminal law — thus the duty arises where, unless D intervenes, his earlier (positive) act will bring about the actus reus.

Note that a defendant's subsequent failure to prevent the risk will not by itself constitute an offence — it must be accompanied by such other elements of the offence as are required, for example mens rea.

It is important to distinguish the basis of liability in *Miller* from the continuing act doctrine (3.2.1(2)(d)). The approach taken in *Miller* is generally to be preferred, and indeed *Fagan* can itself be explained as a case where D created the harm and therefore had a duty to counteract that harm.[42] Nonetheless, it is sometimes necessary to rely on the continuing act doctrine. Because *Miller* imposes liability for an omission, it is inapplicable to those offences that cannot be committed by omission, ie where the terms of the offence exclude liability for omissions. Offences of this type are the subject of the next section.

(3) *Statutory restrictions: offences that cannot be committed by omission*

Some offences exclude liability for omissions by specifying the particular type of behaviour that is required. For example, s 199 creates an offence of, among other things, "throwing" acid. It would seem that this manner of behaving can only be done by a positive act. Similarly, the actus reus of rape and other forms of sexual violation requires an active sexual connection with the victim; an omission cannot suffice.[43]

In these offences, liability for omissions is restricted because the behavioural element of the actus reus has been specified quite precisely by statute. Conversely, omission-based liability should normally be possible where an offence has an unspecific behaviour element, and its actus reus is defined mainly by reference to consequences or circumstances. An example of this is "homicide", in s 158, which is defined as "the killing of a human being by another, directly or indirectly, by any means whatsoever" — in essence, as the causing of death by D.

Homicide is a clear case. It is settled law that culpable homicide can be committed by omission.[44] But what about other offences? Assault, for example, is defined inter alia as the act of intentionally applying force to the person of another. Can this be done by omission? *Adams* is doubtful,[45] a view France shares:[46]

---

40 *R v Miller* [1983] 2 AC 161; [1983] 1 All ER 978 (HL). Cf Smith [1982] Crim LR 527; Williams (letter to the editor) [1982] Crim LR 773. For an extension of this type of case see *R v Speck* [1977] 2 All ER 859; (1977) 65 Cr App R 161 (CA), in which D was convicted of gross indecency because he passively allowed an 8-year-old girl to touch him indecently.

41 *R v Miller* [1983] 2 AC 161; [1983] 1 All ER 978 (HL), 176; 981.

42 Where necessary, however, the two cases can be distinguished, since (unlike *Miller*) in *Fagan* the actus reus had already occurred by the time D acquired mens rea.

43 Section 128.

44 Cf s 160(2)(b); *R v Gibbins and Proctor* (1918) 13 Cr App R 134 (CCA).

45 "The requirement of an 'act' suggests that assault can never be committed by a mere omission": *Adams*, CA196.05 (looseleaf).

49

"Assault is defined as *the act* of intentionally applying force to the person of another. Such a definition leaves little scope for assault by omission although factually it is very easy to conceive of such an event. One who intentionally leaves a leg out to see V fall over it knowing V has not seen the danger surely assaults V as much as by putting the leg out to trip V. The section, however, by employing the term 'act' would not embrace this conduct."

But no authority is cited. With respect to these authors, it seems implausible to say that a parent who intentionally trips his child in the way France describes cannot be convicted of assault. He certainly ought to be. It is submitted that where an offence is unspecific as to the manner of behaviour required, it should be possible to commit that offence by omission. The fact that an offence is defined in terms of "action", as such, should not be determinative. This is especially since positive action is the default requirement of offences with a behavioural element anyway — the entire sphere of omissions liability is predicated on an exception from that requirement.

Sometimes, as we have seen, the action requirement *is* excluded by linguistic considerations. It would be unfair to convict a defendant for conduct the statutory language clearly excludes.[47] But such instances are and should be rare. There is no judicial compunction about saying that a parent can kill a child by failing to feed it, however odd that might sound,[48] and it is submitted that mere linguistic variations, which do not reflect valid moral principles or distinctions, should normally not pre-empt the possibility of liability for omissions.

If such harms as "killing", "wounding",[49] and "injuring"[50] can be done by omission, and if the difference between various offences over whether one can be convicted for an omission is not to be arbitrary and piecemeal, then a coherent general approach should be taken. Unless the Legislature has demonstrated a contrary intention by specifying the particular manner of behaviour in which the offence must be committed, a criminal offence should be capable of being committed by omission. This is the only approach capable of producing predictable and consistent rather than random law. Any concern over the width of that approach should be tempered by the realisation that the defendant would have to be under a legal duty to act, and that mens rea would still have to be proved.

One important point to emphasise is that, even where omission-based liability is excluded by the terms of the offence, a conviction may still be obtained under the continuing act doctrine (3.2.1(2)(d)). Suppose that D and V are having consensual sexual intercourse, and that sexual connection has already occurred. During intercourse, V withdraws her consent. D, however,

---

46 France, "The law of omissions - Proposals for reform" (1992) 7 Otago LR 625, 628.
47 See the fair warning discussion in 2.1.3. (An example might be arson in s 294, which requires that the defendant "sets fire to" the item in question.) For this reason Williams argues in a letter to the editor of the *Criminal Law Review* that "the courts should not create liability for omissions without statutory authority. Verbs used in defining offences and prima facie implying active conduct should not be stretched by interpretation to include omissions": [1982] Crim LR 773. See also his "Criminal omissions - The conventional view" (1991) 107 LQR 86, 87-89 and "What should the Code do about omissions" (1987) 7 LS 92, 94, 95.
48 And for other examples, see *R v Shama* [1990] 2 All ER 602; [1990] 1 WLR 661; *R v Firth* (1990) 91 Cr App R 217; [1990] Crim LR 326.
49 Cf s 188 (wounding with intent), which is expressed in causal terms *simpliciter*, without any restriction regarding the manner of D's behaviour.
50 Section 2(1) Crimes Act 1961, merely "to cause actual bodily harm".

remains in a state of sexual connection with V. His failure to withdraw is a continuation of the original act of having sexual connection with V. Since it is no longer consented to, he commits the actus reus of rape.[51]

(4) *Omissions and consequences: causation*

One problem that arises for omissions is whether or not they can be said to "cause" things. Characteristically, what is significant about omissions is that they fail to prevent *other* factors from bringing about the harm. If D watches from the beach while V drowns, a post-mortem will conclude that V's death was caused by excessive time underwater. D merely failed to intervene: can she truly be said to have caused V's death? We shall consider this question more fully in 3.3.4, when we discuss causation. But it is clear that in the law, omissions can be causes — or perhaps one should say, causal factors. If D could have saved V, then her failure to do so was *a* reason why V died. And if D had a legal duty to save her, then that failure will be a cause of death in law.

(5) *Distinguishing acts from omissions*

Given that, as we have seen, there is normally no liability for omissions, it is important to be able to distinguish acts from omissions in order to decide whether a defendant's behaviour counts as one or the other. Unfortunately, the line between them is not easily drawn:[52]

> "If a doctor is keeping a patient alive by cranking the handle of a machine and he stops, this looks like a clear case of omission. So too if the machine is electrically operated but switches itself off every 24 hours and the doctor deliberately does not re-start it. Switching off a functioning machine looks like an act; but is it any different in substance from the first two cases? On the other hand, is it any different from cutting the high-wire on which a tight-rope walker is balancing? — which is an act, if ever there was one. Is the ending of a programme of dialysis an omission, while switching off a ventilator is an act? Is the discontinuance of a drip feed, which is keeping a patient alive, by withdrawing the tube from his body an act? and failure to replace an emptied bag an omission? It seems offensive if liability for homicide depends on distinctions of this kind; but it appears to be so."

Why is switching off a ventilator an act, and failing to (re)start it an omission? The difference seems to be that the former *requires* certain bodily movements, whereas the latter does not. Switching the ventilator off can be done in only one way,[53] but failing to switch the ventilator on (or off) can be done while doing any number of things — one might be talking to the nurse, reading a journal, taking a walk, booking dinner at a restaurant, etc. Similarly, cranking the handle of a machine and cutting the high-wire are actions because they require very specific behaviour by D: "not cranking the handle" and "not replacing the emptied bag" are not specific about D's behaviour at all.

---

51 R *v Kaitamaki* [1984] 1 NZLR 385, also reported as *Kaitamaki v* R (1984) 1 CRNZ 211; [1985] AC 147 (PC).
52 Smith and Hogan, 86-87. See, in respect of the examples, Williams, *TBCL*, 236, 237; Kennedy, "Switching off life support machines: The legal implications" [1977] Crim LR 443; Benyan, "Doctors as murderers" [1982] Crim LR 17.
53 Or, at most, in only a few ways.

As we saw earlier, this difference is an important facet of the rationale for separating omissions from acts when it comes to criminalisation. Prohibiting omissions rules out many more options than does prohibiting acts. If D is enjoined by law not to strike V, that leaves him with plenty of freedom for legal movement of his arm, not to mention the rest of his body. But if D is *required* to strike V (ie prohibited from omitting to do so) then his freedom of movement is severely curtailed. His options are down to one.

The difference is legally irrelevant, however, where the defendant is held responsible for the actus reus through the existence of a legal duty. With this in mind, we should reconsider Smith and Hogan's remark that "[i]t seems offensive if liability for homicide depends on distinctions of this kind; but it appears to be so". The obvious response is that liability does not *just* depend on the act/omission distinction, but also on the issue in each case whether D is under a duty to intervene. What the examples do suggest, though, is that one might be doubtful of the judicial reasoning in life-and-death medical cases. In *Airedale NHS Trust v Bland*,[54] B had been in a persistent vegetative state for 3 ½ years without medical hope of improvement. Having obtained parental consent, the hospital applied for a declaration that it would be lawful to discontinue artificial feeding and hydration, with the intention that B should be allowed to die. The House of Lords upheld the declaration. Their Lordships affirmed that for the doctors to bring about B's death by lethal injection or suchlike would be murder, but reasoned that (i) what was proposed was an omission rather than an act, and (ii) the legal duty of the doctors did not extend to prolonging treatment of a patient when it was no longer in his best interests to do so.[55]

The difficulty with this reasoning is that ceasing treatment normally involves switching off a ventilator or other life-support machine. Notwithstanding that the House of Lords explicitly countenanced this step,[56] it is an act, not an omission. An intruder who does such a thing commits murder, even though she has no legal duty to save the patient's life. The true explanation of these cases must surely be that there is a limited justification available to doctors, in certain circumstances, to take some quite specific measures toward ending life. Those measures can include particular acts as well as omissions.

3.2.2 Crimes with no (explicit) behaviour element

Some academic writers have suggested that there can be no criminal liability without a "voluntary act" on the part of the defendant; meaning by this that there must be (i) a behavioural element specified in every actus reus, which (ii) must be done "voluntarily" by the defendant.[57] For the most part, the second aspect of this suggestion seems right (see 3.4). The first claim, however, is less plausible.

It is certainly true that crimes such as murder, rape, and assault — with which ordinary citizens are most familiar, and which have the greatest moral resonance — are crimes which require wrong*doing*, and necessarily involve some behaviour (whether act or omission) by the

---

54 *Airedale NHS Trust v Bland* [1993] AC 789; [1993] 1 All ER 821 (HL).
55 *Airedale NHS Trust v Bland* [1993] AC 789; [1993] 1 All ER 821 (HL), 866-868; 867-870 (Lord Goff).
56 *Airedale NHS Trust v Bland* [1993] AC 789; [1993] 1 All ER 821 (HL), 866; 867-868 (Lord Goff), 881-882; 881-883 (Lord Browne-Wilkinson). A similar criticism may be levelled at the underlying thinking in *R v Tarei* 5/8/05, Heath J, HC Tauranga CRI-2004-087-1673, where it was ruled that extubation or other "[w]ithdrawal of any form of life support does not cause death. Rather, it operates to prevent prolongation of life through artifical means". Such conduct is not a failure to prolong life: it is a positive act that causes death (albeit not the only one). See below, 16.2.3(3).

defendant. But many other crimes stipulate no behavioural element on the part of the defendant. These are offences which penalise a defendant on the basis of the situation in which she finds herself. It is the circumstances themselves which make up the harm that the criminal law is designed to address, and so it is possible to specify the actus reus of these crimes solely by reference to those circumstances.

For convenience, we can divide offences of this sort into two main types: crimes where the actus reus specifies only the occurrence of some state of affairs; and crimes of possession.

(1) *Crimes involving states of affairs*

Sometimes known as crimes of "situational liability",[58] these are crimes where the actus reus is simply an event or circumstance that is in some way connected to the defendant. An example is provided by s 57(2) Dog Control Act 1996:

> "The owner of a dog that makes an attack [on any person, stock, or poultry] commits an offence and is liable on summary conviction to a fine not exceeding $3000."

Here the actus reus of the offence is apparently complete without the need to prove any act or omission on the part of the defendant.

Of course, it is not enough for a defendant to be criminally liable for an offence just because something bad happens — for example, because a dog attacks another person. The defendant must in some way be connected to, and responsible for, the actus reus. Normally this connection is through his having a particular status, or relationship, with respect to that actus reus. If a dog attacks someone, it is only the dog's *owner* who is picked out for attention by the criminal law, and not, for instance, every person living on that street. Situational offences are in this respect similar to offences of omission, in that they raise the problem of attribution to defendants, discussed earlier (1.3.2(5)). The potential for over-broad criminalisation means that there is a need on the part of the legislator to contain liability by specifying only defendants who are responsible for, and in a position to control, the prohibited situation.

The requirement for a particular status or relationship is typically found in another type of situational liability, being the vicarious criminal liability sometimes imposed on employers for the acts of their employees. Vicarious liability is dealt with further in chapter 7.[59] A third form of connection may be seen in the notorious English case *R v Larsonneur*.[60] In that case, L was

---

57   For example, Stephen, *A History of the Criminal Law of England* vol II, London, Macmillan, 1883, 97; Cross and Jones, *An Introduction to Criminal Law* (3rd ed), London, Butterworths, 1953, 32; Turner, *Kenny's Outlines of Criminal Law* (17th ed), Cambridge, Cambridge University Press, 1958, 26, 27; O'Connor and Fairall, *Criminal Defences* (2nd ed), Sydney, Butterworths, 1988, 2, 6, 7; Moore, *Act and Crime: The Theory of Action and its Implications for Criminal Law*, Oxford, Clarendon Press, 1993, ch 3. The claim made is normally, in fact, even stronger: that there must be a positive (and voluntary) act by the defendant specified in every actus reus. The phrasing in the text is designed to allow for omissions.

58   Glazebrook, "Situational liability" in Glazebrook (ed), *Reshaping the Criminal Law: Essays in Honour of Glanville Williams*, London, Stevens, 1978, 108; Cohen, "The 'actus reus' and offences of 'situation' " (1972) 7 Israel LR 186. Crimes of this sort are sometimes ruled unconstitutional in the United States: *Robinson v California* 370 US 660; 8 L Ed 2d 758 (1962) (being addicted to narcotics); *Papachristou v City of Jacksonville* (1972) 405 US 156; 31 L Ed 2d 110 (being a vagrant).

59   See also 1.3.2(5).

60   *R v Larsonneur* (1933) 24 Cr App R 74; 149 LT 542 (CCA). See too *Winzar v Chief Constable of Kent* The Times, 28 March 1983; contrast that case with *Palmer-Brown v Police* [1985] 1 NZLR 365, also reported as *Palmer-Brown v Hohaia* (1984) 1 CRNZ 306 (CA); also *O'Sullivan v Fisher* [1954] SASR 33.

convicted of being found in the UK when permission for her to enter the country had previously been refused. It was, however, undisputed that the only reason for her being on UK soil was that she had been brought there against her will by the police. In convicting her of a situational liability offence, the law has picked out Larsonneur because it was she to whom the actus reus happened, and not because of anything she did.[61]

Larsonneur has been widely criticised, and rightly so.[62] But the proper reason for criticising it is less clear. One problem with the case is that the language used in many situational offences does not appear to require any mens rea or fault element on the part of the defendant, and thereby imposes what is known as *absolute liability*. This is an important criticism, and we shall return to it in chapter 5. But that has not been the only ground of opposition. Ashworth, for instance, once disapproved of "defining an offence in a way that seems to require no act by the defendant as a basis for liability".[63] The objection was that, quite apart from there being no mens rea element, there is no behavioural requirement in the actus reus. However, this is not a valid objection. There is nothing inherently defective or unjust about an offence which contains no behaviour element.

To see this, *Larsonneur* may be contrasted with the New Zealand case *Finau v Dept of Labour*,[64] where F was prosecuted under the Immigration Act 1964 for remaining in New Zealand after the expiry of her visitor's permit. The Court of Appeal upheld F's appeal against conviction on the basis that it had been impossible for her to leave the country, owing to her pregnancy and the consequent refusal of any airline to carry her.

At the level of principle, *Finau* and *Larsonneur* are inconsistent decisions. It is, of course, the former which is authoritative in New Zealand. Yet even at the more abstract level of principle, *Finau* is to be preferred. The result in that case demonstrates that there need be no injustice, and there is nothing intrinsically wrong, in criminalising states of affairs, so long as the class of potential defendants is clearly identified. What *Finau* does is to make clear a further proviso: that the defendant could have done something about it. The actus reus, although it specifies no act or omission, must still have been *voluntary*. More on this in 3.4. But it is the failure to observe *this* requirement which is the main problem with *Larsonneur* and (even apart from its inconsistency with *Finau*) the reason why that case should not be followed.

It is submitted that, unless there is a requirement of voluntariness, situational offences are at odds with the deepest presuppositions of the criminal law. The very notion of a trial, of a plea, assumes putative answerability for something. One is not answerable for a state of affairs (for example having red hair), and it should not be the actus reus of an offence, unless one is able to avoid that state of affairs (for example by shaving one's head or dyeing the hair another colour).

---

61   Though see Lanham, "*Larsonneur* revisited" [1976] Crim LR 276, who suggests the possibility of prior fault.
62   For example, Hall, *General Principles of Criminal Law* (2nd ed), Indianapolis, Bobbs-Merrill, 1960, 329, n 14; Williams, *CLGP*, 11; Howard, *Strict Responsibility*, London, Sweet & Maxwell, 1963, 47.
63   Ashworth, *Principles*, 105. Ashworth's discussion of *Larsonneur* has since been moderated, withdrawing the phrasing quoted here: *Principles of Criminal Law* (3rd ed), New York, Oxford University Press, 1999, § 4.3 (a).
64   *Finau v Dept of Labour* [1984] 2 NZLR 396 (CA); also with *Martin v State of Alabama* (1944) 17 So (2d) 427. Contrast the approach of the House of Lords in *Porter v Honey* [1988] 3 All ER 1045; [1988] 1 WLR 1420 (HL).

Where, by contrast with the facts of *Finau* and *Larsonneur*, the defendant *could* have prevented the actus reus from occurring, then situational liability is, in effect, very much like liability for voluntary omissions. Indirectly, it involves the defendant being prosecuted for her failure or omission to prevent the actus reus from happening. A case of this sort is *Tifaga v Dept of Labour*.[65] There D *was* convicted of overstaying, following the termination of his temporary entry permit, because his inability to leave the country was due to his own failure to retain sufficient funds to do so.

(2)   *Crimes of possession*

Possessory offences are a creation of statute. They are not found in the common law.[66] There are a number of such offences on the books, especially relating to drugs, and to weapons or tools of crime.[67] According to s 7 Misuse of Drugs Act 1975, for example, it is a crime for a person to "have in his possession ... any controlled drug". The offence makes no reference to the defendant's conduct.

Characteristically, possession is criminalised as a convenient substitute for the harm that is really objected to, being the *use* of the thing possessed. Criminalisation at the earlier stage both simplifies evidential issues and makes an offence out of behaviour which might otherwise not even count as an *attempt* to do the ultimate crime contemplated. Thus, if offences of this sort did not exist, the police would not be able to intervene at an early stage to prevent many crimes without the prospective offender's escaping the clutches of the criminal law. It is undesirable as well as wasteful of resources that they should have to wait until the contraband is actually used before making an arrest.[68]

In crimes of possession, there is no formal requirement for an act or omission by the defendant.[69] No doubt D put the crowbar in his car before heading out to commit a burglary, but the offence requires only that he *has* it.[70] It does not matter how that situation came about.[71] Nonetheless, like offences of situational liability, possessory offences can be thought of as having an implicit behavioural element, albeit one that the prosecution need not prove. In effect, criminalisation of D's possession of the crowbar may be treated as imposing an

---

65   *Tifaga v Dept of Labour* [1980] 2 NZLR 235 (CA).
66   Cf, for example, *R v Heath* (1810) Russ & Ry 184; 168 ER 750; *Dugdale v R* (1853) 1 E & B 435; 118 ER 499.
67   For example, s 233(1)(a) Crimes Act 1961 (instruments of burglary); s 50 Arms Act 1983 (pistol or restricted weapon).
68   For criticism of this rationale, see Fletcher, *Rethinking Criminal Law*, Boston, Little, Brown & Co, 1978, 197-205.
69   It is otherwise in the US; §2.01(4) Model Penal Code states that possession is established "if the possessor knowingly procured or received the thing possessed or was aware of his control thereof for a sufficient period to have been able to terminate his possession".
70   The physical nature of the possession requirement varies for different offences. It may be enough that the crowbar is held by a third party who will give it immediately to D if asked: *R v McRae* (1993) 10 CRNZ 61 (CA), 66, 67. In the case of drugs, the physical element of possession will be established if the substance is present at a place which is subject to D's dominion or control: *Police v Emirali* [1976] 2 NZLR 476 (CA); *Rose v Loo Kee* [1927] GLR 403.
71   However, the mode of acquisition may be relevant to mens rea. In particular, the possibility of inadvertent possession is usually excluded by the mens rea requirement for knowledge that the courts have held is implicit in the word "possess". Cf *R v Cox* [1990] 2 NZLR 275; (1990) 5 CRNZ 653 (CA); *R v Cugullere* [1961] 2 All ER 343; [1961] 1 WLR 858 (CCA).

indirect liability, *either* for the act of obtaining the crowbar (ie acquiring possession) or for the omission by D to dispose of it.[72]

So possession and situational offences contain no formal requirement for proof of a behavioural element on the part of the defendant. Despite this, criminal convictions in these cases can usually be explained in terms of an implicit act or omission by the defendant. Recognition of this implicit element helps to explain some of the more difficult cases where D did not obtain the prohibited item by dint of his own efforts. Suppose that D is stopped while in his car, and is found to have with him a package containing cannabis. However, he claims that he had nothing to do with the presence of the package in his car and that it had been placed there by a friend. While that claim would suggest that D is not responsible — and therefore should not be criminally liable[73] — for the fact that the cannabis is in his possession, the law may still be justified in imposing criminal liability because of his voluntary failure to dispose of the item.[74] The difficult cases for this analysis occur when D's possession (whether by acquisition or non-disposal) is involuntary. We shall return to this issue in 3.4.2.

3.3 Consequences: the need for causation

Not all consequences involve persons. For example, the unexpected arrival of a very large meteor is thought to have caused the extinction of dinosaurs; and the collapse of many of Napier's buildings in 1931 is ascribed to an earthquake rather than human hand. But for the purposes of the criminal law, consequences are those circumstances, events, or states of affairs which are the result of (ie *caused* by) the defendant's behaviour. Thus, whenever a consequence, such as death, is specified as part of the actus reus of an offence, the prosecution must prove both that the consequence occurred and that the defendant's behaviour caused that consequence.

From this it may be seen that the requirement of causation is fundamental to our understanding of the actus reus in criminal law. Suppose, for example, that V dies. The result, death, is an element of the actus reus of murder. But it would normally be wrong to hold someone guilty of murder who does not cause V's death. Imagine B is a bystander who happens to be standing beside V when, suddenly, D rushes up to V and stabs him fatally. Then it is not B who kills V, but D, because it is D who causes V's death. Here our criminal law takes a very individualistic approach, emphasising the distinctive responsibility of citizens for their own actions. Thus the law does not prosecute D's parents, who brought D up in such a way that he was not adequately instilled with the values that would have stopped him from killing V. Neither would it hold B guilty of murder even if B had, in fact, been planning to kill V himself, and had delightedly stood aside upon perceiving D's murderous intentions.[75] In short, there is no doctrine of

---

72 Cf Williams, *CLGP*, 8; Husak, *Philosophy of Criminal Law*, Totowa, NJ, Rowman & Littlefield, 1987, 12; Moore, *Act and Crime: The Theory of Action and its Implications for Criminal Law*, Oxford, Clarendon Press, 1993, 21.
73 Cf 1.3.2ff; also 3.4.
74 Pace *R v Thomas* (1981) 6 A Crim R 66, in which the disposing of cannabis by D was held to be the assertion of a right of control "amounting to" possession. The decision can be explained on different grounds: that D had knowingly refrained from disposing of the drugs until the police arrived, and that the disposition was not an irrecoverable one; it was, rather, a "secreting".
75 B may, however, become guilty of murder if he manifests his delight in a manner which is intended to encourage D. Not all liability for outcomes is predicated on *the defendant*'s having caused the outcome; he may be held responsible for the consequence of someone else's actions as a secondary party. See ch 6.

collective social responsibility in our criminal law. This reflects the nature of our society. Even in team games, such as a rugby match, the newspaper statistics record the names of those who scored tries. Of course, other approaches are possible.[76] At one time, it was the practice in Greece to hold the entire city punishable for the crimes of its leaders. Similarly, the Chinese doctrine of lian-tsua would result in a whole family or village being punished for the wrongdoing of one of its members. But these are not the ways of modern New Zealand society. Moreover, to impose criminal liability upon someone for the actions of others would not only be out of step with public perceptions, but would also substantially restrict individual liberty.[77] It is inappropriate in a liberal culture to force us to be the guardian of others on pain of criminal conviction.

3.3.1 Rule of thumb

The starting, and frequently finishing, point of any causation problem is the "but for" or sine qua non test: would the consequence specified in the actus reus have occurred *but for* the defendant's behaviour? If it would not have occurred except for the defendant's acting as he did, then prima facie his behaviour caused that consequence. Conversely, if it would have occurred anyway, that is a reason to deny the existence of causation (and consequently to refrain from holding the defendant criminally liable for the occurrence of the actus reus).

Suppose, for example, that a doctor injects his patient with a painkiller, and the patient subsequently dies. Whether or not the doctor is guilty of manslaughter or murder depends upon a number of factors, but he definitely commits neither unless injecting the painkiller caused that patient's death. If the patient would have died when she did whether or not the doctor had injected her (for example of an unrelated heart attack), then the *but for* test is not satisfied and we have grounds for saying that the doctor's actions did not cause her death.[78] Conversely, if it can be proved that (subject to a de minimis exception)[79] she would not have died when she did without the doctor's intervention, then prima facie he killed her.

Most of the time, the sine qua non test will be an entirely adequate yardstick of causation, and in the absence of any unusual circumstances the prima facie answer it gives will be a conclusive one. But it is important to realise that *but for* causation is no more than indicative of true legal causation. Suppose, for instance, that D invites V to meet her for lunch. Unfortunately, while driving to their rendezvous, V's car is hit by a truck, the brakes of which have failed. But for D's inviting V to lunch, the accident would not have occurred. Yet D did not cause the accident. Another useful illustration is *R v Hensler*.[80] D sent V a begging letter in which he misrepresented his plight. V was not deceived, but nevertheless sent D some money. On these facts, although V would not have sent the money but for D's letter, D could not be convicted of obtaining by false pretences, because the false pretence had not caused V to send the money.[81]

So the presence of *but for* causation does not mean that there is true legal causation. Conversely, the absence of *but for* causation does not imply an absence of true legal causation either. Suppose

---

76 See, for example, Fauconnet, *La Responsabilité: étude de Sociologie*, Paris, Alcan, 1920.
77 Cf the argument against liability for omissions at 3.2.1(1); also the discussion in ch 1.
78 Cf *R v Dalloway* (1847) 2 Cox CC 273; *R v White* [1910] 2 KB 124; [1908-10] All ER Rep 340 (CA).
79 See 3.3.2(1).
80 *R v Hensler* (1870) 11 Cox CC 570.
81 D was, however, convicted of an attempt to obtain by false pretences. Cf *R v Mills* (1857) 7 Cox CC 263; 1 Dears & B 205; 169 ER 978.

this time that D sets fire to V's house, razing it. It turns out, however, that there was a faulty electrical circuit in the house that was about to overheat and cause a similar fire. We cannot say that, but for D's conduct, V's house would not have burned down. Yet despite this, it *is* D who causes the damage.

The difficulty arises because so-called *but for* "causation" *is actually not a species of causation at all*. Rather, it is a formula which merely expresses a certain sort of relationship between two things: that, in the circumstances, it was impossible for the second event (the "consequence") to happen without the first action (the "cause") having occurred. As such, the sine qua non relationship simply expresses a proposition of logic, and not of causation. What really matters in the law is not whether there is a logical *but for* relationship between the defendant's behaviour and the prohibited consequence, but whether there is a true causal relationship *at law*.

3.3.2 Causation in law

Some causal relationships are very mechanical, and present no problems for the law. This sort of causation occurs when the action leads to the relevant consequence through the ordinary workings of physics, biology, and the like. Thus the connection between D's knocking over the tumbler and its watery contents pouring out is a simple mechanical one; the consequence follows straightforwardly given the existence of gravity and the fluidity of the liquid inside, without the intervention of subsequent events. The connection between D's shooting V and V's consequential death is normally just as straightforward, something that a pathologist might be able to discuss in technical rather than, say, legal or moral terms.

The real difficulties arise when there are other actions, or events of nature, which *also* play a role in bringing about the relevant consequence. Consider, for example, the facts in *R v Pittwood*,[82] where D failed to close the gate at a railway crossing, with the result that a cart entered the crossing and was hit by a train. One can say, of this case, that the arrival of the train was itself a causal factor in the accident. Yet we can still agree that D's negligence caused the crash. Why?

It is not possible to give a definitive analysis of the principles of causation here.[83] But over the next few pages a number of guiding principles will be suggested. (In the context of homicide, some of these common law principles of causation have been modified by statute: see chapter 16.)

Perhaps the most important point to remember during the discussion which follows is that, while causation frequently depends upon physical, mechanical relationships between actions and outcomes (such as the relationship that D's firing a gun may bear to V's death a moment later), causation is also and very often a function of moral evaluations. When we state that Pittwood's dereliction "caused" an accident, we are articulating a view that his behaviour was responsible for that accident. In other words, the ascription of causation in *Pittwood* is not so much a *prerequisite* of his being held responsible as it is an expression of the moral *conclusion* that, through his behaviour, he is responsible, and legally answerable, for the accident that

---

82 *R v Pittwood* (1902) 19 TLR 37.
83 The classic work is *Hart and Honoré*. See also Kadish, *Blame and Punishment: Essays in the Criminal Law*, New York, Macmillan, 1987, ch 8; Williams, *TBCL*, ch 14. For more philosophical discussion, see Honoré, "Necessary and sufficient conditions in tort law" in Owen (ed), *Philosophical Foundations of Tort Law*, Oxford, Clarendon Press, 1995, 363; Mackie, "Causes and conditions" in Sosa (ed), *Causation and Conditionals*, London, Oxford University Press, 1975, 15.

resulted. The moral considerations underlying that conclusion find legal expression in the guiding principles outlined below.

(1) *Significant cause*

Whatever other causes play a role in bringing the actus reus about, the first requirement is that D's behaviour must contribute in some significant way to its occurrence. In R v White,[84] W gave his mother poison. Before it could take effect, however, she died of an unrelated heart attack. W was guilty of an attempted murder. But he did not commit murder because the poison played no role in his mother's death.

The contribution that D makes must be more than insignificant or de minimis.[85] If a doctor takes a blood sample from a patient who is dying from gunshot wounds, the additional loss of blood for the sample may further weaken the patient and hasten death by a few moments. But the doctor's role in the patient's death is, in this context, causally insignificant, and the law will impute the death solely to the gunshot wounds.[86]

However, the defendant's contribution need not be a substantial one. In R v Hennigan,[87] for example, it was ruled wrong to direct a jury that D was not liable if less than one-fifth to blame for the actus reus. Certainly, D's behaviour need not be the main cause of death. It is enough that her conduct plays a part which is not "insubstantial", or not "insignificant".[88]

(2) *Causal salience*

As well as making a "not insignificant" contribution, D's causal role must also be *salient*. Suppose that D is driving to work at a speed in excess of the speed limit. He slows to the correct speed in advance of an intersection, but is involved in an accident on the intersection with another car. If he had not been speeding he would not have arrived at the intersection when he did, and the accident would not have occurred. But his speeding is not a cause of the accident. Its only role was to ensure that D was present in a particular place at a particular time, and this in no way affected the likelihood of an accident occurring. The risk would have been just as great had he arrived later;[89] indeed, neither would the accident have happened if his speed had been even *more* excessive. A slightly different example is put by Hart and Honoré:[90]

> "If it is negligent of the defendant to hand a child a loaded gun, and the child drops the gun on his foot and injures it, the injury to the foot is not within the risk (shooting) that made it negligent to hand the child the loaded gun. It is also true that the aspect of the defendant's conduct which made it negligent, the fact that the gun was loaded, was not causally relevant to the injury, since that fact did not significantly increase the gun's weight."

---

84 R v White [1910] 2 KB 124; [1908-10] All ER Rep 340 (CA).
85 See R v Cato [1976] 1 All ER 260; [1976] 1 WLR 110 (CA), 265-266; 116-117.
86 Cf Palmer "Dr Adams' trial for murder" [1957] Crim LR 365.
87 R v Hennigan [1971] 3 All ER 133 (CA).
88 R v Myatt [1991] 1 NZLR 674; (1990) 7 CRNZ 304 (CA), 682, 683; 312, 313; R v Cato [1976] 1 All ER 260; [1976] 1 WLR 110 (CA), 266; 117; R v Cheshire [1991] 3 All ER 670; [1991] 1 WLR 844 (CA), 677; 853.
89 Cf Berry v Sugar Notch Borough 43 Atl 240 (1899) (Pa); Hart and Honoré, 168-170; Williams, TBCL, 16.7.
90 Hart and Honoré, lxiii. Cf Gorris v Scott (1874) LR 9 Ex 125; Fleming, The Law of Torts (7th ed), Sydney, Law Book Co, 1987, 174.

Here D, by giving the gun to the child at all (whether loaded or not), played a causal role in V's subsequent injury. But the reasons why D is at fault — which concern the risk that the child will discharge the gun — are in no way salient to the injury that V sustains.[91]

(3) *Multiple causes*

A further principle is that there may be multiple causes. In R *v Pittwood*,[92] both the arrival of the train and the defendant's failure to close the gate were causes of the accident. This may be true even when more than one person is at fault.[93] Suppose that D shoots V, who is taken to hospital. While in hospital, V is attended to by E, an inexperienced doctor who negligently fails to recognise the true extent of her injuries. V dies because those injuries are improperly left untreated. In this case, the actions of both D and E cause V's death, and (depending on mens rea considerations) both D and E may be guilty of homicide-related offences. Similarly, if both A and B simultaneously shoot C fatally through the heart, and C dies instantly, then both A and B kill him; even though we cannot say that "but for" each shot, C would not have died.[94] It is enough that the actus reus or consequence can be attributed to the defendant's conduct as *a*, not *the*, cause. The general test when there are multiple causes is whether the defendant's contribution was, by the time the consequence came about, still a "significant and operating cause".[95] If so, then it is irrelevant whether that same consequence can also be attributed to other defendants.[96]

Neither does it matter whether the consequence can also be attributed to other actions by the defendant himself. In R *v McKinnon*,[97] D struck V on the head, rendering him unconscious. He subsequently manhandled V, eventually leaving him lying on the ground. At some stage V suffered a minor injury to his nose which resulted in bleeding. This injury may have been in itself accidental. Unfortunately, while V was lying on the ground unconscious, the bleeding went into his lung and he suffocated. Had he not been unconscious, the bleeding would have been no serious matter. The Court of Appeal held that, while the injury to V's nose was a cause of death, it was so *concurrently* with the blow to V's head that rendered him unconscious and so unable to deal with the effects of the bleeding. Thus V's death could properly also be attributed to the assault by D.

When multiple causes are concurrently at work, there is no requirement that a defendant's conduct must have been sufficient to cause the prohibited outcome by itself. An example of this is the case of R *v Lewis*,[98] where (on one view of the evidence), two attackers separately injured V, the injuries being fatal only because they were cumulative. In such case *each* attacker

---

91 Cf R *v Fenton* [2003] 3 NZLR 439; (2003) 20 CRNZ 76 (CA), below, 16.5.2(5)(c); also R *v Hawkins* 21/2/01, Goddard J, HC Napier T18/00; noted below, 3.3.4(1).
92 R *v Pittwood* (1902) 19 TLR 37; see 3.2.1(2)(c).
93 Cf R *v Benge* (1865) 4 F & F 504; 176 ER 665.
94 *Jones v Commonwealth* (1955) 281 SW 2d 920, 922-923. From a moral and legal perspective, no other conclusion is possible, even though this type of case presents difficulty for philosophical accounts of causation.
95 Usually "substantial and operating" — cf R *v McKinnon* [1980] 2 NZLR 31 (CA), 37; *Adams*, CA158.07 (looseleaf); R *v Smith* [1959] 2 QB 35; [1959] 2 All ER 193, 42, 43; 198; but see 3.3.2(1).
96 R *v McKinnon* [1980] 2 NZLR 31 (CA); R *v Storey* [1931] NZLR 417 (CA) (even to the defendant's own negligence); *A-G's Reference (No 4 of 1980)* [1981] 2 All ER 617; [1981] 1 WLR 705 (CA). Cf R *v Blaue* [1975] 3 All ER 446; [1975] 1 WLR 1411 (CA).
97 R *v McKinnon* [1980] 2 NZLR 31 (CA).
98 R *v Lewis* [1975] 1 NZLR 222 (CA), 226, 227.

has caused V's death. Once again, the general test is the same: whether the particular defendant's own conduct was a significant contributor in bringing about the actus reus.

3.3.3 Intervening causes

In such cases as *Pittwood*, *McKinnon*, and *Lewis*, the other causal factors operated in tandem with D's conduct to bring about the prohibited harm. Sometimes, however, D's contribution is followed by an action by someone else, or a coincidental event, that is the more immediate (or "proximate") cause of death and which displaces D's causal responsibility for the actus reus. A good example of this is the case of *White*, mentioned earlier. Suppose that in the normal course of events the poison D gave his mother would have caused her death.[99] Nonetheless, it was a subsequent, unrelated heart attack that killed her. The occurrence of the heart attack overtook the effects of D's conduct and usurped his causal responsibility for her death.

Where the later event displaces D's responsibility in this way, it is often called a novus actus interveniens. A novus actus is an action or event which "intervenes" to "break the causal chain" leading from D to the eventual harm. Where the prohibited consequence is attributable to a novus actus, D is not criminally liable for bringing about that consequence. His behaviour is no longer a significant and operating cause.

We look now at the main types of intervening causes in more detail.

(1) *Natural events*

Where the other causal factors involve natural events rather than persons, the basic rule is that causation is attributed to the defendant *unless* the intervening natural event was not reasonably foreseeable. Another way of putting this test is to say that an intervening natural event is a novus actus interveniens only if its occurrence is "something extraordinary" rather than an ordinary occurrence or ordinary fact of life.[100] In *R v Hart*,[101] D assaulted V, leaving her lying unconscious on a beach below the high-water mark. V was subsequently drowned by the incoming tide. The Court of Appeal held that D had caused the death of the victim. It is thought that D would not have killed her had V been left lying above the high-water mark and had only drowned because of a freak tidal wave.[102]

The idea here is that the further cause is not merely a coincidence. Rather, it is the sort of risk that is created or increased by D's initial actions; and the prospect of the prohibited consequence coming about by that further means is one of the reasons we might sensibly give when stating why D should not act as he does.[103] Thus in *R v Forrest*,[104] where D inflicted an injury upon V, thereby making V susceptible to an infection which V later contracted and from which he died, it was held that D's conduct, in rendering V especially vulnerable to the further, immediate cause of death, was a sufficient cause for the death to be attributable to D. A

---

99 In fact, although D probably thought otherwise, it appears that the quantity given was insufficient to cause death, save perhaps as part of a cumulative dose.
100 *Environment Agency v Empress Car Co (Abertillery) Ltd* [1999] 2 AC 22 (HL), 34-36 (Lord Hoffmann). Provided it is borne in mind that what must be foreseeable is events of the same type, rather than the particular intervening event, these alternative ways of phrasing the causation test involve little practical difference.
101 *R v Hart* [1986] 2 NZLR 408; (1986) 3 CRNZ 474 (CA). See also *R v Hallett* [1969] SASR 141; *R v Phillips* [1971] ALR 740; (1971) 45 ALJR 467 (HCA); *R v Hill* [1953] NZLR 688, 694, 695.
102 Perkins, "The law of homicide" (1946) 36 J Crim L & Criminology 391, 393, 394.
103 Cf the requirement for salience at 3.3.2(2).
104 *R v Forrest* (1886) 20 SALR 78.

contrasting case with a different result is *Bush v Commonwealth*.[105] In that case D shot V, who subsequently died of scarlet fever, transmitted to him in hospital by the surgeon who operated on the bullet wound. D was acquitted of unlawful homicide. His attack on V did not substantially increase the risk of V's contracting scarlet fever; neither was that risk a significant reason why we would think D's initial actions wrong.

The outcome in *Bush v Commonwealth* would be different if the fever had caused death only *in conjunction with* the fact that V was weakened by the wound D had inflicted. This would be a case of multiple concurrent causes, rather than of novus actus, since the original injury would still be making an ongoing (operating) contribution to V's death.

There is another important exception to the rule that unforeseeable or extraordinary events are capable of breaking the causal chain linking defendant to eventual outcome. A coincidental or fortuitous route involving natural events will not normally be a novus actus when the ultimate result was *intended* by the defendant.[106] For example:

> D shoots at V on a mountainside, meaning to kill him. She misses, but the noise of her shot triggers an avalanche in which V is swept away and killed. In our view, D is guilty of murder. She has brought about the intended result, and cannot escape responsibility by pointing to the unexpected causal detour of the means that she herself initiated.

This exception is sometimes described as a rule that "intended consequences are never too remote". It is preferable not to characterise the exception in that way, and indeed to do so would be inaccurate. For example, D's intended contribution to an outcome may be superseded by the novus actus of a third party.[107] It is to that possibility that we now turn.

(2) Other persons

In some respects, there are similarities between the causal status of natural events and the intervening actions of third parties. If D stabs V, and V later dies, D is nevertheless not causally responsible if it turns out that V dies because the ambulance within which he was being carried to hospital was crushed by a runaway lorry. Neither does D kill V if, after being fatally wounded and left for dead, V is chanced upon by his old enemy T, who shoots V, killing him instantly.[108] In these situations, the unforeseeable intervention of another breaks the causal chain between D's contribution and the eventual outcome. However, there are also significant differences between the attribution of causation where there are intervening natural events and that where there are intervening actions by other persons. In the former case, the main test is one of "ordinariness" or reasonable foreseeability. In the latter, this is only one aspect of a more complex inquiry.

---

105 *Bush v Commonwealth* (1880) 78 Ky 268.
106 *R v Demirian* [1989] VR 97; (1988) 33 A Crim R 441, 113, 114; 457, 458; *R v Michael* (1840) 9 C & P 356; 173 ER 867. See also *Anon ("The Harlot's Case")* (1560) Crompton's Justice 24, discussed in *TBCL*, 389.
107 The rule would also be subject to a salience requirement regarding unexpected interventions: 3.3.2(2).
108 Cf *State v Wood* (1881) 53 Vt 560; *R v Evans and Gardiner (No 2)* [1976] VR 523, 527, 528. The decision of the Court of Appeal in *R v Lewis* [1975] 1 NZLR 222 (CA), 226, 227 is prima facie contrary to this proposition, in that the language used in the judgment would result in both D and T being guilty of murder. But that case perhaps turns on its facts, which were less than entirely clear. The context appears to have been one in which the injuries inflicted by the second assailant would have compounded rather than superceded those inflicted by D. Moreover, nothing in the judgment of the court suggests an intention to abandon the common law position stated in the text here. See 3.3.2(3).

At a very generalised level, there are two main principles guiding causation when a third person intervenes. First is the proposition that T's intervention which causes the actus reus will normally be a novus actus, and absolve D of responsibility, when that intervention is "free, deliberate and informed".[109] This occurs when T *knowingly* intervenes to bring about the prohibited outcome, without her choice to do so being induced, fettered, or constrained by the situation D has created. In that situation T assumes full responsibility for the outcome, displacing or pre-empting its attribution to D. The rationale for this is ably expressed by Glanville Williams:[110]

> "Underlying this rule there is, undoubtedly, a philosophical attitude. Moralists and lawyers regard the individual's will as the autonomous prime cause of his behaviour. What a person does (if he has reached adult years, is of sound mind and is not acting under mistake, intimidation or other similar pressure) is his own responsibility, and is not regarded as having been caused by other people. An intervening act of this kind, therefore, breaks the causal connection that would otherwise have been perceived between previous acts and the forbidden consequence."

Very often T's knowing intercession will not meet those criteria. The doctor's intervention in treating V is not free or unconstrained, but rather is a justified response to the need for treatment that D has engendered. This point can be stated more generally: T's participation in begetting the actus reus is insufficiently free, and *cannot* be a novus actus, when it is justified or excused by the demands of the situation that D's conduct has placed her in. While T's conduct may itself be a cause of the harm, it is not an independent cause; rather, in law, it has the status of being itself a consequence of D's wrongdoing. Thus, instead of T's becoming fully (and exclusively) responsible for the eventual outcome, D remains at least partly responsible for that intervention by T, and for its effects.

Neither will T's input be "free, deliberate and informed" when T is ignorant of the relevant facts. In this sort of case, T's contribution to the harm is an inadvertent one. Her role may be innocent or accidental, but need not be, and may instead be negligent. Either way, there is no deliberate choice by T to bring the harm about, and so she cannot be said to assume full responsibility for that harm to the exclusion of D.

The second main principle applies where, because of her ignorance or mistake, T's intervention does not meet the "free, deliberate and informed" criteria. In that case the third party intervention is, in effect, no different from a natural event. Thus it is subject to the further tests that govern intervention by a natural event. In particular, it can only count as a novus actus if its occurrence was independent of D's wrongdoing and was not reasonably foreseeable.[111] One new factor in examining this issue will be T's culpability for her conduct: if the harm occurred only following T's gross negligence, it is less likely to be reasonably foreseeable and the sort of risk which provides a reason why D should not have acted as he did in the first place.[112]

---

109 *R v Pagett* (1983) 76 Cr App R 279; [1983] Crim LR 393 (CA), 288, 289; 394; *R v Latif* [1996] 1 WLR 104; [1996] 2 Cr App R 92 (HL), 115; 104. In *Kennedy v R* [2005] EWCA Crim 685, the UK Court of Appeal has suggested a qualification to this principle: that the intervention must not also be done "in concert" with D. This qualification, which is of uncertain status in New Zealand, is critiqued below, at 3.3.3(2)(f).
110 *TBCL*, 391.
111 Or (in Lord Hoffmann's phrasing: *Environment Agency v Empress Car Co (Abertillery) Ltd* [1999] 2 AC 22 (HL), 34-36) if its occurrence was "extraordinary": 3.3.3(1).

As with any intervening cause, whether natural or human, a third principle also applies: that even if the intervention was independent of D and unforeseeable, it will be no more than a concurrent cause if D's contribution is still playing a direct, contributory role at the time the harm eventually occurs. This is a straightforward application of the proposition that there can be multiple causes of an outcome.[113]

In the following subsections, we will consider these rather abstract principles in the more practical context of the leading cases, and in light of judicial dicta.

(a)   Foreseeable and innocent interventions

Cases where another's intervention does not break the causal chain occur in a variety of ways. In some of the most dramatic examples, D will still be ascribed with causal responsibility if the contribution of the other party is both predictable (ie reasonably foreseeable) and itself innocent.

A famous case of this variety is *R v Michael*.[114] D wished to murder her illegitimate child, who was in the care of a foster mother. She gave a bottle of poison to the foster mother, telling her it was medicine and instructing her to administer it to the baby. The foster mother decided not to give the medicine and put it on the mantelpiece. Some days later the foster mother's own 5-year-old child removed the bottle and administered a fatal dose to the child. D was convicted of murder.[115]

The events in *Michael* involved the input of a young child, undoubtedly an innocent for the purposes of legal responsibility. But they would be treated no differently by the law if T were an adult whose foreseeable intervention was inadvertent and blameless. An example of the latter is supplied by *R v Fleeting (No 1)*,[116] where in an altercation D pushed V, who stumbled onto the street and was run over and killed by a passing car. Being a busy street in Auckland, the intervention of the car (unintended by its driver) could not be regarded as a novus actus, and D could properly be treated as having caused V's death.

By contrast, the innocent intervention will be regarded as a novus actus where it is unforeseeable.[117] *Fleeting* may instructively be contrasted with *R v Knutsen*,[118] where D had left V unconscious in a quiet and well-lit street, and could not be held responsible for her death when she was subsequently run over by a drunk driver who had ample opportunity to avoid her.

Where T's actions are not inadvertent but instead justified or excused because of the situation D has created, T will effectively be counted as an innocent intervener. The most important

---

112 See 3.3.3(1). Less likely, but not impossible: cf *R v Fleeting (No 1)* [1977] 1 NZLR 343, 348, where Barker J opined that T's intervention would not necessarily be a novus actus even if negligent or unlawful. Cf *R v Benge* (1865) 4 F & F 504; 176 ER 665; *Smyth v Police* [1973] 1 NZLR 56, 58. See further 3.3.3(2)(c).
113 See 3.2.2(3). This appears to be the best explanation of *Jemielita v R* (1995) 81 A Crim R 409 (WA CCA). Cf *R v Hennigan* [1971] 3 All ER 133 (CA).
114 *R v Michael* (1840) 9 C & P 356; 173 ER 867; see also *Tessymond's Case* (1828) 1 Lew CC 169; 168 ER 1000.
115 It is thought that T's intervention was reasonably foreseeable. (See *TBCL*, 394.) However, even if it were unforeseeable and extraordinary, D's conviction can be justified on the basis that, T's intervention being innocent, it should be treated like a natural event and the rule about intended consequences applied. See 3.3.3(1).
116 *R v Fleeting (No 1)* [1977] 1 NZLR 343.
117 This must be the explanation of *R v Martin* (1827) 3 C & P 211; 172 ER 390.
118 *R v Knutsen* [1963] Qd R 157. See also *Smyth v Police* [1973] 1 NZLR 56, 58.

case of this type is *R v Pagett*,[119] in which the defendant holed up in a building, then emerged firing at police and using his hostage as a human shield. The police returned fire in the dark, killing the hostage. The consequence, that the police would — quite understandably — return fire, and so kill the girl, was an entirely foreseeable upshot of what the defendant did, and so could not break the chain of causation which led from his behaviour to the hostage's death.

It was said in *Pagett* that the policeman's reaction in returning fire was instinctive and "involuntary". But it need not be involuntary. It was enough that the reaction was a reasonable response, justifiable either in terms of self-defence or the execution of a legal duty. Either way, it is not sufficiently "free" to usurp the defendant's causal responsibility for the eventual consequences.

An extension of the decision in *Pagett* may be seen in *R v Tomars*,[120] where D gave chase to a motorcyclist, driving in such a manner that the motorcyclist (V) was caused to swerve in front of another car. V died in the ensuing accident. It was held that D's actions were capable of being a cause of V's death, since V's conduct was reasonably foreseeable. The case is slightly different from *Pagett*, in that V's reaction was a mistake, and as such excusable rather than justifiable.[121] But it was a reasonably foreseeable reaction, and moreover one for which V could not be blamed — a response induced by the circumstances that D himself had generated. Thus V's reaction is allowed to be a mistake, provided it is a reasonable or understandable one made in the heat or emergency of the moment. Although *Tomars* involves an intervention by the victim rather than a third party, and as such may be governed by rules which are even less favourable to the defendant,[122] it is thought that the principle in that case also extends to interventions by strangers.

Another case worth mention is *R v Martin*.[123] Intending to cause confusion and terror, D put out the gaslights on a staircase to the exit of a theatre and placed an iron bar across the exit doorway. In the subsequent panic, a number of persons were seriously injured. D's conviction for inflicting grievous bodily harm was affirmed on appeal — again, rightly so. The immediate cause of injury was no doubt the stampeding of the audience, yet the audience's behaviour was hardly "free, deliberate, and informed". Rather, it was a foreseeable and excusable consequence of the panic induced by D.

(b)   Foreseeable and intentional interventions

The cases above illustrate the general rule that, where the intervention is both innocent and foreseeable, it will not normally suffice to break the causal chain linking the defendant to the actus reus. But what if the third party's free intervention is foreseeable, yet not innocent or blameless? Here things get a little more complicated. The reason for this is the importance of individual autonomy and responsibility in the law. A person's actions are not usually regarded as caused by others, and the law stipulates that a defendant is responsible for her own actions but is normally not responsible for the wrongdoing of a third party even if it was foreseeable, and would not have occurred but for the defendant's contribution. So if D inflicts serious

---

119 *R v Pagett* (1983) 76 Cr App R 279; [1983] Crim LR 393 (CA).
120 *R v Tomars* [1978] 2 NZLR 505 (CA).
121 Cf *R v Williams* [1992] 2 All ER 183; [1992] 1 WLR 380 (CA); *Madison v State* 234 Ind 517; 130 NE 2d 35 (1955).
122 See 3.3.3(3).
123 *R v Martin* (1881) 8 QBD 54.

injuries upon V during a mugging, and another assailant later chances upon and shoots V (killing him instantly) then D does not cause death even if it was foreseeable[124] that another person might subsequently kill V. Similarly, the result in *Michael*[125] would have been different if T had been a mature adult who knew the details of D's plans when she administered the poison to D's baby.[126]

Where the third party's wrongful intervention is itself intentional, something other than causation is required before the outcome can *also* be ascribed to the original actor-defendant. Characteristically, the extra ingredient is supplied when the third party's intervention is in some way induced or underwritten by the defendant. In these cases, D's liability is predicated on a derivative, or secondary party basis, rather than upon causation.[127] Thus when D deliberately incites or assists T to commit a crime, D too will be criminally liable alongside T for its commission. Secondary liability is dealt with separately in chapter 6.

Sometimes an intervention to bring about the actus reus may be intentional without necessarily being culpable. As we saw in the preceding section, where this occurs because of a justification or excuse arising from D's conduct, T is treated as if his were an innocent intervention. However where T's intervention is intentional, free, and unconstrained by justificatory or excusatory circumstances, it will usually break the causal link between defendant and outcome. In *R v Latif*,[128] D was charged, inter alia, with importing a controlled drug. The drug was in fact brought into the country by a customs officer with full knowledge of the contents of the packages he carried. The House of Lords held that the officer's voluntary and knowing intervention relieved D of causal responsibility for importation of the drugs, and that the most he could be convicted of was an attempt to commit the offence.[129]

(c) Foreseeable and culpable interventions

Normally, when there is no *intentional* wrongdoing by the intervener, it is less likely — but not impossible — that the culpable intervention will break the causal link between D and the eventual outcome. This is because, as was stated in 3.3.3(2), T cannot be said to have assumed a full responsibility for the effects of her intervention. Nonetheless, it is still possible for T's conduct to disrupt the causal path joining D with the actus reus. For example, where V is injured by D, but killed in an accident en route to hospital, the fact that the accident was unintended by T is no bar to an application of the novus actus doctrine and denial of D's

---

124 Or even made "likely" by D's actions: *R v Dalby* [1982] 1 All ER 916; [1982] 1 WLR 425 (CA). As Glanville Williams states: "The fact that [D's] own conduct, rightful or wrongful, provided the background for a subsequent voluntary and wrong act by another does not make him responsible for it. What he does may be a but-for cause of the injurious act, but he did not do it." "Finis for novus actus?" (1989) 48 CLJ 391.
125 See 3.3.3(2)(a).
126 *R v Grant* [1966] NZLR 968 (CA), 973, 974; *People v Elder* 100 Mich 515; 59 NW 237 (1894); *Commonwealth v Root* 403 Pa 571; 170 A 2d 310 (1961); cf *Hilton's Case* (1838) 2 Lew CC 214; 168 ER 1132, where a stranger's intervention was a novus actus, with *R v Lowe* (1850) 3 Car & Kir 123; 175 ER 489, where the intermediary was an "ignorant boy" and D was not absolved of responsibility; also *R v Dubois* (1959) 32 CR 187, where T's intervention was provoked by D. Cf the "free, deliberate and informed" criterion in 3.3.3(2).
127 Cf Fletcher, *Rethinking Criminal Law*, Boston, Little, Brown & Co, 1978, 583.
128 *R v Latif* [1996] 1 WLR 104; [1996] 2 Cr App R 92 (HL). To similar effect is *A-G of Hong Kong v Tse Hung-Lit* [1986] AC 876. For another, extraordinary, example, see *People v Campbell* 124 Mich App 333; 335 NW 2d 27 (1983).
129 It is possible that the officer's intervention could be regarded as culpable since the House of Lords treated him as having committed an offence himself. But this was not required in *R v Horsey* (1862) 3 F & F 287; 176 ER 129.

responsibility. The most instructive legal examples of this variety arise in a medical context, where D inflicts injuries upon V the extent of which are at least exacerbated by the medical treatment V subsequently receives.

A case where "palpably" bad medical treatment was held to cause death to the exclusion of D's original actions is *R v Jordan*.[130] In that case the defendant had stabbed V, who was admitted to hospital and died 8 days later. On appeal, evidence was admitted to show that when he died, the original injury had substantially healed. V's death was in fact caused by his allergic reaction to the antibiotic he was given in hospital and by the intravenous administration of too much liquid. Moreover, the antibiotic was introduced to prevent infection only after he had shown he was intolerant of it. The Court of Criminal Appeal, in quashing Jordan's conviction, held that the grossly negligent[131] medical treatment broke the causal link between the stabbing and V's death.

While we submit that *Jordan* was rightly decided, it must be regarded as a very unusual case, distinguished by its rather extreme facts. Acknowledging this, the court was "disposed to accept it as law that death resulting from any normal treatment employed to deal with a felonious injury may be regarded as caused by the felonious injury".[132] Thus where death results from normal treatment applied to the injury, then both the treatment and the injury are causes of death and the treatment does not break the chain of causation from the original injury to death.

Even if the intervening treatment is abnormal, however, it will not necessarily count as a novus actus. In *R v Smith*,[133] V was stabbed by P with a bayonet. His lung was pierced, but this injury went unrecognised by those who attended to him. He was dropped twice on the way to the medical reception station. There the medical officer failed to diagnose the seriousness of the situation and gave the wrong treatment, which very likely increased the risk of death.[134] On appeal, it was held that where the original injury is still an operating and significant[135] cause of death, then — regardless of other contributing causes — the death can still be attributed to the defendant. It is only if the original wound is merely a *historical setting* for the second injury (here, the treatment), which is then the major operating cause of death, that there can be a break in the causal chain. By contrast with the facts in *Jordan*, in *Smith* the stab wound and consequent haemorrhage were still immediate medical factors explaining V's death.

There appear, therefore, to be two conditions that must be satisfied before the intervening behaviour can supersede the defendant's causal role. Loosely stated:

(i)   The original harm inflicted by D must no longer be contributing to the occurrence of the eventual result (ie as a concurrent cause).

This condition applies even if T's wrongdoing is intentional. For example, if D inflicts a non-fatal stab wound upon V, then D (as well as T) causes V's death if T later also stabs V and the loss of blood from both wounds is a contributing factor bringing about V's death.[136] Contrast

---

130   *R v Jordan* (1956) 40 Cr App R 152 (CCA).
131   See Williams, "Causation in homicide" [1957] Crim LR 429.
132   *R v Jordan* (1956) 40 Cr App R 152 (CCA), 157.
133   *R v Smith* [1959] 2 QB 35; [1959] 2 All ER 193.
134   Indeed, it was said in evidence at the trial that V's chances of recovery were 75 percent given proper treatment.
135   "Substantial" in the speech of Lord Parker CJ [1959] 2 QB 35; [1959] 2 All ER 193, 42, 43; 198. But see 3.3.2(1).
136   This may be the best explanation of *R v Dear* [1996] Crim LR 595 (CA).

this example with the example mentioned earlier, where D stabs V and T later chances upon V and shoots her, killing her instantly. In that case T and not D causes V's death.

The second condition is as follows:

(ii) The relevant intervention by T must be independent (ie not itself a consequence) of the original wrongdoing by D.

This condition was pivotal in *R v Kirikiri*.[137] In that case, V was the victim of a serious assault by D, which caused structural damage to her face. At the hospital where she was first treated, a temporary tracheostomy was performed to assist her breathing. She was then transferred to another hospital for reconstructive surgery, which was to take place 4 days later and was not essential to save her life. Before surgery, however, the inserted tracheal tube slipped. Attempts to replace it failed and V died. The High Court held, on a pretrial motion, that there was "ample evidence" on these facts for a jury to hold that D caused V's death. This seems right. The immediate cause of death was the failure of the tracheostomy and of the surgeons' attempts to repair it. But the tracheostomy itself was a medically appropriate response, made necessary by the injuries D had inflicted upon V. D might therefore be regarded as causally responsible for the (necessitous, appropriate) intervention that, in turn, led to V's death.[138]

It may be helpful to illustrate the different legal character of the causal sequences in these cases with diagrams. In *Jordan*, the conduct of the doctor amounted to a novus actus independent of D's actions:

Jordan: D ⟶ stabs V ⊣ T ⟶ injects antibiotics ⟶ V dies

By contrast, in *Kirikiri* the doctor's intervention was a direct response to the injuries D had inflicted, and thus could be treated as a consequence of D's actions:

Kirikiri: D ⟶ attacks V ⟶ T performs tracheostomy ⟶ V dies

In *Smith*, the doctor's conduct made an independent contribution to V's death. But the stab wound inflicted by D remained a concurrent, operating cause of death:

Smith: D ⟶ stabs V ⟶ V dies
T ⟶ exacerbates wounds

One important factor in determining whether the medical intervention counts as a consequence for the purposes of condition (ii) will be the extent to which that treatment is negligent. "Palpably" wrong — ie grossly negligent — treatment is obviously not a consequential intervention falling within condition (ii). (As *Smith* illustrates, the question

---

[137] *R v Kirikiri* [1982] 2 NZLR 648; also in *R v Cheshire* [1991] 3 All ER 670; [1991] 1 WLR 844 (CA), where the doctors' conduct was admittedly negligent. Because of the complexity of *Cheshire*, its analysis is deferred to the end of our discussion of causation, in 3.3.4(3).

[138] Note that s 166, which applies to cases of homicide, was treated for the purpose of argument in *R v Kirikiri* as declaratory of the common law: [1982] 2 NZLR 648, 651. For further discussion of this case, see ch 16.

whether it is a novus actus interveniens will then depend on condition (i).) On the other hand, reasonable, even if ultimately incorrect and harmful, treatment *is* a consequence.[139] However, the status of treatment which is negligent, but not grossly negligent, is not clear. Authority on this question is both obiter and inconsistent.[140] It is submitted that, by analogy with the principles stated in 3.3.3(2)(a) and 3.3.3(3), medically-erroneous treatment that is neither reasonable nor reasonably foreseeable should count as independent action within condition (ii).

(d)   Distinction from the innocent agent doctrine

Sometimes persons bring about outcomes deliberately through the agency of another person. If D gives V's daughter a lethal draught of poison, telling her it is for V's cold, and the daughter administers the poison to V, D is guilty of murder as if he had administered the poison himself.[141] Similarly, D may be convicted of importing prohibited drugs even though the means of conveyance was an airline.[142] The doctrine of innocent agency renders the intervening participant the mere instrument of D, enabling courts to find that D has committed the offence as a principal offender.[143]

Discussion of this doctrine belongs in chapter 6 on secondary parties. It is mentioned here in order to distinguish it from the causation question that arises upon an innocent third party's intervention. Innocent agency requires that D knowingly uses T as his agent to bring about the prohibited result. Thus *Michael*, where a child later and independently administered the poison that D had instructed V's foster-mother to give to V, is not a suitable case for application of the doctrine.

Innocent agency and causal principles nonetheless share some common ground. Like causation, innocent agency requires that T should be ignorant of the true nature of her actions. Where this is not so, and T is aware that her conduct constitutes an actus reus, responsibility for her actions and their result cannot then be imputed back to D.

(e)   Special cases of intentional intervention (1): pollution and the problem of Empress

There are two problematic cases governing deliberate third party interventions. The first is the decision by the House of Lords in *Environment Agency v Empress Car Co (Abertillery) Ltd*.[144] In that case, D had attached a tap to a diesel tank in its yard. The tap overrode existing barriers designed to contain spillage from the tank, meaning that it was possible for overflows from the tap to drain into the nearby river. On 20 March 1995 the tap was opened by an unknown person, with the result that the entire contents of the tank were drained and flowed into the river. D was convicted of "causing polluting matter to enter controlled waters",[145] a conviction that was affirmed by the House of Lords.

The leading judgment, given by Lord Hoffmann, contains a number of useful statements of principle.[146] But it is, in one respect, profoundly unsatisfactory. Apparently, the intervention

---

139 *R v Kirikiri* [1982] 2 NZLR 648; *R v McKechnie* (1991) 94 Cr App R 51, 58.
140 For a survey of the case law, see *Hart and Honoré*, 352ff.
141 *Anon* (1634) Kel 53; 84 ER 1079.
142 *White v Ridley* (1978) 140 CLR 342; 52 ALJR 724 (HCA).
143 *R v Paterson* [1976] 2 NZLR 394 (CA), 396.
144 *Environment Agency v Empress Car Co (Abertillery) Ltd* [1999] 2 AC 22 (HL).
145 Contrary to s 85(1) Water Resources Act 1991 (UK).
146 See, for example, *Environment Agency v Empress Car Co (Abertillery) Ltd* [1999] 2 AC 22 (HL), 29f, 30e-31b.

of the third party was free, deliberate, informed, and indeed malicious. Prima facie, therefore, it was a novus actus. But Lord Hoffman accorded no special status to such interventions and failed to distinguish informed acts by third persons from acts which are either uninformed or unfree, or indeed from interventions of nature. "By parity of reasoning,"[147] the same test was said to apply to all:

> "The true common sense distinction is, in my view, between acts and events which, although not necessarily foreseeable in the particular case, are in the generality a normal and familiar fact of life, and acts or events which are abnormal and extraordinary."[148]

The main effect of this conclusion is to assimilate interventions by third parties with interventions by natural events, thereby extending the appropriate test of the latter (discussed in 3.3.3(1)) also to the former. Hence a normal or foreseeable intervention, even if fully informed and deliberate, would not break the chain of causation linking D to the ultimate outcome.

This holding is contrary both to principle and law. At the level of principle, it is a long-standing precept of causation rules in the criminal law that a person is responsible for his own autonomous actions and not for those of others. As Williams puts it: "What a person does ... is his own responsibility, and is not regarded as having been caused by other people."[149] Otherwise, D's criminal liability for causing an actus reus would not be under his own control but would instead be subject to the autonomous choice of someone else. Giving other citizens the power to render D guilty of a crime not only disempowers D and undermines his autonomy but is also contrary to the importance attached in modern law to an individual's separate identity and responsibility.

The dealer who sells T a gun does not shoot V. T does. It may sometimes be appropriate to criminalise the dealer's actions, but not on the basis of causation. Similarly, in the present case, D did not pollute the river. T did. It was possible for the Legislature to make D responsible for that outcome by stipulating vicarious or situational liability; but the legislation did not do that. The statute requires causation by the *defendant*, in the normal way. The House of Lords trampled on a fundamental precept of criminal law.

Bad principle, then. Bad law, too. The decision is inconsistent with the reasoning in such decisions as *R v Latif*,[150] *Hilton's Case*,[151] and *R v Dalby*,[152] mentioned earlier.[153] Glanville Williams's conclusion on *Dalby* holds just as aptly for *Empress*:[154]

---

147 *Environment Agency v Empress Car Co (Abertillery) Ltd* [1999] 2 AC 22 (HL), 33d, 34.
148 Thus his Lordship eschewed the language of "foreseeability" in favour of "ordinariness", although the distinction is unlikely to be of great practical significance. See 3.3.3(1).
149 *TBCL*, 391; the passage is quoted more fully in 3.3.3(2). Cf *Hart and Honoré*, 364-365.
150 *R v Latif* [1996] 1 WLR 104; [1996] 2 Cr App R 92 (HL); also *A-G of Hong Kong v Tse Hung-Lit* [1986] AC 876.
151 *Hilton's Case* (1838) 2 Lew CC 214; 168 ER 1132.
152 *R v Dalby* [1982] 1 All ER 916; [1982] 1 WLR 425 (CA).
153 See 3.3.3(3). See also *People v Elder* 100 Mich 515; 59 NW 237 (1894); *Commonwealth v Root* 403 Pa 571; 170 A 2d 310 (1961); *People v Campbell* 124 Mich App 333; 335 NW 2d 27 (1983); *R v Horsey* (1862) 3 F & F 287; 176 ER 129. *Empress* is also inconsistent with *Impress (Worcester) Ltd v Rees* [1971] 2 All ER 357, which Lord Hoffmann asserted was wrongly decided, notwithstanding that the result in that case had been endorsed by the House of Lords in *Alphacell Ltd v Woodward* [1972] AC 824 (HL), 835 (Lord Wilberforce), 847 (Lord Salmon).
154 "Finis for novus actus?" (1989) 48 CLJ 391.

"The fact that [D's] own conduct, rightful or wrongful, provided the background for a subsequent voluntary and wrong act by another does not make him responsible for it. What he does may be a but-for cause of the injurious act, but he did not do it."

In *Empress*, D's contribution provided no more than the setting for T's vandalous act. Were it otherwise, the law of complicity would be largely redundant. One who assists another to commit a crime could be held to have caused the prohibited harm and so be convicted of the crime as a principal. Lord Hoffman's analysis virtually demolishes the need for liability of secondary parties.

Yet the decision in *Empress* purports to follow law. Unfortunately, in the face of extensive criminal law precedent to the contrary, the only unequivocal authority Lord Hoffmann cited for his conclusion was a tort case.[155] Moreover, his Lordship placed great weight on the statement attributed to Lord Wilberforce in *Alphacell Ltd v Woodward* that "the *deliberate* act of a third party does not necessarily negative causal connection".[156] But Lord Wilberforce did not use the word "deliberate". During his speech in *Alphacell Ltd v Woodward*, Lord Wilberforce had, obiter, merely rejected the proposition that "in every case the act of a third person necessarily interrupts the chain of causation"; a warranted rejection that provides no support for the reasoning in *Empress*.

It is to be hoped that the decision will be disregarded in New Zealand or, alternatively, regarded as not being of general application but rather confined to regulatory contexts such as pollution. The English Court of Appeal has itself sought to limit the effect of the case, treating it as a matter of specific statutory interpretation.[157] That is, in our view, a suitable analysis.

(f)   Special cases of intentional intervention (2): drug overdoses and acting in concert

The other problematic decision concerning deliberate third party interventions is *Kennedy v R*,[158] the latest in a line of drug overdose cases. D had prepared a heroin mixture for V in a syringe which he then gave to V. V injected himself with the heroin and subsequently died. D was convicted of manslaughter. On appeal,[159] the issue was whether D had caused V's death by an unlawful act. The main difficulty was that, even though D's contribution was unlawful (being the supply of a controlled substance), and had played a part in the events leading to V's death, prima facie there was an intervening act by another, V himself, who had self-administered the injection. The intervention by V was free, deliberate, and informed; as such, it seemed to be a novus actus, absolving D of causal responsibility for the homicide.

---

155 *Stansbie v Troman* [1948] 2 KB 48; [1948] All ER 599.
156 *Environment Agency v Empress Car Co (Abertillery) Ltd* [1999] 2 AC 22 (HL), 33c. See *Alphacell Ltd v Woodward* [1972] AC 824 (HL), 835.
157 *Kennedy v R* [2005] EWCA Crim 685, paras 36-9; below, 3.3.3(2)(f). The Court rejected the wider reading of *Empress* adopted previously in *R v Finlay* [2003] EWCA Crim 3868 (CA).
158 *Kennedy v R* [2005] EWCA Crim 685.
159 In fact, this was D's second appeal. The first saw his conviction upheld: see [1999] Crim LR 65. However, following uncertainty in the subsequent case law, the case was referred back to the Court of Appeal for reconsideration by the UK Criminal Cases Review Commission. Appellate decisions in the more-or-less similar cases of *R v Dalby* [1982] 1 All ER 916; [1982] 1 WLR 425 (CA); *R v Dias* [2002] 2 Cr App R 5, and *R v Richards* [2002] EWCA Crim 3175 had resulted in the defendant's conviction being quashed; whereas in *R v Rogers* [2003] EWCA Crim 945; [2003] 1 WLR 1374 and *R v Finlay* [2003] EWCA Crim 3868 the convictions had been upheld.

The Court circumnavigated this issue by ruling that the relevant act causing death was the administration of a noxious substance, contrary to s 23 of the Offences Against the Person Act 1861 (UK); and that D could be held responsible for that act because D and V had *acted in concert* in administering the heroin:[160]

> "if a defendant is acting in concert with the deceased, what the deceased does in concert with the defendant will not break the chain of causation, even though the general principles as to causation have to be applied.... If Kennedy either caused the deceased to administer the drug or was acting jointly with the deceased in administering the drug, Kennedy would be acting in concert with the deceased and there would be no breach in the chain of causation."

This appears to create a new principle of causation: even where an intervening agent is free, deliberate and informed,[161] the intervention will not break the chain of causation if it is done "in concert" with the defendant.

The idea seems to be that where D's and V's actions are intimately bound together, it is artificial to divide up what in reality is a joint operation, a single "combined" transaction for which both are responsible.[162] In *Kennedy*, the key features that rendered their actions "in concert", thereby invoking this new general principle, were (i) that D was present throughout the events; (ii) that D's own contribution was immediately and intimately connected to V's conduct; and (iii) that D's contribution was pursuant to a shared understanding that encompassed V's subsequent conduct.

The problem with this decision is that, notwithstanding the collaborative nature of the project, it was V, not D, who administered the drug. Properly, cases such as these are the domain of secondary liability: D was a party to the administration of the heroin.[163] To see this, suppose that instead of there being two parties, there had been three. D, let us say, prepared a syringe for P, who injected V — or, indeed, handed over a knife with which P stabbed V. In such cases, D does not cause V's death even though he is criminally responsible for it. Rather, P is straightforwardly guilty of manslaughter as a principal and D as a secondary party.[164] This is the best explanation of the proviso in *R v Latif*, on which *Kennedy* placed great weight.[165] According to Lord Steyn in *Latif*:[166]

> "the free, deliberate and informed intervention of a second person, who intends to exploit the situation created by the first, *but is not acting in concert with him*, is held to relieve the first actor of criminal responsibility."

It is certainly true that, if they are acting in concert, the first is not relieved of criminal responsibility — but this is because he is complicit, not because he causes the outcome personally.

Like *Empress*, it is to be hoped that the decision in *Kennedy* will find no place in New Zealand law, or at least that it will be confined to cases of intervention by the victim. This new doctrine

---

160 *Kennedy v R* [2005] EWCA Crim 685, paras 42-43.
161 Above, 3.3.3(2); *R v Pagett* (1983) 76 Cr App R 279; [1983] Crim LR 393 (CA), 288, 289; 394.
162 *Kennedy v R* [2005] EWCA Crim 685, para 53.
163 Contrary — in New Zealand — to s 7(1)(a) Misuse of Drugs Act 1975. See n 167 below.
164 Pursuant to both s 66(1) and (2). Secondary liability is discussed in detail below, ch 6.
165 *Kennedy v R* [2005] EWCA Crim 685, para 42.
166 *R v Latif* [1996] 1 WLR 104; [1996] 2 Cr App R 92 (HL), 115; 104 (emphasis added).

of causation through another's "acting-in-concert" is no more than a device to evade the problem that arises when D helps P to inflict *self*-harm rather than harm to a third person. Because self-harm is not generally a crime, secondary liability usually does not apply and D cannot be convicted of complicity in P's offence.[167] But general principles of causation should not be invented on an ad hoc basis to deal with specific problems such as this.

(3) *The victim*

What about cases where the intervention is by V himself, rather than by a third party, and D and V are not acting in concert? The general rule is that the consequences of V's intervention are attributable to D provided that:

(i)   V's conduct is in reaction to D's wrongdoing; and

(ii) V's reaction was a reasonably foreseeable possibility.

In *R v Roberts*[168] the defendant made sexual advances to V while driving a car. V leapt out of the moving vehicle and suffered resulting injuries. D's conviction for assault occasioning actual bodily harm was upheld by the English Court of Appeal, which asked whether the injury was "the natural result of what the alleged assailant said and did, in the sense that it was something that could reasonably have been foreseen as the consequence of what he was saying or doing?"[169] The same principle is capable of explaining the American case of *People v Lewis*,[170] in which V, who was dying painfully from a gunshot wound, committed suicide by cutting his throat. D was held to have caused V's death.[171] It would be otherwise, however, if V had killed himself not in reaction to the suffering that D had inflicted, but rather in order to shield D.

The second requirement, of reasonable foreseeability, may not be met where the victim's reaction is disproportionate. Although it is sometimes said that "the victim must be taken as he is found",[172] in *People v Lewis* D would not have been guilty of murder if the wound had merely been painful rather than dangerous, and, knowing this, V had taken his life only in order to escape pain. In general, V's reaction will not be a novus actus where it is "in the

---

167 This was certainly the position under English law in *Kennedy* itself. Because use of a controlled drug is proscribed in New Zealand by s 7(1)(a) Misuse of Drugs Act 1975, in New Zealand D could be convicted straightforwardly on these facts as a secondary party to P's unlawful act and its fatal consequences, without resort to the causal ruse deployed by the Court in *Kennedy*.

168 *R v Roberts* (1972) 56 Cr App R 95; [1972] Crim LR 27. Other cases include *R v Tomars* [1978] 2 NZLR 505 (CA); *DPP v Daley* [1980] AC 237; [1979] 2 WLR 239 (PC); *R v Williams* [1992] 2 All ER 183; [1992] 1 WLR 380 (CA); *R v Pitts* (1842) Car & M 284; 174 ER 509; *R v Halliday* (1889) 61 LT 701; *R v Lewis* [1970] Crim LR 647 (CA). The Crimes Act also sometimes provides for attribution to the defendant where there is indirect causation: for example s 160(2)(d), (inducing self-destruction by threats, fear, or deception).

169 *R v Roberts* (1972) 56 Cr App R 95; [1972] Crim LR 27, 102; 27, 28.

170 *People v Lewis* 124 Cal 551; 57 P 470 (1899).

171 Although the *ratio* of the decision was multiple causes (that V died from loss of blood from the combined wounds), the court would have been prepared to decide the case on this ground if the facts had been clear regarding V's motive for cutting his own throat. See also *State v Angelina* 73 WVa 146; 80 SE 141 (1913); *Jones v State* 220 Ind 384; 43 NE 2d 1017 (1942); *Stephenson v State* 205 Ind 141; 179 NE 633 (1932) (torture).

172 For example *R v Blaue* [1975] 3 All ER 446; [1975] 1 WLR 1411 (CA), 450; 1415; 3.3.4(2).

foreseeable range",[173] and is not "daft".[174] This remains so even if that reaction is negligent or unlawful.[175]

As is the case with third party interventions, the possibility of a victim's contribution being a novus actus interveniens remains subject to the proviso that the original harm inflicted by D must no longer be contributing to the occurrence of the eventual result. In *Wall*,[176] the defendant (a colonial governor) sentenced V to an illegal flogging of some 800 lashes. V died from the punishment. It appeared that V had drunk alcohol after the flogging, which may well have accelerated his death. If so, however, it did so in combination with the effects of the flogging, and so would have been no more than an accompanying rather than overriding causal factor. The defendant therefore remained causally responsible for V's death.

(4)   *Summary of approach to intervening causes*

It is impossible to generalise comprehensively about the principles governing the attribution of causation. The rich detail of the cases defies their reduction entirely to simple rules: sometimes, in analysing new situations, the best technique may be simply to argue by analogy to one or more decided cases. Nonetheless, at the risk of over-simplification we offer the following general guidelines to causation problems where there are intervening causes.

Begin by considering whether D's original act is still making an ongoing contribution, in its own right, to the prohibited result at the time that result occurs (for example where V dies after losing blood from D's wound as well as T's). If so, then, regardless of the other interventions, D's act is a concurrent cause of the result (3.3.2(3)) and the causal chain is not broken by any novus actus interveniens. The analysis is concluded.

If the conclusion is not determined by that first step, it then becomes necessary to inquire whether D's original act is a cause of the prohibited result *through the medium of* T's intervention. This question is approached as follows.

First, assuming T is a human agent, consider whether T's intervention is free, deliberate, and informed (3.3.3(2)). If it meets these criteria in full then, regardless of its predictability, T's intervention is a novus actus interveniens that breaks the causal chain between D's original act and the prohibited result. D is absolved of causal responsibility and the analysis is concluded. (There may be an exception to this where T is the victim and T's action is one of self-harm done in concert with D (3.3.3(2)(f)). But that exception remains controversial.)

Alternatively, if T is not a human agent (3.3.3(1)) or the intervention was not free, deliberate, and informed, consider whether that intervention was reasonably foreseeable, as opposed to unforeseeable and extraordinary. If the former, then it may be expected not to sever the causal chain linking D's original act to the prohibited result; if the latter, then the intervention is a novus actus interveniens.

---

173   *R v Corbett* [1996] Crim LR 594 (CA); pace *R v Dear* [1996] Crim LR 595 (CA). It is submitted that the former case is to be preferred on this point, being consistent with existing case law.
174   *R v Roberts* (1972) 56 Cr App R 95; [1972] Crim LR 27, 102; 28.
175   Cf *R v Fleeting (No 1)* [1977] 1 NZLR 343, 347, 348; *R v Scully* (1824) 1 C & P 320; 171 ER 1213; *R v Swindall and Osborne* (1846) 2 Car & Kir 230; 2 Cox CC 141; 175 ER 95.
176   *R v Wall* (1802) 28 St Tr 51, 145. See also *R v Flynn* (1867) 16 WR 319 (Ir); *R v Mubila* [1956] 1 SA 31.

3.3.4 Omissions

(1) *As causes*

It is sometimes suggested that omissions cannot be causes.[177] This idea is founded on the notion that non-events, like failures to intercede and rescue a drowning victim, cannot bring things about: they are merely failures to prevent. To some extent this is true. If D watches without intervening while in a position to save V, her causal contribution to V's death is not of the same order as that when D herself holds V's head under water. One thing that is distinctive about omissions is that they do not initiate causal processes. Instead, they permit other causal processes to bring about the harm.

Nonetheless, neither ordinary language nor the law has much compunction about attributing causal responsibility to omissions. Both within and outside the courtroom, it is acceptable to say that the railway gatekeeper's failure in *R v Pittwood*[178] to close the gate before the train came through caused the resulting accident. By contrast, it would be misleading just to state that the train's arrival caused the accident, although that was also a causal factor. We tend to reserve the language of causation for those factors which are most relevant to our explanations.

All this reflects the point made earlier in 3.3.2, that causation in law is rarely a simple mechanical issue. Rather, it is intimately connected with the process of ascribing *responsibility* for the actus reus. Active intervention, while an obvious means of "causing" harm in the mechanical sense, is not the only way of being involved in bringing that harm about. In law, responsibility for the consequences of omissions involves a twofold test. D is normally held legally responsible for the consequences of an omission when (i) he has a duty to prevent those consequences from occurring (considered earlier in 3.2.1(2)), and (ii) his omission to intervene made a difference: that is, *if he had intervened, his intervention would have made a difference*. Part (ii) is the causal test.[179] For omissions, it is usually satisfied by proof of "but for" causation. In other words, D's omission causes an outcome if, but for that omission by D, the outcome would not have occurred.[180] If it would have resulted anyway, then D's omission made no difference and D cannot be held causally responsible for that outcome. As an example:

> Suppose that D, a doctor, does not notice that V has stopped breathing and fails to give him artificial respiration. She cannot be held causally responsible for his death unless it can be shown that V would have survived if D had discharged her duty to intervene and artificially respirate him.

---

[177] For example Moore, *Act and Crime: The Philosophy of Action and its Implications for Criminal Law*, Oxford, Clarendon Press, 1993, 267-278. For discussion, see Hughes, "Criminal Omissions" (1958) 67 Yale LJ 590, 627-631; Husak, *Philosophy of Criminal Law*, Totowa, NJ, Rowman & Littlefield, 1987, ch 6; Leavens, "A causation approach to criminal omissions" (1988) 76 Cal LR 547; Beyon, "Causation, omissions and complicity" [1987] Crim LR 539. Fletcher, "On the moral irrelevance of bodily movements" (1994) 142 U Pa L Rev 1443; Hart and Honoré, 38; Fletcher, *Rethinking Criminal Law*, Boston, Little, Brown & Co, 1978, 589ff.
[178] *R v Pittwood* (1902) 19 TLR 37. Cf the discussion in *Hart and Honoré*, 32ff; also Feinberg, *The Moral Limits of the Criminal Law* vol 1: *Harm to Others*, New York, Oxford University Press, 1984, 172ff.
[179] Quaere whether this requirement was overlooked in *R v Stone and Dobinson* [1977] QB 354; [1977] 2 All ER 341 (CA).
[180] *R v Myatt* [1991] 1 NZLR 674; (1990) 7 CRNZ 304 (CA), 682, 683; 312, 313; *R v Morby* (1881-1882) LR 8 QBD 571; *Barnett v Chelsea & Kensington Hospital Mgmt Cttee* [1969] 1 QB 428; [1968] 1 All ER 1068.

A similar example is *R v Dalloway*,[181] in which D was driving a cart without retaining a proper grip on the reins. A young child ran out in front of the cart and was struck and killed. It was ruled that D might be convicted of manslaughter only if it were proved that, had D been using the reins correctly, the child would have been saved.

Note that the prosecution must show, beyond reasonable doubt, that D's intervention *would* — not *might* — have made a difference. This rule is made clear in *R v Morby*, the facts of which were as follows:[182]

> D's child, aged 8, died of smallpox. Owing to D's religious beliefs, he obtained no medical aid for his son. At trial, it was established that proper medical treatment might have saved or prolonged the child's life, and would certainly have increased his chances of survival; but it could not definitely be said that treatment would have made any difference. It might have been of no avail.

On these facts, the Court of Criminal Appeal held unanimously that D's conviction could not be sustained. In this respect, the stringency of the causal test for omissions matches that for acts: it must positively be proved that D's conduct *did* cause death, not that it may have done.

Ex abundante cautela, it is also worth emphasising that even where it can be shown that D's omission is a "but for" cause of the harm, the omission will not be a legal cause if a novus actus intervenes. It is also subject to the requirement of salience.[183] Suppose, for example, that Anne makes a lunch appointment with James. Later, Anne discovers that she will not be free on the day they have arranged. Unfortunately, she discourteously fails to telephone James and cancel the appointment. While *en route* to the restaurant, James is killed in an automobile accident. If Anne had remembered to cancel, James would have eaten lunch at his office. Thus, but for Anne's omission, James would not have died. In this situation, however, Anne's omission is not a cause of death. A good illustration of this possibility is *R v Hawkins*,[184] in which D had a fatal accident while driving without a licence. The court ruled that the unlawful act of driving without a licence was not a cause of death. It was "merely part of the background to the accident".[185]

(2)   *As interventions*

The general rule is that, while an omission by a third party can be a causal factor, it cannot be a novus actus interveniens. Where D omits to prevent harm, his omission may be a legal cause of that harm, but it is normally a *concurrent* cause; ie, alongside those causal processes that the omission has failed to prevent. To illustrate:

> Suppose that D stabs V, who is admitted to hospital with substantial loss of blood and in urgent need of a blood transfusion to save her life. Apart from the loss of blood, V's injuries are not life-threatening. T, the doctor who attends V, recognises that she needs a blood transfusion and prepares to give her one. While waiting for the blood to arrive,

---

181   *R v Dalloway* (1847) 2 Cox CC 273.
182   *R v Morby* (1881-1882) LR 8 QBD 571. See Williams, "What should the Code do about omissions?" (1987) 7 LS 92, 106.
183   See 3.3.2(2).
184   *R v Hawkins* 21/2/01, Goddard J, HC Napier T18/00; below, 16.5.2(1). Cf *R v Little* 12/6/01, William Young J, HC Christchurch T17/01.
185   As was said of a similar case by Blanchard J in *R v Fenton* [2003] 3 NZLR 439, (2003) 20 CRNZ 76 (CA), para 15.

he goes to check on another patient. Unfortunately, he is distracted by a conversation with the patient and forgets to return and administer the transfusion to V. V dies from the loss of blood. Had the transfusion been performed, she would have survived.

In this case, *both* D and T cause V's death. Diagrammatically, their actions are multiple concurrent causes:

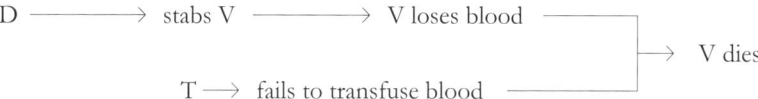

T's omission is not a novus actus that intervenes to break the causal chain from D's conduct to V's death. The whole reason why T's omission is causally significant is that it *fails to break* the causal sequence from D's action's to V's death. Indeed, we fault T and hold him (as well as D) liable for V's death precisely because he should have intervened and broken that chain before it reached its fatal culmination.

The proposition that an omission normally does not break a pre-existing causal chain is the proper explanation of *R v Blaue*.[186] In that case V was stabbed, and was admitted to hospital having lost a large quantity of blood. She was a Jehovah's Witness and refused the blood transfusion that was necessary to save her life. Consequently, the following day she died. D was convicted of her manslaughter. He appealed, contending that V's refusal to have a blood transfusion had broken the causal chain between the stabbing and V's death.

While it was accepted by the Crown that V's refusal to have a transfusion was *a* cause of her death, the English Court of Appeal quite rightly ruled, using an analogy with *Smith*,[187] that the original wound inflicted by D was still an operating cause of death. However, faced with the submission by D's counsel that V's decision was an unreasonable one, the court responded that:[188]

> "It has long been the policy of the law that those who use violence on other people must take their victims as they find them. This in our judgment means the whole man, not just the physical man. It does not lie in the mouth of the assailant to say that his victim's religious beliefs which inhibited him from accepting certain kinds of treatment were unreasonable."

As a general proposition, this is not valid law. Cases such as *R v Roberts*, discussed in 3.3.3(3), establish that an intervening reaction by V *does* break the chain of causation where it is not a reasonably foreseeable possibility — or, as was said in that case, where the reaction is "so daft" that it is really V's own voluntary act.[189] This means that D does not have to take his victim however he finds her, but only in so far as her reaction is a reasonably foreseeable or understandable one.

---

186 *R v Blaue* [1975] 3 All ER 446; [1975] 1 WLR 1411 (CA). Since this is a case involving homicide, in New Zealand it would now be covered by s 165. See ch 16.
187 *R v Smith* [1959] 2 QB 35; [1959] 2 All ER 193.
188 *R v Blaue* [1975] 3 All ER 446; [1975] 1 WLR 1411 (CA), 450; 1415.
189 *R v Roberts* (1972) 56 Cr App R 95; [1972] Crim LR 27, 103; 27-28.

Suppose, then, that V's refusal of a transfusion *was* "daft", and not a sensible or foreseeable possibility (this was not decided by the court). Prima facie, on the authority of *Roberts* and similar cases, this would then be a novus actus for which D was not responsible. In *Blaue*, however, the difference from those other cases was that V's intervening conduct involved not an act but an omission.[190] Thus, while it played a causal role in bringing about her death, and was a factor (unlike *Roberts*) for which D was not responsible, it did not break the causal chain from the stabbing to V's death. D's appeal, in effect, was that by her refusing to break the causal sequence D had set in motion, V broke the chain of causation. But an omission cannot, by itself, do that.[191]

The difference between the two cases can be illustrated, once again, with causal diagrams:

Roberts: D ⟶ frightens V ⟶ V jumps from car ⟶ V is injured

Blaue: D ⟶ stabs V ⟶ V loses blood ⟶ V dies
               V ⟶ refuses transfusion of blood

(3) Two case studies

By way of conclusion, it may be helpful to consider two more complex examples. One case that combines both omissions and the issue of medical interventions is *R v McKechnie*.[192] The facts of the case were as follows:

> D attacked V, inflicting serious head injuries. V was taken, deeply unconscious, to hospital, where he was discovered to be suffering from a duodenal ulcer which required surgery. However, the attending doctors decided not to operate on the ulcer. This decision was taken because, in the doctors' view, administration of the necessary anaesthesia to someone with such extensive head injuries could be fatal. A month later, the ulcer burst, and V died without having regained consciousness.

On these facts, the English Court of Appeal upheld D's conviction for manslaughter. How should the question of causation be analysed? One cause of V's death is, of course, the ulcer. But another, concurrent, causal factor is the doctors' omission to operate: if it had been safe to operate, there was no doubt but that the ulcer would have been removed.[193] What is therefore crucial to D's liability is whether the omission to operate, which *was* a cause of death, can be said in turn to be a consequence of D's actions in inflicting the head injuries on V. It seems clear enough that it was. The doctors' decision not to operate was made because of the injuries D inflicted. Moreover, although expert testimony at trial conflicted over whether it was *possible* to proceed with the operation without endangering V's life, there was no dispute that the decision was a reasonable one to take. Hence, it was not a novus actus interveniens. We may represent the causal analysis as follows:

---

190 More precisely, an action (refusal) whose causal role depends upon an omission (non-transfusion).
191 Contra *Hart and Honoré*, 361. Occasionally, an omission may be a novus actus when *combined* with a positive intervention: for example when the railway gatekeeper fails to close the gate, causing the ambulance taking V to hospital to be hit by a train. The gatekeeper causes V's death, not the original assailant.
192 *R v McKechnie* (1991) 94 Cr App R 51.
193 *R v McKechnie* (1991) 94 Cr App R 51, 57.

McKechnie:

D → injures V → T is deterred from operating ⎤
⎥→ Ulcer bursts → V dies
Growth of duodenal ulcer ⎦

We are also in a position now to consider the difficult case of *R v Cheshire*.[194] The relevant facts of the case were as follows:

> In early December 1987, D shot V in the leg and stomach. V was taken to hospital, where his injuries were operated on, and he was then transferred to the intensive care unit. He developed respiratory problems, and in mid-December a tracheotomy tube was inserted into his windpipe, where it remained for some 4 weeks. In early February his condition began to improve, and it appears that by this time the injuries inflicted by D's bullets had ceased to threaten his life. Unfortunately, he then began to develop breathing difficulties. These arose because his windpipe had narrowed near the site of the tracheotomy — a rare but known side-effect of tracheotomies. The medical staff negligently failed to diagnose the cause of the breathing difficulties, and V died in mid-February.

The Court of Appeal upheld D's conviction for murder, and properly so. Both D and V's doctors caused V's death. The key point is that the tracheotomy and subsequent complication occurred without negligence by the doctors. Thus there is no disruption of the causal chain between D's act of shooting V and the narrowing of V's windpipe. This being so, the question then becomes whether the doctors' subsequent negligence is a novus actus interveniens that breaks the causal chain between the narrowing of the windpipe and V's death. The answer to that question is no — because it constitutes an omission. The complaint against the doctors is that they *failed* to prevent the (natural, albeit rare) complication from causing death. Diagrammatically:

Cheshire:

D → injures V → T performs tracheotomy → Windpipe narrows ⎤
⎥→ V dies
T(2) → fails to rectify windpipe ⎦

3.4 The requirement of voluntariness

It is a fundamental requirement of the criminal law that D cannot be held liable for the occurrence of an actus reus unless he was *responsible* for it; unless its occurrence can in some way be attributed to D.

We noted in chapter 1 that when an actus reus occurs (for example, Jim is murdered), the criminal law begins with every member of society as a potential defendant.[195] The legal criteria that define responsibility for an actus reus also help to tell us which members of society are suitable defendants. Suppose that while investigating Jim's death, the police learn that his daughter Alice had secretly wished him dead because she stood to gain from his will. Despite

---

194 *R v Cheshire* [1991] 3 All ER 670; [1991] 1 WLR 844 (CA).
195 See 1.3.2(5).

her desires, the need for responsibility means that Alice is not guilty of murder unless she actually played some role in bringing about his death.

In respect of consequences, responsibility is established by showing causation. The police may conclude that although Alice wanted Jim's death, she did not cause it. Then she did not murder Jim. More generally, causation is necessary to establish a link between D's behaviour and the prohibited consequences. If an actus reus includes specification of such consequences (for example a person's death), the prosecution must prove causation in order to show that D's behaviour was responsible for that consequence, as part of showing that the actus reus as a whole can be attributed to D.

However, before she can be criminally liable the defendant must also be responsible for the *behaviour* element of the actus reus. This requirement is met when her behaviour is voluntary. Suppose that Alice did in fact cause Jim's death, but that she did so while suffering an epileptic seizure, during which her movements caused a heavy object to fall and crush Jim. Alice's behaviour, which causes Jim's death, is not voluntary. She is not responsible for his death, and cannot be convicted of murder.

Very often, acquittal in these circumstances need not be based upon involuntariness. Crimes such as murder require proof of some mental element on the part of the defendant, ie proof of some form of mens rea.[196] In most cases, murder itself cannot be committed unless D intends or is reckless about the victim's death.[197] Thus, even though Alice's behaviour may have caused death, she lacks the mental element required to be guilty of murder. She lacks mens rea.

But it is important to emphasise that involuntariness is *not* merely a denial of intention, or of other forms of mens rea, or even a denial of fault in general.[198] Alice does not claim that she killed Jim by *accident*. Her denial is much more profound. It is a claim that the movements of her body which caused Jim's death do not belong to Alice as a reasoning person.

This deserves elaboration. As part of our conception of what it is to be a human being, we draw a distinction between a deliberative person and her body. Not all movements of one's body can be identified with the person whose body it is that moves. When the doctor tests Simon's reflexes by tapping him on the knee, the swinging of his leg cannot be attributed to Simon. It is merely an event in the history of his body, rather like the lurching of passengers standing in a crowded bus. These are not actions that a person is answerable for doing. They are things that happen to him, over which he has no control,[199] and for which he is not responsible. So it is with Alice in the example above. Her behaviour is part of her body's history, but is not attributable to her as a reasoning person. It is not produced by any exercise of the capacities that identify Alice as a moral agent. In the words of H L A Hart:[200]

> "What is missing in these cases appears to most people as a vital link between mind and body; and both the ordinary man and the lawyer might well insist on this by saying

---

196 Ch 4.
197 Ch 16.
198 For useful discussion of this point, see Patient, "Some remarks about the element of voluntariness in offences of absolute liability" [1968] Crim LR 23.
199 Cf *R v Milloy* [1993] 1 Qd R 298; (1991) 54 A Crim R 340.
200 Hart, "Acts of will and responsibility" in *Punishment and Responsibility: Essays in the Philosophy of Law*, Oxford, Clarendon Press, 1968, 90, 107.

that in these cases there is not 'really' a human action at all and certainly nothing for which anyone should be made criminally responsible however 'strict' legal responsibility might be."

3.4.1 Involuntary behaviour

In general, D's deliberative control over her behaviour can be lost or impaired in two ways. First, D's normal capacity to reason about her behaviour may be suppressed because of an impaired consciousness. Alternatively, even if D is able to reason normally about her actions, she may have lost physical control over the movements of her body. In either case, her actions are not responsive to reason. They are "where the bodily movements occurred though the agent had no reason for moving his body in that way".[201]

(1) Loss of physical control

Imagine the following assault:

> Deborah is standing between Vicky and Tanya. Suddenly, Tanya grasps Deborah's arm and forces it into Vicky's midriff. Tanya is more powerful than Deborah, and Deborah has no chance to resist her. Vicky is winded.

In this situation, Deborah does not commit an assault on Vicky, because her behaviour is involuntary.[202] The movement of Deborah's arm does not occur under her control, and she cannot prevent its occurrence. Thus she is not responsible for the actus reus which eventuates. (Indeed, it is Tanya who assaults Vicky, using Deborah's arm.) Comparable instances would be where D's arm strikes V as the result of a reflex movement or a muscular convulsion or spasm.[203]

(2) Impaired consciousness

It has also been held that if D, while driving, were to be stunned by a blow and rendered incapable of controlling his car, his consequent failure to give way to a pedestrian at a pedestrian crossing would be involuntary and not subject to criminal liability.[204] An analogous situation is sleepwalking. In *Hughes*, a woman had got out of bed during the night and had gone to the kitchen "to peel potatoes", whence she had taken a knife and returned to the bedroom to stab her husband. She was acquitted of wounding with intent.[205]

Sleepwalking is an instructive case, because D's behaviour in this state may well be purposive,[206] and exhibit many outward signs of intentionality. Glanville Williams makes this point vividly:[207]

---

201 The definition of involuntariness proposed by Hart, *Punishment and Responsibility: Essays in the Philosophy of Law*, Oxford, Clarendon Press, 1968, 255, 256.
202 *R v Farduto* (1912) 10 DLR 669; 21 CCC 144, 673; 149; cf *O'Sullivan v Fisher* [1954] SASR 33, 39, 40; *Purdie v Maxwell* [1960] NZLR 599, 606.
203 *Bratty v A-G for Northern Ireland* [1963] AC 386; [1961] 3 All ER 523 (HL), 409, 532.
204 *Hill v Baxter* [1958] 1 QB 277; [1958] 1 All ER 193, 282-283, 286; 195, 197; *Burns v Bidder* [1967] 2 QB 227; [1966] 3 All ER 29, 240, 36; *Kay v Butterworth* (1945) 61 TLR 452, 453; *R v Spurge* [1961] 2 QB 205; [1961] 2 All ER 688; *McCone v Police* [1971] NZLR 105 (CA), 109; *Sione v Labour Dept* [1972] NZLR 278; *R v Bell* [1984] 3 All ER 842; [1984] Crim LR 685, 846; 686.
205 The Times, 3 May 1978, p 5. Cf *Bratty v A-G for Northern Ireland* [1963] AC 386; [1961] 3 All ER 523 (HL), 403, 409; 528, 532; *R v Carpenter* The Times, 14 October 1976; *R v Carter* [1959] ALR 335; [1959] VR 105; *Fain v Commonwealth* (1879) 39 Am Rep 213.
206 Cf also *R v Charlson* [1955] 1 All ER 859; [1955] 1 WLR 317.

"The sleep-walker does not always proceed as the cartoonists imagine him, with eyes tightly closed and arms outstretched. His eyes may be open and he may appear to be in perfect control. He will open a door and turn a corner, walk downstairs, open a drawer, take out a carving-knife, and return to the bedroom where his wife is asleep. But after waking up he will not remember his deed (except sometimes as a dream). Although his acts have a certain purpose (indeed, he may have an understandable reason for killing his wife), it is the purpose of a dream-state. He is not acting with his normal conscious mind."

When Lady MacBeth is observed "washing" her hands at night,[208] her movements are hardly random or uncontrolled. They exude purpose. Her actions are, in some sense, a subintentional product of her unconscious or subconscious mind. Certainly they are not mere reflex movements. But the control that Lady MacBeth has over them is in no way a conscious control — indeed, she is incapable of acting intentionally at all. Her "acts" are, in law, involuntary.

In the criminal law, these forms of involuntary behaviour are known as automatism. Like Lady MacBeth, the defendant may be unconscious or semi-conscious when she does the actus reus. Where this is so, and her actions are the product of that impaired consciousness, those actions are described as automatic. Automatism will be considered in more detail in chapter 10. However, as the assault example involving Deborah, Tanya, and Vicky shows, automatism predicated upon unconsciousness or impaired consciousness is not *required* for the defendant to be absolved of responsibility for her behaviour. Whether she was conscious or unconscious, what is essential to the denial of responsibility for a defendant's involuntary behaviour is that *she was unable deliberatively to control that behaviour and to prevent it from occurring.*[209]

In most cases, there will be a connection between consciousness and control: the greater the degree of consciousness a defendant has, the greater the degree of conscious or deliberative control she will have over her actions. This raises the further question: where D's claim of involuntariness is based upon automatism and an impaired consciousness, must D have lost *all* conscious control over her limbs?

It would appear not. Certainly there is no requirement that D be altogether unconscious. In *R v Charlson* D was not denied the defence even though he could recall hitting V on the head.[210] Similarly, in *R v Quick*, D was allowed to claim automatism consequent upon hypoglaecemia, notwithstanding that his condition was one of semi-consciousness.[211] North P considered the question in *R v Burr*, where he concluded that the claim of automatism:[212]

---

207 Williams, *TBCL*, 665.
208 Shakespeare, *MacBeth*, Act V, scene i.
209 *R v Milloy* [1993] 1 Qd R 298; (1991) 54 A Crim R 340.
210 *R v Charlson* [1955] 1 All ER 859; [1955] 1 WLR 317, 862I, 863F; 322, 323.
211 *R v Quick* [1973] 1 QB 910; [1973] 3 All ER 347 (CA), 916B; 350. The possibility of semi-conscious automatism appears to have been accepted also in *R v Carter* [1959] ALR 335; [1959] VR 105, 338, 339; 108, 109; *R v Stripp* (1979) 69 Cr App R 318, 320, 321.
212 *R v Burr* [1969] NZLR 736 (CA), 744, 745 (emphasis added). For a somewhat extreme illustration, see *R v T* [1990] Crim LR 256, discussed in Horder, "Pleading involuntary lack of capacity" [1993] 52 CLJ 298, 313-315.

"does not mean that the accused person must be absolutely unconscious because you cannot move a muscle without a direction given by the mind ... all the *deliberative* functions of the mind must be absent so that the accused person acts automatically."

This, with respect, seems correct.[213] What counts is the inability *deliberatively* to control one's conduct — that one's movements are not responsive to a capacity to reason and deliberate about one's conduct. Obviously, where the defendant is altogether unconscious her reasoning capacities will be inactive. But a defendant need *not* be unconscious before those capacities may be suppressed or inoperative. A hypnotised patient who carries out the instructions of the hypnotist must be able to comprehend and implement those instructions at some level of consciousness. Yet he has no capacity to deliberate about what actions to take or his reasons for taking them. He is an automaton, and is not responsible for his behaviour.[214]

Apart from sleepwalking and hypnotism, standard cases of semi-conscious conduct which are capable of qualifying as automatic and involuntary behaviour include acts done while in a state of concussion,[215] dissociation,[216] and advanced stages of hypoglycaemia.[217] (These will be discussed further in chapter 10.) In each of these instances, a loss of the capacity deliberatively to control D's behaviour will mean that he cannot be held criminally responsible for his actions and their consequences.

The view taken here may be contrasted with that found in *Police v Bannin*, where Fisher J suggests that automatism turns on whether D had the capacity to form the mental elements required for the crime:[218]

"the defence of automatism can be reduced to the question whether at the material time the accused had the mental capacity to form the particular mental ingredients of the crime with which he is charged ... The mental ingredients of the crime will vary from one case to another but in every case the accused must have (i) some appreciation of each of the key facts relevant to the crime, (ii) some capacity to make a decision to act with respect to those facts and (iii) some capacity to form each of the residual mental elements of the particular mens rea involved."

---

213 Notwithstanding the suggestion in *Watmore v Jenkins* [1962] 2 QB 572; [1962] 2 All ER 868, 586; 874 that automatic conduct must be "wholly uncontrolled and uninitiated by any function of conscious will"; cf *Re A-G's Reference (No 2 of 1992)* [1994] QB 91; [1993] 4 All ER 683 (CA); *Broome v Perkins* (1987) 85 Cr App R 321; [1987] Crim LR 271. These decisions, which concern driving offences, should be regarded as inconsistent with the case-law and as contrary to general principle (cf Williams, *TBCL*, 679). In *Broome v Perkins*, the prosecution's submission (at 325) that "Automatism meant an act which was done by the muscles without any control by the mind such as a spasm, a reflex action or a convulsion" reveals a fundamental confusion between automatism and loss of physical control over one's limbs (3.4.1(1)). This went unnoticed by the Divisional Court, which repeated (at 330, 331) the characterisation of automatism found in *Watmore v Jenkins* [1962] 2 QB 572; [1962] 2 All ER 868, 586; 874, as connoting no "wider or looser concept than involuntary movement of the body or limbs". Note that *R v Isitt* (1978) 67 Cr App R 44 (CA) is sometimes cited as similar authority, but on the facts appears to have involved action for a purpose, merely without moral inhibition (see 48, 49).
214 For interesting discussion, see Williams, "The actus reus of Dr Caligari" (1994) 142 U Pa L Rev 16667f.
215 Cf *Bratty v A-G for Northern Ireland* [1963] AC 386; [1961] 3 All ER 523 (HL), 403; 528; *R v Quick* [1973] 1 QB 910; [1973] 3 All ER 347 (CA), 918, 920-922; 352, 354-356.
216 Cf *R v Toner* (1991) 93 Cr App R 382; [1991] Crim LR 627; *R v T* [1990] Crim LR 256; *R v Rabey* [1980] 2 SCR 513; (1980) 15 CR (3d) 225.
217 *R v Quick* [1973] 1 QB 910; [1973] 3 All ER 347 (CA).
218 *Police v Bannin* [1991] 2 NZLR 237, also reported as *B v Police* (1991) 7 CRNZ 55, 254; 73.

With respect to his Honour, to claim that D's conduct was involuntary is to make a claim about D's responsibility for the actus reus, not about her capacity to satisfy the mens rea requirements. The test for involuntariness does not, and should not, vary according to the mens rea requirement of each particular offence. Indeed, where an offence includes mental ingredients, it is not necessary to show automatism: D will be absolved of criminal liability so long as one of those mental ingredients was absent, whether or not she had the capacity to form it at the time.[219] Furthermore, it is not at all clear how his Honour's analysis could be applied to offences which do not require proof of mens rea.[220]

In practice, although our approach is based on rather different principles than those embraced by Fisher J, the practical effect will probably be little, at least in respect of offences where proof of a mental element is necessary. Where D is incapable of forming, for example, an intention, she will surely also be incapable of exercising deliberative control over her behaviour, and will thus be automatic. Nonetheless, it is submitted that the approach taken here, which acknowledges the fundamental importance of responsibility and voluntariness, is to be preferred.

(3)   *Imperfect deliberative capacity?*

Although the above cases show that semi-conscious action can be automatic, they all involve a *complete* loss of deliberative control. It must be emphasised, on the other hand, that where D *does* in fact form an intention to commit a crime, then "however clouded, confused, and distant" D's awareness may have been, automatism is excluded.[221] Neither is responsibility for behaviour denied merely because D's deliberative faculties are not "fully functioning",[222] or "not working in top gear".[223] "Not thinking clearly" implies that D is still thinking about his actions, even if not very well. He is still exercising some deliberative control over his conduct, and cannot claim that his conduct was involuntary — it is a far cry from this state to one in which D is not reasoning at all. Rather than automatism, the appropriate defence (if applicable) is one of absence of mens rea. An instructive case is *R v Kingston*, the facts of which were as follows:[224]

> D was invited to a flat for ostensibly innocent purposes. While there, he was given coffee laced with disinhibiting drugs. He was then taken into a bedroom where a 15-year-old boy lay, also drugged, on a bed. D performed sexual acts with the boy, and was subsequently charged with an indecent assault. His conviction was upheld by the House of Lords.

It is quite likely that D would not have acted as he did had he not (unknown to him) ingested the drugs, which may well have affected his judgement by freeing him of his usual self-restraint. But a disinhibited intent is still an intent, and the explanation cannot amount to a denial of responsibility for D. He acts for reasons — albeit perhaps not reasons that would normally motivate him — and thus is not automatic.[225] More generally, it is no defence that D acted

---

219   *R v G* (1984) 1 CRNZ 275; *R v Tucker* (1984) 36 SASR 135, 13 A Crim R 447, 139; 451; *R v Martin* (1983) 32 SASR 419; 9 A Crim R 376.
220   See 3.4.3.
221   *Police v Bannin* [1991] 2 NZLR 237, also reported as *B v Police* (1991) 7 CRNZ 55, 253; 71.
222   *R v Burr* [1969] NZLR 736 (CA), 745.
223   *R v Isitt* (1978) 67 Cr App R 44 (CA), 48.
224   *R v Kingston* [1995] 2 AC 355; [1994] 3 All ER 353 (HL); considered in detail at 11.2.8.

upon an "irresistible impulse", for example, if he knew what he was doing and acted intentionally. An impulsive action is conscious and intentional — it is action for a reason, not action uncontrolled by reason.[226]

(4)   Insane automatism

Whenever a defendant's involuntariness is found to be due to automatism, the court must then determine whether it is to be classified as *sane* or *insane* automatism. This classification depends upon the cause of the automatism. Where the defendant loses consciousness as a result of a blow on the head, for example, his behaviour will be regarded as occurring in a state of sane automatism. By contrast, behaviour occurring during an epileptic fit will be exculpated on the footing of insane automatism.

The test for differentiating these types of automatism will be discussed in chapter 10, where we consider the defence of insanity. The importance of the distinction is that sane automatism operates as a straightforward denial of voluntariness and thus leads to an outright acquittal. By contrast, insane automatism is treated in law as a species of insanity for which there is a special verdict and a different burden of proof upon the defendant.

3.4.2   Omissions, states of affairs, and possession

So far we have considered involuntariness in the context of positive actions by a defendant. However, we saw earlier in this chapter (3.2) that not every actus reus requires a positive action. For example, if D stands by while her child drowns in the bath, her omission to save him is prima facie the actus reus of culpable homicide.[227]

Obviously, the involuntariness of omissions cannot be explained in the same way as actions. It would be odd indeed to talk of a reflex or convulsive omission. Nonetheless, even for omissions the criminal law requires that D must be responsible for her behaviour before she commits the actus reus of a crime. D's omission is involuntary, and her responsibility for the actus reus is negated, when she fails to discharge a duty to intervene because it was *impossible* for her to do so.[228]

Thus, in *Bamber*, a landowner charged with non-repair of a highway across his land was absolved of liability on the ground that repair of the highway was impossible:[229]

> "Both the road which the defendant is charged with liability to repair, and the land over which it passes, are washed away by the sea. To restore the road, as he is required to do, he must create a part of the earth anew … But here all the materials of which a

---

225   Cf *HM Advocate v Kidd* 1960 SLT 82; *R v Burr* [1969] NZLR 736; *R v Isitt* (1978) 67 Cr App R 44 (CA), 49; *A-G for the State of South Australia v Brown* [1960] AC 432; [1960] 1 All ER 734 (PC); *Bratty v A-G for Northern Ireland* [1963] AC 386; [1961] 3 All ER 523 (HL), 409; 532. A similar analysis would apply to provocation; D's provoked intention is still an intention. Thus the defence functions as an excuse rather than as a denial of voluntariness. See ch 16. For an argument that Kingston might deserve an excusatory defence, see Sullivan, "Making excuses" in Simester and Smith (eds), *Harm and Culpability*, Oxford, Clarendon Press, 1996, 131.
226   Cf *R v Burr* [1969] NZLR 736 (CA).
227   See 3.2.1(2)(b).
228   *Stockdale v Coulson* [1974] 3 All ER 154; [1974] 1 WLR 1192; *R v Hogan* (1851) 2 Den 277; 169 ER 504. A valuable discussion is Smart, "Criminal Responsibility for Failing to Do the Impossible" (1987) 103 LQR 532. See also Williams, *CLGP*, 746-748.
229   *R v Bamber* (1843) 5 QB 279; 114 ER 1254, 287; 1257.

road could be made have been swept away by the act of God. Under those circumstances can the defendant be liable for not repairing the road? We want an authority for such a proposition; and none has been found."

In the context of an offence more familiar to students, suppose the following example:

After an earthquake, D observes that his daughter is suffocating under a pile of rubble. D fails to rescue her because he is pinned beneath some collapsed masonry from which he cannot escape. D is not responsible for failing to rescue his daughter, and cannot be attributed with the actus reus of a homicide.

This is true even if, for some reason, D had wanted his daughter dead, and would not have rescued her had it been possible to do so.[230]

In such cases, where a defendant would not have complied with the law even if possible, it is sometimes important to distinguish between involuntary *behaviour* and unavoidable *consequences*. In the earthquake example, D has no control over his behaviour. But imagine the following case:

E is sunbathing on the beach when he observes his young daughter entering the sea and starting to swim in shallow water. Unfortunately, she encounters difficulties and is caught in an outgoing tide. E does not lift a finger to help, despite her cries to him, and watches as she is swept out to sea and drowned.

E may be able to deny responsibility for his daughter's death on the basis of *causation*. In a prosecution for murder or manslaughter, the prosecution must prove that E's omission to intervene caused his daughter's death. If in fact there was a riptide, and E would have been unable to save her anyway, then he is not responsible for the fatal consequence and cannot be convicted of a homicide offence.

The difference between this case and the earthquake example is that E denies responsibility for a *consequence* of his omission, on the basis of causation, while D denies responsibility for his *behaviour*, on the basis of involuntariness. Either way, a vital element of the actus reus of homicide is missing. But unlike D, E may still be criminally liable for any relevant offence where consequences are not part of the actus reus,[231] including an *attempt*. Because E's behaviour was not involuntary, it is capable of constituting the actus reus of an attempted murder. (Whether he would be convicted then depends upon questions of mens rea and proximity.) By contrast, it is impossible for D even to attempt a rescue. Therefore he cannot be held responsible for failing to do so.

(1) *States of affairs*

The test of responsibility is very similar for crimes which specify no behavioural element, and which criminalise states of affairs[232] or possession.[233] This follows from the point made earlier (in 3.2.2(1), 3.2.2(2)) that such offences, while formally needing no proof of particular behaviour by the defendant, can be seen as indirectly imposing liability for a defendant's omission to prevent the actus reus from occurring. In *Kilbride v Lake*,[234] D was charged with

---

230 *Starri v SA Police* (1995) 80 A Crim R 197.
231 Cf *R v Brown* (1841) Car & M 314; 174 ER 522, 318; 524.
232 See 3.2.2(1).
233 See 3.2.2(2).

permitting his car to be on the road without displaying a warrant of fitness. After he had parked and left the car, the warrant somehow became detached. It was conceded that D had no opportunity to rectify this state of affairs, and thus that his omission to do so, and consequently the existence of the actus reus, was involuntary. On this footing Woodhouse J ruled that D should be acquitted. It is a cardinal principle, his Honour said, that:[235]

> "a person cannot be made criminally responsible for an act or omission unless it was done or omitted in circumstances where there was some other course open to him. If this condition is absent, any act or omission must be involuntary ... In the present case there was no opportunity at all to take a different course, and any inactivity on the part of the appellant after the warrant was removed was involuntary and unrelated to the offence."

Without an opportunity to avoid the actus reus, D is not responsible for its occurrence. Similarly, in *Finau v Dept of Labour*[236] the defendant was acquitted of the situational-liability offence of remaining in New Zealand after the expiry of her temporary entry permit. Owing to her pregnancy, she had been refused carriage by an airline. Therefore, even though the actus reus had occurred, Finau was not criminally responsible for that actus, since it was impossible for her to prevent it.[237]

(2) *Possession*

Like situational offences, criminal possession (for example, of an instrument of burglary[238] or of a controlled drug[239]) can be established without proving any behaviour by D. The physical element of "being in possession" is a state of affairs in which D has control, with or without custody,[240] of the prohibited item. It is usually sufficient for the actus reus to show that the item is at a location where it is subject to D's power of control.[241]

Suppose that D acquires possession of controlled drugs but not by means of his own voluntary actions; for example, if a visitor to his house leaves the drugs behind when she departs. D may not be responsible for acquiring possession, but normally he is still responsible for *being* in possession because he fails to divest himself of the drugs. Suppose further, however, that D knows that he has been left the drugs yet happens to be bed-ridden through illness and is thus unable to dispose of them. It is submitted that, by analogy with offences involving states of affairs, D is not responsible for the actus reus and possession should not be attributed to him for the purposes of criminal liability.[242]

---

234 *Kilbride v Lake* [1962] NZLR 590. See Clark, "Accident - Or what became of *Kilbride v Lake*?" in Clark (ed), Essays on Criminal Law in New Zealand, Wellington, Sweet & Maxwell, 1971, 47; Budd and Lynch, "Voluntariness, causation and strict liability" [1978] Crim LR 74.
235 *Kilbride v Lake* [1962] NZLR 590, 593. Contra, in England, *Strowger v John* [1974] RTR 124; [1974] Crim LR 123; *Pilgram v Dean* [1974] 2 All ER 751; [1974] 1 WLR 601.
236 *Finau v Dept of Labour* [1984] 2 NZLR 396 (CA).
237 See also *Tifaga v Dept of Labour* [1980] 2 NZLR 235 (CA), 237-239, 241, 242; *O'Sullivan v Fisher* [1954] SASR 33; *Burns v Nowell* (1880) 5 QBD 444 (CA), 454. English law is rather more draconian than New Zealand law on this point: see the discussion and citations in 3.2.2(1).
238 Section 233 Crimes Act 1961.
239 Section 7 Misuse of Drugs Act 1975.
240 Cf *R v McRae* (1993) 10 CRNZ 61 (CA); *R v Delon* (1992) 29 NSWLR 29; s 2(2) Misuse of Drugs Act 1975.
241 *Police v Emirali* [1976] 2 NZLR 476 (CA); *Rose v Loo Kee* [1927] GLR 403. In some offences control without the availability of imminent custody may not suffice: *R v Rollo* [1956] NZLR 522 (CA); *R v Lester* (1955) 39 Cr App R 157.

(3) Distinction between impossibility and ignorance of duty

Impossibility amounting to involuntariness should be distinguished from situations where D is reasonably unaware of the existence of facts that trigger a duty to act in a certain manner. For example, one does not, apparently, commit an offence of remaining in Singapore when one's presence there becomes unlawful pursuant to an unpublished law.[243] Exculpation in such cases does not depend on any claim of involuntariness, but rather on the source and reasonableness of D's ignorance of law or fact. It is thus a matter for particular defences.

3.4.3 Involuntariness: responsibility by antecedent fault

Sometimes, even though the actus reus occurs involuntarily, D may still be held criminally responsible. One way in which this may occur is through vicarious liability, which is discussed in chapter 7. Leaving that possibility aside, however, D may also be liable for an offence if his involuntariness, and in turn the actus reus, was the consequence of earlier conduct by D at a time when he also had the mens rea required for that offence.

An example might be the phenomenon sometimes called "Dutch courage": where D, planning to perpetrate an assault, drinks himself into a virtual stupor in order to commit it.[244] Even if the court accepts his claim that the assault occurred while D was an automaton, it will not negate his criminal responsibility for the actus reus. Rather than focusing upon D's actions while automatic, his responsibility will be based upon his earlier conduct, which caused the eventual actus reus, and which was itself accompanied by the fault element required for the crime of assault.

This approach was accepted by the Court of Appeal as a possible analysis in *R v Wickliffe*.[245] In that case, D attempted to rob a jeweller's shop. He threatened those in the shop by pointing a loaded and cocked gun at them with his finger on the trigger. It appears that V then sprang at him. D was jolted back against the door, causing his finger to depress the trigger involuntarily. V was killed when the gun went off. Under s 167(d), D is guilty of murder if, for an unlawful object, he "does an act that he knows to be likely to cause death, and *thereby kills any person*". In the court's view,[246] although the immediate cause of death was an involuntary act by D, that was not a novus actus interveniens; his actions leading up to that point, in threatening V and other people in the shop by pointing a gun at them with his finger on the trigger, were still a cause of death.[247] Thus D's earlier conduct, rather than the firing of the gun itself, could be the act for the purposes of s 167(d) which "thereby kills any person".

---

242 As it happens, most offences of possession in New Zealand also require proof of mens rea going beyond mere knowledge of possession: cf *Dong Wai v Audley* [1937] NZLR 290; *R v Cox* [1990] 2 NZLR 275; (1990) 5 CRNZ 653 (CA); *Police v Emirali* [1976] 2 NZLR 476 (CA).
243 *Lim Chin Aik v R* [1963] AC 160; [1963] 1 All ER 223 (PC). Cf *Harding v Price* [1948] 1 KB 695; [1948] 1 All ER 283 (failing to report an accident when D did not know it had occurred). See ch 14.
244 *A-G for Northern Ireland v Gallagher* [1963] AC 349; [1961] 3 All ER 299 (HL), 382; 314 (Lord Denning).
245 *R v Wickliffe* [1987] 1 NZLR 55; (1986) 2 CRNZ 310 (CA), 60; 314. Cf *Ryan v R* (1967) 121 CLR 205; [1967] ALR 577, 218, 219, 231, 233, 239; 586, 594, 596, 600; Elliott, "Responsibility for involuntary acts: *Ryan v The Queen*" (1968) 41 ALJ 497; *R v Howe* [1987] AC 417; [1987] 1 All ER 771, also reported as *R v Burke* [1987] Crim LR 480, 458; 799; 484.
246 At least, on the view of the facts most favourable to the accused.
247 See also the discussion of causation earlier in this chapter, 3.3.3ff.

There is no general doctrine that allows for responsibility to be ascribed to an involuntary or automatic person merely because she was previously at fault for becoming automatic.[248] Consider the facts of *R v Lipman*:[249]

> L and his female friend, V, took a quantity of LSD while in V's flat. During the hallucination which followed, L suffocated V by cramming a bed sheet into her mouth. He believed when he did so that he was fighting snakes while descending to the centre of the earth.

L's behaviour while hallucinating is analogous to sleepwalking. It does not occur under his conscious or deliberative control. However, the automatism is self-induced, and moreover induced by D's own fault in becoming intoxicated. In England, his claim to be exculpated on the basis of automatism was refused, and L was convicted of manslaughter.[250]

In New Zealand, automatism would be available and L would not be convicted.[251] Even though L is responsible for his automatism, becoming automatic is not a criminal offence. It does *not* follow that he is responsible for the further consequences of his automatism. Before that can be the case, L must have the required mens rea not merely in respect of becoming automatic, but also in respect of those further consequences which make up the actus reus. For example, if an offence requires proof that the defendant foresaw the actus reus, the claim of automatism or involuntariness denies responsibility unless she actually foresaw the possibility of her incapacity *and* the resulting offence.[252]

(1)   *Involuntariness and antecedent fault in strict liability offences*

The analysis is perhaps more difficult for offences that do not require proof of mens rea. Such offences, involving what is known as strict or absolute liability, are considered in chapter 5. It is submitted that because voluntariness is fundamental to D's responsibility for the actus reus, and not merely relevant to mens rea, in principle its absence will still result in there being no criminal liability for D's conduct.[253]

---

248   Cf *R v Bailey* [1983] 2 All ER 503; [1983] 1 WLR 760 (CA), overruling the earlier decision in *R v Quick* [1973] 1 QB 910; [1973] 3 All ER 347 (CA), 922; 356, where it was said that automatism would not be available where its onset "could have been reasonably foreseen as a result of either doing, or omitting to do something, as, for example, taking alcohol against medical advice after using certain prescribed drugs, or failing to have regular meals while taking insulin". See generally Ashworth, "Reason, logic and criminal liability" (1975) 91 LQR 102, 106-109; Robinson, "Causing the Conditions of One's Own Defense: A Study in the Limits of Theory in Criminal Law Doctrine" (1985) 71 Virginia Law Review 1.
249   *R v Lipman* [1970] 1 QB 152; [1969] 3 All ER 410 (CA).
250   Approved in *DPP v Majewski* [1977] AC 443; [1976] 2 All ER 142 (HL). See MacKay, "Intoxication as a factor in automatism" [1982] Crim LR 146; Horder, "Pleading involuntary lack of capacity" [1993] 52 CLJ 298, 304ff. The refusal of a defence in England seems to be predicated on the fact that its self-induced cause specifically involves intoxication, rather than some other faultworthy origin. Intoxication does not have the same inculpating status in New Zealand: *R v Kamipeli* [1975] 2 NZLR 610 (CA); *R v Hart* [1986] 2 NZLR 408; (1986) 3 CRNZ 474 (CA); *Steinberg v Police* (1983) 1 CRNZ 129; ch 11.
251   *R v Cottle* [1958] NZLR 999 (CA), 1002, 1007 (Gresson P); *R v O'Connor* (1980) 146 CLR 64; 29 ALR 449 (HCA); *R v Martin* (1984) 51 ALR 540; 16 A Crim R 87 (HCA); Orchard, "Surviving without *Majewski* - A view from down under" [1993] Crim LR 426.
252   *R v O'Connor* (1980) 146 CLR 64; 29 ALR 449 (HCA); 73, 103; 456, 477 (Barwick CJ and Stephen J respectively); cf *R v Egan* (1897) 23 VLR 159; [1897] ALR 37; *Sione v Labour Dept* [1972] NZLR 278; *Ryan v R* (1967) 121 CLR 205; [1967] ALR 577. Thus Lipman might be convicted of manslaughter if the risk of killing someone while under the influence of LSD were such as to make his taking the drug "grossly negligent". (For discussion of the mens rea element in manslaughter, see ch 16.)

Nonetheless, responsibility may again be established antecedently. It will be open to the prosecution to show that earlier, voluntary, behaviour by D is responsible for the later (involuntary) events that brought about the actus reus. As will be seen in chapter 5, in strict liability offences the defendant may exculpate himself by proving that his actions were without fault. It follows that, where D's involuntariness, and in turn the actus reus, *is* a consequence of his earlier, voluntary conduct, then in order to exculpate himself D will be required to show that the later situation in which he found himself was not a foreseeable consequence of earlier behaviour for which he was at fault.

In practice, since D may still be liable where the automatism is his own fault, the requirement of absence of fault is the more important excusing condition for strict liability offences. But it does not entirely subsume the requirement for voluntariness.[254] If the prosecution cannot show that the actus reus was a consequence of earlier voluntary conduct by D, D should be entitled to an acquittal without having to prove an absence of fault.

3.4.4 Evidential issues

A claim of involuntariness or automatism is often described by lawyers as a "defence". In terms of substantive legal doctrine, it is not. It is a denial of the actus reus, rather than a plea that the defendant's actions were justified or excused. As such, it is for the prosecution to prove voluntariness on the part of the defendant alongside the rest of the actus reus. So far as the burden of proof is concerned, however, automatism *is* like a defence. In practice, there is a presumption of deliberative capacity to control one's actions, and voluntariness will become an issue only if there is evidence that genuinely raises the issue.[255] Thus, if the defendant wishes to deny responsibility on this basis, she must point to credible evidence that supports her claim. It is said that "blackout is one of the first refuges of a guilty conscience".[256] In general, since it is so easily feigned, the defendant's testimony of automatism will not be accepted unless it is buttressed by relevant evidence of surrounding circumstances or medical conditions.[257]

---

253 *R v O'Connor* (1980) 146 CLR 64; 29 ALR 449 (HCA); *Hill v Baxter* [1958] 1 QB 277; [1958] 1 All ER 193; Williams, " 'Absolute liability' in traffic offences" [1967] Crim LR 142, 194, 199ff. But see *Keech v Pratt* [1994] 1 NZLR 65, also reported as *Police v Pratt* (1993) 10 CRNZ 659, 72; 666, 667; followed in *Joe v Police* 21/12/95, Goddard J, HC Wellington AP230/95, 11.
254 Contra *MOT v Strong* [1987] 2 NZLR 295. See the criticism of that decision in *Adams*, CA20.47(2) (looseleaf). Note too that if an offence imposes strict liability only as to part of the actus reus, and requires mens rea for some other part, then involuntariness will of course preclude liability in the normal way.
255 *Bratty v A-G for Northern Ireland* [1963] AC 386; [1961] 3 All ER 523 (HL), 406, 407, 413, 416, 417; 530, 531, 535, 536, 537; *R v Cottle* [1958] NZLR 999 (CA), 1025. Similarly for impossibility: cf *R v Bailey* [1983] 2 All ER 503; [1983] 1 WLR 760 (CA), 507, 508; 765, 766. For further discussion of the burden of proof, see 2.3.
256 *Cooper v McKenna, ex p Cooper* [1960] Qd R 406, 419 (Stable J); *Bratty v A-G for Northern Ireland* [1963] AC 386; [1961] 3 All ER 523 (HL), 413, 414; 535, 536 (Lord Denning).
257 *Cook v Atchison* [1968] Crim LR 266; cf *Hill v Baxter* [1958] 1 QB 277; [1958] 1 All ER 193; *R v Stripp* (1979) 69 Cr App R 318; contrast *R v Budd* [1962] Crim LR 49. A more detailed treatment of this point is to be found in *Adams*, CA23.44-46 (looseleaf); also ch 10.

Chapter 4
MENS REA

4.1	Introduction	92
4.2	Intention	93
4.2.1	Ways of speaking about intention (in its core sense)	94
4.2.2	A formal definition of intention in its core sense	95
4.2.3	Foresight of consequences is not enough	97
4.2.4	Virtually certain consequences: the second category of intention	99
(1)	*Objective and subjective virtual certainty?*	103
(2)	*Definitions and evidence*	103
4.2.5	Intention and circumstances	104
4.2.6	Multiple intentions	105
4.2.7	"With intent" or "ulterior intent" crimes	105
4.2.8	Conditional intent	106
4.3	Foresight and recklessness	106
4.3.1	The need for foresight	108
(1)	*An alternative, objective version of recklessness*	109
(2)	*Which alternative? The future of recklessness*	109
4.3.2	Recklessness and circumstances	111
4.4	Why distinguish intention from recklessness?	115
4.5	Knowledge	116
4.5.1	Wilful blindness	116
4.6	Negligence	118
4.6.1	The test for negligence	118
(1)	*Ordinary or gross negligence?*	119
(2)	*Emergency*	119
4.6.2	Abnormal defendants: does the reasonable man share any of their characteristics?	120
4.6.3	Negligence with respect to behaviour rather than consequences or circumstances	123
4.6.4	The place of negligence	124
4.7	Other mens rea states	125
4.8	Transferred mens rea	125
4.9	Concurrence	127

4.9.1   Circumventing the concurrence requirement..128
(1)   *Fresh acts, continuing acts, and subsequent omissions*..128
(2)   *The complex single transaction*..128
(3)   *A causation approach*..130
(4)   *Involuntariness and antecedent fault*..130

4.1   Introduction

The mens rea of a crime is, generally speaking, that part of the offence which refers to the defendant's mental state. Returning to a familiar example from chapter 1, bigamy, consider s 205(1) Crimes Act 1961:

"205 Bigamy defined

"(1)   Bigamy is:

•   •   •   •   •

"(b)   The act of a person who goes through a form of marriage in New Zealand with any other person whom he or she knows to be married or in a civil union... ."

When Tom is charged with an offence against s 205(1)(b), the offence may only be established if Tom *knew that his "bride" was already married or knew that she was already in a civil union*. The italicised part of the last sentence is the mens rea requirement.

In the case of s 205(1)(b), only one mental element is specified. But it is possible for an offence to contain a variety of actus reus elements for which the corresponding mens rea requirements differ. One such offence is that of intentional damage contrary to s 269(1) Crimes Act:

"(1)   Every one is liable to imprisonment for a term not exceeding 10 years who intentionally or recklessly destroys or damages any property if he or she knows or ought to know that danger to life is likely to result."

There are two parts to the mens rea for this offence. A defendant (a) must have *intentionally or recklessly destroyed or* damaged property, and (b) *must have known or ought to have known* that doing so was likely to create a danger to life.

Although mens rea is often regarded as the requirement that the defendant have a "guilty mind", and is taken to contain the fault elements of each offence, it is in practice a rather technical area of law. For a prosecutor, mens rea requires her to establish only that the defendant had the specified mental state toward the actus reus which is required for that crime. In particular, proof that the defendant had the requisite mens rea of an offence does not mean that she must know her conduct is illegal,[1] or wrong. Similarly, a laudable motive which prompts the defendant to commit an offence is no defence. In *R v Smith*,[2] for instance, the defendant offered a bribe to the town mayor. He did so in order to expose the mayor as corrupt. Despite his good motive, he was convicted of offering a bribe to a public servant since he had intentionally (the mens rea) offered the bribe (the actus reus). At that stage the offence was complete, and his motive could not help him.[3]

---

1   Cf s 25 (ignorance of law).
2   *R v Smith* [1960] 2 QB 423; [1960] 1 All ER 256 (CCA). Cf s 105 (corruption and bribery of official).

There are three steps to be taken in establishing whether a defendant has mens rea. The first step is to determine what mens rea standard is required in respect of each separate element of the actus reus. The second is to interpret the criteria of those mens rea element(s). Third is the factual question: did the defendant act with the mens rea element(s) required?

This chapter is concerned with the second of those steps; its purpose is to explain the main types of mens rea which the law might require. There are a great variety of possible mens rea states: the Crimes Act mentions, among others, intention, recklessness, wilfulness, knowledge, belief, the lack of a belief on reasonable grounds, fraudulence, dishonesty, failure to use reasonable care, purpose, calculation, and corruption. However, in this chapter we will confine our discussion to the most common, and most important, types of fault element.

4.2 Intention

The central, and usually the most grave, case of wrongdoing occurs when the defendant's crime is intentional.[4] For the majority of offences, it is not necessary to prove that the actus reus was intended, since recklessness will normally suffice for a conviction. (Intention will therefore, often be most relevant at the sentencing stage.) But this is not always so — the offence of attempting to commit a crime, for example, can only be done intentionally.[5] Similarly, an assault can only be committed by applying force intentionally; recklessness will not suffice.[6] There are other important reasons for distinguishing intention from recklessness, and we shall return to these later.

There is normally no need for an elaborate definition of intention in order to decide whether an actus reus was intended. A few peculiar cases may present difficulty, but usually the analysis will be intuitively obvious: "[t]he general legal opinion is that 'intention' cannot be satisfactorily defined and does not need a definition, since everybody knows what it means."[7] Nonetheless, the fact that some cases are difficult means that we do need guidelines about what intention

---

3   The decision does not sit well with *R v Clarke* (1985) 80 Cr App R 344; [1985] Crim LR 209, which holds that a citizen has a defence if acting honestly and solely to reveal crime and recover its proceeds. However, the view that mens rea means no more than the mental element for the offence is endorsed in *R v Hicklin* (1868) 3 QB 360, 370-372; *Gordon v Schubert* [1956] NZLR 431; *Yip Chiu-Cheung v R* [1995] 1 AC 111; [1994] 2 All ER 924 (PC); also *R v Kingston* [1995] 2 AC 355; [1994] 3 All ER 353 (HL). This approach, which disconnects a finding of mens rea from the presence of fault, is appropriate only if a suitable range of defences is available. See 1.3.2; also Brett, *Inquiry into Criminal Guilt*, Sydney, Law Book Company, 1963. Cf too *R v Gordon* (1993) 10 CRNZ 430 (CA), 438, 439, 441: "sympathy for the appellant cannot prevail over the current statutory provisions."
4   See, for example, Smith, "Intention in criminal law" (1974) 27 CLP 93; White, "Intention, purpose, foresight and desire" (1976) 92 LQR 569; Buzzard, " 'Intent' " [1978] Crim LR 5; Smith, " 'Intent': A reply" [1978] Crim LR 15; Orchard, "Criminal intention" [1986] NZLJ 208; Duff, "The obscure intentions of the House of Lords" [1986] Crim LR 771; Williams, "Oblique intention" (1987) 46 CLJ 417; Buxton, "Some simple thoughts on intention" [1988] Crim LR 484; Duff, "Intentions legal and philosophical" (1989) 9 OJLS 76; Smith, "A note on 'intention' " [1990] Crim LR 85; Simester and Chan, "Intention thus far" [1997] Crim LR 704; Norrie, "After Woollin" [1999] Crim LR 532; Kaveny, "Inferring Intention from Foresight" (2004) 120 LQR 81.
5   See s 72 Crimes Act 1961.
6   Section 2; cf *R v Young* 9/7/92, CA86/92.
7   Williams, *TBCL*, 74. Per Lord Bridge, in *R v Moloney* [1985] AC 905; [1985] 1 All ER 1025 (HL), 926; 1036. "The golden rule should be that ... the judge should avoid any elaboration or paraphrase of what is meant by intent, and leave it to the jury's good sense to decide whether the accused acted with the necessary intent ...". Cf *R v Belfon* [1976] 3 All ER 46; [1976] 1 WLR 741 (CA); *R v Nedrick* [1986] 3 All ER 1; [1986] 1 WLR 1025 (CA), 2, 1027.

means. The legal definition of intention comprises two alternative categories. D may be found to have intended the actus reus if:

(i) D *intended* the actus reus in the ordinary, paradigm sense of "intention"; or

(ii) D recognised that the actus reus was a *virtually certain* consequence of his actions.

The first case, (i), is the standard or core variety and largely reflects the ordinary language meaning of "intention". In this paradigm case, D tries (seeks, attempts) to bring about the relevant outcome. For whatever reason, he wants or needs to bring about that outcome, and that is why he acts as he does. By contrast, in the virtual certainty case, (ii), D does not act in order to bring about the intended outcome; he acts for other reasons. However, he knows that the *actus reus* is a virtually certain consequence of his actions. Though that is not what he is trying to bring about, it is an inescapable concomitant.

We will elaborate on these definitions in the following sections. In 4.2.1-4.2.3, the paradigm category of intention (i) will be discussed. The virtual certainty case (ii) is considered in 4.2.4.

4.2.1 Ways of speaking about intention (in its core sense)

As a starting point, it may be helpful to look at how "intention" has been paraphrased by judges and academic writers. In *Cunliffe v Goodman*, Lord Asquith stated that intention:[8]

> "connotes a state of affairs which the party 'intending' ... does more than merely contemplate: it connotes a state of affairs which, on the contrary, he decides, so far as in him lies, to bring about."

In other words, D generally intends an outcome if it is something that he decides, or seeks, to bring about. Additionally, it seems clear that D intends a result if he acts with the *purpose*,[9] or object, of bringing it about. In Smith and Hogan's useful example:[10]

> "If D has resolved to kill P and he fires a loaded gun at him with the object of doing so, he intends to kill. It is immaterial that he is aware that he is a poor shot, that P is nearly out of range, and that his chances of success are small. It is sufficient that killing is his object or purpose, ... that he acts in order to kill."

At the heart of this approach is a recognition that D intends to kill P if he means to bring about P's death by his actions — if he acts with the aim, object, or purpose of killing P.[11]

Antony Duff has built on this idea. Suppose that D fires a gun knowing that P is nearby, and we are trying to decide whether he intended to kill P. Duff argues that if D aims to cause P's death by his actions, then we can say that D *attempts* to kill P.[12] Furthermore, an attempt can either be a success or a failure. Therefore, Duff shows, one feature of intention is that a defendant who intends (aims, tries, attempts) to kill P would regard himself as having "failed"

---

8   *Cunliffe v Goodman* [1950] 2 KB 237, 253.
9   *R v Burke* [1991] 1 AC 135; [1990] 2 WLR 1313 (HL), 147; 1318.
10 *Smith and Hogan*, 93.
11 Cf *Gollins v Gollins* [1964] AC 644; [1963] 2 All ER 966 (HL), 663; 971 (Lord Reid); *DPP v Smith* [1961] AC 290, also reported as *R v Smith* [1960] 3 All ER 161 (HL), 327 (Viscount Kilmuir LC); *Hyam v DPP* [1975] AC 55; [1974] 2 All ER 41 (HL), 79; 54 (Lord Hailsham).
12 This point was made by the Court of Appeal in *R v Moloney* The Times, 22 December 1983 (May LJ); see *R v Moloney* [1985] AC 905; [1985] 1 All ER 1025 (HL), 919 (Lord Bridge). Cf also *R v Walker* (1990) 90 Cr App R 226, 230.

in some sense if P does not die.[13] By contrast, if he does not intend P's death, then he would not think he has failed if P survives. So this is another way of testing whether D intended P's death.

An illustration of Duff's argument is provided by the case of *Hyam v DPP*.[14] D had poured petrol through the letterbox of V's house and set fire to the petrol, intending only to frighten V but realising her actions risked causing death. Duff remarks:[15]

> "[D] intended to set fire to [V's] house; her action would have failed had the house not caught fire … She intended thereby to frighten [V]: had the fire not frightened [V], her action (though successful as one of 'setting fire to the house') would have failed as one of 'frightening [V]'. But she did not intend to cause death or injury: though she foresaw death or injury as a likely effect of her action, her action would not have been a failure had no one been killed or injured; death or injury were foreseen side-effects, not intended effects, of her action."

By frightening V, the defendant would have succeeded in her purpose; her actions would not have been a failure if no one had died, since it was not part of her purpose to kill. Neither, we would say, was she trying to kill anyone. Thus, the deaths were not intended (at least not in the core sense).

4.2.2 A formal definition of intention in its core sense

The differences noted above between intended and unintended actions can also be set out in terms of means, ends, and side-effects. Things done as means or ends are intended; side-effects are not.[16] In *Hyam v DPP* (see 4.2.1), D set fire to the house as a means of frightening V. Hence, both setting fire to the house and frightening V were intended. But the ensuing fatalities were neither a means nor an end. They were side-effects of her actions, and as such unintended.

Ideas of means, ends, and purpose point to a more formal way of thinking about intention. The purposes or ends for which one acts are the reasons *why* one acts. They motivate and explain one's action. Intention embraces both these and the intermediate steps (the means) that one undertakes in order to achieve those ends. Formally, we can capture the central cases of intention as follows. D intends to do an action (or to bring about some consequence) if he:

(i)   *Wants* to do that action (or to bring about that consequence); or

(ii)   *Believes* it is possible for him to achieve something he wants by doing that action (or by bringing about that consequence); and

(iii)   Behaves as he does *because*[17] of his desire in (i) or his belief in (ii).

Notice that nothing in this definition requires that D should believe the action or consequence is probable, highly likely, or anything more than merely possible. This is shown by Smith and

---

13 Duff, *Intention, Agency and Criminal Liability: Philosophy of Action and the Criminal Law*, Oxford, Basil Blackwell, 1990, 61-63. See now his *Criminal Attempts*, Oxford, Clarendon Press, 1996, ch 1.
14 *Hyam v DPP* [1975] AC 55; [1974] 2 All ER 41 (HL).
15 Duff, *Intention, Agency and Criminal Liability: Philosophy of Action and the Criminal Law*, Oxford, Basil Blackwell, 1990, 61.
16 Finnis, "Intention and side-effects" in Frey and Morris (eds), *Liability and Responsibility: Essays in Law and Morals*, Cambridge, Cambridge University Press, 1991, 32. See also Williams, "Oblique intention" (1987) 46 CLJ 417, 421.
17 Or, at least *in part because*. We consider the possibility of multiple intentions in 4.2.6.

Hogan's example cited earlier, where D attempts to kill P despite the chances of doing so being small. The combination of (i) with (iii) covers actions which are done as ends:

(i)   He *wants* to do that action (or to bring about that consequence); and

(iii) He behaves as he does *because* of that desire.

In *Hyam*, D wanted to frighten V, and she set fire to the house because she wanted to frighten her. Therefore she intended to frighten V. Her desire to frighten, which is the desire contemplated in (i) above, is often termed the defendant's *motive*. But it is important to recognise that a desire, or motive, is not enough by itself to establish intention:[18]

> "It is a dangerous doctrine to lay down that the mere proof of a motive, even in the absence of any apparent motive in any other persons who could have committed the act, is to be held to be conclusive proof of guilt."

Often people want things which they never set out to achieve. If D stands to inherit from his mother's will, he may have a reason for wanting her death. But the mere wish that another person were dead is not an intention to kill that person: "intention is something quite distinct from motive or desire."[19] Distinguishing between desire and intention here is (iii), the requirement that the defendant act because of that motive. A motive is irrelevant to intention unless it is also *why* D did the actus reus.

On the other hand, desire is not an essential component of intention.[20] Often, we bring things about not because we want them, but because they are a *means* to something else (that we do want).[21] The parent who punishes a child for misbehaving may do so regretfully, believing it to be her only option and wishing very much that there were something else she could do; yet she intends to punish him all the same.[22] What she wants, say, is to deter her child from behaving that way again, and she punishes him in order to achieve that aim. But she does not desire his punishment, at least not for its own sake. This sort of case, where the actus reus is done as a means to an end, is captured by the combination of (ii) with (iii):

(ii) He *believes* it is possible for him to achieve something he wants by doing that action (or by bringing about that consequence); and

(iii) He behaves as he does *because* of that belief.

---

18 *Woods v Brown* (1907) 26 NZLR 1312; 10 GLR 70, 1315-1316; 71. Cf Lord Bridge in *R v Moloney* [1985] AC 905; [1985] 1 All ER 1025 (HL), 926; 1037: "intention is something quite different from motive or desire."

19 *R v Moloney* [1985] AC 905; [1985] 1 All ER 1025 (HL), 926; 1037 (Lord Bridge).

20 Cf *R v Mohan* [1976] QB 1; [1975] 2 All ER 193 (CA), 11; 200 (James LJ): intention is "a decision to bring about, in so far as it lies within the accused's power, the commission of the offence ... no matter whether the accused desired that consequence of his act or not".

21 See *Hyam v DPP* [1975] AC 55; [1974] 2 All ER 41 (HL), 74; 62 (Lord Hailsham): intention includes "the means as well as the end". See also Williams, *CLGP*, 16.

22 Cf *Lang v Lang* [1955] AC 402; [1954] 3 All ER 571, 428, 429; 579, 580.

In *Smith*,[23] D believed that by bribing the mayor he would be able to expose him. This was why he acted as he did. Therefore he intended to bribe[24] the official, even though his ultimate aim was to expose him. It may be helpful to show D's reasoning with a diagram:

Smith: S ⟶ Bribe mayor Means ⟶ Expose corruption End

Similarly, in *Hyam*, D believed that by setting fire to the house she would be able to frighten V. That was why she acted as she did. Therefore she intended to set fire to the house:

Hyam: H ⟶ Set fire to house Means ⟶ Frighten V End
                                                 |
                                      Kill V Side-effect

But as this diagram shows, it was no part of her intentions to kill V or do grievous bodily harm to her.

In practice, of course, looking at the defendant's desires and beliefs is an indispensable aid in helping us to ascertain her intentions. Even in (ii), the case of doing something as a means to an end, there must be a motive in the background. And although it does not matter in principle what that background motive is, often it will be important for evidential purposes. "To prove the intention you may show the motive, and this is a link in the chain of evidence."[25]

4.2.3 Foresight of consequences is not enough

The key ingredient of any account of intention is (iii), that the defendant acts because of his desire or belief. Without it, there cannot be intention. If D foresees an outcome, and indeed welcomes it, but that outcome nevertheless plays no part in her decision to act, then she does *not* intend it.[26] The outcome is, for D, incidental. In *Hyam v DPP* (see 4.2.1), D foresaw the possibility of killing V, but she did not set fire to the house *because* of her belief that doing so might bring about V's death. Hence, although she was reckless,[27] she did not intend to kill. Similarly, a judge who awards compensatory damages against a defendant may realise that, in so doing, he might cause the bankruptcy of the defendant, but that has nothing to do with why he awards the damages. The bankruptcy is no more than a foreseen but unintended side-effect.

The law has not always been clear on this point. In *Hardy v Motor Insurers' Bureau*, for instance, it was said of the accused that "he must have foreseen, when he did the act, that it would in all probability injure the other person. Therefore he had the intent to injure the other person".[28] And in *R v Jakac*, the Supreme Court of Victoria was of similar mind: if the defendant "knew what the consequences were likely to be, and with that knowledge he deliberately did

---

23   *Smith* [1960] 2 QB 423; [1960] 1 All ER 256 (CA). See 4.1.
24   Or, more accurately, to "corrupt" the official. In fact s 1(2) Public Bodies Corrupt Practices Act 1889 (UK) requires that the defendant act "corruptly". The Court interpreted this to mean only that he must intend to induce a corrupt bargain. See n 3; Shyllon, "The corruption of 'corruptly' " [1969] Crim LR 250.
25   *R v Heesom* (1878) 14 Cox CC 40, 44 (Lush J).
26   A point made by Kenny, "Intention and purpose in law" in Summers (ed), *Essays in Legal Philosophy*, Oxford, Basil Blackwell, 1968, 146, 155.
27   See 4.3.

the act and if the consequences in fact did follow, he must be taken to intend them".[29] Indeed, in 1960 the House of Lords in *DPP v Smith* simply presumed (among other things) that the defendant intended whatever he foresaw.[30] The Lords later divided on this question in *Hyam*. Although Lord Hailsham declared it "clear that 'intention' is clearly to be distinguished alike from 'desire' and from foresight of the probable consequences",[31] his Lordship's view does not reflect a consensus. Viscount Dilhorne, for instance, remarked that if someone does an act:[32]

> "knowing when he does it that it is highly probable that grievous bodily harm will result, I think that most people would say and be justified in saying that whatever other intentions he may have had as well, he at least intended grievous bodily harm."

Indeed, Lord Diplock felt able, following *Hyam*, to hold that the law was now "well-settled":[33]

> "Where intention to produce a particular result was a necessary element of an offence, no distinction was to be drawn in law between the state of mind of one who did an act because he desired it to produce that particular result and the state of mind of one who, when he did the act, was aware that it was likely to produce that result but was prepared to take the risk that it might do so ... ."

More recently, however, the distinction between intention and mere foresight was accepted in *R v Moloney*, where Lord Bridge expressed himself to be:[34]

> "firmly of opinion that foresight of consequences, as an element bearing on the issue of intention in murder, or indeed any other crime of specific intent, belongs, not to the substantive law, but to the law of evidence."

Similarly, in *R v Hancock*, Lord Scarman stated that "[f]oresight does not necessarily imply the existence of intention".[35] This rule has since been reiterated by the House of Lords in

---

28 Hardy v Motor Insurers' Bureau [1964] 2 QB 745; [1964] 2 All ER 742 (CA), 764; 748 (Pearson LJ); see also 758 (Lord Denning MR). See also Lord Devlin's definition of "purpose" in *Chandler v DPP* [1964] AC 763, 805 to "designate those objects which he knows will probably be achieved by the act, whether he wants them or not".

29 R v Jakac [1961] VR 367, 371. Cf Saunders, *Mozley & Whiteley's Law Dictionary* (9th ed), 1977, 175: "a person contemplates any result, as not unlikely to follow from a deliberate act of his own, he may be said to intend that result, whether he desire it or not."

30 DPP v Smith [1961] AC 290, also reported as R v Smith [1960] 3 All ER 161 (HL). Cf Viscount Kilmuir LC, 326; 166: "the test of what a reasonable man would contemplate as the probable result of his acts, and therefore, would intend." See also R v Ward [1956] 1 QB 351; [1956] 1 All ER 565 (CA); Kenny, "Intention and purpose in law" in Summers (ed), *Essays in Legal Philosophy*, Oxford, Basil Blackwell, 1968, 146.

31 Hyam v DPP [1975] AC 55; [1974] 2 All ER 41 (HL), 74; 52. See also R v Belfon [1976] 3 All ER 46; [1976] 1 WLR 741 (CA).

32 Hyam v DPP [1975] AC 55; [1974] 2 All ER 41 (HL), 82; 59.

33 R v Lemon; R v Gay News Ltd [1979] AC 617; [1979] 1 All ER 898 (HL), 638; 905. See also a similar dictum in Hyam v DPP [1975] AC 55; [1974] 2 All ER 41 (HL), 86; 62.

34 R v Moloney [1985] AC 905; [1985] 1 All ER 1025 (HL), 928; 1038. The defendant was charged with murder after shooting his stepfather during a drunken game. It was not clear that, when he pulled the trigger, he realised the gun was pointing at the victim. His conviction was quashed because the trial judge was ruled to have erred when directing the jury (917; 1030) that "a man intends the consequence of his voluntary act (a) when he desires it to happen, whether or not he foresees that it probably will happen and (b) when he foresees that it will probably happen, whether he desires it or not".

R v Woollin,[36] and it may safely be regarded as prevailing in New Zealand. DPP v Smith itself was effectively overruled by the Privy Council in Frankland and Moore v R.[37]

4.2.4 Virtually certain consequences: the second category of intention

Mere foresight of a consequence, then, does not establish an intention. But one question is still unresolved: what if the consequence is foreseen not merely as possible, but as *certain* to occur — does "intention" include such a case? In R v Richards [aiding and abetting],[38] Fisher J suggested that the answer might be yes when he held that intention includes not only those consequences which are sought, but also those which are foreseen with sufficient certainty. To illustrate this possibility, consider the following example used by a number of philosophers. V, a fat man, is trapped in the mouth of a cave. The waters in the cave are rapidly rising, and the cave will soon be flooded. The trapped man is immovable and is preventing the escape and survival of his fellow spelæologists. The only way of unblocking the exit is by blowing him up with a stick of dynamite. Can they do so without intending his death?[39] The case can be represented as follows:

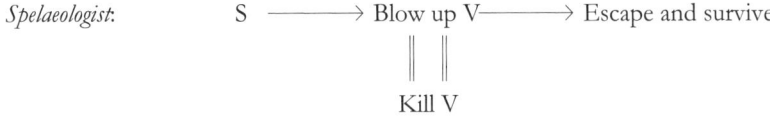

As the example illustrates, some consequences which are not themselves sought (as either means or end) are nevertheless much too close to the intended effects to be separated off as mere side-effects. V's colleagues would be delighted if they could blow him up, and free themselves, without killing V. But they cannot. It is a certainty that V will die. In this context, it is worth noting the definition of intention proposed in the report of the Crimes Consultative Committee.[40] A person intends the result of an act when he does the act:[41]

---

35   R v Hancock [1986] 1 AC 455; [1986] 1 All ER 641 (HL), 472; 649. The defendants, miners who were on strike, pushed concrete blocks off a bridge on to the motorway below. The blocks struck a taxi ferrying another miner to work. The taxi driver was killed. The defendants, it appears, recognised the dangerousness of their actions but claimed they meant only to frighten the miner and prevent him from going to work, and not to harm anyone. Their convictions for murder were quashed. See also at 473-474; 651 (Lord Scarman): "the greater the probability of a consequence the more likely it is that the consequence was foreseen and ... if that consequence was foreseen the greater the probability is that that consequence was also intended ... [T]he probability, however high, of a consequence is only a factor." See also R v Nedrick [1986] 3 All ER 1; [1986] 1 WLR 1025 (CA).
36   R v Woollin [1999] 1 AC 82; [1998] 4 All ER 103 (HL). See also R v Nedrick [1986] 3 All ER 1; [1986] 1 WLR 1025 (CA).
37   Frankland and Moore v R [1987] AC 576; [1987] 2 WLR 1251 (PC). In the *Law Quarterly Review*, Lord Goff concludes that "after the journey through *Smith*, *Hyam*, *Moloney* and *Hancock*, the law is really back where it was ... Foresight of consequences is not the same as intent, but is material from which the jury may, having regard to all the circumstances of the case, infer that the defendant actually had the relevant intent": Goff, "The mental element in the crime of murder" [1988] 104 LQR 30, 41.
38   R v Wentworth [1993] 2 NZLR 450, also reported as R v Richards [aiding and abetting] (1992) 9 CRNZ 355, 456; 361.
39   For philosophical discussion of the case see Geddes, "On the intrinsic wrongness of killing innocent people" (1973) 33 Analysis 93; Duff, "Intentionally killing the innocent" (1973) 34 Analysis 16; Finnis, "The rights and wrongs of abortion: A reply to Judith Thomson" (1973) 2 Philosophy and Public Affairs 117; Hanink, "Some light on double effect" (1975) 35 Analysis 147.

"(a) Meaning to bring about that result; or

"(b) Being aware or believing that that result *will* happen."

It is the second limb which reflects the suggestion in *Richards*, and which captures the case of the spelæologists. The use of the emphatic "will" reflects the need for something more than just foresight that the result is likely or possible; which would be a case of recklessness, something defined in the same report as requiring that the person do an act "being aware that there is a risk that the result will happen".[42]

Until recently, the English Courts, which have considered the definition of intention more fully than have their New Zealand counterparts, were equivocal about this type of case. Although Lord Hailsham did not think that "foresight as such of a high degree of probability is at all the same thing as intention",[43] he nevertheless stated explicitly that intention includes not only those things done as ends or means but also "the inseparable consequences of the end as well as the means". The extension is supported by reference to an example developed by Glanville Williams:[44]

> "suppose that a villain of the deepest dye blows up an aircraft in flight with a time-bomb, merely for the purpose of collecting on insurance. It is not his aim to cause the people on board to perish, but he knows that success in his scheme will inevitably involve their deaths as a side-effect."

According to Lord Hailsham, "if any passengers are killed he is guilty of murder, as their death will be a moral certainty if he carries out his intention".[45] In *Moloney*, Lord Bridge, too, accepted that there may be cases where things which are seemingly not sought as ends or means should be analysed as cases of intention:[46]

> "A man who at London Airport, boards a plane which he knows to be bound for Manchester, clearly intends to travel to Manchester, even though Manchester is the last place he wants to be and his motive for boarding the plane is simply to escape pursuit ... By boarding the Manchester plane, the man conclusively demonstrates his intention to go there, because it is a moral certainty that that is where he will arrive."

In such a case the law would say that the "morally certain" consequence is intended. But the basis on which it does so is unclear.[47] There are two main alternatives: either there is, *by definition*, a second category of (indirect) intention involving morally certain consequences,[48] or there is not and moral certainty is simply evidence of an intention in its core sense. In the

---

40   Crimes Bill Consultative Committee, *Crimes Bill 1989: Report of the Crimes Consultative Committee Presented to the Minister of Justice April 1991*, Wellington, Department of Justice, 1991.
41   Crimes Bill Consultative Committee, *Crimes Bill 1989: Report of the Crimes Consultative Committee Presented to the Minister of Justice April 1991*, Wellington, Department of Justice, 1991, cl 21, 92 (emphasis added).
42   Crimes Bill Consultative Committee, *Crimes Bill 1989: Report of the Crimes Consultative Committee Presented to the Minister of Justice April 1991*, Wellington, Department of Justice, 1991, cl 22, 93.
43   *Hyam v DPP* [1975] AC 55; [1974] 2 All ER 41 (HL), 77; 54.
44   "Oblique intention" (1987) 46 CLJ 417, 423; cf his earlier *The Mental Element in Crime*, Jerusalem, Magnes Press, 1965, 34, 35.
45   *Hyam v DPP* [1975] AC 55; [1974] 2 All ER 41 (HL), 74; 52.
46   *R v Moloney* [1985] AC 905; [1985] 1 All ER 1025 (HL), 926; 1039.
47   Duff, *Intention, Agency and Criminal Liability: Philosophy of Action and the Criminal Law*, Oxford, Basil Blackwell, 1990, 21, 22; also Duff, "The obscure intentions of the House of Lords" [1986] Crim LR 771.

latter case, foresight of a moral certainty is no more than a ground for inferring that the consequence was (directly) intended,[49] and the inference may be rebutted by other evidence.

There is something to be said for thinking the link is merely evidential, and that there is no second category. Even consequences that are certain to occur may appear not to be intended. If D drinks a bottle of scotch one evening, he may be sure that he will get a hangover in the morning, but he does not drink the scotch with the intention of having a hangover.[50] Support for this position is found in decisions subsequent to *Moloney*, where the courts frequently tended to read Lord Bridge's remarks as pertaining to evidential matters. In *R v Nedrick*, Lord Lane CJ held that:[51]

> "if the jury are satisfied that at the material time the defendant recognised that death or serious harm would be virtually certain (barring some unforeseen intervention) to result from his voluntary act, then that is a fact from which they may find it easy to infer that he intended to kill or do serious bodily harm ... ."

Writing extra-judicially in 1987, Lord Goff condemned the extension of intention to embrace moral certainty as "illegitimate".[52]

If Lord Lane and Lord Goff are right, then the explanation of cases like the flight to Manchester has nothing to do with moral certainty. Rather, it is that the fugitive intentionally travels to Manchester as a *means* of leaving London. This is consistent with the account of intention stated earlier, in 4.2.2:

Traveller: T   →   Go to Manchester   →   Leave London

But this answer does not help to deal with the insurance-bombing case proposed by Glanville Williams, where the deaths of the airline passengers are clearly not a means to anything. Despite this, it does seem that the passengers' deaths are so intimately bound up with the villain's intended actions as to be inseparable, and it would be wrong to call them mere side-effects. It appears, therefore, that there is a special category of intention, which falls outside the standard definition given in 4.2.2. This second category arises where the defendant recognises that the additional effect is inseparable from those which he intends. A useful definition of this type of case is the rule proposed by H L A Hart: a foreseen outcome is to be regarded as intended when it:

> "is so immediately and invariably connected with the action done that the suggestion that the action might not have that outcome would by ordinary standards be regarded as absurd, or such as only a mentally abnormal person would seriously entertain."[53]

---

48 Cf Lord Bridge in *R v Moloney* [1985] AC 905; [1985] 1 All ER 1025 (HL), 925; 1036: an overwhelming probability "will *suffice to establish* the necessary intent". (Emphasis added.) Cf also the use of "conclusively" in the quotation at n 46.
49 Cf *R v Nedrick* [1986] 3 All ER 1; [1986] 1 WLR 1025 (CA), 4; 1028: where D realises that a consequence is inevitable, "the inference *may* be irresistible that he intended that result" (emphasis added).
50 Duff, *Intention, Agency and Criminal Liability: Philosophy of Action and the Criminal Law*, Oxford, Basil Blackwell, 1990, 89-90.
51 *R v Nedrick* [1986] 3 All ER 1; [1986] 1 WLR 1025 (CA), 3, 4; 1028. See also the judgment by Lord Scarman in *R v Hancock* [1986] 1 AC 455; [1986] 1 All ER 641 (HL), at n 35.
52 "The mental element in the crime of murder" [1988] 104 LQR 30, 59.

These outcomes are intended even though D is not trying or aiming to bring them about. They represent a supplement to the core definition of intention stated in 4.2.2.

Fortunately, there is now a House of Lords decision that supports this analysis. In *Woollin*,[54] D had lost his temper and thrown his 3-month-old son against a hard surface. The child's skull fractured and death ensued. In D's trial for murder, the prosecution expressly disavowed that D had intended (in the core sense) his son's death or serious injury. His conviction implies, therefore, that foreseeing a result as a virtual certainty is an alternative category of intention and not just evidence from which to infer the core definition of intention. On appeal,[55] Lord Steyn accepted this and explicitly rejected the language of inference. Distilled from his judgment, his Lordship asserts that:[56]

> "in the rare cases where the [standard] direction [that it is for the jury simply to decide whether the defendant intended to kill or to do serious bodily harm] is not enough, the jury should be directed that they are not entitled to find the necessary intention, unless they feel sure that death or serious bodily harm was a virtual certainty (barring some unforeseen intervention) as a result of the defendant's actions and that the defendant appreciated that such was the case."

There are, therefore, two types of intention. First, the normal, core variety is that defined in 4.2.2: where D directly seeks an outcome (because he wants it for its own sake or as a means to something else). Secondly, there are outcomes which, in D's eyes, are so closely bound to normally-intended outcomes that they are virtually certain to occur alongside them. They may also be regarded as (indirectly) intended.

Cases requiring a *Woollin* direction are rare. Normally, as Lord Steyn said, the jury should consider only the core sense of intention.[57] The *Woollin* decision gives the prosecution an alternative way of proving that an outcome was intended; it is supplementary to, and not a substitute for, intention in the core sense.[58]

However, while clarifying the independent status of this second category of intention, *Woollin* does leave its precise definition unresolved. Lord Steyn's model direction is expressed in negative terms:

> "the jury should be directed that they are not entitled to find the necessary intention, unless they feel sure that death or serious bodily harm was a virtual certainty... ."

This suggests that, although foresight of virtual certainty is *necessary* before the alternative category of intention is satisfied, it may not always be *sufficient*.[59] It seems that, where there is

---

53 "Intention and punishment" in *Punishment and Responsibility: Essays in the Philosophy of Law*, Oxford, Clarendon Press, 1968, 113, 120. Hart continues: "the connexion between action and outcome seems therefore to be not merely contingent but rather to be conceptual." See further Simester, "Moral certainty and the boundaries of intention" (1996) 16 OJLS 445. This is a tighter connection (as, with respect, it ought to be) than that required by the Canadian Supreme Court in *R v Chartrand* (1994) 116 DLR (4th) 207 (SCC), 225-230.
54 *R v Woollin* [1999] 1 AC 82; [1998] 4 All ER 103 (HL).
55 Ultimately, D's conviction was quashed and a conviction for manslaughter substituted, because the trial judge had misdirected the jury on the alternative limb by requiring only that D foresaw a "substantial risk" (rather than virtual certainty) of serious injury or death.
56 *Woollin* [1999] 1 AC 82; [1998] 4 All ER 103 (HL), 96; 113.
57 Cf *R v Phillips* [2004] EWCA Crim 112, para 10.
58 *R v D* [2004] EWCA Crim 1391, [2004] All ER (D) 11, para 29.

virtual certainty, the jury is *permitted* to conclude that the defendant intended the outcome and, absent any special considerations, the jury should normally so conclude;[60] but they are entitled not to find intention should there be such considerations. For example, a doctor may know that by injecting a terminally ill patient with the morphine necessary to dull pain, it is virtually certain that she will incidentally shorten the patient's life. The doctor does not aim to shorten the patient's life, and does not intend his death in the core sense. In such a case, notwithstanding that it is a virtually certain side-effect, the jury may well conclude that she does not intend his death, even indirectly.[61]

(1) *Objective and subjective virtual certainty?*

There is another oddity about the *Woollin* direction. Lord Steyn requires not only that the defendant *think* the outcome is virtually certain; it must also *in fact* be virtually certain. Arguably, however, it is only the former that counts. Intention is a measure of the agent's perceptions and mental state, and should be unaffected by facts of which the agent is unaware. Suppose that D is a fugitive who accelerates her car toward a policeman who is blocking her escape. The fugitive, let us say, wishes only to escape but thinks it is virtually certain that, by knocking over the policeman, she will cause grievous bodily harm. In fact, there is a twenty per cent chance in such collisions that the victim will not be seriously injured; but D does not know this and, as it happens, the policeman is severely hurt. In our view, D should be held to have intended the injury.[62]

(2) *Definitions and evidence*

What, then, is the role of evidential inference? Consider Lord Scarman's summary in *R v Hancock*:[63]

> "the greater the probability of a consequence the more likely it is that the consequence was foreseen and ... if that consequence was foreseen the greater the probability is that that consequence was also intended... . [T]he probability, however high, of a consequence is only a factor... ."

At first glance, this may appear inconsistent with Lord Steyn's instruction, in *Woollin*, that no reference should be made to probabilities. However, there need be no inconsistency. *Woollin* pertains to the morally-certain category of intention, while Lord Scarman's summary should be interpreted as referring to the standard, or paradigm, variety of intent discussed in

---

59 Hence the Court of Appeal was right to judge, in *R v Matthews* [2003] EWCA Crim 192; [2003] 2 Cr App R 30, para 43, that "the law has not yet reached a *definition* of intent in murder in terms of appreciation of a virtual certainty." Foresight of virtual certainty is not the same thing as (indirect) intention, but rather grounds from which it may be found.

60 Cf, for example, the analysis of the events in *R v Matthews* [2003] EWCA Crim 192; [2003] 2 Cr App R 30, para 46: "If the jury were sure that the appellants appreciated the virtual certainty of Jonathan's death when they threw him from the bridge and also that they then had no intention of saving him from such death, it is impossible to see how the jury could not have found that the appellants intended Jonathan to die."

61 For a discussion of cases that contain dicta to this effect, see Ashworth, "Criminal Liability in a Medical Context: The Treatment of Good Intentions" in Simester and Smith (eds), *Harm and Culpability*, Oxford, Clarendon Press, 1996, 173. Cf *Re A (Children) (Conjoined Twins: Surgical Separation)* [2001] Fam 147 (CA), 163 (Robert Walker LJ).

62 Cf Simester, "Moral certainty and the boundaries of intention" (1996) 16 OJLS 445, 465-466.

63 *R v Hancock* [1986] 1 AC 455; [1986] 1 All ER 641 (HL), 473-474; 657.

4.2.1-3. Where the prosecution seeks to prove that D intended the actus reus under the standard definition, foresight of a probability is evidence from which that intention may be *inferred*. Notice that reference to probability forms no part of that standard definition (given in 4.2.2). In terms of the paradigm type of intention, there is no reason to require virtual certainty before inferring intent. If D aims a pistol at V and pulls the trigger, it may not be virtually certain, or even very likely, that V will die — perhaps it is a difficult shot — yet we would normally infer that D's intention was to kill; that he was trying to kill. The connection between (standard) intention and foresight of probability is purely evidential.

On the other hand, the connection between foresight of probability and the virtually-certain category of intention is not even evidential. It is non-existent. Without foresight of a virtual certainty, the second category of (indirect) intention is simply not in play.

4.2.5 Intention and circumstances

The account of intention we have given so far needs qualification when applied to any circumstances which form a part of the actus reus. This is best seen by means of an example. Rape can only be committed by D's having sexual intercourse with V without her consent. The circumstance, that V does not consent, is part of the actus reus of the offence. There are two ways in which D's mental state regarding V's non-consent can satisfy the demands of intention. The plain case occurs where D rapes V by intentionally having sexual intercourse with her, *hoping* that she does not consent. In this case D intends "sexual intercourse without consent" in its full sense, because it is part of his purpose not merely to have sexual intercourse with V, but to have it without her consent. Duff's test of failure shows this clearly:[64] D would regard himself as having "failed" if V did in fact consent to having sexual intercourse with him.

Although the clearest sort of case, this is the less common variety of intention where circumstances are at issue, and probably applies only to a pathological or sadistic offender. More often, rape is intentional when D neither intends nor hopes that V is not consenting. (He means to have sexual intercourse, and does not care whether or not his victim consents.) In this situation, he nevertheless intends to have "sexual intercourse without consent", because he intends to have sexual intercourse *believing* that V does not consent.

So there are two ways of showing that an actus reus is intended when it involves circumstances. The first is by showing that the behaviour and consequences are intended, and that D hopes the circumstances are present. The second is by showing that the behaviour and consequences are intended, and that D believes the circumstances are present. What does "believing" mean in this context? In our view "believing" has the same meaning as "knowing", with one exception. We consider the meaning of knowledge below,[65] but in essence what is required is that the defendant hold a positive belief, amounting to an acceptance, that the circumstance exists.

The one difference, in law, between knowledge and belief is that a belief need not be correct. The defendant may believe something wrongly, but she cannot "know" something that is false. Usually the difference will not matter very much. For example, if D wrongly believes that V

---

64 See 4.2.1.
65 See 4.5. We do not endorse Orchard's remark in "Criminal intention" [1986] NZLJ 208, 212, that "it may be that it should suffice [for intention] if D adverted to the *possibility* of the existence of the circumstances."

does *not* consent to sexual intercourse when in fact she *does* consent, then regardless of his mens rea he cannot commit rape, because the actus reus is missing. But sometimes it will still be important to establish whether D has mens rea, since even without the actus reus he might nevertheless be guilty of an attempt. In this example, his false belief that V does not consent will be sufficient to help constitute an intention for the purposes of attempted rape.[66]

4.2.6 Multiple intentions

Very often, a person has more than one reason for acting as he does. By cooking dinner, John might intend not only to assuage his hunger, but also to use up the contents of the fridge, as well as surprise and please his flatmates. All three results are intended. The mere fact that a defendant can point to some other result that he was also trying to achieve does not mean that he cannot have intended the actus reus. It is no answer for a newspaper that deliberately publishes sub judice material to say that it was really trying to increase its circulation. Ignoring extraneous intentions, the criminal law focuses only on the actus reus; and asks, whatever else he intended, did D intend that *actus*?

4.2.7 "With intent" or "ulterior intent" crimes

Sometimes the intentional doing of an actus reus is not itself an offence and becomes criminal only when done for some further purpose. For example, if D carries a crowbar in his bag he does nothing wrong, but if he carries the crowbar with intent to use it in a burglary, he is guilty of an offence.[67] Crimes of this sort require what is often called an "ulterior intent".[68] The main feature of such crimes is that they specify, as part of the mens rea, an intent to do something that is not part of the actus reus. In the example above, the actus reus is simple possession of the crowbar — it does not matter whether the crowbar is actually used in a burglary.[69] This is why such crimes are said to involve "ulterior" intent: because the eventual intention is ulterior to the actus reus.

In other respects, however, these crimes are no different from crimes of ordinary intent. In particular, the ulterior intent must exist at the time when the actus reus is performed. This point is illustrated in *Police v Bannin*,[70] where the defendant appealed against convictions inter alia for three offences of entering a house with intent to commit a crime within it, contrary to s 231. Although he was found to have intended to enter the house, the convictions were quashed on the ground that the prosecution had failed to prove that he had already formed an intent to commit an offence by the time at which he entered the house.

Where a crime specifies an ulterior intent as part of the mens rea, it seems clear that mere foresight of the further consequence will not do. The crime can be committed only if the defendant intends that consequence. This is the explanation of the controversial case of *R v Steane*.[71] Steane had been compelled, through concern for his family's safety, to make broadcasts on behalf of Germany during the Second World War. He was prosecuted under

---

66 The claim here is merely that knowledge or belief satisfies the demands of intention. It is a further question (taken up in ch 8) whether, with respect to circumstances, intention is *required* to establish the mens rea of attempt offences.
67 Section 233(1)(a).
68 Horder, "Crimes of ulterior intent" in Simester and Smith (eds), *Harm and Culpability*, Oxford, Clarendon Press, 1996, 153.
69 Cf *R v Rodley* (1913) 9 Cr App R 69, 76.
70 *Police v Bannin* [1991] 2 NZLR 237, also reported as *B v Police* (1991) 7 CRNZ 55.

English wartime regulations for doing an act likely to assist the enemy (the actus reus) "with intent" to assist the enemy. The Court of Criminal Appeal quashed his conviction for lack of mens rea, and rightly so. Although in making the broadcasts Steane had done an act likely to assist the enemy, the prosecution failed to prove that he intended thereby to assist the enemy (ie that assisting the enemy was a part of his purposes in broadcasting). Notice that the mens rea required is ulterior to the actus reus. The actus reus is "*any act likely* to assist the enemy" and does not involve proof that the defendant in fact did assist the enemy. The mens rea is an intent "to assist the enemy", which goes beyond the actus reus. Steane intended to make the broadcasts, but his ulterior intent in so doing had been to protect his family. It would be otherwise if the foreseen further consequence were "morally certain" to accompany his intended actions, in which case they too would be intended.[72]

4.2.8 Conditional intent

Sometimes a person is willing to commit a crime but her actions will not necessarily result in one. For example, if a thief makes off with a handbag, meaning to keep the contents, she steals those contents only if there are any. In this situation, her intention to take the contents is conditional upon there being anything to steal. Such cases are not uncommon in the criminal law, especially in the context of offences involving an ulterior intent. The general rule is that an intention to do or bring about something only if particular conditions hold remains, in law, an intention. Thus a burglar who enters a flat with intent to steal a television set only if there is one still, in law, enters with intent to steal.[73] Similarly, in *Wicks v Police*[74] it was held that D intended permanently to deprive V of his property even though D meant to keep the item only if V refused to meet his demands.

4.3 Foresight and recklessness

Often people cause injury without intending to — that is, without acting in order to do so. The doctor who injects her patient with a painkiller may unintentionally kill him if the patient proves to be allergic to the drug that she injects. But the fact that an injury is unintended does not mean that the person who causes it is blameless; the doctor may have been aware of the risk of injury, a risk that she nevertheless chose to run. In such cases we would say she *foresaw* but did not intend the harm.

Not every case of foresight amounts to recklessness. In order for a defendant to be reckless, the risk that she chooses to run must also be an unreasonable one. Although in practice this issue does not often arise, the qualification is important. It means that anaesthetists, who knowingly undertake a slight risk that the patient will have a fatal allergic reaction when anaesthetised before an operation, are not automatically guilty of reckless homicide when the patient dies. The question of what is reasonable is an objective question, and it is not an issue of whether the defendant thought the risk was reasonable; rather, it is a question of whether

---

71 *R v Steane* [1947] KB 997; [1947] 1 All ER 813 (CCA). See, for example, Williams, "Oblique intention" (1987) 46 CLJ 417, 428.
72 See 4.2.4; also *R v Chartrand* (1994) 116 DLR (4th) 207 (SCC), 225-230.
73 *A-G's References (Nos 1 and 2 of 1979)* [1980] QB 180; [1979] 3 All ER 143 (CA), distinguishing and confining *R v Husseyn* (1978) 67 Cr App R 131n; [1978] Crim LR 219 (CA); cf *Police v Wylie* [1976] 2 NZLR 167 (CA), 169. See Campbell, "Conditional intention" (1982) 2 LS 77.
74 *Wicks v Police* (1984) 1 CRNZ 328. (D came into possession of a barrister's file and refused to return it until the barrister settled an unrelated claim of D's.) See also *R v Hare* (1910) 29 NZLR 641 (CA).

an ordinary and prudent person would have been prepared to take that risk. To this extent defendants cannot be permitted to displace the law and judge what is right for themselves.[75]

There are several factors for the law to consider when deciding whether a particular risk was reasonable. These include the probability of the risk occurring and the nature and gravity of the harm being risked. Driving at 50 km/h on a busy road may be reasonable; driving at 80 km/h may not be, because of the increased risk of accidents and the more serious injuries that are likely to ensue should there be an accident. Against these considerations should be balanced the value and likelihood of achieving what the defendant was trying to do while running that risk. A high-risk surgical operation may be justifiable when it is done as a last resort or in an emergency to save the patient's life. But the risks involved may not be acceptable if less dangerous alternatives are available, or if the purpose of the operation is trivial, or if reasonable steps were not taken to reduce those risks.[76]

One point that should be made here is that the incorporation of a standard of reasonableness means that there is no need for a separate "threshold" criterion of probability or likelihood.[77] Obviously, if a risk is thought to be minimal or only an "outside chance", running that risk is likely to be unobjectionable.[78] But even a very slight risk will be enough for recklessness if the harm being risked is serious enough and the act concerned has no social value. A game of "Russian roulette" would be reckless even if the chances of being killed were thought to be only one in 200. In such cases, it may be necessary to abandon an activity altogether if the defendant cannot eliminate the risk entirely. One example of this is provided by *Chief Constable of Avon and Somerset Constabulary v Shimmen*.[79] D, a martial arts expert, was demonstrating his skill to friends by kicking close to a window without breaking it. He smashed the window. Even though he thought he had "eliminated as much risk as possible", he was nevertheless guilty of reckless criminal damage since he had chosen to run the slight and unjustifiable risk which remained. Conversely, there may be a very substantial risk of injury or death in certain "last resort" surgical operations, but those operations are not necessarily unreasonable when undertaken.

---

75 Thus we do not entirely concur with the view expressed by Tipping J in *Taylor v Police* (1990) 6 CRNZ 470, 471 that recklessness "is a purely subjective concept". Neither does the Court of Appeal: *R v Tipple* 22/12/05, CA217/05. Cf Eichelbaum J in *Dept of Health v Multichem Laboratories Ltd* [1987] 1 NZLR 334, 339 (a strict liability case): "The defendant's own perception of reasonableness cannot govern the situation." For discussion of such issues in a medical context, see Merry and McCall-Smith, *Errors, Medicine and the Law*, Cambridge, Cambridge University Press, 2001.
76 Cf *Summers v SPCA* [1991] 2 NZLR 469; (1990) 6 CRNZ 201, 474, 475; 207, 208.
77 The view expressed here contrasts with the words used by the Court of Appeal in *R v Tihi* [1989] 2 NZLR 29; (1989) 4 CRNZ 289 (CA), 32; 292, where it was said that "it must be shown that the accused either meant to cause the specified harm, or foresaw that his actions were likely to expose others to the risk of suffering it. This would preserve the subjective test of liability, giving 'likely' the meaning favoured by this Court in *R v Gush* [1980] 2 NZLR 92 (CA)." In *Gush*, the favoured meaning was "such as could well happen"; but the question there arose in the context of a statutory wording rather than a general test of recklessness. There seems no reason in principle why such a threshold should apply to recklessness, and *Adams* accepts that "in some cases it may suffice if there was a realisation that there was some possibility of it eventuating, at least if this was not dismissed as 'altogether negligible'." (*Adams*, CA20.29 (looseleaf).) Cf *R v Whitehouse* [2000] Crim LR 172 (CA), where the question whether an outcome was sufficiently probable to be "likely" depended not just upon its probability but also upon the gravity of the outcome at risk.
78 Cf *Hilder v Police* (1989) 4 CRNZ 232, 236.
79 *Chief Constable of Avon and Somerset Constabulary v Shimmen* (1987) 84 Cr App R 7; [1986] Crim LR 800.

Formally, D does an action recklessly if, in doing it:

(i) He believes his conduct will give rise to a risk of harm; and

(ii) It is unreasonable for D to run the risk that he foresees.

The main difference between intention and recklessness is that while in both cases the defendant must foresee the possibility of doing the actus reus, in recklessness he need not seek or be motivated to bring it about. In recent times, however, there has been a suggestion that element (i), actual foresight of the risk, should not always be required. We consider this possibility in the next section.

4.3.1 The need for foresight

The leading modern case to require that there be actual foresight before a defendant can be reckless is R v Cunningham.[80] In that case, D interfered with the coin-operated gas meter in an unoccupied house in order to steal money from it. The gas escaped, seeped into an adjoining house, and endangered the life of a person living there. Upon his appeal against conviction for maliciously administering a noxious thing so as to endanger life,[81] the Court of Criminal Appeal held that "malice" required either intention or recklessness, and that the latter meant that "the accused has foreseen that the particular kind of harm might be done and yet has gone on to take the risk of it".[82]

On this view, stupidity in failing to think about a risk is not a ground of criminal culpability. An illustration of this principle is found in R v Stephenson,[83] where D lit a fire in order to warm himself while sheltering in a haystack, and was charged with reckless arson after the haystack itself caught fire and was destroyed. Stephenson's conviction was quashed on appeal because (as he suffered from schizophrenia) he might not have been aware of the risk to the haystack.

On the other hand, the law as stated in *Cunningham* does not entitle a defendant deliberately to close her mind to an obvious risk when she is aware of the risk but does not think about it because she does not care. In R v Parker[84] D slammed down a public telephone receiver with such force that he broke it. The Court rejected his defence that he had been too enraged to think about the risk. The inherent association of his violent action with its consequence meant that he could be taken to have appreciated the risk without the awareness of that risk being at the forefront of his mind, and without the need for sober or careful deliberation in advance.

---

80 R v Cunningham [1957] 2 QB 396; [1957] 2 All ER 412 (CCA). Cf R v Briggs [1977] 1 All ER 475 (CA), 477; R v Stephenson [1979] QB 695; [1979] 2 All ER 1198 (CA); R v Mullins [1980] Crim LR 37 (CA); Flack v Hunt (1980) 70 Cr App R 51; [1980] Crim LR 44.
81 Contrary to s 23 Offences Against the Person Act 1861 (UK).
82 R v Cunningham [1957] 2 QB 396; [1957] 2 All ER 412 (CCA), 399; 414. Quoting with approval from Turner, *Kenny's Outlines of Criminal Law* (16th ed), Cambridge, Cambridge University Press, 1952, 186.
83 R v Stephenson [1979] QB 695; [1979] 2 All ER 1198 (CA).
84 R v Parker [1977] 2 All ER 37. Cf Taylor v Police (1990) 6 CRNZ 470, 473.

The inference made in *Parker* is not always appropriate.[85] In *Smith v Police*,[86] D had been served with a High Court summons by V. He attempted to push the documents back through the partly-opened window of V's car. As a consequence of D's actions, and perhaps of the movement of V's car, the car window shattered. On appeal, Barker J ruled that D was not reckless, as he had not necessarily given thought to the risks involved.

Unlike in *Parker*, the risk created by the defendant in *Smith* was not so inherent in his actions that it was inevitable that D had appreciated it. *Smith* reinforces the point that there must be awareness of the risk at some level of the defendant's consciousness before he can be found reckless.

(1) *An alternative, objective version of recklessness*

The above states the traditional position after *Cunningham*. In 1981 the House of Lords invented a second version of recklessness in *MPC v Caldwell*[87] and the companion case of *R v Lawrence*.[88] In *Caldwell*, the defendant set fire to a hotel while intoxicated. He was charged with, among other things, an offence against s 1(1) Criminal Damage Act 1971 (UK), which makes it an offence to damage another's property "being reckless as to whether any such property would be destroyed or damaged". The House of Lords held that a defendant is reckless in law if:[89]

> "(1) he does an act which in fact creates an obvious [and serious][90] risk that property will be destroyed or damaged and (2) when he does the act he either has not given any thought to the possibility of there being any such risk or has recognised that there was some risk involved and has nonetheless gone on to do it."

The essence of the decision was to create a second category of recklessness in criminal law. In addition to the cases of actual foresight covered by *Cunningham*, the defendant would also be treated as reckless if he failed to think of a risk when that risk was a glaring one. In effect, the *Caldwell* definition of recklessness embraces both advertent wrongdoing and gross negligence.[91]

(2) *Which alternative? The future of recklessness*

The extension of recklessness proposed in *Caldwell* was always controversial,[92] and has since been rejected by the House of Lords in *R v G*.[93] It never really took hold in New Zealand.[94] Although the Court of Appeal briefly flirted with *Caldwell* recklessness in *R v Howe*,[95] a decision concerning the offence of riotous damage, the subsequent decision by the Court of Appeal in

---

85 Indeed, it is arguable that the inference was inappropriate in *Parker* itself. As such the decision by the Court of Appeal may be a precursor of *Caldwell*, discussed below in this section. If so, however, the approach in *Parker* is more narrow than that taken by the House of Lords in *Caldwell*; it would justify inferring recklessness only where D "deliberately closes his mind" to obvious consequences because he is "in a self-induced state of temper", or for a similarly discreditable reason. See *R v Parker* [1977] 2 All ER 37, 40.

86 *Smith v Police* (1988) 3 CRNZ 262. Cf *Police v L (a young person)* [1990] DCR 172.

87 *MPC v Caldwell* [1982] AC 341, also reported as *R v Caldwell* [1981] 1 All ER 961 (HL).

88 *R v Lawrence* [1982] AC 510; [1981] 1 All ER 974 (HL). Cf also *R v Miller* [1983] 2 AC 161; [1983] 1 All ER 978 (HL).

89 *MPC v Caldwell* [1982] AC 341, also reported as *R v Caldwell* [1981] 1 All ER 961 (HL), 354; 967.

90 "Interpolated in *R v Lawrence* [1982] AC 510; [1981] 1 All ER 974 (HL), 527; 982. The requirement of obviousness does not apply where the risk is in fact foreseen: *R v Reid* [1992] 3 All ER 673; [1992] 1 WLR 793 (HL), 691; 814.

91 See 4.6.4.

R v Harney made it quite clear that the view taken in *Howe* was specific to its statutory context and not of general application:[96]

> "Subject to the requirements of particular contexts, however, we incline to the view that 'recklessly' has usually been understood in New Zealand to have the meaning given in pre-*Caldwell* textbooks ... That is to say, foresight of dangerous consequences that could well happen, together with an intention to continue the course of conduct regardless of the risk."

Technically, whenever a court comes to interpret the meaning of an offence requiring "recklessness", it always has two options: to follow *Cunningham* and read it as requiring actual foresight, or to require the objective, *Caldwell* version. It therefore remains possible that, in some future context, the courts will interpret a specific statutory requirement of recklessness as entailing *Caldwell* and not *Cunningham* recklessness.[97] Indeed in *Police v Sutherland*,[98] the High Court characterised "objective" recklessness as a "lesser intentionality", which might be applicable to a small number of explicit references to recklessness (such as that in *Howe*). But the likelihood that courts will ever favour *Caldwell* recklessness in a statutory interpretation is surely now remote, notwithstanding that there are some ordinary-language senses of "recklessness" which are not subjective.[99] It is submitted that the definition of recklessness adopted in *Caldwell* has no place in New Zealand law. Even the "particular context" where it first intruded exists no longer: s 90 was amended in 1987 to include damage to "any property", rendering *Howe* "obsolete".[100] An instructive illustration of the present New Zealand approach is to be found in *R v Tihi*, a case similar to *Howe* in that the statute omitted to specify a mens rea element with respect to the causing of injury when done with intent to commit a crime, contrary to s 191(2):[101]

> "Strict liability would run counter to the well-established presumption in favour of mens rea in all criminal offences... . Accordingly, before he can be guilty, it must be shown that the accused either meant to cause the specified harm, or foresaw that his

---

92   See, for example, Dawkins, "Criminal recklessness: *Caldwell and Lawrence* in New Zealand" (1983) 10 NZULR 364; Editorial, "The demise of recklessness" [1981] 5 Crim LJ 181; Fisse, *Howard's Criminal Law* (5th ed), Sydney, Law Book Co, 1990, 444 ("a radical departure from principle"); Smith [1981] Crim LR 393, 410; Williams, "Recklessness redefined" [1981] 40 CLJ 252.
93   *R v G* [2003] UKHL 50; [2004] 1 AC 1034.
94   *R v Tipple* 22/12/05, CA217/05, paras 27-34. Neither elsewhere: *R v Smith* (1982) 7 A Crim R 437; *Sansregret v R* [1985] 1 SCR 570.
95   *R v Howe* [1982] 1 NZLR 618 (CA). Section 90 (as it then read) provided that it was an offence for a member of a riot to damage any of certain specified types of property. D, a rioter, deliberately damaged a vehicle which was, in fact, a police car. The Court held that D would be guilty of an offence against s 90 if he knew or was *Caldwell* reckless that the vehicle was a police car or one of the other types of property specified in the section. The need for recklessness was not explicitly stated in the statute, and the Court noted that one might well expect an extension into Caldwell-style inadvertence to be especially appropriate to such an offence, given that people do not normally stop to ponder the particular nature of the property they are damaging in the midst of a riot.
96   *R v Harney* [1987] 2 NZLR 576 (CA), 579.
97   In *R v G* [2003] UKHL 50; [2004] 1 AC 1034 (HL), this possibility is left open by Lords Bingham (para 28) and Rodger (para 69).
98   *Police v Sutherland* 26/6/06, Clifford J, HC Wellington CRI-2006-435-1, para 18.
99   *Police v Sutherland* 26/6/06, Clifford J, HC Wellington CRI-2006-435-1, para 18.
100 *R v Harney* [1987] 2 NZLR 576 (CA), 579. See also *R v Tipple* 22/12/05, CA217/05, paras 27-34.
101 *R v Tihi* [1989] 2 NZLR 29; (1989) 4 CRNZ 289 (CA), 32; 292.

actions were likely to expose others to the risk of suffering it. This would preserve the subjective test of liability... ."

The tenor of this passage is clear: unless the statute expressly precludes it, the fault element for all criminal offences is a subjective one. Rightly so. As the House of Lords itself acknowledged in *R v G*, convictions of serious crimes should not normally be visited on the inadvertent. In the absence of clear legislative indication, we should not make criminals of those who act without any intent or awareness of wrongdoing, since they may not be sufficiently blameworthy to warrant conviction or punishment:[102]

> "But it is not clearly blameworthy to do something involving a risk of injury to another if ... one genuinely does not perceive the risk. Such a person may fairly be accused of stupidity or lack of imagination, but neither of those failings should expose him to conviction of serious crime or the risk of punishment."

Indeed, especially where the defendant suffers from limitations of age, intellect, or the like, to convict on the *Caldwell* standard would be manifestly unfair:[103]

> "It is neither moral nor just to convict a defendant (least of all a child) on the strength of what someone else would have apprehended if the defendant himself had no such apprehension. Nor, the defendant having been convicted, is the problem cured by imposition of a nominal penalty."

We concur. The justification of *Caldwell*, according to Lord Diplock, was that inadvertence to an obvious risk is frequently just as blameworthy as choosing to run a foreseen risk and so should be treated the same way. There is some force in this: it is an unattractive option to acquit a defendant who did not consider the risks because he was too drunk, too temperamental, or too uncaring a person to bother thinking about them.[104] But it is not obvious that the moral equation Lord Diplock constructed will always (or almost always) hold — which ought to be the case before a court makes such a comprehensive extension. It seems harsh to treat as reckless those whose inadvertence was due to preoccupation or distraction, and who may be utterly horrified when they recognise the consequences of their actions. And it is certainly repugnant to equate with advertent recklessness the actions of those who were incapable of perceiving the risk.[105]

4.3.2 Recklessness and circumstances

Just as with consequences, recklessness as to circumstances requires that the defendant acts believing that there is a possibility, or risk, that the circumstance might exist. This is sometimes called "reckless knowledge", but the term is a misleading one, since "knowledge" as such is not needed, and it will be enough if the defendant merely recognises that the circumstance *may* exist.

The definition just stated is derived from general principles. Recklessness requires that the defendant be aware of the possibility that the actus reus, as a whole, may occur. Hence it requires the defendant to be aware that each element of that actus reus may be present,

---

102 *R v G* [2003] UKHL 50; [2004] 1 AC 1034 (HL), para 32 (Lord Bingham); see also para 55 (Lord Steyn).
103 *R v G* [2003] UKHL 50; [2004] 1 AC 1034 (HL), para 33 (Lord Bingham); see also paras 52-54 (Lord Steyn).
104 Cf Lord Goff in *R v Reid* [1992] 3 All ER 673; [1992] 1 WLR 793 (HL), 687ff; 809ff. This seems to have been the thinking underlying *Parker* above, 4.3.1.
105 As was done in *Elliott v C (a minor)* [1983] 2 All ER 1005; [1983] 1 WLR 939 (DC).

including circumstances. A useful illustration of this can be found in s 135, which creates the offence of indecent assault. One element of that offence is the victim's lack of consent. The mens rea for this element appears to be recklessness.[106] Thus the defendant cannot be guilty if he believes that his victim consents, and may only be convicted if he goes ahead recognising that she may not be consenting. As Lord Bingham put it in *R v G*, a person is reckless with respect to a circumstance "when he is aware of a risk that exists or will exist".[107]

The difference between recklessness and intention can be shown by the following example. If D has sexual intercourse with V recognising (but not caring) that she may not be consenting, then if V does not consent D commits a reckless rape. On the other hand, if D has sexual intercourse *believing* positively that V does *not* consent, he rapes her intentionally. (In either case D will be guilty of an offence against s 128.[108])

The above states the law in principle. Sometimes, however, this definition leads to difficulties where the defendant acts without giving thought to attendant circumstances. This might occur, for example, where D indecently touches another person but claims it did not occur to him that she might not consent. What if D did not think about the possibility because he did not care, and would have gone ahead anyway? Should he be acquitted? In order to deal with such situations, recent cases have suggested two alternative ways of finding recklessness by the defendant.

The first suggested extension is that a defendant may be held reckless about a circumstance, such as non-consent, if he was indifferent to, or could not care less about, whether the victim was consenting. The genesis of this formulation seems to be the "indifference to an obvious risk" test that has informed the law since *Caldwell*. It has received the imprimatur of the New Zealand Court of Appeal at least twice,[109] as well as being endorsed in a number of English and Australian decisions.[110] Nevertheless it must be doubted whether this extension is valid.[111] *Caldwell*, as we have noted, is no longer good law. And in the two cases where

---

106 *R v Nazif* [1987] 2 NZLR 122 (CA), 128; *Police v Bannin* [1991] 2 NZLR 237, also reported as *B v Police* (1991) 7 CRNZ 55, 245; 62. Contrast the application of force itself in an assault, which must be intentional: s 2; *R v Young* 9/7/92, CA86/92. The view taken in *Nazif* may be questionable, since, by contrast with English authorities cited in the case, assault in New Zealand requires intention rather than recklessness on the part of the defendant. The justification for the Court of Appeal's interpretation seems to be that consent is a common law defence, rather than part of the actus reus of assault (cf *Police v Bannin* [1991] 2 NZLR 237, also reported as *B v Police* (1991) 7 CRNZ 55, 245; 62). This is inconsistent with the decision by the House of Lords in *DPP v Morgan* [1976] AC 182; [1975] 2 All ER 347 (HL). See Simester, "Mistakes in defence" (1992) 12 OJLS 295.
107 *R v G* [2003] UKHL 50; [2004] 1 AC 1034 (HL), para 41.
108 Whether D's recklessness would be sufficient for him to be convicted of an attempt (if V in fact does consent) is discussed in ch 8.
109 *Waaka v Police* [1987] 1 NZLR 754; (1987) 2 CRNZ 370 (CA), 759; 375; *Millar v MOT* [1986] 1 NZLR 660; (1986) 2 CRNZ 216 (CA), 678; 236 (Casey J).
110 For example *R v Kimber* [1983] 3 All ER 316; [1983] 1 WLR 1118 (CA), 320; 1123: D's "attitude to [V] was one of indifference to her feelings and wishes. This state of mind is aptly described in the colloquial expression 'couldn't care less.' In law this is recklessness." Cf *R v Pigg* [1982] 2 All ER 591; [1982] 1 WLR 762 (CA) (reversed on a different ground: [1983] 1 All ER 56; [1983] 1 WLR 6); *R v Millard and Vernon* [1987] Crim LR 393 (CA); *R v Khan* [1990] 2 All ER 783; [1990] 1 WLR 813 (CA). Cf, in New South Wales, *R v Tolmie* (1995) 37 NSWLR 660; *R v Kitchener* (1993) 29 NSWLR 696. The approach in *Tolmie* was endorsed by Callinan J in *Banditt v R* [2005] HCA 80, para 86, but not by the majority, which favoured a subjective test: see paras 20, 25, 33-6.
111 Cf *Adams*, CA20.36 (looseleaf).

indifference was contemplated by the Court of Appeal, the remarks made were clearly *obiter* and not demanded by the facts of those cases. Mens rea is not normally concerned with the *attitudes* of defendants; it is concerned with what they intended, knew, and did not know. This is why a worthy attitude, or a good motive, is no defence under the criminal law.[112] It is also why, under the *Cunningham* approach to recklessness, the defendants are not to be convicted on the basis of an unworthy attitude or bad motive, for example for indifference. Correspondingly, the law should not be concerned to enquire *why* D failed to foresee a risk, and whether it was because he did not care. Such fine nuances have no practical place in the law.

The second extension to traditional recklessness is more plausible and is now almost certainly part of New Zealand law. On this test, D will be held reckless about a circumstantial element in an offence *unless* he has a positive belief that the circumstance is lacking. Thus, if D deliberately and indecently touches V, it is an indecent assault unless he believes that V consents. *R v Nazif*[113] supports this analysis. D was charged with indecent assault. He claimed, among other things, that he believed V consented to his actions. The Court of Appeal accepted that such a belief would be a defence:[114]

> "it would be contrary to principle that a person who believes the victim of an assault consented to it should be found guilty of that assault. Where there is evidence of such belief it will be for the Crown to negative it. The reasonableness or otherwise of the grounds of such belief will be material to *the question of whether the accused in fact held it*."

Clearly the Court regarded that question, whether D actually believed that V consented, as legally crucial. The implication of the passage quoted is that a positive belief is required to found D's defence. Thus, for example, where recklessness about non-consent is required to establish mens rea, it suffices *either* if D recognised V might not be consenting *or* if D did *not* believe that she was consenting. This test was also accepted by the House of Lords in *B (a minor) v DPP*.[115] In effect, the prosecution need prove only that D lacked a genuine belief that V consented, without having to prove, in addition, that he believed there was a risk that she did not consent. This formulation of recklessness will not convict defendants who wrongly assume that V consents but will catch those who proceed to harm V without believing (albeit mistakenly) they have V's agreement.

Before moving on, note should be taken of *Waaka v Police*.[116] The case is important but, it is submitted, should be approached with caution. D was charged under s 10 Summary Offences Act 1981 with assault of a constable acting in execution of his duty. While the mens rea for assault is intention,[117] a question arose whether mens rea was required regarding the rest of

---

112 Cf *R v Smith* [1960] 2 QB 423; [1960] 1 All ER 256 (CA); see 4.1, 4.2.2. For the rule that a positive attitude, of hoping the actus reus would not happen, supplies no defence, see *R v Crabbe* (1985) 156 CLR 464; (1985) 16 A Crim R 19, 470; 33.

113 *R v Nazif* [1987] 2 NZLR 122 (CA).

114 *R v Nazif* [1987] 2 NZLR 122 (CA), 128 (emphasis added).

115 *B (a minor) v DPP* [2000] 2 AC 428; [2000] 1 All ER 833 (HL); also *R v K* [2001] 3 All ER 897; [2001] 3 WLR 471 (HL). Cf *R v Satnam; R v Kewal* (1984) 78 Cr App R 149; [1985] Crim LR 236 (CA). Contra *R v Bonora* (1994) 35 NSWLR 74 (CCA), where the Court of Criminal Appeal ruled that D must be aware that V may not be consenting; also *R v G* [2003] UKHL 50; [2004] 1 AC 1034, para 41 (Lord Bingham), quoted in the text above n 107.

116 *Waaka v Police* [1987] 1 NZLR 754; (1987) 2 CRNZ 370 (CA).

117 Section 2 Summary Offences Act 1981; *R v Young* 9/7/92, CA86/92.

the actus reus. In this respect the Court of Appeal's remarks were *obiter*, but they deserve repetition here:[118]

> "In *Millar v Ministry of Transport* [1986] 1 NZLR 660 this Court reviewed generally the position in New Zealand as to mens rea in statutory offences. We laid weight on the general principle that mens rea is an ingredient of criminal liability — guilty intent including in this context indifference or wilful blindness ... the main alternatives for consideration will be a defence of total absence of fault or, more drastic, absolute liability.
>
> "As to s 10 of the Summary Offences Act, there is insufficient reason for not applying the approach in *Millar*. Accordingly we think that mens rea must go to all the ingredients of the offence. The prosecution must prove that the defendant knew that the person assaulted was a police officer and knew that he was acting in the execution of his duty; or that the defendant wilfully shut his eyes to these possibilities or was indifferent to whether or not they were the truth.
>
> "We would leave open for future consideration if need be the position under s 10 of a defendant who knows that the person assaulted is a police constable but gives no thought at all to whether or not he is acting in the execution of his duty."

In accordance with *Millar*, by finding that mens rea was required for the rest of the offence, the Court in effect decides that D must be reckless as to whether V was a constable acting in execution of his duty, since in the absence of express statutory language, recklessness is the basic standard of mens rea.[119] That much is unexceptionable. However, the Court then states that, regarding the victim being a constable, D must "know" that this is so at the time of the assault. This finding must be regarded as doubtful in principle, since full knowledge is not required: recklessness is satisfied if D merely realises that V might be a constable. Yet the Court then watered down the strenuousness of the test by stating that it would be sufficient if the defendant had "wilfully shut his eyes to those possibilities or was indifferent to whether or not they were the truth".[120]

With respect to the Court, the use of the term "know" is unhelpful here. "Knowledge" has its own meaning,[121] and demands a higher standard of belief than mere recklessness. As we shall see, in those offences where knowledge is expressly required by the statute it is certainly not enough to show that D was merely indifferent. We are left, then, with recklessness. It would have been enough for a conviction if D had recognised that V might be a constable acting in execution of his duty. The Court then suggests two additional ways of finding mens rea. The first, wilful blindness, is sufficient to establish recklessness; we shall consider this doctrine below.[122] But for the reasons given earlier, it is submitted that indifference is not enough.

---

118 *Waaka v Police* [1987] 1 NZLR 754; (1987) 2 CRNZ 370 (CA), 759; 375.
119 See 4.4.
120 *Waaka v Police* [1987] 1 NZLR 754; (1987) 2 CRNZ 370 (CA), 759; 375. Followed in *Frost v Police* (1988) 4 CRNZ 539.
121 See 4.5.
122 See 4.5.1.

4.4 Why distinguish intention from recklessness?

In practice, recklessness satisfies the mens rea requirement in most crimes. This raises an obvious question: why bother discussing a separate category of intention at all? There are three reasons for doing so. First, some actions can only be done intentionally. For example, a person attempts to harm another only if he intends to do so. It would be a misuse of language to describe a knowing risk-taker as "attempting" to inflict harm.

Often this linguistic difference reflects a moral distinction,[123] because the presence of intention can alter the very nature of what is done. As Glanville Williams once pointed out: "The act constituting a crime may in some circumstances be objectively innocent, and take its criminal colouring entirely from the intent with which it is done."[124] It was the defendant's intention which changed the action from simple assault to indecent assault in *R v Court*,[125] a case where D spanked a young girl on the seat of her shorts. He was convicted of indecent assault because he had not done so in order to administer discipline, but rather for sexual gratification — his intention made the behaviour "indecent".[126] Similarly, the difference between negligent conversion of property and theft lies not merely in the degree of culpability but also in the nature of the action itself (even though the physical harm may be the same). Theft cannot fully be defined in terms of its consequence because the action itself expresses a certain sort of contempt for property rights, and for the victim, which the mere conversion of property does not.

The second rationale for distinguishing intention from recklessness is that, as we have seen, recklessness is established only if the defendant risked doing the actus reus *unreasonably*. By contrast, there is no condition of unreasonableness attaching to intention. Neither is there a general defence known to the criminal law of reasonable action.[127]

The third ground also involves defences, which is a topic we have not yet discussed. As the law presently stands, in order to claim certain defences, such as self-defence, the defendant must *intend* to defend himself when he does the actus reus. This point is illustrated by the well-known case of *R v Dadson*,[128] in which a policeman shot and wounded a thief who was stealing wood. It was then, as now, an offence intentionally to shoot another, and both the actus reus and mens rea were made out in Dadson's case. However, the thief was in fact a felon, and a defence existed at that time to the effect that the policeman would be justified in shooting to prevent the escape of a felon. The difficulty was that the policeman had not realised that the person he was shooting was a felon. Hence, although he intended to shoot V, he did not intend the justification: ie to prevent the escape of a felon. Therefore, the Court ruled, he was not entitled to claim the defence, and he was convicted.[129]

---

123 See, for example, Duff, "Attempted homicide" (1995) 1 Legal Theory 149; Horder, "Crimes of ulterior intent" in Simester and Smith (eds), *Harm and Culpability*, Oxford, Clarendon Press, 1996, 153.
124 Williams, *CLGP*, 22. See also Lynch, "The mental element in the actus reus" (1982) 98 LQR 109.
125 *R v Court* [1989] AC 28; [1988] 2 All ER 221 (HL).
126 Per Lord Ackner (*R v Court* [1989] AC 28; [1988] 2 All ER 221 (HL), 43; 230): "To decide whether or not right-minded persons might think that assault was indecent, the following factors were clearly relevant - the relationship of the defendant to his victim .... How had the defendant come to embark on this conduct and *why* was he behaving in this way?"
127 For a discussion of this point in the context of medical necessity, see Ashworth, "Criminal Liability in a Medical Context: The Treatment of Good Intentions" in Simester and Smith (eds), *Harm and Culpability*, Oxford, Clarendon Press, 1996, 173.
128 *R v Dadson* (1850) 3 Car & Kir 148; 4 Cox CC 358.

4.5 Knowledge

Where an offence is formulated so as to require that the defendant act "knowing" that some circumstance exists, this requires a positive (and correct)[130] belief on the part of the defendant that the relevant circumstance does indeed exist. If Tom marries Jill suspecting that she is already married, he commits no offence of bigamy because he does not "know" she is married — he merely suspects it. Belief or knowledge that a circumstance *may* obtain, which would be sufficient for recklessness, is not knowledge that it does obtain. Hence it is inadequate to satisfy the mens rea of any offence that requires knowledge or intention that some circumstance exists.[131] In this respect "knowledge" of circumstances is the cognitive cousin of intention, rather than recklessness.

What is not necessary, however, is that the defendant should think that the relevant circumstance exists with provable certainty. In law, it is sufficient that the defendant accepts, or "assumes",[132] and has no serious doubt, at the time he acts, that the circumstance is present.[133] Hence if Tom refrains from investigating further whether Jill is indeed already married, and goes ahead with the ceremony believing that she may well be, he is not guilty of bigamy. It is not enough for him to believe there is a possibility or likelihood that Jill is married.[134] But if, despite the fact that he has not actually seen a marriage certificate, he accepts Jill's disclosure to him that she is already married, then he commits bigamy when he goes ahead with the ceremony.

In sum, "knowing" means "knowing, or correctly believing".[135] The qualification, that the belief be a correct one, is implicit in the meaning of knowledge. Suppose that when Tom marries Jill he is sure that she is already married, but in fact she is not. Tom cannot be guilty of an offence against s 205(1)(b), of marrying someone he knows is already married. This is not only because there is no actus reus, but also because he does not "know" Jill is married, since his belief is wrong.

4.5.1 Wilful blindness

The situation where Tom realises there is a chance Jill is already married, yet deliberately refrains from checking his suspicion, raises the issue of "wilful blindness". Cases of wilful blindness often appear to fall between the mens rea alternatives of (i) recklessness as to the circumstance ("reckless knowledge"), and (ii) (actual) knowledge, which satisfies intention. One alternative is straightforward. *Every* case where a defendant realises or suspects the circumstance might exist and refrains from investigating further is a case of reckless knowledge (i). Even without further investigation, the defendant knows already that there is a risk that

---

129 See also *R v Thain* [1985] NI 457; Sullivan, "Bad thoughts and bad acts" [1990] Crim LR 559; Hogan, "The *Dadson* principle" [1989] Crim LR 679.
130 *R v Crooks* [1981] 2 NZLR 53 (CA); *R v Hall* (1985) 81 Cr App R 260; [1985] Crim LR 377 (CA).
131 *US v Dynar* (1997) 147 DLR (4th) 399; 115 CCC (3d) 481 (SCC), 424; 506.
132 *R v Simpson* [1978] 2 NZLR 221 (CA).
133 Cf Smith's comment on *R v Charles* in [1977] Crim LR 615, 620: "Doubts are inconsistent with belief" — at least if those doubts are serious ones; also Griew, "Consistency, communication and codification: Reflections on two mens rea words" in Glazebrook (ed), *Reshaping the Criminal Law: Essays in Honour of Glanville Williams*, London, Stevens & Sons, 1978, 57, 69ff.
134 Cf *R v Griffiths* (1974) 60 Cr App R 14 (CA); *R v Woods* [1969] 1 QB 447; [1968] 3 All ER 709 (CA).
135 Cf *R v Baird* (1985) 3 NSWLR 331; 32 A Crim R 67, 70; 334. See also the discussion in 19.5.2.

the circumstance is present. So if the mens rea of an offence requires only recklessness, then the defendant may be convicted.[136]

Finding actual knowledge is more difficult. In some cases of deliberate non-inquiry by a defendant, the court will invoke what is known as the "doctrine" of wilful blindness. This doctrine applies where the defendant intentionally chooses not to inquire whether something is true because he has no real doubt what the answer is going to be. Its effect is to attribute knowledge of the circumstance to the defendant. In other words, where the wilful blindness doctrine applies, the law will treat the defendant as having actual knowledge (ii), and not merely the reckless knowledge that he otherwise would have.

The conditions under which the doctrine applies are not capable of being stated precisely.[137] Broadly speaking, if there is an obvious way of finding something out and the defendant deliberately shuts his eyes to a risk by failing to find out, then he will not be permitted to exculpate himself by claiming that he did not know the truth. However, wilful blindness cannot be invoked just because he *should* have inquired into the facts, or even if he suspected the truth;[138] otherwise knowledge would effectively be indistinguishable from recklessness. It appears that the defendant is wilfully blind in only two situations. The first is if he shuts his eyes and fails to inquire "because he knew what the answer was going to be".[139] This approach squares with the test once proposed by the English Law Commission:[140]

> "The standard test of knowledge is — Did the person whose conduct is in issue either know of the relevant circumstances or have no substantial doubt of their existence?"

Alternatively, the wilful blindness doctrine will also apply if the means of knowledge is easily to hand and D realises the likely truth of a matter but refrains from inquiry *in order* not to know.[141] In such circumstances, although D in fact lacks knowledge, there are clear normative grounds for inculpation.

It should be emphasised that wilful blindness is a doctrine of substantive rather than evidential law.[142] It imputes knowledge to the defendant for legal purposes where there is not, in fact, such knowledge. However, even if the doctrine does not apply, there remains the further possibility that a jury may *infer* actual knowledge on the part of the defendant (ie that in fact he accepted the truth and had no serious doubt) from evidence that D recognised the likely

---

136 See 4.3.2.
137 See generally Lanham, "Wilful blindness and the criminal law" (1985) 9 Crim LJ 261; Wasik and Thompson, " 'Turning a blind eye' as constituting mens rea" (1981) 32 NILQ 328; Williams, *CLGP*, 57.
138 *R v Crooks* [1981] 2 NZLR 53 (CA); see also *Millar v MOT* [1986] 1 NZLR 660; (1986) 2 CRNZ 216 (CA), 674; 231.
139 *R v Crooks* [1981] 2 NZLR 53 (CA), 58. See 19.5.2.
140 *Draft Criminal Liability (Mental Element) Bill, Report on the Mental Element in Crime*, No 89, London, HMSO, 1978, cl 3(1). This is a more demanding test than that finally endorsed by the Law Commission: *A Criminal Code for England and Wales*, Law Com no 177, London, HMSO, 1989, cl 18(a). It is also more stringent than the standard set by the House of Lords in *Westminster CC v Croyalgrange Ltd* [1986] 2 All ER 353; [1986] 1 WLR 674 (HL), 359; 684.
141 *Severinsen v DSW* 31/5/94, Penlington J, HC Hamilton AP1/94. Cf *The Zamora No 2* [1921] 1 AC 801 (PC), 812 (Lord Sumner); *Sansregret v R* [1985] 1 SCR 570, 584-6; *R v Camtais Barbeau* (1996) 110 CCC (3d) 69 (Que CA), 92-5.
142 Although a contrary view is expressed in Crimes Bill Consultative Committee, *Crimes Bill 1989: Report of the Crimes Consultative Committee Presented to the Minister of Justice April 1991*, Wellington, Department of Justice, 1991, 14.

circumstances and made no further inquiry. Nonetheless, proof of the latter does not constitute proof of the former.

It will be obvious from all this that, in the bigamy example given earlier, Tom would not be imputed with actual knowledge under the wilful blindness doctrine.

4.6 Negligence

Unlike such mens rea varieties as recklessness, intention, and knowledge, negligence does not presuppose any particular state of mind on the part of the defendant. It is, however, a standard that reflects fault on the part of the defendant, and so it is appropriately discussed alongside the other mens rea categories. The main feature distinguishing negligence from the categories we have mentioned so far is that, in negligence, there is no requirement that the defendant foresee the risk that the actus reus might occur. Sometimes we blame people precisely because they have *failed* to think about something — because they were careless, or thoughtless. It is this sort of case that is captured by negligence.

4.6.1 The test for negligence

Even though negligence permits the finding of fault for inadvertent wrongdoing, it does not actually matter whether the defendant attends to or contemplates the risks. As Glanville Williams asserts, "the essential question, at any rate for legal purposes, is whether it was reasonable for you to go ahead with your conduct in the circumstances".[143] Of course, normally one who foresees and runs an unreasonable risk will be reckless as well as negligent. Negligence does not, however, *require* inadvertence. This is for two reasons. The first is that in the criminal law, the lesser fault standard incorporates the greater. A defendant should not be able to exculpate herself by pleading that her actions were reckless or intentional rather than negligent. It follows that where negligence is enough for criminal liability, then, a fortiori, there is liability for intention or recklessness.

The second reason is that, as we mentioned earlier, a defendant can foresee the actus reus without being reckless, yet may still be negligent. For example, an anaesthetist who recognises there is a slight risk of killing his patient is not normally reckless. But if he has unknowingly miscalculated the dose, then he is negligent even though not reckless. Recklessness involves an objective assessment of the subjectively-perceived risk. Negligence involves an objective assessment of an objectively recognisable risk.[144]

So the emphasis is on the unreasonableness of the defendant's behaviour. Formally, the defendant is negligent if a reasonable person in the same circumstances (i) would have been aware of the risks of doing the actus reus and (ii) would not have run those risks. It does not matter if the defendant herself was unaware of the risks. What counts is that her behaviour falls short of the standard of conduct that we would expect of a reasonable person — that she failed to take reasonable precautions against the harm specified in the actus reus.[145]

---

143 Fitzgerald and Williams, "Carelessness, indifference and recklessness: Two replies" (1962) 25 MLR 49, 57.
144 Although this proposition will be qualified in 4.6.2.
145 Cf *R v Gill* (1999) 19 NZTC 15,526, 15,530.

An example of the negligence standard in operation is provided by *R v Yogasakaran*.[146] D, an anaesthetist, was attending an operation when the patient developed breathing problems. D decided to inject her with a drug known as Dopram. He took a drug container from the drawer marked "Dopram" and, without checking the label on the container, injected its contents into the patient. Unfortunately, the drug he injected was Dopamine. It was correctly labelled but had been placed in the wrong drawer. The patient died in consequence of being injected with the wrong drug. D was convicted of manslaughter, on the footing that a reasonable anaesthetist would be expected to check the label on the drug he was about to inject.

(1) *Ordinary or gross negligence?*

The criminal law knows two types of negligence: ordinary negligence and gross negligence. *R v Yogasakaran*[147] is an instance of ordinary negligence, which — under the law prevailing at the time of that case — was sufficient to ground a conviction for manslaughter.[148] Another offence requiring ordinary negligence is that of careless driving, contrary to s 8 Land Transport Act 1998. D commits the offence by making an error while driving that a reasonably prudent and skilful driver would not make;[149] in other words, by driving in a manner which involves a risk of harm that the reasonable person would regard as unjustifiable.

Sometimes, however, the mens rea of an offence cannot be satisfied by anything less than gross negligence. For example, following amendment of the Crimes Act in 1997, a conviction for manslaughter in circumstances such as those found in *Yogasakaran* now requires proof of gross rather than ordinary negligence: ie "a major departure from the standard of care expected of a reasonable person".[150] While the difference between the two is a matter of degree and judgment in each case, broadly speaking, negligence will be gross if the defendant's conduct not merely fails to meet the standard set by the reasonable person test, but falls short of that standard by a considerable margin — ie if the defendant's conduct is not merely unreasonable, but *very* unreasonable.[151] It may be negligent to drive around a particular bend at 50 km/h; if so, it is grossly negligent to do so at 80 km/h. Hart puts the test another way: "Negligence is gross if the precautions to be taken against harm are very simple, such as persons who are but poorly endowed with physical and mental capacities can easily take."[152]

(2) *Emergency*

One of the features of *R v Yogasakaran* was that the situation was urgent. The test of negligence has sometimes been criticised for being insensitive to circumstances and for assessing

---

146 *R v Yogasakaran* [1990] 1 NZLR 399; (1989) 5 CRNZ 69 (CA). The conclusion of negligence, and the corresponding attribution of blame, is seldom straightforward in such cases. For discussion, see Merry and McCall-Smith, *Errors, Medicine and the Law*, Cambridge, Cambridge University Press, 2001, 12ff.
147 *R v Yogasakaran* [1990] 1 NZLR 399; (1989) 5 CRNZ 69 (CA).
148 See 16.5.2(5).
149 *Police v Chappell* [1974] 1 NZLR 225; *Simpson v Peat* [1952] 2 QB 24; [1952] 1 All ER 447, 27; 449.
150 Section 150A, as inserted by s 2 Crimes Amendment Act 1997. See 16.5.2(5)(c).
151 *R v Burney* [1958] NZLR 745 (CA); Crimes Bill Consultative Committee, *Crimes Bill 1989: Report of the Crimes Consultative Committee Presented to the Minister of Justice April 1991*, Wellington, Department of Justice, 1991, 15, 93. Cf *R v Bateman* (1925) 19 Cr App R 8; [1925] All ER Rep 45 (CCA), 11-12; 48: "in order to establish criminal liability the facts must be such that, in the opinion of the jury, the negligence of the accused went beyond a mere matter of compensation between subjects and showed such disregard for the life and safety of others as to amount to a crime against the State and conduct deserving punishment."
152 "Negligence, mens rea, and criminal responsibility" in *Punishment and Responsibility: Essays in the Philosophy of Law*, Oxford, Clarendon Press, 1968, 136, 149.

emergency judgements in the cold light of the courtroom. Jeremy Horder has argued that in such situations we should not demand clinical accuracy, and that legitimate emotions such as fear and compassion, which sometimes lead us to make mistakes, are not properly allowed for by the orthodox test of negligence.[153] But this underestimates the legal test. We usually excuse a prima facie "negligent" mistake because it was not unreasonable *in the circumstances*. Although the evaluation of a defendant's conduct is done in a courtroom, in each case it must be done in the light of the defendant's particular circumstances and of normal social and personal values — including those of compassion and self-preservation. This is why it is sometimes reasonable to react precipitously.[154] The law does make allowance for emergencies: in *Yogasakaran*, the Court of Appeal pointed out that:[155]

> "instant decisions may have to be taken in an emergency; that must be a major factor to be kept prominently in mind in determining whether there has been a failure to live up to the appropriate professional standard."

Or, as Holmes J has noted, "[d]etached reflection cannot be demanded in the presence of an uplifted knife".[156] Horder claims that negligence in such cases "is not culpable". But if it is not culpable, this will be because it is not negligence at all.

4.6.2 Abnormal defendants: does the reasonable man share any of their characteristics?

The tests of negligence that we have identified seem at first blush to be objective. We complain of the defendant's *conduct*, and decide that she was negligent simply by determining that her conduct does not match a standard of behaviour that would have been acceptable in the circumstances. However, if negligence is truly a measure of culpability, there would seem to be a problem with this approach. In other categories of mens rea, the defendant is blameworthy because she *knowingly* does the wrong thing — not merely because her behaviour is wrong. But that ground of fault cannot apply here. In negligence, the law says that the defendant *should* have done whatever the reasonable man would have done: but why? Why should the defendant be regarded as blameworthy, and attract the odium of criminal culpability, just because her behaviour causes some harm that she did not foresee?[157]

The law's response is to assume that the reasonable person test incorporates the requirements of blame. If the defendant's conduct is objectively unreasonable, then it manifests a failing on the part of the defendant for which she may properly be blamed. Putting things the other way around, had she not been deserving of blame, her behaviour would not have failed the reasonable man test.

---

153 Horder, "Cognition, emotion and criminal culpability" (1990) 106 LQR 469, 482; cf Williams, "Offences and defences" (1982) 2 Legal Studies 233, 242. See also Merry and McCall-Smith, Errors, *Medicine and the Law*, Cambridge, Cambridge University Press, 2001, 58-64.
154 As Bernard Williams notes: *Ethics and the Limits of Philosophy*, Cambridge, Mass, Harvard University Press, 1985, 185. See Horder, "Cognition, emotion and criminal culpability" (1990) 106 LQR 469, 481.
155 *R v Yogasakaran* [1990] 1 NZLR 399; (1989) 5 CRNZ 69 (CA), 405; 74.
156 *Brown v US* 256 US 335, 343 (1921). More prosaically, see *Simpson v Peat* [1952] 2 QB 24; [1952] 1 All ER 447, 28; 449; *Wood v Richards* (1977) 65 Cr App R 300; [1977] Crim LR 295; also Williams, *TBCL*, 90.
157 Simester, "Can negligence be culpable?" in Horder (ed), *Oxford Essays in Jurisprudence*, Fourth Series, New York, Oxford University Press, 2000, 85.

Most of the time this is a satisfactory answer. For example, if D had been a properly attentive and caring parent, she would not have left her child unattended by the swimming pool — we may hold her negligent, and blame her for doing so where a reasonable parent would not. And the fact that D was not a naturally caring parent is no excuse. But not every case is so straightforward. What if D is in some way abnormal? Suppose, for example, that D fails to observe a child climbing into the pool. A normal person would have seen the child. Is D negligent? Perhaps not, if it turns out that D is blind. The example suggests that, although the reasonable person test is mostly independent of the particular defendant, it is not entirely so. We do not expect D to behave as if she were sighted, but rather as a reasonable blind person would.

Generally speaking, the law states that behaviour is negligent if it involves a failure to exercise "care and caution which a reasonable and prudent person ordinarily would exercise under like conditions or circumstances".[158] But what exactly is meant by the "reasonable and prudent person"? The illustration above suggests that we do not replace the defendant altogether with objective characteristics, otherwise the youngest child would receive no allowance for immaturity[159] and the blind would be expected to see.[160] *Adams*, however, characterises the reasonable person standard rather more robustly:[161]

> "The test is 'objective' in that it depends on what the hypothetical reasonable person would have foreseen and done: it does not matter that the individual did not actually advert to the risk, and may have had personal attributes which were such that he or she would not normally be expected to achieve a higher standard of care than was in fact achieved."

It will be clear that we disagree. The test is mostly objective, but it is also, in part, subjective. In particular, the reasonable person should be endowed with any peculiar physical characteristic of the defendant — including sight, hearing,[162] and age.[163] If his colleague's electrocution could have been avoided simply by throwing the mains switch, D is not negligent if he fails to do so because he is a paraplegic. (This partially subjective approach is also, increasingly, favoured in the context of defences such as provocation and duress, which we consider later in this book.)

Sometimes this can work against the defendant. If she has additional knowledge, over and above that which a reasonable person would possess, then she will be held to the standard of that extra knowledge.[164] Thus a driver with abnormally good vision would be expected to avoid the cyclist she espies ahead of her even if ordinary drivers would not see that cyclist in time.

---

158 *Cordas v Peerless Transportation Co* 27 NYS 2d 198, 200 (1941).
159 Gray, "The standard of care for children revisited" (1980) 45 Mo LR 597; Shulman, "The standard of care required of children" (1928) 37 Yale LJ 618. See, for example, *Charbonneau v MacRury* 153 A 457 (1931); *McHale v Watson* (1966) 115 CLR 199; [1966] ALR 513; *Yorkton Agricultural & Industrial Exhibition Assn v Morley* (1967) 66 DLR (2d) 37. Cf *DPP v Camplin* [1978] AC 705; [1978] 2 All ER 168 (HL), 718; 175 (provocation).
160 Cf, in tort law, *Bernard v Russell* 164 A 2d 577 (1960); *Keith v Worcester St RR* 82 NE 680 (1907); *Balcom v City of Independence* 160 NW 305 (1916). See Weisiger, "Negligence of the physically infirm" (1946) 24 NCLR 187; Lowry, "The blind and the law of tort" (1972) 20 Chittys LJ 253.
161 *Adams*, CA20.37 (looseleaf).
162 Cf *SA Ambulance Transport Inc v Wahlheim* (1948) 77 CLR 215; [1949] ALR 1.
163 See n 146. Cf *R v Cox* 7/11/96, CA213/96.
164 Cf *R v Lamb* [1967] 2 QB 981; [1967] 2 All ER 1282 (CA); *R v Gosset* (1993) 105 DLR (4th) 681, 694-696.

And a professional, acting in a professional capacity,[165] will be judged by the standard of "a reasonably skilful and competent practitioner";[166] not by the standard of a layperson.

In what other ways is the reasonable person test to be influenced by facts about the particular defendant? In order to answer that question, consider why we would expect the apparently "objective" standard in negligence to be affected by a defendant's physical limitations. The reason is that to convict a blind person for failing to see would be wrong and unfair. The blind do not deserve blame for failing to see. This, it is submitted, is the right way to approach the question of objectivity in negligence. The reasonable person test should be subjective to the extent that the defendant's shortcomings do not disclose fault. In particular, apart from physical limitations there is one other failing for which an abnormal defendant should not be blamed: intelligence. Consider the facts of *Elliott v C (a minor)*,[167] an English case. C, a 14-year-old girl of low intelligence, had wandered away from home and spent the night outdoors without sleep before ending up in a garden shed. There she found some white spirit, which she poured on to the floor and ignited by dropping lighted matches on it. The shed was destroyed in the ensuing fire. Although someone of normal intelligence would no doubt have appreciated the risk of burning down the shed, it was found as a fact that the risk would not have been obvious to one of her limited capacities. Under the English law of that time, C was convicted of *reckless* criminal damage.[168] But this is a repugnant conclusion. It is submitted that to regard her even as having destroyed the shed *negligently* would be wrong.

That having been said, however, it is not clear whether the criminal law currently makes any allowance for low intelligence when assessing negligence. The above passage from *Adams* suggests not.[169]

Academic argument favours taking account of personal incapacities. Hart has proposed a general precondition for criminal liability of the form: *"Could* the accused, given his mental and physical capacities, have taken [the required] precautions?"[170] The Canadian Supreme Court has endorsed a similar requirement.[171] Otherwise, however, the authorities are unclear. Kirby J in the High Court of Australia has endorsed *obiter* an objective test, disregarding individual capacities.[172] In England, the suggestion of a test like Hart's may be found in *R v Hudson*,[173] but is impliedly excluded by *Elliott v C*.[174] The question awaits definitive resolution by the House of Lords, although there are dicta in *R v Reid* to the effect that fault should be assessed by reference to the capacities of the particular defendant.[175] In New Zealand, there are grounds for optimism: *Elliott v C* seems to have been regarded as "harsh" in *Harney*,[176] and — in a different context — Fisher J suggests in *Police v Bannin*[177] that to be convicted a

---

165 This qualification may not apply in tort: *McComiskey v McDermott* [1974] IR 75.
166 *R v Yogasakaran* [1990] 1 NZLR 399; (1989) 5 CRNZ 69 (CA), 405; 75.
167 *Elliott v C (a minor)* [1983] 2 All ER 1005; [1983] 1 WLR 939 (DC).
168 By application of the *Caldwell* definition of recklessness, now reversed by *R v G*: 4.3.1(1)-(2).
169 Also *Smith and Hogan*, 109 ("If D has less knowledge or capacity for foresight than the reasonable man this, it seems, will not generally help him"); Williams, *TBCL*, 94 ("The reasonable man is not imagined to be substandard in intelligence or foresight"). Note that an objective approach to the absence of fault *is* taken in New Zealand in the context of strict liability offences. See 5.1.1(2).
170 Hart "Negligence, mens rea and criminal responsibility" in *Punishment and Responsibility: Essays in the Philosophy of Law*, Oxford, Clarendon Press, 1968, 136, 154 (emphasis added). See also Simester, "Can negligence be culpable?" in Horder (ed), *Oxford Essays in Jurisprudence*, Fourth Series, New York, Oxford University Press, 2000, 85; Ashworth, *Principles*, 194-5; Orchard, "Culpable homicide: Part II" [1977] NZLJ 447, 451-453.
171 *R v Creighton* (1993) 105 DLR (4th) 632; [1993] 3 SCR 3; (1993) 83 CCC (3d) 346 (SCC).
172 *R v Lavender* [2005] HCA 37, para 128.

defendant should possess the capacity to form the mental elements required for the crime charged. But there is contrary authority in respect of sexual violation,[178] and the position remains uncertain.

It is worth noting that, even if the ordinary negligence test does make allowance for a defendant's low intelligence and similar incapacities, it seems that such an allowance does not apply to the *defence* of absence of fault in strict liability offences. As will be seen in 5.1.1(2) below, a fully objective standard of care is applied in the regulatory context.

4.6.3 Negligence with respect to behaviour rather than consequences or circumstances

Unusually, negligence sometimes operates like an actus reus term. It does so when it qualifies the *behavioural* element in the actus reus, as opposed to elements of consequence or circumstance.[179] So, for example, in an offence of careless driving the carelessness — ie negligence — of the driving is not a mens rea term meaning that a reasonable person would (and the defendant should) have realised that he was driving. Rather, it is effectively an actus reus term: meaning that the defendant was driving in a *manner* that fell short of the standard a reasonable person would set. Thus careless driving is a different type of negligence offence from negligent rape, where the law's concern is not so much with the manner of the defendant's action as with the fact that it was done at all.

Most of the time the difference will not be important, since even as a mens rea term negligence is assessed by reference to the defendant's conduct. However, it seems that the subjective elements of the reasonable person test may not apply when negligence is operating as an actus reus standard. Hence in *McCrone v Riding* it was said that the standard of care in driving:[180]

> "is an objective standard, impersonal and universal, fixed in relation to the safety of other users of the highway. It is in no way related to the degree of proficiency or degree of experience attained by the individual driver."

---

173 *R v Hudson* [1966] 1 QB 448; [1965] 1 All ER 721 (CCA), 455; 724: "There may be cases, of which this is not one, where there is evidence before the jury to show that the defendant himself is a person of limited intelligence or possibly suffering from some handicap which would prevent him from appreciating the state of affairs which an ordinary man might realise." See also *R v Hardie* [1984] 3 All ER 848; [1985] 1 WLR 64 (CA).

174 *Elliott v C (a minor)* [1983] 2 All ER 1005; [1983] 1 WLR 939 (DC); also *R v Stephen* (1984) 79 Cr App R 334; *R v Ward* [1956] 1 QB 351; [1956] 1 All ER 565; *R v Stone and Dobinson* [1977] QB 354; [1977] 2 All ER 341 (CA).

175 *R v Reid* [1992] 3 All ER 673; [1992] 1 WLR 793 (HL), noted by Gardner, "Manslaughter by gross negligence" (1995) 111 LQR 22, 23-24: Lord Keith makes it clear where a defendant should not be liable where his inadvertence is owing to "some condition not involving fault on his part" (675; 796), while Lord Goff refers to "illness or shock" (690; 813), and Lord Browne-Wilkinson to "sudden disability" (696; 819). See also *R v Adomako* [1995] 1 AC 171; [1994] 3 All ER 79 (HL), which suggests that fault should be assessed by reference to the capacities of the particular defendant.

176 *R v Harney* [1987] 2 NZLR 576, 579.

177 *Police v Bannin* [1991] 2 NZLR 237, also reported as *B v Police* (1991) 7 CRNZ 55, 254; 73.

178 See *R v P (T129/92)* (1993) 10 CRNZ 250; 1 HRNZ 417, 252, 253, 255; 419-420, 423, where D's intellectual impairment was said to be irrelevant to the question whether grounds for a belief held by D were reasonable. The unfortunate ruling in *R v P* perhaps depends on the particular wording of s 128(2)(b). See 18.2.2(2).

179 This distinction between types of elements of the actus reus was drawn in 3.1, 3.2.

180 *McCrone v Riding* [1938] 1 All ER 157, 158. See too *Police v Chappell* [1974] 1 NZLR 225; *R v Gosney* [1971] 2 QB 674; [1971] 3 All ER 220 (CA), 680; 224.

The justification for this is the need for a co-operative standard that other drivers can rely upon, together with the fact that driving is a voluntary activity, and those who engage in it may be thought to hold themselves out as being reasonably competent to do so.

4.6.4 The place of negligence

A number of writers have argued that people should never be subject to criminal liability on the basis of negligence,[181] and that its place lies properly in the arena of torts and compensation rather than of crimes and punishment. There is force in this argument, since it would normally be harsh to equate those who do wrong inadvertently with others who break the law intentionally or recklessly. The person who inadvertently does harm might well have refrained from doing so, had she only realised the risk. But the fact that negligence is often not as bad as recklessness or intention does not mean that it is never serious enough to warrant criminalisation. Baker's example is instructive:[182]

> "Carelessly handling loaded firearms in a crowded area, or speeding through a school zone at lunch hour oblivious to the dangers to others because one is absorbed in an interesting conversation, is more culpable ... than deliberately taking a $0.50 store item without payment or than many other knowing offences against property."

Sometimes, one who knowingly takes the risk of a minor crime is not so deserving of a criminal sanction as another who carelessly risks serious harm. It would be wrong for the criminal law only ever to convict in the former case.

However, such instances are properly exceptional, and normally the law is reluctant to inflict serious criminal (rather than civil) sanctions upon people who have merely been negligent. The general rule for serious criminal offences is that, in the few crimes where negligence is a sufficient to meet the mens rea requirements (such as manslaughter), then the negligence must be "gross" before the defendant can be convicted.[183] However, where the statute specifies the standard of care required in its own terms, for example as "reasonable care", then ordinary negligence will suffice.[184]

Although rare among serious crimes, it would be a mistake to discount the significance of negligence. In addition to setting the mens rea standard for manslaughter, sexual violation, and various other statutory offences, it remains very important in the context of defences,

---

181 Hall, "Negligent behaviour should be excluded from penal liability" (1963) 63 Columbia LR 632; Turner, "The mental element in crimes at common law" in Radzinowicz and Turner (eds), *The Modern Approach to Criminal Law*, London, Macmillan and Co, 1945, 195, 207-211; Hall, *General Principles of Criminal Law* (2nd ed), Indianapolis, Bobbs-Merrill, 1960, 138. Hart's refutation of Turner's argument is convincing: "Negligence, mens rea, and criminal responsibility" in Hart, *Punishment and Responsibility: Essays in the Philosophy of Law*, Oxford, Clarendon Press, 1968, 136. See also Moore, "Choice, character, and excuse" in Paul, Miller Jr, and Paul (eds), *Crime, Culpability, and Remedy*, Oxford, Basil Blackwell, 1990, 29, 58; Keedy, "Ignorance and mistake in the criminal law" (1908) 22 Harv LR 75, 83-85.
182 "Mens rea, negligence and criminal law reform" (1987) 6 Law and Philosophy 53, 81. In *Principles*, 199, Ashworth posits the following example: "D, a shotgun champion, fires at a target, knowing that there is a slight risk that the bullet will ricochet and injure a spectator, which it does; E, who rarely handles guns, is invited to participate in a shooting party and fires wildly into bushes, failing to consider the possibility of others being there, and one is injured. Is D manifestly more culpable than E?"
183 *R v Burney* [1958] NZLR 745 (CA); *R v Bateman* (1925) 19 Cr App R 8; [1925] All ER Rep 45 (CCA).
184 *R v Storey* [1931] NZLR 417 (CA); *R v Yogasakaran* [1990] 1 NZLR 399; (1989) 5 CRNZ 69 (CA); *R v P (T129/92)* (1993) 10 CRNZ 250; 1 HRNZ 417.

both common law and statutory: duress of circumstances, for example, is available only if the defendant's response is a reasonable one. Further, as we shall see in chapter 5, it is extremely important in the context of strict liability, where the main ground of exculpation is essentially an absence of negligence.

4.7 Other mens rea states

We have mentioned that there is a variety of other mens rea terms used in the criminal law. Some of these, such as "dishonestly", occur primarily in the context of property crimes such as theft, and will be explored in some detail when we come to look at the specific offences. Another fairly common term is "wilfully", which appears in a number of offences contained in the Crimes Act.[185] In essence, it appears that wilfulness is an alternative term for (subjective)[186] recklessness, and is satisfied if the defendant either intends or foresees the prohibited outcome.[187] Inadvertence will not do.[188]

There may be one distinction. Recklessness, we saw earlier, requires that the actus reus be an unreasonable risk. It is possible that "wilfully" imports no such requirement. If so, then a surgeon who carries out a risky yet medically-justified operation might injure her patient wilfully, even though she is not reckless. Nonetheless, it is submitted that in the context of the criminal law "wilfully" should bear the more restricted meaning, ie of recklessness. The defendant who, without intending the actus reus, takes a reasonable risk of bringing that actus about should not be regarded as having brought it about wilfully.

4.8 Transferred mens rea

It is a general rule that, if the defendant does an actus reus with the required mens rea (and without being able to plead any relevant defence), she is guilty of an offence even though the occurrence of the actus reus may be unexpected in a way which is immaterial to the definition.[189] To illustrate:

> Suppose that Duncan takes aim at Tom with intent to kill him, and pulls the trigger. Just as Duncan shoots, however, Tom bends down to pick a flower. Duncan's shot misses Tom and hits Bill, who was standing behind Tom. Bill is killed instantly. In this situation Duncan is guilty of murdering Bill, notwithstanding that he did not foresee that possible

---

185 See *Adams* (2nd ed), 2263.
186 Pace *R v Sheppard* [1981] AC 394; [1980] 3 All ER 899 (HL), which suggests that *Caldwell* recklessness is sufficient. In general, English case law should not be relied upon for the interpretation of wilfulness, since its meaning appears to vary across the English offences. For discussion, see Andrews, "Wilfulness, A lesson in ambiguity" (1981) 1 LS 303, 315ff.
187 Cf *R v T* [1997] 1 Qd R 623 (CA). An exception is s 201 (infecting with disease), where "wilfully" has been interpreted as requiring an intent to produce the disease: *R v Mwai* [1995] 3 NZLR 149, (1995) 13 CRNZ 273 (CA).
188 *Durey v Police* (1984) 1 CRNZ 392; *Donnelly v CIR* [1960] NZLR 469. See also *Summers v SPCA* [1991] 2 NZLR 469; (1990) 6 CRNZ 201, 475; 207, and the cases there discussed. For consideration of the effect upon "wilfulness" of a mistake of law, see *Police v Cunard* [1975] 1 NZLR 511; *Police v Shadbolt* [1976] 2 NZLR 409; also *Donnelly v CIR* [1960] NZLR 469, 472, 473.
189 For critical discussion, see Ashworth, "Transferred malice and punishment for unforeseen consequences: Essays in honour of Glanville Williams" in Glazebrook (ed), *Reshaping the Criminal Law: Essays in Honour of Glanville Williams*, London, Stevens & Sons, 1978, 77; Ashworth, "The elasticity of mens rea" in Tapper (ed), *Crime, Proof and Punishment: Essays in Memory of Sir Rupert Cross*, London, Butterworths, 1981, 45; Williams, "Convictions and fair labelling" [1983] 42 CLJ 85.

outcome. The actus reus of murder is to kill a *person*.[190] Thus, although Duncan intended to kill Tom rather than Bill, he had the mens rea for murder since he intended to kill a *person*; the identity of that person is immaterial to the definition of the offence.

The doctrine of "transferred malice", as it is popularly known, is not confined to murder.[191] Neither is it a doctrine merely of transferred *intention*. Imagine, this time, that Jane bears a grudge against Daniel. She throws a stone at his house, No 6 King Street. She recognises that the stone might break one of Daniel's windows, although she does not intend it to do so. As it happens, the stone misses the windows of No 6 but ricochets off the brickwork and breaks Pat's window at No 8. Jane's recklessness is sufficient mens rea for the offence of intentional damage[192] and is transferable to the (otherwise unanticipated) result: damage to *Pat's* property.

However, transferred malice does not operate when the divergence between actus reus and mens rea *is* relevant to the definition of the offence. In particular, it is not possible to convict someone on the basis of an actus reus for one offence accompanied by the mens rea for a different offence. If Jane were to throw a stone at Daniel and miss but inadvertently break his window, she is not guilty of intentional damage.[193] Her intent to injure Daniel does not satisfy the mens rea requirement for damage to property.

When malice is transferred, so also are defences. Imagine one last variant: Duncan attempts to shoot Tom only because Tom is attacking him and Duncan is in immediate peril of his life. He misses and unexpectedly kills Bill. Duncan's intention may be transferred, but so too is his claim of self-defence. He is not guilty of murder.[194]

Although the transferred malice doctrine has occasionally had something of a bad press,[195] in its modern incarnation (ie as stated here) the doctrine is unobjectionable. Indeed, it is not a doctrine at all — merely a particular type of immaterial variation. The causal miscarriage of D's actions in transferred malice cases has exactly the same legal status as, for example, cases of immaterial mistake. If Ian steals a cheap painting because he thinks it is a valuable Constable, he has the mens rea (and commits the actus reus) of theft, since the specific identity of the property stolen forms no necessary part of the offence definition. It is enough that he takes something that meets the definition of "property" in s 2 whether or not that thing is of great value.[196] Transferred malice cases are governed by the same principle: D's actions cause an outcome that is in some way unexpected,[197] but not in a way relevant to the offence definition.

---

190 *Agnes Gore's Case* (1611) 9 Co Rep 81; 77 ER 853; *Re A-G's Reference (No 3 of 1994)* [1996] QB 581; [1996] 2 All ER 10; *R v Hopwood* (1913) 8 Cr App R 143. Note that, in s 167(c), explicit statutory provision is made for transferred malice in homicide.

191 For example, *R v Gross* (1913) 23 Cox CC 455; (1913) 77 JP 352; *R v Latimer* (1886) 17 QBD 359; [1886-90] All ER Rep 386; *R v McCullum* (1973) 57 Cr App R 645; [1973] Crim LR 582 (CA).

192 Section 269(2)(a): although the offence is entitled "intentional damage", recklessness suffices.

193 Cf *R v Pembliton* (1874) LR 2 CCR 119; (1874) 12 Cox CC 607; *R v Taaffe* [1984] AC 539; [1984] 1 All ER 747 (HL). However, cf *R v Ellis* (1986) 84 Cr App R 235; [1987] Crim LR 44 (CA), which pays lip service to the principle that the actus reus and mens rea must correspond, but at the same time subverts that fundamental requirement for the sake of enforcement convenience.

194 Cf *Gross* (1913) 77 JP 352 (provocation). Note that the transfer of a defence will not necessarily preclude liability for an independent offence. It may, for example, have been grossly negligent to shoot at Tom because of the risk of hitting Bill.

195 For example *A-G's Reference (No 3 of 1994)* [1998] AC 245; [1997] 3 All ER 936 (HL), 259-262; 950-952 (Lord Mustill).

196 Cf *R v Wrigley* [1957] Crim LR 57. See ch 19.

4.9 Concurrence

As a general rule, the actus reus and mens rea of a crime must coincide in time. That is, the behavioural and circumstantial elements of the actus reus must occur at the same time as the mens rea requirements are satisfied. Unless there is a moment in time, a scintilla temporis, at which these elements are all present, the crime is not committed.[198] Consider the following illustration:

> D is an assassin who has been hired to kill V. One evening she drives over to V's house in order to shoot him when he comes home. On the way, however, she is involved in an accident when she collides with a cyclist who has suddenly cut in front of her car. Upon getting out of the car, D recognises that the cyclist is V. Thinking V is unconscious but alive, she shoots him through the heart. V, however, was already dead as a result of the accident.

D has not murdered V. Although she may have caused his death (the actus reus) by driving into him, when she did so she did not have a present intention to kill. Later, when she shot V, she had the mens rea for murder but her behaviour did not cause his death, so could not constitute the actus reus. Thus there is no moment in time at which both the actus reus and mens rea of murder are present.

Neither can an antecedent mens rea be added to a subsequent actus reus in order to support a conviction. For example:

> D takes a new umbrella to the law library one morning. When she departs, she realises that she cannot remember exactly what her umbrella looked like. However, seeing an attractive umbrella in the stand, she decides to take and keep that one instead — not realising that it is in fact her own umbrella. Later, she begins to feel guilty. She returns to the law library, and replaces the attractive umbrella. In its place, she takes with her a different umbrella which she mistakenly thinks is the one she originally came with.

When D first leaves the library, she attempts to steal an umbrella but fails to do so because the one she takes is her own. She has the mens rea for theft but does not commit the actus reus.[199] Later, when she departs for a second time, she commits the actus reus of theft by taking another person's umbrella, but does so innocently — without an "intent to deprive the owner". There is no scintilla temporis at which all elements of the definition of theft are coexistent.

Where the actus reus includes consequences, the requirement for concurrence applies to the behavioural element rather than its consequence. If D deliberately poisons V, and V takes some hours to die, the fact that D repents in the meantime will not absolve her of murder.[200] Conversely, if D is driving and accidentally hits a cyclist, the fact that she realises the cyclist is V, her enemy, and rejoices while he is dying of his injuries will not make her guilty of a homicide offence. For the purposes of concurrence, the actus reus has already occurred.

---

197 A proviso: transferred malice is unproblematic only if causal principles are properly observed. This explains the otherwise troubling case of *Re Heigho* 18 Idaho 566; 100 P 1029 (1910), discussed in Williams, *TBCL*, 181, n 1. In that case, D assaulted W, and an onlooker died of fright. D was convicted of manslaughter of the onlooker. It is submitted the conviction was wrong; D was not causally responsible for the onlooker's death.
198 Cf *R v Terry* 9/9/96, CA50/96; *R v Scott* [1967] VR 276; *Fowler v Padget* (1798) 7 TR 509; 101 ER 1103.
199 The taking is not a trespass: see 19.3.2.
200 Cf *R v Jakeman* (1983) 76 Cr App R 223; [1983] Crim LR 104 (CA).

Although concurrence is a standard requirement for offences involving mens rea, there are some situations where the need for concurrence does not operate or can be circumnavigated.[201] We consider these below.

4.9.1 Circumventing the concurrence requirement

(1) *Fresh acts, continuing acts, and subsequent omissions*

Where an actus reus by D precedes his having mens rea, one technique available to the prosecutor is to show another, later, occurrence of the actus reus which coincides with D's mens rea — ie to look for a different scintilla temporis at which the offence can be proved to have occurred.

A standard, if unusual, case of this would be where D does a second, positive act which also brings about the actus reus.[202] Suppose that, in the days when tort actions died with the plaintiff,[203] D accidentally runs over V while driving. V, fatally injured, lies dying. D is uninsured and, panicking, she backs up hoping thereby to avoid tortious liability. If the further injuries D inflicts by reversing over V play any causal role in V's death, then D becomes guilty of murder, on the basis of the second and not the first incident.

Absent a fresh causative act by the defendant, the prosecution may try instead to show a *continuing* act: that the actus reus, although initiated by D without mens rea, is still occurring or being perpetrated by D at a later moment when D now has the required mens rea. This type of case is discussed in 3.2.1(2)(d). It is exemplified by *Fagan v MPC*,[204] in which D accidentally stopped his car on a policeman's foot. That itself was no assault, since D did not yet have mens rea. However, when he deliberately refrained from moving his car, an assault was established. There was an ongoing application of force to the policeman by D (the actus reus), which was now accompanied by mens rea.[205]

Alternatively, the prosecution can try to bring its case within the ambit of *R v Miller*.[206] In this situation, a subsequent omission to prevent harm may constitute the actus reus if it amounts to a failure to prevent a danger that D has himself created by his earlier actions. *Miller* is discussed further in 3.2.1(2)(e).

(2) *The complex single transaction*

The law is different when the actus reus of an offence occurs *after* D has mens rea. Here it will sometimes be possible to convict D on the basis that the particular act that caused harm was part of a larger, complex series of actions which should be viewed as a whole, where D has mens rea at some earlier point during that "transaction".

---

201 Marston, "Contemporaneity of act and intention in crimes" [1970] 86 LQR 208. See also White, "The identity and time of the actus reus" [1977] Crim LR 148.
202 Cf, on one view of the facts, *R v Chignell* [1991] 2 NZLR 257, also reported as *R v Chignell and Walker* (1990) 6 CRNZ 103 (CA).
203 Winfield, "Death as affecting liability in tort" (1929) 29 Col L Rev 239.
204 *Fagan v MPC* [1969] 1 QB 439; [1968] 3 All ER 442.
205 See also *R v Kaitamaki* [1984] 1 NZLR 385, also reported as *Kaitamaki v R* (1984) 1 CRNZ 211; [1985] AC 147 (PC); *R v Cooper* [1994] Crim LR 531.
206 *R v Miller* [1983] 2 AC 161; [1983] 1 All ER 978 (HL).

The classic case is *Thabo Meli v R*.[207] In that case, four defendants conspired to kill V and dispose of his body. In accordance with their plan, they struck V on the head (with intent thereby to kill him). Thinking him dead, they rolled him over a cliff. In fact, V was not killed by the blow and died from exposure suffered after falling down the cliff. Prima facie, the act of disposal, which caused V's death, was unaccompanied by the mens rea for murder since the defendants believed he was already dead. Nonetheless, the Privy Council upheld their convictions for murder. Rather than slicing up the events of the killing into component moments of time and then looking for a scintilla temporis at which actus reus and mens rea coincide:[208]

> "It appears to their Lordships impossible to divide up what was really one transaction in this way. There is no doubt that the accused set out to do all these acts in order to achieve their plan and as parts of their plan; and it is much too refined a ground of judgment to say that, because they were under a misapprehension at one stage and thought that their guilty purpose was achieved before in fact it was achieved, therefore they are to escape the penalties of the law."

It is hard to disagree with this decision, which represents a genuine exception to the concurrence requirement. The defendants did exactly what they planned to do, and brought about exactly the result they intended. The fact that the manner in which their success occurred was unexpected seems no ground for exculpation.

As the quotation above emphasises, the defendants' actions were deliberate and pursuant to a preconceived plan. This feature is crucial to the application of *Thabo Meli* in New Zealand. In *R v Ramsay*,[209] D had assaulted and gagged V, whose death was caused by one or other of those acts. However, it appeared that D may not have had the mens rea of murder when gagging V. The Court of Appeal ruled that the assault and the gagging could not be treated as a continuous single course of conduct: there was not a preconceived plan by D to behave as he did, and his conduct could not be regarded as a series of actions governed throughout by a "dominating intention" to produce the actus reus. Hence D's mens rea when he assaulted V could not be combined with the actus reus when he gagged her to satisfy the requirements of murder. Although the rationale underlying *Thabo Meli* might have suggested a different conclusion,[210] the Court of Appeal has taken a firm stance against further exceptions to the concurrence principle.

It follows from the decision in *Ramsay* that the *Thabo Meli* doctrine will not apply to crimes of recklessness or negligence. The New Zealand law on this point differs from applicable law elsewhere,[211] but it is defensible on the basis that it fosters certainty by confining exceptions to the concurrence requirement to those cases where there is a preconceived plan.

---

207 *Thabo Meli v R* [1954] 1 All ER 373; [1954] 1 WLR 228 (PC).
208 *Thabo Meli v R* [1954] 1 All ER 373; [1954] 1 WLR 228 (PC), 374; 230.
209 *R v Ramsay* [1967] NZLR 1005 (CA); cf *R v Chignell* [1991] 2 NZLR 257, also reported as *R v Chignell and Walker* (1990) 6 CRNZ 103 (CA), 265; 111; *R v Dixon* [1979] 1 NZLR 641 (CA), 646, 647.
210 Cf Adams, "Homicide and the supposed corpse" (1968) 1 Otago LR 278, 290. However, as Adams acknowledges, it is arguable that the approach in *Thabo Meli* — that at common law, a homicide committed in such a manner is murder — is less easily adopted where murder has a statutory definition specifying the particular intent(s) required.
211 *Shoukatallie v R* [1962] AC 81; [1961] 3 All ER 966; *R v Church* [1966] 1 QB 59; [1965] 2 All ER 72 (CCA); *R v Moore and Dorn* [1975] Crim LR 229 (CA); *R v Le Brun* [1992] 1 QB 61; [1991] 4 All ER 673 (CA); *A-G's Reference (No 4 of 1980)* [1981] 2 All ER 617; [1981] 1 WLR 705 (CA). For discussion, see Sullivan, "Cause and the contemporaneity of actus reus and mens rea" (1993) 52 CLJ 487, 495-499.

(3) A causation approach

Where the defendant's mens rea precedes the action that most obviously constitutes the actus reus, another way of circumventing concurrence difficulties is to show that some earlier action by the defendant, done at the time when he had mens rea, was *also* a cause of the prohibited harm. An example of this approach is *R v McKinnon*.[212] In that case, D assaulted V and knocked him unconscious. D then manhandled V, apparently causing an accidental nose-bleed, before leaving V lying on the ground and running off. While V was lying unconscious, the blood from his nose entered his lungs and he suffocated. The Court of Appeal upheld D's conviction for murder. Although D may not have had the required mens rea when he caused the injury to V's nose, he did have mens rea when he struck V and knocked him unconscious. Moreover, the Court ruled, D's striking V was a contributory cause of his death, in combination with the nose-bleed, since it rendered V unable to deal with the bleeding. Thus there was no need to invoke a series-of-acts analysis, of the sort found in *Thabo Meli*, since there was already a scintilla temporis at which both an actus reus and the mens rea of murder were present.[213]

(4) Involuntariness and antecedent fault

If D perpetrates an actus reus while in an automatic state, normally the concurrence requirement will not be satisfied. Exceptionally, however, it may be possible to convict D on the basis that his automatism is a consequence of his own earlier actions which occurred at a time when he had the mens rea for the offence. This type of case is discussed more fully in 3.4.3. Suppose, for example, that David is a diabetic. One day he deliberately takes insulin without eating any food. He does this in the hope of reducing himself into a semi-conscious state, where he knows that he is likely to become violent and assault his flatmate whom he does not like. Should his plan be successful, David will be guilty of an intentional assault, notwithstanding his automatism at the time the assault occurs.[214]

Sometimes the offence may be proved without reference to the defendant's subsequent, involuntary conduct. In *Kay v Butterworth*,[215] D fell asleep while driving and collided with soldiers marching on the road. He was convicted of careless driving, but not because he drove into the soldiers. (At that time he was asleep and his behaviour was involuntary.) Rather, the offence was complete when he continued to drive while drowsy — that, in itself, was careless driving. Indeed, D would have committed the offence even if he had not run into the soldiers.[216] Glanville Williams illustrates this point in a lucid example:

---

212 *R v McKinnon* [1980] 2 NZLR 31 (CA). For discussion of multiple causes see 3.3.2(3). Cf *S v Masilela* 1968 (2) SA 558.
213 Indeed, it is arguable that *Thabo Meli* could itself have been decided on a causation basis: Adams, "Homicide and the supposed corpse" (1968) 1 Otago LR 278, 287; Marston, "Contemporaneity of act and intention in crimes" [1970] 86 LQR 208, 218-219; *R v McKinnon* [1980] 2 NZLR 31 (CA), 36, 37; cf *R v O'Brien* (2003) 20 CRNZ 572 (CA), para 21 . On this approach, the *Thabo Meli* doctrine would still be necessary in some cases, but only where the second event was overwhelmingly the cause of death, and amounted to a *novus actus interveniens*. (For example, where V is killed instantly by the impact after he is thrown over a cliff: cf *R v Le Brun* [1992] 1 QB 61; [1991] 4 All ER 673 (CA).)
214 *A-G for Northern Ireland v Gallagher* [1963] AC 349; [1961] 3 All ER 299, 382; 314 (Lord Denning).
215 *Kay v Butterworth* (1945) 61 TLR 452. Cf *Moses v Winder* [1980] Crim LR 232. For a rather more dramatic example, see *People v Decina* 2 NY 2d 133 (1956).
216 *R v Spurge* [1961] 2 QB 205; [1961] 2 All ER 688, 210; 690.

"When, for example, a driver proceeds along Church Lane in a sleepy condition, and falls asleep at the wheel just before entering High Street, where he is involved in an accident, he cannot be convicted of careless driving in High Street, because in contemplation of law he did not 'drive' in High Street, and it makes no difference that his involuntary accident in High Street was the result of his own previous fault. He can, indeed, be convicted of careless driving, but this must be laid as having taken place in Church Lane, when the driver was undoubtedly 'driving'."[217]

The offence occurs in Church Lane.

---

217 Williams, *TBCL*, 682. Obviously, this analysis works only if the time-frame for commission of the actus reus is sufficiently elastic, and not tied to a particular incident. Contrast *Burns v Bidder* [1967] 2 QB 227; [1966] 3 All ER 29 (failing to accord precedence at a pedestrian crossing). A nice illustration is *MOT v Beregi* [1992] DCR 261, in which D had a petit mal epileptic attack while driving. He was convicted on a dangerous driving charge, because it was held reasonably foreseeable that D could endanger others on the road by having an epileptic fit. Nonetheless, he was discharged on the second count of failing to stop after an accident.

Chapter 5

STRICT AND ABSOLUTE LIABILITY

5.1	Strict and absolute liability	133
5.1.1	Strict liability	135
(1)	*Nature of the defence*	136
(2)	*Standard of care required*	137
(3)	*Justification of strict liability*	138
5.1.2	Absolute liability	141
(1)	*The place of absolute liability*	143
5.2	The mens rea categorisation of particular offences	144
5.2.1	Options available before *Millar v MOT*	144
5.2.2	Options available today	146
(1)	*Statutory mens rea elements*	146
(2)	*Implied mens rea*	146
(3)	*Category (3): Strawbridge*	149
(4)	*Strict liability*	149
(5)	*Absolute liability*	149
5.2.3	Deciding which fault standard applies	150
(1)	*Clear cases*	150
(2)	*Guiding principles*	151

5.1 Strict and absolute liability

Not every offence against the criminal law involves the sort of public condemnation that is implicit in a conviction for homicide. We argued in chapter 1 that serious criminal offences, where considerable public stigma attaches to a conviction, should always stipulate some form of mens rea element that must be proved before the defendant may be convicted, in order to avoid inflicting "the disgrace of criminality"[1] upon defendants who are not at fault when harm occurs. By contrast, a parking offence, for instance, involves little or no stigma, so the need for a mens rea element is not as pressing.

In recognition of this, there are many offences of a regulatory nature (sometimes called public welfare regulatory offences) which lack a true mens rea ingredient.[2] These offences fall into two categories: strict and absolute liability. For convenience, we will summarise the two categories before discussing them below:

---

1   *Warner v MPC* [1969] 2 AC 256; [1968] 2 All ER 356 (HL), 272; 360 (Lord Reid).
2   See Simester (ed), *Appraising Strict Liability*, Oxford, Oxford University Press, 2005; Sayre, "Public welfare offences" (1933) 33 Col LR 55; Howard, *Strict Responsibility*, London, Sweet & Maxwell, 1963; Kadish, "Some observations on the use of criminal sanctions in enforcing economic regulations" (1963) 30 U Chicago LR 423.

(i) *Strict liability*: The prosecution is required to prove the actus reus, but, in relation to one or more elements of the actus reus,[3] there is no mens rea element to prove. However, the defendant can prove absence of fault on his part in order to exculpate himself.

(ii) *Absolute liability*: The offence is complete upon proof of the actus reus. There is no requirement to prove mens rea; neither can the defendant claim an absence of fault in his own defence.[4]

(One word of caution. In England, the terms "strict liability" and "absolute liability" are used almost interchangeably, a phenomenon that is likely to mislead the unwary from another jurisdiction. The same is true of cases decided in New Zealand before 1983. A distinction between the two types of regulatory offence was first drawn explicitly in New Zealand by the Court of Appeal in *Civil Aviation Dept v MacKenzie*.)[5]

With isolated exceptions, strict liability offences are a creation of statute rather than the common law.[6] The opportunity to impose them arises from the fact that criminal legislation is very often silent regarding the mens rea element, leaving it to the courts either to infer a mens rea requirement or to interpret the offence literally, ie as one of strict liability. In these circumstances, the courts have long recognised a principle that mens rea was to be regarded as implied: "Acts of Parliament are to be so construed, as no man that is innocent, or free from injury or wrong, be by a literal construction punished or endamaged."[7] Although operation of the principle can be overridden by Parliament, either expressly or impliedly, that conclusion is not lightly to be reached. As we shall see in 5.2, this remains the point of departure for courts when determining whether a particular statute creates an offence of strict liability or one requiring mens rea. But the principle is not absolute, and sometimes the courts are willing to read statutes literally, ie without implying a mens rea requirement. The seeds of this willingness were sewn during the later part of the 19th century, when strict liability offences began to emerge as a convenient means of dealing with rapidly changing social and industrial practices.[8] Most often they owe their existence to a perception that the need to protect the public might on occasion justify convicting people of offences even where they were not necessarily at fault; especially, though not invariably, where the harm involved resulted from

---

3   An offence may properly be regarded as being of strict or absolute liability even though mens rea is required regarding other elements of the actus reus: *R v Lemon; R v Gay News Ltd* [1979] AC 617; [1979] 1 All ER 898 (HL), 656; 920 (Lord Edmund-Davies). This classification will sometimes be misleading, for example where strict liability goes only to a foreseeable consequence of the other actus reus elements, which themselves require mens rea. Operating a vehicle carelessly and thereby causing death, contrary to s 38 Land Transport Act 1998, is an offence of this form: the fact that no additional fault is required about the death itself hardly makes it in substance an offence of strict liability. Indeed, fatalities are precisely the sort of reason why careless driving is culpable.

4   In both strict liability and absolute liability offences the prosecution must still prove the actus reus beyond reasonable doubt.

5   *Civil Aviation Dept v MacKenzie* [1983] NZLR 78, also reported as *MacKenzie v Civil Aviation Dept* (1983) 1 CRNZ 38 (CA).

6   The common law exceptions include contempt of court, together with an employer's liability for public nuisance and criminal libel.

7   *Margate Pier Co v Hannam* (1819) 3 B & Ald 266; 106 ER 661, 270; 663 quoting Lord Coke. Among other cases, see *Fowler v Padget* (1798) 7 TR 509; 101 ER 1103; *R v Tolson* (1889) 23 QBD 168; [1886-90] All ER Rep 26, 187; 37 (Stephen J); *Sherras v de Rutzen* [1895] 1 QB 918; [1895-99] All ER Rep 1167.

8   See, for example, Carson, "Symbolic and instrumental dimensions of early factory legislation: A Case Study in the Social Origins of Criminal Law" in Hood (ed), *Crime, Criminology and Public Policy*, London, Heinemann Educational, 1974; Carson, "The conventionalisation of early factory crime" (1979) 7 Int J Soc Law 37.

a specialised activity, one which might naturally lend itself to control by regulatory rather than "truly criminal" prohibitions. Even the enforcement of such offences tends to be distinctive. They are frequently patrolled not by the police, but by specialist agencies created to monitor and control the effects of particular types of activity such as pollution and industrial safety. Habits of prosecution differ also. In practice, it appears that while prosecution is a typical response of the police to breaches of the law, regulatory agencies by contrast tend to prosecute only for recurring or very serious breaches of the law. Characteristically, in the hands of regulatory agencies, the fact that an offence imposes strict liability operates as an important background consideration in compliance negotiations.[9]

5.1.1 Strict liability

The leading modern case on strict liability is Canadian. Traditionally, English law has consigned regulatory offences to the category of absolute liability unless the offence involved is "truly criminal"[10] in nature (in which case mens rea will be required), or the statute expressly directs otherwise. This approach leaves the courts with only a rather simplistic choice between the extremes of requiring full mens rea and making an offence absolute.[11] In *R v City of Sault Ste Marie*,[12] the Supreme Court of Canada decided that although mens rea need not be an essential ingredient of an offence, an alternative to absolute liability was nonetheless possible: there might be a defence available of "total absence of fault", the onus of proof for which would lie on the defendant. This third category, which the Court named strict liability, was characterised as follows:[13]

> "the doing of the prohibited act *prima facie* imports the offence, leaving it open to the accused to avoid liability by proving that he took all reasonable care. This involves consideration of what a reasonable man would have done in the circumstances. The defence will be available if the accused reasonably believed in a mistaken set of facts which, if true, would render the act or omission innocent,[14] or if he took all reasonable steps to avoid the particular event."

The Supreme Court thus claimed a middle ground that the House of Lords has denied itself. Indeed, it went further and held that public welfare regulatory offences, if they were not found to require proof of full mens rea, should presumptively involve strict rather than absolute liability.[15] In New Zealand, the view of the Canadian Supreme Court was endorsed by the

---

9 See, for example, Hawkins, *Environment and Enforcement: Regulation and the Social Definition of Pollution*, Oxford, Clarendon Press, 1984; Hutter, *The Reasonable Arm of the Law*, Oxford, Clarendon Press, 1988.
10 Cf *Gammon (Hong Kong) Ltd v A-G of Hong Kong* [1985] AC 1; [1984] 2 All ER 503 (PC), 14; 508 (Lord Scarman).
11 *Sweet v Parsley* [1970] AC 132; [1969] 1 All ER 347 (HL).
12 *R v City of Sault Ste Marie* (1978) 85 DLR (3d) 161; [1978] 2 SCR 1299 (SCC) (water pollution). See, for analysis, Hutchinson, "*Sault Ste Marie*, mens rea and the halfway house: Public welfare offences get a home of their own" (1979) 17 Osgoode Hall LJ 415.
13 *R v City of Sault Ste Marie* (1978) 85 DLR (3d) 161; [1978] 2 SCR 1299 (SCC), 181, 182; 1326 (empahsis added).
14 "The *R v Tolson* defence: (1889) 23 QBD 168; [1886-90] All ER Rep 26. Cf, in Australia, *Proudman v Dayman* (1941) 67 CLR 536; [1944] ALR 64, 540; 65 (Dixon J); Howard, "Strict responsibility in the High Court of Australia" (1960) 76 LQR 547. See also Brett, "Strict responsibility: Possible solutions" (1974) 37 MLR 417.
15 *R v City of Sault Ste Marie* (1978) 85 DLR (3d) 161; [1978] 2 SCR 1299 (SCC), 182; 1326. See 5.2.3(2)(d). The policy reasons for preferring strict liability are stated at 171; 1310.

Court of Appeal in *Civil Aviation Dept v MacKenzie*[16] and the other leading case, *Millar v MOT*.[17] A large number of offences have now been held to be of strict liability.[18]

The effect of these decisions is that proof of strict liability offences is prima facie complete as soon as the prosecution proves, beyond reasonable doubt, that the actus reus has occurred. However, it is possible for the defendant to show that the occurrence of the actus reus was not something for which he was at fault. By contrast with the actus reus, and with normal rules about proof of mens rea, the burden of proving absence of fault rests with the defendant, on the balance of probabilities.

(1)   *Nature of the defence*

Usually described as "absence of fault", in essence the defence can be made out by showing that the occurrence of the actus reus was not something the defendant could reasonably have prevented, or — if he in fact caused the actus reus — that he did so without being at fault (ie without being negligent). What counts is not so much how the actus reus occurred but whether the defendant exhibited a reasonable level of care to avoid it.[19] If the actus reus occurred because of factual ignorance or mistake on the defendant's part, then he will be required to prove that his ignorance or mistake was a reasonable one. An example where the facts would support such a defence is provided by *Finau v Dept of Labour*,[20] in which D was prosecuted for remaining in New Zealand beyond the expiry date of her temporary entry permit. D's defence succeeded: owing to pregnancy she had been refused carriage upon an airline, and it was therefore impossible for her to avoid committing the actus reus.

Impossibility is not itself required to sustain the defence; what counts is an absence of fault. In *Dept of Health v Multichem Laboratories Ltd*,[21] D was charged with supplying a medicine to the Auckland Hospital Board Pharmacy before consent to its distribution had been obtained from the Department of Health. Even though it was possible for D to choose not to supply the medicine, and also possible for D to have checked that consent had been obtained, the High Court accepted D's defence that the omission to do so was reasonable.

Although impossibility or involuntariness will generally also deny criminal responsibility for the actus reus,[22] sometimes that impossibility may be a consequence of earlier conduct by D.[23] In such cases the absence of fault defence will still be needed.[24] To illustrate, the facts of *Finau* may be contrasted with those in the earlier case *Tifaga v Dept of Labour*.[25] In *Tifaga*, D's entry permit had similarly expired. He claimed that it had proved impossible for him to leave the country because he had not enough money to purchase an air ticket. Rejecting his claim,

---

16   *Civil Aviation Dept v MacKenzie* [1983] NZLR 78, also reported as *MacKenzie v Civil Aviation Dept* (1983) 1 CRNZ 38 (CA) (dangerous flying).
17   *Millar v MOT* [1986] 1 NZLR 660; (1986) 2 CRNZ 216 (CA) (driving while disqualified).
18   A collection can be found in *Adams*, CA20.45 (looseleaf).
19   *R v Petro-Canada* (2003) 171 CCC (3d) 354 (Ont CA).
20   *Finau v Dept of Labour* [1984] 2 NZLR 396 (CA).
21   *Dept of Health v Multichem Laboratories Ltd* [1987] 1 NZLR 334. Note that the defence in this case was statutory.
22   See 3.4, 3.4.2.
23   See 3.4.3. It has been suggested in *Keech v Pratt* [1994] 1 NZLR 65, also reported as *Police v Pratt* (1993) 10 CRNZ 659; followed on this point in *Joe v Police* 21/12/95, Goddard J, HC Wellington AP230/95, 11, that, in strict liability offences, involuntariness and/or impossibility has been entirely subsumed by the absence of fault defence, with the burden of proof falling on the defendant; but see 3.4.3(1) above, where this view is criticised. In practice, the defence of absence of fault is the more important.

the Court of Appeal opined that D's failure to retain enough funds was his own fault, and therefore a defence did not arise.

(2)   Standard of care required

It may be that a scenario akin to *Tifaga* is what is contemplated when the defence is termed one of *total* absence of fault.[26] Although in considering the phrase Barker J has held that "total" adds nothing to "absence of fault",[27] it does help to emphasise that the defence is not established merely by proving the defendant was not at fault during the very moments that the actus reus occurred. The defendant must show also that he was blameless antecedently,[28] ie that he took "*all* reasonable care", and not merely some reasonable steps. This point was once made by Chapman J in the context of a similarly-worded statutory defence:

> "an acquittal on this ground is not secured by showing that in the ordinary sense reasonable care has been taken; the very words of the section must be pursued, and the defendant must prove that all reasonable steps have been taken to avoid an offence.[29]

If that represents a difference at all from ordinary negligence, it is surely a minor one.[30] More significantly, it also appears that the defence is a purely objective one and seemingly independent of any of the defendant's personal inadequacies. This suggests that the standard of care demanded is more objective than ordinary negligence, which appears to allow for subjective limitations of the defendant.[31] Thus the defence will not be available if the defendant's mistake was one which a person of average intellect should not have made, notwithstanding that the defendant himself was of low intelligence. According to Richardson J, in *MacKenzie*:[32]

> "a high standard of care is properly expected of a defendant in such a case and he must prove that he did what a reasonable man would have done. It would not in our view be appropriate to have a variable standard of negligence depending on subjective considerations affecting the individual concerned, as was suggested in argument at one point."

This statement clearly excludes consideration of the defendant's capacities. It will be no answer for her to claim that because of individual peculiarities he was incapable of attaining the standard of reasonableness that the no-fault defence requires.[33] His Honour cited in support

---

24   Thus it seems that automatism will not excuse a defendant whose automatism is due to antecedent fault, such as self-induced intoxication. *O'Neill v MOT* [1985] 2 NZLR 513 suggests that involuntariness due to intoxication will only be a defence to strict liability offences where the defendant did not know that she was consuming alcohol (or drugs). There is no defence where the defendant ought to have known she could be affected by alcohol; nor where she voluntarily consumes alcohol without knowing that it was too much.
25   *Tifaga v Dept of Labour* [1980] 2 NZLR 235 (CA). Note that this case was decided before *MacKenzie*; thus see also 5.1.2 (absolute liability).
26   Cf *Millar v MOT* [1986] 1 NZLR 660; (1986) 2 CRNZ 216 (CA), 668; 225.
27   *Police v Starkey* [1989] 2 NZLR 373; (1989) 4 CRNZ 400, 379; 405, 406.
28   Cf *Police v Creedon* [1976] 1 NZLR 571 (CA), 582 lines 35-39 (Richmond J).
29   "*Canterbury Central Co-op Dairy Co Ltd v McKenzie* [1923] NZLR 426, 428."
30   Cf *Buchanans Foundry Ltd v Dept of Labour* [1996] 3 NZLR 112, 119.
31   See 4.6.3.
32   *Civil Aviation Dept v MacKenzie* [1983] NZLR 78, also reported as *MacKenzie v Civil Aviation Dept* (1983) 1 CRNZ 38 (CA), 85; 45.

of this proposition the earlier case of *Police v Creedon*,[34] in which Cooke J had approved the assertion by Megaw LJ in R *v Gosney* that fault does not "necessarily involve moral blame":[35]

> "Thus there is fault if an inexperienced or a naturally poor driver, while straining every nerve to do the right thing, falls below the standard of a competent and careful driver. Fault involves a failure; a falling below the care or skill of a competent and experienced driver, in relation to the manner of the driving and to the relevant circumstances of the case."

The "failure", then, need not be one for which the individual is culpable.

(3)   *Justification of strict liability*

(a)   No-fault defence

The argument for having a strict liability fault standard in certain offences is made in two stages. The first step involves arguing that to require something less than full mens rea (intention or recklessness etc) is appropriate in such offences. The second stage is the claim that the other major alternative, absolute liability, is *not* appropriate. This second limb is dealt with in the discussion of absolute liability (5.1.2).

The reason most often given for abandoning a full mens rea requirement is that protection of the public sometimes requires a high standard of care on the part of those who undertake risk-creating activities.[36] Proper care needs to be taken by such persons, and without liability for inadvertence the careless will be able to transfer the considerable costs of their foolishness to the rest of society, without having any serious incentive to reduce or eliminate those risks. The threat of criminal liability supplies a motive for persons in risk-generating activities to adopt precautions, which might not otherwise be taken, in order to ensure mishaps and errors are eliminated.[37] Lady Wootton's writing is a useful example of this type of argument:[38]

> "If the object of the criminal law is to prevent the occurrence of socially damaging actions, it would be absurd to turn a blind eye to those which were due to carelessness, negligence, or even accident[. I]n the modern world ... as much and more damage is done by negligence, or by indifference to the welfare or safety of others, as by deliberate wickedness. If the law says that certain things are not to be done, it is illogical to confine this prohibition to occasions on which they are done from malice aforethought; for at

---

33   Cf France, "Absolute liability since *MacKenzie*" [1987] NZLJ 50, 51; Orchard, "The judicial categorisation of offences" (1983) 2 Canterbury LR 81, 93-94; Orchard, "The defence of absence of fault in Australasia and Canada" in Smith (ed), *Criminal Law: Essays in Honour of J C Smith*, London, Butterworths, 1987, 114, 118.

34   *Police v Creedon* [1976] 1 NZLR 571 (CA), 586, 587. See also 575 line 40 (McCarthy P), 582 line 35 (Richmond J), and 586 lines 38, 39 (Cooke J).

35   R *v Gosney* [1971] 2 QB 674; [1971] 3 All ER 220 (CA), 680; 224.

36   This may help to explain why an objective, rather than subjective, non-fault standard is demanded of the defendant (5.1.1(2)). For an elaboration of the assumption of risk argument, see Honoré, "Responsibility and luck: The moral basis of strict liability" (1988) 104 LQR 530.

37   R *v City of Sault Ste Marie* (1978) 85 DLR (3d) 161; [1978] 2 SCR 1299 (SCC), 171; 1310, 1311.

38   *Crime and the Criminal Law: Reflections of a Magistrate and Social Scientist* (2nd ed), London, Stevens & Sons, 1981, 47ff. The claim of illogicality is, incidentally, false. Sometimes the presence of mens rea is crucial to the wrongfulness of what is done: cf 4.4. Wootton's argument therefore applies only to those harms whose nature is independent of the mens rea with which they are caused, and that (as such) are sufficiently severe to warrant criminalisation.

least the material consequences of an action, and the reasons for prohibiting it are the same whether it is the result of sinister malicious plotting, of negligence or of sheer accident."

In practice, such deterrence-based reasoning seems to be reflected in the law, since regulatory offences are often found where there is a need to protect the public from risks created by industrial and other specialist activities. Particularly where the harmful impact of the actus reus is severe and widespread, the law has reason to provide incentives through criminalisation for persons not only to refrain from advertent wrongdoing, but also to take care against inadvertent harms.

Of course, the public protection/deterrence argument cannot, by itself, be a decisive justification. The public needs also to be protected from assaults, damage to property, and the like, yet these are not strict liability offences; they require proof of mens rea in the ordinary way.[39] The difference, it is said, is that assault is a "true" crime, conviction for which entails serious social stigma — hence the need for a higher standard of fault, which partially overrides the deterrence argument — whereas regulatory offences control "quasi-criminal" (ie not truly criminal) actions.

The force of the deterrence factor is reinforced by other considerations. One is that, in New Zealand, strict liability is a partial substitute for tortious liability for personal injury, which has been displaced by accident compensation legislation. Thus the usual economic incentive to avoid negligent accidents — the prospect of civil liability — is much less effective here than it may be overseas. Additionally, strict liability is particularly appropriate where the offence is directed toward controlling the activity of corporations. There are three reasons for this. First, corporate convictions do not normally involve the same level of stigma as do those attaching to individuals, nor the same practical implications. Secondly, corporate activity is characteristically on a larger scale than that by individuals, and correspondingly creates greater levels of social threat. Finally, and most importantly, the proof of mens rea presents special difficulty in the context of corporate bodies, since there is no one person who can be identified as the agent when a corporation acts. The negligence standard contained in strict liability, by contrast, is much more easily applied to companies and the like, since it can be administered without reference to the defendant's mental state.

All this having been said, it is arguable that there is a case for reform. The above considerations do not establish why *criminal* rather than civil sanctions should be used to regulate the activities involved. Even if private individuals cannot pursue a claim for damages, it may be open to the State, by legislative reform, to pursue miscreants through an administrative system of regulations that applies a standard of strict liability without the accompanying connotations of a criminal conviction. Arguably, as things stand now, the moral authority of the criminal law is being undermined by the extension of liability to what are, in essence, mere regulatory violations.[40]

On the other hand, against this last argument it may be noted that the description "mere regulatory violations" somewhat underplays the vital public protection role that construction

---

39 Cf Mannheim, "Mens rea in German and English criminal law" (1936) 18 J Comp Leg 78, 90: "the number of larcenies committed, *eg*, is also very great; nevertheless, nobody would suggest that acts of larceny should be punished when committed without *mens rea*."
40 Cf Robinson, "The criminal-civil distinction and the utility of desert" (1996) 76 Boston ULR 201, 212-214.

standards, work-safety standards, pollution standards, etc discharge. Setting up a new system to try these matters as civil infractions rather than crimes would be a major task and might be seen as downgrading the importance of effective regulation. There is little evidence that the proliferation of regulatory crimes has blunted the distinction between doing wrong and getting something wrong.

(b)   Burden of proof

While absolute liability is controversial since it involves convicting the blameless, strict liability is primarily a fault-based standard,[41] and the main issue it raises for justification is a different one: is it right to reverse the onus of proof in these offences?

The best argument for abandoning ordinary proof requirements is convenience. Administration of justice would be more expensive and greatly slowed if the prosecution were put to proving mens rea — even negligence — in respect of every minor offence before the courts. This is especially true in areas regulated by public welfare offences, where the defendant may be far better-placed to understand the nature of his own specialist activity (and thus to prevent the occurrence of harm) than is the prosecutor to learn the nature of the defendant's activity in order to prove fault. This is all the more so in the case of activities (and transgressions) by large and complex corporations, where it may be very difficult for an external prosecutor to prove the conduct of particular individuals within such organisations.

Given these factors, it is arguable that, as well as being more efficient, the shift in evidential burdens may also result in better justice. In many cases it may be problematic for the prosecution to disprove a false claim of no fault — even one that would not be established on the balance of probabilities.

Regulatory enforcement needs to be done efficiently — a Government cannot afford to spend large amounts of money on prosecutions, especially where the offences involved are common and involve no serious harm. (Where serious harm does ensue, the prosecution should in any event be for a more serious crime involving mens rea and greater penalties.) Moreover, individual offences that involve no serious stigma can protect against a cumulative harm that may be very substantial indeed. The costs of controlling economic activity are, in truth, part of the costs of carrying on that activity, and it therefore makes some sense that the burden of establishing an absence of fault should be borne as a form of production expense by those who voluntarily initiate risk-creating activities.

Yet it is important to note that, as with a no-fault defence (above), the argument here trades upon the fact that conviction for a strict liability offence does not carry the same moral opprobrium and social stigma as does conviction for an offence that is "truly" criminal in nature. Indeed, that was the basis on which both the New Zealand Court of Appeal and the Supreme Court of Canada distinguished *Woolmington v DPP*.[42] Therefore, a cautionary note is appropriate. In *Woolmington*, Viscount Sankey LC had stated that, apart from insanity and statutory exceptions, the prosecution must prove guilt "no matter what the charge or where the trial".[43] Danger lies in the fact that, if a defendant's interests are to be subordinated to those of the general public in "regulatory" offences, the line denied in *Woolmington* between such

---

41   Though, for exceptions, see 5.1.1(2).
42   *R v City of Sault Ste Marie* (1978) 85 DLR (3d) 161; [1978] 2 SCR 1299 (SCC), 174, 175; 1316; *Civil Aviation Dept v MacKenzie* [1983] NZLR 78, also reported as *MacKenzie v Civil Aviation Dept* (1983) 1 CRNZ 38 (CA), 84, 85; 44, 45.

offences and "true" crimes is not always easy to draw. *MacKenzie* itself involved an offence punishable by imprisonment; surely placing it in the category of serious rather than minor transgressions? It is worth noting that the US Model Penal Code eschews such a possibility, asserting that the possibility of imprisonment should be a conclusive reason against imposing strict liability.[44] We return to the difficulty of categorising offences below (5.2.3). But if a clear distinction between "regulatory" and "truly criminal" offences cannot be drawn, or if that distinction fails to capture the public imagination, then the arguments[45] for retaining the presumption of innocence — and against reversing the onus of proof in strict liability — are much harder to surmount.

Placing the onus upon the defendant in strict liability cases may now be inconsistent with s 25(c) New Zealand Bill of Rights Act 1990, which secures to everyone charged with an offence "the right to be presumed innocent until proved guilty according to law". However, if it does contravene s 25(c), strict liability in its present form had been held by the courts to be saved by s 5 of that same Act, which permits limitations to the rights contained in the Act so long as they "can be demonstrably justified in a free and democratic society".[46]

5.1.2 Absolute liability

In offences of absolute liability, proof beyond reasonable doubt of the actus reus is sufficient to convict the defendant, and even absence of fault is no defence:[47]

> "'absolute liability' entails conviction on proof merely that the defendant committed the prohibited act constituting the *actus reus* of the offence. There is no relevant mental element. It is no defence that the accused was entirely without fault. He may be morally innocent in every sense, yet be branded as a male-factor and punished as such."

An example of such an offence may be found in s 17(1) Machinery Act 1950, which requires owners of machinery to ensure that dangerous parts thereof are securely fenced. In *AHI Operations Ltd v Dept of Labour*,[48] the defendant was convicted under the section notwithstanding that its machine did originally have a guard mechanism, which had been removed (contrary to instructions) by an employee. Heron J held that the offence was complete upon proof merely that the guard was absent.

However, it does appear that a combination of involuntariness (or, as the case may be, impossibility) *and* absence of fault on the part of a defendant will be sufficient to exculpate. The roots of this defence are to be found in *Kilbride v Lake*.[49] In that case, D was convicted at

---

43 *Woolmington v DPP* [1935] AC 462; [1935] All ER 1 (HL), 481; 8; cf *Mancini v DPP* [1942] AC 1; [1941] 3 All ER 272 (HL), 11; 279 (Viscount Simon LC); Orchard, "The judicial categorisation of offences" (1983) 2 Canterbury LR 81, 94.
44 § 6.02(4) US Model Penal Code. Though a contrary statute would not be unconstitutional: *US v Freed* 401 US 601; 28 L Ed 2d 356 (1971).
45 See 2.3, 2.3.1(1).
46 *Joe v Police* 21/12/95, Goddard J, HC Wellington AP230/95; following *R v Wholesale Travel Group Inc* (1991) 84 DLR (4th) 161; [1991] 3 SCR 154 (SCC), a decision by the Supreme Court on corresponding provisions in the Canadian Charter of Rights and Freedoms.
47 *R v City of Sault Ste Marie* (1978) 85 DLR (3d) 161; [1978] 2 SCR 1299 (SCC), 170; 1310.
48 *AHI Operations Ltd v Dept of Labour* [1986] 1 NZLR 645. Criticised by S France, "Absolute liability since *MacKenzie*" [1987] NZLJ 50, 52. The defendant was found in any event not to have been without fault, so would have been convicted even had the offence been one of strict liability. For a survey of other cases imposing absolute liability, see *Adams*, CA20.49 (looseleaf).

first instance of permitting his car to be on the road without displaying a current warrant of fitness.[50] The car had been parked by D on a street. At the time of parking, a warrant of fitness was on display. However, while the car was unattended, the warrant of fitness became detached; hence D's prosecution. His appeal was argued before the Supreme Court on the issue whether the offence was one of absolute liability or mens rea. Woodhouse J, however, decided the case on a different footing. The actus reus of the offence, his Honour said, was "the presence of the car combined with the absence of the warrant".[51] Given the facts, D's liability could only be predicated, if at all, upon his failure immediately to replace the warrant when it became detached. But (it was conceded) that failure was involuntary since D had had no opportunity to rectify the situation. On this basis, D should not be convicted even if the offence was absolute:[52]

> "a person cannot be made criminally responsible for an act or omission unless it was done or omitted in circumstances where there was some other course open to him. If this condition is absent, any act or omission must be involuntary."

The qualification, that the involuntariness must be accompanied by an absence of fault, was articulated by the Court of Appeal in *Tifaga v Dept of Labour*.[53] In that case, the impossible situation in which D found himself was self-induced: his inability to leave the country before his immigration permit expired was attributable to his own failure to retain enough money to buy an air ticket. It would have been different, and he would have escaped conviction, if the impossibility had arisen for reasons beyond his control: if, for instance, D had been robbed of the money while en route to buy his ticket, or had been injured and hospitalised when going to the airport;[54] or if, as in *Finau v Dept of Labour*, she had been refused passage on grounds of pregnancy.[55]

The discussion in *Tifaga* suggests that, in addition to involuntariness or impossibility, necessity may also be available as a defence provided the circumstances of the necessity do not arise through any fault of the defendant.[56] The necessity, however, would have to be such as to leave the defendant with no practical alternative but to permit or bring about the actus reus.[57]

---

49   *Kilbride v Lake* [1962] NZLR 590. Also discussed at 3.4.2.
50   Contrary to reg 52 Traffic Regulations 1976.
51   *Kilbride v Lake* [1962] NZLR 590, 592.
52   *Kilbride v Lake* [1962] NZLR 590, 593.
53   *Tifaga v Dept of Labour* [1980] 2 NZLR 235 (CA).
54   Examples cited by Richardson J in *Tifaga v Dept of Labour* [1980] 2 NZLR 235 (CA), 245, 246. See also *Sione v Labour Dept* [1972] NZLR 278; *Burns v Bidder* [1967] 2 QB 227; [1966] 3 All ER 29; *McCone v Police* [1971] NZLR 105 (CA), 109; *R v Bamber* (1843) 5 QB 279; 114 ER 1254; *Stockdale v Coulson* [1974] 3 All ER 154; [1974] 1 WLR 1192 (distinguishing *Park v Lawton & another* [1911] 1 KB 588 on the basis that the impossibility in the earlier case arose through the defendant's own default); Patient, "Some remarks about the element of voluntariness in offences of absolute liability" [1968] Crim LR 23.
55   *Finau v Dept of Labour* [1984] 2 NZLR 396 (CA). Section 14(5), under which Finau was prosecuted, was held in *Murray v Ongoongo* [1985] BCL 1843 to impose absolute liability — the right decision for the wrong reasons, according to Orchard, "Quasi-absolute liability under the Immigration Act 1964" [1986] NZLJ 66.
56   *Tifaga v Dept of Labour* [1980] 2 NZLR 235 (CA), 243, 244. Cf, in England, *Smith and Hogan*, 156-7; in Canada, *R v Cancoil Thermal Corp & Parkinson* (1986) 27 CCC (3d) 295; 52 CR (3d) 188, 301, 302; 197; *R v Walker* (1980) 48 CCC (2d) 126, 134, 135; *R v Kennedy* (1972) 7 CCC (2d) 42; *R v Breau* (1959) 125 CCC 84; 32 CR 13.
57   Cf *Burns v Nowell* (1880) 5 QBD 444 (CA). There is a brief discussion of these questions in Sayre, "Public welfare offences" (1933) 33 Col LR 55, 75-78.

One question arises regarding the burden of proof. There appears to be no decision on this point, but since absolute liability is not subsumed by *Civil Aviation Dept v MacKenzie*[58] it is prima facie governed by *Woolmington v DPP*,[59] and the prosecution has the burden of disproving any defence suggested by the evidence. Nonetheless it may be arguable, by analogy with the onus upon defendants in strict liability cases, that in offences of absolute liability the defendant should bear the burden of proving his defence to the balance of probabilities.

(1) *The place of absolute liability*

In New Zealand, the conclusion that an offence is of absolute liability should only be made where the statute imposes it "in clear terms or by necessary implication".[60] It is submitted that this approach is the correct one: there is no other justification for a court to hold an offence absolute rather than strict.

It is foolish for the law to demand that defendants do more than what is reasonable. The effect of demanding the unreasonable, through absolute liability, is to force a defendant either to desist from the risk-creating activity altogether, or to persist and accept that he must run all risks, however esoteric and unlikely, of the prohibited harm occurring; and incur the ensuing conviction. The first option cannot be taken seriously. It is surely not the intention of the law to discourage people from entering into productive activity altogether. The nation's economy would not last very long if that were the outcome. Rather, the aim of regulatory laws must be to discourage people from entering into an activity (or from executing it in a manner) which creates *unreasonable* risks of the unwanted harm occurring. But *that* aim can be achieved by strict liability. Absolute liability forces the blameless defendant to become a gratuitous risk-taker, subject to a criminal legal lottery over which she has no reasonable control. If she is unlucky, she will be convicted. A lottery is no basis on which to conduct the nation's criminal law. Such a draconian system, moreover, is likely to promote cynicism and disrespect for the law among innocent people who are labelled criminal "offenders" by their conviction.

It is doubtful whether there are any significant advantages whatsoever to be gained from the device of absolute liability. While it simplifies the prosecution's task, that may also be achieved through the use of strict liability, and since the defendant's lack of fault will still be relevant to any defence of impossibility and (otherwise) to sentencing, the evidence may as well be heard straightforwardly before conviction. Neither is it clear that absolute liability is a more effective deterrent than mens rea offences or strict liability.[61]

---

58   *Civil Aviation Dept v MacKenzie* [1983] NZLR 78, also reported as *MacKenzie v Civil Aviation Dept* (1983) 1 CRNZ 38 (CA).
59   *Woolmington v DPP* [1935] AC 462; [1935] All ER 1 (HL).
60   *Millar v MOT* [1986] 1 NZLR 660; (1986) 2 CRNZ 216 (CA), 660; 225. Cf *B (a minor) v DPP* [2000] 2 AC 428; [2000] 1 All ER 833 (HL). *Millar* was applied in *Jackson v A-G* [2006] 2 NZLR 534 (HC), 541-542, where it was held that the disciplinary offence of having an article in a cell without approval (under s 32(1)(g) Penal Institutions Act 1954) was to be categorised as strict rather than absolute liability. In reaching this determination the Court was influenced by the "not insignificant" penalties, in terms of lost privileges and periods of cell confinement, and by the fact that absolute liability would have rendered an inmate responsible for all items found in his cell without knowledge of their presence and despite all reasonable care on his part.
61   See Jackson, "*Storkwain*: A case study in strict liability and self-regulation" [1991] Crim LR 892; Richardson, "Strict liability for regulatory crime: The empirical research" [1987] Crim LR 295; Baldwin, "Why rules don't work" (1990) 53 MLR 321.

Most importantly of all, it is just wrong to convict the innocent. To do so is a misuse of the criminal law, which is the most condemnatory institution available to society. If someone does not deserve to be convicted then they should not be. To convict innocent people violates this most basic tenet of criminal liability. It is unjust.[62] It also breaches the requirement for fair warning, since citizens have no way of knowing or predicting when they might be about to incur criminal liability.[63] No doubt the public need to be protected from the harms that regulatory offences are designed to prevent. But the public need to be protected, too, from random liability.

To the claim that absolute liability tends to be imposed only for offences which involve little or no public stigma, it may be responded that transgressors still suffer the rigours of the criminal process, with associated costs and loss of time, not to mention the fact of a conviction and a criminal record. And if the conviction is a trivial consideration, why make the wrongdoing a criminal rather than civil or administrative matter? "When it becomes respectable to be convicted, the vitality of the criminal law has been sapped."[64]

5.2 The mens rea categorisation of particular offences

In this and the previous chapter, the discussion of mens rea and strict liability has so far concentrated on defining the leading terms. But a further question arises every time we consider a particular offence. *Which* mens rea state is required to satisfy *that* offence? The answer varies from offence to offence: for rape, negligence will suffice; for assault, intention is required; operating an overloaded vehicle, by contrast, is an offence of strict liability. Often the answer will be found straightforwardly in the explicit words of the statute that creates the offence. For example, s 197 Crimes Act 1961 makes it an offence "wilfully" to disable another person: the offence cannot be committed inadvertently. But, frequently, a statute will specify only the actus reus elements, and be silent regarding whether a form of mens rea is required. In such instances the courts must decide.

5.2.1 Options available before *Millar v MOT*

It now appears that there are four alternative determinations that a court can make regarding a statute that does not itself state what mens rea if any is required. Before the Court of Appeal's decision in *Millar v MOT*, there had been at least seven. The seven categories, which were set out by Cooke P and Richardson J in *Millar*, are differentiated by whether or not mens rea is required, and by various combinations of the burden of proof and the availability of an exculpatory defence:[65]

(1) *Simple mens rea*: This is the standard category for truly criminal offences. Unless there are considerations of statutory interpretation peculiar to the offence under consideration,[66] mens rea here means intention or recklessness (or knowledge or belief,

---

62   See 1.3.2(1).
63   Cf 2.1.3.
64   Sayre, "The present significance of mens rea in the criminal law" in Pound (ed), *Harvard Legal Essays*, Cambridge, Massachusetts, Harvard University Press, 1934, 399, 409.
65   *Millar v MOT* [1986] 1 NZLR 660; (1986) 2 CRNZ 216 (CA), 664-666; 221-223.
66   As in *R v Saengsai-Or* [2004] NSWCCA 108; 147 A Crim R 172, where the Court relied on the legislative history to conclude that a redrafted provision, s 223B(1)(b) Customs Act 1901 (Aust), which previously required intent but is now silent concerning mens rea, continues to require intent — even recklessness does not suffice. Such cases are exceptional.

as appropriate). Actual foresight is required, and negligence will not do.[67] The prosecution has a full probative burden to prove mens rea beyond reasonable doubt. (It should be emphasised that in all seven categories the prosecution has to prove the actus reus beyond reasonable doubt.)

(2) *Assumed mens rea rebutted by an honest belief*: In this type of case the prosecution must prove the actus reus as usual, but mens rea will then be presumed in the absence of any evidence to the contrary. Mens rea once again means intention or recklessness. Thus there is an evidential burden on the defendant to point to evidence suggesting that he did not foresee the possibility of the actus reus (ie that he was not reckless). Upon such evidence being raised, the prosecution then assumes the full burden of proving mens rea beyond reasonable doubt.[68]

(3) *Assumed mens rea rebutted by a defence of honest and reasonable belief*: Here mens rea is once again presumed, and the defendant has an evidential onus to argue that she had an honest and reasonable belief in facts that, if true, would have made her actions innocent. If such evidence is raised, the burden reverts to the prosecution to prove, beyond reasonable doubt, that she did not have an honest and reasonable belief. This category had earlier been recognised by the Court of Appeal in *R v Strawbridge*,[69] in the context of an offence of cultivating prohibited drugs.

(4) *No mens rea required, but a defence is available of honest and reasonable mistake*: In this category the probative burden rests upon the defendant to prove on the balance of probabilities that he had an honest and reasonable belief in facts that, if true, would have made his actions innocent.[70]

(5) *Strict liability*: As in 5.1.1: no mens rea is required, but the defence of absence of fault is available. The burden of proving that defence rests upon the defendant (to the balance of probabilities). This category was regarded by the Court as broader in scope than (4), as it does not confine the available defence to one involving a mistake.

(6) *Assumed mens rea rebutted by a defence of honest belief*: The prosecution need not prove mens rea, and the defendant has the burden of proving, on the balance of probabilities, that she did not advert to the actus reus (in effect, that she lacked mens rea). This category is similar to that in (2), except that the defendant bears a higher onus of proof. It had been applied to the offence of selling an indecent publication[71] by the Court of Appeal

---

67 *R v Walker* [1958] NZLR 810 (CA), 815, 816; also *R v Howe* [1982] 1 NZLR 618 (CA), 623, as modified by *R v Harney* [1987] 2 NZLR 576 (CA).
68 See *R v Wood* [1982] 2 NZLR 233 (CA), 237; *R v Metuariki* [1986] 1 NZLR 488; (1986) 2 CRNZ 116 (CA).
69 *R v Strawbridge* [1970] NZLR 909 (CA). Cf the Australian cases *He Kaw Teh v R* (1985) 157 CLR 523; 59 ALJR 620; *Kidd v Reeves* [1972] VR 563; and *Mayer v Marchant* (1973) 5 SASR 567; and Adams, "Onus of proof in criminal cases" in Clark (ed), *Essays on Criminal Law in New Zealand*, Wellington, Sweet & Maxwell, 1971, 67, 80-82.
70 *R v Tolson* (1889) 23 QBD 168; [1886-90] All ER Rep 26. See Howard, "Strict responsibility in the High Court of Australia" (1960) 76 LQR 547; Campbell, "Crime by omission" in Clark (ed), *Essays on Criminal Law in New Zealand*, Wellington, Sweet & Maxwell, 1971, 1, 16; Orchard, "The defence of absence of fault in Australasia and Canada" in Smith (ed), *Criminal Law: Essays in Honour of J C Smith*, London, Butterworths, 1987, 114.
71 Contrary to the (then) Offensive Publications Act 1892.

in R v Ewart[72] but was disapproved by the Privy Council in *Lim Chin Aik v R*,[73] and was effectively abolished by the Court of Appeal in *Strawbridge*.[74]

(7)　*Absolute liability.*

5.2.2　Options available today

The Court of Appeal in *Millar* then proceeded to abolish three of these categories, by assimilating category (2) with simple mens rea (1), and by absorbing categories (4) and (6) within strict liability (5). Including the case where the statute itself specifies a mens rea requirement, this leaves a total of five options available, as follows.

(1)　*Statutory mens rea elements*

Where the statute explicitly states a mens rea requirement, the situation is like category (1) above. The prosecution must prove that requirement beyond reasonable doubt.[75] This rule was left undisturbed in *Millar v MOT*, since the analysis by Cooke P and Richardson J was concerned only with cases where the statute does not state what, if any, mens rea element is required.[76]

(2)　*Implied mens rea*

It was said in *Millar v MOT* that "if there is any distinction between classes (1) and (2) in the foregoing list, it seems so narrow as not to be worth preserving".[77] Unfortunately, the Court of Appeal did not clearly resolve the further question: if there *is* a difference between the two categories, which one was abolished?

Beginning with the first part of that question, there is indeed a distinction between categories (1) and (2).[78] The difference is that in category (1) the prosecution has both a persuasive and an evidential burden to prove mens rea. In category (2) the evidential burden is on the defendant. This means that, upon proof by the prosecution of the actus reus, mens rea will be *presumed* in the absence of evidence to the contrary. It then falls to the defendant herself to adduce evidence, or point to evidence adduced by the prosecution,[79] which raises a reasonable doubt whether she in fact had mens rea. Once this evidential burden is discharged, the prosecution has the persuasive burden to prove mens rea beyond reasonable doubt.

By contrast, in category (1), the defendant only has a case to answer once the prosecution, besides proving the actus reus, has adduced sufficient evidence from which mens rea can be

---

72　*R v Ewart* (1905) 25 NZLR 709 (CA). Early English authority for this category includes *R v Prince* (1875) LR 2 CCR 154; [1874-80] All ER Rep 881, 161, 162; 890, 891 (Brett J) (now disapproved: *R v K* [2001] 3 All ER 897; [2001] 3 WLR 471 (HL)); *Sherras v de Rutzen* [1895] 1 QB 918; [1895-99] All ER Rep 1167, 921; 1169 (Day J); also *Harding v Price* [1948] 1 KB 695; [1948] 1 All ER 283, 700; 284 (Goddard LCJ).

73　*Lim Chin Aik v R* [1963] AC 160; [1963] 1 All ER 223 (PC), 173, 227, 228 (on appeal from Singapore). Cf *Warner v MPC* [1969] 2 AC 256; [1968] 2 All ER 356 (HL), 303; 386 (Lord Pierce).

74　*R v Strawbridge* [1970] NZLR 909 (CA), 915 lines 24-26.

75　*R v Strawbridge* [1970] NZLR 909 (CA), 915. Cf *R v Kamipeli* [1975] 2 NZLR 610 (CA), 617; *Civil Aviation Dept v MacKenzie* [1983] NZLR 78, also reported as *MacKenzie v Civil Aviation Dept* (1983) 1 CRNZ 38 (CA), 85; 45, 46 (negligence).

76　*Millar v MOT* [1986] 1 NZLR 660; (1986) 2 CRNZ 216 (CA), 664 line 52; 221.

77　*Millar v MOT* [1986] 1 NZLR 660; (1986) 2 CRNZ 216 (CA), 667; 224.

78　For excellent discussion, see Orchard, "The judicial categorisation of offences" (1983) 2 Canterbury LR 81, 87-90.

79　*MacKenzie v Hawkins* [1975] 1 NZLR 165; *Police v Creedon* [1976] 1 NZLR 571 (CA), 584 (Richmond J).

inferred. Often, this will impose upon the prosecution no greater burden than exists in category (2), since proof of the actus reus will usually supply evidence from which mens rea too can be inferred. If D loads his pistol, points it at V, and pulls the trigger, it is a natural inference that D intended to shoot V. Here a presumption adds nothing to the inference. Sometimes, however, the distinction will make a difference. Suppose that D is charged with possession of a prohibited drug, being a "magic mushroom".[80] Evidence is given that D picked the mushroom, which had been growing wild on a beach, just before he was arrested. Such evidence, which establishes the actus reus, might not support the inference that D knew the nature of the mushroom. If the offence falls within category (1), the prosecution will fail unless further evidence is introduced from which mens rea may be inferred as a fact. By contrast, if it belongs in category (2), mens rea will prima facie be presumed, where the presumption is rebuttable by evidence raising a reasonable doubt about the matter.

It might be thought that the upshot of the merger effected by *Millar* was to abolish category (2). In fact, although there is rarely any practical difference, it appears that the Court did away with category (1):[81]

> "absence of guilty knowledge is like the defences of provocation, automatism, self-defence and compulsion. There must be some evidence or material, either from the prosecution case or called by the defence, to raise the issue. In the absence of a foundation for a contrary view the offence will be inferred to have been committed unprovoked, knowingly, not in self-defence, free from compulsion."

It is settled law that the defendant has an evidential onus to raise matters such as provocation, automatism, self-defence etc, and that their absence is presumed unless there is evidence to the contrary.[82] By likening mens rea to these elements, Cooke P and Richardson J seem to have held that where mens rea is an implied and not expressly-stated element of the offence, the defendant has an evidential onus to raise a reasonable doubt about the presence of mens rea. If it appears that the defendant may not have foreseen or intended the actus reus (ie that she did not have mens rea), that onus reverts to the prosecution, who must then prove mens rea beyond reasonable doubt.[83]

Our analysis may be controversial. In particular, note should be taken of Casey J's judgment, in which he said: "I accept the conclusion that there is no practical difference between classes (1) and (2), involving offences in which mens rea is an ingredient ... In such cases both the evidentiary and persuasive onus remain on the Crown."[84] This suggests that it is category (2), rather than (1), which has been displaced. However, the preservation of category (2) is consistent with the earlier decision by the Court of Appeal in *Strawbridge*, where North P had asserted that:[85]

> "in New Zealand we have never interpreted *Woolmington's* case as going any further than determining that the burden of proof at the end of, and on the whole of, the case

---

80 Cf *R v Metuariki* [1986] 1 NZLR 488; (1986) 2 CRNZ 116 (CA).
81 *Millar v MOT* [1986] 1 NZLR 660; (1986) 2 CRNZ 216 (CA), 667, 224.
82 See 2.3, fn 45, 46.
83 Per 2.3.1(4).
84 *Millar v MOT* [1986] 1 NZLR 660; (1986) 2 CRNZ 216 (CA), 678; 236.
85 *R v Strawbridge* [1970] NZLR 909 (CA), 915; concurring with Lord Diplock's dissent in *Sweet v Parsley* [1970] AC 132; [1969] 1 All ER 347 (HL), 164; 362, 363. See too *Sherras v de Rutzen* [1895] 1 QB 918; [1895-99] All ER Rep 1167.

lay on the Crown ... we have however distinguished between cases where the offence consists in 'knowingly' doing an act and cases where the word 'knowingly' has been omitted. In the former class of case the Crown must prove knowledge on the part of the accused before it can be said that a *prima facie* case has been made out. In the latter class of case, on the other hand, knowledge of the wrongful nature of the act will be presumed in the absence of any evidence to the contrary ... it is still true to say that it lies on the accused to point to some evidence which creates a reasonable doubt that he did not have a guilty mind."

The language of *Strawbridge* is unequivocally that of presumption rather than inference. Neither the judgment by Casey J, nor any of the other judgments in *Millar*, purports to overrule *Strawbridge* on this point. Rather, they appear to endorse it.[86] The reality that there is little practical difference between the two approaches can be seen, however, in the judgment of Somers J, who freely intermingles the language of presumption with that of inference.[87] Subsequent cases have been mixed in their analysis of this point. In *Police v Starkey*, Barker J cited Cooke P in *Millar*, and stated:[88]

"Where the necessary mens rea is expressly set out as part of the definition of the offence ... clearly that mental state must be affirmatively proved by the prosecution beyond reasonable doubt, with no evidential onus on the accused. But where, as in the present case, the requisite intention is merely implicit in the section, the necessary mens rea will be assumed in the absence of evidence to the contrary ... It will then be open to the accused to lay a foundation for the defence of lack of mens rea, and the onus will then be on the prosecution to prove mens rea beyond reasonable doubt."

By contrast, in *Police v Bannin*, Fisher J uses the language of inference.[89] However, his Honour was not required to consider the point as carefully as did Barker J, and it is the latter who appears to have stated the law.[90]

For all that, should the issue ever come before the Court of Appeal for authoritative resolution, it is submitted that, to the extent that there *is* a difference between the two approaches, the one taken by Casey J is to be preferred. Suppose a case where proof of the actus reus does not, by itself, unambiguously support the inference that the defendant acted with mens rea.[91] Given that, as was said in *Strawbridge*, the prosecution has the burden of proving mens rea on the whole of, and at the end of, the case, there seems to be no reason why the defendant should bear an evidential onus — why mens rea should be presumed — where the prima facie evidence does not necessarily support that presumption. The language of inference is, in our view, to be preferred.

---

86   See *Millar v MOT* [1986] 1 NZLR 660; (1986) 2 CRNZ 216 (CA), 667; 224 (Cooke P and Richardson J), 675; 232 (McMullin J), 676, 677; 233, 234 (Somers J), 678; 236 (Casey J).
87   *Millar v MOT* [1986] 1 NZLR 660; (1986) 2 CRNZ 216 (CA), 676, 677; 233, 234; cf 678; 236 (Casey J).
88   *Police v Starkey* [1989] 2 NZLR 373; (1989) 4 CRNZ 400, 378; 404, 405.
89   *Police v Bannin* [1991] 2 NZLR 237, also reported as *R v Police* (1991) 7 CRNZ 55, 246; 63: "The fact that the accused physically entered the house would, in the absence of mental abnormality, imply that he intended to do so." Note that the ulterior intention also needed for the offence in that case was an express statutory requirement.
90   Cf *R v Metuariki* [1986] 1 NZLR 488; (1986) 2 CRNZ 116 (CA); *R v Wood* [1982] 2 NZLR 233 (CA), 237; *Summers v SPCA* [1991] 2 NZLR 469; (1990) 6 CRNZ 201, 473-475; 205-208. See generally *Adams*, CA20.40-42 (looseleaf).
91   Cf *R v Keane* [1921] NZLR 581 (CA), 584.

(3) Category (3): Strawbridge

Category (3) occurs in *R v Strawbridge*.[92] D was prosecuted for cultivation of cannabis. She sought to deny knowledge of the nature of the plant. The Court of Appeal held that, while the prosecution did not need to prove knowledge in order to make out a prima facie case, and knowledge should be presumed in the absence of evidence to the contrary, it was open to the defendant to point to evidence that she honestly believed on reasonable grounds that her act was innocent.

This class of offence was described in *Millar v MOT* as "a troublesome anomaly, probably best done away with or severely confined".[93] Even by the time of *Millar*, most cases falling within its scope had already migrated to category (2), which "may be called *Strawbridge* without reasonable grounds".[94] The requirement that D's belief be reasonable was abandoned by the Court of Appeal following the English case of *DPP v Morgan*;[95] and it is now said that the reasonableness of D's claimed belief is relevant only to the evidential question whether that belief was in fact honestly held by D.

It seems, therefore, unlikely that an offence will now be held to fall within the *Strawbridge* category. Yet we cannot say for sure that this class of offence has been abolished. *Millar* does not expressly take that step. Moreover, the offence in *Strawbridge* is unlike those found in categories (4) through (6), which are now absorbed by strict liability. Strict liability is inappropriate because the case involves a serious criminal offence, punishable by a maximum of 14 years' imprisonment. Thus, it should now either become a full mens rea offence, or remain sui generis.

Strawbridge may be contrasted with *Police v Creedon*,[96] a case in which D was prosecuted for failing to yield the right of way at an intersection, in circumstances where (it was conceded) he was not at fault. Although the case was said in *Millar* to belong properly in category (5), the original decision fell within category (3), since the Court of Appeal in fact held that D bore only an evidential onus to suggest a lack of fault.[97] It is clear that *Creedon*, a mere traffic offence, does not survive *MacKenzie* and *Millar*.

(4) Strict liability

See 5.1.1. In *Millar*[98], strict liability was endorsed by the Court of Appeal as being best placed to achieve "the object of justice aimed at by the other three classes" of offence, viz (3), (4), and (6).

(5) Absolute liability

See 5.1.2. This category of offence has survived unmolested. However, as was made clear in *Millar*, "there is a good deal less room for class 7, absolute liability, once it is accepted that

---

92 *R v Strawbridge* [1970] NZLR 909 (CA).
93 *Millar v MOT* [1986] 1 NZLR 660; (1986) 2 CRNZ 216 (CA), 668; 224, 225 (Cooke P).
94 *Millar v MOT* [1986] 1 NZLR 660; (1986) 2 CRNZ 216 (CA), 667; 224.
95 *DPP v Morgan* [1976] AC 182; [1975] 2 All ER 347 (HL). See *R v Wood* [1982] 2 NZLR 233 (CA), 237; *R v Metuariki* [1986] 1 NZLR 488; (1986) 2 CRNZ 116 (CA), 490, 493, 497; 118, 120, 125.
96 *Police v Creedon* [1976] 1 NZLR 571 (CA).
97 *Police v Creedon* [1976] 1 NZLR 571 (CA), 575, 576, 584, 586. See *Civil Aviation Dept v MacKenzie* [1983] NZLR 78, also reported as *MacKenzie v Civil Aviation Dept* (1983) 1 CRNZ 38 (CA), 83; 43.
98 *Millar v MOT* [1986] 1 NZLR 660; (1986) 2 CRNZ 216 (CA).

class 5 is an available alternative under which the onus is on the defendant of proving total absence of fault".[99]

5.2.3 Deciding which fault standard applies

(1) *Clear cases*

The starting place is the statute that creates the offence. If the statute specifies a particular mens rea standard, that is decisive. Even where it does not do so explicitly, the scheme of the statute may give a clear indication of the Legislature's intent. France cites, by way of example, s 56(4) Dog Control and Hydatids Act 1982 (now repealed), which provides that:

> "The owner of any dog that makes any such attack [specified in s 56(1)] commits an offence and is liable on summary conviction to a fine not exceeding $500 ...; and, where the dog has not been destroyed, the Court may, on convicting the owner, make an order for the destruction of the dog."

According to France, this created an absolute liability offence by necessary implication:[100]

> "The drafting of this provision makes the Court's ability to order destruction of the dog dependent upon conviction of the owner. If an owner were allowed a no-fault defence, the Court would become unable to deal with the animal. Yet, if the dog has attacked even though the owner has done all that could reasonably be expected, that would seem exactly the situation when a Court may wish to order destruction. This could only be achieved by holding the offence to be absolute."

We agree, although this manner of drafting is very unfortunate.

Absent clear legislative guidance, there may be an "overriding judicial history".[101] That is to say, the mens rea standard for the offence may have been settled by judicial precedent. For example, the offence of operating an overloaded vehicle has been held to impose strict liability in *S M Savill Ltd v MOT*[102] and *MOT v Coastal Carriers Ltd*.[103] In light of this, and unless the offence becomes altered by legislation, there would seem to be no reason for another court to reconsider the question in future.

It is worth remembering that different parts of the actus reus may correspond to different standards of mens rea. In the previous chapter we discussed an example where the statute was explicit.[104] But the situation may arise even where the statute is silent. An illustrative case is *Police v Starkey*,[105] which involved an offence against s 55 Local Elections and Polls Act 1976 (now repealed). Section 55 prohibited (a) publication of a document containing (b) an untrue (c) and defamatory statement (d) which was calculated to influence the vote of any elector. Barker J held that the mens rea requirements are, as to (a) intention; (b) strict liability; (c) none, since it was a question of law; and (d) knowledge of likelihood to influence.

---

99   *Millar v MOT* [1986] 1 NZLR 660; (1986) 2 CRNZ 216 (CA), 668; 224.
100 France, "Absolute liability since *MacKenzie*" [1987] NZLJ 50, 53. See now s 57(2) Dog Control Act 1996, which is expressed in almost identical terms.
101 *Millar v MOT* [1986] 1 NZLR 660; (1986) 2 CRNZ 216 (CA), 668, 225.
102 *S M Savill Ltd v MOT* [1986] 1 NZLR 653.
103 *MOT v Coastal Carriers Ltd* [1990] DCR 529.
104 Section 205(1)(b) Crimes Act 1961.
105 *Police v Starkey* [1989] 2 NZLR 373; (1989) 4 CRNZ 400.

(2)   Guiding principles

If the mens rea standard for the offence is not settled by statute or case law, the court will have to make a fresh decision. The guiding principles affecting that decision are stated in 5.2.3(2)(a)-(d).

(a)   The initial presumption

The basic presumption from which one starts is that mens rea is required for every offence.[106] Traditional authority for this presumption is *Sherras v de Rutzen*:[107]

> "The presumption is that mens rea ... is an essential ingredient in every offence; but that presumption is liable to be displaced either by the words of the statute creating the offence or by the subject matter with which it deals, and both must be considered."

The justification for this starting-point rests in the issues discussed earlier in this chapter, and in chapters 1 and 2. According to Lord Diplock, in *Sweet v Parsley*:[108]

> "the mere fact that Parliament has made the conduct a criminal offence gives rise to *some* implication about the mental element of the conduct proscribed ... This implication stems from the principle that it is contrary to a rational and civilised criminal code ... to penalise one who has performed his duty as a citizen to ascertain what acts are prohibited by law (*ignorantia juris non excusat*) and has taken all proper care to inform himself of any facts which would make his conduct lawful."

Parliament normally does not, and indeed should not, intend to make criminals of those who are not blameworthy and do not warrant that label.

In most cases, the presumption in *Sherras v de Rutzen* will operate as a point of departure, a prelude to assessment of further considerations (noted below). But its substantive force is that mens rea is the default position for an offence unless its implication is *clearly* outweighed by other factors. This implication is buttressed by the passage from Lord Reid's judgment in *Sweet v Parsley*, which finds recitation in both *Civil Aviation Dept v MacKenzie* and in *Millar v MOT*:[109]

> "it is a universal principle that if a penal provision is reasonably capable of two interpretations, that interpretation which is most favourable to the accused must be adopted."

Thus the presumption for mens rea is abrogated, in favour of strict or absolute liability, only when it would be positively unreasonable[110] (in light of the factors stated below) to interpret the offence as requiring mens rea. In practice, this constraint is not as forceful as it sounds. Usually, according to the courts, it turns out that the only reasonable construction of public welfare regulatory offences is that they are intended to be of strict liability.[111]

---

106   Endorsed as the "ordinary rule" by Cooke P and Richardson J (668; 224), and as the "starting point" by Somers J (676; 234), in *Millar v MOT* [1986] 1 NZLR 660; (1986) 2 CRNZ 216 (CA).

107   *Sherras v de Rutzen* [1895] 1 QB 918; [1895-99] All ER Rep 1167; 921, 1169.

108   *Sweet v Parsley* [1970] AC 132; [1969] 1 All ER 347 (HL), 162, 163; 361, 362. See also 148; 349 (Lord Reid), 153; 353 (Lord Morris); *B (a minor) v DPP* [2000] 2 AC 428; [2000] 1 All ER 833 (HL).

109   *Sweet v Parsley* [1970] AC 132; [1969] 1 All ER 347 (HL), 149; 350. See *Civil Aviation Dept v MacKenzie* [1983] NZLR 78, also reported as *MacKenzie v Civil Aviation Dept* (1983) 1 CRNZ 38 (CA), 81; 41; *Millar v MOT* [1986] 1 NZLR 660; (1986) 2 CRNZ 216 (CA), 668; 224.

It should be emphasised that, as was said earlier, the presumption of mens rea generally means intention or recklessness (or, as appropriate, knowledge or belief). Negligence is thought to be not blameworthy enough to warrant criminal sanctions for "truly criminal" offences. In *R v Walker*, the Court of Appeal adverted to this point expressly: "negligence or inadvertence is in general insufficient to constitute the guilty mind, which is necessary where mens rea is not ruled out by the words of the section creating the offence."[112]

(b)   Whether to override the presumption

In deciding whether to override the presumption in favour of mens rea, the courts have had regard to various considerations.

Put most broadly, the main concern is whether the offence is "serious" or "truly criminal", as opposed to a "public welfare or regulatory" offence. At the heart of this issue is the nature of the mischief the offence is designed to suppress. Very obviously, an offence will be of the truly criminal variety, and require mens rea, when it prohibits an activity that is, in itself, overtly wrongful (for example murder and assault).[113] In these cases the activity might occasion moral condemnation even without being criminalised, and a conviction is therefore likely to attract a substantial level of moral stigma. By contrast, where conviction for the offence is likely to occasion little or no public stigma (as in the case of a parking infringement), the courts will be more willing to find strict liability. Such instances are said to fall within the "class of acts … which are not criminal in any real sense, but are acts which in the public interest are prohibited under a penalty".[114]

More difficult are cases where the defendant's activity is not necessarily or inherently wrongful, but becomes the actus reus of an offence when done in a particular manner. Driving a vehicle may be a legitimate activity, but driving a vehicle while overloaded is a strict liability offence.[115] Factors relevant to the assessment of such offences include whether the offence is directed at regulating trades, activities, and the like, especially those which involve specialist

---

110   In England, the general rule is that, at least in principle, the presumption of mens rea is to be overridden only if there is a *necessary implication* that Parliament intended the offence to be (what in New Zealand is known as) absolute: *B (a minor) v DPP* [2000] 2 AC 428; [2000] 1 All ER 833 (HL). This is the same standard as is required to find absolute liability in New Zealand. Seemingly, it is a more stringent standard than is required to find strict liability here; presumably because this middle ground is unavailable in England, where the only alternative to mens rea is absolute liability (cf 5.1.1). On this point, see the quotation from *Millar* in 5.2.2(5): the greater willingness of the Courts to find that an offence is of strict liability reflects the fact that it is a less Draconian alternative.

111   Cf *R v City of Sault Ste Marie* (1978) 85 DLR (3d) 161; [1978] 2 SCR 1299 (SCC), 182; 1326: public welfare offences would "prima facie" involve strict liability. In *Millar v MOT* [1986] 1 NZLR 660; (1986) 2 CRNZ 216 (CA), 668; 224, it was stated that "the qualification *reasonably* is also important and prevents an overweighting in favour of the accused".

112   *R v Walker* [1958] NZLR 810 (CA), 816; *MacKenzie v Hawkins* [1975] 1 NZLR 165, 167, 168; *Civil Aviation Dept v MacKenzie* [1983] NZLR 78, also reported as *MacKenzie v Civil Aviation Dept* (1983) 1 CRNZ 38 (CA), 84; 44; *R v City of Sault Ste Marie* (1978) 85 DLR (3d) 161; [1978] 2 SCR 1299 (SCC), 170; 1309, 1310; see 5.2.1.

113   For example, assault on a constable in the execution of his duty: *Waaka v Police* [1987] 1 NZLR 754; (1987) 2 CRNZ 370 (CA), 758, 759; 373-375; also possession of a controlled drug: *R v Cox* [1990] 2 NZLR 275; (1990) 5 CRNZ 653 (CA).

114   *Sherras v de Rutzen* [1895] 1 QB 918; [1895-99] All ER Rep 1167, 922.

115   *S M Savill Ltd v MOT* [1986] 1 NZLR 653.

skills and those for which one must be licensed. Where this is the case, it is more likely to be treated as a public welfare offence:[116]

> "the essentially regulatory nature of the legislation justifies the interpretation that proof or an inference of mens rea is not required as part of the prosecution's case."

An example of this reasoning can be seen in *Re Wairarapa Election Petition*.[117] In that case, speaking about the prohibition of expenditure in excess of $5,000 on a candidate's electoral campaign, the High Court said:[118]

> "This is not an offence such as the other corrupt practices of bribery or treating which import moral turpitude and which have all the attributes of true criminal offending ... Rather this is a means of controlling the conduct of an election to prevent excesses and to avoid unfair competition and unfair advantage simply because of the more ready availability of money in one case than in another."

Unlike other corrupt practices, the offence was held to impose strict liability because it regulates and controls excesses in an otherwise acceptable practice.

The fact that the activity is a specialist one increases the probability that its regulation will involve strict liability. One reason for this is that the use of strict liability simplifies prosecutions, a factor that is especially salient when the defendant may be expected to know far better than the prosecutor what went wrong and how to prevent it. According to the Court of Appeal:[119]

> "there are a significant group of statutory provisions, aimed at regulating the carrying on of various trades or activities, where ... it may be unreasonable to read in the ordinary implication of mens rea. For instance, ... it may be unreasonable to suppose that the prosecutor will be able to acquire any accurate knowledge of the workings of the defendant's business organisation. The object of this type of provision is best served by imposing liability prima facie if the defendant or his or its servants or agents are shown to have committed the unlawful act, while allowing exculpation if the defendant can prove total absence of fault."

This reasoning is reinforced by the fact that regulation of a voluntary specialist activity does not lead to the conviction of citizens for doing ordinary things without being on notice that their conduct was in danger of breaching the criminal law. Concerns about fair warning[120] are thus less pressing where the defendant may be said to some extent to have assumed the risks of liability by voluntarily bringing herself within the particular sphere of operation of a regulatory law. A similar point was made in *Sweet v Parsley* by Lord Diplock:[121]

---

116 *Millar v MOT* [1986] 1 NZLR 660; (1986) 2 CRNZ 216 (CA), 669; 226.
117 *Re Wairarapa Election Petition* [1988] 2 NZLR 74, 117, 118.
118 *Re Wairarapa Election Petition* [1988] 2 NZLR 74, 117, 118. The remarks are made apropos of distinguishing the offence from one of absolute liability, but are relevant also to the distinction from mens rea offences — cf also 118 lines 33-39, 119 lines 12-15.
119 *Millar v MOT* [1986] 1 NZLR 660; (1986) 2 CRNZ 216 (CA), 668; 225. Per *Civil Aviation Dept v MacKenzie* [1983] NZLR 78, also reported as *MacKenzie v Civil Aviation Dept* (1983) 1 CRNZ 38 (CA), 85; 45, "the defendant will ordinarily know far better than the prosecution how the breach occurred and what he had done to avoid it". Cf *Helleman v Collector of Customs* [1966] NZLR 705.
120 See 2.1.3.

"Where penal provisions are of general application to the conduct of ordinary citizens in the course of their everyday life, the presumption is that the standard of care required of them in informing themselves of facts which would make their conduct unlawful, is that of the familiar common law duty of care. But where the subject-matter of a statute is the regulation of a particular activity involving potential danger to public health, safety or morals, in which citizens have a choice whether they participate or not, the court may feel driven to infer an intention of Parliament to impose, by penal sanctions, a higher duty of care on those who choose to participate."

As Lord Diplock contemplates, the likelihood of a law's being declared strict is also increased if the activities it regulates have a tendency to endanger sections of the public[122] (or, in recent times, the environment[123]). Obvious places for such laws are health and safety regulations, governing the quality of food products or safety in a workplace.[124]

Another consideration is the range and severity of punishments prescribed upon conviction. In *Strawbridge*, for example, it was said by the Court of Appeal to be "unthinkable that Parliament ever intended to expose citizens to a liability of up to fourteen years' imprisonment where the accused person did not know that the plant he or she was cultivating was a prohibited plant".[125] In general, where the offence is punishable by imprisonment, the presumption that mens rea is an implied element is very unlikely to be overridden.[126] The force of this point is further strengthened, it seems, if the actus reus is specified in terms of the defendant's *actions*, rather than prohibiting a mere state of affairs.[127]

Further, if one element of the actus reus involves the arbitrary drawing of a line over such matters as time, quantity, or size, mens rea may be less likely to be required in respect of that particular aspect.[128] The most obvious case is a speeding offence, where the difference between

---

121 *Sweet v Parsley* [1970] AC 132; [1969] 1 All ER 347 (HL), 163; 362. One interesting philosophical discussion which makes a point of this type is Honoré, "Responsibility and luck: The moral basis of strict liability" (1988) 104 LQR 530.
122 *Millar v MOT* [1986] 1 NZLR 660; (1986) 2 CRNZ 216 (CA), 669; 226.
123 Cf *Hastings CC v Simons* [1984] 2 NZLR 502 (CA). This notwithstanding that environmental offences now appear to involve significant social stigma.
124 Cf *Civil Aviation Dept v MacKenzie* [1983] NZLR 78, also reported as *MacKenzie v Civil Aviation Dept* (1983) 1 CRNZ 38 (CA), 85 line 15ff; 45.
125 *R v Strawbridge* [1970] NZLR 909 (CA), 916. Cf *R v Tihi* [1989] 2 NZLR 29; (1989) 4 CRNZ 289 (CA), 32; 292.
126 At times, the position has appeared to be otherwise in English law. Cf *Gammon (Hong Kong) Ltd v A-G of Hong Kong* [1985] AC 1; [1984] 2 All ER 503 (PC), 17; 511: "The severity of the maximum penalties [a $250,000 fine and imprisonment for 3 years] is a more formidable point. But ... there is nothing inconsistent with the purpose of the ordinance in imposing severe penalties for offences of strict liability." (One may ask whether the Privy Council missed the point. Perhaps one may have reason to impose strict liability if it is inconsistent with the purpose of a statute *not* to do so. But surely not the other way round? The mere fact that strict liability is "not inconsistent" with the purpose of the statute is hardly a reason to impose it.) More recently, however, the mens rea presumption has been reaffirmed by the House of Lords as one that is not to be overridden except by necessary implication: *B (a minor) v DPP* [2000] 2 AC 428; [2000] 1 All ER 833 (HL); *R v K* [2001] 3 All ER 897; [2001] 3 WLR 471 (HL).
127 *R v Gedson* 4/12/97, Fisher J, HC Rotorua T51/97 (carrying out unapproved modifications to an aircraft, contrary to reg 173(2) Civil Aviation Regulations 1953).
128 See the references collected in *Adams*, CA20.12 (looseleaf). An example where this point might have been relevant (but was not considered) is *Re Wairarapa Election Petition* [1988] 2 NZLR 74.

50 and 51 km/h may have a significance that is purely the result of law. It seems unnecessary to require knowledge of one's speed in such cases.[129]

At the other end of the spectrum, if an element of the actus reus involves the legal assessment of certain facts, then the defendant need only possess whatever mens rea is required regarding the facts themselves; their legal assessment will be, in effect, a matter of absolute liability — a legal conclusion in the nature of a value judgment that the defendant is not permitted to second-guess.[130] In *Police v Starkey*, D was prosecuted for publishing matter defamatory of a candidate in an election.[131] Barker J held, inter alia, that while D must have intended to publish the material, whether the material was defamatory was a question of law, regarding which no fault element was required.

(c)   Inferring mens rea from statutory language

Sometimes, rather than being presumed or explicit, or established by the judicial history, the legislative intent to include a mens rea requirement can be *inferred* directly from the words of the statute. For example, s 306 creates an offence of threatening to kill another person. Although the section contains no express mention of mens rea, it has been held that the word "threaten" itself involves an intention to influence the mind of another — simply as a matter of ordinary language. Absent that intention, the defendant's conduct could not be described as a "threat".[132] Similarly, it has been held that the action of "publishing" defamatory matter, contrary to s 55 Local Elections and Polls Act 1976, can only be done intentionally. It is not possible to "publish" a document inadvertently.[133]

(d)   When mens rea is not implied, and the presumption is overridden

If the presumption of mens rea is overridden, the court must then decide whether the offence is of strict or absolute liability.[134] Factors in that determination are as follows. First, and most importantly, absolute liability ought to be very rare, especially in light of ss 25(c) and 27(1) New Zealand Bill of Rights Act 1990.[135] The courts should find that an offence is one of absolute liability only when it is imposed in express terms or by necessary implication.[136] An example of the former, where the language of the statute evinces a clear intention by Parliament to impose absolute liability, was said in *Millar* to reside in ss 17 and 27 Machinery Act 1950:

---

129 By contrast, this argument does not apply to a victim's age in the context of sexual offences, where that age has independent moral significance. See *B (a minor) v DPP* [2000] 2 AC 428; [2000] 1 All ER 833 (HL); *R v K* [2001] 3 All ER 897; [2001] 3 WLR 471 (HL). The earlier, contrary, case of *R v Prince* (1875) LR 2 CCR 154; [1874-80] All ER Rep 881 is no longer good authority.

130 Cf *R v Lemon; R v Gay News Ltd* [1979] AC 617; [1979] 1 All ER 898 (HL) (whether a statement is "calculated to outrage the feelings of Christians"). But compare the dissent on this point by Barwick CJ in *Iannella v French* (1968) 119 CLR 84; [1968] ALR 385, 97; 393. The presence of a legal assessment within the actus reus raises conflicting concerns; between the need to prevent individuals from "second guessing" the law's values, and the need to give them fair warning of the criminal implications of their conduct. See further the discussion of ignorance of law, at 14.2.

131 *Police v Starkey* [1989] 2 NZLR 373; (1989) 4 CRNZ 400. Other cases are noted in *Adams*, CA20.12 (looseleaf).

132 *R v Meek* [1981] 1 NZLR 499 (CA).

133 *Police v Starkey* [1989] 2 NZLR 373; (1989) 4 CRNZ 400. In *Jackson v A-G* [2006] 2 NZLR 534, 538, the High Court held that most of the offences created in s 32(1) Penal Institutions Act 1954 provided, expressly or by necessary implication, for proof of some form of mens rea, notwithstanding that the offence in hand, s 32(1)(g) (having an article in a cell without approval), was found to impose strict liability.

134 Cf *Millar v MOT* [1986] 1 NZLR 660; (1986) 2 CRNZ 216 (CA), 668; 225 (Cooke P and Richardson JJ), 676; 233, 234 (Somers J).

amendment of that Act to require "due" and not merely "faithful" compliance with the obligations therein has been held to indicate that no defence should be available.[137] Perhaps more important is the alternative possibility, that absolute liability may be a necessary implication, particularly in light of the scheme and purpose of the Act. In *IRD v Thomas*,[138] Barker J held that failing to file a tax return elicited absolute liability, since otherwise the purpose of the offence would be frustrated by the ability of a taxpayer to shelter behind the failings of his accountant.[139]

The reluctance to find that an offence imports absolute liability is surely right, both on principles of strict construction[140] and because strict liability will normally achieve the desired object of an offence anyway. In addition, there are at least three specific features that will further incline a court away from imposing absolute liability. The first is the presence of an evaluative term in the actus reus, such as "fair" or "reasonable". Because this type of element cannot be determined by the defendant, in advance, with total certainty, but must always await the subsequent assessment of a judge, it raises a problem of fair warning.[141] Absolute liability, if it is imposed at all, should be threatened only in the clearest terms, so that it is at least possible for a defendant to know in advance what the boundaries of the offence are. This argument was recognised by the High Court in *Re Wairarapa Election Petition*:[142]

> "the provisions of subs (4) of s 139 provide that a fair proportion of expenses when carried on earlier than the three months period may be attributed to that period as election expenses. It would be wrong that, no matter how conscientiously a candidate had assessed that fair proportion, he should be absolutely liable for the excess of payment if in the end the Electoral Court concluded that his fair proportion was erroneous. When there is absolute liability there ought to be absolute certainty as to the ingredients of the offence so that the offender cannot say that he was unable beforehand to conduct himself so as to avoid the offence."

For similar reasons, the courts are very reluctant to ascribe absolute liability in cases where the defendant's activity is affected by what others are doing. This principle was recognised in *Jackson v A-G*,[143] where the High Court held that one reason for not imposing absolute liability

---

135 These sections, which codify respectively the presumption of innocence and the right to natural justice, were said in *Hamilton CC v Fairweather* [2002] NZAR 477 (HC), 494 to "point against absolute liability on the part of one who is without fault." Although the presumption of innocence was thought to be compatible with absolute liability in *Barnfather v London Borough of Islington Education Authority* [2003] EWHC (Admin) 418; [2003] 1 WLR 2318, that decision may be defensible in light of the panoply of measures that must be taken in the UK before a prosecution for truancy can be brought: Horder, "Whose Values Should Determine When Liability is Strict" in Simester (ed), *Appraising Strict Liability*, Oxford, Oxford University Press, 2005, 105. See generally, in the same volume, Sullivan, "Strict Liability for Criminal Offences in England and Wales following Incorporation into English Law of the European Convention on Human Rights", 195. However, the analysis in *Barnfather* has since been affirmed by *R v G* [2006] EWCA Crim 821.
136 *Millar v MOT* [1986] 1 NZLR 660; (1986) 2 CRNZ 216 (CA), 668; 225.
137 *AHI Operations Ltd v Dept of Labour* [1986] 1 NZLR 645. See the criticism by France, "Absolute liability since *MacKenzie*" [1987] NZLJ 50, 52, 53.
138 *IRD v Thomas* (1989) 13 TRNZ 697.
139 Cf 5.2.3(1). It is arguable that this case could have been decided differently, on the basis that the offence imported strict liability but that D may vicariously be liable for the fault of his agent.
140 Cf the principle asserted by Lord Reid in *Sweet v Parsley* [1970] AC 132; [1969] 1 All ER 347 (HL), 149; 350; 5.2.3(2)(a). See also 2.2.3.
141 See 2.1.3.
142 *Re Wairarapa Election Petition* [1988] 2 NZLR 74, 117.

for an offence under s 32 Penal Institutions Act 1954 was that imposition of absolute liability would tend to encourage inmates to take retribution against another inmate by placing cannabis or other drugs in the other's cell. In *Police v Creedon*, a prosecution for failing to yield the right of way at an intersection, McCarthy P emphasised the importance of the fact that "the regulation requires a driver of a motor vehicle to take a specific course of action if, and only if, something else is being done by someone else".[144] By contrast, say, with failing to stop at an intersection governed by a stop sign, the offence in *Creedon* does "not impose an omnipresent and unvarying obligation".[145] Its uncertain boundaries thus militate against absolute liability. An additional and buttressing rationale is that the regulation, in effect, gives another person the power to place the defendant under a criminal legal duty (in this case, by approaching the intersection from another direction). The vesting of such powers in third parties should never be accompanied by absolute liability on the part of the defendant.[146]

Another factor is the severity of the penalty prescribed for a breach. In *Re Wairarapa Election Petition*, where the mandatory penalty was described as "truly draconian", this was taken to be a reason against imposing absolute liability: "It is contrary to sense and justice that a person should be liable to the ultimate penalty, no matter how careful or innocent he may be."[147]

On the other hand, one consideration in favour of implying absolute liability arises if the statute itself designates a more specific defence, such as the taking of detailed steps by the defendant. *McLaren Transport Ltd v MOT* provides one such example: offences against s 23(2)(a) Road User Charges Act 1977 were held to be of absolute liability, subject to particular statutory defences contained in the Act. According to Hardie Boys J, "the statute itself prescribes 'avenues of escape' which are of limited availability and which would be entirely subverted were absence of fault in a more general sense to be available as a defence".[148] Where the function of the more specific defences is not "entirely subverted", of course, this argument would not apply.[149]

---

143 *Jackson v A-G* [2006] 2 NZLR 534 (HC), 542.
144 *Police v Creedon* [1976] 1 NZLR 571 (CA), 573.
145 *Police v Creedon* [1976] 1 NZLR 571 (CA), 574.
146 Cf *Re Wairarapa Election Petition* [1988] 2 NZLR 74, 117 lines 36-38. For related discussion of this point, see 3.2.2(1).
147 *Re Wairarapa Election Petition* [1988] 2 NZLR 74, 117.
148 *McLaren Transport Ltd v MOT* [1986] 2 NZLR 81, 83. Cf *McKnight v NZ Biogas Industries Ltd* [1994] 2 NZLR 664 (CA), 667-669; *Hamilton CC v Fairweather* [2002] NZAR 477 (HC).
149 Hence, in *Pickering v Ministry of Agriculture* 4/3/98, Hammond J, HC Hamilton AP5/97, the Court (obiter) was prepared to allow a general defence of absence of fault to supplement the statutory defence specifically provided for the offence itself.

Chapter 6

SECONDARY PARTICIPATION

6.1	Derivative liability	160
6.2	Modes of participation	162
6.3	The principal: s 66(1)(a)	163
6.3.1	Innocent agents	164
6.4	Secondary parties who assist or encourage crime: s 66(1)(b)-(d)	166
6.4.1	The conduct element	167
(1)	*Aiding*	167
(2)	*Abetting*	168
(3)	*Inciting*	170
(4)	*Counselling*	170
(5)	*Procuring*	170
6.4.2	The need for a connection	171
6.4.3	Omissions	172
6.4.4	Mens rea for participation under s 66(1)(b)-(d)	175
(1)	*S's own contribution: the intention to aid, abet, incite, or counsel*	175
(2)	*S's own contribution: the intention to procure*	176
(3)	*P's criminal conduct: "knowledge" of essential matters*	177
(4)	*P's criminal conduct: what "essential matters" must S know about?*	178
6.5	Secondary parties pursuant to a common intention: s 66(2)	181
6.5.1	A common unlawful purpose	182
6.5.2	Known to be a probable consequence	183
6.5.3	In the prosecution of the common purpose	184
(1)	*Conviction for a lesser offence?*	185
6.5.4	Applying s 66(2) where the offence committed was the object of the common purpose	186
6.6	General principles applying to all secondary parties	187
6.6.1	Liability normally depends on commission of the offence	187
6.6.2	Exceptions: Secondary liability without the primary offence	188
(1)	*When S is responsible for P's excuse*	188
(2)	*When S procures P to act without mens rea*	188
(3)	*No requirement that P be charged and convicted*	191
6.6.3	Conviction for different offences with the same actus reus	191

159

6.6.4 Limitations on the application of s 66...192
(1) *The Tyrrell principle*..193
(2) *Specific or implicit legislative identification of parties*..193
6.6.5 Secondary liability and inchoate offences..194
6.6.6 Withdrawal..194
(1) *Withdrawal from participation by common intention under s 66(2)*..195
(2) *Withdrawal from assistance or encouragement under s 66(1)(b)-(d)*......................................196

6.1 Derivative liability

In chapter 1, we considered the following example:[1]

> One fine September morning, Jim is discovered dead in his home. His skull has been crushed by a blow inflicted with a heavy object. The police are called. Upon investigation, they establish that he was murdered by his daughter, Alice, who killed him in order to receive her inheritance under his will.

This, as we said earlier, is a paradigm case of criminal wrongdoing by Alice, involving deliberate, culpable infliction of the sort of serious harm that the criminal law is meant to prevent. Alice is precisely the sort of person who deserves the condemnation of a criminal conviction. But she may not be the only person culpable in respect of Jim's death. Imagine the following additional details:

> During the course of their investigation, the police unearth a number of related facts. Frank, Jim's cousin, had learned by accident of Alice's plan to murder Jim, but had done nothing because he, too, stood to inherit under the will. Alice had planned the murder with the help of Gertrude, whom she had consulted about possible methods of carrying out the killing. The baseball bat that Alice eventually used belongs to Harry, who lent it to Alice for the purpose.

When an offence is committed it is not only the immediate perpetrator of the actus reus who may incur criminal liability. Others may also be held accountable by the criminal law. Usually, this will occur when those others have participated in the commission of the crime, albeit without themselves carrying out the actus reus. Such persons, when they are held to be criminally accountable, are said to be *parties* to the offence.

The difficult question, for both theory and doctrine in criminal law, is *when* persons other than the perpetrator of a crime should be held liable. When Jim dies the criminal law begins with every person within the jurisdiction as potential defendants, yet it is inappropriate to regard every member of society as involved in the crime that Alice commits. But how do we narrow the field in a principled way? In short, when a crime occurs, who are the suitable defendants?

In chapter 3 we considered the criminal law's doctrines of omission and causation, which play a vital role in identifying those persons who may be attributed with legal responsibility for committing a crime. Because of the law regarding omissions, for example, Frank will not be held responsible for Jim's death. On the other hand, these are not the only doctrines of

---

1 See 1.3 and, especially, 1.3.2(5).

responsibility in criminal law. Gertrude and Harry did not cause Jim's death: Alice's action was free and unconstrained.[2] Yet they, as well as Alice, will be held guilty of Jim's murder.

In this and the next chapter, we consider the doctrines by which a defendant may be held responsible for a crime she does not herself commit.[3] There are two main ways in which this may occur. The first gives rise to *secondary liability*. Although they did not perpetrate the crime, Gertrude and Harry have participated in Jim's murder by rendering aid and encouragement to Alice. Hence, they are known as secondary parties to the murder and are guilty of the offence alongside Alice. The second doctrine of responsibility occurs when a person is held responsible, at large, for the various acts of another person. This is known as *vicarious liability* and is much more common in civil than in criminal law. For example, an employer may sometimes be sued in tort for the damage its employee causes to P's property, but cannot itself be prosecuted for vandalism.

Both forms of liability are *derivative*. The defendant is indirectly held responsible for a crime committed by another and, as such, her liability is dependent upon the criminal actions of that other person. If no crime is committed, there is nothing of a criminal character that can be secondarily or vicariously attributed to the defendant.[4] As was noted in 1.3.2(5), and will be seen below, the fact that liability is derived from the crime of another raises difficult questions of policy. The level of involvement required to make D guilty when P commits a crime must balance the consideration that D is often just as culpable as P (and indeed sometimes more culpable), even though it was not D who pulled the trigger, against the difficulty that derivative liability casts the net of criminalisation well beyond the direct infliction of criminal harms, to catch ostensibly innocent conduct such as lending (or selling)[5] Alice a baseball bat or even sitting as a passenger in a car.[6] It is for this reason that the mens rea requirements of secondary liability, in particular, are generally more stringent than those for the underlying offence.

For similar reasons, vicarious liability is normally to be avoided altogether in criminal law, since it arises simply out of a pre-existing relationship between the defendant and the actual perpetrator of a crime, and so is not specific to the crime or to any conduct by D relevant to that crime. It follows that D risks being convicted of a crime to which he has not contributed and for which he is in no way at fault. As chapter 1 argued, that would be an undesirable outcome, especially in the context of stigmatic crimes. Consequently, it will be seen in chapter 7 that vicarious liability is normally restricted to regulatory offences,[7] and is imposed only when it is found that Parliament must have intended it.

---

2   See 3.4ff. Their assistance need not even be a sine qua non of the crime — Alice, we may suppose, would have received the same advice and aid from others had Gertrude and Harry been unavailable or unwilling.
3   A classic discussion is Sayre, "Criminal responsibility for the acts of another" (1930) 43 Harv LR 689. See also Perkins, "Parties to crime" (1941) 89 U Pa LR 581; Dressler, "Reassessing the theoretical underpinnings of accomplice liability: New solutions to an old problem" (1985) 37 Hastings LJ 91.
4   Kadish, *Blame and Punishment: Essays in the Criminal Law*, New York, Macmillan, 1987, ch 8, 146ff. This proposition is subject to certain exceptions, for example where S has procured P to do the actus reus of an offence without mens rea, or under duress. See 6.6.2(2).
5   Cf *National Coal Board v Gamble* [1959] 1 QB 11; [1958] 3 All ER 203. See, for example, Duff, " 'Can I help you?': Accessorial liability and the intention to assist" (1990) 10 LS 165; G Williams, "Complicity, purpose and the draft code" [1990] Crim LR 4.
6   For example *Ashton v Police* [1964] NZLR 429; *Du Cros v Lambourne* [1907] 1 KB 40; 6.4.3.
7   Cf *S M Savill Ltd v MOT* [1986] 1 NZLR 653. See also 7.1.

In the second part of chapter 7, we will turn our attention to the liability of corporations. Although corporations are sometimes credited with a legal capacity to act, or omit, and to commit crimes directly, as will be seen, corporate liability is often to be explained as a specialised variety of vicarious liability.

6.2 Modes of participation

The law governing forms of participation in a crime is stated in s 66 Crimes Act 1961.[8] The section reads as follows:

"66 Parties to offences

"(1)   Every one is a party to and guilty of an offence who—

"(a)   Actually commits the offence; or

"(b)   Does or omits an act for the purpose of aiding any person to commit the offence; or

"(c)   Abets any person in the commission of the offence; or

"(d)   Incites, counsels, or procures any person to commit the offence.

"(2)   Where 2 or more persons form a common intention to prosecute any unlawful purpose, and to assist each other therein, each of them is a party to every offence committed by any one of them in the prosecution of the common purpose if the commission of that offence was known to be a probable consequence of the prosecution of the common purpose."

Conventionally, we distinguish between the *principal* — the person or persons who actually perpetrate the crime — and the *secondary party*. In general, D will be a principal offender if he personally fulfils the actus reus and mens rea requirements of the crime. Secondary parties are those persons whose assistance, abetment, etc is sufficient under s 66 to make them also participants in, and guilty of, the crime committed by the principal, notwithstanding that the secondary party does not herself commit that crime.[9]

A secondary party should be distinguished from an *accessory after the fact*. The latter is a person who assists someone else (who may be either a principal or secondary party) who has committed an offence, *after* the crime has been completed. Thus the accessory after the fact does not participate in the crime itself, and his liability is not for the original crime committed, but instead arises independently as an offence under ss 71 and 312. By contrast, participation by a party to the offence must occur before that offence is completed.[10]

---

8   Except in the case of a crime committed outside New Zealand, for which the liability of parties is pursuant to ss 68 and 69.

9   At common law, secondary parties were further categorised as "principals in the second degree" or as "accessories before the fact", depending whether their participating conduct occurred while present at (rather than before) the commission of the relevant crime. The finer point is now of mere terminological interest.

10 *R v Beuth* [1937] NZLR 282 (CA); *R v Gosney* [1977] 2 NZLR 130 (CA); *Larkins v Police* [1987] 2 NZLR 282; (1987) 3 CRNZ 49; *S v Thomo* [1969] (1) SA 585 (AD). In the case of a continuing offence, such as rape (cf *R v Kaitamaki* [1984] 1 NZLR 385, also reported as *Kaitamaki v R* (1984) 1 CRNZ 211; [1985] AC 147 (PC)), the participation may occur after commencement of the offence but must happen before its completion (ie prior to withdrawal by the rapist): *R v Mayberry* [1973] Qd R 211. For discussion, see *Adams*, CA66.18 (looseleaf).

As s 66 makes clear, the distinction between principals and secondary offenders is now of little practical significance in criminal law, since each is deemed to be guilty of the full offence. Thus it will not affect his resulting conviction for, say, murder, whether D himself killed another person or was simply a secondary party. Indeed, it can be very difficult on the facts of some cases to differentiate between principals and secondary parties,[11] and the form of charge need not reveal the nature of D's participation, but may simply allege guilt.[12]

Nonetheless, the terminology is still to be found in the case law. One reason for this is that the distinction is still crucial to the operation of s 66 itself. If D was not a principal, the inquiry whether D was a secondary party will depend in part upon the existence of a principal who did perpetrate the offence, and will take a different form (with a different actus reus and different mens rea) from the inquiry into the principal's liability. The elements of the principal's liability are specific to each offence: in murder, for example, they will be as set out in s 167 (and surrounding sections) and s 66(1)(a). By contrast, the elements of the secondary party's liability are set out in s 66(1)(b)-(d) and (2).

The difference between principals and secondary parties matters for at least two other reasons. First, some offences are defined so that certain participants are excluded from liability, either because only a named class of persons may commit the offence as a principal or (more rarely) because the possibility of secondary participation is excluded.[13] Secondly, there is no vicarious liability for the acts of secondary parties.[14]

6.3 The principal: s 66(1)(a)

Before considering the varieties of secondary participation falling within s 66, it is necessary to make some observations regarding the participation of principal offenders. First, there may be more than one principal offender. If P and Q assault V by jointly raining blows on him, they are each principals. If V dies from the combination of blows, they will each be guilty of manslaughter or murder.[15] There are two ways in which multiple defendants may be held to be principals. First, each may separately satisfy all the required ingredients of the relevant offence. In the above example, P and Q are each independently guilty of an assault. This form of liability requires no reference to s 66, although it falls within the scope of s 66(1). Alternatively, under s 66(1)(a) each may separately satisfy *some* part of the actus reus for the offence where their actions, in combination, fulfil the complete actus reus requirement and each has the requisite mens rea. The latter is a true case of joint principals, in that it is sufficient for liability that each party does a part of the actus reus.[16]

Note, however, that normally there must be *some* contribution to the occurrence of the actus reus before one can be held to have committed the offence as a principal.[17] This requirement

---

11 Consider, for example, the facts of *R v Samuels* [1985] 1 NZLR 350 (CA); *Abbott v R* [1977] AC 755; [1976] 3 All ER 140 (PC); *R v Lewis* [1975] 1 NZLR 222 (CA).
12 Section 343 Crimes Act 1961; s 76 Summary Proceedings Act 1957. It is desirable wherever possible for the prosecution to specify the form of participation when laying the charge: *DPP for Northern Ireland v Maxwell* [1978] 3 All ER 1140; [1978] 1 WLR 1350 (HL). However, this is not common practice.
13 See 6.6.2.
14 *Ferguson v Weaving* [1951] 1 KB 814; [1951] 1 All ER 412.
15 Cf *R v Lewis* [1975] 1 NZLR 222 (CA).
16 *R v Wyles* [1977] Qd R 169 (CA); *R v Bingley* (1821) Russ & Ry 446; 168 ER 890 (each forged part of a banknote); *R v Cornwall* (1730) 2 Str 881; 93 ER 914 (breaking and entering); Williams, *TBCL*, 330; Lanham, "Complicity, concert and conspiracy" (1980) 4 Crim LJ 276.

was disregarded — it is submitted, wrongly — by the Court of Appeal in *R v Harawira*,[18] in which D had been present during an attack on V by a number of assailants, and had assaulted but not injured V. Nonetheless, her conviction for injuring with intent as a principal under s 66(1)(a) was upheld, the Court of Appeal stating that it was sufficient that she had "participated in concert" with the persons who actually injured the victim.

Harawira and the Australian case of *Osland v R*[19] suggest a new rule that, at least until recently, was not part of the common law: that where D and others form a common purpose to commit a crime, D is guilty, as a principal, of all the crimes committed in her presence that fall within the scope of that common purpose, regardless of whether D actually contributed to the commission of a particular offence. With respect, however, it is submitted that there is no such principle in the common law.[20] Neither should there be. Although D's conviction for injuring with intent in *Harawira* was obviously warranted, the proper basis for the conviction is clearly one of secondary participation (through aiding and abetting or common unlawful purpose), rather than the actual commission of the offence. Moreover, whatever may be the law in Australia, the terms of s 66(1)(a) (especially when contrasted with s 66(2), which deals explicitly with common purpose liability) impliedly exclude such a principle by requiring that D "actually commits" the offence. D does not actually commit an offence when she plays no part in its actual commission.

6.3.1 Innocent agents

Sometimes the actus reus is not perpetrated personally by the defendant, but is instead brought about by another who is unaware of the significance of his actions. Where the defendant deliberately[21] *uses* an "innocent agent" to bring about the actus reus, the intervening actor is not regarded as a participant in the crime, and the law treats the defendant as the principal.[22] Conceptually, it is as if D "stands in the shoes" of the innocent agent. An example is when the host at a party gives a waiter a glass of wine to take out to the victim, when only the host knows that the wine contains poison. Although the waiter gives the victim poison, he is merely an innocent agent and it is the host who is the perpetrator of the crime.[23] This rule was applied by the Court of Appeal in *R v Paterson*,[24] in which D, who procured T to uplift a television for

---

17 Cf *R v Demirian* [1989] VR 97; (1988) 33 A Crim R 441; but this aspect of *Demirian* has been rejected by the High Court of Australia in *Osland v R* (1998) 197 CLR 316; 159 ALR 170 (HCA). For criticism of *Osland* see Gray, " 'I didn't know I wasn't there': Common purpose and the liability of accessories to crime" (1999) 23 Crim LJ 201.

18 *R v Harawira* [1989] 2 NZLR 714; (1989) 4 CRNZ 348 (CA).

19 *Osland v R* (1998) 197 CLR 316; 159 ALR 170 (HCA).

20 Cf Smith and Hogan, *Criminal Law* (9th ed), London, Butterworths, 1999, 124; Smith, "Joint enterprise and secondary liability" (1999) 50 NILQ 153.

21 Exceptionally, an actus reus brought about by an innocent agent may also be attributed to D if it resulted from D's negligence, when negligence is sufficient to establish mens rea: *Tessymond's Case* (1828) 1 Lew CC 169; 168 ER 1000.

22 For discussion, see Alldridge, "The doctrine of innocent agency" (1990) 2 Crim L Forum 45; Williams, "Innocent agency and causation" (1992) 3 Crim L Forum 289; Alldridge, "Common sense, innocent agency, and causation" (1992) 3 Crim L Forum 299; Orchard, "Criminal responsibility for the acts of innocent agents" [1977] NZLJ 4. By contrast, secondary liability is thought to depend upon the existence of a principal offender: see, for example, *R v Bowern* (1915) 34 NZLR 696 (CA). This requirement is considered at 6.6.1.

23 Cf *Anon* (1634) Kel 53; 84 ER 1079; *R v Michael* (1840) 9 C & P 356; 173 ER 867; *R v Butt* (1884) 15 Cox CC 564; *White v Ridley* (1978) 140 CLR 342; 52 ALJR 724 (HCA); *R v Franklin* (2001) 119 A Crim R 223 (Vic CA), para 23ff per Brooking JA.

him from V's flat by pretending the flat was his, was held "actually" to have committed the offence of burglary within the terms of s 66(1)(a).

The doctrine of innocent agency does not apply if the intervening agent is herself guilty of the offence; consequently, it will often be inapplicable to strict liability offences.[25] Further, it may only be invoked, and the agent can only be categorised as an *innocent* agent, either if she does not know that she is doing the *actus reus* or if she lacks criminal capacity, in particular through being insane.[26] At common law, it is also sufficient if the intervening agent lacks criminal capacity through being an infant.[27] In New Zealand, however, the test appears to be a substantive one, of whether the intervener is "lacking intent or understanding" of her actions, rather than whether she is "merely incapable of being convicted" for those actions. As such, a young child who knows what she is doing is not an innocent agent for the purposes of the doctrine, notwithstanding that she may not herself be convicted.[28]

There are also some crimes for which the doctrine is excluded altogether because, by the nature of those crimes, it cannot be said that D has personally committed the actus reus. This will depend on the particular statutory language used to specify each offence, but in general such cases are of two types.

First, innocent agency is more likely to be excluded where the essence of the crime is specified *behaviour* by the criminal, rather than the bringing about of some *consequence*.[29] In bigamy, for example, it seems impossible to say that D has gone through a ceremony of marriage with V (the actus reus) when he has procured T to do so. The same is true for rape,[30] and for crimes such as careless driving[31] and driving with excess alcohol.[32] The doctrine of innocent agency operates only where it is possible for D to fulfil the elements of the actus reus by the instrument of some other person. That is straightforwardly done where the actus reus does not specify particular behaviour by the defendant. For example, in murder, which requires the causing of another's death, it is apt to view D as having killed V herself, even though she in fact procures

---

24 *R v Paterson* [1976] 2 NZLR 394 (CA).
25 Where, despite her innocence, the intervening agent is guilty of an offence, D should be convicted as a secondary party: *A-G's Reference (No 1 of 1975)* [1975] QB 773; [1975] 2 All ER 684 (CA).
26 Cf *R v Tyler* (1838) 8 C & P 616; 173 ER 643; notwithstanding that the insane "innocent agent" in that case was the ringleader!
27 *R v Manley* (1844) 1 Cox CC 104; *R v Mazeau* (1840) 9 C & P 676; 173 ER 1006.
28 *R v Ngatai* 9/4/01 Williams J, HC Auckland T001864. In such cases, D may nonetheless be convicted as a secondary party, by virtue of ss 21(2) or 22(2).
29 See the distinction made between behavioural, circumstantial, and consequential elements of the actus reus in ch 3.
30 Notwithstanding *R v Cogan; R v Leak* [1976] QB 217; [1975] 2 All ER 1059 (CA); see the commentary in [1975] Crim LR 584. *Cogan* was followed by the Victorian Supreme Court in *R v Hewitt* (1996) 84 A Crim R 440 (Vic SC) but should now be explained on the basis of procurement: 6.6.2(2). The language of s 128(5)(a) ("any other person") seemingly admits of "sexual connection" by an innocent agent: *R v Cooper* 29/6/88, Williamson J, HC Christchurch T16/88. By contrast, the definition of rape in s 128(2) ("his penis") appears to exclude innocent agency.
31 *Thornton v Mitchell* [1940] 1 All ER 339; see also 6.6.1 Cf *R v Harrison* [1941] NZLR 354 (CA); *Sweetman v Industries and Commerce Dept* [1970] NZLR 139, 146, 147.
32 Cf *A-G's Reference (No 1 of 1975)* [1975] QB 773; [1975] 2 All ER 684 (CA), in which D secretly laced P's drink. (Note that the offence in that case was held to be one of absolute liability, and that P was therefore guilty of committing the offence as a principal, notwithstanding his "innocence". D, in turn, was a secondary party.)

the waiter to deliver the poison. It is rather less easy to treat D as having done the actus reus personally when the gist of the wrong is T's actual conduct, rather than its consequence.[33]

However, while the distinction may seem clear enough in principle, the question whether the conduct element of a particular offence requires D's direct, personal involvement can involve fine — indeed, seemingly arbitrary — distinctions. For instance, it is apparently possible to "enter" premises as a burglar through the agency of another,[34] which is arguably as much a behaviour crime as is rape. Thus the range of offences to which the innocent agent doctrine applies is uncertain.[35] Since the reason for excluding innocent agency rests purely on the linguistic peculiarities of a statute, and does not reflect any underlying moral distinction, it is unsurprising that few offences have been held to be incompatible with the innocent agency doctrine.[36]

Secondly, innocent agency is also excluded if D is not a member of the class of persons eligible to commit the offence as a principal. A typical example is an offence that can only be committed by a licensee. *Adams* observes:[37]

> "If A, who is not a licensee, procures B, an innocent licensee, to commit such an offence, it seems inappropriate to say that A 'actually commits' the offence. To do so implies that A is a licensee when that is not so. However, A may properly be regarded as having actually committed the offence in the reverse situation where, being a licensee, A procures B, an innocent non-licensee, to perform the physical acts constituting the offence."

6.4 Secondary parties who assist or encourage crime: s 66(1)(b)-(d)

Persons who involve themselves in a crime by giving assistance or encouragement to its commission are deemed to be parties if they fall within the terms of s 66(1)(b), s 66(1)(c), or s 66(1)(d). These subsections mention five varieties of conduct counting as secondary participation: aiding, abetting, inciting, counselling, and procuring. Apart from incitement (which in any event overlaps with abetment, counselling, and procurement), these are also the categories of participation recognised at common law, and the common law applicable to these concepts necessarily informs their interpretation in s 66. Because, as we shall see, the categories overlap, it appears that they effectively include the actus reus of any form of assistance, encouragement, contribution to, or causing of a crime by the principal.

---

33 This difficulty may be thought a reason to doubt the extension of the innocent agency doctrine to assault, notwithstanding its application in *R v S* [1994] DCR 76. See Dawkins, "Criminal law" [1995] NZ Law Review 34, 51.
34 *R v Paterson* [1976] 2 NZLR 394 (CA).
35 See generally Orchard, "Criminal responsibility for the acts of innocent agents" [1977] NZLJ 4.
36 Innocent agency has been applied in such contexts as gaining access to a computer system (*Police v B* [1990] 2 NZLR 504; (1990) 5 CRNZ 575, affirmed [1991] 2 NZLR 527, also reported as *B v Police* (1990) 7 CRNZ 607 (CA)); making a false return of income (*Adair v Leigh Hotel Ltd* (1984) 6 NZTC 61,853); using a document with intent to defraud (*R v Gunthorp* [2003] 2 NZLR 433, CA); and engaging in misleading or deceptive conduct (*Goldsbro v Walker* [1993] 1 NZLR 394; (1992) 5 TCLR 46 (CA)).
37 *Adams*, CA66.16(1) (looseleaf).

6.4.1 The conduct element

Although s 66(1) identifies five disparate types of conduct constituting participation, it is arguably a mistake to treat them as independent, alternative, actus reus elements,[38] and it is not necessary in the charge to specify which type of conduct is relied on. The section is clearly designed to capture all forms of non-trivial assistance or encouragement for crimes committed by others, when rendered with the requisite mens rea,[39] and it may be artificial to analyse the terms separately. Nonetheless, the manner in which the statute is drafted, by dividing the alternatives into different subsections, makes this unavoidable.

(1) Aiding

S aids P by assisting, helping, or giving support to P in the commission of a crime. There must be actual assistance: merely trying to help is not enough.[40] If S, knowing that P is going to rob a bank, plans to lend P her gun, she does not aid the offence if her car breaks down on the way over to P's house and P leaves to commit the robbery before S arrives. On the other hand, the assistance need not be substantial.[41] Merely being available as a back-up person in the event of need would be sufficient.[42] By implication, it is not necessary that the assistance should take place at the actual scene of the offence. A helpful illustration of these principles may be found in the facts of *R v Turanga*.[43] Two secondary parties aided the perpetrators of an aggravated robbery by supplying a second getaway car, for use in completing the escape after the robbers had abandoned their first getaway car (utilised to flee the scene of the robbery itself). In the event, the second car was never used, because the principal robbers were arrested first. Despite the fact that their agreed role was never performed, and despite their distance from the scene of the crime, the defendants' applications for discharge on counts of aiding the robbery were refused. The accused had helped the principals by providing their *means* of escape.

Neither is it always necessary that the principal should be aware of the assistance, provided she is in fact assisted.[44] Neither need she be agreeable to it.[45] Suppose that P plans a robbery, intending to use her gun. The day before the robbery takes place, S notices that P's gun is missing from its drawer. Without telling P, he places his own gun, a similar model, in the drawer for P to use instead. P carries out the robbery using S's gun. In this case S has aided P and is a party to the robbery even though P is ignorant of S's contribution.[46]

Sometimes, however, the question whether assistance is actually provided may be more difficult because the principal is unaware of the assistance. Consider the following facts, which arose in *Larkins v Police*.[47] Some associates of S had decided to burgle a bottle store. After they

---

38   Cf *Adams* (2nd ed), para 648.
39   Outlined at 6.4.4.
40   *Larkins v Police* [1987] 2 NZLR 282; (1987) 3 CRNZ 49. See Smith, "Secondary participation and inchoate offences" in Tapper (ed), *Crime, Proof and Punishment*, London, Butterworths, 1981, 21, 36-39.
41   Cf *Pou v Police* 6/7/00, Laurenson J, HC Whangarei AP22/000, paras 21-23; *R v Giannetto* [1997] 1 Cr App R 1 (CA), 13.
42   *R v George* 16/5/96, CA550/95. But see the discussion of *Larkins v Police* [1987] 2 NZLR 282; (1987) 3 CRNZ 49, in the text below.
43   *R v Turanga* [1993] 1 NZLR 685.
44   *Larkins v Police* [1987] 2 NZLR 282; (1987) 3 CRNZ 49; *Hobart v R* (1982) 25 CR (3d) 214 (Ont CA), 236.
45   An unusual case is considered in *R v Zizov* 12/11/03, Williams J, HC Auckland T031264, paras 32-34.
46   See *State v Talley* 102 Ala 25 (1894): S prevented a third party from warning V of the danger, thereby making it easier for P to kill V. S was guilty of aiding murder, notwithstanding that P was unaware of the assistance.

had broken into the rear of the store, S, who was on the street fronting the store, decided to act as a lookout in case the police arrived. The persons inside the store were unaware of S's decision to keep watch. As it happened, however, he made no contribution to events, since someone else saw the police arrive and called out the warning. S was charged with (being a party to) the offence of breaking and entering. Although his conviction was quashed on another ground,[48] Eichelbaum J considered that:[49]

> "the appellant's action in providing the principal offenders with, as counsel put it, an extra pair of eyes was at least evidence of actual assistance regardless whether those offenders were aware of its availability."

Adams doubts this view, describing the case as one:[50]

> "[o]f completely ineffectual aid which might have had some effect only if events had turned out differently ... His act amounted to no more than a completely ineffective attempt to aid, and attempting to aid is not an offence."

But, it is submitted, Eichelbaum J's analysis is plausible. Where the participation of a lookout is known by the principal offenders, *Adams* seems to suggest the principals are aided because they rely on the presence of the lookout, whether or not the lookout has cause actually to give any warning. Yet it is arguable that reliance does not constitute assistance. Consider the case where S tricks P by promising to act as lookout but not in fact doing so. Although P relies on S to keep watch, it would be odd to say that S "aids" (as opposed to abets) P. Either way, moreover, it *adds* something to the assistance P receives if S *does* in fact supply P with an extra pair of eyes. And this occurs in *Larkins v Police* even though P is unaware that S does so. This case is not like the example given earlier, in which S attempts but fails to lend P her gun.

(2) *Abetting*

In terms of its dictionary definition, "to abet" means to incite by aid, to instigate, or to encourage. In practice, because of its overlap with the other forms of participation in s 66(1), abetment is typically associated with encouragement.[51] Even so, there is an extensive overlap with other forms of participation in crime. For example, as was suggested in 6.4.1(1), in cases where S is alleged to "assist" P by providing support on which P relies, the reliance itself may be sufficient for P to be abetted, whether or not any further assistance is in fact provided. Similarly, encouragement of P to commit an offence is likely also to constitute counselling.

The encouragement may be by words or conduct: nodding one's head in endorsement of a plan may be just as effective as a verbal indication of agreement. Indeed, mere presence as part of a group can constitute abetment where the group as a whole encourages the principal to go

---

47 *Larkins v Police* [1987] 2 NZLR 282; (1987) 3 CRNZ 49.
48 Namely, that S's assistance occurred after the break-in was complete. Thus the offence had already been committed and S could only be charged with being an accessory after the fact. See 6.2.
49 *Larkins v Police* [1987] 2 NZLR 282; (1987) 3 CRNZ 49, 290; 57.
50 *Adams*, CA66.17(1) (looseleaf). See Dawkins, "The unknown look-out and liability for 'aiding' an offence" [1989] NZLJ 30. For the rule that attempting to be a party to an offence is not itself an offence, see 6.6.3.
51 Cf *R v Schriek* [1997] 2 NZLR 139; (1996) 14 CRNZ 449 (CA); *R v Galey* [1985] 1 NZLR 230 (CA).

ahead.[52] For example, in *R v Coney*[53] it was said that attendance at an illegal prize fight might be evidence of abetting battery by the fighters, since as Mathew J observed:[54]

> "the chief incentive to the wretched combatants to fight on until (as happens too often) dreadful injuries have been inflicted and life endangered or sacrificed, is the presence of spectators watching with keen interest every incident of the fight."

Simply by watching, S and others may encourage the fighters (although, as we shall see below, the mens rea requirement means that S must also *intend* this result).

Indeed, arguably there could even be situations where the mere presence of another *individual* — say, a trusted confidant — reassures and encourages P's commission of a crime. There seems no reason why P cannot be abetted in such a case. Notwithstanding statements by the Court of Appeal that mere presence is not enough,[55] the additional consideration that, say, S is someone in whom P places great faith may suffice to establish the required encouragement.

However, such cases are exceptional, because it is necessary to show that S (whether individually or as part of a group) *did in fact* encourage P to commit a crime. Mere presence *by itself*, which does not encourage, is insufficient.[56] The inference of encouragement requires something further, such as proof of some additional action by S or of a particular circumstance that implies support, for example that P and S are members of the same gang or that S's presence is pursuant to some prior arrangement.[57] Alternatively, as we have noted, it is sufficient that S is part of a group offering encouragement and that P is aware of the group's behaviour, albeit unaware of S's individual conduct.[58]

By contrast with aid, which can be rendered to P without P's knowledge (6.4.1(1)), it is essential that the encouragement be communicated successfully to P. There cannot be "encouragement in fact" by S unless P knows of it.[59] Suppose, for example, that S knows P intends to commit a robbery. S posts a letter to P in which she encourages P to commit the robbery, but the letter is never delivered. On these facts alone, S cannot be a party to the robbery because her encouragement, although offered, is not received by P.

This point, which applies also to incitement and counselling, is considered further at 6.4.2. But it is important to emphasise that the requirement that S's encouragement be communicated to P is *not* a requirement that the encouragement had any effect on P by inducing him to commit the offence. It is unnecessary to show that P would not have offended but for the

---

52 Cf *R v Schriek* [1997] 2 NZLR 139; (1996) 14 CRNZ 449 (CA), 150; 459.
53 *R v Coney* (1882) 8 QBD 534.
54 *R v Coney* (1882) 8 QBD 534, 544 (dissenting). See also *R v Young and Webber* (1838) 8 C & P 644; 173 ER 655.
55 *R v Schriek* [1997] 2 NZLR 139; (1996) 14 CRNZ 449 (CA), 149-50; 459; *R v Loper* 22/5/00, CA502/99, para 12; *R v Briggs* 29/11/01, CA244/01, para 14.
56 *R v Schriek* [1997] 2 NZLR 139; (1996) 14 CRNZ 449 (CA); *R v Atkinson* (1869) 11 Cox CC 330; *R v Clarkson* [1971] 3 All ER 344; [1971] 1 WLR 1402 (CA); *R v Allan* [1965] 1 QB 130; [1963] 2 All ER 897 (CCA).
57 See, for example, *Innes v Police* 24/4/91 Williamson J, HC Invercargill AP 17/91 and *R v Pene* 1/7/80, CA63/80 (accompanying P to the scene of the crime); also *Wilcox v Jefferey* [1951] 1 All ER 464 (S attended an unlawful concert performance in his capacity as a jazz critic and, further, paid a fee to attend).
58 *R v Schriek* [1997] 2 NZLR 139; (1996) 14 CRNZ 449 (CA).
59 *R v Thomson* 14/6/05, CA1/05, para 38.

encouragement, or even that P was influenced by it. These principles emerge from *R v Schriek*,[60] where the Court of Appeal confirmed the trial judge's directions that P must be aware of his being encouraged (the encouragement "must be communicated") but that it is not necessary to prove that P "was actually encouraged to go on and commit the offence".

(3) *Inciting*

The meaning of incitement, which is also an inchoate offence, is considered in 8.4. In essence, incitement requires an instigation or urging, something that seeks to induce or encourage P to commit the offence. It therefore overlaps with abetting. To the extent that there is any practical difference between the two terms, participation by incitement may more naturally refer to cases where the pressure or influence exerted by S is more substantial than mere encouragement, especially where P has not already determined to commit the offence.[61]

(4) *Counselling*

"Counselling" has two varieties of meaning which both overlap with the other terms used in s 66(1). First, it includes the provision of advice or information, though such conduct may also amount to aiding or abetting.[62] Alternatively, counselling may contemplate "urging" someone to commit an offence[63] — in which context the overlap is with incitement of the offence.

(5) *Procuring*

By contrast with the other varieties of secondary participation, procurement of an offence requires that the secondary party deliberately *causes* the principal to commit the offence. Therefore the requisite connection between S and the commission of the offence must be rather stronger than for aiding, abetting, counselling, or incitement. By contrast with those other terms, which require only that S play some part in the crime:[64]

> "To procure means to produce by endeavour. You procure a thing by setting out to see that it happens and taking the appropriate steps to produce that happening."

Thus the perpetration of the principal crime must in some sense be a consequence of the procurement by S.[65] However, S's contribution need not be a decisive, or sine qua non ingredient of the decision by P to commit the offence: it is enough that the procurement was influential. Even if there were other reasons why, without S's contribution, P might have chosen to commit the offence anyway, that does not matter. Provided that S's conduct in fact played some part in influencing P, S will be guilty of procurement.[66]

---

60 *R v Schriek* [1997] 2 NZLR 139; (1996) 14 CRNZ 449 (CA). Cf, on the facts, *Wilcox v Jefferey* [1951] 1 All ER 464.
61 Cf *R v Hendrickson* [1977] Crim LR 356 (CA); *Burnard v Police* [1996] 1 NZLR 566; *R v Tamatea* (2003) 20 CRNZ 363 (HC).
62 Cf *R v Baker* (1909) 28 NZLR 536 (CA); *Martyn v Police* [1967] NZLR 396. *Baker* is criticised by Williams, *CLGP*, para 125, but only on the issue of mens rea.
63 *Stuart v R* (1974) 134 CLR 426; 4 ALR 545 (HCA). The second interpretation is preferred in Canada: *R v Hamilton* (2005) 255 DLR (4th) 283 (SCC).
64 *A-G's Reference (No 1 of 1975)* [1975] QB 773; [1975] 2 All ER 684 (CA). See also *Cardin Laurant Ltd v Commerce Commission* [1990] 3 NZLR 563; (1989) 3 TCLR 470; *MOT v Barnett* (1986) 3 DCR 382; *R v Bryce* [2004] EWCA Crim 1231, [2004] 2 Cr App R 35.
65 See the summary by Smith, "Aid, abet, counsel, or procure" in Glazebrook (ed), *Reshaping the Criminal Law: Essays in Honour of Glanville Williams*, London, Stevens & Sons, 1978, 120, 134.

Normally, procurement by S will take the form of persuasion, inducement, or threats. Sometimes, however, the causation element of a procurement may operate without influencing P's reasons; indeed, P may be entirely ignorant of S's role. In cases where an offence can be committed without mens rea, and the innocent agent doctrine does not apply,[67] S may become a secondary party to an offence by causing P to commit it. In *A-G's Reference (No 1 of 1975)*[68] S secretly laced the drinks of P, who was subsequently convicted of driving with excess alcohol (in that jurisdiction, an absolute liability offence). S was guilty of procuring the offence.

6.4.2 The need for a connection

Secondary liability is derived from S's *involvement* in the principal offence, and not merely her attempt to become involved. It follows that S's conduct must somehow be connected to the commission of the offence by P. As we have seen, in the case of aiding this requirement is manifested by the need to demonstrate that assistance of some sort *was in fact* provided to P; similarly, in the case of procuring, it is reflected in the need to show a causal link between S's conduct and perpetration of the offence. The same is true for abetting, inciting, and counselling. Although causation need not be shown, it must be established by the prosecution that the principal *received* encouragement, incitement, or advice, before S's conduct may count as participation falling within s 66.[69]

This point is sometimes misunderstood, and was left open by the Court of Appeal in *R v Padlie*.[70] Nonetheless, it is fundamental to the nature of secondary participation. Derivative liability is *not* a form of inchoate liability. Liability is not based on S's act of incitement (for example) *per se*, as it is in the corresponding inchoate offence punishable under s 311(2). Rather, it is derived from S's *participation in* the offence perpetrated by P. If P is not aware of the encouragement, incitement, or advice, S necessarily fails to participate in the commission of the offence. In such a case, S cannot be a party to its commission.

The result is the same if the encouragement was so long ago that P has forgotten about it by the time she resolves to commit the offence; in which case S will not be a party to the offence.[71] This type of "forgotten advice" case is covered by a further *connection-based* requirement, suggested in the extraordinary case of *R v Calhaem*.[72] P must be aware not only of S's encouragement (for example), but also that he is acting in accordance with, or within

---

66 *Blakey v DPP* [1991] RTR 405; [1991] Crim LR 763. For a civil law illustration of this possibility, see *Barton v Armstrong* [1976] AC 104, 121 (execution of deed voidable for duress, even though P had other reasons to execute the deed apart from D's threat): "the illegitimate means used was a reason (not the reason, nor the predominant reason nor the clinching reason) why the complainant acted as he did. We are also prepared to accept that a decisive answer is not obtainable by asking the question whether the contract would have been made even if there had been no threats because, even if the answer to this question is affirmative, that does not prove that the contract was not made because of the threats."
67 See 6.3.1.
68 *A-G's Reference (No 1 of 1975)* [1975] QB 773; [1975] 2 All ER 684 (CA). The decision has considerable untapped potential for the liability of hosts and publicans: see, for example, Williams, *TBCL*, 339, 341.
69 *R v Schriek* [1997] 2 NZLR 139; (1996) 14 CRNZ 449 (CA); *R v Clarkson* [1971] 3 All ER 344; [1971] 1 WLR 1402 (CA) (abetting); *R v Calhaem* [1985] QB 808; [1985] 2 All ER 266 (CA) (counselling). Cf Smith, "Aid, abet, counsel, or procure" in Glazebrook (ed), *Reshaping the Criminal Law: Essays in Honour of Glanville Williams*, London, Stevens & Sons, 1978, 120, 131-134.
70 *R v Padlie* 28/11/95, CA209/95; CA232/95; CA237/95: the Court chose not to decide the question whether abetting requires proof that the principal was aware of the encouragement.
71 Cf *A-G v Able* [1984] QB 795; [1984] 1 All ER 277.

the scope of, the endorsement provided by S's encouragement. The Court of Appeal provided the following illustration:[73]

> "For example, if the principal offender happened to be involved in a football riot in the course of which he laid about him with a weapon of some sort and killed someone who, unknown to him, was the person whom he had been counselled to kill, he would not, in our view, have been acting within the scope of his authority; he would have been acting entirely outside it, albeit what he had done was what he had been counselled to do."

This is not to require that the encouragement, counselling, etc actually "made a difference" in influencing P to commit the offence: "it does not make any difference that the person [counselled] would have tried to commit suicide anyway."[74] As was stated in 6.4.1(2), P must have received and been aware of, say, encouragement by S, but the encouragement need not have played any further role.

6.4.3 Omissions

S may aid or abet an offence by omission.[75] Most obviously, this may occur where S's failure to discharge a legal duty assists P to commit an offence: for example, when the security guard at a warehouse deliberately fails to lock a door, intending that P may readily gain entry into the building and steal some of the goods stored inside.

Rather more problematic are cases where a person is held liable as a party for omitting to interfere and prevent an offence when she has a duty to do so and/or a power of control over the principal or the victim. Standard examples of this variety of abetment are said to occur if a parent permits another to commit an offence against her child, or if the owner of a car, while sitting in the passenger seat, permits the driver to break the law. However, these are not the same type of case.

Consider, first, the case where S, a parent, permits another to inflict fatal injuries upon his child when he is in a position to prevent the assault from taking place. In *R v Witika*,[76] the Court of Appeal had stated that such a person would be party to a culpable homicide if, by not intervening, S encouraged (and — the mens rea element — intended to encourage) the principal offender. As far as secondary liability is concerned, this understates the position. It is submitted that where S has a legal duty and the present ability to prevent V's death, his failure to do so, *in itself*, constitutes *aiding*, and not merely evidence of encouragement. The case is analogous to that of the warehouse security guard (above); in both examples, the conduct would be aiding whether or not P knew of the decision by S to refrain from performing

---

72   *R v Calhaem* [1985] QB 808; [1985] 2 All ER 266 (CA). S had hired P to murder her rival, V. It was said that P, after having second thoughts, had decided not to kill V but went to V's house in order to act out a pretence so that both S and V would think an attempt had been made to kill V. However, after V screamed, P apparently went "berserk" and killed V by hitting her several times with a hammer. On these facts, the Court of Appeal upheld S's conviction for counselling murder.
73   *R v Calhaem* [1985] QB 808; [1985] 2 All ER 266 (CA), 813; 269.
74   *A-G v Able* [1984] QB 795; [1984] 1 All ER 277, 812; 288 (Woolf J).
75   See, for example, *Ashton v Police* [1964] NZLR 429; *Theeman v Police* [1966] NZLR 605; *Cooper v MOT* [1991] 2 NZLR 693. For general discussion, see Finn, "Culpable non-intervention: Reconsidering the basis for party liability by omission" (1994) 18 Crim LJ 90.
76   *R v Witika* (1991) 7 CRNZ 621 (CA); *R v Witika* [1993] 2 NZLR 424; (1992) 9 CRNZ 272 (CA).

his duty. This view is now confirmed by the more recent decision of the Court of Appeal in *R v Brough*, where it is said:[77]

> "An intention to encourage is normally an essential ingredient: *R v Witika* (1991) 7 CRNZ 621 Cooke P at 622. However, this element is not always necessary. Liability for an omission will arise where A, who has a legal duty to act and a right or power of control over B, fails to observe or discharge the duty by exercising that control to prevent B committing an offence."

Indeed, arguably S is not merely a secondary party; he may be independently guilty of homicide as a principal. Provided that his intervention would have been causally efficacious in preventing the actus reus from occurring, it seems open to conclude that death results from his culpable failure to discharge his duty as a parent to intervene,[78] in which case this is a case of direct liability, as principal, for murder or manslaughter resulting from his omission to perform a legal duty.[79]

At the other end of the scale is the case where S, a stranger, chances upon the commission of a crime and remains to watch. As we have noted already (6.4.1(2)), such facts by themselves are insufficient to make S a party to the crime. In *R v Clarkson*,[80] two soldiers entered a room where a rape was taking place. They stayed to observe the events, purportedly without either encouraging or discouraging commission of the offence. The English Court of Appeal quashed their convictions for aiding and abetting. In the absence of actual and intended encouragement, their failure to intervene attracted no criminal liability, since they were under no duty to intervene.

The difficult case arises when S is not under a duty but has a legal power to control P's activity. Consider the facts of *Du Cros v Lambourne*, an English case.[81] S was the owner of a car that had been driven dangerously, but it was not clear whether S or his companion, P, was driving at the time. Nonetheless, S was convicted of being a party to dangerous driving, it being irrelevant whether he was principal or abettor. If P was driving, S had the legal power to direct the manner in which P drove; his acquiescence in the manner of P's driving was therefore held to constitute abetment of the offence of dangerous driving.

In England, *Du Cros v Lambourne* is generally taken as authority that failure by S to exercise a legal *power* (not duty) of control over P's activity may be, without more, constitutive of secondary participation in crime.[82] Hence there is no need to show that S's non-intervention actually assisted or encouraged P.

---

77 *R v Brough* 27/2/97, CA507/96, 10; followed in *R v Crossan* 7/7/98, Chisholm J, HC Invercargill T980970. Cf *R v Zizov* 12/11/03, Williams J, HC Auckland T031264, para 33.
78 This would require analysis of the case as involving concurrent causes (ie P's action and S's omission), rather than a novus actus by P. Yet such an approach seems plausible, provided that S is able to prevent P's conduct. This is not to criticise the actual outcome in *Witika*, as opposed to the legal analysis. Arguably (albeit a question of fact for the jury), on the particular facts of the case, one of the defendants was not in a position to prevent the violence. As such, her liability would have to be predicated on secondary participation.
79 The existence of such a duty is discussed at 3.2.1(2)(b).
80 *R v Clarkson* [1971] 3 All ER 344; [1971] 1 WLR 1402 (CA).
81 *Du Cros v Lambourne* [1907] 1 KB 40; followed in New Zealand in *Ashton v Police* [1964] NZLR 429. In New Zealand, owner-passengers in a vehicle may be a special case, in that they may fall within the scope of the statutory duty — not mere power — created by s 156 (duty of persons in charge of dangerous things). Cf *R v Crossan* 7/7/98, Chisholm J, HC Invercargill T980970.

However, is this the law in New Zealand? In 1964, the Supreme Court applied *Du Cros v Lambourne* without qualification.[83] But the implication of the Court of Appeal's decision in R v *Witika*[84] (above) is a resounding no. Not only must there be a failure to intervene, but the non-intervention must in fact encourage (and be intended to encourage) P in her commission of the offence. The scope of *Witika* has been limited by the subsequent decision in R v *Brough*,[85] so that a failure to intervene is sufficient *per se* when S is under a duty; but *Witika* — which, it must be emphasised, is a Court of Appeal decision and is therefore authoritative save to the extent that it is qualified by *Brough* — appears still to govern the case where S merely has a power to control P's conduct.

In light of *Witika* and *Brough*, we conclude that the current New Zealand law regarding omissions is as follows:

(i) If S has a *legal duty* to prevent an offence (for example, in the case of a parent to protect his child), then a failure by S to take reasonable steps to intervene *in itself* constitutes the actus reus of aiding. (Indeed, if causation can be established, S may be guilty as a principal.)

(ii) If S has neither a duty nor a particular power, then he must intend by his non-intervention to encourage P and, in fact, his inaction must also encourage P.

(iii) If S has a power of control over P, but no particular legal duty, it seems that the position is the same as in (ii): he must intend by his non-intervention to encourage P and, in fact, his inaction must also encourage P.

It is category (iii) that is controversial. If *Witika* is right, such persons are in exactly the same legal position as the onlookers to the rape in *Clarkson* or the casual spectators at a prizefight in R v *Coney*.[86]

There are arguments in favour of this conclusion. To impose liability in such cases is, effectively, to extend criminal liability for omissions. As we saw in chapter 3, the law is reluctant to impose liability for omissions, and for good reason. Forcing persons to intervene and regulate the actions of others (for example, requiring property owners to police the actions of users) substantially widens the umbrella of criminal responsibility for wrongdoing and, in turn, risks intruding severely upon the autonomy of citizens.[87] Thus the New Zealand position, as asserted in R v *Witika*, is not without justification.

---

82   In fact, the judgments in *Du Cros v Lambourne* are equivocal on the point. Darling J appears to have regarded non-intervention as abetment per se ([1907] 1 KB 40, 46-47); Lord Alverstone CJ, with whom Ridley J agreed, refused to "attempt to lay down any general rule or principle, but having regard to these findings of fact, it is, in my opinion, impossible to say that there was in this case no evidence of aiding and abetting" (at 46). Compare too *Cassady v Reg Morris Transport Ltd* [1975] RTR 470; [1975] Crim LR 398, where it was held that an employer's failure to forbid an offence by its employee was merely *evidence* (and not constitutive) of encouragement.

83   *Ashton v Police* [1964] NZLR 429. Cf *Cooper v MOT* [1991] 2 NZLR 693, 698; contrast, however, *George v Police* (1989) 5 CRNZ 411, 413.

84   R v *Witika* (1991) 7 CRNZ 621 (CA); R v *Witika* [1993] 2 NZLR 424; (1992) 9 CRNZ 272 (CA).

85   R v *Brough* 27/2/97, CA507/96.

86   R v *Coney* (1882) 8 QBD 534; see 6.4.1(2).

87   For elaboration of this argument, see 3.2.1(1), 1.3.1, 1.3.2(5). See also S Bronitt, "Defending *Giorgianni*: Part two: New solutions for old problems in complicity" (1993) 17 Crim LJ 305, 310-311.

On the other hand, it is arguable that the English position is to be preferred. In the difficult case, S is not a mere stranger, a passer-by who stumbles upon a crime that she is under no duty to prevent. Although there is no general obligation to prevent crime,[88] it seems reasonable to conclude that those with the legal power to prevent a crime *do* contribute to — hence, participate in — the wrongdoing by refraining from exercising their authority and, thus, deliberately permitting that crime to occur.[89]

6.4.4 Mens rea for participation under s 66(1)(b)-(d)

The mens rea for secondary participation (by assisting or encouraging)[90] is intention: S must intend to participate in the crime committed by P. Stated in this way, the fault element appears straightforward. However, it is in fact quite complex, because the mens rea element must relate to two different matters: S's own conduct, in assisting or encouraging P, and the fact that P's actions are criminal in nature. We may summarise the mens rea requirement as follows.

(i) S must intend his own contribution (ie to aid, abet, incite, counsel, or procure P); and

(ii) S must know the nature of P's actions. That is, S must know the "essential matters" relating to P's actions which make those actions an offence.

(1) *S's own contribution: the intention to aid, abet, incite, or counsel*

The essence of aiding and abetting is intentional help or encouragement.[91] This means that not only must S intend her actions, but she must also act with the intent thereby to aid, abet, incite, counsel, or procure P's conduct. It is therefore insufficient that S is reckless whether P is assisted or encouraged: mere knowledge that her actions are likely to aid or abet P's conduct does not establish the intent required under s 66(1).[92]

The criteria of intention are considered at 4.2. In the context of s 66(1), there is no requirement for S to desire that P commit the offence she aids (abets, etc). It is the *assistance* or the *encouragement*, not the ultimate crime, that must be intended by S.[93] Consider, for example, the following facts, which are based on *R v Wentworth*:[94]

> S is a pharmacist. He sells large quantities of Panadeine tablets to P, which he knows P will use to try to manufacture heroin. S does not sell the Panadeine because he wants P

---

88 Cf *R v Allan* [1965] 1 QB 130; [1963] 2 All ER 897 (CCA).
89 In any event, the gulf between power and duty is easily bridged. Where S has a supervisory role, for example as the instructor of a learner-driver, it seems that a mere omission to intervene is sufficient to establish liability as a secondary party and that the instructor is under a duty (and does not merely have a right) to intervene and prevent a dangerous manoeuvre by the learner-driver: *Rubie v Faulkner* [1940] 1 KB 571; [1940] 1 All ER 285; see Wasik, "A learner's careless driving" [1982] Crim LR 411; Lanham, "Drivers, control, and accomplices" [1982] Crim LR 419. In *Tuck v Robson* [1970] 1 All ER 1171, 1175, a public house licensee was held to have assisted others in drinking after hours through "passive assistance", which the Court defined as "presence with no steps being taken to enforce his right either to eject the customers or at any rate to revoke their licence to be on the premises". The decision is problematic: although the Court relied on the publican's "right" (ie power) and did not use the language of duties, the decision effectively imposes a duty on the publican to revoke his customers' licence. Seemingly, that duty rests on nothing other than the existence of a corresponding power.
90 For the mens rea requirements of participation by joint enterprise, see 6.5.1-6.5.2.
91 *R v Samuels* [1985] 1 NZLR 350 (CA).
92 *R v Pene* 1/7/80, CA63/80, p 5. For the distinction between intention and foresight, see 4.2.3.
93 *R v Singh* 10/12/03, CA53/03; CA67/03.
94 *R v Wentworth* [1993] 2 NZLR 450, also reported as *R v Richards [aiding and abetting]* (1992) 9 CRNZ 355.

to manufacture heroin, but rather because he wants the money that P is prepared to pay for the tablets.

The claim that S does not want or intend P to manufacture heroin is irrelevant. It may be characterised as a claim about S's motive, or ultimate purpose, which is of course to make money. But what matters is whether he intended to assist P. The answer to that question is yes: S intended to provide P with the essential ingredient for manufacturing heroin, *knowing* that this very act would, without more, assist P in his efforts. It is that *help*, not the ultimate offence, that must be intended;[95] whether that aid is itself rendered for the further purpose of bringing about the offence is simply beside the point.

It might be thought that s 66(1)(b) imposes a narrower requirement than intention, at least in respect of participation by aiding. The subsection specifies that every person is a party to an offence if she "does or omits an act *for the purpose* of aiding any person to commit the offence". In *Wentworth*, counsel for the defendant sought to argue that use of the term "purpose" implies a stricter mens rea standard: that S's assistance should be motivated by a desire that the offence itself be committed.

Fisher J rejected counsel's submission,[96] and rightly so. The crucial test under s 66(1)(b) is whether S's action is taken for the purpose of aiding. In this context, "purpose" adds nothing to "intention", and, like intention, S may have more than one purpose when she acts. There is no requirement under s 66(1) that S's purpose of aiding be the sole, primary, or motivating reason for her behaviour — indeed, the limitation proposed by counsel in *Richards* would deprive s 66 of much of its role, excluding secondary parties whenever they have some further reason (for example payment or fear)[97] explaining why they assisted.

On the other hand, the help must be *intended*; that is, as we saw in chapter 4, S must act either in order to help P or being virtually certain that P will be aided by that act. Recklessness is insufficient. Thus it would not be enough for secondary liability that S merely thinks it is likely P may be assisted. Suppose, for example, the following variation:

> S is an auctioneer of various goods. At auction, she sells an unlabelled box of goods to P, a wholesaler. Because the goods are in bond, she is unsure (ie reckless) whether the box contains Panadeine. S knows that P has plans to manufacture heroin.

On these facts, S lacks the mens rea for secondary participation because she is merely reckless whether P is assisted or encouraged.

(2)   *S's own contribution: the intention to procure*

In respect of S's intending her own contribution, procurement is a special case. By contrast with assistance and encouragement, the connection is necessarily tighter. S must still be proved to have intended her act of procurement. However, because procurement requires a causal contribution that influences or induces P to commit the crime, it follows that S must intend to help bring it about that P will commit the crime itself. For this reason, it was said by the

---

95   Cf *National Coal Board v Gamble* [1959] 1 QB 11; [1958] 3 All ER 203; *Lynch v DPP for Northern Ireland* [1975] AC 653; [1975] 1 All ER 913 (HL); *A-G v Able* [1984] QB 795; [1984] 1 All ER 277.
96   *R v Wentworth* [1993] 2 NZLR 450, also reported as *R v Richards* (1992) 9 CRNZ 355, 454-455, 458; 362, 363.
97   Cf *R v Joyce* [1968] NZLR 1070 (CA); *R v Pollock* [1973] 2 NZLR 491 (CA). However, such fear may be sufficient to underpin a defence of compulsion within s 24: see chapter 12.

English Court of Appeal in *A-G's Reference (No 1 of 1975)*[98] that, unlike aiding, abetting, inciting, or counselling, procuring an offence requires an "endeavour" or "setting out" to cause the commission of the offence.

(3) *P's criminal conduct: "knowledge" of essential matters*

The classic statement of this requirement is to be found in *Johnson v Youden*, where it was said that:[99]

> "Before a person can be convicted of aiding and abetting the commission of an offence he must at least know the essential matters which constitute that offence."

Two issues arise: (i) what degree of "knowledge" must S have, and (ii) what "essential matters" of an offence must S know about?

The meaning of "knowledge" is considered at 4.5: S must accept, or assume, and have no substantial doubt that the relevant facts are true.[100] There must be actual knowledge: it is not enough that S *ought* to have known the facts.[101] Neither is it sufficient if S *suspects* that they may well be true, even if accompanied by a failure to inquire into the facts;[102] although in the special case of wilful blindness, S will be treated as having knowledge.[103]

This analysis would exclude from liability a person who renders assistance to P believing that P may be about to commit a crime but not knowing that he will. Mere belief in the possible existence of a set of facts amounts to recklessness, not intention.[104] Consider the following variant of an example used in 6.4.4(1):

> S is a pharmacist. He sells a quantity of Panadeine tablets to P. S does not sell the Panadeine because he wants P to manufacture heroin, but rather because he wants the money that P is prepared to pay for the tablets. However, this time S is unsure whether P intends to use the Panadeine to treat her and her family's illnesses or to manufacture heroin. In fact, P does use the Panadeine (combined with tablets purchased elsewhere) to manufacture heroin.

On these facts, S is merely reckless about the essential facts of the crime ultimately committed by P. Assuming S does not satisfy the criteria of wilful blindness,[105] he does not *know* those facts. As such, according to the criteria laid down in *Johnson v Youdan* (above), S is innocent of secondary participation in P's crime.

There appears to be one qualification to this requirement, applying to knowledge in respect of facts that are unknowable to S, such as future circumstances or P's future conduct. In these instances, it seems that knowledge of the probable existence of such facts will suffice.[106]

---

98 *A-G's Reference (No 1 of 1975)* [1975] QB 773; [1975] 2 All ER 684 (CA), 779.
99 *Johnson v Youden* [1950] 1 KB 544; [1950] 1 All ER 300, 546; 302. Cf *R v Churchill* [1967] 2 AC 224 (HL), 236-7; *DPP for Northern Ireland v Maxwell* [1978] 3 All ER 1140; [1978] 1 WLR 1350 (HL). For general discussion of this requirement in New Zealand, see *Cooper v MOT* [1991] 2 NZLR 693.
100 *Giorgianni v R* (1985) 156 CLR 473; 58 ALR 641 (HCA).
101 *Halaunga v Police* 17/12/04, Winkelman J, HC Auckland CRI-2003-404-232, para 25.
102 *R v Crooks* [1981] 2 NZLR 53 (CA); *Millar v MOT* [1986] 1 NZLR 660; (1986) 2 CRNZ 216 (CA), 674; 230.
103 The doctrine of wilful blindness is examined at 4.5.1.
104 See 4.2.3, 4.5.
105 See 4.5.1.

Although the foregoing states the relevant law, the merits of requiring knowledge rather than recklessness have been doubted. *Adams* questions:[107]

> "whether, as a general requirement, such a degree of knowledge should be necessary for there to be an intention to help or encourage the principal party.... While a secondary party must know of any relevant circumstance where knowledge is required of the principal party, it is difficult to see why recklessness should not be sufficient for a secondary party when it suffices for the principal party. A fortiori, belief in the probable existence of a circumstance [ie an 'essential matter'] should satisfy the mental element for a secondary party where neither knowledge nor recklessness in respect of that circumstance is required of the principal party."

With respect, however, the basis of secondary liability is different from that of a principal. There is no suggestion that the secondary party actually commits the offence himself or that he satisfies the actus reus requirements of the relevant crime. The actus reus element of secondary participation is entirely independent of the actus reus of the principal offence. This being so, there seems no reason why the mens rea requirement for participation should be determined by that principal offence. Moreover, derivative liability of any variety involves widening the net of the criminal law beyond those who actually perpetrate offences: not only may S not strike V, she may not do anything to help anyone else strike V either.[108] Because of this widening, the grounds of derivative liability ought correspondingly to be constricted, in order to prevent excessive criminalisation of conduct that does not itself cause a criminal harm. Otherwise, over-criminalisation may lead, in turn, to a disproportionate intrusion upon the freedoms of citizens who do not themselves commit crimes, forcing them constantly to modify their own actions because of the potential conduct of others.

(4)   *P's criminal conduct: what "essential matters" must S know about?*

It is also a difficult question what aspects of P's crime count as "essential matters", such that they must be known by S. The following propositions may be asserted.

First, S must know that P intends or contemplates doing actions which constitute the actus reus of an offence, although S need not recognise that those actions in fact constitute an offence.[109] Secondly, S need not know all the details of the proposed offence, such as the time or place of its commission.[110] However, mere knowledge that "something illegal" is intended by P is not enough.[111] S must at least know either:

(i)   The *type* of offence intended (and eventually committed) by P;[112] or

---

106 See *Cooper v MOT* [1991] 2 NZLR 693, which otherwise appears to accept the requirement of knowledge in *Giorgianni v R* (1985) 156 CLR 473; 58 ALR 641 (HCA); *R v Rees* [1990] 1 NZLR 555; (1990) 5 CRNZ 487 (CA), 558; 489. In *R v Bryce* [2004] EWCA Crim 1231, [2004] 2 Cr App R 35, para 49, it is suggested that foresight of a "real possibility" will suffice in respect of crimes yet to be committed; but see Simester, "The Mental Element in Complicity" (2006) 122 LQR 578, 585-7.
107 *Adams*, CA66.19(1)(b) (looseleaf).
108 See 1.3.2(5).
109 *Cardin Laurant Ltd v Commerce Commission* [1990] 3 NZLR 563; (1989) 3 TCLR 470, 569; 477.
110 *R v Baker* (1909) 28 NZLR 536 (CA); *R v Witika* [1993] 2 NZLR 424; (1992) 9 CRNZ 272 (CA). Cf s 70(1), discussed at 6.4.4(4)(a).
111 *R v Bainbridge* [1960] 1 QB 129; [1959] 3 All ER 200 (CCA); *R v Scott* (1979) 68 Cr App R 164 (CA).
112 *R v Baker* (1909) 28 NZLR 536 (CA); *R v Bainbridge* [1960] 1 QB 129; [1959] 3 All ER 200 (CCA).

(ii) That P was likely to commit any one of a number of offences, the "list" of which includes the type of offence that eventually was committed.[113]

The leading decision which states these criteria is that of the Court of Appeal in *R v Kimura*.[114] In that case, S was charged with aiding and abetting aggravated burglary, as defined now in s 240A(1)(b). The principal offence consisted, essentially, of burglary accompanied by possession or use of a weapon by P, and the Court of Appeal ruled that it was a misdirection for the trial judge to state that S need not know P had a weapon with him. Instead, the Court held that possession or use of a weapon was an "essential element" of the offence of aggravated burglary, and that aggravated burglary could therefore not be regarded as being of the same *type* as simple burglary. S could only be convicted as a party to aggravated burglary if, as well as knowing that P contemplated a burglary, he also knew that P would have a weapon with him at the time.[115]

(a) Other variations within a type

Suppose that P plans to set fire to V's house. Knowing the details of the plan, S helps P by giving him V's address. P goes to the house, then changes his mind and instead sets fire to V's car. Is S guilty of arson? Yes. At common law, incidental variations of detail such as time and place are immaterial since they do not alter the type of crime committed by P (and assisted by S).[116] Therefore, because P commits the same offence (arson) either way, S's liability is normally unaffected by this variation. This conclusion is reinforced by s 70(1), which confirms that a secondary party remains liable even though the principal commits the offence "in a way different from that which was incited, counselled, or suggested."

The exception is if S's assistance or encouragement is directed specifically to the aspect of P's offence that was varied. In such cases, even though that aspect be immaterial to P's guilt, it becomes essential to S's complicity. For example, suppose that S counsels P to murder a particular person, V; but P, having set out to kill V, then changes his mind and decides instead to kill W. At common law, S is not a party to the murder of W.[117] It is otherwise if the identity of the victim to be killed — or the identity of the property to be fired, in our earlier example — were of no particular relevance to S's intervention. Thus, for instance, if P were to receive S's help with obtaining a weapon in order to kill someone ("as it happens, X"), S would still be liable when Y is shot instead.

It is undecided whether in New Zealand this common law exception is overridden by s 70(1). It is submitted, however, that s 70(1) *should* extend to such cases, so that S is nonetheless liable despite the variation. Since the difference between shooting V and shooting W is

---

113 *DPP for Northern Ireland v Maxwell* [1978] 3 All ER 1140; [1978] 1 WLR 1350 (HL); *R v Wentworth* 26/5/93, CA10/93, 12-13.
114 *R v Kimura* (1992) 9 CRNZ 115 (CA).
115 While the decision in *Kimura* was restricted to participation under s 66(1), the same conclusion was reached in respect of s 66(2) participation in *R v Mokaraka* [2002] 1 NZLR 793, (2001) 19 CRNZ 316 (CA), paras 22-23; below, 6.5.2.
116 *R v Bainbridge* [1960] 1 QB 129; [1959] 3 All ER 200 (CCA); *R v Baker* (1909) 28 NZLR 536 (CA); *R v Witika* [1993] 2 NZLR 424; (1992) 9 CRNZ 272 (CA).
117 *R v Saunders and Archer* (1573) 2 Plowd 473, 75 ER 706; *R v Leahy* [1985] Crim LR 99; *S v Robinson* 1968 (1) SA 666; Hawkins, 2 PC ch 29, ss 20, 21; Foster, *Crown Law*, Oxfordshire, Professional Books Ltd, 1982, 369; Stephen, *A Digest of the Criminal Law (indictable offences)* (5th ed), London, Sweet and Maxwell Ltd, 1894, art 43. For criticism of this rule, see Smith, *A Modern Treatise on the Law of Criminal Complicity* (1991) 200ff; Clarkson, "Complicity, Powell and Manslaughter" [1998] Crim LR 556, 559.

immaterial to the definition of murder, the variation would seem to be covered by the doctrine of transferred malice.[118] It is murder of any human being, and participation therein, that the law criminalises; not murder of a particular person. In principle, since the identity of the victim does not matter to P's liability for murder, neither should it make a difference to the liability of S.[119]

In any event, S remains liable if the variation is unintentional. Suppose that P does not change his mind, and carries out his attempt to shoot V. Unfortunately, he mistakes W for V and kills W. Here, the transferred malice doctrine applies to S as well as P, and both S and P are guilty of murdering W.

(b)   Mens rea of the principal

P's mens rea is also an essential matter. S must know that P will do the actus reus with the level of mens rea required for it to amount to an offence. S cannot abet murder, for example, if S recognises that P is likely to kill V negligently, since negligence is insufficient mens rea for P to be guilty of murder.[120] Similarly, if P's offence requires proof of an ulterior intention, S must be aware of that intent by P.[121] To illustrate: on a charge of abetting possession of a controlled drug for sale or supply,[122] S would have to know not only about P's possession, but also about her purpose of sale or supply.[123]

(c)   Strict liability for consequences of P's conduct

Many offences contain a mixture of actus reus elements where, for some of those elements, the prosecution must prove mens rea on the part of the principal and, for other actus reus elements, no mens rea is required. In the context of secondary liability, those consequences to which the fault requirement does not extend are not normally regarded as essential matters of the offence. For example, S need not foresee the consequence (death) in order to abet the offence of "dangerous driving causing death". For the purposes of secondary participation, only the dangerous driving counts as an essential element.[124] Effectively, this means that the strict liability element (ie the fatal consequence) is not regarded as changing the type of offence. Thus "dangerous driving" and "dangerous driving causing death" are variant offences within the same type, and application of the principle in *Kimura*[125] means that S need only anticipate P's dangerous driving in order to be exposed to liability for either offence.

However, the rule applies even in offences where the strict liability element arguably does change the type of offence. If S aids or abets P to inflict a common assault upon V, and V dies, both S and P are guilty of manslaughter even though neither may have foreseen the

---

118   See 4.8.
119   One possible distinction, which would confine the common law exception, might be drawn between assistance and encouragement. Arguably, assistance should always be covered by the transferred malice doctrine, but encouragement (say) to murder V can be expressed in such confined terms that it does not encourage murder generally, ie of anyone else.
120   *R v Chignell* [1991] 2 NZLR 257, also reported as *R v Chignell and Walker* (1990) 6 CRNZ 103 (CA); *R v Hamilton* [1985] 2 NZLR 245 (CA). See Dennis, "The mental element for accessories" in Smith (ed), *Criminal Law: Essays in Honour of J C Smith*, London, Butterworths, 1987, 40, 46-47, 55.
121   *DPP for Northern Ireland v Maxwell* [1978] 3 All ER 1140; [1978] 1 WLR 1350 (HL).
122   Contrary to the Misuse of Drugs Act 1975.
123   *R v Samuels* [1985] 1 NZLR 350 (CA); followed in *R v Hill* [2004] 2 NZLR 145 (CA).
124   *Giorgianni v R* (1985) 156 CLR 473; 58 ALR 641 (HCA).
125   *R v Kimura* (1992) 9 CRNZ 115 (CA); above, 6.4.4.

prospect of V's death. P is guilty because causing death by an unlawful act satisfies the required elements of manslaughter as a principal;[126] upon proof of the criminal assault, death is a strict liability element. Correspondingly, death is not an "essential matter" for the purposes of S's secondary liability.[127] Thus V's death need be foreseen by neither P nor S.

(d)   Strict liability for circumstantial elements of the actus reus

The foregoing rule about strict liability elements is restricted to *consequences*. It does not apply to any circumstances which form part of the gravamen of the principal's actus reus, even if those circumstantial elements are a matter of strict liability vis-à-vis the principal.[128] Thus, in the offence of making a false representation in the course of trading in supply of goods or services, contrary to s 13(a) Fair Trading Act 1986, it is not necessary to prove that the principal knew the representation to be false. Nonetheless, in *Megavitamin Laboratories (NZ) Ltd v Commerce Commission*, Tipping J followed common law authority in ruling that it was not "necessary or desirable to extend the concept of strict liability to secondary offenders".[129] This seems right in principle. Secondary liability extends the net of the criminal law beyond direct wrongdoing, to ensnare parties whose conduct is ostensibly innocent — those who, for instance, merely typeset the representation, or carry the proofs to the printer. Such persons should not be required to go about their ordinary activities at the risk of being made criminals when, in the absence of mens rea, they have no way of knowing or controlling their liability.[130]

6.5   Secondary parties pursuant to a common intention: s 66(2)

In 6.4, we considered the standard forms of secondary participation that are mentioned expressly in s 66(1). Under that section, liability is established on the basis that the offender assists or encourages the principal by aiding, abetting, inciting, counselling, or procuring the relevant offence. As an accessory, S knows the essential facts of the offence charged and intends to assist or encourage the principal in committing the offence.

In principle, s 66(1) involves a single offence: ie, the offence that is both deliberately aided (or abetted, etc) by S and ultimately committed by P. Section 66(2) contemplates "joint enterprise" liability in a different situation, typically involving two offences: ie an offence (A) that S and P jointly undertake, and the offence (B) that P commits. The secondary party need not know the facts that constitute the offence (B) with which, ultimately, he is charged. He becomes a party to the offence if he foresaw that its commission was a "probable consequence" of proceeding with the original plan to commit some different crime (A), even though he may not have intended or even been directly involved in the commission of that further, or "collateral", offence that P perpetrated. For example:

> P and S agree to commit a burglary. Together they break into V's home. In the course of the burglary, P is challenged by V whom he attacks. S does not participate physically in the assault. However, S knew that P had a propensity toward violence and realised that

---
126   See 16.5.2(1).
127   *R v Rapira* [2003] 3 NZLR 794; (2003) 20 CRNZ 396 (CA); *R v Renata* [1992] 2 NZLR 346; (1991) 7 CRNZ 616 (CA). Cf *R v Creamer* [1966] 1 QB 72; *R v Swindall and Osborne* (1846) 2 Car & Kir 230; 2 Cox CC 141; 175 ER 95.
128   *Callow v Tillstone* (1900) 83 LT 411, 19 Cox 576; *Yorke v Lucas* (1985) 158 CLR 661 (HCA).
129   *Megavitamin Laboratories (NZ) Ltd v Commerce Commission* (1995) 6 TCLR 231; 5 NZBLC 103,834, 249; 103,849.
130   Simester, "The Mental Element in Complicity" (2006) 122 LQR 578.

P was likely to attack the occupier of the house were they to be confronted. S is guilty, with P, of assault.

It matters not that S did not intend that an assault should be committed; nor that S was uncertain whether the assault would occur; nor that S did not intend to help or encourage its commission. Liability arises because S has participated in a criminal enterprise with P, pursuant to which P has committed a further, "collateral", offence which S knew might occur. In simple terms, we may say that the parties set out to commit one crime and become liable for a different one. The difference between the two varieties of secondary participation, in so far as the mental element is concerned, is that assisting or encouraging under s 66(1) requires knowledge plus an intention to assist or encourage, whereas for joint enterprise within s 66(2), a knowledge of probability suffices.[131] It is irrelevant under s 66(2) that S did not intend to assist or encourage crime B.[132] In so far as the conduct element is concerned, the difference is that there is no need to show specifically that S assisted or encouraged the second offence.

Under s 66(2), the elements of joint enterprise liability are:

(i) S and P form a joint enterprise ("a common purpose") to commit crime A;

(ii) S foresees that, in the course of the joint enterprise to commit crime A, P may well commit the essential elements of crime B (with the requisite mens rea for that crime);

(iii) P commits crime B;

(iv) The commission of crime B occurs as an incident of ("in the prosecution of") the joint enterprise and not in a manner that departs completely from the prosecution of S and P's common purpose.

If these requirements are met, then in addition to any liability S may have for conspiracy to commit a crime, and as a principal or secondary party to crime A (should that crime be perpetrated), S will be liable as a party to crime B. Indeed, where S and P form a common purpose to commit a crime, S is liable for every offence P committed in carrying out that purpose which S knew to be a probable consequence of carrying out the common purpose.

We discuss the main elements of s 66(2) in 6.5.1-6.5.3.

6.5.1 A common unlawful purpose

Section 66(2) requires that there be a common intention between the parties "to prosecute any unlawful purpose, and to assist each other therein". S and P must, therefore, share an intention to commit a crime.[133] However, there is no need for the prosecution to prove a formal or explicit agreement, or any prearrangement at all: it is sufficient even if the mutual intention between S and P arises only at the time the offence is being committed.[134]

Nonetheless, it is not enough that S and P both happen to have the same intention at the same time. That intention must be shared. Consider the following example, put by Sir John Smith:[135]

---

131 See Orchard, "Parties to an offence: The function of s 66(2) of the Crimes Act" [1988] NZLJ 151.
132 *R v Curtis* [1988] 1 NZLR 734 (CA); *R v Hamilton* [1985] 2 NZLR 245 (CA).
133 In principle, a civil wrong (such as a tort) is insufficient. Cf *R v Seiffert* (1999) 104 A Crim R 238; *R v Franklin* (1883) 15 Cox CC 163.
134 *R v Vang* (1999) 132 CCC (3d) 32; 21 CR (5th) 260 (Ont CA); *R v O'Flaherty* [2004] EWCA Crim 526; [2004] 2 Cr App R 20.

"S and P see a policeman [V] approaching, they exchange glances, and S goes for the officer while P stands by, ready to intervene if S seems to need his assistance. There is now evidence on which a jury could find an agreement to collaborate in the commission of the offence, a joint enterprise. If P knocks down the second approaching policeman, S will be liable for that assault."

Here, there is no difficulty about finding that S and P had a *common* intention. But suppose, in Smith's example, there had been no mutual understanding reached between P and S but that P had merely decided, spontaneously, to assist S by knocking down the second policeman and preventing him from stopping S's assault. In that case, each would intend that V be assaulted by S, yet there would be no joint enterprise. P would be liable for S's assault under ordinary principles of aiding and abetting. However, S would not be liable for the assault committed by P.

6.5.2 Known to be a probable consequence

The mens rea requirement is subjective: S must actually foresee the likelihood that P will commit the essential matters of the collateral offence (crime B).[136] A convenient illustration of this is provided by *R v Mokaraka*.[137] S, P, and others jointly committed a burglary by unlawfully entering a house in Auckland in an attempt to steal drugs. P, however, carried with him a knife, which made his offence one of aggravated burglary.[138] The Court of Appeal ruled that possession of a weapon was an essential element of aggravated burglary. Hence, for S also to be guilty of the greater offence, he must have foreseen the probability that one of the group would be carrying a weapon. Since S may have been unaware that P or anyone else had brought a weapon with him, his conviction was quashed and a retrial ordered.

On the other hand, in the context of s 66(2) knowledge of probability does not require S to think that P's commission of the offence is "more likely than not". It is sufficient that S recognises that the offence may well be committed; that it is "a substantial or real risk" or an event that "could well happen".[139] However, S will lack mens rea under s 66(2) if she thinks the risk is negligible or only remotely possible.[140]

There are two qualifications to this general rule. First, there is no requirement that S must have foreseen the precise manner in which crime B is committed. She need only recognise that an offence of that type is probable.[141]

Secondly, there is Court of Appeal authority that S's foresight of crime B need not include foresight of any consequences that are actus reus elements of crime B but for which no mens rea element is required of P. Just as under s 66(1), such elements are not regarded as "essential"

---

135 *R v Petters and Parfitt* [1995] Crim LR 501 (CA), 502. (The characters' names are substituted.)
136 In earlier Acts, the predecessor of s 66(2) included offences that "ought to have been" known to be a probable consequences. These words were omitted in s 66(2). See *R v Pope* 31/5/88, CA305/87.
137 *R v Mokaraka* [2002] 1 NZLR 793; (2001) 19 CRNZ 316 (CA).
138 Contrary to then s 240A(1)(a), which made it an offence if a person "while ... unlawfully entering a building ... with intent to commit a crime therein, has any weapon with him." Contrast the lesser offence under the then s 242, committed if a person "unlawfully enters ... any building ... with intent to commit any crime therein."
139 *R v Gush* [1980] 2 NZLR 92 (CA); *R v Tomkins* [1985] 2 NZLR 253; (1985) 1 CRNZ 627 (CA); *R v Hamilton* [1985] 2 NZLR 245 (CA), 250-252.
140 *R v Piri* [1987] 1 NZLR 66 (CA), 79; *R v Hamilton* [1985] 2 NZLR 245 (CA), 250-252.
141 *R v Emery* [1996] DCR 374.

for the purposes of secondary liability.[142] In *R v Tuhoro*,[143] P had shot V while robbing a bottlestore, intending to cause V grievous bodily harm. V died. Under s 168(1)(a), these facts were sufficient to make P guilty of murder irrespective of whether he foresaw the risk that V may die. S, a participant in the joint enterprise of robbery, was also charged with murder. The jury was directed that S was guilty of murder by virtue of s 66(2) if he knew that it was probable (ie there was a real risk) that P would cause grievous bodily harm to facilitate the robbery. On appeal, the Court of Appeal affirmed the correctness of this direction. Since there is no requirement that P foresees death in s 168(1)(a), in the Court's view there should be no such requirement for S either.[144]

6.5.3 In the prosecution of the common purpose

Section 66(2) makes S party to only those offences P commits *in the prosecution of* their common purpose; ie, as an incident of or adjunct to their pursuit of that purpose. It follows that S is not guilty of offences P commits after the joint enterprise has been concluded.[145] In *R v Hubbard*,[146] S and P had agreed to burgle premises but had not agreed to set fire to those premises once the burglary was completed. S was held not to be a party to the arson by P.

As well as temporal contiguity, the requirement that crime B be committed in the prosecution of the common purpose generates one further constraint. P's actions must be of the same *type* that S foresees and must not be "fundamentally different" from those S recognises to be possible incidents of the enterprise. According to the Court of Appeal in *R v Te Moni*:[147]

> "It is of course possible for the principal offender to step right outside the boundaries of the common purpose, for example by committing a rape while engaged in a routine robbery. In order to fulfil the object of subs (2), that is to fix secondary parties with liability for offences within their contemplation, carried out in the prosecution of the common unlawful purpose, the 'prosecution' should encompass everything the particular secondary party contemplated as a reasonable (although not a remote) *adjunct* of the core of the unlawful enterprise. See *R v Powell*, per Lord Hutton at pp 556-557."

Where P's actions depart completely from the common design, therefore, it appears S is not liable as a party to those egregious actions. This appears to have happened in the House of Lords case of *R v English*, one of the appeals decided together with *R v Powell*,[148] to which reference is made in *Te Moni*. The facts of *English* were as follows:

> "S and P jointly attacked a police officer with wooden posts, causing injury. During the attack, P produced a knife and stabbed the police officer. The officer died of the

---

142 Above, 6.4.4(4)(c)-(d).
143 *R v Tuhoro* [1998] 3 NZLR 568; (1998) 15 CRNZ 568 (CA). Cf *R v Rapira* [2003] 3 NZLR 794; (2003) 20 CRNZ 396 (CA), paras 21-7.
144 Notwithstanding the attractive argument to the contrary by Orchard, "Strict liability and parties to murder and manslaughter" [1997] NZLJ 93, which was not accepted by the Court.
145 Note that the duration of the *common purpose* includes acts subsequent to the purposed *crime* but which are integral to the common purpose, such as escaping from the scene: cf *R v Raw* (1984) 12 A Crim R 299 (WA CA); *R v Seiffert* (1999) 104 A Crim R 238.
146 *R v Hubbard* (1990) 6 CRNZ 80.
147 *R v Te Moni* [1998] 1 NZLR 641; (1997) 15 CRNZ 439 (CA), 650; 448. (Emphasis added.)
148 *R v Powell*; *R v English* [1999] 1 AC 1; [1997] 4 All ER 545 (HL) (6.5.2). Cf *R v Gamble* [1989] NI 268.

stab wound. Apparently S had not known that P was carrying a knife and had not foreseen the stabbing."

The House of Lords ruled that the stabbing was not incidental to the joint enterprise, as contemplated by S. According to Lord Hutton:[149]

> "the secondary party must foresee an act of the type which the principal party committed, and in the present case the use of a knife was fundamentally different to the use of a wooden post."

The courts have not yet specified with precision the test of when P's actions fall outside the prosecution of the common purpose. One example of an offence falling outside the scope of s 66(2) is given in *Te Moni*,[150] when, during an agreed robbery, P unexpectedly commits a rape. Perhaps the same conclusion would be reached if, during the robbery, P encounters an old enemy and murders her in order to satisfy a grudge (ie for reasons unconnected to the robbery). Conversely, the infliction of bodily injury likely to cause death has been held to be a foreseeable adjunct to the parties' common unlawful purpose of burglary, kidnapping, and robbery.[151]

So far as can be discerned from the cases to date, there seem to be two types of situations where P's acts will be regarded as a fundamental departure from the common purpose. The first, illustrated by the example given in *Te Moni*, occurs where P unexpectedly commits a crime of a completely different type from that purposed. In this situation S will be acquitted of the further offence by P, unless the risk of such a crime is a natural or inherent risk of the prosecution of their common purpose (and is foreseen as such by S). The second type of case is that seen in *English*, where P perpetrates an act of a type contemplated by S, but in an unexpected and radically more dangerous fashion (eg by using a knife instead of a fencepost to commit an assault, with death resulting).[152] However, at least under New Zealand law,[153] in this latter case S may still be convicted of a lesser offence in respect of the consequence caused by P.

(1)   *Conviction for a lesser offence?*

Even where P goes beyond the scope of the common purpose, S may still be guilty of a lesser offence if that lesser offence was known to be a probable consequence of the prosecution of their common purpose. In *R v Tomkins*,[154] for example, S planned with P and another to rob a taxi driver. They armed themselves with knives, apparently solely in order to intimidate and without any intent to kill. After the robbery was carried out, they forced the driver to drive to a deserted spot where P stabbed and killed him while S stood alongside. On these facts, P was convicted of murder and S of manslaughter. Even though S apparently had not known that P

---

149   *R v Powell; R v English* [1999] 1 AC 1; [1997] 4 All ER 545 (HL), 20; 564.
150   *R v Te Moni* [1998] 1 NZLR 641; (1997) 15 CRNZ 439 (CA), 650; 448. S's liability in that case was upheld, on somewhat bizarre facts: although P appeared *also* to have a plan of his own (suicide), he was still prosecuting the agreed-upon robbery when he killed the bank teller who sought to overpower him.
151   *R v Pham* 6/7/98, Williams J, HC Auckland T98/98.
152   The relative dangerousness of P's actions is emphasised not only in *R v Powell; R v English* [1999] 1 AC 1; [1997] 4 All ER 545 (HL), 30; 566, but also in *R v Greatrex* [1999] 1 Cr App R 126 (CA), 135ff and *R v Uddin* [1999] QB 431; [1998] 2 All ER 744 (CA), 437; 750-751.
153   And perhaps in England too: in *R v Gilmour* [2000] 2 Cr App R 407; [2000] Crim LR 763 (NI CA), where S foresaw the use of a small petrol bomb, not normally dangerous to life, and P used a much larger bomb to lethal effect, a conviction of manslaughter was held to be appropriate.
154   *R v Tomkins* [1985] 2 NZLR 253; (1985) 1 CRNZ 627 (CA); cf *R v Hamilton* [1985] 2 NZLR 245 (CA).

was likely to murder the driver, his conviction was upheld. Their plan contemplated actions that, should death result, evinced sufficient culpability to warrant a conviction for manslaughter:[155]

> "The availability of manslaughter as a verdict in such cases gives effect to the community's sense that a man who joins in a criminal enterprise with the knowledge that knives (or other weapons such as loaded guns) are being carried should bear a share of criminal responsibility for an ensuing death; but that, if he did not think that the weapons would be intentionally used to kill, it may be unduly harsh to convict him of murder."

In cases where P is guilty of murder and S failed to foresee the essential elements of murder — eg by failing to foresee the likelihood that P would act with sufficient mens rea for murder — S may nonetheless be convicted of manslaughter if she foresaw the probability that P may act with the culpability required for a manslaughter conviction:[156] for example, by committing an unlawful act, such as an assault, that involved some risk of physical harm to another person.[157] Because death is not an essential element of unlawful-act manslaughter (being a strict liability element), S need *not* foresee that death was a likely consequence of carrying out the joint enterprise.[158]

6.5.4 Applying s 66(2) where the offence committed was the object of the common purpose

Although, typically, the collateral offence (crime B) is different in character from the offence that the parties planned to commit (crime A), this is not necessary. The subsection is not phrased in terms limited to offences strictly collateral to the main purpose.[159] Indeed, in *R v Currie*,[160] the Court of Appeal noted that the words "to every offence committed by any one of them" in s 66(2) do not exclude the very offence that was the immediate object of the common purpose. So if the immediate object of the common purpose was to administer a severe beating to the victim and included an intention to cause bodily injury that the accessories knew was likely to cause death, together with a reckless disregard as to whether death ensued, evidence that one of the accessories struck a blow with the necessary knowledge of its consequences would be sufficient to bring the case within the terms of s 66(2).[161]

Nonetheless, where the parties achieve what they set out to do, s 66(2) should not normally be invoked. This is because s 66(1) is concerned with *intentional* acts of aiding, abetting, etc, whereas s 66(2) contemplates the situation where certain consequences are merely foreseen. In *R v Curtis*,[162] the Court of Appeal said that s 66(2):

---

155   *R v Tomkins* [1985] 2 NZLR 253; (1985) 1 CRNZ 627 (CA), 255; 629. See further 6.6.3.
156   Cf the hypothetical contemplated in *Day* [2001] Crim LR 984.
157   Below, 16.5.2(1).
158   *R v Rapira* [2003] 3 NZLR 794; (2003) 20 CRNZ 396 (CA), paras 28-35; *R v Renata* [1992] 2 NZLR 346; (1991) 7 CRNZ 616 (CA).
159   *R v Nathan* [1981] 2 NZLR 473, 475 (Prichard J).
160   *R v Currie* [1969] NZLR 193 (CA).
161   *R v Nathan* [1981] 2 NZLR 473, 475. But see *R v Simpson* (1988) 46 DLR (4th) 466; [1988] 1 SCR 3 (SCC), where the Supreme Court of Canada held that "unlawful purpose" must be different from the "offence" charged. See also *R v MacDonald* (1990) 54 CCC (3d) 97; 75 CR (3d) 238.
162   *R v Curtis* [1988] 1 NZLR 734 (CA), 739, 740.

"is concerned, not with an act which is the very unlawful act to which an offender lends his aid or his encouragement, but with any act done by the principal party which, while not the result aimed at, was a probable consequence of the prosecution of the unlawful common purpose ... Liability turns on the contemplated, albeit unwanted, consequences of the criminal enterprise."[163]

Contemplating consequences that are unwanted (crime B) will normally be incompatible with an intention to do the very thing which is the object of the criminal enterprise (crime A), so that in putting its case the prosecution will need to choose between s 66(1) or s 66(2). Both bases of accessory liability cannot be alleged together in respect of the same facts.[164]

6.6 General principles applying to all secondary parties

Whether it arises on the basis of assistance or encouragement under s 66(1)(b)-(d) or on the basis of joint enterprise under s 66(2), secondary liability is subject to certain general doctrines. These doctrines are discussed below, in the remainder of this chapter.

6.6.1 Liability normally depends on commission of the offence

As we have observed already, and unlike inchoate crimes such as attempt, secondary participation is derivative and not itself an offence. Rather, it involves S in being ascribed, alongside P, with legal responsibility for the offence that P commits. It follows that, subject to certain exceptions, S may be liable as a secondary party only *if the offence actually is committed*.[165] For example:

> S urges P to shoot V, a common enemy. P purchases a gun, but before he has the opportunity to purchase any ammunition the gun dealer becomes suspicious and alerts the police, who cancel P's gun licence and confiscate the weapon.

S is guilty of the inchoate offence of incitement to commit a crime but, since P does not actually commit the crime, S cannot be a party to murder.[166] In these standard examples, there can be no secondary liability because there is no actus reus by the principal. Consider the facts of *Thornton v Mitchell*:[167]

> S, a bus conductor, negligently directed the bus driver to reverse. Two pedestrians were in consequence hit by the bus. However, the driver was acquitted of careless driving, since he had quite properly relied upon the instructions of the conductor.

In these circumstances, S was acquitted of aiding and abetting the offence of careless driving. There was no actus reus by the bus driver — he had not been driving carelessly[168] — and thus nothing at all of a criminal character from which S's liability might derive.

---

163 See *R v Hamilton* [1985] 2 NZLR 245 (CA), 250 (Cooke J); also *R v Gush* [1980] 2 NZLR 92 (CA); *Chan Wing-Siu v R* [1985] AC 168; [1984] 3 All ER 877 (PC); *R v Powell; R v English* [1999] 1 AC 1; [1997] 4 All ER 545 (HL).
164 *R v Curtis* [1988] 1 NZLR 734 (CA), 740.
165 Cf *R v Demirian* [1989] VR 97; (1988) 33 A Crim R 441; Lanham, "Primary and Derivative Criminal Liability: An Australian Perspective" [2000] Crim LR 707.
166 *R v Bowern* (1915) 34 NZLR 696 (CA); *R v Harrison* [1941] NZLR 354 (CA); *R v Paterson* [1976] 2 NZLR 394 (CA); *R v Nathan* [1981] 2 NZLR 473.
167 *Thornton v Mitchell* [1940] 1 All ER 339. See also *R v Loukes* [1996] Crim LR 341; R D Taylor, "Complicity and Excuses" [1983] Crim LR 656.
168 For explanation, see 4.6.3.

6.6.2 Exceptions: Secondary liability without the primary offence

The case is straightforward where P does not commit an actus reus at all. However, there are certain circumstances where something less than the full offence by P is required. The first occurs when P commits the actus reus of the offence, but is not criminally responsible for doing so because of infancy (ss 21 and 22)[169] or insanity (s 23). In these cases, S may still be convicted of the offence, both pursuant to express provisions in ss 21(2), 22(2), and 23(4), and under common law principles. To illustrate, consider the following facts from the Australian case of *Schultz v Pettit*:[170]

> D allowed P, his five-year-old daughter, to operate a power boat. P pushed the throttle too far and the boat plowed into another boat. D was charged with carelessly operating the boat.

Prima facie, P operated the boat carelessly. However (as we shall see in chapter 9), she could not be convicted because of her infancy. Therefore, no offence was committed by P. Despite this, Cox J would have been willing to uphold D's conviction as a secondary party.[171] The same analysis applies in New Zealand, by virtue of s 21(2).

It seems that there are at least two further exceptions to the requirement that P be guilty of an offence, although the scope of those exceptions is not fully settled. We consider them in the following subsections.

(1) When S is responsible for P's excuse

The first exception is for other possible defences, apart from infancy and insanity, that P may claim which will not negate S's liability as a secondary party. There is at least one such general defence:[172] that of compulsion, when S is the source of compulsion. In *R v Bourne*,[173] S forced his wife to have sexual connection with an animal. S was convicted of abetting her to commit buggery notwithstanding that it was assumed his wife, had she been charged with the same offence, would have been acquitted owing to the availability of a defence of coercion. It appears that this defence operates only as a personal excuse, and similar reasoning would not, therefore, carry over to situations where (for example) P acted in justifying self-defence.[174]

(2) When S procures P to act without mens rea

The second exception arises when P does the actus reus of an offence but lacks mens rea. In limited circumstances, S may be liable as a secondary party when she procures P to commit the actus reus of an offence for which P lacks mens rea. In the English case of *R v Cogan; R v Leak*,[175] P had sexual intercourse with S's wife, apparently believing (on the basis of what S told

---

169   Cf *DPP v K and B* (1997) 1 Cr App R 36.
170   *Schultz v Pettit* (1980) 25 SASR 427. Note that the innocent agency doctrine was held not to apply: see 6.3.1, 6.6.2(2).
171   As it happened, this ground for upholding the conviction failed on the facts, because the father apparently lacked the mens rea required for secondary participation.
172   And see also 6.6.1.
173   *R v Bourne* (1952) 36 Cr App R 125 (CCA). See Edwards, "Duress and aiding and abetting" (1953) 69 LQR 226; Cross, "Duress and aiding and abetting (a reply)" (1953) 69 LQR 354.
174   Cf *R v Howe* [1987] AC 417; [1987] 1 All ER 771 (HL), 458; 799, where Lord Mackay highlighted the fact that duress involved a "reason special to [P] himself". *Bourne*, a common law decision, is confirmed in New Zealand by the wording of s 24(1), which states that the defence of compulsion protects from criminal responsibility "a person who commits an offence".

him) that the wife was consenting. On appeal, P's conviction for rape was quashed, but S's conviction was upheld. The main ground for upholding his conviction was said to be that P was an innocent agent through whom S had acted as a principal in committing the offence. However, as Smith and Hogan point out, "[t]he agency theory is misconceived. If it were right, a woman could be convicted of rape as the principal and it is plain that she cannot commit that offence."[176] Rape is one of a variety of offences that cannot be committed through an innocent agent.[177]

Alternatively, the Court of Appeal reasoned that S was guilty of procuring rape, since even though P could not be convicted, S's wife had "clearly" been raped: "Cogan had had sexual intercourse with her without her consent. The fact that Cogan was innocent of rape because he believed that she was consenting does not affect the position that she was raped."[178]

This, with respect, is also problematic. Rape is not an absolute liability crime, constituted simply by its actus reus. The fact that P was innocent of rape because of his belief means that, for the purposes of the criminal law (and by contrast with ordinary language), no rape occurred.[179] Nonetheless, S's conviction seems a just result. If so, the better analysis seems to be that, where S *procures* P to commit the actus reus of an offence without mens rea, S may be convicted of procuring that offence. The English Court of Appeal subsequently accepted this account in *R v Millward*,[180] the facts of which were as follows:

> S instructed P, his employee, to driv0e S's tractor on the highway. The tractor was in a defective condition, and by driving it on the highway P (the Court assumed)[181] committed the actus reus of reckless driving. S knew, and P did not know, that the vehicle was unroadworthy. While on the highway, the tractor's condition caused an accident, killing the passenger of another car.

On these facts, P was acquitted of causing death by reckless driving, but S was convicted as a party to the offence. The Court of Appeal upheld S's conviction explicitly on the basis that he had procured P's commission of the actus reus.

It is submitted that this is the preferable approach to the difficulty seen in cases such as *Cogan* and *Millward*, notwithstanding the language of s 66(1).[182] S should not be permitted to evade conviction by the vagaries of the innocent agency doctrine, especially where S has created the circumstances of his own exculpation by inducing P to perform the actus reus without mens rea. Rather than seeking (as in *Cogan*) to shoehorn such cases within existing doctrines,

---

175 *R v Cogan; R v Leak* [1976] QB 217; [1975] 2 All ER 1059 (CA).
176 *Smith and Hogan*, 205.
177 See 6.3.1.
178 *R v Cogan; R v Leak* [1976] QB 217; [1975] 2 All ER 1059 (CA), 223; 1062.
179 A similar example of this reasoning appears in *R v Bourne* (1952) 36 Cr App R 125, discussed in 6.6.2(1). Lord Goddard asserted (128) that the fact that P would have been acquitted of buggery presented no impediment to S's conviction for complicity because "that [P] could have set up duress ... means that she admits that she has committed the crime but prays to be excused from punishment". Yet an acquittal would mean that she committed no crime. The better explanation of *Bourne* is that given in 6.6.2(1).
180 *R v Millward* [1994] Crim LR 527 (CA). See also *R v Wheelhouse* [1994] Crim LR 756 (CA).
181 Erroneously. In fact, the case was like *Thornton v Mitchell*, discussed in 6.6.1, where no actus reus occurred. See the acceptance of this criticism of *Millward* by Smith, in his discussion of *R v Loukes* [1996] Crim LR 341, 343.
182 By contrast with the common law, the New Zealand statute poses the difficulty that, for s 66(1)(d) to apply, S must have procured P "to commit the offence".

it is better openly to recognise a qualification to the general rule that secondary liability requires a guilty principal. Certainly that would be consonant with justice. If they show nothing else, cases like *Cogan* demonstrate that unwavering adherence to the general rule is unwarranted.

Nonetheless, the propriety of this common law exception to the rule that P must be guilty of the offence has been doubted,[183] and it remains to be seen whether this analysis will be accepted by the Court of Appeal in New Zealand.[184] The High Court has effectively allowed such an exception in *van Niewkoop v Registrar of Companies*,[185] although part of the analysis in that case may be doubted. S was the mortgage broker for a company which arranged public contributory mortgages. The advertising for some of the mortgages contained false statements, wherefore the directors of the company were prosecuted as principals under s 58 Securities Act 1978. It seems that while the actus reus of the offence had been committed, they were entitled to a defence under s 58(2) that they had reasonable grounds to believe the statements contained in the advertisements were true. Nonetheless, S's convictions as a secondary party to the offences were upheld.

The ground on which those convictions were upheld was that the actus reus of the offence had been upheld and the defence under s 58(2), being personal to the principals and something for which the burden of proof was reversed, was irrelevant to S's liability. According to Laurenson J:[186]

> "all the elements necessary to prove the actus reus of the strict liability offending by the directors was proved.... The trial Judge in that case had also found that the directors had made out the defence under s 58(2). That, in my view, so far as the prosecution against the appellant is concerned, is irrelevant. Although the defence relates to mens rea it is not an ingredient requiring proof in the first instance by the prosecution."

With respect to his Honour, this reasoning is too broad. It falls into the same error as did the English Court of Appeal in *R v Cogan; R v Leak*, discussed above. If the directors reasonably believed the statements were true, no offence was committed. Neither is this a case of a personal excuse unavailable to S, of the sort contemplated in 6.6.2(1). The reversal of the burden of proof is irrelevant to either of these points. Nonetheless, it is arguable that S's convictions were rightly upheld because, as his Honour notes but does not emphasise, the foundation for the s 58(2) defence was that the principals "had relied on the appellant to ensure the statements were true".[187] As such, S may have procured the principals to commit the actus reus of the offence, in which event the case comes within the narrower scope of the true exception recognised in *R v Millward* (above).

In any event, cases of this sort will be rare, since whenever the actus reus involves consequences, S may normally be convicted as a principal offender (either on the basis of having caused the actus reus personally or by means of the innocent agent doctrine). subsections.

---

183   See, for example, Kadish, *Blame and Punishment: Essays in the Criminal Law*, New York, Macmillan, 1987, ch 8, 135, 180.
184   The issue was undecided by the Court of Appeal in *R v Lewis* [1975] 1 NZLR 222 (CA).
185   *van Niewkoop v Registrar of Companies* [2005] 1 NZLR 796 (HC).
186   *van Niewkoop v Registrar of Companies* [2005] 1 NZLR 796 (HC), para 50(f).
187   *van Niewkoop v Registrar of Companies* [2005] 1 NZLR 796 (HC), para 51.

(3) No requirement that P be charged and convicted

It is worth emphasising that the general principle, to which the above paragraphs state exceptions, is that there must *be* a principal who commits the offence to which S is party, not that P must be convicted — or even identified or charged. So, for example, in *R v Kimura*[188] S was charged with aiding and abetting aggravated burglary committed by a person unknown. It must be proved in such a case that the aggravated burglary was committed, but not by whom.

Even if another person *is* charged as the principal and is acquitted, it will not follow that the secondary party must be acquitted also.[189] The apparent inconsistency may be explained by other factors: for example, different evidence may be admissible against the secondary party than was admissible against the principal. The only exception to this is if, on the same evidence as is used to convict the secondary party,[190] the acquittal of the principal implies that the elements of the offence cannot be proved, so that the offence was not actually committed.[191] To convict in such a case would be an "unjust inconsistency".[192]

6.6.3 Conviction for different offences with the same actus reus

A variant situation arises when there are two offences constituted by the same actus reus and differentiated only by degree of culpability. The leading example of this is murder and manslaughter. Suppose, for instance, the following situation:

> S lends P a cosh, which he knows P plans to use to assault V. S knows that the blow may cause V's death, but believes P intends only to knock V out and does not mean to kill him. In this, however, S is mistaken. P intends to kill V. Unfortunately, although P hits V no harder than agreed, she succeeds in her aim of killing him.

It appears that, in circumstances of this sort, S and P need not be convicted of the same offence and that, where P is guilty of murder, it is possible to convict S only of manslaughter.[193] In the case of s 66(2), this possibility has already been noted in 6.5.3(1).[194] Under s 66(1), the basis of such a finding would be that S acted with the intention of assisting or encouraging P, whose envisaged conduct was such that, were V to die, P would be guilty of manslaughter; but where, ultimately, P performed the envisaged conduct with sufficient mens rea for murder.[195]

The fact that these offences share the same actus reus means that any incursion upon the principle that S's liability is derivative upon P's is minimal. Indeed, manslaughter may be regarded as a lesser included offence within murder. Moreover, arguably the jury has a constitutional power on a charge of murder (improperly) to return a verdict of manslaughter,

---

188 *R v Kimura* (1992) 9 CRNZ 115 (CA).
189 See, for example, *R v Wahrlich* [1976] 2 NZLR 9 (CA).
190 *Sweetman v Industries and Commerce Dept* [1970] NZLR 139 (SC), 148.
191 Especially in a case where the acquitted person was the only possible principal: *R v Waaka* 9/7/01, Hammond J, HC Hamilton T010076.
192 *Sweetman v Industries and Commerce Dept* [1970] NZLR 139 (SC), 148; citing *Surujpaul v R* [1958] 3 All ER 300; (1958) 42 Cr App R 266 (PC).
193 *R v Tomkins* [1985] 2 NZLR 253; (1985) 1 CRNZ 627 (CA); *R v Hamilton* [1985] 2 NZLR 245 (CA); *R v Te Moni* [1998] 1 NZLR 641, (1997) 15 CRNZ 439 (CA); *R v Rapira* [2003] 3 NZLR 794; (2003) 20 CRNZ 396 (CA); *R v Kopelani* 23/11/05, CA79/05.
194 See also Orchard, "Joint and several murder and manslaughter" [1986] NZLJ 45, 47, 48.
195 Cf *R v Gilmour* [2000] 2 Cr App R 407; [2000] Crim LR 763 (NI CA); *R v Murtagh* [1955] Crim LR 315; *R v Malcolm* [1951] NZLR 470 (CA), 485.

even though the jury is satisfied that every element necessary to constitute the crime of murder has been established.[196]

However, the reverse is not true, and it does not follow from the above that S may be convicted of murder if the principal party is guilty only of manslaughter. This possibility requires separate consideration. Imagine the following example:

> S encourages P to punch V. S knows, and P does not, that V has an "egg-shell skull", and she hopes that the blow will cause V's death. (P does not foresee any risk of serious injury to V.) P strikes V, killing him.

P is guilty of manslaughter. But is S guilty of murder, or only of manslaughter? In *R v Hartley*,[197] the Court of Appeal answered: no. S may not be convicted of murder when the principal party is guilty only of manslaughter.

At the time, the view adopted in *Hartley* appeared to be in line with the common law.[198] But that view has been powerfully criticised,[199] and was subsequently disapproved in England and Australia.[200] Therefore it is possible that New Zealand law may yet reconsider the position stated in *Hartley*.

Moreover, there are good reasons why it should, and why in the example above S should be convicted of murder. It is true that P has acted without the mens rea for murder, but it is misleading to present murder and manslaughter as independent offences. The core of the wrong is identical. The dominant rationale for each offence is the protection of life. Indeed, it is generally appropriate to think of manslaughter as an alternative rather than a separate charge, available when the mens rea of murder cannot be proved or when the defendant has some limited defence such as provocation. Arguably therefore, in the context of derivative liability, these offences should not be regarded as separate.

There is, in any event, one other and uncontroversial exception. Consistent with the case of compulsion in 6.6.2(1), it arises when a personal excusatory defence is available to P. Culpable homicide admits of palliative defences: especially, for provocation, suicide pacts, and infanticide. Where such a defence is open to the principal, the secondary party's liability for murder will not correspondingly be reduced.[201]

6.6.4 Limitations on the application of s 66

Sometimes party liability is excluded explicitly by statute. An example is provided by s 131(4), in the context of sexual conduct with a dependent family member, which provides that the dependent "cannot be charged as a party to the offence." Prima facie, consensual

---

196 For discussion of this point, see *Adams*, CA171.15-17 (looseleaf); also Snelling, "The alternative verdict of manslaughter" (1958) 32 ALJ 137.
197 *R v Hartley* [1978] 2 NZLR 199 (CA). See *R v Lewis* [1975] 1 NZLR 222 (CA); *Remillard v R* (1921) 59 DLR 340; 62 SCR 21 (SCC).
198 *R v Richards* [1974] QB 776; [1973] 3 All ER 1088 (CA).
199 Smith, "Aid, abet, counsel, or procure" in Glazebrook (ed), *Reshaping the Criminal Law: Essays in Honour of Glanville Williams*, London, Stevens & Sons, 1978, 120, 128-130; Williams, *TBCL*, para 15.18. Contrast Kadish, *Blame and Punishment: Essays in the Criminal Law*, New York, Macmillan, 1987, ch 8, 135, 184-186.
200 *R v Howe* [1986] QB 626; [1986] 1 All ER 833 (CA), 641, 642; 839, 840, affirmed *R v Howe* [1987] AC 417; [1987] 1 All ER 771 (HL); *Warren v R* [1987] WAR 314; (1985) 15 A Crim R 317.
201 Cf s 169(7) (provocation); s 178(8) (infanticide); s 180(5) (suicide pact). In the case of infanticide, S's liability may be for either murder or manslaughter.

intercourse with a dependent child would involve the child's being a party under s 66 to the offence committed by her adult partner. The express legislative exception reflects the fact that the relevant offence exists for the *protection* of such persons, even "against themselves", and that they are regarded by the statute as victims rather than co-offenders.

(1) *The Tyrrell principle*

Arguably, express statutory exceptions, while welcome, are not required to achieve this result. The same principle excepting victims from participation in crimes against themselves exists at common law. In *R v Tyrrell*, it was held that D, a girl under the age of 16 years, could not be convicted of abetting unlawful sexual intercourse with herself, because the Act that created the offence "was passed for the purpose of protecting women and girls against themselves".[202] However, the common law principle espoused in *Tyrrell* is of uncertain scope[203] and its application may be doubtful in areas other than offences against young persons and persons suffering from a disability.

The possibility of applying the *Tyrell* principle depends on the purpose of the relevant legislation, and arises only if the statute is directed toward protecting an identified class of persons. There is certainly no *general* exception for "victims" of crime. Thus, for example, if S asks P to inflict a wound on him, it seems that both P and S commit an offence.[204]

(2) *Specific or implicit legislative identification of parties*

On occasion, the relevant primary offence may be defined by statute in such a way that it specifies the class of participants who may commit that offence. In such instances, participation under s 66 may be excluded except in so far as such participants qualify within the class stipulated by the primary offence. One example is the former offence of keeping a brothel, which under (then) s 147(1)(a) was committed by any person "who keeps, or manages or acts or assists in the management of, any brothel". Evidently Parliament intended thereby to make guilty of an offence those involved in running a brothel; but not, by the principle expressio unius est exclusio alterius, those who simply work there as prostitutes and are not in any way involved in its management. It follows that the latter cannot be convicted as secondary parties.[205]

However, cases of this type are rare. More commonly, the statute may define a class of persons who may commit the offence *as a principal*, without restricting the range of persons who may be guilty of the offence as a secondary party.[206] A good example is the offence of rape within s 128(1)(a), which can be committed only by a "male" against a "female". The definition makes clear that a female cannot commit rape as a principal party (though she may commit sexual

---

202 *R v Tyrrell* [1894] 1 QB 710; [1891-94] All ER Rep 1215, 712; 1215 (Lord Coleridge CJ). See also *Scott v Killian* (1985) 40 SASR 37; 19 A Crim R 187; *R v Whitehouse* [1977] QB 868.
203 Williams, "Victims and other exempt parties in crime" (1990) 10 LS 245; Hogan, "Victims as parties to crime" [1962] Crim LR 683; Williams, "Victims as parties to crimes: A further comment" [1964] Crim LR 686.
204 *R v Brown* [1994] 1 AC 212; [1993] 2 All ER 75 (HL); below, 17.2.4(1)-(3). Cf *R v Ngamoki* 7/11/97, Heron J, HC Palmerston North T5/97 (supply of drugs), which, it is submitted, is to be preferred on this point to *R v Willoughby* [1980] 1 NZLR 66. Cf also *Angland v Hosken* [1935] NZLR 71 (sale of liquor).
205 *R v Mickle* [1978] 1 NZLR 720 (SC).
206 For example, *Sweetman v Industries and Commerce Dept* [1970] NZLR 139; *van Niewkoop v Registrar of Companies* [2005] 1 NZLR 796 (HC). See also *R v Sockett* (1908) 72 JP 428.

violation under s 128). But she may nonetheless aid and abet a rape committed by someone else.[207]

6.6.5 Secondary liability and inchoate offences

Section 66 does not create offences. It operates as a conduit to S's responsibility for some other crime. Therefore, since aiding and abetting is not per se an offence, it follows that S cannot commit an inchoate crime of attempting, inciting, or conspiring to aid and abet.[208] Conceptually, this seems right. If S has failed to participate in a crime, she has no connection to it and should not be convicted. Her conduct is, one might say, too remote from manifest criminality to warrant the attention of the criminal law; attention that would be tantamount to punishing for little more than wrongful thoughts.[209]

Conversely, however, the inchoate offences *are* offences independent of the further crime that is attempted, incited, or conspired toward. Therefore, S may be a party to (aid, abet, etc) an attempt,[210] incitement, or conspiracy[211] by P to commit an offence. The exception to the latter rule is that S may not be a party under s 66(2) to a conspiracy. In view of the overlap between that subsection and the requirements of conspiracy, S will be liable in such cases only if she is in fact a member of the conspiracy itself.[212]

One situation where the general rule, that there is no inchoate liability for participation, does not apply is where assistance or encouragement is itself made a substantive offence by legislation. For example, the offence of aiding suicide under s 179(b) is defined in terms of aiding and abetting. Under this section, the aiding or abetting is not a secondary form of participation in some further offence; it is an offence in its own right. Consequently, S may be guilty of attempting to commit an offence against s 179(b).[213]

6.6.6 Withdrawal

When perpetrating the principal offence, P cannot undo his crime. Once the elements of the offence are concurrently satisfied the offence is committed and cannot be "uncommitted". By contrast, participation *can* be undone. S may withdraw her participation, although she must do so before the crime is committed or attempted.[214] Withdrawal, however, is not easy.

---

207 See *R v Ram* (1893) 17 Cox CC 609.
208 Smith, "Secondary participation and inchoate offences" in Tapper (ed), *Crime, Proof and Punishment*, London, Butterworths, 1981, 21; 6.4.1(1).
209 Fletcher, *Rethinking Criminal Law*, Boston, Little, Brown & Co, 1978, 680, 681: "there is no social wrong in acting to aid the crime of another, unless the aid actually furthers the criminal objective." See also Dawkins, "The unknown look-out and liability for 'aiding' an offence" [1989] NZLJ 30, 34, 35.
210 *R v Baker* (1909) 28 NZLR 536 (CA); *R v Mackie* [1957] NZLR 669 (CA); *Drewery v Police* (1988) 3 CRNZ 499; cf *R v Hapgood* (1870) LR 1 CCR 221; 11 Cox CC 471.
211 *R v Anderson* (1984) 80 Cr App R 64; [1984] Crim LR 550 (CA); *R v McNamara (No 1)* (1981) 56 CCC (2d) 193. Cf *R v Gemmell* [1985] 2 NZLR 740; (1985) 1 CRNZ 496 (CA).
212 *R v Gemmell* [1985] 2 NZLR 740; (1985) 1 CRNZ 496 (CA); Orchard, "The mental element of conspiracy" (1985) 2 Canterbury LR 353.
213 *R v Stack* [1986] 1 NZLR 257; (1986) 2 CRNZ 238 (CA); *R v McShane* (1978) 66 Cr App R 97; [1977] Crim LR 737 (CA).
214 *R v Pink* [2001] 2 NZLR 860, 862, in a paragraph that appears to draw upon the corresponding passage from the first edition.

Repentance is insufficient.[215] The participation must not merely be discontinued. It must be countermanded.

The leading New Zealand statement of the requirements of withdrawal is found in *R v Pink*:[216]

> "As a matter of legal doctrine, it seems to me that the following conditions must be met:
>
> • First, there must in fact be a notice of withdrawal, whether by words or actions.
>
> • Secondly, that withdrawal must be unequivocal.
>
> • Thirdly, that withdrawal must be communicated to the principal offenders. There is some debate as to whether the communication must be to all the principal offenders, but here all were told.
>
> • Fourthly, the withdrawal may only be effected by taking all reasonable steps to undo the effect of the party's previous actions. (See *R v Menniti* [1985] 1 Qd R 520.) As with any test of "reasonableness", it is impossible to divorce that consideration from the facts of a given case. The accused's actions may have been so overt and influential that positive steps must be taken by him to intercede, and prevent the crime occurring. There is at least one authority (*R v Grundy* [1977] Crim LR 534 (CA)) which suggests that where the accused's participation was in the form of counselling, attempts by the accused to dissuade the principal offenders from proceeding with the crime are sufficient."

For convenience, we can elaborate these requirements according to the subsection of s 66 within which S's participation falls.

(1) *Withdrawal from participation by common intention under s 66(2)*

Where S has participated simply by joining in a common intention to commit a crime, the common intention may be abandoned by S's communicating his withdrawal in an unequivocal and timely way. Established authority for this requirement is found in the Canadian case of *R v Whitehouse*:[217]

> "where practicable and reasonable there must be timely communication of the intention to abandon the common purpose from those who wish to dissociate themselves from the contemplated crime to those who desire to continue in it."

As was emphasised in *R v Pink* (above), the notice of withdrawal, whether made by words or actions, must be unequivocal; a perfunctory disclaimer is likely to be insufficient,[218] as is merely leaving the scene,[219] standing a distance apart,[220] or simply not turning up.[221] It must also be

---

215 *R v Croft* [1944] 1 KB 295; [1944] 2 All ER 483 (CCA).
216 *R v Pink* [2001] 2 NZLR 860, 864; endorsed by the Court of Appeal in *R v Ngawaka* 6/10/04, CA111/04; CA146/04; CA174/04, paras 14-15.
217 *R v Whitehouse* [1941] 1 DLR 683; (1940) 75 CCC 65 (BC CA), 685; 67. See also *Henderson v R* [1949] 2 DLR 121; (1948) 91 CCC 97 (SCC); *R v Becerra* (1975) 62 Cr App R 212 (CA); *R v Wilcox* [1982] 1 NZLR 191 (CA). For discussion of the common law and recommendations for reform see Smith, "Withdrawal in Complicity: A Restatement of Principles" [2001] Crim LR 769.
218 *R v Malcolm* [1951] NZLR 470 (CA).
219 *R v Ngawaka* 6/10/04, CA111/04; CA146/04; CA174/04.

timely, occurring before the crime is committed,[222] and perhaps before its commission is even commenced.[223]

There is no general requirement that S must, in addition to withdrawing unequivocally, also take reasonable steps to prevent P from committing the offence.[224] However, where the situation is such that communication of withdrawal to the other parties is impossible or impractical, withdrawal may alternatively be effected by taking steps to prevent the commission of the offence, for example by warning the victim or the police.[225] There may come a point when events are so far advanced that efficacious withdrawal by S is impossible.[226]

(2) *Withdrawal from assistance or encouragement under s 66(1)(b)-(d)*

When S has actually provided assistance or encouragement toward the commission of a crime, countermanding that participation is more onerous. Mere cessation of further participatory activity will be insufficient.[227] Withdrawal may only be effected by taking all reasonable steps to undo the effect of his previous actions.[228] What steps are sufficient will, it seems, depend upon the circumstances and upon the extent of S's prior participation: the greater the involvement, the more S must do to withdraw.[229] Incitement or encouragement can normally be undone by an express statement to the opposite effect.[230] However, if material assistance has been rendered, there may have to be some form of physical intervention to impede the crime. For example, S may have to try to recover the weapon loaned to P or attempt to protect the victim, perhaps even by restraining P physically.[231] Advice or counsel, on the other hand, cannot as such be undone, but may be countermanded by attempts to dissuade P from proceeding with the crime.[232]

---

220   R v *Whitehouse* [1941] 1 DLR 683; (1940) 75 CCC 65 (BC CA).
221   R v *Goodspeed* (1911) 6 Cr App R 133; R v *Rook* [1993] 2 All ER 955; [1993] 1 WLR 1005 (CA).
222   R v *Witika* [1993] 2 NZLR 424; (1992) 9 CRNZ 272 (CA).
223   A possibility raised in R v *Perman* [1996] 1 Cr App R 24 (CA), 34.
224   R v *O'Flaherty* [2004] 2 Cr App R 314, paras 60-61.
225   R v *Becerra* (1975) 62 Cr App R 212 (CA); R v *Jensen* [1980] VR 194.
226   As appears to have occurred in *White v Ridley* (1978) 140 CLR 342; 52 ALJR 724 (HCA).
227   R v *Johnson* (1841) Car & M 218; 174 ER 479.
228   R v *Pink* [2001] 2 NZLR 860, 864; R v *Menniti* [1985] 1 Qd R 520; (1984) 13 A Crim R 417; R v *Wilton* (1993) 64 A Crim R 359.
229   For discussion of variant cases, see *Adams*, CA66.14 (looseleaf).
230   R v *Saunders and Archer* (1573) 2 Plowd 473, 75 ER 706. Cf R v *Croft* [1944] 1 KB 295; [1944] 2 All ER 483; R v *Rook* [1993] 2 All ER 955; [1993] 1 WLR 1005 (CA).
231   R v *Becerra* (1975) 62 Cr App R 212 (CA); R v *Baker* [1994] Crim LR 444 (CA).
232   R v *Grundy* [1977] Crim LR 534 (CA).

Chapter 7

Vicarious and Corporate Liability

7.1	Vicarious liability	197
7.1.1	"Delegation" theory	198
7.1.2	"Scope of employment"	200
(1)	*A due diligence defence?*	201
7.2	Liability of corporations	201
7.2.1	Presumed criminal liability of corporations	204
7.2.2	Distinguishing between direct and vicarious liability of companies	205
7.2.3	Vicarious liability of corporations	205
7.2.4	Rules for attributing direct (non-vicarious) liability to a company	206
(1)	*"Alter ego" v "embodiment" or "identification"?*	209
(2)	*Liability for negligence in failing to supervise a company's activities*	211
(3)	*Mens rea offences*	212
7.2.5	Personal liability of company employees	212
7.2.6	Reform of corporate liability	213
(1)	*Aggregation*	213
(2)	*Safety cultures*	214
(3)	*Reactive fault*	215

7.1 Vicarious liability

Unlike secondary liability, which involves *participation* by the defendant in the crime of another, vicarious liability involves the *attribution* to one individual or corporation of criminal liability for the acts of another. The defendant bears liability *on behalf of* another. In general, the possibility of vicarious liability is rejected at common law, the basic rule being that a master or principal is not criminally liable for an offence committed by his servant or agent: "they must each answer for their own acts, and stand or fall by their own behaviour."[1] The courts have resiled from the idea that D might be held criminally responsible for an event brought about by another which it was impossible for him to prevent, in circumstances where he could not personally take the precautions enjoined upon by the relevant statute.[2] In effect, vicarious liability imposes criminal responsibility on the basis of status; yet, unlike ordinary "state-of-affairs" offences that may be committed by a principal,[3] there is no implicit behavioural element

---

1 *R v Huggins* (1730) 2 Stra 883; 93 ER 915, 885; 917 (Raymond CJ). See *Woodgate v Knatchbull* (1787) 2 Term Rep 148; 100 ER 80; *Smith and Hogan*, 174ff.
2 *Hardcastle v Bielby* [1892] 1 QB 709, 713 (Collins J).
3 Discussed at 3.2.2(1).

of the offence and no defence of involuntariness. Such liability is, therefore, repugnant to the fundamental principles of criminal law.

Nonetheless, vicarious liability may sometimes be imposed by the express terms or necessary implication of a statute, and occasionally on the basis of a master-and-servant or principal-and-agent relationship.[4] At common law, there were two notable exceptions to the principle that a master could never be liable for the criminal acts of his servant. They concerned public nuisance and criminal libel, where a master could be held liable for his servant's acts even though he was completely innocent. However, these exceptions were overtaken in the late 19th century, when it became increasingly common to use vicarious liability to regulate the activities of persons and corporations who held licences to perform specific activities, in circumstances where it was common practice to delegate the statutory functions and responsibilities of the licensee to an employee or agent. In limited circumstances of this type, it was considered not unreasonable to make the principal liable for those acts of her employee committed within the scope of employment.[5]

To determine whether a statute impliedly imposes vicarious liability, it is necessary to consider the object of the statute, the words used, the nature of the duty laid down, the person upon whom it is imposed, the person by whom it would in ordinary circumstances be performed, and the person upon whom the penalty is imposed.[6] Where the duty is one which would ordinarily be performed by a servant of the owner or other person having responsibility, the courts have often been willing to find an intention by the Legislature to impose vicarious liability. The rationale for this willingness is that, where a penalty is imposed for a breach of duty, it may be reasonable to infer that the penalty was imposed for a default of the person by whom the duty would ordinarily be performed, namely the employee, regardless of the state of mind of the employer. This point is buttressed by the fact that it is normally the employer who is best placed to ensure her employee complies with the law.[7]

Once an offence is held to import the doctrine, there are two principal bases upon which vicarious liability may be established: the "delegation" principle, and the "scope of employment" principle. According to the delegation principle, which applies in the case of mens rea offences, a person may be held liable for the acts of another where he has delegated the performance of statutory duties to that other person. According to the scope of employment principle, which applies to strict and absolute liability offences, a master may be held liable because the servant has been given authority to do the very kind of act involved in the offence.

7.1.1 "Delegation" theory

The delegation principle only applies in those cases where, by the terms of the relevant statutory provision, "knowledge" or some similar mens rea element is required as a condition of liability. In such a case, liability may be imposed where the principal knows the relevant facts, or where she has delegated her powers and duties. In *Vane v Yiannopoullos*[8] the licensee of a restaurant had been granted a licence subject to the condition that liquor was only to be sold to persons

---

4 See *Crawford v Haughton Ltd* [1972] 1 All ER 535.
5 *Mousell Brothers v London and North-Western Railway Co* [1917] 2 KB 836.
6 *Mousell Brothers v London and North-Western Railway Co* [1917] 2 KB 836, 845 (Atkin J).
7 For the moral objection to an analogous argument, see the discussion of absolute liability at 5.1.2.
8 *Vane v Yiannopoullos* [1965] AC 486; [1964] 3 All ER 820 (HL).

ordering meals. A waitress, despite being instructed only to serve drinks to customers ordering meals, had served drinks to two youths who had not ordered meals while the licensee was in another part of the restaurant and knew nothing of the sale. Upon an appeal against the dismissal of an information alleging that the licensee had "knowingly" sold intoxicating liquor contrary to the conditions of the licence, it was held that since there had been no delegation and the licensee had no knowledge of the offence, he was rightly acquitted. However, a delegation was found to have occurred in *Allen v Whitehead*[9] where the occupier of a cafe had been charged and convicted of "knowingly permitting" prostitutes to remain in a place where refreshments were sold and consumed. He had left his manager in charge of the business with instructions that no prostitutes were to be allowed to congregate on the premises. However, on a number of occasions this instruction was ignored and a number of prostitutes had been allowed to remain on the premises contrary to the statutory requirements. On appeal, it was held that D's ignorance of the facts was no defence. The manager's acts and his mens rea were to be imputed to the occupier because it was found that the management of the cafe had been delegated to him.[10]

The distinction between these two cases suggests that for vicarious liability to arise there must be a real and effective delegation of powers and the corresponding duties, such that the activity delegated is under the exclusive control of the delegate, free from the principal's supervision.[11]

The delegation principle has been described as "anomalous"[12] and as "hard to justify".[13] It allows a person to be liable for an offence requiring mens rea on the basis that the defendant had put in her own place a substitute who did the proscribed acts and had the relevant mental element at the time. The defendant is thus made answerable for the acts and mental element of another.[14] Perhaps, however, it can be said that the defendant voluntarily assumes that risk by her act of delegation? As such, vicarious liability by delegation may be justifiable on the basis that, in certain areas of regulatory activity, legislative compliance would be difficult to achieve if the person upon whom certain statutory duties have been cast were able to avoid responsibility for ensuring compliance by choosing not to exercise the requisite control, and simply passing to a delegate the control of the premises.[15] It is arguable that in those areas in which it has traditionally been applied, vicarious liability is a useful vehicle for ensuring that a master is answerable for her servant's actions and, particularly in the area of liquor licensing, that it serves the interests of public policy. However, it remains a controversial form of criminal liability, which probably should not be extended beyond the area it has traditionally occupied, namely liquor licensing.[16]

---

9   *Allen v Whitehead* [1930] 1 KB 211; [1929] All ER Rep 13.
10 See also *Linnet v CMP* [1946] KB 290; [1946] 1 All ER 380, in which a co-licensee was held liable for acts of the other licensee for "knowingly permitting disorderly conduct", on the basis of delegation in keeping the premises.
11 See *Somerset v Hart* (1884) 12 QBD 360.
12 *Adams*, CA2.28.09 (looseleaf).
13 Cf the comments of Lord Reid in *Vane v Yiannopoullos* [1965] AC 486; [1964] 3 All ER 820 (HL); *Smith and Hogan*, 177.
14 For trenchant criticism of *Allen v Whitehead*, see Williams, *TBCL*, para 43.3.
15 On the other hand, perhaps the tactic mentioned in the text could often be outflanked by the (preferable) use of strict liability offences.
16 See *Bradshaw v Ewart-James* [1983] QB 671; [1983] 1 All ER 12. For New Zealand cases in which the delegation principle has been applied, see *Gifford v Police* [1965] NZLR 484 (CA); *Murphy v Weir* [1968] NZLR 657.

7.1.2 "Scope of employment"

Where a vicarious liability offence imposes strict[17] or absolute[18] liability and is not one to which the delegation principle applies, the defendant may alternatively be liable for the conduct of any person who has been authorised to do the very type of act involved in the offence. In these circumstances, the principal is held liable because the acts done physically by the servant may, in law, be considered the master's acts. The basis of liability under the "scope of employment" rule is that authority has been vested in a substitute, regardless of the nature of the relationship existing between the parties.

The scope of employment rule reflects the practical reality that, in most cases, the business of selling, for example, liquor by a licensee holding a licence to do so is carried on by other persons on behalf of the licensee. Consequently, it is thought that unless the licensee is held responsible for the behaviour of his servants when acting within the scope of their employment, the object of the legislation would be defeated. Thus, in *Gifford v Police*,[19] the appellant was held liable for the act of a friend, whom he had temporarily authorised to supervise a hotel bar, after the friend supplied beer to a person under the age of 21.

However, where the substitute acts outside the scope of his employment or of the authority conferred, the defendant will not be liable. For example, if a cleaner, lacking any authority to do so, opens a hotel bar outside the legal hours and sells liquor to customers, the licensee will not be liable.[20] The cleaner's acts are clearly outside the scope of his employment and cannot bind the licensee who employs him. Similarly, in *Adams v Camfoni*[21] it was held that a master was not liable when a servant boy, who had no authority to do so, supplied his master's liquor to a customer out of hours. On the other hand, a servant will not necessarily go outside the scope of his authority simply because he acts in a way contrary to instructions given. Accordingly, an assistant's selling hams as "scotch ham", despite the employer's express instructions that they were only to be sold as "breakfast hams", was held in *Coppen v Moore (No 2)*[22] to constitute a prima facie case of an offence vicariously committed by the employer.

Whenever an employee acts within the scope of her employment, the act of the employee is deemed to be the act of the master. The standard cases of this variety arise where the legislation prohibits the performance of a particular type of activity like "selling" or "possessing". These offences typically involve strict or absolute liability, where it is not necessary for the prosecution to prove that the offender knew the relevant facts. Liability attaches to the master or employer because, using a broad construction of the words which constitute the actus reus of the offence, the employer is treated as performing the relevant acts through the employee's actions. Smith and Hogan observe:[23]

> "Now a 'sale' consists in the transfer of property in goods from A to B and the seller, in law, is necessarily the person in whom the property is vested at the commencement of the transaction. It is not a great step, therefore, for the court to say that the employer

---

17 Cf *S M Savill Ltd v MOT* [1986] 1 NZLR 653.
18 *Barker v Levinson* [1951] 1 KB 342; [1950] 2 All ER 825, 345; 827; *Bradshaw v Ewart-James* [1983] QB 671; [1983] 1 All ER 12, 676; 14.
19 *Gifford v Police* [1965] NZLR 484 (CA). See also *Sivyer v Taylor* [1916] NZLR 586.
20 See *Jull v Treanor* (1896) 14 NZLR 513.
21 *Adams v Camfoni* [1929] 1 KB 95.
22 *Coppen v Moore (No 2)* [1898] 2 QB 306.
23 Smith and Hogan, *Criminal Law* (7th ed), London, Butterworths, 1992, 175.

has committed the *actus reus* of 'selling' even though he was nowhere near when the incident took place."

Analogously, on the basis of the scope of employment principle, a company as the "master" was held liable for the acts of an employee who "used" a motor vehicle with defective brakes contrary to regulations.[24] Similarly, in *Sopp v Long*[25] the defendant, a licensee of a number of railway refreshment rooms, was held liable for the acts of a waitress, whom he had never met, for "causing" to be delivered to a customer whisky short of the measure purported to be sold. The Court held that, being absent from the premises the licensee sold through his servant, the waitress, and that by every sale he conducted through her, he "caused" to be delivered that which was sold.[26]

(1) *A due diligence defence?*

Where the relevant offence is one of strict liability, the Canadian Supreme Court has suggested that an employer would have the usual strict liability defence of due diligence, if charged as vicariously responsible for that offence committed by an employee, provided the defendant had set up and monitored a system intended to prevent the offence.[27] Although inconsistent with the principles of vicarious liability, this is a development to be welcomed. However, the substance of any such defence may well depend on the degree to which the preventive system is actually monitored. It would seem that merely drafting and circulating instructions to managers aimed at ensuring strict compliance with the law will not suffice.[28] The issue has yet to be decided in New Zealand.

7.2 Liability of corporations

For a long time the common law considered that corporations were beyond the reach of the criminal law.[29] There were many reasons why this was thought to be the case. A principal difficulty concerned the meaning given to the word "person". Where "persons" could be punished for offences committed by them, the phrase seemed inapt to include an incorporated association.[30] This merely linguistic difficulty was eventually overcome by legislation, which stipulated that the word "person" may be construed to include a legal, as well as a natural, person.[31] A further problem was that because personal appearance was necessary at assizes and quartersessions, a company, which lacked a physical existence, could not appear. However, this perceived difficulty was eventually overcome by the practice of having a representative appear and enter a plea on behalf of the company, for which provision is now made in legislation.[32]

---

24 *James & Son Ltd v Smee* [1955] 1 QB 78; [1954] 3 All ER 273.
25 *Sopp v Long* [1970] 1 QB 518; [1969] 1 All ER 855 (CA).
26 *Sopp v Long* [1970] 1 QB 518; [1969] 1 All ER 855 (CA), 526; 860 (Edmund Davies LJ). See also *Strutt v Clift* [1911] 1 KB 1 ("keeps").
27 *R v City of Sault Ste Marie* (1978) 85 DLR (3d) 161; [1978] 2 SCR 1299 (SCC).
28 See *Sopp v Long* [1970] 1 QB 518; [1969] 1 All ER 855 (CA); *Coppen v Moore (No 2)* [1898] 2 QB 306; *Director General of Fair Trading v Pioneer Concrete (UK)* [1995] 1 AC 456; [1994] 3 WLR 1249 (HL).
29 In the famous words of Edward, First Baron Thurlow, a company has "no soul to be damned and no body to be kicked": Mencken, *New Dictionary of Quotations* (1942), 223.
30 See, for example, *Pharmaceutical Soc v London Provincial Supply Assn Ltd* (1880) 5 App Cas 857, 869, where it was held that "person" in the Act under consideration did not include an incorporated company.
31 See s 2 Interpretation Act 1889 (UK): "person" is defined to include "a body of persons corporate or unincorporate". A similar stipulation is now made in s 2 Crimes Act 1961.

In addition, at one time a major obstacle to the prosecution of corporations for crimes (felonies) was that all felonies were punishable by death, and since a corporation could not be put to death it was, in that sense, incapable of committing a crime. This objection has been overcome by legislation enabling a court to sentence the offender to pay a fine in lieu of imprisonment.[33] In other cases, the court may be justified in disregarding the fact that the provision creating a particular offence imposes a mandatory penalty that cannot be imposed on a company.[34] Furthermore, the objection that a corporate body has no mind or soul and, as such, is incapable of possessing the mental element necessary for most serious offences, can be met by saying that a corporation can have knowledge and form an intention *through its human agents*, so that the knowledge and intention of its agents may be *imputed* to the body corporate.[35]

The general position at common law today is that a corporation is in the same position in relation to criminal liability as a natural person, and may be convicted of common law and statutory crimes including those requiring mens rea.[36] In a now celebrated passage in *Lennard's Carrying Co Ltd v Asiatic Petroleum Co Ltd*, Viscount Haldane said:[37]

> "A corporation is an abstraction. It has no mind of its own any more than it has a body of its own; its active and directing will must consequently be sought in the person of somebody who for some purposes may be called an agent, but who is really the directing mind and will of the corporation, the very ego and centre of the personality of the corporation ... [T]he fault or privity [of the company] is the fault or privity of somebody who is not merely a servant or agent for whom the company is liable upon the footing of respondeat superior, but somebody for whom the company is liable because his action is the *very action* of the company itself."

In New Zealand there are now only a few crimes for which a company may not be convicted.[38] For example, a corporation cannot, by its nature, commit the offence of perjury (an offence which cannot be committed vicariously) or bigamy, which can only be committed by a natural person.[39] Homicide, including both murder and manslaughter, cannot be committed by a company as a principal because of its definition, in s 160 Crimes Act 1961, as the "killing of one human being by another".[40] For this reason, it was held in *R v Murray Wright*[41] that the defendant company, which conducted a chemist business, could not be liable as a principal offender on a charge of negligent manslaughter when the incorrect preparation

---

32 See s 361 Crimes Act 1961 (plea on behalf of corporation).
33 Section 39 Sentencing Act 2002.
34 See *Police v Purser Asphalts & Contractors Ltd* [1990] 1 NZLR 693, also reported as *Purser Asphalts and Contractors Ltd v Police* (1988) 3 CRNZ 540 (mandatory period of disqualification from driving did not prevent imposition of corporate liability).
35 *DPP v Kent and Sussex Contractors Ltd* [1944] 1 KB 146; [1944] 1 All ER 119, 155; 123 (Viscount Caldecote CJ). No distinction is drawn here between corporations and companies: *R v Church of Scientology of Toronto* (1997) 116 CCC (3d) 1; 33 OR (3d) 65 (Ont CA), 69-73; 131.
36 *Halsbury's Laws of England* vol 11(1) (4th ed reissue), London, Butterworths, 1990, para 35.
37 *Lennard's Carrying Co Ltd v Asiatic Petroleum Co Ltd* [1915] AC 705; [1914-15] All ER Rep 280 (HL), 713; 283 (emphasis added).
38 *Police v Purser Asphalts & Contractors Ltd* [1990] 1 NZLR 693, also reported as *Purser Asphalts and Contractors Ltd v Police* (1988) 3 CRNZ 540, 695; 543 (Eichelbaum J).
39 *R v ICR Haulage Ltd* [1944] 1 KB 551; [1944] 1 All ER 691 (CA), 554; 693.
40 *R v Murray Wright Ltd* [1970] NZLR 476 (CA).
41 *R v Murray Wright Ltd* [1970] NZLR 476 (CA).

of a prescribed medicine was the cause of death. However, this is not to deny that a company may be liable as a party to homicide. Liability as a principal is merely limited by s 160 in respect of the act causing death, which must be committed by a "human being". Section 66, governing secondary participation, contains no such limitation. Hence a company may still be held liable as a party to offences committed by an individual. In *R v Robert Millar (Contractors) Ltd*,[42] the company was convicted of counselling and procuring the death by dangerous driving of six occupants of a car, which had been struck by a truck owned and operated by the company. The accident was caused by a tyre blowing out on the truck. The company was jointly charged with one of its directors, who had instructed an employee to drive the truck knowing that it had a dangerously defective tyre and that there was a serious risk of harm resulting to other road users. Rejecting the company's appeal, the Court approved the view that where a corporate employer, with imputed knowledge of the defective mechanical state of the vehicle, permits an employee to take that vehicle out on the road, it is counselling and procuring the employee to drive the vehicle in that state.

Indeed, it is arguable that corporate liability should be more wide-ranging than it presently is, in that the current barrier to liability as principal for homicide is anachronistic and out of step with the law in other jurisdictions.[43] There is no obvious reason why a company should avoid liability as a principal on a charge of manslaughter. Indeed, the potential for serious injury and death that may be caused by negligent and wilful corporate activity powerfully supports amending the law to allow such prosecutions to proceed. Growing concern about the need to establish a corporate "safety culture"[44] and the emerging view that corporations should be culpability-bearing agents in their own right, as implied in the notion of personal corporate liability, hint in the direction of future reform, considered further in 7.2.6.

Although it is sometimes argued that a punitive approach to corporate responsibility is inappropriate[45] and does little to ensure compliance with the law,[46] it seems plausible to assume that corporate liability coupled with the doctrine of strict liability in public welfare regulatory offences, with its defence of lack of fault, means that the management of a corporation has a real incentive to make diligent efforts to ensure compliance with the law. It may be that a variety of approaches, including both punitive and preventive, are needed to restrain the immense power of corporations in modern society and to protect citizens from the effects of misuse, or careless use, of that power.

---

42 *R v Robert Millar (Contractors) Ltd* [1970] 2 QB 54; [1970] 1 All ER 577 (CA).
43 See, for example, *Re A-G's Reference (No 2 of 1999)* [2000] QB 796; [2000] 3 All ER 182 (CA); Brookbanks, "Corporate manslaughter: *Attorney General's Reference (No 2 of 1999)* [2000] 3 WLR 195" (2000) 6 NZBLQ 228.
44 Trotter, "Corporate manslaughter" (2000) 150 NLJ 454; Maakestad, "Corporate homicide" (1990) 140 NLJ 356.
45 Some commentators have challenged the efficacy of a "blaming" approach in corporate prosecutions altogether. They prefer to concentrate on organisational or systems analysis, noting that individual human errors are inevitable and arguing that a better approach is to pursue a policy of continuous improvement. On this basis, errors are seen not so much as negative events as opportunities for open disclosure and remedial action. See Wells, *Corporations and Criminal Responsibility* (2nd ed), Oxford, Oxford University Press, 2001, 16-17; Merry and McCall-Smith, *Errors, Medicine and the Law*, Cambridge, Cambridge University Press, 2001, 26-40.
46 See, for example, Fisse, "Responsibility, prevention and corporate crime" (1973) 5 NZULR 250, 253.

7.2.1 Presumed criminal liability of corporations

As was noted above, corporate criminal liability has been provided for by extending the meaning of the word "person" to include bodies corporate,[47] implying that all criminal statutes are presumed to apply to artificial as well as natural legal persons. This presumption can be overridden, especially if the particular statute indicates a contrary intention. For example, a company cannot be nominated as a "pharmacist" for the purposes of certain proceedings under the Misuse of Drugs Act 1975.[48] The definition of "pharmacist" in the Act is clearly limited to a "*person* for the time being registered as a pharmacist", which necessarily excludes a corporation.[49] We have already noted another statutory exception, that a company cannot, by definition, be guilty of homicide as a principal. The presumption of corporate liability may also be rebutted for most sexual offences, at least in respect of liability as a principal.

Sometimes legislation requires that a mandatory penalty be imposed in respect of certain offences which, by its nature, is inapplicable to a corporation. In the rare cases where this occurs, it may not be possible to prosecute a corporation, and the presumption in favour of corporate liability may be rebutted. This might occur where, for example, legislation prescribes a mandatory minimum sentence of imprisonment or community service for a particular offence. However, as was noted earlier, exclusive minimum sentences are rare and in almost every case the courts may alternatively impose a fine in lieu of imprisonment.[50]

Even in cases where the legislation imposes a mandatory form of penalty that is not amenable to a company (for example, a mandatory period of disqualification), the presumption will not necessarily be rebutted if other penalties may be imposed such that the mandatory penalty may be regarded in the context as "mere surplusage" to the other penalties available. An illustrative case is *Police v Purser Asphalts & Contractors Ltd*,[51] where a company was charged under s 56 Transport Act 1962 with causing death by the careless use of a motor vehicle. The mandatory period of disqualification from driving, which can apply only to a natural person convicted of the offence, was held simply to be inapplicable to the company, which would nonetheless be subject to other penalties under the statute. The Court was influenced to reach this result by the fact that any other outcome would be inconsistent not only with the legislative presumption in favour of including companies, but also with the very purpose of s 56. As Eichelbaum J observed:[52]

> "It is notorious that numerous vehicles on the roads are in commercial use and owned by companies. There would be a significant gap in the scope of s 56(1) if incorporated owners were exempt from prosecution. The general direction of the Transport Act toward promotion of road safety is therefore in favour of the applicability of the section to bodies corporate."

---

47   See ss 29 and 30 Interpretation Act 1999 and s 2 Crimes Act 1961.
48   See *R v Wentworth* [1993] 2 NZLR 450, also reported as *R v Richards [aiding and abetting]* (1992) 9 CRNZ 355.
49   Section 2 Misuse of Drugs Act 1975 (emphasis added).
50   Section 39 Sentencing Act 2002.
51   *Police v Purser Asphalts & Contractors Ltd* [1990] 1 NZLR 693, also reported as *Purser Asphalts and Contractors Ltd v Police* (1988) 3 CRNZ 540.
52   *Police v Purser Asphalts & Contractors Ltd* [1990] 1 NZLR 693, also reported as *Purser Asphalts and Contractors Ltd v Police* (1988) 3 CRNZ 540, 696; 543.

We may therefore state, as a general principle, that where legislation expressly mandates a particular penalty which is apposite only to natural persons, a company may still be prosecuted, provided at least one other penalty (applicable to companies) is available. This requirement is usually met by the possibility of imposing a fine, which for most offences is available by way of alternative to imprisonment.

7.2.2 Distinguishing between direct and vicarious liability of companies

Because a company is a legal person without a physical existence, it is incapable of acting or forming an intention to act other than through its human agents. There are two ways in which a corporation may be liable for an offence. First, it may be liable for the conduct of employees or agents through the doctrine of *vicarious* liability (7.1), at least whenever a statute admits of vicarious liability. Alternatively, the corporation may be liable because acts done by its agents, servants, or directors are treated as acts done by the corporation itself, in circumstances where the human agents are deemed to be the "directing mind and will" of the company. In a sense, this is a false distinction, since under either approach the liabilities of the company are vicarious, being based upon an identification of the defendant company with the conduct of its agents, rather than upon any acts by the defendant itself. Nonetheless, although there is potential for confusing the two doctrines, their distinction reflects some important differences in the manner in which the acts of the human agents of a corporation may become, in law, the acts of the company itself. Whereas corporate liability depends upon an *identification* being made between the acts of a human agent and the company itself, vicarious liability involves the *attribution* of criminal liability to one individual or corporation for the acts of another.

7.2.3 Vicarious liability of corporations

Normally, vicarious liability, which makes the defendant answerable for the acts of its deputy, will not be imposed unless there are in the statute creating the offence very clear words imposing responsibility upon a defendant for the acts of its servant or agent. It should be remembered that vicarious liability was virtually unknown in the criminal law until quite recently, even though civil law has long held that an employer may be responsible for the torts of its employees acting in the course of their employment. In the criminal law, a defendant will normally only be liable for the actions of its servants on the basis of being a party to those actions. For the most part offenders are answerable only for their own acts.[53]

However, vicarious liability may be found where to fail to hold a master liable for the acts of its servant would be to "render nugatory" the statute and thus defeat the will of Parliament.[54] Especially in the context of regulatory offences, a particular statute may be open to the interpretation that it was the Legislature's intention to regulate certain types of activity by making the defendant liable for the acts of a servant, on the presumed basis that imposing liability on employers for contraventions by employees will more effectively achieve compliance with the legislation. The issue in each case will be whether the relevant statutory provision, which imposes a penalty on (say) an owner, is capable of making the defendant liable for an act of its employee when that act is done within the scope of employment but without the knowledge or instructions of the defendant. Because, in such cases, liability may be established without mens rea on the part of the defendant, it follows that this form of

---

53 *R v Huggins* (1730) 2 Stra 883; 93 ER 915, 885; 917.
54 Allen, *Textbook on Criminal Law* (3rd ed), London, Blackstone Press, 1995, 200.

liability is likely to be relatively rare. However, as we saw in 7.1 there are some limited areas of commercial activity where, historically, the Legislature has sought to regulate the activity by imposing vicarious liability. There does not appear to be any legislative tendency to expand the scope of vicarious liability.

A company may become vicariously liable for the actions of its servant (provided she is acting within the scope of her employment[55] or pursuant to a delegation)[56] in any circumstances in which vicarious liability may be imposed on an individual defendant. Typically, vicarious liability is found in legislation which regulates the sale or distribution of foodstuffs and other related activities, and in the area of liquor licensing. In such activities, it is not uncommon for the Legislature to attach criminal responsibility to an employer, whether or not a company, for the acts done by an employee in the course of his employment, or (in the case of mens rea offences) pursuant to a delegation of the employer's powers and duties, even though the particular acts were not authorised by the master, and may even have been expressly prohibited.[57] The details of this doctrine are considered in 7.1.

7.2.4 Rules for attributing direct (non-vicarious) liability to a company

Any proposition about a company necessarily involves reference to a set of rules. A company exists because there is a statutory rule which says that a fictional person is deemed to exist and which has the powers, rights, and duties of a natural person.[58] However, the creation of such a fictional person is only meaningful if rules exist that are able to tell us which acts count as acts of the company. Such rules are called "the rules of attribution". Their particular form depends upon the constitutional rules of the company, rules ordinarily implied in company law, and other rules which have been formulated by the courts in order to distinguish between employees and other company officials whose acts may be attributed to the company itself. The application of these rules determines the circumstances in which a company may be liable for the acts and mental state of an individual.

The basic rule of attribution is that, for an individual's conduct and state of mind to be identified with the company, *she must be in control of the company or a sphere of its activities*. However, this rule, as we shall see, is no more than a generalisation.

It is tempting to argue that the rules of attribution are general and invariant in nature, so that the liability of corporations for the acts of wayward employees or agents could be conveniently limited to acts done within the permissive powers of the company: for example, where the act is specifically authorised by a resolution of the board or a unanimous agreement of shareholders. Unfortunately, issues of liability are seldom as simple as this. First, where nominal and effective authority within a company differ, the courts will attribute on the basis of the particular company's actual as well as legal management structures. For example, in *Meridian Global Funds Management Asia Ltd v Securities Commission*[59] the company was held liable for the activities of employees who were left in de facto control of an area of the company's activities, though nominally authority was in the hands of a superior. It was held that the fact that an

---

55 See 7.1.2.
56 See 7.1.1.
57 See, for example, *Coppen v Moore (No 2)* [1898] 2 QB 306, where vicarious liability was found to exist in relation to the offence of selling goods to which a forged trademark or false trade description is applied.
58 See *Meridian Global Funds Management Asia Ltd v Securities Commission* [1995] 3 NZLR 7; [1995] 2 AC 500 (PC), 11; 506 (Lord Hoffmann). See ss 29 and 30 Interpretation Act 1999.

investment manager had undertaken a deal to purchase shares for a corrupt purpose, and did not give notice as required by the New Zealand Securities Amendment Act 1988 because he did not want his employers to find out, did not prevent that knowledge and the duty to give notice from being attributed to the company. Provided the person speaks and acts as the company, and is in actual control of company operations, liability may attach to the company.[60]

Secondly, and perhaps even more importantly, a simple insistence upon generalised rules of attribution would sometimes defeat the legislative intention that a particular law was intended to apply to companies. In such cases the court must fashion a special rule of attribution "tailored ... to the terms and policies" of the particular substantive rule.[61] In *Meridian*, Lord Hoffman set out this approach, in a passage that has since been adopted and applied by the Court of Appeal:[62]

> "In such a case, the Court must fashion a special rule of attribution for the particular substantive rule. This is always a matter of interpretation: given that it was intended to apply to a company, how was it intended to apply? Whose act (or knowledge, or state of mind) was *for this purpose* intended to count as the act etc of the company? One finds the answer to this question by applying the usual canons of interpretation, taking into account the language of the rule (if it is a statute) and its content and policy."

We may see the tailoring of generalised attribution principles in a number of recent decisions, considered in the following paragraphs.

In *Linework Ltd v Department of Labour*,[63] the employer, L, was a company that installed and maintained electricity distribution networks. V, an employee who worked in one of its installation teams, was seriously injured while removing a disconnected cable which came into contact with live cables. L was convicted under s 6 Health and Safety in Employment Act 1992, on the basis that the team's foreman had failed to take all practicable steps to ensure V's safety. The foreman had failed to ensure that V had adequately secured the cable before moving it. Affirming L's conviction, the Court of Appeal ruled that, in the context of the 1992 Act, the foreman's acts and omissions could be attributed to L:[64]

> "The Act is concerned with safety of the employees at work — for example, on the floor of the factory, on building sites, and while operating vehicles, plant and machinery. In practical terms, this is a world far removed from administrative offices which are the natural habitat of senior or middle level management. The statutory obligations upon an employer and, in particular, its obligation to provide on-the-job supervision of safety practices, must be viewed with this setting in mind. It is difficult to believe

---

59 *Meridian Global Funds Management Asia Ltd v Securities Commission* [1995] 3 NZLR 7; [1995] 2 AC 500 (PC). See also *Morris v Wellington City Corp* [1969] NZLR 1038. Cf *John Henshell (Quarries) Ltd v Harvey* [1965] 2 QB 233; [1965] 1 All ER 725: knowledge of an employee (a weighbridge operator) who has no real control over the company's activities is not enough.
60 See *Nordik Industries Ltd v Regional Controller of Inland Revenue* [1976] 1 NZLR 194.
61 *Meridian Global Funds Management Asia Ltd v Securities Commission* [1995] 3 NZLR 7; [1995] 2 AC 500 (PC), 16, 17; 512 (Lord Hoffmann).
62 *Meridian Global Funds Management Asia Ltd v Securities Commission* [1995] 3 NZLR 7; [1995] 2 AC 500 (PC), 12; 507; *Linework Ltd v Department of Labour* [2001] 2 NZLR 639 (CA), paras 12, 23-24.
63 *Linework Ltd v Department of Labour* [2001] 2 NZLR 639 (CA), paras 12, 23-24.
64 *Linework Ltd v Department of Labour* [2001] 2 NZLR 639 (CA), paras 12, 23-24.

that Parliament would have intended that the relevant acts and omissions of the person in charge of a work site should not be attributable to the employer.... We agree with the lower Courts that the acts and omissions of the person in effective charge of a work site, in this case the foreman who had a supervisory capacity, should be attributed to Linework. In applying the test proposed by the Judicial Committee in *Meridian* at p 12, it was [the foreman's] actions or inactions that, for the purpose of taking all practicable steps to ensure the safety of employees, were 'intended to count' as the acts of the company."

In earlier cases, the courts often utilised a distinction between individuals who were the "brains" or "minds" of the company and those who were merely its "hands", implying that inferior employment status may never bind a company in respect of unauthorised acts done within the scope of an individual's employment.[65] The analogy of "brains" and "hands" was applied in *Tesco Supermarkets Ltd v Nattrass*.[66] Tesco had been prosecuted under the Trade Descriptions Act 1968 for displaying a notice that goods were being offered at a price less than that at which they were in fact being offered. The prosecution had arisen because the shop manager of one of the 200-odd supermarket branches had negligently failed to notice that he had run out of specially marked low-price packets of washing powder, one of which was sold to a customer at a price higher than that stated on the display notice. The Act provided a defence for a shop owner who could prove that the commission of the offence was caused by "another person" and that he took "all reasonable precautions ... to avoid the commission of such an offence by himself or anyone under his control". The House of Lords held that the branch manager could not be considered a controlling mind of the company, such that his negligence could be attributable to the company (he was, in law, "another person"), and that the precautions taken by the board of directors were sufficient to count as precautions taken by the company. However, while the decisions in *Meridian* and *Linemark* make clear that attribution is no longer restricted to the "brains" of the company, it is important to notice that *Tesco* was not resolved simply at the level of general principle, by distinguishing between "brains" and "hands", but also by examining the substantive rule in the particular statute which, the Court concluded, was intended to give effect to a policy of consumer protection, the rationale for which did not require the conclusion that the acts and defaults of the manager were to be attributed to the company. It is this particularised element that makes the modern cases on corporate attribution distinguishable from each other.

In contrast with *Tesco* is the decision in *Director General of Fair Trading v Pioneer Concrete (UK)*.[67] There a restrictive arrangement, in breach of an undertaking by a company to the Restrictive Practices Court, was made by executives of the company acting within the scope of their employment. The board of directors knew nothing of the arrangement and had given instructions to company employees that they were not to make such arrangements. However, the House of Lords held that for the purposes of deciding whether the company was in contempt, the act and the state of mind of an employee who entered into an arrangement in the course of his employment should be attributed to the company. Again, the particular attribution rule was derived from a construction of the undertaking against the background

---

65 See *H L Bolton (Engineering) Co Ltd v T J Graham & Sons Ltd* [1957] 1 QB 159; [1956] 3 All ER 624 (CA), 172; 630.
66 *Tesco Supermarkets Ltd v Nattrass* [1972] AC 153; [1971] 2 All ER 127 (HL).
67 *Director General of Fair Trading v Pioneer Concrete (UK)* [1995] 1 AC 456; [1994] 3 WLR 1249 (HL).

of the Restrictive Trade Practices Act 1976. The Court concluded that such undertakings would be worth little if the company could avoid liability for what its employees had actually done on the ground that the board did not know about it. An uncritical application of the *Nattrass* rule, the Court found, would effectively mean that the "higher management" of a company could benefit from restrictive arrangements, outlawed by Parliament, by hiding behind the actions of an employee who had individually accepted, implemented, and arranged prohibited activities which benefited the company, while claiming that he was not authorised to do so.[68]

The conclusion which emerges from these cases is that it will be a question of construction in each case whether enforcement of the particular statute or regulation requires that knowledge of an act, or the state of mind with which it is done, should be attributed to the company. In particular, it should not be assumed that whenever a servant of a company has authority to do an act on the company's behalf, knowledge of that act will for all purposes be attributed to the company.[69] For example, the fact that a company authorises an employee to drive a heavy vehicle does not automatically imply that, if he kills someone by reckless driving, his actions and state of mind must be attributed to the company for the purposes of establishing its criminal liability. Conversely, it should not be assumed that direct attribution of liability to the company can be avoided simply because company directors have no actual knowledge of the unlawful activities of a company employee.[70] In each case, the rule of attribution must be tailored to the terms and policies of the substantive rule.[71]

(1) *"Alter ego" v "embodiment" or "identification"?*

In older case law it is sometimes suggested that identification between the company and its human agents was based on the theory that when speaking and acting for the company, the agent was acting as the "alter ego" of the company. In *Tesco Supermarkets Ltd v Nattrass* Lord Pearson indicated that he saw a place for the phrase "alter ego":[72]

> "A company may have an alter ego, if those persons who are or have its ego delegate to some other person the control and management, with full discretionary powers, of some section of the company's business."

However, in the same case Lord Reid deprecated the use of the phrase "alter ego" in this context:[73]

---

68 See the comments of Lord Templeman, *Director General of Fair Trading v Pioneer Concrete (UK)* [1995] 1 AC 456; [1994] 3 WLR 1249 (HL), 465; 1254-1255.
69 *Meridian Global Funds Management Asia Ltd v Securities Commission* [1995] 3 NZLR 7; [1995] 2 AC 500 (PC), 16, 17; 512.
70 Cf *R v Forges du Lac Inc* (1997) 117 CCC (3d) 71, 84 (failure by a company employee with significant authority over the management of a company's finances to file tax returns in respect of money diverted from the company to privately controlled bank accounts). The imposition of corporate criminal liability in such circumstances should stimulate shareholders to exercise stricter supervision and control in the selection of company directors and, in turn, compels directors to be alert to the corporate practices of its senior personnel: *R v McNamara (No 1)* (1981) 56 CCC (2d) 193.
71 *Meridian Global Funds Management Asia Ltd v Securities Commission* [1995] 3 NZLR 7; [1995] 2 AC 500 (PC), 16, 17; 512; *Linework Ltd v Department of Labour* [2001] 2 NZLR 639 (CA), paras 23-24.
72 *Tesco Supermarkets Ltd v Nattrass* [1972] AC 153; [1971] 2 All ER 127 (HL), 193; 150.
73 *Tesco Supermarkets Ltd v Nattrass* [1972] AC 153; [1971] 2 All ER 127 (HL), 171-172; 132-133 (emphasis added).

"I think it is misleading. When dealing with a company the word alter is I think misleading. The person who speaks and acts as the company is not alter. *He is identified with the company.* And when dealing with an individual no other individual can be his alter ego. The other individual can be a servant, agent, delegate or representative but I know of neither principle nor authority which warrants the confusion ... of two separate individuals."

The essence of corporate personality, as Lord Reid notes in an earlier passage in the judgment,[74] is that when a person acts or speaks for a company he is acting *as* the company and his mind which directs his acts is the mind of the company:[75]

"There is no question of the company being vicariously liable. He is not acting as a servant, representative, agent or delegate. He is an embodiment of the company or, one could say, he hears and speaks through the persona of the company, within his appropriate sphere, and his mind is the mind of the company."

In *Meridian Global Funds Management Asia Ltd v Securities Commission*,[76] the New Zealand Court of Appeal based attribution upon the notion that the investment manager was the "directing mind and will" of the company.[77] The concept of a "directing mind and will" is closer to Lord Reid's idea that the person acting for the company is "an embodiment of the company" and is, with respect, to be preferred to the "alter ego" theory. However, as has been noted, whether a particular individual can be described as the "directing mind and will" whose knowledge that an act has been done may be attributed to a company, remains a matter for construction in each case. In *Meridian*, the Privy Council said:[78]

"In such a case, the court must fashion a special rule of attribution for the particular substantive rule. This is always a matter of interpretation: given that it was intended to apply to a company, how was it intended to apply? Whose act (or knowledge, or state of mind) was *for this purpose* intended to count as the act etc of the company? One finds the answer to this question by applying the usual canons of interpretation, taking into account the language of the rule (if it is a statute) and its content and policy."

The notion of the "directing mind" is the basis of the "identification" doctrine in Canada. In *R v Church of Scientology of Toronto*[79] the Ontario Court of Appeal applied the identification doctrine to a non-profit religious corporation on the basis that since corporations (including non-profit corporations) occupy such a central role in society, it would be "intolerable" to leave them outside the purview of the criminal law.[80] Of the identification doctrine itself, the Court said:

"The identification doctrine is a pragmatic, but rational, way of making a corporation liable for criminal acts committed on its behalf or at least partly for its benefit ... It imposes liability only for the acts of the corporate governing body and those to whom

---

74 *Tesco Supermarkets Ltd v Nattrass* [1972] AC 153; [1971] 2 All ER 127 (HL) 170; 131.
75 *Tesco Supermarkets Ltd v Nattrass* [1972] AC 153; [1971] 2 All ER 127 (HL).
76 *Meridian Global Funds Management Asia Ltd v Securities Commission* [1994] 2 NZLR 291 (CA).
77 The phrase "directing mind and will" comes from a celebrated speech of Viscount Haldane in *Lennard's Carrying Co Ltd v Asiatic Petroleum Co Ltd* [1915] AC 705; [1914-15] All ER Rep 760 (HL).
78 *Meridian Global Funds Management Asia Ltd v Securities Commission* [1995] 3 NZLR 7; [1995] 2 AC 500 (PC), 12, 13; 507.
79 *R v Church of Scientology of Toronto* (1997) 116 CCC (3d) 1; 33 OR (3d) 65 (Ont CA).
80 *R v Church of Scientology of Toronto* (1997) 116 CCC (3d) 1; 33 OR (3d) 65 (Ont CA), 69-73; 131.

that body has delegated executive authority. Moreover, even if the employee is deemed to be a directing mind of the corporation, the corporation will not be liable for that employee's acts if they are in total fraud of the corporation."

The reason for the latter limitation would seem to be that an employee who acts in fraud of a company cannot be said to be carrying out his assigned function in the corporation and, as such, is acting outside the scope of his authority. In *R v Safety-Kleen Canada*[81] it was held that where the identification theory applies in the absence of a statutory basis for corporate liability, the inquiry is a "fact-driven" one which looks beyond titles and job descriptions to the reality of any given situation.

(2) *Liability for negligence in failing to supervise a company's activities*

Alternatively, depending upon the particular statute, a company may be directly liable for offences of negligence in failing to prevent the actus reus from occurring. Because negligence liability does not require proof either of particular acts or of a particular state of mind, the company is more easily affixed with responsibility for its omission to prevent harm. In these cases, the company will normally escape criminal liability if it has acted reasonably to select suitable persons to oversee the corporation's activities and to carry out a reasonable policy to ensure compliance with the law. Conversely, in the absence of a reasonable standard of conduct and management, liability may be imputed to a company. In *The Lady Gwendolen*[82] the defendant company was the owner of a ship which had been involved in a collision with another vessel. The collision occurred because the master, as was his practice, had taken his fully-laden vessel up the Mersey Channel at full speed in dense fog without more than an odd glance at his radar. Owning ships was a subsidiary part of the company's activities. It had a traffic department which managed the ships under the overall supervision of a member of the board who was a brewer and took little interest in the safety of their navigation. The marine superintendent, who was below the traffic manager in the company's hierarchy, failed to observe that the ship's master was given to dangerous navigation. In attributing liability to the company, the Court said:[83]

> "In their capacity as shipowners they must be judged by the standard of conduct of the ordinary reasonable shipowner in the management and control of a vessel ... ."

The Court found that a reasonable shipowner would have realised what was happening and would have given the master proper instruction in the use of radar.

While a corporation will not normally be liable for the negligent conduct of junior employees, the breach, by a superior officer of a company, of a duty to check the conduct of a junior may result in liability being attributed to the company itself. However, such a duty would not normally arise where the junior employee is experienced at the work in question, unless there were special facts to suggest a need for closer oversight.[84] Such a person could properly be described as the "hands" of the company, whose actions would not normally be attributable to the company because they do not represent the mind and will of the company.[85]

---

81 *R v Safety-Kleen Canada* (1997) 145 DLR (4th) 276; 114 CCC (3d) 214.
82 *Arthur Guinness, Son, and Co (Dublin) Ltd v Owners of the Motor Vessel Freshfield (The Lady Gwendolen)* [1965] P 294; [1965] 2 All ER 283 (CA).
83 *Arthur Guinness, Son, and Co (Dublin) Ltd v Owners of the Motor Vessel Freshfield (The Lady Gwendolen)* [1965] P 294; [1965] 2 All ER 283 (CA), 333; 288 (Sellers LJ).
84 See *Lewin v Bland* [1985] RTR 171.

(3) Mens rea offences

Where the offence committed requires proof of a specific intent, a corporate defendant cannot be found guilty unless the requisite intent was a state of mind of one or more of the natural persons who constituted the company's directing mind and will.[86] By contrast, where the offence is one of strict or absolute liability, the company may be held liable for the acts of any of its servants or agents once those acts are proved to be, in law, the company's acts.[87] Where (a third alternative) it is a defence for an employer to prove that the offence was due to the act or default of another, and that the employer took all reasonable precautions, this defence is available to a corporation. In such circumstances, "another person" is any person other than the directors or other superior officers who control the corporation's affairs.[88]

If a defence requires evidence of a belief or other state of mind, this must normally be the belief or state of mind of the controlling officer[89] since she is acting as the company and it is her mind which directs the company.[90] However, such a belief may be negated if another superior officer knows that the belief is ill-founded.[91] This is because the supervening belief held by the superior officer becomes the knowledge or belief of the corporation itself, provided that officer at the point at which he acquires the knowledge is acting within the scope of his employment.

Relevant knowledge or beliefs may also be attributed to the company, even where the impugned individual cannot be described as a or the "directing mind and will" of a company, provided it is established that the individual concerned had been delegated the "governing executive authority" of the company within the scope of her authority: that is to say, where she has been left with the decision-making power in a relevant sphere of corporate activity.[92]

7.2.5 Personal liability of company employees

As a general rule, a director or controlling member of a company is not criminally liable for the acts of the company simply because of his position. Liability is not automatically vicarious. Furthermore, it does not follow that because a company may be criminally liable for the acts of its officers acting within the scope of their employment, an individual officer must be criminally liable because the company has been found to be criminally liable. The company's acts are defined by the actions of those who are identified as the "directing mind and will" of the company. But an individual officer of the company may avoid liability if he did not know of the facts which were constitutive of the offence or offences committed by other senior officials of the company and by which the company was itself impugned. In *Cardin Laurant Ltd v Commerce Commission*,[93] which involved a prosecution under the Fair Trading Act 1986

---

85   See *H L Bolton (Engineering) Co Ltd v T J Graham & Sons Ltd* [1957] 1 QB 159; [1956] 3 All ER 624 (CA), 172; 630 (Denning LJ).
86   *Wings Ltd v Ellis* [1984] 1 All ER 1046, 1053; and see *Tesco Supermarkets Ltd v Nattrass* [1972] AC 153; [1971] 2 All ER 127 (HL).
87   Smith and Hogan, *Criminal Law* (7th ed), London, Butterworths, 1992, 182.
88   *Tesco Supermarkets Ltd v Nattrass* [1972] AC 153; [1971] 2 All ER 127 (HL).
89   *G F Coles & Co Ltd v Goldsworthy* [1958] WAR 183.
90   *Nordik Industries Ltd v Regional Controller of Inland Revenue* [1976] 1 NZLR 194, 203.
91   *Brambles Holdings Ltd v Carey* (1976) 15 SASR 270.
92   *Rhone (The) v Peter AB Widener (The)* (1993) 101 DLR (4th) 188; [1993] 1 SCR 497 (SCC), 209, 210; 520, 521 (Iacobucci J).
93   *Cardin Laurant Ltd v Commerce Commission* [1990] 3 NZLR 563; (1989) 3 TCLR 470.

for offering to supply a garment which failed to comply with product safety standards, the High Court held that the principal in a company could not be held a party to any offence committed by the company unless he had knowledge of the essential matters which constitute the offence.[94] However, where the principal of a company is knowingly concerned in the commission of offences committed by the company, there can be no objection to prosecuting the principal personally for the identical acts and decisions that were relied on as the acts of the company.[95] There is nothing conceptually wrong with such a course because a person may function in two capacities.[96] The relevant principle has been expressed in these terms:[97]

> "the company, being a legal entity apart from its members, is also a legal person apart from the legal personality of the individual controller of the company, and that he in his personal capacity can aid and abet what the company speaking through his mouth or acting through his hand may have done."

But the same principle does not apply when a conspiracy is alleged. The basis of conspiracy is the acting in concert of two or more persons. Although a company is a separate legal entity, where the sole responsible person in a company is the defendant herself, there cannot be two or more persons or minds and so there can be no conspiracy between the defendant and the company.[98] On the other hand, this rationale does not exclude the possibility of a conspiracy involving the company where two or more directors have agreed together to do an unlawful act, since the guilty mind of only one human agent, acting within the scope of his employment, is necessary to impugn the company.

Individual liability may also attach to the directors of a company in respect of an offence committed by a corporation where the statute creating the offence specifically provides, for example, that the directors or persons involved in the management of the corporation are liable unless they can prove that they did not know that the offence was being committed or that they took reasonable steps to prevent its commission.[99]

7.2.6 Reform of corporate liability

(1) *Aggregation*

Because of the high incidence of employment-related injuries and deaths, there are growing calls for reform of the law regarding the liability of companies, especially in respect of homicide.[100] In order to deal with the problem that corporate actors seldom act in isolation when seeking to advance a corporation's interests, some commentators have proposed an

---

94 *Cardin Laurant Ltd v Commerce Commission* [1990] 3 NZLR 563; (1989) 3 TCLR 470, 569; 477 (Fisher J). Of course, the person need not actually know that an offence has been committed, because he may not know that the facts constitute an offence and ignorance of the law is not a defence: *Johnson v Youden* [1950] 1 KB 544; [1950] 1 All ER 300, 546; 302.
95 See *Hamilton v Whitehead* (1988) 166 CLR 121; 82 ALR 626 (HCA), 125; 628; *Linework Ltd v Department of Labour* [2001] 2 NZLR 639 (CA), paras 38, 47.
96 *Hamilton v Whitehead* (1988) 166 CLR 121; 82 ALR 626 (HCA), 128; 630.
97 *R v Goodall* (1974-1975) 11 SASR 94, 101 (Bray CJ).
98 *R v McDonnell* [1966] 1 QB 233; [1966] 1 All ER 193 (CCA).
99 See, for example, s 340 Resource Management Act 1991; *Machinery Movers Ltd v Auckland Regional Council* [1994] 1 NZLR 492; (1993) 2 NZRMA 661.
100 See, for example, Ashworth, *Principles*, 117. See also Lederman, "Models for Imposing Corporate Criminal Liability: from adaptation and imitation towards aggregation and the search for self-identiy" [2001] Buff Crim LRev 641, for a thoughtful account of recent theorising on corporate liability.

"aggregation" of the knowledge and attitudes of employees as a whole. Thus no single, individual controlling officer need be proved to have the relevant knowledge of wrongdoing by the corporation — thereby avoiding the problem of making liability contingent upon finding one individual who, by herself, satisfies the entire mens rea requirement.[101] This approach would require legislative reform: although aggregation does not appear to have been considered judicially in New Zealand, the courts elsewhere have not endorsed it.[102] Nonetheless, the English Law Commission has recently recommended an aggregative approach of corporate fault as part of its proposed reforms of manslaughter.[103] In a movement away from common law doctrines, the Law Commission has recommended a new offence of corporate killing where a cause of death is "management failure by the corporation" and where "that failure constitutes conduct falling far below what can reasonably be expected of the corporation in the circumstances". A "management failure" would comprise a failure to organise the company so as to ensure the health and safety of employees or others affected by the company's activities.

This approach is consistent with the view that many harms involve a contribution from more than one person. Thus it avoids the tendency to blame the last identifiable element in the chain of causation — the so-called "smoking gun". In the context of medical errors, it has been suggested that a more comprehensive approach would identify the relative contributions of other failures in the system apart from the last medical actor, including failures in the conduct of other individuals.[104] A similar analysis might be applied in the present context.

(2) *Safety cultures*

Other law reform proposals urge a movement away from the concept of attribution towards a change in "safety culture". It has been argued that merely fining corporations — the principal form of punishment for companies which breach the law — fails adequately to deter multinational corporations and, moreover, neither compensates the victim nor improves the company's safety system. To counter deficits in corporate safety management, it has been suggested that company legislation should be amended to require the appointment of a "Safety Director", whose name must be shown on the company letterhead and registered at the Companies Office. Such a person would have a defence to liability for safety failures provided that he raised the need for safety measures that were unquestionably refused by directors.[105] Other proposals include the appointment of independent directors to monitor corporate behaviour.[106] In general, preventive sanctions along these lines are increasingly favoured in the regulation of corporate activity.[107]

One advantage of such proposals is that they represent a movement away from a purely individualistic approach to corporate liability, toward a model that acknowledges a holistic

---

101 Wells, *Corporations and Criminal Responsibility* (2nd ed), Oxford, Oxford University Press, 2001, 156.
102 See *R v HM Coroner for East Kent, ex parte Spooner and others* (1989) 88 Cr App R 10, 16; *Re A-G's Reference (No 2 of 1999)* [2000] QB 796; [2000] 3 All ER 182 (CA).
103 *Legislating the Criminal Code: Involuntary Manslaughter*, Law Com no 237, 1996, paras 8.1-8.77.
104 Merry and McCall-Smith, *Errors, Medicine and the Law*, Cambridge, Cambridge University Press, 2001, 14.
105 Trotter, "Corporate manslaughter" (2000) 150 NLJ 454.
106 Stone, *Where the Law Ends: The Social Control of Corporate Behaviour*, New York, Harper & Row, 1975.
107 Cf the US Sentencing Guidelines, which encourage compliance through rewarding monitoring and self-reporting: Wells, *Corporations and Criminal Responsibility* (2nd ed), Oxford, Oxford University Press, 2001, 38.

form of corporate agency and corporate culpability, one which need not be derived from the fault of particular individuals associated with the company.

(3) *Reactive fault*

Another, more radical, proposal for reforming corporate liability is Fisse and Braithwaite's notion of "reactive fault". Reactive fault is "unreasonable corporate failure to devise and undertake satisfactory preventive or corrective measures in response to the commission of the actus reus of an offence by personnel acting on behalf of the organisation".[108] Building on community values which are critical of corporate irresponsibility and the perceived uselessness of criminal prosecutions of corporations, reactive fault claims to offer a way of attributing culpability to a company in a manner that is workable and corporate in orientation. Thus a company could be held liable where, having committed the actus reus of an offence, it fails to respond by subsequently implementing satisfactory corrective measures designed to prevent a recurrence. Fisse and Braithwaite argue that the concept of reactive fault allows the issue of blameworthiness to be approached through a corporation's internal decision structures and facilitates an examination of how and why a corporation has failed to adapt its policies in the light of past errors. As such, it may be a useful model in the areas of health and safety for employees, product safety, and pollution regulation, where it may be easy to refute an allegation of recklessness if each offence is considered in isolation.[109] However, in addition to in-principle objections to abandoning the concurrence principle,[110] by using subsequent culpability to support convictions for antecedent harms, there are practical difficulties associated with the reactive fault model. For example, how would it be determined whether the degree of reactive fault proved against D Ltd merited, say, a conviction for manslaughter? The issues arising at trial would not centre on the culpability at the time of a particular incident but would require a review of corporate safety and other procedures within an open-ended time-frame. The prosecutorial and forensic burden would be enormous — indeed, prohibitive.

---

108 Fisse and Braithwaite, *Corporations, Crime and Accountability*, Cambridge, Cambridge University Press, 1993, 48.
109 Cf Wells, *Corporations and Criminal Responsibility* (2nd ed), Oxford, Oxford University Press, 2001, 159.
110 See 4.9.

Chapter 8

THE INCHOATE OFFENCES

8.1	Introduction	218
8.2	Attempts	219
8.2.1	Mens rea	220
8.2.2	Actus reus	222
(1)	*Modes in which attempts may be made*	224
(2)	*"For the purpose of accomplishing his object"*	227
8.2.3	From preparation to attempt	227
(1)	*Common law tests for proximity*	227
(2)	*Inadequacy of proximity theory*	236
(3)	*A way forward?*	237
(4)	*"Dangerous" proximity*	237
8.2.4	Withdrawal	240
8.2.5	Impossibility	241
(1)	*"Legal" impossibility as a defence*	242
(2)	*Factual impossibility*	244
(3)	*The "imaginary crime" exception*	245
8.2.6	A crime of attempted conspiracy?	246
8.3	Conspiracy	248
8.3.1	Scope of conspiracy	248
8.3.2	When is a conspiracy complete?	250
8.3.3	Elements of conspiracy	251
8.3.4	Actus reus of conspiracy	252
(1)	*Acts subsequent to the formation but during the continuation of the conspiracy*	253
(2)	*Proof of the agreement*	254
(3)	*Conspiring with "persons unknown"*	254
(4)	*The "wheel" conspiracy*	255
(5)	*The "chain" conspiracy*	256
(6)	*Purely "internal" conspiracies?*	257
8.3.5	Mens rea of conspiracy	258
(1)	*Agreements and acquiescence*	259
(2)	*Partial conspiracy?*	260
8.3.6	Variations in details of the conspiracy	262
8.3.7	Attempted conspiracy?	263

8.3.8   Conspiracy and party liability 263

8.3.9   Extraterritorial conspiracies 264

8.3.10   Acquittal of other conspirators 265

8.3.11   Impossibility and conspiracy 266

(1)   *Conduct wrongly believed to be an offence* 266
(2)   *Desired end impossible to produce* 267
(3)   *Merits of excluding liability for impossibility* 268

8.3.12   Charging conspiracy together with the substantive offence 269

8.4   Incitement 270

8.4.1   Actus reus 271

(1)   *Communication of incitement* 272
(2)   *Renunciation of incitement* 273
(3)   *Attempted incitement* 273

8.4.2   Mens rea 274

8.4.3   Incitement to murder 274

(1)   *Inciting "any person"* 275
(2)   *To murder "any other person"* 275

8.4.4   Impossibility 275

8.1   Introduction

Attempt, conspiracy, and incitement are inchoate crimes. Their designation as "inchoate" reflects the fact that they criminalise conduct by D which is incomplete or imperfect, in the sense that it has not resulted in the commission of some particular, substantive offence. Thus they criminalise the conduct of a person who has the purpose of committing a substantive offence, where her conduct has the potential to culminate in that offence, without the need for the offence actually to occur.[1]

In general, the rationale for having inchoate crimes is derivative from the rationale for criminalising a substantive offence. If particular conduct — say, causing another's death — is sufficiently harmful to warrant criminalisation, it is thought that so, too, is the attempt (conspiracy, incitement) to bring that harm about. It may not be so bad to try unsuccessfully to kill V as it is to succeed, but it is both culpable and wrongful to do so all the same. It would be odd if V were to react as if nothing untoward had happened. Society endorses this view, by recognising that the proximity of her attempt to the substantive crime gives D's behaviour and intentions a criminal character in their own right.

Moreover, there are deterrence and law-enforcement reasons for criminalising inchoate activity. In order to deter persons from killing others, it seems desirable also to deter them from attempting (plotting, inciting others) to do so.[2] Having inchoate offences also enables the police to intervene and prevent crime before it occurs, without foregoing the chance of a

---

1   Gillies, *Criminal Law* (1st ed), Sydney, The Law Book Company, 1985, 512.
2   See *DPP v Nock* [1978] AC 979; [1978] 2 All ER 654 (HL), 997; 661 (Lord Scarman).

conviction. It would be bizarre indeed if the police were, in order to save V's life, forced to arrest D and in so doing enable her to escape criminal liability.

On occasion, the inchoate offence of "attempt" may also be charged where the defendant's attempt was successful but, because of evidential difficulties, only an attempt, not the consummated offence, can be proved. Formally, every successful crime is also an attempt. In such cases, the law of "attempt" is employed, not for the purpose of deterring offenders from committing offences (which may actually have been committed), but rather to ensure that an offender does not avoid criminal conviction because of a technical inability to prove, for example, the concurrence of actus reus and mens rea.[3]

8.2 Attempts

Section 72 Crimes Act 1961 provides:

"(1) Every one who, having an intent to commit an offence, does or omits an act for the purpose of accomplishing his object, is guilty of an attempt to commit the offence intended, whether in the circumstances it was possible to commit the offence or not.

"(2) The question whether an act done or omitted with intent to commit an offence is or is not only preparation for the commission of that offence, and too remote to constitute an attempt to commit it, is a question of law.

"(3) An act done or omitted with intent to commit an offence may constitute an attempt if it is immediately or proximately connected with the intended offence, whether or not there was any act unequivocally showing the intent to commit that offence."

The law of attempts has a long history, dating back at least to the ancient Greek and Roman civilisations. However, it is noticeably absent from early common law, where it was generally said that "a miss is as good as a mile". Only in 1801 was the general principle established that an attempt to commit a crime is, itself, a crime.[4]

Section 72 does not create offences, but rather defines the circumstances in which an attempt may be committed. Punishment for attempts is found under a number of other provisions in the Crimes Act 1961, most of which criminalise attempts to commit specific offences.[5] The general provision punishing attempts is contained in s 311, which covers every situation falling within s 72 where no punishment is otherwise provided for. The effect of s 311 is to criminalise any attempt to commit a criminal offence (including all summary offences). In general, a person guilty of an attempted crime under s 311 is liable to one half of the maximum penalty to which a person guilty of the completed offence is liable.[6]

---

3 Thus in R v Williams (2002) 176 CCC (3d) 449 (SCC), para 64, failure to prove endangerment to life (because it was possible the victim was already infected with HIV before the respondent knew he was HIV positive) was fatal to a prosecution for aggravated assault, requiring proof of actual endangerment, but was not fatal to a conviction for attempted aggravated assault.
4 See R v Higgins (1801) 2 East 5; 102 ER 269.
5 See s 95 (attempts to commit piracy); s 129 (attempt to commit sexual violation); s 173 (attempt to murder); s 295 (attempted arson); s 302 (attempting to wreck).
6 Regarding the summary trial of offences under s 311, see s 6(2) Summary Proceedings Act 1957, as amended by s 3(1) Summary Proceedings Amendment Act 1961 and s 4(2) Summary Proceedings Amendment Act 1973.

The law of attempts focuses on four principal types of element: mens rea, actus reus, proximity, and impossibility. Each of these aspects will be discussed below. The first three relate to the minimum requirements for a criminal attempt; the fourth, impossibility, represents an important limitation on liability for an attempt.

8.2.1 Mens rea

Mens rea is the most important element of criminal attempts, because the actus reus does not, as a matter of definition, require proof of a completed crime. Indeed, although some conduct by the accused is required before there can be an attempt, that conduct need not be obviously criminal in nature; and the criminal element of the offence may lie solely in the intent.[7] In many attempts, the actus reus may be a quite harmless act which, of itself, would not attract any adverse comment were it not for the intention of the offender to commit a crime.

Therefore, it is essential to determine the precise state of mind of the accused at the time of the act which allegedly constituted the attempt. The phrase in s 72(1) "having an intent to commit an offence" prima facie suggests that only an intention to commit the offence will suffice. In most jurisdictions, the meaning of intent in relation to attempts is construed quite narrowly. In England, for example, whereas recklessness is sufficient mens rea for most non-fatal offences against the person, and for offences of criminal damage, it is not a sufficient mens rea on a charge of attempting to commit any of those offences.[8] This is almost certainly the position in New Zealand, although the point has not been formally decided upon by the courts.

However, while it appears that the mens rea element of the crime of attempt is unaffected by the mens rea required to be convicted of the relevant full offence, and is specific to s 72, it cannot be said for certain that *only* intent suffices for the mens rea requirements of s 72. There is some debate on this point.

There is authority in England to the effect that while intent is required regarding the behaviour and consequence elements of the full offence, recklessness will be sufficient regarding any *circumstances* specified in the actus reus.[9] Similarly, it has been argued by Smith and Hogan that merely because the notion of attempt requires an intended result, it does not necessarily require intention with respect to material circumstances.[10] The authors contend that the mens rea of a completed crime should be modified only in so far as it is necessary in order to accommodate the concept of attempt; and that if recklessness as to circumstances is a sufficient mens rea for the complete crime, so also should it be for an attempt.[11] On the other hand, Professor Griew has argued that the phrase "with intent to commit an offence" requires, as a matter of construction, that the intention must apply to the whole situation necessary to constitute the offence.[12] According to this analysis a man attempting to have sexual intercourse with a woman who does not in fact consent will not be guilty of attempted rape if he is merely reckless whether

---

7   R v Ancio [1984] 1 SCR 225; (1984) 10 CCC (3d) 385 (SCC), 248; 402.
8   Smith and Hogan, *Criminal Law* (9th ed), London, Butterworths, 1999, 306.
9   For example R v Khan [1990] 2 All ER 783; [1990] 1 WLR 813 (CA). See also White, "Three points on Pigg" [1989] Crim LR 539.
10 Smith and Hogan, *Criminal Law* (9th ed), London, Butterworths, 1999, 307-308.
11 Smith and Hogan, *Criminal Law* (9th ed), London, Butterworths, 1999, 307-308.
12 Griew, *Current Law Statutes*, cited in Smith and Hogan, Criminal Law (5th ed), London, Butterworths, 1983, 257. The wording is that of s 1 Criminal Attempts Act 1981 (UK), and parallels the requirements of s 72 Crimes Act 1961: "having an intent to commit an offence."

she is consenting or not. His aim must be not merely sexual intercourse, but non-consensual intercourse.

The latter, seemingly narrow, approach to the mens rea requirements of attempt has been criticised on the ground that it creates an absurdity when applied to crimes such as rape, in which the circumstantial element of non-consent is central to the offence. Ashworth[13] gives the example of two men who set out to have sexual intercourse with two women, not caring whether they consent. He notes that it would be absurd if the one who achieved penetration was convicted of rape, while the other, who failed to achieve penetration despite trying, was not even liable for attempted rape. In both cases the degree of moral culpability is identical, yet the attempter would avoid conviction because, being reckless, he failed to achieve his objective.

In other jurisdictions, the approach to the mens rea requirement for attempts varies. The Court of Criminal Appeal of South Australia has taken an approach similar to the English Court of Appeal, holding that the mens rea of attempted rape is an intention to have sexual intercourse being recklessly indifferent whether there is absence of consent.[14] However, in *R v Colburne*[15] the Quebec Court of Appeal has held that an attempt requires a specific intent to carry out the crime, even if the completed offence requires a lesser intent. This has led one commentator to suggest that, arguably, an attempted sexual assault in Quebec must be based on D's subjective intent to engage in non-consensual sexual activity, even though a person could now be convicted of the completed offence of sexual assault on the basis of recklessness, wilful blindness, or a failure to "take reasonable steps, in the circumstances known to the accused at the time, to ascertain that the complainant was consenting".[16] That would be to adopt the "narrow" approach advocated by Griew.

The theoretical basis for the narrow approach is, in essence, that where attempt is in issue, "the intent is the essence of the crime";[17] hence the conviction that the mental element in an attempt should be expressed as an intent to bring about each of the constituent elements of the offence attempted.[18] Anything less would be to create a very different inchoate offence from attempt, in which the marque of criminality was not supplied by D's *seeking through his actions* to commit a crime, but by the fact that his conduct merely ran the risk of being wrongful.

However, while there would seem to be little merit in any proposal to amend the New Zealand law of attempts to establish a more general doctrine of "reckless attempts", and indeed the problems presented by criminal attempts in New Zealand are not so grave as to justify such an extension to the reach of the criminal law, Ashworth's example makes a powerful case for accepting recklessness as sufficient mens rea for the *circumstantial* elements of the offence attempted.[19] It makes little sense if an offender could be convicted of rape for failure to take "reasonable steps" to ascertain a victim's consent,[20] while his counterpart, unsuccessfully

---

13 Ashworth, *Principles of Criminal Law* (3rd ed), Oxford, Oxford University Press, 1999, 465.
14 *R v Evans* (1987) 30 A Crim R 262. Cf *R v Zorad* [1979] 2 NSWLR 764 (CCA), 773.
15 *R v Colburne* (1991) 66 CCC (3d) 235 (Que CA), 240, 248, 249.
16 Section 273.2 Criminal Code (Can). See Roach, *Criminal Law* (1st ed), Toronto, Irwin Law, 1996, 72.
17 *R v Whybrow* (1951) 35 Cr App R 141 (CA), 146, 147 (Lord Goddard CJ).
18 English Law Commission, *Criminal Law: Attempt, and Impossibility in Relation to Attempt, Conspiracy and Incitement*, report no 102, London, HMSO, 1980, 10, 11.
19 For further discussion of "reckless attempts", see Moloney, "Attempts" (1991) 15 Crim LJ 175, 179; Duff, "The circumstances of an attempt" [1991] 50 CLJ 100, and now his *Criminal Attempts*, Oxford, Clarendon Press, 1996.

attempting the same offence and despite even recognising that the victim may not be consenting, could avoid conviction because the prosecution had been unable to prove "subjective intent" (ie purpose, knowledge, or belief that consent was absent).[21] The issue, however, has not yet been considered by a New Zealand court.[22]

Ultimately, the law's willingness to extend attempts liability to include reckless attempts is likely to be determined as a matter of public policy. The issues that need to be considered are as follows. First, should liability for an attempt depend principally on the meaning of particular words, like "intent"? Should the fact that attempt normally connotes trying and, by extension, purposeful behaviour, necessarily imply that all other elements of mens rea in an attempt must also conform to the same linguistic limitation? Secondly, is the fact that the law has historically given "intent" a narrow meaning in relation to attempts a sufficient reason for rejecting the concept of reckless attempts? Finally, would a more broadly-based mens rea for attempts be better able to protect the public against those who *would* cause harm apart from the fortuities of insufficiency of means, incompetence, or factual impossibility?

8.2.2 Actus reus

From the discussion above, it will be apparent that the mens rea of an attempt is of paramount importance. This is not to say that the actus reus is a trivial matter, but rather that it is D's mens rea that will determine whether a particular act relied on by the prosecution amounts to an attempt. For example, to enter a bank with a motorcycle helmet in one's hand may or may not constitute an attempt to rob the bank, depending on whether there is an intent to rob the bank or merely to make a withdrawal. It is the intent which determines the character of the act. The actus reus of an attempt, on the other hand, determines when acts done by the accused in pursuit of that intention are sufficiently proximate to the envisaged crime to warrant criminal liability.[23] In a pragmatic sense, the task of the courts here is to determine when an act is sufficiently close to the intended offence to constitute a real danger to the public and justify intervention by enforcement agencies.

Under s 72(1), the actus reus of an attempt is an act or omission done "for the purpose of accomplishing his object". However, not every act or omission done for the purpose of accomplishing the criminal object will necessarily be sufficient to lead to a conviction. It has been observed that the quoted words are so general by themselves that they would include

---

20 Sufficient mens rea for the completed crime: see s 128(2)(b) Crimes Act 1961.
21 See 4.2.5, 4.5. Conversely, this argument would not apply for attempts to commit offences where recklessness does not suffice for the complete offence; in which case it should not suffice for the attempt. Accordingly, where D attempts to receive property, being reckless whether it is stolen, he cannot be guilty of an attempt to receive "anything stolen" because the full offence of receiving requires knowledge that the goods are stolen. See s 258(1) Crimes Act 1961; 19.4.
22 Neither have the New Zealand courts yet ruled on the question whether foresight of consequences as a "moral" or "virtual" certainty will be sufficient mens rea for an attempt. In principle, this issue should be approached on the basis discussed in 4.2.4. In practice, the question is unlikely to arise, since foresight of certainty, or even of probability, will be a fact from which a jury may anyway find it easy to infer direct intent. Suppose that D, charged with attempting to injure V with intent, is apprehended before he is able to deliver a blow to the unsuspecting V's head with a heavy piece of timber. His protestations that he was not "100 percent sure" that the blow, had it been delivered, would have injured V should hardly be a ground for avoiding conviction on the attempt charge. Every normal instinct would inform us that D had intended to injure V.
23 Cross and Jones, *Criminal Law* (10th ed), London, Butterworths, 1984, 419, para 17.32.

acts of mere preparation.[24] It is necessary, therefore, in applying the section, to read subs (1) subject to the statutory limitation placed on those words by the rest of s 72. It must be shown that the criminal intent has been accompanied by an act or omission which is "immediately or proximately connected with the intended offence";[25] it is not sufficient to prove activity which is "only preparation for the commission of that offence, and too remote".[26]

Conduct which constitutes mere preparation, as opposed to an actual attempt, is on display in the facts of *R v Wilcox*.[27] In that case, the appellant had been charged with attempted aggravated robbery of a suburban post office. He admitted that he had planned to rob the post office, and that two air rifles and two balaclavas had been purchased for that purpose. He also admitted that he had arranged with a friend for transportation and had embarked on the journey. His plan was, however, frustrated: the police had received a warning of the planned robbery from an associate of the appellant, and stopped the car carrying the offenders when it was about 1 km from the post office.

In directing the jury, the trial judge had ruled that the evidence of purchasing the weapons and balaclavas, giving false names, persuading someone to act as a driver, loading the weapons, and travelling to within a kilometre of the objective were not simply matters of preparation and were not too remote to constitute an attempt. The judge also implied that the individual acts could be regarded *cumulatively* as acts done for the purpose of accomplishing the object of robbery and as such sufficient to amount to an attempt.

The Court of Appeal rejected this approach. It held that independent acts of mere preparation cannot take on the quality of attempt merely by being added together. Although the Court's decision appears to leave open the question whether a judge may direct a jury to consider the whole pattern of conduct and not any individual parts of it as constituting an attempt, the Court was nevertheless satisfied on the facts of this case that the purchase of weapons and balaclavas were only acts of preparation and were incapable of giving "increased significance" as a matter of law to the car journey. It concluded, in allowing the appeal, that the appellant, at the point that he was apprehended — still some distance away from the post office — was doing no more than *getting himself into a position* from which he could embark on an actual attempt at robbery.

In reaching its decision, the Court was influenced by the reasoning of Taschereau J in a dissenting opinion in *Henderson v R*, where his Honour said:[28]

> "I do not believe that it can be held that the mere fact of going to the place where the contemplated crime is to be committed, constitutes an attempt. There must be a closer relation between the victim and the author of the crime; there must be an act done which displays not only a preparation for an attempt, but *a commencement of execution, a step in the commission of the actual crime itself*."

Thus, at least for the purposes of New Zealand law, it is possible to discern two preliminary threshold tests for determining the point at which an act of mere preparation *may* become an attempt. Each may be postulated as a question:

---

24 *R v Wilcox* [1982] 1 NZLR 191 (CA), 193.
25 Section 72(3).
26 Section 72(2).
27 *R v Wilcox* [1982] 1 NZLR 191 (CA).
28 *Henderson v R* [1949] 2 DLR 121; (1948) 91 CCC 97 (SCC), 128; 105 (emphasis added).

(i) Has the offender done anything more than *getting himself into a position* from which he could embark on an actual attempt? Or,

(ii) Has the offender actually commenced execution; that is to say, has he taken a step in the actual crime itself?

If the answer to either question is "yes", then we may safely say that there has been an attempt as a matter of law. Otherwise, the conduct remains in the realm of preparation and is not a crime.

In most cases, applying either of these tests should straightforwardly resolve whether relevant conduct amounts to an attempt without the necessity of being drawn into a discussion of the complex and often inconclusive threshold tests developed at common law. Nonetheless, because some cases do present difficulty, it will be necessary to consider the other threshold tests which have been developed at common law and which continue to be applied by the courts. However, before doing so, we first consider the circumstances in which, under New Zealand law, either an act or an omission may provide the basis of a prosecution for attempt.

(1) *Modes in which attempts may be made*

(a) Words

As was noted above, the actus reus of an attempt may be either an act or omission. Where the attempt is by a positive act, it may include words used as a means of accomplishing the offence and indicating the criminal attempt. However, as with other forms of conduct, the courts distinguish between words which are *mere propositions* and at worst preparation for an attempt, and words which are *constitutive* of an attempt. In the celebrated case of *R v Barker*, Salmond J observed that in certain kinds of crime, words used by the accused which are expressive of his criminal purpose may be themselves the means or part of the means by which he endeavours to fulfil his purpose.[29] For example, D's words themselves may be the overt acts which constitute her attempt. However, before words alone will be constitutive of an attempt there must be a clear proximity between the words uttered and the offence contemplated, such that it can be said that the words constitute an attempt or part of an attempt to commit the offence. Accordingly, there will be a significant difference between the words "meet me at the park at 6 o'clock, and we will have some fun" in the context of a charge of attempted sexual indecency, and the words "come with me and we will commit a burglary". In the former example, liability for an attempt may be established, because the nearness to consummation of the crime and the accused's ability to control the course of events should the invitation be accepted suggest that there is a substantial likelihood of success. In the other example, however, the lack of specificity of time and place and the number of acts required to transform the proposition into a consummated act would strongly suggest the existence of mere words too remote to constitute even preparation, let alone an attempt. In *R v Barker*, a letter delivered to a 16-year-old boy inviting him to meet at a park with a view to "some good fun" was held to be a sufficiently overt act to constitute attempted sodomy. Similarly, in *R v Yelds*,[30] the accused's words to a girl, "you are getting a big girl now. Have you got hair growing there?" while pointing to his private parts was held, together with evidence that he had accosted the child and endeavoured to entice her to accompany him to a park, to be evidence of an attempt.

---

29   *R v Barker* [1924] NZLR 865 (CA), 876.
30   *R v Yelds* [1928] NZLR 18 (CA).

In these examples, D's spoken or written words amounted to an attempt partially because they made a link, explicit or implicit, with the substantive offence being attempted. By contrast, this link was missing in *R v Rowley*.[31] In that case, D was convicted of attempted incitement to commit gross indecency. He had left a number of notes in different public places designed to lure young boys for immoral purposes. In allowing D's appeal, the English Court of Appeal held the notes could not be regarded as more than a preparatory act because they went no further than to seek to meet with the boy or boys in question. To constitute an attempt at incitement to commit gross indecency would have required a proposition to be made *for that specific purpose*.[32] The Court differentiated between letter-writing that sought merely to engineer a preliminary meeting, and letter-writing in which a specific invitation to commit gross indecency is made. Only the latter would amount to an attempt, since only then would D have done all he could towards inciting the commission of an offence.[33]

(b) Possession

There has been some judicial debate on the question whether the status of possession, or other criminal status created by unlawful involvement in defined factual circumstances, could be the subject of an attempt charge. The status of possession is, strictly speaking, neither an act nor an omission. Accordingly, since s 72 requires proof of "do[ing] or omit[ting] an act for the purpose" of committing an offence, the acquisition of a particular status as the basis of an attempt may seem to be inconsistent with the express wording of the statute.

This issue arose in *R v Grant*,[34] which involved a prosecution for attempted possession of marijuana. The accused had picked up a bag which he thought contained marijuana. However, the police had removed the drug and replaced it with newspaper and had the bag under surveillance when the accused uplifted it. Mahon J, noting that the offence of having in possession does not entail an act by the defendant but a status created by involvement with specified factual circumstances, held that possession is itself an inchoate offence and cannot be attempted. His Honour's reason for so holding was that since the offence of possession is itself an "inchoate attempt", it would seem contrary to policy to further create an offence of attempting to be in possession.[35]

Arguably, Mahon J's reasoning reflects an unnecessarily doctrinaire approach to the requirement for an "act". In particular, he cites approvingly the statement of Glanville Williams that the actus reus of an attempt is the commission of an act and is almost always an overt act, concluding that because s 72 requires as a criterion of liability an act coupled by an intention on the part of the offender to commit an offence, it can only refer to the commission of an *act* as opposed to the acquisition (by design or otherwise) of some criminal status, created by unlawful involvement in defined factual circumstances; ie possession. Yet in *Grant*, the accused had sought to acquire (the criminal status of) possession *by an act*; ie by picking up the bag. The act requirement in s 72 was clearly satisfied.

---

31 *R v Rowley* [1991] 4 All ER 649; [1991] 1 WLR 1020 (CA).
32 *R v Rowley* [1991] 4 All ER 649; [1991] 1 WLR 1020 (CA), 654; 1025.
33 See *R v Ransford* (1874) 13 Cox CC 9; 31 LT 488.
34 *R v Grant* [1975] 2 NZLR 165.
35 *R v Grant* [1975] 2 NZLR 165, 169, 170.

The decision in *Grant* should be contrasted with that in R v *Willoughby*,[36] a prosecution for attempting to have possession for supply. There the Court took a broader view of the meaning of "act", at least for the purposes of attempts liability. Speight J reasoned that the notion of possession can be both "active" and "passive", and since it may include both the positive conduct of holding or transporting the thing in possession, and the passive recognition that an article is within one's power and control while permitting it to remain there, it is possible to say that an act or omission demonstrating control must always be proved in a case of possession.[37] In addition, the Court noted that the wording of the Misuse of Drugs Act 1975 referred, in the relevant section, to the conduct of possessing heroin for supply as an "offence". His Honour concluded that if, in terms of s 72, D has an intention to commit that offence (ie intends to have heroin in his possession), and does an act such as purchasing or attempting to purchase to that end, then he comes within the plain wording of s 72.

This reasoning is similar to the approach taken in Canada.[38] It is, with respect, to be preferred to Mahon J's approach in *Grant*. It is consistent with the theory of criminal attempts, and avoids ascribing too narrow a scope to the concept of an attempt. Even though statutory language is sometimes infelicitous in its insistence on using language that fails to reflect important developments in criminal jurisprudence, it is the task of the courts to apply the law in a manner which respects and gives expression to the policy behind the provision in question.[39]

(c)   Omissions

We have noted that s 72 allows a prosecution for attempt based on an omission by D as opposed to a positive act. It follows that where D deliberately omits to perform a legal duty but fails to bring about the (intended) consequence specified in the principal offence, the failure may constitute an attempt. However, because omissions liability is by its nature rare, an omission will seldom be the basis of an attempt prosecution.

By way of example, attempt liability may occur where D, an anaesthetist, owing V a duty to avoid omissions dangerous to life, deliberately fails to supply oxygen when V begins to turn blue in the course of an operation; but D's plan to cause the death of V is foiled before V can succumb to oxygen starvation.

This analysis applies in those rare cases where a *result* crime may be committed by an omission. However, it will not apply where the offence charged alleges a simple omission that does not require any consequences for its commission. For example, it would not normally be possible to be convicted of the offence of attempting to fail to stop after an accident, or of attempting to fail to permit a blood specimen to be taken.[40] In such cases, D's omission constitutes not merely an attempt but a successful commission of the full offence. There is no middle ground.

---

36   R v *Willoughby* [1980] 1 NZLR 66.
37   R v *Willoughby* [1980] 1 NZLR 66, 68. See 3.2.2(2).
38   See R v *Codina* (1999) 132 CCC (3d) 338 (Ont CA).
39   For a more detailed discussion see Dawkins, "Attempting to have in possession" (1981) 5 Otago LR 172. See 2.2.
40   See ss 22 and 60 Land Transport Act 1998.

(2) "For the purpose of accomplishing his object"

Before moving on to discussion of the boundary between attempt and preparation, it is necessary briefly to consider the phrase "for the purpose of accomplishing his object" which appears in s 72(1). The phrase limits the types of acts or omissions which may properly be considered as the basis of a charge of attempt.

The fact that D intends to commit an offence does not mean that every act she subsequently does is directed toward commission of that offence. In order to establish the actus reus of an attempted crime, there must be an act (or omission) by D which is done *for the purpose* of committing that offence. Unrelated actions, even actions coincidentally proximate to execution of the intended offence,[41] do not count.

For example, imagine a variation of the facts of *R v Wilcox* (8.2.2). Suppose that D intended to rob Bank V. He proceeded to the scene of the robbery, alighted from his car, and was apprehended by police as he proceeded up the steps of the neighbouring Bank X with a loaded air rifle under his jacket. Assuming that walking up the steps would normally be an act going beyond mere preparation,[42] D should still avoid liability for attempted robbery on the basis that he approached the bank not (yet) in order to rob, but rather to meet his girlfriend beforehand. Whatever offences the accused may be guilty of in such circumstances, attempted robbery is not one of them.

8.2.3 From preparation to attempt

(1) Common law tests for proximity

At the heart of any discussion of criminal attempts is the question where to set the threshold between an attempt and an act of "mere" preparation. To set the threshold too high means that many people who may have come dangerously close to achieving their criminal objective will avoid criminal liability, thus compromising public safety. To set it too low presents the danger of penalising those whose criminal "conduct" may have proceeded not much further than unexecuted thoughts. Unfortunately, judicial debate on this question has not always been enlightening, and many of the judicial attempts to define the threshold do little more than state the obvious in terms that are often trite and tautological. Glanville Williams notes that:[43]

> "Almost all the judgments content themselves with elaborate tautologies, reiterating in an infinite variety of language the basic rule that the attempt must be 'proximate' and not 'mere preparation', but furnishing no helpful definition of the meaning of these terms. Where a test is indicated by the judges it turns out on examination to be useless."

In addition, statutory tests are often unhelpful in providing guidance on the issue of proximity. For example, the test contained in the English Criminal Attempts Act 1981, which has been described as "a triumph of trumpery and triviality",[44] asks simply whether "a person does an act which is more than merely preparatory to the commission of the offence",[45] and gives no guidance about when that line between preparation and attempt might have been crossed.

---

41 See 8.2.3.
42 *R v Campbell* (1991) 93 Cr App R 350 (CA), a decision of dubious application (see 8.2.3(4)). Cf *R v Kelly* [1992] Crim LR 181.
43 "Police control of intending criminals" [1955] Crim LR 66, 68.
44 Meehan, *The Law of Criminal Attempt: A Treatise*, Alberta, Carswell, 1984, 92.
45 Section 1(1) Criminal Attempts Act 1981 (England).

Arguably, the test in the New Zealand Crimes Act 1961,[46] which defines an attempt in terms of an act or omission that is "immediately or proximately connected with the intended offence", is equally trite and inconclusive. Such vague standards make the application of the law very difficult, and indeed risk leaving D without fair warning that his next step may be illegal.[47] To aggravate the difficulty, judicial dicta are often contradictory and confusing. For example, it is difficult to reconcile the statement "all acts done for the purpose of committing a crime are not attempts, for they may be merely acts of *preparation*"[48] with the proposition that "preparation is not an attempt. But *some* preparations may amount to an attempt".[49]

While both statements are true, they may, taken together, seem to suggest that the accumulation of independent acts of mere preparation may be sufficient to constitute an attempt, a proposition clearly rejected by the New Zealand Court of Appeal.[50]

The truth is that the mere language of proximity, as reflected in phrases like "proximately connected", "immediately connected", "more than preparation", "too remote to constitute an attempt" etc conveys much less legal meaning than might be expected of a code, and raises a serious question about the utility of attempting to define liability for attempts at all. The lack of specificity in these terms creates real problems for judges endeavouring to locate impugned conduct within notions of preparation, proximity and remoteness. The problems are illustrated in *R v B*,[51] where the accused made an unsuccessful application to remove a charge of attempted murder from an indictment. B separated from his wife following a violent altercation, and it was contended by the Crown that he planned his wife's murder and his own suicide. He allegedly broke into his wife's house where, according to her account, he tied her up, raped her, and told her he would kill her. The Court observed that the real problem in the case related to s 72(2) and whether B's alleged actions were "only preparation" and "too remote to constitute an attempt" or were alternatively, "immediately or proximately connected with the offence". There was no actual point in the process where B did an act with the immediate intention of killing his wife, although he had taken some substantial steps towards achieving that end. Nonetheless, the proximity issue was resolved in favour of the Crown, and B's alleged actions were ruled sufficiently proximate to the crime to warrant leaving the case to the jury.

If, as has been suggested, endeavours to define the difference between a proximate attempt and preparation are efforts to define the indefinable and are doomed to failure,[52] efforts to do so may be discounted as being at best unenlightening and at worst irrelevant. As the Court of Appeal observed in *R v Wilcox*,[53] the "broad" answer by D that his alleged conduct amounted to nothing more than preparation depends simply on an assessment of that conduct; and since the question whether preparation or attempt is one of law, it ought to be possible for judges to direct themselves on that issue having regard to the quality of the accused's acts, and the time and circumstances of their occurrence, without the need to resort to an abstract test. Thus

---

46   See s 72(3).
47   Cf 2.1.3.
48   *R v Linneker* [1906] 2 KB 99, 104 (Walton J) (emphasis added).
49   *Commonwealth v Peaslee* (1901) 177 Mass 267; 59 NE 55 (1900), 272; 56 (Holmes CJ) (emphasis added).
50   *R v Wilcox* [1982] 1 NZLR 191 (CA), 194 (Woodhouse J). See also *R v Campbell* (1991) 93 Cr App R 350 (CA), 355, per Watkins LJ.
51   *R v B (No 5)* 7/9/01, William Young J, HC Christchurch, T19/01.
52   *Adams* (2nd ed), para 700.
53   *R v Wilcox* [1982] 1 NZLR 191 (CA), 193.

the Supreme Court of Canada has stated that ultimately the distinction involves a "commonsense" judgment, in which there are a number of factors:[54]

> "[T]he distinction between preparation and attempt is essentially a qualitative one, involving the relationship between the nature and quality of the act in question and the nature of the complete offence, although consideration must necessarily be given, in making that qualitative distinction, to the relative proximity of the act in question to what would have been the completed offence, in terms of time, location and acts under the control of the accused remaining to be accomplished."

Nevertheless, the courts continue to assess liability for attempts with reference to various tests for proximity, despite the fact that liability invariably turns on the facts and circumstances of each case. It is necessary, therefore, to examine more closely the different tests that have been developed by the judges.

(a)   The tests in *Eagleton*

It is sometimes suggested that, at common law over the last 100 years, two different tests as to the actus reus of attempt have predominated.[55] The first was exemplified by the decision in *R v Eagleton*.[56] In that case, the defendant was alleged to have attempted to obtain money from the guardians of a parish by falsely pretending to the relieving officer that he had delivered loaves of bread of the proper weight to the poor, when in fact the loaves were deficient in weight. In giving the judgment of the Court, Parke B said:[57]

> "Acts *remotely leading* towards the commission of the offence are not to be considered as attempts to commit it, but acts *immediately connected* with it are; and if, in this case, after the defendant had obtained the credit with the relieving officer for the fraudulent overcharge, any further step on the part of the defendant had been necessary to obtain payment, as the making out a further account or producing the vouchers to the Board, we should have thought that the obtaining credit in account with the relieving officer would not have been sufficiently proximate to obtaining the money. But, on the statement in this case no other act on the part of the defendant would have been required. It was the *last act*, depending on himself towards the payment of the money, and therefore, it ought to be considered as an attempt."

Eagleton has had an important influence on the law of criminal attempts in common law jurisdictions, and the dictum quoted above is probably more often cited than any other authority in this area of the criminal law. For over 100 years, the passage has been quoted as representing a correct statement of the law, and has been adopted by law-makers in crafting statutory tests for attempts liability. Yet its use of such broad concepts as "acts remotely leading towards" and "acts immediately connected with", which purport to state a legal rule, begs the question of how to distinguish mere preparation from attempt.[58] The truth is that despite its obvious appeal to generations of judges, the dictum has served to inhibit the development of

---

54   *Gladstone v R* (1996) 109 CCC (3d) 193 (SC), 202 (Lamer CJ), applying the distinction articulated earlier in *R v Deutsch* (1986) 30 DLR (4th) 435; [1986] 2 SCR 2 (SCC).
55   See *R v Gullefer* [1990] 3 All ER 882; [1990] 1 WLR 1063, 884; 1065; *R v Jones* [1990] 3 All ER 886; [1990] 1 WLR 1057 (CA), 888; 1060.
56   *R v Eagleton* (1855) Dears CC 515; [1843-60] All ER Rep 363.
57   *R v Eagleton* (1855) Dears CC 515; [1843-60] All ER Rep 363, 538; 367 (emphasis added).
58   Meehan, *The Law of Criminal Attempt: A Treatise*, Alberta, Carswell, 1984, 90.

the law of attempts by limiting the conceptual framework within which the doctrine has developed.

In practice, apart from these broad conceptual phrases, the most influential aspect of the *Eagleton* approach has been its endorsement of the so-called "last act" test. As we will demonstrate later in this discussion, this test, together with other "final stage theories",[59] presupposes that attempt liability can only exist where the accused has completed the last necessary act needed for the offence to occur, or has set in motion events which would normally result in an offence, without further action on his part. So, for example, in *R v Susak*[60] it was held that the offender's endeavouring to open the rear door of a cinema, which was locked, with the intention of entering the cinema and robbing the cashier, did not constitute the actus reus of an attempted robbery. The Judge took the view that the actions of the accused were not sufficiently proximate to enable it to be characterised as an attempt to commit the crime: "The accused had not yet entered the premises, he had not reached the location where the crime was to be committed and he was still approaching the point where he could be said to have embarked upon the commission of the crime."[61]

(b) The "series of acts" test

The second major approach as to the actus reus in attempt focuses not on the requirement for a discrete act that is sufficiently proximate to amount to an attempt, but rather on the question whether a "series" of acts, if uninterrupted, would amount to the crime sought. This approach is attributed to Stephen, in whose view:[62]

> "An attempt to commit a crime is an act done with intent to commit that crime, and forming part of a series of acts which would constitute its actual commission if it were not interrupted."

According to Stephen, the point at which such a series of acts begins cannot be defined, but depends on the circumstances of each case. On the face of it, this suggests a very loose test of liability and allows for the threshold for liability to be constantly shifted according to the fact situation in each case. Indeed, in one passage of an earlier edition of the *Digest*, Stephen appears to imply that there may be some situations where even an act of preparation could make a person criminally liable.[63] Such an approach to attempts liability may be characterised as a radical "first stage" theory, because it offers a basis for liability much earlier than other conventional theories would allow. And for that reason we think it must be rejected. As one commentator has observed, if *any* act were a sufficient actus reus for attempt, when combined with the presence of mens rea, the non-criminal preparation/criminal attempt dichotomy would disappear, because all acts of "preparation" would suffice for an attempt.[64] This would effectively amount to punishing for mens rea alone.

---

59 The phrase is due to Meehan, who formulated it to describe those theories of attempt liability which focus on conduct occurring at a late stage of a transaction or series of events and which indicate the existence of an attempt. See Meehan, *The Law of Criminal Attempt: A Treatise*, Alberta, Carswell, 1984, 103ff.
60 *R v Susak* (1999) 105 A Crim R 592 (NTSC).
61 *R v Susak* (1999) 105 A Crim R 592 (NTSC), 597, per Riley J. See further below, 8.2.3(1)(e).
62 *A Digest of the Criminal Law (Indictable Offences)* (5th ed), London, Sweet & Maxwell, 1894, art 50.
63 "I should hesitate to say no act leading up to a crime could be criminal unless it amounted to an attempt": Stephen, *A Digest of the Criminal Law (Indictable Offences)* (1st ed), London, Macmillan & Co, 1877, Note IV, 337.
64 Meehan, *The Law of Criminal Attempt: A Treatise*, Alberta, Carswell, 1984, 99.

Despite its approval in a number of English cases since 1906,[65] Stephen's test must be criticised for lacking practical usefulness, and for its ambiguity, since it fails to define the exact point at which a series of acts can be said to begin.

(c)   The "Rubicon" test

Other tests have sometimes gained judicial currency. The first of these derives from the judgment of Lord Diplock in *DPP v Stonehouse*.[66] There the accused, an English member of Parliament and Privy Councillor, staged his own drowning in order to effect a false insurance claim. Lord Diplock held that before an act of preparation may be held to be sufficiently proximate to amount to an attempt, it must indicate a "fixed irrevocable intention to go on to commit the complete offence unless involuntarily prevented from doing so".[67] Quoting Parke B's classic words in *R v Eagleton* ("Acts remotely leading towards the commission of the offence are not to be considered as attempts to commit it, but acts immediately connected with it are"),[68] Lord Diplock then summarised the test in the now-celebrated phrase: "In other words, the offender must have crossed the Rubicon and burnt his boats."[69] The Rubicon is the ancient name of a small stream which formed part of the boundary between Italy and Cisalpine Gaul; Caesar's crossing of the stream marked the beginning of the war with Pompey. The phrase "to cross the Rubicon" thus signifies the making of a decisive or final step. In *Stonehouse*, the House of Lords held that D's staging of his own drowning was sufficiently proximate to the commission of a complete offence of obtaining property by deception to amount to an attempt to commit that offence. His acts were held not to be mere preparatory steps towards the commission of the complete offence, since he had done all the physical acts *in his power* necessary for completion of the full offence.

(d)   The "commencement of execution" test

This test, various formulations of which have proved popular in both common law and civil law jurisdictions,[70] falls somewhere between *Eagleton*'s "last act" test and Stephen's "uninterrupted series of acts" test. Typical statutory formulations of this test make it a crime where a person, intending to commit a crime, *begins to put his intention into execution*.[71] Arguably, a form of the "commencement of execution" test is also implicit in *Eagleton* in the assertion that "acts immediately connected with it" are to be considered attempts to commit the offence. What the commencement of execution test requires is an act (or omission) which indicates that the accused has started to do the very thing which he had planned. However, the test attracts the same criticism as does Stephen's test, in that it tends to beg the question whether the conduct is preparation or attempt, and, as the cases demonstrate, is not easy to apply to a particular set of facts. Consider the following example:

> D decides to commit an aggravated robbery, having a particular victim in mind. To this end he acquires a large hunting knife, locates a map indicating the victim's address and

---

65 See *R v Linneker* [1906] 2 KB 99; *Hope v Brown* [1954] 1 All ER 330; [1954] 1 WLR 250, 332; 253; *Davey v Lee* [1967] 2 All ER 423; [1967] 3 WLR 105, 425; 108 (Lord Parker CJ).
66 *R v Susak* [1978] AC 55; [1977] 2 All ER 909 (HL).
67 *R v Susak* [1978] AC 55; [1977] 2 All ER 909 (HL), 68; 917.
68 *R v Eagleton* (1855) Dears CC 515; [1843-60] All ER Rep 363, 538; 367.
69 *DPP v Stonehouse* [1978] AC 55; [1977] 2 All ER 909 (HL), 68; 917.
70 See Meehan, *The Law of Criminal Attempt: A Treatise*, Alberta, Carswell, 1984, 101.
71 See, for example, Criminal Code 1899 (Qld), as amended, s 4 (1964); Criminal Code (WA), as amended, s 4 (1978).

likely walking route, purchases a carry-bag to carry the anticipated "spoils", and having disguised himself with a balaclava purchased for the purpose, lies in wait for his victim. The victim is seen walking towards D, but when she is 100 metres from where the offender is hiding, she, for no apparent reason, turns around and begins to retrace her steps. Because he considers it too risky to attack the victim in the changed circumstances, D abandons his plan.

Is he guilty of an attempt? We could not say that, because he has made elaborate preparations for the crime and has got himself physically into a position from which the crime may be launched, he has done an act forming part of a series of acts which would constitute the commission of the crime of aggravated robbery if not interrupted. He would not satisfy the test in Stephen's *Digest*. By the same token, can we really say he has commenced "execution" of the crime intended? The specific elements of the crime of aggravated robbery require theft accompanied by violence or the use of a weapon. Has D come so close that he can be said to have commenced the execution of that crime? The notion of "execution" implies a degree of propinquity that goes beyond acts that are merely suggestive of criminal intent. But how far beyond? In the dissenting dictum of Taschereau J in *Henderson v R*,[72] his Honour required a "closer relation between the victim and the author of the crime" than D's merely going to the place where the contemplated crime was to be committed; but his Honour gave no guidance about the point at which the required "closer relation" was established.

In all probability, on the facts given, D would be judged not to have attempted an aggravated robbery. This conclusion is certainly consistent with the commencement of execution test in principle. But at a pragmatic level, the test appears to offer little guidance for triers of fact, and leaves the threshold question substantially unresolved. It has, nonetheless, been approved in principle by the New Zealand Court of Appeal, and may be regarded as an applicable test for determining the threshold question in New Zealand.[73] Further support for the test has also been given by the High Court in *Drewery v Police*, where Williamson J approved Lord Reid's dictum in *Haughton v Smith*[74] that for an act to be proximate for the purposes of attempt, "the accused must have *begun to perpetrate* the crime".[75]

(e) The "last act" test

As we have noted, the "last act" test has its origins in the dictum of Lord Parke in *R v Eagleton*.[76] The true significance of the test is that it nominates the "last act depending on [the defendant]" as the threshold at which an act of preparation becomes an attempt. According to this test an accused commits an attempt when she does the last act necessary to be done, or has set in motion physical or human factors which in the normal course of events would result in an offence, without her doing anything further.[77] The test was approved and applied by the English Court of Appeal in *R v Ilyas*,[78] where the accused had falsely reported his car stolen and had obtained, but not completed, an insurance claim form. In allowing the appeal, the Court held that the appellant had not done every act which it was necessary for

---

72 *Henderson v R* [1949] 2 DLR 121; (1948) 91 CCC 97 (SCC).
73 See *R v Wilcox* [1982] 1 NZLR 191 (CA), 195.
74 *Haughton v Smith* [1975] AC 476; [1973] 3 All ER 1109 (HL), 499; 1120, 1121.
75 *Drewery v Police* (1988) 3 CRNZ 499, 502 (emphasis added).
76 *R v Eagleton* (1855) Dears CC 515; [1843-60] All ER Rep 363, 538; 367.
77 Meehan, *The Law of Criminal Attempt: A Treatise*, Alberta, Carswell, 1984, 103, 104.
78 *R v Ilyas* (1984) 78 Cr App R 17.

him to do in order to achieve the result he intended, and as such his conduct, in so far as it had gone, was merely preparatory and too remote from the contemplated offence.

The "last act" test was also applied in the controversial decision in *R v Robinson*,[79] a case involving facts reminiscent of *Ilyas*. R was a jeweller who, having insured himself against theft, simulated a robbery against himself with a view to falsely claiming the insurance money. He concealed some of his stock, tied himself up with string, and called for help. He told a policeman who broke in to "rescue" him that he had been knocked down and his safe robbed. However, the policeman was not satisfied with the story, and while searching the premises discovered the concealed property. In allowing his appeal against conviction, the Court of Appeal held, applying the approach in *Eagleton*, that because R had taken no steps towards communicating the claim to the insurers his act of faking the robbery was an act only remotely connected with the commission of the full offence, and was not immediately connected with it. Furthermore, it was not the last act that depended on R himself to achieve the intended result.

It could be argued that the "last act" test is overly generous to those accused of crimes, and that it has the potential to allow too many criminals to escape liability. The test does, after all, allow potential criminals to proceed dangerously close to achieving their criminal purpose before enforcement authorities may intervene. This is certainly true where the sequence of events between the consummated crime and the acts of preparation is foreshortened, as may be likely to occur in crimes such as attempted rape or attempted murder. In these instances, the last act depending on the accused is likely to be the very act constituting the crime itself — ie pulling the trigger in attempted murder, and achieving penetration in the case of rape or sexual violation. In such cases, application of the last act standard appears to be inappropriate because of its tendency to leave the public unprotected against clearly dangerous conduct. This can be illustrated with reference to the case of *R v Linneker*.[80] L had drawn a loaded revolver from his pocket during an argument, but his arm was seized before he could take aim. His conviction for attempting to discharge a revolver with intent to cause grievous bodily harm was upheld on the basis that L's act in drawing the revolver from his pocket was sufficiently proximate to constitute the actus reus of an attempt. However, had the last act test been applied, at least two further stages would have had to be passed; namely, taking aim and pulling the trigger. On this basis, L would have been acquitted. It is submitted that his conviction was correct.

The better view, it is submitted, is that the "last act" is a *sufficient* but not a *necessary* basis for attempts liability. The mere fact that the accused gets so close to achieving her object but fails to complete the last act dependent on her does not necessarily imply that every act before the last act is an act of mere preparation. This analysis is supported by *O'Connor v Killian*,[81] a decision of the Supreme Court of South Australia. The appellant had received cheques sent to the previous occupant of the house in which she lived. She went to a building society and tried unsuccessfully to cash the cheques, and then opened an account in the name of the previous occupant and deposited the cheques. The appellant did not make any request to withdraw the money because she realised that she was unable to produce appropriate identification. Her defence, when charged with attempting to obtain money by false pretences, was that the

---

79 *R v Robinson* [1915] 2 KB 342; [1914-15] All ER Rep Ext 1299 (CCA).
80 *R v Linneker* [1906] 2 KB 99.
81 *O'Connor v Killian* (1985) 15 A Crim R 353. See also commentary on the case at (1985) 9 Crim LJ 367.

conduct alleged was not sufficiently proximate to the completed offence. In particular, the defence argued, applying *Eagleton*, that because identification and a further demand for money was required, the last act depending on the appellant herself had not occurred, and therefore the offence was not made out.

In response, the Court refused to rely on the last act theory, which it held was not a condition precedent to conviction. Observing that the fact D had more to do did not prevent her attempt to commit the offence from being commenced,[82] the Court preferred the view of Salmond J in *R v Barker* that:[83]

> "to constitute a criminal attempt the first step along the way of criminal intent is not necessarily sufficient and the final step is not necessarily required."

The Supreme Court concluded that the appellant's conduct was purposive, and that the prosecution had proved a sufficiently proximate act to warrant conviction. It dismissed D's appeal. The decision is surely correct. To have conceded D's argument would have meant the appellant would virtually have to have committed the intended offence before she could be guilty of an attempt. In such circumstances there is, as one writer has observed, a consequential risk for the victim; since completion of the last act before success will often be followed by complete success.[84] The consequences of setting the threshold of attempt liability at a very late stage in a series of acts could be disastrous for the victims of attempted crimes, and may be one reason why the courts have appeared unwilling to fully embrace the "last act" test. This appears from the facts in *R v Jones*.[85] D, a married man, had formed a relationship with another woman who, despite a strong attachment to D, had decided to break off the relationship in favour of another man. Subsequently, D climbed into the back seat of a car driven by his former mistress's new lover, whom he had never met, and pointed a loaded sawn-off shotgun at him, saying "You are not going to like this". The victim managed to grab the gun and push it away, and in the course of a struggle threw the gun out of the car window. The victim then escaped and rang the police.

At his trial for attempted murder, there was evidence that the safety catch of the gun was on at the time of the attack, and the victim was unable to say that the appellant's finger had ever been on the trigger. It was argued that since D would have had to perform at least three more acts before the full offence could have been completed (ie remove the safety catch, put his finger on the trigger, and pull it), the evidence was insufficient to support the charge. However, the trial judge ruled against the submission and, after D had given evidence, the jury convicted him of attempted murder.

In construing the meaning of the corresponding attempts provision in the English Criminal Attempts Act 1981,[86] the Court of Appeal rejected D's contention that the *Eagleton* "last act" test should have been adopted by the trial judge. Neither did it consider itself bound by the test derived from *Stephen's Digest of the Criminal Law*. Rather, the Court appeared to deny the relevance of both tests, preferring the approach taken in *R v Gullefer* that the Criminal Attempts

---

82   Cf *R v Page* [1933] ALR 374; [1933] VLR 351.
83   *R v Barker* [1924] NZLR 865 (CA), 874.
84   Meehan, *The Law of Criminal Attempt: A Treatise*, Alberta, Carswell, 1984, 106.
85   *R v Jones* [1990] 3 All ER 886; [1990] 1 WLR 1057 (CA).
86   Section 1(1) Criminal Attempts Act 1981 (UK) provides: "If with intent to commit an offence to which this section applies, a person does an act which is *more than merely preparatory to the commission of the* offence, he is guilty of attempting to commit the offence." (Emphasis added.)

Act steers a "midway course" between the two: an attempt "begins when the merely preparatory acts come to an end and the defendant embarks on the crime proper", ie on the actual commission of the offence.[87]

There can be little doubt that Jones ought to have been convicted. However, the approach taken by the Court to justify that conclusion is hardly satisfactory. In reality, the distinction articulated by the Court is a non-distinction. It tells us nothing further about where the line is to be drawn and reduces analysis to mere casuistry. It certainly does not tell us *why* Jones's acts were an attempt to kill, as opposed to preparation to do so.

(f)   The "equivocality" test

One theory of proximity, which dominated attempts theory in New Zealand for many years, was the so-called "equivocality" rule. The rule derives from a threshold theory developed by Salmond J in *R v Barker*.[88] Salmond J held that in order to be sufficiently proximate, the acts relied on as constituting an attempt must be "sufficient in themselves to declare and proclaim the guilty purpose with which they are done". That is to say, the case must be one of res ipsa loquitur. The "equivocality" rule was accepted by *R v Yelds*[89] as stating the law in New Zealand in 1928. It remained as the principal threshold test for attempts in New Zealand until being criticised by Adams J in *Campbell v Ward*,[90] on the grounds that it tended to exclude overt acts that were proximate and which were proved by other evidence to have been done with the necessary intent.[91] The rule was explicitly abrogated by s 72(3) Crimes Act 1961,[92] which provides that an intentional act immediately or proximately connected with the intended offence may be an attempt, regardless whether there was any act "unequivocally showing the intent to commit that offence". However, it seems the unequivocality rule may not be completely dead. A partial revival of the theory would seem to be implicit in comments of Williamson J in *Drewery v Police*.[93] In that case, his Honour suggested in construing s 72(3), that in any case where the act is one which *does* unequivocally show intent to commit an offence, the question whether the act is only preparation or is too remote cannot be answered by inquiring only whether that act was *immediately* or *proximately connected* with the intended offence:[94]

> "It would seem to be a matter of degree so that if the evidence of intent is strong and clear the proximity or immediacy may not have to be as great as in cases where evidence of intent is reliant upon inferences to be drawn from the nature of the act itself."

That is to say, where D's actions unequivocally disclose a criminal purpose, that factor may be taken into account when deciding whether D's actions were sufficiently proximate to commission of the full offence to count as an attempt. In our view, this proposition cannot be accepted without reservation.[95] First, the suggested qualification to subs (3) would seem to

---

87 *R v Gullefer* [1990] 3 All ER 882; [1990] 1 WLR 1063 (CA), 885; 1066.
88 *R v Barker* [1924] NZLR 865 (CA).
89 *R v Yelds* [1928] NZLR 18 (CA).
90 *Campbell v Ward* [1955] NZLR 471. See also *R v Mackie* [1957] NZLR 669 (CA); Sim, "The actus reus in criminal attempt" (1955) 8 MLR 620.
91 *Campbell v Ward* [1955] NZLR 471, 476.
92 *Adams*, CA72.10 (looseleaf).
93 *Drewery v Police* (1988) 3 CRNZ 499, 503.
94 *Drewery v Police* (1988) 3 CRNZ 499, 503.
95 *Adams*, CA72.10 (looseleaf).

introduce new, extra-statutory criteria for determining proximity, when the Legislature had been concerned to limit the effect of such criteria by deliberate abrogation of the equivocality rule. Secondly, it is arguable that s 72(3) is not only or primarily concerned with situations where the nature of the act fails unequivocally to show an intent to commit a crime, and that it stipulates a general test of proximity whether or not there was any act unequivocally showing the intent to commit the offence.[96] Williamson J's interpretation of s 72(3) has itself been questioned. In R v Drummond,[97] a prosecution for attempting to manufacture amphetamine, Holland J queried the approach of Williamson J in the passage quoted. Noting that subs (3) does not apply unless the act has been proved to have been done or omitted with the necessary intent, his Honour expressed difficulty in seeing how the strength of the evidence of the intent can affect the interpretation of the subsection if the Court must be satisfied about D's intent even before the subsection applies.[98] We agree. It seems unnecessarily confusing to reintroduce, in any form, the language of unequivocal acts when the Legislature has clearly been at pains to avoid the complications implicit in such an approach.[99]

(2)   *Inadequacy of proximity theory*

Proximity has always been "of the essence" in determining liability for an attempt. In the Crimes Act 1961, the notion of "proximity" stands opposed to that of "remoteness", suggesting the conceptual threshold between an act of preparation and an attempt. However, it is a circular and an ultimately unhelpful distinction because an attempt is intentional conduct which is sufficiently proximate to the intended crime and not so remote as to be regarded as mere preparation; preparation is intentional conduct which is insufficiently proximate to an intended crime and too remote to be regarded as an attempt. Neither proposition gets us very far. Neither tells us what it is about the *character* of an act that allows us to say "that act is only preparation" or "that act is an attempt".

One of the factors that has bedevilled the law's attempts to articulate a simple, universal test to determine the threshold question in attempts is its insistence on identifying discrete "acts" or "omissions" as the harbingers of criminal conduct, rather than considering the character of the conduct taken as a whole. Yet, this is done freely in other areas of the criminal law. For example, we do not insist on a minute analysis of each separate act or omission preceding the prohibited event to determine whether an accused was acting voluntarily. Rather, we examine the whole context of events to determine whether the accused's "behaviour" was consistent with the claim that he was acting involuntarily.[100] Similarly, when determining liability in respect of result crimes such as murder, we do not analyse the multiplicity of individual acts and omissions that comprise the actus reus. We usually simply ask the jury, "did D 'kill' V?" We know, as a matter of common understanding, that the act of killing has composite elements which must necessarily occur before the crime of murder can be said to be complete. And while each element is susceptible to proof or disproof, liability ultimately turns on the existence of broad patterns of conduct which establish the accused's responsibility for the crime. It seldom turns on the existence or non-existence of a particular bodily movement.

---

96 *Adams*, CA72.10 (looseleaf).
97 R v *Drummond* (1993) 9 CRNZ 228.
98 R v *Drummond* (1993) 9 CRNZ 228, 233.
99 Regarding the impact of the equivocality rule outside New Zealand, see the brief discussion in *Adams*, CA72.14 (looseleaf).
100 See, for example, *Ryan v* R (1967) 121 CLR 205; [1967] ALR 577.

Nonetheless, it seems that this is just what attempts "theory" seeks to do. As long as we continue to insist on a fine line being drawn between attempt and mere preparation, we necessarily consign ourselves to the sorts of analyses discussed above that are ultimately incapable of clear or definite resolution. In fact we are no closer to determining the point at which preparation ends and an attempt begins than when that inquiry first began in earnest over 100 years ago. This truth, it is submitted, reveals something about the theoretical tools being used.

(3) *A way forward?*

The difficulty involved in devising an adequate abstract test to determine whether, in a particular case, the accused has gone beyond mere preparation, has led some judges to conclude that the issue must be determined by "common sense".[101] This was the Court of Appeal's preferred approach in *Police v Wylie*.[102] On a charge of attempting to procure cocaine, D had got as far as inspecting the drugs but had not agreed on the price or made an actual offer to purchase. For these reasons the Supreme Court on appeal quashed D's conviction, holding that there had been nothing more than an invitation to trade. The Court of Appeal, on the contrary, held there was an attempt, applying its "common sense" to decide that D's conduct amounted to a "real and practical step" towards the actual commission of the crime rather than mere preparation.[103] Yet "common sense" is itself a very elusive concept. What may appear to one judge as a solution based on practical wisdom, may appear to another as unreasonable. Each will bring her own values and preconceptions to the determination of "common sense". It is a highly subjective criterion.

It seems that something more than "common sense" or epithets like "real and practical step", "commencement of execution", "last proximate act", "a step in the actual crime itself" etc may be necessary if we are to make any headway in accounting for the proximity of attempts. The problem, as one writer has observed,[104] is finding the mean that is compatible with the requirement for clear legislative definition of punishable conduct, and yet consistent with the practical value of early police intervention. Many legal systems have now moved away from the view that to be guilty of an attempt one must do everything in one's power to effectuate the offence, on the basis that it is incompatible with the policy of early intervention and the prevention of harm.[105] If, as may be thought, early intervention and prevention of harm are cardinal criminal justice values that the law on criminal attempts seeks to uphold, a threshold test which best supports those values might seem to be worth considering. In our view, a test of "dangerous proximity" is well suited to uphold those values, while providing a fair threshold for marking out punishable conduct.

(4) *"Dangerous" proximity*

A theory of "dangerous" proximity focuses on the *character* of the conduct we judge to be proximate, in order to determine whether it is the sort of preparatory conduct that ought to

---

101 See *Haughton v Smith* [1975] AC 476; [1973] 3 All ER 1109 (HL), 499; 1121 (Lord Reid). See also *Drewery v Police* (1988) 3 CRNZ 499; *R v Peneha* (1993) 11 CRNZ 183, 502; 184.
102 *Police v Wylie* [1976] 2 NZLR 167 (CA).
103 *Police v Wylie* [1976] 2 NZLR 167 (CA), 170.
104 Fletcher, *Rethinking Criminal Law*, Boston, Little, Brown & Co, 1978, 136.
105 Fletcher, *Rethinking Criminal Law*, Boston, Little, Brown & Co, 1978, 136.

be visited with criminal sanctions. There are two ways in which relevant "dangerousness" may be judged by considering the:

(i) *Degree* of closeness to completion of the intended crime; or

(ii) *Nature* of the preparatory conduct undertaken, in terms of the actual risk presented to public health or safety.

Either criterion or both criteria may be considered in evaluating the proximity of the alleged conduct to the intended offence. If, for example, on an altered version of the facts in *R v Wilcox*,[106] the offenders had been stopped by the police as their car pulled up outside the bank, it could be argued that, on both counts, they were *dangerously* close to achieving their object. Regardless of how many discrete acts may have been required to have effected the actual robbery, the degree of closeness inherent in driving to within metres of the planned crime would suggest that a major issue of prevention of harm had arisen, justifying immediate (early) intervention. Assuming the robbers were armed and intent on completing their object, their presence could be said to have posed an immediate and serious threat to any innocent person within the immediate vicinity of the bank, a threat which the police may justifiably act to eliminate.

A similar analysis could be applied to the facts of *Police v Wylie*.[107] At the point at which the prospective purchaser of cocaine was holding the cash in his hands and was proceeding to examine the cocaine with a view to its purchase, it could be said that he was "dangerously close" to achieving his object. (Bear in mind that he must *intend* to commit the crime.) At any moment he could simply have extended his hand with the cash in it and said "I'll have it". At that point, the crime of procuring would have been complete. Had he done so, it would not have been necessary to ask whether the appellant's conduct would also have presented an actual risk to public health or safety, since the threshold for an attempt had already been established. Arguably, even without doing so, a person who so determinedly pursues the object of purchasing dangerous narcotic drugs represents a similar social threat.

The test of "dangerous proximity" may be more difficult to apply in factual situations where the accused has done everything in his power to assist another in the commission of a crime, but more steps remained to be undertaken by others before the substantive offence is complete. The problem is demonstrated in *Drewery v Police*,[108] where D was charged with arson and attempted false pretences after he had destroyed the vehicle owned by the principal offender as part of a fraudulent insurance claim. There D carried out the only and final act he was to perform in the offence, namely destroying the principal's car, while more steps remained to be taken by the principal to effect the false claim. It is arguable in such a case that it is not straining language to say that D came "dangerously close" to achieving his object because there was nothing more he could have done or was required to do as part of the agreement. However, although it does not affect the theory of proximity being advocated here, it has been suggested that *Drewery* may have been wrongly decided. D did not intend to commit the offence himself, and he could only be guilty of an attempt on the basis that he was a secondary party to a sufficiently proximate act by the owner of the car who was the intended principal.[109] Since the

---

106 *R v Wilcox* [1982] 1 NZLR 191 (CA).
107 *Police v Wylie* [1976] 2 NZLR 167 (CA), 170.
108 *Drewery v Police* (1988) 3 CRNZ 499.
109 *Adams*, CA72.13 (looseleaf).

owner did not appear to have gone beyond arranging for D to destroy the car (a mere preparation), it may be doubted whether D himself could be said to have proceeded beyond mere preparation.

In spite of the difficulties presented in cases such as *Drewery*, where the liability of a secondary party for attempt may depend on whether the principal has committed an act sufficiently proximate to amount to an attempt,[110] the test of dangerous proximity would seem to work well in other situations of attempt. For example, it is appropriate to the facts of a case like *R v Jones*,[111] where the accused, apparently intent on murdering his putative victim, had entered the victim's car and pointed a loaded shotgun at him at a range of 10 to 12 inches, while saying "You are not going to like this". It would seem an inescapable conclusion that the accused was "dangerously close" to achieving his object of killing the victim, regardless of whether there were one, two, three, etc discrete acts required to be performed by him before the full offence could be completed.[112] Indeed, it may be argued that the application of threshold tests like the "last act" test to such a case make a mockery of prevention of harm policies, and establish an impossibly narrow "window of opportunity" for police intervention.

The problem is illustrated in the English case of *R v Campbell*,[113] where the accused, who was in possession of an imitation firearm, was arrested just before entering a post office that he intended to rob. His conviction for attempted robbery was quashed on the basis that, however close he had come to committing robbery, he was not yet in a position to carry out the offence. The Court of Appeal noted that execution of the robbery still required further uncompleted acts; namely, entering the post office, going to the counter, and making some kind of hostile act directed to whoever was behind the counter and in a position to hand over money. As such the acts preceding those conclusive steps could only indicate preparation, not attempt. A standard of "dangerous proximity", however, would have enabled the fact-finder to assess whether the *completed* acts were, of themselves, sufficiently close to the completion of the ultimate objective (the robbery) to establish a truly dangerous proximity to the commission of a serious crime. If the answer to that question was "yes", then it would be possible, without having to examine the *uncompleted* acts necessary to execute the crime, to say that the conduct thus far undertaken constituted, by extension, an attempt.[114]

---

110 But see *R v Peneha* (1993) 11 CRNZ 183, where Williamson J was "unrepentant" in his view that if a person intends to be a party to an offence and then carries out the physical act which is his part in the offence then the tests in s 72(1) are met, regardless of whether the principal has carried out the physical act necessary to complete the offence. However, with respect, the essential issue in the statute (s 72(2)) is whether the act done or omitted "with intent" was sufficiently proximate to the "commission of [the] offence" intended, not whether the party, whether secondary or principal, had done all that she could to complete the offence.
111 *R v Jones* [1990] 3 All ER 886; [1990] 1 WLR 1057 (CA).
112 *R v Jones* [1990] 3 All ER 886; [1990] 1 WLR 1057 (CA), 887; 1059.
113 *R v Campbell* (1991) 93 Cr App R 350 (CA). Cf *R v Susak* (1999) 105 A Crim R 592 (NTSC), where D had armed himself with a knife and returned to a cinema he had previously been inside but, on finding the rear door to the cinema locked, had returned to his car and left the scene. It was held that D's actions were not capable of constituting an attempt.
114 Such an analysis conforms well to the facts in *R v Tosti* [1997] Crim LR 746 (CA), where D had been observed hiding oxyacetylene cutting equipment behind a hedge, approaching a barn door, and bending down to examine a padlock. In sustaining D's conviction, the English Court of Appeal achieved a result which, as Sir John Smith has commented, was "highly desirable" (at 747): "The appellants had set out to commit the offence and would no doubt have done so if they had not been thwarted. They were as dangerous to society and as deserving of punishment as if they had succeeded."

The theory of "dangerous proximity" aims to make clearer when the threshold between proximity and attempt has been reached, by focusing on the point at which it may be said the accused's conduct has become "dangerous". It seeks to capture the point of difference between acts of preparation which, while notionally close to the complete offence, are in themselves innocuous and unthreatening, and acts which, by their nature, demonstrate that the accused is significantly close to success and may even be endangering the lives/interests of other people already. It is this element of propinquity and threat, coupled with an intention to commit a crime, that justifies the attribution of attempt and calls for the intervention of the police.

8.2.4 Withdrawal

Once the threshold from preparation to attempt is crossed, the attempt is committed and cannot be undone. The accused is then unable to withdraw, or to seek to distance himself from the enterprise by a change of heart or repentance, and the intervention of others into the enterprise before completion of the crime cannot affect its character as an attempt.

Therefore, the crucial question is up until what time does an accused have a locus poenitentiae[115] during which he may withdraw from the enterprise without attracting criminal liability? Applying the "dangerous proximity" analysis, we may say that a locus poenitentiae should remain so long as the accused's acts of preparation are merely innocuous and unthreatening, and do not represent a threat to the safety or interests of other persons. So, in *R v Page*,[116] the Australian Court rightly found an attempt proved where the accused had inserted a tyre lever to break open a window, but changed his mind before applying any force. Similarly, when the defendant in *R v Taylor*[117] approached a stack of corn with a lighted match in his hand for the purpose of setting the stack on fire, but abandoned the plan once aware that he was being watched, he was properly convicted of an attempt. In principle, withdrawal should make no difference to liability for an attempt where the accused, by her conduct up until the time of withdrawal, has demonstrated a contumelious disregard for the safety or interests of others and has demonstrated a fixed determination to achieve her object. Withdrawal, signalling a change of heart, may be a factor relevant to sentencing but does not affect liability for an attempt where the accused has already shown her hand, and demonstrated a dangerous willingness to harm the interests of others. New Zealand law does not recognise any defence of free and voluntary desistance; nor, in our view, should it. Repentance and desistance is always available while conduct remains in the realm of preparation. Once an accused moves into the uncharted waters of the threshold between preparation and attempt she takes the risk that she may already have gone too far, and cannot be heard to plead, after the event: "I'm sorry. I wish I had abandoned the plan earlier."

The argument against allowing a defence of free and voluntary desistance may be illustrated by a simple example. D, intent on raping P, has pinned her to the ground by the weight of his own body. She is terrified and alone. But before he has touched her in any indecent manner or attempted to remove her clothes, he suddenly has a change of heart and decides to abandon the assault. Should he be able to avoid liability on a charge of attempted rape simply because he has voluntarily desisted? The answer must surely be "no". D has callously inflicted P's plight. Even though he has not physically harmed her, the emotional scars of his conduct — which

---

115 Literally, a place of repentance.
116 *R v Page* [1933] ALR 374; [1933] VLR 351.
117 *R v Taylor* (1859) 1 F & F 511; 175 ER 831.

is recognised by P as an attempted rape, and which will affect her as such — will remain with P for a long time.

8.2.5 Impossibility

The issue of impossible attempts has been a subject of fascination for generations of criminal law students.[118] Although it provides an excellent framework in which to tease out fascinating theoretical issues of criminal responsibility, and indeed to set examination questions, the issue of impossibility does, periodically, give rise to important practical questions that are reflected in the case law. In cases of attempts to do the impossible, the defendant was labouring under some kind of mistake, since no sane person will intend to do what he knows to be impossible.[119] In so far as impossible attempts always involve a mistake of some kind, the legal status of relevant mistakes depends on whether the mistake gives rise to a situation of "factual" impossibility, or to one of "legal" impossibility.

Section 72(1) includes the phrase "whether in the circumstances it was possible to commit the offence or not". The phrase, which has appeared in New Zealand criminal legislation since 1893, was intended to express the common law as stated in *R v Ring*.[120] In that case, the accused was convicted of attempted theft after he placed his hand in an empty pocket with a view to stealing the purse he hoped was there. The impossibility of success was no impediment to his conviction. At the same time, the subsection abrogates the effect of *R v Collins*[121] where, on facts similar to those in *Ring*, it was held that a person who put his hand into the pocket of another was not guilty of an attempt to steal because, as it happened, no theft was possible since the pocket was empty. In favouring *Ring* over *Collins*, Parliament has foreshadowed that mere "factual" impossibility will not be a bar to conviction.

This approach is generally consistent with the position in other jurisdictions, where the common law defence of impossibility has been largely foreclosed by legislation. In *United States of America v Dynar*,[122] for example, D's extradition from Canada was sought on a charge of attempting to launder money. As part of an FBI "sting" operation, a police informer called him in Canada and asked if he would launder drug money obtained from illegal trafficking in the United States. D agreed to do so. Under Canadian law, the offence requires that the money be the proceeds of crime; in fact, however, the money which the FBI planned to transfer to him had not been obtained from criminal activities. Nonetheless, the Supreme Court held that, while he could not be guilty of the full offence, he could be convicted of an attempt:[123]

---

118 See Smith, "Attempts, impossibility and the test of rational motivation" in *Auckland Law School Centenary Lectures*, Auckland, Legal Research Foundation, 1983.
119 Smith, "Attempts, impossibility and the test of rational motivation" in *Auckland Law School Centenary Lectures*, Auckland, Legal Research Foundation, 1983, 27.
120 *R v Ring* (1892) 17 Cox CC 491.
121 *R v Collins* (1864) 9 Cox CC 497.
122 *US v Dynar* (1997) 147 DLR (4th) 399; 115 CCC (3d) 481 (SCC). Cf *R v Kerster* (2003) 175 CCC (3d) 28 (BCCA).
123 *US v Dynar* (1997) 147 DLR (4th) 399; 115 CCC (3d) 481 (SCC). Cf *R v Kerster* (2003) 175 CCC (3d) 28 (BCCA), para 50. Under the s 24(1) Criminal Code 1985 (Canada): "Every one who, having an intent to commit an offence, does or omits to do anything for the purpose of carrying out his intention is guilty of an attempt to commit the offence *whether or not it was possible under the circumstances to commit the offence*." (Emphasis added.)

"In our view, s 24(1) is clear: the crime of attempt consists of an intent to commit the completed offence together with some act more than merely preparatory taken in furtherance of the attempt ... In this case, sufficient evidence was produced to show that Mr. Dynar intended to commit the money-laundering offences, and that he took steps more than merely preparatory in order to realize his intention. That is enough to establish that he attempted to launder money contrary to s 24(1) of the Criminal Code."

The same conclusion would now be reached in England, where s 1(2) Criminal Attempts Act 1981 (which has abolished the offence of attempt at common law and substituted a statutory offence) contains an expression similar to s 72(1), according to which a person may be guilty of attempting to commit an offence "even though the facts are such that the commission of the offence is impossible". The effect of this provision is that a person may be convicted of an attempt where she has accomplished that which she set out to do, but because of some mistake on her part her conduct does not after all amount to an offence. This is demonstrated in the House of Lords decision in *R v Shivpuri*.[124] In that case, D was charged with attempting to be knowingly concerned in dealing with a prohibited drug. While on a visit to India, D had been approached by a man who offered him a sum of money if, on return to England, he would receive a suitcase containing packages of "drugs" and then distribute them. Having duly received the suitcase, D arranged to meet a third person with a view to delivering a package of drugs. While they were meeting, the police arrested them. D frankly admitted his involvement in receiving and distributing the drug, which he believed was either cannabis or heroin. However, on a scientific analysis the packages were found to contain only a harmless vegetable substance.

In upholding D's conviction, the House of Lords overruled its earlier decision in *Anderton v Ryan*,[125] in which it had held that a person could not be liable for conviction of an attempt where his actions were "objectively innocent" even though he erroneously believed in facts which, if true, would make those actions criminal. In *Shivpuri*, Lord Bridge declared that the concept of "objective innocence" is "incapable of sensible application in relation to the law of criminal attempts".[126]

(1) *"Legal" impossibility as a defence*

It is sometimes said that a distinction should be drawn between attempts which are impossible owing to some "physical" or "factual" impediment (for example D's crowbar is in fact not strong enough to lever open V's safe), and those which are impossible owing to some required legal status or element (for example because V — though D does not know it — is already dead, he is no longer a human being within the meaning of s 158, and therefore cannot be murdered).

One significant implication of *Shivpuri*, which interprets statutory language similar to that found in s 72, is that United Kingdom law no longer recognises any distinction between situations of "legal" and "physical" impossibility. A person will be guilty of an attempt provided simply that she has an intent to commit an offence, and has done an act which is more than merely preparatory to the commission of that offence.[127]

---

124 *R v Shivpuri* [1987] AC 1; [1986] 2 All ER 334 (HL).
125 *Anderton v Ryan* [1985] AC 560; [1985] 2 All ER 355.
126 *R v Shivpuri* [1987] AC 1; [1986] 2 All ER 334 (HL), 21; 344.
127 See s 1(1) Criminal Attempts Act 1981 (UK).

However, it appears that New Zealand law still recognises a distinction between "legal" and "factual" impossibility. Its recognition derives from the seminal case of *R v Donnelly*.[128] D had been charged with attempted receiving after he had presented a ticket at the left luggage office of the Auckland Railway Station with a view to collecting some gramophone records which he believed had been stolen. In fact, the records had been uplifted earlier by the police, after being identified by their owner as property stolen from her home. It was held that, in those circumstances, it was impossible *in law* for D to commit the offence of receiving, because of the operation of s 261 Crimes Act 1961, which states that it is not an offence to receive property once it has been restored to its owner.

The Court of Appeal agreed that the fact that the goods had been *physically* removed from the place where D believed them to be did not affect his liability for attempt, because such a case of *factual* impossibility was clearly covered by s 72(1). However, the majority held that this was a case of *legal* impossibility, which precluded the appellant's liability for an attempt. Since he could not have been convicted of the completed offence of receiving, it was held that he could not be convicted of attempt. The Court identified six situations in which a person who sets out to commit a crime might fail.[129] They are:

(i)   Change of mind before committing an act sufficiently "overt" to amount to an attempt;

(ii) Change of mind but too late to deny an attempt;

(iii) Prevention by some outside agency from doing an act necessary to complete the crime;

(iv) Ineptitude, inefficiency, or insufficiency of means;

(v)   Physical impossibility; and

(vi) Legal impossibility.

Only in respect of the first and sixth categories can there be no liability for attempt under the present New Zealand law. It was into the sixth category that the case was held to fall.

The approach taken in *Donnelly* has been criticised on the grounds that it admits a technical and unmeritorious defence, based on fortuitous circumstances unrelated to D's social dangerousness and moral blameworthiness.[130] Furthermore, the decision implicitly endorses the theory of "objective innocence", now rejected in the English courts, by emphasising that the appellant's actions, considered alone, "would leave him guiltless in the eyes of the law".[131] Yet, as Haslam J rightly points out in his dissenting judgment, the concluding phrase in s 72(1) — "whether in the circumstances it was possible to commit the offence or not" — makes "objective impossibility" an irrelevant consideration.[132]

In our view, the Court's conceptualisation of D's intention is flawed, leading it falsely to attribute him with intention to do something which was not an offence. The Court said:[133]

---

128 *R v Donnelly* [1970] NZLR 980 (CA).
129 *R v Donnelly* [1970] NZLR 980 (CA), 990, 991 (Turner J).
130 See Dawkins, "Parties, conspiracies and attempts" in Cameron and France (eds), *Essays on Criminal Law in New Zealand: Towards Reform?*, VUW Law Review monograph no 3, Wellington, Victoria University of Wellington Law Review, 1990, 141. For further criticism of the "illusory and analytically suspect" distinction between factual and legal impossibility, see Meehan, *The Law of Criminal Attempt: A Treatise*, Alberta, Carswell, 1984, 151-153.
131 *R v Donnelly* [1970] NZLR 980 (CA), 992 (Turner J).
132 *R v Donnelly* [1970] NZLR 980 (CA), 994.

"What the appellant intended to do, therefore, was *to do something which was not an offence*. If he is to be convicted of a criminal attempt, it must be simply because of his erroneous belief that what he was attempting to do was an offence in law, when actually it was not one."

This would be true if the appellant's intention had been "to receive [previously] stolen goods *that had been restored to their owner*". But that was *not* his intention. His intention was "to receive stolen goods" simpliciter. That is an intention to do something which is an offence.

Indeed, the Canadian Supreme Court has described the distinction between factual and legal impossibility as untenable:[134]

"There is no legally relevant difference between the pickpocket who reaches into the empty pocket and the man who takes his own umbrella from a stand believing it to be some other person's umbrella. Both have the mens rea of a thief. The first intends to take a wallet that he believes is not his own. The second intends to take an umbrella that he believes is not his own. Each takes some steps in the direction of consummating his design. And each is thwarted by a defect in the attendant circumstances, by an objective reality over which he has no control: the first by the absence of a wallet, the second by the accident of owning the thing that he seeks to steal."

Quite so. The complexity of these cases arises in part because the legal status of the goods (ie as no longer stolen) depends itself on the presence of relevant facts (ie that the goods have been recovered on behalf of their owner). It may be a failure to recognise this connection that explains why the majority judgment seems to contain a confusion between "imaginary crimes", which we shall discuss below and which can never be attempted, and the situation in which the defendant's objective, if it could be attained, would be a crime but where, because he is making a mistake *of fact*, he believes it to be possible when it is not. In relation to the latter, impossibility should not be a bar to conviction. It is a case of failure where, if the accused had succeeded and the facts been as he thought they were, he would have committed a crime.[135]

(2) *Factual impossibility*

By contrast, as we stated at the beginning of 8.2.5, factual impossibility has never been a bar to conviction in New Zealand. In *Police v Jay*,[136] a conviction for attempting to receive cannabis was upheld when the accused received hedge-clippings by deception. This was held to fall within the fifth category in *Donnelly*. In *Jay*, the Court followed R *v Austin*,[137] where a person was found guilty of attempting to unlawfully supply a pregnant woman a "noxious thing" knowing that it was intended to be used to procure a miscarriage. The thing was not noxious at all. In *Higgins v Police*,[138] factual impossibility was held to be no defence to a charge of attempting to cultivate cannabis, in circumstances where positive identification of the seedlings was not possible because of their immaturity.

---

133 R *v Donnelly* [1970] NZLR 980 (CA), 992 (Turner J).
134 *US v Dynar* (1997) 147 DLR (4th) 399; 115 CCC (3d) 481 (SCC), para 62, per Iacobucci J. Cf *Regina v Dalaney and Budge* (1982) 69 CCC (2d) 276 (Al QB), a decision on very similar facts to *Donnelly* but to opposite effect.
135 Smith, "Attempts, impossibility and the test of rational motivation" in *Auckland Law School Centenary Lectures*, Auckland, Legal Research Foundation, 1983, 30.
136 *Police v Jay* [1974] 2 NZLR 204.
137 R *v Austin* (1905) 24 NZLR 983 (CA).
138 *Higgins v Police* (1984) 1 CRNZ 187; and see *Collector of Customs v Kozanic* (1983) 1 CRNZ 135.

In such cases, liability follows because the accused, intending to commit an offence, does *something* (going beyond preparation) for the purpose of accomplishing the offence. Although the means chosen was not sufficient for the object sought, or a supervening event made completion impossible, the accused nevertheless did a relevant act for the purpose of accomplishing her object, fulfilling the essential requirements for an attempt.

While the distinction between factual and legal impossibility remains in New Zealand, it is difficult to justify in the light of the reasoning in *Shivpuri*. In particular, the decision in *Donnelly* has been the subject of strong criticism, and although the decision has thus far survived challenge in the Court of Appeal, its continuing usefulness as an authority on impossibility must be doubted.[139] Above all, the distinction drawn between legal and factual impossibility lacks a clear or coherent basis and is contrary to the plain meaning of the words in s 72(1).

The category of "legal impossibility" is anomalous. It is predicated upon an "act-centred" approach to liability, which is inconsistent with the prevailing general principle governing impossible attempts, namely that a person is judged on the facts as she believes them to be. Provided the offender intended to commit an offence (as opposed to an imaginary crime, a special case considered in the next section), there is no reason in principle why liability should not follow, regardless of whether it was possible to commit that offence in contemplation.[140] This analysis of impossible attempts is supported also by the Supreme Court of Canada in *US v Dynar*.[141] In rejecting the factual/legal impossibility distinction as "not tenable", the Court concluded that the only relevant distinction for the purposes of s 24(1) Criminal Code (Can) is between imaginary crimes and attempts to do the factually impossible.[142]

(3)   *The "imaginary crime" exception*

A noteworthy feature of common law developments elsewhere is that they signal a clear movement away from a focus on the objective quality of the act, toward an emphasis on the subjective intention of the accused coupled with proof of a relevant post-preparatory act. However, although *Shivpuri* appears to have foreclosed virtually all situations that might previously have qualified (at common law) as exculpatory "impossible" attempts,[143] there is one remaining situation where it would seem an attempt cannot be committed.

The exception occurs when the accused makes no mistake about any material fact, but wrongly believes that what he is attempting to do is a crime. His object need not be impossible to attain yet, when it is attained, no crime will have been committed. In such a case, even if his "attempt" is successful, it is not a proximate step toward the commission of a crime.[144] Consider the following examples:

---

139 See Orchard, "Impossibility and inchoate crimes: Another hook in a red herring" [1993] NZLJ 426.
140 For discussion, see Ashworth, *Principles of Criminal Law* (3rd ed), Oxford, Oxford University Press, 1999, 469-471; McAuley, "Relational liability in criminal law" (1999) 34 The Irish Jurist 132-140.
141 *US v Dynar* (1997) 147 DLR (4th) 399; 115 CCC (3d) 481 (SCC), 418-428; 500-510.
142 *US v Dynar* (1997) 147 DLR (4th) 399; 115 CCC (3d) 481 (SCC), 421; 503. See also *R v English* (1993) 68 A Crim R 96.
143 For example, the man who attempts to steal from an empty pocket, or attempts to steal his own umbrella, or who attempts to receive an item he believes to be stolen which is not: see *R v Collins* (1864) 9 Cox CC 497; *Anderton v Ryan* [1985] AC 560; [1985] 2 All ER 355.
144 Smith, "Attempts, impossibility and the test of rational motivation" in *Auckland Law School Centenary Lectures*, Auckland, Legal Research Foundation, 1983, 27.

"(i) D has sexual intercourse with a 17-year-old girl. He believes that the criminal law prohibits sexual intercourse with girls under the age of 18. However, contrary to his belief, the relevant age is 16. He has not committed a crime or an attempted crime.

"(ii) D believes that it is unlawful to shoot opossums without a licence. She shoots six opossums which are eating turnips in a farm paddock. There is nothing unlawful in her actions."

These do not amount to attempts to commit crimes in law. There is no actus reus, because the act done is lawful; there is no crime that D's conduct can be an attempt to commit. Neither is there mens rea, because the mens rea of an attempt requires an intention to cause a result forbidden by law. A mere belief by D that her act is a criminal offence is insufficient.[145]

In these cases, the language of impossible attempts is inapt, because impossibility in this context implies the existence of an offence the completion of which is impossible in the circumstances. Similarly, applying the test of "dangerous proximity" postulated earlier, the conduct described in the examples above could not amount to an attempt because the conduct is neither *inherently* dangerous nor can it be said to be *dangerously* close to achieving the object sought, since the object is already accomplished and is not per se criminal. Most jurisdictions recognise that the "imaginary crime" is a legitimate exception in cases of liability for impossible attempts.[146]

8.2.6 A crime of attempted conspiracy?

Recent case law in Canada has suggested that conduct which falls short of a conspiracy to commit a substantive offence may, nevertheless, be prosecuted as an attempt to conspire. Although academic opinion is divided over whether such "doubly inchoate" offences serve any useful public policy purpose, judicial authority supports the proposition that in some circumstances, namely where conspiracy is codified as a substantive offence in itself, a person may be convicted of an attempt to commit that offence.[147] The analysis supporting this view is that where, through evidence of conversations between putative conspirators, evidence exists that the parties' actions were more than merely preparatory, there is a basis to find an attempt to conspire. In R v Dery,[148] the three accused had numerous conversations about the possibility of stealing road trailers loaded with alcohol. It was held that an attempt to conspire had been established on the basis that, although there was reasonable doubt as to the existence of one of the conditions for the formation of a criminal conspiracy, discussions between the parties concerning "upfront" payment to one of them constituted an illegal act. The sole element said to be missing was a clear consensus on the proposition regarding the advance

---

145 Smith, "Attempts, impossibility and the test of rational motivation" in *Auckland Law School Centenary Lectures*, Auckland, Legal Research Foundation, 1983, 28.
146 See, for example, *Britten v Alpogut* [1987] VR 929; (1986) 23 A Crim R 254. See also *R v Sew Hoy* [1994] 1 NZLR 257; (1993) 10 CRNZ 581 (CA), 267; 591: "But certainly it cannot be a crime to agree to commit an 'imaginary crime'" (Hardie Boys J); *US v Dynar* (1997) 147 DLR (4th) 399; 115 CCC (3d) 481 (SCC), 424; 506: "Only attempts to commit imaginary crimes fall outside the scope of the provision" (Cory and Iacobucci JJ). The concept of "imaginary crime" is also discussed by Glanville Williams in "The Lords and impossible attempts, or *quis custodiet ipsos custodes*" (1986) 45 CLJ 33, 55ff.
147 *R v Dery* (2005) 197 CCC (3d) 534 (QCA).
148 *R v Dery* (2005) 197 CCC (3d) 534 (QCA).

payment which, had it been forthcoming, would have completed the substantive offence of conspiracy, contrary to s 465(1)(c) of the Canadian Criminal Code.

The decision in *Dery* is problematic. While it is a decision of a distinguished appellate Court, in our view it is based on a flawed principle and should not be followed. The first difficulty concerns the value of permitting "doubly inchoate" offences at all. The crimes of conspiracy and attempt are auxiliary or relational to the substantive law creating the crime agreed or attempted to be committed. In the case of a conspiracy, the object of making a conspiratorial agreement punishable is to prevent the commission of the offence aimed at (the substantive offence) before it has even reached the stage of an attempt. On this basis there can be little justification in criminalising conduct that falls short even of being a conspiracy to commit a substantive offence. The issue is one of remoteness. Since all inchoate offences are necessarily auxiliary, the danger is in permitting the law to reach too far back to attach liability for conduct which merely expresses a criminal intent and which could never supply the actus reus component of a substantive offence.

A second difficulty is one of analysis. The principle basis upon which the decision in *Dery* proceeds is that, because under Canadian law conspiracy is a substantive offence, there is nothing wrong in principle in prosecuting for an attempt to commit that substantive offence. However, as has been noted,[149] there is an incongruity in "attempting simply to conspire", since a person cannot simply conspire, but only conspire to do something unlawful, namely, to commit a further substantive offence. Since conspiracy only has meaning in relation to the substantive offence intended, it makes little sense to postulate the legitimacy of an attempt to conspire *simpliciter*.

A third difficulty is linguistic. Conspiracy is an agreement between two or more persons to commit an offence. There is either an agreement or there is not. Linguistically one does not generally "prepare" to agree or, to bring it within the realm of attempts liability, take a step that is "proximate" to the commission of an agreement. The difficulty is compounded when we acknowledge that the essence of a conspiratorial agreement includes an intention to agree.[150] An attempt to conspire suggests an attempt to intend to agree — clearly a nonsensical idea. Furthermore, before such agreement there is only conversation, which has its own specific forms of criminalisation through incitement and complicity, and which otherwise has never been a sufficient basis for criminal liability.[151]

The essential question is whether it can be argued that conspiracy is a complete substantive offence as opposed to being a step towards the commission of another offence. There is general academic agreement that one should not combine inchoate crimes in order to constitute complete crimes. The danger is that by doing so we arrive at "preposterously wide" definitions of offences,[152] leading to a potentially infinite regression of inchoate offences, including attempting to attempt, counselling an attempt, attempted incitement, and so on.[153]

---

149 See Meehan and Currie, *The Law of Criminal Attempt* (2nd ed), Scarborough, Carswell, 2000, 264-265; cited in *R v Dery* (2005) 197 CCC (3d) 534, 558, para 94 per Forget JA (dissenting).
150 *R v Gemmell* [1985] 2 NZLR 740; (1985) 1 CRNZ 496 (CA), 743; 500.
151 "Counselling" the commission of a crime, which may involve only spoken words, is a basis for secondary liability, provided the offences aimed at is ultimately committed. See ch 6. Incitement is discussed below, 8.4.
152 See Stuart, *Canadian Criminal Law* (2nd ed), Toronto, Carswell, 1987, 592-593. See also Mewett and Manning, *Mewett & Manning on Criminal Law*, 3rd ed, Toronto, Butterworths, 1994, 344.

In our view, the idea of attempting to agree is legal obfuscation that serves no useful social purpose.

Implicit in this last objection is a definitional problem. As we know, all offences must have an actus reus and a mens rea element, save offences of absolute or strict liability. The difficulty in defining an offence of attempted conspiracy is to assign it an actus reus element. Since the actus reus of a conspiracy is the act of agreeing itself, it is virtually impossible to imagine a prior event which bears any of the hallmarks of culpable conduct sufficient to be called an actus reus. If there are no steps taken that could be designated as being in furtherance of a design and no event signifying a "step" towards committing a crime, then where does the actus reus element lie. In mere conversation? In being in corsortium with someone who articulates criminal designs? In signifying by signs a criminal intent? While consorting may, in particular circumstances, constitute a separate offence, none of these modes of "acting" could reasonably be described as the actus reus of an inchoate offence, let alone a substantive crime. In the absence of a clearly defined actus reus element, the offence of attempted conspiracy breaches the fair labelling and fair warning principles (above, 2.1.3-4). The law needs precision in order to identify exactly what offence the wrongdoer has committed, and in order to forewarn citizens of exactly which actions will get them into trouble. Without clear actus reus boundaries, the "offence" of attempted conspiracy can do neither.

8.3 Conspiracy

The last section leads us to consideration of the next form of inchoate liability: conspiracy. A person does not become guilty of a crime by merely thinking about it. There must always be some external manifestation of conduct to transform a criminal thought into culpable conduct. Even more than attempts and incitement, however, conspiracy, by its nature, is a crime that comes very close to punishing a person for his thoughts alone. Yet even here mere evidence of a criminal intention, in the absence of an actual *agreement* between two or more persons to commit a crime, will be insufficient to constitute an offence. On the face of it the reason seems clear enough. If two people have actually agreed on a course of conduct it is much more likely that it will be carried out than if one person, scheming alone in the solitude of his mind, merely imagines the completion of a criminal enterprise.

The question whether conduct amounts to a conspiracy is not, like criminal attempts, merely a difficult threshold problem of determining when there is sufficient proximity to the intended crime. Instead, the focus of the wrongdoing is quite sharply defined: what must be proved is an actual agreement to commit an offence. However, while defining the elements of a conspiracy has all the appearance of simplicity, the jurisprudence of conspiracy is quite complex and requires careful analysis. Conspiracy has been described as one of the most difficult and controversial branches of the criminal law.[154] To say that the essence of conspiracy is agreement is very much to oversimplify the relevant law.

8.3.1 Scope of conspiracy

Although successive New Zealand criminal codes have established liability for conspiracy, neither the elements nor the scope of the offence has ever been defined by statute.[155] The principal substantive provision, s 310 Crimes Act 1961, is primarily a penalty provision.

---

153 Stuart, *Canadian Criminal Law: A treatise*, 2nd ed, Toronto, Carswell, 1987, 592-593.
154 *Kamara v DPP* [1974] AC 104; [1973] 2 All ER 1242 (HL), 116; 1248 (Lord Hailsham).

However, it does clarify the rule that conspiracy is only a crime in New Zealand if the conspiracy is to commit a statutory offence or "to do or omit, in any part of the world, anything of which the doing or omission in New Zealand, would be an offence".[156] By contrast, where the Crimes Act 1961 defines particular conspiracies, for example conspiracy to defraud in s 257, it is clear that the conspiracy need not be aimed at the commission of an offence.[157] Similarly, the offence of conspiring to defeat justice[158] is not limited to conspiracies to commit offences per se, and includes conspiracies to do acts that if done by individuals might not be offences.[159] Nonetheless, in the vast majority of cases, the conduct impugned as conspiracy will comprise an agreement to commit an offence; and, if impugned under s 310, it *must* do so.

The reasons for this are historical. When the Criminal Code Bill Commissioners presented their report containing the Draft Code,[160] they recommended that crimes should no longer be indictable at common law.[161] One effect of this recommendation was to prevent indictments at common law for conspiracy. Having identified the individual conspiracies that could be prosecuted under the Draft Code,[162] the Commissioners expressed doubt whether there was any "distinct authority" that other common law conspiracies exist. They did concede, however, that a "degree of obscurity exists on the subject".[163] Consequently, the decision to abolish common law conspiracies reflects a perception that it is unsatisfactory to have any indictable offence where the elements are left in uncertainty and doubt.[164]

This is in contrast to the position in the United Kingdom, where the courts have held that the common law definition of conspiracy does not limit liability to agreements to commit crimes but may also include agreements to commit some torts, to defraud, to corrupt public morals, and to outrage public decency.[165] While in England the categories of conspiracy to effect a public mischief may not be closed, the House of Lords has cautioned that any extension should be closely and jealously watched by the courts because of the difficulty of "riding the horse of public policy".[166]

---

155 Dawkins, "Parties, conspiracies and attempts" in Cameron and France (eds), *Essays on Criminal Law in New Zealand: Towards Reform?*, VUW Law Review monograph no 3, Wellington, Victoria University of Wellington Law Review, 1990, 130.
156 Section 310(1). See *R v Gemmell* [1985] 2 NZLR 740; (1985) 1 CRNZ 496 (CA), 743; 499.
157 See 20.4; also *Adams*, CA310.02.
158 Section 116.
159 See *Adams* (2nd ed), para 880; also *R v Newland* [1954] 1 QB 158; [1953] 2 All ER 1067.
160 See Criminal Code Bill Commission, *Report of the Royal Commission Appointed to Consider the Law Relating to Indictable Offences: With an Appendix Containing a Draft Code Embodying the Suggestions of the Commissioners*, London, Eyre & Spottiswoode for HMSO, 1879, C2345, C.2345.
161 See s 5 Draft Code (offenders to be tried under this Act) and see Crimes Act 1961; also s 9 Crimes Act 1961 (offences not to be punishable except under New Zealand Acts).
162 Including treasonable conspiracies, seditious conspiracies, conspiracies to bring false accusations, to pervert justice, to defile women, to murder, to defraud, to commit indictable offences, and to prevent by force the collection of rates and taxes. See ss 79, 102, 126, 127, 149, 180, 284, 419, 420, and 421 Draft Code.
163 See Criminal Code Bill Commission, *Report of the Royal Commission Appointed to Consider the Law Relating to Indictable Offences: With an Appendix Containing a Draft Code Embodying the Suggestions of the Commissioners*, London, Eyre & Spottiswoode for HMSO, 1879, C2345, 16.
164 Criminal Code Bill Commission, *Report of the Royal Commission Appointed to Consider the Law Relating to Indictable Offences: With an Appendix Containing a Draft Code Embodying the Suggestions of the Commissioners*, London, Eyre & Spottiswoode for HMSO, 1879, C2345, 16. Cf discussion of the Rule of Law, 2.1.
165 Allen, *Textbook on Criminal Law* (2nd ed), London, Blackstone Press, 1993, 202. See 2.1.2-2.1.3.

In New Zealand, then, all conspiracies are necessarily statutory. Under s 310 Crimes Act 1961, where the conspiracy is to commit a summary offence, the conspiracy itself is a crime and may be tried indictably. Suppose, for example, that A and B conspire to light a fire in a rubbish skip belonging to their neighbour X, with whom they have had a long-running feud. Even though the summary offence[167] they plan to commit is punishable only by a fine of $200 and carries no right of election, the conspiracy becomes an electable offence; albeit that the penalty for conspiracy is limited to the maximum for the substantive offence, ie $200.[168]

8.3.2 When is a conspiracy complete?

Before examining the elements of conspiracy, it may be useful to reflect on the question: "when is a conspiracy complete?" Because the actus reus in a conspiracy is an agreement to execute an offence, it is now settled law that a conspiracy is complete when the agreement is made.[169] "Complete", in this sense, means "constituted" — ie, that all the elements necessary for the offence have occurred. The offence has been committed and all the conspirators can be prosecuted, even though no performance may have taken place. But it does not mean that the conspiratorial agreement is finished with.[170] As long as the conspirators continue to perform their agreement the conspiracy remains alive and operating and it continues to operate until it is discharged by being performed in full or until it is abandoned or frustrated.[171] So if A and B agree together to commit a robbery, but before the robbery actually commences B is shot and killed by a security guard, then while A may still be guilty of conspiracy to rob, the conspiracy itself would be deemed to have terminated because it is incapable of further agreement. Any further acts of A in pursuance of the common design would necessarily be the acts of A alone and not pursuant to a continuing agreement.

It follows that, where the conspiracy has been conceived and commenced in one jurisdiction but acts necessary to its execution are committed in New Zealand, it is open to a court to find that the conspiracy continues and is not discharged until all that is necessary for the offence has occurred. This is illustrated in R v Johnston.[172] In that case D, while on holiday in England, had arranged to send some Class A drugs to New Zealand. His appeal was based on the fact that he never received the drugs, which were intercepted by customs officers, and did not plan the operation in New Zealand. He argued that the New Zealand courts had no jurisdiction. In rejecting these arguments and dismissing the appeal against conviction, the Court of Appeal held that the use of the New Zealand Customs and Postal Services was part of the conspiracy, which brought the offence within the jurisdiction of the New Zealand courts. The Court was

---

166 *Kamara v DPP* [1974] AC 104; [1973] 2 All ER 1242 (HL), 123; 1254 (Lord Hailsham). See, in particular, *DPP v Withers* [1975] AC 842; [1974] 3 All ER 984.
167 See s 36 Summary Offences Act 1981 (lighting fires).
168 Section 310(1).
169 See *Kamara v DPP* [1974] AC 104; [1973] 2 All ER 1242 (HL), 119; 1251; *R v Gemmell* [1985] 2 NZLR 740; (1985) 1 CRNZ 496 (CA), 744; 500. See also the *Poulterer's Case* (1610) 9 Co Rep 55b; 77 ER 813.
170 *R v Johnston* (1986) 2 CRNZ 289 (CA), 291; *DPP v Doot* [1973] AC 807; [1973] 1 All ER 940 (HL), 827; 951.
171 *DPP v Doot* [1973] AC 807; [1973] 1 All ER 940 (HL), 827; 951 (Lord Pearson). There may, however, be special occasions where a narrower view should be taken and the conspiracy regarded as complete at the time of the agreement. Such a case might be where the sentence for an offence has changed as a result of statutory amendment after the agreement but before all overt acts in furtherance of the agreement are completed. In these circumstances fairness would dictate either that the conspiracy be coterminous with the agreement or two separate conspiracies be charged. See *R v Hobbs* [2002] 2 Cr App R 324 (CA), 329.
172 *R v Johnston* (1986) 2 CRNZ 289 (CA). Cf also *R v Greenfield* 5/2/02, CA322/01.

influenced by the fact that s 7 Crimes Act 1961 confers jurisdiction and deems an offence to be committed in New Zealand:

> "where [i] any act or omission forming part of any offence, or [ii] any event necessary to the completion of any offence, occurs in New Zealand, the offence shall be deemed to be committed in New Zealand, whether the person charged with the offence was in New Zealand or not at the time of the act, omission, or event."

(Item numbering added.) In the Court's words:[173]

> "It is well settled that though the offence of conspiracy is complete when the agreement to do the unlawful act is made a conspiracy does not end with the making of the agreement. The conspiratorial agreement continues in operation and therefore in existence until it is ended by completion of its performance or abandonment or in any other manner by which agreements are discharged."

Richardson J, delivering the judgment of the Court, noted that the expressions "complete" and "completion" may be used in the different sense of having come into existence and having been at an end.[174] The Court ruled that in the context of the phrase "any event necessary to the completion of any offence" under limb (ii) of s 7, "completion" must be read as meaning "coming into existence" — ie *formation* of the conspiracy. The use of the post office therefore fell outside the second limb, since the conspiracy had already been formed. However, D's conviction stood, because the handling of the letter by the post office fell within limb (i). It constituted an action "forming part of the offence [of conspiracy]" — ie an action within the envisaged conduct of the conspiracy, which occurred before the conspiracy was terminated.

8.3.3 Elements of conspiracy

In *R v Gemmell*,[175] the Court of Appeal approved the following statement from *Mulcahy v R*,[176] as being the "locus classicus" of the definition of conspiracy:[177]

> "A conspiracy consists not merely in the intention of two or more, but in the agreement of two or more to do an unlawful act, or to do a lawful act by unlawful means. So long as such a design rests in intention only, it is not indictable. *When two agree to carry it into effect, the very plot is an act in itself, and the act of each of the parties, promise against promise, actus contra actum, capable of being enforced, if lawful, punishable if for a criminal object or for the use of criminal means.*"

This statement, while useful, is not exhaustive. For example, it fails to identify the fact, implicit in s 310, that a conspiracy may have as its object an omission. Thus, a couple conspire to commit an offence by omission if they agree not to feed their young child, or not to provide it with medical attention when ill, thereby intending to cause the child's death.[178] Of course, it

---

173 *R v Johnston* (1986) 2 CRNZ 289 (CA), 290-291.
174 See, for example, *R v Kaitamaki* [1984] 1 NZLR 385, also reported as *Kaitamaki v R* (1984) 1 CRNZ 211; [1985] AC 147 (PC).
175 *R v Gemmell* [1985] 2 NZLR 740; (1985) 1 CRNZ 496 (CA).
176 *Mulcahy v R* (1868) LR 3 HL 306, 317.
177 *R v Gemmell* [1985] 2 NZLR 740; (1985) 1 CRNZ 496 (CA), 743; 499.
178 The example is due to Dawkins, "Parties, conspiracies and attempts" in Cameron and France (eds), *Essays on Criminal Law in New Zealand: Towards Reform?*, VUW Law Review monograph no 3, Wellington, Victoria University of Wellington Law Review, 1990, 130, 131.

would still be necessary in such a case to establish the existence of a plot — an actual agreement to effect the child's death by a wilful omission. Mere negligence in failing to provide the necessaries of life[179] accompanied by the intention of one party to injure the child by such neglect would not, without more, amount to a conspiracy.

Nonetheless, as the quotation makes clear, at the heart of a criminal conspiracy is "the very plot", the element of agreement or consensus, ie the joint resolution of two or more persons. This is nicely illustrated in R v Greenfield,[180] where the Court of Appeal held that the essence of a conspiracy is an agreement to pursue a course of conduct which, if carried out, would amount to or involve the commission of an offence by one or more parties to the agreement. The offence turns on the agreement itself and does not necessitate any further involvement in the commission of the crime.[181]

Every conspiratorial agreement is entered into by the operation of both physical and mental faculties and consists, as with all true crimes, in an actus reus and mens rea. Other important elements within the nature of conspiracy concern parties' liability and the circumstances which pertain following the acquittal of other alleged conspirators. We will look at each element in turn.

8.3.4 Actus reus of conspiracy

It is common ground that the actus reus of a conspiracy is the agreement to execute the illegal conduct, and not the execution of it. The crime is complete when the agreement is made. The actual conduct comprising the actus reus consists in the physical acts, words, or gestures whereby the conspirators indicate their agreement. The agreement may be express or implied, or in part express and in part implied.[182] However, for a conspiracy to exist, it is not necessary for the prosecution to establish that the individuals are in direct communication with each other, or that they directly consulted together. It is enough that they entered into an agreement with a common design.[183]

A conspiracy will not necessarily be present simply because two or more persons pursued the same unlawful objects at the same time or in the same place; it is necessary to show a meeting of minds, a consensus to effect an unlawful purpose. In R v Walker,[184] it was held that mere negotiation of an agreement was insufficient for a conspiracy. In that case, D's conviction was quashed because, although D had discussed with the others the idea of stealing a payroll, it was not proved that the alleged conspirators had got beyond the stage of negotiation when D withdrew.

For a conspiracy to exist it is not necessary that each conspirator should have been in communication with every other. In R v Parnell, Grose J said:[185]

---

179 Section 151 Crimes Act 1961.
180 R v Greenfield 5/2/02, CA322/01, para 18. Cf R v Cuthbertson [1980] 2 All ER 401, 403.
181 R v Greenfield 5/2/02, CA322/01, para 18.
182 Halsbury's Laws of England vol 11(1) (4th ed reissue), London, Butterworths, 1990, para 64.
183 R v Gemmell [1985] 2 NZLR 740; (1985) 1 CRNZ 496 (CA), 744; 500. Because direct evidence of the making of the agreement and its nature and terms is rarely available, proof will almost always depend on evidence of subsequent acts or declarations by persons alleged to be parties to the conspiracy, and on the inferences to be drawn from them (for example that the acts are pursuant to a concluded agreement). However, it is important to note that those acts do not themselves constitute the conspiracy. They are only the evidence from which the agreement may be inferred.
184 R v Walker [1962] Crim LR 458 (CA). See also R v Mills [1963] 1 QB 522; (1962) 47 Cr App R 49 (CCA).

"It may be that the alleged conspirators have never seen each other, and have never corresponded, one may have never heard the name of the other, and yet by the law they may be parties to the same common criminal agreement. Thus, in some of the Fenian cases tried in this country, it frequently happened that one of the conspirators was in America, the other in this country; that they had never seen each other, but that there were acts on both sides which led the jury to the inference, and they drew it, that they were engaged in accomplishing the same common object, and when they had arrived at this conclusion, the acts of the one became evidence against the other."

From this statement it is clear that persons may conspire together, even though there is no direct communication between each and all of them. What must be established is that they entered into an agreement with a common design.[186] In describing the different ways in which such agreements may be made the courts have resorted to the use of various metaphors, including those of a "wheel" and of a "chain". We shall consider these particular varieties in 8.3.4(4)-(5).

(1) *Acts subsequent to the formation but during the continuation of the conspiracy*

It has been held that any subsequent acts performed in the commission or attempted commission of the unlawful object are not part of the actus reus of conspiracy, although they may be evidence from which an inference can be drawn regarding the existence of an illegal agreement.[187] While this is clearly true in the case of a simple conspiracy which is complete on the agreement's being made, it is also apparent from cases like *R v Johnston*[188] and *R v Sanders*,[189] involving extraterritorial conspiracies, that subsequent acts may be regarded as part of the actus reus of a *continuing* conspiracy. Indeed, unless such acts were treated as part of the continuing actus reus, it would be impossible to obtain convictions of co-conspirators who reside outside the jurisdiction in which the conspiracy is initially formed.

However, if the alleged agreement is identical to and coterminous with the very crime which is the object of the conspiracy (the "object crime") there cannot be a conspiracy because the agreement must precede, or be anterior to, the object crime contemplated in the agreement; it cannot be synonymous with the object crime itself.[190] For this reason, particular problems may arise in determining the appropriate charge where the statute, in addition to nominating conspiracy as a possible offence, specifies other general offences like "supplying", which is capable of being interpreted to include "*agreeing* to supply".[191] Where the Crown, in such a case, relies on a form of "supply" consisting of the act of entering into an agreement to sell drugs, there can be no charge of conspiracy because there would be no agreement anterior in time to the object crime (the agreement to supply).[192]

---

185 *R v Parnell* (1881) 14 Cox CC 508, 515.
186 *R v Meyrick* (1929) 21 Cr App R 94, 102.
187 See *R v Janis* 28/5/92, Heron J, HC Wellington T91-95/91.
188 *R v Johnston* (1986) 2 CRNZ 289 (CA); above 8.3.2.
189 *R v Sanders* [1984] 1 NZLR 636; (1984) 1 CRNZ 194 (CA).
190 *R v Richards [conspiracy]* (1992) 9 CRNZ 403, 407. See also *R v Chow* (1987) 11 NSWLR 561; 30 A Crim R 103 (CA).
191 *R v Richards [conspiracy]* (1992) 9 CRNZ 403, 407. See s 6(1)(c) and (2A) Misuse of Drugs Act 1975.
192 *R v Richards [conspiracy]* (1992) 9 CRNZ 403.

(2) Proof of the agreement

As was noted above, the essence of conspiracy is an *agreement* or *consensus* between two or more persons in certain terms. The actus reus consists in the physical acts, words, or gestures by which the conspirators indicate their agreement.

Often, however, it may be unenlightening to talk of the actus reus of conspiracy, in so far as actus reus typically speaks of the acts or omissions of an accused that are proscribed by law. Realistically, to establish conspiracy such acts or omissions need not necessarily be proved. Indeed, in many criminal conspiracies the actual agreement will not be capable of identification or proof. The precise manner in which agreement was reached may even be irrelevant, provided the fact of an agreement in the terms alleged can be established.[193] The formation of the agreement can be proved *either* (i) by evidence that the parties actually met together and concluded an agreement, or (ii) indirectly, by proof of the overt acts done in the transaction of the agreement — provided these acts are sufficient, when taken with any relevant surrounding circumstances, to compel the inference that their commission was the product of concert between the alleged parties.[194] One consequence of this possibility is that the prosecution need not prove the exact moment at which the conspiracy began.

(3) Conspiring with "persons unknown"

There must be at least two parties to a conspiracy. But it is not essential to prove the actual number and identity of the co-conspirators. An accused may be convicted of conspiring "with a person or persons unknown" to commit an unlawful act.[195] For example, in *R v Savage*[196] the accused received a text message from an unknown person asking where he was. He replied that he was "on his way down" and that he had a "whole one" and asked the caller whether he wanted him to save it for him. It was accepted by the defendant that the message meant that he was in possession of one gram of methamphetamine and that he would save it for the caller. The unknown person replied that he only had $300, whereupon the accused arranged to meet the person later in the day. This was held to be evidence of a conspiracy to supply methamphetamine with a person unknown.

On the other hand, the number and identity of the co-conspirators may be relevant or even essential to the identification of the subject matter of the alleged conspiracy and to the proof of its actual existence. For example, the question whether the intended perpetrator of an unlawful act is actually a party to a conspiracy is likely to be of critical importance to the question whether the relevant conspiracy is a conspiracy to commit the act as distinct from a conspiracy to procure its commission by another.[197] In *Gerakiteys*,[198] the identity of the alleged co-conspirators was of importance in determining whether the conspiracy charged was a conspiracy to make fraudulent claims, or a conspiracy to procure or enable the making of those claims by persons who were not conspirators.

---

193 *R v Richards [conspiracy]* (1992) 9 CRNZ 403.
194 *R v Janis* 28/5/92, Heron J, HC Wellington T91-95/91, 3. See also Gillies, *The Law of Criminal Conspiracy*, Sydney, The Law Book Company, 1981, 13.
195 See *R v Howes* (1971) 2 SASR 293; *R v Anthony* [1965] 2 QB 189. Sometimes a statute may depart from this rule, and specify that a person can be charged as having conspired with various people, provided that at least one of them is named. See, for example, s 393 Crimes Act 1900 (NSW).
196 *R v Savage* 21/7/06, Lang J, HC Whangarei CRI-2005-029-1267.
197 *Gerakiteys v R* (1984) 153 CLR 317; 51 ALR 417, 334; 431 (Deane J).
198 *Gerakiteys v R* (1984) 153 CLR 317; 51 ALR 417, 334; 431.

One co-conspirator is always enough. Thus, where an indictment alleges multiple conspiracies involving co-conspirators in different combinations in each conspiracy alleged, it is not a misdirection for the judge to direct the jury that each conspirator had only to conspire with one of the co-conspirators named in the count in question for the conviction to be valid.[199]

However, where an indictment alleges conspiracy with "a person or persons unknown", there must be some evidence from which a conspiracy could be inferred.[200] In *White*, where W appealed against a conviction for conspiring with L and other persons unknown to utter forged petrol coupons, Myers CJ stated:[201]

> "The charges however in the present case are not confined to a conspiracy ... with the other and with other persons unknown. It follows, therefore ... that even if there were no evidence against *White* of having conspired with L and there were no evidence ... of his having conspired with other persons unknown and if in consequence of there being no evidence against him he is entitled to be acquitted, L might still be convicted if the evidence showed that *he* had conspired with other persons unknown, that is to say, persons other than White whose identity the evidence did not disclose."

Often, inferences of conspiracy may legitimately be drawn from the criminal acts of the parties accused, done in pursuance of an apparent common purpose. But mere conjecture is insufficient. A court must be careful to ensure that a person is not convicted of a crime simply on suspicion, speculation, or guesswork.[202] Thus, in *White*,[203] it was held that evidence that one accused was seen to pass his wallet into the pocket of another alleged conspirator, and that the wallet contained what looked like folded cards of coupons, was not evidence that they were forged coupons sufficient to infer a conspiracy to utter forged coupons. A mere series of assumptions, each in the nature of a guess unsupported by other evidence, is insufficient to prove a conspiracy charge.[204]

(4) *The "wheel" conspiracy*

The essence of this kind of conspiracy is the notion that there is one global agreement made by all the conspirators, through the intermediary of a central person or group of persons. The persons at the centre (hub) form links (spokes) to the other individual members of the conspiracy, each of whom has no contact with any other conspirator apart from the central persons. However, there are some important limitations to this analysis. First, a person should not be joined in a charge alleging a *general* conspiracy unless there is real evidence from which a jury can infer that their minds went beyond a conspiracy to do a particular act or acts. This objection may be illustrated by the following example:[205]

> "A employs an accountant, C, to prepare his tax return. He and his clerk B are present when A is about to sign the return. A notices and queries an item in his expenses of

---

199 R v *Georgiadis* (2002) 133 A Crim R 152.
200 R v *White* [1945] GLR 108, 112.
201 R v *White* [1945] GLR 108, 111-112.
202 R v *White* [1945] GLR 108.
203 R v *White* [1945] GLR 108, 112. Cf R v *Drummond* (1993) 9 CRNZ 228, 231, where on a charge of conspiring with persons unknown to manufacture amphetamine, the Court concluded that, while there may well have been reason to suspect that D must have needed the help of another person, mere suspicion is not proof on a criminal charge and the reasonable possibility that D had acted on his own had not been disproved.
204 R v *Sadler* (1911) 14 GLR 117, 123 (Denniston J).
205 R v *Griffiths* [1966] 1 QB 589; [1965] 2 All ER 448, 598, 599; 454.

$100 and indicates that he doesn't remember incurring the expense. B concedes that A did not put the item in but that it had been added by B on his own initiative on the basis that A 'would not object to a few dollars being saved'. The accountant agrees with the arrangement and after some hesitation A also agrees to let it stand."

On those bare facts A and B could be charged with conspiring with C to defraud the Inland Revenue Department. However, the same evidence could not justify a charge against A of conspiring with 20 other people to defraud the Inland Revenue Department of $10,000 simply because the accountant and B had persuaded 100 other clients to make false returns. A would not be guilty of the general conspiracy because he has not knowingly attached himself to a general agreement to defraud.

In *R v Griffiths*,[206] the Court of Criminal Appeal allowed appeals against conviction on the grounds that there was no evidence that the appellants, a group of farmers who had allegedly conspired to defraud the Government by inducing a department of State to pay excessive contributions under an Agriculture Lime Scheme, had any link with each other or knew what contracts other than their own had been entered into by the principal alleged conspirator to supply lime.

A second objection is that, with both "wheel" and "chain" conspiracies (8.3.4(5)), the concept of "agreement" is replaced by "common design".[207] Yet for the common design to become a common agreement, there must have been some manifestation of assent to the agreement.[208] Where wheel or chain conspiracies are in issue, it appears that the courts sometimes derive the necessary manifestation of assent by treating some conspirators as making the agreement on behalf of themselves and others.[209] This approach is problematic. It is probably going too far to suggest that the concept of a "wheel conspiracy" is not known to the criminal law, as was suggested in the headnote to one English case.[210] However, it is equally clear that a person should not be convicted of complicity in a "wheel" conspiracy unless the trier of fact is convinced that each alleged conspirator was a party to a single, common conspiracy.[211] This implies that individual conspirators must at least have *knowingly* attached themselves to a conspiracy, whether or not their minds have gone beyond a conspiracy to do a particular act or acts. A person cannot enter a conspiracy inadvertently.

(5) *The "chain" conspiracy*

In a "chain" conspiracy, the overall agreement is made by a series of groups of conspirators. Each group includes only some of the people who are members of the other groups. Thus, A communicates with B, B with C, C with D, and so on until the end of the list of conspirators. What has to be ascertained is whether the acts of the accused were done in pursuance of a criminal purpose held in common between the individual conspirators.[212] The courts treat each conspirator as being a party to the common design, and therefore as being a party to the agreement or conspiracy. On this basis, direct communication between all the co-conspirators

---

206 R v Griffiths [1966] 1 QB 589; [1965] 2 All ER 448.
207 *Adams*, CA310.06 (looseleaf).
208 *Adams*, CA310.06 (looseleaf).
209 *Adams*, CA310.06 (looseleaf).
210 See R v Griffiths [1966] 1 QB 589; [1965] 2 All ER 448, and see discussion in R v Ardalan [1972] 2 All ER 257; [1972] 1 WLR 463, 262; 470.
211 R v Ardalan [1972] 2 All ER 257; [1972] 1 WLR 463, 262; 470.
212 R v Meyrick (1929) 21 Cr App R 94, 102.

is unnecessary. Neither is it required that any one co-conspirator knows of the existence of all the others.[213] What must be established is that the individual conspirators did have the common purpose to achieve some unlawful end. But if two conspirators agree to effect several unlawful objects and a third person agrees with them to effect only some of those objects, there are two conspiracies, not one. The original conspirators are parties to both conspiracies, the third person is party only to the conspiracy with the more limited objects.[214]

Note that where a single conspiracy has been charged, it is not open to the jury to find the accused guilty of a consequential but different conspiracy which flowed from that which is the subject of the actual charge.[215]

(6) *Purely "internal" conspiracies?*

It may be that the actus reus of a criminal conspiracy is subject to a further restriction. There is some authority that an agreement between two people to do particular criminal conduct will not constitute a conspiracy where that activity is for the sole benefit of the alleged conspirators and does not involve third parties.

The issue has arisen in relation to the charge of conspiring to supply class A drugs. In *R v Lang*,[216] the appellant, D, telephoned N, her alleged co-conspirator, seeking to buy for her own use one tab of LSD. She then went to N's address and was there supplied with the LSD. On the question of whether a person can conspire to supply a drug to herself, the Court of Appeal, while mindful of authority suggesting that a person could so conspire,[217] was influenced by the wording of the relevant statutory provision, which makes it an offence to supply or offer to supply a class A controlled drug "to any other person".[218] Henry J observed that the offence D supposedly conspired to do — the supply of a controlled drug to another person, namely D — was on its face self-contradictory. His Honour expressed "serious reservations" about endorsing the proposition that D could be convicted of a conspiracy to supply LSD to herself, particularly where the conspiracy did not form part of any wider agreement involving other persons and did not embrace any transactions other than the one actually effected as a direct, and the only, intended result of D's request for drugs for personal use.

Although the Court did not rule conclusively on the issue and has left it open for reconsideration, an important issue of principle is at stake. Conspiracy is a "relational" offence, the aim of which is to pre-empt serious offending before members of the public are placed at risk of harm. Conspiracy law empowers the police to anticipate sources of criminal wrongdoing and nip them in the bud.[219] It is, arguably, inapt to prosecute an agreement to commit an offence as a conspiracy where the only possible victims are the conspirators;[220] especially where there is ample evidence to sustain a prosecution for the full offence. A consequence of the proposition that a person can conspire to supply drugs to himself would be that every person who possesses a controlled drug supplied by another would be guilty of conspiracy to

---

213 *Adams*, CA310.06 (looseleaf).
214 *Gerakiteys v R* (1984) 153 CLR 317; 51 ALR 417, 327; 425.
215 *Gerakiteys v R* (1984) 153 CLR 317; 51 ALR 417, 334; 431 (Deane J).
216 *R v Lang* (1998) 16 CRNZ 68 (CA).
217 See *R v Richards [conspiracy]* (1992) 9 CRNZ 403; *R v Wrenn, Ross and Thomas* (1989) 4 CRNZ 165 (CA).
218 Section 6(1)(c) Misuse of Drugs Act 1975.
219 See McAuley, "Relational liability in criminal law" (1999) 34 The Irish Jurist 100.
220 Cf the *Tyrrell* principle in complicity, whereby, in certain classes of offences, the victim cannot be a party to the crime committed against her: *R v Tyrrell* [1894] 1 QB 710; [1891-94] All ER Rep 1215; see 6.6.2.

supply.²²¹ Such an outcome would demean the useful social purpose played by conspiracy prosecutions, namely to impugn criminal associations which threaten harm to other members of the community. Moreover, it would improperly target persons who, while perhaps a danger to themselves, do not represent the sort of risk to public health or safety that a conspiracy prosecution typically aims to prevent.

8.3.5 Mens rea of conspiracy

In general, the mens rea for conspiracy is present where there is an intention to agree coupled with an intention that the requisite course of conduct shall be pursued.²²² The intention to carry out a crime is an essential element in conspiracy; a mere expectation or anticipation that a crime will be carried out is insufficient.²²³ There must be a common design to commit some offence and an intention that the design be put into effect.²²⁴

Correspondingly, it is no defence for the accused to plead that the intended course of conduct was ultimately proved impossible to pursue; because the essence of conspiracy is what the accused *agreed to do*, not what was *achieved*. In *R v Sew Hoy*,²²⁵ the Court of Appeal held that it is the making of the agreement that is inimical to the public good, regardless of whether it proceeds further.²²⁶

In *R v Gemmell*²²⁷ it was held that, to have the necessary knowledge for conspiracy, a person must know what he is supposed to have agreed to do. That is, D must intend to be a party to an agreement to commit the specific offence to which the conspiracy is directed.²²⁸ However, it is not necessary that the accused should know the intended conduct will amount to an offence.²²⁹ Thus if A and B agree together to take a 15-year-old girl out of the possession of her parents, the fact that B believed the girl to be 17 would be no defence to a charge of conspiracy to abduct.²³⁰ However, if on the same facts the evidence was that B believed the girl was a family friend of A's, and that the parents had consented to A and B having the temporary custody of the child, he would not be guilty of conspiracy because it could not be said that on the facts known to B what they agreed to do amounted to an unlawful act.²³¹ In *Churchill v Walton*, Viscount Dilhorne held:²³²

---

221 See *R v Lang* (1998) 16 CRNZ 68 (CA), 71 (Henry J).
222 *Halsbury's Laws of England* vol 11(1) (4th ed reissue), London, Butterworths, 1990, para 65.
223 *Yip Chiu-Cheung v R* [1995] 1 AC 111; [1994] 2 All ER 924 (PC), 118; 927; *R v Trudgeon* (1988) 39 A Crim R 252; *R v Genser* (1986) 27 CCC (3d) 264.
224 Cf *R v Morris (Lee)* [2001] 3 NZLR 759, para 15.
225 [1994] 1 NZLR 257; (1993) 10 CRNZ 581 (CA).
226 This is in contrast to the position at common law, where if the conspiracy could not possibly have been successful, the parties were not guilty of conspiracy though they believed otherwise. See *DPP v Nock* [1978] AC 979; [1978] 2 All ER 654 (HL); *R v Bennett* (1978) 68 Cr App R 168; [1979] Crim LR 454 (CA). However, in the United Kingdom, the common law position has now been reversed by statute, to the effect that a person may be guilty of conspiracy even though the facts were such that the commission of the offence was impossible. See s 1(1) Criminal Law Act 1977 (UK), as amended by the Criminal Attempts Act 1981 (UK).
227 *R v Gemmell* [1985] 2 NZLR 740; (1985) 1 CRNZ 496 (CA), 744; 500.
228 *R v Gemmell* [1985] 2 NZLR 740; (1985) 1 CRNZ 496 (CA). See also *Churchill v Walton* [1967] 2 AC 224; [1967] 1 All ER 497 (HL), 237; 503.
229 *R v Gemmell* [1985] 2 NZLR 740; (1985) 1 CRNZ 496 (CA).
230 Section 210. This is because, for an offence to be committed under s 210, it is not necessary that D should know the age of the girl (s 210(2)).
231 Cf s 210(3).

"If what they agreed to do was, on the facts known to them, an unlawful act, they are guilty of conspiracy and cannot excuse themselves by saying that, owing to their ignorance of the law, they did not realise that such an act was a crime. If, on the facts known to them, what they agreed to do was lawful, they are not rendered artificially guilty by the existence of other facts, not known to them, giving a different and criminal quality to the act agreed upon."

It follows, therefore, that while a mistake of law will not afford a defence, an honest belief in a state of facts which, if true, would render the conduct lawful, will be an answer to any charge of conspiracy.[233] It would also follow, for example, that if T, charged with conspiracy to trespass, asserted a belief in a state of facts which would give rise to an enforceable right-of-way, that too would deny mens rea. Similarly, on a charge of conspiracy to publish defamatory matter during an election campaign,[234] it would normally be a defence that the accused genuinely believed in facts which would establish a privilege.[235] In these examples the burden of proof would rest on the prosecution to exclude the defences.[236]

(1)   *Agreements and acquiescence*

While an accused need not know that what she has agreed to do is unlawful, an apparent agreement which stops short of an intention to carry the offence through to completion is generally regarded as being insufficient for a conspiracy.[237] For example, if B and C, while having a quiet drink at the local pub, begin to discuss the possibility of committing a burglary, but before they can agree on the location and timing of the crime there is a disturbance in the hotel and they have to vacate the bar, there will be no conspiracy because there has been no intention manifested to carry the offence through to completion.

In this example, the charge of conspiracy would seem to be doomed because of the apparent absence of any agreement. One might think that merely discussing, in a speculative and abstract way, the possibility of committing an offence at an undefined future date defies the notion of agreeing to carry a criminal design into effect. Is it not the fact of consensus to participation in a common design that transforms mere discussion into a conspiracy? At first blush, it would seem reasonable to suggest that an accused person should not be guilty of conspiracy if she has not agreed and intended to do something of a positive nature herself to further the criminal design.

However, the authorities are not easily reconcilable on this point. In *Mulcahy v R*, in the dictum quoted earlier,[238] Willes J noted that the agreement to carry a criminal design into effect is a "plot" which constitutes the actus reus of conspiracy. A plot, by its nature, is a plan to carry something out or to accomplish something. Nevertheless, it appears that a requirement that the accused, to be a conspirator, must have intended *to play some part* in the agreed course of conduct,[239] may overstate the legal requirements. If it were to be insisted on, it would effectively confer impunity on the organiser of a crime who recruited others to carry it out. Such a person

---

232   *Churchill v Walton* [1967] 2 AC 224; [1967] 1 All ER 497 (HL), 237; 503.
233   *Kamara v DPP* [1974] AC 104; [1973] 2 All ER 1242 (HL), 119; 1252.
234   See s 55 Local Elections and Polls Act 1976; *Police v Starkey* [1989] 2 NZLR 373; (1989) 4 CRNZ 400.
235   *Kamara v DPP* [1974] AC 104; [1973] 2 All ER 1242 (HL), 120; 1252.
236   *Kamara v DPP* [1974] AC 104; [1973] 2 All ER 1242 (HL).
237   *R v Gemmell* [1985] 2 NZLR 740; (1985) 1 CRNZ 496 (CA), 744; 500.
238   *Mulcahy v R* (1868) LR 3 HL 306; see 8.3.3.
239   See *R v Anderson* [1986] AC 27; [1985] 2 All ER 961 (HL), 39; 965 (Lord Bridge).

would, on this view, not herself be guilty of conspiracy unless it could be proved that she also intended to play an active part thereafter.[240]

On the other hand, acquiescence in a course of conduct over which a person would in any event have no influence does not qualify as an agreement for the purposes of conspiracy. The agreement should at least require that an accused assent to something in circumstances where, had he withheld assent, the withholding would have been of practical consequence.[241]

Accordingly, there is no conspiracy where a prospective offender has merely discussed with another person his own intention to commit an offence, to which course of conduct the other person acquiesces. The absence of a causal nexus between the discussion and any offence that follows would seem to defeat the possibility of a conspiracy charge.[242] However, where the second person, as a consequence of the conversation, offers to provide equipment or tools for the commission of the "object" crime, or otherwise intentionally encourages the intending offender to proceed with the crime, the act of expressing agreement in such practical terms might well amount to the real nexus required for a conspiracy charge.[243]

(2)   *Partial conspiracy?*

As we have seen, New Zealand courts have held that there must be an intention that the agreement be carried out, and that the agreement must be common to the minds of the conspirators. This requirement presents difficult problems in cases where D "agrees" with two or more others, who themselves intend to pursue a course of conduct which will necessarily involve the commission of an offence, but where D in fact has a secret intention to participate in only part of that course of conduct. Is D also guilty of conspiracy to commit an offence?

Commonwealth courts have diverged from the English courts on this question. In *Gemmell*, the Court of Appeal approved the decision of the Supreme Court of Canada in *R v O'Brien*,[244] where the majority agreed that because one of the co-conspirators did not have any intention to carry though the common design he could not be a party to the conspiracy. In *O'Brien*, this mental element was expressed as the *intention to put the common design into effect*. So if A and B purport to enter into an agreement to manufacture a Class A prohibited drug but B, acting as an informer for the police, has determined that he will have no part in the manufacture of drugs and will pull out of the agreement as soon as certain information has been disclosed, there is no conspiracy because, in reality, there is no common intention to put the design into effect. It has also been held that where a criminal enterprise is well advanced in the course of preparation, and it comes to the notice of the police or some other honest citizen in such circumstances that the only prospect of exposing and frustrating the criminals is that some innocent person should play the role of an intending collaborator in the proposed criminal conduct, the innocent person will be regarded as being innocent of conspiracy even though that person may be obliged to agree to a course of conduct involving the commission

---

240 See *R v Siracusa* (1990) 90 Cr App R 340 (CA), 349, where the English Court of Appeal "explained" Lord Bridge's dictum.
241 *R v Richards [conspiracy]* (1992) 9 CRNZ 403, 411.
242 *R v Richards [conspiracy]* (1992) 9 CRNZ 403.
243 This causal link must be both present and intended (*R v Richards [conspiracy]* (1992) 9 CRNZ 403, 412).
244 *R v O'Brien* [1954] SCR 666; (1954) 110 CCC 1 (SCC).

of a crime.[245] Public policy reasons dictate that an intention to frustrate the objects of a conspiracy ought to be allowed as a special defence.[246]

In *R v Anderson*,[247] the House of Lords took a different approach. The defendant was convicted of conspiring with a number of other men to effect the escape of one of them from jail. For a fee of £20,000 he had agreed to supply diamond wire to cut through metal cell bars, but claimed that he never intended the plan to be put into effect and did not believe that the plan could succeed. In rejecting this defence, it was held that it was sufficient that the accused agreed to perform certain of the acts contemplated for the achievement of an illegal end, even though he did not intend to go further with the scheme or believe that the offence could be committed.

Lord Bridge pointed out that to find in favour of the defendant would lead to an absurdity, because it would mean that a person could assist in aiding and abetting the commission of a crime by supplying the means to effect it and be fully aware of the agreed course of conduct yet be able to avoid a conviction for conspiracy on the basis that he was completely indifferent whether the offence was committed or not and therefore could not be said to have intended that the offence be committed. In Lord Bridge's view, a person who is fully aware of the circumstances of the commission of an offence and has provided assistance instrumental for its successful completion is "plainly" a party to the conspiracy to commit the offence.

The suggested justification for this approach is the fact that, in these days of highly organised crime, the most serious statutory conspiracies will frequently involve an elaborate and complex agreed course of conduct in which many will consent to play necessary but subordinate roles, which do not involve any direct participation in the commission of the offence at the heart of the conspiracy:[248]

> "Parliament cannot have intended that such parties should escape conviction of conspiracy on the basis that it cannot be proved against them that they intended that the relevant offence or offences should be committed."

However, while the policy argument appears sound it may also be criticised as producing an absurdity. It has been observed that if no intention need be proved on the part of one alleged principal offender in conspiracy, it need not be proved on the part of another. Yet a conspiracy which no one intended to carry out is an absurdity, if not an impossibility.[249] For these reasons it is suggested that *Anderson* should not be followed on this point.[250]

However, a conspiracy may be committed if a person acts with an intention to carry out the object of the conspiracy even though the ulterior motive is to gather evidence as part of a surveillance operation and where the party would not have been prosecuted if he carried out the plan agreed to. In *Yip Chiu-Cheung v R*,[251] A met N in Thailand and arranged to act as a courier to carry heroin from Hong Kong to Australia, for which he was to be paid US$16,000. N was, in fact, a United States undercover drug enforcement officer whom the Australian and Hong Kong authorities had permitted to carry drugs from Hong Kong to Australia in the hope

---

245 *R v Anderson* [1986] AC 27; [1985] 2 All ER 961 (HL).
246 See Smith and Hogan, *Criminal Law* (9th ed), London, Butterworths, 1999, 277.
247 *R v Anderson* [1986] AC 27; [1985] 2 All ER 961 (HL).
248 *R v Anderson* [1986] AC 27; [1985] 2 All ER 961 (HL), 38; 965 (Lord Bridge).
249 Smith and Hogan, *Criminal Law* (9th ed), London, Butterworths, 1999, 276.
250 Smith and Hogan, *Criminal Law* (9th ed), London, Butterworths, 1999, 276.
251 *Yip Chiu-Cheung v R* [1995] 1 AC 111; [1994] 2 All ER 924 (PC).

of breaking the drug ring to which the appellant belonged. Although the plan was not carried through and N did not fly to Hong Kong, the appellant A was arrested in Hong Kong and charged with conspiring with N to import heroin.

The Privy Council upheld the appellant's conviction for conspiracy. Their Lordships held that the fact that N would not have been prosecuted if he had carried out the plan to import the drugs into Australia as intended did not mean that he did not intend to commit the criminal offence, even though this was part of a wider scheme to combat drug dealing. Since N intended to commit the drug importation offence, it followed that there had been a conspiracy and A was properly convicted. The existence of a good motive did not negate the mens rea for the conspiracy. Suppose that N's undeclared intention had been to abscond to South America with the heroin upon successfully importing it into Australia and that he had, unknown to his superiors, arranged for an innocent "mule" to undertake the actual importation. Would these facts have negated the existence of a conspiracy to traffic in heroin? On the grounds of general principle N would have been regarded as the principal and the act of importing by the innocent agent would have been deemed to be his act.[252] The existence of the conspiracy would have been unaffected by the fact that N had acted with an impure motive.

8.3.6 Variations in details of the conspiracy

Should the parties still be guilty of conspiracy where both agree to commit the same offence but each contemplates committing the offence in a different way? In *R v Broad*,[253] D and E agreed to manufacture drugs. D thought they had agreed to produce heroin, whereas E thought their agreement was to produce cocaine. The English Court of Appeal held that the difference was immaterial, since on either view of the agreement both parties had the objective of producing a class A drug. Arguably, *Broad* establishes a general principle that differences over the content of an agreement between the parties do not vitiate the agreement between them if the variant courses of conduct contemplated by each party will still result in the commission of the same offence. However, the generality of the decision in *Broad* has been queried on the basis of a hypothetical case in which D, agreeing with E to murder V, is later horrified to learn that the victim E intends is W. Sir John Smith suggests that differences concerning the type of class A drug are immaterial, whereas the identity of the murder victim is a matter of substance and, in the latter case, D would not be liable for conspiracy to murder.[254] There are two possible approaches to this problem.

First, it could be argued that, since the mens rea for murder does not take any account of the identity of the victim, it is enough that D and E agreed to murder someone. Liability in this case would be based on a similar premise to the case where the accused, by mistake, kills someone other than the person he meant to kill.[255] Such cases are normally governed by the doctrine of "transferred malice": the accused is guilty of an offence if he brings about the actus reus of an offence in respect of which he had the required mens rea, notwithstanding that the result may be unintended and unforeseen in a way which is immaterial to the definition of the offence.[256] An alternative approach would be to say that, since a conspiracy involves "common

---

252 *R v Paterson* [1976] 2 NZLR 394 (CA). See also *R v Jakeman* (1983) 76 Cr App R 223; [1983] Crim LR 104.
253 *R v Broad* [1997] Crim LR 666 (CA).
254 *R v Broad* [1997] Crim LR 666 (CA), 668.
255 See s 167(c).
256 See 4.8.

design" and "a meeting of the minds directed to the crime which is to be committed",[257] a mistake regarding the identity of the victim is a matter of substance that goes to the heart of what has been agreed and, by its nature, vitiates the agreement between the parties.

The first option focuses on the policy undergirding the offence of homicide, namely to protect innocent members of the public from life-threatening acts of violence; while the second focuses on what it means to "agree" and gives weight to the requirement that there must be a "meeting of minds" before there can be a true conspiracy to commit a crime. It is not yet clear which is preferred in New Zealand.

8.3.7 Attempted conspiracy?

The language of the Crimes Act 1961 appears not to exclude the possibility that one may be convicted of attempting to form a conspiracy to commit an offence, and it seems that it was possible at common law to attempt to conspire.[258] Moreover, as we saw in 8.2.6, there is modern Canadian authority favouring such an offence. However, it remains possible for the courts to refrain from acknowledging the possible "offence" in New Zealand and, for the reasons given in 8.2.6, it is submitted that it is undesirable to extend the ambit of the criminal law by heaping preliminary crime upon preliminary crime.[259]

8.3.8 Conspiracy and party liability

The essence of a conspiracy is two or more persons participating in a common agreement to commit a crime. In that sense conspirators may properly be described as "parties" to a conspiracy. They are co-participants in a joint enterprise. Strictly speaking, this is where any assumed similarity between party liability and conspiracy should rest.

However, because New Zealand's statutory provision governing party liability refers, in one subsection, to person who "form a common intention to prosecute an unlawful purpose",[260] it has sometimes been assumed that liability as a secondary party to an offence will necessarily make an offender liable as a party to conspiracy. In *R v Gemmell*,[261] the Court of Appeal rejected this approach, emphasising that a conspiracy is not the same thing as aiding and abetting, since the two offences have different ingredients. The Court approved the view that a person who knows other persons have agreed to commit a crime, but who is not a party to the agreement, and who does certain acts designed to assist in carrying out the crime, is not an accomplice to the offence of conspiracy. The person may, of course, be an accomplice to the substantive offence (the "object offence") if it is committed.[262]

---

257 *R v Gemmell* [1985] 2 NZLR 740; (1985) 1 CRNZ 496 (CA), 748; 504.
258 Smith and Hogan, *Criminal Law* (9th ed), London, Butterworths, 1999, 270, although there is some debate over whether the offence of attempting to conspire exists at common law. In any event, the offences of incitement and attempt to conspire were abolished in England by s 5(7) Criminal Law Act 1977 (UK).
259 See Orchard, "Impossibility and the inchoate crimes" [1978] NZLJ 403, 412. In practice, because liability for the attempt to commit a crime requires an intention to carry out that crime, at least in cases where the absence of intention to carry the offence through to completion is a bar to the substantive crime of conspiracy, it would seem also to debar a successful prosecution for attempt.
260 Section 66(2) Crimes Act 1961.
261 *R v Gemmell* [1985] 2 NZLR 740; (1985) 1 CRNZ 496 (CA), 746; 502.
262 *R v Gemmell* [1985] 2 NZLR 740; (1985) 1 CRNZ 496 (CA), 747; 502. See also *R v Clark* [1951] OR 791; (1951) 101 CCC 166; *Koury v The Queen* (1964) 43 DLR (2d) 637; [1964] SCR 212, 650; 217 (Spence J).

The reason why the accomplice should not be guilty of conspiracy in such a case is that, although she may do or have done things which assist the principal to commit the object offence, the agreement is complete before those things are done and it cannot be said that there is a causal nexus between the agreement and the acts of the accomplice done in pursuance of the substantive offence.[263]

Regarding the specific relationship between conspiracy and the notion of common intention in s 66(2), the Court said:[264]

> "Viewed simply in conceptual terms we incline to the view that s 66(2) has no application to a conspiracy charge for the reason that the concept of probable consequences of a common purpose used in that provision is inconsistent with the concept of conspiracy. It is of the essence of a conspiracy that there must be a common design, a meeting of minds directed to the crime which is to be committed. That points to a state of knowledge on the part of the accused at the time the agreement is made between the conspirators. Reference to an offence which is a probable consequence of the crime which the conspirators have actually agreed to commit is at odds with an agreed common design to commit an agreed particular crime."

8.3.9 Extraterritorial conspiracies

It was noted in 8.3.2 that a conspiracy may be conceived and commenced in one jurisdiction while acts necessary to its completion are committed in another. These are called "extraterritorial" conspiracies. It is clear from s 310(3) that the New Zealand courts have jurisdiction in respect of an agreement made in New Zealand to commit an offence overseas. However, difficulties may arise where the alleged conspiracy is an agreement to commit an offence in New Zealand but the agreement is made outside the country. A fundamental requirement of criminal liability in New Zealand is that a person may not be tried in respect of any "act done or omitted" outside New Zealand, unless the act or omission is an offence by virtue of the Crimes Act itself or some other enactment.[265] But where an act or omission forming *part of* an offence, or an event necessary to complete any offence, occurs in New Zealand, the offence is *deemed* to be committed in New Zealand, regardless whether the person charged was in New Zealand at the time of the act or omission.[266] The effect of these provisions taken together is to give the New Zealand courts jurisdiction over all offences completely performed in this country and also over offences where any act or omission forming part of the offence occurs here. Relying on these provisions, the Court of Appeal in *R v Sanders*[267] found that New Zealand courts had the jurisdiction to try conspirators who formed an agreement in Australia to import drugs into New Zealand because the conspirators had gone on to perform acts in New Zealand in furtherance of the execution of the conspiracy. D and E had agreed in Australia to import heroin into New Zealand. D then came to New Zealand and, after speaking with E by telephone, went to the airport to meet E. E arrived with the drug but was apprehended at the airport. In affirming D's conviction for conspiracy to import heroin, the Court held that conspiracy is a continuing offence, which is committed when the

---

263 *R v Richards [conspiracy]* (1992) 9 CRNZ 403, 411.
264 *R v Gemmell* [1985] 2 NZLR 740; (1985) 1 CRNZ 496 (CA), 748; 504.
265 Section 6.
266 Section 7.
267 *R v Sanders* [1984] 1 NZLR 636; (1984) 1 CRNZ 194 (CA).

agreement is made but which continues as long as the agreement is in existence. Considering the effect of s 7, the Court said:[268]

> "the agreement in the present case had its origins in Australia but remained effective as a continuing agreement in New Zealand. In the words of s 310 the offenders were continuing to conspire at the moment the applicant was apprehended at the Auckland airport."

Similarly, in *R v Darwish*[269] part of the agreement to commit certain drug importation offences was made during telephone conversations between the accused (in New Zealand) and his alleged co-conspirator or co-conspirators (outside New Zealand). It was held that the agreement was formed in both New Zealand and the country in which the co-conspirator was at the time.

The reasoning in *Sanders* was extended in *R v Johnston*,[270] where the Court of Appeal affirmed the view of the trial judge that a conspiracy to import a controlled drug was within the jurisdiction of the New Zealand courts. In that case, although the agreement had been formed abroad, one of the conspirators had come to New Zealand and a drug had been sent pursuant to the conspiracy. In such a case jurisdiction might be established on the basis that a conspiracy can be held to be committed wherever *anything* occurs pursuant to it in New Zealand during its continuance.[271] In *Johnston*, the only acts done in New Zealand (including the handling of a letter containing hashish sent by a co-conspirator in England) were done by innocent agents, namely members of the Customs and Post Office. Nevertheless, these were held to be acts "within the contemplation of the conspirators in the performance of the continuing conspiracy" and were part of the continuing offence.

With respect to the Court of Appeal, it is arguable whether acts of innocent agents that are done in furtherance of the common object are to be regarded as constituting the offence, since they are not essential ingredients of the offence of conspiracy — which, of course, consists in a formed and continuing *agreement* between two or more people. The better approach may be to regard them as acts and events which provide *evidence* of the continued existence and performance of the agreement, rather than as constituent elements of the offence itself.[272]

8.3.10 Acquittal of other conspirators

If A is charged with conspiring with B and B is acquitted, can A be convicted? At common law there was some doubt whether a jury trying several conspirators could convict one and acquit the others. To convict A and acquit B would contravene the requirement that the verdicts on co-conspirators be formally consistent.[273] However, there are good reasons why it may be appropriate to convict one conspirator and acquit the other(s). For example, A may

---

268 *R v Sanders* [1984] 1 NZLR 636; (1984) 1 CRNZ 194 (CA), 640; 198 (McMullin J). The objection that a conspiracy to import is completely performed the moment the drug is brought within the territory, may be answered by noting that although this constitutes importing, that process also continues for a time, at least until the goods are released by the carrier, Customs, or the Post Office. See *Purdy v Collector of Customs* 25/10/78, White J, SC Wellington M459/78, noted [1979] NZ Recent Law 43.
269 *R v Darwish* [2006] 1 NZLR 688, 701.
270 *R v Johnston* (1986) 2 CRNZ 289 (CA). See discussion at 8.3.2.
271 See Orchard, "Jurisdiction over extraterritorial conspiracy" [1986] NZLJ 185.
272 See Orchard, "Jurisdiction over extraterritorial conspiracy" [1986] NZLJ 185, 186. And see further discussion in Orchard, "Jurisdiction over extraterritorial conspiracy: an addendum" [1986] NZLJ 335.
273 See *Kannangara Aratchige Dharmasena v R* [1951] AC 1.

have made a confession which is admissible against him but not against B, which indicates that A conspired with B. Similarly, if A and B are tried separately the evidence presented at each trial may be different in some material respect, or the cases may be conducted differently, producing inconsistent verdicts.[274] It may also be that the convicted co-conspirator had conspired with a person other than the one acquitted.[275]

It is doubtful whether the strict rule requiring consistency of verdicts for co-conspirators now applies in New Zealand following its rejection at common law. In the United Kingdom, the question has been put beyond doubt by the Criminal Law Act 1977 (UK), which provides that the mere fact that the others, supposedly party to an agreement on which the conviction of one conspirator is based, are acquitted, is not a ground for quashing the one conviction unless the conviction is inconsistent with the acquittal of the others.[276]

The effect of this rule is that where the evidence against C and D is of equal weight the judge should direct the jury that they must either acquit both or convict both, and if they are in any doubt, to acquit both.[277] There is no comparable rule under New Zealand statute law. It is suggested that the law in New Zealand is likely to follow the approach taken by the High Court of Australia, to the effect that there need be no impermissible inconsistency where there is a *significant difference* in the evidence admissible against the co-accused.[278] If there is a significant difference in the evidence admissible against the co-conspirators, or if the findings are by different tribunals, different verdicts are not necessarily inconsistent.[279]

8.3.11 Impossibility and conspiracy

Impossibility in the inchoate crimes of conspiracy, incitement, and attempts is conceptually distinct from the defence of impossibility of compliance and the related defence of necessity. Obviously, where a crime is impossible to commit, no one can be convicted of it. However, the law has long recognised that a person may, in some circumstances, still be convicted of conspiring to commit an offence even though the commission of that offence was impossible. Impossibility may be relevant to conspiracy in two situations:

(i) Where the agreement made was to perform conduct which was wrongly believed to amount to an offence; or

(ii) Where the agreement was to perform only certain types of conduct which could not, in fact, produce the desired end result.

(1) *Conduct wrongly believed to be an offence*

This case is reasonably straightforward: no offence is committed. Thus if A comes to New Zealand believing that opossums are a protected species which it is illegal to kill, because it is a crime in some Australian states, he may freely agree to kill opossums for commercial gain. In fact the offence which he contemplates does not exist, its "commission" is legally impossible, and he has committed no offence.[280]

---

274 Allen, *Textbook on Criminal Law* (2nd ed), London, Blackstone Press, 1993, 205. See *DPP v Shannon* [1975] AC 717; [1974] 3 WLR 546.
275 *R v Ahearne* (1852) 6 Cox CC 6.
276 Section 5(8) and (9) Criminal Law Act 1977 (UK).
277 *R v Longman* (1981) 72 Cr App R 121; [1982] Crim LR 38.
278 *Adams*, CA310.10 (looseleaf).
279 *Adams*, CA310.10 (looseleaf).

(2) Desired end impossible to produce

At common law, impossibility was generally an answer to a charge of conspiracy. In *DPP v Nock*,[281] the accused persons had agreed to attempt to produce cocaine from a certain substance in their possession by subjecting it to a particular chemical process. In reality the substance did not contain cocaine. They were held not guilty of conspiracy to produce a controlled drug since the performance of the agreement could never have resulted in the commission of an offence.

By contrast, *Nock* was not applied by the New Zealand Court of Appeal in *R v Sew Hoy*.[282] In that case, the company owned by the respondent had imported a shipment of clothing, described on accompanying documents as women's clothing. A customs inspection revealed it was men's clothing, and it was so classified by the Customs Department. The duty payable was higher for men's clothing and the company held insufficient import licences for the clothing. When asked to produce further documentation the accused again produced documents showing the clothing to be women's clothing. However, the false documents would not have affected the classification because the classification decision had already been made.

The trial judge applied *Nock* and held that because at all material times the documents could not have deceived the Customs Department in the way intended, the agreement was incapable of commission from the outset. However, the Court of Appeal distinguished *Nock*. It distinguished between an agreement which, if carried out, *could not* result in the commission of the alleged offence because of legal or physical impossibility, and an agreement which would result in the commission of the crime alleged if carried out in accordance with the intention of the parties but which cannot be carried out because some person not a party to the agreement is unwilling or unable to do something necessary for its performance.[283]

The Court held that in this case the respondents intended to defraud and did all they intended to do to realise that intention. They failed because the means they adopted were inappropriate to realise their intention. Whereas in *Nock* the substances employed were incapable under any circumstances of achieving the narrow purpose of the conspiracy, in *Sew Hoy* the means employed *were* capable of deceiving. The respondents were frustrated in achieving their purpose simply because the Customs Department instituted its own assessment procedures to prevent this kind of fraud. The case was held to fall within the fourth category of attempts identified by Turner J in *R v Donnelly*,[284] namely inefficiency or insufficiency of means, and therefore the respondents were guilty of both an attempt and conspiracy.

The decision indicates the Court's approval of an approach to conspiracy which emphasises the inherent *culpability* of the criminal agreement, rather than an approach which focuses on *results* that may or may not happen.[285] In *Sew Hoy* Hardie Boys J said:[286]

---

280 See *R v Taaffe* [1984] AC 539; [1984] 1 All ER 747 (HL). D imported packages into the United Kingdom thinking they contained foreign currency which he believed (wrongly) it was a crime to import. Since there was no such crime, he could not be convicted of an offence even though the packages in fact contained cannabis. Although he committed the actus reus of importing cannabis he had no mens rea to do so.
281 *DPP v Nock* [1978] AC 979; [1978] 2 All ER 654 (HL).
282 *R v Sew Hoy* [1994] 1 NZLR 257; (1993) 10 CRNZ 581 (CA).
283 *R v Bennett* (1978) 68 Cr App R 168; [1979] Crim LR 454 (CA), 178; 455. See also *R v Harris* (1979) 69 Cr App R 122.
284 *R v Donnelly* [1970] NZLR 980 (CA), 990.
285 See *Maxwell v HM Advocate* 1980 SLT 241.

"The essence of conspiracy is an intention to agree coupled with a common design to commit an offence, that is, to put the design into effect. The mens rea is the intention to achieve the common design, the actus reus is the fact of the agreement ... The offence is therefore complete when the agreement is made. *It is the making of the agreement itself that is seen as inimical to the public good,* whether it proceeds further or not. It should therefore be irrelevant that it may not be possible in fact to carry out the agreement. This does not mean that the parties are punished on the basis of guilty intention alone. They will have gone further, and have acted upon their intention by making their agreement."

(3)   *Merits of excluding liability for impossibility*

Where the conspiracy is to do actions that are wrongly believed to be an offence (8.3.11(1)), the conspiracy involves what is known as an "imaginary crime" and rightly does not attract liability. Conspiracy to commit such fanciful, non-existent offences does not give rise to criminal liability for the simple reason that the agreement can never involve the commission of an offence known to the law, even if fully and successfully implemented. It would be contrary to public policy to punish people merely for being willing to break the law if, in fact, no legal infraction has occurred. There is now a view in some jurisdictions that impossibility can be a defence to a charge of conspiracy only where the conspirators intend to commit an "imaginary" crime.[287] In other jurisdictions, however, the courts have continued to characterise as "legally impossible" conspiracies to commit crimes that are not merely imaginary, such as those considered in 8.3.11(2).[288] Thus judicial agreement on the scope of truly impossible conspiracies remains uncertain, although in the light of *Sew Hoy* it appears that the New Zealand courts are distancing themselves from exculpatory impossibility, save in relation to "imaginary" crimes.

It is for sound reasons of principle that so-called impossible conspiracies may be successfully prosecuted. Conspiracy, like attempt, is an inchoate crime of intention. The actus reus of the offence is satisfied by a mere *agreement* to commit the substantive offence: it does *not* have to correspond with the actus reus elements of the substantive offence. For example, if A, B, and C agree to rob X using physical violence, it is not necessary, to prove the conspiracy, to establish that actual force was applied to X's person. It will be enough to prove that the conspirators agreed to do so. It is the agreement, and their intent to implement it, that is wrong and that triggers the law's intervention, not its implementation.

All this is inherent in the inchoate nature of conspiracy. Because the offence of conspiracy requires only an agreement with intention to commit a substantive offence, and not the commission of the offence itself, it is of no consequence that the commission of the offence may be impossible.[289] Since the subjective perspective is a critical element of a conspiracy, we may say that conspirators who intend to commit an indictable offence intend to do everything necessary to satisfy the conditions of the offence. The mere fact that they cannot do so, because an objective circumstance is not as they believe it to be, in no way changes the prior intention.

---

286   R v Sew Hoy [1994] 1 NZLR 257; (1993) 10 CRNZ 581 (CA), 267; 591 (emphasis added).
287   See, for example, US v Dynar (1997) 147 DLR (4th) 399; 115 CCC (3d) 481 (SCC), 434; 516 (Cory and Iacobucci JJ).
288   See, for example, R v Barbouttis (1995) 37 NSWLR 256; 82 A Crim R 432 (NSW CA).
289   US v Dynar (1997) 147 DLR (4th) 399; 115 CCC (3d) 481 (SCC), 435; 517 (Cory and Iacobucci JJ).

On the basis of this analysis, it is submitted that it would be contrary to public policy to permit some defect in the accompanying circumstances to defeat a charge of conspiracy on the grounds that the conspiracy was "legally impossible". Culpability for such conspiracies would depend in this way on a matter of pure luck, divorced from the conspirators' true intentions. The purpose of inchoate liability generally is to pre-empt wrongful activities that, if left to be completed, are of a *type* that risks significant harm to the community, whether or not ultimately they cause harm in this particular case. Thus inchoate liability, including conspiracy, derives its justification from broad notions of social defence and the need to prevent crime. That justification extends also to impossible conspiracies (and attempts), save only where the conspiracy involves an imaginary crime.

8.3.12 Charging conspiracy together with the substantive offence

Generally, it is inappropriate to include a charge of conspiracy in an indictment alleging the substantive offence.[290] The reasons commonly given for this are that evidence admissible only on the conspiracy count could have a prejudicial effect in relation to other counts. In particular, by bringing a conspiracy count the prosecution can combine into an indictment a variety of offences. If two or more persons are arraigned on an indictment which includes a conspiracy count, everything said or done by either accused which is relevant to that count is admissible in evidence against both accused at their joint trial. However, without the conspiracy count, even though an application for separate trials may not succeed, the trial judge must be careful in directing the jury about which evidence is admissible against each individual accused. In addition to these considerations, adding a count of conspiracy may unnecessarily complicate and prolong a trial.[291]

Another objection to the joinder of conspiracy and substantive counts in the same indictment concerns the risk of unfairness to an accused because of the different evidentiary rules which apply. In particular, evidence admissible only on the conspiracy count can have a prejudicial effect in respect of other counts. Statements made by other persons about what they are intending to do, against the background of statements about what they have done, may be admissible even where they involve statements about what another alleged conspirator said. In these circumstances such statements are not hearsay if they are received as evidence of their purposes and intentions at the time of speaking.[292] So the existence of a conspiracy can be shown by such statements, including what they have said about the accused. The words of others in this context are sometimes referred to as "verbal acts".[293] However, an accused's membership of a conspiracy cannot be proved by reference to what other conspirators have said about the accused in his or her absence. To admit such evidence for that purpose would be hearsay.[294] The proper approach is for the Crown, having shown that there is evidence of

---

290 A conspiracy count should certainly not be added as an alternative charge simply in order to circumvent a limitation period which prevents the laying of substantive charges: *R v Nichols* [1998] 1 NZLR 608; (1997) 15 CRNZ 350, 620; 362, where it was held that any time limit applicable to a prosecution for committing a primary offence applies equally to a conspiracy to commit that offence, on the basis that conspiracy liability is "parasitic" upon the primary offence.
291 *R v Humphries* [1982] 1 NZLR 353 (CA), 355. See also *Verrier v DPP* [1967] 2 AC 195; [1966] 3 All ER 568 (HL).
292 *R v Morris (Lee)* [2001] 3 NZLR 759, 763, para 17, per Blanchard J.
293 *R v Qiu Jiang* 3/5/06, CA495/05, para 32. See also *R v Jackson* (1987) 11 NSWLR 318, 324.
294 *Ahern v R* (1988) 165 CLR 87, 93.

a conspiracy, to prove the accused's membership of it to the requisite standard by reference to matters external to the statements which have been made in the accused's absence.[295]

Including conspiracy and a substantive count in one indictment will normally be justifiable only where there is real evidence from which a jury may infer that the alleged conspirators were acting in pursuance of a criminal purpose held in common between them.[296] However, a charge of conspiracy might properly be included in an indictment where the substantive offences charged do not represent the total criminality,[297] particularly where the criminality allegedly comprehended by the conspiracy count is wider and more extensive than that reflected in the discrete substantive counts.[298] Joinder may also be appropriate where the prosecution sets out to show that there was a continuing conspiracy of which the substantive offences were no more than incidents, or "milestones along the way".[299] Where there is a joinder of substantive offences and conspiracy the correct approach is to deal with the substantive charges first, before deciding whether the conspiracy charge should be considered.[300]

8.4 Incitement

Incitement is not defined in the Crimes Act 1961, but a general provision governing the penalty for the offence is provided in s 311(2).[301] If D incites *any* person to commit *any* offence *which is not in fact committed*, she is liable to the same punishment as if she had attempted to commit that offence, except where a punishment for that offence is expressly provided by statute.[302] "Offence" may be taken to include all penal offences and not merely crimes defined in the Crimes Act.[303] The reason why the offence created by s 311(2) applies only where the incited offence is not committed, is that, if the offence is committed, a person who incites, counsels, or procures the commission of an offence will be liable as a secondary party under s 66(1)(d). The provision thus supplements the rules on parties by providing for the situation where, because no principal offence has actually been committed, secondary liability cannot be imposed under s 66.

In addition to the general offence of incitement, punishable under s 311(2), certain grave incitement offences are punished independently by specific provisions. For example, s 68(2) provides for a prison term not exceeding 10 years for every person who incites the commission of an act outside New Zealand which would be murder if done or omitted in New Zealand, where no such act is done or omitted.[304] Separate provision is also made for the crime of inciting the murder of any other person in New Zealand, when murder is not in fact committed.[305]

---

295 *R v Morris (Lee)* [2001] 3 NZLR 759, 763, para 18.
296 *R v Griffiths* [1966] 1 QB 589; [1965] 2 All ER 448.
297 *R v Jones* (1974) 59 Cr App R 120; [1974] Crim LR 663.
298 *Western Australia v Oates* (2004) 148 A Crim R 202, [2004] WASC 170.
299 *R v Humphries* [1982] 1 NZLR 353, cited with approval in *Western Australia v Oates* (2004) 148 A Crim R 202, [2004] WASC 170, 206.
300 *R v Dawson and Wenlock* [1960] 1 All ER 558; [1960] 1 WLR 163.
301 The offence is electable: s 6(2) Summary Proceedings Act 1957, as amended by s 3 Summary Proceedings Amendment Act 1961.
302 Section 311(2) Crimes Act 1961.
303 See s 2. See also *Clyne v Bowman* (1987) 33 A Crim R 280, 285, 286.
304 See also s 69 (party to any other crime outside New Zealand).
305 Section 174.

There is one special case. In all these varieties of incitement, incitement may be charged only where the substantive offence is *not* committed. By contrast, the crime of inciting suicide is committed only if the person *actually commits* or attempts to commit suicide in consequence of the incitement.[306] This is because if the suicide is committed, the inciter cannot be charged as a party to the commission of an offence, since suicide itself is no longer a crime. Accordingly incitement becomes, in effect, the substantive offence. This means that advising V to commit suicide does not amount to incitement unless and until V does commit or attempt suicide.[307] In turn, since incitement is the principal offence, it has been accepted that an offence exists of attempting to incite suicide; thus D's "unsuccessful" advice or encouragement, which does not result in a suicide attempt by V, may be punishable as an attempt by D.[308]

8.4.1 Actus reus

As has been remarked, incitement is not defined in the Crimes Act. Its meaning is derived from the common law. A person who incites:[309]

> "is one who reaches and seeks to influence the mind of another to the commission of a crime. The machinations of criminal ingenuity being legion, the approach to the other's mind may take various forms, such as suggestion, proposal, request, exhortation, gesture, argument, persuasion, inducement, goading or arousal of cupidity."

In *Young v Cassels*,[310] "incite" was held to mean "to rouse", "to stimulate", "to urge or spur on", "to stir up", "to animate". In that case, the appellant had been charged with inciting persons to resist constables in the execution of their duty when, in a speech to striking waterside workers, he had used the words, "if a police constable uses his baton to you, give him one back, and if one won't do, make it a double header". Stout CJ held that there is no requirement that the incited actors must be ready to commit the crime, or that anyone must have acted on the incitement before D could be convicted of inciting; rather, what was required, generally speaking, was simply that the time of the incitement was antecedent to the time when the crime was to be committed or attempted. On the facts of *Young v Cassels*, this meant that it was not necessary for an arrest to be about to take place before the offence of inciting to resist arrest could be committed.[311]

As the quotation above makes clear, the modes and forms of incitement are many and varied. For example, incitement may be committed where D threatens or puts pressure on another to commit an offence. The incitement does not have to take the form of persuasion.[312] Additionally, the target of the incitement may be a particular individual or people generally.[313] In *R v Most*,[314] the defendant published an article urging readers throughout the

---

306 Section 179(a).
307 Smith and Hogan, *Criminal Law* (9th ed), London, Butterworths, 1999, 383.
308 Smith and Hogan, *Criminal Law* (9th ed), London, Butterworths, 1999, 383. See *R v McShane* (1978) 66 Cr App R 97; [1977] Crim LR 737 (CA).
309 *S v Nkosiyana* [1966] (4) SA 655, 658 (Holmes JA); cited in Smith and Hogan, *Criminal Law* (9th ed), London, Butterworths, 1999, 267.
310 *Young v Cassels* (1914) 16 GLR 391, 392.
311 *Young v Cassels* (1914) 16 GLR 391, 393.
312 *Race Relations Board v Applin* [1973] 1 QB 815; [1973] 2 All ER 1190, 825; 1194 (Lord Denning MR).
313 *Walsh v Sainsbury* (1925) 36 CLR 464; [1925] ALR 343, 476; 347 (Isaac J).
314 *R v Most* (1881) 7 QBD 244 (prosecution under s 4 Offences Against the Person Act 1861 (UK)).

world to follow the example of Russian revolutionaries and murder their heads of State. This was held to be an incitement to murder.

Further, incitement need not be express but may be implied. This includes a disguised or encoded invitation in a letter to commit an offence that can only be understood by the recipient.[315] So advertising a police radar detection device in a magazine, emphasising its value in detecting police radar traps, was held in *Invicta Plastics Ltd v Clare*[316] to amount to inciting the offence of using unlicensed apparatus for wireless telegraphy contrary to the Wireless Telegraphy Act 1949. However, it is not incitement *per se* to manufacture and sell a device which has no function other than one involving the commission of an offence.[317] There must be a promotion of the offence; unless D actually seeks to persuade or encourage another, there can be no incitement.[318] On this basis an advertisement for a product which was known to be capable of assisting people to break the law, but in which no words of endorsement, inducement, or encouragement appear, would not amount to incitement to commit an offence.[319]

Another limitation is that since the terms of s 311(2) are confined to persuasion and attempted procuring, the offence does not include assistance to commit an offence.[320] Thus, if P, intent on committing a crime, asks D to supply him with services or materials to be used in the commission of the offence, the supply of those materials or services would not make D liable under s 311(2) when B does not in fact commit the offence.

(1) *Communication of incitement*

For an incitement to be complete there must be some form of actual communication with a person whom it is intended to incite. Where a communication is sent with a view to incite, but does not reach the intended recipient, the sender can be guilty only of an attempt to incite.[321] Accordingly, in *R v Banks*,[322] where the accused sent a letter to her niece advising her how to kill her infant using poison, it was held that even though the letter was intercepted D could be convicted of an attempt to incite her niece to murder the child.

Banks illustrates the requirement that a criminal incitement must be communicated to the other party. However, it need not in fact influence the recipient.[323] In *R v Dimozantos*,[324] which involved an appeal against conviction for incitement to murder, the Court of Criminal Appeal of Victoria had to construe a provision in the Crimes Act 1958 (Vic) which provided that a person will be guilty of incitement "if the inciting *is acted on* in accordance with the inciter's intention".[325] The Court agreed with the interpretation of the trial judge who held that it was not necessary to prove that the person incited *in fact* acted upon the incitement, but rather that

---

315 *R v Cope* (1921) 16 Cr App R 77.
316 *Invicta Plastics Ltd v Clare* [1976] RTR 251; [1976] Crim LR 131. The point here is not that D was inciting speeding, but that D was inciting *use* of the radar detector, which itself constituted an offence.
317 *R v James* (1985) 82 Cr App R 226; [1986] Crim LR 118, 232; 119.
318 *Halsbury's Laws of England* vol 11(1) (4th ed reissue), London, Butterworths, 1990, para 58.
319 See *R v Dionne* (1987) 38 CCC (3d) 171 (CA).
320 *Adams*, CA311.04 (looseleaf).
321 See *R v Cope* (1921) 16 Cr App R 77; *R v Ransford* (1874) 13 Cox CC 9; 31 LT 488.
322 *R v Banks* (1873) 12 Cox CC 393.
323 *R v Krause* (1902) 66 JP 121.
324 *R v Dimozantos* (1992) 56 A Crim R 345.
325 Section 321G Crimes Act 1958 (Vic) (emphasis added).

it was essential to prove that the course of conduct urged would, *if* it had been acted upon as the inciter intended, amount to the commission of the offence. In the view of the Victorian Court, the offence of incitement is constituted "solely by what the inciter says or does and intends".[326]

This interpretation is consistent with the common law, which has held that incitement is complete even though the mind of the person incited is unaffected.[327] The law has never required any consequent step towards the completion of the substantive offence before incitement may be established. Thus incitement would be complete even if the person incited (for example) intended to inform on the inciter.

(2) *Renunciation of incitement*

Similarly, in *R v Gonzague*[328] D was charged with procuring C to commit murder after he had allegedly arranged for C to have a business competitor "wiped off the mat". The Ontario Court of Appeal held that the offence of procuring (the equivalent of inciting) is complete when the solicitation or incitement occurs, even though it is immediately rejected by the person solicited, or even though the person solicited merely pretends assent and has no intention of committing the offence. The Court rejected the appellant's contention that a renunciation by the appellant of a previous act of incitement constituted a defence, stating that there is no authority supporting the view that renunciation of the criminal purpose constitutes a defence to a charge of inciting.[329] The rationale for this rule would appear to be that the essence of the crime of incitement lies in D's seeking to influence the mind of another, and that this action is complete once the solicitous words have been uttered or otherwise articulated, regardless of their eventual impact on the mind of the audience. Subsequent renunciation of the criminal purpose cannot retrieve those words already uttered, whether or not they actually incite the commission of an offence.

(3) *Attempted incitement*

An attempt to incite the commission of an offence requires proof of an act which is more than merely preparatory to the commission of the full offence. In *R v Rowley*,[330] the accused was charged, among other things, with attempting by written notes to incite a child under the age of 14 to commit an act of gross indecency. However, the fact that the notes relied on went no further than seeking to meet with the boys in question, and contained nothing "lewd, obscene or of a disgusting nature", led the Court to find that the acts were no more than preparatory even on the assumption that the appellant's ultimate intention was gross indecency. It was held that incitement to commit gross indecency would require a proposition to be made for that specific purpose.[331]

---

326 *R v Dimozantos* (1992) 56 A Crim R 345, 349.
327 See *R v Diamond* (1920) 84 JP 211.
328 *R v Gonzague* (1983) 4 CCC (3d) 505, 508.
329 *R v Gonzague* (1983) 4 CCC (3d) 505, 508, 509. See also Wasik, "Abandoning criminal intent" [1980] Crim LR 785.
330 *R v Rowley* [1991] 4 All ER 649; [1991] 1 WLR 1020 (CA).
331 *R v Rowley* [1991] 4 All ER 649; [1991] 1 WLR 1020 (CA), 654; 1025.

8.4.2 Mens rea

To prove incitement, it is necessary to show that the accused sought to persuade or encourage another to commit an act that would constitute a crime if done by that other.[332] Thus the offence requires two mental elements, which correspond to those necessary to establish secondary liability under s 66(1):

"(i) Knowledge of the circumstances which would make the act of the person incited an offence; and

"(ii) An intention that the person incited should commit the act constituting the offence."

In relation to (i), the meaning of knowledge has been considered earlier in this book, and would include cases of wilful blindness where the accused deliberately closed his eyes to the circumstances of the act incited which are elements of the crime in question.[333] The relevant circumstances include the mens rea of the incitee. For example, if D incites V to commit theft by representing to her that the item to be stolen actually belongs to D, and V believes D, D could not be guilty of incitement to steal (assuming the item is not actually stolen), because V, the innocent agent, will have acted without any mens rea for theft. Of course, D would be liable as the principal if the offence is committed, or otherwise for attempted theft if the venture has proceeded beyond mere preparation.

In relation to (ii), D must intend the consequences specified in the actus reus of the offence incited. Suppose that D, walking with his girlfriend, comes across two men arguing in the street. D yells out to them both, "give him one from me!", being indifferent whether a fight ensues but intending to show off to his girlfriend. On these facts, D is not guilty of inciting to assault. He is reckless whether an assault results but does not intend that it should do so. It is an *intention* to bring about the criminal result, when coupled with an act of persuasion, that is the essence of incitement.[334]

8.4.3 Incitement to murder

This offence is defined separately in s 174 Crimes Act 1961. The elements of the offence are:

(i) Inciting any person,

(ii) To murder any other person in New Zealand,

(iii) The murder is not in fact committed.

Where the murder is committed, there is no offence under s 174, although if there has been counselling or inciting s 66(1) will apply, and the offender may be liable for the substantive offence of murder. Where the murder incited is attempted but not committed, the inciter may be charged with attempted murder under s 173 in addition to inciting murder under s 174. So, if D publishes an article in a "hard-core" nationalist magazine extolling the virtues of those who kill "white" politicians, which inspires P to attempt to kill such a person, D may be guilty

---

332 *R v Curr* [1968] 2 QB 944; [1967] 1 All ER 478 (CA).
333 See 4.5.
334 Smith and Hogan, *Criminal Law* (9th ed), London, Butterworths, 1999, 271.

of both attempted murder and incitement.[335] In such circumstances it is not necessary that the proposed victims be named, provided they form a sufficiently well-defined class.[336]

As with incitement generally, it must be proved that communication of the incitement to murder reached a person whom D intended to incite, although it is not necessary to show that the recipient's mind was affected thereby.[337]

It remains unclear from the cases whether it is necessary that the person being incited should actually understand the communication, ie that they are being solicited to commit a particular offence. However, it is arguable that since the essence of incitement is what the inciter says or does (and intends),[338] it does not matter whether the person being incited actually understands the communication, provided it is proved to have reached her.

(1)   *Inciting "any person"*

It is submitted that the words "any person" in s 174 may be given their natural meaning, and may therefore include an "innocent agent" or a person who is incapable of understanding the solicitation. However, if D knew that P (the person incited) was mentally disordered and lacked the capacity to understand that what he was being incited to do was an offence, it could not be said that D had knowledge of the circumstances which would make P's act an offence.[339] On the other hand, if the intended offence is committed D may still be guilty as the principal.

(2)   *To murder "any other person"*

In *R v Shephard*,[340] the Court of Criminal Appeal held that the phrase "any other person"[341] applied when D solicited a pregnant woman (P) to kill her child when it was born. At the time of D's writing the solicitous letter, P was only 6 weeks pregnant. The proposed victim did not have to exist as a human being at the date of the incitement, but the Court left open the question whether the offence could be committed if the child had not been born alive, and thus could never have been a potential victim of murder. However, since incitement is a relational crime and is not dependent on any "permissive" facts being in existence before the crime may be committed (the person inciting need only believe that the crime incited is capable of being committed at some future time), there would seem to be no reason why incitement could not be committed even if the child were stillborn. The requirement that the child be born alive is a necessary condition for murder. It is not an element of incitement to do the same. In New Zealand, this analysis is reinforced by the fact that s 174 expressly excludes the commission of the substantive offence as an element of incitement. Given this, it would seem to be of no consequence whether the intended victim is ultimately capable of being killed.

8.4.4 Impossibility

Although s 311 makes no direct reference to impossibility, it is clear that situations may and do arise where one person incites, counsels, or attempts to procure another to commit an

---

335   *R v Diamond* (1920) 84 JP 211.
336   Smith and Hogan, *Criminal Law* (9th ed), London, Butterworths, 1999, 379. See *R v Most* (1881) 7 QBD 244; *R v Antonelli and Barberi* (1905) 70 JP 4.
337   *R v Fox* (1870) 19 WR 109 (CCR); *R v Krause* (1902) 66 JP 121.
338   *R v Dimozantos* (1992) 56 A Crim R 345, 349.
339   See *Adams*, CA311.09 (looseleaf).
340   *R v Shephard* [1919] 2 KB 125 (CA).
341   Also contained in s 4 Offences Against the Person Act 1861 (UK).

offence which it is impossible in law or in fact to commit. In *R v Fitzmaurice*,[342] the appellant's father conceived a plan to defraud a security firm of reward money by informing the police of a plan to rob a security van and then simulating a street robbery to make it appear that the advice was instrumental in preventing a major robbery from occurring. The appellant, believing the plan to commit the street robbery was genuine, had secured the services of two men to rob a woman carrying wages between a factory and a bank. However, before the "robbery" could take place the two men were arrested and charged with conspiracy to rob. The appellant was charged with and convicted of unlawfully inciting the two men to rob the woman. In dismissing the appeal, the Court of Appeal held that in approaching an inchoate crime at common law it was necessary to decide in each case what was the course of conduct incited, agreed, or attempted. In particular, the evidence might establish incitement in general terms, while the subsequent agreement might be directed at a specific crime in greater detail. In such a case, although a successful committal of the specific crime (in the manner agreed) may be impossible, it might nonetheless be possible for the inciter to be convicted. This occurred in *Fitzmaurice* itself. Because D had taken steps to recruit the men at a time when he *believed* that there was to be a robbery, he was encouraging the men to participate in a robbery, and accordingly there was incitement to commit an offence which was not, in itself, an impossible offence to carry out.

This analysis is consistent with the general principle concerning incitement, that it is what the accused does or says with intent that constitutes the wrongdoing—not whether her incitement has any effect on the mind of the incitee, nor whether it is capable of fulfilment. For this reason, in *R v McDonough*,[343] on a charge of incitement to receive stolen goods, it was held to be unnecessary that any stolen goods should be in existence as envisaged at the time of the incitement.

---

342   *R v Fitzmaurice* [1983] 1 QB 1083; [1983] 1 All ER 189 (CA).
343   *R v McDonough* (1962) 47 Cr App R 37 (CCA).

Chapter 9

INFANCY

9.1	Rational capacity	277
9.2	Young children: an irrebuttable presumption	278
9.2.1	Other forms of intervention	279
9.2.2	Proposed reform	280
9.3	Children over 10 years of age	280
9.3.1	Care and protection proceedings	281
9.3.2	Burden of proof in rebutting the doli incapax presumption	282
9.4	A case for reform	283
9.4.1	Proposed reforms: turning more children into criminals	284

9.1 Rational capacity

A hallmark of criminal responsibility is that at the time of the alleged offence the offender possessed the rational capacity to be charged with and convicted of a crime. Rational capacity generally requires that the person be capable of understanding what she is doing, in the sense of being able to understand the nature, circumstances, and consequences of her actions and of having the ability to control those actions. It follows that criminal culpability should not attach to a person who at the time of an alleged offence was incapable of understanding either what she was doing, or the legal and social significance of her conduct, and/or who was unable to control her actions.[1] The principle of rational capacity is thus a *precondition* of one's eligibility for punishment.[2] Defences based on the absence of rational capacity include infancy, insanity, and automatism. They operate on a different theoretical basis to those "defences", including intoxication and certain mistakes of fact,[3] which gainsay criminal liability by denying some (usually, mens rea) element of the offence charged. For example, intoxication is not a defence of incapacity under New Zealand law because the essential question is not whether the accused was *incapable* of forming the necessary intent, owing to the effect of alcohol or drugs, but instead whether the requisite intent or recklessness by D *was in fact* present.[4] Intoxication is merely evidence from which a tribunal of fact may infer that the mens rea for an offence was lacking. It is therefore inapt to describe it as a fundamental incapacity.

---

1   See Barlow, "Drug intoxication and the principle of capacitas rationalis" (1984) 100 LQR 639.
2   Regarding the distinction between conditions and preconditions in the criminal law, see Duff, "Law, language and community: Some preconditions of criminal liability" (1998) 18 OJLS 189, 192 et seq. A precondition is a condition that must be met if the trial is to be possible, or legitimate, at all.
3   See ch 14.
4   *R v Kamipeli* [1975] 2 NZLR 610 (CA), 616.

Similarly, defences like self-defence, compulsion, duress of circumstances, and necessity are not based on a claim of rational incapacity. Rather, they operate as justification or excuse. They depend upon a different sort of claim, namely, a "compelling 'hard choice' situation"[5] — a recognition that although the accused was capable of understanding relevant actions, circumstances, and consequences, his free choice was circumscribed by threats or exigent circumstances so that he had no reasonable choice but to break the law.

Lack of rational capacity is not the only form of incapacity known to the law. As we saw in 3.4, in cases of impossibility or physical involuntariness, responsibility for the actus reus is avoided because of the operation of imperious forces over which the accused had no control. The defence is one of involuntariness based not on *rational incapacity* but rather on *causative impotence*. The accused is simply *physically* incapable of conduct that would result in compliance with the law, or of avoiding the circumstances which constitute a criminal offence.

9.2 Young children: an irrebuttable presumption

By contrast, when we consider the criminal responsibility of children and young persons we are concerned with the mental developmental capacity of a person to engage in criminal conduct. While it is clear that some children may have a reasonably sophisticated understanding of right and wrong, sufficient to inform a basic understanding of both the actus reus and mens rea elements of a crime, the law, nonetheless, proceeds on the basis that children do not have the same level of development of their mental and intellectual capacities as adults. As such we consider it unfair to subject young children to criminal punishment.[6] At common law the rule was that children under the age of 7 years were doli incapax. This meant that they were considered to be incapable of crime, regardless of evidence of actus reus or mens rea. Under s 21 Crimes Act 1961, which is otherwise declaratory of the common law,[7] the triggering age is now 10 years. While the age of 10 is sometimes said to be the age of criminal responsibility, in reality in New Zealand there is no fixed age at which children face prosecution for their criminal behaviour.[8] Section 21 lays down an irrebuttable presumption that a person *under* the age of 10 years is incapable of committing an offence:

> "**21 Children under 10**
>
> "(1) No person shall be convicted of an offence by reason of any act done or omitted by him when under the age of 10 years."

Consequently, where an offender is under 10 years of age, the State is absolutely prohibited from acting against that child in respect of any "offence" committed by him, regardless of the degree of understanding in fact possessed by the child regarding the nature and consequences of his offending. The formula in s 21, "no person shall be convicted", does not alter the common law by suggesting that a criminal offence *is* committed by the infant but that he is merely exempted from being convicted. A child of relevant age is by stipulation incapable of *committing* a crime.

---

5 Morse, "The Mind of a Child: The Relationship between Brain Development, Cognitive Functioning, and Accountability under the Law: Brain Overclaim Syndrome and Criminal Responsibility: A Diagnostic Note" (2006) 3 Ohio St J Crim L 397, 399.

6 See Maher, "Criminal Responsibility: Age and Criminal Responsibility" (2005) 2 Ohio State J Crim L 493, 495.

7 *R v Brooks* [1945] NZLR 584 (CA), 595 (Myers CJ).

8 *Brookers Family Law — Child Law* vol 2, Wellington, Brookers, 2005, YJ2.1.02A

9.2.1 Other forms of intervention

However, immunity from prosecution for children and young persons exists along a graduated continuum, so that while young children (those under 10) are absolutely incapable of crime, children between the ages of 10 and 14 may be "dealt with" as responsible agents, but generally not in a manner that involves the imposition of punishment per se. Beyond the age of 14 young persons are increasingly amenable to adult punishments, although sentencing concessions based on an offender's young age may be made until an offender has reached the age of 18. When we think of the "age of responsibility" in this way, it is clear that there are two contrasting senses of criminal responsibility. The first, already noted, is the capacity of the child or young person to engage in criminal conduct. The second concerns the process by which a person is held to be answerable for such conduct. This second sense concerns the special provisions made within the youth justice system for dealing with children and young people who commit what would otherwise be criminal offences. In New Zealand, these matters are governed by the Children, Young Persons, and Their Families Act 1989, which provides for jurisdictional separation between children and young persons in need of care and protection, and those who have offended against the law.[9]

Because at common law a child cannot commit a crime, it would normally follow that someone who instigates the commission of an offence by a child cannot be a party to that offence. This exclusion appears to be overridden by s 21(2), which provides that s 21 "shall not affect the question whether any other person who is alleged to be a party to that offence is guilty of that offence". However, reliance on s 21(2) is generally not necessary, since even at common law any person acting through the child to commit a crime would be liable as the principal offender under the doctrine of innocent agency.[10] This might occur where, for example, D, an adult, instructs C, a child aged 7, to steal an item from a shop. In those circumstances D would be deemed to be the principal offender because C is presumptively incapable of committing an offence. In law, C's body is merely the "agency" through which D has acted to commit the offence. In such a case C is not criminally responsible, not because she lacked mens rea, but because (as with the defence of insanity) she lacked the legal capacity to commit a crime.

However, this does not mean that the State is powerless to intervene in any way in respect of a young child who is suspected of having deliberately committed an offence. Where there is evidence that the child under the age of 10 is behaving in a way which is harmful to the child's well-being, or where the child's parent, guardian, or other person having the care of the child is unwilling or unable to care for the child, proceedings for "care and protection" may be commenced under Part II of the Children, Young Persons, and Their Families Act 1989.[11] The purpose of this jurisdiction is not to punish but rather to protect such children from harm and to promote their welfare.[12]

---

9   For a detailed discussion of these provisions *Brookers Family Law — Child Law* vol 2, Wellington, Brookers, 2005, NT1.2.01-10 (looseleaf).
10 See 6.3.1.
11 See s 14(1)(d) and (f) Children, Young Persons, and Their Families Act 1989.
12 Section 13 Children, Young Persons, and Their Families Act 1989. For a comprehensive discussion of the principles underlying the protective jurisdiction for children and young persons, see *Brookers Family Law — Child Law* vol 2, Wellington, Brookers, 2005, NT4.1 (looseleaf).

9.2.2 Proposed reform

While the foregoing states the current legal position, reform is in the air. There has been a recent initiative to extend the criminal liability of children, in a manner that would substantially modify New Zealand's existing youth justice system. The initiative, which is contained in the Young Offenders (Serious Crime) Bill, is noted below in 9.4.1.

9.3 Children over 10 years of age

Under existing law, a child in the "twilight zone"[13] between the ages of 10 and 14 cannot be convicted unless it is proved not only that the child did the act in circumstances which would involve an adult in criminal liability, but also that he knew that he was doing wrong. That is to say, for children aged between 10 and 14 years there is a rebuttable presumption that they are doli incapax.

Another way of expressing this rule is to say that, in the case of wrongdoing by such a child, knowledge that her act or omission was wrong becomes a necessary ingredient of the charge against her, and the existence of this necessary ingredient must be proved by the Crown before the child can be convicted.[14] Criminal responsibility would result upon proof of actus reus and mens rea together with what was known at common law as "mischievous discretion".[15] The relevant principles are defined in s 22 Crimes Act 1961:

> "**22 Children between 10 and 14**
>
> "(1) No person shall be convicted of an offence by reason of any act done or omitted by him when of the age of 10 but under the age of 14 years, unless he knew either that the act or omission was wrong or that it was contrary to law."

In effect, a child between the ages of 10 and 14 will be presumed to be incapable of committing an offence, but this presumption may be rebutted by proof that the child "knew" her act or omission was "wrong" or that it was "contrary to law".[16] The onus of such proof lies on the prosecution.[17] As we shall see in 9.3.2, the court, in determining whether that burden is discharged, will "look to something beyond mere naughtiness or childish mischief";[18] in effect, the child must have known that his act was seriously wrong.[19]

Although s 22(1) implies that a child may be prosecuted where such knowledge is present and the doli incapax presumption is rebutted, in practice such prosecutions are uncommon because of the operation of s 272(1) Children, Young Persons, and Their Families Act 1989. Section 272(1) stipulates that a child over the age of 10 shall not be subject to proceedings brought under the Summary Proceedings Act 1957, except where the charges involve murder or manslaughter. (However, as will be noted in 9.4.1, this provision will change significantly if the Young Offenders (Serious Crime) Bill becomes law.) Under existing law, in the event of

---

13 Stuart, *Canadian Criminal Law: A Treatise* (3rd ed), Toronto, Carswell, 1995, 336. See also Williams, "The criminal responsibility of children" [1954] Crim LR 493.
14 *R v Brooks* [1945] NZLR 584 (CA), 595.
15 Stuart, *Canadian Criminal Law* (3rd ed), 1995, 336. See also 1 Hale PC 630.
16 Section 22(1) Crimes Act 1961.
17 *R v Brooks* [1945] NZLR 584 (CA).
18 *J M (a minor) v Runeckles* (1984) 79 Cr App R 255, 259.
19 See *R v Gorrie* (1918) 83 JP 136 (Salter J) and see *C (a minor) v DPP* [1996] 1 AC 1; [1995] 2 WLR 383 (HL).

a prosecution for murder or manslaughter, the preliminary hearing must take place before a Youth Court under the terms of the Children, Young Persons, and Their Families Act 1989. Where the defendant is a child, the European Commission of Human Rights has stated that the procedures adopted "must be conducive to an active participation, as opposed to passive presence"[20] if the trial is not to prevent the appearance of an exercise in the vindication of public outrage. It is a standard that commands respect in New Zealand also.

9.3.1 Care and protection proceedings

While prosecution of children between 10 and 14 is very rare, such child offenders may, like those under 10, be subject to care and protection proceedings pursuant to the Children, Young Persons, and Their Families Act 1989, where the offending by the child is such as to give "serious concern for the well-being of the child".[21] These proceedings are focussed around the family group conference, a statutory mechanism that enables families to participate in care and protection decisions and to resolve difficulties or problems.[22] The Family Court has jurisdiction to make orders ensuring, as far as possible, that children and young persons are safely supported in the care of families or family groups.[23]

Since the child cannot normally be charged with the relevant offence (except where the offence is murder or manslaughter), the commission of the offences by the child will seldom be established by criminal conviction.[24] This means that any applicant for a declaration that the child is in need of care or protection will have to prove the commission of the offences during the civil proceedings, either by proving that the child admitted the offences or by calling evidence.[25] In any case where application has been made for a declaration that the child is in need of care and protection, where the application is based on the fact of offending by the child, a declaration cannot be made unless the following conditions are met:[26]

(i) It must be established that the court would have found the child guilty of an offence if the proceedings had been pursuant to an information laid under the Summary Proceedings Act 1957, charging the child with an offence; and

(ii) The court must be satisfied the child knew either that the act or omission constituting the offence was wrong or that it was contrary to law.

The criminal standard of proof and rules of evidence apply in such proceedings.[27]

Note that, in the case of children under the age of 10, the police or a social worker cannot apply for a declaration that a child is in need of care and protection on the grounds that the child has committed an offence giving serious concern as to the child's well-being. Such a course of action is only available in respect of children in the 10 to 13 age range.[28] However, as was mentioned in 9.2.1, a declaration under the Children, Young Persons, and Their Families

---

20 *T v UK; V v UK* [1999] Crim LR 579. See also McDiarmid "Age of criminal responsibility: Raise it or remove it?" [2001] The Juridical Review 243.
21 Section 14(1)(e) Children, Young Persons, and Their Families Act 1989.
22 *Brookers Family Law — Child Law* vol 2, Wellington, Brookers, 2005, NT1.2.01 (looseleaf).
23 *Brookers Family Law — Child Law* vol 2, Wellington, Brookers, 2005, NT1.2.01 (looseleaf).
24 *Trapski's Family Law* vol I, Wellington, Brooker's, 1991, CP.1 (looseleaf).
25 *Trapski's Family Law* vol I, Wellington, Brooker's, 1991, CP.1 (looseleaf).
26 Section 198 Children, Young Persons, and Their Families Act 1989.
27 Section 198(2) Children, Young Persons, and Their Families Act 1989.
28 Section 14(1)(e) Children, Young Persons, and Their Families Act 1989.

Act 1989 may nonetheless be sought by police or a social worker in respect of a child under 10 on the basis of any of the other grounds listed in s 14(1).

9.3.2 Burden of proof in rebutting the doli incapax presumption

At common law, the presumption that a child between the ages of 10 and 14 was *doli incapax* at the time of the alleged offending can be rebutted only by clear positive evidence that the child knew that her act was *seriously* wrong, and evidence of acts amounting to the offence itself will not be enough to rebut the presumption.[29] In *C (a minor) v DPP*, evidence that the 12-year-old offender had done substantial damage to a motorcycle that he was intending to steal and the fact that he ran from the police leaving behind a crowbar was held by the House of Lords not to be sufficient of itself to rebut the presumption.

Although "conceptually obscure", the meaning of the common law test, which requires that the child should know that her act is "seriously wrong" in a moral sense,[30] is reasonably clear when the phrase is contrasted with "merely naughty or mischievous".[31] Mere knowledge of illegality will not necessarily suffice. It is only if there is evidence which satisfies the jury beyond reasonable doubt that the child knew the act was wrong or contrary to law that he or she may be convicted.[32]

While it appears generally to be accepted that, in modern times, the presumption of incapacity is not always appropriate, especially in the case of older children within the range to which it applies, it provides a "benevolent safeguard" against children being treated as if they ought to know the wrongfulness of their acts when, in reality, they may not. The safeguard may, however, be overcome by the prosecution's positively proving that the child was of normal mental capacity and as such was able to distinguish right from wrong and to form a criminal intent.[33] But it is *not* for the child to disprove the presumption that she is a normal child of her age; the courts will not countenance, as a means of rebutting the presumption, the "sensible" argument that any child of the defendant's age would know what she was doing was wrong.[34]

In *R v Rapira*[35] the Court of Appeal observed that the evidence relied on to establish knowledge of wrongfulness under s 22 must go beyond mere evidence that D did the acts forming the offence. Mere proof of participation in the offence cannot give rise to any inference that D knew of its wrongfulness.[36] However, in order to prove such knowledge the Crown can lead a variety of evidence, including opinion evidence relevant to whether D would have understood the wrongfulness or unlawfulness of the particular criminal act alleged. Such evidence can include anything the child may have said or done before or after the conduct in question; the results of an interview or psychiatric examination; and the evidence of someone who knows the child well (eg a teacher).[37] Evidence of normal development is admissible, but may not be

---

29 *C (a minor) v DPP* [1996] 1 AC 1; [1995] 2 WLR 383 (HL).
30 See *J B H and J H (Minors) v O'Connell* [1981] Crim LR 632, where Donaldson J described the relevant test as being that the prosecutor had to prove the appellants knew that what they were doing was wrong morally, whether or not they knew it was an offence.
31 *C (a minor) v DPP* [1996] 1 AC 1; [1995] 2 WLR 383 (HL), 33; 397.
32 *R v Rapira* [2003] 3 NZLR 794, (2003) 20 CRNZ 396 (CA), para 78.
33 *R v Rapira* [2003] 3 NZLR 794, (2003) 20 CRNZ 396 (CA), para 78.
34 See *I P H v Chief Constable of South Wales* [1987] Crim LR 42.
35 *R v Rapira* [2003] 3 NZLR 794; (2003) 20 CRNZ 396 (CA).
36 *R v Rapira* [2003] 3 NZLR 794; (2003) 20 CRNZ 396 (CA), paras 75 and 77.
37 *R v Rawiri* 9/8/02, Fisher J, HC Auckland T014047, para 18

"really cogent", at least without further evidence that a normal child of D's age would have understood the wrongfulness of his acts.[38]

For the purposes of ascertaining a child's knowledge, evidence of prior misconduct is generally not relevant. However, it may become relevant and admissible where, in spite of its otherwise prejudicial effect, there is a commonality with the current offence and the accused knew or was told that such conduct was wrong or unlawful at that time.[39] It is important, however, that the prior misconduct be relevant. For example, at common law on a charge of blackmail, evidence of a conviction for assault or for riding a bicycle on a footpath would normally be excluded as irrelevant, whereas a conviction for theft may be relevant.[40] Other relevant evidence may include anything the child said or did before or after the conduct in question, the results of an interview or psychiatric examination, and evidence from someone who knows the child well.[41]

Evidence that the child ran away following detection may be equivocal, because it shows that the child appreciated the conduct was "naughty" but does not necessarily establish knowledge that the conduct was "seriously wrong". What is required is proof of knowledge of wrongfulness that is clear "and beyond all possibility of doubt", or evidence that is "very clear and complete",[42] so that there is no danger of merely naughty children being convicted of crimes.

9.4 A case for reform

Despite the existence of quite sophisticated law on the matter, for the purposes of criminal law, because of the operation of the Children, Young Persons, and Their Families Act 1989, the defence of infancy based upon a child's lack of knowledge that the act or omission was wrong is seldom likely to be advanced. Under present law, it will only ever be relevant in a case where the offence charged is murder or manslaughter. For practical purposes, the presumption of incapacity by infants has such a narrow scope of operation in New Zealand that its utility as a general defence must be doubted. The increasingly common criticisms that the rule "reflects an outworn mode of thought", "is stepped in absurdity", is "unreal" and "contrary to common sense" may foreshadow its future demise.[43] In 2002 the Scottish Law Commission recommended the abolition of an age-related capacity test for criminal responsibility, on the grounds that the existence of a rule on immunity for prosecution, prohibiting the prosecution in the criminal courts of children under the age of 16, meant that there was no need to retain the rule on age in the capacity sense.[44] The doli incapax rule has also been criticised in both England and Australia in recent years on the grounds that it was developed at a time before free and compulsory education and that young people today are

---

38 Cf R v Rapira [2003] 3 NZLR 794; (2003) 20 CRNZ 396 (CA), para 85.
39 Cf R v Rapira [2003] 3 NZLR 794; (2003) 20 CRNZ 396 (CA), para 22.
40 C (a minor) v DPP [1996] 1 AC 1; [1995] 2 WLR 383 (HL), 35; 398 (Lord Lowry).
41 Adams, CA22.03 (looseleaf).
42 R v Gorrie (1918) 83 JP 136.
43 See, for example, Law Commission (UK), *Criminal Law, Codification of the Criminal Law: A Report to the Law Commission*, no 143, London, HMSO, 1985, paras 11.22, 11.23. Indeed, in the United Kingdom the rebuttable presumption that a child aged 10 or over is incapable of committing an offence has now been abolished: s 34 Crime and Disorder Act 1998 (UK). The defence itself has not been abolished, but the burden of establishing doli incapax now lies upon the defendant. For discussion, see the United Kingdom Government White Paper, *No More Excuses: A New Approach to Tackling Youth Crime In England and Wales*, Cm 3809; Walker, "The end of an old song?" (1999) 149 NLJ 64.

better educated and more sophisticated and that it should not be necessary to prove that they knew there offending behaviour was wrong or unlawful.[45] Nevertheless, a comprehensive review of the rule by the Criminal Law Review division of the Attorney-General's Department in New South Wales in February 2001, has recommended that the rule be retained and incorporated into legislation in that jurisdiction. The rule was considered to be a recognition that younger children may lack the developmental maturity to understand that their actions are wrong. The report considered that the better education of today's children did not necessarily mean that they were better able to tell right from wrong,[46] a conclusion evidently disputed by the drafters of the New Zealand Young Offenders (Serious Crimes) Bill.

Yet it may be, as the Scottish Law Commission has concluded, that procedural questions are of much greater practical importance when judging the criminal responsibility of a child or young person: in particular, whether the child or young person can *understand* the proceedings, in the sense of being able to understand the "language" of the law and thereby meaningfully to participate in the proceedings against her. Arguably, this ability is an essential precondition of the legitimacy of the trial.[47]

In accordance with this, there is much to commend the suggestion[48] that all juvenile offences should be tried in the Youth Court, without exception, both because of the desirability of preserving the child's privacy and future development and because of the need to conduct proceedings against children in an atmosphere that allows the child to participate and express herself freely.[49] More generally, there is now widespread acceptance in international law that children's interests should be approached and treated differently to those of adults. New Zealand law already requires, by virtue of s 25(i) New Zealand Bill of Rights Act 1990, that child defendants be dealt with "in a manner that takes account of the child's age". This would seem to suggest that a complete separation of adults and children in adjudicative curial settings is both desirable and necessary if minimum standards of juvenile justice are to be met. That, at least, would seem to be a direction of necessary reform in this area.

9.4.1 Proposed reforms: turning more children into criminals

Sadly, the increasing incidence and seriousness of offences committed by children and young persons has led, in some jurisdictions, to a growing trend towards prosecuting children in adult criminal courts. These developments represent a disturbing shift in juvenile criminal proceedings in which children, apparently regardless of their age and mental competency, are being tried as adults in cases where the crime is sufficiently serious to give rise to public outrage and debate.[50] While New Zealand's youth justice legislation significantly limits the ability of the State to prosecute children as adults, it is also evident that attitudes amongst some public

---

44   See Scottish Law Commission, Discussion Paper No 185, Report on Age of Criminal Responsibility (2002), discussed in G Maher, "Symposium: Criminal Responsibility: Age and Criminal Responsibility" (2005) 2 Ohio St J Crim L 493, 498.
45   *Brookers Family Law — Child Law* vol 2, Wellington, Brookers, 2005, YJ2.1.06.
46   *Brookers Family Law — Child Law* vol 2, Wellington, Brookers, 2005, YJ2.1.06.
47   Duff, "Law, language and community: Some preconditions of criminal liability" (1998) 18 OJLS 189, 198.
48   Noonan, "Children who kill: Wolves in sheep's clothing or deeply disturbed lambs?", unpublished research paper, University of Auckland, 2000.
49   See also the *United Nations Standard Minimum Rules for the Administration of Juvenile Justice* ("the Beijing Rules"), para 14.2; *T v UK; V v UK* [1999] Crim LR 579, 580 (commentary).
50   E D Sentlinger, "Comment: *V v United Kingdom*: Is it a 'New Deal' for Prosecuting Children as Adults" (2000) 16 Conn J Int'l L 117.

officials are hardening. In a private Members Bill currently before the New Zealand Parliament,[51] it is proposed, in order to address the problem of serious crimes being committed by young offenders, to make such offenders accountable for their crimes "more or less" in the same way as adult offenders.[52] The stated principle behind the Bill is that there should be "adult punishment" for "adult crimes". Several measures are advanced to deal with serious crimes committed by young people. First, the Bill changes the legal position with respect to the age of criminal responsibility where serious offences are committed by children. In particular, the addition of a new category of "any other serious offence"[53] significantly expands the range of offences (currently limited to murder and manslaughter) in respect of which proceedings against a child may be commenced under the Summary Proceedings Act 1957.[54] The Bill would also broaden the circumstances in which young offenders can be sentenced to imprisonment, to include cases where the offender has been convicted of a "serious offence".

These amendments, should they become law, will expose large numbers of children to the risk of criminal prosecution in adult courts and would seriously impact the restorative and protective mandate of existing youth justice legislation.

---

51   See Young Offender's (Serious Crimes) Bill 2006, a Private Members Bill put forward by NZ First list MP Ron Mark, 30 March 2006.
52   Young Offenders (Serious Crimes) Bill 2006, Explanatory Note.
53   "Serious offence" is defined in the Bill to mean "any offence (a) for which the maximum penalty is imprisonment for a term of not less than 3 months or a fine of not less than $2,000; or (b) that is, in the case of any other offence, committed by an offender ... who has previously been convicted of an offence to which paragraph (a) applies or has more than 3 previous convictions for offences other than those to which that paragraph applies".
54   See s 272(1) Children, Young Persons, and Their Families Act 1989.

Chapter 10

INSANITY

10.1	**Introduction**	288
10.1.1	Unfitness to stand trial	288
10.1.2	Mental disorder at sentencing	290
10.1.3	Mental disorder during incarceration	292
10.2	**The insanity defence: Origins**	292
10.2.1	Insanity defence during the 18th and 19th centuries	293
10.2.2	M'Naghten Rules	294
10.3	**Elements of insanity in New Zealand**	295
10.3.1	Presumption of sanity and burden of proof	298
10.3.2	Natural imbecility	300
10.3.3	Disease of the mind	301
(1)	*Disease of the mind: origins or effects?*	303
(2)	*What counts as a disease of the mind?*	304
(3)	*"Internal v external cause" test*	306
(4)	*Automatism*	308
10.3.4	"Nature and quality" of the act or omission	313
(1)	*Incapable*	313
(2)	*Nature and quality*	314
10.3.5	Knowledge of wrongfulness of act	315
10.3.6	Insanity and strict liability	318
10.3.7	Delusions	318
10.3.8	Diminished responsibility	320
10.3.9	Irresistible impulse	321
10.3.10	Role of expert evidence	322
10.4	**Raising and determining insanity**	324
10.4.1	Raising insanity "where it appears from the evidence"	325
10.4.2	New procedure for determining insanity by consensus	325
10.5	**Disposition of the criminally insane**	326
10.5.1	The range of orders	327
10.5.2	Detention as a "special patient"	328

10.5.3 Detention as a "patient" under the Mental Health (Compulsory Assessment and Treatment) Act 1992 or "special care recipient" under the Intellectual Disability (Compulsory Care and Rehabilitation) Act 2003...329
10.5.4 Immediate release..330

10.1 Introduction

The defence of insanity is concerned with an individual's mental capacity for crime. Although it is commonly conceptualised as a "defence", in earlier textbooks on criminal law it was common to treat insanity as an instance of legal incapacity, a status shared at common law by the Sovereign, children, corporations, and clerks in holy orders.[1] On this basis, criminal responsibility was denied because the offender was said to lack the legal *capacity* to be held responsible for a crime, rather than because the prosecution had failed to prove an essential element in the definition of the offence. For practical purposes, the distinction may have little significance, because it will often be the case that an "insane" offender, on account of the relevant mental disorder, did not possess whatever mens rea is required to establish the charge. We will, therefore, adopt the common convention of referring to insanity as a defence. Nonetheless, it is important to acknowledge that in some instances of insanity the *mens* may not be *rea* not because the accused did not know or intend what he was doing, but rather because the mental illness has removed part of the very foundation for criminal responsibility, ie moral rationality.[2]

Although in the courtroom we continue to use the word "insanity", it is important to realise that it is not a medically recognised concept, and does not fit within any diagnostic standard. It is a legal term of art, and is used exclusively to describe the state of mind which, in a criminal prosecution, will produce a verdict of not guilty by reason of mental disorder.

10.1.1 Unfitness to stand trial

Mental disorder or incompetence other than at the time of committing the offence may also be relevant during the trial process. Before briefly considering these situations, some comment about language is appropriate. In New Zealand, the term "insanity" refers exclusively to the insanity defence. In the past, "insanity" also included the mental state of a person who had been found by a court to be unfit to plead or unfit to be tried, which in New Zealand was referred to as being "under disability". The "under disability" provisions formerly in Part 7 of the Criminal Justice Act 1985 have now been repealed and replaced by the Criminal Procedure (Mentally Impaired Persons) Act 2003 (CP(MIP)A).[3] To be under disability or, as it is now said, "unfit to stand trial", a person must necessarily be "mentally impaired" to such a degree as to be unable to conduct a defence or instruct counsel (s 2, CP(MIP)A).

However, it by no means follows that, because an offender is unfit to stand trial, he must also be legally insane. Indeed, it is possible and may often be the case that an offender is mentally impaired and unfit to stand trial at the time of trial but legally sane at the time of the commission of the crime. Conversely, a person may be proven to have been insane when the offence was committed yet be fit to stand at the time of the trial. It is, therefore, essential to separate

---

1 See, for example, Turner, *Kenny's Outlines of Criminal Law* (19th ed), Cambridge, Cambridge University Press, 1966, 74ff.
2 For example, where D decides that his wife and daughter must die "in order [to] destroy the evil spirits within them": *Wihongi v Police* 10/5/99, Fisher J, HC Auckland T990080, 1.

carefully the particular context and purpose for which mental state is being assessed, appreciating that mental abnormality is not a unitary concept in criminal law and that it is capable of broad and diverse applications.[4]

Under s 2 CP(MIP)A, a person may be found "unfit to stand trial" where, as a result of mental impairment, he is unable to conduct a defence or instruct counsel, so as to be incapable of pleading, understanding the nature or purpose and possible consequences of the proceedings, or of communicating adequately with counsel for the purposes of conducting a defence. The evidence of two health assessors is required.[5] If satisfied that the person is unfit to stand trial, having previously conducted a "special hearing" to determine the accused's responsibility for the physical ingredients of the offence, the court is required to make an order that she be detained either as a "special patient" or as a "special care recipient".[6] Alternatively, provided the Court is satisfied that it is safe in the interests of public safety to do so, it can order the offender's detention as a "patient" under mental health legislation or as a "care recipient" under the Intellectual Disability (Compulsory Care and Rehabilitation) Act 2003 (ID(CCR)A). Where the interests of public safety are satisfied, the court has a discretion to order a person's immediate release.[7]

In New Zealand the question whether D is unfit to stand trial is always determined by a judge alone.[8] However, there is still some debate whether a jury may be empanelled to determine the preliminary issue of muteness, where a person "wilfully refuses to plead". The better view seems to be that in order to achieve conformity of practice between the High Court and the District Court the jurisdiction to determine muteness should lie, as it does in determining fitness to plead, with a judge alone and that the procedure should be identical to that prescribed for determining whether an offender is under disability.[9]

---

3   The Act redefines "under disability" as "unfitness to stand trial" and alters the threshold criteria for being found unfit to stand trial. In addition, the legislation adds a new procedure, called a "special hearing" which must be held prior to a hearing to determine trial competence in order to establish whether the accused caused the acts or omissions constituting the offence. A negative response to that inquiry mandates the accused's immediate discharge from the proceedings (s 9 CP(MIP)A). For a full discussion of the origins of the law governing fitness to plead in New Zealand, see Brookbanks, "A contemporary analysis of the doctrine of fitness to plead" [1982] NZ Recent Law 84. For a full account of the current law in this area see *Adams*, CM4.17.01-CM4.17.07, CM7.01-CM17.03. See also Brookbanks, "Judicial determination of fitness to plead: The fitness hearing" [1992] 7 Otago LR 520; Brookbanks, "Fitness to plead and the intellectually disabled offender" [1994] Psychiatry, Psychology and Law 171; commentary on special patients in *Trapski's Family Law* vol III, Wellington, Brooker's, 1993, MH2.25.04 ff (looseleaf); Legal Research Foundation, *Fitness to Plead: Under Disability in the 90's*, Auckland, 1995.
4   The phrase "mental abnormality" does not appear in New Zealand law but may be used to describe the broad range of aberrant mental states encompassed by the legal concepts of insanity, disability, and mental disorder.
5   See s 14 CP(MIP)A. Note, however, that their evidence must address the legal criteria provided by s 14 This requires a finding that the offender is "mentally impaired". The Court must then decide if the impairment is such as to prevent the offender's effective participation in the trial. See *R v Duval* [1995] 3 NZLR 202; (1995) 13 CRNZ 215.
6   See CP(MIP)A ss 24, 25.
7   Section 25(1)(d) CP(MIP)A . See *Police v R* [1997] DCR 431 regarding the circumstances in which immediate release may be appropriate.
8   Contrast the position in the United Kingdom, where the issue of an accused's fitness to plead is always determined by a jury: s 4(5) Criminal Procedure (Insanity) Act 1964 (UK).
9   See discussion in *Adams*, CA356.08-09 (looseleaf).

10.1.2 Mental disorder at sentencing

The question of the mental state of an accused person may also be relevant at the sentencing stage. However, New Zealand courts have been reluctant to permit the issue of competence to be sentenced to be tested in a formal inquiry, despite the approval of such a process in other common law jurisdictions.[10] (Similarly, the courts have doubted whether a trial court has jurisdiction to hear an application concerning the issue of unfitness to be tried between depositions and trial, on the basis that the legislative scheme requires such applications to be determined within a specified formal stage of the proceedings.[11]) Sometimes the issue of mental illness or disorder, not evident during the trial or in the remand period, may flare up after the offender has been convicted, perhaps as a traumatic reaction to the fear of imprisonment or to the experience of custodial detention while awaiting sentence. There are two main ways in which the legal process may be affected by the intervention of mental illness or disorder at this stage.

First, where an accused has pleaded guilty to an imprisonable offence but appears to be unfit to proceed either at the time the sentence is imposed or when the sentence is about to commence, the implementation of the sentence should be deferred and the accused's mental capacity to be sentenced determined by the court.[12] Although the question whether the accused is unfit to stand trial normally arises before or during the course of the trial or hearing,[13] it is arguable that the common law continues to apply to the effect that the question of fitness to plead may be raised at any stage of the proceedings, including verdict and sentencing. In *R v Skokolic*[14] the Supreme Court noted that the practice of deferring sentence where, after conviction, a criminal becomes "insane" was designed to protect a prisoner who had become incapable of advancing "some plea which if sane he could urge in stay of execution". A more practical argument favouring extension of the unfitness provisions post-conviction lies in the fact that under the Sentencing Act 2002 provision is now made for a "disputed facts" hearing where, at sentencing, the prosecution or defence seek to adduce evidence in support of a disputed fact relevant to sentence.[15] On the basis that the "evidence" in the trial could not be said to have been "concluded", in terms of s 7 CP(MIP)A, until the disputed facts have been determined, the unfitness to stand trial procedure must extend at least until any disputed facts hearing has been concluded. Logic would suggest that it should extend to the whole of the sentencing phase of the proceedings. This approach is supported by Canadian jurisprudence where the courts have emphasised that all of the accused's procedural rights that exist at trial

---

10   *A-G of Canada v Balliram* (2003) 173 CCC (3d) 547 (Ont SC) (McWatt J). See also Manson, "Fitness to be sentenced: A historical, comparative and practical review" (2006) 29 International Journal of Law and Psychiatry 257.
11   *R v Codd* 5/5/06, Simon France J, HC Auckland CRI-2005-004-12997. See also *P v Police* 14/9/06, Baragwanath J, HC Auckland CRI-2006-404-203.
12   The legislation does not define the procedure to be followed in these circumstances. It is debatable whether the issue of unfitness to stand trial can be determined in the post-conviction phase The legislation permits the issue to be raised "at any stage after the commencement of the proceedings and until all the evidence is concluded" (CP(MIP)A, s 7(1)). For a fuller discussion of this issue, see Schneider, "Fitness to be Sentenced" (1998) 41 Crim LQ 261 and see Manson, above, note 10.
13   Section 7 CP(MIP)A specifies that a court may make a finding of unfitness to stand trial "at any stage after the commencement of the proceedings and until all the evidence is concluded".
14   *R v Skokolic* [1929] NZLR 521, 523 (Blair J). See also *R v Berry* (1876) 1 QBD 447, 449, where the Court held that the accused could not be *convicted* because he was incapable of understanding the proceedings.
15   See s 24 Sentencing Act 2002.

continue in the sentencing process. In *R v Gardiner*[16] the Supreme Court of Canada stated that "ordinary legal principles governing criminal proceedings" apply and, "[u]pon conviction the accused is not abruptly deprived of all procedural rights existing at trial: he has a right to counsel, a right to call evidence and cross-examine prosecution witnesses, a right to give evidence himself and to address the Court." We would venture to suggest that this continuation of procedural rights should also extend to a requirement that the accused be competent to be sentenced.

The second way in which the sentencing process may be affected by the intervention of mental disorder is where, having convicted the accused, the court is concerned that the offender's mental state is such that treatment for mental impairment is *required*, either in the person's own interests or for the safety of the public or of a person or class of persons. In these circumstances s 34 CP(MIP)A empowers a judge to make one of two types of orders. First, assuming the offender presents a high level of risk to public safety and deserves punishment, the court can make a "hybrid" order by sentencing her to imprisonment while also ordering the person's detention as a special patient or special care recipient, according to the nature of the relevant mental impairment (s 34(1)(a)). Alternatively, and as a "benevolent alternative to a custodial sentence in a penal institution",[17] the Court may order that the offender be detained in a hospital as a patient or in a care facility as a care recipient (s 34(1)(b)). The latter order is only one of the possibilities for consideration by the judge in determining what if any sentence to impose on an offender, and "[i]ts function in the statutory scheme is to provide a more suitable individualised sentence operating in the interests of the offender and in the wider public interest than would otherwise be available".[18] However, its companion order in s 34(1)(a) is clearly punitive and is likely to be used for very serious offenders, where the need for punishment outweighs the case for a purely therapeutic option.

In *R v Elliot* the Court of Appeal held that the purely therapeutic hospital order option should not be used to detain a minor offender as a committed patient,[19] and should not be invoked without regard to the gravity of the offending because of the need to maintain a reasonable proportionality between the offending and the "severe curtailment of liberty inherent in an order for detention as a committed patient".[20] The correct approach in deciding, after conviction, whether a person is mentally impaired and should be detained in hospital is to decide whether there is jurisdiction to make an order under s 34: that depends, in turn, on the evidence of two health assessors. If there is jurisdiction to make the order, the court still has absolute discretion to decide whether, on the facts of the particular case, it is appropriate to use the more severe option under s 34(1)(a) or whether the circumstances justify the making of a purely therapeutic order under s 34(1)(b).[21] A hospital order will not necessarily be

---

16   *R v Gardiner* [1982] 2 SCR 368; (1982) 68 CCC (2d) 477 (SCC), 415; 514.
17   *R v Elliot* [1981] 1 NZLR 295 (CA), 302.
18   *R v Elliot* [1981] 1 NZLR 295 (CA), 302. For a more thorough discussion of the law and practice in relation to therapeutic orders in New Zealand, see Brookbanks, "The sentencing and disposition of mentally disordered offenders" in Brookbanks (ed), *Psychiatry and the Law: Clinical and Legal Issues*, Wellington, Brooker's, 1996, 308ff. See also the useful discussion of s 34 orders in Hall, *Sentencing Law and Practice*, Wellington, LexisNexis, 2004, para IV, 7.2 ff, D/1076-D/1081.
19   *R v Elliot* [1981] 1 NZLR 295 (CA), 302.
20   *R v Elliot* [1981] 1 NZLR 295 (CA), 302.
21   *Police v Travers* [1996] DCR 671. See also *R v Redmile* [1987] 1 NZLR 157 (CA); *R v Royce* 1/7/82, CA203/81; *R v Batt* [1987] 1 NZLR 760 (CA); *R v Mason* [1987] 2 NZLR 249; (1987) 3 CRNZ 7 (CA); *R v Rolander* [1989] 1 NZLR 366; (1988) 3 CRNZ 603 (CA).

preferred simply because an offender suffers from a very severe mental illness. A prison sentence, untagged to any particular therapeutic option, may still, for example, be justifiable in order to maintain control over the offender under the criminal justice system, especially where the offender would be able to receive appropriate treatment in prison.[22] We will consider the appropriateness of detaining mentally disturbed offenders in hospitals later in the chapter, where we examine the issue of disposition.

10.1.3 Mental disorder during incarceration

Frequently, sentenced offenders, or those in custody on remand pending either trial or the hearing of charges, become mentally unwell while in a penal institution. Mental illness or disorder in such circumstances may be the product of stress caused by the isolation and harshness of the prison environment or anxiety at the outcome of legal proceedings. Where the superintendent of a prison has reasonable grounds to believe that an inmate may be mentally disordered she may apply for the person to be assessed under the provisions of the Mental Health (Compulsory Assessment and Treatment) Act 1992.[23] In the event that the assessment confirms the superintendent's belief that the inmate is mentally disordered, she may be formally transferred to a hospital to be detained for as long as is necessary to treat the illness. If the patient responds to treatment and recovers her mental health she may be returned to the institution in which she was previously detained to undergo the remainder of the sentence.[24] Offenders dealt with in this manner are designated "special patients"[25] because, unlike offenders committed under s 34(1)(b) CP(MIP)A, their mental health status does not represent a final disposition of the matter and will change upon return to the penal institution or upon reclassification if the sentence expires while the patient is still detained in hospital.[26] Similarly, where the offender is intellectually disabled and has been detained under mental health legislation as a special patient for treatment of a mental illness or disorder, provision is made for such a person to be transferred from a hospital to a care facility under the ID(CCR) A.[27]

10.2 The insanity defence: Origins

The foundations of the insanity defence can be traced back at least to the 13th century. Prior to this, in the period of pre-Norman English law, there was no insanity defence as such because contemporary practice required the family of an insane person who committed a serious offence to pay compensation to the family of the victim, without presenting the offender for trial.[28] Early formulations of a test for legal insanity, such as Bracton's idea that an insane

---

22 *Arthur v Police* 13/12/93, Tipping J, HC Christchurch AP369/93; *Laing v Police* 28/3/00, Gendall J, HC Wellington AP19/00.
23 Section 45(3) Mental Health (Compulsory Assessment and Treatment) Act 1992.
24 Section 47(1) Mental Health (Compulsory Assessment and Treatment) Act 1992.
25 "Special patient" is defined in s 2 Mental Health (Compulsory Assessment and Treatment) Act 1992. Essentially, the classification encompasses offenders found unfit to stand trial, those acquitted on account of insanity, those remanded for psychiatric assessment, and those detained in a hospital under ss 45 and 46 of that Act. For a comprehensive account of special patient status, see *Trapski's Family Law* vol III, Wellington, Brooker's, 1993, MH2.25.04-31 (looseleaf); Bell and Brookbanks, *Mental Health Law In New Zealand* (2nd ed), Wellington, Brookers, 2005, ch 5.
26 Section 48(3) Mental Health (Compulsory Assessment and Treatment) Act 1992.
27 Section 47A Mental Health (Compulsory Assessment and Treatment) Act 1992.
28 Walker, *Crime and Insanity in England*, Edinburgh, Edinburgh University Press, 1968, 26, discussed in McAuley, *Insanity, Psychiatry and Criminal Responsibility*, Dublin, Roundhall Press, 1993, 18 fn 1.

person was "one who does not know what he is doing, who is lacking in mind and reason, and who is not far removed *from the brutes*",[29] tended to draw descriptive analogies with the mental capacities of children and animals.[30] While these descriptions were intended as metaphors for a radical want of reason and not as prosaic descriptions of a subhuman species,[31] their effect was to limit the availability of exculpatory insanity to evidence of unrestrained irrationality, so that as late as 1723, in R v *Arnold*, the jury was properly directed that to be found insane, "it must be a man that is *totally deprived* of his understanding and memory and doth not know what he is doing, no more than an infant, than a brute, or a wild beast".[32] It is safe to assume that only very serious mental disorder would have been recognised as giving exemption from serious crime, particularly homicide.[33]

10.2.1 Insanity defence during the 18th and 19th centuries

A succession of cases during the 18th and early 19th centuries appeared to harden the notion that only those who were completely bereft of reason were entitled to the defence of insanity.[34] However, towards the end of the 18th century there was a growing acceptance amongst commentators that if the purpose of punishment is the prevention of offences, the punishment of a person mentally ill at the time of the crime simply fails to achieve its object. Accordingly, by 1800, when James Hadfield was tried for the attempted murder of George III, there had been a softening of the rigid test applied in *Arnold*, such that the jury was now able to acquit upon being satisfied that the defendant suffered from a delusion which prompted his act.[35] On this basis, Hadfield was acquitted after firing a pistol at George III as he entered his box in the Drury Lane Theatre.[36]

However, the acquittal of Hadfield immediately highlighted an important lacuna in the legislation, in that there existed no statutory means of securing Hadfield's safe keeping following the finding of insanity. Accordingly, in 1800 the English Legislature passed the Criminal Lunatics Act, described in its Long Title as "an Act for the Safe Keeping of Insane Persons Charged with Offences". The statute was passed in great haste and made retrospective. It provided that if any person charged with treason, murder, or felony was found to be insane at the time of committing the offence and acquitted, "the Court shall ... order such Persons to be kept in strict custody, in such place and in such Manner as to the Court shall seem fit, until His Majesty's Pleasure shall be known".

---

29 Henri de Bracton, *On the Laws and Customs of England* (trans Thorne), Cambridge, Belknap Press, 1977, vol IV, 308.
30 See also Hale, who suggested that the insane are not criminally responsible "for they have not the use of understanding, and act not as reasonable creatures, but their actions are in *effect in the condition of brutes*": 1 Hale PC 31 (emphasis added).
31 McAuley, *Insanity, Psychiatry and Criminal Responsibility*, Dublin, Roundhall Press, 1993, 19.
32 R v *Arnold* (1724) 16 St Tr 695, 765 (emphasis added).
33 Prins, *Offenders, Deviants or Patients? An Introduction to the Study of Socio-forensic Problems* (2nd ed), London, Tavistock Publications, 1995, 13.
34 See R v *Ferrers* (1760) 19 St Tr 886; R v *Hadfield* (1800) 27 St Tr 1281; R v *Bellingham* Coll Lun 636; R v *Oxford* (1840) 4 State Tr (NS) 498.
35 McAuley, *Insanity, Psychiatry and Criminal Responsibility*, Dublin, Roundhall Press, 1993, 21.
36 It has been suggested that an important factor in securing Hadfield's acquittal may have been public sympathy engendered by the long-standing intermittent mental illness of King George III. See Prins, *Offenders, Deviants or Patients? An Introduction to the Study of Socio-forensic Problems* (2nd ed), London, Tavistock Publications, 1995, 13.

Hadfield's case is noteworthy in that it provided for the first time for a special verdict "Not guilty, he being under the influence of Insanity at the time the act was committed" and created a new category of offenders, to be known as "criminal lunatics".[37]

10.2.2 M'Naghten Rules

The most significant development in the insanity defence came in 1843 with the decision of the House of Lords in *M'Naghten's Case*.[38] M'Naghten, a former woodcarver who suffered from paranoid delusions, was charged with murder when he shot and killed Edward Drummond, having mistaken him for the then Prime Minister of England, Sir Robert Peel. M'Naghten believed, among other things, that the Tories were conspiring to kill him. Although he was acquitted at his trial on the grounds of insanity, the furore created by his acquittal led the House of Lords to demand of the 15 common law judges a statement of the law governing such cases. The judges, summoned under considerable pressure, were required to answer, in the abstract, five questions on the subject of insanity as a defence to criminal charges. In answering on behalf of the other judges, Lord Chief Justice Tyndal laid out two rules which have become the basis of the legal test for insanity in many Western jurisdictions. Those rules are as follows:[39]

"(1) The jurors ought to be told in all cases that ... to establish a defence on the ground of insanity, it must be clearly proved that, at the time of committing the act, the party accused was labouring under such a defect of reason, from disease of the mind, as not to know the nature and quality of the act he was doing, or if he did know, that he did not know he was doing what was wrong.

"(2) Where one labours under partial delusions only and is not in other respects insane, and commits an offence due to that fact, he must be considered in the same situation as to responsibility as if the facts with respect to which the delusion exists were real."

This statement of the law has been followed in most common law jurisdictions and has remained substantially unchallenged as the test for legal insanity for over 150 years. The M'Naghten Rules emphasise the importance of the patient's notions of right and wrong, the causal relationship between the content of delusions and the crime, and the status of the offence if the content of the delusions is true. Interestingly, it has been observed that the "rules" were more stringent in their formulation than the guides given in the earlier cases, such that if the "right from wrong" test had been applied at the time of M'Naghten's trial, he could *not* have been found not guilty on the grounds of insanity.[40] Yet *M'Naghten* demonstrates, and subsequent cases have also shown, that a person may know precisely what she is doing and even be aware that she is committing a criminal act, yet be excused because her firmly-held delusions have compelled her to act as she did. The strength of delusions may be such as to force the conclusion that the offender did not know the *moral quality* of the act she is charged with committing. Delusions which appear to be limited to an isolated topic (as with

---

[37] See Forshaw and Rollin, "The history of forensic psychiatry in England" in Bluglass and Bowden (eds), *Principles and Practice of Forensic Psychiatry*, Edinburgh, Churchill Livingstone, 1990, 84.
[38] *M'Naghten's Case* (1843) 10 Cl & Fin 200; 8 ER 718; [1843-60] All ER Rep 229 (HL).
[39] *M'Naghten's Case* (1843) 10 Cl & Fin 200; 8 ER 718; [1843-60] All ER Rep 229 (HL).
[40] Forshaw and Rollin, "The history of forensic psychiatry in England" in Bluglass and Bowden (eds), *Principles and Practice of Forensic Psychiatry*, Edinburgh, Churchill Livingstone, 1990, 84.

M'Naghten), may in reality be symptoms of a more general condition and indicate a diseased condition of the brain which is said to affect the *volition* of the person exhibiting them.[41] While the concept of mens rea, technically, refers to the mental state, such as intention or recklessness, required to commit a particular crime, in a looser sense it may be thought of as referring to mental states consistent with moral and/or legal blame. So a killing motivated by insane delusional beliefs may meet the requirements for mens rea in the first sense but not in the looser, underlying second sense.[42]

Another point to note is that the Rules do not address the issues of lack of control, irresistible drives, or impulses.[43] The mere claim that the impulse to kill or seriously injure someone was *irresistible* or *uncontrollable* will not excuse in the absence of evidence that the accused was suffering from a mental disease at the time of the crime.[44] We will examine the claims of irresistible impulse in more detail later in the chapter.

10.3 Elements of insanity in New Zealand

The essential elements of the M'Naghten Rules were first incorporated into New Zealand's criminal law in the Criminal Code Act 1893. The Criminal Code Act was itself based upon the Draft Code of the English Criminal Code Bill Commission, published in 1879, and indeed s 23 of the 1893 Act enacted in almost identical terms the text of s 22 of the Draft Code, although the arrangement of the text differed in some respects. Because of the close linguistic relationship which exists between the two provisions, it may be instructive to consider the comments made in relation to s 22 by the drafters of the Draft Code,[45] bearing in mind also that New Zealand's insanity defence has been relatively unaffected by subsequent revisions of our criminal legislation.

Acknowledging that s 22 expresses the existing law, the Commissioners conceded, perhaps somewhat despairingly, that:[46]

> "The obscurity which hangs over the subject cannot be altogether dispelled until our existing ignorance as to the nature of the will and the mind, the nature of the organs by which they operate, the manner and degree in which those operations are interfered with by disease, and the nature of the diseases which interfere with them, are greatly diminished. The framing of the definition has caused us much labour and anxiety; and although we cannot deem the definition to be altogether satisfactory, we consider it as satisfactory as the nature of the subject admits of. Much latitude must in any case be left to the tribunal which has to apply the law to the facts in each particular case."

---

41 See, for example, *R v Monkhouse* [1923] GLR 13 (Chapman J).
42 Goldstein, Morse, and Shapiro, "Evaluation of Criminal Responsibility" in Goldstein (ed), *Forensic psychology* vol 11, New York, Wiley, 2003, 381-406; cf Greene and Cohen, "For the law, neuroscience changes nothing and everything" (2004) 359 Phil Trans R Soc Lond B 1775.
43 Forshaw and Rollin, "The history of forensic psychiatry in England" in Bluglass and Bowden (eds), *Principles and Practice of Forensic Psychiatry*, Edinburgh, Churchill Livingstone, 1990, 84, 88.
44 *R v Deighton* (1900) 18 NZLR 891.
45 See Criminal Code Bill Commission, *Report of the Royal Commission Appointed to Consider the Law Relating to Indictable Offences: With an Appendix Containing a Draft Code Embodying the Suggestions of the Commissioners*, London, Eyre & Spottiswoode for HMSO, 1879, C2345.
46 See Criminal Code Bill Commission, *Report of the Royal Commission Appointed to Consider the Law Relating to Indictable Offences: With an Appendix Containing a Draft Code Embodying the Suggestions of the Commissioners*, London, Eyre & Spottiswoode for HMSO, 1879, C2345, 17.

Three points in particular deserve comment. First, the alleged "obscurity" which hangs over the subject of exculpatory insanity still remains. One reason for this is that, despite the developments in medical science over the last 150 years our knowledge of the nature and causes of mental illness is still limited and subject to ongoing change. But perhaps even more importantly, there seems to be little interest in handing over the judicial task of determining the legal status of mental illness or disease exclusively to medical experts.[47] While judges continue to be invested with the responsibility of determining the legal content of insanity, the "obscurity" will continue, simply because a judge's function is not to declare the *clinical parameters* of a particular disease process but rather to state whether a mental disease fits within the legal criteria for insanity laid down by Parliament. Ultimately, medical evidence on such matters provides useful guidance for a judge but is never determinative of the issues to be decided by the court.[48]

Secondly, it is probably impossible to formulate a perfect legal test of insanity. There have been many attempts over the years to recast the law's insanity criteria to reflect modern psychiatric developments and understanding. Few of the formulations that have departed radically from the M'Naghten Rules have survived, and most modern Western versions of the insanity defence are modelled on the Rules in one form or another. They are for the most part thoroughly cognitive in emphasis, notwithstanding the ongoing debate over whether they give adequate consideration to disorders of the will or the emotions. In recent years some jurisdictions have conceded the claim that the test for insanity ought to include volitional disorders,[49] although professional opinion on this question is strongly divided. Many commentators agree that "[s]o-called volitional or control problems are generally and notoriously difficult conceptually to define and practically to apply",[50] and there is no immediate proposal to revisit this limitation in the New Zealand defence. The main focus of current debate tends to be not on whether the M'Naghten Rules should be replaced, but on whether they ought to be supplemented by statutory rules which are better able to reflect differing levels of criminal culpability of those affected by mental illness falling short of legal insanity.

Thirdly, because the M'Naghten Rules are very narrowly formulated, it is not uncommon for judges to interpret them liberally in order to accommodate difficult but deserving cases. This being the case, it might be argued that any attempt to redefine insanity according to a detailed prescriptive formula may inhibit the ability of trial judges to apply the law generously in order to ensure that severely mentally disordered offenders are not unfairly treated by the courts.

---

47 For a directly opposing view, see Nygaard, "On responsibility: Or the insanity of mental defences and punishment" (1996) 41 Villanova LR 951, 952.
48 This is likely to continue to be the case despite fascinating new discoveries in neuroscience which, arguably, have radical implications for criminal responsibility. See Morse, "The Mind of a Child: The Relationship between Brain Development, Cognitive Functioning, and Accountability under the Law: Brain Overclaim Syndrome and Criminal Responsibility: A Diagnostic Note" (2006) 3 Ohio St J Crim L 397.
49 In the Commonwealth of Australia and most of its States, legislation includes a "volitional" arm which asks whether or not the accused lacked the capacity to control his or her conduct. See Criminal Code 1995 (Cth), s 7.3, Crimes Act 1900 (ACT), s 428N; Criminal Code 2002 (ACT), s 28; Criminal Code (NT), s 43C; Criminal Code (Qld), s 27; Criminal Law Consolidation Act 1935 (SA), s 269C; Criminal Code Act 1924 (Tas), s 16; Criminal Code (WA), s 27.
50 Morse, "Fear of Danger, Flight from Culpability" (1998) 4 Psych PPL 250, 262; Yeo, "Rethinking the Capacities of Insanity" (2000) 36 The Irish Jurist 275.

To the extent that these observations are accurate it could be said that the comments of the Commissioners reflect even present realities, and remind us of the thoroughly elusive nature of legal insanity. The following discussion will demonstrate that insanity is a remarkably fluid concept.

New Zealand's current version of the Rules is set out in s 23 Crimes Act 1961, although important rules governing the operation of the defence in practice are also set out in criminal procedure legislation, which should also be consulted when determining a defence strategy involving the insanity defence.[51] In Australia, the common law States of New South Wales, Victoria, and South Australia still follow the M'Naghten Rules, although statutory provisions in these jurisdictions also deal with ancillary matters. Under the Criminal Codes of Queensland, Western Australia, the Northern Territory, and Tasmania, provision is also made for a volitional criterion, based on the capacity of the accused to control his actions; as noted above, this is not part of the common law criteria for insanity.

Section 23 states:

"**23 Insanity**

"(1) Every one shall be presumed to be sane at the time of doing or omitting any act until the contrary is proved.

"(2) No person shall be convicted of an offence by reason of an act done or omitted by him when labouring under natural imbecility or disease of the mind to such an extent as to render him incapable—

  "(a) Of understanding the nature and quality of the act or omission; or

  "(b) Of knowing that the act or omission was morally wrong, having regard to the commonly accepted standards of right and wrong.

"(3) Insanity before or after the time when he did or omitted the act, and insane delusions, though only partial, may be evidence that the offender was, at the time when he did or omitted the act, in such a condition of mind as to render him irresponsible for the act or omission.

"(4) The fact that by virtue of this section any person has not been or is not liable to be convicted of an offence shall not affect the question whether any other person who is alleged to be a party to that offence is guilty of that offence."

The principal difference between the M'Naghten Rules and s 23 is that the New Zealand Parliament has defined insanity in terms of the accused's *capacity* to understand the nature and quality of an act or omission, or to know that it was morally wrong; whereas the M'Naghten Rules were concerned with the accused's *actual knowledge* of those matters. In addition, the Criminal Code Act 1893 added "natural imbecility" as one of the factors which might bring an accused within the scope of the insanity defence.

The M'Naghten Rules and earlier New Zealand legislation contained a provision that persons suffering "specific delusions", but otherwise sane, were not to be acquitted on the ground of insanity unless the delusions would, if true, have justified or excused the act.[52] However, as

---

51   See s 20 Criminal Procedure (Mentally Impaired Persons) Act 2003.
52   See s 22 Draft Criminal Code 1879; s 23(3) Criminal Code Act 1893; s 43(2) Crimes Act 1908.

was recognised in *R v Monkhouse*[53] (where the accused was charged with the attempted murder of a farm manager after he had been heard to mutter "Him and I for it. If I don't kill him he'll kill me"), delusions that appear to be limited to an isolated topic may really be symptoms of a more general condition and possibly indicative of deep-seated insanity. In that case, the evidence of delusions was accepted as being evidence of insanity and the accused was acquitted on the ground of insanity. The provision concerning delusions was not re-enacted in the present New Zealand provision, in part because s 23(2) probably covers such cases, and also because its insistence on legal justification or excuse might conflict with the introduction of "moral" wrongness in s 23(2)(b).[54]

10.3.1 Presumption of sanity and burden of proof

Section 23 commences with a presumption that "every one" is sane at the time of doing or admitting any act "until the contrary is proved".[55] This is where any inquiry concerning insanity must begin.[56] Every person is deemed to be sane until he is proved to be insane. The *accused* must show (has the burden of proving) that he was insane when he committed the relevant act. This implies that the accused has both an evidentiary burden to point to direct evidence that amounts to more than a mere allegation of the existence of a defence at law ie sufficient evidence to put the defence "in play", and the legal burden of establishing the defence case.[57] Apart from statutory exceptions and case law developments in relation to public welfare regulatory offences, insanity is the only qualification to the general rule that it is the duty of the prosecution to prove an accused's guilt.[58] The accused must persuade the court of his insanity, on the balance of probabilities, which will normally mean adducing medical testimony regarding his state of mind at the time. A mere assertion that he was insane, without more, will not be sufficient to discharge the duty. However, the onus on the accused to prove insanity is not as heavy as that which remains on the prosecution to establish other elements of the offence charged. The accused is not required to prove insanity beyond reasonable doubt, but only need prove it to the satisfaction of the jury on the balance of probabilities, the standard of proof required of a plaintiff in a civil action.[59] Thus the accused must be acquitted if the jury think it more likely than not that he was insane at the relevant time.

It has been held in South Africa that even where sufficient evidence has been led to show that there was a *reasonable chance* that the accused may have suffered from a mental disease which prevented him from knowing what he was doing, the accused must nevertheless prove the alleged mental disease on the balance of probabilities. There can be no obligation, in such a case, for the prosecution to prove that the mental disease did not have the effect claimed.[60] New Zealand courts have also held, in relation to proof of disease of the mind, that it is not enough for the accused to provide evidence that merely indicated such a disease. It is necessary to prove the *probable presence* of a disease of the mind.[61] In *Proctor v Police*[62] evidence that the

---

53 *R v Monkhouse* [1923] GLR 13.
54 *Adams* (2nd ed), para 414. Delusions are considered further at 10.3.7.
55 Section 23(1) Crimes Act 1961.
56 See *R v Deighton* (1900) 18 NZLR 891, 892.
57 See *R v Fontaine* (2004) 183 CCC (3d) 1 (SCC), para 68, (Fish J).
58 *Woolmington v DPP* [1935] AC 462; [1935] All ER 1 (HL). See 2.3.
59 *R v Cottle* [1958] NZLR 999 (CA), 1014, 1022 (Gresson P); *Sodeman v R* (1936) 55 CLR 192; [1936] ALR 156 (HCA).
60 *S v Kennedy* (1951) 4 SA 431 (A).
61 *R v Roulston* [1976] 2 NZLR 644 (CA); *Proctor v Police* 5/4/84, Vautier J, HC Auckland M1333/83.

accused had probably inhaled quantities of paint vapour prior to consuming liquor was insufficient to show the probable presence of disease of the mind even though the evidence was led by witnesses who included both members of the police and psychiatrists.

Similarly, in New Zealand the courts have rejected the proposition that the accused need only lay some foundation for the defence of insanity and when that is done the general burden of proving the charge would require the Crown to prove it beyond reasonable doubt. In *R v Roulston*,[63] the Court of Appeal approved the view that while the *ultimate* burden rests on the Crown to prove every element essential in the crime, in order to prove that the act was voluntary, the Crown may rely on the presumption of sanity and if the defence wishes to displace the presumption they must give some evidence from which the contrary may reasonably be inferred.

Sometimes the fact that the burden of proving insanity is on the accused may create difficulties, particularly where joint defences of insanity and involuntariness are raised. This will include situations where there is an evidential foundation for both insanity and sane automatism to be considered. Involuntariness (sane automatism) places only an evidentiary burden on the accused, and the defence must be negatived by the prosecution beyond a reasonable doubt, whereas insanity must be affirmatively proved by the accused. One approach to this difficulty suggested by the High Court of Australia is that the accused should receive an unqualified acquittal if the evidence leaves the jury in a reasonable doubt on the issue of sane automatism. The issue of whether insanity has been proved should be considered only if the prosecution excludes such reasonable doubt.[64]

The requirement that a defendant must affirmatively prove insanity derives, as has been observed, from the common law presumption that an accused is legally sane until the contrary is proved. In Canada a similar statutory presumption in s 16(4) Criminal Code (Can) has been criticised as being a historical anomaly, unfair to the accused, unnecessary as a matter of policy, and an irrational exception to the ordinary onus of proof. Nonetheless, in that jurisdiction the Supreme Court has held, in a majority decision, that although the reverse onus in insanity violates the presumption of innocence in s 11(d) Canadian Charter of Rights and Freedoms, it is nevertheless a "reasonable limitation" under s 1 of the Charter.[65]

The argument that the burden on the accused to prove insanity is both anomalous and without justification has some powerful supporters, and indeed the English Criminal Law Revision Committee in its 11th report (1972) and 14th report (1980)[66] recommended that the burden of proof be changed so that the accused need only raise a reasonable doubt to support the insanity verdict. However, despite these objections to the reverse onus, the predominant direction of legal reform seems to be towards retention of the traditional burden of proof rules for insanity. In the US, as a result of reforms made since the Hinckley trial, approximately two-thirds of the States which accept the insanity plea place the burden of proof on the defendant, usually by a preponderance of the evidence.[67]

---

62 *Proctor v Police* 5/4/84, Vautier J, HC Auckland M1333/83.
63 *R v Roulston* [1976] 2 NZLR 644 (CA), 648. See also *Bratty v A-G for Northern Ireland* [1963] AC 386; [1961] 3 All ER 523 (HL); *R v Cottle* [1958] NZLR 999 (CA), 1029; *R v Burr* [1969] NZLR 736 (CA), 743.
64 See *R v Falconer* (1990) 171 CLR 30; 65 ALJR 20 (HCA), 63; 34.
65 *R v Chaulk* [1990] 3 SCR 1303; (1991) 62 CCC (3d) 193 (SCC).
66 Criminal Law Revision Committee, *Offences Against the Person*, 14th report, Cmnd 7844, London, HMSO, 1980.

Although the common law burden of proof requirements for insanity have been criticised for having the effect of making exculpation more difficult for the insane than the sane defendant, ultimately where the burden of proof lies will depend on policy considerations prevailing in particular jurisdictions, and public perceptions of how readily defendants are able to avoid conviction through "unconvincing" insanity defence pleas. In New Zealand, there has been no pressure upon the Legislature to abolish the presumption of sanity, presumably because the insanity defence is numerically insignificant in this country and has not given rise to the perceived social and legal injustices which have accompanied recent American show trials involving the insanity defence. However, in Scotland it has been argued that the reverse onus is incompatible with the European Convention on Human Rights and that the accused should only bear an evidential burden of raising insanity as a live issue for consideration by the tribunal of fact. The essential difficulty with requiring an accused person to prove insanity, according to the Scottish Law Commission, is that where an accused bears the legal burden of proof, there exists a likelihood of conviction despite the presence of evidence in favour of his defence, because that evidence did not meet the standard of balance of probabilities.[68] Consequently, the Commission has recommended that, where an accused pleads insanity at the time of an offence, he or she should bear only an evidential burden of establishing it.[69]

10.3.2 Natural imbecility

Proof of either natural imbecility or disease of the mind is the necessary foundation of any insanity defence in New Zealand. The expression "natural imbecility" (which may be translated as "subnormality" or "mental retardation") clearly includes a congenital defect, as well as a disorder which develops later in life. In Australia the expression has been equated with "arrested or retarded development of mind".[70] In practice, the defence of insanity is seldom based on the presence of natural imbecility. However, natural imbecility may provide the foundation for an insanity defence where its effect is to deprive the offender of the capacity to know facts relevant to a complainant's capacity, for example, to consent, and thereby depriving the accused of the ability to know his acts were wrong. In such a case the presence of intellectual impairment need not be advanced as a claim of "global" and permanent incapacity, but rather as a contextualised claim that, in the circumstances, the absence of the ability to access knowledge of certain facts relevant to an appreciation of the legal quality of an offender's acts, may have affected his or her criminal responsibility. In *R v Mrzljak*[71] the appellant, who spoke little English and was mildly intellectually disabled, was convicted of two counts of rape of an intellectually disabled female complainant. Although on appeal the Court was divided on the question whether the accused's intellectual impairment affected his cognitive capacity to a sufficient degree to deprive him of the capacity to understand what he was doing, there was agreement that the presence of intellectual impairment (whether or not coupled with language difficulties) could inhibit an offender's ability to pick up cues which might have led another person to appreciate that the complainant was intellectually impaired and not consenting. In such circumstances, provided the evidence was capable of supporting

---

67 See Mackay, "Post-*Hinckley* insanity in the USA" [1988] Crim LR 88, 93.
68 Scottish Law Commission, *Discussion Paper on Insanity and Diminished Responsibility* (Discussion Paper No 122), Edinburgh, The Stationery Office, 2003, para 5.16.
69 Scottish Law Commission, *Discussion Paper on Insanity and Diminished Responsibility* (Discussion Paper No 122), Edinburgh, The Stationery Office, 2003, para 5.19.
70 *R v Rolph* [1962] Qd R 262, 271 (Qld CA).
71 *R v Mrzljak* (2004) 152 A Crim R 315.

a conclusion that the offender was in such a state of natural imbecility as to deprive him of the capacity to understand what he was doing or knowing that it was wrong, it might be capable of supporting a conclusion that the offender was legally insane.[72]

Like the phrase "disease of the mind", "natural imbecility" is a legal concept and it is therefore a question of law for the trial judge whether particular mental conditions are included within the term.[73] The concept is wider than disease or "injury" in that it does not necessitate permanence, though it does connote durability.[74] The condition of autism, for example, which is a chronic, lifelong disorder characterised by impaired social interactions and impaired ability to communicate, could fall within the definition of "natural imbecility" for the purposes of the insanity defence, even though it is not uniformly associated with mental retardation.[75]

In Canada, legislative changes have meant that the term "insane" has been replaced with the term "not criminally responsible". In addition, the phrase "state of natural imbecility or has disease of the mind" has been replaced with the term "mental disorder", which in turn is defined as meaning "disease of the mind".[76] Prior to these modifications, "natural imbecility" had been held to involve an "imperfect condition of mental power from congenital defect or natural decay as distinguished from a mind once normal which has become diseased".[77] This unfortunate circularity left the status of "natural imbecility" somewhat uncertain in that jurisdiction, although it is thought that with the re-adoption of the phrase "disease of the mind" in the definition of "mental disorder", much of the case law decided under the predecessor legislation is applicable to the new provision[78]. While it is not clear that the Canadian case law on "natural imbecility" will necessarily carry over to the new provision, it would seem to follow that a mentally retarded person should be granted protection within the defence of "mental disorder" if her mind is affected to such a degree that she cannot appreciate the nature and quality of her act or know the act is wrong. As most psychiatrists distinguish subnormality from other forms of mental disorder, any legal standard ought also to reflect that distinction.

10.3.3 Disease of the mind

Under existing law, medical witnesses are permitted to give an opinion whether a disorder may be regarded as a "disease of the mind". They may also testify to the causes and symptoms of the condition diagnosed. Since "disease of the mind" (or natural imbecility) is a necessary, though not a sufficient, requirement for legal insanity, such testimony will always be crucial in an insanity trial. However, as has been noted already, disease of the mind is a legal not a medical concept and it is therefore a question of law what mental abnormalities are included within the term. While it is for the jury, not medical experts, to decide whether the particular mental

---

72 R v Mrzljak (2004) 152 A Crim R 315, 319, para 15 (Williams J). Yet, perhaps paradoxically, it has been held that a mildly intellectually disabled 15-year-old youth, with an IQ of an 8-year-old, did not lack the mental capacity to participate effectively in a criminal trial. See R (TP) v West London Youth Court [2006] Mental Health LR 40.
73 See Bratty v A-G for Northern Ireland [1963] AC 386; [1961] 3 All ER 523 (HL), 412; 534 (Lord Denning).
74 Campbell, *Mental Disorder and Criminal Law in Australia and New Zealand*, Wellington, Butterworths, 1988, 126.
75 Andreasen and Black, *Introductory Textbook of Psychiatry*, Washington, American Psychiatric Press, 1991, 439: up to 70 percent of autistic patients show some evidence of mental retardation, although others have normal intelligence and may demonstrate very specific talents or abilities.
76 See s 2 Criminal Code (Can).
77 R v Cooper (1978) 40 CCC (2d) 145, 159.
78 Greenspan (ed), *Martin's Annual Criminal Code 1997*, Aurora, Ontario, Canada Law Book Co, 1996, cc/48.

disease the accused suffered from rendered her incapable of knowing the nature and quality of her actions or of knowing that they were morally wrong, the jury's verdict must be founded on evidence. Medical evidence supported by other relevant evidence cannot arbitrarily be put aside.[79]

In New Zealand, disease of the mind is said to be "a term which defies precise definition and which can comprehend mental derangement in the widest sense".[80] Our courts have never attempted to define it precisely or comprehensively. However, because (as we shall see below) it has been legally defined as being caused by an "internal" condition, arising from an "underlying pathological infirmity of mind",[81] it is apt to include all physiological conditions that may impact the operation of the mind. Included amongst these are conditions like epilepsy, somnambulism, hyperglycaemia, and cerebral arteriosclerosis.[82]

Even so, the inclusion of non-psychiatric pathological conditions within the ambit of disease of the mind is problematic. It has been argued, in the context of English criminal law, that the effect of their inclusion is to render the M'Naghten Rules incompatible with the European Convention on Human Rights. This is on the basis that, since the Convention only permits the lawful detention of "persons of unsound mind"[83] where medical evidence "establish[es] that his mental state is such as to justify his compulsory hospitalisation",[84] the specialised definition of disease of the mind does not comport with medical science.[85] In particular, conditions like hyperglycaemia and epilepsy are impossible to square with the requirement for objective medical evidence supporting the fact that the accused is of unsound mind.[86]

It has correspondingly been suggested that current versions of the insanity defence in Australia and New Zealand may breach the right to liberty set out in article 9(1) of the international Covenant on Civil and Political Rights.[87] While it is not appropriate to debate this issue at length in the present context, it is a matter that needs to be carefully considered in any future reforms of the insanity defence in these jurisdictions.

---

79 R v Rotana (1995) 12 CRNZ 650 (CA). See further 10.3.10.
80 R v Cottle [1958] NZLR 999 (CA), 1011 (Gresson P). In two Australian jurisdictions, legislation refers to "mental disease" in place of the concept "disease of the mind", but the two have been held to mean the same. See Criminal Code (Qld), s 27; Criminal Code (Tas), s 16; R v Falconer (1990) 171 CLR 30; 65 ALJR 20 (HCA).
81 See R v Radford (1985) 42 SASR 266, 247 (King CJ); McSherry and Naylor, Australian Criminal Laws: Critical Perspectives, Melbourne, Oxford University Press, 2004, 532.
82 McSherry and Naylor, Australian Criminal Laws: Critical Perspectives, Melbourne, Oxford University Press, 2004, 532.
83 European Convention of Human Rights, Article 5(1).
84 Winterwerp v The Netherlands (1979) 2 EHRR 387, para 39.
85 Scottish Law Commission, Discussion Paper on Insanity and Diminished Responsibility (Discussion Paper No 122), Edinburgh, The Stationery Office, 2003, para 2.61.
86 For further development of this argument see Sutherland and Gearty, "Insanity and the European Court of Human Rights" [1992] Crim LR 418; Baker, "Human Rights, M'Naghten and the 1991 Act" [1994] Crim LR 84; Mackay and Gearty, "On Being Insane in Jersey — the case of the Attorney-General v Jason Prior" [2001] Crim LR 560; Ashworth, Principles of Criminal Law (3rd ed), Oxford, 1999, 215-217.
87 See Hopper and McSherry, "The Insanity Defence and International Human Rights Obligations" (2001) 8 Psychiatry, Psychology and Law 161, and see discussion in Brookbanks, "Insanity in the Criminal Law: Reform in Australia and New Zealand" (2003) The Juridical Review 81.

(1) *Disease of the mind: origins or effects?*

When considering the meaning of "disease of the mind" it is important to understand that the criminal law is not concerned with the *origin* of the disease so much as with its *effects*.[88] This means that it is unimportant whether the relevant incapacity is due to degeneration of the brain, or to some other form of mental derangement, or to a physical disorder, such as arteriosclerosis or brain tumour, provided it has the effect of impairing the *reasoning* process. It follows that the law will normally only accommodate those disorders which affect the mind, that is to say the faculties of reasoning, memory, and understanding; it is unconcerned with disorders which simply produce disturbed *behaviour*. This analysis has important implications when considering the impact of mind-altering substances like mephamphetamine. This substance, commonly described as "P" (*pure* methamphetamine), is capable of causing a syndrome similar to acute schizophrenia, accompanied by auditory hallucinations, delusions and thought disorder. However, this aberrant mental state is often accompanied by severe personality disorder and raises a question as to whether the psychosis induced by P should be considered a disease of the mind. Professional opinion is divided on the point. On one view, if it cannot be shown that the state represents more than a state of intoxication (albeit prolonged), and there is no clear indication of the need for treatment and rehabilitation in a hospital, then the condition should not be considered a disease of the mind.[89] According to another view, a diagnosis of major psychosis should not be excluded unless there is compelling evidence that the symptoms are entirely attributable to drugs.[90] Drawing a distinction between patients experiencing drug-induced psychosis and those with "real" mental illness, may be ethically questionable, since both types suffer psychological distress.[91]

Psychiatrists distinguish between *psychoneurosis* and *psychosis*, conditions which cause subjective distress in patients, and are professionally committed to treating both. However, neurotic disorders, including such conditions as anxiety states, obsessional states, hysteria, various mood (affective) disorders, and most personality disorders, are normally excluded from the category "disease of the mind". Most psychoses, on the other hand, satisfy the criteria for legal insanity.[92] Because a psychiatrist operates from a professional desire to assist in the alleviation of subjective mental distress, she may have difficulty in accepting the law's insistence that only mental states which affect the accused's rationality are fit candidates for inclusion within this archaic legal category. She may legitimately reason that any aberrant mental state that produces distress and affects individual behaviour should be considered in evaluating an offender's criminal responsibility, and may seek to introduce evidence to this effect. However, to do so would be to misconceive the purpose of the insanity defence, which is designed not only for the therapeutic benefit of the offender, but as a measure and symbol of criminal responsibility and as a means of protecting the public against the recurrence of dangerous conduct.[93] The role of the psychiatrist in giving evidence of insanity has been well expressed in the following passage from Gunn and Taylor:[94]

---

88 *Halsbury's Laws of England* vol 11(1) (4th ed reissue), London, Butterworths, 1990, para 31.
89 See Tapsell, "Forensic Psychiatry and Law: A Judicial Update", Institute of Judicial Studies, High Court Update, 7 & 14 November, 2005.
90 See Poole and Brabbins, "Drug Induced Psychosis" (1996) 168 British Journal of Psychiatry 135-138.
91 Poole and Brabbins, "Drug Induced Psychosis" (1996) 168 British Journal of Psychiatry 135-138.
92 Allen, *Textbook on Criminal Law*, London, Butterworths, 1991, 106.
93 See *R v Sullivan* [1984] 1 AC 156; [1983] 2 All ER 673 (HL), 172; 677-678 (Lord Diplock).

"The psychiatrist should resist, within the bounds of propriety, the temptation to give a medical view on the question of the level of responsibility. Instead, he should set out the medical evidence, give an account of the relationship of the killing (if admitted) to those medical facts (especially the mental state) and indicate how far, in his opinion, the medical features and/or diagnosis influenced the aggressive and other relevant behaviour. The reply to direct questioning about the diminution of responsibility should reiterate the nature of any mental disorder discovered and then the point should be made that only a layman's view about the ultimate question can be given."

The danger is that if the psychiatrist attempts to translate medical terms into legal terms, or to act as a patient advocate out of a desire to achieve optimal treatment opportunities for the offender, he may subvert the role of the jury by being tempted to answer questions that are for their sole consideration.[95] Alternatively, he may, out of a humane desire to help his sick patient, endeavour to place clinical information before a jury which is irrelevant to the determination of criminal responsibility and which may only serve to confuse the jury and skew the direction of the trial.

(2)   *What counts as a disease of the mind?*

All this still leaves us with the underlying question: what constitutes, in law, a "disease of the mind"? We may accept that the term embraces any illness, disorder, or abnormal condition which actually impairs the human mind and its functioning, although this must be taken to exclude self-induced intoxication caused by alcohol or drugs, as well as transitory states such as hysteria or concussion.[96] The status of *alcoholism* is problematic. Where a history of alcoholism produces an independent and recognised pathological condition, it seems that this may form the foundation of an insanity defence.[97] On this basis, both delirium tremens and alcohol withdrawal psychosis have successfully underpinned claims to the defence.[98] However, it is not clear whether alcoholism per se, together with states of intoxication resulting from it, can form the basis of insanity. In practice, even though a state of "sober alcoholism" might amount to a disease of the mind if it is sufficiently chronic, particularly if accompanied by brain damage, such a condition is unlikely ever to be sufficiently severe to raise the insanity defence because alcoholism alone is unlikely to impair a defendant's cognitive functions to such a degree that he is incapable of understanding the nature and quality of his acts or of knowing that they are wrong.[99] Tolmie suggests that if alcoholism is analysed as a disease, then not only can an alcoholic's state of mind be viewed as abnormal but, also, his intoxication may in principle fall within the ambit of his mental condition as a symptom of it.[100] Analysing alcoholism as a disease may be contrasted with the "habit" model of alcoholism, which, if it were adopted, would leave little scope for alcoholism to provide a foundation for an insanity defence.

---

94   Gunn and Taylor, *Forensic Psychiatry: Clinical, Legal and Ethical Issues*, Oxford, Butterworth Heinemann, 1993, 54.
95   Allen, *Textbook on Criminal Law*, London, Butterworths, 1991, 106.
96   Greenspan (ed), *Martin's Annual Criminal Code 1997*, Aurora, Ontario, Canada Law Book Co, 1996, cc/48.
97   See Tolmie, "Alcoholism and criminal liability" [2001] MLR 688, 703.
98   *R v Davis* (1881) 14 Cox CC 563; *R v Kina* 23/5/96 (NSW SC). See Tolmie, "Alcoholism and criminal liability" [2001] MLR 688, 703.
99   Tolmie, "Alcoholism and criminal liability" [2001] MLR 688, 703-704.
100 Tolmie, "Alcoholism and criminal liability" [2001] MLR 688, 704.

Concussion might qualify as a disease of the mind if it was associated with an enduring brain injury which caused the offender to act irrationally at the relevant time. Similarly, in *R v Kemp*,[101] where the accused, in an entirely motiveless attack, struck his wife with a hammer severely injuring her, it was held that arteriosclerosis, from which he suffered and which caused a restriction of the flow of blood to his brain producing a temporary loss of consciousness, was a disease of the mind for the purpose of the insanity defence. In that case Lord Devlin made the following important observation:[102]

> "The law is not concerned with the brain but with the mind, in the sense that 'mind' is ordinarily used, the mental faculties of reason, memory and understanding. If one read for 'disease of the mind' 'disease of the brain', it would follow that in many cases pleas of insanity would not be established because it could not be proved that the brain had been affected in any way, either by degeneration of the cells or in any other way."

This recognises the fact that while psychiatry may, for classification and therapeutic purposes, distinguish between *functional* and *organic* mental "diseases",[103] these distinctions are of no consequence for legal purposes, because the law's concern is not with the origin of the disease or the cause of it but simply with the mental condition that has brought about the act.[104]

The decision in *Kemp* may be compared with the case of *R v Charlson*.[105] In the latter case a father, without any provocation or motive, struck his 10-year-old son with a mallet and threw him out of a window. The defence was non-insane automatism. Insanity was not raised as a defence, although medical evidence revealed a possibility that the accused had a brain tumour which, if it existed, could have caused an outburst of impulsive violence over which he would have no control. The jury followed the judge's direction that unless they were satisfied, when he struck his son, that the accused was acting consciously knowing what he was doing, they should return a verdict of "Not guilty", and acquitted him. The case turned on the fact that it had not been "given in evidence"[106] that the accused was insane; indeed, the evidence of the only medical witness was that he was sane. Clearly, the case turned on its own facts and should not be taken as any authority that a cerebral tumour can never be a disease of the mind. Had there been probative evidence going beyond mere speculation that the accused did suffer from a brain tumour, it would have been open to Barry J to conclude that he was suffering from a disease of the mind such that at the time of the assault he did not know what he was doing.

In *R v Sullivan*,[107] which also involved an unprovoked and apparently motiveless attack on an innocent victim, the issue was whether psychomotor epilepsy constituted a disease of the mind for the purpose of determining whether the accused could rely on a defence of "non-insane"

---

101 *R v Kemp* [1957] 1 QB 399; [1956] 3 All ER 249 (CA).
102 *R v Kemp* [1957] 1 QB 399; [1956] 3 All ER 249 (CA), 407; 253.
103 In fact, modern psychiatry knows nothing of the concept of mental "disease" as such, but does distinguish between functional and organic mental psychoses — psychological or behavioural abnormalities associated with serious mental dysfunction. See *Bratty v A-G for Northern Ireland* [1963] AC 386; [1961] 3 All ER 523 (HL), 412; 534, where Lord Denning noted that the *major* mental diseases (psychoses), such as schizophrenia, are "clearly" diseases of the mind.
104 *Bratty v A-G for Northern Ireland* [1963] AC 386; [1961] 3 All ER 523 (HL).
105 *R v Charlson* [1955] 1 All ER 859; [1955] 1 WLR 317.
106 As required by s 2 Trial of Lunatics Act 1883 (UK), as amended by s 1 Criminal Procedure (Insanity) Act 1964 (UK). The phrase "appears in evidence" also occurs in s 113(3) Criminal Justice Act 1985, as a condition of the provision allowing a judge to direct a jury to consider the question of insanity.
107 *R v Sullivan* [1984] 1 AC 156; [1983] 2 All ER 673 (HL).

automatism. The accused, apparently in the post-ictal phase of a petit mal seizure, had struck the elderly victim and knocked him to the ground and then proceeded to kick him about the head and body, causing him severe injuries. Lord Diplock, with whom the other Law Lords agreed, concluded that psychomotor epilepsy was a disease of the mind constituting insanity because it impaired the mental faculties of reason, memory, and understanding to the extent that the sufferer did not know what he was doing.[108] Provided such a disease subsists at the time of the commission of the act, it does not matter whether the origin of the impairment is organic, as in epilepsy, or functional; or whether the impairment itself is permanent, or transient, or intermittent.[109]

One suggested means of identifying a disease of the mind is to ask: is it a mental disease which has "manifested itself in violence" and is it "prone to recur"? This test was first formulated by Lord Denning in *Bratty v A-G for Northern Ireland*.[110] It has, however, been criticised as being "ill considered"[111] and possibly too sweeping.[112] The difficulty with this test is that it appears to exclude mental diseases which manifest in ways that do not include violence, such as pyromania or kleptomania, and fails to recognise that some conditions which manifest themselves in violence may not legally be diseases of the mind.[113] However, Lord Diplock's statement in *R v Sullivan* that the purpose of the legislation relating to the defence of insanity "has been to protect society against the recurrence of dangerous conduct"[114] has been judicially interpreted as endorsing the consideration of recurrence as a relevant if non-determinative factor in the insanity inquiry.[115] The danger of recurrence has also been approved recently by the English Court of Appeal as an "added reason" for categorising sleepwalking as a disease of the mind.[116] Perhaps the proper conclusion to draw from this discussion is that while recurrence is one of a number of policy factors to be considered in the disease of the mind inquiry, the absence of a danger of recurrence will not automatically exclude the possibility of a finding of insanity.[117]

(3)   *"Internal v external cause" test*

At the same time, some conditions which do manifest themselves in violence may not fall within the definition of disease of the mind. This is because of a distinction recognised at law between "external" and "internal" causes when determining the existence of legal insanity. A temporary mental aberration may be caused by some factor "external" to the accused. This could include a blow on the head, consumption of alcohol or drugs, absorption of an anaesthetic, hypnotism, hypoglycaemia, or delirium produced by the toxins of infection.[118] In

---

108   Lord Diplock stated that the expression "He did not know what he was doing" was a more apt way to explain to a jury the expression in the M'Naghten Rules "as not to know the nature and quality of the act he was doing", which may also be taken to include the case of a person who does an act while unconscious: R v Sullivan [1984] 1 AC 156; [1983] 2 All ER 673 (HL), 173; 678. See also the discussion on this point in R v Cottle [1958] NZLR 999 (CA), 1009.
109   R v Sullivan [1984] 1 AC 156; [1983] 2 All ER 673 (HL), 173; 678.
110   Bratty v A-G for Northern Ireland [1963] AC 386; [1961] 3 All ER 523 (HL).
111   Allen, *Textbook on Criminal Law*, London, Butterworths, 1991, 107.
112   *Adams*, CA23.09 (looseleaf).
113   Allen, *Textbook on Criminal Law*, London, Butterworths, 1991, 107.
114   R v Sullivan [1984] 1 AC 156; [1983] 2 All ER 673 (HL), 172; 678.
115   R v Parks (1992) 95 DLR (4th) 27; [1992] 2 SCR 871 (SCC), 50; 906 (La Forest J).
116   See R v Burgess [1991] 2 QB 92; [1991] 2 All ER 769 (CA), 99; 774.
117   R v Parks (1992) 95 DLR (4th) 27; [1992] 2 SCR 871 (SCC), 50; 906 (La Forest J).
118   R v Rabey (1977) 79 DLR (3d) 414; 37 CCC (2d) 461.

such cases, the aberrant mental state is properly regarded as externally *imposed* upon the offender's otherwise normal and rational mental state. Accordingly, any act committed while in that state would be treated as involuntary for the purposes of criminal responsibility and would lead to an unqualified acquittal. An offender would be said to have been acting as a "sane" automaton. Such mental states are distinguishable from those contemplated by the phrase "disease of the mind", which uniformly embraces mental or bodily disorders endemic to the physical or psychological make-up of the offender herself which affect the balance of her mind and/or produce a state of automatism. Because these states of mental aberration arise from within the individual herself and are unrelated to any external causality, they are referred to as "internal" causes. In this regard the concepts of insanity and automatism merge, and a person so afflicted would be detained subject to the special verdict of "not guilty by reason of insanity". This is so even if her actions were done in an automatic state (a case of "insane automatism").

The gravamen of "internal" causes is that the malfunction or abnormality of the mind arises from some cause *within the individual herself*, and has its source in the person's psychological or emotional make-up, or in some organic pathology. Included within the concept of an "internal cause" are purely functional disorders which, so far as is currently known, have no physical cause. Generally speaking, any malfunctioning of the mind which has its source primarily in some subjective condition or weakness that is internal to the accused (whether or not it is fully understood) may be a disease of the mind.

Because it cannot be limited to a clinical model of mental illness, the concept of "disease of the mind" is capable of extension by the courts. The types of mental disorder it embraces have never been closed. It certainly includes medically recognised mental disorder or mental illness, but may also embrace subjective states of mind that would not normally be associated with mental disorder or illness. This may be because the notion of legal insanity serves public policy goals other than therapy. The case of *Rabey v R*[119] illustrates the point. The accused had struck a fellow student with a rock after he became aware that she thought little of him. Psychiatric evidence was given that the act was involuntary and was done while the accused was in a state of dissociation caused by a "psychological blow" following discovery of the young woman's rejection of him. A majority of the Supreme Court of Canada, while rejecting the accused's claim of *sane* automatism, acknowledged that transient disorders caused by "specific external factors" are not within the concept of disease of the mind:[120]

> "Any malfunctioning of the mind or mental disorder having its source primarily in some subjective condition or weakness internal to the accused (whether fully understood or not) may be 'a disease of the mind' if it prevents the accused from knowing what he is doing, but transient disturbances of consciousness due to certain specific external factors do not fall within the concept of disease of the mind."

The Court held that the notion of an "external factor" did not apply to a case like the present one where dissociation resulted from "the ordinary stresses and disappointments of life which are the common lot of mankind". Such a condition, including the claimed dissociation, was to be considered as having its source principally in the accused's psychological or emotional make-up and was to be regarded as a disease of the mind. However, Dickson J, in his dissenting

---

119 *Rabey v R* (1980) 15 CR (3d) 225; [1980] 2 SCR 513 (SCC).
120 *Rabey v R* (1980) 15 CR (3d) 225; [1980] 2 SCR 513 (SCC), 233; 519.

judgment, suggests that proof of a disease of the mind would normally require evidence of an "underlying pathological condition *which points to a disease requiring detention and treatment*".[121] For the reasons discussed above, we suggest that this represents an incorrect view of the role played by the disease of the mind concept, and confuses the requirement of therapy, which may be an *outcome* of an insanity plea, with legal responsibility and public protection, arguably the principal rationales for the rule.

A point of some interest is whether or not "disease of the mind" includes personality disorders. There does not appear to be a clear view on this. On one view, personality or behavioural disorders classified as "psychopathy" or "neuroses" will not suffice.[122] Other writers suggest that severe personality disorders may be included because they are regarded as functional psychoses.[123] The real issue is simply whether there is medical evidence that the condition should be regarded as a mental illness, regardless whether the defence is able to satisfy the additional tests in s 23(2).[124] Because the notion of insanity serves social and legal purposes quite distinct from other legal standards of mental disorder and capacity, the attitudes of clinicians to personality disorder in other mental health contexts should not determine its acceptability in this context. It is ultimately for the courts to determine whether it qualifies as mental disease, and for the tribunal of fact to decide whether it affected the accused's mental capacity in a relevant way.

(4) *Automatism*

The distinction between "internal" and "external" causes has become critical for courts in relation to claims that the accused was acting as an automaton at the relevant time. Automatism, which, like "disease of the mind", is a legal rather than a medical concept, signifies "action without conscious volition" or an act "which is done by the muscles without any control by the mind".[125] Where the defence of automatism is raised by a defendant, two questions must be decided by the judge before the defence can be left to the jury. The first is whether a proper evidential foundation for the defence of automatism has been laid. The second is whether the evidence shows the case to be one of insane automatism, ie whether it is a case which falls within the M'Naghten Rules, or one of non-insane automatism. As we have noted, cases do periodically arise where the issue of insanity is closely linked to a claim that the offender had acted without conscious awareness, and the main medico-legal question concerns what *caused* the state of altered consciousness. Automatism caused by disease of the mind is subsumed under the insanity defence and will ultimately lead to the special verdict of not guilty on account of insanity.[126] It is often described as "insane" automatism. On the other hand, where automatism is produced by concussion or the consumption of drugs, it may be characterised as "non-insane" or "sane" automatism and constitutes a complete defence to a charge.

The principal cases of non-insane automatism which have been considered by the courts include concussion, and situations where a person has experienced involuntary intoxication

---

121 *Rabey v R* (1980) 15 CR (3d) 225; [1980] 2 SCR 513 (SCC), 260; 552 (emphasis added).
122 See Williams, *CLGP*, paras 146, 170 and 171.
123 See Greenspan (ed), *Martin's Annual Criminal Code 1997*, Aurora, Ontario, Canada Law Book Co, 1996, cc/ 48; also Allen, *Textbook on Criminal Law*, London, Butterworths, 1991, 106.
124 *Adams*, CA23.08 (looseleaf).
125 *Bratty v A-G for Northern Ireland* [1963] AC 386; [1961] 3 All ER 523 (HL). See 3.4.
126 Section 20(1) CP(MIP)A.

due to drugs administered medically.[127] However, there are two additional areas where major difficulties have arisen. They concern, first, the problem of diabetes leading to either *hypoglycaemia* (low blood sugar caused by excessive insulin) or *hyperglycaemia* (elevated blood sugar caused by a failure to take insulin) and, secondly, the case of sleepwalking.

(a) Diabetic automatism

R v Quick[128] concerned a diabetic man who, while employed as a charge nurse, committed an assault upon a disabled patient. At the time of the assault he was suffering from hypoglycaemia caused by his failure to eat and subsequent deficiency of blood sugar. The trial judge ruled that the defence of automatism amounted to a plea of insanity, whereupon Q, not wanting to put forward a defence of insanity, changed his plea to one of guilty. In quashing his conviction, the Court of Appeal ruled that because the appellant's mental condition was not caused by his diabetes "but by his use of the insulin prescribed by his doctor" such malfunctioning of the mind as there was was caused by an *external* factor and not by a bodily disorder in the nature of a disease which disturbed the working of his mind.[129] The Court concluded that he was entitled to have his defence of non-insane automatism left to the jury.

In contrast to this case is the decision in *R v Hennessy*.[130] H, also a diabetic, was charged with taking a conveyance without authority and driving while disqualified. At his trial, he attempted to raise a defence of non-insane automatism. However, the trial judge ruled that any impairment of the appellant's mind could not have been caused by anything but diabetes, a disease. H then changed his plea to guilty and was sentenced to imprisonment for 9 months. Dismissing the appeal against conviction, the Court of Appeal agreed with the trial judge. It held that hyperglycaemia caused by an inherent defect (diabetes), and not corrected by insulin, is a disease; and if it does cause a malfunction of the mind, the case falls within the M'Naghten Rules. This means, in effect, that automatism in a case involving hyperglycaemia is attributable to an "internal" cause and for legal purposes is treated as insanity.

The use of the "internal/external cause" test to distinguish insanity from automatism has been described as "fatuous"[131] and, it is suggested, may cause ordinary people to regard with incredulity those decisions which endorse the distinction — contrary to the warning of Lawton LJ in *Quick* that "the law should not give the words 'defect of reason from disease of the mind' a meaning that would be regarded with incredulity outside a court".[132] Allen asks:[133]

> "Is the distinction between a diabetic in hyperglycaemic coma and one in hypoglycaemic coma so marked in its dangers, consequences and risk of recurrence that the former should be found insane while the latter goes free?"

The answer is clearly "no", yet the distinction is upheld by the courts. We cannot escape the fact that both hypoglycaemia and hyperglycaemia are conditions derivative of the same medical disease, namely diabetes. The only basis of the differing policy approach to the cases is the

---

127 See, for example, *R v King* (1962) 35 DLR (2d) 386; [1962] SCR 746 (SCC).
128 *R v Quick* [1973] 1 QB 910; [1973] 3 All ER 347 (CA).
129 *R v Quick* [1973] 1 QB 910; [1973] 3 All ER 347 (CA), 923; 356.
130 *R v Hennessy* [1989] 2 All ER 9; [1989] 1 WLR 287 (CA).
131 See Allen, *Textbook on Criminal Law*, London, Butterworths, 1991, 107.
132 Allen, *Textbook on Criminal Law*, London, Butterworths, 1991, 107. See *R v Quick* [1973] 1 QB 910; [1973] 3 All ER 347 (CA), 919; 353 (Lawton LJ).
133 Allen, *Textbook on Criminal Law*, London, Butterworths, 1991, 109.

occurrence, at different stages of the disease's progression, of low blood sugar as opposed to low insulin. It seems problematic, to say the least, that important legal consequences should turn upon such serendipitous medical episodes. It is enough to observe that the hypoglycaemic (non-insane) automaton one day could become a hyperglycaemic (insane) automaton the next, depending simply upon his failure to take or, alternatively, over-absorption of insulin.[134]

On the other hand, while it seems that a more medically and legally appropriate means of dealing with the problem of hyperglycaemic automatism is called for, it is not at all clear what the solution to the problem should be. A possible answer would be legislatively to declare all diabetes-related automatisms to be the result of (say) "external" causes, thus eliminating, for legal purposes, the distinction between *hyper*glycaemia and *hypo*glycaemia. However, an objection to this solution might be that it unfairly discriminates against other automatistic actors who also suffer from organic disorders but which have been characterised as "internal" causes. Another possible solution is to do nothing, on the basis that cases of diabetic automatism are rare and that any unfairness resulting from the attribution of a diabetic condition as an "internal" cause can be dealt with by dispositional solutions that restrict the offender's freedom to the least extent possible.

(b)   Sleepwalking and automatism

Another area of current difficulty concerns the correct characterisation of sleepwalking (somnambulism) as a defence to crime. Traditionally, people who committed offences while asleep were entitled to an unqualified acquittal provided there was no evidence of a condition which could be regarded as a disease.[135] In *Bratty v A-G for Northern Ireland* Lord Denning considered that sleepwalking should be treated in the same way as concussion:[136]

> "No act is punishable if it is done involuntarily: and an involuntary act in this context — some people nowadays prefer to speak of it as 'automatism' — means an act which is done by the muscles without any control by the mind such as a spasm, a reflex action or a convulsion; or an act done by a person who is not conscious of what he is doing such as an act done whilst suffering from concussion *or whilst sleepwalking.*"

Such dicta in this and other decisions clearly characterise violence in sleepwalking as illustrations of non-insane automatism. However, in *R v Burgess*,[137] the English Court of Appeal held that the case of violence occurring during a sleepwalking episode amounted to insanity under the M'Naghten Rules and was not sane automatism. The Court held that the accused, who had struck the victim on the head with a video recorder while unconscious and sleepwalking, was to be treated as though insane because medical evidence suggested that the

---

134 For a more comprehensive discussion of the problems with the insane/non-insane automatism distinction, see Padfield, "Exploring a quagmire: Insanity and automatism" [1989] 48 CLJ 354, 354-355. See also McDonald, "Acquittal for the intoxicated automaton?" [1993] NZLJ 44, 46.
135 See *R v Tolson* (1889) 23 QBD 168; [1886-90] All ER Rep 26, 187; 37, where Stephen J said: "can any one doubt that a man who, though he might be perfectly sane, committed what would otherwise be a crime in a state of somnambulism, would be entitled to be acquitted? And why is this? Simply because he would not know what he was doing."
136 *Bratty v A-G for Northern Ireland* [1963] AC 386; [1961] 3 All ER 523 (HL), 409; 532 (emphasis added). See also Viscount Kilmuir LC, who opined (403; 528) "[where] a defence of insanity is raised unsuccessfully [there may be] ... room for an alternative defence based on automatism. For example, [if] ... the accused ... was a sleep-walker."
137 *R v Burgess* [1991] 2 QB 92; [1991] 2 All ER 769 (CA).

sleepwalking was an abnormality resulting from an internal factor which, although transitory, might recur. The appellant had stated that he and the victim had fallen asleep on the evening of the alleged assault and that when he awoke he felt confused, realising at the same time that he was holding the victim down on the floor. He claimed he did not recall hitting the victim and argued that, because he was sleepwalking when he attacked her, he was suffering from non-insane automatism and accordingly, lacked the mens rea for the offence. In dismissing the appeal, the Court agreed that sleep was a normal condition. However, it was satisfied, on the basis of the medical evidence presented, that in this case the appellant was suffering from a sleep *disorder* which was an abnormality of the brain function and could properly be regarded as a pathological condition. As such it was an internal factor, and because the disorder had manifested itself in violence, and even though the recurrence of serious violence was unlikely, the trial judge had been right to direct the jury that the defence was one of insanity. Even if, as the prosecution medical witness had opined, this was not a case of sleepwalking but a case of *hysterical dissociation* (where for psychological reasons, such as being overwhelmed with his emotions, a person's brain works in a different way), the disorder would still have been treated as an internal cause with the consequential features of an insanity verdict.

However, the decision in *Burgess* is open to criticism. It has been argued that the judges' reasoning on the issue whether B suffered from a disease of the mind was flawed,[138] because in claiming to have adopted the definition of "disease of the mind" put forward by Lord Denning in *Bratty*, there was no evidence upon which it could be properly concluded that B suffered from a mental disorder or illness of any kind.[139] In reality, all that was established was that B had suffered from some sort of transitory abnormality of the brain function; and because the evidence fell far short of a disorder that was "prone to recur", it is argued that their Lordships were wrong to conclude that B suffered from a disease of the mind, and the issue of insanity should have ended there.[140] To the extent that the Court was concerned to pursue a social defence policy, it was unnecessary to do so, because this was not the sort of case where the accused should be detained in hospital in order to protect the public.[141]

Burgess contrasts with the decision in *R v Parks*.[142] The appellant in *Parks*, while asleep, had driven 23 km and then killed his mother-in-law by stabbing and beating her, and seriously injured his father-in-law. The defence of automatism was left to the jury, on the basis of a direction that if the jury decided that the appellant was in a state of somnambulism at the time of the killing, he was entitled to be acquitted on the basis of non-insane automatism. The Ontario Court of Appeal found the case very troubling but dismissed the Crown's appeal against P's acquittal.

In the Supreme Court of Canada, on a further appeal by the Crown against the acquittals, it was held that sleepwalking was a common disorder in children, occasionally found in adults, which involved no neurological, psychiatric, or other illness and which was not treatable. It did not arise from a disease of the mind and, therefore, entitled the accused to a complete acquittal. While the uncontradicted evidence was that the respondent's faculties of reason, memory, and understanding were impaired at the relevant time, there was no evidence that

---

138 Mackay, "The sleepwalker is not insane" [1992] 55 MLR 714.
139 Mackay, "The sleepwalker is not insane" [1992] 55 MLR 714, 717.
140 Mackay, "The sleepwalker is not insane" [1992] 55 MLR 714, 718.
141 Mackay, "The sleepwalker is not insane" [1992] 55 MLR 714.
142 *R v Parks* (1990) 56 CCC (3d) 449 (Ont CA).

this was because he was suffering from any illness. P's awareness of his actions was impaired (ie he was unconscious) because he was asleep, not because his sleep was disordered. It could not be said, therefore, that there was a causal connection between the impairment of P's faculties and the sleep disorder, and thus his inability to know what he was doing could not be due to a "disease of the mind". The Court found that sleep impairs the human mind and its functioning, but cannot be called an illness, disorder, or abnormal condition because it is a perfectly normal condition.

However, it has been observed that *Parks* is "more striking for its unusual facts than for its advancement of the law".[143] It is not easy to discern the clear basis of the Court's reasoning. For example, Lamer CJC concluded that, because sleep was the cause of the accused's mental state and is a normal condition, P did not suffer from a disease of the mind. His Lordship then stated that for there to be a finding to the contrary, the record would need to disclose evidence that sleepwalking was the cause of the respondent's state of mind which, he concluded, was not the case with P. Yet he intimated that sleepwalking might be a disease of the mind "in another case on different evidence",[144] although the Court did not give any indication what evidence might lead to the classification of sleepwalking as a disease of the mind. Furthermore, La Forest J appears to reject the internal/external cause criterion as a universal approach to the disease of the mind inquiry, and relegates it the status of an analytical tool rather than an all-encompassing methodology.[145] Again, no clear alternative analysis is offered in the judgment.

Some of the uncertainty created by *Parks* and the cases that preceded it has been addressed by the decision of the Supreme Court of Canada in *R v Stone*,[146] which establishes that in future only in the most exceptional of cases will an outright acquittal result from a finding that an accused person has committed criminal acts while sleepwalking. In *Stone*, Bastarache J, writing for the majority, defines automatism as "a state of impaired consciousness, rather than unconsciousness, in which an individual, though capable of action, has no voluntary control over that action".[147] Thus his Honour concluded that "voluntariness, rather than consciousness, is the key legal element in automatistic behaviour since a defence of automatism amounts to a denial of the voluntariness component of the actus reus."[148] Non-mental-disorder automatism is defined in a derivative fashion, as "involuntary behaviour which does not stem from disease of the mind",[149] and results in the acquittal of the accused: mental disorder automatism, which is caused by a disease of the mind, comes within the scope of the insanity defence.

The analysis in *Stone* completely recasts the approach to be taken by trial judges to automatism in Canada. The approach involves a reconsideration of issues of burden of proof and prescribes a two-step approach for judges to follow whenever the defence raises automatism. Essentially,

---

143 Grant and Spitz, "Case comment: *R v Parks*" (1993) 72 Can Bar Rev 224.
144 *R v Parks* (1992) 95 DLR (4th) 27; [1992] 2 SCR 871 (SCC), 40; 891.
145 *R v Parks* (1992) 95 DLR (4th) 27; [1992] 2 SCR 871 (SCC), 47; 902.
146 *R v Stone* [1999] 2 SCR 290; (1999) 134 CCC (3d) 353 (SCC). The accused had stabbed his wife numerous times after she had verbally insulted and criticised him. He claimed to have been overcome by a "whooshing" sensation, after which he had no recollection of the events which then transpired. When the sensation had passed he looked down and saw his wife slumped over, dead, and a knife in his own hand.
147 *R v Stone* [1999] 2 SCR 290; (1999) 134 CCC (3d) 353 (SCC), 367; 417.
148 *R v Stone* [1999] 2 SCR 290; (1999) 134 CCC (3d) 353 (SCC), para 170.
149 *R v Stone* [1999] 2 SCR 290; (1999) 134 CCC (3d) 353 (SCC), 369; 418.

the court is required to presume that a person has acted voluntarily. The onus lies on the accused to establish, on the balance of probabilities, that she acted involuntarily.

This "presumptive" approach to the disease of the mind inquiry requires trial judges to start "from the proposition that the condition the accused claims to have suffered from is a disease of the mind".[150] Only after beginning their analysis with this proposition are trial judges permitted to "determine whether the evidence in the particular case takes the condition out of the disease of the mind category".[151] Furthermore, Bastarache J specifies a "holistic approach" to the disease of the mind inquiry in cases involving automatism. This suggests that all relevant factors must be considered, including "internal cause", "continuing danger", and other policy considerations.[152]

A reading of *Stone* in the light of *Parks* and earlier cases on sleepwalking suggests that, in Canada at least, where an accused performs criminal acts while sleepwalking, prima facie the proper verdict is not guilty on grounds of mental disorder. It is likely that a verdict of outright acquittal will now be available only in the most exceptional of circumstances.[153]

The effect of these decisions on New Zealand law is unclear. Even though both *Burgess* and *Stone* suggest that somnambulistic automatism is typically insane automatism, it is difficult to reconcile the divergent approaches in these cases. Indeed, they illustrate how mental abnormality "defences" may be used to serve a variety of diverse and sometimes apparently contradictory social purposes, and to reflect significant differences in criminal justice values. Resolution of the difficulties in future cases may require a more accurate understanding of the underlying mental infirmity.

10.3.4 "Nature and quality" of the act or omission

If the disease of the mind or natural imbecility suffered by the accused is to be effective in establishing a defence of insanity, it must affect her responsibility by producing a relevant incapacity in one of the two ways specified in the Crimes Act 1961. Accordingly, the accused must prove that she was "incapable" *either* "of understanding the nature and quality of the act or omission; ... *or* of knowing that the act or omission was morally wrong having regard to the commonly accepted standards of right and wrong".[154]

(1) Incapable

Before examining the alternative elements of this test, it is necessary to say something concerning the threshold for a proven incapacity. Does "incapable of understanding" in s 23 imply a total or absolute inability to understand the relevant considerations, or is some lesser degree of incapacity sufficient? The issue was considered by the New South Wales Court of Criminal Appeal in *R v Cheatham*.[155] The accused had been convicted of murdering his wife and older daughter and of attempting to murder his infant daughter. He claimed that, at the time of the offences, he had been suffering from a hypochondriacal delusion or from a severe kind of melancholic depression, both of which were said to be diseases of the mind for the

---

150 *R v Stone* [1999] 2 SCR 290; (1999) 134 CCC (3d) 353 (SCC), 388; 433.
151 *R v Stone* [1999] 2 SCR 290; (1999) 134 CCC (3d) 353 (SCC).
152 *R v Stone* [1999] 2 SCR 290; (1999) 134 CCC (3d) 353 (SCC), 390; 434.
153 See *R v Campbell* (2000) Ont Sup CJ LEXIS 1180 16.
154 Section 23(2)(a) and (b) Crimes Act 1961.
155 *R v Cheatham* [2000] NSWCCA 282.

purposes of legal insanity. On appeal, the appellant argued that the trial judge had been wrong in directing the jury that, in order to excuse, they had to find that a disease of the mind must have "prevented the accused ... knowing that what he was doing was wrong"[156] or that he was "disabled from knowing that it was a wrong act to commit".[157] The appellant argued that the words "prevented" and "disabled" were too absolute, and that the true test was not a "total absence of knowledge of wrongness" but "difficulty with the reasoning process".[158]

In rejecting this submission, the Court held that a mere "difficulty" with reasoning processes is far too low a standard and that the words "incapable" and "quite incapable", used in earlier judicial formulations of the threshold test, had a degree of absoluteness that is properly implied in the language of "prevented" and "disabled". This suggests that the relevant threshold imposes a high standard of cognitive impairment, to a degree sufficient to eliminate an accused's capacity to reason coherently about the circumstances of the alleged offence. Generally, the fact that a person was merely excitable, lacking in self-control, or impulsive will be insufficient to establish a relevant incapacity.

Defendants with identity disorders are not necessarily incapable either. For example, in *R v Hamblyn*,[159] D suffered from dissociative identity disorder (sometimes referred to as multiple personality disorder). While this was, undoubtedly, a disease of the mind, it did not follow that the alter personalities, through whose agency the offences were committed, were legally insane for the purposes of s 23. They were still aware of the "nature and quality" or "wrongness" of the acts, even though this knowledge was kept from the consciousness of D's main, or host, personality. Accordingly, a defendant can be mentally diseased but criminally responsible.

(2) *Nature and quality*

In most jurisdictions the "nature and quality" of an act refers exclusively to the physical character of the act concerned.[160] It includes cases where the accused is not conscious of acting and situations where the accused is mistaken, through some delusional process, as to the character of the act he is doing. The phrase does not involve any consideration of the accused's moral perception, his knowledge of the moral quality of his act. To succeed under this limb it is necessary for the accused to prove that he did not know what he was doing, or did not appreciate the consequences of his act, or did not appreciate the circumstances in which he was acting.[161] Traditional, if unlikely, examples include someone's strangling the victim while believing he is squeezing a lemon, or cutting a person's throat believing he is slicing a loaf of bread. However, because, outside of an encapsulated delusional system,[162] an offender's logic and train of ideas are generally unimpaired, it is highly improbable that an offender could be so deluded as to fail to appreciate the essential character of conduct in the manner suggested by these traditional examples. The older texts are littered with bizarre examples of incapacity

---

156 *R v Cheatham* [2000] NSWCCA 282, para 8.
157 *R v Cheatham* [2000] NSWCCA 282, para 9.
158 *R v Cheatham* [2000] NSWCCA 282, para 13.
159 *R v Hamblyn* (1997) 15 CRNZ 58 (CA). For a useful critique, see Orchard, "Criminal responsibility for the other self" [1997] NZLJ 431.
160 *R v Codere* (1916) 12 Cr App R 21.
161 Allen, *Textbook on Criminal Law*, London, Butterworths, 1991, 110.
162 A technical term, indicating that apart from the delusion or its ramifications, the patient generally behaves in a normal manner.

to understand the nature and quality of the act, such as the person who cuts off a sleeper's head because "it would be great fun to see him looking for it when he woke up"[163] or the woman who put her child on the fire thinking she was putting on a log of wood. Perhaps these examples reflect the earlier perception that true insanity can only be found where the person was totally devoid of rational capacity. However, as we shall see, the demands of the present law are much less rigorous than this view would suggest.

Virtually all cases falling under the "nature and quality" limb involve (insane) automatism, where D's behaviour is not under his conscious control at all, rather than cases where D's behaviour is voluntary but misunderstood by him. Because this limb of the insanity test is concerned with the incapacity of the accused to appreciate the *physical* consequences of his act, an accused would be unable to rely on this limb of the insanity defence where, for example, he was aware that he was killing the victim and knew that killing was a crime, but believed that the victim was "Satan" and that in killing the deceased he was acting under divine orders.[164] (Such a case would fall under s 23(2)(b), covering "knowledge of … wrong".) In reality, a determination of insanity very seldom turns on whether the defendant understood the "nature and quality of his act". Apart from instances of automatism, in almost all litigated insanity cases, it is the second limb that is in dispute (ie whether the defendant knew the wrongfulness of the criminal act).

10.3.5 Knowledge of wrongfulness of act

Under the second "limb" of the insanity test a defendant must establish that she did not know that the act was wrong. Historically, there has been much debate over whether, in formulating the test in these terms, the judges intended to inquire into the defendant's knowledge of *legal* or *moral* wrong. Before the 1961 Act there was particular doubt about this because of earlier English authority which had held that "wrong" means contrary to law.[165] In *R v Windle*, W had been charged with murder when he killed his wife after having been coaxed by his workmate to "give her a dozen aspirin". He gave her 100. His wife was always talking of committing suicide and was certifiably insane. When he gave himself up to the police W said "I suppose they will hang me for this". At his trial evidence was led that W suffered from a form of communicated madness called folie a deux whereby if a person was in constant attendance of another person who was mentally ill in some way, insanity can be communicated to the attending person. Experts on both sides agreed that he knew that he was doing an act prohibited by the law, as a result of which the judge withdrew the issue of insanity from the jury and he was convicted.

On appeal to the Court of Appeal, Lord Goddard CJ held that it was not the function of a jury to determine whether a particular act was morally right or wrong and that the test of "wrong" in the M'Naghten Rules means *contrary to law*. Since the appellant knew what he was doing was contrary to law it was appropriate for the defence of insanity to be withdrawn from the jury. The appeal was dismissed.

Some years earlier in the case of *R v Porter*,[166] an Australian judge had directed a jury, in what has come to be regarded as a classic direction in this country, in the following terms:[167]

---
163 Stephen, *A History of the Criminal Law of England* vol II, London, Macmillan, 1883, 166.
164 Greenspan (ed), *Martin's Annual Criminal Code 1997*, Aurora, Ontario, Canada Law Book Co, 1996, cc/49.
165 See *R v Windle* [1952] 2 QB 826; [1952] 2 All ER 1 (CA).
166 *R v Porter* (1933) 55 CLR 182; [1936] ALR 438 (HCA), 189-190; 441 (Dixon J).

"We are not dealing with right or wrong in the abstract. The question is whether he was able to appreciate the wrongness of the particular act he was doing at the particular time. Could this man be said to know in this sense whether his act was wrong if through a disease or defect or disorder of the mind *he could not think rationally of the reasons which to ordinary people make that act right or wrong?* If through the disordered condition of the mind he could not reason about the matter with a moderate degree of sense and composure it may be said that he could not know what he was doing was wrong. What is meant by 'wrong'? *What is meant by wrong is wrong having regard to the everyday standards of reasonable people.*"

This approach to the meaning of "wrong" was later endorsed by the High Court of Australia in *Stapleton v R*.[168] Rejecting *Windle*, the Court held that in applying the second branch of the legal test of insanity in *M'Naghten's Case*, the question is "whether the accused knew that his act was wrong according to the ordinary principles of reasonable men, not whether he knew it was wrong as being contrary to law".[169]

This has always been the approach taken by New Zealand courts,[170] and in *R v Macmillan*[171] the Court of Appeal affirmed that what was intended by s 23(2)(b) was to adopt the *Stapleton* direction as appropriate in future trials in New Zealand.[172] The question of the meaning of "wrong" has been put beyond debate in New Zealand by the express language of the statute, which requires proof of knowledge that the act or omission was "*morally* wrong, having regard to the commonly accepted standards of right and wrong".[173] The meaning of the phrase was discussed at length in *Macmillan*. M, who suffered from paranoid schizophrenia, pleaded insanity to a charge of attempting to break out of Mt Eden jail. The essence of his defence was that he did not regard the act as wrong for him to do, although he would have known that people generally would regard it as wrong. At the trial, counsel for the prosecution argued that the inclusion in the statute of the words "having regard to the commonly accepted standards of right and wrong" signified the Legislature's intention to substitute an objective for a subjective standard by which to judge whether an act was morally wrong; a conclusion which, if pressed, would have meant that a large group of persons suffering from paranoia would have been excluded from the defence of insanity.[174]

In rejecting this approach, the Court held that in enacting the present section the Legislature did not intend to change the law as it was understood at the date of its enactment, but rather clearly to indicate its preference for the decision in *Stapleton* over *Windle*. The introduction of the word "morally" simply reflects this preference.[175] In other words, it seems that insanity will be established in New Zealand even where the accused perceived that the act was "morally wrong in the eyes of other people", if he thought the act was right himself, or thought that his own acts were "above judgment on moral standards".[176] The practical effect of this decision has been to affirm that the statutory test for insanity in New Zealand is based on a *subjective*

---

167 *R v Porter* (1933) 55 CLR 182; [1936] ALR 438 (HCA), 189-190; 441 (Dixon J).
168 *Stapleton v R* (1952) 86 CLR 358; [1952] ALR 929 (HCA).
169 *Stapleton v R* (1952) 86 CLR 358; [1952] ALR 929 (HCA). This quote is from the CLR headnote.
170 See *Murdoch v British Israel World Federation (NZ) Inc* [1942] NZLR 600 (CA), 630.
171 *R v Macmillan* [1966] NZLR 616 (CA), 622.
172 *R v Macmillan* [1966] NZLR 616 (CA), 622.
173 Section 23(2)(b) Crimes Act 1961 (emphasis added).
174 *R v Macmillan* [1966] NZLR 616 (CA), 620.
175 *R v Macmillan* [1966] NZLR 616 (CA), 621.

moral standard. This implies that an accused will not be criminally responsible for his acts if, as a result of mental disease, he believes he is morally justified in his behaviour even though he may have known that his acts were illegal and/or contrary to public standards of morality (ie that he would be condemned in the eyes of "right-thinking people").

Although the New Zealand approach has been criticised as being "directly contrary to the words of the Act",[177] it is clear that the Court in *Macmillan* was concerned to avoid an interpretation which would have excluded the defence from a significant class of persons who are clearly insane. The reason why this approach may now be accepted is that it conforms both with the way in which exculpatory insanity has been understood historically, and that it reflects sound common sense. No person should be convicted of a crime whose mind is so disordered that he is unable to make the moral judgments which, in "sane" people, enable them to live socially integrated lives and to choose conduct which conforms with both moral and legal norms. It is that capacity which is so radically lacking in an "insane" person. Indeed, it is difficult to imagine a class of persons less mentally equipped to perform such tasks than those diagnosed as paranoid schizophrenics — whether or not they comprehend the applicable law.

What constitutes a relevant lack of mental "composure" for the purposes of legal insanity is a matter to be considered in the light of the facts of a particular case. There is no formula that can be applied. However, since the test approved in *Stapleton* requires only an ability to reason about a matter with a "moderate" degree of sense and composure, it would seem that not every degree of mental perturbation or upset is necessarily an indication of a relevantly disordered mind. In *Macmillan*[178] the Court indicated that the fact that an accused may have methodically and logically planned a crime, such that there was "method in his madness", was not necessarily inconsistent with insanity "but might in fact support it".[179] However, a lack of "appropriate feelings", as in the case of a psychopath who kills a person but lacks a normal person's emotional and affective appreciation of the wrongness of the act, will not secure an insanity acquittal where the psychopath has an intellectual awareness that his act is wrong.[180] What is normally required is that the accused acted "in a state of frenzy, uncontrolled emotion, or suspended reason".[181] The defence will fail if the evidence merely establishes an "absence of moral inhibition, restraint, or conscience" falling short of a state of suspended reason.[182] Therefore if, because of a disease of the mind, D is unable to restrain himself from killing V because he is subject to an emotional impulse which he cannot control (a so-called "irresistible impulse") but, nevertheless, understands the nature of his act and that it is morally wrong, he would not be able to take advantage of the insanity defence.[183] Provided a person's cognitive processes are functioning at a level sufficient to enable the accused to grasp the nature and wrongfulness of his act, the fact that his emotional and volitional capacities are abnormal will not detract from the judgment that he was legally sane.[184]

---

176 *R v Macmillan* [1966] NZLR 616 (CA), 622. There is some evidence that, even in England, "wrongness" is being interpreted in psychiatric reports in a manner consistent with "common sense folk psychology" approaches. This may, it seems, effectively have expanded the scope of the Rules in that jurisdiction: Mackay and Kearns, "More fact(s) about the insanity defence" [1999] Crim LR 714.
177 *Adams* (2nd ed), para 418.
178 *R v Macmillan* [1966] NZLR 616 (CA), 625.
179 *R v Macmillan* [1966] NZLR 616 (CA), 625.
180 See *Willgoss v R* (1960) 105 CLR 295 (HCA).
181 *Willgoss v R* (1960) 105 CLR 295 (HCA), 301.
182 *R v Brown* [1968] SASR 467, 475.
183 See Gillies, *Criminal Law* (1st ed), Sydney, The Law Book Company, 1985, 177.

This is a further indication of the fact that the insanity defence is grounded in an exclusively cognitive model of rational capacity to know right and wrong and is largely unconcerned with disorders which have their impact principally upon the will or the emotions. Whether this is fair may well be debated, although there is insufficient space to do so here. Yet it is apt at this point to highlight a need for further discussion on how best to accommodate, within the criminal justice system, those offenders who are not insane in this narrow sense yet who suffer from mental abnormalities which impair their ability to conform to the law's requirements.

10.3.6 Insanity and strict liability

The question whether insanity is available on a charge of strict liability does not appear to have been considered judicially in New Zealand. However, in *MOT v Strong*,[185] it was held that the defence of automatism is available only to charges in which "intent" is an ingredient. Sinclair J ruled that automatism is no defence to a charge of driving a motor vehicle while under the influence of drink or drugs because mens rea is not an element of the offence. This view has been challenged as "controversial".[186] The prevailing view in New Zealand is that where the offence is a public welfare regulatory offence of strict liability, the defence of automatism *is* still available but that its operation has, in practice, been subsumed by the defence of absence of fault.[187] In principle, the same is true of insanity, despite contrary English authority in *DPP v H*[188] — which, like *Strong*, held that, since driving with excess alcohol is an offence of strict liability, the defence of insanity has no relevance. This decision has rightly been criticised. The essence of H's defence was that his state of manic-depressive psychosis was such that he did not know that drunken driving was either morally or legally wrong. Such knowledge is not part of the mens rea of any offence. Since, therefore, the "wrongness" limb of the insanity defence does not negate mens rea, it is nonsensical to say that it cannot apply where there is no mens rea to negate.[189] In line with this analysis, it is submitted that, so far as New Zealand law is concerned, insanity ought to be a defence to a strict liability offence.

In any event, since absence of fault is a defence to strict liability offences, proof of insanity would in effect also establish that the defendant is not morally culpable for the actus reus (because not a morally responsible agent); whereupon an acquittal should follow. As with automatism, the defendant would have the legal burden of proving insanity on the balance of probabilities.

10.3.7 Delusions

A delusion is an abnormality in the content of thought. Delusions, particularly persecutory and religious delusions, are commonly associated with the insanity defence and have been a feature of legal insanity throughout its history: for example, Daniel M'Naghten suffered from the delusion that he was being persecuted by Tories, while Edward Oxford, who in 1840 fired two pistols at Queen Victoria while she was travelling in her coach, suffered from the grandiose delusion that he was to be the instrument of a plot of an imaginary secret society.[190] In a more

---

184 Gillies, *Criminal Law* (1st ed), Sydney, The Law Book Company, 1985, 177. See also *Sodeman v R* (1936) 55 CLR 192; [1936] ALR 156 (HCA).
185 *MOT v Strong* [1987] 2 NZLR 295.
186 *Adams*, CA23.39 (looseleaf).
187 *Adams*, CA23.39 (looseleaf). See 4.5.
188 *DPP v H* [1997] 1 WLR 1406.
189 Ward, "Magistrates, insanity and the common law" [1997] Crim LR 796, 802.

recent case the accused shot and killed, without apparent motive, a young female friend because of a delusion that members of a local union had conspired to "destroy" him and that they had commissioned the victim to kill him.[191]

One of the questions posed to the judges in *M'Naghten's Case* concerned the liability of a person who, under an insane delusion about existing facts, commits an offence as a consequence of the delusion. The judges replied:[192]

> "the answer must, of course, depend on the nature of the delusion: but making the same assumption as we did before, namely, that he labours under such partial delusion only, and is not in other respects insane, we think he must be considered in the same situation as to responsibility as if the facts with respect to which the delusion exists were real. For example, if under the influence of his delusion he supposes another man to be in the act of attempting to take away his life, and he kills that man, as he supposes in self-defence, he would be exempt from punishment. If his delusion was that the deceased had inflicted a serious injury to his character and fortune, and he killed him in revenge for such supposed injury, he would be liable to punishment."

In some jurisdictions which follow the M'Naghten Rules, this supplementary rule regarding insane delusions has been retained. The effect is that a person will be responsible for an act committed under an insane delusion on the basis that the facts with respect to which the delusion exists were real. Although this rule still applies in the United Kingdom, it may be that it adds nothing to the Rules because the situation is already covered by the test relating to the nature and quality of the act.[193] In effect, the rule simply emphasises the fact that delusions which do not prevent D from having mens rea will not afford a defence.[194]

Various forms of this rule appear in the criminal legislation of Queensland, Western Australia, Northern Territory, and Tasmania. A similar version appeared in s 16(3) Criminal Code (Can) but was repealed in 1991 on the ground that it was superfluous.[195] The formulation as to insane delusions has been criticised as being far too mechanical to be capable of sensible application, and in any event does not appear to have been applied in any of the reported cases subsequent to *M'Naghten*.[196] Another criticism is that the rule concerning insane delusions is obsolete and outmoded in that it assumes that a person may be sane in every respect except for a specific delusion. It is suggested that this is faculty psychology at its worst.[197]

The rule has never been part of the law in New Zealand. The matter falls to be decided on ordinary principles. Thus the fact an accused knew that he was killing a person and that killing was wrong, while labouring under a delusion caused by mental disease, will not necessarily exclude him from the protection of the insanity defence. Indeed, under s 23(3) "insane delusions", whatever their character, may be evidence that the offender was mentally

---

190 Forshaw and Rollin, "The history of forensic psychiatry in England" in Bluglass and Bowden (eds), *Principles and Practice of Forensic Psychiatry*, Edinburgh, Churchill Livingstone, 1990, 84.
191 *R v Oommen* (1993) 21 CR (4th) 117 (CA).
192 *M'Naghten's Case* (1843) 10 Cl & Fin 200; 8 ER 718; [1843-60] All ER Rep 229 (HL), 211; 723; 234.
193 See Allen, *Textbook on Criminal Law*, London, Butterworths, 1991, 110; also Smith and Hogan, *Criminal Law* (7th ed), London, Butterworths, 1992, 203.
194 *Smith and Hogan*, 204.
195 *Chaulk v R* (1991) 62 CCC (3d) 193; (1990) 2 CR (4th) 1 (SCC).
196 Gillies, *Criminal Law* (1st ed), Sydney, The Law Book Company, 1985, 185.
197 O'Connor and Fairall, *Criminal Defences* (2nd ed), Sydney, Butterworths, 1988, 249.

irresponsible for his act or omission. The question, as always, is whether he is able to think *rationally* of the reasons which to ordinary people make his act right or wrong. However, in *R v Green*,[198] the New Zealand Court of Appeal expressed doubt whether delusions as to factual matters which, if true, would make an act morally justifiable, can by themselves be sufficient to show that a person is incapable of knowing that an act or omission is morally wrong. While acknowledging that there was some authority for a contrary view,[199] the Court concluded that ultimately the issue was one for the jury to decide. It is, nevertheless, of interest that in *R v Chaulk*[200] the Supreme Court of Canada was satisfied that such a person does not know and is incapable of knowing that the conduct is wrong in the circumstances.

10.3.8 Diminished responsibility

Diminished responsibility is a statutory defence in a number of Commonwealth jurisdictions including Barbados, Bahama, England, New South Wales, Queensland, and the Northern Territory. The defence in each jurisdiction is substantially the same and is based on the English defence defined in s 2 Homicide Act 1957 (UK). Diminished responsibility is only a defence to murder and may reduce what would otherwise be murder to manslaughter. The defence has never been part of New Zealand law, the view having been taken at the time the Crimes Act 1961 was passed that since there was no longer a death penalty in New Zealand there was no need for a separate diminished responsibility defence.[201] Its non-availability as a defence has been recently reaffirmed in a case where psychological evidence was admitted in support of the defence claim that the accused had arranged for her husband's murder while suffering from post-traumatic stress disorder, battered wife syndrome, and depression.[202] In *R v Gordon* the Court of Appeal held that sympathy for the appellant could not prevail over the current statutory provisions,[203] and that it was unable to accept expert testimony that the accused "had diminished responsibility because of her mental state at the time [of the offence]".[204] The Court did find, however, that where an accused person is suffering from an illness that might affect her responses or judgment, its consequences may be beyond the experience and knowledge of a jury, and so expert evidence may be adduced to show that those consequences may be such as to weaken or negate the inference of intent that could properly be drawn in the case of a normal person.[205] In such a case a jury might acquit, not on the grounds of diminished responsibility, but simply because it is not satisfied beyond a reasonable doubt that the accused possessed mens rea at the relevant time.

It may be argued that in New Zealand there is a "de facto" defence of diminished responsibility, which has been acknowledged by the courts but not yet endorsed by the Legislature. This

---

198 *R v Green* [1993] 2 NZLR 513; (1993) 9 CRNZ 523 (CA), 525; 535-536.
199 See *Murdoch v British Israel World Federation (NZ) Inc* [1942] NZLR 600 (CA).
200 *R v Chaulk* [1990] 3 SCR 1303; (1991) 62 CCC (3d) 193 (SCC), 1361-1362; 235-236. See also *R v Oommen* [1994] 2 SCR 507; (1994) 91 CCC (3d) 8 (SCC).
201 Brookbanks, "Diminished responsibility: Balm or bane" in Legal Research Foundation, *Movements and Markers in Criminal Policy*, Auckland, 1984, 30. More recently, the New Zealand Law Commission has rejected the idea of introducing a partial defence of diminished responsibility, arguing that such matters would be better dealt with through discretionary sentencing. See Law Commission, *Some Criminal Defences with Particular Reference to Battered Defendants*, NZLC R73, Wellington, 2001, paras 121-140.
202 *R v Gordon* (1993) 10 CRNZ 430 (CA).
203 *R v Gordon* (1993) 10 CRNZ 430 (CA), 441.
204 *R v Gordon* (1993) 10 CRNZ 430 (CA), 439.
205 *R v Gordon* (1993) 10 CRNZ 430 (CA), 437.

possibility was first alluded to by the Court of Appeal in *R v Aston*.[206] In that case, the respondent had been convicted of arson and manslaughter following an incident in which he had shot and killed the proprietor of a service station then set fire to the service station, a museum, and a private home. Under the legal guise of a provocation defence, psychiatric evidence was led at the trial that the respondent was suffering from paranoia at the time and had been provoked into losing his self-control by suggestions from the deceased that he was homosexual. It was accepted by the trial judge that the respondent's mental illness played a significant part in the crimes.

In surveying sentencing issues, the Court alluded to three Australian cases of manslaughter on the ground of diminished responsibility, observing that this was "in substance" the present case.[207] But, apart from additional comparisons drawn from other jurisdictions regarding the sentencing of persons who commit grave crimes while suffering from mental disorder, there is no further reference to a substantive diminished responsibility defence in the judgment. However, in *R v McCarthy*[208] the Court of Appeal suggested that the availability of diminished responsibility, while it has never been expressly accepted by a New Zealand Parliament, may nevertheless, within the limited field of the provocation defence, be seen as the "*inevitable and deliberate effect* of the statutory changes embodied in s 169 of the Crimes Act 1961".[209] The full implications of this concession are not yet entirely clear. Nonetheless, one may safely say that the judicial expansion of the scope of relevant "characteristics"[210] to include such matters as mental deficiency, or a tendency to excessive emotionalism as a result of brain injury,[211] as factors relevant to the determination whether murder should be reduced to manslaughter, clearly foreshadows the emergence of a type of diminished responsibility defence, albeit still under the banner of provocation.[212]

In those jurisdictions in which a diminished responsibility defence is currently available, the "abnormality of mind" which is essential to establish the defence need not be a generally recognised type of "insanity"[213], provided it is a state of mind so different from that of ordinary human beings that the reasonable man would term it abnormal.[214]

10.3.9 Irresistible impulse

Because diminished responsibility also extends to an accused's inability to exercise willpower to control physical acts in accordance with a rational judgment, it may be established where there is evidence that the accused acted under an irresistible impulse. Again, however, apart from the statutory provisions relating to infanticide in s 178 Crimes Act 1961 which arguably allow a limited form of diminished responsibility defence,[215] in New Zealand irresistible

---

206   *R v Aston* [1989] 2 NZLR 166; (1989) 4 CRNZ 241 (CA).
207   *R v Aston* [1989] 2 NZLR 166; (1989) 4 CRNZ 241 (CA), 170; 245.
208   *R v McCarthy* [1992] 2 NZLR 550; (1992) 8 CRNZ 58 (CA).
209   *R v McCarthy* [1992] 2 NZLR 550; (1992) 8 CRNZ 58 (CA), 558; 66 (emphasis added).
210   See s 169(2)(a) Crimes Act 1961. Within the statutory scheme a relevant "characteristic" may be added to the profile of an ordinary person in deciding whether some idiosyncratic personal trait may have made the offender more susceptible to a loss of self-control caused by provocation than if that characteristic had not been present. For detailed discussion see 16.5.1(5)(c).
211   *R v McCarthy* [1992] 2 NZLR 550; (1992) 8 CRNZ 58 (CA), 557; 65-66.
212   See also Brown, "Provocation: Characteristics, diminished responsibility and reform" in *Movements and Markers in Criminal Policy*, Auckland, Legal Research Foundation, 1984, 40.
213   *R v Rose* [1961] AC 496.
214   *R v Byrne* [1960] 2 QB 396; [1960] 3 All ER 1 (CA).

impulse is not a defence even if caused by disease of the mind. In *R v Deighton*[216] the accused was charged with the murder of his 3-month-old son. Although evidently fond of the child, the accused had become depressed at the state of his home and his wife's continual drunkenness. However, there was no evidence that he was suffering from any mental disease at the time. The only evidence was that, on the day in question, he may have become "excited" and formed a fixed idea to kill the child while claiming to suffer from an impulse which he could not control. In rejecting the defence of irresistible impulse, Stout CJ held that if the accused knew he was killing the child, and knew that it was wrong, he could not be acquitted on the ground of insanity. The other matters, including his fixed idea to kill his child, his wife, and himself, and the claimed impulse which he could not control, could not assist him.

It would seem, therefore, that the only circumstances in which an irresistible impulse may assist a defendant in New Zealand is where there is evidence that an irresistible impulse is a symptom of a mental disease sufficient to exclude knowledge of the physical or moral quality of the act, amounting to legal insanity.[217]

10.3.10 Role of expert evidence

Once a court has ruled on the question whether the particular disorder from which the accused suffered was a disease of the mind, it is for the jury to determine whether he was legally insane at the time of the commission of the offence. The courts have stated on numerous occasions that this function cannot be usurped by medical experts. In *R v Rotana*[218] the appellant had been convicted of the murder of his wife after he had struck her about the head with an axe. At the trial, evidence was given by two psychiatrists to the effect that he was suffering from a disease of the mind at the time of the killing, and although he knew the nature and quality of his actions, he was incapable of knowing they were morally wrong. The Crown did not call rebutting evidence, but extensively cross-examined the defence witnesses in order to provide another explanation for the killing. On appeal it was held that it was for the jury, not medical witnesses, to make a decision in such cases. The fact that the verdict is inconsistent with medical evidence given at the trial will not necessarily provide grounds for holding that a verdict is unreasonable. Nevertheless, the verdict must be based on evidence, and medical evidence which is supported by other relevant evidence cannot arbitrarily be put aside. While a jury may disagree with expert opinions, there has to be some rational basis for doing so, otherwise their decision amounts to an arbitrary substitution of their own view for what appears to be uncontradicted evidence from well qualified professionals.[219]

If, in an appeal against conviction, it "appears" to the Court of Appeal that the appellant was insane at the time of the commission of the offence and should have been acquitted on account of his insanity, the court may quash the conviction and substitute a special verdict of not guilty on account of insanity.[220] However, this procedure will only be adopted where the Court of Appeal is of the opinion that the jury's verdict was unreasonable and unable to be supported having regard to the evidence[221] — ie where the only available evidence points conclusively to

---

215 See 16.6.
216 *R v Deighton* (1900) 18 NZLR 891.
217 *A-G for the State of South Australia v Brown* [1960] AC 432; [1960] 1 All ER 734 (PC), 449-450; 742-743.
218 *R v Rotana* (1995) 12 CRNZ 650 (CA).
219 *R v Rotana* (1995) 12 CRNZ 650 (CA), 654-655.
220 Section 386(4).
221 Section 385(1)(a).

the fact that the accused was insane, particularly where the nature of the offence suggests an "insane driving force at work".[222] Such a case was *R v Clark*.[223] The accused had killed and mutilated the body of a middle-aged man in a motel lavatory. The victim's eyes had been torn out and he was cut or torn in the area of the testicles, although death was caused by strangulation. The unchallenged medical evidence from two psychiatrists suggested that the accused was suffering from schizophrenia and was legally insane at the time of the attack. In allowing the appeal against conviction for murder and substituting an insanity verdict, the Court of Appeal noted that, while a verdict inconsistent with medical evidence was not necessarily unreasonable, the verdict must still be founded on evidence. Where doctors' evidence on insanity is not only unchallenged but also actually receives support from the surrounding facts, it cannot be rejected. In such circumstances an insanity verdict is unavoidable.[224]

This does not mean a jury may never challenge expert psychiatric testimony. A jury must weigh expert evidence as it weighs the probative value of other evidence. It is entitled, when doing so, to examine the factual foundations of expert opinions and is entitled to afford less weight to an opinion where it is not based on facts proved at trial and/or where it is based on factual assumptions with which the jury disagrees.[225] But there must be a rational foundation, in the evidence, before the jury may reasonably reject the experts' opinion, especially where the experts are unanimous and uncontradicted by other experts. This could occur, for example, where an expert's opinion, as expressed in her evidence-in-chief, is substantially qualified and diluted by her evidence given in cross-examination.[226] In *R v Molodowic*, the issue was summarised as follows:[227]

> "A proper understanding and weighing of expert opinion often plays a central role in the determination of whether or not an accused should be found not guilty by reason of mental disorder. The absence of a Crown rebuttal expert to contradict an accused's psychiatric evidence is not in itself sufficient to conclude that a verdict of guilty was unreasonable if that conclusion remained reasonably open to the jury on the totality of the evidence. However, it may be unreasonable for a jury to disregard the expert evidence put before it, particularly where all the experts called were in agreement with each other, when their evidence was 'uncontradicted and not seriously challenged' ... and when there was nothing in the 'conduct of the commission of the crime which would raise any serious question as to the validity of the psychiatrists' conclusion'."

At the same time, the mere fact that, on the basis of expert evidence, the jury concludes that at the time of the crime an accused suffered from mental abnormality, and deviated in material medical respects from a condition of complete sanity, will not necessitate an insanity verdict if the jury is not satisfied that the abnormality amounted to *legal* insanity.[228] Suppose, for

---

222 *R v Rotana* (1995) 12 CRNZ 650 (CA), 655.
223 *R v Clark* (1983) 1 CRNZ 132 (CA).
224 *R v Clark* (1983) 1 CRNZ 132 (CA), 133. However, an appellate court ought not to interfere with the verdict of a jury unless, on consideration of all the evidence, it is satisfied that the verdict is one which no jury acting judicially and properly instructed could have reached: *R v Mailloux* (1985) 25 CCC (3d) 171 (Ont CA), 177 (Lacourciere J).
225 See *R v Lavallee* [1990] 1 SCR 852; (1990) 76 CR (3d) 329 (SCC), 896-897; 362-363; *R v Ratti* [1991] 1 SCR 68 (SCC), 81.
226 *R v Mailloux* (1985) 25 CCC (3d) 171 (Ont CA), 173.
227 *R v Molodowic* (2000) 143 CCC (3d) 31 (SCC), 38.

example, that D, while in a state of mild depression, kills V, his anorexic daughter, to "put her out of her misery and save the family further heartache". The depression represents a material deviation from complete sanity. However, it is doubtful whether it could it be said that these circumstances led inevitably to the conclusion that the accused was driven by a deranged mind into a course of conduct about which he was incapable of forming a rational moral judgment.[229] D may have been deeply distressed at V's self-destructive conduct, but that would not of itself be sufficient to constitute a disease of the mind for the purposes of legal insanity. However, it might, as in *R v Gordon*,[230] be sufficiently serious to justify the conclusion that, were a defence of diminished responsibility available in New Zealand, such a defence might well have availed D.

Note that the ability to challenge expert opinion evidence of insanity necessarily imports the right to cross-examine the author of an assessment report which concludes that an offender may have been legally insane at the time of the offence. In such circumstances and where the accused has deliberately refrained from raising insanity at the trial, principles of natural justice and fairness require that the accused be provided with the opportunity to cross-examine an expert witness, especially where any such report is likely to be relied on by the court in determining the outcome of the trial.[231]

10.4 Raising and determining insanity

For much of the history of insanity in New Zealand, acquittal on account of insanity resulted in automatic indefinite detention with no right of appeal from the verdict. This remained the position until 1969, when the Criminal Justice Amendment Act of that year introduced a range of new disposal options. However, a consequence of the harsh position prevailing until 1969 was the establishment of a rule that the issue could only be raised by the accused, or by the court where it "appears from the evidence"[232] that the defendant may have been insane at the time the offence was committed. The practice that developed at common law was that the Crown should place in the hands of the accused such evidence of insanity as it possesses, but should not adduce evidence of insanity unless the defence is raised or indicated.[233] However, once the accused had adduced evidence of insanity there could be no objection to the Crown's calling further evidence in support.[234] The Crown was also entitled to call evidence in rebuttal of a claim of insanity[235] and, where the defence is clearly foreshadowed in the cross-examination of prosecution witnesses but no supporting evidence is called, the prosecution may call evidence of sanity as part of its own case, or with the leave of the Court after the close of its own case.[236]

Even following the 1969 amendments, the longstanding authority that the prosecution is not entitled to initiate evidence of insanity was affirmed in *R v Green*.[237] In *Green*, the Court of

---

228 See *R v Bransgrove* [1954] NZLR 1076 (CA), 1080.
229 See *R v Smith* (1995) 12 CRNZ 616 (CA), 623 (Casey J).
230 *R v Gordon* (1993) 10 CRNZ 430 (CA), 441.
231 See *R v Langlois* (2005) 195 CCC (3d) 152 (BCCA).
232 See s 20(4) CP(MIP)A.
233 *R v Brooks* [1945] NZLR 584, 596-597 (Myers CJ). See also *R v Dixon* [1961] 3 All ER 460.
234 See eg *R v Clark* (1983) 1 CRNZ 132 (CA).
235 See *R v Gilbert-Smith* (1912) 8 Cr App R 72.
236 *R v Abramovitch* (1912) 7 Cr App R 145.
237 *R v Green* [1993] 2 NZLR 513; (1993) 9 CRNZ 523 (CA).

Appeal allowed a case-stated appeal against the trial judge's decision to permit the prosecution to raise insanity, despite unanimous psychiatric evidence that the appellant was insane, where the accused had given written instructions that insanity would not be relied on. In so ruling, the Court referred to other statutory options which would provide protection to the public offered by an insanity verdict. In particular, it was noted that the MH(CAT)A now allowed a Judge considering making a compulsory treatment order to refer a case to the Director of Mental Health with a view to the Director applying to the court for a "restricted patient" order. This may be an appropriate course where defendants present special difficulties because of the danger they pose to others.[238]

10.4.1 Raising insanity "where it appears from the evidence"

The power of the judge to put the issue of insanity before the jury is vested by s 20(4) CP (MIP)A, which permits her to do so where it "appears from the evidence", and even though the defendant may have expressly disclaimed it. The rationale for this rule is that the interests of justice require that a defendant should not be convicted if he was insane at the time of the offence.[239] As the rule has developed in New Zealand, it imposes a duty on the court to ask the jury to find whether the defendant was insane, even though the statute formally confers a discretion.[240] As such, the rule is consistent with the general obligation on judges to direct a jury on any matter of defence which is reasonably open to a jury to consider in reaching their verdict,[241] and reflects the principle that it is for the court and not the parties to determine the nature of any of the defence supported by the evidence.[242]

10.4.2 New procedure for determining insanity by consensus

The power of a court to record an insanity verdict is now contained in s 20 CP(MIP)A. The possibility of such a verdict is no longer restricted to hearings or trials for an offence punishable by death or imprisonment. In principle, insanity may be pleaded at any "hearing or trial"[243] although, in practice, it is typically raised only where the offender is at risk of imprisonment. Where the offender indicates an intention to raise insanity at the trial, the prosecution agrees that acquittal on account of insanity is the only reasonable verdict, and the judge is herself satisfied that the defendant was insane at the relevant time, the Court is now mandated to record a finding of not guilty on account of insanity.[244]

Section 20 deals only with defendants found not guilty on account of insanity. While the section largely restates the substance of the previous law, it adds a new provision in subs (2). The section allows the judge to bring in an insanity verdict before or at a hearing or trial whenever the defendant indicates an intention to raise insanity, the prosecution agrees with the plea and the judge is satisfied on expert evidence the defendant was insane when the offence was committed.

---

238 *R v Green* [1993] 2 NZLR 513; (1993) 9 CRNZ 523 (CA). See s 54(1) Mental Health (Compulsory Assessment and Treatment) Act 1992.
239 See *R v Green* [1993] 2 NZLR 513; (1993) 9 CRNZ 523 (CA), 521; 531.
240 See s 20(4) CP(MIP)A. Cf (now repealed) s 113(3) Criminal Justice Act 1985.
241 See *R v Tavete* [1988] 1 NZLR 428; (1987) 2 CRNZ 579 (CA).
242 However, the circumstances where a judge may raise the issue of insanity are "exceptional and very rare": *R v Dickie* [1984] 1 WLR 1031; 3 All ER 173 (CA), 1036; 178 (Watkins J).
243 Section 20(1) CP(MIP)A.
244 Section 20(2) CP(MIP)A.

In effect, the new procedure allows for the entry of a "not guilty on account of insanity" verdict by consent (see s 20(2)), although the judge is still required to consider the evidence in favour of insanity and satisfy himself that the offender was insane at the relevant time. The provision has been actively used by the courts since the legislation came into force and has already generated a number of appeals to the Court of Appeal.[245] An emerging consensus approach to the provision suggests a simple procedure that is to be followed once there is agreement between the forensic experts that the offender was insane at the time of the crime. Upon such agreement, the judge must determine whether he is "satisfied" of the relevant facts in terms of s 20(2)(c). There is no limitation to the number of health experts the court may hear from for this purpose, since the judge need only be satisfied "on the basis of expert evidence".[246]

The judge's role at the hearing is then to assess the evidence in favour of insanity and to make a judicial decision whether the evidence supports the conclusion that the offender is insane. This will normally involve evaluating the evidence given by psychiatrists for both the defence and the Crown in relation to the principal elements of s 23 Crimes Act 1961 and being satisfied that the offender:

"(1)   suffered from a 'disease of the mind' and;

"(2)   either was incapable of understanding the nature and quality of the act, or was incapable of knowing the act was morally wrong"

Once the judge is satisfied that these elements are established by the evidence of all the medical experts, she must conclude that the person was legally insane.

The new procedure will have at least two important consequences. First, it will eliminate the need for lengthy and possibly traumatic jury trials by permitting an insanity verdict to be recorded, without the need for the judge or jury to determine the factual issues concerning the accused's insanity. Secondly, it will reduce the risk of juries entering perverse verdicts of guilty against defendants who are clearly legally insane, but where the horror of the alleged offence has generated substantial popular prejudice against the defendant.[247]

10.5   Disposition of the criminally insane

Prior to 1969, an accused person acquitted on account of insanity was required to be kept in strict custody "until the pleasure of the Minister of Justice is known".[248] This invariably meant indefinite detention in a mental hospital, there being no other form of disposition available to the courts. However, an amendment to the Criminal Justice Act 1954 in 1969[249] inserted s 39G into the principal Act, which gave the courts an additional range of dispositional options. These options were carried over to s 115 Criminal Justice Act 1985, which allowed for four possibilities once a person had been either found to be "under disability" or "acquitted on account of his or her insanity". They were:

(i)   An order that the person be detained as a "special patient" (s 115(1));

---

245   See *R v B* 21/4/05, CA4/05; *R v Barnes* 16/6/05, CA69/05.
246   For example, in *R v B* 21/4/05, CA4/05, the Court accepted as evidence psychiatric reports produced from three psychiatrists, two of whom also gave oral evidence at the hearing.
247   See eg *R v Clark* (1983) 1 CRNZ 132; *R v Smith* 5/4/95, CA271/94.
248   Section 31 Mental Health Act 1911.
249   See s 2 Criminal Justice Amendment Act 1969

(ii) An order that the person be detained in a hospital as a committed patient (s 115(2)(a));

(iii) An order for the person's immediate release (s 115(2)(b)); and

(iv) To make no order at all, where the person is already subject to a full-time custodial sentence (s 115(2)(c)).

However, more recently, these disposal options have been modified by new legislation, in the form of the CP(MIP)A. The new provisions are broadly similar in the range of available disposal options to those in the previous legislation, save that express provision is now made for offenders with an intellectual disability.[250] The orders applicable to intellectually disabled offenders essentially track the range of orders that are applicable to other mentally impaired offenders. However, apart from modifying the options themselves, the Act makes important changes to the criteria for determining the appropriate disposition.

10.5.1 The range of orders

Section 24 of the CP(MIA)A provides for orders to detain defendants found unfit to stand trial or insane as special patients under the Mental Health (Compulsory Assessment and Treatment) Act 1992 or as special care recipients under the Intellectual Disability (Compulsory Care and Rehabilitation) Act 2003. The court must make such an order if, having considered all the circumstances of the case, it is satisfied, on the evidence of one or more health assessors, that the order is necessary in the interests of the public or the person or group that may be affected.

Section 25, on the other hand, allows for a range of "alternative" dispositions where the security needs of the offender are less pressing. In *R v Bayford*,[251] Young J noted that under the previous legislation there was a presumption that a person acquitted on account of insanity would be detained as a special patient. This presumption no longer applies. The correct course now is for the court to consider all the circumstances of the case together with the evidence of the health assessors and then decide if it is necessary to make an order that the offender be detained as a special patient in the interests of the public or any class of persons affected by the court's decision.[252] If the court concludes that it is not necessary to make such a decision, then the alternative ways of dealing with the accused, outlined in s 25, may be considered.

In *R v B* Young J decided that a special patient order was necessary on the basis of the seriousness of the offending (a serious unprovoked attack on a young girl with a knife) and the continuation of a high level of risk. In reasoning described by the Court of Appeal as "unimpeachable",[253] these factors were held to indicate the need for long-term in-patient treatment better suited to a special patient order.

Where the Court is not satisfied that a security order is "necessary" in the interests of the public or any person or class of persons who may be affected by the court's decision, the Act specifies a range of alternative orders that may be imposed. Under the new scheme a court may only make an alternative order once it has satisfied itself that a security order is not necessary. However, once it is so satisfied the Court must make an alternative order. The importance of

---

250 See ss 24(2)(b) and 25(1)(b) CP(MIP)A 2003.
251 *R v Bayford* 9/12/04, Ronald Young J, HC Palmerston North CRI-2004-254-97.
252 See s 24(1) CP(MIP)A.
253 See *R v B* 21/4/05, CA4/05, para 22 (Hammond J).

compliance with the strict terms of the legislation has been emphasized in a number of recent cases.[254]

There is therefore no fall back position whereby a court, not satisfied that a security order is necessary, nevertheless decides to impose one because it considers it would be helpful for the management of the patient, or because it satisfies some broader notion of the public interest. Indeed, the provisions must be regarded as having, by implication, overruled the decision in *R v GH*,[255] in which the Court had held that there was "some wider element of public interest, quite apart from its safety, and quite apart from what might be in the interests of the individual involved" which justified the making of a special patient order in the case of a young offender acquitted on account of insanity.

10.5.2 Detention as a "special patient"

As we have noted, a person acquitted on account of insanity can be detained in a hospital as a "special patient" under the Mental Health (Compulsory Assessment and Treatment) Act 1992.[256] Special patient status is an intermediate designation that describes a range of offenders who have been made subject to therapeutic intervention at various stages of the prosecution process. As applied to an insanity acquittee, it may signify that the person represents a serious danger to the public and must be kept in secure detention and be subject to non-clinical control. Under s 33 CP(MIP)A, a defendant acquitted on account of insanity and detained under a special patient or special care recipient order continues under that status until the defendant is "reclassified" as a committed "patient" or as a "care recipient", or is discharged. In either event, the direction can only be made by the Minister of Health who, after having received appropriate certification under either mental health or intellectual disability legislation, forms the opinion that further secure detention is no longer necessary either in the defendant's own interests or for the safety of the public or the safety of a person or class of persons.[257] However, it should be noted that disposition under s 33 is distinct from disposition under s 25. The former presupposes that the defendant has already been made a special patient or special care recipient and is subject to non-clinical oversight. However, where a defendant is made subject to an order under s 25 the court is given the immediate power either to make the offender a committed patient or care recipient or to immediately release. The matter is not subject to the Minister's discretion.

In the past judges have been generally reluctant to impose special patient status because of its indeterminate character and the difficulties that may be faced by an offender in ultimately achieving reclassification; with the exception of homicide cases. Prior to the 2003 enactment, in cases involving homicide it was said to be an "invariable" practice for judges to make a special patient order following an insanity acquittal and that it was inappropriate to take any other course.[258] In such cases a "wider element of public interest, quite apart from its safety, and quite apart from what might be in the best interests of the individual", was thought to justify detaining an offender as a special patient, even though he may no longer be a public danger.[259]

---

254 See eg *Police v L* 11/12/01, Doogue J, HC Masterton M21/2001, paras 6-7; *Trow v Police* 4/4/05, Nicholson J, HC Auckland CRI-2004-404-208, para 15.
255 *R v GH* [1977] 1 NZLR 50, 52.
256 Section 115(1)(b) Criminal Justice Act 1985 (now repealed).
257 Section 33(3) CP(MIP)A.
258 See *R v GH* [1977] 1 NZLR 50.

However, in light of the changes effected in s 24 CP(MIP)A, this approach appears no longer to be appropriate. The presumption that a person found to be insane and therefore acquitted will be detained as a special patient no longer applies.[260] The appropriate course is to consider all the circumstances of the case and the evidence from health assessors and then decide whether it is necessary to make an order that the person be detained as a special patient in the interests of the public or any class of persons that may be affected by the Court's decision. If the Court concludes that it is not necessary to make such a decision, then other alternative ways of dealing with an accused person must be considered.[261]

In *Wihongi v Police*,[262] Fisher J observed that the paramount consideration in determining whether to depart from special patient status is whether it would be "safe in the interests of the public" in terms of the language of the earlier provision.[263] At root, this involves considering the likelihood of a recurrence of the aberrant behaviour and the seriousness of the form that it may take. The High Court found the following matters to be relevant:[264]

(i) The nature and seriousness of the conduct for which the patient was acquitted (the more serious the aberrant behaviour, the less likely the court could be satisfied under the statutory test);

(ii) Whether there was a unique combination of causes unlikely to recur;

(iii) The reliability and certainty of the diagnosis and its relationship to treatment and recurrence;

(iv) The reliability and effectiveness of provisions for future care and supervision; and

(v) Expert opinion regarding the necessity for special patient treatment.

These matters will remain relevant under the new law.

10.5.3 Detention as a "patient" under the Mental Health (Compulsory Assessment and Treatment) Act 1992 or "special care recipient" under the Intellectual Disability (Compulsory Care and Rehabilitation) Act 2003

Detention as a special patient or special care recipient is the appropriate form of disposition where a person has been acquitted on account of insanity whose conduct represents a serious threat to public safety. However, where the court is satisfied that there is no such threat and is not satisfied that such secure detention is necessary, it may, as an alternative to special patient or special care recipient status, order the person's detention as a patient in a hospital or as a care recipient in a facility for the care of persons with an intellectual disability.[265]

An order that a person be detained in hospital as a patient or in a facility as a care recipient opens up the possibility of a number of distinct disposition options. Where ordered to be

---

259 *R v GH* [1977] 1 NZLR 50, 52.
260 See *R v Bayford* 9/12/04, Ronald Young J, HC Palmerston North CRI-2004-254-97.
261 *R v Bayford* 9/12/04, Ronald Young J, HC Palmerston North CRI-2004-254-97, para 21.
262 *Wihongi v Police* 10/5/99, Fisher J, HC Auckland T990080.
263 See s 115(2) Criminal Justice Act 1985.
264 See also Brookbanks and Simpson, "Restricted patients in New Zealand: A legal and clinical overview", (1996) 3 JLM 336, 343-344; also *Rini v Police* 12/11/98, Fisher J, HC Whangarei T981696.
265 Section 25 (1)(a) and (b) CP(MIP)A and s 9 ID(CCR)A.

treated as a "patient",[266] a person may be detained either as an inpatient or as an outpatient subject to a community treatment order.[267] An order made under s 25(1)(a) is to be regarded as a compulsory treatment order.[268] What will be determinative of the type of "patient" order that is appropriate will be whether the court is satisfied that services for care and treatment on an outpatient basis appropriate to the needs of the patient are available and that the social circumstances of the patient are adequate for his care in the community.[269]

10.5.4 Immediate release

If the form of disability suffered by the "patient" is not of a type that would justify detention and treatment in a mental hospital and the person does not represent a danger to the public, then it may be appropriate to order the person's immediate release.[270] However, because most persons acquitted on account of insanity will have committed serious crimes and are likely to pose a danger to the public, this option will seldom be appropriate. A difficulty, recognised by the courts in the use of this option, is that the order for immediate release under s 25(1)(d) is a somewhat blunt instrument that does not allow the court any supervisory control of the offender once discharge into the community has taken place.[271] It may, nonetheless, be appropriate where the offender has been acquitted of an offence that did not involve injury or violence or was otherwise of a relatively minor nature.[272] Such was the case in *Police v T*,[273] where the intellectually disabled 19-year-old first offender was found unfit to plead to charges of cannabis-related offences and burglary. In finding that an order for immediate release was appropriate, the Court observed that the offender could not yet be regarded as a particular risk to the safety of the public, despite the seriousness of the charges. There were no particularly aggravating features to the alleged burglary, and no violence. Of importance was the additional fact that the offender would have benefited from the involvement of Intellectual Disability Services who would assist him and his family.

---

266 Section 25(1)(a) CP(MIP)A.
267 Section 26 CP(MIP)A
268 Section 26(1) CP(MIP)A
269 Section 28(2) Mental Health (Compulsory Assessment and Treatment) Act 1992.
270 *R v S (No 2)* (1991) 7 CRNZ 576.
271 See *Rini v Police* 12/11/98, Fisher J, HC Whangarei T981696.
272 See, for example, *Police v XYZ* [1994] DCR 401.
273 *Police v T* [2004] DCR 311.

Chapter 11

INTOXICATION

11.1	Background	331
11.1.1	Intoxication in English law	335
(1)	*"Basic" v "specific" intent distinction*	335
(2)	*DPP v Majewski*	338
11.2	Intoxication defence in New Zealand	341
11.2.1	R v Kamipeli	341
(1)	*Guiding the jury*	342
(2)	*Evidential considerations*	343
11.2.2	Capacity and intent	345
11.2.3	Intoxication and recklessness	346
11.2.4	Intoxication and mistake	346
11.2.5	Negligence and strict liability offences	348
11.2.6	Intoxication and automatism	348
11.2.7	Manslaughter	349
(1)	*Intoxication and provocation*	351
11.2.8	Involuntary intoxication: a new excuse?	351
(1)	*Breath-alcohol offences*	354

11.1 Background

Alcohol, crime and social disorder exist within a complex relationship.[1] The nexus between aggression and substance use may be mediated by personality and expectancy factors, situational factors and socio-cultural factors, although the association between intoxication and aggressive conduct is far from consistent and the reasons are diverse and poorly understood.[2] A British Crime Survey in 2001 reported that a third of violent incidents between strangers and a fifth of violent incidents between acquaintances take place in or around a pub or club.[3] No doubt similar figures apply in New Zealand. The relationship between intoxication and aggression can be examined from a range of perspectives, including biological and physiological, pharmacological, psychological and psychiatric, and social and cultural. However, as a legal paradigm, intoxication is more closely associated with a psychological and

---

1 Richardson and Budd, "Young adults, alcohol, crime and disorder" (2003) 13 *Criminal Behaviour and Mental Health* 5, 6.
2 Fagan, "Intoxication and Aggression" (1990) 13 *Crime and Justice* 241, 243-244.
3 Richardson and Budd, "Young adults, alcohol, crime and disorder" (2003) 13 *Criminal Behaviour and Mental Health* 5, 6.

psychiatric perspective, in that quite apart from their role in stimulating aggressive behaviours, alcohol or drug use may sometimes generate a "defence", to excuse behaviour or deny responsibility for aggression,[4] by permitting an offender to claim that while her conduct was objectively wrongful, she was acting unawares or not as a moral agent at the relevant time.[5] On this basis, and perhaps paradoxically, even though offending is more prevalent in heavy drinkers,[6] the law continues to allow evidence of intoxication to negate responsibility for such offending committed under the influence of alcohol (or drugs). This incongruity means that there are two broad themes which any discourse on alcohol and crime must ultimately address. First is the extent of social toleration of alcohol and other mind-altering substances, together with the official measures undertaken to tackle alcohol-related problems. Second is the extent to which alcohol may be called in aid as an excusing condition in criminal prosecutions. While the first theme involves matters of great public importance, it is not the concern of this chapter. Rather, our concern is to examine the law around the "defence" of intoxication, in an attempt to discern relevant guiding principles and to consider their application in practice.

In New Zealand, the defence of incapacity or lack of mens rea owing to intoxication is based on the English common law defence preserved by s 20 Crimes Act 1961. However, the New Zealand defence has developed along different lines to its English forebear, and is less restrictive than the common law defence. While intoxication is currently capable of underwriting a complete defence to most crimes that may be committed intentionally, that was not always the case, and for many centuries intoxication was regarded simply as an aggravating factor in assessing criminal liability. A brief overview of the history of intoxication may assist our understanding of some recent developments in the theory of the defence.

A preliminary note: throughout this chapter we will refer to the "defence" of intoxication, although strictly speaking intoxication amounts to a claim that the prosecution has failed to prove an essential element of the crime: namely, mens rea. As such, a claim of intoxication represents a denial that D is guilty of the offence charged, not simply that his conduct should be excused.

The earliest reference to drunkenness and the criminal law occurs in the *Penitential of Theodore, Archbishop of Canterbury*, 668-690 AD. According to Theodore:[7]

> "whosoever shall have killed a man while drunk shall be guilty of homicide; he commits one fault by self-indulgence and another by killing a Christian."

---

4 Fagan, "Intoxication and Aggression" (1990) 13 *Crime and Justice* 241, 258-259. This "defence" model of intoxication must be differentiated from intoxication as a cultural defence, whereby intoxication is used as an excuse for behaviour which is socially disapproved or controlled. According to the latter approach, aggressiveness while intoxicated may involve a highly ritualised set of learned behaviours and specific social rules that dictate the conditions for becoming intoxicated and the participants in episodes of aggression (273). To the extent that "cultural defence" intoxication operates to embolden planning of asocial or antisocial acts and then drinking as an "excuse" for the behaviours that follow, it is antithetical to the "excuse" model considered in this chapter.

5 See Morse, "Excusing and the new Excuse Defenses: A Legal and Conceptual Review" (1998) 23 *Crime and Justice* 329, 333.

6 McMurran, "Editorial: Alcohol and Crime" (2003) 13 *Criminal Behaviour and Mental Health* 1, and see Fergusson, Lynskey and Horwood, "Alcohol misuse and juvenile offending in adolescence" (1996) 91 *Addiction* 483-494.

7 Cited in Singh, "History of the defence of drunkenness in English criminal law" (1933) 49 LQR 528.

The theme of intoxication amounting to fault *of itself* is picked up in later expositions on the subject, and tends to explain the fact that before the 19th century intoxication was no defence to a criminal charge. Writing in 1643, Dalton remarked that "if a man that is drunk killeth another, that is felony of death, for it is a *voluntary ignorance* in him, insomuch as ignorance cometh to him by his own act and folly".[8] (Indeed, that is still the character of legislation in some jurisdictions, where evidence of "self-induced" intoxication is to be ignored when determining issues of voluntariness or intention.[9])

Many early commentators regarded drunkenness as an *aggravation* of an offence, as the following extract from *Beverley's Case* in 1603 illustrates:[10]

> "although he who is drunk is for the time *non compos mentis*, yet his drunkenness does not extenuate his act or offence … but it is a great offence … and therefore aggravates his offence, and doth not derogate from the act which he did during that time."

The law's unbending condemnation of drunkenness during this period is reflected in an early 17th century statute described in its Short Title as "an Act for repressing the odious and loathsome Sin of Drunkenness",[11] which identified drunkenness as the single cause of a range of additional "enormous sins" including "bloodshed, stabbing, murder, swearing, fornication, adultery". It was also blamed for the "overthrow" of various arts and manual trades, and for the general disablement and impoverishment of the workforce. In such a climate of condemnation, it is not difficult to imagine why it was regarded as an aggravation rather than a mitigation of crime.

For all this, it is unclear what practical effect was actually given to the notion of drunkenness as an aggravation of crime, and whether, in truth, penalties were harsher for those who committed offences while drunk. Even in the 17th century, some qualifications to the strict rule that intoxication was an aggravation of an offence had begun to emerge, presaging the future direction of the defence at common law. In a chapter of Sir Matthew Hale's *Historia Placitorum Coronae* entitled "Concerning the defect of ideocy, madness and lunacy",[12] a separate section was devoted to a discussion of *"Dementia affectata, namely Drunkenness"*. The gist of this passage was that at English law, voluntary drunkenness was not a "privilege", and that, legally, it left D in the same position as if he were in his right senses. However, certain mitigations were recognised, in particular the acknowledgement that if a person by the "contrivance" of his enemies had eaten or drunk something which caused a temporary or permanent "phrenzy", this put him into the same condition as any other "phrenzy" and equally excused him. Thus the law began to recognise an important distinction between *voluntary* and *involuntary* intoxication. Furthermore, in a later passage discussing *"Dementia accidentalis"*, which might be taken to include cases of involuntary intoxication, Hale appears to lay the groundwork for the future exculpatory defence of intoxication when he contemplates a state of involuntary

---

8   Singh, "History of the defence of drunkenness in English criminal law" (1933) 49 LQR 528, 531.
9   See eg ss 428G and 428H Crimes Act 1900 (NSW) and see *Hadba v The Queen* (2004) 146 A Crim R 291.
10 *Beverley's Case* (1603) Co Rep 123b; 76 ER 1118, 125a; 1123. See also Sir Edward Coke, *The First Part of the Institutes of the Laws of England* (1832 ed), New York and London, Garland Publishing Inc, 1979, vol II, 247a, who noted that a drunkard was a "voluntarius daemon", who gained no "privilege" from that status, and if any "hurt or ills" were occasioned thereby, "his drunkenness doth aggravate it".
11 4 Jac 1, c5.
12 Hale, "Concerning the defect of ideocy, madness and lunacy" *Historia Placitorum Coronae* 1694, 29ff.

intoxication so profound as to amount to temporary insanity, such that if the accused was rendered incapable of forming the necessary intent the crime was not made out.[13]

Other early authority on intoxication, which tended to suggest that evidence of intoxication may be relevant to the question whether the accused had the requisite intent for certain grave crimes like homicide, has tended to be discounted by some commentators who argue that the relevant dicta were uttered at a time when the law concerning the mental element of crime, and in particular the place of intoxication within it, was at an early stage of development.[14] However, during the 19th century the original common law rule suggesting that intoxication was, if anything, an aggravation of crime, came significantly to be relaxed. In a line of cases, judges accepted that drunkenness could be relied upon to support a defence that the defendant had not formed the intent required to commit the crime charged.[15] During this period a clear distinction began to emerge between criminal liability and moral delinquency, to the extent that intoxication was increasingly allowed as an indirect defence which negatived the existence of a specific intent required for certain serious crimes. This approach is illustrated in *R v Grindley*,[16] where Holroyd J held that, although voluntary drunkenness could never excuse the commission of a crime, on a murder charge, where the material question was whether the act was premeditated or done in the heat of the moment, the fact of intoxication was a relevant consideration to take into account. The case, despite its subsequent overruling,[17] represents a watershed in the development of the intoxication defence and shows the emergence of a change in attitude towards drunkenness and the beginning of judicial resistance to Establishment disapproval of drunkenness.

By the time Stephen J delivered his celebrated dictum in *R v Doherty*,[18] there had been a significant turning of the tide of opinion towards drunkenness, and the broad parameters of a future exculpatory defence could now be seen:[19]

> "Although you cannot take drunkenness as any excuse for crime, yet when the crime is such that the intention of the party committing it is one of its constituent elements, you may look at the fact that a man was in drink in considering whether he formed the intention necessary to constitute the crime."

---

13 See *R v Kingston* [1995] 2 AC 355; [1994] 3 All ER 353 (HL), 368; 363 (Lord Mustill). However, Lord Mustill cautions that while the extract from Hale is consistent with the existing law, legal concepts of criminal responsibility in the 17th century were so different from those of today that there may be danger in placing too much reliance on them as a starting point for the development of the modern doctrine of intoxication.
14 See, for example, *Pearson's Case* (1835) 2 Lew CC 144; 168 ER 1108, where Park J suggests that drunkenness may be taken into consideration to explain the probability of a party's intention in the case of violence committed on sudden provocation. See also Singh, "History of the defence of drunkenness in English criminal law" (1933) 49 LQR 528; also the discussion in *R v Kingston* [1995] 2 AC 355; [1994] 3 All ER 353 (HL), 367; 363 (Lord Mustill).
15 A suggested explanation for this was that in the 19th century, judges began to relax the strict common law rule in cases of murder and serious violent crime where the penalties were perceived to be particularly harsh or where there was likely to be much sympathy for the accused. See *DPP v Majewski* [1977] AC 443; [1976] 2 All ER 142 (HL), 456; 153, (Lawton LJ).
16 *R v Grindley* (1819), cited in *Russell on Crime* (12th ed), London, Stevens & Sons, 1964, vol 1, 80.
17 *Grindley* was, however, overruled in *R v Carroll* (1835) 7 C & P 145; 173 ER 64, where the court held that the language in *Grindley* was capable of such wide application that "there would be no safety for human life if it were to be considered as law".
18 *R v Doherty* (1887) 16 Cox CC 306.
19 *R v Doherty* (1887) 16 Cox CC 306, 308.

Stephen J's apparent purpose in making this concession was to ensure that in prosecutions for very serious crimes, ie those that required proof of an additional mens rea element (usually intention) going to consequences and beyond the mere intention to behave as D did, evidence of intoxication could be admitted by the trial judge for the purpose of negating the "ulterior" mens rea element, thus reducing the level of culpability of the offender. As one commentator has observed, Stephen J's formulation established the emerging rationale for the "long-desired mitigation of punishment" of grossly inebriated homicides.[20]

11.1.1 Intoxication in English law

In English common law, intoxication is normally irrelevant in determining criminal liability. It is suggested that this is because there are varying degrees of intoxication, and the issue can only be relevant in those relatively rare cases where the intoxication is so serious that it prevents the formation of a mental element.[21] In itself, intoxication has never been a defence to a criminal charge. Crucially, English law has always held that criminal intent and a state of intoxication can be compatible, a view captured in the phrase "a drunken intent is nevertheless an intent".[22] That is to say, provided she had the necessary mens rea for the offence, D cannot avoid criminal liability by saying that intoxication impaired her ability to distinguish between right and wrong, or weakened her inhibitions so that she behaved impulsively or in a way she would not have done if she had been sober.[23] Similarly, the fact that D intentionally committed an offence while intoxicated will be no defence even though he cannot remember what he did.[24] Amnesia is not per se a defence to crime, and does not become one simply because it is associated with intoxication.

Nevertheless, in crimes where proof of a subjective mental element is required, evidence of intoxication may, in very limited circumstances, be relevant to the question whether the required state of mind was present. Intoxication may have the effect of impairing awareness, perception, or foresight; and thus result in the absence of the requisite state of mens rea.[25] Equally, however, for certain crimes, including strict liability offences and other offences requiring proof of negligence or objective recklessness, even extreme intoxication is irrelevant. The rationale for this is, as the case may be, either that there is no mental element to be proven, or that the defendant must comply with the standard of the reasonable person, who would not have been intoxicated and so would not be prevented thereby from foreseeing the risk of harm.[26]

(1) *"Basic" v "specific" intent distinction*

In England, the concept of a "specific intent" has been used by the courts to limit the availability of the defence of lack of intent based on intoxication. For those crimes requiring proof of a subjective mens rea, extreme intoxication (such that D lacked mens rea) *may* be

---

20   Hall, *General Principles of Criminal Law* (2nd ed), Indianapolis, Bobbs-Merrill, 1960, 532, 533.
21   Virgo, "Reconciling principle and policy" [1993] Crim LR 415.
22   *R v Doherty* (1887) 16 Cox CC 306, 308; *R v Sheehan* [1975] 2 All ER 960; [1975] 1 WLR 739 (CA), 964; 744.
23   Criminal Law Reform Committee, *Report on Intoxication as a Defence to a Criminal Charge*, Wellington, Government Printer, 1984, 44.
24   Criminal Law Reform Committee, *Report on Intoxication as a Defence to a Criminal Charge*, Wellington, Government Printer, 1984, 44.
25   Criminal Law Reform Committee, *Report on Intoxication as a Defence to a Criminal Charge*, Wellington, Government Printer, 1984, 44.
26   Virgo, "Reconciling principle and policy" [1993] Crim LR 415, 416.

relevant, depending on whether the offence is characterised as one of "basic" intent or one of "specific" intent.

It is not entirely clear how the distinction originated. It seems that it may have had its origins in the judicial decisions of the late 19th century, where certain judges were concerned to devise a means of partial exculpation for offenders charged with capital offences who, because of the effects of intoxication, were incapable of forming the particular intent required for grave crimes like murder. Where evidence of intoxication was sufficiently powerful to negate the specific mens rea for murder, the offender was eligible for the lesser verdict of manslaughter, and thus able to avoid the mandatory penalty of capital punishment for murder. Initially, intoxication seemed to be relevant only to the question whether an act was premeditated or done only with "sudden heat or impulse" for the purposes of the provocation defence.[27] However, in due course it became common in homicide cases for evidence of intoxication to be admitted, and for judges to direct juries to the effect that although drunkenness is no excuse for crime, it may be of great importance in cases where it is "a question of intention".[28] In such cases, a person may be so drunk as to be utterly unable to form any intention at all, yet be guilty of very great violence.[29] The connection between intoxication and its ability to negate the *specific* mens rea for certain grave crimes is made explicit by the judgments of Patterson J and Coleridge J in R v Monkhouse:[30]

> "if the defendant is proved to have been intoxicated, the question becomes a more subtle one; but it is of the same kind, namely, was he rendered by intoxication entirely incapable of forming the intent charged.... Drunkenness is ordinarily neither a defence nor excuse for crime, and where it is available *as a partial answer* to a charge, it rests on the prisoner to prove it, and it is not enough that he was excited or rendered more irritable, unless the intoxication was such as to prevent his restraining himself from committing the act in question, or to take away from him the power of forming any *specific intention.*"

Two things emerge from this extract. First, on the question of exculpation, intoxication was perceived only to be a *palliative* defence, capable of reducing the crime charged to one of lesser seriousness. It was never perceived as a complete defence. Secondly, as to responsibility, its effect, in those rare cases where intoxication was legally relevant, must be to negate the *capacity* to form the intention required for certain crimes. This implies that intoxication was only ever relevant in cases where an offender had reached an advanced state of drunkenness and in that state had committed an act of great violence. It seems that intoxication was only ever intended to provide a narrow release from criminal culpability for offenders charged with grave crimes like murder and attempted murder who, while in a state of profound intoxication, had committed some violent act while lacking the mental capacity to premeditate or otherwise intend that act. It was, arguably, never meant by early jurists to have any wider application, and certainly not to provide a complete exculpation from criminal responsibility.

---

27 See, for example, *R v Grindley* (1819), cited in *Russell on Crime* (12th ed), London, Stevens & Sons, 1964, vol 2, 8; also in Singh, "History of the defence of drunkenness in English criminal law" (1933) 49 LQR 528, 537.
28 *R v Cruse* (1838) 8 C & P 541; 173 ER 610.
29 Singh, "History of the defence of drunkenness in English criminal law" (1933) 49 LQR 528, 539.
30 *R v Monkhouse* (1850-1851) 4 Cox CC 55, 56 (Coleridge J) (emphasis added).

Thus voluntary (self-induced) intoxication was generally regarded as being presumptively incapable of conferring either justification or excuse for *any* crime. At best, in those relatively rare cases where it was pleaded in extenuation of an offence, it was regarded as being available only as a "partial answer" to a charge.[31] What is contemplated by the notion of a "partial answer" is not absolutely clear, but the best view may be that the negation of mens rea in certain crimes did not lead to avoidance of criminal responsibility altogether but rather only to avoidance of the harsh consequences of conviction for a mandatory capital offence. The importance of the passage from *Monkhouse*, we submit, lies not only in the fact that it is the first direction to point out that evidence of drunkenness is admissible to negative *specific* intent,[32] but also in the apparent analogy it creates between provocation and intoxication as *palliative* defences. The passage as a whole indicates that whether as extenuation of homicide in provocation or as a limited negation of mens rea, intoxication can never excuse and can only ever have the effect of lowering an accused's culpability from the capital offence charged to one involving a lesser degree of culpability.

Until 1920, when the decision of the House of Lords in *DPP v Beard*[33] was handed down, there was no clear authority contradicting the view that intoxication was never intended to allow for more than extenuation of certain grave crimes, and that its application was probably limited to homicide. In respect of lesser crimes the general rule was consistently applied; namely, that drunkenness is ordinarily neither a defence nor excuse for crime.

However, the decision in *Beard* irrevocably altered the common law on intoxication. Although the case was an appeal against conviction on a prosecution for murder, certain dicta in the case suggested the basis for a much more broad-based defence of intoxication. Lord Birkenhead asserted the general proposition that evidence of drunkenness which renders the accused incapable of forming a specific intent essential to constitute the crime should be taken into consideration with other facts proved in order to determine whether the accused had that required intent. He proceeded to articulate a significantly wider rule for intoxication; indeed, one which has been criticised on the ground that it extends the defence of drunkenness far beyond the limits assigned to it by the common law and which is opposed to the weight of authority on the point.[34] According to Lord Birkenhead:[35]

> "I do not think that the proposition of law deduced from these earlier cases is an exceptional rule applicable only to cases in which it is necessary to prove a specific intent in order to constitute the graver crime — for example wounding with intent to do grievous bodily harm or with intent to kill. It is true that in such cases the specific intent must be proved to constitute the particular crime, but this is, on ultimate analysis, only in accordance with the ordinary law applicable to crime, for, speaking generally (and apart from certain special offences), a person cannot be convicted of a crime unless the *mens* was *rea*."

The implication that intoxication may affect ordinary mens rea has become the conceptual foundation of the intoxication defence as it has developed in New Zealand law. We will

---

31 *R v Monkhouse* (1850-1851) 4 Cox CC 55, 56 (Coleridge J).
32 See Singh, "History of the defence of drunkenness in English criminal law" (1933) 49 LQR 528, 540.
33 *DPP v Beard* [1920] AC 479; [1920] All ER Rep 21 (HL).
34 Singh, "History of the defence of drunkenness in English criminal law" (1933) 49 LQR 528, 544, 545.
35 *DPP v Beard* [1920] AC 479; [1920] All ER Rep 21 (HL), 504; 30 (emphasis added).

consider these developments shortly. However, before doing so it is necessary to make some further brief observations about the development of the common law defence since *Beard*.

Beard appeared to leave open the possibility that a person charged with *any* offence requiring proof of intention could plead intoxication as evidence going to prove that he was *incapable* of forming the intention essential to constitute the crime charged. This implied, in theory at least, that a person charged with a relatively minor crime, say a simple assault, could plead intoxication in order to show that he lacked the capacity to form the intent to assault his victim. Consequently, however, if such a defence were available to a lesser crime like assault, the accused would have to be acquitted altogether — because there would be no lesser crime for which liability could attach once intoxication had been allowed to palliate his liability for assault.

(2) *DPP v Majewski*

This possibility existed in English law until 1977, when the window of opportunity left open by *Beard* was conclusively shut by the decision of the House of Lords in *DPP v Majewski*.[36] In that case, the accused had been involved in a bar-room brawl as a result of which he was convicted on three counts of assault causing actual bodily harm and on three counts of assault on a police constable in the execution of his duty. There was evidence that at the time of the alleged assaults Majewski was acting under the influence of a combination of voluntarily-consumed alcohol and drugs, and it was suggested that he may not have known what he was doing. The trial judge directed the jury that the effect of the drink and drugs could provide no defence and should be ignored. On appeal, this ruling was unanimously approved by both the English Court of Appeal and the House of Lords. It was held to be established law in England that the effects of self-induced intoxication could provide a defence only if the offence charged required a "specific" intent; and that intoxication, however extreme it might be, could never support a defence when the mental element was no more than a "basic" intent. In the words of Lord Elwyn-Jones LC:[37]

> "In the case of these offences it is no excuse in law that, because of drink or drugs which the accused himself had taken knowingly and willingly, he had deprived himself of the ability to exercise self-control, to realise the possible consequences of what he was doing or even to be conscious that he was doing it."

Because the offences charged in *Majewski* required proof only of a "basic intent" on the part of the accused, it was held that the jury had been properly directed to ignore intoxication as the possible basis for a defence.

There are three things to be noted here. The first is that a formal distinction between offences of "basic" and "specific" intent did not exist before *Majewski*. It does not represent a logical development of the common law. Secondly, the distinction would be unnecessary if the common law defence had been confined to cases involving really serious physical violence. Thirdly, the distinction does not detract from the widely accepted view that intoxication, of itself, is not a defence to crime but merely evidence from which a lack of intent to commit a serious crime may be inferred. Liability may still attach for any offence for which proof of that intent is not required.

---

36   *DPP v Majewski* [1977] AC 443; [1976] 2 All ER 142 (HL).
37   *DPP v Majewski* [1977] AC 443; [1976] 2 All ER 142 (HL), 476; 151.

The rule in *Majewski* has its most important impact in cases involving personal violence or damage to property.[38] In such cases, the intoxicated actor may take advantage of a defence of lack of intent in relation to the most serious offences, where intent is of primary importance. However, the rule ensures that voluntary intoxication cannot support a defence of lack of intent to a range of lesser charges which will generally be available.[39] This means that under English law, D may be acquitted of murder by pleading intoxication, but will then be convicted of manslaughter, a "basic" intent crime.

One explanation of the distinction is that specific intent offences are those offences always requiring proof of intention, while offences of basic intent are those offences which can be committed recklessly. In practice, however, the distinction is quite arbitrary, and does not imply, as might be expected, that crimes of specific intent are necessarily more serious than crimes of basic intent. For example, while theft is characterised as a crime of specific intent, regardless of the seriousness of the particular charge, rape is characterised as a crime of basic intent,[40] in respect of which intoxication cannot be relied upon to negate mens rea. Furthermore, if the defendant is charged with a basic intent crime then, even if when the harm was caused he could not have foreseen that harm because he was intoxicated, recklessness is deemed to exist from the time the intoxicating substance was taken.[41] In *Majewski*, Lord Elwyn-Jones said that the defendant's course of conduct in reducing himself by drugs and drink to a state of intoxication itself supplies evidence of mens rea sufficient for crimes of basic intent.[42] At common law the very taking of an intoxicating substance is deemed to be reckless, and to be sufficiently culpable to justify conviction for a basic intent charge. However, where intoxication has been caused by a drug whose effects are not well known, recklessness cannot be presumed and the prosecution must prove that the defendant foresaw the risk of unpredictable and uncontrollable conduct as a result of intoxication.[43]

In an attempt to mitigate the harshness of the basic intent rule, it has been held that the jury should discount the fact that the defendant was intoxicated and ask whether, if the defendant had been sober, he would have foreseen the risk that the victim was not consenting.[44] However, this approach merely demonstrates the oddity of the basic/specific intent distinction because, as Virgo notes,[45] it means that the defendant may still be acquitted if the jury accepts that he would have lacked the necessary mental element for the offence *had he been sober*! One is bound to ask, if it is necessary to contrive a means of exculpating the drunken defendant on a basic

---

38 Criminal Law Reform Committee, *Report on Intoxication as a Defence to a Criminal Charge*, Wellington, Government Printer, 1984, 10.
39 Criminal Law Reform Committee, *Report on Intoxication as a Defence to a Criminal Charge*, Wellington, Government Printer, 1984, 10.
40 See *R v Fotheringham* (1989) 88 Cr App R 206; [1988] Crim LR 846 (CA).
41 Virgo, "Reconciling principle and policy" [1993] Crim LR 415, 416.
42 *DPP v Majewski* [1977] AC 443; [1976] 2 All ER 142 (HL), 474-475; 150. As Ashworth points out, this is "plainly a fiction": *Principles*, 211.
43 *R v Bailey* [1983] 2 All ER 503; [1983] 1 WLR 760 (CA); *R v Hardie* [1984] 3 All ER 848; [1985] 1 WLR 64 (CA).
44 *R v Woods* (1981) 74 Cr App R 312; [1982] Crim LR 42 (CA), discussed in Virgo, "Reconciling principle and policy" [1993] Crim LR 415, 417. See also *R v Richardson* (1999) 1 Cr App R 392 (CA). It has been suggested that, as a result of *Richardson*, it may be argued that intoxication will be a defence if it caused D to believe that V was consenting — even though, had D been sober, he would have known V was not. See the commentary on the case at [1999] Crim LR 494.
45 Virgo, "Reconciling principle and policy" [1993] Crim LR 415, 417.

intent crime by postulating a *sober* defendant, what is the point of continuing the distinction at all?

The unsatisfactory nature of the current English position is well illustrated by the decision in *Jaggard v Dickenson*.[46] The accused had gained entry to a house which she believed belonged to her friend, whose licence she had to occupy the house and treat it as her own. She broke a window and damaged a curtain. In fact the house belonged to someone else. Her mistake was the result of intoxication. Charged with criminal damage under the Criminal Damage Act 1971 (UK) the justices held that her belief in lawful excuse was negated by the fact that it was induced by intoxication and she was convicted.[47] The Divisional Court overturned her appeal, on the basis that the Act directed the court to consider the existence of the belief and not its intellectual soundness: "a belief can be just as much honestly held if it is induced by intoxication, as if it stems from stupidity, forgetfulness or inattention".[48] Bizarrely, if the woman had stumbled against the window in a blind intoxicated stupor, she would have had no defence — the offence being one of basic intent. But because her defence was based on a claim of right which required only an honestly held belief, she was acquitted.[49]

The English Law Commission recently proposed the abolition of the basic/specific intent distinction, and its replacement with a new offence.[50] The effect of this change would have been that there would be a return to fundamental principles of criminal liability; namely, that the accused should be acquitted if she lacked the relevant mental element for an offence. However, in order to reflect public policy concerns that voluntarily intoxicated people who commit the actus reus of a crime should not escape punishment, an offender acquitted of the principal substantive offence on grounds of intoxication would still be liable for the offence of causing harm while intoxicated. The mens rea of the new offence would be "deliberate" intoxication, meaning that the accused took the intoxicant of her own will, being aware that, in the quantity she knowingly took, it would or might cause her to become intoxicated. Intoxication would not, however, be deliberate if the intoxicant was taken for medicinal, sedative, or soporific purposes, or if it was taken involuntarily.[51]

Although the Law Commission subsequently resiled from these proposals,[52] they reflect a growing disillusionment with the *Majewski* approach in England.[53] In particular, they evince a concern with its illogicality, and its incompatibility with accepted theory. What, then, is the "accepted theory" concerning the modern defence of intoxication? We illustrate this with reference to New Zealand law.

---

46 *Jaggard v Dickinson* [1981] QB 527; [1980] 3 All ER 716.
47 In general, defences (such as self-defence, necessity, and the like) are disallowed if they are predicated on a mistake arising from voluntary intoxication: *R v O'Grady* [1987] QB 995, [1987] 3 All ER 420 (CA); *R v O'Connor* [1991] Crim LR 135; below, 11.2.4.
48 *Jaggard v Dickinson* [1981] QB 527; [1980] 3 All ER 716, 532; 719 (Mustill J).
49 See Reed, "Court of Appeal — Criminal Damage: Defences" (2004) 68 Jo CL 463.
50 Law Commission (UK), *Intoxication and Criminal Liability*, Consultation Paper no 127, London, HMSO, 1993, para 6.30.
51 For a detailed discussion of these proposals and comments on them, see Virgo, "Reconciling principle and policy" [1993] Crim LR 415, 421ff.
52 Law Commission (UK), *Legislating the Criminal Code: Intoxication and Criminal Liability*, no 229, London, HMSO, 1995. See Paton, "Reformulating the intoxication rules: The Law Commission's report" [1995] Crim LR 382.
53 An exception is Gardner, "The importance of *Majewski*" (1994) 14 OJLS 279.

11.2 Intoxication defence in New Zealand

There is at present no statutory provision that governs the extent to which intoxication may support a defence to a criminal charge. As will be seen, the approach taken to intoxication in New Zealand is significantly different to that taken in other jurisdictions, including the United States, Canada, and the United Kingdom.

Judicial development of the defence in New Zealand effectively begins with *DPP v Beard*.[54] New Zealand judges have never sought to limit the availability of the defence to grave crimes, nor to limit its scope by reference to the basic/specific intent distinction. *Beard* was considered in *R v Kamipeli*,[55] the leading authority on intoxication in New Zealand, and from that analysis certain principles emerged which continue to govern the defence. The Court of Appeal's approach in *Kamipeli* is consistent with the Australian High Court's approach in *R v O'Connor*,[56] still the leading Australian authority on intoxication. *O'Connor* upheld the fundamental common law principle that the prosecution bears the burden of proving beyond reasonable doubt that the accused committed an offence voluntarily and intentionally. In both Australia and New Zealand, where self-induced intoxication is relevant, it is open to counsel for the defence to cast doubt on whether the accused's acts were willed and conscious and whether the accused possessed the requisite mental element.[57]

In the following section, we examine the decision in *Kamipeli* and outline the guiding principles identified in that case.

11.2.1 *R v Kamipeli*

The accused was charged with murder, following an incident in which he attacked another man in the street and, after knocking him to the ground, continued to punch him and allegedly kicked him in the head. The prosecution argued that he intended to cause the death of the victim, or that he intended to cause the victim bodily injury known to the offender to be likely to cause death and was reckless whether death ensued.[58] There was no suggestion that the accused had struck the victim unintentionally. Indeed, the appellant claimed in evidence that he thought the deceased was about to assault one of his friends, implying that he struck the deceased in order to defend another. It was argued that he should be convicted only of manslaughter because he had not acted with the intent required for murder.

Evidence that the accused was heavily intoxicated was relied on in support of his defence of lack of intent. However, the trial judge directed the jury that the accused must have been so drunk that his mind had "ceased to function, that he was acting as a sort of automaton"[59] without his mind functioning. On appeal, the Court of Appeal held that this was a misdirection because it would have left the jury with the impression that anything less than being so drunk that the accused's mind had ceased to function could not, as a matter of law, leave them with

---

54 *DPP v Beard* [1920] AC 479; [1920] All ER Rep 21 (HL).
55 *R v Kamipeli* [1975] 2 NZLR 610 (CA).
56 *R v O'Connor* (1980) 146 CLR 64 (HCA).
57 Bowman, "Dealing with the 'drunk's defence'" (1999) 24 Alt LJ 233. In a recent report, the Victorian Law Reform Committee endorsed the decision in *O'Connor*, stating that its principles should continue to state the law in Victoria. However, certain procedural changes are recommended in order to safeguard the integrity of the Victorian criminal justice system. See Bowman, 234.
58 See s 167(a) and (b) Crimes Act 1961.
59 *R v Kamipeli* [1975] 2 NZLR 610 (CA), 612.

a proper doubt whether intent had been established on all the evidence. The court made the following observation about the true effect of evidence of intoxication:[60]

> "Drunkenness is not a defence of itself. Its true relevance by way of defence ... is that when a jury is deciding whether an accused has the intention or recklessness required by the charge, they must regard all the evidence, including evidence as to the accused's drunken state, drawing such inferences from the evidence as appears proper in the circumstances. *It is the fact of intent rather than the capacity for intent which must be the subject matter of the inquiry.*"

This has been approved as a standard direction on intoxication,[61] and a direction in these terms is necessary within the wider duty of directing the jury on the Crown's burden of proving all elements of the charge including the mental element.[62] Thus, in a case like *Kamipeli*, a drunken offender might have known what he was doing when he attacked the victim, and he might have intended such an attack, but his intoxication remains relevant to the further question whether he meant to kill or foresaw the risk of causing death. (Indeed, Kamipeli was subsequently retried and acquitted of murder but convicted of manslaughter.)

At common law, judges must now direct a jury on intoxication whenever there is evidence from which a jury might conclude that there is a reasonable possibility that the accused did not form the requisite mens rea.[63] This almost certainly reflects the position in New Zealand. In *R v Tavete*,[64] it was held that when the evidence led by either side discloses a credible narrative that might lead the jury to entertain the reasonable possibility of self-defence, the defence must be put to the jury, even if the accused does not rely on it or expressly disavows it. This rule applies equally to intoxication and other defences recognised at common law, except insanity and absence of fault.

(1) *Guiding the jury*

In *R v Tihi*,[65] the Court of Appeal approved the following direction on the relevance of intoxication to mens rea in the context of a murder prosecution:[66]

> "It has to be shown that in the state of mind that the offender was in, he recognised the real possibility that what he was doing could lead to death ... [W]e do not judge it by an objective standard. If we are considering each man's position ... with the age that he is, what sort of man we judge him to be and his state of mind ... including how drunk he might have been, must he, in the state that he then was, have realised that there was this risk of death as a real possibility?"

The task of the jury in such a prosecution is to have regard to all the evidence, including that relating to drink, in order to determine whether, at the material time, the accused had the requisite intent. The judge is not entitled to give an opinion on the evidence about the degree of the accused's intoxication. That is exclusively a jury question, and no more than one matter

---

60 *R v Kamipeli* [1975] 2 NZLR 610 (CA), 616 (emphasis added).
61 In *R v Tihi* [1990] 1 NZLR 540; (1990) 5 CRNZ 472 (CA), 544; 476 and *R v Tukaki* 14/6/06, CA360/05, para 20.
62 *R v Storer* 2/5/06, CA368/05, para 17 (Harrison J).
63 *R v Bennett* [1995] Crim LR 877; see also *R v Brown and Stratton* [1998] Crim LR 485 (CA).
64 *R v Tavete* [1988] 1 NZLR 428; (1987) 2 CRNZ 579 (CA).
65 *R v Tihi* [1990] 1 NZLR 540; (1990) 5 CRNZ 472 (CA).
66 *R v Tihi* [1990] 1 NZLR 540; (1990) 5 CRNZ 472 (CA), 545; 476.

to be taken into account in considering all the circumstances when reaching a verdict.[67] Nevertheless, the manner in which the direction to juries on intoxication is formulated continues to trouble trial judges. The most common sources of misdirection are (1) to direct the jury that the issue is whether the accused was *incapable* of forming the necessary intent; and (2) to require that, as a result of intoxication, he must have been acting, in effect, as an automaton.[68] But is it clear that such directions set the bar too high. Even if evidence falls short of proving that an accused is so drunk that his mind is no longer functioning, it is still open to a jury to conclude on all the evidence that the Crown has failed to prove the necessary intent.[69] There is judicial agreement that the question is:[70]

> "[W]hether he *had in fact formed* the intent necessary to constitute the particular crime. If he was so drunk that he was incapable of forming or did not in fact form the intent required, he could not be convicted of a crime which is committed only if intent is proved. The onus is upon the Crown to establish his guilt in these circumstances, it is not for the accused to prove that he lacked such an intent. Such is often wrongly referred to as a defence, but it does not mean that drunkenness in itself is an excuse for the crime but that the state of drunkenness may be incompatible with the actual crime charged and may therefore negative the commission of that crime."

In addition to this general obligation, a court may also be required to clarify the relevance of intoxication to specific mens rea elements within the definition of an offence, especially elements other than intention. In particular, where the question is whether the defendant(s) had knowledge of a probable consequence in terms of party liability under s 66(2), the judge's direction should be quite specific. The jury should be told that, when considering an accused's knowledge of probable consequences, the effect of alcohol on her actual knowledge of what could well happen should be examined. If they were left with a reasonable doubt whether the accused, by reason either of alcohol or anything else, did have actual knowledge of what could well happen, they must acquit that accused on the count.[71] In such a case it is important to distinguish between intent relating to the execution of a common purpose and actual knowledge of a probable consequence; the judge may therefore need to direct on the relevance of intoxication to each element distinctly.[72] A similar principle applies where the judge directs a jury on the relevance of intoxication to intent under s 167(b).[73]

(2) Evidential considerations

Of course, the claim that D was too drunk to understand the consequences of his actions may usually be regarded with some scepticism. In any case where the defence of intoxication is

---

67 *R v Tihi* [1990] 1 NZLR 540; (1990) 5 CRNZ 472 (CA), 546; 477.
68 See *R v Purcell* 20/6/05, CA42/05, para 17 (Goddard J). The Court found a misdirection when the trial judge referred to the defence theory on the effect of intoxication requiring that the offender was "effectively a robot — a brainless so intoxicated robot" and as a situation where "a person really does not know what they are doing to the point that they cannot form an intention". See also *R v Boardman* 29/10/03, CA173/03: "a person is so intoxicated that he or she is incapable of forming the necessary intent ..." (para 19).
69 *R v Purcell* 20/6/05, CA42/05, para 17 (Goddard J).
70 *R v Storer* 2/5/06, CA368/05, para 17 (Harrison J) (emphasis added). See also *R v Farrell* [1964] NSWR 1143; *R v Gordon* [1963] SR (NSW) 631, 635-636; *R v Kamipeli* [1975] 2 NZLR 610, 616.
71 *R v Hagen* 4/12/02, CA195/02, para 38 (Anderson J).
72 *R v Hagen* 4/12/02, CA195/02, para 40.
73 See below, 11.2.3.

raised by the accused but there is no evidence of intoxication which could reasonably be thought to have affected the accused's awareness or formation of an intent, a trial judge should so rule and thereby exclude drunkenness from the jury's consideration.[74] For example, where the appellant had admitted deliberately slashing the victim's face with a knife, thereby in effect admitting intending to cause serious bodily harm, evidence of intoxication could not be admitted as preventing him from forming this intention.[75] Equally, however, general principle would seem to require that wherever evidence of intoxication does arise in the course of a trial which may have a bearing on the question of the accused's intent or foresight, the defence must be put to the jury even where the accused has not pleaded it or even expressly disavowed it.[76] It is always a question of law to be determined by the judge whether there is sufficient evidence of intoxication for the matter to go before the jury. Such evidence should state, at the very least, how much alchol the defendant had consumed, and over what period of time, and whether the accused had consumed other drugs in addition to alcohol.[77]

However, the question of the sufficiency of evidence of intoxication to raise the defence as a live issue should not be confused with the question of sufficiency of evidence of intoxication to justify an acquittal. Because intoxication is always a threshold question, it is quite possible that there will be enough evidence to persuade the jury that the accused was indeed intoxicated at the time she committed the offence but insufficient to persuade it that at the time the offence was committed the accused had not formed the intent necessary to constitute the particular crime. It has been observed on many occasions that the mere fact that a defendant was affected by drink so that she acted in a way that she would not have done had she been sober, will not assist her provided the necessary mens rea is present. As has already been remarked, "a drunken intent is nevertheless an intent".[78] Neither is the defence established by the fact that the offender was so intoxicated that he could not remember what he was doing.[79]

It is for the jury, using its common sense and experience of life, to discern (for example) whether a person using violence in a drunken state possessed an intention to kill.[80] In the absence of proof of such an intent, manslaughter would be a proper verdict. However, intoxication is seldom the only relevant consideration and other circumstances, including the duration and degree of violence required to inflict extensive injuries or to cause death, may well weigh with a jury in finding a murderous (albeit drunken) intent proved.[81] So, in a situation where D, in a drunken state, attacks V with an iron bar, without any provocation on V's part,

---

74 *R v Kamipeli* [1975] 2 NZLR 610 (CA), 617 and see *R v Chandra* (2005) 198 CCC (3d) 80. See also *R v Cinous* [2002] 2 SCR 3. Held that if a defence lacks an "air of reality" and should never have been put to the jury, any errors in the charge relating to it are irrelevant.
75 *R v Hayes (Dennis Francis)* [2002] EWCA Crim 1945, discussed in James, "Court of Appeal — Murder: Direction to Jury" (2003) 67 Jo CL 83. See *R v Cooper* (2005) 190 CCC (3d) 342 (BCCA).
76 See *R v Tavete* [1988] 1 NZLR 428; (1987) 2 CRNZ 579 (CA). In so doing, it may be necessary to direct on manslaughter as an alternative verdict to murder: *R v Porter* (2003) 138 A Crim R 581, 602.
77 *R v Chandra* (2005) 198 CCC (3d) 80, 91.
78 *R v Sheehan* [1975] 2 All ER 960; [1975] 1 WLR 739 (CA), 964; 744; and see *R v Doherty* (1887) 16 Cox CC 306, 308 (Stephen J): "A drunken man may form an intention to kill another, or to do grievous bodily harm to him, or he may not; but if he did form that intention, although a drunken intention, he is just as much guilty of murder as if he had been sober."
79 See Coutts, "Judicial Committee of the Privy Council — Constructive Malice: The Felony/Murder Rule" (2000) 64 Jo CL 317.
80 *R v Tihi* [1990] 1 NZLR 540; (1990) 5 CRNZ 472 (CA), 546; 477.
81 *R v Tihi* [1990] 1 NZLR 540; (1990) 5 CRNZ 472 (CA), 546; 477.

D's liability for the murder of V may well depend in practice as much on the nature of the assault as upon the fact of intoxication. If the assault is prolonged and deliberate, the jury may well conclude that its severity negates the claim that the killing was unintentional, despite D's intoxicated state. A single blow, on the other hand, may suggest an impulsive act in which an intention to kill is properly negated by evidence of heavy intoxication.

11.2.2 Capacity and intent

Some earlier judgments on intoxication appear to suggest that intoxication will justify an acquittal only if the accused is "incapable" of forming a required intent. In *DPP v Beard*, Lord Birkenhead said:[82]

> "evidence of drunkenness which renders the accused *incapable* of forming the specific intent essential to constitute the crime should be taken into consideration with the other facts proved in order to determine whether or not he had this intent."

In *A-G for Northern Ireland v Gallagher*, Lord Denning made a similar observation when he asserted:[83]

> "If a man is charged with an offence in which a specific intention is essential (as in murder, though not in manslaughter), then evidence of drunkenness, which renders him *incapable* of forming that intent, is an answer."

However, in *Broadhurst v R*,[84] where the Privy Council was required to interpret an express provision in the Malta Criminal Code governing the defence of intoxication, Lord Devlin observed that the passage from *Beard* cited above "is not altogether easy to grasp". He went on to state:[85]

> "If an accused is rendered incapable of forming an intent, whatever the other facts in the case may be, he cannot have formed it; and it would not therefore be sensible to take the incapacity into consideration together with the other facts in order to determine whether he had the necessary intent."

If a rigid standard for the defence of incapacity to form intent were insisted upon, it would be open to the criticism that an offender might be *capable* of forming the required intent yet fail *in fact* to form it. That would result in the jury being deprived of its proper function of deciding on all the evidence, including that of intoxication, whether the Crown has in fact discharged its onus of proving mens rea.[86] For that reason, it is submitted, the Court of Appeal was right to hold that it is the *fact* of intent rather than *capacity* for intent which is the crucial inquiry.

This means that in a case like *Kamipeli*, an intoxicated offender may have known what he was doing when he attacked the victim, and may even have intended the attack. Nevertheless, intoxication will still be relevant to the essential questions, in a charge of murder, whether he either *meant* to kill, or meant to cause bodily injury *foreseeing* the risk of causing death.

---

82   *DPP v Beard* [1920] AC 479; [1920] All ER Rep 21 (HL), 501-502; 29 (emphasis added).
83   *A-G for Northern Ireland v Gallagher* [1963] AC 349; [1961] 3 All ER 299 (HL), 381; 313 (emphasis added).
84   *Broadhurst v R* [1964] AC 441; [1964] 1 All ER 111 (PC).
85   *Broadhurst v R* [1964] AC 441; [1964] 1 All ER 111 (PC), 461; 122.
86   *R v Kamipeli* [1975] 2 NZLR 610 (CA), 614.

11.2.3 Intoxication and recklessness

When a statute fails to define the mental element required for a "true" crime it is generally held that either intention or recklessness will suffice.[87] Sometimes the statute will explicitly specify that recklessness is sufficient mens rea. We saw in chapter 4 that New Zealand has traditionally regarded recklessness as a subjective mental state, requiring that the defendant actually foresee that the particular offence might result from her conduct. At the same time, it is clear from *R v Kamipeli* that the Court of Appeal anticipated that intoxication might in some circumstances exclude the mens rea for an offence that could be committed recklessly.[88] The implications of intoxication for recklessness, therefore, are straightforward: if D fails to foresee a risk of causing some element of the actus reus because she is too drunk, she is not to be held reckless.

This, at least, is the position for consequences. Where a circumstance is an element of the actus reus, it now appears sufficient to establish recklessness in respect of that circumstance if D lacks a positive belief that the circumstance is not present.[89] Hence, if D fails to think about the possibility of that circumstance because she is too drunk, she will be held reckless about that element.

Sometimes care will be needed to emphasise this, especially where an offence contains multiple mens rea elements. Thus, where evidence of intoxication is relevant to the question whether the accused had the mens rea for murder as defined in s 167(b) Crimes Act 1961, the judge's direction must distinctly explain how drunkenness could have an effect on the three elements of s 167(b), namely, intention, knowledge and recklessness.[90] In *R v Tukaki* it was held to be insufficient for the trial judge to direct the jury that the accused's drunkenness was a factor to be taken into account "in the general mix".[91] Similarly, a direction that "drunkenness was no defence but … [was] a factor to take into account" has been held to a misdirection.[92] Where they are relevant, failure to specify intoxication's relevance to knowledge and recklessness, and not just intention, will raise a concern about the safety of a guilty verdict.[93]

11.2.4 Intoxication and mistake

In adopting a predominantly subjective approach to mens rea, New Zealand law has accepted as a cardinal principle of criminal responsibility that people are to be judged according to the facts as they believed them to be. As such, if D genuinely believed in a set of facts which, if true, would have made her act innocent, the cause of her mistaken belief ought, strictly speaking, to be irrelevant. Normally, the law does not inquire why D was mistaken, and concerns itself only with the inquiry whether D was *in fact* mistaken; rather less frequently does it ask whether her mistake was *reasonable*.

Intoxication adds a complicating element to this inquiry because, arguably, a person who acts dangerously while voluntarily intoxicated is per se acting unreasonably, and ought not for

---

87   See 5.2.
88   *R v Kamipeli* [1975] 2 NZLR 610 (CA), 617.
89   *B (a minor) v DPP* [2000] 2 AC 428; [2000] 1 All ER 833 (HL); *R v K* [2001] 3 All ER 897; [2001] 3 WLR 471 (HL). See 4.3.
90   *R v Tukaki* 14/6/06, CA360/05, para 29 (Chambers J).
91   *R v Tukaki* 14/6/06, CA360/05, para 29 (Chambers J).
92   *R v Hagen* 4/12/02, CA195/02, para 42 (Anderson J).
93   *R v Tukaki* 14/6/06, CA360/05, para 31. See also *R v Hagen* 4/12/02, CA195/02, para 40.

reasons of public policy to be able to take advantage of a mistake made while in that state. This may be the reason why the English Court of Appeal has held that evidence of voluntary intoxication cannot support a plea of absence of mens rea by reason of mistake unless it negates a specific intent — even when the statute itself provides that the question whether there were reasonable grounds for a mistake is of evidential significance only.[94] Moreover, when it comes to claiming supervening defences, such as necessity and self-defence, the general approach in England is that if the defendant made a mistake of fact when intoxicated, such a mistake should be ignored, regardless whether the offence charged is one of specific or basic intent.[95] The approach is illustrated in *O'Grady*,[96] where D's claim of self-defence failed because D had been drunk when he mistakenly believed he needed to defend himself.

The approach to intoxicated mistakes in New Zealand is somewhat analogous, in that the standard of performance expected of a defendant varies according to whether the mistake is one about the *essential circumstances* (ie the actus reus elements), or about *some matter of defence*. The former can be illustrated with reference to the case of *R v Thomas*.[97] The defendant, having been drinking with friends, was driving down a suburban road in the early hours of the morning when she came upon what she mistook to be a police "beating up". In fact the police were attempting to effect a quite lawful arrest. The defendant investigated and intervened in the mistaken belief that the police were using excessive force. Upholding her appeal against conviction, the Court of Appeal held that her honest belief negated the mens rea required for a charge of obstructing a police officer in the execution of his duty. According to the defendant's honestly-held belief, the police were effecting an unlawful arrest, and therefore she did not intend "to obstruct the police while they were acting lawfully".

Concerning the second category, the general rule is that a mistaken belief as to a matter of defence will exclude liability only if it is based on reasonable grounds. So if D, mistakenly believing that his safety is seriously under threat from an imminent hurricane, breaks into V's house in order to take shelter, the defence of duress of circumstances will be unavailable unless, inter alia, D can point to evidence that his belief was based on reasonable grounds.[98]

Where an excusing mistake is required to be both honest and reasonable, D's voluntary intoxication will be relevant to the determination whether the mistake might actually have been made, but it will be disregarded in assessing the reasonableness of any such mistake.[99] The reasonable person is not drunk. Thus, in the duress example above, if D's mistake arises owing to his intoxication, his intoxication will be relevant to the issue *whether* he mistakenly believed his safety was being threatened. However, if a reasonable sober person would not have made the same mistake, D cannot call his intoxication in aid to explain *why* he made the mistake. Hence, unless there are other grounds for his belief, D will be unable to claim the defence.

---

94 *R v Woods* (1981) 74 Cr App R 312; [1982] Crim LR 42 (CA). But cf *Jaggard v Dickinson* [1981] QB 527; [1980] 3 All ER 716 (above, 11.1.1(2)), where it was held that if a statute expressly provides that some honest but mistaken belief is a defence, such a belief suffices even though it is induced by voluntary intoxication and the offence requires no specific intent.
95 Virgo, "Reconciling principle and policy" [1993] Crim LR 415, 417.
96 *R v O'Grady* [1987] QB 995; [1987] 3 All ER 420 (CA); cf *R v O'Connor* [1991] Crim LR 135.
97 *R v Thomas* [1991] 3 NZLR 141; (1991) 7 CRNZ 123 (CA).
98 *Kapi v MOT* [1992] 1 NZLR 227; (1991) 7 CRNZ 481, 230; 484, affirmed (1991) 8 CRNZ 49 (CA).
99 Orchard, "Surviving without Majewski: A view from down under" [1993] Crim LR 426, 428. See also *R v McCullough* (1982) 6 A Crim R 274 (Tas CCA); *R v Clarke* [1992] 1 NZLR 147 (CA).

There are exceptions to this rule governing defences, which typically arise from the statutory wording of specific defences. For example, where an accused person relies on a mistaken belief in relation to self-defence, the statutory definition of self-defence in s 48 Crimes Act 1961 justifies such defensive force as is reasonable "in the circumstances as the accused believes them to be". (Another example is s 24, governing compulsion.) This statutory formula overrides the general rule, and allows a defendant to rely on a mistaken view of the circumstances even when the mistake is attributable to self-induced intoxication; contrary to the position at common law.[100] Indeed, this was an alternative ground for the decision in *R v Thomas*, since (as the Court of Appeal recognised) D's mistaken belief that the police were using unlawful force also supported the justificatory claim of lawful defence of another under s 48.

11.2.5 Negligence and strict liability offences

Where the mens rea of an offence requires only negligence, rather than intention or recklessness, the approach of the law is similar to that taken to reasonable mistakes (11.2.4). Evidence of voluntary intoxication will generally be irrelevant, even in circumstances where the accused claims he was mistaken as to the strength of the alcohol consumed.[101] Once again, the reasonable person is not drunk, and the accused's intoxication is disregarded when determining whether his conduct is reasonable. The same rule applies to the defence of absence of fault in strict liability offences. This principle operates most commonly in the context of offences involving impaired driving, where it reflects the commonsense view that where intoxication is of the essence of the offence it would be contrary to public policy to confer impunity simply because, as a consequence of intoxication, the defendant lacked the relevant awareness or intention to drive while impaired.

11.2.6 Intoxication and automatism

An area of some continuing uncertainty concerns the question whether a person who, through voluntary consumption of alcohol or drugs, becomes an automaton ought to be able to plead automatism as a defence to a charge based on absence of fault.

Automatism at law is action without conscious volition and connotes the state of a person who, though capable of physical movements, is not deliberatively able to control those movements.[102] As such, actions performed in an automatic state are generally said to be "involuntary", and normally attract no criminal liability. The ground for exculpation is twofold: (i) the accused lacks mens rea because she acted without intention or foresight, and (ii) she was not responsible for producing the actus reus because her acts (or omissions) were involuntary.[103]

While automatism, including intoxicated automatism, is a well-established ground of defence in respect of crimes requiring proof of mens rea, its status in the context of public welfare offences, and in offences where intoxication is of the essence of the offence charged, remains

---

100 Cf R v O'Grady [1987] QB 995; [1987] 3 All ER 420 (CA).
101 See *MOT v Crawford* [1988] 1 NZLR 762; (1988) 3 CRNZ 163; *MOT v Strong* [1987] 2 NZLR 295.
102 *Bratty v A-G for Northern Ireland* [1963] AC 386; [1961] 3 All ER 523 (HL), 401; 527. See 3.4.1.
103 It is accepted by the courts that intoxication may produce a state of automatism sufficient to excuse D from criminal responsibility. See, for example, *R v Cottle* [1958] NZLR 999 (CA), 1007; *R v Kamipeli* [1975] 2 NZLR 610 (CA), 612. In *Kamipeli*, intoxicated automatism was not discussed directly by the Court of Appeal, but is implicit in the direction of the trial judge, who is not criticised on that point.

unclear. While in principle intoxicated automatism will deny the accused's responsibility for the actus reus, she may nonetheless be liable for her subsequent, involuntary, behaviour, on the basis that it was a foreseeable consequence of her becoming intoxicated beforehand.[104] If so, then although a general defence of "total absence of fault" is available to the accused, it will be difficult to establish given that she became drunk voluntarily.

11.2.7 Manslaughter

Another difficult issue is whether voluntary intoxication should be a defence to a charge of manslaughter. In England, the rule in *Majewski* does not permit evidence of self-induced intoxication to support a defence to manslaughter. This is because manslaughter has been characterised as a crime of *basic* intent.[105] However, this may be thought to be an unsatisfactory situation for two reasons. First, there is the general objection that it is possible to convict a defendant simply for bringing about the actus reus, even though intoxication prevented the formation of mens rea. Second is the more particular objection that manslaughter is itself a very grave crime that requires proof of an unlawful act (and often, in turn, mens rea) or, at least, that the offender acted voluntarily. Because of its seriousness, it seems odd to allow evidence of intoxication to reduce an offender's culpability for murder but not for manslaughter.

The position in both Australia and New Zealand remains unsettled on this point, although arguments from general principle would seem to favour allowing intoxication to support a defence to unlawful act manslaughter. The decision in *Kamipeli* establishes the general principle that, on a charge of any criminal offence, evidence of voluntary intoxication may be relied upon to support a defence that the accused lacked a mens rea component required by the definition of the crime, or that she acted unconsciously. Prima facie, this principle would include manslaughter and not merely crimes requiring proof of intent or recklessness.

The general principle has also been endorsed by the majority in the Australian High Court decision in *R v O'Connor*.[106] In that case, D had stabbed a police officer in the arm. There was evidence that a state of voluntary intoxication, produced by alcohol in combination with a hallucinogenic drug, may have meant that D did not intend to act as he did. On appeal, a majority of the High Court refused to apply *Majewski*, and held that in the Australian common law jurisdictions, evidence of self-induced intoxication could support the denial of any requirement that conduct, circumstances, or consequences be intended, known, or foreseen; also of any requirement that the conduct be conscious and voluntary.[107] Further, the High Court endorsed the judgment of the Court of Appeal in *Kamipeli*, which had held that there should be no distinction between offences of "general" intent and offences where a "particular" intent was required, and that evidence of intoxication was relevant even if the mens rea requirement for the crime was only recklessness.[108]

In *O'Connor* itself, because of the existence of earlier common law authorities (predating *Majewski*) to the effect that voluntary intoxication can never support an acquittal of

---

104 See 3.4.3, 5.1.1(1).
105 See *DPP v Beard* [1920] AC 479; [1920] All ER Rep 21 (HL), 499, 500; 27, 28; *R v Howell* [1974] 2 All ER 806, 810; *R v Lipman* [1970] 1 QB 152; [1969] 3 All ER 410 (CA).
106 *R v O'Connor* (1980) 146 CLR 64 (HCA).
107 See Orchard, "Surviving without Majewski: A view from down under" [1993] Crim LR 426, 426.
108 *R v Kamipeli* [1975] 2 NZLR 610 (CA), 614.

manslaughter,[109] the High Court acknowledged that manslaughter may be an exception, albeit an "entrenched anomaly".[110] But in a more recent decision, the High Court of Australia has held that, because *O'Connor* establishes that evidence of intoxication is relevant in any case where it is necessary to prove the mental element of a crime, intoxication is therefore available to support an acquittal even of manslaughter in a case where the accused's conduct might have been involuntary.[111] It thus appears that in the Australian common law jurisdictions, evidence of intoxication will now support a defence of automatism in a prosecution for manslaughter; although, where the accused was not so drunk as to be an automaton, intoxication may (anomalously) still be inadmissible to support a simple denial of the mens rea for manslaughter.

In New Zealand, the Court of Appeal in *R v Grice*[112] left open the question whether self-induced intoxication can ever support a defence to manslaughter. In *Grice*, D, who was intoxicated, had been fighting with his father. When his father continued shouting at him after D had threatened otherwise to "throw something", D threw a large bottle which struck his father above the left eye. The father later died as a result of the injuries he received. One ground of appeal against a conviction for manslaughter was that the trial judge had been wrong in declining to put the defence of drunkenness to the jury. D sought to persuade the court that there was a proper foundation in the evidence for an inference that, although conscious of what he was doing, D may have been so affected by alcohol that he did not appreciate the risk or intend to injure or frighten his father. However, this argument was rejected on the basis that, because D had threatened to throw something at his father unless he left D alone, there was an "inevitable inference" that D intentionally applied force directly to his father, which was sufficient to constitute assault and, in turn, the requisite unlawful act for a manslaughter prosecution.

However, when the decision is examined in the light of *Kamipeli*, decided 4 months later by a differently-constituted court, it appears that the court in *Grice* stated the wrong test in finding, as it did, that there was no evidence to go to the jury that D was "incapable of forming any intent" to apply force to his father. It is clear from *Kamipeli* that the proper inquiry is whether the accused actually possessed the relevant intent, not whether he was "capable" of forming the necessary intent. Accordingly, it is arguable that the Court of Appeal in *Grice* may have overstated the legal requirements when it concluded that there was no evidentiary foundation for a defence that drunkenness might have completely precluded D from *having any mens rea whatever*. In truth, D was not contending for such a broad proposition, but simply that he lacked the mens rea to make his act an assault (ie unlawful); for which, it could be argued, there was at least some evidence to enable intoxication to go to the jury.

On the broader policy question whether intoxication can ever be a defence to manslaughter, the court in *Grice* ventured the very tentative view that "it *may prove to be* the law that, putting aside only rare cases of drunken stupor so complete as to result in automatism, intoxication can never be a defence to manslaughter".[113] However, this view finds support only from the broad proposition from *DPP v Beard*[114] that drunkenness can never do more than reduce the

---

109 *DPP v Beard* [1920] AC 479; [1920] All ER Rep 21 (HL), 499, 500; 27, 28; *R v Howell* [1974] 2 All ER 806, 810.
110 *R v O'Connor* (1980) 146 CLR 64 (HCA), 86.
111 *R v Martin* (1984) 51 ALR 540; 16 A Crim R 87 (HCA).
112 *R v Grice* [1975] 1 NZLR 760 (CA).
113 *R v Grice* [1975] 1 NZLR 760 (CA), 767 (emphasis added).

crime from murder to manslaughter. That this fails to adequately represent the current jurisprudence on the intoxication defence hardly need be stated, and certainly does not reflect the trend to expand rather than narrow the scope of exculpatory intoxication. However, the issue still awaits an authoritative ruling from the Court of Appeal.

(1) Intoxication and provocation

In New Zealand, intoxication is irrelevant to the objective test of provocation in s 169(2)(b). That is to say, evidence of intoxication may not be led on the question of whether the provocation given was sufficient to deprive of self-control a person who has the power of self-control of an ordinary person but otherwise has the offender's characteristics. Generally, the effect of alcohol will be regarded as being of a "transitory" nature, lacking the permanence and significance necessary to qualify it as a characteristic for the purposes of s 169(2)(a).[115] However, it is a reviewable error for a judge to say that a defendant may not "call in aid any effects that liquor might have had and it is no help to her on [a] defence of provocation" or that "intoxication is not a factor which can be taken into account when considering whether the defence of provocation can succeed".[116] The true significance of intoxication where provocation is concerned is that it can be a factor to be taken into account in determining whether the defendant *actually* lost her self-control and consequently acted with murderous intent. In *Makoare v R*,[117] the Court of Appeal noted that, where a jury is told simply that intoxication is not relevant to provocation, there is a real danger that the jury will first go to the question of whether self-control was actually lost — the issue in s 169(2)(b) — and, taking the direction to refer also to that paragraph rather than only to s 169(2)(a), will consider the question of actual loss of self-control on the assumption that the drunken defendant was in fact sober. This could lead the jury to conclude, wrongly, that there was no actual loss of self-control and to not consider para (a) at all.

11.2.8 Involuntary intoxication: a new excuse?

In recognising defences, the law allows that, in very limited circumstances, D may be entitled to an acquittal if there is a possibility that although her act was intentional, the intent itself arose out of circumstances for which she bears no blame. Despite its hostility to voluntary intoxication, English law does extend this rationale to situations where D's intoxication was not deliberate. Hale observed that although drunkenness per se was no excuse because it was a "voluntary contracted madness",[118] nonetheless a person might be excused a crime if his intoxication was the result of the "unskilfulness of his physician" or "the contrivance of his enemies".[119] The principle is one which reflects "common justice".[120] Although there is little case law, it appears to be a settled principle that *involuntary* intoxication may be taken into account in determining the existence of a subjective mens rea.[121]

---

114   *DPP v Beard* [1920] AC 479; [1920] All ER Rep 21 (HL), 500; 28.
115   See *R v Fryer* [1981] 1 NZLR 748 (CA), 753.
116   See *R v Barton* [1977] 1 NZLR 295 (CA), 297; *Makoare v R* 20/10/99, CA469/99, para 10 (Blanchard J).
117   *Makoare v R* 20/10/99, CA469/99, para 14.
118   See 1 Hale PC 32. See also *Pearson's Case* (1835) 2 Lew CC 144; 168 ER 1108 (Park J): "If a party be made drunk by stratagem, or the fraud of another, he is not responsible."
119   1 Hale PC 32.
120   *R v Kingston* [1994] QB 81; [1993] 4 All ER 373 (CA), 87; 378 (Lord Taylor).

The distinction between voluntary and involuntary intoxication is, of course, irrelevant in New Zealand — where the law simply asks, whatever the reason, *did* D have mens rea? However, it is worth paying some attention to a recent case that suggests the possibility of an excuse-based defence of involuntary intoxication, which would be available even when D does have mens rea. The suggestion is made by the English Court of Appeal in R *v Kingston*.[122]

In *Kingston*, K, a paedophiliac homosexual, was invited by P to P's flat, ostensibly to discuss business matters. While there, he was given coffee laced with soporific drugs. He was then invited into a bedroom where a boy of 15, also drugged, was lying unconscious on the bed. K, at P's instigation, committed indecencies upon the boy. At trial, K's defence was that his actions, although intentional, had been done in a state of involuntary intoxication. The judge directed the jury that they could convict if they were sure that despite the effect of any drugs he still intended to commit an indecent assault, because a drugged intent is still an intent. The Court of Appeal held that this amounted to a misdirection. Lord Taylor CJ said:[123]

> "A man is not responsible for a condition produced 'by stratagem, or the fraud of another.' If ... drink or a drug, surreptitiously administered, causes a person to lose his self-control and for that reason to form an intent which he would not otherwise have formed, it is consistent with the principle that the law should exculpate him because the operative fault is not his. The law permits a finding that the intent formed was not a criminal intent or, in other words, that the involuntary intoxication negatives the mens rea ... [T]here must be evidence capable of giving rise to the defence of involuntary intoxication before the judge is obliged to leave the issue to the jury. However, once there is an evidential foundation for the defence, the burden is upon the Crown to prove that the relevant intent was formed and that notwithstanding the evidence relied on by the defence it was a criminal intent."

This excuse-based defence of involuntary intoxication, so formulated, is quite different from the defence of intoxication that we been considering in this chapter. As we have seen, the essence of ordinary intoxication as a "defence" is that evidence of intoxication is evidence from which a jury *may* infer that D lacked the mens rea for the crime charged (or, in an extreme case, that D was in a state of automatism). That is, mens rea may be absent because D, being drunk, did not form the required intent. The prosecution is judged to have failed to prove an essential element of the crime charged.

By contrast, where involuntary intoxication is pleaded it may be conceded that an intent is formed to do an act that would otherwise be criminal, but the intent is not attributed to the accused as mens rea because it is not an intent he would have formed had he not been surreptitiously plied with drink. Yet to say that an intent formed as a result of involuntary intoxication is not a criminal intent, or that involuntary intoxication negatives mens rea, is problematic. If an intent is present then a formal element of criminal responsibility has been established. Non-culpability must, therefore, be related to some factor other than the *absence* of mens rea. In *Kingston*, the Court of Appeal hinted that the true basis of exculpation is an analogy to the rationale underlying the defence of duress, although this is not developed in

---

121 See Smith and Hogan, *Criminal Law* (7th ed), London, Butterworths, 1992, 220, 228; cited with approval in R *v Kingston* [1994] QB 81; [1993] 4 All ER 373 (CA), 88; 378; also Law Commission (UK), *Intoxication and Criminal Liability*, Consultation Paper no 127, London, HMSO, 1993, para 2.28.
122 R *v Kingston* [1994] QB 81; [1993] 4 All ER 373 (CA), 88; 378.
123 R *v Kingston* [1994] QB 81; [1993] 4 All ER 373 (CA), 89; 380 (Lord Taylor CJ).

the judgment. If it is desirable as a matter of legal policy to excuse people who commit offences only because of the deliberate actions of other people, the theoretical basis and scope of such a defence needs to be clearly articulated.[124] It should be made clear that, in excusing a person who commits a crime while involuntarily intoxicated, the judgment of non-culpability relates not to the fact that no offence is committed, but rather that punishment in such circumstances is both pointless and unfair. We may excuse because of the commonsense recognition that anyone whose inhibitions may have been involuntarily taken away by the use of unsolicited alcohol or drugs might act with the same degree of disinhibition and commit an offence. It is, strictly speaking, a case of confession and avoidance rather than a claim that an essential element of the offence, namely mens rea, was lacking.

This approach to involuntary intoxication has two important consequences. First, it recognises the error of saying that a person who forms an intent that they would not have formed but for being plied with drink, does not have a criminal intent. If a drunken intent is still an intent,[125] then an involuntarily induced drunken intent must also be an intent, albeit perhaps not one which the law regards as criminally culpable.

Secondly, its recognition as an excuse, of confession and avoidance, does not imply that involuntary intoxication should be an unqualified defence. Arguably, there must be limits to the extent to which conduct should be excused on the basis that D deliberately committed the crime only because P had laced his drink. Consider the following variant on the facts in *Kingston*. Imagine that, in addition to the indecencies committed, D also beat the boy with a baseball bat so that he suffered very serious injuries from which he nearly died. Should involuntary intoxication provide a defence? According to the theory of the defence as outlined by the Court of Appeal in *Kingston*, if the drink surreptitiously administered causes D to lose control *and to form an intent he would not have otherwise formed*, he is entitled to an acquittal because the "operative fault" is not his.[126] Yet this seems an outrageous result. While accepting that D intended, albeit drunkenly, to inflict a serious beating on the boy, this view would suggest that he may do so with impunity. In its decision, the Court of Appeal does not suggest that there is any limit to the operation of the doctrine.

The decision of the Court of Appeal in *Kingston* was overturned by the House of Lords,[127] which ruled, first, that the existence of mens rea is a purely formal question, and is not dependent upon whether the accused is blameworthy: an involuntarily-drugged intent is still an intent, and there is no distinction between "intent" and "criminal intent". Secondly, it held that there is no confession-and-avoidance defence of the type the Court of Appeal purported to recognise. Arguably, however, it is open to the New Zealand Court of Appeal to prefer the analysis of the English Court of Appeal to that of the House of Lords were such a case to come before our courts. Yet, without wanting to deny sympathy for one in Kingston's position, objections to recognising an "excuse" of involuntary intoxication are powerful.

---

124 For discussion of one possible theoretical basis for the defence, see Sullivan, "Making excuses" in Simester and Smith (eds), *Harm and Culpability*, Oxford, Clarendon Press, 1996, 131.
125 In the sense that it is no defence that intoxication removed the defendant's inhibitions and caused him to act in a way he would not have done when sober: *R v Sheehan* [1975] 2 All ER 960; [1975] 1 WLR 739 (CA).
126 *R v Kingston* [1994] QB 81; [1993] 4 All ER 373 (CA), 89; 380.
127 *R v Kingston* [1995] 2 AC 355; [1994] 3 All ER 353 (HL).

First, it seems to strain credulity somewhat to suggest that *only* because a person was involuntarily subject to the effects of drink or drugs, did he deliberately commit a crime he would not otherwise have done. Arguably, the propensity to commit the crime *must already have been present*. The alcohol or drugs merely took away D's inhibitions that would otherwise have suppressed those propensities *on that occasion*.

Secondly, for the reasons outlined above, the defence must be subject to restrictions. There are many situations where a person is placed in a situation (for example temptation, duress) where, if she chooses to commit a crime, she may say that she would not have done so but for her being *involuntarily* placed in that situation. In our view, there is no practical way of drawing a boundary around which crimes may be excused, and under what circumstances. Therefore, in our view, the defence of *exculpatory* involuntary intoxication should be limited to those cases where, because of the effects of intoxication, mens rea is lacking so that the accused is entitled to an unqualified acquittal in any case where mens rea is an element of the offence to be proved by the prosecution. Where, however, the involuntary intoxication merely causes disinhibition such that the accused commits a crime he would otherwise not have committed, we submit that intoxication should not be a complete defence, but rather a factor to be considered by the court in mitigation of sentence. We do not believe that involuntary intoxication should be endorsed in New Zealand as an exculpatory defence which in some fictional sense negates mens rea in circumstances where clearly there was an intention to commit an offence, albeit drunkenly.

(1) *Breath-alcohol offences*

"Involuntary intoxication" is sometimes also used in another sense in New Zealand. There is a line of cases, involving excess breath-alcohol offences, which suggests that a defence may exist where a person was unaware that she was consuming drink or drugs — the availability of the defence depending on whether the accused had notice of the possible effect of the substance, and whether she had an opportunity of avoiding its effects. However, because the offences concerned have now been formally classified as public welfare regulatory offences,[128] they are now governed by ordinary principles of strict liability. Thus the defence of involuntary intoxication, where it is relevant, will be available only where the defendant is able to prove (on a balance of probabilities) that she was totally without fault. Such a defence will not succeed where a person concerned knew, or ought to have known, that she was affected by alcohol.[129]

Intoxication may be relevant in another sense in cases where alcohol has affected the manner of an offender's driving. Evidence that the defendant drove a motor vehicle while under the influence of drink, to such an extent as to be incapable of having proper control of the vehicle and thereby caused the death of another person, may in some circumstances support a prosecution for manslaughter under s 160(2)(a). However, in such a case the jury must be warned of the danger of using evidence of intoxication improperly to elevate any carelessness found to such a degree as to bring it within the scope of a major departure from the standard of care required from a driver of a motor vehicle.[130] The jury should look at the carelessness

---

128 See *O'Neill v MOT* [1985] 2 NZLR 513.
129 See *O'Neill v MOT* [1985] 2 NZLR 513. See also *Flyger v Auckland CC* [1979] 1 NZLR 161; *Rooke v Auckland CC* [1980] 1 NZLR 680.
130 *R v Paenga (No 4)* 22/2/06 Heath J, HC Tauranga, CRI-2004-070-2905, para 51 (Heath J).

of the driving, not at the level of intoxication per se. This is consistent with the principle that matters which are merely part of the background to an accident and which go to prove acts or omissions which were not, whatever their character, wholly or partly causative of the fatality, may be inadmissible. The reason is that such matters may not be relevant because their probative value is slight and exceeded by their potential for unfairly prejudicing the defendant in the eyes of the jury.[131]

---

131 R v Fenton [2003] 3 NZLR 439, (2003) 20 CRNZ 76 (CA), para 15 (Blanchard J).

Chapter 12

COMPULSION

12.1	Introduction	358
12.2	Historical background behind the statutory defence	358
12.3	Theoretical basis (or bases) of compulsion	359
12.3.1	Involuntariness as an element of compulsion	361
12.4	The statutory definition of compulsion	363
12.5	Elements of compulsion	363
12.6	A threat to kill or cause grievous bodily harm	364
12.6.1	Implied threats	366
12.6.2	Mistaken perceptions of threats and mistaken inferences of danger	367
12.7	Immediately following refusal to commit an offence	368
12.8	Person making threat present during commission of offence	371
12.9	Honest belief that the threat will otherwise be carried out	373
12.10	Further restrictions on the defence	374
12.10.1	Opportunity to escape or seek protection	374
12.10.2	Threats to others apart from the accused	377
(1)	*What if the person threatened is not present?*	377
12.10.3	Volunteers: parties to conspiracies or association	378
(1)	*Foreseeability or actual knowledge?*	379
12.10.4	Excluded offences	379
(1)	*Should compulsion be available for murder?*	381
12.11	The burden of proof	383
12.12	Compulsion and self-defence	384
12.13	Battered women who commit offences under compulsion	385
12.14	Reform: the Law Commission's recommendations	387
12.14.1	Non-specific threats	387
12.14.2	Immediacy or inevitability	388
12.14.3	A reasonableness test	388

12.1 Introduction

The criminal law concept of compulsion, together with its cognate expression, duress, has been described as an "extremely vague and elusive juristic concept".[1] This may be partly because the defence has developed on an insecure theoretical footing and partly on account of imprecision in the use of definitions. For example, in legal literature the concept of compulsion may be referred to by a bewildering variety of expressions, and it is not always clear from the context in what sense the concept is being employed. The foundational notion of overbearing physical or psychological pressure may be implied in any of the following expressions: physical causation, physical compulsion, causal necessity, absolute causation, coercion, duress per minas, duress of circumstances, teleological necessity, and coactus volui.[2] Some of these expressions will be explained below and in the chapter following, as the discussion proceeds. All represent different ways of conceptualising compulsion and show that there is a strong linguistic connection between compulsion and related notions of necessity and duress, such that the concepts are often confused in legal discussion. In this chapter, we will confine ourselves to the statutory defence of compulsion. Common law defences of necessity and duress will be analysed in the next chapter.

Although the expressions "compulsion" and "duress" overlap extensively, and are often used interchangeably in the case law, compulsion appears to have been the expression first used in the context of overbearing threats which induce criminal action, and is the expression commonly used by common law commentators.[3] It is also the expression preferred by Sir James Fitzjames Stephen and, through his influence on the Draft Criminal Code of 1879, is the expression adopted in s 24 Crimes Act 1961 and in its antecedents.[4] To some extent, as we shall note in 12.3 below, the common law defence of duress has since developed beyond the scope of New Zealand's compulsion defence; but we shall defer a fuller consideration of that separate development until the chapter following.

12.2 Historical background behind the statutory defence

The law has, from a very early period, endorsed the view that a person is entitled to preserve his life and limb. The right is recognised and preserved in a variety of ways, including the statutory defences of compulsion and self-defence, and the common law defence of necessity. Contrasting somewhat with this rich palette, the statutory defence of compulsion is designed to provide relief from criminal liability only in fairly closely circumscribed situations in which an offender has been "forced" to commit an offence because of the overbearing threats or violence of another person. Moreover, it is clear that not every threat or situation of anxiety generating an apprehension of personal violence will raise the defence. The relevant threats must be immediately to kill or seriously injure the person claiming compulsion, and the person must apprehend a real risk that unless she cooperates the threatener will deliver on the threats.

As the law has developed, it has been established that compulsion is a defence only where the crime is not of a heinous character.[5] In particular, English common law has insisted — an insistence reflected in many modern statutory formulations of the compulsion defence — that

---

1 *Lynch v DPP for Northern Ireland* [1975] AC 653; [1975] 1 All ER 913 (HL), 686; 931 (Lord Simon).
2 Literally, "by his will but coerced".
3 See 1 Hale PC 49; 1 East PC 70.
4 See s 24 Criminal Code Act 1893; s 44 Crimes Act 1908; s 24 Crimes Act 1961.

the killing of an innocent person can never be justified.[6] This rule dates back at least to the writings of Lord Hale, who said:[7]

"if a man be desperately assaulted, and in peril of death, and cannot otherwise escape, unless to satisfy his assailant's fury he will kill an innocent person then present, the fear and actual force will not acquit him of the crime and punishment of murder, if he commit the fact; for he *ought rather to die himself, than kill an innocent*."

Many of the early cases involved offenders who sought to defend charges of treason on the grounds that the commands of an invading enemy or rebels backed by threats of force constituted compulsion. In a number of trials for high treason in 1746, the defence of the prisoners was that they were compelled to serve in the rebel army.[8] In these cases the law was fairly generous, and provided that the defence of compulsion applied not only to furnishing provisions to the rebel army, but also to joining and serving in that army.[9] Relief was nonetheless conditional:[10]

"The only force that doth excuse is a *force upon the person and present fear of death* and this force and fear of death *must continue all the time the party remains with the rebels*. It is incumbent on every man who makes force his defence, to show an *actual force*, and that he quitted the service as soon as he could."

New Zealand law does not require actual force as an element of compulsion because the defence, as defined in s 24, is concerned with *moral* force, ie with threats as opposed to direct physical force. However, the other elements in italics generally reflect present requirements of statutory compulsion.

12.3 Theoretical basis (or bases) of compulsion

The defence of compulsion operates on the basis of "confession and avoidance"; although the accused may have intentionally committed an offence, she is excused because her will or freedom of choice has been "overborne" by threats from another. Where compulsion is established, it does not operate to negative any legal ingredient of the crime committed by the defendant.[11] Nor is it regarded as justifying the conduct of the defendant. It is now properly

---

5 Criminal Code Bill Commission, *Report of the Royal Commission Appointed to Consider the Law Relating to Indictable Offences: With an Appendix Containing a Draft Code Embodying the Suggestions of the Commissioners*, London, Eyre & Spottiswode for HMSO, 1879, 43.
6 Criminal Code Bill Commission, *Report of the Royal Commission Appointed to Consider the Law Relating to Indictable Offences: With an Appendix Containing a Draft Code Embodying the Suggestions of the Commissioners*, London, Eyre & Spottiswode for HMSO, 1879, 43. See also s 24(2)(e) Crimes Act 1961; s 17 Criminal Code (Can); s 94 Indian Penal Code; s 31 Criminal Code (Qld); s 31 Criminal Code (WA).
7 1 Hale PC 51 (emphasis added).
8 Criminal Code Bill Commission, *Report of the Royal Commission Appointed to Consider the Law Relating to Indictable Offences: With an Appendix Containing a Draft Code Embodying the Suggestions of the Commissioners*, London, Eyre & Spottiswode for HMSO, 1879, 43.
9 Criminal Code Bill Commission, *Report of the Royal Commission Appointed to Consider the Law Relating to Indictable Offences: With an Appendix Containing a Draft Code Embodying the Suggestions of the Commissioners*, London, Eyre & Spottiswode for HMSO, 1879, 43.
10 Criminal Code Bill Commission, *Report of the Royal Commission Appointed to Consider the Law Relating to Indictable Offences: With an Appendix Containing a Draft Code Embodying the Suggestions of the Commissioners*, London, Eyre & Spottiswode for HMSO, 1879, 43 (emphasis added).
11 Cf *R v Fisher* [2004] Crim LR 938, where the English Court of Appeal rightly rejected the proposition that the common law defence of duress attaches only to the actus reus of the offence.

regarded as a defence which, if established, excuses what would otherwise be criminal conduct.[12] Typically, a person claiming compulsion is told: "Do this [an act that would amount to a crime in the absence of a defence of compulsion] or you will be killed." In fear for her life, D does what she is commanded to do. At the heart of the defence is the motive of *fear* that certain consequences will occur if the threat is not obeyed. As such, the defence represents an exception to the general rule that motive is never an element of an offence.[13] It is the fact that an offender has acted out of a well-grounded fear in succumbing to illegal threats that provides the true basis of exculpation, since it is argued that anyone of like fortitude would have acted in the same way and, therefore, D should not be punished. Unlike defences which operate to negate *mens rea* (as in the cases of mistake and intoxication) or *actus reus* (as with the defences of involuntariness, automatism, and impossibility) compulsion provides a supervening excuse which negates criminal responsibility for an offence that prima facie *has been committed*. That is to say, in the case of compulsion, the elements of both *actus reus* and *mens rea* are in place, but criminal liability is overridden because D's choice to commit the offence was a constrained one. Exceptionally, therefore, motive may be regarded as an (exculpatory) element of an offence committed under compulsion. One way of thinking of compulsion is as a species of temptation, in which a person is motivated to do and to refrain from doing that which one believes is in some way wrong or bad, reflecting a measure of volitional ambivalence. Since agents motivated by strong temptations are not fully free, they are not fully responsible for the actions they perform as a result of such temptations.[14] The essence of compulsion, according to this approach, is the undermining of autonomy caused by irresistible temptations.[15]

Under English common law, the defence of compulsion is embraced under the name "duress per minas" ("duress by threats") or, sometimes, just "duress". Traditionally this extended, as the expression "per minas" suggests, only to threats made by another person; and it is this historical understanding of the defence that informs the statutory defence of compulsion that has been codified in New Zealand.

However, in recent years the English courts have recognised another form of duress, duress of *circumstances*; which also depends on the accused committing a crime out of fear, but in circumstances where there was no *person* demanding that she do it. The defence of duress of circumstances is still in its infancy in England, but in that jurisdiction it is developing by analogy to duress by threats. It is thought that considerations of policy suggest that both defences should be governed by the same principles.[16] While this approach has much to commend it, it is not currently the position in New Zealand, where the tests for duress of circumstances and compulsion remain distinct. The former is a common law defence; the latter is statutory.

---

12 Cf *R v Hasan* [2005] 2 WLR 709; [2005] 2 AC 467; [2005] UKHL 22, para 18 (Lord Bingham). See also *R v Hibbert* (1995) 99 CCC (3d) 193, paras 21, 38, 47 (Lamer CJC).
13 See, for example, Smith and Hogan, *Criminal Law* (7th ed), London, Butterworths, 1992, 79: "If D causes an *actus reus* with *mens rea*, he is guilty of the crime and it is entirely irrelevant to his guilt that he had a good motive."
14 See Hughes, "Temptation and Culpability in the Law of Duress and Entrapment" [2006] 51 Crim LQ 342, 343.
15 See Hughes, "Temptation and Culpability in the Law of Duress and Entrapment" [2006] 51 Crim LQ 342, 344.
16 Smith and Hogan, *Criminal Law* (9th ed), London, Butterworths, 1999, 231.

At the same time, common law decisions on the former may be authorities, by analogy, for the scope of the latter. It is, unfortunately, a recipe for confusion.[17]

In New Zealand, although the courts have recognised the common law evolution of duress of circumstances,[18] the position is complicated by the fact that compulsion here is codified, while duress of circumstances remains as a common law defence of uncertain scope. It seems that duress of circumstances will only be available in New Zealand to the extent that the threat which underlies the claim of duress does not issue from any human agency, on the basis that s 24 Crimes Act 1961 exhaustively defines the extent to which human agent threats are available as a means of exculpation.[19] This issue will be considered in more depth in the next chapter.

The matter is also complicated by the fact that "duress of circumstances" is often used interchangeably with "necessity", and the two are often thought to be analogous or even identical defences. Not so. As we shall see in chapter 13, the modern defence of necessity is a fundamentally different defence — a justification, not an excuse — and it has a rationale quite distinct from the underpinnings of compulsion and duress.

12.3.1 Involuntariness as an element of compulsion

It is sometimes said that a person who acts under compulsion acts "involuntarily". However, this is merely a shorthand way of saying that the threat *substantially impaired* the person's free choice, so that he acted purposively but unwillingly. Such a person, though doing an act under compulsion, may still act voluntarily. In the criminal law, many acts are done under pressure. This does not mean that there was no mens rea or that the act was not voluntary. With compulsion, the element of involuntariness lies in threats which "overbear the ordinary power of human resistance".[20] To say that D's will is "suppressed" or "overborne" in this context is not the same as saying that D acted involuntarily; because the latter would normally imply that D's will had not merely been overpowered but had ceased to be operative at any conscious level.

Furthermore, attributing involuntariness to acts done under compulsion makes it difficult to distinguish conceptually between conduct which is *constrained* (as with compulsion by threats) and conduct which is *driven* by a superior force (as in cases of physical causation). So we may properly say that D acted involuntarily when T, using superior force, shouldered D who in turn struck V, causing V to fall to his death from a narrow walkway. This is qualitatively different to E's claim to have acted "involuntarily" when he succumbed to P's threat to shoot him unless he drove the getaway car for an armed robbery. One person acts involuntarily; the other's choices are merely constrained by threats. Unlike the person "acting" while under physical compulsion (for example the person whose hand is held and directed by superior force to perform some criminal act), the person acting under compulsion is unable to say "I had no choice" (or, indeed, that "my conduct occurred outside my control"). The alternative

---

17 See, eg, *Police v Matsubara* [2004] DCR 385, discussed below at 12.6.
18 See *Kapi v MOT* (1991) 8 CRNZ 49 (CA), affirming [1992] 1 NZLR 227; (1991) 7 CRNZ 481.
19 *Kapi v MOT* (1991) 8 CRNZ 49 (CA), 54, 55 (Gault J): "When s 24 provides a defence of compulsion (or duress) where the criminal act is done under threat of death or grievous bodily harm from a person who is present when the offence is committed, we do not consider s 20 [Crimes Act] can be said to preserve a common law defence of duress by threat or fear of death or grievous bodily harm from a person not present."
20 *A-G v Whelan* [1934] IR 518 (CCA), 526 (Murnaghan J).

to not committing the crime may have been extremely unpleasant, but it would be untrue to say there was no choice.

The nature of the choice that is exercised in cases of compulsion can be demonstrated in the following example. D is standing at the window of her room on the third floor of a 20-storey hotel. The hotel is ablaze and fire is threatening to consume her room. D may choose to stay in the hotel and almost certainly burn to death or she may jump, risking serious injury and possibly death. Her decision to jump is the result of a choice in which she weighs the dangers of remaining in the hotel against the risks inherent in jumping and concludes that the odds of surviving the fall are greater than remaining in the burning building. It is truly a choice between evils. Yet it is a choice. This type of invidious decision-making is sometimes referred to as "normative" or "moral" involuntariness, because it is typical of what anyone with normal fortitude could be expected to do under such terrible pressure, even though an ability to choose remains.[21] The heart of the compulsion defence is that no person should be *forced* by threats to have to make such awful choices and be held criminally responsible when they do.

In the case of compulsion it is, therefore, possible that the offender may *intend* to commit the prohibited act yet not *wish*, or desire, that it should happen. Compulsion is consistent with voluntary and deliberate action. What allows exculpation in such cases is not the fact that the accused acted involuntarily but rather the fact that the power of choice — axiomatic to the notion of freedom of the human will and to criminal responsibility — was substantially impaired.[22] However, as Smith and Hogan note,[23] a defence of compulsion should never be available where the prosecution is able to prove that the accused would have done the same act even if the threats had not been made. Where the accused's acts are attributable to other motives in addition to threats, the question that will determine the availability of the defence is whether he would have acted as he did but for the threats.[24]

At common law, compulsion developed under the rubrics "duress per minas"[25] and "coercion"; the latter was a limited defence available to a wife who committed an offence while subject to the influence of her husband. In New Zealand there is no longer any presumption that a woman who commits an offence in her husband's presence was subject to compulsion by him. Some writers prefer to reserve the expression "compulsion" to situations of overpowering physical force, where there is arguably neither mens rea nor actus reus. However, this usage is inappropriate in New Zealand where the expression as used in statute is clearly limited to situations where D is constrained by threats to act as he does. It is this element which distinguishes statutory compulsion from the emerging common law defence of "duress of circumstances" — where disobedience of the law is compelled by dangers other than a threat from a human agent.

---

21 The notion of "normative involuntariness" has developed from Canadian criminal jurisprudence. See *R v Perka* [1984] 2 SCR 232, also reported as *Perka v R* (1984) 14 CCC (3d) 385 (SCC). It is said that an accused whose offence is normatively involuntary cannot be said to be personally at fault because it "is axiomatic that in criminal law there should be no responsibility without personal fault": *R v DeSousa* [1992] 2 SCR 944; (1992) 76 CCC (3d) 124 (SCC), 956; 134 (Sopinka J), discussed in *R v Langlois* (1993) 80 CCC (3d) 28, 33 (Fish JA).

22 *Lynch v DPP for Northern Ireland* [1975] AC 653; [1975] 1 All ER 913 (HL), 689; 933 (Lord Simon).

23 Smith and Hogan, *Criminal Law* (9th ed), London, Butterworths, 1999, 232.

24 Smith and Hogan, *Criminal Law* (9th ed), London, Butterworths, 1999, 234. See *R v Valderrama-Vega* [1985] Crim LR 220; also *DPP v Bell* [1992] RTR 335; [1992] Crim LR 176.

25 See 12.1.

12.4 The statutory definition of compulsion

The defence of compulsion is defined in s 24 Crimes Act 1961, which states:

"**24 Compulsion**

"(1) Subject to the provisions of this section, a person who commits an offence under compulsion by threats of immediate death or grievous bodily harm from a person who is present when the offence is committed is protected from criminal responsibility if he believes that the threats will be carried out and if he is not a party to any association or conspiracy whereby he is subject to compulsion."

The remaining subsections itemise the offences which are excluded from the operation of the statutory defence (subs (2)), and repeal the presumption of marital coercion (subs (3)). These will be considered later in this chapter.

Unlike the modern common law defence of duress of circumstances, the statutory defence in s 24 is concerned primarily with the verbal threats of human agents, although threats implicit in the *conduct* of persons present at the commission of a crime will also qualify, provided they have the consequences defined in the section.[26] However, the defence is not to be viewed as a general catch-all provision to assist offenders of frail personality who crumble at the slightest pressure and are especially susceptible to the threatening behaviour of others. Indeed, the provision has been tightly drawn to prohibit its use in all but the most exigent of circumstances. The Court of Appeal has said:[27]

"The legislation provides a *narrow release from criminal responsibility where its strict requirements are met*. It reflects a policy decision that in those limited circumstances (and where the offence is not in the gravest category excluded from the application of the defence under s 24(2)) a person faced with the threat of immediate death or grievous bodily harm may properly be excused if he chooses the lesser evil of committing the offence."

12.5 Elements of compulsion

The scope of the statutory provision was examined by the Court of Appeal in *R v Teichelman*,[28] where it was noted that four ingredients were contemplated by the Legislature:

(1) There must be a threat to kill or cause grievous bodily harm;

(2) The threat must be to kill or inflict that serious harm immediately following a refusal to commit an offence;

(3) The person making the threat must be present during the commission of the offence; and

(4) The accused must commit the offence in the belief that otherwise the threat will be carried out.

---

26 An analogy may be drawn with the cases on self-defence, in which context it has been held that threats to use physical power, as well as the actual use of physical power, are included in the notion of "force" within s 48 Crimes Act 1961. See *R v Terewi* (1985) 1 CRNZ 623 (CA).
27 *R v Teichelman* [1981] 2 NZLR 64 (CA), 66 (emphasis added).
28 *R v Teichelman* [1981] 2 NZLR 64 (CA), 66 (emphasis added).

We might elaborate on these ingredients with the following, more or less implicit, qualifications:

(5) There must be no reasonable opportunity to avoid the threat;

(6) The threat may, it is submitted, be to kill or inflict serious harm upon someone other than the accused;

(7) The accused must not have voluntarily exposed herself to the threat by becoming party to a conspiracy or association whereby she is subject to the compulsion that follows; and

(8) The offence committed by the accused must fall outside the list of offences for which availability of compulsion is excluded by s 24(2).

We shall consider each of these elements in turn.

12.6 A threat to kill or cause grievous bodily harm

In *R v Teichelman*[29] the Court of Appeal, interpreting the phrase "immediate death or grievous bodily harm" in s 24, held that it is the "belief in the inevitability of immediate and violent retribution for failure ... to comply with the threatening demand", that constitutes the gravamen of the defence.[30] In that case the accused, a drug dealer, claimed compulsion on the basis that a drug dealing associate had allegedly made threats to a third person to "blow [his] head off" if he refused to put him in contact with suppliers of drugs; and on the further ground that he "felt frightened" and thought the associate would attack him if he did not supply drugs. On appeal the Court held there was an insufficient evidential foundation for compulsion to be considered by the jury, in particular because there was no evidence, on any of the occasions the appellant had been requested to supply drugs, that threats had been uttered or "threatening gestures" made.[31]

The inclusion of "threatening gestures" in this context may be taken to imply that the requirement in the statute for "threats of immediate death" will be satisfied where there is relevant threatening behaviour that causes the accused to believe that he will be subjected to inevitable and immediate violent retribution if he fails to comply with the threatening demand.[32] This is also consistent with the common law defence of duress per minas, which is taken to include "threats and menaces, which induce a fear of death or other bodily harm".[33] In *R v Raroa*[34] the Court of Appeal confirmed that a threat need not be in words for the purpose of s 24. On the other hand, it must still be a particular kind of threat associated with a particular demand. Therefore mere apprehension, leading an offender to feel "threatened" in some general sense, will be insufficient to satisfy the statutory test in the absence of a clear demand. Yet if D is faced with a large and intimidating aggressor holding a dangerous weapon in a menacing manner, the sense of threat and the felt need to comply with any implicit demand is likely to be as powerful as any imperious verbal command. It is proper that the law should

---

29 R v Teichelman [1981] 2 NZLR 64 (CA), 66.
30 R v Teichelman [1981] 2 NZLR 64 (CA), 67.
31 R v Teichelman [1981] 2 NZLR 64 (CA), 67.
32 R v Teichelman [1981] 2 NZLR 64 (CA), 67.
33 Blackstone, *Commentaries on the Laws of England* (19th ed), London, Sweet & Maxwell, 1836, Book IV, chapter II, 30 (emphasis added).
34 R v Raroa [1987] 2 NZLR 486; (1987) 2 CRNZ 596 (CA), 493; 602 (Bisson J).

acknowledge this in interpreting "threats". This approach may be further reinforced by the Court of Appeal's insistence, in *Teichelman*, that in the final analysis it is the accused's *belief* in the inevitability of immediate and violent retribution that determines the ground for exculpation, rather than the manner in which the threat is delivered. Despite this, in *Teichelman* itself the Court found that the highest it could reasonably be put on the evidence was that, because of the previous menacing conduct of the associate, the appellant felt that if he did not cooperate he would be in some danger. This, the Court found, fell far short of acting under a continuing threat of immediate grievous bodily harm as contemplated by the section.

The emphasis in *Teichelman* on the "strict requirements" of the statute would seem to require that the threats are actually aimed at forcing the accused to commit an offence. If "mere apprehension" on the part of an accused or an honest belief in non-existent threats is insufficient to provide a defence,[35] it may be difficult to contend that the defence ought to be available to a defendant who is not actually forced to commit an offence. In *R v Raroa*,[36] it was precisely because there was no evidence of any demand, accompanied by threats, having been made on the accused to assist in the disposal of two bodies following an execution-style killing that the Court of Appeal disallowed compulsion and dismissed the appeal. It is arguable that such a requirement is implicit in the insistence by s 24 that the accused act "under compulsion". However, this element was left unresolved in *R v Lamont*.[37] In that case, the appellant sought to defend a charge of causing death by careless use of a motor vehicle on grounds of compulsion. The alleged compulsion had been generated by another's car driving up behind him and maintaining a close proximity, in circumstances in which the defendant believed he was being chased and needed to take evasive action to avoid the "threat" of a collision. The Court did not consider it necessary to deal with the issue whether s 24 necessarily requires a "demand" element, because of the appellant's failure to provide any evidence of threats of, and a genuine fear of, immediate death or serious bodily harm.

Compulsion was, however, allowed in *Police v Matsubara*,[38] a District Court decision of doubtful authority. In a prosecution for driving with excess breath alcohol, D had driven his car a short distance after he had been drinking and was admittedly incapable of driving. He had done so in order to put some distance between himself and some youths who had set upon him while he was resting in his car, stealing his glasses and wallet and subjecting him to racial slurs and other verbal abuse. Although the Court characterised the active element of the claimed defence of compulsion under s 24 as a "threat" from third persons, it is not clear that the defendant was actually subjected to threats of death or grievous bodily harm normally required to establish an evidential foundation for the defence. Nonetheless, the Court found that he had presented such an evidential foundation, despite the absence of evidence of actual threats of death or bodily injury.[39] The finding was based on the judgment that the defendant had "reasonable grounds" to believe that he could suffer serious bodily injury if he attempted to remain in his car, even if it was locked; and that his reaction was "proportionate" to the threat because he

---

35   *R v Raroa* [1987] 2 NZLR 486; (1987) 2 CRNZ 596 (CA), 494; 604 (Bisson J).
36   *R v Raroa* [1987] 2 NZLR 486; (1987) 2 CRNZ 596 (CA), 494; 604 (Bisson J). See also *R v Dawson* [1978] VR 536, where the common law defence was held to be available only when threats were aimed at forcing the accused to commit an offence.
37   *R v Lamont* 27/4/92, CA442/91.
38   *Police v Matsubara* [2004] DCR 385.
39   *Police v Matsubara* [2004] DCR 385, para 18.

drove only a sufficient distance to be out of sight and away from the group. The Judge concluded that the defence of compulsion had been made out under s 24 and the prosecution was dismissed.

The difficulty with this decision is that, while the initial discussion concerned the availability of a common law defence of "duress of circumstances", for which an evidential foundation may well have existed, the decision in favour of the defendant is made on the basis of the statutory defence of compulsion, for which the evidence in support is non-existent. The Court appears to have (wrongly) assumed, that the elements for both defences are the same and has used the expressions "compulsion" and "duress of circumstances" interchangeably, with a consequential confusion of the defence requirements.

The "strict requirements" approach to interpreting s 24 precludes the acceptance in New Zealand of lesser threats, including threats of serious "hurt" to a person's "comfort", or threats to property, since the statute expressly requires threat of "death or grievous bodily harm",[40] an element that was seemingly absent in *Police v Matsubara*. It is now established that these words should be given their ordinary meaning of "really serious bodily harm" or "really serious hurt".[41] However, the words of the statute are sufficiently broad to include threats to inflict a person with a fatal disease and would extend to the situation where, for example, a person is threatened with the infliction of the Aids virus either through an act of sexual violation or through a contaminated syringe, if he fails to comply with the demand made.[42] Since the expression "grievous bodily harm" now includes serious psychiatric injury,[43] it is arguable that the defence could be made out where there is evidence that an accused genuinely believed that the threatener had the power to inflict psychological devastation upon him unless he complied with the demand.[44] However, such an extension to the law has yet to be tested by the courts.

12.6.1 Implied threats

Under the present law, "mere apprehension" is not enough to give rise to the defence of compulsion.[45] The person must fear the particular type of harm set out in s 24. Often, this will involve proof of a verbal threat communicated to the offender. However, as we have seen there is at present no requirement that the threat must be communicated verbally.[46] At common

---

40 It is a misdirection to direct the jury that the threatener might bring pressure on the defendant "of any kind": "The possible pressure of which a defendant is to be aware is pressure of a violent kind in the form of violence or threats of death or violence to the defendant or a member of his immediate family." *R v Baker & Ward* (1999) 2 Cr App R 335 (CA), 344 (Roch LJ). For a thoughtful discussion of the arguments in favour of allowing lesser threats, see Aldridge, "Developing the defence of duress" [1986] Crim LR 433, 435-437.
41 *DPP v Smith* [1961] AC 290, also reported as *R v Smith* [1960] 3 All ER 161 (HL); *R v Metharam* [1961] 3 All ER 200; (1961) 45 Cr App R 304 (CA); *R v Mwai* [1995] 3 NZLR 149; (1995) 13 CRNZ 273 (CA), 155; 280.
42 For a discussion of the general issues involved in this example, see Kirby, "Legal implications of Aids" in *Legal Implications of Aids*, Auckland, Legal Research Foundation, 1989, 3.
43 *R v Mwai* [1995] 3 NZLR 149; (1995) 13 CRNZ 273 (CA), 155; 280.
44 Such an extension of the defence would still not assist the defendant in *Salaca v R* [1967] NZLR 421 (CA), because his fear that "something might happen to me" would be insufficient to establish serious psychiatric injury.
45 *R v Frickleton* [1984] 2 NZLR 670 (CA), 672. See *R v Tyler* (1838) 8 C & P 616; 173 ER 643, 620; 645: "[fear of the other] has never been received by the law as an excuse for his crime."
46 See 1 Hale PC 51; *M'Growther's Case* (1746) Fost 13, 14; Stephen, *A Digest of the Criminal Law (Indictable Offences)*, London, Macmillan & Co, 1877, art 10; also *Lynch v DPP for Northern Ireland* [1975] AC 653; [1975] 1 All ER 913 (HL), in which evidence of duress was allowed to go to the jury although there had been no express threat.

law it could be express or implied by words or conduct. There is no reason to suppose that s 24 does not include implied threats, although such cases may provide more room for disputing whether the threat was of the kind required by statute.[47] We have seen from *R v Raroa*[48] that a threat need not be in words for the purposes of s 24, notwithstanding that it must be a particular kind of threat associated with a particular demand. Consequently, it seems that threats implied and "inherent in the situation" in which the defendant found herself would support a compulsion defence, in appropriate circumstances.[49] This might include a situation where, for example, the threateners, who are present in the courtroom, have previously threatened the accused that she will be beaten up unless she gives perjured evidence.[50]

12.6.2 Mistaken perceptions of threats and mistaken inferences of danger

The difficulty arises when D makes a mistake about the existence of a threat. There are two types of mistake that may be made:

(i) A mistake about what T has done or said, so that D believes he has been threatened; and

(ii) A mistaken inference that D is in danger, when the facts as D perceives them to be do not disclose a threat (at least, a threat qualifying under s 24).

The first variety of mistake might occur, for example, when D mishears T, and thinks that T has threatened to shoot him unless he commits a specified crime, when in fact T has merely asked D the time. Although at common law such mistakes must be reasonable to exculpate,[51] under s 24 a subjective belief is sufficient, and D will qualify for the defence of compulsion.[52]

However, in the second case, in the absence of an *actual threat*, an honest (and even reasonable) belief that D is in danger will not be a sufficient basis for a defence of compulsion. The language of s 24 requires "threats of immediate death or grievous bodily harm", which excludes mere inferences of danger to life or limb based on non-existent threats.[53] If D mistakenly thinks there is an implied threat by T to shoot him unless D offends, that will be a mistake of the first variety and may exculpate. But if D merely infers a risk of danger to himself without thinking that he has, as yet, expressly or impliedly actually been threatened in a manner qualifying within s 24, the inference falls within the second category and will not be compulsion. Section 24, it seems, requires that D subjectively believe that T has, explicitly or implicitly, *issued* a threat to kill or cause grievous bodily harm. Thus D must believe not only that his life or limb is at risk, but that the risk is pursuant to a demand by T.

An example of the second category, where the requisite demand was absent, is *R v Raroa*.[54] D was charged with being an accessory after the fact with murder, after he had assisted the killers

---

47 Orchard, "The defence of compulsion" (1980) 9 NZULR 105, 112.
48 *R v Raroa* [1987] 2 NZLR 486; (1987) 2 CRNZ 596 (CA), 493; 602.
49 *R v Raroa* [1987] 2 NZLR 486; (1987) 2 CRNZ 596 (CA), 493; 603.
50 See *R v Hudson; R v Taylor* [1971] 2 QB 202; [1971] 2 All ER 244 (CA).
51 *R v Graham* [1982] 1 All ER 801; [1982] 1 WLR 294 (CA).
52 *R v Raroa* [1987] 2 NZLR 486; (1987) 2 CRNZ 596 (CA), 492; 602; *R v Teichelman* [1981] 2 NZLR 64 (CA), 67; below, 12.9.
53 *R v Raroa* [1987] 2 NZLR 486; (1987) 2 CRNZ 596 (CA), 494; 603, 604.
54 *R v Raroa* [1987] 2 NZLR 486; (1987) 2 CRNZ 596 (CA), 494; 603, 604.

to dispose of two bodies. Although the Court of Appeal acknowledged that "the accused was no doubt very frightened, frightened of what had happened and frightened of what he would see, frightened at the men who could have done such a thing",[55] it endorsed the refusal of the trial judge to allow a defence of compulsion:[56]

> "He was fearful of the possibility of harm because of what had happened and because they still had three shells left. He may even have gone [with the killers] because he feared what would happen if he did not but the law is clear that fear is not enough. To be excused under s 24 there must be a particular kind of threat and there is no evidence that there was in this case."

Raroa, then, tightly circumscribes the law governing when D may claim the defence.

But it must be said that this is hardly a satisfactory position. If D accompanies T because, even in the absence of an actual threat, she reasonably fears for her life were she not to volunteer, her moral position is just the same as if she acts under a "compulsion" falling within s 24. Given that s 24 applies according to what D believed the facts to be, rather than what the facts are in reality, it would seem that the difference between a belief in implied threats and a belief in danger from non-existent threats is likely in many cases to be marginal. It is certainly doubtful that culpability should turn upon such a tenuous distinction.[57] It is the belief in the imminent risk that T poses to D's life, which prompts D's response, that should determine liability; not the technical question whether D believes T has actually issued the threat. The pressure on the accused is the same.[58] Suppose D believes, rightly, that T is not likely to bother with issuing a threat: he will simply kill D if he does not act as expected. D falls squarely within the moral foundations of the compulsion defence. His life is threatened, and the law should acknowledge it.

It is worth observing that to allow an honest, albeit mistaken, belief in the existence of a danger to life and limb (even without actual threats) to support a compulsion defence does not threaten the integrity of the statutory provision.[59] The defendant would still be required to discharge an evidentiary onus that she genuinely believed she was in such danger. Evidence of a belief that was simply the product of the defendant's over-anxious imagination or her unreasonable fears would be relevant to the issue whether or not the belief was in fact held.

12.7 Immediately following refusal to commit an offence

In *R v Teichelman*[60] the Court of Appeal noted that s 24(1) requires a threat to kill or cause grievous bodily harm "immediately following a refusal to commit the offence", and that the accused must offend "in the belief that otherwise the threat will be carried out immediately". It is not sufficient that the threat was "immediate" in the sense that it was made or continued at the time of the offence. It must also be a threat that the harm will follow immediately on

---

55 R v Raroa [1987] 2 NZLR 486; (1987) 2 CRNZ 596 (CA), 493; 602.
56 R v Raroa [1987] 2 NZLR 486; (1987) 2 CRNZ 596 (CA), 494; 603.
57 See also 12.5(4). A similar criticism is made of the English decision in *Martin (Anthony)* [2002] 2 WLR 1; [2002] 1 CAR 27; [2002] Crim LR 136, a decision concerning self-defence, below, 15.1.3.
58 Cf Orchard, "The defence of compulsion" (1980) 9 NZULR 105, 113.
59 See *R v Williams* [1987] 3 All ER 411; (1983) 78 Cr App R 276, where it was held in the context of private defence that D should be judged on the facts as he believed them to be: "it seems inconsistent in principle to apply a different test for duress."
60 R v Teichelman [1981] 2 NZLR 64 (CA), 66, 67.

non-compliance with the threatener's demand.[61] In *Salaca v R*,[62] a defence of compulsion was disallowed on a charge of bigamy because there was insufficient evidence that at the time of the ceremony of marriage the appellant was under compulsion of threats of immediate death or grievous bodily harm. S claimed he had bigamously married K because she had, some time before the ceremony, threatened that if he did not marry her she would get the witch doctor "to do something" to him, a threat which he believed. Despite the Court's decision, it may be observed that, while in many cases a threat that "something" will happen will not sufficiently suggest death or serious injury, in the circumstances of *Salaca* such harm might well have been impliedly threatened, at least in the accused's mind.[63] Orchard suggests that the facts of the case provide a good illustration of the desirability of rejecting any legal requirement that a mistake must be reasonable.[64]

At least in the context of the offence of supplying drugs, it is not necessary that the person making the threat be present from the making of the threat onwards while the accused does everything directed towards carrying out the offence up to its completion.[65] A threat antecedent to the commission of the crime will still support a defence of compulsion provided it continues as a threat of immediate violence at the time of the offence.[66] (In this context it is the actual supplying which is the essence of the offence and the critical time for the alleged threat to be operative.) Conversely, the mere presence of the threatener at the time of the offence will not establish compulsion in the absence of relevant threats.

In determining the immediacy of the alleged threats, it is impossible to ignore the accused's beliefs on the matter. Although *Teichelman* requires a belief on the part of the accused that she will be instantly killed or really seriously injured if she does not do what she is told, the question of when and how the threat will be executed is a question of fact and degree. This may mean that, although the accused believes the threat will be executed, it may not be necessary for her to believe that this is inevitable, or that she believes the threatened injury may not follow instantly but after an interval. Much common law authority supports this view, as is illustrated by *Subramaniam v Public Prosecutor*.[67] The appellant had been charged in Malaya with unlawful possession of ammunition. He defended on the basis that he had been captured by terrorists and at all material times was acting under duress. The statute under which he was charged required that the threats "reasonably cause the apprehension [of] *instant death*".[68] The Privy Council held that there was evidence of compulsion because the appellant had acted as a result of the terrorists' threats, who, although absent at the time he committed the offence, "may have come back at any moment".

It is possible that the accused may put a wrong interpretation upon the actions of those putting him under compulsion, or even attribute a time framework to events that may be completely misconceived. On this basis, an accused may either underestimate or overestimate the relative immediacy of the execution of the threats. However, it would surely be quite wrong to deprive him of the defence of compulsion because he thought there might be a small time delay in the

---

61 Orchard, "The defence of compulsion" (1980) 9 NZULR 105, 113.
62 *Salaca v* R [1967] NZLR 421 (CA).
63 Orchard, "The defence of compulsion" (1980) 9 NZULR 105, 113.
64 Orchard, "The defence of compulsion" (1980) 9 NZULR 105, 113.
65 *R v Teichelman* [1981] 2 NZLR 64 (CA), 66.
66 *R v Teichelman* [1981] 2 NZLR 64 (CA), 66.
67 *Subramaniam v Public Prosecutor* [1956] 1 WLR 965 (PC).
68 Section 94 Penal Code (Malay) (emphasis added).

execution of the threat when, in reality, he had no means of knowing the actual intentions of the threateners. What is important is that he believed the threats were imminent, and that they were compelling.

How imminent must the threats be? At one time, a generous allowance was made in R v Hudson; R v Taylor,[69] where the English Court of Appeal held that threats of future harm suffice where their effect is to neutralise the accused's freedom of choice at the time of the offence. The defendants, two young women, were charged with perjury by not identifying W at his trial on a charge of wounding. They admitted their evidence was false, but claimed compulsion on the grounds of having been threatened that they would be "cut up" if they testified against W. The threat was reinforced by the presence of a man in the public gallery who had a reputation for violence and was one of the group who had threatened them. The Court, following *Subramaniam*, held that the Recorder was wrong in ruling that as a matter of law the threats were not sufficiently present and immediate to support the defence of duress, and found that it should have been left to the jury to decide whether the threats had overborne the will of the appellants at the time they gave their evidence. The Court said:[70]

> "When ... there is no opportunity for delaying tactics, and the person threatened must make up his mind whether he is to commit the criminal act or not, the existence at that moment of threats sufficient to destroy his will ought to provide him with a defence even though the threatened injury may not follow instantly but after an interval."

However, whether this commonsense view represents the New Zealand position is doubtful. The problem is the requirement of threats of *immediate* death. On the face of it, this would appear to exclude the defence if the accused knows that a significant time must elapse before the harm is inflicted. Yet if the requirement of strict immediacy is insisted upon in such a case, it would mean that compulsion will never be a defence to oral perjury, even though that is not an offence listed in s 24(2).[71] A possible solution is to ask: "what does the Legislature seek to achieve in its insistence on the immediacy of the threat?" A plausible answer is that what is being aimed at is an assurance that the threat be "present" in the sense that it is effective to neutralise the free will of the accused at the relevant time. If the real issue is the effectiveness of the threat on the accused's mind, and that is certainly the moral crux of the matter, then it cannot matter whether she believes it will be carried out immediately upon non-compliance or after an interval, provided she believes it *will* be carried out and has complied because of that belief.

Nonetheless, the issue would seem to have been put beyond debate by the decision of the Court of Appeal in R v Joyce.[72] There the accused, who had been charged with assault with intent to rob under s 237 Crimes Act 1961, gave evidence that at the time the robbery was attempted he had been compelled by threats to keep watch in the street, although he was not physically proximate to the perpetrator of the offence. Citing as authority the Canadian decision of R v Carker (No 2),[73] the Court held that the evidence did not disclose threats of

---

69 R v Hudson; R v Taylor [1971] 2 QB 202; [1971] 2 All ER 244 (CA), confirmed in R v Abdul-Hussain [1999] Crim LR 570 (CA), where it was said that the threat must be "imminent" rather than immediate; but disapproved in R v Hasan [2005] 2 WLR 709; [2005] 2 AC 467; [2005] UKHL 22, below in this section; see also 12.10.1.
70 R v Hudson; R v Taylor [1971] 2 QB 202; [1971] 2 All ER 244 (CA), 207; 247.
71 Orchard, "The defence of compulsion" (1980) 9 NZULR 105, 114.
72 R v Joyce [1968] NZLR 1070 (CA).

"immediate" death or grievous bodily harm from a person present[74] when the appellant did the acts which made him a party to the offence, and held that compulsion had properly been withdrawn from the jury by the trial judge. A similar approach has been taken by the House of Lords in *R v Hasan*,[75] where Lord Bingham of Cornhill criticised the decision in *R v Hudson and Taylor* as having weakened the requirement that execution of the threat must be imminent and immediate in order to support the defence.

12.8 Person making threat present during commission of offence

R v Joyce is also authority for the proposition that threats must come from a person who is actually present at the time of the commission of the offence and in a position to execute the threats. When D said he wanted to withdraw from the planned robbery on becoming aware that P proposed to use a rifle to achieve his object, P threatened to shoot D unless he continued with the arrangement. In complying with the threat, D had gone with P to the garage. While P went inside and committed the robbery, D remained outside as a lookout. In this capacity as a party to the robbery, D prima facie committed the offence for which he claimed compulsion. Moreover, it was held that because at the time D was offending he was on the street while P was inside, compulsion necessarily failed. It could not be said that D was being threatened with "immediate" harm from a person who was "present". This was decided on the basis that there was no evidence of any threat of immediate death or grievous bodily harm once P left D on the street and entered the building to carry out the robbery. The Court reached this strict interpretation of the meaning of "presence" after reviewing the relevant provisions of the earlier Codes and noting that the word "actually" had been deleted from the original phrase "a person *actually* present" when the provision was re-enacted in 1961. The Court said:[76]

> "In our poinion [sic] ... there is no justification for concluding that the Legislature in making this amendment intended to include as a good defence anything less than threats by a person actually present when the accused committed such acts as were alleged against him, for the very object of the section is to provide a defence to persons who commit offences under 'immediate' threats of death or grievous bodily harm from persons who are in a position to execute their threats."

The implicit limitation of the meaning of "present" to physical presence only was affirmed by the decision in *R v Teichelman*,[77] where the Court of Appeal said:[78]

> "there must be evidence of a continuing threat of immediate death or grievous bodily harm made by a person who is present while the offence is being committed and so is in a position to carry out the threat or have it carried out *then and there*."

While the meaning of "present" now seems clear, the strict insistence on physical proximity is likely to produce anomalies in future applications of the rule. For example if, assuming the

---

73 *R v Carker (No 2)* [1967] SCR 114; (1968) 2 CRNS 16 (SCC).
74 Although the lack of "presence" of the threatener may be a ground for distinguishing *Joyce*, as we shall see (when discussing the requirement for presence in 12.5(3)), the tenor of the decision essentially precludes that possibility.
75 *R v Hasan* [2005] 2 WLR 709; [2005] 2 AC 467; [2005] UKHL 22.
76 *R v Joyce* [1968] NZLR 1070 (CA), 1077.
77 *R v Teichelman* [1981] 2 NZLR 64 (CA).
78 *R v Teichelman* [1981] 2 NZLR 64 (CA), 67 (emphasis added).

facts in *Joyce*, D had been present inside the service station so that P was clearly in view and capable of carrying out the threat when P committed the robbery, the presence requirement would have been satisfied and D would have had a defence of compulsion. But what if D was standing on the threshold of the door to the service station, so that in theory he could have fled and avoided the operation of P's threats? Would he still have a defence of compulsion? Or, to take the scenario a step further, what would be the position if the service station room in which D and P were "present" was divided by a large fixture separating the door and D from the counter where the robbery occurs? In the physical circumstances which pertain, P would be prohibited by the obstruction of the fixture from shooting D were D to essay a sudden departure. Can we say P is "present" in these circumstances for the purpose of conferring a defence of compulsion on D?

Alternatively, and perhaps more importantly, what if D is a person who is psychologically weak and easily intimidated and more likely to submit to and to be held in thrall by threats of death or injury, even where the law insists that the threatener was not "present" at the relevant time? Since the standard for belief in the carrying out of the threats is subjective and the belief itself need not be reasonable,[79] it must matter that the accused believed that the threatener was effectively "present" and able to carry out the threats even if the requirements of strict physicality of presence cannot be met. In these circumstances, a concept of "constructive" or "psychological" presence may be better able to do justice to defendants who find themselves in situations of compulsion, without seriously damaging the "strict requirements" test. Moreover, such a concept would give some effect to the Legislature's deletion, in 1961, of "actually" from the requirement of presence under s 24.

At common law there is no requirement that the threatener be "actually" present, and a notion of "constructive" presence appears to undergird the relevant case law. In *R v Williamson*[80] the appellant was charged with being an accessory after the fact to murder. The murder had occurred on a Wednesday and W was threatened with death unless he helped to dispose of the body, which he did on the following Sunday. W claimed that throughout the intervening 4-day period the original threat remained operative. He was under constant pressure to comply by the persons who had issued the original threat and, while they had left him alone for most of the period, they had visited him from time to time to reiterate the threat. The New South Wales Court of Appeal held that the issue of duress should have been left to the jury even though the threateners were "not actually present and in a position to execute the threats".

A case in which the parameters of "constructive" presence are more clearly identified is the South Australian case of *Goddard v Osborne*.[81] There a wife, who claimed she was acting under duress from her husband, attempted to obtain a welfare benefit by presenting false documents, while her husband remained outside in the street. The Supreme Court held that the wife was entitled to an acquittal by reason of duress *and* the statutory defence of marital coercion, which required that the offence be committed "in the presence of" the husband. It was held that the

---

79   *R v Raroa* [1987] 2 NZLR 486; (1987) 2 CRNZ 596 (CA), 491; 600; see also 12.6, 12.6.1, 12.6.2 above. But see *R v Atofia* [1997] DCR 1053, 1055. In light of *Raroa*, the observation in *Atofia* that the defendant's belief that the threats would be carried out must be "reasonably based on an objective standard" is clearly wrong. No authority is cited in support of the observation. However, the Court of Appeal has upheld the judge's ruling: *R v Atofia* 15/12/97, CA453/97; CA455/97.
80   *R v Williamson* [1972] 2 NSWLR 281.
81   *Goddard v Osborne* (1978) 18 SASR 481.

husband was "present" if he was "close enough to influence the wife into doing what he wants done, even if he is not physically present in the room".[82] It has been noted that such constructive presence was probably sufficient to raise the common law presumption of marital coercion and, in view of the deletion of the word "actually", that it should be enough for the purposes of compulsion in s 24.[83]

Despite all this, it seems that the New Zealand courts will continue to insist that "actual presence" is required and, at the present time, it is an apparently inescapable feature of New Zealand law that nothing less than the physical presence of the threatener in close proximity to the accused or the ability, in an exceptional case, of instantly executing the threat from a distance, will suffice.[84] This interpretation of the New Zealand position is reinforced by the gloss in *Teichelman*, suggesting the necessary capacity of the threatener to carry out the threat "then and there".

12.9 Honest belief that the threat will otherwise be carried out

The fourth critical feature of statutory compulsion identified in *Teichelman* is that the accused must commit the offence in the belief that otherwise the threat will be carried out. This raises a difficult issue regarding the subjective nature of the accused's belief.

In *Teichelman*, the Court of Appeal characterised the required belief as "belief in the inevitability of immediate and violent retribution for failure ... to comply with the threatening demand".[85] In New Zealand there is no requirement that the accused's belief be subject to an objective test of whether a person of reasonable firmness of character could have been expected to resist the threat, by contrast with the common law.[86]

Moreover, at common law it is also required that D's belief in the existence of the threat must itself be reasonable.[87] Yet this requirement, too, is no part of New Zealand law. However, it has been held that although an objective test is not open in New Zealand because the wording of s 24 specifically refers to the belief of the accused, thereby requiring a subjective test, a question of fact still arises about whether the belief is genuinely held. This must be negated by the prosecution beyond reasonable doubt.[88] Whether such a belief is reasonable or well-grounded will be relevant to the question whether it was genuinely held.[89]

This would seem to suggest that an accused may unreasonably believe that he is facing inevitable and immediate violence if he does not comply with the threatener's demands, even if a sober person of reasonable firmness, sharing the accused's characteristics, would not have acted in the same way. The accused is to be judged simply on the basis of what he actually believed and what he actually feared.[90] Consider, then, the following example:

---

82 *Goddard v Osborne* (1978) 18 SASR 481, 493.
83 Orchard, "The defence of compulsion" (1980) 9 NZULR 105, 116.
84 G Orchard suggests that such an exceptional case might be where the threat can be instantly executed; where, for example, a rifle is aimed at the accused from a distance (116).
85 *R v Teichelman* [1981] 2 NZLR 64 (CA), 67.
86 *R v Howe* [1987] AC 417; [1987] 1 All ER 771 (HL), 426; 775 (Lord Hailsham), affirming *R v Graham* [1982] 1 All ER 801; [1982] 1 WLR 294 (CA).
87 *R v Howe* [1987] AC 417; [1987] 1 All ER 771 (HL), 436, 438, 446, 458-9; 782, 784, 790, 799-800 ,affirming *R v Graham* [1982] 1 All ER 801; [1982] 1 WLR 294 (CA), 806; 300; confirmed in *R v Hasan* [2005] 2 WLR 709; [2005] 2 AC 467; [2005] UKHL 22, para 23.
88 *R v Raroa* [1987] 2 NZLR 486; (1987) 2 CRNZ 596 (CA), 492; 602.
89 *R v Raroa* [1987] 2 NZLR 486; (1987) 2 CRNZ 596 (CA), 492; 602.

T, in D's presence, points a shotgun and shoots and kills V. She then waves the shotgun in the air while performing a dance around V's body. Next, she turns to D and asks him to help dispose of the body. D, who is an associate of T but had no part in or knowledge of the intended shooting, thinks that if he doesn't comply T will shoot him also. In the circumstances, should D have a defence of compulsion if he then assists T with disposal of the body?

It may seem that, according to the subjective test, the answer ought to be "yes": he is to be judged according to the facts as he believed them to be. If D honestly believed that he was under a threat of death if he failed to comply with T's request, he should be excused. It is not necessary to ask whether a person of reasonable firmness could have been expected to resist. The only question should be, what did D believe? However, as we saw in 12.6.2, when we examine the actual approach taken by the courts to the "subjective" test its efficacy seems to evaporate.

Consider the example above. It is instructive to ask, "how does one characterise the 'threat'"? Is it primarily an implied threat that D honestly believed to exist, or is it simply a "non-existent" threat? If the facts as D observes them disclose no belief that T has issued a threat (above, 12.6.2), then it cannot assist D, however earnestly he believes in its existence, because a non-existent threat cannot give rise to compulsion under s 24.[91] If, on the other hand, the case is characterised as an implied threat which D honestly believed to exist, how is that state of mind different from "mere apprehension" that, unless he co-operates, he will be shot? "Mere apprehension", unaccompanied by the type of threat set out in s 24, is similarly not enough to raise a defence of compulsion.[92]

Because non-existent threats — even if D honestly believes himself to be "threatened", in the sense of being in danger — are excluded from the operation of compulsion, the utility of the subjective standard in s 24 must be in doubt. It is arguable that in refusing to allow compulsion to operate in purely subjective circumstances the New Zealand courts have determined that the defence be "shackled" by requirements that are relevant to only the most obvious, but less likely, forms of compulsion, requirements which fail to recognise that there are many subtle forces by which people are compelled to betray their own will, including their own subjective fears.[93]

12.10 Further restrictions on the defence

12.10.1 Opportunity to escape or seek protection

At common law, the defence will fail if the accused did not avail herself of an opportunity which was reasonably open to her to render the threat ineffective.[94] However, this requirement is qualified by the further rule that it is essentially a jury question whether the accused had a reasonable opportunity to render the threat ineffective. In determining this question, the jury may have regard to other factors, including the offender's age and circumstances, the ability

---

90   Smith and Hogan, *Criminal Law* (9th ed), London, Butterworths, 1999, 239.
91   *R v Raroa* [1987] 2 NZLR 486; (1987) 2 CRNZ 596 (CA), 494; 603.
92   See *R v Frickleton* [1984] 2 NZLR 670 (CA), 672; *R v Raroa* [1987] 2 NZLR 486; (1987) 2 CRNZ 596 (CA), 494; 603; *R v Atofia* [1997] DCR 1053.
93   See Coolican, "Compulsion and duress as an excuse for the commission of a criminal offence" (1966) 2 CRNS 21, 28.
94   *R v Hudson; R v Taylor* [1971] 2 QB 202; [1971] 2 All ER 244 (CA).

of the police to provide effective protection, and the risks or costs of D's alternatives.[95] Consequently, many common law courts have generously assessed the reasonableness of D's opportunity to escape. In *Goddard v Osborne*,[96] for instance, the Supreme Court of South Australia was unimpressed by the fact that the wife could have called the police or sought the help of an official in the Social Services Department by whom she was being interviewed. It accepted that seeking such protection could have terminated the accused's marriage, and concluded that a court should not require a wife to terminate her marriage in order to escape bodily injury and compulsion. Thus, the preservation of marriage was seen to be a consideration relevant to the question whether the accused could reasonably have avoided committing the offence.

The view taken in Australia may be contrasted, however, with that of the House of Lords in *R v Hasan*. In Lord Bingham's view:[97]

> "if the [threat] is not such as he reasonably expects to follow immediately or almost immediately on his failure to comply with the threat, there may be little if any room for doubt that he could have taken evasive action, whether by going to the police or in some other way, to avoid committing the crime with which he is charged."

His Lordship took a stringent approach to the earlier decision in *R v Hudson; R v Taylor*,[98] where the Court of Appeal had held that failure to seek the protection of the court and the police was not a bar to the defence, unless the jury decided that the accused had failed to take an opportunity to render the threat ineffective which was "reasonably open to him". While agreeing that the defence was lost where such an opportunity was available, Lord Bingham demurred on the facts:[99]

> "I cannot, consistently with principle, accept that a witness testifying in the Crown Court at Manchester has no opportunity to avoid complying with a threat incapable of execution then or there ... ."

One might, however, express some reservations about the logic of this analysis of "avoidability". Suppose that T threatens to murder D's family unless D commits a burglary. D has a day or two to comply. Of course D can go to the police; so D can avoid *compliance*, which is the test that Lord Bingham states. Yet if the safety of D's family cannot be guaranteed, how does this evade the *threat*? There is a serious analytical error here. Lord Bingham points out that "he could have taken evasive action ... to avoid committing the crime". But one can always avoid committing the crime, even if the threat is immediate — it's just that the consequences are rather severe. That isn't the test. What counts is whether one can avoid the *threat* save *by* committing the crime. Lord Bingham's argument therefore contains a non-sequitur. It cannot be too hard to imagine, as the Court of Appeal was willing to conjecture, that effective witness protection would not have been available to the defendants in *Hudson and Taylor*. Surely, if that is true, the rationale behind the duress defence extends to such cases?

---

95 *R v Hudson; R v Taylor* [1971] 2 QB 202; [1971] 2 All ER 244 (CA). However, there is no burden on the accused to prove that he or she did not have a safe avenue of escape. The burden remains on the Crown: *R v Williams* (2003) 168 CCC (3d) 67, 73 (BCCA).
96 *Goddard v Osborne* (1978) 18 SASR 481.
97 *R v Hasan* [2005] 2 WLR 709; [2005] 2 AC 467; [2005] UKHL 22, para 28.
98 *R v Hudson; R v Taylor* [1971] 2 QB 202; [1971] 2 All ER 244 (CA), 207; 247. See also above, 12.7.
99 *R v Hasan* [2005] 2 WLR 709; [2005] 2 AC 467; [2005] UKHL 22, para 27.

In New Zealand, by contrast, s 24 makes no reference to the accused's having a "safe avenue of escape" or a means of "seeking effective protection", and the strict terms of the section would seem to militate against importing into the statute a further qualification which Parliament has not seen fit to impose.[100] It is, therefore, arguable that the statutory test is less rigorous in this regard than the common law. However, it appears that this may have little effect in practice, because the necessity for actual threats, and the requirements of immediacy and presence, will operate to exclude the defence where there is a reasonable chance of escape.[101]

Some clarification of these requirements has been achieved in *R v Raroa*.[102] In proposition 3 of the trial judge's summary of the statutory requirements it was stated that there must be, inter alia, "no chance of escape".[103] The inclusion of this phrase in the required elements, together with the requirement in proposition 2 that "there is no opportunity of seeking help or protection", were challenged by the defence on the grounds that they were unnecessary restrictions upon the application of s 24 and that they were restrictions that did not appear in *Teichelman* when the Court of Appeal outlined the "critical features" of s 24(1). It was submitted that their inclusion, were they to be regarded as "elements" of compulsion, might be taken to mean that if there is an opportunity of seeking help or protection the claim that one was acting under compulsion might be rejected.

In dealing with this issue, Bisson J referred to *DPP for Northern Ireland v Lynch*,[104] in which Lord Morris had cited with approval a statement of the Court of Appeal in *Hudson*:[105]

> "it is always open to the Crown to prove that the accused failed to avail himself of some opportunity which was reasonably open to him to render the threat ineffective, and that upon this being established the threat in question can no longer be relied upon by the defence. In deciding whether such an opportunity was reasonably open to the accused the jury should have regard to his age and circumstances, and to any risks to him which may be involved in the course of action relied upon."

His Honour concluded that whether there is a "continuing threat" when there is an opportunity of seeking help or protection or of escaping is a question of fact in each case, the answer to which is relevant to the accused's belief.[106] That is to say, if D recognises the existence of a viable escape route, then his beliefs may not disclose a continuing threat sufficient to qualify as compulsion within s 24.

All this suggests that, under New Zealand law, the stricture suggested in *A-G v Whelan*,[107] that "if there were reasonable opportunity for the will to reassert itself, no justification can be found in antecedent threats", and the suggested limitation of the trial judge in *Raroa* that "there is no opportunity of seeking help or protection", are not to be taken as absolute requirements of the defence of compulsion, but rather as factors to be taken into account by a judge or jury in determining the belief of the accused.[108] However, this qualification will not alter the practical

---

100   See Orchard, "The defence of compulsion" (1980) 9 NZULR 105, 117.
101   Orchard, "The defence of compulsion" (1980) 9 NZULR 105, 117.
102   *R v Raroa* [1987] 2 NZLR 486; (1987) 2 CRNZ 596 (CA).
103   *R v Raroa* [1987] 2 NZLR 486; (1987) 2 CRNZ 596 (CA), 490; 600.
104   *Lynch v DPP for Northern Ireland* [1975] AC 653; [1975] 1 All ER 913 (HL).
105   *Lynch v DPP for Northern Ireland* [1975] AC 653; [1975] 1 All ER 913 (HL), 675; 922.
106   *R v Raroa* [1987] 2 NZLR 486; (1987) 2 CRNZ 596 (CA), 491; 601.
107   *A-G v Whelan* [1934] IR 518 (CCA), 526.

reality that, in the majority of cases, if the accused clearly had a chance of escape or ability to seek protective custody, the efficacy of "immediate" threats and the threatener's "presence" will be called seriously into doubt. Conversely, as was recognised in R v Hasan, it is where the threat is immediate that the availability of alternatives is likely to be restricted.

12.10.2 Threats to others apart from the accused

The paradigm situation in coercion is where T threatens D with death or grievous bodily harm unless she commits a crime nominated by T. As we have seen, the essence of the defence is the pressure that the threat exerts on D herself. Yet the pressure on D may be equally or even more intense should the threat be made against E, the husband or daughter, or any other person closely connected with D. There is nothing in the statutory defence that excludes such threats. Section 24 requires only that D act "under compulsion by threats of immediate death or grievous bodily harm from a person who is present when the offence is committed"; it does not require that D act under "threats of her immediate death" or of "grievous bodily harm to *her*". At common law, too, there is authority that the defence of duress will accommodate such situations,[109] and there is every reason in principle why it should. D may be able to resist a threat to herself yet be unable to allow her resistance to initiate death or serious harm to a loved one.

What about threats to strangers? In *R v Hasan*, the House of Lords restricted the common-law scope of duress per minas to threats "directed against the defendant or his immediate family or someone close to him", or perhaps "to a person for whose safety the defendant would reasonably regard himself as responsible".[110] But no reasons were given for this *obiter* limitation,[111] and it is submitted that the defence of coercion should not be constrained by any closed list of relationships. Suppose that T, a bank robber, threatens to shoot a customer unless D, a bank employee, hands over the key to the safe. It is easy to imagine how D may feel constrained to comply. To deny the defence in such cases is not required by the terms of s 24, and would seriously disadvantage genuine defendants whose only reason for complying with the demands of criminals is to protect innocent parties whose lives are threatened in the event of non-compliance.

(1) *What if the person threatened is not present?*

In our example above, T, D, and the victim of the threat (V) are all together at the scene of the crime. A difficulty will arise, however, where D and V are separated, because of the statutory requirement for the person making the threat to be "present". The form of words in the 1961 Act has changed from "a person actually present *at* the commission of the offence" to "a person who is present when the offence is committed". While this formula does not specify *where* the person must be present, we saw in 12.8 that *R v Joyce* ordinarily requires that T be with V when he offends. However, it is not so clear what "present" means when the threat is to harm V, who is somewhere else, should D not comply. If the presence of T with D is insisted

---

108 *R v Raroa* [1987] 2 NZLR 486; (1987) 2 CRNZ 596 (CA), 491; 601.
109 *R v Hurley and Murray* [1967] VR 526 (Vic SC) (threats to de facto wife); *R v Ortiz* (1986) 83 Cr App R 173 (CA) (assumption that threats to wife and daughter would suffice).
110 *R v Hasan* [2005] 2 WLR 709; [2005] 2 AC 467; [2005] UKHL 22, para 21.
111 Indeed, in one of the authorities decisions cited for the restriction, *R v Conway* [1989] QB 290 (CA), the threat (constituting duress of circumstances) was to D's passenger rather than D, yet the Court did not investigate the nature of the relationship between D and the passenger.

upon, that would appear to exclude situations where a threat is made to kill V and T is with V rather than D; say, where T is holding V hostage in order to ensure that D commits the offence.[112]

Arguably, s 24 is ambiguous about the scope of "presence". In light of the revised wording, which no longer requires that T be "at" the commission of the offence (a requirement suggesting location, as opposed to "when", which emphasises the time), it is submitted that the section should be interpreted so as to extend the defence to such cases. Thus T is "present when the offence is committed" if T is either with D at the time, or present with V in order to execute the threat. However, the matter has not yet been directly considered by a New Zealand court and, in the absence of statutory reform, we await an authoritative ruling on the matter.

12.10.3 Volunteers: parties to conspiracies or association

Broadly speaking, the defence of compulsion is lost if D voluntarily associates herself with those who threaten her. This restriction is contained in s 24, where it is stipulated that the defence will be available only if an accused person "is not a party to any association or conspiracy whereby he is subject to compulsion". The limitation is aimed at preventing the situation where a gang leader threatens an associate with physical violence unless he complies with a criminal demand, thereby effectively conferring immunity on him. However, it does not mean that the defence must fail simply because the compulsion comes from a member of a criminal enterprise which the accused has voluntarily joined. In *R v Joyce*[113] the Court of Appeal held that the limitation only operated where it is proved that:[114]

> "the very nature of the association was such that the offender, as a reasonable man, should have been able to foresee that the association was of a kind which at least rendered it possible that at a later stage he might be made subject to compulsion."

On this basis, casual criminal associations in which a group of offenders decide spontaneously to commit an offence like burglary or car theft will seldom qualify for exclusion, because they will fail to meet the "nature of the association" test and will not usually be the type of association for which violence is a foreseeable prospect. However, liability in each case will still turn on the particular features of the group's modus operandi. In *R v Sharp*[115] the appellant was a member of a gang which, to his knowledge, used loaded firearms to carry out robberies of post offices. During one such robbery, in which the appellant was involved, a post office employee was killed. At his trial for murder he pleaded duress, on the basis that he did not want to take part in the robbery when he realised loaded guns were to be used, but did so when the gang leader pointed a gun at him and threatened to "blow his head off" if he did not participate. The Court of Appeal, dismissing the appeal, held that where a person has voluntarily, with knowledge of its nature, joined a criminal organisation or gang which he knew might put him under pressure to commit an offence and was an active member when put under such pressure, he could not rely on duress as a defence to an offence committed as a member of the gang.

---

112 Cf *R v Hurley and Murray* [1967] VR 526 (Vic SC), 543 (Smith J, dissenting).
113 *R v Joyce* [1968] NZLR 1070 (CA).
114 *R v Joyce* [1968] NZLR 1070 (CA), 1076.
115 *R v Sharp* [1987] QB 853; [1987] 3 All ER 103 (CA).

Where the organisational and initiatory structure of an organisation is such that violence and threatening behaviour is an endemic characteristic of its identity and social purpose, it will always be more difficult for an offender to avoid the conclusion that in joining the group he must have known that it was one "whereby he [would be] subject to compulsion". This restriction would apply to many ethnic gangs and other organised criminal associations whose existence depends on their ability to threaten and intimidate for the purpose of achieving various social and economic advantages. However, where the accused has been subject to compulsion from the outset of the association, so that it cannot be said that he has voluntarily joined it, the defence will not fail on that account alone.[116]

(1) *Foreseeability or actual knowledge?*

Notwithstanding the language of foreseeability used in *R v Joyce* (above), there is no New Zealand case in which the facts have required a determination whether, in voluntarily joining a group, D must have actual knowledge that its members were ready to use violence to further their criminal purposes, or whether he loses the defence if violence was merely reasonably foreseeable. However, the standard of foreseeability in *Joyce* is in line with the common law, where it has been held that the defence is lost if D "voluntarily becomes or remains associated with others engaged in criminal activity in a situation where he knows or ought reasonably to know that he may be the subject of compulsion by them or their associates".[117] (paras 38, 39). Indeed, there is no requirement that the anticipated coercion be to commit crimes,[118] let alone crimes of the type ultimately committed. In gist, D loses the defence because he voluntarily associates himself with generally violent and coercive people.

12.10.4 Excluded offences

A feature of s 24, which it shares with other codified versions of the compulsion defence but which distinguishes it from the common law, is the inclusion of a list of "grave" offences that compulsion never excuses. The excluded offences are listed in s 24(2), which provides:

"(2)   Nothing in subsection (1) of this section shall apply where the offence committed is an offence specified in any of the following provisions of this Act, namely:

"(a)   Section 73 (treason) or s 78 (communicating secrets):

"(b)   Section 79 (sabotage):

"(c)   Section 92 (piracy):

"(d)   Section 93 (piratical acts):

"(e)   Section 167 and 168 (murder):

"(f)   Section 173 (attempt to murder):

"(g)   Section 188 (wounding with intent):

---

116 *R v Hurley and Murray* [1967] VR 526, 544.
117 *R v Hasan* [2005] 2 WLR 709; [2005] 2 AC 467; [2005] UKHL 22, paras 38, 39.
118 *R v Hasan* [2005] 2 WLR 709; [2005] 2 AC 467; [2005] UKHL 22, paras 38, 39, rejecting *R v Baker & Ward* (1999) 2 Cr App R 335 (CA).

"(h) Subsection (1) of section 189 (injuring with intent to cause grievous bodily harm):

"(i) Section 208 (abduction):

"(j) Section 209 (kidnapping):

"(k) Section 234 (robbery):

"(ka) Section 235 (aggravated robbery):

"(l) Section 294 (arson)."

When the list was first compiled, it was generally agreed that certain "heinous"[119] offences should be excluded from the defence, although in reality the compilation of the list appears to have been somewhat arbitrary. In particular, there is no evidence that all the offences listed in subs (2) ever fell outside the common law defence, which, on the contrary, has allowed it in respect of a number of those offences. For example, it is now recognised that the common law defence of duress per minas is available for some forms of treason,[120] and it has been allowed for arson.[121] The current position at common law is that duress may now excuse any crime except murder, attempted murder, and possibly some forms of treason.[122] Although in New Zealand the Crimes Bill 1989 proposed to drop the list of excluded offences, this recommendation has not become law and the statutory exclusions remain. These exclusions are anomalous, and as well as being historically unjustified, they produce arbitrary distinctions.[123]

Because s 24(2) precisely identifies each excluded offence by reference to the specific section creating the offence, the courts are prevented "by necessary implication" from adding other offences to the list.[124] This produced the absurdity, in R v Joyce,[125] that the defence was available to a charge of aggravated robbery (s 235) but not to robbery simpliciter because that is an excluded offence (s 24(2)(k)). It might be thought that this result was so bizarre that it should have prompted a review at least of s 24(2). However, the response of the Legislature was simply to add aggravated robbery to the list[126] while ignoring other important and arguably unjust distinctions. For example, while the defence is apparently available on a charge of assault with intent to rob (s 237), injuring (s 189(2)), and aggravated wounding or injury (s 191), all of which are not listed offences, it is excluded from wounding with intent (s 188) and injuring with intent (s 189(1)).

---

119 See Criminal Code Bill Commission, *Report of the Royal Commission Appointed to Consider the Law Relating to Indictable Offences: With an Appendix Containing a Draft Code Embodying the Suggestions of the Commissioners*, London, Eyre & Spottiswode for HMSO, 1879, 43.
120 See *M'Growther's Case* (1746) Fost 13; *R v Purdy* (1946) 10 J Cr L 182.
121 See Orchard, "The defence of compulsion" (1980) 9 NZULR 105, 108, and cases cited at 12.3, n 18. But not attempted murder: *R v Gotts* [1992] 2 AC 412; [1992] 1 All ER 832 (HL).
122 *R v Hasan* [2005] 2 WLR 709; [2005] 2 AC 467; [2005] UKHL 22.
123 Orchard, "The defence of compulsion" (1980) 9 NZULR 105, 108. The Law Commission has recommended that the exclusions be limited to murder and attempted murder: Law Commission, *Some Criminal Defences with Particular Reference to Battered Defendants*, NZLC R73, Wellington, 2001, para 215. See also 12.6.
124 Orchard, "The defence of compulsion" (1980) 9 NZULR 105, 108.
125 *R v Joyce* [1968] NZLR 1070 (CA).
126 See s 24(2)(ka), as inserted by s 2 Crimes Amendment Act 1973.

Prior to February 1986, when an important statutory amendment came into force, another puzzling exclusion was the offence of "aiding or abetting rape". The offence of rape itself was not listed, which meant that compulsion could have been relied upon if the actual commission of rape was alleged, but not if the charge was of aiding or abetting! The reference to aiding or abetting rape has now been deleted by s 7 Crimes Amendment Act (No 3) 1985, with the result that compulsion may now be a defence to a charge of sexual violation,[127] regardless whether the accused actually committed the offence or was a secondary party.

With the possible exceptions of murder and attempted murder (regarding which see 12.10.3(1)), there would seem to be scant justification for maintaining the list of excluded offences, given the anomalies that the list, by its nature, creates. In Canada it has been held that the exclusion, in s 17 Criminal Code, of certain offences from the operation of the compulsion defence is unconstitutional, because it violates the principle of fundamental justice that a person should not be found guilty of a crime if she is morally blameless.[128] In *Langlois*, the accused had been charged with conspiracy, possession of drugs, and trafficking in drugs. Claiming to have been acting under compulsion, he brought drugs into a penitentiary where he worked as a recreation officer. The trial judge held that s 17 Criminal Code, which would have deprived him of a defence of compulsion by threats, was unconstitutional and permitted the accused to rely on a common law defence of duress. The trial judge's ruling was upheld on appeal to the Quebec Court of Appeal, which was concerned that because of its narrow scope, s 17 had the potential of allowing a conviction despite the "normatively involuntary" character of the accused's actus reus.

It is arguable that the New Zealand position is even more restrictive than that which existed in Canada, given that in New Zealand a defendant is debarred from taking advantage of any residual common law defence of duress by threats even if she is also excluded from the terms of s 24.[129] However, it has been observed[130] that while a similar criticism might be levelled at the statutory exclusions in s 24(2), the current formulation reflects a policy decision that compulsion will only be available as "a narrow release from criminal responsibility where its strict requirements are met".[131] Any existing unfairness is statutory and therefore can only be removed by the Legislature. In any event, a review of the provision would be timely in the light of recent calls for a fresh parliamentary look at the defence of duress in both England and Canada.[132]

(1)   Should compulsion be available for murder?

We have noted that s 24(2) currently excludes the availability of compulsion as a defence to the offences specifically listed and that cl 31 Crimes Bill 1989, by deleting the list of exclusions, would make compulsion available "in all cases".[133] This must be taken to include murder and attempted murder, for which the defence is unavailable even at common law.

---

127   The crime of rape was replaced by the generic crime of "sexual violation" in s 2 Crimes Amendment Act (No 3) 1985. "Rape" is retained as an included offence by s 128(1)(a). See chapter 16.
128   R v Langlois (1993) 80 CCC (3d) 28, 33.
129   Kapi v MOT (1991) 8 CRNZ 49 (CA), 55.
130   Adams, CA24.18 (looseleaf).
131   R v Teichelman [1981] 2 NZLR 64 (CA), 66.
132   See R v Langlois (1993) 80 CCC (3d) 28, 53.
133   See Crimes Bill 1989, Explanatory Note, vii.

In R v Howe,[134] the House of Lords in a unanimous decision ruled that the defence of duress is unavailable either to a principal in the first degree to murder (the actual killer) or to the principal in the second degree (the aider and abetter).[135] Essentially, their Lordships were of the opinion that the loss of any right to a defence justifying or excusing the deliberate taking of an innocent life was a proper price to pay in order to emphasise the sanctity of a human life.[136] Lord Hailsham spoke of the availability of administrative as distinct from purely judicial remedies for the hardships that might otherwise occur in the most agonising cases.[137] Lord Griffiths considered it "inconceivable" that in extreme situations involving innocent persons, for example, a woman motorist being hijacked and forced to act as a getaway driver, such persons would be prosecuted.[138]

Two major grounds of objection have been suggested by critics of the decision in Howe. First, it is argued that a "morally innocent person" should not be left to the mercy of administrative discretion on a murder charge, if indeed it is realistic to suppose that Parliament intended to leave it to the discretion of the police not to prosecute in such cases.[139] Secondly, it may be thought that there is an "indefensible anomaly" in allowing a defence of duress if, with the mens rea for murder, the defendant only injures his victim, while taking the defence away if the victim dies within a year and a day.[140]

Dealing with the first of these objections, it seems a rather startling proposition that a person, who with full mens rea kills another innocent person, should be deemed to be innocent, simply because what is done is done out of fear, however well-grounded. Compulsion cannot here be a justification, but, at most, an excuse. Moreover, the fact that it may seem pointless to punish in such cases is not to say that the actor is morally blameless. Such a judgment could be made only if the interests of the victim in a coerced attack represented a value that was not worth preserving. That is clearly not the case. Considered in this light, it is not unreasonable for the law to declare that taking innocent life under compulsion is morally reprehensible, regardless of the options that may be available to reflect the diminished culpability of the offender.

As for the "indefensible anomaly" argument, their Lordships concede that there are anomalies inherent in their decision, but that these are a consequence of the fact that murder is a result-related crime with a mandatory penalty.[141] The anomaly is not one specific to compulsion, but

---

134 R v Howe [1987] AC 417; [1987] 1 All ER 771 (HL).
135 Expressly overruling its earlier decision in Lynch v DPP for Northern Ireland [1975] AC 653; [1975] 1 All ER 913 (HL), while approving and applying the Privy Council decision in Abbott v R [1977] AC 755; [1976] 3 All ER 140 (PC). The decision in Lynch had precluded the defence only for principals in the first degree.
136 See R v Howe [1987] AC 417; [1987] 1 All ER 771 (HL), 433; 781 (Lord Hailsham). Lord McKay emphasised that "repugnance" of the law's recognising in any individual "in any circumstances" the right to choose that one innocent person should be killed rather than another (456; 798).
137 R v Howe [1987] AC 417; [1987] 1 All ER 771 (HL), 433; 781.
138 R v Howe [1987] AC 417; [1987] 1 All ER 771 (HL), 433; 781. As a reason for not extending duress to murder, this prognosis is criticised as being "over-optimistic" and a "complete evasion of the responsibilities of the House of Lords to avoid dealing with difficult cases". See Milgate, "Duress and the criminal law: Another about turn by the House of Lords" [1988] CLJ 61, 70, 71.
139 See the commentary on Howe (sub nom R v Burke) at [1987] Crim LR 480, 481-485.
140 [1987] Crim LR 480, 481- 485; cf s 162 Crimes Act 1961.
141 R v Howe [1987] AC 417; [1987] 1 All ER 771 (HL) (Lord McKay). For a full discussion of the other anomalies created by the decision, see Milgate, "Duress and the criminal law: Another about turn by the House of Lords" [1988] CLJ 61, 74, 75.

inherent in any legal system where the actual occurrence of results affects one's criminal liability. As Lord Hailsham observes, consistency and logic, though inherently desirable, are not always prime characteristics of a penal code based on custom and common sense.[142] This may be an area where the demands of "consistency" must defer to other moral principles aimed at maximising the protection of innocent persons. In any event, as an ethical principle, it is very doubtful whether automatic priority should be given to saving one's own life, or whether a person ought always to be entitled to protect her own bodily integrity at any cost.

Given that the clear weight of common law authority has been against extending exculpatory defences to those who, in situations of extremity, consider themselves forced to take innocent life, the arguments in favour of extending the defence of duress to persons charged as parties to murder become less persuasive. For New Zealand to maintain the status quo in this regard establishes consistency with other common law jurisdictions, which generally exclude murder or attempted murder from the ambit of compulsion.[143]

12.11 The burden of proof

Where a defendant relies on the defence of compulsion, in practice the burden lies upon him to adduce sufficient evidence to raise compulsion as a "live issue". The possibility of compulsion cannot be considered by the jury unless an evidential foundation for the defence exists.[144] Thus the trial judge, in her gatekeeping function, must decide whether there is evidence reasonably capable of supporting all of the constituent elements of the defence.[145] Where the defendant does not testify, the necessary evidential basis for the defence must be found in the evidence of other parties, if the defence is not to be rejected as a meritless defence.[146]

By way of example, evidence that the accused had been "pressured" or was being "hassled" to supply heroin to a third party, or that he was merely frightened by the actions of another into doing so, will be insufficient to raise the defence of compulsion.[147] However, once compulsion becomes a live issue, the burden is on the prosecution to negative the defence beyond reasonable doubt.[148] In *R v Bone*[149] the English Court of Appeal, in considering the question of burden of proof in cases of duress, said:[150]

> "Duress, like self-defence and drunkenness, is something which must in the first instance be raised by the defence, but at the end of the day it is always for the prosecution to prove their case, which involves negativing the defence which has been set up ... to ensure that the jury are not confused it is not sufficient to give the general

---

142 *R v Howe* [1987] AC 417; [1987] 1 All ER 771 (HL), 432; 780.
143 See s 17 Criminal Code (Can); s 94 Indian Penal Code; s 20 Criminal Code (Tas); s 31 Criminal Code (Qld); s 31 Criminal Code (WA).
144 *R v Teichelman* [1981] 2 NZLR 64 (CA), 66.
145 *R v Cinous* (2002) 162 CCC (3d) 129 (SCC), 170-1; *R v Savoury* (2005) 200 CCC (3d) 94 (Ont CA), 108.
146 Canadian courts have held that meritless defences that could only confuse juries and lead to improper acquittals cannot be left with the jury, since an acquittal premised on a legally meritless defence is a miscarriage of justice. See *R v Cinous* (2002) 162 CCC (3d) 129 (SCC), 170-71; *R v Gunning* [2005] SCJ No 25 (QL), 196 CCC (3d) 123.
147 See *R v Frickleton* [1984] 2 NZLR 670 (CA).
148 *R v Gill* [1963] 2 All ER 688; [1963] 1 WLR 841 (CCA). See also *Salaca v R* [1967] NZLR 421 (CA), 422.
149 *R v Bone* [1968] 2 All ER 644; [1968] 1 WLR 983 (CA).
150 *R v Bone* [1968] 2 All ER 644; [1968] 1 WLR 983 (CA), 645; 985.

direction at the beginning in regard to the burden and standard of proof, but the jury should be told specifically that it is for the prosecution to negative in that case, the self-defence."

In New Zealand there has been some debate whether this rule applies equally to summary trials as to trials on indictment. Adams argued that the rule only applied to trials on indictment, and that in summary proceedings the onus of proof (on the balance of probabilities) rests on the accused.[151] This was based on the assumption that s 67(8) Summary Proceedings Act 1957, which requires the defendant in a summary proceeding to prove any "exception, exemption, proviso, excuse, or qualification, whether it does or does not accompany the description of the offence in the enactment creating the offence", necessarily required the defendant to prove compulsion, which constituted an "excuse" within the meaning of the subsection. However, it may be doubted whether the provision was ever intended to apply to general defences, since the exception, in terms of its common law origins, is limited to "offences arising under enactments which prohibit the doing of an act save in specified circumstances or by persons of specified classes or with specified qualifications or with the licence or permission of specified authorities",[152] language which seems inapt to describe a general statutory defence like compulsion. It is arguable that the principle espoused in s 67(8) applies only to statutory provisions that provide limited exceptions to what would otherwise be unlawful conduct *within that same provision*, and not to a provision that negatives criminal responsibility for other offences in general.

12.12 Compulsion and self-defence

Occasionally, the facts of a case may give rise to both compulsion and self-defence. In these circumstances it may be necessary to make difficult decisions as to whether to run both defences simultaneously or whether, and in what circumstances, one defence should yield to the other. There are no clear rules to assist in making such determinations and, in the final analysis, it is counsel's decision whether to leave both defences to the jury or, if not, which one should be left.[153]

The issue arose in an interesting way in the English case of *R v Burley*.[154] The police arrested B for offences allegedly committed earlier in the year. As he got into his car he was approached by two police officers, who had previously been observing him. During the course of the arrest he drove his motor vehicle at the two officers, who took evasive action. He was then charged with attempted wounding with intent to resist arrest and attempting to cause grievous bodily harm. Among the issues for consideration by the jury was whether the appellant reasonably believed that he was being subjected to a violent attack and was at risk of death or serious injury. The trial judge directed the jury that, in the event that the appellant had recognised his assailants as police officers, neither self-defence nor duress of circumstances would be available to him, and withdrew duress from the jury. The Court of Appeal allowed an appeal in which B contended that the defence of duress should not have been withdrawn from the jury. The

---

151 *Adams* (2nd ed), para 482.
152 *R v Edwards* [1975] QB 27; [1974] 3 WLR 285 (CA), 40; 295 (Lawton LJ).
153 As a matter of practice, it is desirable that where both defences are available the court should discuss with counsel, at the end of the evidence and before the closing speeches, whether it is necessary to leave both defences to the jury and, if not, which one should be left. See the commentary to *R v Burley* [2000] Crim LR 843, 844.
154 *R v Burley* [2000] Crim LR 843.

Court of Appeal held that it was not the law that, where a person is assaulted by the police, he cannot plead self-defence or raise duress of circumstances. It held that the judge should have directed the jury that, even if they found that the appellant knew the men in the car park were police officers, they still had to consider whether the prosecution had proved that the appellant was not acting in self-defence. The convictions were held to be unsafe.

Knowledge that a victim of an alleged offence is a police officer should not affect the availability of defences of duress and self-defence any more than if the victim were a known member of the public. However, knowledge that the victim was a particular type of public official whose duties would have justified the action in question (for example a police officer or a bailiff) would undermine such a defence because the official status itself would normally legitimate the action taken, provided it was not unlawful or excessive.[155]

12.13 Battered women who commit offences under compulsion

Generally, mere fear will be insufficient to ground the defence if the strict requirements of the test are not satisfied.[156] The fact that the defendant may have been suborned in her judgment by a stronger, violent man whom she feared, will not provide evidence of compulsion in the absence of threats of the nature and quality contemplated by the Legislature. This has become an issue of some significance in relation to battered women who commit offences while ostensibly under a form of duress. However, the arguments in favour of allowing compulsion in such circumstances are sometimes less than convincing and fail to support the case being contended for. For example, the view has been advanced in New Zealand that *every* action a battered woman takes is coerced because of the overwhelming need, in most aspects of daily living, to placate the batterer.[157] It is claimed that crimes (without apparent differentiation) committed by the abused woman are simply an extension of the same duress that leads her to cook the batterer's favourite meal or keep the children quiet.[158] That is to suggest that the whole matrix of a battered woman's life is one of coercion and that every offence committed by her, whatever its nature, is presumptively coerced. Such a claim is overly broad,[159] inasmuch as the vast majority of women who might be classified as battered women do not commit crimes. Furthermore, even if there were evidence to support such a claim, it by no means follows that compulsion is a necessary element of every offence so committed. The acceptance of this argument would lead to the startling view that a person could claim global immunity from criminal liability for every criminal act committed by her (or him) on the basis simply of her status as a battered partner, regardless of the existence or otherwise of a proven causal link between the alleged offence and the fact of abuse. This raises the important question whether the law should be any more inclined to grant immunity to battered women who offend than to other oppressed and marginalised groups within the community who offend under pressure of need or disability, yet who are uniformly prosecuted for their offending (for example persons who shoplift to supplement their low incomes, substance abusers who steal or rob to support

---

155 For an illustrative case, see *Blackburn v Bowering* [1994] 3 All ER 380 (CA).
156 *R v Frickleton* [1984] 2 NZLR 670 (CA); cf *R v Thomson* 2/3/06, CA406/05.
157 New Zealand Law Society, *New Zealand Law Society Seminar: Women in the Criminal Justice System*, Wellington, 1997, 66.
158 New Zealand Law Society, *New Zealand Law Society Seminar: Women in the Criminal Justice System*, Wellington, 1997, 66.
159 Quite apart from the fact that the tenor of the claim runs contrary to the abolition of the marital coercion presumption by s 24(3).

their drug addiction, or compulsive gamblers who commit serious fraud to support their gambling addictions). *That* is an important question, requiring careful debate. Yet prima facie, it may be thought that such special immunity as may be justified would be available only to crimes of violence *directed against the batterer*.

Where the facts of a case, involving the prosecution of an offence committed by a battered woman, raise the possibility of compulsion as a live issue, that defence ought to be put to the jury together with any other defence for which there is an evidentiary basis. However, the fact that the defence contains elements that "cannot be easily satisfied by women who are abused"[160] puts battered women at no greater disadvantage than other defendants seeking to plead compulsion. As has already been noted, the statutory defence of compulsion has been crafted within clear and precise limits in order to provide a "narrow release from criminal responsibility where its strict requirements are met".[161] If this is perceived to be unfair for battered women who offend, then it is a statutory unfairness that can only be resolved by Parliament as a matter of law reform. Moreover law reform, if effected, ought to be based on an assessment of the specific needs of battered women — an assessment that ought not to be *avoided* by the pretence that the present, unspecific defence of compulsion is appropriate.[162]

Be that as it may, it is important to note that a substantial consensus has grown in Canada and Australia[163] to the effect that the strict criterion of "immediacy" is no longer a generally accepted component of the common law defence of duress. Moreover, the requirement in duress that the threat be immanent has been interpreted and applied in a relatively flexible manner.[164]

It has been suggested that the focus on an "instantaneous connection" between the threat and the commission of the offence misses the point in the case of a battered woman who is coerced by her abusive partner to break the law. Even though her partner is not present when she commits the offence and is therefore unable to execute the threat immediately, a battered woman may nonetheless believe she has no safe avenue of escape: "Her behaviour is morally involuntary, yet the immediacy and presence criteria ... would preclude her from resorting to [the statutory defence]."[165] But this analysis overgeneralises. The broadly inclusive proposition that "her behaviour is morally involuntary" appears to attribute normative involuntariness to all battered women who may be coerced by their partners to act unlawfully. Yet in some cases, a woman may simply have been frightened of her partner's perceived possible reaction and apprehensive of his anger. This would not constitute a well-grounded fear of death or bodily harm and, in this country, mere fear has never been sufficient to ground a defence of compulsion.[166] More generally, such cases should not normally be characterised as involuntary conduct, even in the normative sense of having "no true choice at all" or of being "remorselessly compelled by normal human instincts" of self-preservation. Battered women are moral agents and not non-responsible, involuntary actors.[167]

---

160 New Zealand Law Society, *New Zealand Law Society Seminar: Women in the Criminal Justice System*, Wellington, 1997, 66.
161 R v *Teichelman* [1981] 2 NZLR 64 (CA), 66.
162 For a comprehensive discussion of these and related issues, see Law Commission, *Some Criminal Defences with Particular Reference to Battered Defendants*, NZLC R73, Wellington, 2001; see 12.6.
163 But not, perhaps, in England: R v *Hasan* [2005] 2 WLR 709; [2005] 2 AC 467; [2005] UKHL 22, para 28.
164 R v *Ruzic* (2001) 197 DLR (4th) 577, 615 (Le Bel J).
165 R v *Ruzic* (2001) 197 DLR (4th) 577, 616.
166 See R v *Frickleton* [1984] 2 NZLR 670 (CA); 12.6.1.

12.14 Reform: the Law Commission's recommendations

In its 2001 report *Some Criminal Defences with Particular Reference to Battered Defendants*,[168] the New Zealand Law Commission has recommended amendments to the current statutory defence of compulsion, the better to accommodate the claims of battered women who commit offences while under coercion from their batterers. Because of the nature and scope of the recommended changes, it is necessary to consider them in some detail.

In its earlier report,[169] the Law Commission considered whether s 24 should be replaced by a proposed revision of cl 31 of the Crimes Bill 1989, which defined "duress" in the following terms:

"(1) A person is not criminally responsible for any act done or omitted to be done because of any threat of immediate death or serious bodily harm to that person or any other person from a person who he or she believes is immediately able to carry out that threat.

"(2) Subclause (1) does not apply where the person who does or omits the act has knowingly and without reasonable cause placed himself or herself in, or remained in, a situation where there was a risk of such threats.

"(3) Subclause (1) does not apply to the offences of murder or attempted murder."

In considering the broader question of whether s 24 should now be replaced by cl 31, the commission posed four questions for further public discussion and submission.[170] Assuming s 24 should be replaced by clause 31:

"(a) should clause 31 be amended so that:

"(i) The definition of 'threat' includes non-specific threats arising from the circumstances of the violent relationship?

"(ii) The immediacy requirement is replaced with an 'inevitability' requirement?

"(iii) The defendant's beliefs about the existence of a threat and whether it will be carried out must be reasonable?

"(b) What offences, if any, should be excluded from the defence?"

12.14.1 Non-specific threats

On this issue the commission noted the argument that, in violent relationships, non-specific threats tend to predominate over specific threats and that, accordingly, a "well founded fear" of immediate death or serious bodily harm should be sufficient. However, ultimately this argument was rejected. Although the commission considered that s 24 should be replaced by cl 31, it was not persuaded that a "reasonably based belief that a threat exists and that it will be carried out" was a standard preferable to a "specific threat of immediate harm":[171]

---

167 See *R v Ruzic* (2001) 197 DLR (4th) 577, 595.
168 Law Commission, *Some Criminal Defences with Particular Reference to Battered Defendants*, NZLC R73, Wellington, 2001.
169 *Battered Defendants: Victims of Domestic Violence Who Offend*, NZLC PP41, Wellington, 2000.
170 *Battered Defendants: Victims of Domestic Violence Who Offend*, NZLC PP41, Wellington, 2000, 56.

"It is right to expect them to refrain from offending until a demand is made and until the danger is immediate, despite the high level of risk that this may incur. Compulsion that does not fit within the terms of the defence can be taken into account in mitigation of sentence."

12.14.2 Immediacy or inevitability

The commission recognised that replacing the immediacy requirement in subcl (1) with an inevitability requirement would be consistent with the broader common law[172] understanding of duress. It also noted an objection to an "inevitability" test, as being too open-ended a concept to be deployed in a defence that operates as a complete excuse for causing harm to an innocent third party. Ultimately, the commission did not support the adoption of an inevitability standard. No further reasons were given for that conclusion. However, the fact that the proposal was supported by a "large majority" of commentators[173] justifies some further comment here. While "immediacy" in this setting involves a temporal and subjective judgment about the closeness of an anticipated event, one that makes no claims about precisely when or definitely whether the threatened event will happen, "inevitability" is a different kind of claim. It is a claim that the anticipated event *will* happen in the ordinary course of events. It involves, therefore, a metaphysical judgment about the certainty of a proposed risk of harm occurring. While some events are so predictable that such judgments are possible (for example knowledge that a pilotless plane will crash or that exploding a bomb in a crowded mall will kill shoppers), that degree of certainty is relatively uncommon. Since the criminal law normally eschews reliance on metaphysical judgments about the certainty or inevitability of events as a basis for criminal liability (the main exception being the modern definition of "intention", which includes knowledge that a prohibited event is a virtual certainty),[174] it is unclear why it should now, for excusatory purposes, either attribute or require such certain knowledge in one class of defendants but not in all others. A battered woman, despite the dreadful and often enduring situation in which she finds herself, may be in no better position to predict the inevitability of future physical violence than are other members of the community to predict the certainty of profoundly feared but seemingly unavoidable events. Indeed, neither should she or anyone else be required to do so: the fact that she has thus far survived the previous abuse is itself evidence that the "inevitability" of death in the near future is, in all likelihood, a misconceived claim.

12.14.3 A reasonableness test

Under current law, there is no requirement that the defendant's belief that threats of life-threatening violence will be carried out must be reasonably based. The test is entirely subjective. However, in proposing that the requirements for a specific threat and for immediacy of harm be removed from cl 31 to better accommodate the needs of battered defendants, some submissions to the Law Commission recommended that an objective test of belief be incorporated into the test. The rationale for these submissions is that, with the removal of

---

[171] Law Commission, *Some Criminal Defences with Particular Reference to Battered Defendants*, NZLC R73, Wellington, 2001, para 196.
[172] See *R v Hudson; R v Taylor* [1971] 2 QB 202; [1971] 2 All ER 244 (CA).
[173] Law Commission, *Some Criminal Defences with Particular Reference to Battered Defendants*, NZLC R73, Wellington, 2001, para 188.
[174] See 4.2.4.

those elements, the defence would become very broad and its application would depend largely on the defendant's subjective judgment. Incorporation of a standard of reasonableness, against which the defendant's beliefs and actions could be measured, would be a desirable limitation of the defence.

However, in supporting the adoption of cl 31, the Law Commission considered that the potential breadth of compulsion as an excuse to a wide range of conduct means it should continue to be confined to limited, tightly defined circumstances.[175] It concluded that this can best be achieved by continuing to require a specific threat of immediate harm, rather than a reasonably-based belief that a threat exists and that it will be carried out. Any potential risk to the defendant in some cases must be balanced against the harm that a defendant causes to an innocent third party. Nevertheless, in order to achieve a desirable conformity with the way in which the common law defence of necessity is structured, the Law Commission recommends that reform proposals for compulsion should include a requirement that the threat be one which in all the circumstances (including any of the defendant's personal circumstances that affect its gravity) the defendant cannot reasonably be expected to resist.[176] While this additional requirement would place a greater burden on defendants whose actions are coerced, it would not exclude the use of expert evidence in cases of domestic violence to support a battered defendant's claim that there was a threat of immediate death or serious injury and to explain why the defendant may genuinely have believed that the threat would be carried out.

---

175 Law Commission, *Some Criminal Defences with Particular Reference to Battered Defendants*, NZLC R73, Wellington, 2001, para 195.
176 Law Commission, *Some Criminal Defences with Particular Reference to Battered Defendants*, NZLC R73, Wellington, 2001, para 205.

Chapter 13
DURESS OF CIRCUMSTANCES, NECESSITY, AND IMPOSSIBILITY

13.1 Duress, necessity: separate defences..392
13.1.1 Distinction from impossibility..393
13.2 Duress of circumstances..394
13.2.1 Development of the common law doctrine..395
13.2.2 Development of duress of circumstances in New Zealand..398
13.2.3 Parameters of the defence in New Zealand..400
(1) *Characteristics of the accused*..400
(2) *Imminence*..403
(3) *Danger from human agents: exclusion by s 24*..404
13.2.4 Conclusion: synthesising elements of duress of circumstances..405
13.3 Necessity..406
13.3.1 Does necessity exist?..406
13.3.2 Denial and recognition in the case law..407
13.3.3 Problems with necessity doctrine..408
(1) *The Rule of Law*..410
13.3.4 Recognition of necessity in New Zealand law..410
(1) *Specific statutory defences of necessity*..411
(2) *Trespass offences*..411
(3) *Emergency operations*..414
(4) *Moral imperatives?*..414
13.3.5 The rationale and scope of the common law defence..414
(1) *A lesser-evil justification*..415
(2) *Best interests medical treatment*..416
(3) *Lesser-evils necessity and homicide*..418
13.4 Strict liability offences..420
13.5 Some codification proposals..421
13.5.1 A generic "necessity" proposal..421
13.5.2 A specific duress of circumstances recommendation..422
13.6 Impossibility of compliance..423
13.6.1 Absolute impossibility..423
(1) *Impossibility given ignorance of duty*..425

13.6.2 Antecedent fault..425
13.6.3 Public policy...426
13.6.4 Inconsistency with the statute?...427

13.1 Duress, necessity: separate defences

The common law defences of duress of circumstances and necessity have never been codified in New Zealand. In fact, until quite recently their status as separate defences was seriously in doubt. There appeared to be a general perception that because many of the early instances of necessary action, including self-defence and compulsion, had acquired recognition as separate defences, there was little need to recognise general defences of duress of circumstances or necessity. However, this perception has now changed and New Zealand courts have begun to recognise the existence of separate duress and necessity defences. Importantly, the courts have recognised that in determining what "rules and principles of the common law"[1] may give rise to a defence, the principle that the law is always speaking must be borne in mind, suggesting that common law defences which would have been recognised at an earlier period by s 20 of the Crimes Act 1961 should not be regarded as frozen in time.[2] Instead, they should be developed with regard to evolutions in other common law jurisdictions, to the extent that inconsistency with other legislation is avoided.[3] This suggests that the categories of exculpatory circumstances are not closed. Rather, they are developing in response to new and emerging social demands.

The evolutionary nature of the common law has generated one particular source of confusion in the present context. In the case law, the same term, "necessity", is often applied interchangeably to different sets of exculpatory conditions as if they all constituted just the one, unitary defence. This is not the case. Duress of circumstances and necessity are separate defences, albeit that they sometimes overlap. They have different criteria, different ranges of application, and different rationales.[4] Therefore, notwithstanding the fact that, in practice, the cases sometimes use "necessity" to refer to either or both defences, *in this chapter we will adopt separate terminology in order to distinguish them.*

The first variety of necessity, "necessity" properly so-called, is concerned with the *avoidance of the greater harm* or the *pursuit of some greater good*. This is also sometimes known as "lesser-evils" necessity. The second variety, duress of circumstances, concerns the *difficulty of compliance with the law in emergencies.*

Because the first type often involves situations in which citizens are compelled to break a specific law in order to preserve a greater good, these situations are sometimes said to be "justified"; as when a mother breaks the speed restrictions in order to rush her sick child to hospital, or a house is demolished in order to prevent the spread of a fire.[5] In such situations we consider D's actions lawful and, indeed, very often worthy of praise. D's conduct is permitted and punishment is an inappropriate response.

---

1   See s 20 Crimes Act 1961 (NZ).
2   R v Hutchinson 7/7/03, CA92/03.
3   R v Hutchinson 7/7/03, CA92/03, para 44.
4   For a fuller discussion see Chan and Simester, "Duress, Necessity: How Many Defences?" (2005) 16 KCLJ 121.
5   Williams, "The Defence of Necessity" (1953) 6 CLP 216.

By contrast, duress of circumstances is not a defence of justification. It recognises that while the accused's actions are "wrong", and may well violate another's legal rights, it would be pointless or even inhumane to punish in such circumstances. Examples might include a backpacker who breaks into a Department of Conservation hut and smashes the lock of a cupboard in order to find food; or a prisoner who escapes from jail because he fears, on good grounds, a severe attack by other inmates. Whether or not such actions are also justified (and sometimes they will be, when they overlap with necessity), they are *at least* excused. We excuse because, although the conduct is not permissible or endorsed, we are not prepared to say that it should be punishable. Our reluctance is because, although D's reason for acting was (objectively speaking) inadequate, we can quite understand that it was good enough *for D*. She feared for her life. Any reasonable person might have been impelled by such a fear;[6] where this is so, we cannot make the inference of fault that would normally entitle us to blame D for her actions. In duress cases, the pressure on D directly explains her motivation. D is right to fear for her life: her only mistake is to treat that as a good reason for doing the actus reus (say, harming V). But that mistake merely discloses an imperfect virtue — a limitation — not a fault. We do not count, among the qualities reasonably expected of D, the levels of self-control and altruism that would be needed for D to refrain from acting.[7]

The role of the "pressure" in necessity, understood as a lesser-evils defence, is not like this. Rather, it is a rule-of-law constraint. One cannot raze V's house in order to create a fire break, and thereby preserve the village, without official authority *unless* the fire is at hand — otherwise, where the situation is not urgent and recourse to State authority is readily available, D will not be allowed to take the law into her own hands.

"Pure" necessity, thus, is not about self-preservation but about doing the right thing. Correspondingly, the scope of necessity is wider than duress. What makes duress exculpatory is the understandable difficulty of resisting the threat to D, so it is no surprise that qualifying threats must be severe; and this is formalised in a legal requirement (discussed below) that the threat must be of death or serious injury. Necessity, however, exculpates because D has, all things considered, good reasons for acting as she does. Thus it may be available even where there is no threat to life or limb. Moreover, as we shall see, it may even extend exceptionally to murder; something that duress can never do.

13.1.1 Distinction from impossibility

Like compulsion, necessity and duress of circumstances refer to cases where D is not completely deprived of control over her behaviour but is faced with a choice between evils. She may simply do nothing and allow a harm to occur, or she may "choose" to commit an offence in order to avoid the harm. In a sense, these situations may be characterised as involving "normative" involuntariness; because, in practical terms, the accused had no true choice.

Yet, as Fletcher notes, this "normative" conception of involuntariness must be sharply distinguished from physical involuntariness or impossibility, even though both expressions may be involved in any talk of "circumstances overpowering the will" or the actor's having

---

6 Cf *Graham* [1982] 1 All ER 801; [1982] 1 WLR 294; (1982) 74 Cr App R 235 (CA), 806, requiring that the threat in duress be such as to overcome the resistance of a "sober person of reasonable firmness".

7 It is, in this sense, apt to describe the defence of duress as a "concession to human frailty" (eg *Howe* [1987] AC 417, 432-435) — ie, in the sense that it is an imperfection characteristic of humans in general, and not particular to D.

"no choice".[8] Stressing the element of involuntariness in a claim of compulsion, duress, or necessity is simply a way of emphasising the moral claim that the offender should not be blamed for (inevitably) making the same choice that other people would make under similar circumstances.[9] This is very different from a claim of physical involuntariness or impossibility. Where the notion of involuntariness strictu sensu[10] is employed, there is not merely a claim that the offender's choices were overridden; it is also implicit that the offender has not acted at all, at least not in any sense that would be of interest to the criminal law, because he is entirely unable consciously to control the course of events.[11]

Hale described impossibility by the maxim "quicquid necessitas cogit, defendit" (that may be lawfully done which cannot be forborne).[12] By contrast, we cannot say the same of a person acting "involuntarily" in the normative sense. Such a person has clearly acted and deliberately so. We recognise defences in such cases not because there was no choice at all, but because we do not fault them for the choice they did make.

13.2 Duress of circumstances

The common law of crimes has long recognised a supervening[13] defence of duress by threats,[14] available in situations where D commits a prima facie crime in response to threats from another person, T, to cause death or serious injury should D not act as instructed. As we saw in chapter 12, this common-law defence is supplanted in New Zealand by its statutory alternate, compulsion.[15] More recently, however, English courts have also begun to grant exculpation in situations where D commits a prima facie crime in response to circumstances that pose a serious risk of harm should D not act as he does. Known as "duress of circumstances", this defence is now uncontroversial at common law. Its criteria have been developed by analogy to duress by threats, and they are in essence the same. Indeed, one may fairly describe the two as complementary versions of a generic defence of duress, which is available (subject to various restrictions) when D commits an offence in order to avoid death or serious injury.

The evolution of duress of circumstances is a simple matter of analogy. The main rationale behind the exculpatory force of compulsion or duress by threats is that, depending on the circumstances, it can be unfair to expect D to refrain from criminality when faced with grave threats to life or limb. In such cases D's action may be wrongful, in that it violates the rights of an innocent victim, but we do not fault D for doing it. Complying with T's threat, and allowing the scale of that threat to outweigh the interests of the victim, is not merely understandable but reasonable. The same rationale extends to duress of circumstances. Hence,

---

8   Fletcher, *Rethinking Criminal Law*, Boston, Little Brown, 1978, 803.
9   Fletcher, *Rethinking Criminal Law*, Boston, Little Brown, 1978, 856.
10   Hart, *Punishment and Responsiblity: Essays in the Philosophy of Law*, Oxford, Clarendon Press, 1968, 22-24. See 3.4.
11   For a useful discussion of the various ways in which the notion of involuntariness may be conceptualised with reference to necessity and related concepts, see *Tifaga v Dept of Labour* [1980] 2 NZLR 235 (CA), 241 (Richardson J).
12   1 Hale PC 54.
13   By "supervening", we mean a defence that does not deny proof of actus reus or mens rea, but arises once those elements are established (eg self-defence).
14   See, eg, *Oldcastle's case* (1491) 1 Hale PC 50, 1 East PC 70; *Crutchley* (1831) 5 C & P 133; *A-G v Whelan* [1934] IR 518; *Purdy* (1946) 10 JCL 182.
15   Section 24.

the law has good reason to afford a defence of duress independent of the source of the threat, whether it be a third party or extraneous events. It is the risk, not its source, that does the exculpatory work.

Duress of circumstances was first recognised, sub silentio, in *R v Willer*.[16] The appellant had been charged with reckless driving after he had driven very slowly on a pavement while attempting to escape from a gang of youths who were intent on subjecting him and his passengers to violence. The trial judge ruled that the defence of necessity was not open to him. The Court of Appeal quashed the conviction and said that the issue of necessity did not, in any event, arise. Rather, it considered that the appropriate defence to raise was duress, which was not pursued. The foundation of the defence would have been: "I could do no other in the face of this hostility than to take the right turn as I did, to mount the pavement and to drive through the gap out of further harm's way, harm to person and harm to my property."[17] However, as the authors of Smith and Hogan properly observed,[18] this was not an instance of the previously recognised defence of duress by threats (or "duress per minas"), which in New Zealand is codified as compulsion. Rather, the Court was allowing a new version of duress which arose from the circumstances, not from a specific (conditional) threat: "It should surely make no difference whether D drove on the pavement to escape from the youths, or a herd of charging bulls, a runaway lorry, or a flood, if he did so in order to escape death or serious bodily harm."[19] Conceived of in these terms, the case for a defence of duress of circumstances might seem so strong as to be unarguable when the emergent peril involves the threat of death or serious bodily harm. (However, as will be seen in 13.2.3(3), the existence of s 24 makes it doubtful whether any separate defence of duress may be raised in New Zealand where it arises from threatening *human* behaviour.)

13.2.1 Development of the common law doctrine

In *R v Conway*[20] the English Court of Appeal first coined the expression "duress of circumstances". The appellant, D, had been convicted of reckless driving. His evidence was that a passenger, T, had a few weeks earlier narrowly escaped being shot with a shotgun. When on this occasion two young men in civilian clothes had come running towards his car, T screamed "drive off!" and D did so, fearing that the men were potential assassins intent on attacking T. They were in fact police officers, who wanted to talk to T for whom a bench warrant was outstanding. In allowing D's appeal, the Court concluded that only where the facts establish "duress of circumstances" could necessity be a defence to a charge of reckless driving. The defence would be established where, as in *R v Willer*, the defendant was constrained by circumstances to drive as he did, in order to avoid death or serious bodily harm to himself or some other person. On the facts alleged, the trial judge was bound to leave the defence to the jury and because he failed to do so the conviction was quashed.

The Court in *Conway* accepted that the admission of a defence of duress of circumstances is a logical consequence of the existence of the defence of duress by threats, in its commonly understood sense of a conditional threat requiring D to "do this or else".[21] The only difference

---

16 *R v Willer* (1986) 83 Cr App R 225 (CA).
17 *R v Willer* (1986) 83 Cr App R 225 (CA), 227.
18 Smith and Hogan, *Criminal Law* (9th ed), London, Butterworths, 1999, 242.
19 Smith and Hogan, *Criminal Law* (9th ed), London, Butterworths, 1999, 242.
20 *R v Conway* [1988] 3 All ER 1025; [1988] 3 WLR 1238 (CA).
21 *R v Conway* [1988] 3 All ER 1025; [1988] 3 WLR 1238 (CA), 1029; 1244.

between the two defences is that, whereas duress arises from wrongful threats of violence by *another human being*, duress of circumstances arises from other (*"objective"*, as opposed to human) *dangers* which threaten the accused.[22] In the view of Lord Hailsham, the distinction is one without a relevant difference.[23] Duress by threats may be viewed as simply a species of the genus of duress from any source. In either case, the type of pressure on a person's free will is precisely the same.

In *Conway*, the Court of Appeal concluded that necessity could only be a defence to a charge of reckless driving where the facts establish "duress of circumstances", ie where the defendant is constrained to drive as he did to avoid *death or serious bodily harm* to himself or to some other person. It appears from the discussion that there is, in law, no difference between duress by threats and duress of circumstances, in that the latter defence is subject "to the same limitations as the 'do this or else' species of duress".[24]

In any event, the Court was unwilling to recognise any wider defence to a charge of reckless driving, which would imply that where duress of circumstances is invoked it must always be possible to point to an "objective danger" if not actual threats. What constitutes a relevant "objective danger" is not at all clear. However, by analogy with the common law governing duress of threats, it appears that the feared danger must be either real or, if not, at least reasonably perceived.[25] Mere anxiety that the accused *might* be attacked, or a claim that she was forced to drive recklessly because she wanted to escape the effects of a tidal wave that she feared *might* eventuate, when none in fact existed and there was no reasonable basis for her concern, would not seem to meet the "objective" requirement.

The scope of duress of circumstances was also considered in *R v Martin*,[26] where the disqualified defendant drove his son to work because he feared that his wife, who was mentally disturbed, would commit suicide if he refused. The son had overslept and his wife was obsessively fearful that he would lose his job. The Court of Appeal held that the possibility of the defence should have been left to the jury. The Court summarised the relevant principles:

(i) English law recognises a defence where actions are undertaken in *extreme circumstances*. The defence most commonly arises as duress, ie pressure on the accused's will from the wrongful threats or violence of others. However, it may arise from other objective dangers threatening the accused or others. In this form it is referred to as "duress of circumstances".

(ii) The defence is only available if, from an *objective* standpoint, the accused can be said to be acting *reasonably* and *proportionately* to avoid the threat of death or serious injury.

(iii) Where the defence is available on the facts, the jury must determine two questions:

---

22 *R v Howe* [1987] AC 417; [1987] 1 All ER 771 (HL), 429; 777 (Lord Hailsham LC).
23 *R v Howe* [1987] AC 417; [1987] 1 All ER 771 (HL), 429; 777.
24 *R v Conway* [1988] 3 All ER 1025; [1988] 3 WLR 1238 (CA), 1029; 1244.
25 *R v Graham* [1982] 1 All ER 801; [1982] 1 WLR 294 (CA). Contra *R v Martin* (2000) 2 Cr App R 42 (CA), where it was said by the Court of Appeal to be sufficient that D honestly, even if unreasonably, believes a threat exists. The latter view, however, is contrary to authority and was based on a misreading of the Court of Appeal's own decision in *R v Cairns* (1999) 2 Cr App R 137 (CA), a duress of circumstances case. *Martin* must be doubted, at least in the absence of endorsement from the House of Lords.
26 *R v Martin* [1989] 1 All ER 652; (1989) 88 Cr App R 343 (CA).

(a) Was the accused impelled to act as he did because, given what he *reasonably believed to be the situation*,[27] he had good cause to fear that death or serious physical injury may otherwise result?

(b) If so, would a sober person of reasonable firmness, *with the accused's characteristics*, have responded to the situation by acting as the accused did?

(iv) Where the answer to both questions is "yes", the jury should acquit.

In considering the availability of the defence to a charge of driving while disqualified, the Court stated:[28]

"We see no material distinction between offences of reckless driving and driving whilst disqualified so far as the ... scope of this defence is concerned. Equally we can see no distinction in principle between various threats of death; it matters not whether the risk of death is by murder or by suicide or indeed by accident. One can illustrate the latter by considering a disqualified driver being driven by his wife, she suffering a heart attack in remote countryside and he needing instantly to get her to hospital."

While the principles seem clear enough, it is strange that the situation in *Martin* should have been characterised as one of *duress of circumstances* since it appears to have been a case of duress by threats ("do this or else").[29] However, its characterisation as duress of circumstances may be of little consequence for English law because, as we have seen, the principles governing each defence are identical.[30]

Despite early predictions that the defence of duress of circumstances in England would be restricted in its application to road traffic offences, this has not proved to be the case. In *R v Cole*[31] duress of circumstances was held to be a possible defence to a charge of theft and in *R v Pommell*[32] it was applied to unlawful possession of firearms. The appellant in *Pommell* had been charged with the possession of a loaded sub-machine-gun which, he told police, he had persuaded another person to give him, in order to prevent that person from shooting some others. He told the police he intended to wait until morning to give the gun to his brother to hand in to the police. The trial judge ruled that the appellant's failure to go to the police immediately deprived him of the defence of necessity. On appeal, it was held that the defence of duress of circumstances was open to the appellant in respect of his acquisition of the gun, although a person in possession in such circumstances must desist from committing the crime as soon as he reasonably can.

There are two important points to note about *Pommell*. First, the offence under the Firearms Act 1968 (UK) was one of absolute liability.[33] As such, it would have been no defence for the

---

27 There need not actually *be* a threat, provided D reasonably believes there is: *R v Cairns* (1999) 2 Cr App R 137 (CA), 141.
28 *R v Martin* [1989] 1 All ER 652; (1989) 88 Cr App R 343 (CA), 654; 346.
29 Smith and Hogan, *Criminal Law* (9th ed), London, Butterworths, 1999, 242.
30 Yet the characterisation would be critical in New Zealand. As we see in 13.2.3(3), where any duress situation arises from a danger posed by "human agency", it falls outside the scope of the duress of circumstances defence under New Zealand law, and must, instead, comply with the strict terms of s 24 Crimes Act 1961.
31 *R v Cole* [1994] Crim LR 582.
32 *R v Pommell* (1995) 2 Cr App R 607.
33 See *R v Bradish* [1990] 1 QB 981; (1990) 90 Cr App R 271 (CA); *R v Waller* [1991] Crim LR 381 (CA); also comments in *R v Pommell* (1995) 2 Cr App R 607 (CA), 613.

defendant to maintain that he did not know or could not reasonably have been expected to know that the gun was a sub-machine-gun as defined in s 5(1) of the Act.[34] Secondly, among the recent English cases on duress of circumstances this was the first case not involving a road traffic offence. In delivering its judgment, the Court observed that there are no grounds for supposing the defence is limited to road traffic cases. On the contrary, the defence, being closely related to the defence of duress by threats, appears to be general, applying to all crimes except murder, attempted murder, and some forms of treason.[35]

This expansive view was adopted in R v Abdul-Hussain[36] where the Court of Appeal approved the view that the defence of duress (whether by threats or from circumstances) was generally available to all substantive offences, except those expressly nominated in *Pommell*. In *Abdul-Hussein*, the Court of Appeal held that the trial judge had interpreted the law too strictly in refusing to allow a defence of duress to go to the jury on a charge of hijacking a plane. Rose LJ affirmed the test established in R v Martin,[37] albeit noting that the defence of duress had been developed by English courts on a case by case basis and remained imprecise in its scope.

13.2.2 Development of duress of circumstances in New Zealand

In New Zealand, the statutory defence of compulsion has developed along different lines from the common law defence of duress by threats, so that it cannot be said that their criteria are identical. Nonetheless, the New Zealand courts have now also acknowledged the existence of a defence of duress (albeit sometimes called "necessity") analogous to duress of circumstances, in respect of which the English cases on duress of circumstances have been considered and approved. The critical issue in New Zealand concerns the content and scope of the new defence, an issue which has yet to fully be determined by the courts.

The status of duress in New Zealand was considered in *Kapi v MOT*.[38] The defendant was charged in the District Court with failing to stop after an accident and failing to ascertain injury. He had been driving home along a suburban street following a rugby practice when he collided with the rear of a parked vehicle which he said he failed to see because of oncoming headlights. He argued that he should not be convicted because he held an honest belief that he might be beaten up if he stopped to ascertain whether any person had been injured, which made it reasonable for him not to do so. His defence was thus one of duress of circumstances.

The District Court judge accepted that although there was no authority in New Zealand regarding traffic offences, a common law defence of duress may be available under s 20 Crimes Act 1961. His Honour concluded, however, that the defence required evidence of an immediate threat of death or serious bodily injury; because there was no reason why the defendant was prevented from at least stopping and backing up, without getting out of the car, to ascertain whether anyone had been injured, it was held there was no reasonable basis for him to be apprehensive for his safety. The defence failed.

In the High Court, the appeal was argued on the assumption that the defendant had an honest belief that he was in danger of an assault by persons unknown if he stopped following the

---

34 R v Bradish [1990] 1 QB 981; (1990) 90 Cr App R 271 (CA), 992; 280 (Auld J).
35 R v Pommell (1995) 2 Cr App R 607, 615. See the comments of Sir John Smith at [1992] Crim LR 176.
36 R v Abdul-Hussain [1999] Crim LR 570.
37 R v Martin [1989] 1 All ER 652; (1989) 88 Cr App R 343 (CA).
38 Kapi v MOT (1991) 8 CRNZ 49 (CA), affirming [1992] 1 NZLR 227; (1991) 7 CRNZ 481. See also *Police v Anthoni* [1997] DCR 1034.

collision. The defendant contended that for the defence to succeed his belief did not need to be based on reasonable grounds. Jeffries J accepted that a defence of duress of circumstances (albeit called "necessity" in the judgment) does exist in New Zealand and that the "prospective legislative provision" of a general defence in cl 30 Crimes Bill 1989 "means to put the existence of the defence beyond question for New Zealand".[39]

Concerning the requirement for "reasonable grounds", the Court acknowledged that the defence of self-defence, to which counsel sought to draw an analogy, required only an honest belief that the person was being attacked, regardless whether that belief was reasonable, and that the defence would only be lost on objective grounds if the *reaction* in self-defence was unreasonable. Counsel then argued that in the case of duress of circumstances, the honest belief being the subjective element, the objective element is supplied by measuring the response against what a person of ordinary common sense and prudence would do in the circumstances. The Court disagreed. After reviewing the authorities, Jeffries J held that:[40]

> "On close analysis most, if not all the cases, reveal three elements. First, a really extraordinary emergency; secondly an honest belief, and thirdly reasonable grounds. There is no authority for an honest belief and an ordinary commonsense and prudence test to the circumstances. The general rule in the decided cases in all countries is that honest belief is firmly limited to reasonable grounds before the honest belief itself can be accepted."

On appeal on a question of law, the Court of Appeal affirmed the approach taken by the High Court and identified three key elements of the defence:[41]

(i) A belief formed on reasonable grounds, of imminent death or serious injury;[42]

(ii) Circumstances in which the accused has no realistic choice but to break the law; and

(iii) A breach of the law proportionate to the peril involved.

To these has been added a fourth element:[43]

(iv) The need to establish a nexus between the imminent peril of death or serious injury and the choice to respond to the threat by unlawful means.

In agreeing with the High Court's analysis of the objective component, the Court of Appeal in *Kapi* adverted to the fact that, in *Conway*, the argument that the duress of circumstances defence should be based upon subjective belief was expressly rejected.[44]

A useful illustration of the foregoing requirements is *R v Lamont*,[45] in which the appellant appealed against conviction on two counts of causing death by careless use of a motor vehicle.

---

39 *Kapi v MOT* [1992] 1 NZLR 227, (1991) 7 CRNZ 481, 230; 483.
40 Ibid, at 230; 484.
41 *Kapi v MOT* (1991) 8 CRNZ 49, 57: "We consider on the authorities cited to us that a defence of [duress of circumstances], if available in New Zealand, requires at least a belief formed on reasonable grounds of imminent peril of death or serious injury. Breach of the law then is excused only where there was no realistic choice but to act in that way. Even then the response can be excused only where it is proportionate to the peril."
42 In *R v Hutchinson* 7/7/03, CA92/03, para 34 per Heath J, the Court interpolated "genuine" before "belief", although this is an addition of emphasis rather than substance.
43 In *R v Hutchinson* 7/7/03, CA92/03, the Court of Appeal, in considering *Kapi*, considered that this additional element was necessarily implicit.

The principal ground of appeal was the trial judge's failure to allow a defence of duress of circumstances to go to the jury. The appellant had driven at an excessive speed and ultimately lost control of and crashed his vehicle after another vehicle had allegedly "tailgated" him, causing him to panic. The judge refused to allow the defence of duress of circumstances to go to the jury, principally on the basis that there was no evidence that he feared death or serious injury, simply that he feared there would be a collision. The Court of Appeal agreed and dismissed the appeal:[46]

> "The type of emergency situations for which these defences may be available are those in which fear for life and limb is such as to compel breach of the law. If a breach of the law is by way of response to such threats and fear it is to be expected that the attribution would be immediate. Yet in this case ... despite it being put to him more than once the appellant gave no evidence that he feared death or serious injury.... A concern at having his car hit or even shunted in the rear does not amount to fear of death or serious injury."

13.2.3 Parameters of the defence in New Zealand

So far, the senior courts have left it there. *Kapi v MOT* does not explore all the parameters of the defence. One thing that is certain, however, is that for such a defence to be available in New Zealand, the defendant must possess a belief formed on reasonable grounds of *imminent peril of death or serious injury*, notwithstanding that this may appear unreasonably to limit the availability of the defence in respect of relatively trivial offences. A breach of the law is excused where there is no realistic choice but to act as does the accused, because of imminent risk of death or serious injury, and where the accused's response is proportionate to the peril.[47] While there is no requirement to prove there was in fact a "really extraordinary emergency", the absence of actual peril will of course be relevant to an assessment of the reasonableness and honesty of the belief.

Three further qualifications emerge, nonetheless, from the case law.

(1) *Characteristics of the accused*

An issue which has proved to be of some importance in the development of the English defence of duress by threats and, by extension, duress of circumstances, concerns the extent to which particular characteristics possessed by the accused, for example low intelligence or voluntary consumption of drink or drugs, are relevant in assessing the proportionality of the accused's reponse in yielding to the threat, and whether he had any realistic alternative but to yield. A requirement of "reasonable firmness" is imposed on the accused, so that his interpretation of and response to the peril is assessed objectively. This raises the question:

---

44 *Kapi v MOT* (1991) 8 CRNZ 49 (CA), 54. "It follows that a defence of 'duress of circumstances' is available only if from an objective standpoint the defendant can be said to be acting in order to avoid a threat of death or serious injury": *R v Conway* [1988] 3 All ER 1025; [1988] 3 WLR 1238 (CA), 1030; 1244 (Woolf LJ). See also *Perka v R* (1984) 14 CCC (3d) 385, 406, also reported as *Perka v R* [1984] 2 SCR 232 (SCC), 259 (Dickson J): "involuntariness is measured on the basis of society's expectation of appropriate and normal resistance to pressure." See also *R v Latimer* (2001) 193 DLR (4th) 577, 593.
45 *R v Lamont* 27/4/92, CA442/91. See also *Cooke v Police* 7/11/02, HC Christchurch AP118/02.
46 *R v Lamont* 27/4/92, CA442/91, paras 8-10.
47 *R v Lamont* 27/4/92, CA442/91, para 57.

what are the relevant characteristics of the accused to which the jury should have regard when considering whether his yielding to the danger was reasonable?

The question was considered by the English Court of Appeal in *R v Bowen*.[48] In that case, the appellant had been convicted of obtaining services by deception after he had purchased various items by paying a proportion of the cost by way of deposit, but had never completed payment on any item purchased. He claimed that throughout the period in question (a period of over 2 years) he had acted under duress imposed by two men, who had accosted him in a public house and had threatened him that he and his family would be petrol-bombed if he did not obtain goods for them. Defence evidence was presented at the trial that the appellant was a man of low intelligence (with an IQ of 68 and reading age of a child of 6 years, 8 months) and that he was abnormally suggestible. The Court of Appeal held that in most cases the only relevant "characteristics", for the purposes of the second objective element, were the offender's age and sex.[49] The Court also took the view that low IQ, short of mental impairment or mental defectiveness, could not be a characteristic that makes those who have it less courageous and less able to withstand threats and pressure. It held that since the objective test predicates a "sober person of reasonable firmness", there could be no scope for attributing to that sober and reasonable person the offender's low intelligence, since it was difficult to see how the person of reasonable firmness could be invested with the characteristic of a personality which lacks reasonable firmness.[50] The Court of Appeal identified seven general principles, derived from the relevant authorities:

(i) The fact that the accused is more pliable, vulnerable, timid, or susceptible to threats than a normal person is not a characteristic that may legitimately be invested in the reasonable person for the purpose of considering the objective test.

(ii) The defendant may be in a category of persons whom the jury think is less able to resist pressure than people not within that category. Relevant factors for this purpose include *age* (a young person is not so robust as a mature one); *sex* (though many women would probably consider they had as much moral courage to resist pressure as men); *pregnancy*; *serious physical disability* (which inhibits self-protection); and *recognised mental illness or psychiatric condition* (for example post-traumatic stress disorder).

(iii) Characteristics relevant in considering provocation,[51] relating to the nature of provocation itself, will not necessarily be relevant in cases of duress. This would include homosexuality, since there is no reason to think that homosexuals are less robust in resisting threats of the kind that are relevant in duress cases.

(iv) Self-induced characteristics such as those owing to abuse of alcohol, drugs, and glue are not relevant.

---

48 *R v Bowen* [1996] 4 All ER 837; (1996) 2 Cr App R 157 (CA).
49 In making this determination, the Court was influenced by authorities on provocation — which it considered were similar to duress — where it had been consistently held that age, sex, physical health, and disability may be relevant characteristics. See *R v Howe* [1987] AC 417; [1987] 1 All ER 771 (HL), 459; 800; *R v Morhall* [1996] AC 90; [1995] 3 All ER 659 (HL), 97, 98; 665, 666.
50 *R v Bowen* [1996] 4 All ER 837; (1996) 2 Cr App R 157 (CA), 845; 164-165. See also *R v Hegarty* [1994] Crim LR 353; *R v Horne* [1994] Crim LR 584 (CA); *R v Hurst* (1995) 1 Cr App R 82.
51 See chapter 16.

(v) Psychiatric evidence may be admissible to show that the accused suffered from a *mental illness, mental impairment*, or *recognised psychiatric condition*, provided, generally, persons suffering from such a condition may be more susceptible to pressure and threats, and to assist the jury in deciding whether a reasonable person suffering from such a condition might have been impelled to act as the defendant did.

(vi) Where counsel wishes to submit that the accused has a relevant characteristic, this must be made plain to the judge who must then rule on the admissibility of supporting medical evidence.

(vii) In most cases it is probable that the age and sex of the accused will be the only characteristics capable of being relevant.

In New Zealand it must be regarded as an open question whether, in an appropriate case, a court would consider itself limited, in determining the second objective limb, to the sorts of characteristics listed in (ii) and (vi) above. To the (partial) extent that provocation and duress are analogous for the purposes of determining the scope of the objective element, a court in ruling on the availability of a defence of duress of circumstances in New Zealand may need to be mindful of the local developments regarding "characteristics" in the defence of provocation.[52] In particular, the New Zealand Court of Appeal has expressed the view that the ambit of provocation in New Zealand may have been "unduly restricted" by observations in earlier case law,[53] such that they "go somewhat too far and add needless complexity to the application of [s 169 Crimes Act 1961]".[54] It has been held, for the purposes of New Zealand law, that an accused's racial characteristic, her age and sex, any mental deficiency, or her tendency to excessive emotionalism as a result of brain injury, are all examples of characteristics of the offender to be attributed to the hypothetical person for the purposes of s 169.[55]

However, it is doubtful whether, if a case involving facts similar to *Bowen* had to be determined in New Zealand, the accused's low intelligence would amount to a characteristic under the title of "mental deficiency". The English courts have ruled that "mental impairment" or "mental defectiveness", which may be regarded as analogous to the New Zealand expression "mental deficiency", are to be distinguished from low intelligence which, in itself, is not a characteristic that makes those who have it less courageous and less able to withstand threats and pressure.[56] Nevertheless, it is clearly a question of degree. In each case it will be necessary to ask whether the deficit in intelligence amounted to an intellectual disability so that it can be said that the defendant was "mentally deficient". It will then be up to the jury or trier of fact to determine whether the measure of coercion brought to bear on the mind of the defendant

---

52　See Salmon J's remarks in *Police v Kawiti* [2000] 1 NZLR 117; (1999) 17 CRNZ 88, 123; 93, 94, where his Honour indicates that it seems likely that in New Zealand a parallel will be drawn with the consideration of a defendant's characteristics in provocation, as is suggested here.
53　See *R v McCarthy* [1992] 2 NZLR 550; (1992) 8 CRNZ 58 (CA), 558; 66, commenting on the limitations suggested in *R v McGregor* [1962] NZLR 1069 (CA), 1080-1083.
54　*R v McCarthy* [1992] 2 NZLR 550; (1992) 8 CRNZ 58 (CA), 558; 67.
55　*R v McCarthy* [1992] 2 NZLR 550; (1992) 8 CRNZ 58 (CA), 558; 67. For a powerful critique of the relevance of "characteristics" when evaluating steadfastness and the nature of actions performed under duress, see Smith, "Duress and steadfastness: In pursuit of the unintelligible" [1999] Crim LR 363. Smith argues that limiting the common law defence of duress with an objective requirement of reasonable steadfastness, in order to satisfy public policy limitations on the defence, is logically and morally incoherent as well as being superfluous.
56　*R v Bowen* [1996] 4 All ER 837; (1996) 2 Cr App R 157 (CA), 845; 167.

was such as would influence the reaction of a sober person of reasonable firmness, having the characteristic of the defendant as a person of low intelligence; mindful of course that mere pliancy or vulnerability to pressure are not relevant characteristics.[57]

(2) *Imminence*

It is also uncertain whether the risk of death or serious injury must be "immediate" or whether an "imminent" peril will suffice. While s 24 expressly requires threats of "immediate" death to ground a defence of compulsion, the Court of Appeal in *Kapi* identifies a genuine belief, formed on reasonable grounds, of "imminent" peril as a condition for the defence.[58] Yet, in a later passage of the judgment, the Court uses the expressions "feared imminent death or serious injury" and "fear of immediate serious injury" as though "imminent" and "immediate" were synonyms.

In England, the requirement of immediacy in duress has in the past been interpreted expansively, so that it was equated more precisely with "imminence".[59] In *R v Abdul-Hussain*,[60] for instance, the appellants had formed the idea to hijack a plane to avoid being deported to Iraq where they feared persecution. Upon landing in England they were charged under the Aviation Security Act 1982. The trial judge refused to allow duress to go to the jury on the basis that the threat was insufficiently close and immediate to give rise to a spontaneous reaction to the risk arising. In quashing the convictions, on the basis that the judge had interpreted the law too strictly, the Court of Appeal accepted a distinction between an immediate and an imminent peril:[61]

> "[The peril must] operate on the mind of the defendant at the time he committed the act, so as to overbear his will but the execution of the threat need not be immediately in prospect."

However, in *R v Hasan* the House of Lords has revisited duress and, obiter, reconfigured it more narrowly, requiring execution of the threat to follow "immediately or almost immediately".[62] Yet, as we saw in chapter 12,[63] in their Lordships' analysis the key issue is not so much whether the threat must be immediately at hand, but whether the offender has an available alternative for taking evasive action.

Considered in this way, the immediacy requirement is in England a practical consideration, one that assists in establishing D's lack of alternatives. As such, in New Zealand it may anyway be implicit in the requirement, in *Kapi*, that the accused have no realistic choice but to break

---

57 *R v Horne* [1994] Crim LR 584 (CA), 585, 586; *R v Bowen* [1996] 4 All ER 837; (1996) 2 Cr App R 157 (CA), 843; 165. However, where the offender is intellectually disabled, but not sufficiently so to be found unfit to plead, susceptibility to pressure and suggestibility will normally be a feature of his emotional make-up that may make him more readily amenable to threats and compulsion.
58 *Kapi v MOT* (1991) 8 CRNZ 49, 57; above, 13.2.2.
59 Irish Law Reform Commission, Consultation Paper, Duress and Necessity, Dublin, 2006, at para 2.109.
60 *R v Abdul-Hussain* [1999] Crim LR 570.
61 *R v Abdul-Hussain* [1999] Crim LR 570.
62 *R v Hasan* [2005] 2 WLR 709; [2005] 2 AC 467; [2005] UKHL 22.
63 Above, 12.10.1. As Ryan and Ryan put it, although the earlier Court of Appeal decision in *R v Hudson; R v Taylor* [1971] 2 QB 202; [1971] 2 All ER 244 (CA) (discussed above, 12.7) was not expressly overruled in *Hasan*, it was "the subject of such disapproving comment as to effectively render the decision no more than a historical anomaly": Ryan and Ryan, "Resolving the Duress Dilemma: Guidance from the House of Lords" (2005) 56 NILQ 421, 427.

the law.[64] If that is right, there may be no need to insist on "immediacy" rather than "imminence".

Nonetheless, in R v Hutchinson the same Court questioned whether, in light of the limitations imposed by s 24(1), any accepted defence of duress of circumstances could legitimately include a threat that was not immediate.[65] The Court further observed that there is a "serious argument" that s 20(1) should not preserve a common law defence which is inconsistent with statutory codification; an argument which, if accepted, suggests that in New Zealand "imminent" should be interpreted as "immediate".[66]

(3)   *Danger from human agents: exclusion by s 24*

Concerning the scope of the generic defence of duress, the Court of Appeal has also described it as "probable" that, in New Zealand, the scope of the defence was considered by the Legislature and that s 24 Crimes Act 1961 reflects the extent to which the defence of duress by threats was adopted in this country. After quoting the text of s 24(1), the Court said:[67]

> "In this respect, in *R v Willer* (1986) 83 Cr App R 225 there was evidence of direct threats to kill. In *Conway* there was evidence of people running at the accused (in fact they were plain clothes policemen) and claimed fear of a fatal attack and in *Martin* there was evidence of a threat of suicide. So far as such fact situations would not fall within s 24 this might be said to result from deliberate legislative intent to restrict the scope of the defence of duress or compulsion."

The Court reasoned that because s 24 provides a defence of compulsion (duress by threats) where the criminal act is done under threat of death or grievous bodily harm from a person who is present when the offence is committed, s 20 cannot be said to preserve a common law defence of duress by threat or fear of death or grievous bodily harm from a person not present.[68] The appeal was determined against the appellant on this basis, the clear implication being that in the absence of persons actually present making threats, there was no emergency that could give rise to a defence of duress of circumstances, since it was not claimed that the threat came from an "objective" (ie non-human) "danger".

Kapi was further considered in *Police v Kawiti*,[69] where, on a case stated from the District Court, the High Court was invited to rule on whether the common law defence of "duress of circumstances" was available on charges of driving while disqualified and driving with excess blood alcohol. The defendant had driven a vehicle while disqualified and under the influence of alcohol because she was suffering severe pain as a result of an earlier assault and feared further assault if she did not leave and seek medical help at a hospital. Salmon J ruled that, following *Kapi*, "in so far as the duress or compulsion arises from threats from persons the codification of the law in s 24 limits the availability of the defence to the circumstances there set out."[70]

---

64   *Kapi v MOT* (1991) 8 CRNZ 49, 57; above, 13.2.2.
65   R v Hutchinson 7/7/03, CA92/03, para 54.
66   R v Hutchinson 7/7/03, CA92/03, para 55. In the event, the Court disallowed the defence of duress of circumstances to the charge of wilfully damaging pellets designed for a drop of 1080 poison, because the appellant had failed to adduce any evidence that he had no realistic choice other than to break the law
67   *Kapi v MOT* (1991) 8 CRNZ 49 (CA), 54.
68   *Kapi v MOT* (1991) 8 CRNZ 49 (CA), 54, 55.
69   *Police v Kawiti* [2000] 1 NZLR 117; (1999) 17 CRNZ 88.

13.2.4 Conclusion: synthesising elements of duress of circumstances

Where, however, the peril to life and limb arises from a non-human source, Salmon J was willing to contemplate a defence:[71]

> "In my view, it is a reasonable conclusion to be drawn from *Kapi* and the subsequent decision of [R *v Lamont* 27/4/92, CA442/91] that the defence of necessity of circumstances is available in New Zealand, but only where the perceived threat is one of imminent death or serious injury to the defendant or some other person."

Such cases might arise if, for example, the partner of a disqualified driver has a heart attack in a location where there is no telephone and no person to provide assistance, whereupon, in reasonable fear of his imminent death, she drives him to the nearest hospital.[72] His Honour concluded by approving the synthesis of the New Zealand and English case law principles offered in (i)-(vi) below.

While New Zealand lacks an authoritative statement of the criteria of duress of circumstances, it appears from the foregoing discussion that, by synthesising the New Zealand case law with such English case law as is consistent, the following observations, at least, may be made about the operation of the defence in New Zealand:

(i)   The perceived threat must be one of imminent death or serious injury.

(ii) D's perception of the threat must be either correct or reasonably based.

(iii) D's action must be in response to that perceived threat.

(iv) D's response to the threat must be proportionate, in the sense that a sober person of reasonable firmness, sharing certain characteristics of D, would have responded in like manner. (Which characteristics qualify to be shared is not yet authoritatively decided in New Zealand.)

(v)   The defence is not available to murder or attempted murder.

(vi) The defence is not available whenever the source of the threat is another person (such cases being covered by s 24).

(vii) The defence is not available where D has a realistic, law-abiding alternative available to him.

Item (vii) is also implicit in (iv), the requirement of proportionality, but is included for emphasis, since it is expressly stipulated in *Kapi* and was regarded as determinative of the appeal in *Cooke v Police*.[73] In that case, D pleaded duress of circumstances on a charge of dangerous driving. He claimed to have been rammed and side-swiped by another vehicle while he was attempting to drive to a police station and to avoid further conflict. Evidence given at the trial suggested that there may have been a series of rammings and counter-rammings before both vehicles ultimately crashed into a ditch. In following *Kapi*, the Court disallowed the appeal,

---

70 *Police v Kawiti* [2000] 1 NZLR 117; (1999) 17 CRNZ 88, 120; 91.
71 *Police v Kawiti* [2000] 1 NZLR 117; (1999) 17 CRNZ 88, 122; 93. See, too, *R v Atofia* [1997] DCR 1053, 1059; *Kelt v Police* 21/2/03, Durie J, HC Napier, AP57/2002, para 3.
72 *Police v Kawiti* [2000] 1 NZLR 117; (1999) 17 CRNZ 88, 122; 93.
73 *Cooke v Police* 7/11/02, HC Christchurch AP118/02.

ruling that there had been an opportunity for D to disengage from the conflict with the other driver, which he failed to take.

13.3 Necessity

13.3.1 Does necessity exist?

It seems that, at common law, a long-standing debate over whether a general defence of necessity exists has now been largely resolved in favour of the defence; albeit that its parameters are still being explored by the courts. In this regard, it seems that modern judges have finally begun to catch up with earlier visionaries and law reformers like Sir Samuel Griffith, who chose to specify a general defence of necessity in his Criminal Code (which provides the basis of the Criminal Codes in the states of Queensland, Western Australia, and Papua New Guinea). Griffith intended to make the statement of common law justification or excuse in his Code comprehensive by including a provision dealing with "sudden or extraordinary emergency" as a residual defence to protect the "morally innocent" where other defences did not apply.[74]

While some modern academics, like the late Professor Glanville Williams, also supported the view that there is a general defence of necessity, other commentators have argued that no such defence exists, or that it is unnecessary.[75] The evidence, however, is broadly in favour of the defence.[76] Over the years, varying measures of recognition have been granted to the concept in a variety of circumstances involving "criminal" behaviour, although acceptance of necessity in particular instances has tended to wax and wane. For example, in 1803, East suggested that "taking upon necessity" was a defence to larceny,[77] a view which had earlier been condemned by Sir Matthew Hale[78] and one which is not supported by modern authorities.[79] However, if we accept, as Sir William Scott suggests, that even the law must sometimes yield to necessity, where to force compliance would compel someone to "impossibilities",[80] then it is difficult to say that necessity may *never* be a defence to offences such as theft. Each case would depend on the *nature* of the circumstances at hand, whether the alleged "harm" (eg theft, property damage, or traffic violation) has made possible the preservation of some greater interest or value (eg physical health and integrity), and whether committing the offence was the only means of conserving that value.[81]

---

74 O'Regan, *New Essays on the Australian Criminal Codes*, Sydney, Law Book Co, 1988, 50, 51.
75 See O'Connor and Fairall, *Criminal Defences* (2nd ed), Sydney, Butterworths, 1988, 105.
76 It is well established in the US, where necessity has been successfully claimed for offences as diverse as escaping from prison and unlawfully withdrawing a child from school. See LaFave, *Criminal Law* (3rd ed), St Paul, Minnesota, West Group, 2000, 479ff.
77 11 East PC 656, cited in O'Connor and Fairall, *Criminal Defences* (2nd ed), Sydney, Butterworths, 1988, 105. East is supported in this view by Bacon, who asserted that "If a man steale viands to satisfie his present hunger, this is no felony nor larceny" (cited in *DPP for Northern Ireland v Lynch* [1975] AC 653; [1975] 1 All ER 913 (HL), 691; 935 (Lord Simon)).
78 1 Hale PC 54.
79 See *DPP for Northern Ireland v Lynch* [1975] AC 653; [1975] 1 All ER 913 (HL), 691; 935.
80 Sir William Scott in *The Generous* (1818) 2 Dods 322; 165 ER 1501; discussed in *Broom's Legal Maxims* (10th ed), London, Sweet & Maxwell, 1939, 162, and cited in *Tifaga v Dept of Labour* [1980] 2 NZLR 235 (CA), 243.
81 See Hall, *General Principles of Criminal Law* (2nd ed), Indianapolis, Bobbs-Merrill, 1960. See also *R v Lalonde* (1995) 37 CR (4th) 97, 108 (defence of necessity allowed to charges of fraud on the basis that in the mind of the accused, a battered woman, there was no reasonable alternative and the need to put food on the table for her children, in her financial circumstances, was pressing).

13.3.2 Denial and recognition in the case law

Periodically, celebrated cases have given rise to important debates concerning the scope of the defence of necessity. In the late 1800s the case of *R v Dudley and Stephens*[82] raised the intriguing question whether necessity could ever be a defence to murder, arising out of circumstances which would, undoubtedly, have tested the fortitude of even the most "staunch" of sea-faring adventurers. The merits of the case have been analysed at length by numerous commentators.[83] The accused were the survivors of a shipwreck. After having drifted in an open boat for 8 days, without food and with no immediate prospect of rescue, they killed and ate the cabin boy in order to save their own lives. They were rescued 4 days later and subsequently tried for murder.

Lord Coleridge, speaking on behalf of a distinguished bench, completely repudiated the defence of necessity, at least in relation to murder. He considered that to apply the doctrine in a case like this, where no wrongful act had been committed by the deceased, who was "the weakest, the youngest, the most unresisting", would be preposterous.[84] He considered the doctrine of necessity "at once dangerous, immoral, and opposed to all legal principle and analogy"[85] and, repudiating the alleged "duty" of self-preservation, said that the "plainest and the highest duty" may sometimes be to sacrifice one's own life.[86]

The effect of the decision in *Dudley and Stephens* was to leave the English law on necessity in a very unsatisfactory state. In 1883, Sir James Fitzjames Stephen expressed the view that the law on necessity was so vague that the judges were virtually free to lay down any rule they thought expedient. In his view, the expediency of breaking the law might occasionally be so great that a defence should be allowed, but such cases could not be defined in advance.[87]

Notwithstanding *Dudley and Stephens*, however, the common law has recognised necessity in a variety of circumstances, even when life and limb are not at stake. This is not merely a recent innovation. As far back as the sixteenth century it was thought that a prima facie offence may sometimes be committed "to avoid greater inconveniences, or through necessity, or by compulsion ...",[88] and the common law seems to have accepted the possibility of necessary action in specific contexts, such as the demolition of a house in order to prevent the spread of fire, and prison officials force-feeding prisoners to preserve their health.[89] In *R v Vantandillo*[90] it was held to be lawful to carry an infected child through the streets to seek medical aid, even though such conduct would normally have amounted to the common law

---

82   *R v Dudley and Stephens* (1884) 14 QBD 273; [1881-85] All ER Rep 61.
83   See, for example, Hall, *General Principles of Criminal Law* (2nd ed), Indianapolis, Bobbs-Merrill, 1960, 430-436. For a full account of the tragic last voyage of *The Mignonette* and of the ensuing legal issues, see Simpson, *Cannibalism and the Common Law*, Harmondsworth, Penguin, 1986.
84   Hall, *General Principles of Criminal Law* (2nd ed), Indianapolis, Bobbs-Merrill, 1960, 431.
85   Hall, *General Principles of Criminal Law* (2nd ed), Indianapolis, Bobbs-Merrill, 1960, 431.
86   Hall, *General Principles of Criminal Law* (2nd ed), Indianapolis, Bobbs-Merrill, 1960, 431, 432.
87   Stephen, *A History of the Criminal Law of England* vol II, London, Macmillan, 1883, 109-110.
88   *Reniger v Fogassa* (1550) 1 Plowd 1; 75 ER 1, 18; 29. The fuller quotation appears in the text below, 13.3.3.
89   Cf Williams, "The Defence of Necessity" (1953) 6 CLP 216. Admittedly, many of these cases involve risks to life, and would fall within the ambit of duress of circumstance. But the cases also embrace necessary action to avert property damage. See, eg, *Tolson* (1889) 23 QBD 168, 172 (Wills J); *Cope v Sharpe* [1912] 1 KB 496; *Johnson v Phillips* [1975] 3 All ER 682; [1976] 1 WLR 65; [1975] Crim LR 580; *Wood v Richards* (1977) 65 Cr App R 300; [1977] Crim LR 295.
90   *R v Vantandillo* (1815) 4 M & S 73; 105 ER 762.

misdemeanour of public nuisance. A constable, it seems, also has the right to direct a driver to disobey traffic regulations where it is necessary to protect life *or property*.[91]

At the same time, whether these instances could be generalised was in the past doubtful, and the existence of a general defence of necessity had been denied in a variety of English decisions.[92] Yet the courts have now begun to recognise a defence of necessity in a wide variety of contexts. In decisions such as *Re F*[93] and *R v Bournewood Community and Mental Health NHS Trust*,[94] the House of Lords has been willing to countenance the compulsory sterilisation of a woman with low mental capacity, and the detention of a person with a mental disorder, on grounds of necessity. And, in *Re A (Children)*,[95] it was ruled lawful for surgeons to operate in order to separate conjoined twins, notwithstanding that the operation was certain to cause the death of one twin and, being prima facie a murder, would be ineligible for the duress of circumstances defence.

In these and other cases, the courts have used the term "necessity" candidly and, frequently, interchangeably with "duress". Nonetheless, taken as a whole, the cases suggest a distinct, more general defence of necessity, one that goes beyond its occasional and somewhat ad hoc recognition in the old cases. What is not yet entirely clear, however, is the basis upon which the defence will in future be available, and the rationale on which it rests.

13.3.3 Problems with necessity doctrine

Early attempts in New Zealand to conceptualise a necessity defence by reference to specific examples were viewed as the product of a "fertile imagination",[96] based on situations in which it was impossible to believe that the person concerned would ever be prosecuted, or if prosecuted, that a jury would ever convict him. Adams gives the example of A, who sees a crane about to drop a heavy load on B. He pushes B aside just in time to save B from being killed. Adams observes that it is difficult to visualise A's ever being convicted of assault or of assault causing grievous bodily harm in the event of B being seriously injured, even though A may technically be guilty of either offence. The unlikelihood of prosecution in such cases is supported with reference to ancient authorities like *Reniger v Fogassa*,[97] where the Court said:[98]

> "[I]n every law there are some things which when they happen a man may break the words of the law, and yet not break the law itself; and such things are exempted out of the penalty of the law, and the law priviledges [sic] them although they are done against the letter of it, for breaking the words of the law is not breaking the law, so as the intent of the law is not broken. And therefore the words of the law of nature, of the law of this realm, and of other realms, and of the law of God also will yield and give way to

---

91 *Johnson v Phillips* [1975] 3 All ER 682; [1976] 1 WLR 65; [1975] Crim LR 580. See also Smith and Hogan, *Criminal Law* (9th ed), London, Butterworths, 1999, 245 and other examples given there.
92 See, eg, *R v Kitson* (1955) 39 Cr App R 66 (CCA); *Buckoke v GLC* [1971] 1 Ch 655 (CA); also *Southwark London Borough Council v Williams* [1971] Ch 734; [1971] 2 All ER 175 (CA), where Lord Denning held that the law may permit an encroachment on private property only in order to preserve life in a case of "great and imminent danger".
93 *Re F (Mental Patient: Sterilisation)* [1990] 2 AC 1; [1989] 2 WLR 1025 (HL); below, 13.5.2.
94 *R v Bournewood Community and Mental Health NHS Trust* [1998] 3 All ER 289 (HL); below, 13.5.2.
95 *Re A (Children) (Conjoined Twins: Surgical Separation)* [2001] Fam 147 (CA).
96 *Adams* (2nd ed), para 491.
97 *Reniger v Fogassa* (1550) 1 Plowd 1; 75 ER 1.
98 *Reniger v Fogassa* (1550) 1 Plowd 1; 75 ER 1, 18; 29 (Pollard, Sergeant at Law).

some acts and things done against the words of the same laws, and that is, where the words of them are broken to avoid greater inconveniences, or through necessity, or by compulsion."

While it is true that jurists and legal commentators have long maintained that in some situations the force of circumstances makes it unrealistic and unjust to attach criminal liability to actions which, prima facie, violate the law,[99] such broad statements of principle often fail to appreciate the complexity of the situations and forms in which a claim of necessity may arise. Neither do they give guidance on how the "defence" ought informally to be applied. In such cases, non-prosecution can never be guaranteed.[100] In particular, to the extent that "extraordinary circumstances" of necessity in the examples commonly given often involve *real* situations of *extreme* pressure (for example the lost alpinist forced to break into a mountain chalet to escape a storm) which invoke immediate sympathy for the imperilled defendant, they fail to take account of the fact that many modern claims of necessity are based upon a *mistaken* belief, or upon less perilous circumstances where life may not be at stake. Such cases may invoke considerably less sympathy than do the classic examples. It would be unrealistic to hope that prosecutors will always act with absolute fairness, and be able to accommodate the complex jurisprudential issues inherent in a claim of mistaken necessity, when deciding whether or not to prosecute in such a case. The proper place to address such issues is in the courtroom.

It is regrettable that much of the early debate in New Zealand concerning the merits of the necessity defence was highly rhetorical and tended to falter upon the perception that early examples of necessity (for example the moral duties of two persons in the water struggling for the possession of a plank capable of supporting only one) simply existed for the whimsical amusement of "casuists" who have "for centuries" amused themselves with such moral teasers.[101] A similar view is expressed by Adams, who suggests that the courts cannot be drawn into "a morass of moralising" which is the product of the "endless argument" to which the (often unrealistic) classic cases of necessity give rise.[102] However, it should be noted that the claims of casuistry and moralising have largely been associated with a discussion of the merits of necessity as a defence to murder. They bear little relationship to the modern defence, which typically concerns such practical questions as whether necessity should be available to a mother who runs a red light while rushing a sick child to hospital, or to a doctor performing an operation without consent, or to an offender who causes an accident when he speeds to avoid the threatening behaviour of the occupants of another car. These questions, we suggest, involve issues of principle that have *real* importance, and should not be dismissed as mere casuistry.

The complexity of modern society demands a more considered and rational response to the claims of justifying necessity than that suggested by the early commentators. Traditional accounts of the doctrine have allowed necessity to excuse conduct that would otherwise be

---

99   See, for example, the comments of Dickson J in *R v Perka* [1984] 2 SCR 232, 241, also reported as *Perka v R* (1984) 14 CCC (3d) 385 (SCC), 392.

100 Lamentably, defendants are on occasion found guilty of offences even though, in the view of the Court, a prosecution should not have been brought: see, eg, *Smedleys Ltd v Breed* [1974] AC 839; *Hart v Bex* [1957] Crim LR 622.

101 See Criminal Code Bill Commission, *Report of the Royal Commission Appointed to Consider the Law Relating to Indictable Offences: With an Appendix Containing a Draft Code Embodying the Suggestions of the Commissioners*, London, Eyre & Spottiswode for HMSO, 1879, note A to p 10, 44.

102 *Adams* (2nd ed), para 492.

criminal in exceptional cases based on the maxim "in casu extremae necessitatis omnia sunt communia" (in cases of extreme necessity all things are common).[103] However, such broadly expressed principles do not reflect the intricacy of a modern doctrine of necessity and fail to give any guidance about how it should be applied in circumstances where the merits of a claim are not intuitively clear. In our view, the now-accepted, common-law doctrine should be clearly expressed in statutory form and should be available in New Zealand as a general defence.

(1) The Rule of Law

But before we move on to this new development, it is important to recognise the concern underlying the earlier decisions since, as we shall see, it may help to illuminate current difficulties raised by the recognition of a general plea of necessity. Earlier rejection of the defence was driven by an understandable reluctance to allow individuals to be the judge of when to dispense with the letter of the law:[104]

> "[T]he law regards with the deepest suspicion any remedies of self-help, and permits those remedies to be resorted to only in very special circumstances. The reason for such circumspection is clear — necessity can very easily become simply a mask for anarchy."

This is a Rule of Law argument. The legal system will simply not work if its authority is optional. Derogation from its rules is not permitted save in specific, confined circumstances. It is clearly in the public interest that traffic signals be rigidly obeyed: general security would be much diminished if overriding discretions were allowed. The use of vacant council properties is best resolved by political decision-making processes, implemented by consistent administration rather than ad hoc self-help. And so on. The drawback produced by this unyielding stance is that it exposes to criminal liability persons whose conduct may have brought about significant benefit and whose motivation may have been impeccable. This is a powerful consideration and warrants the admissibility of a necessity plea, which has rightly now been recognised. Yet it is a plea that imports considerable difficulties of definition and ambit.

13.3.4 Recognition of necessity in New Zealand law

The first explicit reference to a defence of necessity in New Zealand occurs in *R v Woolnough*,[105] where the Court of Appeal alluded to the "extreme vagueness of necessity" as a general defence in English criminal law and observed that the defence, if it existed at all, would be available by virtue of s 20 Crimes Act 1961. In *Tifaga v Dept of Labour*,[106] an immigration case in which the accused pleaded "impossibility of compliance" to a charge of overstaying, the Court of Appeal again, somewhat tentatively, conceded the existence of necessity, endorsing its preservation under s 20. Noting that necessity and impossibility are distinct but related concepts, Richardson J approved the dictum of Lord Simon in *DPP for Northern Ireland v Lynch*[107] that, although an action constrained of "true" necessity is one made without any choice of action at all, necessity has come to denote the situation where circumstances present a person not with no choice at all, but with a choice between two evils such that he cannot be

---

103 See 1 Hale PC 54, 55.
104 *Southwark London Borough Council v Williams* [1971] Ch 734; [1971] 2 All ER 175 (CA), 745-6; 181 (Edmund Davies LJ). Cf Brudner, "A Theory of Necessity" (1987) 7 OJLS 339, 342-4.
105 *R v Woolnough* [1977] 2 NZLR 508 (CA), 516.
106 *Tifaga v Dept of Labour* [1980] 2 NZLR 235 (CA), 242.
107 *DPP for Northern Ireland v Lynch* [1975] AC 653; [1975] 1 All ER 913 (HL), 690, 691; 934, 935.

blamed if he chooses the lesser. By contrast, impossibility involves the inability to comply with the law at all.

(1) Specific statutory defences of necessity

At present the Crimes Act 1961 does not provide a general defence of necessity, although, as has been noted, other defences analogous to necessity have been codified, including compulsion (s 24), self-defence (s 48), and defence of property (ss 52-56). There is also provision in ss 61 and 61A for those who perform surgical operations to be protected from criminal responsibility where the operation is performed with "reasonable care and skill". In addition, legislation occasionally provides that a particular emergency or danger may excuse a specified offence. An example is s 183, which, in combination with s 187A, prohibits procuring the miscarriage of any woman or girl by certain "unlawful" means. Pursuant to s 187A(3), the procurement will not be done "unlawfully" if the person doing it believes the miscarriage is "necessary to save the life of the woman or girl". It has been suggested that the word "necessary" as used in this context may require proof that the danger to the woman could not reasonably be averted by any means other than an abortion.[108] However, the use of the word "necessary" alone does not of itself imply that the section must be interpreted in light of established principles governing the operation of the defence at common law. Rather, the meaning of necessity must be judged by the context in which it occurs, which may in turn be affected by particular case law developments. For example, the interpretation of s 187A, in particular of the term "unlawfully", has been largely influenced by the decision in *R v Woolnough*,[109] where the Court of Appeal held that an abortion would not be performed "unlawfully" for the purposes of s 183(1) if the accused believed in good faith that there was a real risk of danger to the mother's life or of serious harm to her mental and physical health if she continued with the pregnancy.

(2) Trespass offences

The question of the relationship of the word "necessary" appearing in a statutory definition with the common law defence of necessity has been considered in New Zealand in relation to the offence of trespass as defined by s 3 Trespass Act 1980. That section states:

"(1) Every person commits an offence against this Act who trespasses on any place and, after being warned to leave that place by an occupier of that place, neglects or refuses to do so.

"(2) It shall be a defence to a charge under subsection (1) of this section if the defendant proves that it was necessary for him to remain in or on the place concerned for his own protection or the protection of some other person, or because of some emergency involving his property or the property of some other person."

In *Wilcox v Police*,[110] the appellant and nine other persons had gone to a Christchurch hospital with the purpose of preventing the entry of women who were intending to have abortions that day. They were warned to leave, but refused to do so and were then charged under s 3(1) with trespass. They argued that since unlawful abortions were going to be performed at

---

108 *Adams*, CA187A.07 (looseleaf).
109 *R v Woolnough* [1977] 2 NZLR 508 (CA).
110 *Wilcox v Police* [1994] 1 NZLR 243; (1993) 10 CRNZ 704 (Tipping J).

the hospital that morning, they were justified in refusing to leave because it was *necessary* for them to remain for the protection of the unborn children and the mothers concerned.

One issue for the Court to determine was whether the provision of a statutory defence of necessity in subs (2) "overwhelmed" the common law defence of necessity as it applied to trespass or whether the common law defence operated in tandem with the statutory defence. The Court held that under s 3 the question of necessity should be considered only under the defence available in subs (2) and not, additionally, when determining whether there had been a breach of subs (1). If necessity were to arise twice, first within the concept of trespass under subs (1) and then again under the statutory defence in subs (2), it was likely, the Court held, that the statutory defence would become a dead letter in most cases.

In ruling that the defence of necessity in s 3 was limited to its statutory form, Tipping J considered and distinguished the Court of Appeal decision in *Kapi v MOT*.[111] It was argued by counsel for the appellants that the decision in *Kapi* (in which the possibility of a defence of necessity had been acknowledged, but ruled out where the statutory defence of compulsion governed), read together with s 20 Crimes Act 1961, supported the proposition that necessity arises twice, ie under each subsection. His Honour made the following observations:[112]

> "The fact that necessity, properly understood, is a justification for trespass at common law is not in doubt. When acting by force of necessity the person concerned does not commit a trespass at all ... [H]owever, ... this principle of the common law does not continue to apply if altered by, or inconsistent with, any other enactment. In my judgment the common law principle of justification by necessity is inconsistent with s 3(2) of the Trespass Act 1980 and has in substance been altered thereby. Section 3(2) is in large measure a statutory enactment of the common law doctrine of necessity. While it may not be exactly the same, Parliament has clearly codified in statutory form the essential aspects of the doctrine of necessity.

> "Necessity has been made a statutory defence to a charge of trespass under s 3(1). It is a defence in respect of which the defendant has the onus of proof on the balance of probabilities. That in my judgment is quite inconsistent with the proposition that the informant must, for the purposes of s 3(1), negative any question of necessity beyond reasonable doubt in order to establish that there has been a trespass. Accordingly, while s 20 ... prima facie preserves the concept of necessity for the purpose of the law of trespass, s 3 of the Trespass Act has expressly altered the position and is inconsistent with the prima facie preservation. There is nothing in the decision ... in *Kapi's case* which ... assists the appellants on this point."

The result is that facts raising necessity which do not fall within the terms of s 3(2) Trespass Act fail to exculpate, arguably as a result of a deliberate legislative intent to restrict the scope of the defence of necessity in that regard.[113] Unfortunately, the decision does not attempt to define the *elements* of necessity within the offence of trespass. Is one to suppose, for example, that the Legislature intends, in defining necessity within the terms of s 3(2), to provide a *narrow* release from criminal responsibility where the strict terms of the statutory requirements are met, as in the case of statutory compulsion?[114] If so, what is implied in the expression

---

111 *Kapi v MOT* (1991) 8 CRNZ 49 (CA). See 13.2.2.
112 *Wilcox v Police* [1994] 1 NZLR 243; (1993) 10 CRNZ 704, 247; 707, 708.
113 *Kapi v MOT* (1991) 8 CRNZ 49 (CA), 54 (Gault J).

"necessary ... to remain"? Does the defence require an honest and reasonable belief that there was, say, an emergency justifying the accused's actions — or must a *factual* emergency be proved regardless of the accused's belief? By analogy with the statutory defence of compulsion, it could be argued that mere apprehension of an emergency in the absence of a (factually) critical situation will be insufficient to establish a necessity to remain.[115]

Some of these questions were addressed by the Court of Appeal in *Bayer v Police*,[116] which also concerned the actions of anti-abortionists who entered the premises of the Auckland Medical Aid Trust and effectively blocked access. The question of the proper interpretation of s 3(2) Trespass Act 1980 was again in issue. The Court noted that, although the requirement to prove necessity was expressed in absolute terms, the implication of an objective standard of reasonableness qualifying the word "necessary" was called for in order to give realistic scope to the beneficial operation of the subsection. Therefore, the standard was whether a reasonable person aware of all the circumstances would have thought it necessary to remain for the protection of some other person.[117]

Given this objective standard, is there any scope within the statutory defence under s 3(2) for a *mistaken* belief in the existence of an emergency justifying the accused's remaining in or on the place, whether or not that belief is based on reasonable grounds? It would seem not. In *Bayer* the Court held that the language of the section "does not admit of any allowance" for the defendant's honest belief in circumstances justifying necessity.[118] The apparent rationale for this approach is that a statutory defence such as that provided for in s 3(2) confers a "benefit" on an accused and there is no warrant for reading into its terms those common law considerations which are appropriate to "penal" provisions. In particular, the specific references to the accused's belief, made in those sections of the Crimes Act 1961 dealing with matters of justification or defence,[119] by implication excludes consideration of the matter in a "statutory" defence that makes no such mention.

This approach has more recently been affirmed in *Wilcox v Police*.[120] Yet the rationale is surely a dubious one. The actual distinction, if any, between a "statutory" defence and a "penal" provision is not made clear, and it is submitted that ordinary principles of criminal responsibility regarding exculpatory mistakes should apply also to the former case. Criminal defences, whether statutory or not, are part of penal provisions. It could also be argued that all defences, statutory and common law based, confer a "benefit" on an accused and in that regard are, or ought to be, indistinguishable. In any event, it does not follow that the sort of benefit conferred by a "statutory" defence is such as to justify the exclusion of other possible exculpatory provisions, particularly where the offence, in respect of which the statutory defence is claimed, is itself truly "penal" and carries the possibility of loss of liberty.[121]

---

114   See *R v Teichelman* [1981] 2 NZLR 64 (CA), 66 (Richardson J).
115   See *R v Frickleton* [1984] 2 NZLR 670 (CA), 672 (McMullin J): "once it is shown that an accused person intended to do the act which is forbidden by law mere apprehension is not enough to provide a defence."
116   *Bayer v Police* [1994] 2 NZLR 48 (CA).
117   *Bayer v Police* [1994] 2 NZLR 48 (CA), 50. See also *R v Gough* [1993] AC 646; [1993] 2 All ER 724 (HL).
118   See also *O'Neill v Police* 22/11/93, CA392/93, on appeal from *Police v O'Neill* [1993] 3 NZLR 712. The same principle was held to apply.
119   See, for example, s 41 (prevention of suicide or injury), ss 44-46 (suppression of riot), and s 48 (self-defence).
120   *Wilcox v Police* [1995] 2 NZLR 160; (1995) 12 CRNZ 468 (CA), 165; 474.
121   The offence defined in s 3(1) Trespass Act 1980 is punishable either by a fine not exceeding $1,000 or by imprisonment for a term not exceeding 3 months.

(3) Emergency operations

It has been noted that the standard of "reasonable care and skill" mentioned in ss 61 and 61A should be read in the light of the duty imposed by s 155.[122] This section provides that, *except in the case of necessity*, every one who undertakes to administer surgical or medical treatment is under a legal duty to have and to use reasonable knowledge, care, and skill in administering the treatment. In R v Yogasakaran,[123] the Court of Appeal rejected a submission that the qualification "except in the case of necessity" had any bearing on the situation where an anaesthetist had to act in haste when an emergency arose during an operation. Of the expression, the Court said:

> "That exception is plainly intended to cover the case of persons unqualified or insufficiently qualified who in emergencies undertake surgical or medical treatment or the like. It is not intended to emancipate a professional medical practitioner from the exercise of reasonable professional care and skill in an emergency. Instant decisions may have to be taken in an emergency; that must be a major factor to be kept prominently in mind in determining whether there has been a failure to live up to the appropriate professional standard."

There may be many situations in which an emergency dictates the need for immediate medical intervention and treatment. Almost invariably, it will not be possible to obtain the consent of the patient concerned and obtaining the consent of someone able to give consent on the patient's behalf may be impracticable. If actual patient consent were required for every medical procedure without exception, the administration of emergency medicine would be seriously impaired and doctors would face a choice between operating without such consent (with a possible prosecution for criminal assault to follow) and refusing to operate at all.[124]

(4) Moral imperatives?

Necessity, however, is not available where the claim is presented as a "perceived moral imperative", namely, of being "driven by love and compassion" to end the life of the accused's terminally ill mother.[125] In *Martin* the Court refused to accept that a "perceived moral imperative" ("whatever that might be"[126]) could equate with any notion of necessity, or normative involuntariness (above, 13.1.1), for the purposes of what was in effect a mercy killing; it could not be said that the accused had no choice but to end her mother's life.

13.3.5 The rationale and scope of the common law defence

The idea behind the defence is simple and beguiling: achieve the greater good rather than slavishly follow the letter of the law. There will be occasions where following this injunction will produce incontrovertible gains in welfare and an absence of countervailing harms. Yet an absence of countervailing harms is not a necessary condition for establishing the defence. A balance of harms test may be allowed in some circumstances; whereas in other situations vested

---

122 See *Adams*, CA61.02 (looseleaf).
123 R v Yogasakaran [1990] 1 NZLR 399; (1989) 5 CRNZ 69 (CA), 405; 74.
124 Collins notes that if consent were mandatory in every case of medical intervention it would jeopardise the ethical obligation of doctors to "render all assistance possible to any patient where an urgent need for medical care exists": Collins, *Medical Law in New Zealand*, Wellington, Brooker & Friend, 1992, para 3.4.1.
125 R v *Martin* 24/3/04, Wild J, HC Wanganui, CRI-2003-083-432B.
126 R v *Martin* 24/3/04, Wild J, HC Wanganui, CRI-2003-083-432B, para 6.

legal rights will be given priority, thereby precluding on those occasions a necessity defence based on a balance of harms test. The devil is in the detail. The leading cases are short on guidance about these issues. In what follows, we will do what we can to delineate the ambit of this defence.

There is no unitary rationale of the necessity defence. Rather, within the general rubric of "necessity", the defence cloaks at least two intertwined justifications (below). What they have in common is at least a degree of urgency, which may fall short of immediate emergency. Sometimes it may be possible to seek the assistance of the courts ex ante to determine the legality of a proposed course of action. In medical cases, the courts have shown a commendable degree of procedural flexibility in advising on the legality of proposed surgery; surgery which would constitute a criminal (and tortious) act unless warranted by necessity. Where prior guidance of the courts is feasible, the Rule of Law concerns about necessity (above, 13.3.3(1)) become less pressing; yet there will be occasions where immediate action is called for — unless D takes V's car she will not be able to rescue T. Nowadays, a court may rule, ex post facto, that D was entitled to drive V's car, without prior permission from V, to avert harm to T. But what must be present in every case is a harm which can only be avoided if, in the near future, the letter of the law is breached.

If the harm is more remote than that (particularly where the harm has a degree of conjecture and imprecision), D cannot take the law into her own hands and must address her concerns in some other fashion. In *Shayler*,[127] D, a civil servant employed in MI5, was concerned that the kind of covert actions supported by the service threatened rather than enhanced public security. He was held to be in breach of the Official Secrets Act 1989, consequent on sharing secret information with a newspaper. Even on the assumption that his concerns were warranted, he was not attempting to avert some imminent catastrophe by the only possible and proportionate means. There was no forthcoming incident his actions were intended to avert, merely a fear that the covert operations of MI5 threatened public security generally. Since necessity has an uncertain scope and is not tightly confined in the way that other defences generally are, its recognition could potentially undermine the authority of law. If defendants were permitted to break laws *whenever* there was, say, a lesser-evils justification (below), the generality of those laws would be undermined and their application would have to be reassessed on a case-by-case basis. It is for the legal system to determine when its prima facie laws may be broken.

Ideally, in a democracy, the freedom of action that a perceived necessity requires should be afforded by legislative change. Yet constraints of time may preclude resort to legislation. In those circumstances, wherever possible, guidance from a court should be sought before the putatively illegal action is taken, as was done, for instance, in the conjoined twins separation case of *Re A (children)*.[128] Where that is impossible and the only recourse is direct action by D, D may be found to have been justified by necessity.

(1)   *A lesser-evil justification*

The most obvious rationale for allowing necessity is a recognition that, on occasion, more welfare may ensue from breaking the law than keeping it. The defence looks to the consequences of particular episodes of conduct rather than to the desert of the actor. To be

---

127   *R v Shayler* [2001] 1 WLR 2206.
128   *Re A (Children) (Conjoined Twins: Surgical Separation)* [2001] Fam 147 (CA).

sure, on many occasions where a necessity defence may be invoked, the defendant is meritorious or blameless. Yet if, say, a driver of a fire-engine decides to pass a red light with complete safety on a clear road in order to effect a life-saving rescue, it misses the point to say that a conviction for a road traffic offence is not merited because the driver has an exculpatory excuse. The gain in welfare arising from saving a life rather than opting for pedantic compliance with regulatory law is so salient that it eclipses any issues of culpability and blame typically associated with law-breaking. The conduct in question is incontrovertibly worthwhile, like giving to charity or researching cures for deadly diseases. It is not that D acted wrongly and is insufficiently culpable: it is that D did the right thing.

The fire-engine case is an easy example because the offence in question was a victimless offence; no-one's rights or interests were overridden when making the rescue. Yet even where another person's rights are violated, necessity may be available, at least where those rights are of a lesser order of importance by comparison with the value being protected. Thus it may be necessary to trespass across land to effect the rescue of T. Or it may be necessary to break into the absent V's house in order to telephone an ambulance required to take D to hospital for vital emergency treatment. In each of these cases, provided the situation is an emergency, such minor infringements of rights are compatible with allowing a necessity plea. Sufficient regard of V's interests will be offered if he is entitled to full compensation for any loss sustained.[129] The key criteria of the defence, drawn from the work of Stephen, are set out by Brooke LJ in *Re A (children)*:[130]

(i) The act is needed to avoid inevitable and irreparable evil.

(ii) No more should be done than is reasonably necessary for the purpose to be achieved.

(iii) The evil inflicted must not be disproportionate to the evil avoided.

If this analysis is correct, D may, say, pick up V's mobile phone from the table to alert emergency services even if V should decline D's request to use the phone. It may well be that D is entitled to use a reasonable degree of force should V attempt to take back the phone until the emergency call is made. Indeed, as we shall see in 13.3.5(3), in special circumstances the lesser-evils defence of necessity may stretch even to homicide.

(2) *Best interests medical treatment*

Lesser-evils necessity overlaps with a second type of necessity, which is a form of "best-interests" intervention. The latter is exemplified by *Re F (Mental Patient: Sterilisation)*.[131] F was a sexually active woman, aged 36 but with the mental age of a young child. It was judged that a pregnancy would be extremely detrimental to her well-being, but ordinary contraception techniques were apparently either ineffective or impracticable. The House of Lords ruled that it would be permissible, on grounds of necessity, to conduct a sterilization operation. Unlike duress, the principle "is one of necessity, not of emergency."[132] But neither is this a

---

129   Cf the famous tort case of *Vincent v Lake Erie Transportation Co* (1910)124 NW 221, in which D tied his yacht to P's jetty during a storm, thereby saving the yacht but damaging the jetty.
130   *Re A (Children) (Conjoined Twins: Surgical Separation)* [2001] Fam 147 (CA), 240.
131   *Re F (Mental Patient: Sterilisation)* [1990] 2 AC 1; [1989] 2 WLR 1025 (HL).
132   *Re F (Mental Patient: Sterilisation)* [1990] 2 AC 1; [1989] 2 WLR 1025 (HL), 75 (Lord Goff): "[e]mergency is however not the criterion or even a pre requisite; it is simply a frequent origin of the necessity which impels intervention." In particular, it may be the reason why there is no opportunity to consult with V before intervening.

straightforward case of lesser evils. The principle is one of acting on behalf of another to preserve their life, health, or wellbeing, in circumstances where there is no opportunity to consult with the beneficiary. As such, according to Lord Goff, the defence contains two key and distinctive ingredients:[133]

(i) First, there must be a necessity to act when it is not practicable to communicate with the other person;

(ii) Secondly, the action taken must be such as a reasonable person would, in all the circumstances, take action in the best interests of the person being assisted.

The principle of necessity, so formulated, will not justify mere officious intervention.[134] Neither will it justify a medical intervention without consent when another more appropriate person is available and willing to act or when it is contrary to the known wishes of the person in need of assistance (to the extent that the person is rationally capable of forming such a wish).[135] However, provided the above criteria are fulfilled, interference with the person or property of the person being assisted will not be unlawful. So, in the event of a railway accident or plane crash where injured passengers lie trapped in the wreckage, the principle of necessity will render lawful the actions of other persons who seek to help the victims, even where reasonable assistance given in good faith actually accelerates the death of the person being assisted. This might occur where, for example, a victim is trapped in a fiercely burning carriage and amputation of a limb is necessary to remove him from the immediate threat to his life; notwithstanding that the victim may later die as a result of complications caused by blood-loss from the amputation before intensive life-saving treatment could be administered.

The same principle would also cover the treatment by a doctor or nurse of an elderly person who suffers a stroke which renders him incapable of speech or movement. Any touching or movement of his person aimed at assisting or caring for him will be lawful. Clearly, this situation, although embraced by necessity, is not strictly an emergency and is characterised as a permanent or semi-permanent state of affairs. In *Re F*,[136] Lord Goff suggested that the principle of necessity should also be applicable to a case of a mentally disordered person who is disabled from giving consent. In such a case, as with a stroke victim, the permanent state of affairs may call for a wider range of care than may be needed in an emergency which arises from accidental injury.[137]

> "When the state of affairs is permanent, or semi-permanent, action properly taken to preserve the life, health or well-being of the assisted person may well transcend such measures as surgical operation or substantial medical treatment and may extend to include such humdrum matters as routine medical or dental treatment, even simple care such as dressing and undressing and putting to bed."

A situation or state of affairs characterised as permanent or semi-permanent, as with a mentally impaired person or a patient in a "permanent" coma, may justify a doctor's moving with despatch to do the thing which secures the patient's best interests, without the need to obtain the patient's consent. However, this stands in contrast to the situation where a doctor performs

---

133 *Re F (Mental Patient: Sterilisation)* [1990] 2 AC 1 (HL), 75.
134 *Re F (Mental Patient: Sterilisation)* [1990] 2 AC 1 (HL), 76.
135 *Re F (Mental Patient: Sterilisation)* [1990] 2 AC 1 (HL), 76.
136 *Re F (Mental Patient: Sterilisation)* [1990] 2 AC 1 (HL), 76.
137 *Re F (Mental Patient: Sterilisation)* [1990] 2 AC 1 (HL), 76.

an operation without consent on a patient temporarily rendered unconscious as a result of an accident. In these circumstances the doctor should do no more than is reasonably essential, in the best interests of the patient, before he recovers consciousness.[138] The latter restriction derives from the expectation that the patient will, before long, regain consciousness, and may then be consulted about longer-term measures. Therefore, the doctrine of necessity may not cover medical interventions where the attending physician does more than is reasonably required to secure the patient's immediate needs. Suppose, for example, that V is severely injured in a motor accident. While V is comatose, D, a surgeon, performs surgery to repair a compound fracture to V's upper left leg. Although the primary operation without V's consent may well be justified on grounds of necessity, D is not at liberty to perform additional surgery of a cosmetic nature to eliminate "ugly scarring" without V's consent, particularly where this involves the surgical removal of skin tissue from some other part of V's body.[139] The suggested standard, that any treatment which is "clearly to the medical benefit of the patient" may be given where there is no reasonable likelihood of the patient regaining competency,[140] clearly needs elaboration in cases where the patient is in fact expected to recover competency.

(3) *Lesser-evils necessity and homicide*

To the extent that necessity excuses otherwise unlawful conduct performed during a medical procedure, it normally implies action aimed at fostering life, not destroying it. And as we have seen, the defence of duress of circumstances does not apply to cases of murder or attempted murder. The question which therefore arises is whether there are any circumstances, apart from self-defence, in which human life may lawfully be destroyed in the face of necessity. The answer to that question must be a qualified "yes". For while the notion of "lawfully destroying" human life must be treated with great circumspection, the decision in Re *A (children)*[141] clearly admits of that possibility, albeit in very narrow and fact-specific circumstances.

Re A (children) concerned two infants (J and M) who were born conjoined. The English Court of Appeal was asked to determine whether it would be lawful for surgeons to operate on the twins to separate them. The implications of separation were that one twin, Mary, would certainly die within minutes and that the other, Jodie, would most probably live. If the operation had not been performed, both twins were expected to die within a matter of months. The difficulty was that M's own heart and lungs were inadequate to sustain M's life, so that her survival depended on J; in particular, on J's heart continuing to pump the blood oxygenated by J through both twins' bodies. Unfortunately, sustaining both lives was imposing an excessive strain on J's heart. It was common ground that J's heart would fail within a few months, and that M's death would inevitably follow J's.

The Court held that it would be lawful (though not required) for surgeons to undertake the operation. The decision seems to establish the general proposition that a defence of necessity can extend to lethal acts undertaken in order to negate a threat to life, even where that threat is an innocent one. Prima facie, this general proposition, that a necessitous killing can be lawful, is difficult to reconcile with the existing case law. The rule in *R v Dudley and Stephens*,[142] which

---

138 *Re F (Mental Patient: Sterilisation)* [1990] 2 AC 1 (HL), 76, 77.
139 For further discussion of the issues arising see *Marshall v Curry* [1933] 3 DLR 260; (1933) 60 CCC 136; *Murray v McMurchy* [1949] 2 DLR 442; also the discussion in Collins, *Medical Law in New Zealand*, Wellington, Brooker & Friend, 1992, paras 3.4.4, 3.4.5.
140 Gostin, *Mental Health Services: Law and Practice*, Shaw & Sons, 1986, paras 20-16.
141 *Re A (Children) (Conjoined Twins: Surgical Separation)* [2001] Fam 147 (CA).

is still a binding authority in New Zealand, clearly states that necessity is not a defence to murder. Yet the surgeons' acts would prima facie amount to murder because of the presence of both actus reus and mens rea elements.

The Court of Appeal sought to avoid the implications of *Dudley and Stephens* by a variety of routes. For the purposes of this discussion, we will limit ourselves to Brooke LJ's approach. His Lordship held that the case fell within the defence of lesser-evils necessity:[143]

> "The claim is that [D's] conduct was not harmful because on a choice of two evils the choice of avoiding the greater harm was justified."

As we noted in 13.3.5(1), his Lordship set out the three essential common law requirements for the defence, according to which the intervention in *Re A* would be permissible:[144]

(i)   The act is needed to avoid inevitable and irreparable evil.

(ii) No more should be done than is reasonably necessary for the purpose to be achieved.

(iii) The evil inflicted must not be disproportionate to the evil avoided.

Brooke LJ characterised the situation as one of a choice of evils. His Lordship then sought to distinguish *Re A* from the troublesome implications of *Dudley and Stephens* by arguing that M was "self-designated for a very early death",[145] thereby eliminating, it was hoped, the difficult legal and ethical implications associated with the issue of human choice in selecting a candidate for death. Brooke LJ also suggested that the balance of evils was tilted in J's favour by the fact that "the principles of modern family law point irresistibly to the conclusion that the interests of [J] must be preferred to the conflicting interests of [M],"[146] because J had a good prospect of living a happy, fulfilled life while M had no prospects at all.

There are difficulties with Brooke LJ's analysis, in that, if the "lesser-evils" approach is to be used to deal with the complexities of a case like *Re A*, its requirements need to be augmented. The limitation of these criteria is that, without more, they would also exculpate the defendants in *Dudley and Stephens*. Moreover, it will not do the trick to point out that "Mary is, sadly, self-designated for a very early death." So was the cabin-boy in *Dudley and Stephens*, whose condition was far more acute than that of the others. Similarly, the same doctors who operated in *Re A* would not have been free to accelerate M's death in order to, say, facilitate the early transplant of one of her working organs into P, some otherwise healthy patient.[147]

What makes the difference is that the doctors did what was necessary, and proportionate, purely in order to protect J. Although Brooke LJ did not rely on this point explicitly, it matters that M was the source of the threat to J's life, a feature absent in *Dudley and Stephens*. This did not entitle the doctors to kill M in order to save J. (Such a response may be permissible when the defence is self-defence. But, while Ward LJ adopted a self-defence approach, Brooke LJ categorically rejected it, being unwilling to characterise M as an "unjust aggressor" for the purposes of applying a self-defence model.) Nonetheless, according to Brooke LJ, the doctors

---

142 R v Dudley and Stephens (1884) 14 QBD 273; [1881-85] All ER Rep 61; above, 13.3.2.
143 Re A (Children) (Conjoined Twins: Surgical Separation) [2001] Fam 147 (CA), 236.
144 Re A (Children) (Conjoined Twins: Surgical Separation) [2001] Fam 147 (CA), 236, citing Sir James Stephen.
145 Re A (Children) (Conjoined Twins: Surgical Separation) [2001] Fam 147 (CA), 239.
146 Re A (Children) (Conjoined Twins: Surgical Separation) [2001] Fam 147 (CA), 238.
147 For that matter, neither would it be relevant in the context of duress (for example, when D complies with a threat from gangsters by shooting a policeman known to be dying from cancer).

were entitled to act in order to save J's life,[148] by protecting her from the threat to her life, even though their doing so would have the side-effect of accelerating M's death.[149]

Brooke LJ's analysis points up a significant distinction between the doctrines of self-defence and lesser-evils necessity. One may directly intend to kill in self-defence. One may only *obliquely* intend death in necessity.[150] In *Dudley and Stephens*, the cabin boy's death was directly intended: the defendants aimed to kill him, in order to then eat him. In *Re A*, M's death was no part of the doctors' aim or purpose, although it was an inevitable consequence of what they sought to achieve. It is only by supplementing Brooke LJ's analysis with these considerations that the rule in *Dudley and Stephens* can safely be distinguished.

Be that as it may, it is an inescapable conclusion of *Re A* that M's death is obliquely intended, once it is accepted that the actus reus of killing M is a virtually certain[151] consequence of the surgeons' actions. Given this, there can be no plausible claim that the duress of circumstance defence was applicable. It is an inescapable conclusion that necessity, at common law, has a separate existence.

13.4 Strict liability offences

Where the relevant offence is characterised as a public welfare regulatory offence, the defences of duress of circumstances and necessity are subsumed by the general defence of absence of fault. The test to be applied in such cases is whether in all the circumstances the accused did what a reasonable person would have done.[152] The defence of absence of fault is one of due diligence or absence of negligence, and extends to situations where the accused reasonably, but mistakenly, believed in facts which, if true, would have made the conduct innocent.[153] Given that duress and necessity are subsumed under absence of fault in relation to public welfare offences, it would appear that an honest but reasonably mistaken belief that the offender is, say, threatened with death or serious injury, mandating action in breach of the law, will be a good defence to a public welfare offence; even though not to a true crime. This would suggest that the defence has a different, perhaps more liberal, character when applied to public welfare offences. However, in the regulatory context, the accused is required to prove absence of fault, which would include duress of circumstances, on the balance of probabilities. In addition, before a trial judge is required to leave the defence to the jury there must be a credible or plausible narrative which might lead the jury to entertain the reasonable possibility of the defence.[154] These requirements would tend to eliminate any notorious or unmeritorious claims.

---

148 Subject, of course, to their satisfying the other criteria of necessity, in particular those identified by Brooke LJ.
149 It is here (and, more generally, in decisions about which life to save) that the matter of M's life expectancy may be a consideration, going to assessment of the proportionality criterion.
150 See above, 4.2.1-4.
151 See above, 4.2.4.
152 See *Civil Aviation Dept v MacKenzie* [1983] NZLR 78, 81, also reported as *MacKenzie v Civil Aviation Dept* (1983) 1 CRNZ 38 (CA), 41 (Richardson J); also *Tifaga v Dept of Labour* [1980] 2 NZLR 235 (CA), 242, 243 (Richardson J); *R v Slovack* [1980] 1 WWR 368; *R v Gonder* (1981) 62 CCC (2d) 326.
153 See 5.1.1(1); *Adams*, CA20.46 (looseleaf).
154 *R v Joyce* [1968] NZLR 1070 (CA), 1077; *R v Grice* [1975] 1 NZLR 760 (CA), 765.

13.5 Some codification proposals

Since the early 1970s, the tide of both law reform and judicial developments has been moving in favour of the recognition of duress and necessity as defences.

13.5.1 A generic "necessity" proposal

In New Zealand, the draft Crimes Bill 1989 contains a proposal for a codification of "necessity" (cl 30). The proposal is expressed in sufficiently amorphous terms that it might effectively embrace both necessity and duress. Clause 30, as originally drafted, provided:

> "*Necessity*
>
> "A person is not criminally responsible for any act done or omitted to be done under such circumstances of sudden and extraordinary emergency that a person of ordinary commonsense and prudence could not reasonably be expected to act otherwise."

The clause aimed to protect a person from criminal responsibility for anything done in an emergency, if a person of ordinary common sense and prudence could not reasonably be expected to have acted otherwise. It was based broadly on cl 46 of the proposed Criminal Code (UK) and on § 3.02 of the Model Penal Code (US).[155] The draft reflects the common law position that where duress of circumstances is advanced as a defence to crime it must be established by reference to objective facts or beliefs. This would imply that a mistaken belief, wholly unfounded in fact, in circumstances of necessity, will be insufficient to give rise to the defence.[156]

The position of mistaken but reasonable beliefs is unclear. The wording of the original cl 30 does not even mention the accused's state of mind, and appears to require only an objective situation of emergent peril, regardless of whether it is perceived as such. However, this interpretation, which excludes consideration of the defendant's subjective belief concerning the emergency, is both inconsistent with principle and contrary to the approach taken in respect of other defences recognised under New Zealand criminal law, and must be regarded as unlikely.

This anomaly was rectified when the Crimes Consultative Committee recommended a significant redraft of cl 30,[157] in order to incorporate some "useful features" of the English Draft Code provision.[158] The redrafted clause now reads:

> "**30 Necessity**

---

155 Crimes Bill 1989, Explanatory Note. However, unlike the Crimes Bill proposal, the Model Penal Code envisages that the defence of necessity is available for homicide: American Law Institute, *Model Penal Code and Commentaries*, 1985, para 3.02, 14-15. See also the discussion in *R v Latimer* (2001) 193 DLR (4th) 577, 596, regarding the difficulty about reconciling necessity as a defence to homicide with the requirement of proportionality. However, further weight to the proposition that necessity should be available for homicide is now added by the decision *Re A (Children) (Conjoined Twins: Surgical Separation)* [2001] Fam 147 (CA), discussed at 13.3.5(3); see also Rogers, "Necessity, private defence and the killing of Mary" [2001] Crim LR 515.
156 See *R v Conway* [1988] 3 All ER 1025; [1988] 3 WLR 1238 (CA), 1029; 1244: "necessity can only be a defence ... where the facts establish 'duress of circumstances'" (emphasis added).
157 See Crimes Bill Consultative Committee, *Crimes Bill 1989: Report of the Crimes Consultative Committee Presented to the Minister of Justice April 1991*, Wellington, Department of Justice, 1991, 95, 96.

"(1) A person is not criminally responsible for any act done or omitted to be done under circumstances of emergency in which—

"(a) The person *believes* that it is immediately necessary to avoid death or serious bodily harm to that person or any other person; and

"(b) A person of ordinary common sense and prudence could not be expected to act otherwise.

"(2) Subclause (1) does not apply where the person who does or omits the act has knowingly and without reasonable cause placed himself or herself in or remained in, a situation where there was a risk of such an emergency.

"(3) Subclause (1) does not apply to the offences of murder or attempted murder." [Emphasis added]

The revised version now clearly includes a subjective element, which, should it ever become law, would bring the statutory defence broadly into line with the other defences already contained in the Crimes Act. But, as will be apparent, the redraft essentially abandons the original idea of necessary and proportionate action, in favour of the duress of circumstances model.

13.5.2 A specific duress of circumstances recommendation

More recently, the Law Commission has addressed some problems identified in recent cases in which necessity or duress of circumstances has been raised. The principal focus of its report *Some Criminal Defences with Particular Reference to Battered Defendants*[159] is on defendants who are the victims of domestic violence. However, it contains recommendations concerning the reform of the defence of compulsion (s 24) and specifically recommends that a new general defence of duress of circumstances be created. The Law Commission recognises that the terms "duress of circumstances" and "necessity" are often used interchangeably. However, this may create confusion. If "necessity" is used also to mean "duress of circumstances" then we are left with no expression to describe those cases where the defendant's will is not overborne and there is no crisis demanding an immediate response, but where the defendant makes a considered and rational decision deliberately to commit a prima facie offence to prevent the occurrence of a greater harm. As we saw earlier (13.000), an extreme example of such conduct, justified not on grounds of duress of circumstances but as necessity, is *Re A (children)*.[160] Such cases do not constitute an emergency in the accepted sense. Neither do they encompass the actor's choices being irresistibly overborne. For these reasons, the Law Commission has recommended that "duress of circumstances" be reserved for situations where the actor's choices are overborne in the face of an emergency and "necessity" be preserved to cover situations of "choice of evils", absent overbearing mental pressure.[161]

---

158 See Crimes Bill Consultative Committee, *Crimes Bill 1989: Report of the Crimes Consultative Committee presented to the Minister of Justice April 1991*, Wellington, Department of Justice, 1991, 20.
159 Law Commission, *Some Criminal Defences with Particular Reference to Battered Defendants*, NZLC R73, Wellington, 2001.
160 *Re A (Children) (Conjoined Twins: Surgical Separation)* [2001] Fam 147 (CA). See also *Re F (Mental Patient: Sterilisation)* [1990] 2 AC 1; [1989] 2 WLR 1025 (HL) (sterilisation of mentally disabled but sexually active hospital patients); *R v Bournewood Mental Health Trust, ex p L* [1999] 1 AC 485 (HL) (detention without statutory authority of mentally disabled people in order to protect them).

The Law Commission's recommended new statutory defence of duress of circumstances is based, with some modifications, on the Crimes Consultative Committee's version of the necessity provision, first proposed in the Crimes Bill 1989.[162] Its effect would be to clarify the scope of the defence in New Zealand and remove the limitation imposed in *Kapi*, which excludes common law necessity in cases where the threatened danger comes from a human source. The defence proposed by the Law Commission is:[163]

"(1) A person is not criminally responsible for any act done or omitted to be done under circumstances of emergency in which—

"(a) That person believes that such act or omission is immediately necessary to avoid death or serious bodily harm to that person or any other person; and

"(b) In all the circumstances (including any of his or her personal circumstances that affect their gravity) that person cannot reasonably be expected to act or omit to act otherwise."

13.6 Impossibility of compliance

A defence which is closely related to necessity is that of impossibility. To distinguish it from impossibility in attempts, which has an entirely different conceptual basis, the defence is sometimes called impossibility of compliance. Impossibility in this sense may arise where, at the time of the prohibited conduct or event, it was not possible to comply with the law. However, there are two important qualifications to the doctrine:

(i) The impossibility must not be attributable to the accused's own fault.

(ii) The claimed impossibility must not create an inconsistency with the enactment creating the particular offence or any other statutory provision.

We examine each of these qualifications below.

13.6.1 Absolute impossibility

Impossibility operates by negativing the actus reus of an offence, in the same way as does physical involuntariness.[164] The essence of the analysis in such cases is that the performance of a legal duty was impossible because of circumstances which absolutely physically prevented the accused from doing the thing required by law. It is a case of actus reus for which the accused is not responsible. Unlike the defences of duress of circumstances and necessity, it is not simply a case of choice between evils. In *Tifaga v Dept of Labour*, Richardson J stated, "[i]n contemporary usage *inability to comply at all* is the subject of ... impossibility".[165] There would seem, therefore, to be no room for a mistaken belief in impossibility as a defence to a charge

---

161 Law Commission, *Some Criminal Defences with Particular Reference to Battered Defendants*, NZLC R73, Wellington, 2001, paras 177, 229.
162 Law Commission, *Some Criminal Defences with Particular Reference to Battered Defendants*, NZLC R73, Wellington, 2001, paras 230, 231.
163 For a comprehensive critique of the Law Commission's proposals, see Dawkins and Briggs, "Criminal law" [2001] NZ Law Review 328. See also Dawkins, "The Defence of Duress of Circumstances in New Zealand" in J B Robertson (ed) *Essays on Criminal Law: A Tribute to Professor Gerald Orchard*, Wellington, Brookers, 2004, 96.
164 See 3.4.
165 *Tifaga v Dept of Labour* [1980] 2 NZLR 235 (CA), 243 (emphasis added).

that the accused had failed to perform a duty prescribed by law. Either the duty was impossible to fulfil or it was not, in which case the defence must fail.

Similarly, the notion of impossibility, being a species of involuntariness, does not allow for a qualification based on reasonableness. It does not make sense to say that a proscribed omission was "reasonably impossible" any more than it makes sense to say that the accused's acts were "reasonably involuntary". Conduct was either impossible or it was not. It does not assist analysis to ask whether a reasonable person would have considered the duty impossible to fulfil. The essence of the claim is that the defendant was prohibited from fulfilling her legal responsibilities by exigent events.

This may assist us in understanding why some claims of impossibility must fail. The availability of an alternative course of action militates against the notion of impossibility, because it suggests that the course of conduct required by the law was merely *difficult* to fulfil and not impossible. An opportunity to abide by the law is an essential basis for testing responsibility for acts and omissions,[166] and its absence denies D's responsibility for the actus reus of a crime. Any qualification to the exculpatory defence based on *difficulty* of compliance, as opposed to *impossibility*, would negate the purpose of the doctrine and would decrease the effectiveness of criminal sanctions. Many people find difficulty in complying with the law's demands, but that has never seriously been advanced as a reason for reducing the high standard of compliance expected of all responsible citizens.

The *absolute* character of impossibility may be demonstrated by reference to cases. In the old English case of *R v Bamber*,[167] the defendant was indicted for failure to repair a road adjoining the sea. It was held that the accused was not guilty because, as the result of an "act of God", the road, and all the materials with which a road could be made, had been washed away in a storm. Sometimes a defence akin to impossibility is claimed but not expressed as such. For example, in *Stockdale v Coulson*,[168] where the defendant company director had been charged with failing to annex copies of the company's balance sheet to annual returns as required by the Companies Act 1948 (UK), it was held that since there were no balance sheets in existence which had been laid before the company in a general meeting the defendant was not guilty of the offence charged. The Court said that "you cannot be punished for failing to annex something which does not exist".[169]

By contrast, as was noted above, mere difficulty of compliance is no defence. This is demonstrated in *Tifaga v Dept of Labour*,[170] where impossibility had been claimed as a defence to a charge of overstaying under s 14 Immigration Act 1964. The defendant had come to New Zealand on a temporary entry permit. During the period in which the permit was still current, the defendant was convicted of an offence and sentenced to imprisonment for 6 months. While in prison he was advised that his permit was to be revoked. At about the time of his release from prison he received a formal notice which required him to leave New Zealand within 21 days of that date. He failed to do so and was charged with overstaying his permit. His defence was that at the time of his release from prison he had neither savings nor recourse to funds to meet the cost of departing from New Zealand and in the time available to him had

---

166 *Tifaga v Dept of Labour* [1980] 2 NZLR 235 (CA), 238 (Woodhouse J).
167 *R v Bamber* (1843) 5 QB 279; 114 ER 1254.
168 *Stockdale v Coulson* [1974] 3 All ER 154; [1974] 1 WLR 1192.
169 *Stockdale v Coulson* [1974] 3 All ER 154; [1974] 1 WLR 1192, 158; 1196 (Melford Stevenson J).
170 *Tifaga v Dept of Labour* [1980] 2 NZLR 235 (CA), discussed at 5.1.2.

been unable to earn a sufficient amount. He argued that he had no choice about leaving or remaining in New Zealand so that his conduct in that regard was involuntary. Rejecting that argument, the Court of Appeal held that it was the appellant's responsibility to provide the practical means to enable him to leave the country. He had chosen not to have sufficient funds available to meet the fare from New Zealand. Since there was no evidence that it had been impossible to maintain a reserve fund for that purpose, it could not be said that his conduct was involuntary. The appeal was dismissed. Woodhouse J pointed out that it could not be said that some "extraneous cause" produced the situation whereby he was unable to leave, and that having the practical means to leave the country was the continuing responsibility of the defendant throughout his visit. The conviction and subsequent imprisonment of the appellant made compliance with the law more difficult and may have generated some sympathy for the defendant, but did not justify a finding that he was not criminally responsible.[171]

(1)   *Impossibility given ignorance of duty*

Impossibility of the variety being considered here should be distinguished from a different type of case which arises where D is unaware of his legal duty to act. In *Harding v Price*,[172] it was held that a driver is not liable for failure to report an accident if he does not know the accident has happened. Similarly, in an early case in which the defendant was charged with failing to give notice to a police constable that some animals of his were infected with a contagious disease, it was held that since the defendant did not know the animals were infected he could not be convicted.[173] As Keating J said:

> "I cannot understand how ... it can be said that a man can neglect to give notice with all practicable speed without knowledge of the fact of which he is to give notice."

In these cases exculpation is predicated not on physical impossibility of compliance but upon the meaninglessness of demanding compliance with a duty when D does not know that facts exist which give rise to the duty.

13.6.2 Antecedent fault

As such, however, the determination of D's liability will, like physical impossibility, depend upon the absence of fault or mens rea in respect of those underlying facts. In *Tifaga v Dept of Labour*,[174] Richardson J noted that a requirement that the accused be free from fault in order to avoid criminal responsibility is implicit in the line of authorities on impossibility. In particular, the law looks first at the defendant's conduct leading up to, and his responsibility for the existence of, the impossibility; and, secondly, at the defendant's efforts and ability to overcome the situation he found himself in, ie whether he used "all practical endeavours" to overcome the difficulties of his situation but which, in the event, he found insurmountable.[175] A person cannot rely on impossibility of compliance which she has knowingly brought about by her own actions.[176] It is only where the impossibility has arisen

---

171 See *Oakley-Moore v Robinson* [1982] RTR 74 in which it was held that where "parking" was caused by running out of petrol, no excuse was available to the regulatory offence of parking in the approach limits to a pedestrian crossing.
172 *Harding v Price* [1948] 1 KB 695; [1948] 1 All ER 283. See 3.4.2(3).
173 *Nichols v Hall* (1873) LR 8 CP 322.
174 *Tifaga v Dept of Labour* [1980] 2 NZLR 235 (CA).
175 See *The Generous* (1818) 2 Dods 322; 165 ER 1501 (Sir William Scott), quoted in *Tifaga v Dept of Labour* [1980] 2 NZLR 235 (CA), 243, 244.

in circumstances which are outside the person's "reasonable or possible control" and in which she is not at fault, that liability is negated.[177]

Note that the limitation concerning "reasonable control" should be viewed as attaching only to the first limb of the test, namely, whether the defendant's conduct leading up to and perhaps generating the necessity was reasonable;[178] not to the second limb, concerning her ability to overcome the situation she found herself in (ie the situation of impossibility itself). For the reasons mentioned earlier, impossibility is an absolute concept. A thing cannot be impossible in degrees: it is either impossible or it is not. An objective evaluation is unhelpful on this second question.

13.6.3 Public policy

The doctrine of impossibility proceeds from the premise that the Legislature is not to be assumed to have intended to punish for failure to perform the impossible. Of course, there will always be a point in a chain of events after which it may be said that the proscribed result is "inevitable".[179] However, the defence of impossibility is unavailable if the prohibited event is *not* caused by circumstances beyond the accused's ability to control:[180]

> "A defendant who by due diligence could have avoided the position from which there is no escape does not have a claim in justice for exemption from criminal responsibility for his conduct."

Accordingly, mere inability due to financial stringency to comply with a statutory requirement will not amount to impossibility[181] where the shortage of funds has not been produced by circumstances beyond the defendant's control. For example, D should not park in a metered space unless he has money to feed the meter; and E, on a charge of failing to stop at a controlled intersection, should not drive a car which he knows has brakes that may fail at any time.

The essential principle may be described thus: impossibility is present where there is a complete inability on the part of the defendant to control events at the point at which, without fault on her part, she has acquired a duty to perform an act or avoid an omission prescribed by law. It does not matter that the situation of impossibility may, at some earlier point, not have existed, provided the impossibility pertaining has not been generated by a lack of due diligence on the part of the defendant. Thus, in *Finau v Dept of Labour*,[182] it was held that the defendant had a defence of impossibility to a charge of overstaying when, at the time she was due to leave New Zealand, medical advice concerning her pregnancy triggered a refusal by the only available airline carrier to fly her to her destination. It might have been different, however, if there had

---

176 A general principle: cf Robinson, "Causing the Conditions of One's Own Defense: A Study in the Limits of Theory in Criminal Law Doctrine" (1985) 71 Virginia Law Review 1.
177 *Burns v Bidder* [1967] 2 QB 227; [1966] 3 All ER 29, 240; 36 (James J).
178 This may explain the much criticised decision in *R v Larsonneur* (1933) 24 Cr App R 74; 149 LT 542 (CCA), despite its being described by one commentator as "the acme of strict injustice!": Hall, *General Principles of Criminal Law* (2nd ed), Indianapolis, Bobbs-Merrill, 1960, 329, n 14. Cf Lanham, "*Larsonneur* revisited" [1976] Crim LR 276; 3.2.2(1).
179 *Tifaga v Dept of Labour* [1980] 2 NZLR 235 (CA), 245.
180 *Tifaga v Dept of Labour* [1980] 2 NZLR 235 (CA), 245 (Richardson J).
181 See *MV Yorke Motors v Edwards* [1982] 1 All ER 1024; [1982] 1 WLR 444 (HL): a defendant cannot complain because a financial condition is difficult for him to fulfil; he can only complain when a financial condition is imposed which it is impossible for him to fulfil.
182 *Finau v Dept of Labour* [1984] 2 NZLR 396 (CA).

been evidence that the pregnancy or other matters, for example leaving a booking to such a late stage that it was impossible to obtain a seat, had simply been manoeuvres by the appellant to circumvent the legislation.[183] Such evidence would tend to negate the defendant's claim that the situation was one she was powerless to avoid.

13.6.4 Inconsistency with the statute?

The common law defence of impossibility is available in New Zealand by virtue of s 20 Crimes Act 1961, which preserves all common law defences to the extent that they are not "altered by or are inconsistent with" the express terms of legislation. In addition, however, the defence reflects deeper principles of legal policy embodied in the maxims impotentia excusat legem (the law does not punish a person for not doing what he lacked the power to do or for being in a situation he was powerless to avoid), lex non cogit ad impossibilia (the law does not compel the impossible), and necessitas non habet legem (necessity knows no law).[184] While the availability of any common law defence in New Zealand will prima facie be determined by whether it conflicts with the express terms of the Crimes Act or with any other legislation, these deeper principles imply that, as a general rule, no-one should ever be compelled by the threat of legal sanctions to do something that he is powerless to do, or be punished when he fails to do the thing he cannot avoid.

As we have seen, the proviso in s 20 has been invoked to prevent the common law defence of duress of circumstances from being available in New Zealand when based on direct or indirect wrongful threats of violence made by persons not present, on the basis that the statutory defence of compulsion in s 24 Crimes Act reflects the extent to which the Legislature was willing to countenance any such common law defence.[185] Similarly, in *Bayer v Police*,[186] the Court of Appeal, without referring to the express terms of s 20, refused to allow a defence of honest belief in the existence of circumstances justifying the need for protection of another to a charge of trespass on the grounds that the language of s 3(2) Trespass Act 1980 did not make any allowance for the defendant's belief.

By contrast, it was held in *Finau v Dept of Labour*[187] that allowing the defence of impossibility does not create an inconsistency with the terms of s 14(5) Immigration Act 1964. In the High Court, on an appeal by the Crown, it had been held that to allow an acquittal on the basis of impossibility would have entitled the appellant to a plea of autrefois acquit in the event of a fresh prosecution. It would, in effect, have conferred on her a new immigration status, contrary to the scheme of the Immigration Act under which only the Minister could confer a new status upon an immigrant. However, in allowing the appeal, the Court of Appeal rejected this argument and held that a plea of autrefois acquit would not have been a defence to a subsequent charge of remaining in New Zealand beyond the expiry of the permit, once it became possible for the appellant, after the birth of her child, to leave the country.

---

183 *Finau v Dept of Labour* [1984] 2 NZLR 396 (CA), 397.
184 *Halsbury's Laws of England* vol 44(1) (4th ed reissue), London, Butterworths, 1990, para 1448. For discussion of general principles regarding involuntariness and impossibility, see 3.4ff.
185 *Kapi v MOT* (1991) 8 CRNZ 49 (CA), 54. See also *R v Witika* [1993] 2 NZLR 424; (1992) 9 CRNZ 272 (CA), 433ff; 281ff.
186 *Bayer v Police* [1994] 2 NZLR 48 (CA), 50.
187 *Finau v Dept of Labour* [1984] 2 NZLR 396 (CA).

It is submitted that, wherever possible, the latter approach to interpretation is to be preferred. While a relevant statutory inconsistency may mandate refusing to allow a common law defence in an appropriate case, this step should not be lightly taken. The importance of preserving the fundamental principles of responsibility and culpability in the law require that a statutory inconsistency should only be found where the interests of the State clearly outweigh the interests of personal liberty, so that it is necessary to deprive a defendant of a defence which would otherwise be available.

Chapter 14

MISTAKE

14.1 Introduction 429
14.2 Mistake of fact 430
14.2.1 Mistake negativing mens rea 432
(1) *The burden of persuasion* 435
(2) *Mistake and recklessness* 436
(3) *Mistake and negligence* 437
14.2.2 Mistake about a claim of justification 438
14.2.3 Mistake about a claim of excuse 439
14.2.4 Mistake and regulatory offences 440
14.2.5 Mistake and statutory defences 440
14.3 Ignorance of law 443
14.3.1 Mistake of law and mens rea 445
14.4 Exceptions to the "ignorance of law" principle 448
14.4.1 Officially induced error 449
(1) *Officially induced error in New Zealand* 453
14.4.2 Non-publication 455

14.1 Introduction

It has been said that: "The most difficult problems in criminal theory are generated by dissonance between reality and belief, between the objective facts and the actor's subjective impression of the facts."[1] Faulty impressions give rise to mistakes which may cause an actor to believe that he/she is acting in response to a particular set of facts, when the facts are not, in reality, what the actor thinks they are. This problem is covered by the doctrine of mistake of fact.

Generally, the law regarding mistakes in the criminal law gives expression to two fundamental principles of criminal responsibility. The first is that moral obligation is determined not merely by the actual facts but also by the actor's perception of them.[2] D should be acquitted of theft if, mistakenly believing an umbrella in a stand to be his own, he walks off with it. He lacks the mens rea, of intent permanently to deprive the owner of possession, because he believes he is

---

1 Fletcher, *Rethinking Criminal Law*, Boston, Little, Brown & Co, 1978, 683; cf Christopher, "Criminal Law — Mistake of Fact in the Objective Theory of Justification: Do Two Rights make Two Wrongs make Two Rights…?" (1994) 85 J L & Criminology 295.
2 Hall, *General Principles of Criminal Law* (2nd ed), Indianapolis, Bobbs-Merrill, 1960, 363.

the owner. The second is that, subject to two principal exceptions,[3] ignorance of the law (that is, of the content of a penal statute) is no excuse for an offence committed against that express prohibition. The fact that D did not know, for example, that theft was a crime in the jurisdiction in which she is charged is no excuse at law. The doctrine concerning ignorance of law gives support to the principle of legality by declaring, in effect, that no person may substitute her own mistaken view of the penal law for what the law has been declared to be by competent officials:[4]

> "To permit an individual to plead successfully that he had a different opinion or interpretation of the law would contradict the ... postulates of a legal order."

These principles define the parameters of mistake as an exculpatory condition in the criminal law, although it is by no means clear that all mistakes of fact are relevant in assessing criminal liability. Some may be disregarded because even when taken into account, the offender still had the mens rea to commit the crime in question. Suppose, for example, that D, having determined to — commit theft in house X, enters house Y mistakenly believing it to be house X. He is still liable for conviction for burglary because, despite his mistaking the identity of the house, he committed the very offence that he intended. His mistake is, therefore, irrelevant for purposes of exculpation. This type of mistake is sometimes characterised as a mistake as to a *quality* of an element of the actus reus, as opposed to a mistake as to the actus reus *element* itself.[5] The mistake is irrelevant because it does not affect the attribution of mens rea, since A intended to commit the crime regardless of his mistake. Conversely, as we shall see, there may be other situations involving mistake of law where both mens rea and actus reus are present yet for other reasons it is determined that conviction is inappropriate. This applies particularly to situations involving "officially induced" error of law.

In the course of this chapter both of these principles will be examined in greater depth, in order to ascertain the scope of exculpatory mistakes and to locate the concept of mistake within a broader theory of criminal responsibility.

14.2 Mistake of fact

We have seen in our discussion of mens rea that a necessary element of most offences, other than those of "strict" or "absolute" liability, is a proposition concerning the particular state of mind that must be proved before the offence can be said to have been committed. The principal mens rea "types" relevant to mistakes concerning elements of the actus reus are intention, knowledge, and recklessness, although sometimes negligence may be sufficient mens rea for a crime. Where the required state of mind is absent at the time the offence was committed, the offender is entitled to be acquitted, even where the absence of mens rea was the result of a mistake of fact. For this reason it is sometimes said that mistake of fact is a good *defence* to a criminal charge in that it may be effective in negating the mens rea in respect of the offence charged. Imagine, for example, that D, whose eyesight is not the best, while walking in the park in the early evening sees a "stick" lying at the base of a tree. Without examining it, he breaks it in half intending to take it home for firewood. There is no prohibition against gathering firewood in the park. Unfortunately, it turns out the "stick" which D breaks is a

---

3   The two exceptions are "officially induced error" and "non-publication". See below, 14.4.
4   Hall, *General Principles of Criminal Law* (2nd ed), Indianapolis, Bobbs-Merrill, 1960, 383.
5   Allen, *Textbook on Criminal Law* (2nd ed), London, Blackstone Press, 1993, 72. See also R *v McCullum* (1973) 57 Cr App R 645; [1973] Crim LR 582 (CA); R *v Ellis* (1986) 84 Cr App R 235; [1987] Crim LR 44 (CA).

valuable carved walking stick owned by V, who had placed it on the ground while he climbed the tree to retrieve his hat blown off by the wind. D cannot be guilty of the crime of wilful damage[6] because he lacked the necessary knowledge that the "stick" was a valuable artifact and therefore had no intention to damage property. The mistake negated the mens rea for the offence.

However, to suggest that mistake is a "defence" to a crime is likely to be misleading, because it may suggest that the accused has an evidentiary burden to discharge in order to raise the defence of "mistake" as a live issue before his defence can be considered by the jury. That is not the case. Mistake, being a denial of the accused's belief in the facts which would otherwise make his actions a crime, is a mens rea element which must be disproved by the prosecution beyond a reasonable doubt. Of course, it may be incumbent on the accused to draw the Court's attention to the possibility of a mistake, since otherwise the Court may never know of it; but once this is done, the onus lies on the prosecution to refute that possibility. There is no legal burden of proof on the defence.[7]

The general rule concerning mistake of fact has long been recognised at common law, where mistake is seen being embodied in the maxim actus non facit reum nisi mens sit rea. In *R v Tolson*,[8] Cave J said:

> "At common law an honest and reasonable belief in the existence of circumstances, which, if true, would make the act for which a prisoner is indicted an innocent act, has always been held to be a good defence. This doctrine is embodied in the somewhat uncouth maxim, Actus non facit reum, nisi mens sit rea. Honest and reasonable mistake stands in fact on the same footing as absence of the reasoning faculty, as in infancy, or perversion of that faculty, as in lunacy."

Although the Judge uses the language of "defence", it is implicit in this passage that mistake goes to the very heart of mens rea, since an honest belief in the existence of circumstances which, if true, would make an act innocent, represents the very absence of a culpable mental state to which criminal liability may attach. It follows that if D, as a result of a factual error, honestly believes that the act he performs is no crime because he believes it to be a *wholly different kind of act* — for example, shooting at a "stump" in the forest for target practice, the "stump" being a crouching person, or putting "sugar" into another's tea, the "sugar" being caustic soda — he should not be liable for the crime charged where conviction depends on proof of an intention to do the unlawful act. In both of the examples, D's act would have been completely innocent if the facts had been as he believed them to be. He may, conceivably, be guilty of an offence of negligence if his mistake was also related to a failure to perform some legal duty which he had acquired. But that would be an issue quite independent of his liability for the offences requiring proof of intention or recklessness.

---

6   Section 11 Summary Offences Act 1981.
7   See 2.3, 14.2.1(1). The need for D to point to some evidence as a basis for the defence is sometimes referred to as the "tactical burden" (2.3, n 46). For reasons of credibility, in practice the need for D plausibly to raise the possibility of the defence requires more than a mere assertion — there must be some support for it in the circumstances. Where independent evidence exists to support the accused's testimony, this will generally improve the defence's chances: *R v Park* [1995] 2 SCR 836; (1995) 99 CCC (3d) 1 (SCC) (L'Heureux-Dubé J); *R v Esau* (1997) 116 CCC (3d) 289, 295 (Major J). In any event, there must generally be some evidence supporting an inference of such belief, so as to give the possibility of an honest mistaken belief an "air of reality": *R v Livermore* (1995) 43 CR (4th) 1; 102 CCC (3d) 212; [1995] 4 SCR 123 (SCC).
8   *R v Tolson* (1889) 23 QBD 168; [1886-90] All ER Rep 26, 181; 34.

In the now celebrated case of *DPP v Morgan*,[9] where the three accused had claimed, implausibly, that they honestly believed the victim was consenting to intercourse with them because her husband, who was present, had said that she "enjoyed a struggle", the House of Lords considered the relevance of mistake in the context of the common law crime of rape. Lord Hailsham said:[10]

> "Once one has accepted ... that the prohibited act in rape is non-consensual sexual intercourse, and that the guilty state of mind is an intention to commit it, it seems to me to follow as a matter of inexorable logic that there is no room either for a 'defence' of honest belief or mistake, or of a defence of honest and reasonable belief and mistake. Either the prosecution proves that the accused had the requisite intent, or it does not. In the former case it succeeds, and in the latter it fails. Since honest belief clearly negatives intent, the reasonableness or otherwise of that belief can only be evidence for or against the view that the belief and therefore the intent was actually held."

Morgan continues to be the principal authority on exculpatory mistakes in the English common law jurisdictions, although its authority in the context of rape has, as we shall see, been seriously eroded by statutory developments.[11]

An exculpatory mistake will be relevant in one of two situations:

(i) Where it relates to a *definitional element* of the offence; or

(ii) Where it relates to an *excusatory claim*.

In New Zealand it is not possible to say with any certainty what the principal difference between these categories is. Typically, a mistake as to a definitional element would need, as in *Morgan*, only to be honestly made to negate the mens rea for the particular offence. For the reasons expressed by Lord Hailsham in the passage cited, the reasonableness of the mistake is irrelevant. Conversely, a mistake as to an excusatory claim, being a mistake as to a *non-definitional element* of the offence involving an admission that the accused had performed the actus reus and mens rea of the offence but was seeking to avoid liability of other grounds (for example duress of circumstances), would normally be required to be reasonable.[12] However, in each case significant exceptions to the general rule have now so undermined the foundation for the distinction that it is no longer possible to articulate a clear principle for distinguishing between mistakes in each class. It is necessary to look at each case in the light of its own facts to determine which category it falls within, then decide whether a subjective or objective approach to the particular mistake is required.

14.2.1 Mistake negativing mens rea

Where the mistake goes to a definitional element of the offence, *Morgan* is authority for the general principal that if the law requires intention or recklessness with respect to some element

---

9 *DPP v Morgan* [1976] AC 182; [1975] 2 All ER 347 (HL).
10 *DPP v Morgan* [1976] AC 182; [1975] 2 All ER 347 (HL), 214; 361.
11 Below, 14.2.1(3) and ch 18. Compare too the Canadian Criminal Code, s 273.2, which requires the accused to take "reasonable steps, in the circumstances known to the accused ... at the time, to ascertain that the complainant was consenting"; *R v Cornejo* (2003) 181 CCC (3d) 206.
12 See, for example, *R v Graham* [1982] 1 All ER 801; [1982] 1 WLR 294 (CA), where it was held that the accused may only rely on a common law defence of duress where his belief, that he would be killed or seriously injured unless he committed the offence, was reasonable.

in the actus reus, a mistake, whether reasonable or not, which precludes both states of mind will deny criminal liability.[13] In *Morgan* the three accused sought, unsuccessfully, to deny the mens rea of rape by claiming that because of a mistake honestly made by them, they believed the victim was consenting to intercourse when she was not. However, had their claim been believed, their convictions would have been quashed. The mens rea for rape at common law was intention to have sexual intercourse with a woman without consent, or being indifferent whether the woman was consenting, absence of consent being an element in the actus reus of the offence; therefore their mistake, if believed, would have meant that they lacked mens rea. Their claim was not that V had consented; but, that by erroneously believing she had consented, they lacked mens rea.

In New Zealand, an honest belief in consent, simpliciter, will no longer be a good defence to a charge of rape by sexual violation, because the Legislature has moved to close the perceived gap left by *Morgan* by requiring that the accused have "reasonable grounds" for believing that the woman is consenting to "sexual connection".[14] This move is discussed further in 14.2.1(3): its effect is to change the mens rea requirement in sexual violation, so that the crime in New Zealand is now one of negligence, rather than of recklessness or intent. As such, apart from manslaughter, it is virtually the only serious crime in New Zealand where a mistake negativing mens rea must be "reasonable" as opposed to being simply "honestly" held.[15] In every other serious crime, where the offence requires proof of recklessness or intent, a mistake, to exonerate, need only be honest (although it has been said that the reasonableness or otherwise of a belief may be an important index as to whether the belief was genuinely held[16]).

This principle has been firmly established in a line of decisions of the High Court and Court of Appeal, although the line itself is a somewhat circuitous one. In *R v Wood*,[17] the appellant had been charged with cultivating cannabis. Her defence was that she believed that the seeds from which the plants had been grown were "supertom" tomato seeds. The case was decided on an evidentiary point which need not concern us. However, in a postscript to the decision the Court was required to reconsider its earlier decision in *R v Strawbridge*,[18] concerning the nature of the belief required where an exculpatory mistake arises. *Strawbridge* involved similar facts to *Wood*. The accused had been charged with cultivating prohibited plants, namely cannabis. She admitted cultivating a number of plants which it was accepted were cannabis but said that she honestly believed they were not cannabis plants. The Court concluded for various reasons, including the severity of the penalty, that the offence created under the Narcotics Act 1965 was not one of absolute liability and adopted a "half-way house" approach. It said that in order to present a prima facie case it is not necessary for the Crown to establish knowledge on the part of the accused and in the absence of evidence to the contrary knowledge on her part will be presumed, "but if there is some evidence that the accused believed *on reasonable grounds* that her act was innocent, then she is entitled to be acquitted unless the jury

---

13   Smith and Hogan, *Criminal Law* (7th ed), London, Butterworths, 1992, 216.
14   Section 128 Crimes Act 1961.
15   For a discussion of the significance of "honest" in this context, see *Adams*, CA20.33 (looseleaf). It is doubtful whether "honest" adds anything to the subjective test of belief, but for a contrary opinion see *Millar v MOT* [1986] 1 NZLR 660; (1986) 2 CRNZ 216 (CA), 678; 236 (Casey J).
16   *R v Wood* [1982] 2 NZLR 233 (CA), 237.
17   *R v Wood* [1982] 2 NZLR 233 (CA), 237.
18   *R v Strawbridge* [1970] NZLR 909 (CA), 916.

is satisfied beyond reasonable doubt that this was not so".[19] In *Strawbridge* the Court adopted the reasoning of Lord Diplock in *Sweet v Parsley*[20] that "it is open to an accused person to point to evidence which tends to show that he or she did not know that the plant which was being cultivated was a prohibited plant".[21]

This reasoning was implicitly adopted in *Wood*. However, on the question of the *nature* of the belief required in such a case (ie whether reasonable or not), the Court of Appeal concluded that in view of the decision in *Morgan* it was clear that there was no obligation on the part of a defendant to prove that she had reasonable grounds for the "honest" belief that the plants were other than cannabis plants. The conviction was quashed and a retrial was ordered.

Since *Wood*, the matter has been regarded as settled in New Zealand law. Wherever an offence requires proof of a subjective mens rea element, the absence of that mens rea element due to an honest mistake will lead to an acquittal. This rule applies, for example, where the defendant honestly, albeit mistakenly, believes that the constable she is charged with resisting is not "acting in the execution of his duty".[22] Resisting a constable in the execution of his duty is a mens rea offence. Therefore, if the prosecution cannot negative the reasonable possibility that the accused (genuinely) believed that the constable was not acting in the execution of his duty, the accused is entitled to have the information dismissed.[23]

However, in *Clarke*, William Young J intimated that although the current law is that offences of resisting are mens rea offences, this issue may warrant reconsideration:[24]

> "A person who is told by a police officer that he or she is under arrest should comply with the requirements of the police officer and leave any arguments about the reasonableness or otherwise of the police officer's actions for later debate. Treating a thoroughly unreasonable although genuine belief that a constable is not acting in the execution of his duty as a defence to a resisting charge has a tendency to promote physical violence."

Yet it is precisely in situations of this kind, where emotions may be running high and the opportunities for "detached reflection" substantially reduced, that offenders are most likely to act impulsively and make mistakes about a developing fact situation. In such cases, it may be a counsel of perfection to expect them to disengage from the conflict and resolve to pursue their legal remedies after the event. It is arguably better that the law provides protection, in the form of an excusatory claim that the defendant honestly thought that the officer was acting unreasonably.

Of course, before any mistake of fact will excuse, it must be a *relevant* mistake: it must relate to relevant facts at the material time. Accordingly, a mistake about facts that the accused anticipated would come into existence (for example that a licence would in future be granted

---

19 *R v Strawbridge* [1970] NZLR 909 (CA), 916. The present status of this case is discussed at 5.2.2(3).
20 *Sweet v Parsley* [1970] AC 132; [1969] 1 All ER 347 (HL).
21 *R v Strawbridge* [1970] NZLR 909 (CA), 916.
22 Section 23(a) Summary Offences Act 1981.
23 *Clarke v Police* 18/11/03, William Young J, HC Wellington CRI-2003-485-28, para 56. See also *Mackley v Police* (1994) 11 CRNZ 497 and *ITW v Police* 11/09/03, William Young J, HC Christchurch CRI-2003-409-35.
24 *Clarke v Police* 18/11/03, William Young J, HC Wellington CRI-2003-485-28, para 57.

authorising the export of certain goods) is no defence to a charge based on *current* facts (for example, a charge of exporting goods without a current licence).[25]

(1) *The burden of persuasion*

These cases alert us to an important qualifying principle concerning exculpatory mistakes. Where the mistaken belief attaches to an actus reus element of a crime in which mens rea is an essential ingredient of the offence, the accused's belief in relevant facts need only be subjectively honest (unless the crime is one of negligence; for example, sexual violation). In such cases where intention or its counterpart, knowledge, is an express element in the definition of the offence, the Crown must affirmatively prove the existence of such intention or knowledge, and negate any exculpatory belief held by the accused, beyond a reasonable doubt. Strictly speaking, in a case where the prosecution must prove mens rea, it is unnecessary for the accused to discharge even an evidentiary burden in respect of such knowledge or intention, because it is the obligation of the prosecution to prove all aspects of mens rea, including the negation of any affirmative exculpatory belief.[26]

Nevertheless, it is difficult to see how, in such a case, the Crown could acquire awareness of such an exculpatory belief in order to negate it, unless the accused herself had adduced some evidence of it in the first instance. In practice, it is only when there is some evidence of an exculpatory belief that the Crown will be called on to negate it.[27] In R v Thomas,[28] which involved a prosecution for obstruction of a police officer in the execution of duty (a crime requiring proof of mens rea), the Court of Appeal held that where "honest belief" is an available defence, it is for the prosecution to prove that the accused had no such belief *once an evidentiary basis for it has been established*. This is clearly the case where the offence has been characterised as a "true" crime but the mens rea requirement is not stated expressly in the statute. In such a case, in the absence of some evidence to the contrary it may be assumed that mens rea, in the form of intention or guilty knowledge, existed; but if there is any evidence to the contrary (for example, the accused adduces evidence of an honest belief in facts which, if true, would make his act innocent) the onus falls on the prosecution to prove such knowledge affirmatively in the normal way.[29]

This is demonstrated in R v *Metuariki*.[30] There the appellant was appealing against his conviction for supplying a class A controlled drug to an undercover constable. He had gathered, and sold to the constable, a bag of mushrooms which he knew as "magic mushrooms" and had been told that he could get high on them. However, he denied any knowledge that the mushrooms contained a controlled drug (psilocybine) under the Misuse of Drugs Act 1975. His defence was that he honestly believed on reasonable grounds that he could quite innocently have possession of the mushrooms with their particular properties. Applying *Strawbridge* as modified

---

25 *Arnold v Wood* (1996) 89 A Crim R 264.
26 See 2.3.
27 R v *Nazif* [1987] 2 NZLR 122 (CA), 128.
28 R v *Thomas* [1991] 3 NZLR 141; (1991) 7 CRNZ 123 (CA), 143; 126; cf R v *Christiansen* 24/10/01, CA196/01. See also *Waaka v Police* [1987] 1 NZLR 754; (1987) 2 CRNZ 370 (CA), 759; 375. Discussing the mental elements of the offence of assault on a police officer under s 10 Summary Offences Act 1981 the Court of Appeal said: "Knowledge or its equivalent may be assumed ... unless there is a foundation in the evidence for a contrary view."
29 See *Millar v MOT* [1986] 1 NZLR 660; (1986) 2 CRNZ 216 (CA), 665; 221. Also 2.3.1(4), 5.2.2(2).
30 R v *Metuariki* [1986] 1 NZLR 488; (1986) 2 CRNZ 116 (CA).

by *Wood*, the Court of Appeal held that to establish a prima facie case against the accused, the Crown had to prove that the accused supplied the mushrooms and that they were a controlled drug. His knowledge that he was dealing with such a drug would then be presumed unless he could point to some evidence that he *honestly* believed his action to be innocent. The Court accepted that the appellant had made a "good faith" mistake as to an element in the definition of the offence. His mistake was not one of law; rather, he was asserting an honest, but mistaken, belief as to the character of the plant material and it was for that reason a mistake of fact.

In such cases, involving true crimes, although reasonableness is not a required element of the accused's belief, it will be relevant to the credibility of the claim.[31] So if D breaks into the home of V, a complete stranger, in the early hours of the morning while V is still asleep, it would be straining the credulity of the jury for him to assert, on a charge of indecent assault, that he honestly believed that V was consenting to the conduct, despite the fact that honest belief in consent is a defence to such a charge.[32] The patent unreasonableness of the claimed belief will be the strongest evidence that it was not in fact held by the accused at the time of the act of assault.

(2) *Mistake and recklessness*

Mistake may also be relevant to whether an accused has acted recklessly, in cases where recklessness is sufficient mens rea for the offence charged. The issue arose in an interesting way in *R v Hay*.[33] In that case the accused, together with some associates, had removed a stolen car to a workshop owned by the employer of one of the associates with a view to stripping the car. While the accused was working with a grinder, sparks from the machine had ignited petrol on the floor of the workshop, which the offenders had spilt while siphoning the car's petrol tank. H was charged with arson in relation to the damage to the building, which required proof that he caused the event "by an act which he *knew* would probably cause it, being reckless whether that event happens or not".[34] His defence was that although he turned his mind to the possibility, he did not go ahead with an act which he knew would probably cause damage; rather, he went ahead with an act that he *thought would not* cause damage.[35] Recognising that the sparks might ignite the petrol, he had (he said) turned the machine in a different direction to avoid that possibility. The Court accepted this argument, on the basis that a person who adverts to the question of risk and decides (mistakenly) that there is none should not be held reckless: "The fact that a person is mistaken in that belief does not mean that he is reckless".[36]

This implies that where a person consciously addresses a particular risk but honestly (if wrongly) concludes that it does not exist or will not eventuate, she cannot be guilty of reckless conduct.[37] Recklessness, as we saw in 4.3, requires that a person foresees a risk (which it is unreasonable to run), and chooses to run it: a definition that is incompatible with a positively held belief that there is no risk. However, in any case where the risk is adverted to but the

---

31 *R v Metuariki* [1986] 1 NZLR 488; (1986) 2 CRNZ 116 (CA), 490; 118. See also *R v Nazif* [1987] 2 NZLR 122 (CA), 128 (Somers J): "The reasonableness or otherwise of such the grounds of belief will be material to the question of whether the accused in fact held it."
32 *R v Nazif* [1987] 2 NZLR 122 (CA), 128.
33 *R v Hay* (1987) 3 CRNZ 419.
34 Section 293(1) Crimes Act 1961 (repealed).
35 *R v Hay* (1987) 3 CRNZ 419, 421.
36 *R v Hay* (1987) 3 CRNZ 419.
37 See *R v Stephenson* [1979] QB 695; [1979] 2 All ER 1198 (CA), 703; 1203.

defendant concludes it is negligible only, as opposed to being non-existent, there is always a danger that she may be wrong in her judgment and the risk, considered objectively, is an unreasonable one to run. So in *Jefferson v Ministry of Agriculture and Fisheries*,[38] where the accused was charged with applying a herbicide in a reckless manner so that damage resulted to vegetation on a neighbouring property, it was held that the accused had been reckless. Upholding the conviction Barker J decided that the District Court Judge had been correct to hold that the risk of damage to other properties was more than negligible and that the appellant had erred in deciding to proceed after considering the risks. The point here is that while a mistake about the *amount* of risk will be taken into account by the Court, the Court imposes its own judgment about the *reasonableness* of running the risk that the accused perceives. A mistaken *evaluation*, whether the perceived risk is a reasonable one, affords the accused no defence.

(3) *Mistake and negligence*

Most serious offences, we have said, require proof of a subjective mens rea condition, such as recklessness. The seminal case of *Morgan*, discussed above in 14.2, was a classic example. Much of the disapproval of that decision was misguided. If, in law, the mens rea requirement really was recklessness (and it was), a genuine[39] mistake of fact mandates an acquittal for lack of mens rea, whether or not the mistake was reasonable. To this extent, their Lordships were right. The proper target of the criticism was the mens rea requirement in the offence: it should have been negligence. *That* criticism should have been directed at the legislature. New Zealand law is to be commended for reforming the law to specify that the mens rea of sexual violation is now negligence.[40]

Once the required mens rea is negligence, a mistake of fact no longer implies lack of mens rea. The mistake must also be reasonable; it must be the sort of mistake that a reasonable person in the same circumstances may also make. The consequent rejection of mistake of fact as a denial of mens rea, except where the D believes on reasonable grounds that the V was consenting to the activity in question, combines subjective and objective fault elements "in a novel and creative manner."[41] Again, however, this is not a matter of defences, but remains a matter of proving mens rea: thus the onus lies on the prosecution to prove, beyond reasonable doubt, that the defendant's mistake was unreasonable.

Negligence as a mens rea state is analysed in more detail in 4.6 above.[42] It is important to observe, however, that the solution to *Morgan* is not an appropriate response to all serious offences. Generally speaking, individuals cannot always be aware of all the surrounding facts of the world. As such, the law is rightly reluctant to impose a duty on citizens to always verify

---

38 *Jefferson v Ministry of Agriculture and Fisheries* 12/8/86, Barker J, HC Rotorua M286/85.
39 In *Morgan* it was not, which was why the convictions ultimately were upheld.
40 Below, ch 18.
41 Roach, *Criminal Law* (2nd ed), Toronto, Irwin Law, 2000, 157-158; cited in *R v Cornejo* (2003) 181 CCC (3d) 206, 214.
42 It has been suggested that, in order to determine whether the accused took reasonable steps, or (in terms of the New Zealand provision) possessed a reasonable belief that the complainant was consenting, much will depend on the Court's view about what is a reasonable belief. Some judges are likely to find that positive steps are required in most, if not all situations, regardless of the accused's subjective perception of the circumstances. Other judges may only require such steps if the complainant has indicated resistance or lack of consent in some way that is subjectively known to the accused. See Roach, *Criminal Law* (2nd ed), Toronto, Irwin Law, 2000, 157-158.

whether the current state of the world is such that it may render their conduct criminal. They need first some *cue*, some signal that puts them on notice that criminal liability is a real prospect, so that the law is then *entitled* to expect them to enquire further.

In the absence of some reason for further enquiry, to impose criminal liability on inadvertent wrongdoers generally would place an almost impossible burden on citizens. In particular, in many of the mundane activities which we daily undertake, we would be effectively robbed of the freedom to act freely,[43] since we would constantly be expected to stop what we are doing and enquire into the possible and no doubt esoteric consequences. Suppose that D places a cigarette into a waste-paper basket, which she mistakenly thinks is extinguished, and causes a fire of the basket and its contents. In such circumstances, we would not normally want to punish the insufficiently aware D, unless there was in existence a specific legal duty to avoid hypothetical dangers of the sort which the conduct in fact created. The want of sufficient culpability in situations like this is reflected in the fact that such a mistake negates the intentional endangerment of property, necessarily implicit in a charge of wilful damage or destruction of property. If the facts had been as D believed them to be, namely that the cigarette was extinguished, the act would have been innocent, indeed laudatory. She is an environmentally "friendly" person.

In serious offences, then, a person who is subjectively unaware of the actus reus should not bear criminal liability even if it would have been possible, by checking, to determine the existence of facts which would render the conduct criminal. However, this principle is not universal. There are particular contexts where we may conclude that D is more or less on notice of the need to check her environment. For example, if D, mistakenly believing the cigarette extinguished, was walking through a petrol refinery compound, we might think she had a duty to take reasonable care to ensure the cigarette was truly extinguished before tossing it into what appears to be a rubbish bin. Clearly, the nature of the physical environment creates a duty to use reasonable care to avoid the risk of a major fire.

A similar argument applies in respect of sexual violation. Sexual offences are special, in that the absence of consent makes for a grave wrong whereas the presence of consent ensures respect for autonomy and the absence of any form of harm. So crucial is the presence or absence of consent that D must, as Gardner and Shute put it, be "astute" to the state of V's consent.[44] Given the issues at stake, this is not asking for too much.[45] The very activity puts D on notice about the need to be sure of V's consent. And D only has to ask. Not to ask is wrong, and if D has sexual connection with someone who was not asked, who did not consent, and whose non-consent was reasonably apparent, D should be found guilty of a crime.

14.2.2 Mistake about a claim of justification

It is commonly said that where an accused asserts an honestly held belief as to a matter of justification, the belief need not be reasonable. This is the position in the United Kingdom[46] and in New Zealand, at least as regards self-defence.[47] However, this principle does not apply

---

43 Cf Gur-Arye, "Reliance on a Lawyer's Mistaken Advice - Should it be an Excuse from Criminal Liability?" (2002) Am J Crim L 455, 463.
44 Gardner and Shute, "The Wrongness of Rape", Horder (ed), *Oxford Essays in Jurisprudence* (4th Series), Oxford, Oxford University Press, 2000, 193.
45 Pickard, "Culpable Mistakes and Rape: Relating Mens Rea to the Crime" (1980) 30 U Toronto LJ 75.
46 See *Albert v Lavin* [1982] AC 546; [1981] 3 All ER 878 (HL).

to defence of a dwellinghouse (also a matter of justification), because the statute requires that D's belief that there is no lawful justification for the breaking and entering be based on "reasonable and probable" grounds.[48] On the other hand, where the defence is one of compulsion under s 24 Crimes Act 1961 — a matter of excuse rather than justification — the "belie[f] that the threat will be carried out" need not be reasonable, although its reasonableness or otherwise will be relevant to whether it was honestly held.

The reason why only a subjectively "honest" belief is required in respect of self-defence is because, under the statutory framework, the justification of self-defence goes to the core of the charge. A person acting in self-defence does not intend to act *unlawfully*, whether or not his belief in the circumstances giving rise to the need to use defensive force is reasonable. Indeed, if the facts are as D believes them to be, provided he does not use excessive force, then judged objectively, he is deemed to be upholding a fundamental value of the criminal law by preventing what he believes to be an unlawful assault. That belief negates the intent to act unlawfully and as such need only be honest.[49]

14.2.3 Mistake about a claim of excuse

Unless a statute commands otherwise, where a defence is characterised as a matter of excuse rather than justification, and the offence is intentionally committed but is sought to be excused because there was no choice (as in cases of "duress of circumstances" or necessity), the issue of mistake or honest belief is treated differently to cases where the justification goes to an element of the mens rea.[50] In *Kapi v MOT* the Court of Appeal held that the common law defence of necessity, to the extent it is available in New Zealand, requires at least a belief formed on reasonable grounds of imminent peril of death or serious injury. The Court was unwilling to contemplate judicially amending the mental element in necessity to bring it into line with the self-defence test, because that would effect a change in the law which the Court considered was the Legislature's responsibility.

This type of defence is sometimes termed "confession and avoidance", because prima facie commission of an offence is conceded but criminal responsibility is avoided because of the exigent circumstances or threats.[51] Where an accused makes a mistake in relation to an element of an *excusatory* defence, it has been held at common law that the mistake must be reasonable.[52] The reasons why the belief must be reasonable in such circumstances are seldom clearly articulated. Nonetheless, the law requires that if a person is to be excused for a crime which, but for the element of overwhelming fear and compulsion, they would otherwise have been judged to be fully responsible for, the belief which motivated such a clear breach of the law must be objectively reasonable.

One reason why the belief in necessity must be reasonable appears to be that, unlike other cases where an honest mistake defence might excuse by negating the mens rea of the offence in question, the claimed belief in circumstances justifying necessity does not actually negate

---

47   *R v Thomas* [1991] 3 NZLR 141; (1991) 7 CRNZ 123 (CA), 144; 127 (Casey J): "Subjective honest belief ... is sufficient."
48   Section 55 Crimes Act 1961.
49   Cf *Beckford v R* [1988] AC 130; [1987] 3 All ER 425 (PC).
50   *Kapi v MOT* (1991) 8 CRNZ 49 (CA), 56 (Gault J).
51   The concept is summed up in the Latin aphorism coactus volui. Literally, "at his will but coerced".
52   See *R v Graham* [1982] 1 All ER 801; [1982] 1 WLR 294 (CA); *R v Howe* [1987] AC 417; [1987] 1 All ER 771 (HL).

mens rea for the offence in the sense of creating a belief in a state of affairs which if true would make the act innocent. The effect of the belief is simply to establish the existence of an additional exculpatory condition on account of which the act done with intent may be judged to be non-culpable. It would seem perfectly acceptable to say that the additional exculpatory belief, if it is to have this effect, should be reasonable.

14.2.4 Mistake and regulatory offences

In New Zealand, reasonable mistake of fact is a good defence to a public welfare regulatory offence.[53] The Court of Appeal in *Millar v MOT*[54] has held that a defence of honest and reasonable mistake is available in respect of some modern statutory offences and is incorporated within the general defence of total absence of fault which is available in New Zealand for all public welfare regulatory offences.[55] However, the recognition by the Court of a separate category of absolute liability would seem to imply a narrow band of liability in respect of which even a reasonable mistake of fact will not support a defence. Fortunately, with recognition of the category of strict liability, absolute liability offences are likely to be rare.[56]

14.2.5 Mistake and statutory defences

Occasionally a case may arise where the statute creating an offence provides that specified facts provide a defence, but makes no express provision for mistaken belief in the existence of such facts. This may occur in respect of both statutory offences of strict liability and statutory offences requiring proof of mens rea. An example of the former would be a prosecution under s 15 Resource Management Act 1991 for discharging a contaminant into the environment. A charge under s 15 alleges an offence of "strict" liability, in respect of which it is not necessary for the prosecution to prove that the defendant intended to commit the offence.[57] Section 341 of the Act sets out a number of statutory defences, including necessity, natural disaster, mechanical failure, and the defence that the defendant's "conduct" was reasonable in the circumstances.[58] However, there is no provision that "reasonable belief" or "reasonable mistake" is a defence to such a charge. It may be argued that in this case a mistake of fact defence is excluded both as a matter of necessary implication from the structure of the statutory defences and as a matter of construction concerning the importance attached to protection of the country's natural and physical resources in the Resource Management Act. Arguably, it would contradict the purposes of the Act if a defendant was able to defend herself on the basis that she honestly and reasonably believed that her actions would not allow contaminants to escape into water, when that Act has expressly provided that a person may discharge a contaminant without intending to do so,[59] and still be guilty of an offence under the Act. Since belief is a cognate of intention it would seem highly likely that the Legislature also intended to exclude any defence based on a mistaken belief.

---

53 *Civil Aviation Dept v MacKenzie* [1983] NZLR 78, 81, also reported as *MacKenzie v Civil Aviation Dept* (1983) 1 CRNZ 38 (CA), 41 (Richardson J).
54 *Millar v MOT* [1986] 1 NZLR 660; (1986) 2 CRNZ 216 (CA).
55 *Millar v MOT* [1986] 1 NZLR 660; (1986) 2 CRNZ 216 (CA), 665; 222.
56 *Civil Aviation Dept v MacKenzie* [1983] NZLR 78, also reported as *MacKenzie v Civil Aviation Dept* (1983) 1 CRNZ 38 (CA), 85, 45. See 5.2.3(2)(d).
57 Section 341 Resource Management Act 1991.
58 Section 341(2) Resource Management Act 1991.
59 See *McKnight v NZ Biogas Industries Ltd* [1994] 2 NZLR 664 (CA).

14.2.5 MISTAKE AND STATUTORY DEFENCES

An example of the second variety, involving an offence of mens rea, is provided by *Bayer v Police*,[60] a case concerning a prosecution for trespass under s 3 Trespass Act 1980. The accused, an opponent of abortion, had entered the premises of an organisation licensed to perform abortions and, with some fellow protesters, had effectively blocked access and refused to move when warned to leave by the occupier. Continuing to remain on any place after having been so warned is an offence under s 3(1) of the Act. However, by subs (2) it is a defence if the accused proves that it was "necessary for him to remain" for the protection of himself or another or for some other emergency. The accused's counsel argued that since the justification to use force in the defence of another (the accused believed that her actions were aimed at the protection of unborn children) provided by s 48 introduced a subjective element of "honest belief", the accused should, under s 3(2) Trespass Act, also be able to rely on an honest if mistaken belief in the existence of circumstances which, if true, would provide a defence to a charge laid under s 3(1). The Court of Appeal rejected this argument and held that the language of the subsection, creating a limited defence in defined circumstances, does not make any allowance for the defendant's belief. The Court has since reiterated this approach in *O'Neill v Police*.[61]

This means that not only will an honest but mistaken belief in the necessity to remain on property be irrelevant on a charge of trespass, but so will a belief formed on reasonable grounds.[62] Although it would seem that the courts have adopted this narrow approach in order to prevent the kind of interference with lawful processes associated with abortions,[63] the approach taken in *Bayer* and *O'Neill* necessarily applies to all cases of trespass under s 3. Consider the following example. D, having trespassed onto V's land in order to bypass a flooded stream, then concludes on reasonable grounds that it is necessary to remain on V's land in order to avoid being trapped by the rising waters of the stream. V warns him to leave but he remains and is eventually arrested and charged with trespass. According to the authority of *Bayer* and *O'Neill*, D's belief in the necessity to remain is wholly irrelevant. What determines liability is simply the question whether it was "necessary" to remain, seemingly a purely objective test. If, however, D had unlawfully entered V's house in order to seek protection from what he honestly and reasonably believed to be the imminent arrival of an overwhelming flood, his honest belief on reasonable grounds of imminent peril of death or serious injury would have been a good defence to the charge of being found on property without reasonable excuse.[64]

Such a distinction is clearly unsatisfactory. It has been correctly observed that if there is a principle of the common law by which belief in facts which would constitute a defence is itself a defence, this should be available *generally* under s 20 Crimes Act 1961, unless such a principle is inconsistent with the relevant legislation.[65] On the facts given in the example above it is difficult to imagine how allowing a defence of honest and reasonable belief in the necessity to remain on land could possibly create an inconsistency with the Trespass Act 1980.

---

60   *Bayer v Police* [1994] 2 NZLR 48 (CA).
61   *O'Neill v Police* 22/11/93, CA392/93, on appeal from *Police v O'Neill* [1993] 3 NZLR 712.
62   See Orchard, "Mistake and statutory defences" [1994] NZLJ 92.
63   Orchard, "Mistake and statutory defences" [1994] NZLJ 92, 94.
64   See s 29 Summary Offences Act 1981; *Kapi v MOT* (1991) 8 CRNZ 49 (CA).
65   Orchard, "Mistake and statutory defences" [1994] NZLJ 92, 93.

However, there is a more fundamental objection to the Court of Appeal's approach in these cases. It is arguable that necessity is not a concept that can be completely objective. Whether something is "necessary" is, by its nature, a matter of perception. As a criminal law concept, the doctrine of necessity is a tacit admission of a person's impotence against some great evil, *or what he perceives to be a great evil*, assailing him, and a measure of that person's moral obligation *in extremis*.[66] It is surely unavoidable that, in determining whether something is "necessary", an accused must address his mind to the conditions which dictate that judgment and decide, as a matter of reflection and intuition, that a particular response is called for. The relevant ethical principle is that moral excuse is determined not by the actual facts but *by the actor's reasons for acting*.[67] In turn, the reasons for which the accused acts can only be supplied by his beliefs. Accordingly, to require a person to make a determination that a course of conduct is necessary without the person's subjective belief intruding into that process is both logically unsound and ethically questionable. It effectively imposes absolute liability in respect of a mistake, contrary to general principles of criminal responsibility; since, if the actual facts determine our duties, we will be under a moral obligation without knowing it and perhaps even without being able to discover it.[68]

In the case law, the most frequent situation that arises involving the defence of mistake of fact concerns apparently necessary self-defence.[69] In these cases, as has been noted, if D's mistake stimulates his attack, undertaken in apparently necessary self-defence, he may claim a defence. This should alert us to the possibility that in any case where necessity is claimed, there is a similar danger that the individual's perception of the relevant "necessity" may also be driven by a fundamental mistake of fact. If the courts insist that the determination of necessity under s 3 Trespass Act is to be based on a purely objective standard, the effect will be to deny the "scope for the beneficial operation intended for the subsection"[70] contrary to the apparent intention of the Legislature. It is surprising that even an unreasonable mistake should excuse the serious harms inflicted by self-defensive measures, while the trespasser, who causes a much less serious harm, is put to the strict burden of proving her defence to a rigid objective standard.

It is not clear from the trespass cases whether the limitation on a "subjective mistake" defence, implied where the underlying defence is specified by statute, is created, operates as a general rule. However, for the reasons given here, such a limitation should not be supported on general principles.[71] Consistency with other general statutory defences, in particular self-defence, defence of property,[72] and compulsion would seem to demand that a defence of mistaken belief in facts constituting a defence ought to be a defence, even if it is necessary to incorporate within it an objective requirement of reasonableness.

---

66 Hall, *General Principles of Criminal Law* (2nd ed), Indianapolis, Bobbs-Merrill, 1960, 416.
67 Hall, *General Principles of Criminal Law* (2nd ed), Indianapolis, Bobbs-Merrill, 1960, 363.
68 Hall, *General Principles of Criminal Law* (2nd ed), Indianapolis, Bobbs-Merrill, 1960, 363.
69 Hall, *General Principles of Criminal Law* (2nd ed), Indianapolis, Bobbs-Merrill, 1960, 364.
70 *Bayer v Police* [1994] 2 NZLR 48 (CA), 50.
71 Orchard, "Mistake and statutory defences" [1994] NZLJ 92, 94. Orchard argues that there is authority from which it is possible to extract support for the existence of a common law principle that an honest but mistaken belief in facts which would constitute a statutory defence may itself be a defence if it is based on reasonable grounds.
72 See *R v Keating* (1992) 76 CCC (3d) 570 and *R v Born with a Tooth* (1992) 76 CCC (3d) 169 (CA), where it was held that necessary defence of property included cases where the accused reasonably believed, or honestly believed, in the existence of the requirements for a defence.

14.3 Ignorance of law

It is a general principle of law that ignorance of the law does not excuse, and that an honest and reasonable, but mistaken, belief that conduct is not criminal is no defence.[73] While there are exceptions to this general principle, the availability of defences owing to mistake of law is much more limited than it is following a mistake of fact. The distinction between the two is, therefore, vitally important. It is summarised by Gur-Arye in the following terms:[74]

> "A person who mistakenly believes that the law does not forbid killing trespassers (mistake of law) will feel free to kill trespassers. Until informed otherwise, such a person will enjoy greater freedom to fend off trespassers than a person who knows that the law does not permit killing trespassers. By contrast, a person who kills a trespasser in the mistaken belief that the trespasser is an animal (mistake of fact) does not assume a greater measure of freedom. She continues to restrict herself and refrain from knowingly killing trespassers. In order to ensure that individuals assume similar scopes to their freedom, they should be required to investigate the limits imposed by the criminal law."

In New Zealand, the principle that legal ignorance is no excuse is reflected in s 25 Crimes Act 1961, which states:

> **"25 Ignorance of law**
>
> "The fact that an offender is ignorant of the law is not an excuse for any offence committed by him."

The principle derives from the natural law precept that every person who has attained the age of reason is supposed to know that he should not do to another what he would not have done to himself.[75] In the context of modern criminal law, the principle can be traced back to the Latin maxim ignorantia juris neminem excusat and relies on an obvious fiction, namely, that everyone is presumed to know the law. Despite the fiction, however, the rule reflects a commonsense principle that incorrectly thinking that something is legal should be no defence to a person who violates a rule of law.[76] One reason for this is the requirement for certainty in adjudication. The requirements of a legal order necessitate that no one individual should be permitted to substitute his or her view of the criminal law for what the law has been declared to be. To allow such a concession arguably contradicts the principle of legality.[77] For this reason, reliance on a lawyer's mistaken advice is seldom an excuse. In part, this is because of the possibility of abuse; in particular, the concern that granting the excuse might lead people toward purchasing custom-made legal opinions in order to acquire immunity from criminal prosecutions.[78] But more generally, such reliance is excluded because, while a lawyer's task may be to present legal arguments for one party before a court, the power and the right to adjudicate between those arguments lies with judges alone.[79]

---

73 See *Johnson v Youden* [1950] 1 KB 544; [1950] 1 All ER 300.
74 Gur-Arye, "Reliance on a Lawyer's Mistaken Advice - Should it be an Excuse from Criminal Liability?" (2002) Am J Crim L 455, 464.
75 Hobbes, *Leviathan* (Oakeshott ed), Oxford, Basil Blackwell, 1955, 191.
76 *Anon* (1871) 7 Mad 35, cited in 14(1) *English and Empire Digest* (1977 reissue), para 124.
77 Hall, *General Principles of Criminal Law* (2nd ed), Indianapolis, Bobbs-Merrill, 1960, 382, 383.
78 "Reliance on a Lawyer's Mistaken Advice - Should it be an Excuse from Criminal Laibility?" (2002) 29 Am J Crim L 455, 466.

Operation of the principle concerning ignorance of law is confined to ignorance of criminal laws, and may include misapprehensions concerning either the existence of the law or its meaning, scope, or application.[80] By contrast, misunderstandings of civil law rights may often lead to acquittal. If D takes V's umbrella, believing that it is rightfully his and not realising that the "contract" under which he bought it was invalid for some reason, his mistake about his rights under property law may be introduced in denial that he had the mens rea for theft.[81]

In practice, situations involving ignorance of law seldom involve clear-cut cases where the accused claims ignorance of a penal provision that is well-known to almost everyone — for example, that taking the property of another without their consent is an offence, or that striking someone with the intention of injuring them is a crime. For the most part, the issues arise in circumstances where the boundaries between mistake of fact and ignorance of law seem to merge, so that it is not clear whether the honest belief arises from a mistake of fact, a mistake of law, or a combination of the two. In *De Malmanche v McKenzie*,[82] the issue was whether the accused's honest belief that games of chance (which he had permitted on premises he occupied) were not illegal was a defence to prosecutions under s 7(1) Gaming and Lotteries Act 1977. The accused believed that because certain modifications had been carried out to gaming machines in his tavern and they were operated in a particular way, the machines complied with the law. However, Judge Kerr held that a mistake in interpreting the law or failing to read and understand the appropriate law was no defence and said:[83]

> "[He] is not saying that he did not know there were gaming machines in the tavern. He is saying he did not know the machines in the tavern were machines prohibited by the law ... [A]lthough [he] might be said to have an 'honest and reasonable, but mistaken belief' that belief is not in a state of facts, but rather in the application of the law to what he had allowed to occur in the tavern."

A mistake of law may be found where an accused either misreads a statute or fails to read it carefully.[84] Additionally, where an accused knowingly handles a substance which she knows to have particular characteristics but which she does not know to be a statutory poison, it will be no defence that she knew it by another name. That is ignorance of the law.[85] However, where an accused attributes her lack of guilty knowledge to something other than mere ignorance that a particular substance is proscribed, her mistake may qualify as a mistake of fact but not ignorance of law. An example of a mistake of fact would occur if the accused were to say, "I did not know that it was the controlled plant cannabis; I thought it was a tomato plant". It would, however, be a mistake of law if the defendant were to say, "I knew it was cannabis, but did not know that cannabis is a controlled plant".[86]

---

79 Cf *R v Daly* (2005) 198 CCC (3d) 185 (BCCA), 194, rejecting the proposition that obtaining legal advice may negate mens rea.
80 For example, a belief that silence, passivity, or ambiguous conduct constitutes consent for the purposes of the crime of rape is a mistake of law and no defence: *R v Ewanchuk* (1999) 131 CCC (3d) 481 (SCC), 501; cf *R v M (ML)* [1994] 2 SCR 3; (1994) 89 CCC (3d) 96.
81 There might also be a "claim of right": below, 19.4.2.
82 *De Malmanche v McKenzie* [1989] DCR 567.
83 *De Malmanche v McKenzie* [1989] DCR 567, 570.
84 *Johnson v Youden* [1950] 1 KB 544; [1950] 1 All ER 300, 547; 303.
85 *Police v Taggart* [1973] 1 NZLR 732.
86 *Police v Taggart* [1973] 1 NZLR 732.

Similarly, where (for example, on an immigration charge) an accused honestly, but mistakenly, believes in a set of facts which if true would constitute a legal entitlement — for example that he had permission to enter the jurisdiction — it would not be a question of his not knowing that there was a prohibition on entering the jurisdiction without a permit. His belief would simply be mistake of fact, in that the facts that he believed existed were inconsistent with the application of the prohibition.[87] This type of case may be contrasted with *R v Watson*,[88] where the mistake related not to the actus reus but to a claim of legal justification. D, an environmental activist and the captain of a vessel, was charged with mischief that caused danger to life when he used his vessel in an attempt to force another vessel to stop fishing. It was held that D's belief that his actions were justified under the World Charter for Nature, an international convention, in effect constituted a mere mistake of law and could not support a defence under the relevant provision of the Canadian Criminal Code.[89]

14.3.1 Mistake of law and mens rea

In general, we have observed that a mistake of law cannot excuse a crime. So if D, with mens rea, causes the actus reus of an offence she is, according to normal principles of criminal liability, guilty of an offence. She cannot then claim that she did not know that the actus reus was prohibited by the criminal law. In *R v Custance*,[90] the accused was charged with failing to comply with a condition of bail that he live at a specified address. The person who was to meet him at the address where he was supposed to live could not obtain appropriate keys and he was unable to access the building. Instead he decided to sleep in his car in the building's car park until his next court appearance 3 days later. It was held that the accused's belief that he could comply with the bail terms by sleeping in his car for 3 nights amounted to a mistake of law. The Court rejected his claim that he believed that the Court's direction, "you must to live *there*", could be met if he had stayed on the front lawn of the apartment or, as he did, remained in the car park. By sleeping in the car, the accused was mistaken about the legal consequences of his actions and was operating under a mistake of law, a mistake which was incapable of negativing the mens rea for breach of bail. As the Court put it, "the interests of the justice system are not best served by allowing individuals to decide for themselves the legal parameters of compliance with the conditions of a recognizance".[91]

However, it is sometimes contended that, in certain circumstances, a mistake of law may negative the mens rea of an offence. For example, the actus reus may be defined in such a way that a mistake of law may result in D's act not being intentional with respect to some element of it, so that D lacks mens rea.[92] In these cases the accused's mistake, reasonable or otherwise, may be a defence.[93] The principles and constraints under which this concession operates are not always clearly articulated in the case law, and there is potential for confusion. In *Booth v MOT*,[94] the appellant had been charged with driving while disqualified. After the

---

87 See *Kumar v Immigration Dept* [1978] 2 NZLR 553 (CA), 557 (Richardson J). Similarly, *R v Latouche* (2000) 147 CCC (3d) 420 (Can CMAC), 435 (Ewaschuk JA): "It appears that the specific nature of official documents is most likely a question of mixed fact and law allowing an accused to raise the defence of mistake of fact."
88 *R v Watson* (1999) 137 CCC (3d) 422.
89 The Court went on to hold, further, that D's ignorance that the Criminal Code applied to his activity, which took place outside Canada's 200 mile exclusive economic zone, also constituted mere ignorance of law.
90 *R v Custance* (2005) 194 CCC (3d) 225.
91 *R v Custance* (2005) 194 CCC (3d) 225, 234 (Steel JA).
92 Smith and Hogan, *Criminal Law* (9th ed), London, Butterworths, 1999, 82.

disqualification had been pronounced in open court, no one had taken the appellant's licence from him, and after waiting half an hour he left the Court. Two days later he was stopped by a traffic officer and charged with the offence. His defence was that he believed he was entitled to drive a motor vehicle as he was still in possession of his driver's licence. The trial Judge treated the mistake as one of law and convicted the appellant. On appeal, the issue was whether the appellant's mistake was one of law and whether the prosecution had established mens rea.

It was conceded that the appellant knew that he had been disqualified from driving, but believed that the disqualification did not commence until he had surrendered his licence or had been requested to do so. There was no doubt as a matter of law that the disqualification commenced at the making of the order.[95] In formulating its approach, the Court considered a passage from Smith and Hogan in which the authors suggest that in certain circumstances a mistake of law might negate the mens rea for a particular offence.[96] The view of the Court was that since the offence of driving while disqualified was one requiring proof of mens rea, the issue was whether the Crown had proved as a fact that the appellant was disqualified and that he *knew* he was disqualified. Holland J said:[97]

> "Although the time of the commencement of the disqualification was a matter of law which the appellant in some circumstances must be deemed to know, the issue before the Court on a charge of driving while disqualified was what was the actual state of mind of the accused. If there is evidence from which a Court can infer that the accused did not know that the disqualification was in force at the time, and the Crown has failed to prove his state of knowledge to the contrary, then the Crown has failed to prove that element of mens rea which is a necessary ingredient of the crime."

The critical question, it would seem, is whether the appellant's mistake about the time of *commencement* of the disqualification was a relevant mistake of law sufficient to justify an acquittal. Clearly the Court thought it was a relevant mistake about legal rights sufficient to negative mens rea, on the basis that the mens rea for the offence is an intention "to drive [conduct] while disqualified [circumstance]". By implication, the Court rejected the alternative view, that the "mens rea" was in two parts, comprising (i) an intention to drive, and (ii) strict liability as to being disqualified.

However, in so deciding, the Court did not consider whether the mistake about disqualification was one about rights under the civil or criminal law. In our view, this distinction is crucial. It is perhaps unfortunate that, in citing the passage from Smith and Hogan, Holland J failed to include the following section which, with respect, does clarify the distinction being advocated here and which, if applied to the facts of *Booth*, may have produced a different outcome. The authors say:[98]

---

93 See *R v Barrett & Barrett* (1981) 72 Cr App R 212; [1980] Crim LR 641 (CA), 216; 642. In that case, the Court affirmed that an honest but mistaken belief about one's legal rights can afford a defence. However, the Court was clearly of the view that the relevant mistaken belief would be a mistake about civil law rights, rather than about the criminal law. In any event, the defence does not extend to situations where the rights in question have been the subject of litigation and a court of competent jurisdiction has stated what the rights are, but the losing party "out of obstinate blindness" continues to behave as if the Court has never declared those rights.
94 *Booth v MOT* [1988] 2 NZLR 217.
95 See s 36 Transport Act 1962 (repealed).
96 Smith and Hogan, *Criminal Law* (9th ed), London, Butterworths, 1999, 82.
97 *Booth v MOT* [1988] 2 NZLR 217, 220.

14.3.1 MISTAKE OF LAW AND MENS REA

"The crucial question will be, what is the *mens rea* required by the crime? A mistake negativing *mens rea* as to some element of the *actus reus* is no defence if the law does not require *mens rea* as to that element ...

"This principle will operate only when the definition of the *actus reus* contains some legal concept like 'property belonging to another'. It has no application where the law fixes a standard which is different from that in which D believes .... The principle is probably also confined to the case where the legal concept belongs to the civil law — as the notion of property ownership does — and not to the criminal law. Suppose that X obtains goods from P by deception and gives them to D, who knows all the facts. We have already seen that it will not avail D to say he does not know handling stolen goods is a crime. Equally, it is thought it will not avail him to say that he did not know that it is against the criminal law to obtain goods by deception and that goods so obtained are 'stolen' for this purpose. 'Stolen' is a concept of the criminal, not the civil law, and ignorance of it is no defence."

Taking up Smith and Hogan's example, even though the legal status of property as "stolen" has civil law implications, it is a designation that arises primarily from the application of the relevant criminal law rules. Similarly, disqualification is a legal status that arises primarily as a consequence of criminal activities and legal processes. Applying this rationale to the facts in *Booth*, it surely must be said that the appellant's mistake was about a concept of penal law. It was not the same sort of mistake about civil law as that contemplated in the example given. As such, it could even be said that it was a "pure" mistake of law, because there was no factual error,[99] for example, concerning the date when the period of disqualification began, but simply an erroneous opinion about certain legal requirements of the disqualification order itself.

Whatever sympathy the Court may have felt for the appellant, it is doubtful whether his was the sort of legal mistake that justified an acquittal. It is, in any event, a result which is difficult to reconcile with the express terms of s 25 Crimes Act.

However, there is a more fundamental objection to the decision in *Booth*. By allowing the appeal and quashing the conviction, the Court effectively permitted the appellant to substitute his erroneous view of the penal law ("disqualification commences when the licence is physically removed from the defendant") for what the law has been declared to be by competent officials ("the period of disqualification shall commence on the date of the making of the order") thus arguably challenging the Rule of Law itself.[100]

Some support for the approach contended for here may be derived from *MOT v Wilke*,[101] where on a prosecution for driving while disqualified it was held that mens rea related to factual beliefs and not to a belief in, or knowledge of, the law. There the District Court refused to follow *Booth*, preferring the view that the application of ignorance of law as an aspect of mens rea is probably confined to ignorance of civil law.[102] More generally, the courts are unwilling

---

98   Smith and Hogan, *Criminal Law* (7th ed), London, Butterworths, 1992, 84, 85.
99   Unlike *Millar v MOT* [1986] 1 NZLR 660; (1986) 2 CRNZ 216 (CA).
100 See Hall, "General Principles of Criminal Law" (2nd ed), Indianapolis, Bobbs-Merrill, 1960, 383: "A legal order implies the rejection of such contradiction. It opposes objectivity to subjectivity, judicial process to individual opinion, official to lay, and authoritative to non-authoritative declarations of what the law is. This is the rationale of *ignorantia juris neminem excusat*." See too *R v Custance* (2005) 194 CCC (3d) 225, 234, quoted in the text above, 14.3.1.
101 *MOT v Wilke* [1992] DCR 104.

447

to contemplate defences that may be characterised as "pure" mistakes of law. So it will not be a defence that the defendant, while aware that the person being assaulted was a police constable, entertained an incorrect understanding of the law regarding the extent of a constable's powers.[103] Similarly, where the appellant, on a charge of unlawfully conducting a bingo hall, claimed that his belief that the Criminal Code was inoperative in certain circumstances was a mistake of fact, it was held that the mistake was one of law and as such no defence.[104]

Neither is it a defence to a prosecution under the Arms Act 1983 for the defendant to claim that he did not know that an air-powered machine gun was a restricted weapon contrary to s 50(1)(b). In *R v Foox*,[105] the Court of Appeal held that such ignorance is simply ignorance of law and falls within s 25. For a charge of possession of a restricted weapon to succeed, all the prosecution needs to establish is knowledge that the weapon possesses the particular characteristics described in the relevant Order in Council and that the offender intended to possess a weapon of that character. Were knowledge of the weapon's legally restricted status an element of the offence, serious problems might arise. As Thomas J noted,[106] having regard to the purpose of the Arms Act it would be remiss to accept that a person who had possession of, for example, a device like a Molotov cocktail could defend such a charge on the basis that she did not know that such devices were listed as restricted weapons under the relevant legislation. Underpinning this limitation is the public policy rationale that it leads to better protection of the public.

Similarly, in *R v Cave*[107] the Court of Appeal rejected an appeal against conviction on a charge of driving with excess breath alcohol. The appellant claimed that he did not know that the paddock in which he had driven his car had been designated a "place to which the public have access" for the purposes of a one day agricultural show. The Court accepted that while the appellant would not have had the "faintest idea" that the law would regard the carpark as a road, the mistake was essentially one of law in not understanding the scope of the Land Transport Act and therefore no defence.

14.4 Exceptions to the "ignorance of law" principle

The case law supports two major exceptions to the principle that ignorance of the law is no excuse.[108] These exceptional defences, according to which the state is, in a sense, estopped from prosecuting an offence for which it is partially responsible, concern so-called "officially

---

102 *MOT v Wilke* [1992] DCR 104, 112.
103 *Waaka v Police* [1987] 1 NZLR 754; (1987) 2 CRNZ 370 (CA).
104 *R v Jones* (1991) 8 CR (4th) 137 (SCC). See also *Inspector of Factories v Tarbert St Food Centre (1985) Ltd* [1989] DCR 471, where an error was ruled to be a "pure" mistake of law when the accused took advice from a senior employee of a large wholesale concern as to the legal requirements of the Shop Trading Hours Act 1977.
105 *R v Foox* [2000] 1 NZLR 641; (1999) 17 CRNZ 216 (CA).
106 *R v Foox* [2000] 1 NZLR 641; (1999) 17 CRNZ 216 (CA), 649; 224, 225. See too *R v Leolahi* [2001] 1 NZLR 562; (2001) 18 CRNZ 505 (CA): lack of knowledge that it was a "criminal wrong" corruptly to use official information was held to be ignorance of law and no excuse.
107 *R v Cave* 1/08/05, CA393/04. Canadian courts have also shown reluctance to extend the mistake defence in cases where mistakes are made about the expiration or commencement of vehicular licensing requirements, especially where the mistake, or ignorance, is rooted in the defendant's passive failure to enquire concerning his true legal obligations: cf *Levis (City) v Tetreault; Levis (City) v 2629-4470 Quebec Inc* (2006) 207 CCC (3d) 1.

induced" error, and ignorance of laws that have not been published or are "non-discoverable". We will briefly consider each exception.

14.4.1 Officially induced error

Although ordinarily a mistake of law cannot be successfully raised as a defence to a criminal or *quasi*-criminal charge or regulatory offence, an officially induced error of law may, in some circumstances, constitute a valid defence.[109] In particular, an overly inflexible approach to the principle that ignorance of the law is no excuse becomes cause for concern where the error in law of the accused arises out of an error of an authorised representative of the state and the state then demands, through other officials, that the criminal law be applied strictly to punish the conduct of the accused.[110] Moreover, the complexity of modern legislation makes it unrealistic to assume that a responsible citizen will have a comprehensive knowledge of all the criminal law and, in the circumstances, good faith reliance on an official's advice as to the scope of a particular statutory prohibition, may not be unreasonable.

However, this complexity does not justify completely abandoning the rule that "ignorance of the law is no excuse", which encourages citizens to be responsible, and which is an essential foundation to the rule of law.[111] Rather, the complexity and extensiveness of regulation should be seen as one motive for creating a limited exception to the ignorantia juris rule, in the form of officially induced error. As the State's involvement in the day-to-day lives of people increases, and as the number of officials from whom advice can potentially be sought increases, the likelihood multiplies that an official will be relied on for advice about an enactment which has criminal implications.[112]

The claim that an accused was induced to commit a crime by relying on the erroneous advice of an official responsible for the administration of the law in question has found favour in appellate courts in both the United States and Canada, but has not found ready acceptance in the United Kingdom and the Australian states. Its status as a defence in New Zealand is currently uncertain. The "defence" raises a number of important questions. First, should an official ever have the power to declare authoritatively what the law is? Secondly, if it is permissible for officials effectively to declare the law in certain defined situations, who qualifies as a relevant official for the purposes of the rule? What obligations lie on a defendant to ascertain whether the interpretation of the law offered by an official is correct? Should the giving of such erroneous advice amount to an excuse or is it best left as a matter going to penalty in an appropriate case?

---

108 It is sometimes suggested that "claim" or "colour" of right is also an exception to the general principle that ignorance of law is no excuse. However, since claim of right relates principally to a mistake in relation to non-penal law which has induced an offender to act unlawfully, it is best regarded as sui generis and not to be confused with "pure" mistakes of law. For discussion of claim of right as an element of theft, see below, 19.4.2.
109 For a more comprehensive treatment of this topic see Brookbanks, "Officially induced error as a defence to crime" (1993) 17 Crim LJ 381. A valuable discussion of the principles at work is found in Ashworth, "Testing Fidelity to Legal Values: Official involvement and Criminal Justice" in Shute S and Simester A (eds), *Criminal Law Theory: Doctrines of the General Part*, Oxford, Oxford University Press, 2002, 299.
110 *Levis (City) v Tetreault; Levis (City) v 2629-4470 Quebec Inc* (2006) 207 CCC (3d) 1, 13.
111 *R v Jorgensen* [1995] 4 SCR 55; (1996) 102 CCC (3d) 97 (SCC), 77; 111 (Lamer CJ).
112 *R v Jorgensen* [1995] 4 SCR 55; (1996) 102 CCC (3d) 97 (SCC), 77; 111 (Lamer CJ).

The principal rationale for the rule is that a person should not be held to be criminally liable where his conduct is in direct consequence of an authoritative declaration of what the law is, albeit a declaration that is wrong. It is arguable that the doctrine of ignorantia juris actually upholds the rule of law (the principle of legality) by requiring that only formal or authoritative declarations can give expression to what the law is, and not leaving the determination of law to the discretion of officials. It follows that, to permit an individual to plead successfully that he had a different interpretation of the law, even if officially induced, would contradict the Rule of Law. Nonetheless, in our view the challenge to the principle of legality is insufficient to justify convicting the blameless when a person acts in good faith on the advice of a "law-declaring" official; because the person is not purporting to substitute his view of the law for what the law actually is. Rather, he is acting on an interpretation of the law which has been presented as authoritative.

Moreover, although the basic policy behind the mistake of law doctrine is that all people should know and obey the law at their peril, in certain situations there may be an overriding societal interest in having individuals rely on authoritative pronouncements of officials whose decisions we wish to see respected. Therefore a rule which states, "a person ought not to be punished who reasonably relies on a judicial decision or other official declaration of the law later held to be erroneous", may constitute a valid exception to the general principle. It would, we think, be unjust if a person were to be held criminally responsible who had acted in reasonable reliance on judicial or other official opinion advising that such conduct is legal. A test question is revealing: could the individual reasonably be expected to have been more conscientious or dutiful?[113]

An example illustrating the application of our test question is *R v Laniel Canada Ltd*.[114] In that case, the appellant had been convicted of having kept devices for gambling contrary to the Criminal Code. He argued that he had obtained a licence to conduct and manage a lottery scheme, which included gambling in a public place of amusement, from the Lottery and Races Board. The licence authorised the company to "carry on the business of amusement machines". The Court noted that the regulation concerned *amusement* machines, without mentioning *gambling* machines; which, it held, did not exclude the possibility that an amusement machine within the meaning of the provincial regulation could, for the purposes of the criminal law, be a gambling machine and not only an amusement machine. The Court refused to accept the appellant's argument that he had been "led into error by an official" who only gave him a licence for an amusement machine. The Court said:[115]

> "The provincial statute and relevant regulation in the present case cannot be interpreted as permitting the licensee to carry on the business of amusement machines to successfully argue that he was led into error by a civil servant who acted under a statute whose area of concern is clearly distinguishable from that of the criminal law."

Evidently, the appellant had failed to make a reasonable inquiry whether the licence it had obtained included the right to possess machines used specifically for gambling

---

113 See Briggs, "Mistake of law", Master of Laws thesis, University of Otago, 1994, 67.
114 *R v Laniel Canada Ltd* (1991) 63 CCC (3d) 574.
115 *R v Laniel Canada Ltd* (1991) 63 CCC (3d) 574, 576.

By contrast is the case of *R v Dubeau*.[116] There the accused had been charged, among other things, with carrying on a business including selling firearms and ammunition without a permit. He pleaded officially induced error, on the basis that before he had commenced the garage sales at which these weapons and ammunition were to be sold, he had made inquiries of the local police firearms officer concerning the legality of selling firearms at a garage sale and, if permissible, how many could be sold without obtaining a "dealer's permit". He was told by the firearms officer that selling guns at a garage sale could be done without a permit and that there was no limit on the number of guns sold. In addition, the appellant had written to the head office of the police department requesting information about a dealer's permit, but because of an oversight, the request had been overlooked.

In the Ontario Court (General Division), Ferguson J held that the appellant's reliance on the advice from the firearms officer was reasonable, taking into account (1) the *complexity* of the relevant law, and (2) the *duty* of the firearms officer to respond to general inquiries from the public. The Court held that the appellant's failure to disclose the fact that he intended to conduct a series of garage sales did not amount to a deliberate withholding of information and that he was not "careless or negligent" in failing to make that disclosure. In finding in the appellant's favour on the issue of officially induced error, the Court acknowledged that the defence had been "clearly recognised" by the Ontario Court of Appeal in *R v Cancoil Thermal Corp & Parkinson*,[117] where the Court of Appeal said:

> "The defence of 'officially induced error' is available as a defence to an alleged violation of a regulatory statute where an accused has reasonably relied upon the erroneous legal opinion or advice of an official who is responsible for the administration or enforcement of the particular law. In order for the accused to successfully raise this defence, he must show that he relied on the erroneous legal opinion of the official and that his reliance was reasonable. The reasonableness will depend upon several factors including the efforts he made to ascertain the proper law, the complexity or obscurity of the law, the position of the official who gave the advice, and the clarity, definitiveness and reasonableness of the advice given."

The defence of officially induced error has been given further endorsement by the Supreme Court of Canada in *R v Jorgensen*.[118] It would now seem, contrary to some early opinions about the scope of the defence, that officially induced error is equally applicable to "true crimes" with a "full *mens rea* component"[119] as it is to regulatory offences, although for certain crimes, such as those involving "moral turpitude" the chances of success of such an excuse will be negligible.[120] The Court in *Jorgensen* established a number of criteria which must be satisfied before the defence will be available.[121] They are summarised as follows:

---

116 *R v Dubeau* (1993) 80 CCC (3d) 54.
117 *R v Cancoil Thermal Corp & Parkinson* (1986) 27 CCC (3d) 295; 52 CR (3d) 188, 303; 199. For a more detailed analysis of that case see Brookbanks, "Officially induced error as a defence to crime" (1993) 17 Crim LJ 381, 388.
118 *R v Jorgensen* [1995] 4 SCR 55; (1996) 102 CCC (3d) 97 (SCC). See also *Postermobile plc v Brent London Borough Council* 8/12/97 (QBD), where local authority officers represented that planning consent was not required for temporary advertising hordings. It was held that subsequent prosecutions for failing to obtain planning consents were an abuse of process: "It was not as if they had requested planning advice from one of the council's gardeners" (Schiemann LJ).
119 *R v Jorgensen* [1995] 4 SCR 55; (1996) 102 CCC (3d) 97 (SCC), 77; 111 (Lamer CJC).
120 *R v Jorgensen* [1995] 4 SCR 55; (1996) 102 CCC (3d) 97 (SCC), 78; 112.

(1) Once the Court has determined the error is one of law, the accused must demonstrate that she considered the legal consequences of her actions. Requiring an accused to consider whether her conduct might be illegal and seek advice as a consequence, ensures that the incentive for a responsible and informed citizenry is not undermined.

(2) It must be demonstrated that the advice came from an appropriate official. This avoids the obvious injustice of the State approving conduct on the one hand and seeking to impose a criminal sanction for that conduct with the other. Generally, Government officials who are involved in the administration of the law in question will be considered appropriate officials. The official must be one whom a reasonable individual in the position of the accused would normally consider responsible for advice about the particular law in question (for example a Motor Vehicle Registrar). The advice of officials at any level of government may induce an error of law, provided that a reasonable person would consider that particular Government organ to be responsible for the law in question.

(3) Once an accused has established that he sought advice from an appropriate official, he must demonstrate that the advice was reasonable in the circumstances. Since an individual relying on advice has less knowledge of the law than the official in question, the individual must not be required to assess reasonableness at a high threshold. Thus, if an appropriate official is consulted, the advice obtained will be presumed to be reasonable unless it appears on its face to be utterly unreasonable.

(4) The advice obtained must have been erroneous, a fact which does not have to be demonstrated by the accused. In proving the elements of the offence, the prosecution will have already established what the correct law is, from which the existence of the error can be deduced. Nevertheless, it is important to note that when no erroneous advice has been given, the excuse cannot operate.

(5) To benefit from the excuse, the accused must demonstrate reliance on the official advice. This may be shown by proving that the advice was obtained before the actions in question were commenced and by showing that the questions posed to the official were specifically tailored to the accused's situation.

(6) Officially induced error of law functions as an excuse rather than a full defence. It can only be raised after the Crown has proven all elements of the offence. To rely on the excuse, an accused must show, after establishing that she made an error of law, that she considered her legal position, consulted an appropriate official, obtained reasonable advice, and relied on that advice in her actions. The accused, who is the only one capable of bringing this evidence, is solely responsible for it. Ignorance of the law is not encouraged because informing oneself about the law is a necessary element of the excuse.

(7) As the excuse does not affect the determination of culpability, it is said to be procedurally similar to entrapment. As excuses, both claims concede the wrongfulness of the action but assert that under the circumstances it should not be attributed to the actor. The successful raising of an officially induced error of law argument will lead to a judicial stay of proceedings rather than an acquittal. Because a stay can only be entered

---

121 R v Jorgensen [1995] 4 SCR 55; (1996) 102 CCC (3d) 97 (SCC), 78-81; 112-114.

in the clearest of cases, an officially induced error of law argument will only be successful in the clearest of cases.

(8) The question whether officially induced error constitutes an excuse in law is a question of law or of mixed law and fact. While a jury may determine whether the accused is culpable, and hence whether the argument is necessary, it is for a judge to determine whether the precise conditions for the excuse are made out. Only the trial Judge is in a position to determine if a stay should be entered. The elements of the officially induced error excuse are to be proven on a balance of probabilities by the accused.

By general agreement the criteria in *Jorgensen* may be reduced to five key steps, which may be summarized as follows:[122]

(i) The accused must have considered the legal consequences of his/her actions;

(ii) The advice given came from an appropriate official;

(iii) The advice received must be reasonable;

(iv) The advice must have been erroneous; and

(v) The accused must have relied on the official advice.

Once each of these steps is satisfied, the defence is available under Canadian law.

(1) *Officially induced error in New Zealand*

Notwithstanding overseas developments, the availability in New Zealand of a common law defence of officially induced error remains unclear. There is very little appellate authority. In *Tipple v Police*,[123] involving prosecutions for sales in breach of the Arms Act 1983, which had allegedly been condoned by the police, Holland J suggested, somewhat tentatively, that "such a principle" may need to be applied in an appropriate case if there was no other way of achieving justice. In the event, he preferred to apply s 19 Criminal Justice Act 1985.

While this hardly represents a strong endorsement of the doctrine, neither is it excluded. In *MaCrae v Buller District Council*,[124] where the appellant had sought unsuccessfully to rely on the defence of officially induced error in defending a charge of carrying out building work without a building consent, Chisholm J criticised the trial Judge's reliance on *Tipple v Police* to support the proposition that officially induced error is not a defence to a criminal or quasi criminal charge. His Honour doubted that the decision was capable of supporting any such proposition.[125] The Court assumed, without deciding the point, that officially induced error was capable of providing a defence in New Zealand, but found that the evidence presented by the appellant fell well short of establishing a plausible foundation.

A possible obstacle to the development of the defence in New Zealand is the ruling in *Waaka v Police*,[126] to the effect that the defence of total absence of fault cannot extend to pure mistakes of law. Where a court has categorised an officially induced error as a pure mistake of law, in

---

122 See *R v Charles* (2005) 197 CCC (3d) 42 (Sas CA), 62. See also *Maitland Valley Conservation Authority v Cranbrook Swine Inc* (2003), 225 DLR (4th) 255 (Ont CA).
123 *Tipple v Police* [1994] 2 NZLR 362; (1993) 11 CRNZ 132.
124 *MaCrae v Buller District Council* 12/12/05, Chisholm J, HC Greymouth CRI-2005-418-1.
125 *MaCrae v Buller District Council* 12/12/05, Chisholm J, HC Greymouth CRI-2005-418-1, para 40.
126 *Waaka v Police* [1987] 1 NZLR 754; (1987) 2 CRNZ 370 (CA), 759; 375.

the context of a public welfare regulatory offence, it may therefore be difficult to contend that the mistake ought to be excused. However, since officially induced error is distinct from a defence of due diligence[127] or absence of fault, its application to situations involving pure mistakes of law may be unobjectionable. Indeed, the essence of the claim, and a principal rationale for the doctrine, is that the offender was misled about the scope or content of a particular law by one who, in the nature of her office, ought to have been better informed — a very different explanation than absence of fault. There would seem to be little justification for limiting the operation of the doctrine to mixed mistakes of law and fact. Doing so would seem to undermine the foundation of the excuse.

It must be doubted, therefore, whether in light of the Canadian developments the District Court decision in *Inspector of Factories v Tarbert St Food Centre (1985) Ltd*[128] can stand. In that case it was held, applying the dictum of Cooke P in *Waaka v Police*,[129] that since the defence of officially induced error rested on a pure error of law, it was unavailable to the defendant. Two comments should be made.

First, it is clear from recent developments in Canadian criminal law that any attempt to limit the operation of the defence of officially induced error to mixed mistakes of law and fact is misconceived. It is clear that the doctrine, which operates as a carefully carved exception to the ignorantia juris principle, applies to any relevant mistake of law, subject to the limitation mentioned above that its likelihood of success with crimes involving moral turpitude will be nearly nil.

Secondly, the comments of Cooke P in *Waaka* were limited by the context to a consideration of the general principle concerning ignorance of law, and did not address the specific claims of officially induced error. In any event, it is arguable that Cooke P was doing no more than reiterating, in a different form of words, the statutory requirements of s 25 Crimes Act, which prevents mistakes regarding the content or effect of penal law from being a defence to crime. Taken at its face value, the statement "the defence of total absence of fault cannot extend to pure mistakes of law" would seem to eliminate all defence claims involving any error of civil or criminal law, including those which give right to such defences as colour of right. Given the context in which the statement was made, and the lack of a clear signal to this effect, it is unlikely this was the Court's intention.

Officially induced error was considered in *Diriye v Police*,[130] which involved a prosecution under Land Transport Regulations for operating a commercial vehicle with "mixed" tyres on the front wheels. The appellant had sought assistance from three tyre supply specialists in equipping the vehicle with a new tyre before the vehicle was finally given a certificate of fitness by the Vehicle Testing Station, under delegated authority of the Land Transport Safety Authority. Although the Court doubted the availability of officially induced error as an excuse,[131] it achieved effectively the same result by exercising its sentencing discretion to discharge the offender without conviction.[132]

---

127 *R v Jorgensen* [1995] 4 SCR 55; (1996) 102 CCC (3d) 97 (SCC), 78; 112 (Lamer CJC).
128 *Inspector of Factories v Tarbert St Food Centre (1985) Ltd* [1989] DCR 471.
129 *Waaka v Police* [1987] 1 NZLR 754; (1987) 2 CRNZ 370 (CA), 759; 375.
130 *Diriye v Police* 20/07/06, Baragwanath J, HC Auckland CRI-2006-404-7.
131 "To do so would not only fly in the face of the clear language of s 25, but would run counter to a clear line of authority in New Zealand, England and Australia ... Without argument on the appellant's side I do not comment further on this topic" para 17.

14.4.2 Non-publication

There is some authority at common law for the view that inability to know of the existence of a statutory prohibition, either because it has not been published or because the accused was physically absent from the jurisdiction when the law was passed, may be a defence to a criminal charge.[133] However, the better view would seem to be that a criminal intent need not involve knowledge on the part of an accused that his acts were against the law and constituted a crime.[134] In *R v Bailey*, D, the captain of a ship at sea, fired on another ship, unaware of a new law which rendered firing on another ship unlawful. He was convicted, even though it was impossible for him to know the law. The Judges recommended a pardon. The principle which justifies conviction in such a case is that the prosecution is only required to prove that the accused brought about the actus reus of the particular offence with the required mens rea. It is not necessary to prove that the accused knew that what he was doing was contrary to law. So, in *Barronet's Case*,[135] where the accused, French nationals, were charged with duelling, the fact that they did not know that duelling was an offence in the United Kingdom was held to be no defence to the charge. It has also been held that a mistaken belief that a prosecution will not be instituted in respect of the offence is not a defence.[136]

In all these cases, however, the relevant law had at least been published. Moreover, in the modern age of sophisticated access to information, merely being outside the jurisdiction is today no bar to knowing the law. By contrast, when it is *impossible* for the accused to become aware of what the law is because, for example, a particular regulation has not been issued at the time of the alleged offence, it may be a defence that the accused was unaware that the particular prohibition applied to him or her.[137] In Canada, the rigours of the principle concerning ignorance of law have been relaxed where commission of the offence is dependent on a regulation which has not been published in the Canadian *Gazette*. In those circumstances, no person can be convicted of an offence consisting of a contravention of the regulation unless reasonable steps have been taken to bring the purport of the regulation to the notice of the persons likely to be affected by it.[138] There does not appear to be any comparable provision under current New Zealand law, although the current proliferation of regulatory legislation containing penal provisions may indicate a need to consider the creation of a similar rule for New Zealand.

In our view, non-publication of a law should afford a defence. In substance if not in form, it amounts to retrospective criminalisation. Arguably, conviction for contravening an unpublished law may be inconsistent with s 27 New Zealand Bill of Rights Act 1990, which enshrines a right to observance of the principles of natural justice by any tribunal. It would certainly be inconsistent with the Rule of Law, which, as we saw in chapter 2, demands that

---

132 Section 106 Sentencing Act 2002. See also *R v Goldstone* 17/06/97, Williams J, HC Auckland T74/97, where officially induced error was discussed, although it was not determinative on the facts of the case. The status of the doctrine in New Zealand was considered to be "at its highest, uncertain".
133 See *Burns v Nowell* (1880) 5 QBD 444 (CA).
134 *Halsbury's Laws of England* vol 11(1) (4th ed reissue), London, Butterworths, 1990, para 20.
135 *Barronet's Case* (1852) 22 LJ MC 25.
136 *R v Arrowsmith* [1975] QB 678; [1975] 1 All ER 463 (CA). However, a promise to that effect made by a police officer, which is then broken, could conceivably provide a ground to challenge the proceedings on the basis of abuse of process.
137 See *Lim Chin Aik v R* [1963] AC 160; [1963] 1 All ER 223 (PC).
138 *R v Molis* [1980] 2 SCR 356; (1980) 55 CCC (2d) 558.

MISTAKE

the State give citizens fair warning of offences, so that they may have a proper opportunity to comply with the law.[139]

---

139 See 2.1.3.

Chapter 15

SELF-DEFENCE AND DEFENCE OF PROPERTY

15.1	Self-defence	457
15.1.1	Legislative history	458
15.1.2	The statutory test	460
(1)	*A broad application*	460
15.1.3	Belief in circumstances justifying force	462
(1)	*Psychological abnormalities*	463
(2)	*Variety of circumstances justifying force*	465
(3)	*Where the offence does not involve force*	466
(4)	*Unreasonable mistakes*	467
(5)	*Mistakes induced by intoxication*	468
15.1.4	Reasonable force	469
(1)	*Proportionality*	471
(2)	*Requirement that the threat be unjust*	473
(3)	*Retreat*	474
(4)	*Pre-emptive strike*	476
(5)	*Self-defence and battered women*	479
(6)	*Importance of imminence*	483
15.1.5	Excessive force	484
15.1.6	Proving self-defence	486
15.2	**Defence of property**	487
15.2.1	Structure of the current New Zealand law	489
15.2.2	Defence of land or building and defence of movable property: ss 52, 53, 56	489
(1)	*"Reasonable force"*	490
(2)	*No "striking" or "bodily harm"*	491
(3)	*"Peaceable possession"*	492
(4)	*"Claim of right"*	492
15.2.3	Defence of dwellinghouse: s 55	494
15.2.4	Reform	495

15.1 Self-defence

The law of self-defence reflects the commonsense notion that a person who is attacked may defend herself and will be legally justified in repelling force with force. This is regarded as one of the great principles of the common law.[1] However, questions remain about the nature of the justification which self-defence confers and about whether, for example, the actions of a person who falsely believes she is acting in self-defence can ever be justified. While New

Zealand law admits a justification for all acts done in legitimate self-defence, there is still an arguable case for saying that a person who mistakenly thinks she is justified should merely be excused — because justification, by its nature, renders an act permissible.[2] By contrast, a person who kills someone whom she mistakenly believes was threatening her life should hardly be told that her act is permissible; yet at the same time, it may be equally counter-intuitive to suggest that she should be held responsible for a crime.

Despite the fact that these sorts of questions abound in self-defence theory, and that they are an ongoing source of controversy for legal philosophers, the *availability* of self-defence is essentially a very practical matter. According to one writer, it is grounded in the "morally distinctive" feature of the use of defensive force against an unjust immediate threat. That is to say, D's act is one of self-defence when it directly blocks the infliction of unjust harm, regardless of whether the relevant harm is, or is not, a bodily injury.[3] It would seem to follow that defensive force may be permissible even when the person posing the threat is not culpable. Even a child, a sleepwalker, or an insane person can compromise his right to life simply by becoming an unjust immediate threat to the life of another person.[4] Self-defence preserves the right, though not the unqualified right, of any person to protect himself against a perceived unjustified threat to life or limb.

Because the employment of *lawful* force is not an offence, it is sometimes said that D should be acquitted because an element of the actus reus is missing, namely an *unlawful* act.[5] This analysis applies regardless of whether the assailant is killed or merely injured. However, the law has always required that wherever force is used to prevent the infliction of harm, the force used is limited to that which is *necessary* to prevent the mischief threatened. Thus there is a tension between the justified use of force, and its limitation to what is necessary or reasonable.

This tension defines the principal elements of self-defence. Where D uses more force than the law allows in what would otherwise be legitimate self-defence, he is liable for the excess of force used.[6] In such circumstances, the force is deemed to be unlawful, and D's act is deprived of the legal status of having been committed in self-defence. In New Zealand there is no intermediate category of exculpation. His conduct either qualifies as self-defence or he is liable for the full consequences of whatever offence he may have committed.

15.1.1 Legislative history

Prior to 1 January 1981, the New Zealand law on self-defence was characterised by a series of complex statutory provisions originating in the Criminal Code Act 1893 and re-enacted in the Crimes Act 1908.[7] A Bill introduced into Parliament in 1959 slightly modified the provisions in the 1908 Act relating to self-defence, and the resulting law was duly re-enacted as

---

1   See Criminal Code Bill Commission, *Report of the Royal Commission Appointed to Consider the Law Relating to Indictable Offences: With an Appendix: Containing a Draft Code Embodying the Suggestions of the Commissioners*, London, Eyre & Spottiswode for HMSO, 1879, 11.
2   Husak, "The complete guide to self-defence" (1996) 15 Law and Phil 399, 402.
3   Uniacke, *Permissible Killing: The Self-Defence Justification of Homicide*, Cambridge, Cambridge University Press, 1994 and see R v Kingi 10/8/05, CA122/05, paras 61-63, per Glazebrook J.
4   Husak, "The complete guide to self-defence" (1996) 15 Law and Phil 399, 401.
5   *Beckford v R* [1988] AC 130; [1987] 3 All ER 425 (PC); Allen, *Textbook on Criminal Law* (3rd ed), London, Blackstone Press, 1995, 164.
6   See s 62 Crimes Act 1961 and discussion at 15.1.5.
7   Sections 73-76 Crimes Act 1908.

ss 48-50 Crimes Act 1961. In their various re-enactments, these provisions distinguished between provoked and unprovoked assaults, and contained separate provisions for the defence of persons under protection. The laws were difficult to apply in practice and left defendants who were responsible for minor acts of provocation largely unprotected by the law if they chose to defend against an anticipated retaliation. Furthermore, the old law was unclear regarding by what standard the need for defensive force was to be judged — ie according to the subjective perceptions of the defendant, or by an objective test.

However, the greatest problem in the old law was the inherent difficulty in any fact situation of deciding who started the particular incident,[8] which meant that it was often very difficult for a judge to decide whether to direct a jury to proceed under s 48 (self-defence against unprovoked assault) or s 49 (self-defence against provoked assault). The judges were unusually critical of the provisions. In *R v Kerr*[9] Richmond J, delivering the judgment of the Court of Appeal, spoke of the "quite incomprehensible" tests and distinctions laid down by the former ss 48 and 49, and urged that the sections be replaced by a simpler form of legislation that could be applied in a "commonsense" way. An earlier memorandum prepared by Richmond J and Speight J at the request of the then Chief Justice, Sir Richard Wild, had also called for a simplification of the law.

Of course, and as the memorandum acknowledged, the then-existing law had been drafted as it was for a reason: to prevent juries from having too much latitude when determining the availability of the defence, particularly in cases where D's actions caused death or grievous bodily harm. It was recognised that changing the law would require a policy decision whether it was desirable to seek greater simplicity at the price of fewer statutory constraints.[10] After considering various options for reform, the Criminal Law Reform Committee eventually opted for simplification, through the codification of a comprehensive provision to the effect that, *whatever the antecedent circumstances,* the use of force is justified in self-defence or in the defence of another, provided the amount of force used is (objectively) reasonable in light of the defendant's (subjective) perception of the circumstances. This option was favoured because it would "require no abstruse legal thought and no set words or formula to explain it; and only commonsense is needed for its understanding".[11] It was anticipated that the new formulation would simplify the task for both judge and jury. The jury would be required to decide the question of reasonableness in the light of the judge's summing up of the evidence, while the judge would no longer be faced with varying statutory tests and distinctions which were perceived to be extremely difficult to explain to a jury.[12]

---

8   See Criminal Law Reform Committee, *Report on Self-Defence*, Wellington, 1979, 4.
9   *R v Kerr* [1976] 1 NZLR 335 (CA), 344.
10 Memorandum of the Judges prepared for the Criminal Law Reform Committee, cited in Criminal Law Reform Committee, *Report on Self-Defence*, Wellington, 1979, 4, 5.
11 Memorandum of the Judges prepared for the Criminal Law Reform Committee, cited in Criminal Law Reform Committee, *Report on Self-Defence*, Wellington, 1979, 8.
12 The Committee rejected the notion of providing, additionally, a list of evidentiary guidelines for the court, on the basis that doing so could introduce into the law complexities of interpretation and a further body of case law when the question in self-defence is one of fact to be decided in the light of an infinite variety of circumstances in different cases.

15.1.2 The statutory test

The present test for self-defence is defined in s 48 Crimes Act 1961, as amended by the Crimes Amendment Act 1980. It provides:

"Everyone is justified in using, in the defence of himself or another, such force as, in the circumstances as he believes them to be, it is reasonable to use."

Essentially, the section comprises two elements, one subjective and the other objective. The first part of the section poses a subjective question: what did the accused *believe* the circumstances to be? If the accused is able to establish a sufficient evidential foundation to the effect that she believed the circumstances were such that she was about to be killed or seriously injured, the trial judge is bound to put the defence to the jury.[13] Once it has been accepted that the jury could at least entertain a reasonable doubt about the accused's state of mind, then that becomes a material issue in relation to the second, objective element of the section, which requires the jury to consider whether the force used was *reasonable* given the circumstances that the accused thought existed.[14]

The courts have approved a format for directing juries on these elements. In R v Li, the Court of Appeal paraphrased Tipping J's approach in *Shortland v Police*,[15] and stated:[16]

"In summary ... the jury is asked to consider first what the accused believed the circumstances to be, from his or her point of view. The second question is whether, bearing in mind that belief of the accused about what was happening, he or she was acting in self-defence (again considered from his or her point of view). The last question is whether, given that belief, the force used in self-defence was actually reasonable."

This formula has been approved in a line of cases.[17] The essential aspect is that both the subjective and objective elements of the test are to be assessed in the light of the circumstances as the accused saw them. It is "axiomatic" that a trial judge sitting alone should also direct him or herself along the lines of the approved formula.[18] However, in approving the Shortland direction, the Court of Appeal has cautioned against the use of the terms "subjective" or "objective" to describe the different elements of the self-defence test, since they are terms that may not be familiar to all jury members. The courts have emphasised that s 48 is a simple comprehensive provision, which judges should be wary of giving unnecessary embellishment. Generally, they should read the terms of s 48, direct the jury to the three questions noted above and make any necessary linkages to the evidence.[19]

(1)   *A broad application*

Because of the very broad way in which the current statutory test has been formulated, it has given juries significantly more latitude when considering claims of self-defence. This can be

---

13   See R v Tavete [1988] 1 NZLR 428; (1987) 2 CRNZ 579 (CA); also R v Ranger (1988) 4 CRNZ 6 (CA).
14   R v Ranger (1988) 4 CRNZ 6 (CA), 9.
15   Shortland v Police 23/4/96, Tipping J, HC Invercargill AP74/95.
16   R v Li 28/6/00, CA140/00; CA141/00, 6. See also R v Bridger [2003] 1 NZLR 636; (2002) 19 CRNZ 676 (CA) and R v Howard (2003) 20 CRNZ 319 (CA).
17   See R v Hackell 10/10/02, CA131/02; R v Bridger [2003] 1 NZLR 636; (2002) 19 CRNZ 676 (CA); R v Reyland 13/7/04, CA439/03.
18   R v Sarich 16/5/05, CA407/04, per Goddard J.
19   R v Howard (2003) 20 CRNZ 319, 325, per Keith J.

illustrated by considering the case of *R v Ranger*.[20] At first instance, the appellant was convicted of the murder of her de facto husband. She had armed herself with a kitchen knife following an argument in the bedroom, during the course of which she was struck by the deceased. Carrying the knife behind her back, the appellant had returned to the bedroom where she used it to stab the deceased in the shoulder. The deceased left the house with the knife still in his body and died a short time later.

At trial, defence counsel did not raise the defence of self-defence, preferring to rely on provocation. However, evidence was given by the accused at the trial that during the struggle the deceased had reached under the bed, where the accused knew firearms were kept, having immediately beforehand threatened to blow both the appellant's and her son's heads off. On appeal, the Court of Appeal held that although this evidence would be far from adequate to discharge a legal burden of proof, because the accused was required to establish only an evidential foundation for the defence, no burden of proof fell on her.[21] Therefore, because there was evidence properly capable of establishing a foundation for the defence, even though it had not been put forward by defence counsel, the trial Judge had a responsibility to place it before the jury.

The Court allowed the appeal and ordered a new trial. It accepted that in the circumstances, in which the accused believed that the lives of herself and her son were in peril because of the deceased's threats to shoot them, it was not impossible that a jury could be left in reasonable doubt whether a pre-emptive strike with a knife would be reasonable force in the circumstances.

The case demonstrates that under the present law, an intention to kill or cause serious bodily injury is consistent with legal self-defence. A deliberate causing of injury may well be justified on the basis that it is a reasonable response to a believed threat.[22] A person may even intend to *kill* her assailant if she believes that killing the assailant is the only means of avoiding the threatened harm; although the use of fatal force will necessarily give rise to careful consideration by the jury of the issue of proportionality. On the basis that an agent intends those aspects of her act which in the circumstances she believes are necessary for the achievement of her aim,[23] many of the deaths caused by self-defence may be described as intentional, since they are necessary to attain the end of self-preservation.[24]

Accordingly, it has been held to be a "false dichotomy" to direct a jury that they must decide whether the accused intended to assault or intended to act in self-defence.[25] It follows too that, in a case where self defence is pleaded, for a judge to direct a jury that the defence accepts that the accused killed the victim "by an unlawful act" will constitute an incorrect premise since, if the act meets the legal test of self-defence, the act is justified and, by definition, lawful,[26] whether or not there is an intention to kill.[27]

---

20 *R v Ranger* (1988) 4 CRNZ 6 (CA).
21 See 2.3.
22 *R v Howard* (2003) 20 CRNZ 319, 324, per Keith J.
23 Cf Uniacke, *Permissible Killing: The Self-Defence Justification of Homicide*, Cambridge, Cambridge University Press, 1994, 405.
24 For fuller discussion, see 4.2.
25 *R v Styles* 6/11/03, CA 297/03, para 31.
26 *R v Seu* 8/12/05, CA81/05, para 69, per Glazebrook J.

Ranger also demonstrates that far from requiring retreat as a legal element, it is clearly open for those employing self-defence sometimes to use pre-emptive force (below, 15.1.4(4)), and even to benefit from the defence in cases where it has not been expressly pleaded (below, 15.1.5).

15.1.3 Belief in circumstances justifying force

Although self-defence might be characterised as an "actus reus" defence (since it prevents D's conduct from being "unlawful"), the mental element is nonetheless critical. The question which necessarily arises is, *what were the circumstances believed by the accused to exist?* A cardinal principle of criminal responsibility is that moral obligation is dependent not merely upon the actual facts but also upon the actor's perception of them.[28] This principle is of particular importance in the context of self-defence where, typically, the stress of a violent confrontation or emergent threat becomes a fertile environment for mistakes to be made. Often an offender, mistakenly believing he is about to be unjustly attacked, may use or threaten the use of lethal force when, in reality, the victim's conduct is lawful. Self-defence in such circumstances may be characterised as *putative* self-defence, because it is supposed or imagined.

In order to deal with problems that can arise with putative self-defence, the Law Reform Commission of Victoria recommended in a 1991 report that the common law condition that the victim's conduct be unlawful should no longer be a requirement of the plea of self-defence.[29] Fortunately, the same reform is not required in New Zealand. Section 48 contains no requirement that the victim's actions be unlawful; rather, it allows the use of putative self-defence in any circumstances where the accused believes he is about to be unjustly assaulted. An illustrative case is *R v Terewi*,[30] in which the appellant had threatened to shoot police officers who visited his home, thinking they were people he had earlier met at a hotel and who had caused him trouble. Although the question of mistake was not directly in issue, the Court of Appeal, in allowing the appeal against conviction for threatening to cause grievous bodily harm, held that it was "totally unlikely that the Legislature intended the new section to restrict the former availability of selfdefence".[31] The Court may be taken implicitly to have approved the notion that a mistake of fact will not necessarily negate a claim of self-defence. This approach has been confirmed in subsequent case law.[32] Because s 48 is no longer confined to defence against unlawful assault, even in cases where the victims are police officers acting lawfully, the accused may be justified in using reasonable force in self-defence or defence of another, if as a result of a mistake of fact the accused believes the force used by the police is such that it

---

27 Generally, this will mean that a jury should have considered self-defence before it considers the question of intent. However, the failure of a judge to direct a jury to consider self-defence before considering intent will not create a difficulty provided the judge makes it clear that self-defence is a complete answer to the charges: *R v Seu* 8/12/05, CA81/05, para 70, per Glazebrook J.

28 Cf Hall, *General Principles of Criminal Law* (2nd ed), Indianapolis, Bobbs-Merrill, 1960, 363; also 1.3.2(1)-(2). See too Wright, "The circumstances as she believed them to be: A reappraisal of section 48 of the Crimes Act 1961" (1998) 7 Waikato LR 109. Since D's belief is the crucial thing, rather than the truth of that belief, the term "mistake" need not even be used; although, where D claims that he correctly perceived justifying circumstances, the possibility that he mistakenly did so should be put to the jury as an alternative. See *R v Joyce* 24/2/98, CA364/97.

29 Law Reform Commission of Victoria, *Homicide*, report no 40, Melbourne, 1991, 99, cited in Uniacke, *Permissible Killing: The Self-Defence Justification of Homicide*, Cambridge, Cambridge University Press, 1994, 37.

30 *R v Terewi* (1985) 1 CRNZ 623 (CA).

31 *R v Terewi* (1985) 1 CRNZ 623 (CA), 624.

32 See, for example, *R v Thomas* [1991] 3 NZLR 141; (1991) 7 CRNZ 123 (CA); *R v Petel* [1994] 1 SCR 3; *R v Nelson* (1992) 71 CCC (3d) 449; 13 CR (4th) 359.

would be unlawful. In *R v Thomas*[33] the accused had intervened to assist the "victim" of what she believed to be an unlawful police "beating". In fact the police were conducting a lawful arrest. However, because the accused had an honest, albeit mistaken, belief that the police were using excessive force, the Court of Appeal held that the defence in s 48 was available.[34]

Nonetheless, there is still a need for caution in such circumstances. To afford a *Thomas*-type of defence, the mistake must be one of fact and not a mistake of law, for example as to the authority of a person acting in an official capacity. In *R v Lee*[35] the defendant, while being arrested after testing positive for excess breath alcohol, had punched the two arresting officers and was charged with assault with intent to resist lawful apprehension for failing a roadside breathalyser. He appealed on the ground that the Judge had erred in failing to direct the jury that it was a defence genuinely, albeit mistakenly, to believe that the purported arrest was unlawful. Rejecting the appeal, the English Court of Appeal observed that neither public order nor the clarity of the criminal law would be improved if juries were required also to consider the impact of the defendant's belief as to the *lawfulness* of his arrest in cases where a lawful arrest was being properly attempted on reasonable grounds.

(1) *Psychological abnormalities*

One issue that has arisen in both New Zealand and England concerns the status of an accused's subjective belief in facts where that belief has been influenced by psychological factors affecting the accused's perception of the emergent threat. The question is whether such factors, or other personal characteristics, should be considered as a legitimate feature of the accused's subjective makeup, and relevant to the beliefs held by him or her, or whether they should be disregarded.

The issue arose in *R v Bridger*,[36] where the accused had appealed against conviction on a charge of causing grievous bodily harm with intent, after he had struck the complainant unconscious with a rake. The appeal was based, inter alia, on the ground that psychiatric evidence, not available to defence counsel or the trial Judge until the sentencing hearing, revealed the possibility that at the time of the incident the appellant was suffering from a mental disorder which may have heightened his subjective perception of danger from the complainant. Although the Court acknowledged that the trial Judge had not appropriately considered the effect of undiagnosed bipolar affective disorder in the assessment of culpability, it found that there was no evidence that the accused's mental disorder had affected his subjective perception of danger. The Court was, therefore, not required to address the question of whether mental disorder might have affected the appellant's subjective perception of danger. Neither did it offer an opinion on the Crown's contention that s 48 must be read alongside s 23(1) Crimes Act 1961, with the suggested outcome that "the circumstances as [an accused] believes them to be applies to sane beliefs only."[37] The issue remains undecided in New Zealand.

---

33 *R v Thomas* [1991] 3 NZLR 141; (1991) 7 CRNZ 123 (CA).
34 However, compare *Williams v Police* [1981] 1 NZLR 108, 113-115 where it was held that an accused was not justified in interfering with the arrest of another even if it was unlawful. This authority must be regarded as having been overtaken by *R v Thomas* [1991] 3 NZLR 141; (1991) 7 CRNZ 123 (CA).
35 *R v Lee* [2000] NLJ 1491.
36 *R v Bridger* [2003] 1 NZLR 636; (2002) 19 CRNZ 676 (CA).
37 *R v Bridger* [2003] 1 NZLR 636; (2002) 19 CRNZ 676 (CA), para 34.

One possible rationale for disregarding such subjective beliefs might be that the assessment of the dangerousness of believed facts is an objective matter that should not be influenced by psychological matters personal to the accused. In *R v Martin (Anthony)*,[38] the English Court of Appeal considered this issue in a case where the accused had shot two burglars who had entered his isolated farmhouse at night, killing one and seriously injuring the other, On appeal against his conviction for murder, D sought to adduce fresh evidence that he suffered from paranoid personality disorder, an effect of which was that he would have perceived someone breaking into his house as presenting a greater threat to his safety than a normal person.

The English Court rejected this evidence as having any relevance to self-defence. It drew a three-fold distinction between (1) the facts, (2) the danger presented by those facts, and (3) D's response to those facts. While, for purposes of self-defence, the facts must be taken to be as D saw them, the assessment of the dangerousness of those facts was, like the assessment of D's response, an objective matter. Thus personal characteristics such as personality disorder are to be disregarded in so far as they affect (2) and (3).

This approach to the subjective limb of self-defence would seem to directly contradict the unitary approach to the accused's belief in facts taken by New Zealand courts and, in our view, undermines the rationale of modern self-defence theory. To require an objective assessment of the dangerousness of believed facts subverts the very notion of a subjective belief and imports into the accused's perception a reasonableness requirement that is both unrealistic and unwarranted. For the purposes of self-defence, the distinction drawn between categories (1) and (2) appears to be false. Consider: what is it for a person to think that the situation is dangerous? It is to think that there is a risk of something harmful happening. That is a belief about the facts, and it is the crucial belief in any claim of self-defence. Diane does not act in self-defence when she thinks to herself, "Victor has a gun, therefore I shall shoot him." That is never enough. Self-defence requires that she think, "Victor has a gun, so there is a real risk that Victor is about to kill me, therefore I shall shoot him." In other words, action is taken in self-defence only when it is motivated by and responds to a *subjectively perceived threat*. Not by the facts that give rise to the threat: it must respond to the threat itself.

Significantly, the approach of the Court of Appeal in *Martin* is contradicted by the Privy Council's advice in *Shaw v R*,[39] an appeal from Belize. D had also shot two men, killing them both in purported self-defence. The appeal against the murder conviction was on the basis that the trial Judge had misdirected the jury by inviting it to assess the reasonableness of the defence of self-defence on the basis of the facts as they were, rather than as D believed them to be. The Privy Council affirmed the generally accepted test for self-defence in suggesting the necessity for the trial Judge "to pose two essential questions ... for the jury's consideration. (1) Did the appellant honestly believe or may he honestly have believed that it was necessary to defend himself? (2) If so, and taking the circumstances *and the danger* as the appellant honestly believed them to be, was the amount of force which he used reasonable?"[40]

Although *Shaw* does not directly address the issue raised in Bridger, the decision is consonant with the approach taken by New Zealand courts and in our view represents the correct approach to the subjective element in self-defence.

---

38   *R v Martin (Anthony)* [2002] 2 WLR 1; [2002] 1 Cr App R 27; [2002] Crim LR 136.
39   *Shaw v R* [2001] 1 WLR 1519; [2002] 1 Cr App R 10; [2002] Crim LR 140. *Martin* was decided on 30 October 2001; the Privy Council's advice, to which *Martin* does not refer, was handed down on 24 May 2001.
40   *Shaw v R* [2001] 1 WLR 1519; [2002] 1 Cr App R 10; [2002] Crim LR 140, para 19 (emphasis added).

(2) Variety of circumstances justifying force

The text of s 48 makes it clear that self-defence is not limited to the use of force or the threat of it in the defence of oneself. The addition of the words "or another" in the section allow self-defence to be used for the protection of a third party who may or may not be related to the person claiming the defence. The common law has always recognised the right of a person to protect himself from attack or to act in defence of others and if necessary to inflict violence on another in doing so.[41] In *R v Portelli*[42] the Supreme Court of Victoria affirmed this principle, noting that the privilege of a person to respond to the attack of another should not be confined to attacks directed at the accused or a person in some defined relationship to the accused, but should be equally applicable whenever response is made to an attack upon any person, whether relative, friend or stranger.

Neither is self-defence restricted to cases where the person anticipates an assault involving physical harm. In principle, it is also available as a defence to assaults where bodily harm may not be threatened.[43] It is now clear that if a person uses force against another in the genuine belief that such force is necessary to protect a third party from a really serious *psychiatric* injury, the person is entitled to rely on s 48, provided, of course, that the defence lays down a sufficient evidentiary foundation.[44] Therefore if, for example, a mother believes her infant daughter is in danger of suffering serious psychiatric injury as a result of the child's father attempting to remove the child from her custody, she would be justified in using reasonable force in defence of the embattled child. However, for psychiatric injury to constitute a relevant anticipated harm for the purposes of s 48, the consequences must involve more than raised emotions, such as inducing intense fear in a person or feelings of panic or distress. The courts have set a high threshold for what will constitute actual bodily harm of a psychological nature.[45]

It is not necessary that the defensive action be motivated by fear. Where the law justifies repelling force by force, as in s 48, it is clearly implied that the right to repel force includes the right to strike back. There is no requirement that self-defence be limited simply to defensive, warding-off, bodily movements. In *R v Doherty*[46] the appellant, a bouncer in a nightclub, returned a blow delivered by a former patron whom earlier he had evicted from the nightclub and who had returned and assaulted the appellant. As a result of the blow by the appellant, the victim fell and hit his head on the road. He managed to walk home but was later found dead as a result of a major head injury. On appeal, it was held that the accused had been unlawfully assaulted. He had not intended to cause death or grievous bodily harm and had used no more force than was necessary to enable him to defend himself. He was justified in repelling unlawful force by force even though he was not in fear of his life or health when he did so.[47]

---

41 *Beckford v R* [1988] AC 130; [1987] 3 All ER 425 (PC), 144; 431, per Lord Griffiths.
42 *R v Portelli* (2004) 148 A Crim R 282.
43 *R v Howard* (2003) 20 CRNZ 319, 325, per Keith J.
44 See *R v Kneale* [1998] 2 NZLR 169; (1997) 15 CRNZ 392 (CA), 179; 402; also *R v Young* 8/3/06, CA266/05, per O'Regan J.
45 *R v Kneale* [1998] 2 NZLR 169; (1997) 15 CRNZ 392 (CA), 177; 400.
46 *R v Doherty* (2000) 146 CCC (3d) 336. Cf *R v Deana* (1909) 2 Cr App R 75; *R v Loo Manson* (1925) 43 CCC 30 (Alta CA).
47 Cf *McKay v Police* [1997] 3 NZLR 199, 201, per Hammond J: "[the] punches have to be weighed in the circumstances that ... the complainant had launched a gratuitous and unprovoked attack on the appellant."

The issue of fear notwithstanding, it will be a misdirection for a judge to say that the law does not protect a person from the consequences of acting out of revenge, or retribution, or spite, or anger. In *R v Howard*[48] the Court of Appeal held that self-defence is concerned with meeting future possibilities. It cannot solely take the form of retaliation for past grievances. Nevertheless, it may be the case that someone who is angry or spiteful may also fear a future assault. Such an additional mindset should not prevent the accused from availing herself of the defence.[49] At the same time, an assault intended to teach the victim a lesson is not self-defence, and feelings of anger may in some circumstances support an inference of excessive force.[50]

(3) *Where the offence does not involve force*

It seems that self-defence is not ordinarily available unless the offence charged involves the use of force. In *R v Busby*[51] the appellant had been convicted on a charge of possessing an offensive weapon, namely a large knife, contrary to s 202A(4)(b) Crimes Act 1961. He appealed on the basis that his conviction on the possession charge was inconsistent with his acquittal on a charge of wounding with intent and that self-defence ought to have been put to the jury in respect of the possession count as well as the count on which he was acquitted. The Court rejected that claim. Gault J held that the offence charged was an offence of possession in specified circumstances. It was not an offence specifying, as one of its elements, the use of force. Where the offence is complete upon proof of possession together with circumstances that prima facie show an intention to use it to commit an offence, there is no room for self-defence. The Court acknowledged that its decision was contrary to the approach taken in *Tuli v Police*,[52] where self-defence had earlier been recognised in respect of offences under s 202A(4)(b). The Court concluded that the approach in *Tuli* was wrong.

We must accept that this is the correct position. Because "force" is specified in the definition in s 48, it appears an unavoidable conclusion that, as a matter of ordinary language, s 48 will not cover acts (and offences) that lack a violent element. In *Blake v DPP*,[53] where a vicar appealed against a conviction for criminal damage after he had written a protest note with felt tip pen on a public building, it was similarly held that the statutory defence of self-defence was unavailable because the relevant section of the Criminal Law Act 1967 (UK), s 3, was only available for crimes committed by the use of force. However, it is a position that produces some paradoxical results. It has been commented, with reference to *Blake*, that if the vicar had inscribed his protest message with a hammer and chisel he might have had a defence, but he did not because a felt pen could not, by its nature, generate relevant force.[54] In *Busby*, an analogous result might occur where, instead of merely possessing the knife, the appellant had threatened the victim with it. In those circumstances he might conceivably have a defence to the more serious offence of threatening behaviour but not to the lesser offence of possession. It is established law that "force" in s 48 can include threats of force.[55] There seems to be no

---

48 *R v Howard* (2003) 20 CRNZ 319, 325, per Keith J.
49 *R v Howard* (2003) 20 CRNZ 319, 325, per Keith J.
50 *R v De Mey* 17/12/04, CA169/04.
51 *R v Busby* 26/9/01, CA211/01. But see *Thompson v Police* 6/5/96, Tipping J, HC Invercargill AP35/96 (self-defence allowed where D had entered a public place for an apparently innocent purpose, carrying a baseball bat); also Orchard, *Crimes Update*, NZLS Seminar, Wellington, 2001, 27.
52 *Tuli v Police* (1987) 2 CRNZ 638.
53 *Blake v DPP* [1993] Crim LR 586.
54 *Blake v DPP* [1993] Crim LR 586, 588.

reason in principle why, in an appropriate case, it should not extend to conduct where an element of force is implicit in the thing possessed (for example an offensive weapon) albeit not actuated in physical conduct or the threat of it. This follows from the well-known principle in criminal law that the greater (the use or threat to use an offensive weapon) includes the lesser (its mere possession).

It should not be assumed from this discussion that self-defence can never be available as a defence to a charge of possession of an offensive weapon, despite the existence of an "uneasy synergy" between the law prohibiting offensive weapons and the defence of self-defence.[56] In each case it will be necessary to examine the wording of the legislation prohibiting offensive weapons to determine the extent to which self-defence is excluded or, alternatively, accommodated. Lanham has identified seven general principles derived from the authorities relating to self-defence in the context of legislation prohibiting the possession of offensive weapons:[57]

(1) Where offensive weapons legislation contains generally-worded defences like reasonable excuse or good reason, the courts interpret these words to include self-defence and like defences.

(2) The defence of self-defence is limited to prevent its defeating the purpose of the prohibition.

(3) Imminence is an important but not universal limitation.

(4) Where the legislation contains defences like lawful purpose or lawful object these defences, which taken literally could defeat the purpose of the prohibition are either given limited scope or are held inapplicable to self-defence.

(5) Even in the absence of statutory defences the limited defence of self-defence is available at common law unless excluded by legislation.

(6) The common law defence is not superseded by statutory defences but co-exists with them.

(7) Even where the legislation places the legal burden of proving the statutory defence on the defendant, the better view, following from (6) above, is that the burden of proof in relation to self-defence, as it is a common law defence, is on the prosecution.

To the extent that they are consistent with s 48, these principles may be regarded as providing a relevant guide to the law in New Zealand. Note, too, that where the defence is precluded, the possibility of necessity should also be considered.[58]

(4) Unreasonable mistakes

There is no requirement that D's mistake must be a reasonable one. But it must, of course, be genuine. Although the judge must rule on whether there is evidence of self-defence to go to the jury and is bound to put the defence where there is a sufficient evidential foundation, the jury may still reject the defence if the evidence fails to disclose a reason for the accused to

---

55 See *R v Terewi* (1985) 1 CRNZ 623 (CA).
56 See Lanham, "Offensive Weapons and Self-Defence" [2005] Crim LR 85.
57 See Lanham, "Offensive Weapons and Self-Defence" [2005] Crim LR 85, 97.
58 See *R v Kerr* [2004] SCC 44, para 76 , per Le Bel J; above, chapter 13.

believe that the victim was posing the danger claimed.[59] An unreasonable belief is not *per se* fatal to the defence, although the more unreasonable the accused's belief is that he is under attack, the less likely the jury is to believe it.

In this context, the meaning given to "believe" is critical. That it is a subjective mental state is not in dispute. But what it implies *as* a subjective state of mind does not appear to have been judicially considered in respect of self-defence in New Zealand. To believe is to have faith in, or to put trust in, the existence of something. It is the acceptance of a state of affairs as true or existing.[60] Such a state of mind would seem normally to be inconsistent with a fanciful, unreasonable judgment that a person may be under attack by an unjust immediate threat. In *Burns v HM Advocate*,[61] the appeal was disallowed because although the trial Judge misdirected himself in requiring that the accused must not have instigated the trouble in order to be able to claim self-defence, there was in fact no miscarriage of justice since there was no evidence to suggest that the accused *had* been acting in self-defence. The case could also have been decided, it is submitted, on the basis that D did not "believe" that the deceased was about to kill or seriously injure him, and therefore D could not be said to have been defending himself against an unjust threat.

(5) *Mistakes induced by intoxication*

The rule that a mistake of fact does not necessarily negate the availability of self-defence is now well established in English common law. In *R v O'Grady*,[62] the English Court of Appeal held that a sober man who mistakenly believes he is in danger of immediate death at the hands of an attacker is entitled to be acquitted of both murder and manslaughter if his reaction in killing his supposed assailant was a reasonable one. However, the same case makes clear that in England a defendant is not entitled to rely on a mistake of fact which has been induced by voluntary intoxication.[63] The reason for this ruling appears to lie in public policy concerns that a person who has voluntarily consumed alcohol should not be able to take advantage of mistakes made by him while in that state — which, by its nature, involves an element of dangerousness.[64] Nevertheless, English authority on this point has never been accepted in New Zealand as determining the relevance of the defendant's intoxication.[65] It is doubtful whether, in the context of self-defence, there is any room in New Zealand for the approach taken in *O'Grady*, given that s 48 expressly requires the conduct to be assessed according to the circumstances as the accused believed them to be. The question does not appear to have been directly discussed in the Court of Appeal. However, there are cases where self-defence has been held to be available, despite the fact that the accused was intoxicated when using force and was mistaken as to the circumstances.[66]

---

59 *Burns v HM Advocate* (1996) The Juridical Review 416.
60 See 4.5.
61 *Burns v HM Advocate* (1996) The Juridical Review 416.
62 *R v O'Grady* [1987] QB 995; [1987] 3 All ER 420 (CA).
63 *R v O'Grady* [1987] QB 995; [1987] 3 All ER 420 (CA).
64 See *DPP v Majewski* [1977] AC 443; [1976] 2 All ER 142 (HL).
65 See also chapter 11.
66 *R v Ranger* (1988) 4 CRNZ 6 (CA); *R v Thomas* [1991] 3 NZLR 141; (1991) 7 CRNZ 123 (CA); *R v Terewi* (1985) 1 CRNZ 623 (CA). See also *Tuialli v Police* 19/3/87, Greig J, HC Auckland AP310/86; *Deans v Police* 5/3/87, Holland J, HC Christchurch AP7/87; *King v Police* 5/8/87, Quilliam J, HC Dunedin AP11/87.

In principle this seems to be correct. If, as is the case in New Zealand, a defendant may adduce evidence of intoxication to support her claim that the required state of mens rea was absent,[67] it would seem appropriate to allow the same evidence on the question of a mistake about the necessary use of force in self-defence.

15.1.4 Reasonable force

As was noted above, the test for self-defence in New Zealand involves both a subjective and an objective element. The subjective element, we have seen, concerns the actual belief of the defendant about the circumstances confronting her. The objective element concerns the requirement that the defensive force must have been "reasonable",[68] albeit reasonable in the circumstances as perceived by the defendant.

Generally, in a jury trial it will be for the jury to determine whether the force used was reasonable (or whether there is at least a reasonable doubt about this). Indeed, the question of the reasonableness of the force used may be regarded as exclusively a jury question and never a point of law for the Judge to decide.[69] Indeed, it will not be a misdirection for the Judge to ask the jury to consider "was the force used reasonable ... from your point of view, not his".[70] In *R v Hackell* the Court of Appeal rejected defence counsel's submission that a direction in those terms erroneously encouraged the jury to substitute their collective subjective view as to what was reasonable and that the test of what is "reasonable" was determined by a reference point external to the jury itself. The Court held that it was unnecessary and unhelpful to direct the jury to determine whether the force used was more than reasonable by reference to some elusive external criterion such as community standards: "Collectively the jury fix the standard in the particular case."[71]

By the same token, to the extent that the reasonableness of force used is a jury question, it cannot be open to a defendant to claim that she *thought* the force used was reasonable. To allow such a concession would largely defeat the purpose of the objective element. Earlier judicial dicta which suggested that the test is whether the defendant believed the force used was reasonable must now be regarded as wrong.[72] In *R v Murray*,[73] Eichelbaum J stated:

> "It would be a startling, not to say dangerous, proposition that the assessment of reasonable force was left subjectively to each individual accused."

Accordingly, the suggestion in *R v Scarlett*,[74] that the accused's belief that the force was reasonable constitutes a defence, does not represent the law in New Zealand.

---

67 See *R v Kamipeli* [1975] 2 NZLR 610 (CA).
68 Section 48 Crimes Act 1961.
69 *A-G for Northern Ireland's Reference (No 1 of 1975)* [1977] AC 105; [1976] 3 WLR 235 (HL), 137; 246 (Lord Diplock). See also *R v Hackell* 10/10/02, CA131/02, para 27: "Reasonableness, or more accurately whether the Crown has proved the use of unreasonable force in the circumstances as the accused believed them to be, is a straightforward question of fact for the jury to determine." Per Hammond J.
70 *R v Hackell* 10/10/02, CA131/02, per Hammond J.
71 *R v Hackell* 10/10/02, CA131/02, para 26, per Hammond J.
72 See *R v Robinson* (1987) 2 CRNZ 632 (CA), 635. The aberrant dictum in *Robinson* has been explained as being "clearly a slip in quoting s 48". See *R v Wang* [1990] 2 NZLR 529; (1989) 4 CRNZ 674 (CA), 534; 678.
73 *R v Murray* 22/10/87, Eichelbaum J, HC Wellington T26/87.
74 *R v Scarlett* [1993] 4 All ER 629; (1994) 98 Cr App R 290 (CA), 636; 296.

However, an accused's unreasonable belief that the force was *necessary* may still support the defence, provided the belief is honestly held.[75] That is to say, a belief may support the defence where an accused has unreasonably, albeit honestly, thought that the facts of the situation were such that force was his only option. Similarly the expression, "such force as ... it is reasonable to use", has been held to include force which otherwise is not in reasonable balance with the believed threat where, for example, the accused has no real choice of means, other than a means which might be seen in the normal course as out of balance with the threat.[76] This might arise where V is approached by D, who is large and aggressive and proceeds to attack V, overpowering him. V grabs for the only item at hand, which happens to be a loaded rifle, and shoots and kills D.[77] What is a "reasonable balance" in the circumstances will depend on the circumstances as the accused believed them to be and on the perceived threat. The question of balance is not to be assessed in the abstract and divorced from the perceived facts.[78]

At the same time, the defence will be negated where the accused acts independently of the claimed belief and in a manner which suggests that it was not the belief, but rather revenge or retaliation, that was the true motivation for an act of aggression. In *R v Savage*,[79] the deceased, a hotel patron, had been violent and abusive toward the accused. Before the fatal incident the accused had asked another patron for a knife. A fight ensued, in which the accused was seen to deliver an upward blow to the chest of the deceased who was not in possession of a weapon at the time of the killing. The accused claimed to have been acting in self-defence when he saw the deceased pull a knife from his back pocket. In rejecting the appeal, the Court of Appeal said:[80]

> "when the knife was used, the accused must have seen himself as under a real threat of danger, and not *merely think there may be* some future danger to him."

The dictum implies that "merely thinking that there may be" danger does not satisfy the requirements in s 48 that the accused "believes" danger exists, and that he acts "in the defence" of himself.

Generally, however, New Zealand courts have shown a remarkable degree of liberality in determining the nature and degree of force that is consistent with lawful self-defence, and have readily acknowledged that extreme circumstances may demand extreme measures.[81] In *Dixon v Police*,[82] for example, it was held that striking the victim in the arm with a knife in response to an attack with a heavy electric flex was consistent with a genuine belief that the defendant was in danger. The Court appeared to be uninfluenced by the fact that the defendant had a ready means of escape and could have avoided the confrontation.[83] Similarly, in *King v Police*[84] Quilliam J held the accused was justified when he smashed a beer handle in the face of his assailant, inflicting severe injuries. The assailant had grabbed the accused, who had a broken arm, by the throat while he was seated. In *Deans v Police*,[85] an appeal against conviction on a

---

75 See *Tuialli v Police* 19/3/87, Greig J, HC Auckland AP310/86. See also the commentary on *R v Scarlett* in [1994] Crim LR 288; White, "Going over the top: Self-defence and excessive force" (1994-95) 5 King's College LJ 112.
76 *R v Howard* (2003) 20 CRNZ 319, para 26.
77 See *Melrose v R* 26/3/03, HC Auckland, T022282, per Potter J.
78 *R v Kingi* 10/8/05, CA122/05, para 65, per Glazebrook J.
79 *R v Savage* [1991] 3 NZLR 155 (CA).
80 *R v Savage* [1991] 3 NZLR 155 (CA), 158 (emphasis added).
81 *Jenkins v Police* (1986) 2 CRNZ 196.
82 *Dixon v Police* 13/2/86, Jeffries J, HC Palmerston North AP5/86, noted [1986] NZ Recent Law 233.

charge of assault was allowed on the basis that there was a reasonable doubt whether the complainant (a hotel bouncer) may have been pushed through a hotel window justifiably as a result of a "pushing off" by the accused that was no more than a reasonable response to an unlawful assault. The Court held that the District Court Judge had misdirected himself because he had only satisfied himself as to the physical fact that the defendant had pushed the complainant through the window and had not considered whether the Crown had disproved self-defence.

These cases illustrate the diverse range of actions that may constitute legitimate force in self-defence. In *R v Kissling*[86] the Court of Appeal appears to support the proposition that reasonable force might even include biting a Constable's finger, in circumstances in which an unlawful search would have constituted an assault.[87]

(1) *Proportionality*

The moral right to self-defence is not unlimited. It is confined to the use of reasonably necessary force.[88] This means that the law does not permit a person to use *any* means to ward off unjust harm. The qualifying principle is that of proportionality. Suzanne Uniacke illustrates this principle by suggesting that a defender is not entitled to aim at an attacker's heart if she can shoot him in the leg and doing so is, in the circumstances, sufficient to defend herself.[89] Of course, the example presupposes that the accused is aware that the lesser degree of force will disable the aggressor and terminate the attack, and chooses instead to use a significantly greater measure of (lethal) force. It leaves open the possibility that D may shoot to kill if she (perhaps wrongly) believes that the degree of force used *is* necessary to repel the attack and that shooting V in the leg will not stop him (for example because she thinks he has a gun).

The need for proportionality dictates that there is no general right to use force in self-defence irrespective of other morally relevant considerations. For example, D cannot use lethal force against V as a means of preventing V from stepping on D's toe — even if that means is the only one available.[90]

In addition, to be reasonable within the scope of s 48, the force used must also be *indispensable* or *unavoidable*; because necessity is, together with proportionality, an essential element in self-defence. This principle is expressed at common law on the basis that the mischief sought to be prevented could not be prevented by less violent means; and that the mischief done by, or which might reasonably be anticipated from, the force used is not disproportionate to the injury or mischief which it is inflicted to prevent.[91] In practice, the

---

83 The Court's approach could not be justified on the ground that a homeowner has no duty to retreat from his own home, since the right of a householder to "stand fast" only applied where it was necessary to use deadly force against an intruder. There was no evidence here that the victim intended to break into the defendant's home.
84 *King v Police* 5/8/87, Quilliam J, HC Dunedin AP11/87.
85 *Deans v Police* 5/3/87, Holland J, HC Christchurch AP7/87.
86 *R v Kissling* 4/5/05, CA403/04.
87 *R v Kissling* 4/5/05, CA403/04, para 12.
88 Uniacke, *Permissible Killing: The Self-Defence Justification of Homicide*, Cambridge, Cambridge University Press, 1994, 31.
89 Uniacke, *Permissible Killing: The Self-Defence Justification of Homicide*, Cambridge, Cambridge University Press, 1994, 31.
90 Uniacke, *Permissible Killing: The Self-Defence Justification of Homicide*, Cambridge, Cambridge University Press, 1994, 31, 32.

requirement for necessity operates as an important litmus test for the dictates of proportionality. While it is true to say "if stunning one's assailant will suffice for self-defence, one must not shoot him through the heart" because that offends against the proportionality principle,[92] the action is legally countermanded more specifically because it is unnecessary. In practical terms the more extreme an action taken in self-defence is, relative to the threat offered, the easier it is to conclude that the action was unnecessary. Conversely, it would seem that the more extreme the danger facing the accused (or facing someone under his protection), the less the courts will be inclined to minutely examine issues of proportionality, and the more inclined they will be to accept the necessity of the accused's actions. Thus, in one case where an elderly man attacked, and unintentionally killed, his son-in-law with a wooden baton in order to protect his daughter from physical abuse, the Court, in directing the accused's discharge, stated that "actions are not to be weighed too finely or nicely".[93] Similarly, in R v Murray,[94] in an oral ruling on whether the defence of self-defence should be put to the jury, Eichelbaum J stated:

> "one is reluctant to give any encouragement to the notion that the production of a dangerous knife or other weapon can be regarded as a reasonable response to an attack by a single person using bare hands. However, here there is available evidence of additional elements, namely a disparity in size and age, that the accused had rapidly got the worst of the encounter, the other party's known karate skills ... do not think I can go so far as to say that it is impossible that a jury would entertain a reasonable doubt."

In that case, the accused had fatally stabbed the deceased in the neck with a knife after he had been severely assaulted. He had escaped from the attack and had gone into a bedroom where he obtained a hunting knife with the aim of "scaring off" the deceased. The fatal stabbing occurred when a further fight took place, in which the accused received a number of solid blows. Although the force used was fatal, it could not be said that it was irrefutably disproportionate, given the exigencies of the situation.

The need for a proper synthesis of the elements of necessity and proportionality has been recognised by the Privy Council in R v Palmer, in a well-known passage from the judgment of Lord Morris:[95]

> "If there is some relatively minor attack it would not be common sense to permit some action of retaliation which was *wholly out of proportion* to the *necessities* of the situation. If an attack is serious so that it puts someone in immediate peril then immediate defensive action may be necessary. If the moment is one of crisis for someone in imminent danger he may have to avert the danger by some instant reaction. If the attack is all over and no sort of peril remains then the employment of force may be by way of revenge or punishment or by way of paying off an old score or may be pure aggression. There may no longer be any link with a *necessity* of defence. Of all these matters the good sense of a jury will be the arbiter. There are no prescribed words which must be employed in or adopted in a summing-up. All that is needed is a clear exposition, in relation to

---

91 Criminal Code Bill Commission, *Report of the Royal Commission Appointed to Consider the Law Relating to Indictable Offences: With an Appendix Containing a Draft Code Embodying the Suggestions of the Commissioners*, London, Eyre & Spottiswode for HMSO, 1879, 11.
92 Finnis, *Fundamentals of Ethics*, Oxford, Clarendon Press, 1983, 85.
93 See R v Brown 20/5/87, Smellie J, HC Auckland, T51/87.
94 R v Murray 22/10/87, Eichelbaum J, HC Wellington T26/87.
95 Palmer v R [1971] AC 814; [1971] 1 All ER 1077 (PC), 831-832; 1088 (emphasis added).

the particular facts of the case, of the conception of *necessary* self-defence. If there has been no attack then clearly there will have been no need for defence. If there has been attack so that defence is reasonably necessary it will be recognised that a person defending himself *cannot weigh to a nicety the exact measure of his necessary defensive action*. If a jury thought that in a moment of unexpected anguish a person attacked had only done what he honestly and instinctively thought was necessary that would be most potent evidence that only reasonable defensive action had been taken."

The passage affirms the conventional requirements of self-defence, namely, necessity and proportionality; but allows a degree of latitude to the defendant who, faced with a grave threat, must determine for herself the measure of force necessary to repel the threatened attack — without the advantage of on-the-spot guidance from a court. That is not a matter which can be weighed with fine scales.

(2)   *Requirement that the threat be unjust*

Although the case law is not clear on this point, it would seem implicit in the notion of necessary self-defence that the accused must have been or have believed herself to be the victim of an *unjust* threat. This appears to be a necessary qualification of the right of self-defence. Uniacke gives the example of a hijacker who is holding hostages at gunpoint as human shields and picks off a police sharpshooter about to fire at him.[96] Such a person may act out of fear, may have a very strong, even an irresistible, desire to defend his life, but cannot plead self-defence. It is generally accepted that self-defence is not legally permissible against the necessary and proportionate self-defence by the victim of D's culpable attack.[97] To allow an aggressor the *right* to use self-defence against a person defending herself against an unjust attack is inconsistent with a fundamental justification for killing in self-defence, namely that an aggressor killed in self-defence has compromised his right not to be attacked. V, in turn, cannot both be justified in using necessary defensive force and at the same time be said to have forgone his right to be free of attack. Public policy, too, would seem to demand that an unjust aggressor not be entitled to plead self-defence. To not enforce such a limitation on the defence would imply that the State is willing to offer impunity to any unjust aggressor simply because her victim used force to defend himself.

This is not to say, however, that force, or a threat to use it, is necessarily unjust because it arises in the context of a broader enterprise of an unlawful nature. Unjust aggression against D may occur even where D herself is already engaged in criminal activity. Suppose, for example, that in the course of their committing a violent assault on an innocent victim, A, the principal offender, turns and begins to attack B, a co-offender (whom he perhaps perceives to be unwilling to enter fully into the assault in progress). In these circumstances, the fresh assault of A upon B is clearly *unjust* and there would seem no reason in principle why B should be deprived of the right to use necessary and proportionate force to defend against A's attack; regardless of his complicity in the original assault. The determinative questions are likely to be whether D has *foreseeably* and *wrongfully* created the circumstances in which he is endangered by

---

96   Uniacke, *Permissible Killing: The Self-Defence Justification of Homicide*, Cambridge, Cambridge University Press, 1994, 36.
97   See, for example, LaFave and Scott, *Criminal Law* (2nd ed), St Paul, Minnesota, West Publishing Co, 1986, 455, 459.

V,[98] and whether the danger is being posed by V's justified response to those wrongfully-created circumstances.

(3) Retreat

Under New Zealand law there is no absolute rule that a threatened person has a "duty to retreat", although failure to show an unwillingness to fight, or failure to take an opportunity of avoiding the use of force, will be relevant to the question whether the accused acted in reasonable self-defence. According to natural law theorists, such as Samuel von Pufendorf,[99] self-defence should always be tempered by restraint, and should be available as a last resort only when one's safety cannot otherwise be secured. However, even natural lawyers qualify this proposition. Pufendorf stated that a person is not required to flee imminent danger where this would expose the person to attack from behind. Neither, he suggested, is a person always *required* first to retreat rather than stand and fight, because to do so might weaken the position from which she is able to defend herself.

Pufendorf suggests another useful qualification. While the criterion that defensive force be necessary and proportionate does not mean that D must never expose himself to danger by simply going about his business, it does mean that if a person *impermissibly* courts a risk to his life, he cannot plead self-defence when it then comes to the point that he must kill to save himself. This implication was relevant in R v Savage,[100] where the accused, following extreme provocation by the deceased, but before the fatal incident, had asked another hotel patron for a knife. In a subsequent fist fight the deceased was stabbed fatally. In disallowing the appeal against conviction, the Court of Appeal stated:[101]

> "The law is that a threat which does not involve a present danger can normally be answered by retreating or adopting some other method of avoiding the present danger."

The Court of Appeal went on to say that:[102]

> "whether a person was justified in fighting or should have retreated depends on the jury's view of what was reasonable in the circumstances."

Rather than exercising restraint, D had sought out the very danger that he claimed in justification. His claim must therefore fail: D may not deliberately generate his own defence.[103]

At common law it had been held, in R v Julien, that while a person threatened need not "take to his heels and run",[104] it is necessary that he demonstrate that he is prepared to temporise and disengage and perhaps make some physical withdrawal. This approach aims to prevent the application of force wherever possible, and requires retreat, rather than force, as a first

---

98 Uniacke, *Permissible Killing: The Self-Defence Justification of Homicide*, Cambridge, Cambridge University Press, 1994, 84.
99 *De Officio Hominis et Civis Juxta Legem Naturalem Libri Duo* vol 2, New York, Oxford University Press, 1927, ch V, 3-36, cited in Uniacke, *Permissible Killing: The Self-Defence Justification of Homicide*, Cambridge, Cambridge University Press, 1994, 66.
100 R v Savage [1991] 3 NZLR 155 (CA). See 15.1.4.
101 R v Savage [1991] 3 NZLR 155 (CA), 158.
102 R v Savage [1991] 3 NZLR 155 (CA), 159.
103 Cf Robinson, "Causing the Conditions of One's Own Defense: A Study in the Limits of Theory in Criminal Law Doctrine" (1985) 71 Virginia Law Review 1.
104 See R v Julien [1969] 2 All ER 856; [1969] 1 WLR 839 (CA), 858; 843.

resort. However, in *R v McInnes*,[105] the English Court of Appeal qualified its earlier ruling in *Julien*, by holding that a direction on the requirement to retreat should not be in "too inflexible terms". The Court expressed its preference for the view that failure to retreat is only *an element* in the consideration upon which the reasonableness of an accused's conduct is to be judged. While, as noted earlier, there is no statutory duty to retreat in New Zealand, the approach taken in *McInnes* is relevant in this country also, in that failure either to show an unwillingness to fight or to take the opportunity to avoid using force will be relevant to the question whether the defendant acted in reasonable self-defence.[106] In *R v Terewi*,[107] for example, it was held that retreating from, or some other method of avoiding, a threatened danger will normally be appropriate where the threat does not involve immediately present danger. A proper jury direction would include a statement that ease of escape is one of the factors which the jury should consider when determining whether D's actions were reasonable in the circumstances.[108]

Despite all this, it appears that a person may still be justified in holding her ground, even when an opportunity for escape exists, where the aggressor is actively using a weapon and is in an aggressive and hostile mood. In *Dixon v Police*,[109] the victim had stood in front of the accused, who was standing on his front doorstep, and had swung a heavy electric flex at him. The accused had then struck the victim in the forearm with a knife. In holding that the appellant had acted reasonably in the circumstances as he believed them to be, the Court acknowledged that:[110]

> "He was being attacked by a man wielding a heavy electric cord which is not an ineffective weapon. He had a genuine belief he was in danger and I think rightly so."

However, while the Judge was no doubt justified in finding that the appellant genuinely believed himself to be in danger, it is arguable that the Judge may have misdirected himself by failing to give adequate consideration to the issue of necessity. The issue, as was noted above, is not just whether the force used was proportionate (arguably the case here) but also whether it was *necessary* or *unavoidable*. Yet on the facts of the case it apparently *was* avoidable, since the appellant had available the option of walking back into his house and shutting the door, thereby disengaging from the conflict. In these circumstances consideration of the related issue of proportionality becomes unnecessary, since the failure of the appellant to satisfy the requirements of necessity should have meant the defence was unavailable.

The facts of *Dixon* may for illustration be contrasted with those of the Canadian case of *R v Weshaver*,[111] in which failure to retreat was also held not to preclude the accused from relying on statutory self-defence. There the accused, who had been convicted on a charge of assault causing bodily harm, had struck the assailant three times with a heavy wooden doorstop. His appeal against conviction was allowed on the basis that the accused was being threatened by

---

105 *R v McInnes* [1971] 3 All ER 295; [1971] 1 WLR 1600 (CA), 300; 1607.
106 See also *R v Bird* [1985] 2 All ER 513; [1985] 1 WLR 816 (CA).
107 *R v Terewi* (1985) 1 CRNZ 623 (CA), 625.
108 *R v Whyte* [1987] 3 All ER 416; (1987) 85 Cr App R 283 (CA), 419; 286; *R v Savage* [1991] 3 NZLR 155 (CA).
109 *Dixon v Police* 13/2/86, Jeffries J, HC Palmerston North AP5/86, noted [1986] NZ Recent Law 233.
110 *Dixon v Police* 13/2/86, Jeffries J, HC Palmerston North AP5/86, noted [1986] NZ Recent Law 233, 234. See 15.1.4 generally and n 83.
111 *R v Weshaver* (1993) 17 CR (4th) 401 (SCC).

a powerful and aggressive adversary who had consumed a large quantity of alcohol and was in an uncontrollable rage. The Court held that no properly directed jury could have been satisfied beyond reasonable doubt that the accused had used more force than necessary to defend himself. It appears in that case that the requirement of necessity was satisfied, because there was no clear option available that would have enabled the appellant to disengage from the conflict. The force used was indispensable.

Clearly, failure to show an unwillingness to fight or to take an opportunity of avoiding the use of force may be relevant to the question whether the accused acted in reasonable self-defence. However, it has been acknowledged by the courts that seriousness, in terms of anticipated injury, is often a matter in the eye of the beholder.[112] It may be argued that a person cannot be blamed who, in an intuitive response to threatened violence, uses a degree of force that would have been unacceptable if there had been opportunity for cool reflection and careful deliberation. In a simple case like *Jenkins v Police*,[113] where the Court allowed that throwing a milk bottle at the feet of pursuing assailants was a reasonable response to the fear of further serious assault and a legitimate basis for claiming self-defence on a charge of disorderly behaviour, the principle is capable of a straightforward application. However, it is not an unqualified principle and, arguably, the more violent the response to the perceived aggression, the more carefully a jury will be required to look at whether the accused actually *believed* that the force was necessary against an unjust assault, or whether he *merely thought that there may be some future danger to him*.[114]

(4) Pre-emptive strike

The formal requirements for self-defence allow the use of force to resist or repel an unjust immediate threat. This does not necessarily imply, however, that the defender must have begun to experience an actual assault before the use of self-defensive force can be justified. In some circumstances the law allows the use of pre-emptive force to repel or disable the aggressor before he is able to mount an attack. The theoretical basis for allowing a pre-emptive strike is that the person who intends to launch an unjust attack and has armed himself for that purpose, is an aggressor even before having struck a blow.[115] It follows that such a person may also be resisted before the blow is struck. The critical question is, then, at what point may an intended victim use force to prevent an anticipated unlawful attack from occurring? On this point the law in most jurisdictions is unclear, although it now seems to be generally conceded that a pre-emptive strike is sometimes permissible, at least in principle.

Amongst the early natural law accounts of self-defence, Grotius takes the view that while the threatened injury must constitute "a present danger", "imminent in point of time", this condition may be fulfilled where there is a manifest intention to kill on the part of someone who takes up weapons.[116] Uniacke suggests that the condition could also be fulfilled where the victim of an ongoing or intermittent attack uses force against an aggressor who has paused to

---

112 *Jenkins v Police* (1986) 2 CRNZ 196, 198.
113 *Jenkins v Police* (1986) 2 CRNZ 196, 198.
114 *R v Savage* [1991] 3 NZLR 155 (CA).
115 Uniacke, *Permissible Killing: The Self-Defence Justification of Homicide*, Cambridge, Cambridge University Press, 1994, 70.
116 Grotius, *De Juri Belli et Pacis (The Rights of War and Peace)*, transl William Whewell, Cambridge, Parker, 1853, 61-68, cited in Uniacke, *Permissible Killing: The Self-Defence Justification of Homicide*, Cambridge, Cambridge University Press, 1994, 70.

reload a weapon, or has stumbled, or temporarily lost consciousness.[117] It is important to note that while Grotius appears to endorse the view that self-defence is sometimes permissible to anticipate an unlawful attack, he warns that in general *mere fear* does not give a right of killing for prevention.[118] The reason for this limitation is that where the danger is uncertain, or can otherwise be averted, recourse should be had to other means of avoidance (such as retreat) or to legal remedies. These limitations suggest that the right of pre-emptive strike is of limited application and should not be used as a mask for retaliation or as a means of resolving D's misplaced anxiety concerning a future, possible, or even imaginary attack. Because it is a representative form of self-defence, it must also be subject to the same essential elements: necessity and proportionality.

The case law on pre-emptive strike in New Zealand, although scanty, has laid down some clear limits to the doctrine. The issue appears first to have been considered by the Court of Appeal in *R v Terewi*.[119] There the Court cited with approval a passage in Glanville Williams' *Textbook on Criminal Law* to the effect that pre-emptive strike is allowable, subject to the qualification that the danger threatened must be or appear imminent.[120] This is consistent with the first of Grotius' suggested limitations. In *Terewi*, the Court emphasised that there was no general right of pre-emptive attack in self-defence; rather, any right of pre-emptive strike must exist only within the wider rule that the force used in self-defence must not exceed what is reasonable in the circumstances. Accordingly, we may state these limitations in terms of two broad conditions. Pre-emptive strike should not be allowed where:

(i) The danger is not imminent; or

(ii) Retreat or disengagement is a reasonable possibility.

The permissibility of pre-emptive strike has already been discussed in relation to *R v Ranger*.[121] There the Court of Appeal stated:

"If this accused did really think that the lives of herself and her son were in peril because the deceased, enraged after the struggle, might attempt to shoot them with a rifle near at hand, then it would be going too far, we think, to say that the jury could not entertain a reasonable doubt as to whether a pre-emptive strike with a knife would be reasonable force in all the circumstances."

In allowing the appeal and ordering a new trial, the Court emphasised that it was *the circumstances as the accused believed them to be* which were determinative whether the force used was reasonable.

The issue of pre-emptive strike also arose in *R v Wang*.[122] In that case, the accused had stabbed her husband to death while he was asleep in a drunken state after he had threatened to kill the accused and her sister and after threatening to blackmail another sister. The question on appeal

---

117 Grotius, *De Juri Belli et Pacis (The Rights of War and Peace)*, transl William Whewell, Cambridge, Parker, 1853, 61-68, cited in Uniacke, *Permissible Killing: The Self-Defence Justification of Homicide*, Cambridge, Cambridge University Press, 1994, 70.
118 Grotius, *De Juri Belli et Pacis (The Rights of War and Peace)*, transl William Whewell, Cambridge, Parker, 1853, 61-68, cited in Uniacke, *Permissible Killing: The Self-Defence Justification of Homicide*, Cambridge, Cambridge University Press, 1994, 70.
119 *R v Terewi* (1985) 1 CRNZ 623 (CA).
120 See Williams, *TBCL*, 503.
121 *R v Ranger* (1988) 4 CRNZ 6 (CA), 9. See 15.1.2(1).
122 *R v Wang* [1990] 2 NZLR 529; (1989) 4 CRNZ 674 (CA), 535; 679.

was whether the trial Judge was right to refuse to allow self-defence to go to the jury. The trial Judge had found that, having regard to the fact that the accused's husband was asleep and intoxicated, and that she was able to tie him up without waking him, "a reasonable person in her position had a number of alternative courses open to her". By implication, she was in no immediate danger and killing her husband could not be regarded as a reasonable course of action. Significantly, the trial Judge did not rule out the possibility that a pre-emptive strike, even with a knife, could in certain circumstances qualify for consideration as self-defence. Instead, he held that to accede to the accused's suggestion that such an action was justified in the present circumstances would have amounted to "a return to the law of the jungle". Even giving the jury every latitude in taking the most favourable view of the accused's honest, if mistaken, view of the circumstances, no jury could regard the accused's reaction as a reasonable one.

The Court of Appeal agreed, and for the same reasons as the trial Judge found that self-defence was not open to the appellant. Regarding the issue of pre-emptive strike, the Court held that what is reasonable force must depend on the *imminence* and *seriousness* of the threat, and upon the *opportunity to seek protection* without recourse to the use of force. If a person has alternative courses of action other than the use of force, and the threat by V cannot be carried out immediately, then it would be unacceptable to make a pre-emptive attack.

At the same time, the Court did not seek to generalise its refusal in *Wang*, and indeed approved the dictum of Lord Griffiths in *Beckford v R*, that "a man about to be attacked does not have to wait for his assailant to strike the first blow or fire the first shot: circumstances may justify a pre-emptive strike".[123] However, in order properly to reflect society's concern for the sanctity of human life, the Court concluded that where there has not been an assault, but merely a *threatened* assault, killing in self-defence or in defence of another can only be justified where there is an *immediate* prospect of *life-threatening violence*.

It would seem, therefore, that while pre-emptive strike may be permissible in certain circumstances, it cannot be used as a mask for revenge or retaliation. Neither may it be employed as a means of eliminating a future anticipated lethal attack that is not imminent in point of time and where other means of avoidance are available. Thus self-defence will not be a justification for criminal conduct where there was merely a threat that the offender or a third person would be harmed at some indeterminate future time by an unspecified person.[124]

There is no positive obligation on a judge to raise, in terms, the issue of a pre-emptive strike.[125] It will be sufficient that the judge, while not expressly referring to a pre-emptive strike, allows for the possibility in his or her direction, by asking the jury to consider, for example: "Was it a reasonable response to the total circumstances that he thought was confronting him?"[126] The issue for the jury will be whether it accepted the accused's account as to what she believed, and whether, on her belief, she acted reasonably, if pre-emptively, in self-defence.[127]

---

123 *Beckford v R* [1988] AC 130; [1987] 3 All ER 425 (PC), 144; 431.
124 Cf *R v Leuta* [2002] 1 NZLR 215, 220, where it was held that no properly instructed jury could entertain the possibility that stabbing an unarmed man in the chest, in response to a claimed threat to the appellant's life by someone yet to be hired as a contract killer, could amount to reasonable force.
125 *R v Hackell* 10/10/02, CA131/02, para 18, per Hammond J.
126 *R v Hackell* 10/10/02, CA131/02, para 19.
127 *R v Hackell* 10/10/02, CA131/02, para 20.

(5) Self-defence and battered women

One particularly troubling area, in which the issue of pre-emptive strike frequently arises, concerns situations where battered women have killed their sleeping spouses in circumstances where the victim does not pose an objective imminent threat to their life or safety. In some Canadian and United States jurisdictions, courts have been willing to extend the self-defence doctrine to cover these situations, on the grounds that a battered woman should not have to wait until a deadly attack occurs before she can act in self-defence.

Suppose the following scenario:

"D is a battered woman who has lived in an abusive relationship for a period of years. After a bout of drinking the abusing male partner, P, returns home and commences physically and mentally abusing D. P then announces that he is going to bed, or simply falls asleep in a drunken stupor on the couch, having previously warned D that he intends to 'deal' with her in the morning. D, by now emotionally and mentally exhausted, and fearing the prospect of another violent beating the next day, decides that the only way to deal with the problem is to kill P while he is unconscious and not presenting an immediate threat to her. She takes a kitchen knife and stabs P to death while he sleeps."

Is this self-defence? According to conventional self-defence theory the law must say no. The danger to D is not immediate in point of time, and it cannot be said that she is without recourse to other means of avoidance. She could, for example, leave the house, or even seek assistance from the police. Even granted that she is to be judged by the circumstances as she believes them to be, it is impossible to view her response as either *necessary*, in the sense of being unavoidable and indispensable, or *proportionate*, in the sense that a reasonable person in the accused's position would not have considered that the injury inflicted in avoiding the threatened harm was disproportionate.

Despite these implications of the conventional analysis, the approach of the Courts to this problem has varied significantly in different jurisdictions. In the now celebrated case of *R v Lavallee*,[128] the Supreme Court of Canada appeared to lend its weight to the notion of "battered woman syndrome", characterised by a condition of "learned helplessness", when allowing the appeal of a woman who had shot her abusive partner in the back of the head as he was leaving a room, after he had issued the challenge "either you kill me or I'll get you". The question on appeal (against the decision of the Manitoba Court of Appeal overturning the accused's acquittal) was whether there was sufficient evidence of self-defence, in the form of expert psychological evidence regarding "battered woman syndrome" ("BWS") to allow the defence to be put to the jury.

In allowing the appeal and reinstating the acquittal, the Supreme Court held that the definition of what was a reasonable response to the apprehension of death must sometimes be adapted to circumstances which are foreign to the hypothetical reasonable man. The Court held that, in light of the condition of the defendant, it might not be unreasonable to apprehend death or grievous bodily harm before the physical assault is in progress.

However, there are problems with this analysis. In giving more weight to the accused's subjective beliefs and to the somewhat imprecise concept of "learned helplessness", the Court

---

[128] *R v Lavallee* [1990] 1 SCR 852; (1990) 76 CR (3d) 329 (SCC).

appears to have overlooked, or at least heavily discounted, the formal requirements of necessity, proportionality, and an objectively imminent threat. Arguably, rather than applying existing law, it has tailored a new defence specific to battered women. The High Court of Australia emphasised the need for caution in the reception of testimony concerning BWS in *Osland v R*,[129] where Kirby J made the following observations which are pertinent to self-defence:

> "[BWS] is not a universally accepted and empirically established scientific phenomenon. Least of all does the mere raising of it, in evidence or argument, cast a protective cloak over an accused, charged with homicide, who alleges subjection to a long-term battering or other abusive relationship. No civilised society removes its protection to human life simply because of the existence of a history of long-term physical or psychological abuse. If it were so, it would expose to unsanctioned homicide a large number of persons who, in the nature of things, would not be able to give their version of the facts. The law expects a greater measure of self-control in unwanted situations where human life is at stake. It reserves cases of provocation and self-defence to truly exceptional circumstances. While these circumstances may be affected by contemporary conditions and attitudes, there is no legal carte blanche, including for people in abusive relationships, to engage in premeditated homicide."

Kirby J emphasised the importance, in cases where evidence about BWS might bear on the claim of self-defence, of focusing not on who the woman is but on what she did. His Honour endorsed the observation of L'Heureux-Dube J in *R v Malott* that:[130]

> "The legal inquiry into the moral culpability of a woman who is, for instance, claiming self-defence must focus on the *reasonableness* of her actions in the context of her personal experiences, and her experiences as a woman, not on her status as a battered woman and her entitlement to claim that she is suffering from 'battered woman syndrome'."

New Zealand courts have been slow to accommodate the claims of battered women within the rules of self-defence. In *R v Wang*,[131] the Court of Appeal rejected self-defence because the wife was not held hostage and was free to seek protection in other ways. The Court emphasised the need for "immediacy of life-threatening violence", in any case where an assault is merely threatened, to justify killing in self-defence.[132] Under New Zealand law the courts, when considering the use of pre-emptive force by battered women who kill their abusers, seem to be more inclined to ask whether there was a crystallised, immediate danger that needed to be averted by instant action. If the circumstances are such that no jury could entertain a reasonable doubt on the point, the defence should be withdrawn from the jury.[133]

Of course, the Court must still consider the circumstances believed by the accused to exist, when determining the reasonableness of the force used. Thus evidence that the accused suffered from BWS may be relevant in determining the imminence and degree of force that the accused might have anticipated, and also as part of a response to any suggestion that the

---

129 *Osland v R* (1998) 197 CLR 316; 159 ALR 170 (HCA), 375; 216.
130 *R v Malott* (1998) 155 DLR (4th) 513, 529.
131 *R v Wang* [1990] 2 NZLR 529; (1989) 4 CRNZ 674 (CA).
132 *R v Wang* [1990] 2 NZLR 529; (1989) 4 CRNZ 674 (CA), 539; 683.
133 See *R v Ranger* (1988) 4 CRNZ 6 (CA), 9; *R v Wang* [1990] 2 NZLR 529; (1989) 4 CRNZ 674 (CA), 535; 679.

accused should simply have left the victim.[134] However, the question whether her response was reasonable remains ultimately *objective*. By continually relating the issue of the accused's subjective belief back to an objective evaluation of the reasonableness of the force used in light of that belief, New Zealand's judges have sought to give proper weight to the requirements of necessity and proportionality, while not entirely ignoring the special claims presented by these cases.

(a)   A self-preservation defence?

Nonetheless, the question remains whether the existing self-defence rules are adequate to deal with the unique difficulties presented by cases of BWS. Indeed, it is doubtful whether they should be characterised as cases of self-defence at all, since the formal requirements of unjust aggression, imminence of threat, necessity, and proportionality seem to be lacking in each case. Yet this is one area where "conflicting moral and ideological forces [have driven] the law in [a] particular direction".[135] It might be preferable to think of these cases as situations of (say) *self-preservation*, which raise legal considerations different to those typically presented by cases of self-defence against immediate unjust aggression. Given the fact that cases of spousal killings involving BWS do not really fit happily within the conventional canons of self-defence, a case might even be made for the return to a form of the old common law plea of *se defendendo*, which provided for the concept of *excusable* homicide, a category of liability occupying a halfway house between total liability and total acquittal.[136] The plea operated by way of confession and avoidance; asserting *se defendendo* conceded the illegality of the killing, but sought to avoid the capital penalty, routine for ordinary cases of murder.[137] Applied in the context of BWS killings, the defence would be required to concede the illegality of the killing, but evidence of BWS could be adduced on the question whether the offender was fully culpable for the offence, in much the same way as evidence of "abnormality of mind" is used in the English defence of diminished responsibility to reduce murder to manslaughter.[138] It is interesting to observe that in *R v Gordon*,[139] where the appellant sought to introduce BWS as evidence supporting self-defence to a charge that she murdered her husband, the Court of Appeal noted that if New Zealand had had a statutory defence of diminished responsibility, the appellant would have been a candidate for it. Although self-defence failed in that case, and the murder conviction was upheld because of evidence that the appellant intended to kill her husband and had arranged for a "hit man" to do so, the judgment helpfully shows the unsatisfactory state of the law, which currently imposes a mandatory punishment for culpable homicide, even though it is acknowledged that the offender may not have been fully responsible for her crime.

It is submitted that there is room for acceptance of a new palliative defence of *excusable self-preservation*, supplementing the existing rules on self-defence, which would allow juries more latitude in dealing with spousal homicides involving BWS, and would overcome some of the

---

134   See *R v Oakes* [1995] 2 NZLR 673 (CA); also *R v Gordon* (1993) 10 CRNZ 430 (CA).
135   Fletcher, *A Crime of Self-Defense: Bernard Goetz and the Law on Trial*, New York, University of Chicago Press, 1988, 27.
136   Fletcher, "Defensive force as an act of rescue" in E Paul, F Miller Jr, and J Paul (eds), *Crime, Culpability, and Remedy*, Oxford, Basil Blackwell, 1990, 171.
137   Fletcher, "Defensive force as an act of rescue" in E Paul, F Miller Jr, and J Paul (eds), *Crime, Culpability, and Remedy*, Oxford, Basil Blackwell, 1990, 171.
138   Section 2 Homicide Act 1957 (UK).
139   *R v Gordon* (1993) 10 CRNZ 430 (CA).

anomalies created by the present law, without compromising the elements of statutory self-defence.

The New Zealand Law Commission considered the idea of enacting such a defence in its report on battered defendants.[140] Several versions of a "self-preservation" defence have been proposed, including an extended form of self-defence proposed by the Western Australia Task Force for Gender Violence and Tyrannicide.[141] The Western Australian proposal would have operated as a complete defence, extending and complementing traditional self-defence. By contrast,[142] the model of self-preservation discussed by the Law Commission was intended only as a partial defence to murder and would be available to:

"any woman causing the death of a person:

"(a) with whom she has, or had, a familial or intimate relationship; and

"(b) who has subjected her to racial, sexual and/or physical abuse and intimidation to the extent that she:

"(i) honestly believes there is no protection nor safety from the abuse; and

"(ii) is convinced the killing is necessary for her self preservation."

However, public reaction to the proposal was generally negative, either because it was considered unnecessary or because it was thought that a satisfactory defence would be too difficult to draft.

In its final report, the Law Commission concluded that, rather than creating a special complete defence for victims of domestic violence who kill or assault their abusers, it would be preferable to interpret reasonableness in self-defence to incorporate the use of force against violence that may not be imminent but where the force was necessary to save life or limb.[143] This move could be supplemented by relevant expert evidence regarding the nature and dynamics of battering relationships and the effects of battering, judicial directions, and other reforms proposed by the commission in order to overcome the difficulties presented by the traditional self-defence rules. Further, the Law Commission chose not to support the creation of a special partial defence because of its recommendation that the mandatory life sentence for murder be replaced with a sentencing discretion.[144]

---

140 See Law Commission, *Some Criminal Defences with Particular Reference to Battered Defendants*, NZLC R73, Wellington, 2001, 27.
141 See Law Commission, *Battered Defendants: Victims of Domestic Violence Who Offend*, NZLC PP41, Wellington, 2000, 22-25.
142 Unsurprisingly, the commission never seriously entertained the proposal for a defence of "tyrannicide". The difficulties that would be associated with proving a regime of private "tyranny" are considerable. For a full discussion of the theory of such a defence, see Cohen, "Regimes of private tyranny: What do they mean to morality and for the criminal law?" (1996) 57 U Pitt LR 757.
143 Law Commission, *Some Criminal Defences with Particular Reference to Battered Defendants*, NZLC R73, Wellington, 2001, 30.
144 Law Commission, *Some Criminal Defences with Particular Reference to Battered Defendants*, NZLC R73, Wellington, 2001, 30.

(6) Importance of imminence

The legal issues associated with pre-emptive strikes and battered women highlight a more general issue when assessing the reasonableness of self-defensive force: how important is it that the threat to which D responds be imminent?

Imminence is not a distinct formal requirement but rather an ingredient in the melting pot of reasonableness. It is simply the quality of being close at hand. As such, imminence is a measure of proximity; although, because self-defence depends on subjective personal perception (the facts as D believes them to be), imminence must also be measured, at least in part, by how close D *believed* the threatening event to be. Traditionally, the imminence of danger has been held to be a question of fact and degree and not a requirement of law.[145] Nevertheless, in deciding whether self-defence is legitimate, the issue of imminence may not be ignored but must be weighed together with the seriousness of the threat and opportunity to seek protection without resorting to the use of force. The sense of the present urgency of the threat is captured in the requirement that D must see herself (or the person being protected) as being in "real", or crystallised, danger — and not merely think that there may be some future danger to her.[146]

The law's insistence that the threat of danger be real, in the sense of close at hand and not merely anticipated in some general sense, has created difficulties in some cases where battered women have resorted to fatal violence to protect themselves against anticipated future violence from a violent and abusive partner. Because the danger faced by a battered woman is often characterised as "ongoing" rather than a "one-off" incident of violence, it is sometimes suggested that the concept of imminence is an inappropriate measure of the necessity to use force. For this reason, the Law Commission has recommended that s 48 be amended to make it clear that there can be circumstances in which the use of force is reasonable where the danger is not imminent but is inevitable.[147] The commission reasoned that, in many situations, the use of force will be reasonable only if the danger is immediate because the defendant will have an opportunity to avoid the danger and seek effective help: but this may not be the case where the defendant has been subject to ongoing physical abuse within a coercive intimate relationship and knows that further assaults are inevitable, even if help is sought and the immediate danger avoided.[148]

There is much to be said for this reasoning, in so far as imminence serves at least in part as an indicator of unavoidability when assessing self-defence, especially for pre-emptive strikes. Nonetheless, there are major difficulties with displacing the ingredient of imminence with a test of inevitability. First, there is the problem of ascribing juridical force to a concept so elusive as "inevitability". Whereas imminence is a measure of proximity, inevitability is a measure of moral certainty and, as such, a metaphysical not a temporal judgment. Risks of non-imminent harms are always contingent (at the very least, upon extraneous events) and uncertain, even in contexts where there is a previous history of violence. Many unforeseen events may intervene to prevent an anticipated remote harm from occurring, thus defeating the judgment of

---

145 *R v Wang* [1990] 2 NZLR 529; (1989) 4 CRNZ 674 (CA), 534-535; 680.
146 See *R v Savage* [1991] 3 NZLR 155 (CA).
147 Law Commission, *Some Criminal Defences with Particular Reference to Battered Defendants*, NZLC R73, Wellington, 2001.
148 Law Commission, *Some Criminal Defences with Particular Reference to Battered Defendants*, NZLC R73, Wellington, 2001, para 30.

inevitability. By contrast, it is precisely the element of propinquity between the threatened danger and the agent's response to that perceived danger that the policy of self-defence aims to capture; and moreover, to capture in a way that mediates between D's right of self-protection, V's right not to be harmed, and the risk that D may be mistaken. Any attempt to attenuate the urgent relationship between the agent's fear of harm and the threatener's crystallised ability to execute the threat subverts the character of the self-defence claim.

Consider the following example. D, the diminutive victim of an intoxicated bully's assaulting behaviour, stabs the victim to death while he is seated drinking and, at the time, showing no aggression. D's explanation for his actions, and the basis of his claim of self-defence, is that he knew the victim was violent and a bully and that it was "inevitable" that he would be beaten up "later on". Clearly, under current self-defence standards, such a claim of self-defence must fail because of the lack of imminence of life-threatening violence, lack of proportionality between the threat offered and the force used in self-defence, and the availability of other options to the accused. However, characterised as a claim based on the inevitability of future violence, who is to say that the offender's apprehension was not justified or the force used unreasonable in the circumstances that D perceived? How is inevitability to be measured? Is it sufficient to say that the defendant believed (subjectively) that a future assault was certain and, if so, how could the prosecution ever contradict such a claim? These questions reflect some of the difficulties to which a standard of inevitability would give rise.

For these reasons, it is submitted that imminence should remain an important consideration in self-defence and, in particular, that it should not be substituted by a standard of inevitability. Such a substitution would render self-defence a dangerously open-ended defence and would expose persons erroneously perceived to be aggressors to the risk of life-threatening violence without good cause.

15.1.5 Excessive force

In a sense, the law gives conflicting signals concerning the degree of force that is permissible in self-defence. On the one hand it states that the defence must fail if the force used by the accused is excessive. On the other hand, the courts will not "weigh to a nicety" what is reasonable defensive force.[149] However, the underlying principle would seem to be that because a person who repels an unjust attack is upholding the law, and as such is justified, where force used in self-defence is disproportionate to the threat offered, the defender himself acts unlawfully and may forfeit the protection that the law otherwise confers. Such a person is then liable for using an excess of force beyond that which the law allows. In New Zealand, authority for punishing excess force is provided by s 62 Crimes Act 1961, which indicates that wherever the law permits someone to use force, she is liable for the consequences of force used beyond that which the law allows. In *R v Godbaz*,[150] the Court of Appeal held that excessive force in repelling an assault was not protected by self-defence and itself constituted an assault. Thus, applying s 62 in a case where excessive force has been used in self-defence resulting in the death of the original aggressor, the offender will be liable for murder (unless she can avail herself of some other defence, such as provocation). For example, this may occur where the original aggressor (V) unjustly attacked D with fists, whereupon D responded by shooting V with a pistol.

---

149 See *Palmer v R* [1971] AC 814; [1971] 1 All ER 1077 (PC), 832; 1088.
150 *R v Godbaz* (1909) 28 NZLR 577 (CA).

To say that the force used was excessive is to say that D's response to the unjust attack was disproportionate to the threat it presented. In either case, D has proceeded beyond the status of a victim to become an aggressor and as such is liable for the consequences of his unlawful acts.[151] Of course, as we saw in 15.1.3, the test of excessive force is not *purely* objective (ie whether the force used was more than was in fact necessary). The issue under s 48 is whether the force used was (objectively) excessive in the circumstances as D (subjectively) believed them to be.[152]

In recent years, there have been moves in some jurisdictions to introduce, or reintroduce, a partial defence based on excessive self-defence in cases of murder. Typically, this partial defence would reduce the defendant's conviction from murder to manslaughter. In England, both the Criminal Law Revision Committee of England and Wales and the Law Commission (England and Wales) have in the past recommended the introduction of versions of an excessive self-defence rule into English law.[153] Introducing such a rule would deal with the problem, identified by some commentators, of the "all or nothing" quality of the decision in a murder case where self-defence is pleaded. It is argued that the introduction of a special defence would have the dual benefits of enabling convictions in cases where juries might otherwise return perverse or dubious acquittals and reductions in the gravity of homicide convictions where the defendant has substantial grounds for mitigation.[154]

The New Zealand Law Commission, in its preliminary paper on battered defendants, proposed a version of excessive self-defence based on the wording of s 48:[155]

> "It is a partial defence to a charge of murder (reducing the offence to manslaughter) if, in the defence of himself or herself or another, a person uses more force than it is reasonable to use in the circumstances as he or she believes them to be."

The suggested advantage of the defence was that it would recognise that a person who kills, believing wrongly that this is necessary in self-defence, would be less culpable than a person who kills with no such belief. A partial defence of excessive self-defence was thought to be capable of taking into account the subjective perception and motivation that prompted the defendant's action without abandoning the boundaries of acceptable conduct that society has a right to expect from all citizens.[156] However, in its later report the Law Commission resolved not to endorse the introduction of such a defence in New Zealand.[157] Although the commission

---

151 Uniacke notes that the designation "aggressor" can shift during the course of a conflict from the instigator to the other party, for example when the instigator publicly and sincerely attempts to withdraw, or to introduce peaceful negotiations aimed at settlement, and the victim then unreasonably continues the hostility: Uniacke, *Permissible Killing: The Self-Defence Justification of Homicide*, Cambridge, Cambridge University Press, 1994, 71.
152 Cf *R v Edgar* (2000) 142 CCC (3d) 401, 416 (Charron JA).
153 See Criminal Law Revision Committee, *Offences Against the Person*, 14th report, Cmnd 7844, London, HMSO, 1980, recommendation 73, 138; Law Commission (England and Wales), *A Criminal Code for England and Wales*, Law Com No 177, London, HMSO, 1989, 68. The text of both versions is reproduced in Law Commission, *Some Criminal Defences with Particular Reference to Battered Defendants*, NZLC R73, Wellington, 2001, 21, 22. The Law Commission for England and Wales did not, however, recommend a specific separate defence in its 2004 report, *Partial Defences to Murder*, Law Com No 290, part 4, mainly for the reason that its proposed reformulation of the provocation defence would, it thought, "be the simplest and most effective way of ameliorating the deficiencies of the present law", para 4.30.
154 See Editorial, "What should be done about the law of self-defence?" [2000] Crim LR 417.
155 Law Commission, *Battered Defendants: Victims of Domestic Violence Who Offend*, NZLC PP41, Wellington, 2000, 18-21.

was sympathetic to the case for recognising the partial defence, ultimately it chose instead to endorse a sentencing discretion for murder. The commission preferred that approach because of its more general ability "to accommodate the many and various situations when a lesser culpability in intentional homicide should be recognised".[158]

15.1.6 Proving self-defence

Where evidence has been adduced by the defence or the prosecution which establishes a credible or plausible narrative which might lead a jury to entertain the reasonable possibility of self-defence, the defence must be put to the jury.[159] This obligation pertains even where the offender does not rely on self-defence or has expressly disavowed the defence. However, a Judge may properly direct the jury to ignore the possibility of self-defence if it is not a reasonable possibility arising from the evidence and is simply speculation.[160] But in deciding the threshold issue of whether there is a credible or plausible narrative, a judge must avoid making factual findings which are properly in the domain of the jury.[161] For a trial judge to say, in deciding whether self defence should be put to the jury that "[i]t had to be put to the complainant that he was acting in an aggressive way towards your man before he could even justifiably raise self-defence", fails to reflect the "subtle and complex" character of self-defence.[162] Where such a rationale is used as a basis for refusing to allow self defence to go before a jury, particularly where some evidential base for the defence has been laid, the Court on appeal may find that the refusal results in a miscarriage of justice.[163] It is for the Crown to prove beyond reasonable doubt that at the time of the force used the accused was not acting in self-defence. Thus it will not be a misdirection for the judge to direct the jury to consider "whether the Crown have excluded, as a *reasonable possibility*, that the accused was acting in self defence".[164]

Sometimes self-defence may be claimed in circumstances where there may be no direct evidence of circumstances justifying the use of self-defensive force, yet the defendant believed he was subject to a threat of death or grievous bodily harm and that he was acting in self-defence. In such situations, where evidence of necessary defensive force is objectively weak, evidence of a complainant's convictions may be relevant in order to substantiate a claim of self-defence. The courts have observed that convictions for violent crimes can suggest a propensity for violence and that knowledge of a complainant's violent disposition in relevant circumstances may be helpful to the jury in assessing the veracity of an accused person's claim to self-defence.[165]

---

156 Law Commission, *Battered Defendants: Victims of Domestic Violence Who Offend*, NZLC PP41, Wellington, 2000, 20.
157 Law Commission, *Some Criminal Defences with Particular Reference to Battered Defendants*, NZLC R73, Wellington, 2001, 25-26.
158 Law Commission, *Some Criminal Defences with Particular Reference to Battered Defendants*, NZLC R73, Wellington, 2001, 26.
159 *R v Tavete* [1988] 1 NZLR 428; (1987) 2 CRNZ 579 (CA). See also *R v Grayson* 4/7/05, CA436/04, para 18, per Potter J.
160 See *R v Winterburn* 8/10/98, CA30/98.
161 *R v Ronaki* 13/5/04, CA451/03.
162 *R v Miller* 16/6/06, CA26/06, per Priestly J.
163 *R v Miller* 16/6/06, CA26/06, para 24, per Priestly J.
164 *R v van der Hulst* 18/5/06, CA469/05 para 9, per Pankhurst J.
165 *R v Davis* [1980] 1 NZLR 257 (CA); *R v Farquhar* 20/3/06, CA4/06.

In directing on self-defence it will be a misdirection for a trial judge to say that where there are two quite different accounts of the event, that it is up to the jury to sort out where the truth lies. It is not the jury's task to work out who to believe. Its task is to decide whether the Crown had proved its case to the requisite standard.[166] However, such a misdirection will not necessarily amount to a miscarriage of justice, provided further adequate directions preceded the contested direction and the judge has properly directed the jury on the onus of proof. The issue is whether the jury has been left in no doubt about their role and the role of the Crown.[167]

15.2 Defence of property

The traditional response of the common law to the right of an individual to protect his property is reflected in the following statement:[168]

> "the house of every one is to him as his castle and fortress, as well for his defence against injury and violence, as for his repose."

The maxim, "an Englishman's home is his castle", survives today in common speech and is a principle still recognised by the courts.[169] In *McLorie v Oxford*,[170] Donaldson LJ observed that the rule is subject to exceptions, but that they are few; even in the context of search and seizure, it is for the police to justify a forcible entry. As his Honour said:[171]

> "Such is the importance attached by the common law to the relative inviolability of a dwelling house that we cannot believe that there is a common law right without warrant to enter one either in order to search for instruments of crime, even of serious crime, or in order to seize such an instrument which is known to be there. Certainly if there were, we would expect it to be reflected in the books and it is not."

Generally, the right to defend property reflects the commonsense notion that a person who owns or has an interest in land as an occupier should have the right forcibly to remove an intruder, even though the force used may otherwise be an assault. The cases, for the most part, fall into two categories: (a) where an occupier uses force to prevent the entry of an intruder, who may or may not be known to the occupier; and (b) where the occupier seeks to prevent an unlawful intrusion upon his rights by agents of the State (including police, customs, or immigration officers). At the heart of the "right" to defend property is the interest of civilised society in upholding and protecting the legal institution of ownership, which itself implies the right to exclude all others lacking a legal interest from that property, either with the assistance of the State or by resort to self-help. Similarly, the law grants security of possession to a possessor, including the right to exclude all others, save perhaps the owner, from entry to the property possessed.

The issue of defence of property brings into focus a difficult question of how to balance the interests of the community in peace and good government, and the interests of a private occupier in protecting his personal space. In general, the balance is found by distinguishing

---

166 *R v Boardman* 29/10/03, CA173/03, para 12.
167 *R v Boardman* 29/10/03, CA173/03, para 14.
168 *Semayne's Case* (1604) 5 Co Rep 91a; 77 ER 194, 91b; 195.
169 *R v Stanley* (1977) 36 CCC (2d) 216, 226; *Morris v Beardmore* [1981] AC 446; [1980] 2 All ER 753 (HL).
170 *McLorie v Oxford* [1982] QB 1290; [1982] 3 WLR 423, 1296; 427.
171 *McLorie v Oxford* [1982] QB 1290; [1982] 3 WLR 423, 1298; 429.

between using force to *claim* property, and using force to *defend* property already in D's possession. Blackstone expressed the basic philosophy of the law in these terms:[172]

> "the public peace is a superior consideration to any one man's private property; and as, if individuals were once allowed to use private force as a remedy for private injuries, all social justice must cease, the strong would give law to the weak, and every man would revert to a state of nature: for these reasons it is provided, that this natural right of recaption shall never be exerted, where such exertion must occasion strife and bodily contention, or endanger the peace of society."

Normally, in respect of both movable and real property, disputes should be resolved by the courts rather than by resort to self-help. However, where there is an imminent danger of damage to or loss of property or possession at the hands of a wrongdoer, the courts may be unable to provide the relief needed in time, and the occupier/owner of property may find herself so placed that the exigencies of the situation demand immediate action to protect the interests threatened. What should be the response of the law in such circumstances?

The law recognises the paramountcy of human life and safety, even for a wrongdoer, over the security of another's property. For this reason, the provisions in the Crimes Act 1961 governing defence of property, as we shall see, generally limit the use of force in protecting property to that which does not actually cause bodily harm to the trespasser.[173] The only exception to this rule concerns the defence of a dwellinghouse, whereby a person in "peaceable possession of a dwellinghouse" may use "such force as is *necessary*" to prevent the forcible breaking and entering into the house.[174] The reasons for this exception will be discussed below. More generally, the rationale for limiting the permissible use of force to protect property is expressed in the following passage:[175]

> "the life of a man is a thing precious and favoured in law; so that although a man kills another in his defence, or kills one *per infortun*, without any intent, yet it is a felony, and in such a case he shall forfeit his goods and chattels for the great regard which the law has to a man's life."

Similarly, while no longer asserting that people have quite so absolute a right to life, when drafting the provisions of the Draft Code of 1879,[176] the Criminal Code Bill Commissioners were concerned to ensure that the Code reflected the proposition that force used in defence of person, liberty, or property against illegal violence must be proportionate to the injury or mischief which it is intended to prevent.[177] It followed that the use of lawful force was subject to the restriction that the force used was necessary, that is to say that the mischief sought to

---

172 Morrison (ed), *Blackstone's Commentaries on the Laws of England (1765-1769)*, London, Cavendish Publishing Ltd, 2001, vol 3, ch I, 5.
173 See, for example, ss 52 (defence of movable property against trespasser), 53 (defence of movable property with claim of right), and 56 (defence of land or building).
174 Section 55 Crimes Act 1961 (emphasis added).
175 *Semayne's Case* (1604) 5 Co Rep 91a; 77 ER 194, 91b; 195.
176 Criminal Code Bill Commission, *Report of the Royal Commission Appointed to Consider the Law Relating to Indictable Offences: With an Appendix Containing a Draft Code Embodying the Suggestions of the Commissioners*, London, Eyre & Spottiswode for HMSO, 1879, C-2345. The Draft Code was the basis of the Criminal Code Act 1893 and of subsequent enactments of the Crimes Act.
177 Criminal Code Bill Commission, *Report of the Royal Commission Appointed to Consider the Law Relating to Indictable Offences: With an Appendix Containing a Draft Code Embodying the Suggestions of the Commissioners*, London, Eyre & Spottiswode for HMSO, 1879, C-2345, 44.

be prevented could not be prevented by less violent means.[178] This principle still informs the current approach of the law in this area.

15.2.1 Structure of the current New Zealand law

The present New Zealand law concerning defence of property has remained largely unchanged since 1893, when the Criminal Code Act was first enacted. The relevant statutory provisions, now contained in ss 52-56 Crimes Act 1961, have been subject to minimal revision over the last 100 years. It is arguable that the present law is unnecessarily cumbersome and complex, with five sections dealing with defence of property, and three devoted exclusively to defence of movable property. In addition, the legislation makes separate provision for the peaceable entry on any land or buildings and the right to exercise a right of way.[179] The law could surely be rendered in a more compendious and simple form, consistent with the reforms that have significantly simplified the law on self-defence. However, the relative dearth of reported cases where the defence of property has been judicially considered would suggest that this is not a controversial area of law and that, despite their relative complexity, the provisions are readily applied.

15.2.2 Defence of land or building and defence of movable property: ss 52, 53, 56

Because of the common limitations on the use of force which apply to these sections, it is convenient to deal with them together. The defence provided in ss 52, 53, and 56 allows everyone "in peaceable possession of any movable thing" (ss 52 and 53) or "land or building" (s 56) to use "reasonable force" to defend such property provided the force used does not include striking or doing bodily harm to the trespasser.

Taking as representative of these the defence of movable property, allowed by s 52, the section contains four elements. This means that before an accused can benefit from it, the jury must at least have a doubt about all four. If a jury is convinced beyond any reasonable doubt that any one element is missing the defence must fail.[180] The four elements are:

(i) The accused must be in possession of a movable thing.

(ii) His possession must be *peaceable*.

(iii) He may use *reasonable force* to resist the taking of the thing by a trespasser, or to retake the thing from any trespasser.

(iv) He may not *strike* or *do bodily harm* to the trespasser.

"Movable property" is not defined in the Act but would seem to encompass tangible personal property. Although the section is silent on the point, it is submitted that a subjective standard is be applied in determining whether the nature of the situation that is claimed to justify the use of reasonable force does justify it; thus if D honestly believes V is a trespasser and meets the other criteria of the subsection, the actions taken by D in defence of property will be justified.

---

178 Criminal Code Bill Commission, *Report of the Royal Commission Appointed to Consider the Law Relating to Indictable Offences: With an Appendix Containing a Draft Code Embodying the Suggestions of the Commissioners*, London, Eyre & Spottiswode for HMSO, 1879, C-2345, 11.
179 Sections 57 and 58 Crimes Act 1961.
180 See *R v Born with a Tooth* (1992) 76 CCC (3d) 169 (CA), 177.

(1) *"Reasonable force"*

Assuming the accused honestly believes the circumstances are such that some force is justified, the force used to resist the trespasser must be objectively reasonable. It will not be enough that the accused *herself* thought the force used was reasonable, if an ordinary person in the same circumstances as the accused perceives would not have used that degree of force.[181] As a general rule, in a jury trial it will be for the jury to determine whether the force used was reasonable (or whether there is at least reasonable doubt about this).[182] So if D, resisting what she rightly believes to be an attempt to execute an invalid search warrant, pushes V, a police constable, in the chest, that will not be an unreasonable use of force.[183] Further, some degree of manhandling may well come within the definition of reasonable force if a person has already been requested to leave, provided the trespasser is neither struck nor injured.[184] The force used must be reasonable. There is some authority for the view that the pointing of a gun by a physically weak person may be justifiable to prevent the taking of property,[185] although firing at a person to prevent him from taking the property would probably constitute an unreasonable use of force, whether or not the trespasser is injured.[186] Depending on the circumstances, when taking back something from a trespasser, it may be necessary for D to request its return before using force.[187]

The Canadian equivalent of s 52 contains a provision that where a person in peaceable possession of personal property lays hands on it, a trespasser who persists in attempting to keep it or take it from him will be deemed to have committed an assault without justification or provocation.[188] Although the New Zealand section does not contain the same provision in express terms, it is arguably an implicit element. Where an issue of defence of property has degenerated into physical conflict between the trespasser and the person in possession, the continued unlawful attempts by the trespasser to gain possession may become a criminal assault against which the possessor may use reasonable force in self-defence.[189] This situation was contemplated by the drafters of the Draft Code, who said:[190]

> "If the trespasser resists, and in so doing assaults the party in possession, that party may repel the assault and for that purpose may use any force which he would be justified in using in defence of his person."

It is submitted that this statement reflects the current law.

---

181 *R v Wang* [1990] 2 NZLR 529; (1989) 4 CRNZ 674 (CA), 534; 679.
182 See *R v Ranger* (1988) 4 CRNZ 6 (CA), 9.
183 *Galvin v Police* 22/4/86, Bisson J, HC Rotorua M44/85.
184 See *Deans v Police* 5/3/87, Holland J, HC Christchurch AP7/87.
185 See Greenspan (ed), *Martin's Annual Criminal Code 1997*, Aurora, Ontario, Canada Law Book Co, 1996, CC/83.
186 See *R v Baxter* (1975) 27 CCC (2d) 96 (Ont CA); also *R v Figueira* (1982) 63 CCC (2d) 409 (Ont CA).
187 *Goundan v Police* 28/5/99, Durie J, HC Wellington AP97/99. Cf *Deans v Police* 5/3/87, Holland J, HC Christchurch AP7/87: in a case under s 56, it is unreasonable force to manhandle a person who has not first been asked to leave.
188 Section 38(2) Criminal Code (Can).
189 Section 48 Crimes Act 1961.
190 Criminal Code Bill Commission, *Report of the Royal Commission Appointed to Consider the Law Relating to Indictable Offences: With an Appendix Containing a Draft Code Embodying the Suggestions of the Commissioners*, London, Eyre & Spottiswode for HMSO, 1879, 45.

(2) No "striking" or "bodily harm"

In *Hastings v Police*,[191] D had been convicted of assault following an incident when he went to reclaim a motorcycle wheel that V had rebuilt for him. When he went to collect the wheel, D took the view that the amount charged for the work done was too high. D, who was by then in possession of the wheel, attempted to tender a sum that he considered was reasonable for what was done. V refused to let him leave until the full sum demanded had been paid. Physical contact ensued, during which D thrust his elbow into V's chest, knocking him backwards. This was done to prevent V from reasserting control over the wheel.

On appeal, Priestley J held that the trial Judge had been wrong to reject D's defence. In particular, his Honour found that although the intentional contact between the parties amounted to an assault, it did not constitute a "strike" for the purposes of s 52. While a push or a shove *can* reach a level at which it might constitute a striking, that is an issue of proportionality, the threshold of which was not reached by the shove or push from D's elbow. Neither, the Court found, was the force used by D unreasonable. On this basis D should have been entitled to the defence contained in s 53. His conviction was quashed.

There is no direct authority on the meaning of "do bodily harm" in s 52. However, case law on the meaning of "actual bodily harm" may be relevant. "Actual bodily harm" comprises any type of injury, however minor or temporary, though more than transient or trifling,[192] which is calculated to interfere with the health or comfort of the complainant.[193] In *R v McArthur*,[194] McMahon J held that a victim could not be said to be "injured" when there was no evidence of broken bones, cuts, lacerations, or bruising.

Although the provisions clearly allow the use of *some* physical force, the degree of permissible force used must necessarily be minimal if it excludes such injuries as cuts and (non-trivial) bruising, and if it must also fall short of any "striking". It may be that the only types of force contemplated by the sections are minor technical assaults in the nature of pushing, or the confrontational standing of one's ground to physically prevent the trespasser achieving his object. The Criminal Code Commissioners suggested that the defence of possession of either goods or land against a mere trespass does not, strictly speaking, justify even a breach of the peace: the party in lawful possession "may justify gently laying his hands on the trespasser and requesting him to depart".[195] However, even this attempt partially to stipulate the ambit of the defence in advance may be unhelpful, since the availability of the defence will depend on the facts of each case. It is possible, for example, that even a mild push or the threat to use force could be unreasonable, when a simple request might have persuaded the trespasser to leave the premises or to desist from asserting a claim to property. In the absence of a striking or an infliction of bodily harm, whether the force used was permissible will ultimately depend upon what the tribunal of fact considered was reasonable in the circumstances of the case.[196]

---

191 *Hastings v Police* 19/7/01, Priestley J, HC Whangarei AP24/01.
192 *R v Donovan* [1934] 2 KB 498 (CCA), 509.
193 *R v Miller* [1954] 2 QB 282; [1954] 2 All ER 529. See also *R v Dawson* (1985) 81 Cr App R 150; [1985] Crim LR 383 (CA) (emotional disturbance not itself actual bodily harm but shock causing physical harm is).
194 *R v McArthur* [1975] 1 NZLR 486, 487.
195 Criminal Code Bill Commission, *Report of the Royal Commission Appointed to Consider the Law Relating to Indictable Offences: With an Appendix Containing a Draft Code Embodying the Suggestions of the Commissioners*, London, Eyre & Spottiswode for HMSO, 1879, 45. See also *De Lambert v Ongley* [1924] NZLR 430.

(3) "Peaceable possession"

Another element common to the defences in ss 52-56 is the requirement that the person defending be in "peaceable possession" of the property concerned. The meaning of the phrase does not appear to have been considered directly by a New Zealand court. However, it is thought that "peaceable possession" need not be lawful possession. It suffices that the accused has actual control of the property.[197] In Canada, "peaceable possession" has been held to mean a possession hitherto not seriously challenged by others.[198] In *R v Born with a Tooth*,[199] the appellant together with a group of Peigan Indians had confronted police and environmental officers who had crossed land occupied by the Indians, in order to repair a dyke on land that had been surrendered to the Alberta Government. The appellant's defence to a charge of pointing a rifle at police officers was that he was in peaceable possession of the land and that the officers had not given reasonable notice of their intention to come on the land. He claimed he was entitled to use reasonable force to eject the trespassers. Because a proper explanation of the defence had not been put to the jury, the Court allowed the appeal and ordered a new trial. However, the Court observed that the demand that possession be "peaceable" greatly limits the defence. It is not enough for an accused to show that he kept the peace while on the land. Peaceable possession means that the possession has not provoked a breach of the peace[200] and that it is acquiesced in by all other persons.[201] For the purposes of the Code, it was held to mean a possession not seriously challenged by others before the incident in question. The key to peaceable possession is whether the possession is such, and the challenge to it is such, that the situation is unlikely to lead to violence.[202]

(4) "Claim of right"

An element common to the defences in ss 53 and 54, and specifically exempted in s 54, is the requirement that there be peaceable possession of a movable thing with "claim of right". Claim of right is not defined in the Crimes Act 1961. However, it is generally thought that the expressions "colour of right" and "claim of right" are synonymous, and that in defining "colour of right" the statute also defines "claim of right".[203] If so, in the context of ss 53 and 54, claim of right requires an honest belief that D's possession is justified and encompasses not only a belief in a state of facts which would at law justify or excuse the possession, but also a belief

---

196 But see *R v Dupuis* [1974] RL 379 (Que Prov Ct), where a restaurant owner threw an 11-year-old boy out of his establishment, the boy having made a nuisance of himself. The boy fell and broke his wrist, yet it was held the force used was reasonable. See also *Marguson v Grant* (1921) 57 DLR 710 (CA): a woman who refused to quit the defendant's premises on request suffered a wrenched arm when turned out by the defendant. Use of force held not unreasonable.
197 *Adams*, CA56.02 (looseleaf). See also *Paxhaven Holdings Ltd v A-G* [1974] 2 NZLR 185; *Foster v Warblington Urban Council* [1906] 1 KB 648; [1904-07] All ER Rep 366 (CA).
198 *R v Born with a Tooth* (1992) 76 CCC (3d) 169 (CA).
199 *R v Born with a Tooth* (1992) 76 CCC (3d) 169 (CA).
200 See Stephen, *A History of the Criminal Law of England*, vol III, London, Macmillan, 1883, 13.
201 *Black's Law Dictionary* (6th ed) St Paul, Minnesota, West Publishing Co, 1990.
202 *R v Born with a Tooth* (1992) 76 CCC (3d) 169 (CA), 178. See also Law Reform Commission of Canada, report no 30, Ottawa, 1987, 35.
203 *Adams* (2nd ed), para 48. For discussion of "colour of right", see 19.4.2. The Crimes Amendment Bill (No 6) 1999 proposes to replace "colour of right" with "claim of right" throughout the Act. The resulting definition would be similar to that currently given to "colour of right" except that "justifiable" will be replaced by "lawful". The proposed new definition is consistent with the interpretation of the term in *Singh v Police* 22/2/00, Williams J, HC Auckland A185/99.

based on ignorance or mistake of law. The test is a purely subjective test, of the honesty of D's claim. In *Murphy v Gregory*,[204] Henry J said:

> "Where an accused person really believes he has the right asserted, it is a good defence even if he is mistaken both in fact and in law … It is for the prosecution to prove there was no colour of right. If a prisoner puts forward, however wrongheadedly, an honest claim of right, he ought to be acquitted."

As *Murphy v Gregory* indicates, even a "wrongheaded" claim of right will suffice: thus the "claim of right" requires only an honest belief that D has a lawful right to do what she is doing, not a belief in a right that is actually recognised by law.[205] However, an honest belief that the accused had a *moral* right to act as she did, as opposed to an honest belief in a *legal* right, will not suffice.[206] So if D, seeking to prevent police officers from seizing his car as evidence in a hit and run accident in which D was not involved, asserts that such a seizure may occur only "in the hours of daylight", his honest, albeit wrongheaded, belief would constitute a claim of right and may underwrite his defence to a charge of obstruction arising out of his refusal to let an officer enter the car at 9 pm for the purposes of removing it into police custody. If, on the other hand, he asserts that, whatever the powers of the police, they ought not to be allowed to take the car "because he had paid for it", that would constitute a claim of moral right which is no defence.

In the example above, where D has a valid claim of right, D has not simply made a mistake of law, which would be no excuse (as s 25 makes clear).[207] This is because his mistake is not about the specific law of the offence with which he is charged (ie obstruction). Rather, the mistake relates to the general enforcement powers of a constable, which forms the backdrop of his defence, and not to an element of the offence of obstruction. Thus, in our view, the situation in our example is distinguishable from the facts of *Van Gaalen v Police*.[208] In that case, the Court of Appeal held that s 53 could not create a defence to a charge of assaulting a traffic officer under s 63(1) Transport Act 1962. The Court held that to give effect to s 53 in the circumstances in which the appellant had grabbed the traffic officer to prevent him from removing the rotor arm from his car's engine, would defeat the intention of Parliament to empower officers to take appropriate steps where necessary to immobilise vehicles for reasons of public safety. By contrast, in the example above, it is precisely in such circumstances that s 53 is designed to provide protection to someone seeking to protect his interests in private property. Since the context did not involve any issues of public safety, it could not be claimed that D's assertion of the statutory defence defeated the legislative intention inherent in the offence of obstruction. Indeed, it is arguable that in the circumstances contemplated by our example, the interests of the police in law enforcement and the interests of D in protecting his property are evenly matched. The issue for the Court should then simply be to determine whether it is satisfied beyond reasonable doubt that all the elements of the defence are present. Only if it is convinced beyond reasonable doubt that one or more of the elements are missing should D be convicted.[209]

---

204 *Murphy v Gregory* [1959] NZLR 868, 872. See also *R v Bernhard* [1938] 2 KB 264; [1938] 2 All ER 140 (CA); *Wicks v Police* (1984) 1 CRNZ 328; *Brown and Edney v Police* (1984) 1 CRNZ 576.
205 *Walden v Hensler* (1987) 163 CLR 561; 75 ALR 173 (HCA).
206 See *R v Hemmerly* (1976) 30 CCC (2d) 141 (Ont CA); *Harris v Harrison* [1963] Crim LR 497 (PC).
207 See further chapter 14 (mistake of law).
208 *Van Gaalen v Police* [1979] 2 NZLR 204 (CA).

15.2.3 Defence of dwellinghouse: s 55

The elements of the defence defined in s 55 are different to those in the other sections. They are as follows:

(i) The accused must be in possession of a *dwellinghouse*.

(ii) His possession must be peaceable.

(iii) He may use force to prevent forcible breaking and entry of the dwelling.

(iv) The force used must be *necessary* for that purpose.

(v) He must believe on *reasonable and probable grounds* that there is no lawful justification for the breaking and entry.

Of note under this section is the fact that the peaceful possessor may use *necessary* (not just reasonable) force to prevent forcible entry. The use of "necessary" without any words of qualification implies a subjective standard (ie what the accused considered was necessary). Unlike s 48, there is no statutory requirement that the force used be reasonable. It is implicit, however, that the force must be necessary *for the specified purpose*, ie to prevent the break-in and for no other reason. For example, if D, exercising lawful force to prevent V from breaking into his home, then inflicted a severe beating on V in order to punish him for upsetting the tranquillity of D's otherwise peaceful existence, the beating clearly would be unnecessary and that element of the defence would not be established. D would be liable to prosecution for assault to the extent that the injury inflicted during the beating exceeded what was necessary to prevent the break-in.[210] Indeed, in R v Frew[211] Tipping J held that although the expression used in s 55 is not "*reasonably* necessary", that may nonetheless be the effect of the provision. His Honour doubted whether any difference was intended between the "reasonable" force in s 56 and the "necessary" force in s 55. He did not, however, attempt to offer any guidance on the question of what constituted necessary force.

In our view, the question of the correct categorisation of the standard to be applied in determining whether force is necessary (ie whether it is objective or subjective) is of some importance. The pattern of s 55 is not similar to that of the amended s 48.[212] There is, we submit, no warrant for importing an objective standard of liability into a penal statute in the absence of a clear justification for doing so. In the absence of qualifying words the Legislature must be presumed to have intended to differentiate between ss 55 and 56 by imposing an objective test of force in one context but not in the other. In the circumstances, given the lack of clarity in the statute, "necessary" should be given its natural meaning of "needful to be done", which is, with respect, an eminently subjective determination. This approach also makes sense in the context of the provision itself. Once the occupier has determined, reasonably, that the breaking and entering is unlawful, she may use whatever force is "needful" to prevent the breaking and entering from occurring or continuing, subject to her considering whether the mischief could be prevented by less violent means. Failure to assess whether a less violent solution was available could be evidence from which the tribunal of fact may infer that the accused did not really believe the force used was necessary at all. But at all points the inquiry

---

209 See R v Frew [1993] 2 NZLR 731; (1992) 9 CRNZ 445, 734; 448.
210 See s 62 Crimes Act 1961.
211 R v Frew [1993] 2 NZLR 731; (1992) 9 CRNZ 445, 736; 451.
212 See *Adams*, CA55.01 (looseleaf).

should be a subjective one, which does not depend on inquiring whether a reasonable person in the shoes of the accused would have considered the force necessary.

Although the statute does not attempt to define what counts as necessary force, as a matter of general principle the force used in defence of the dwelling must be proportionate to the mischief sought to be prevented, and must be such that the mischief could not be prevented by less violent means.[213] The question of the nature and degree of force permissible in the defence of a dwellinghouse was considered in *R v Frew*.[214] There the accused was charged with wounding with intent to injure. After having been burgled, and anticipating the return of the burglars, he hid in his house with two loaded guns. When the burglars returned, D, without warning, shot one of them in the knee. At a police interview he claimed that he was trying to stop the burglars, retrieve stolen property, and make the house safe for his children. At the trial the Crown sought to have the accused's defence under s 55 withdrawn from the jury on the basis that no jury properly directed could see the accused's actions as being "to prevent" the forcible breaking and entering of the dwellinghouse.

The Court observed that it is only within the time-frame between when the forcible breaking and entering begins and ends that the person in peaceable possession can logically take action to prevent such breaking and entering. It held that, whereas in the crime of burglary the entry may be complete upon "penetration" (of the house), the same analysis cannot apply to breaking and entering under s 55: "to hold that the breaking and entering was already complete at [the point of penetration] would be to rob s 55 of most of its intended effect. It would put a quite unreal premium on the precise timing of the force used by the householder."[215] The Judge then directed the jury that at the time the shot was fired, the breaking and entering was still occurring and, subject to the other constraints in the section, the accused was entitled to use force to prevent its continuance. He concluded that the section was not limited to repelling intended burglars from entering, but included the prevention of their continuing with the burglary after having entered.

15.2.4 Reform

In *R v Frew*, Tipping J observed that the ground covered by s 55 and the adjoining sections of the Act would benefit from legislative clarification and harmonisation at an early date.[216] We agree. There would seem to be little justification for having five separate statutory provisions dealing with defence of property when the subject-matter is substantially the same. What is needed is a simple form of words that is capable of being readily explained to a jury, and which encompasses the essential elements of defence of movable property, land, and buildings. Whether there is a need for a separate generic defence of "defence of dwellinghouse" is debatable, when the modes of modern habitation are so diverse. A defence that seeks to preserve the interests of all citizens to secure *habitation*, as opposed to the protection of only one particular form of residence, would seem to be preferable. A more open-ended defence would also enable well-intentioned third parties, for example neighbours or members of a neighbourhood watch group, to take appropriate action to prevent entry or occupation of a

---

213 Criminal Code Bill Commission, *Report of the Royal Commission Appointed to Consider the Law Relating to Indictable Offences: With an Appendix Containing a Draft Code Embodying the Suggestions of the Commissioners*, London, Eyre & Spottiswode for HMSO, 1879, 11.
214 *R v Frew* [1993] 2 NZLR 731; (1992) 9 CRNZ 445.
215 *R v Frew* [1993] 2 NZLR 731; (1992) 9 CRNZ 445, 735; 450.
216 *R v Frew* [1993] 2 NZLR 731; (1992) 9 CRNZ 445, 736; 451.

residential home where the owners are absent and known not to have consented to the entry on to their property by named or unnamed persons.

Chapter 16

CULPABLE HOMICIDE

16.1 Introduction 498
16.2 Elements of homicide 498
16.2.1 The offender 498
16.2.2 The victim 499
16.2.3 Causation 501
(1) *Year and day rule* 501
(2) *Killing by influence on the mind* 502
(3) *Acceleration of death* 502
(4) *Causing preventable death* 504
(5) *Death resulting from treatment* 504
(6) *Inducing victims to kill themselves* 506
16.3 Culpable homicide 508
16.4 Mens rea of murder 508
16.4.1 Intentional killing 508
16.4.2 Reckless killing 509
16.4.3 Transferred mens rea 510
16.4.4 Killing in furthering an unlawful object 511
16.4.5 Further definition of murder 513
16.4.6 Concurrence of mens rea and actus reus 514
16.5 Manslaughter 515
16.5.1 Provocation 515
(1) *Function of judge and jury and burden of proof* 516
(2) *Anything done or said* 517
(3) *Cooling time* 518
(4) *Actual loss of self-control* 520
(5) *The objective test* 521
(6) *Accident and mistake* 532
(7) *Self-induced provocation* 534
16.5.2 Involuntary manslaughter 534
(1) *Killing by an unlawful act: s 160(2)(a)* 535
(2) *Inducing victims to kill themselves: s 160(2)(d)* 539
(3) *Killing by frightening: s 160(2)(e)* 540
(4) *Killing by unlawful omission: s 160(2)(b)* 541
(5) *Fault required for manslaughter by omission* 548
(6) *Duties of care and unlawful acts* 554

497

| (7) | Lawful excuse | 555 |
| (8) | Killing by unlawful act and omission | 557 |

16.6 Infanticide 558

16.6.1 Scope of infanticide 558

16.6.2 Insanity 559

16.6.3 Conclusion 560

16.1 Introduction

Part 8 of the Crimes Act 1961 provides for various crimes against the person. These include three which are described generally as "culpable homicide", and more specifically as murder, manslaughter, and infanticide. While anyone who commits murder is liable to life imprisonment (s 172(1)), life imprisonment is no longer the mandatory penalty for murder. Under s 102(1) Sentencing Act 2002, a person convicted of murder must be sentenced to life imprisonment unless "given the circumstances of the offence and the offender, a sentence of imprisonment for life would be manifestly unjust." A court must also give written reasons for not imposing a sentence of life imprisonment.[1]

Manslaughter carries a maximum sentence of life imprisonment, the penalty in a particular case being at the discretion of the Court (s 177).[2] The maximum penalty for infanticide is three years' imprisonment (s 178). When an accused is charged with murder, if the evidence warrants it, she may be acquitted of murder but convicted of manslaughter, or infanticide, but not, on that charge, of any other offence (s 339).

Homicide that is not culpable is not an offence (s 160(4)),[3] but homicide is, of course, an essential element of any offence of culpable homicide.

16.2 Elements of homicide

Homicide is defined by s 158 as "the killing of a human being by another, directly or indirectly, by any means whatsoever". There are three important elements of this definition: (i) the causing of death (ii) of a person (iii) by another person. We shall consider these elements separately.

16.2.1 The offender

In s 158, "by another" means "by another human being", so that a corporation cannot actually commit homicide.[4] Probably a corporation can be guilty of manslaughter as a *secondary* party,

---

1   Sentencing Act 2002, s 102(2). Where a court does impose a sentence of life imprisonment, provision is made for a minimum period of 10 years' imprisonment before eligibility for parole under the Parole Act 2002. However, a minimum period of more than ten years may be imposed if the Court is satisfied that the circumstances of the offence are sufficiently serious to justify doing so: Sentencing Act 2002, s 103. Where certain aggravating circumstances (specified in s 104) are implicit in the murder, including a high degree of brutality, an especially vulnerable victim, or calculated or lengthy planning, a minimum period of at least 17 years must be imposed unless it would be manifestly unjust to do so.
2   Manslaughter is a crime which varies enormously in gravity, and the Judge's discretion as to penalty is correspondingly large; in exceptional cases the maximum of life may be justified: *R v Wickliffe* [1987] 1 NZLR 55; (1986) 2 CRNZ 310 (CA) , 62-65; 316-320, or, at the other extreme, no penalty: *R v Yogasakaran* [1990] 1 NZLR 399; (1989) 5 CRNZ 69 (CA).
3   But in addition to murder, manslaughter, and infanticide, some unlawful killings may be offences under other legislation: for example, ss 36, 38 and 39 Land Transport Act 1998; s 53 Arms Act 1983.

but possibly not murder, for it cannot be subject to imprisonment,[5] which remains the mandatory penalty for murder, even though the term need no longer be for life. The general power to impose a fine under s 39 Sentencing Act 2002, as an alternative to imprisonment, applies where a court "may" sentence an offender to imprisonment[6] and is therefore not available where imprisonment is mandatory.[7]

16.2.2 The victim

The victim must be a living human being at the time of the killing. The destruction of a child before or in the course of birth, or of a foetus, may be the offence of killing an unborn child (s 182),[8] or procuring abortion (s 183), but it is not homicide. This follows from s 159:

> "**159 Killing of a child**
>
> "(1) A child becomes a human being within the meaning of this Act when it has completely proceeded in a living state from the body of its mother, whether it has breathed or not, whether it has an independent circulation or not, and whether the navel string is severed or not.
>
> "(2) The killing of such child is homicide if it dies in consequence of injuries received before, during, or after birth."

Subsection (1) follows common law authority in requiring that the child be wholly expelled from the mother's body,[9] but need not have breathed,[10] and the umbilical cord need not have been severed.[11] Whether a child is born "in a living state" may depend on whether its heart was functioning,[12] and there is no requirement that it had any hope of survival.[13] In Australia it has been held that any indicia of independent life will suffice, and it is neither necessary nor helpful to align the meaning of "born alive" with any statutory definition of death.[14]

---

4   *R v Murray Wright Ltd* [1970] NZLR 476 (CA). It is otherwise at common law: Cf *R v P & O European Ferries (Dover) Ltd* (1990) 93 Cr App R 72; [1991] Crim LR 695; *R v AC Hatrick Chemical Pty Ltd* (1995) 152 A Crim R 384.
5   Cf *R v Murray Wright Ltd* [1970] NZLR 476 (CA), 480 (North P).
6   Sentencing Act, s 39(1).
7   Section 44(3) Criminal Justice Act 1954 expressly provided for fining a corporation when imprisonment was the only prescribed penalty. This was overlooked in *R v Murray Wright Ltd* [1970] NZLR 476 (CA), but s 39 Sentencing Act 2002 does not include such a provision, and applies only when imprisonment "may" be imposed.
8   See *R v Henderson* [1990] 3 NZLR 174; (1990) 6 CRNZ 137 (CA) for the uncertain scope of s 182, which depends on when a foetus becomes a "child" within the "ordinary and natural meaning of the word" (26 weeks' gestation was clearly enough).
9   *R v Poulton* (1832) 5 C & P 329; 172 ER 997.
10   *R v Brain* (1834) 6 C & P 349; 172 ER 1272; but cf *R v Handley* (1874) 13 Cox CC 79.
11   *R v Trilloe* (1842) 2 Mood CC 260; 169 ER 103; the provision as to circulation is now seen as based on a misconception as it is established that a living child has an independent circulation before birth: Royal Commission of Inquiry into Contraception, Sterilisation and Abortion, *Contraception, Sterilisation and Abortion in New Zealand: Report of the Royal Commission of Inquiry*, Wellington, Government Printer, 1977, 279, quoted in *R v Henderson* [1990] 3 NZLR 174; (1990) 6 CRNZ 137 (CA), 181; 144.
12   Williams, *TBCL*, 290. Difficulties of proof are likely: *Adams*, CA159.04 (looseleaf); *R v Castles* [1969] QWN 36.
13   *R v West* (1848) 2 Car & K 784; 2 Cox CC 500.
14   *R v Iby* (2005) 154 A Crim R 55 (NSW CCA): evidence of a child having breathed independently of its mother, even where the child's breathing was assisted by mechanical respiration, was evidence that the child was born alive.

Subsection (2) allows a case to be homicide if a born and living child dies as a result of events before, during, or after birth. This too is consistent with the common law, but it applies only when death results from "injuries". Thus it covers the case where the child was directly injured before birth, or suffered physical injury,[15] including infection,[16] as a result of injury to the mother. However, doubts may arise if D induces premature birth and the child then dies because of inadequate development,[17] including cases where this results from injury to the mother (the most natural interpretation of "injuries" in s 159(2) requiring injuries to the child).[18] But even in these cases the death of the child will be the result of physiological processes, and perhaps these may be sufficient post-natal "injury" for s 159(2) to apply. At common law, however, it was not regarded as manslaughter if death resulted from a mother's inadequate preparation before birth,[19] and in such a case there might not be a "killing" under the Act.

By contrast, where an assault has caused the death of a foetus or unborn child, subs (2) has no application, since it is concerned with the death of a "child". In such circumstances liability may instead exist for an offence of causing bodily harm to the mother.[20] It seems that, in this context, the foetus is to be regarded as part of the mother, so that harm to the former is, in law, harm to the latter.[21]

If the child suffered a fatal injury as a result of an unlawful and dangerous act aimed at either the mother or the unborn child the killing will be manslaughter, although the House of Lords has held that it cannot be murder at common law unless, perhaps, D intended that the child should die or suffer serious harm after birth.[22] However, the terms of the codification of the doctrine of transferred malice in s 167(c) appear to allow a finding of murder if D acts with murderous mens rea towards the mother, but by accident that conduct brings about the death of the child after a live birth.

The question may also arise whether V was no longer alive when D acted. In the past, death was often equated with the cessation of heartbeat and breathing, but these may stop temporarily and developments in medicine and technology enable them to be maintained mechanically. The generally accepted medical opinion now is that death occurs when none of the vital centres in the brain stem is functioning (in which case, in the absence of mechanical intervention, there will be an irreversible loss of heartbeat and breathing).[23] There is no doubt that such "brain death" will mean that in law a person is dead, but it is uncertain whether it is essential for legal death.[24] The Crimes Consultative Committee recommended that the Act provide that a person is dead if there is either irreversible cessation of all brain stem functions or irreversible cessation of all spontaneous circulatory or respiratory functions.[25] However, in

---

15 For example *R v Martin* (1995) 13 WAR 472.
16 *R v Prince* (1988) 44 CCC (3d) 510 (Man CA).
17 Cf *R v West* (1848) 2 Car & K 784; 2 Cox CC 500.
18 Cf *A-G's Reference (No 3 of 1994)* [1998] AC 245; [1997] 3 All ER 936 (HL).
19 *R v Izod* (1904) 20 Cox CC 690.
20 For example, under s 188 (wounding with intent).
21 *R v King* (2004) 150 A Crim R 409. See also *Harrild v Director of Proceedings* [2003] 3 NZLR 289.
22 *A-G's Reference (No 3 of 1994)* [1998] AC 245; [1997] 3 All ER 936 (HL).
23 For a brief discussion, see Skegg, "The edges of life" (1988) 6 Otago LR 517, 519-522.
24 There are suggestions that it is in *Airedale NHS Trust v Bland* [1993] AC 789; [1993] 1 All ER 821 (HL) 856; 859 (Lord Keith), 863; 865 (Lord Goff); but Thomas J regarded it as an open question in *Auckland Area Health Board v A-G* [1993] 1 NZLR 235; (1992) 8 CRNZ 634, 246-247; 645-646.

the absence of brain death it may be doubted whether a finding of death would ever be possible if circulation and breathing are artificially maintained,[26] although it has been anticipated that there will be increasing pressure to treat as dead those whose brain stem has not been destroyed but whose brain has been so damaged that they are irreversibly unconscious, a condition known as "persistent vegetative state".[27] Ultimately, the question whether a person in a persistent vegetative state is dead for legal purposes calls for a legislative decision.

16.2.3 Causation

The definition of homicide requires that an offender "kill" another, which means "cause the death" of another,[28] although this may be done "directly or indirectly, by any means whatsoever". In most cases no issue of causation will arise, and it will not be necessary for the Judge to give directions on it.[29] Where, however, causation is in issue the Judge should explain the applicable principles,[30] it being a question for the jury whether D's conduct was a factual and sufficient cause of death.[31] But if on the evidence or admitted facts the only reasonable view is that D's conduct was a significant cause the Judge may so direct and withdraw the issue from the jury.[32] Conversely, a conviction cannot be sustained if on the evidence a reasonable jury could not have found sufficient cause established.[33]

In the case of unlawful act manslaughter, the unlawfulness of the act must also be *salient* to the causing of death. Thus, in *R v Hawkins*,[34] the unlawful act of driving without a licence could not support a charge of manslaughter because the absence of a licence was not the operative and substantial cause of death.

The general principles of causation apply to homicide, and these have already been examined.[35] In summary, while there may be other causes of death, an offender's act or omission must contribute to it in a significant way. There are also a number of particular statutory provisions, which will now be considered.

(1) Year and day rule

Section 162 retains the ancient common law rule that there is no criminal responsibility for a killing unless death occurs within a year and a day after the cause of death.[36] This period is reckoned inclusive of the day of the last contributing unlawful act, or on which a relevant omission ceased. Modern developments in medicine make long postponement of death

---

25 Crimes Bill Consultative Committee, *Crimes Bill 1989: Report of the Crimes Consultative Committee Presented to the Minister of Justice April 1991*, Wellington, Department of Justice, 1991, 42, 103.
26 Cf the definition of death quoted by Facer, "Do we need a legal definition of death" [1975] NZLJ 171, 173.
27 Skegg, "The edges of life" (1988) 6 Otago LR 517, 522.
28 *R v Storey* [1931] NZLR 417 (CA), 465 (Reed J); *R v Grant* [1966] NZLR 968 (CA) , 973-974.
29 *R v Pagett* (1983) 76 Cr App R 279; [1983] Crim LR 393 (CA) , 288; 394.
30 *R v Pagett* (1983) 76 Cr App R 279; [1983] Crim LR 393 (CA), 288; 394.
31 *R v Storey* [1931] NZLR 417 (CA); *R v Fleeting (No 1)* [1977] 1 NZLR 343, 346; *R v Tomars* [1978] 2 NZLR 505 (CA) , 511-512; *R v Kirikiri* [1982] 2 NZLR 648, 651.
32 *R v Blaue* [1975] 3 All ER 446; [1975] 1 WLR 1411 (CA); *R v Malcherek* [1981] 2 All ER 422; [1981] 1 WLR 690 (CA); in such a case, absence of causation directions will not involve a miscarriage of justice: *R v McKinnon* [1980] 2 NZLR 31 (CA).
33 *R v Jordan* (1956) 40 Cr App R 152 (CCA).
34 *R v Hawkins* 21/2/01, Goddard J, HC Napier T18/00. See above, 3.3.2(2).
35 See 3.4.
36 *R v Dyson* [1908] 2 KB 454; [1908-10] All ER Rep 736 (CA); Yale, "A year and a day in homicide" (1989) 48 CLJ 202.

possible, but D will not be freed from responsibility merely because survival beyond the statutory period was precluded by the withdrawal in good faith of life support.[37] There is no obligation on the Crown to prove that a victim would not have survived beyond a year and a day had life support not been removed.[38]

The abolition of this arbitrary rule was proposed in the Crimes Bill 1989, and by the Crimes Consultative Committee,[39] and has been effected in England.[40]

(2)   *Killing by influence on the mind*

Although psychiatric injury can constitute the "injury" or "actual bodily harm" required for some offences, mere emotions such as fear, distress, or panic will not,[41] and in the context of homicide a special rule is imposed by s 163. It provides that there is no criminal responsibility for killing by "any influence on the mind alone", or by causing some fatal disorder or disease by such influence; unless it is done by wilfully frightening a child under 16[42] or a sick person,[43] in which case the killing is culpable homicide.[44]

An illustration is the Canadian case of *R v Powder*.[45] The deceased had died from acute heart failure, precipitated by the fear and emotional stress of a burglary perpetrated by the accused and the ensuing struggle. D's conviction for manslaughter was quashed, on the grounds that fear and emotional stress were excluded causal means of killing by influence on the mind.[46] It would have been different if the physical exertion, or the assault, during the struggle had contributed to the victim's death, since then causation could have been proved on ordinary principles without resort to the special provision; but there was no evidence of this (even though V did have a pre-existing heart condition).

(3)   *Acceleration of death*

Insofar as everyone dies at some time, every killing is an acceleration of death. This is recognised by s 164, under which D kills V although the effect of the "bodily injury" caused to V "was merely to hasten his death while labouring under some disorder or disease arising from some other cause". The same rule applies at common law. It is a particular application of the principles that independent contributing causes do not excuse, and D must take the victim as he finds him. Causation is not excluded merely because V would not have died but for some disorder,[47] or because a disorder would have soon caused death in any event.[48]

Even so, V's ill-health may be relevant to whether D is criminally responsible. Ignorance of it may result in absence of the fault needed for liability,[49] and in some cases the shortening of

---

37   *R v Trounson* [1991] 3 NZLR 690; (1991) 8 CRNZ 491 (CA) , 696; 497-498.
38   *R v Tarei* 5/8/05, Heath J, HC Tauranga CRI-2004-087-1673.
39   Crimes Bill Consultative Committee, *Crimes Bill 1989: Report of the Crimes Consultative Committee Presented to the Minister of Justice April 1991*, Wellington, Department of Justice, 1991, 51-52.
40   Law Reform (Year and a Day Rule) Act 1996 (UK).
41   *R v Mwai* [1995] 3 NZLR 149; (1995) 13 CRNZ 273 (CA), 153-155; 278-280; *R v Ireland; R v Burstow* [1998] AC 147; [1997] 4 All ER 225 (HL).
42   Cf *R v Towers* (1874) 12 Cox CC 530.
43   Cf *R v Hayward* (1908) 21 Cox CC 692.
44   Section 160(2)(e); see 16.5.2(3).
45   *R v Powder* (1981) 29 CR (3d) 183 (Alta CA).
46   Per s 228 Criminal Code (Canada), which is similar to the New Zealand provision in s 163.
47   Cf *R v Renata* [1992] 2 NZLR 346; (1991) 7 CRNZ 616 (CA).
48   For example *R v Dyson* [1908] 2 KB 454; [1908-10] All ER Rep 736 (CA).

life in the course of medical treatment will be lawful. As to this, s 164 expressly applies to causing death by act or omission, but on the issue of lawfulness the law draws a distinction according to whether conduct is classed as an act or omission. Both withholding and withdrawing treatment are classified as omissions, and even though quick death may be inevitable, and intended, a doctor may lawfully withdraw life support if a competent patient consents, or if the patient is unconscious and according to responsible medical opinion its continuation would not benefit the patient.[50] In contrast, even with the consent of the patient it is not lawful for a doctor, or anyone, to do a positive act (such as injecting a drug) in order to bring about death, notwithstanding that the motive is to end suffering.[51] Such an act is, however, lawful if the doctor's purpose is to relieve pain, even though a known incidental effect will be to shorten life, provided the doctor acts in the patient's best interests and in accordance with responsible medical opinion.[52] In directing the jury in *R v Adams*[53] Devlin J appeared to distinguish between a doctor accelerating death permissibly by "minutes or hours" and impermissibly by "weeks or months". In either case there may be a significant acceleration of death and it is doubtful whether principles of causation, or mens rea, satisfactorily explain these instructions.[54] But the more quickly death is accelerated the more likely is the inference that the real purpose was to kill, and that makes the act unlawful, even if the motive is to end suffering.

Granted that "any" act or omission may be a relevant cause of death sufficient to give rise to homicide, it would seem difficult to contend that withdrawal of a patient's life support does not cause death. Yet the High Court so held in *R v Tarei*,[55] where the victim had suffered a subdural haematoma on the right hand side of his head as a result of D's assault. The Court ruled that such withdrawal, rather than causing death, operates to prevent the prolongation of life through artificial means, and therefore could not amount to an intervening cause — a novus actus interveniens — so as to supplant or negate the accused's original blow as a cause of the victim's ultimate death.[56]

The correctness of this ruling as a general proposition has rightly been challenged.[57] If a patient has already died, or is no longer dependent upon life-support, no doubt death cannot be caused.

49　Cf *R v Dawson* (1985) 81 Cr App R 150; [1985] Crim LR 383 (CA).
50　*Airedale NHS Trust v Bland* [1993] AC 789; [1993] 1 All ER 821 (HL); *Auckland Area Health Board v A-G* [1993] 1 NZLR 235; (1992) 8 CRNZ 634; Skegg, "Omissions to provide life: Prolonging treatment" (1994) 8 Otago LR 205. When a competent patient requests discontinuance there will also be a duty to comply; such duty may also exist when the treatment is of no benefit to the incompetent: *Bland* 883; 882 (Lord Browne-Wilkinson).
51　Section 63 Crimes Act 1961; *Airedale NHS Trust v Bland* [1993] AC 789; [1993] 1 All ER 821 (HL), 859, 865-866, 892-893; 867, 890, 891.
52　*Airedale NHS Trust v Bland* [1993] AC 789; [1993] 1 All ER 821 (HL), 867-870 (Lord Goff); in his seminal directions in *R v Adams* [1957] Crim LR 365, 375, Devlin J put it succinctly: "he was entitled to do all that was proper and necessary to relieve pain and suffering even if the measures he took might incidentally shorten life".
53　*R v Adams* [1957] Crim LR 365, 375.
54　Cf Smith and Hogan, *Criminal Law* (9th ed), London, Butterworths, 1999, 334; Williams, *TBCL*, 385; Beynon, "Doctors as murderers" [1982] Crim LR 17, 18; "a few moments" would no doubt be insignificant: see 3.3.2(1).
55　*R v Tarei (No 3)* 5/8/05, Heath J, HC Tauranga CRI-2004-087-1673.
56　*R v Tarei (No 3)* 5/8/05, Heath J, HC Tauranga CRI-2004-087-1673, paras 17-18.
57　See Skegg, "Omissions to Prolong Life" in Skegg and Paterson (eds), *Medical Law in New Zealand*,Wellington, Brookers, 2006, 536.

But where any person positively intervenes to change a patient's existing physical environment, with the direct result that death comes sooner than otherwise it would, that person causes (accelerates) death. To rule otherwise is to indulge in legal fictions. And unnecessary ones, at that. There is no rule in the law that says there cannot be more than one cause of death. The fact that the removal of life support was *also* a causal factor in no way implies that D's actions did not cause death.

(4) *Causing preventable death*

Section 165 provides that:

"Every one who by any act or omission causes the death of another person kills that person, although death from that cause might have been prevented by resorting to proper means."

For example, an injury which results in death kills V even though death could have been prevented by proper treatment, which is not provided because of a doctor's negligence,[58] or even because V refuses treatment in the knowledge that death might follow.[59] Everyone has the right to refuse medical treatment,[60] and the exercise of it does not relieve another of responsibility for the result. Neither is the chain of causation broken by the lawful withdrawal of life sustaining treatment.[61] This might also be the case when treatment was unlawfully prevented or terminated by another, and injuries caused by D were the physiological cause of death ("that cause" in s 165). Such intervening unlawful conduct would, however, also be a cause of death,[62] and if it was intentional and truly voluntary it might arguably prevent attribution to D.[63]

(5) *Death resulting from treatment*

What is the position if the most immediate cause of death was treatment which was applied in response to injury inflicted by D? The general principles governing intervening causes have been outlined earlier.[64] Nineteenth century case law suggested that medical treatment might never break the chain of causation, but it has since been recognised that there may be exceptional cases where it does. The question is governed by s 166:

"**166 Causing injury the treatment of which causes death**

"Every one who causes to another person any bodily injury, in itself of a dangerous nature, from which death results, kills that person, although the immediate cause of death be treatment, proper or improper, applied in good faith."

---

58   R v *Evans and Gardiner (No 2)* [1976] VR 523; R v *Bristow* [1960] SASR 210.
59   R v *Blaue* [1975] 3 All ER 446; [1975] 1 WLR 1411 (CA); R v *Holland* (1841) 2 Mood & R 351; 174 ER 313.
60   Section 11 New Zealand Bill of Rights Act 1990.
61   R v *Trounson* [1991] 3 NZLR 690; (1991) 8 CRNZ 491 (CA), 696; 497; R v *Malcherek* [1981] 2 All ER 422; [1981] 1 WLR 690 (CA). A failure to realise this point seems to explain the ruling in R v *Tarei (No 3)* 5/8/05, Heath J, HC Tauranga CRI-2004-087-1673, that the withdrawal of a life support system could not cause death. See above, 16.2.3(3).
62   *Airedale NHS Trust v Bland* [1993] AC 789; [1993] 1 All ER 821 (HL), 866; 868 (Lord Goff).
63   See 3.3.3(2)(b). But it is doubtful whether a mere omission to perform a legal duty could have this effect: see s 160(2)(c); 16.5.2(5); also 3.3.4(2).
64   See 3.3.3(2)(a) (foreseeable and innocent intervention), 3.3.3(2)(c) (foreseeable and culpable intervention).

This has been regarded as declaratory of the common law,[65] but as it applies only if death "results" from injuries caused by D, its only clear effect is that causation is not necessarily excluded when proper or improper treatment is the immediate cause of death. There may, however, be cases where treatment does have this effect.

Two types of case are to be distinguished. First, the killing is attributable to D's conduct if injury inflicted by D was a significant physiological cause of death, even if its effect was aggravated or accelerated by treatment, and even if that treatment was "thoroughly bad".[66] Such a case is at most one of multiple *concurrent* causes and resort to s 166 is unnecessary. In principle D should be responsible (in terms of causation) even if the original injury was not dangerous, and even if the subsequent "treatment" was not applied in good faith, and may have been intended to kill.[67] Secondly, the harm inflicted by D may not be a physiological cause and may have resulted in death only in the sense that had it not been for that harm V would not have been subjected to the treatment which killed. At common law there is authority that D is responsible in such a case even if the treatment was negligent,[68] but this is qualified by *R v Jordan*.[69] There the wound inflicted by D was held not to have caused death, it having practically healed at the time of death, which resulted from pneumonia caused by "palpably wrong" treatment. This has always been regarded as a very exceptional case,[70] and its effect was further confined in *R v Cheshire*,[71] where it was said that negligent treatment should not relieve D of responsibility unless it "was so independent of his acts, and itself so potent in causing death, that [the jury] regard the contribution made by his acts as insignificant".

The only reported New Zealand decision on the application of s 166 to this type of case is the pretrial ruling in *R v Kirikiri*,[72] where the original injury seems not to have been a physiological cause of death (which resulted from asphyxiation caused by a mishap in the course of treatment). Jeffries J held that it was a question for the jury whether the injury remained "an operating cause of death", rather than merely part of the history. This test is open to the criticism that it allows the jury to find that the chain of causation was broken by treatment directed at the injury notwithstanding that the treatment was not negligent. The issue involves a question of policy as well as fact, and other authority would allow such a result only if the treatment was at least negligent, and probably grossly negligent.[73]

Section 166 applies only if the injury was "in itself of a dangerous nature". In *Kirikiri* this was also treated as a question of fact for the jury, and the meaning of the term was not discussed.

---

65   *R v Kirikiri* [1982] 2 NZLR 648, 651.
66   This was the position in the leading case of *R v Smith* [1959] 2 QB 35; [1959] 2 All ER 193; 3.3.3(2)(c); the position is the same when V's own imprudent conduct, such as drinking or physical exertion, worsened his condition: *R v Wall* (1802) 28 St Tr 51; *R v Flynn* (1867) 16 WR 319 (Ir).
67   See 3.3.2(3).
68   *R v Cheshire* [1991] 3 All ER 670; [1991] 1 WLR 844 (CA); *R v Davis and Wagstaffe* (1883) 15 Cox CC 174; 6 C & P 177; 172 ER 1196.
69   *R v Jordan* (1956) 40 Cr App R 152 (CCA); 3.3.3(2)(c).
70   *R v Smith* [1959] 2 QB 35; [1959] 2 All ER 193, 43; 198; *R v Evans and Gardiner (No 2)* [1976] VR 523, 531 (where it was unsuccessfully argued that negligent failure to diagnose and treat broke the chain of causation).
71   *R v Cheshire* [1991] 3 All ER 670; [1991] 1 WLR 844 (CA). This judgment provides excessively uncertain guidance: Smith and Hogan, *Criminal Law* (9th ed), London, Butterworths, 1999, 351, 352.
72   *R v Kirikiri* [1982] 2 NZLR 648; 3.3.3(2)(c).
73   *Cameron* (1983) 7 Crim LJ 168, where it is also noted that the jury acquitted D of murder and convicted of attempted murder only. As well as its major effect on penalty such a result can allow an offender to benefit under the victim's will, intestacy, or insurance cover.

It may require an injury which would create a real risk of death if untreated. When the injury was not itself dangerous, and did not actually contribute to death which was caused by treatment, it seems to be implicit from the terms of s 166 that the chain of causation will be broken,[74] although in principle this should not be the case when the treatment was a reasonably foreseeable response to the injury.[75]

(a)   The scope of "treatment"

The "treatment" referred to in s 166 means treatment directed at the dangerous injury. The expression necessarily implies therapeutic intervention intended for the patient's benefit. As a medical concept, "treatment" means management in the application of remedies and includes the whole management of a patient, including decisions not to administer drugs. Indeed, in *R v Tarei*[76] it was held that a decision not to perform surgery was part of the process of "treatment" under s 166.

That may be relatively uncontroversial. However, the Court went on to rule that implementation of the further decision to withdraw any form of life support system is *not* "treatment" falling within the section. Given that such withdrawal constitutes an intervention motivated by medical decisions about the best interests of the the patient, it might reasonably have been thought also to be a form of treatment.[77] Once it is accepted that the decision not to perform surgery is treatment, one is committed to an understanding of treatment in terms of a patient's medical management. Thus, while "treatment" *typically* is aimed at enhancing of the prospects of recovery, it need not always hold that sense. For example, few would contend that mopping the brow, administering water, or binding a wound on a dying patient following a motor vehicle accident is any the less treatment, simply because the patient has no chance of recovery. Arguably, it is difficult to materially distinguish between putting a patient on a life support system, which is clearly treatment for the purposes of s 166, and the withdrawal of such support, which amounts to the cessation of treatment — a form of treatment in its own right.

(6)   *Inducing victims to kill themselves*

This kind of case is expressly provided for in the definition of culpable homicide. Under s 160(2)(d), culpable homicide includes the killing of a person "by causing that person by threats or fear of violence, or by deception, to do an act which causes his death". Although this is a rule of causation as well as of culpability, it is convenient to leave examination of it to the discussion of involuntary manslaughter.[78] However, it is necessary at this point to consider the case where D induces V to commit suicide.

At common law suicide by a sane person of responsible age was a felony, being regarded as self-murder. It followed that secondary parties to it were guilty of murder.[79] In New Zealand, suicide has not been a crime since the enactment of the Code of 1893, for the statutory definition of homicide has always been confined to the killing of a human being "by

---

74   Common law authorities on this are inconsistent: *R v McIntyre* (1847) 2 Cox CC 379; *R v Clark and Bagg* (1842) 6 JP 508; cf *R v Davis and Wagstaffe* (1883) 15 Cox CC 174; 6 C & P 177; 172 ER 1196.
75   See 3.3.3(2), 3.3.3(2)(c).
76   *R v Tarei (No 3)* 5/8/05, Heath J, HC Tauranga CRI-2004-087-1673.
77   The point was left open in *R v Trounson* [1991] 3 NZLR 690; (1991) 8 CRNZ 491 (CA).
78   See 16.5.2(2).
79   *R v Croft* [1944] 1 KB 295; [1944] 2 All ER 483 (CCA).

another".[80] If, however, D actually kills V with the latter's consent that will be homicide, and V's consent to death provides no defence to a charge of murder or manslaughter (s 63). It has also been argued that a person who deliberately assists or induces another to commit suicide might still be convicted of murder, on the basis that this can be regarded as a "killing" of another within s 158.[81] However, it is submitted that as a general rule this is wrong. At common law, liability of a party assisting or procuring suicide did not depend on D being held to have "killed", but rather on the theory that D was a secondary party to the suicide's crime.[82] If a person deliberately kills herself by an act which is "free, deliberate and informed", there is a novus actus interveniens which breaks the chain of causation and prevents a secondary party being held to have "killed".[83] It may, however, be otherwise if V was insane, or below the age of responsibility, and it may be culpable homicide under s 160(2)(d) if D induces suicide by threats or fear of violence, or by deception. In such circumstances the coercer could be regarded as the principal offender in a prosecution for murder.

In the English case of *R v Dhaliwal*,[84] the victim had committed suicide by hanging herself. Police discovered evidence that she had endured psychological and physical abuse over a number of years by her husband, who was then charged with manslaughter and inflicting grievous bodily harm. The Court of Appeal upheld the trial Judge's ruling that D could not be convicted. The Crown had failed to establish the presence of an identifiable clinical condition that could have amounted to a psychiatric injury sufficient to establish actual bodily harm, the essential element of the unlawful act upon which the Crown relied. However, the Court of Appeal observed that, subject to the issue of causation, unlawful violence on an individual with a fragile and vulnerable personality which was proved to be a material cause of death (even if the result of a suicide) could potentially constitute manslaughter.[85] Toczek suggests that, to prove manslaughter resulting from suicide due to domestic abuse, the prosecution would have to obtain medical evidence that ther abuse caused the victim to develop a recognised psychiatric illness, and establish beyond reasonable doubt that the abuse thereby caused the victim's death.[86]

Such a case is exceptional. So far as more typical cases are concerned, since the Crimes Act also makes specific provision for parties to suicide, this reinforces the conclusion that such parties are not generally guilty of homicide. Under s 179, a secondary party to suicide is guilty of a crime punishable by up to 14 years' imprisonment and, under s 180(2), if someone kills herself pursuant to a suicide pact, a survivor of the pact is punishable by a maximum of 5 years' imprisonment.

---

80   Attempt to commit suicide was an offence under the Acts of 1893 (s 173) and 1908 (s 193), but this is not retained in the 1961 Act.
81   *Adams* (2nd ed), paras 1211-1213; in *R v Hinchcliffe* (1906) 8 GLR 652, Cooper J directed that the Code provisions had not excluded such liability.
82   *R v Croft* [1944] 1 KB 295; [1944] 2 All ER 483 (CCA); *R v Dyson* (1823) Russ & Ry 523; 168 ER 930; *R v Russell* (1832) 1 Mood & R 356; 168 ER 1302.
83   See 3.3.3(2). It is this principle which creates the need for rules governing secondary liability.
84   *R v Dhaliwal* [2006] EWCA Crim 1139; [2006] All ER (D) 236.
85   *R v Dhaliwal* [2006] EWCA Crim 1139; [2006] All ER (D) 236, para 32.
86   Toczek, "Driven to Suicide?" (2006) NLJ 1205.

16.3 Culpable homicide

For a homicide to be an offence, it must be "culpable homicide" within s 160(2). In most cases this will require that a person is killed by an unlawful act or an omission to comply with a legal duty. Apart from cases of infanticide, any culpable homicide will be the offence of manslaughter or, if it is committed with the appropriate mens rea and not under provocation, it will be murder: s 160(3). Issues as to the scope of culpable homicide under s 160(2) will almost always arise when a killing might not have been murder or manslaughter under provocation, and the question is whether it was at least manslaughter (or "involuntary manslaughter"). Detailed consideration of the scope of s 160(2) will, therefore, be deferred until after discussion of the mens rea of murder, and manslaughter under provocation.

16.4 Mens rea of murder

Historically, at common law the mens rea of murder was described as "malice aforethought". This included a number of different states of mind, but in England the effect of s 1 Homicide Act 1957 (UK) is that some of these no longer suffice, and there it is settled that it now consists of an intention to kill or cause grievous bodily harm to a person.[87] In New Zealand, however, the relevant states of mind are specified in four paragraphs in s 167, and in a "further definition of murder" contained in s 168. The scope of the crime depends on the interpretation of these provisions.[88] They are alternatives so that, subject to any defences, an unlawful killing is murder if any one of them applies. Because common law definitions of the mens rea of murder have yet to be reduced to statutory form, they are of limited significance in the construction of the definitions in ss 167 and 168.

16.4.1 Intentional killing

Section 167(a) provides that culpable homicide is murder "if the offender means to cause the death of the person killed". This requires "an actual intent to kill".[89] There is an absence of authority, but "means" in its ordinary sense would appear to require that the killing be a purpose and object of the offender, although perhaps it would suffice that he knows it to be an inseparable consequence of his object.[90] Where D seeks to injure or to achieve an "unlawful object", it will not be necessary to resolve this question because, in such cases, the effect of the further provisions of s 167 is that a killing is murder where D deliberately takes the risk of causing death.[91] However, if D has no such purpose, it may be that mere knowledge that death is virtually certain to result will not bring the case within s 167, although such knowledge may be sufficient mens rea for murder at common law.[92] This reasoning has special significance in

---

87 R v Cunningham [1982] AC 566; [1981] 2 All ER 863 (HL), applying R v Hyam [1975] AC 55; [1974] 2 All ER 41 (HL) and R v Vickers [1957] 2 QB 664; [1957] 2 All ER 741 (CCA); see also A-G's Reference (No 3 of 1994) [1998] AC 245; [1997] 3 All ER 936 (HL), 258; 944-948.
88 Cf R v Piri [1987] 1 NZLR 66 (CA), 76-83.
89 R v Aramakutu [1991] 3 NZLR 429; (1991) 7 CRNZ 114 (CA), 432; 117; R v Juanetty (2005) 200 CCC (3d) 116.
90 Cf 4.2.4.
91 R v Piri [1987] 1 NZLR 66 (CA), 82.
92 R v Woollin [1999] 1 AC 82; [1998] 4 All ER 103 (HL); above, 4.2.4. Woollin was followed in R v Matthews and Alleyne [2003] Crim LR 553 (CA), where it was noted that the law had not yet reached a definition of intent in murder in terms of a virtual certainty, although the Court observed (para 45) that "once what is required is an appreciation of a virtual certainty of death, and not some lesser foresight of merely probable consequences, there is very little to choose between a rule of evidence and one of substantive law."

some medical contexts where, for example, knowledge that the administration of effective doses of pain relief to patients is virtually certain to hasten death might otherwise lead to the (erroneous) conclusion that the medical professional therefore intends to kill.[93]

16.4.2 Reckless killing

Under s 167(b), culpable homicide is murder "if the offender means to cause to the person killed any bodily injury that is known to the offender to be likely to cause death, and is reckless whether death ensues or not". At common law, it suffices that death was caused by an act done with intent to cause grievous bodily harm (meaning "really serious" bodily harm),[94] and it is not necessary that D intended to endanger life.[95] By contrast s 167(b) expressly requires that the intended injury be "known to the offender to be likely to cause death". This was given a strict interpretation by the Court of Appeal in *R v Dixon*,[96] where V had died as a result of a series of assaults by D, including punching and kicking. It was held that under s 167(b), at the time of conduct contributing to death, D must have "actually appreciated", or had a "conscious appreciation of", the likelihood of causing death; it was not enough that D ought to have been aware of this, or had "the necessary general knowledge to have appreciated the risk if he had paused to think about it". The Court doubted whether the additional requirement that the offender be "reckless whether death ensues or not" really adds anything, although it might emphasise the "conscious appreciation" required.[97]

This interpretation was reaffirmed in *R v Harney*,[98] where D had killed V by stabbing him in a street brawl. It was held that in s 167(b) "reckless" could not refer to a failure to give thought to an obvious risk, but rather "means that there must be a conscious taking of the risk of causing death". The Court added that the inclusion of the term points up the contrast between paras (a) and (b): "The one is aimed at deliberate killing, the other at deliberately taking the risk of killing." On the other hand, "likely" does not mean that D must have thought that a killing was more likely than not, it sufficing that it was recognised as a "real or substantial" risk, as "something that might well happen", or as a risk which was more than negligible or remote.[99]

Neither is it enough that the accused should have known that death was a likely consequence. The accused's actual "subjective" state of mind must be established. In *R v Meads and Smith*[100] the Court of Appeal affirmed that "reckless" in s 167(b) simply means "that there must be a conscious taking of the risk of causing death". The Court held that it was unwise for a judge to say it meant "careless", since that expression obscures the need for conscious awareness of risk.

---

93 For a detailed discussion of this issue in the context of medical acts which may hasten death, see Skegg, "Medical Acts Hastening Death" in Skegg and Paterson, *Medical Law in New Zealand*, Wellington, Brookers, 2006, 519.
94 *DPP v Smith* [1961] AC 290, also reported as *R v Smith* [1960] 3 All ER 161 (HL); *R v Cunningham* [1982] AC 566; [1981] 2 All ER 863 (HL), 574; 865.
95 *R v Cunningham* [1982] AC 566; [1981] 2 All ER 863 (HL), 574; 865.
96 *R v Dixon* [1979] 1 NZLR 641 (CA), 647.
97 Cf *R v Cooper* [1993] 1 SCR 146; (1993) 18 CR (4th) 1 (SCC), 153; 7.
98 *R v Harney* [1987] 2 NZLR 576 (CA), 579-580.
99 *R v Piri* [1987] 1 NZLR 66 (CA), 78-79; *R v Harney* [1987] 2 NZLR 576 (CA), 581; cf *R v Gush* [1980] 2 NZLR 92 (CA), 96. It may be prudent to use one or both forms of words when directing a jury. See *R v Meynell* [2004] 1 NZLR 507; (2003) 20 CRNZ 526 (CA).
100 *R v Meads and Smith* 20/4/00, CA514/99.

The requisite knowledge and intent may be determined by inference from the nature of the act and the circumstances that D must have known.[101] If D had launched a sustained attack on V, it may be open to the jury to infer that whichever act caused death was accompanied by mens rea, even if the particular act cannot be identified.[102] However, given that s 167(b) needs to be relied on only if D might not have meant to kill, it will often be at least arguable that D lacked the requisite knowledge, even if a weapon was used, especially if the act may have been an instinctive, unthinking reaction in the heat of the moment.[103] If the injury intended was not of a kind which would normally be expected to kill it is likely that the inference of knowledge will not be possible.[104]

16.4.3 Transferred mens rea

Paragraphs (a) and (b) of s 167 are in terms confined to cases where D means to kill or injure the person killed. However, the principle of transferred mens rea (see 4.8) is applied by s 167(c), under which it is murder if D acts with one of the states of mind specified in paras (a) and (b) "and by accident or mistake kills another person, though he does not mean to hurt the person killed". A case will be one of mistake when D injures the intended victim, except that he mistook the latter's identity, and it will be a case of accident when D aimed at one person but unintentionally killed another.[105] The Supreme Court has held that the concept of "accident or mistake" is also applicable where a murder prosecution is based on s 167(d) and where the offender pleads provocation in reliance on s 169(6).[106]

Three particular cases require further mention.

First, there may be cases where D has no particular victim in mind and indiscriminately attacks a group (perhaps by shooting or the use of explosives). If someone is killed, it is neither necessary nor appropriate to rely on para (c), for if D meant to kill or injure anyone she will have meant to kill or injure whoever was in fact killed.[107]

Secondly is the case of bungled suicides. Homicide is confined to the killing of a human being other than the offender (s 158), from which it follows that paras (a) and (b) of s 167 require an intention to kill or injure someone other than D. There is little doubt that this is the state of mind required for para (c) to operate, in which case it will not apply if D's object was confined to suicide or self-injury and another was accidentally killed.[108]

Thirdly, if an attack on a pregnant woman is followed by the birth of a live child, and the child then dies as a result of injury to it before or after birth, this is homicide of the child.[109] It should

---

101   R v Leaaetoa 30/6/94, CA520/93.
102   R v Ryder [1995] 2 NZLR 271; (1995) 13 CRNZ 81 (CA); Meyers v R (1997) 71 ALJR 1488; cf R v McKeown [1984] 1 NZLR 630 (CA). For the limits on the extent to which expert evidence might be admissible on the issue of mens rea, see R v Makoare [2001] 1 NZLR 318; (2000) 18 CRNZ 511 (CA), 323-325; 516-518.
103   R v Harney [1987] 2 NZLR 576 (CA), 581-582.
104   Cf R v Pira (1991) 7 CRNZ 650; difficulties of proof may also arise from the requirement that the prescribed mens rea must accompany an act which contributes to the death: see 16.4.6.
105   For example R v Droste (1984) 6 DLR (4th) 607; [1984] 1 SCR 208 (SCC); this may include a case where the death results from the intervening act of another which is not such as to break the chain of causation between D's act and the death: Adams, CA167.07 (looseleaf), citing R v Pagett (1983) 76 Cr App R 279; [1983] Crim LR 393 (CA); R v Mitchell [1983] QB 741; [1983] 2 All ER 427 (CA).
106   Timoti v R [2005] NZSC 37, paras 25, 28.
107   A-G's Reference (No 3 of 1994) [1998] AC 245; [1997] 3 All ER 936 (HL), 261; 948.
108   Adams, CA167.08 (looseleaf); contra Re Brown and R (1983) 4 CCC (3d) 571.

be noted, in contrast to the view stated here, that in *A-G's Reference (No 3 of 1994)*[110] the House of Lords held that at common law the fact that D acted with murderous intent directed at the mother would not make such a killing of the child murder, it being thought that the "fiction" or "doctrine" of transferred mens rea should not be taken so far. But such a case would seem to be within the natural and ordinary meaning of the terms of s 167(c), which do not suggest that V must have been a living human being at the time D acts. On the other hand, if the only injury intended by D was to the foetus and not the mother, and the later birth and death of the child was an unintended (though possibly foreseen) result, none of paras (a), (b), and (c) would apply, for D did not mean to kill or injure a "human being".[111] It appears, however, that such a case could be within s 167(d), which is now to be considered.

16.4.4 Killing in furthering an unlawful object

Section 167(d) provides that culpable homicide is also murder:

"If the offender for any unlawful object does an act that he knows to be likely to cause death, and thereby kills any person, though he may have desired that his object should be effected without hurting any one."

Like s 168 below (16.4.5), this provision is a qualified application of the old common law "felony murder" rule.[112] Under this provision, D may be guilty of murder even though she did not intend to kill, or even injure, anyone, if she deliberately risked life for an unlawful end. For example, if D sets an explosion in a jail with the object of enabling prisoners to escape and the explosion kills a guard (or a prisoner), D will be guilty of murder if she foresaw a killing as a real risk, although she may have hoped it would not eventuate. Such killings were murder at common law, although in England legislative and judicial developments have meant that this is no longer the case.[113]

The earlier New Zealand codes included the words "or ought to have known" after "knows", but these words were dropped in 1961, it being evidently decided that objective tests of the kind endorsed in *DPP v Smith*[114] should be eschewed.[115] Now, as under para (b), liability under s 167(d) requires that in doing the act which causes death D consciously appreciates that death might well result, or that death is a real or substantial risk.[116] It suffices, however, that the death of anyone is known to be a real risk, so that there is no need for a separate provision for cases of transferred mens rea.

Common to both provisions, therefore, is the running of a known risk of causing death.[117] With the adoption of a subjective test of knowledge, the essential difference between

---

109 See 16.2.2.
110 *A-G's Reference (No 3 of 1994)* [1998] AC 245; [1997] 3 All ER 936 (HL); see commentary in [1997] Crim LR 829; contra *R v Kwok Chak Ming (No 1)* [1963] HKLR 226, 349; cf *R v Martin* (1995) 13 WAR 472.
111 The position at common law was left open in *A-G's Reference (No 3 of 1994)* [1998] AC 245; [1997] 3 All ER 936 (HL), 254, 265; 942, 952; it was said to be murder in *R v West* (1848) 2 Car & K 784; 2 Cox CC 500, but this was an effect of the defunct felony murder rule, which does not apply in New Zealand. As to manslaughter, see 16.5.2(1).
112 *Timoti v R* [2006] 1 NZLR 323; (2005) 21 CRNZ 804 (CA), para 11.
113 See *R v Piri* [1987] 1 NZLR 66 (CA), 79-82.
114 *DPP v Smith* [1961] AC 290, also reported as *R v Smith* [1960] 3 All ER 161 (HL).
115 *Downey v R* [1971] NZLR 97 (CA); *R v Piri* [1987] 1 NZLR 66 (CA), 77.
116 *R v Fryer* [1981] 1 NZLR 748 (CA); *R v Piri* [1987] 1 NZLR 66 (CA), 77, 79, 82, 84.
117 *Timoti v R* [2006] 1 NZLR 323; (2005) 21 CRNZ 804 (CA), para 15.

paras (b) and (d) of s 167 is that para (b) applies where D means to cause bodily injury to someone, whereas para (d) applies although D has some other unlawful object.[118] Paragraph (d) will be most clearly appropriate when D's unlawful object does not include any form of personal injury, but the courts have not confined it to such cases. If the only identified unlawful object is the same personal injury which in fact caused death it would be confusing to attempt to apply para (d) as well as para (b), and it has been held that as the concluding words of para (d) would make no sense in such a case this paragraph cannot be applied to it.[119] However, para (d) will apply if D, with the requisite knowledge, causes death by an assault, and does this act with the unlawful object of effecting some further hurt or injury. In *R v McKeown*,[120] D bound and gagged V with the object of then indecently assaulting her. V subsequently died of asphyxiation as a result of the gag. It was possible that para (b) did not apply, for in binding and gagging the victim D might not have meant bodily injury; but it was held that, if the required knowledge accompanied the conduct, para (d) did apply, notwithstanding that the unlawful object included hurt or injury to V. There was, moreover, no requirement that D foresaw precisely how death would occur (in this case, by asphyxiation).

For para (d) to apply there must have been both a fatal act and an unlawful object, but these need not involve two different offences, or even be "clearly distinct". In *R v Aramakutu*[121] D lit a fire with the unlawful object of damaging a house, and an occupant died as a result. Provided the requisite knowledge was proved, this was murder under s 167(d), even though the act and the object were aspects of the one offence of arson. In Canada it has been suggested that in this context an "unlawful object" must involve "a serious crime, that is an indictable offence requiring mens rea".[122] It is doubtful whether such a precise definition would be regarded as appropriate in New Zealand, but it may be that it does require some kind of criminal offence.[123] On the other hand, para (d) can apply even though the object was capable of being lawful, but on the facts is unlawful because of the means used to try to achieve it. For example, in *R v Piri*[124] D's object was to obtain information from V, which in itself could have been lawful, but was not because of the means used to achieve it (tying V to a tree, and leaving her exposed to the elements, which caused death).

Liability under paragraph (d) is not inconsistent with the defence of provocation, where the accused claims that he or she was provoked by one person, but by accident or mistake killed

---

118 *R v Aramakutu* [1991] 3 NZLR 429; (1991) 7 CRNZ 114 (CA), 432; 117.
119 *Downey v R* [1971] NZLR 97 (CA), as explained in *R v McKeown* [1984] 1 NZLR 630 (CA), 634-635; in *Adams*, CA167.12 (looseleaf) it is further suggested that para (d) cannot apply if the fatal injury was one of two or more objects D sought to achieve by the act which caused death. If D's only object was to apply unlawful force, but not to injure, it may also be doubted whether para (d) can apply, given the requirement of an intent to injure in para (b): Cf *R v Woollin* [1999] 1 AC 82; [1998] 4 All ER 103 (HL).
120 *R v McKeown* [1984] 1 NZLR 630 (CA); cf *R v Hakaraia* [1989] 1 NZLR 745 (CA).
121 *R v Aramakutu* [1991] 3 NZLR 429; (1991) 7 CRNZ 114 (CA); see also *Stuart v R* (1974) 134 CLR 426; 4 ALR 545 (HCA); *R v Gould and Barnes* [1960] Qd R 283. The latter decision held that murder could be found under an equivalent provision when an unlawful abortion resulted in the death of the mother; if such an act resulted in the birth of a living child who then died as a result of injuries caused by the abortion, it appears that that could also be murder, provided D had known that the act was likely to cause the death of a human being: Cf n 91.
122 *R v Vasil* [1981] 1 SCR 469; (1981) 58 CCC (2d) 97 (SCC).
123 Cf the discussion of "unlawful act" in s 160(2)(a): 16.5.2(1).
124 *R v Piri* [1987] 1 NZLR 66 (CA); see also *R v Hakaraia* [1989] 1 NZLR 745 (CA); conversely the fact that the object involved an offence may show that the fatal act was unlawful: *R v Hamilton* [1985] 2 NZLR 245 (CA), where the act was firing a gun with the object of frightening another.

another person.[125] In *Timoti v R*[126] the accused set fire to premises in which the person killed was present. He was acquitted on charges of attempted murder in relation to the two people said to have provoked him. The acquittal (which rejected any intention to kill) meant that the murder conviction must have been based on s 167(d) and, in particular, on a finding that the accused knew his lighting the fire with the object of burning down the building was likely to cause death, even though he may have desired that his object should be effected without hurting anyone. The Court rejected the Crown's submission that provocation could never reduce to manslaughter what would otherwise be murder under paragraph (d) of s 167. The fact that death was merely foreseen and not intended did not itself preclude the operation of s 169(6) and, therefore, provocation was held to be available in a prosecution under s 167(d).[127]

16.4.5 Further definition of murder

At common law, under what was known as the felony murder rule, a killing while furthering another offence was murder even though neither death nor personal injury was intended, although ultimately this was restricted to killings in the course of violent felonies.[128] In England this principle was abolished by s 1 Homicide Act 1957, but a much modified version of it survives in New Zealand in s 168 Crimes Act 1961.[129]

Section 168 significantly enlarges the crime of murder by expressly providing that certain unlawful killings are murder whether or not the offender meant to kill or knew that death was likely to ensue. The effect of the rather precise provisions of s 168(1) is that an unlawful killing is murder if the following conditions are met:

(a) Death resulted from grievous bodily injury which D had meant to cause, or from D's administering any stupefying or overpowering things to, or wilfully stopping the breath of, any person; and

(b) D acted for the purpose of either

 (i) Resisting lawful apprehension in respect of any offence; or

 (ii) Facilitating the commission of a listed offence, or facilitating the flight or avoidance of detection of the offfender on the commission or attempted commission of a listed offence.

The listed offences are found in s 168(2), and are treason (s 73), communicating secrets (s 78), sabotage (s 79), piracy (ss 92 and 93), escape from prison, lawful custody or detention (ss 119-122), sexual violation (s 128), murder (s 167), abduction and kidnapping (ss 208 and 209), robbery (s 234), burglary (s 241), and arson (s 294).

In contrast to the felony murder rule at common law, under s 168 it is not enough that D kills while committing one of the specified offences, or while resisting arrest. It is also essential that D meant to cause grievous bodily injury (that is, really serious bodily harm),[130] or did one of the other specified acts for a prescribed purpose. So, for example, killing as a result of the

---

125 See s 169(6).
126 *Timoti v R* [2006] 1 NZLR 323; (2005) 21 CRNZ 804 (CA).
127 *Timoti v R* [2006] 1 NZLR 323; (2005) 21 CRNZ 804 (CA), para 21 et seq.
128 *A-G's Reference (No 3 of 1994)* [1998] AC 245; [1997] 3 All ER 936 (HL), 257-258; 945.
129 *R v Piri* [1987] 1 NZLR 66 (CA), 79-82; s 167(d) can also be traced to this rule: *Downey v R* [1971] NZLR 97 (CA), 100.

accidental discharge of a gun during a robbery is not murder under s 168, although D may be convicted under s 167(d) if, in presenting the gun, he knew that there was a real risk of accidental discharge and consequent death.[131] Although it is not made express, the terms of s 168 appear to extend to a case where D aims at one person but accidentally kills another.[132] Additionally, where the provisions as to flight or avoidance of detection are relied on, it will not be necessary to show that D was in fact being pursued, and the killing need not occur "immediately" after the offence.[133]

Although s 168(2)(k) refers only to "robbery," there is no reason to exclude reliance on s 168(1)(a) where the offence is aggravated robbery. In *R v Rapira*[134] the Court of Appeal concluded that the specific reference to aggravated robbery in subs (2) is unnecessary because that offence includes the qualifying offence of robbery.

Where the actual killer is guilty of murder under s 168, a secondary party may be equally guilty under s 66(1) if he intentionally assisted or encouraged the intentional infliction of grievous bodily injury, or one of the other specified acts, knowing that one of the specified objects was being pursued, even if he may not have foreseen a killing.[135] The Court of Appeal has also held that a killing need not be foreseen when s 66(2) is relied on.[136]

16.4.6 Concurrence of mens rea and actus reus

The general need for such concurrence has already been considered in 4.9. In the context of murder, it requires that an offender had one of the required states of mind when she was responsible for an unlawful act or omission which caused or significantly contributed to the death. This can cause difficulty when there were a number of violent acts, for it may be necessary for the jury to identify which act or acts caused death, and to determine D's state of mind at that time, something that may be an impossible task.

There are a number of ways in which this problem may be overcome. It will not be necessary to identify the particular act which caused death if it can be inferred that, whichever act it was, it was accompanied by murderous mens rea.[137] If death resulted from a continuing act (for example, strangulation), it will suffice that the actor had such mens rea at some point during that act,[138] and if there is nothing to suggest that D's state of mind varied during a rapid series of acts, one of which caused death, it will be enough if the jury find that D acted with mens rea during those acts.[139] Moreover, it will be murder if mens rea accompanied an act of D

---

130 See *DPP v Smith* [1961] AC 290, also reported as *R v Smith* [1960] 3 All ER 161 (HL), and the definition of "to injure" in s 2; *R v Mwai* [1995] 3 NZLR 149; (1995) 13 CRNZ 273 (CA).
131 *R v Wickliffe* [1987] 1 NZLR 55; (1986) 2 CRNZ 310 (CA).
132 Cf *R v Rowe* [1951] 4 DLR 238; [1951] SCR 713 (SCC).
133 *R v Rowe* [1951] 4 DLR 238; [1951] SCR 713 (SCC).
134 *R v Rapira* [2003] 3 NZLR 794; (2003) 20 CRNZ 396 (CA).
135 *R v Hardiman* [1995] 2 NZLR 650; (1995) 13 CRNZ 68 (CA).
136 *R v Tuhoro* [1998] 3 NZLR 568; (1998) 15 CRNZ 568 (CA); Orchard, "Strict liability and parties to murder and manslaughter" [1997] NZLJ 93.
137 *R v Ryder* [1995] 2 NZLR 271; (1995) 13 CRNZ 81 (CA); *Meyers v R* (1997) 71 ALJR 1488.
138 *R v Cooper* [1993] 1 SCR 146; (1993) 18 CR (4th) 1 (SCC); see 4.9.1(1).
139 *R v McKeown* [1984] 1 NZLR 630 (CA): this applied where D had struck, bound, and gagged V, who died of asphyxiation caused by the gag. Where the possible causes of death were distinct events, in which D may have had a different involvement, or which may have been accompanied by different states of mind, jury unanimity on the issue of causation may be necessary: *R v Chignell* [1991] 2 NZLR 257, also reported as *R v Chignell and Walker* (1990) 6 CRNZ 103 (CA); *R v Boreman* [2000] 1 All ER 307 (CA).

which was a contributing cause of death, even if it did not exist when D did another (and possibly the last) contributing act;[140] and the earlier act will be a sufficient contributing cause if its effect was to incapacitate, and thus prevent V from escaping the effects of the later conduct.[141]

In addition, strict concurrence might not be required if death followed a series of acts which constituted "one transaction", which included acts which contributed to death as well as acts which did not, if, before the killing, D acted with mens rea during part of the transaction. However, as has been explained, this principle has been allowed only restricted application in New Zealand. In *R v Ramsay*[142] the Court of Appeal thought that it can apply only if one or more offenders carried out the single transaction in furtherance of a "preconceived plan". Moreover, although the Court accepted that the principle might apply if D had meant to kill, so that s 167(a) applied, it held that the principle could not apply when para (b) or para (d) was relied upon; for their terms require knowledge of the risk of killing at the time of the act which caused or contributed to death. The force of both these aspects of *Ramsay* has been doubted,[143] but the judgment appears to remain authoritative.

16.5 Manslaughter

Apart from the special case of infanticide,[144] any culpable homicide which is not murder is manslaughter. Although it is not terminology used in the Act, an unlawful killing is commonly called "involuntary" manslaughter if it is not murder because of the absence of a required intent, and "voluntary" manslaughter if it is not murder despite the fact that D may have killed with such intent. In many jurisdictions legislation provides for a verdict of (voluntary) manslaughter in cases of diminished responsibility, where the person who killed was not insane within s 23 but nevertheless suffered such abnormality of mind that his mental responsibility was substantially impaired.[145] This partial defence is not recognised in New Zealand,[146] where there are only two forms of voluntary manslaughter: unlawful killings under provocation (s 169), and killing pursuant to a suicide pact (s 180). Only the first will be examined here.

16.5.1 Provocation

As a general rule, the fact than an accused's conduct was provoked by another is no defence to any crime. Murder is the single exception, in that, although it is not a complete defence, a killing which would otherwise be murder is reduced to manslaughter if it is committed as a result of provocation. This common law rule is codified in s 169.[147]

---

140 *R v Wickliffe* [1987] 1 NZLR 55; (1986) 2 CRNZ 310 (CA): pointing a loaded gun was a contributing cause, although the final cause was an unintended firing of it; cf *R v Cooper* [1993] 1 SCR 146; (1993) 18 CR (4th) 1 (SCC).
141 *R v McKinnon* [1980] 2 NZLR 31 (CA), 36, 37; see 4.9.1(3).
142 *R v Ramsay* [1967] NZLR 1005 (CA); see 4.9.1(3).
143 *Adams*, CA167.14 (looseleaf); in *Ramsay* it was also held that whether a series of acts was "indivisible" was for the jury. The *Thabo Meli* approach (*Thabo Meli v R* [1954] 1 All ER 373; [1954] 1 WLR 228 (PC)) involves "pitfalls" which a judge may be wise to avoid: *R v Menzies* 16/10/97, CA222/97.
144 See 16.6.
145 For example, in England, s 2 Homicide Act 1957.
146 For example *R v Burr* [1969] NZLR 736 (CA); diminished responsibility was provided for in the Crimes Bill 1961, but was deleted when Parliament rejected capital punishment: (1961) 328 NZPD 2680, 2990, 2991. The Law Commission has also declined to recommend its introduction: Law Commission, *Some Criminal Defences with Particular Reference to Battered Defendants*, NZLC R73, Wellington, 2001.

The partial defence of provocation developed at common law from the late 16th century.[148] Initially the judges ruled on a case by case basis whether particular conduct amounted to sufficient provocation, but in the 19th century a general rule was articulated: there had to be "a serious provocation ... which might naturally cause an ordinary and reasonably minded man to lose his self-control and commit such an act".[149] In addition, however, the judges continued to rule that some acts might or might not justify a verdict of manslaughter. In particular, as a general rule some physical violence was required, and words alone could never suffice "save in circumstances of a most extreme and exceptional character".[150] Section 169(2) largely dispenses with particular rules of this kind, and instead provides two general tests which have to be satisfied:

"(2) Anything done or said may be provocation if—

"(a) In the circumstances of the case it was sufficient to deprive a person having the power of self-control of an ordinary person, but otherwise having the characteristics of the offender, of the power of self-control; and

"(b) It did in fact deprive the offender of the power of self-control and thereby induced him to commit the act of homicide."

Paragraph (a) imposes an objective, or evaluative, condition that requires an estimation of the effect of the provocation on the self-control of a hypothetical "ordinary" person, and para (b) requires that the provocation actually deprived the offender of the power of self-control, and by that means led to the killing.[151] Before considering these in more detail, it is convenient to deal with three more particular matters.

(1) *Function of judge and jury and burden of proof*

It is expressly provided by s 169(3) that whether there is any evidence of provocation is a question of law, meaning that it is a question for the trial judge, and by s 169(4) that, if there is such evidence, whether the requirements of subs (2) are met is a question of fact, meaning that it is a question for the jury.

The judge should not leave provocation to the jury unless there is sufficient evidence to raise the issue, or evidence supporting "a credible narrative of causative provocation".[152] This will require some evidence of specific acts or words of provocation resulting in a loss of self-

---

147 Section 169(1) says that this "may" be the effect of provocation, but it is not discretionary: *R v Leblanc* (1985) 22 CCC (3d) 126 (Ont CA). It has been suggested that provocation within s 169 should also reduce attempted murder to attempted manslaughter, for murder is not "the offence intended": Cf s 72(1). The weight of authority is against such a possibility: *R v Laga* [1969] NZLR 417; *McGhee v R* (1995) 183 CLR 82; 69 ALJR 650 (HCA); *R v Campbell* (1977) 38 CCC (2d) 6 (Ont CA); *R v Bruzas* [1972] Crim LR 367; but see *R v Smith* [1964] NZLR 834; *R v Duvivier* (1981) 5 A Crim R 89, 107.
148 Kaye, "The early history of murder and manslaughter" (1967) 83 LQR 365, 569, 589.
149 *R v Welsh* (1869) 11 Cox CC 336, 339 (Keating J).
150 *Holmes v DPP* [1946] AC 588; [1946] 2 All ER 124 (HL), 600; 128, where it was held that a spouse's confession of adultery could not be enough, although the finding of a man committing adultery with the accused's wife had long been sufficient, for "there could not be greater provocation than this": *R v Manning* (1672) T Raym 212; 83 ER 112, sub nom *Maddy's Case* 1 Vent 158; 2 Keb 829; 86 ER 108.
151 A similar dual test applied under the developed common law: *Holmes v DPP* [1946] AC 588; [1946] 2 All ER 124 (HL); and under the rather differently worded provisions of the earlier codes: s 165 Criminal Code Act 1893; s 184 Crimes Act 1908.

control,[153] although in some cases it will suffice that the nature of the conduct or words can be inferred from the evidence.[154] The accused is not, however, required to prove the defence,[155] and neither is it essential that D should give evidence of provocation and loss of self-control: in some cases, even if it is inconsistent with evidence from D, there may be sufficient material supporting the defence within the evidence adduced by the prosecution, the defence, or a combination of both.[156] The question for the judge is whether the evidence is reasonably capable of leading a jury to find it reasonably possible that both the tests in s 169(2) are satisfied. If, but only if, this is the case, the jury should be directed on the defence, which succeeds if the jury finds that both tests are satisfied or is of the view that this is a reasonable possibility.[157] This rule as to onus applies to all ingredients, including the evaluative question of whether the provocation was sufficient to deprive the hypothetical person of the power of self-control.[158] If, on the evidence, the issue is fit to be left to the jury, the judge should direct on it even if it was not raised as an issue during the trial.[159]

(2)   Anything done or said

Under s 169(2), "anything done or said" may be provocation, provided only that the two general tests are satisfied. This broadens the defence in a number of ways.

Some formulations of the common law required acts done "to the accused",[160] but this is not required by s 169. So, for example, an assault on another may constitute provocation to D;[161] and it is not necessary that it be intended or foreseen that D might be provoked.[162] An

---

152 *R v Matoka* [1987] 1 NZLR 340 (CA), 344; this is a favoured formula in New Zealand, apparently designed to prevent speculation; cf *Lee Chun-Chuen v R* [1963] AC 220; [1963] 1 All ER 73 (PC), 229; 77: "All that the defence need do is to point to material which could induce a reasonable doubt."
153 *R v Acott* [1997] 1 All ER 706; [1997] 1 WLR 306 (HL); under New South Wales legislation it seems that "a specific triggering incident" is not needed if loss of control follows a history of abuse: *R v Muy Ky Chhay* (1994) 72 A Crim R 1 (NSW CCA), 13, 14. It is unlikely that this can apply in New Zealand. See 16.5.1(3).
154 *R v Anderson* [1965] NZLR 29 (CA), 35.
155 *R v Kahu* [1947] NZLR 368 (CA).
156 *R v Nepia* [1983] NZLR 754 (CA), 756; *R v Matoka* [1987] 1 NZLR 340 (CA).
157 *R v Nepia* [1983] NZLR 754 (CA); in England the effect of s 3 Homicide Act 1957 (UK) is that the defence must be left to the jury if on the evidence D may have been provoked actually to lose self-control: *DPP v Camplin* [1978] AC 705; [1978] 2 All ER 168 (HL), 716; 173; in New Zealand the defence should be withdrawn either if there is no evidence supporting this (for example *R v Matoka* [1987] 1 NZLR 340 (CA); *R v Mita* [1996] 1 NZLR 95), or if no reasonable jury could find that the objective test may have been satisfied: for example *R v Anderson* [1965] NZLR 29 (CA), 38, 39; *R v Tai* [1976] 1 NZLR 102 (CA); *R v King* (1987) 7 CRNZ 591 (CA). However, the defence is not lightly to be taken away from the jury: *R v Taaka* [1982] 2 NZLR 198 (CA); *R v Nepia* [1983] NZLR 754 (CA); *R v Makoare* [2001] 1 NZLR 318; (2000) 18 CRNZ 511 (CA).
158 *R v Rongonui* [2000] 2 NZLR 385; (2000) 17 CRNZ 310 (CA), paras 234, 235 (Tipping J). Contra *R v Smith (Morgan)* [2001] 1 AC 146; [2000] 3 WLR 654 (HL), 174; 679 (Lord Hoffmann).
159 *R v Sarah* (1990) 5 CRNZ 663 (CA); but if counsel consider that there may be such evidence they have a duty to draw this to the judge's attention: *R v Cox* (1995) 2 Cr App R 513; [1995] Crim LR 741 (CA).
160 For example *R v Duffy* [1949] 1 All ER 932 (CCA); but sexual conduct with, or violence against, a spouse, child, or sibling could suffice: *R v Manning* (1672) T Raym 212; 83 ER 112; *R v Fisher* (1837) 8 C & P 182; 173 ER 452; *R v Harrington* (1866) 10 Cox CC 370; *R v Terry* [1964] VR 248; or a false imprisonment of a stranger: *R v Tooley* (1709) 2 Ld Raym 1296; 92 ER 349.
161 For example *R v Taaka* [1982] 2 NZLR 198 (CA); cf *R v Pearson* [1992] Crim LR 193 (CA).
162 *R v Campbell* [1997] 1 NZLR 16; (1996) 14 CRNZ 117 (CA); *R v Taaka* [1982] 2 NZLR 198 (CA); *R v Twine* [1967] Crim LR 710 (CA); cf *R v McGregor* [1962] NZLR 1069 (CA), 1073.

act of provocation need not be violent (for example, it might be a gesture), and a requirement in the earlier Codes that it be "wrongful" has not been retained. This may have merely meant that there had to be an element of "offensiveness",[163] but with its deletion there is no doubt that lawful conduct may be provocation, although s 169(5) expressly provides that the lawful exercise of any "power conferred by law" cannot suffice.[164]

The earlier Codes qualified the common law rule that words alone were not enough, by allowing an "insult" as possible provocation. Now, under s 169, "anything ... said" may qualify; thus the defence may be based, for example, on verbal taunts, threats of violent or non-violent action,[165] or even on the reporting of a provocative incident.[166]

Of course, the mere fact that the possibility of the defence is not excluded does not mean that it will necessarily be viable when D reacts violently to lawful or verbal conduct. In each case, the two tests in s 169(2) must still be met, and, although the particular circumstances must be considered, it may well be found that the objective test could not be satisfied if, for example, the provocation was a mere admission of unfaithfulness,[167] or an intimation of a decision to end a relationship,[168] or took the form of force in self-defence.[169]

(3)   *Cooling time*

Classic provocation directions require "a sudden and temporary loss of self-control" which may be negated by a lapse of time between the provocation and the killing.[170] A time lapse has dual relevance. Together with the offender's behaviour during the interval, it may indicate that she was not in fact deprived of self-control at the time of the killing.[171] Alternatively, it may be such that an ordinary person would have regained control.[172] This aspect of the law has been criticised for failing to recognise sufficiently that people's reaction times vary. In particular, it has been said that by reason of national or racial temperament some people are "slow burning" and prone to brood for a time before losing control,[173] and that delayed reaction is also typical of battered women.[174]

The previous Codes expressly required that the offender act "in the heat of passion caused by sudden provocation ... on the sudden and before there has been time for his passion to cool". The 1961 Act contains no reference to suddenness or time lapse, but in *R v McGregor*[175] the

---

163   *Stingel v R* (1990) 171 CLR 312; 97 ALR 1 (HCA), 322; 7.
164   This will include lawful arrest; in the case of illegal arrest, s 170 provides that this does not necessarily suffice, but if the illegality is known to D it may be evidence of provocation; even if D does not know of the illegality no doubt the manner of such arrest might also provide such evidence.
165   For example *R v Nepia* [1983] NZLR 754 (CA) (revelation of adulterous relationship plus a threat of loss of access to children).
166   Cf *R v White (Shane)* [1988] 1 NZLR 122 (CA) (a report to D of the rape of his sister, plus an insulting reference to her).
167   *R v Anderson* [1965] NZLR 29 (CA).
168   *R v Tai* [1976] 1 NZLR 102 (CA).
169   *R v Fryer* [1981] 1 NZLR 748 (CA).
170   For example *R v Duffy* [1949] 1 All ER 932 (CCA).
171   For example *R v Mita* [1996] 1 NZLR 95.
172   For example *R v Erutoe* [1990] 2 NZLR 28; (1990) 5 CRNZ 538 (CA), 35; 545.
173   Marsack, "Provocation in trials for murder" [1959] Crim LR 697.
174   Nicholson and Sanghvi, "Battered women and provocation: The implications of *R v Ahluwalia*" [1993] Crim LR 728; *R v Muy Ky Chhay* (1994) 72 A Crim R 1 (NSW CCA), 11.
175   *R v McGregor* [1962] NZLR 1069 (CA), 1078, 1079.

Court of Appeal rejected a submission that this had become irrelevant, and upheld directions requiring that the provocation and the killing be "reasonably related in time". But the Court did accept that it is not necessary as a matter of law that the provocation occur "immediately" before the killing, and other cases confirm that "cooling time" is a flexible and uncertain consideration. The heat of anger may be "more enduring than fleeting moments".[176] When there has been more than one provocative incident, anger may smoulder "from the repetition of affronts until fanned into flame by an incident which, taken out of context, would not excuse the response."[177] In such cases, it is the period after the last provocative incident which is important[178] and, although the longer the delay the more likely it is that the defence will fail, there are cases where the defence is for the jury even though a few hours pass before the killing.[179]

In cases where time lapse is regarded as significant, the courts also commonly have regard to how the offender acted in that time, even when the objective test is emphasised;[180] although neither the lapse of some hours nor intervening conduct of some complexity and apparent deliberation are necessarily fatal to the defence.[181]

Notwithstanding this flexibility, the courts continue to hold that "a sudden and temporary loss of self-control" is essential,[182] although with the abandonment of a requirement of immediacy the meaning of this is obscure. In *R v Mita*[183] Fisher J suggests that the defence will be "untenable" unless it was a real possibility that between the provocation and the killing the offender "was in a continuous state of hot blood", or "uncontrolled anger", but this deprives rejection of the need for an immediate response of much of its effect, and seems incompatible with some cases where the defence has been held viable.[184] Alternatively, in *R v McGregor*[185] there is a suggestion that "a sudden transition" to loss of control is necessary, but this would not allow for those whose emotions are "slow burning" and develop gradually before control is eventually lost.[186] The better view seems to be that such directions merely serve to emphasise that it is not enough that the offender was made extremely angry, and that true "loss of self-control" is needed.[187]

---

176 *R v Timoti* [2005] 1 NZLR 466; (2004) 21 CRNZ 90 (CA), para 52.
177 *R v Timoti* [2005] 1 NZLR 466; (2004) 21 CRNZ 90 (CA), para 52.
178 For example *R v Taaka* [1982] 2 NZLR 198 (CA), where a fight between D and the victim may have "revived" provocation from 13 days before.
179 *R v Mita* [1996] 1 NZLR 95, 101 (Fisher J), citing *R v Taaka* [1982] 2 NZLR 198 (CA); cf *R v Ahluwalia* [1992] 4 All ER 889; (1993) 96 Cr App R 133 (CA).
180 For example *R v Anderson* [1965] NZLR 29 (CA), 38-39; *R v Erutoe* [1990] 2 NZLR 28; (1990) 5 CRNZ 538 (CA), 35; 544-545; *R v King* (1987) 7 CRNZ 591 (CA).
181 For example *R v Taaka* [1982] 2 NZLR 198 (CA); *R v Ahluwalia* [1992] 4 All ER 889; (1993) 96 Cr App R 133 (CA).
182 *R v McGregor* [1962] NZLR 1069 (CA), 1079; *R v Ahluwalia* [1992] 4 All ER 889; (1993) 96 Cr App R 133 (CA), 895; 138; *R v Thornton (No 2)* [1996] 2 All ER 1023; [1996] 1 WLR 1174 (CA), 1030; 1181.
183 *R v Mita* [1996] 1 NZLR 95, 99-100.
184 For example *R v Taaka* [1982] 2 NZLR 198 (CA); *R v Ahluwalia* [1992] 4 All ER 889; (1993) 96 Cr App R 133 (CA).
185 *R v McGregor* [1962] NZLR 1069 (CA), 1078; cf *R v Thornton (No 2)* [1996] 2 All ER 1023; [1996] 1 WLR 1174 (CA), 1031; 1183.
186 In *R v Tai* [1976] 1 NZLR 102 (CA), 107 it was recognised that such an attribute might be relevant to the time factor; and the 1961 Act was intended to allow for "brooding" offenders: (1961) 328 NZPD 2681. Under s 169(2)(a), a personal characteristic is relevant to objective *sufficiency* of provocation only if it affects its gravity: 16.5.1(5)(c); but this rule need not affect its relevance to a "cooling time" issue: 16.5.1(5)(f).

(4) Actual loss of self-control

This is the most fundamental requirement and, notwithstanding the different order in the statute, it is best to deal with it before the objective test, which imposes a limit on the defence.[188]

Under s 169(2)(b), the provocative conduct or words must "in fact deprive the offender of the power of self-control", and in that way bring about the killing. The jury should have regard to any fact, circumstance, or personal attribute of the offender which makes this more likely, whether or not it is relevant to the objective test. This may include, for example, the offender's ill-temper, irascibility, or voluntary intoxication,[189] her history or psychological condition,[190] or mistaken belief regarding the circumstances.[191]

It is not, however, possible to describe precisely what is involved in loss of "the power of self-control". The criterion will be negatived if the killing was "deliberate and premeditated", but positive descriptions of what is required always employ highly metaphorical language: for example, D must act "in hot blood", "in the heat of passion", "while not master of his or her mind".[192] The precipitating emotion will often be anger or resentment, but it may be fear or panic.[193] However, in no case is any such feeling sufficient in itself, it being essential that the result is "an emotional state which the jury are prepared to accept as a loss of self-control".[194] Nor will the defence be assisted by expert evidence which suggests an abnormal propensity to choose to act violently, rather than a propensity to lose self-control.[195]

Overseas authority suggests that the loss of self-control is a matter of degree, in that the defendant's loss of self-control must have been sufficient to cause her to act as she did.[196] In New Zealand, however, it seems that the language of s 169 mandates a less nuanced, an all-or-nothing approach, since it requires simply that D be deprived "of the power of self-control".[197]

While it may seem odd, loss of self-control is consistent with D's acting with intent to kill, or with other murderous mens rea.[198] Indeed, if D acts without the mens rea required for murder, an unlawful killing will be manslaughter whether or not provoked.[199] The defence only applies to "culpable homicide that would otherwise be murder" (s 169(1)), and strictly it should not

---

187   Cf R v McGregor [1962] NZLR 1069 (CA), 1078; R v Ahluwalia [1992] 4 All ER 889; (1993) 96 Cr App R 133 (CA), 895; 138.
188   Cf R v McCarthy [1992] 2 NZLR 550; (1992) 8 CRNZ 58 (CA), 558; 67; R v Mita [1996] 1 NZLR 95, 99; R v Rongonui [2000] 2 NZLR 385; (2000) 17 CRNZ 310 (CA), para 234 (Tipping J).
189   R v Barton [1977] 1 NZLR 295 (CA); R v Makoare 18/4/00, CA469/99; Orchard, "Provocation: The subjective element" [1977] NZLJ 77.
190   R v Thornton (No 2) [1996] 2 All ER 1023; [1996] 1 WLR 1174 (CA), 1030; 1182 (battered woman syndrome); cf R v Taaka [1982] 2 NZLR 198 (CA) (a "brooding" temperament, which could explain delayed reaction).
191   R v White (Shane) [1988] 1 NZLR 122 (CA), 126.
192   R v Muy Ky Chhay (1994) 72 A Crim R 1 (NSW CCA), 8, 9; cf R v Mita [1996] 1 NZLR 95, 100.
193   Packett v R (1937) 58 CLR 190, 217 (Dixon J); Van Den Hoek v R (1986) 161 CLR 158; 69 ALR 1 (HCA), 167-168; 8 (Mason J); from which it follows that provocation is not inconsistent with self-defence: R v Pita (1989) 4 CRNZ 660 (CA); cf R v Oakes [1995] 2 NZLR 673 (CA); R v Thornton (No 2) [1996] 2 All ER 1023; [1996] 1 WLR 1174 (CA).
194   R v Muy Ky Chhay (1994) 72 A Crim R 1 (NSW CCA), 14.
195   R v Makoare [2001] 1 NZLR 318; (2000) 18 CRNZ 511 (CA).
196   Phillips v R [1969] 2 AC 130; [1969] 2 WLR 581 (PC), 137-138; 585.
197   Timoti v R [2005] NZSC 37, para 44. See further below, 16.5.1(5)(a).

be considered before murderous intent is found to be established.[200] Furthermore, as is implicit in the rule that provocation merely reduces the crime to manslaughter, a finding that provocation "did in fact deprive the offender of the power of self-control" does *not* prevent him from being responsible for his conduct, since that conduct was nonetheless deliberate and voluntary. In *R v Campbell*[201] D had killed the victim after conduct which D interpreted as a sexual advance. He gave evidence that he was unable to stop what he was doing, and there was medical evidence that it was unlikely that he could control his actions, because of the effects of post traumatic stress disorder from which he suffered after being sexually abused as a child. The Court of Appeal held that the evidence justified a verdict of manslaughter as a result of provocation, but that the accused remained criminally responsible unless he was insane or had acted in a state of automatism, which required conduct that was "not subject to any conscious control". Neither of these defences was available. Despite the medical evidence, the accused had been aware of his acts, which could only be regarded as "deliberate voluntary acts".

(5) *The objective test*

What was done or said must also have been, in the circumstances of the case, sufficient to deprive of the power of self-control "a person having the power of self-control of an ordinary person, but otherwise having the characteristics of the offender": s 169(2)(a).

The Act appropriately applies the standard of an "ordinary", not a "reasonable", person. The test is not concerned with reasoning or reasonable conduct (needless killing in the throes of passion is the antithesis of reasonable conduct).[202] The purpose of this additional test is to keep the defence within bounds by ensuring that a killing will not be reduced from murder to manslaughter unless the provocation was "grave and weighty".[203] It does this by imposing a standard which denies the defence "not to all those who react unreasonably to provocation, but only to those whose reactions show a lack of self-control falling outside the ordinary or common range of human temperaments".[204] Application of the test requires the jury to make a decision on a question of opinion.[205] In the following sections, we consider the factors relevant to that decision.

---

198 *R v Barton* [1977] 1 NZLR 295 (CA), 299; see also *A-G for Ceylon v Perera* [1953] AC 200; [1953] 2 WLR 238 (PC); *Lee Chun-Chuen v R* [1963] AC 220; [1963] 1 All ER 73 (PC); *Parker v R* [1964] AC 1369; [1964] 2 All ER 641 (PC), 1391; 651; in *Holmes v DPP* [1946] AC 588; [1946] 2 All ER 124 (HL), 598; 127 there was a dictum to the contrary, which perhaps echoed the historical theory that provocation rebutted the "presumption of malice" which the early common law applied to render voluntary killings murder: 1 Hale PC 455.
199 *R v Bruzas* [1972] Crim LR 367.
200 *Johnson v R* (1976) 136 CLR 619; 11 ALR 23 (HCA), 633, 643; 33, 41; *Masciantonio v R* (1995) 183 CLR 58; 129 ALR 575 (HCA), 66; 580.
201 *R v Campbell* (1997) 15 CRNZ 138 (CA); this was an appeal following a conviction of manslaughter on a retrial ordered in *R v Campbell* [1997] 1 NZLR 16; (1996) 14 CRNZ 117 (CA).
202 Cf *R v Morhall* [1996] AC 90; [1995] 3 All ER 659 (HL), 97-98; 665-666; *Stingel v R* (1990) 171 CLR 312; 97 ALR 1 (HCA), 328-329; 11-12.
203 *R v McGregor* [1962] NZLR 1069 (CA), 1075; *Johnson v R* (1976) 136 CLR 619; 11 ALR 23 (HCA), 635; 35.
204 *R v Enright* [1961] VR 663, 669; *Stingel v R* (1990) 171 CLR 312; 97 ALR 1 (HCA).
205 *Phillips v R* [1969] 2 AC 130; [1969] 2 WLR 581 (PC), 137; 585.

(a) Proportionality

The terms of s 169(2)(a) require only that the hypothetical person might have been deprived of "the power of self-control". Traditionally, however, the question was held to be a more particular one. The traditional approach was that the provocative conduct should be compared with the offender's reaction, and the test to be applied was whether a person of ordinary self-control might have so lost control as a result of that provocation as to form a murderous intent, and also to act on it in a way *akin to the offender's reaction*. For example, in *R v Anderson*[206] the woman with whom the accused lived made a remark which indicated that she had been unfaithful. The accused responded with a brutal and prolonged beating, which continued for up to an hour in more than one location, and which resulted in death. The defence, it was held, was not available because no person of ordinary self-control could have been led by this kind of provocation "to the degree and method and continuance of violence" which had killed the victim.

Similarly, the High Court of Australia has suggested that one should ask whether an ordinary person could (not would) have so acted, and it is the "kind and degree" of violence which matters, rather than its continuance or precise physical form.[207]

The position in New Zealand law has now changed, as a result of the decision of the Supreme Court in *Timoti v R*.[208] It now seems that earlier authority, such as *Anderson*, may be of doubtful application in New Zealand. In particular, it has been suggested that the decision in *Anderson* may have been influenced by the statutory language of s 3 Homicide Act 1957 (UK). By contrast, the common law rule, that the jury had to bring to account "the degree and method and continuance" of the violence which produced death, was not the correct approach under s 169, which requires only that there be the loss of self-control:[209]

> "There is a material difference between provocation which is sufficient to deprive the statutory hypothetical person of the power of self-control on the one hand and provocation which is sufficient to make that person do as the accused did on the other."

The Court further held that, since a culpable homicide which would otherwise be murder necessarily involves action causative of death accompanied by murderous intent, provocation, to be successful, must have been sufficient to cause in the hypothetical person loss of self-control inducing both a murderous act and murderous intent. The degree of the loss of self-control beyond that point is not relevant to the evaluative question, and so the extent of loss of self-control manifested by the accused is no longer a relevant consideration.[210] The question for analysis now is whether the provocation was sufficient to cause a hypothetical person to lose self-control inducing both a murderous act and murderous intent. Beyond that it is not necessary to go.

Accordingly, it will be a misdirection for a trial judge to direct the jury in terms of whether the provocative words were bad enough to cause "the kind of reaction" rather than whether they were sufficient to cause a loss of self-control.[211]

---

206 *R v Anderson* [1965] NZLR 29 (CA), 38.
207 *Masciantonio v R* (1995) 183 CLR 58; 129 ALR 575 (HCA), 69-70; 582-583.
208 *Timoti v R* [2005] NZSC 37.
209 *Timoti v R* [2005] NZSC 37, para 44.
210 *Timoti v R* [2005] NZSC 37, para 46.
211 *Timoti v R* [2005] NZSC 37, para 48.

At one time it was further suggested that the defence could succeed only if there was some "reasonable relationship" or "proportion" between the provocation and the offender's reaction.[212] "Fists might be answered with fists, but not with a deadly weapon."[213] However, it is clear that there is no such rule of law, although such relationship or proportion has been said to be "a factor, and indeed a weighty factor, to be considered by the jury in determining whether there was provocation".[214] The jury is entitled to take the view that people are liable to react with more or less violence according to the gravity of the provocation.[215]

It may now be arguable whether lack of proportion will ever justify withdrawing the defence from the jury, and even whether it is relevant in applying the "ordinary person" limb. In *R v Rongonui*,[216] the victim had refused to help D by babysitting and had presented a knife. D responded by seizing the knife, and in killing the victim she inflicted more than 150 wounds (some with a second knife which she got when the first broke). The Court of Appeal was primarily concerned with the relevance of D's personal "characteristics", but it is noteworthy that the majority did not discuss the possible significance of the sustained and ferocious nature of the attack and did not question whether provocation was open on the facts.[217] Elias CJ (with whom Thomas J agreed) did discuss the relevance of disproportion in response, but in terms which suggest it has a limited role. Her Honour accepted that it may sometimes provide compelling evidence that a killing was not induced by the provocation[218] but added that it will usually be unnecessary to mention this possibility and that, if it is, the judge should also point out that such disproportion is equally capable of supporting the defence because it suggests lack of control.[219] While not explicitly ruling out the possibility of it being relevant to the objective question, the Chief Justice further noted that, unlike s 3 Homicide Act 1957 (UK), s 169(2)(a) does not in terms require that the hypothetical person might have acted as D did and (following the wording of the paragraph) said that it "is concerned only with the sufficiency of the provocation to deprive the accused of self-control".[220] This approach is endorsed by the Supreme Court in *Timoti v R*.[221]

(b) Circumstances of the case

The objective test requires the jury to consider the provocation in its context and to assess its gravity. Section 169(2)(a) expressly incorporates "the circumstances of the case".[222] This will

---

212 *Mancini v DPP* [1942] AC 1; [1941] 3 All ER 272 (HL), 9; 277: "the mode of resentment must bear a reasonable relationship to the provocation."
213 *R v Duffy* [1949] 1 All ER 932 (CCA), 933.
214 *R v Noel* [1960] NZLR 212 (CA), 219; *R v Dougherty* [1966] NZLR 890 (CA); in *Phillips v R* [1969] 2 AC 130; [1969] 2 WLR 581 (PC), 138; 586 the Privy Council was less emphatic in describing it as "merely a consideration which may or may not commend itself to them". It may not always be an appropriate or useful consideration: *R v Campbell* [1997] 1 NZLR 16; (1996) 14 CRNZ 117 (CA), 26; 127.
215 *Phillips v R* [1969] 2 AC 130; [1969] 2 WLR 581 (PC), 137, 138; 584, 586; *Masciantonio v R* (1995) 183 CLR 58; 129 ALR 575 (HCA), 67; 581.
216 *R v Rongonui* [2000] 2 NZLR 385; (2000) 17 CRNZ 310 (CA).
217 On a retrial the defence succeeded, it being held that a sentence of 10 1/2 years' imprisonment was appropriate in view of D's diminished responsibility: *R v Rongonui* 9/5/01, CA321/00.
218 Cf *R v Savage* [1991] 3 NZLR 155 (CA), 160; *R v Campbell* [1997] 1 NZLR 16; (1996) 14 CRNZ 117 (CA), 25, 26; 127, 128.
219 Cf *Masciantonio v R* (1995) 183 CLR 58; 129 ALR 575 (HCA), 68-69; 582; *R v R* (1981) 28 SASR 321; 4 A Crim R 127, 327; 132; Orchard, "Provocation: The subjective element" [1977] NZLJ 77, 79, 80.
220 *R v Rongonui* [2000] 2 NZLR 385; (2000) 17 CRNZ 310 (CA), paras 137-142.
221 *Timoti v R* [2005] NZSC 37.

include information given to the accused, by the victim or others, about surrounding circumstances or earlier events,[223] as well as the past and present relationship between the victim and the offender, which may be important. For example, a history of antagonism between them, or abuse by V, may lead to a build-up of emotion and so aggravate the effect of an ultimate provocative incident that, even if the incident by itself may appear comparatively trivial, it may in the context be serious, and cause "slumbering fires of passion to burst into flame".[224] Alternatively, D's experience of V's past conduct may lead to anticipation of a particular degree of violence and abuse.[225]

(c) Characteristics of the offender[226]

After the adoption of the "reasonable man" test, English judges consistently held that the reasonable man was not to be invested with any particular features of the accused's personality. In particular, it was irrelevant to the test that the accused was unusually excitable or pugnacious, or bad-tempered and wanting in "mental balance";[227] and this was so whatever the cause: for example, whether it be mental deficiency,[228] pregnancy,[229] or drunkenness.[230] In *Bedder v DPP*[231] it was confirmed that the same was true of physical disability, it being held that the offender's sexual impotence was to be ignored in assessing a reasonable person's likely response to taunts of impotence. For Lord Simonds LC this followed from the purpose of the reasonable man test:[232]

> "Its purpose is to invite the jury to consider the act of the accused by reference to a certain standard or norm of conduct and with this object the 'reasonable' or the 'average' or the 'normal' man is invoked. If the reasonable man is then deprived in whole or in part of his reason or the normal man endowed with abnormal characteristics, the test ceases to have any value."

There seems to be no doubt that the same principle applied in New Zealand to the unqualified "ordinary person" test in the statutes of 1893 and 1908,[233] but in 1961 Parliament refined the test so that it requires the provocation to be sufficient to deprive of the power of self-control "a person having the power of self-control of an ordinary person, but otherwise having the characteristics of the offender".[234] The intention was at least to overturn the effect of *Bedder*,

---

222 Cf *R v Morhall* [1996] AC 90; [1995] 3 All ER 659 (HL), 98-99; 666-667 ("the entire factual situation").
223 *R v White (Shane)* [1988] 1 NZLR 122 (CA), 126-127; *R v Matoka* [1987] 1 NZLR 340 (CA), 344; but see 16.5.1(6), regarding mistake.
224 *R v McGregor* [1962] NZLR 1069 (CA), 1080; *R v Pita* (1989) 4 CRNZ 660 (CA), 665-666; *R v Tai* [1976] 1 NZLR 102 (CA), 107; cf *R v Thornton (No 2)* [1996] 2 All ER 1023; [1996] 1 WLR 1174 (CA), 1030; 1182-1183; Wasik, "Cumulative provocation and domestic killing" [1982] Crim LR 29.
225 Briggs, "Provocation re-assessed" (1996) 112 LQR 403.
226 Orchard, "Provocation: Recharacterisation of 'characteristics' " (1996) 6 Canterbury LR 202.
227 *Mancini v DPP* [1942] AC 1; [1941] 3 All ER 272 (HL), 9; 277; *R v Lesbini* [1914] 3 KB 1116 (CCA).
228 *R v Alexander* (1913) 9 Cr App R 139 (CCA).
229 *R v Smith* (1914) 11 Cr App R 36 (CCA).
230 *R v McCarthy* [1954] 2 QB 105; [1954] 2 All ER 262 (CCA).
231 *Bedder v DPP* [1954] 2 All ER 801; [1954] 1 WLR 1119 (HL).
232 *Bedder v DPP* [1954] 2 All ER 801; [1954] 1 WLR 1119 (HL), 804; 1123; cf *R v Raney* (1942) 29 Cr App R 14, 17, where the fact that D was one-legged was regarded as relevant to whether a blow to his crutch might be provocation.
233 As to ill-temper and drunkenness, see *R v Jackson* [1918] NZLR 363.
234 Section 169(2)(a) Crimes Act 1961.

and it was described as an "important clarification".[235] But the courts have experienced some difficulty in interpreting and applying this revised test.

The Court of Appeal first considered it in *R v McGregor*,[236] where it described the relevance of an offender's "characteristics" with two different propositions: (i) they might weaken the power of self-control otherwise to be expected of an ordinary person,[237] but (ii) they may be taken into account only insofar as they made the words or conduct more provocative to the offender.[238] The Court also thought it necessary to impose various limitations on the meaning of "characteristics", in order to prevent the unintended obliteration of the ordinary person test.

The dual approach to relevance in *McGregor* was confusing, and the judgment was severely criticised by Sir Francis Adams. He regarded it as introducing unnecessary complexity and objected that proposition (i) gave no effect to the words "but otherwise". Sir Francis reasoned that a homicide committed under provocation results from a conflict between (a) the offender's sensitivity or susceptibility to the provocation and (b) his power of self-control. The words "but otherwise" make it clear that an offender's personal characteristics may be relevant to the assessment of (a), but the offender is to be judged as if she possessed normal self-control.[239]

On this reading of s 169(2)(a) the offender's actual power of self-control, or level of self-restraint, is irrelevant and the jury is required to imagine a person with the power of self-control of an "ordinary person", or "normal self-control". The offender's personal characteristics are not relevant to this, and characteristics which do no more than negate the possession of such a level of self-control must be ignored: these include, for example, a disposition to lose one's temper readily, unusual pugnacity, or excitability.[240]

However, a particular characteristic may be relevant to an assessment of the gravity of the provocation in a particular case, or how sensitive a person might be to it, and, therefore to how she might react to it, even if she has an ordinary power of self-control. The nature and degree of a person's mental and emotional response to the provocation may be affected by a personal attribute of the offender. It may so aggravate the effect of the provocation that even normal self-control might be overcome, although such control would not be in the absence of such aggravation. For example, a young man who is impotent and sensitive about this may feel taunts about it differently, and perhaps more deeply, than one who was not in fact impotent. Indeed, there may be cases where the very nature of the provocation cannot be properly understood without regard to some personal attributes: for example, the offender's race in the case of a racial slur, the offender's ability to understand the meaning and significance

---

235 (3 October 1961) 328 NZPD 2681.
236 *R v McGregor* [1962] NZLR 1069 (CA).
237 *R v McGregor* [1962] NZLR 1069 (CA), 1081: "The offender must be presumed to possess in general the power of self-control of the ordinary man, save insofar as his power of self-control is weakened because of some particular characteristic possessed by him."
238 *R v McGregor* [1962] NZLR 1069 (CA), 1082: "The words or conduct must have been exclusively or particularly provocative to the individual because, and only because, of the characteristic."
239 *Adams*, CA169.12-13 (looseleaf).
240 *R v McGregor* [1962] NZLR 1069 (CA), 1081; *R v Fryer* [1981] 1 NZLR 748 (CA), 752; cf *DPP v Camplin* [1978] AC 705; [1978] 2 All ER 168 (HL), 716; 173.

of allegedly provocative words,[241] or the gender of the parties in the case of a sexual assault or advance.[242]

The Court of Appeal gave somewhat equivocal support to this interpretation in *R v McCarthy*[243] and more clearly adopted it in *R v Campbell*.[244] A full Court then reviewed the issue exhaustively in *R v Rongonui*.[245]

D was a woman who had suffered historical and recent physical abuse. She was brain damaged, she suffered from post-traumatic stress disorder and depression, and her self-esteem largely arose from the mothering of her children. In the belief that the children were about to be removed by a welfare agency, she said that she went to a female neighbour to ask her to babysit while she resolved the issue with the agency. It was claimed that the neighbour refused to help and presented a knife. D responded by seizing the knife and stabbed the victim to death.

D was convicted of murder, but the Court of Appeal was unanimous that a retrial was required because of an error in a ruling of the trial judge. However, the Court was divided on the interpretation of s 169(2)(a). The majority held that it means that personal characteristics are relevant only to the gravity of the provocation to the offender and may not be regarded as reducing the general power of self-control of the hypothetical person whose imagined reaction to the provocation provides the test for liability. The minority accepted that a characteristic would not be relevant if it was no more than "the ill-temper, irascibility, impulsiveness, violence, or intoxication an ordinary man may experience and which he is expected to keep under control".[246] But they held that the jury should take into account other characteristics which diminished the accused's power of self-control and ask itself whether the provocation was sufficient for an ordinary person with that characteristic and reduced self-control to lose it, or whether the accused "ought" to have exercised self-control.

At the time of decision, the majority conclusion was consistent with decisions (on various statutes) of the House of Lords, Privy Council, High Court of Australia, and Supreme Court of Canada.[247] However, subsequently in *R v Smith (Morgan)*,[248] the House of Lords by a 3 : 2 majority adopted an interpretation of s 3 Homicide Act 1957 (UK) consistent with the minority view in *Rongonui*. Yet in turn, *Smith* has itself been disapproved by the Privy Council in *A-G for Jersey v Holley*[249] and, consequently, was not followed by the English Court of Appeal.[250] In *Holley*, and extraordinary sitting of nine Law Lords held (by a majority of six to three) that, under art 4 of the Homicide (Jersey) Law 1986, which is identical to s 3 of the Homicide Act 1957 (UK), loss of self-control for the purposes of provocation must be judged by a uniform, objective standard of self-control to be expected of an ordinary person. This rejects the more

---

241 Cf *R v Lafaele* (1987) 2 CRNZ 677 (CA).
242 *R v Hill* (1986) 25 CCC (3d) 322 (SCC).
243 *R v McCarthy* [1992] 2 NZLR 550; (1992) 8 CRNZ 58 (CA).
244 *R v Campbell* [1997] 1 NZLR 16; (1996) 14 CRNZ 117 (CA), 25; 126-127.
245 *R v Rongonui* [2000] 2 NZLR 385; (2000) 17 CRNZ 310 (CA).
246 *R v Rongonui* [2000] 2 NZLR 385; (2000) 17 CRNZ 310 (CA), para 120 (Elias CJ).
247 *R v Morhall* [1996] AC 90; [1995] 3 All ER 659 (HL); *Luc Thiet Thuan v R* [1997] AC 131; [1996] 2 All ER 1033 (PC); *Stingel v R* (1990) 171 CLR 312; 97 ALR 1 (HCA); *Masciantonio v R* (1995) 183 CLR 58; 129 ALR 575 (HCA); *R v Hill* (1986) 25 CCC (3d) 322 (SCC).
248 *R v Smith (Morgan)* [2001] 1 AC 146; [2000] 3 WLR 654 (HL); see [2000] Crim LR 1004 (critique by Sir John Smith).
249 *A-G for Jersey v Holley* [2005] UKPC 23; [2005] 3 WLR 29 (PC).
250 *R v James* [2006] 2 WLR 887; [2006] 1 All ER 759 (CA).

"flexible" approach which would permit a jury to take account of the accused's particular characteristics and abnormalities. The Privy Council's approach, which was said by their Lordships to be a definitive clarification of the present state of English law, is consistent with the majority approach in *Rongonui*.

In the meantime, prior to the determination in *Holley*, the Court of Appeal had declined to revisit the issue in *R v Makoare*,[251] so it may safely be concluded that *Rongonui* states the law in New Zealand. The analysis of the majority in *Rongonui* accords with the natural meaning of the terms of s 169(2)(a). It also provides an objective criterion for the jury to apply in assessing the sufficiency of provocation, whereas the minority approach would leave this to their "essentially subjective judgment", without any such measure.[252]

On the other hand, this comes at a price: the minority objected that unfairness might result from discounting a diminished power of self-control, for which an accused may not be to blame. It was also thought that the distinction required by the majority view is artificial, is too hard for jurors to understand, and leads to excessively complex directions.[253] So it may be no surprise that, in *R v Timoti*,[254] the Court observed that the division of opinion in *Rongonui* was testament to the "wholly unsatisfactory nature of the statutory concept of provocation." It suggested that jury verdicts on provocation are more likely to have been reached by the "application of common-sense, community values and a wise and merciful appreciation that a case which would otherwise be one of murder, may nevertheless have extenuating circumstances or a diminution of responsibility which, as a matter of justice, warrant a verdict of manslaughter."[255]

Where there is evidence of a relevant characteristic which might affect the gravity of the provocation for the defendant, this should be explained to the jury,[256] and if the jury are invited to take into account proportionality of provocation and loss of self-control the judge will need to make it clear that it is the provocation as affected by any relevant characteristics which needs to be considered.[257]

(1) *Normal and abnormal characteristics*. In *R v McGregor*[258] it was recognised that a "characteristic" might be either a physical or a mental quality, or an attribute such as colour, race, or creed. But it was also said that it "must be something definite and of sufficient significance to make the offender a different person from the ordinary run of mankind", or different from "the ordinary man of the community".[259] This is

---

251 *R v Makoare* [2001] 1 NZLR 318; (2000) 18 CRNZ 511 (CA). See also *R v Warren* 20/11/00, CA315/00, para 21.
252 *R v Smith (Morgan)* [2001] 1 AC 146; [2000] 3 WLR 654 (HL), 206; 710 (Lord Hobhouse dissenting).
253 Tipping J suggested a model, which is complex: *R v Rongonui* [2000] 2 NZLR 385; (2000) 17 CRNZ 310 (CA), para 235; cf the simpler proposal in *R v Smith (Morgan)* [2001] 1 AC 146; [2000] 3 WLR 654 (HL), 205; 709 by Lord Hobhouse (dissenting).
254 *R v Timoti* [2005] 1 NZLR 466; (2004) 21 CRNZ 90 (CA).
255 *R v Timoti* [2005] 1 NZLR 466; (2004) 21 CRNZ 90 (CA), para 47.
256 *R v Morhall* [1996] AC 90; [1995] 3 All ER 659 (HL), 100; 668; *R v Thornton (No 2)* [1996] 2 All ER 1023; [1996] 1 WLR 1174 (CA), 1031; 1183. The judge will have to decide whether a suggested characteristic could be held to qualify, it being for the jury to decide whether it might in fact have affected the gravity of the provocation: Cf *R v Rongonui* [2000] 2 NZLR 385; (2000) 17 CRNZ 310 (CA), paras 234-235 (Tipping J).
257 *R v Campbell* [1997] 1 NZLR 16; (1996) 14 CRNZ 117 (CA), 26, 27; 128, 129; in *R v Oakes* [1995] 2 NZLR 673 (CA), 681, 682 a very brief and general explanation was held acceptable, when the point had been at the forefront of the defence.
258 *R v McGregor* [1962] NZLR 1069 (CA), 1081.

misconceived. Although s 169(2)(a) refers to an "ordinary person", what is required is an assessment of the effect of particular provocation on a hypothetical person who has one particular human capacity — an "ordinary" power of self-control.[260] Provided that a personal attribute affects the content or gravity of provocation it may be a relevant "characteristic" even though it is not "peculiar" or other than normal or ordinary.[261] For example, in appropriate cases the offender's race or gender may qualify, as might love for a spouse and children.[262] If fear may have contributed to loss of self-control the comparative size and strength of the parties may be relevant.[263]

(2) *Temporary attributes (including drunkenness).* It was also said in R v McGregor that a characteristic must have a sufficient degree of permanence to be part of an offender's "character or personality", so that temporary or transitory states of mind (such as a mood of depression, excitability, or irascibility), or conditions (such as drunkenness) were excluded.[264] New Zealand courts have yet to question this,[265] but it raises a difficult question of degree, and reflects a rather narrow interpretation of "characteristics" which ignores the fact that in the assessment of gravity of provocation it is the time of the killing which is important.[266] In R v Morhall,[267] Lord Goff considered that some temporary physical conditions may be characteristics (eczema being given as an example), at least if the subject of taunts. He accepted that drunkenness is plainly excluded, but suggested that the basis for this might be the rule of policy that intoxication does not itself excuse offending. The courts have consistently held that drunkenness on the occasion of the killing is irrelevant to the objective test,[268] although a self-induced addiction or other discreditable attribute, or even intoxication on another occasion, may be a characteristic, if relevant to the gravity of the provocation.[269]

---

259 In R v Tai [1976] 1 NZLR 102 (CA), 106, this was expanded to "an ordinary person in terms of [New Zealand's] mixed society".
260 R v Morhall [1996] AC 90; [1995] 3 All ER 659 (HL), 97-98; 665-666; Masciantonio v R (1995) 183 CLR 58; 129 ALR 575 (HCA), 66-67; 581; this standard is sometimes expressed in normative terms: "such powers of self-control as everyone is entitled to expect that his fellow citizens will exercise in society as it is today": DPP v Camplin [1978] AC 705; [1978] 2 All ER 168 (HL), 716-717; 173-174 (Lord Diplock).
261 R v Hill (1986) 25 CCC (3d) 322 (SCC), 335, 336.
262 Cf R v Nepia [1983] NZLR 754 (CA), 757.
263 Cf R v Oakes [1995] 2 NZLR 673 (CA), 676 (in the context of self-defence).
264 R v McGregor [1962] NZLR 1069 (CA), 1081.
265 In R v McCarthy [1992] 2 NZLR 550; (1992) 8 CRNZ 58 (CA), 558; 66-67 the Court excluded the effect of alcohol, "being transitory and not a characteristic"; and Adams, CA169.14ff (looseleaf) thought it implicit in "characteristics" that "merely temporary or transitory" conditions did not qualify.
266 Orchard, "Provocation: Recharacterisation of 'characteristics' " (1996) 6 Canterbury LR 202, 208; Brown, "Killings non sedato animo: A new test" [1962] NZLJ 489, 491.
267 R v Morhall [1996] AC 90; [1995] 3 All ER 659 (HL), 99; 667; cf Luc Thiet Thuan v R [1997] AC 131; [1996] 2 All ER 1033 (PC), 142; 1042; R v Rongonui [2000] 2 NZLR 385; (2000) 17 CRNZ 310 (CA), para 236 (Tipping J).
268 This has not been doubted since R v McCarthy [1954] 2 QB 105; [1954] 2 All ER 262 (CCA); cf Sir John Smith [1995] Crim LR 891, 892; Orchard, "Provocation: Recharacterisation of 'characteristics' " (1996) 6 Canterbury LR 202, 213; intoxication is relevant to the subjective question under s 169(2)(b): R v Barton [1977] 1 NZLR 295 (CA).
269 R v Morhall [1996] AC 90; [1995] 3 All ER 659 (HL), 99, 100; 667, 668 (addiction to glue sniffing, which was the subject of taunts).

(d)   Relationship between the provocation and a characteristic

In *R v McGregor*, the Court of Appeal stated that there must be some "real" or "direct" connection between the nature of the provocation and the characteristic relied on; the two must be "related", or the provocation must be "directed at" the characteristic.[270] It was apparently thought that a characteristic could not influence the provocative effect of conduct unless such a test was met.

In *R v McCarthy*,[271] however, the Court indicated that the whole of this passage had caused difficulty, and clearly rejected the suggestion that provocation must be "directed at" a characteristic for it to be relevant. In *Luc Thiet Thuan v R*[272] the Privy Council said that such a requirement "may be misleading". It accepted that it would be met "in the great majority" of cases where a characteristic is relevant to the gravity of the provocation to D, but observed that this need not be so, instancing a case where D interprets a remark as referring to a characteristic, when this was not in fact intended. Whether the provocation be by words or conduct, it is clear that it is not essential that the author of the provocation have in mind the characteristic or, indeed, the accused. For example, in *R v Taaka*[273] the primary provocation arose when D discovered V attempting to have intercourse with D's wife, and the characteristic which increased the gravity of the provocation was described by a psychiatrist as "an obsessively compulsive personality ... directed to his child, his wife [and V]".

However, in *R v Rongonui*[274] the need for a characteristic to affect the gravity of the provocation was said to mean that there must be some "perceptible connection" or "sufficient relationship" between the two. It may be that this means no more than that the characteristic, when fully understood, must be logically relevant to the assessment of gravity. Thus there may be cases where D's susceptibility to the provocation is affected even though the victim may not have had the characteristic in mind and may not have overtly referred to it. For example, D's "cultural values and mores" might affect the degree of shame and humiliation caused by particular conduct.[275]

(e)   Mental abnormality

In *R v McGregor*,[276] it was also said that "special difficulties" arise when "purely mental peculiarities" are relied on. This is likely to be so for a number of reasons. How such a condition is likely to affect the gravity of provocation may not be a matter of common sense or ordinary experience, so that expert evidence about this will be needed.[277] Much will depend on the expert's diagnosis and description of the condition. If this identifies a facet of D's personality

---

270   *R v McGregor* [1962] NZLR 1069 (CA), 1081, 1082.
271   *R v McCarthy* [1992] 2 NZLR 550; (1992) 8 CRNZ 58 (CA), 557-558; 66-67; cf *R v Campbell* [1997] 1 NZLR 16; (1996) 14 CRNZ 117 (CA), 25; 127.
272   *Luc Thiet Thuan v R* [1997] AC 131; [1996] 2 All ER 1033 (PC), 148; 1048.
273   *R v Taaka* [1982] 2 NZLR 198 (CA).
274   *R v Rongonui* [2000] 2 NZLR 385; (2000) 17 CRNZ 310 (CA), para 215 (Blanchard J), para 226 (Tipping J); *R v Makoare* [2001] 1 NZLR 318; (2000) 18 CRNZ 511 (CA), 320-321; 513-514.
275   *R v Abebe* [2000] 1 VR 429.
276   [1962] NZLR 1069 (CA), 1082.
277   At least as a general rule such evidence should not extend to an opinion as to how a person of ordinary self-control might react to the provocation: *R v Turner* [1975] QB 834; [1975] 1 All ER 70 (CA); *DPP v Camplin* [1978] AC 705; [1978] 2 All ER 168 (HL), 716, 727; 173, 182-183. However, when understanding of a condition requires specialised knowledge, expert evidence of its nature and possible effects will be permitted: *R v Makoare* [2001] 1 NZLR 318; (2000) 18 CRNZ 511 (CA).

or mental make-up which would aggravate his emotional response to the particular provocation, it will be evidence of a relevant "characteristic".[278] But if in substance it is no more than evidence of a short temper or unusual pugnacity, it will not. That was the conclusion in *R v Fryer*,[279] where a psychiatrist had described D as suffering from "a severely disordered personality marked by lack of control when frustrated, violent response to physical threat, and emotional immaturity".[280] Similarly, in *Luc Thiet Thuan v R*[281] brain damage causing "episodic dyscontrol" did not qualify.

It has been suggested that *Luc Thiet Thuan* holds that mental abnormality is not a relevant characteristic unless the subject of taunts.[282] Certainly, it will be much easier to establish increased provocative effect when a characteristic ("purely mental" or otherwise) is overtly referred to, but such a requirement is not imposed by *Luc Thiet Thuan*, where the evidence did not go beyond identifying a condition which deprived D of a normal power of self-control. We submit that there is no such requirement, although, in the absence of taunts or the like, cases of mental abnormality are liable to present difficulty. If the condition is such that D would feel all or any provocation unusually deeply, it may well be that it should be regarded as in substance no more than evidence of a reduced power of self-control.[283] Even if the abnormality might enhance the provocative effect of only some provocative conduct it might also produce a general reduction in D's power of self-control. Artificial though it might be,[284] the objective test in its present form requires that account be taken only of the enhancement of provocative effect, and not the reduction in the power of self-control.[285]

Section 169(2)(a) does not allow any concession based on reduced self-control even if this arises from brain damage or some other condition which cannot be attributed to any fault of D, and even if it would support a finding of diminished responsibility where that is a defence. In *R v McCarthy*[286] Cooke P remarked that within the limited field of provocation, the unheralded introduction of diminished responsibility may have been the "inevitable and deliberate effect" of allowing for personal characteristics.[287] No doubt this is its effect in those cases where a mental condition increases the gravity of particular provocation, but it does not mean that mere diminution of self-control renders such abnormality relevant.[288]

---

278 Cf the identification of the wife and victim as particular subjects of D's obsession in *R v Taaka* [1982] 2 NZLR 198 (CA); and battered woman syndrome may qualify on the basis that it heightens awareness of or sensitivity to threatening behaviour: *R v Oakes* [1995] 2 NZLR 673 (CA), 676.
279 *R v Fryer* [1981] 1 NZLR 748 (CA), 752.
280 Even so, it has been suggested that evidence of an appellant's obsessive and jealous nature may be a relevant matter for consideration in an appropriate case. In *R v Zhou* 11/9/06, Potter J, HC Auckland, CRI-2005-092-10395, the Court appeared to accept that Klinefelter syndrome, a chromosome anomaly, and morbid jealousy could in appropriate circumstances amount to "characteristics", although they failed to do so on the facts of the case.
281 *Luc Thiet Thuan v R* [1997] AC 131; [1996] 2 All ER 1033 (PC).
282 *Smith and Hogan*, 370-371.
283 Cf *R v Fryer* [1981] 1 NZLR 748 (CA); Orchard, "Provocation: Recharacterisation of 'characteristics'" (1996) 6 Canterbury LR 202, 210.
284 Yeo, "Power of self-control in provocation and automatism" (1992) 14 Syd LR 3.
285 *Stingel v R* (1990) 171 CLR 312; 97 ALR 1 (HCA), 332; 14.
286 *R v McCarthy* [1992] 2 NZLR 550; (1992) 8 CRNZ 58 (CA), 558; 66.
287 See *R v Rongonui* [2000] 2 NZLR 385; (2000) 17 CRNZ 310 (CA). To be a "characteristic" a mental state should amount to a "professionally recognised form of mental disease, disability or disorder", and recognition of mental diseases or disorders as "characteristics" could be seen as "acceptance of diminished responsibility in the circumstances of provocation." (Per Tipping J.)

(f) Age, gender, and race

In England, Canada, and Australia there is one established exception to the insistence of an unvarying standard of an "ordinary" power of self-control: when D is young, the standard is the power of self-control of an ordinary person of D's age.[289] It appears that this will be applied to qualify the "ordinary person" in s 169(2)(a),[290] although age can probably be significant only "at the extremes of senility or obvious youthful immaturity".[291]

There has also been support for including in the description of the applicable standard such other normal attributes as D's gender,[292] and race or "ethnic or cultural background",[293] although it may be misleading to describe these as "characteristics" per se. In *R v Rongonui*[294] it was suggested that age and gender are better regarded as "variable features of the ordinary person, and thereby relevant to the power of self-control of an ordinary person."[295] As to gender, it would seem neither politic nor justifiable to suppose that the level of normal self-control varies according to sex, although gender may sometimes be relevant to the assessment of the nature and gravity of particular provocation. Regarding D's racial or ethnic background, in *R v McGregor*[296] the Court of Appeal had no doubt that it would be irrelevant for D to claim that he belongs to an "excitable race", or a nationality readily accustomed to resort to lethal weapons, and this seems clearly correct unless D's race affects the nature or gravity of the provocation.

However, the position may be different if the issue is whether sufficient time had elapsed for the passion of an ordinary person to cool. If there is evidence that persons of D's gender or race, or with a particular condition (such as battered woman's syndrome), will commonly react to the kind of provocation in question by losing their self-control after a delay, such attributes should be characteristics relevant to the question of "cooling time".[297] If the issue is whether

---

288 Pace the interpretation of New Zealand law, before *Rongonui*, in *Luc Thiet Thuan v R* [1997] AC 131; [1996] 2 All ER 1033 (PC), 143-145; 1043-1045; Orchard, "Provocation: Recharacterisation of 'characteristics' " (1996) 6 Canterbury LR 202, 206, 207; cf *R v Parker* [1997] Crim LR 760, and commentary. There may be some decisions which are difficult to reconcile with confining the relevance of mental abnormality to an evaluation of the provocative effect of conduct: for example *R v McCarthy* ("excessive emotionalism as a result of brain injury"); *R v Aston* [1989] 2 NZLR 166; (1989) 4 CRNZ 241 (CA) ("paranoid disorder" resulting in distortion of grievances); cf *R v Leilua* 20/9/85, CA19/84, see *R v Leilua* [1986] NZ Recent Law 118; Stanish, "Whither provocation" (1993) 7 AULR 381, 393, 395.
289 *DPP v Camplin* [1978] AC 705; [1978] 2 All ER 168 (HL); *R v Hill* (1986) 25 CCC (3d) 322 (SCC); *Stingel v R* (1990) 171 CLR 312; 97 ALR 1 (HCA).
290 *R v Rongonui* [2000] 2 NZLR 385; (2000) 17 CRNZ 310 (CA), para 231 (Tipping J); *R v Makoare* [2001] 1 NZLR 318; (2000) 18 CRNZ 511 (CA), 322; 515.
291 *R v Trounson* [1991] 3 NZLR 690; (1991) 8 CRNZ 491 (CA), 693; 494, where the fact that D was 18 was not regarded as significant, although it was otherwise in *DPP v Camplin* [1978] AC 705; [1978] 2 All ER 168 (HL), where D was 16; *R v Rongonui* [2000] 2 NZLR 385; (2000) 17 CRNZ 310 (CA), para 231 (Tipping J) (age and gender are relevant on the basis that they are "variable features of an ordinary person"). Abnormal immaturity must probably be treated like any other mental abnormality: *Luc Thiet Thuan v R* [1997] AC 131; [1996] 2 All ER 1033 (PC), 145; 1045, doubting *R v Raven* [1982] Crim LR 51.
292 *DPP v Camplin* [1978] AC 705; [1978] 2 All ER 168 (HL), 718; 175; *R v Trounson* [1991] 3 NZLR 690; (1991) 8 CRNZ 491 (CA), 693; 494; cf Williams, *TBCL*, 538, 539.
293 *Masciantonio v R* (1995) 183 CLR 58; 129 ALR 575 (HCA), 73-74; 586-587 (McHugh J dissenting).
294 *R v Rongonui* [2000] 2 NZLR 385; (2000) 17 CRNZ 310 (CA).
295 *R v Rongonui* [2000] 2 NZLR 385; (2000) 17 CRNZ 310 (CA), para 231 (Tipping J).
296 *R v McGregor* [1962] NZLR 1069 (CA), 1082.

an ordinary person might have so lost control as to use a weapon, as D did, the comparative stature and strength of the parties might also be relevant.[298]

(6) *Accident and mistake*

Section 169(6) was a new provision introduced in 1961. It provides that:

> "This section shall apply in any case where the provocation was given by the person killed, and also in any case where the offender, under provocation given by one person, by accident or mistake killed another person."

This codifies the common law, which allowed the defence in cases of "accident", where D aims retaliation at a person who has provided provocation but unintentionally strikes another,[299] and in cases of "mistake", where D intentionally strikes V in the mistaken belief that V is the person, or one of the persons, who provided the provocation.[300] However, when neither of these possibilities applies the Court in *R v McGregor*[301] thought it inherent in the word "provocation", and the unambiguous effect of subs (6), that the provocation must emanate from the victim. This approach was consistent with such common law authority as there is,[302] although the restriction is not imposed under modern English legislation.[303] The defence may, however, still succeed if V was one of a number who acted provocatively (for example, by attacking D),[304] and provocation will be "given by" anyone who is a party to provocative conduct by acting in concert with, or by aiding, abetting, or inciting, another,[305] or who is "sufficiently associated" with the conduct so that in the jury's view it may be attributed to him.[306] Participation in an armed attack would suffice in that regard.[307]

However, the ambit of accidental or mistaken killings under provocation has been significantly expanded in New Zealand as a result of the decision in *Timoti v R*.[308] In particular, the Court of Appeal has rejected the proposition in *McGregor* that the provocation must come from the deceased, on the grounds that it is irreconcilable with the plain terms of the second half of s 169(6). In *Timoti* the appellant had set fire to the house occupied by members of his immediate family and others after a violent argument, as a result of which D was evicted from his place of residence. After securing the safety of his infant daughter, he had poured petrol through

---

297 This possibility was not excluded in relation to a "brooding personality" associated with race in *R v Tai* [1976] 1 NZLR 102 (CA), 107; see also Nicholson and Sanghvi, "Battered women and provocation: The implications of *R v Ahluwalia*" [1993] Crim LR 728; Tarrant, "The 'specific triggering incident' in provocation: Is the law gender biased?" (1996) 26 WAL Rev 190.
298 Cf *R v Oakes* [1995] 2 NZLR 673 (CA), 676, in relation to self-defence.
299 *R v Gross* (1913) 23 Cox CC 455; (1913) 77 JP 352; *R v Porritt* [1961] 3 All ER 463; [1961] 1 WLR 1372 (CA).
300 *R v Brown* (1776) 1 Leach 148; 168 ER 177.
301 *R v McCarthy* [1962] NZLR 1069 (CA), 1080; see also *R v Matoka* [1987] 1 NZLR 340 (CA), 344.
302 *R v Simpson* (1915) 84 LJKB 1893 (CCA); cf *R v Scriva (No 2)* [1951] ALR 733; [1951] VLR 298; see also the terms of the "classic direction" in *R v Duffy* [1949] 1 All ER 932 (CCA).
303 *R v Davies* [1975] QB 691; [1975] 1 All ER 890 (CA); *R v Twine* [1967] Crim LR 710 (CCA); Smith, "Provocation: The widened ambit" [1975] 34 CLJ 188.
304 *R v Brown* (1776) 1 Leach 148; 168 ER 177; *R v Hall* (1928) 21 Cr App R 48 (CCA).
305 *R v Kenney* [1983] 2 VR 470; *R v Tumanako* (1992) 64 A Crim R 149, 155; *R v Manchuk* [1937] 4 DLR 737; [1938] SCR 18 (SCC).
306 *R v Paniani* [2000] 1 NZLR 234; (1999) 17 CRNZ 519 (CA).
307 *R v Turaki* 23/6/05, CA405/04, para 80 (Glazebrook J).
308 *Timoti v R* [2005] NZSC 37.

the house, causing his mother, step-father and one other adult to flee for their lives, but causing the death of the victim who succumbed to the fire before he could escape. D was charged with murder under s 167(d). Although he pleaded provocation, the provocation relied on was given by D's mother and stepfather, whereas it was V who was killed. The essential question then became whether D had killed him "by accident or mistake". Unless that was so, provocation was unavailable to D because the wording of s 169(6) only permitted provocation in circumstances where the offender, under provocation given by one person, had killed another "by accident or mistake".

In the Court of Appeal it had been held that the killing of the victim could not in law be an accident or mistake because the foresight of death inherent in s 167(d), upon which the prosecution for murder was based, meant that the death could not be regarded as accidental or mistaken. The essence of the Court of Appeal's argument was that any person or class of persons whom the offender knows to be likely to be killed cannot be the object of an accident or mistake because they must have been specifically envisaged as potential victims.[309]

However, the Supreme Court rejected that reasoning. Allowing the appeal, it accepted that foresight of death did not of itself preclude a killing that was accidental or mistaken. It reasoned that it is just as appropriate, both conceptually and in policy terms, to transfer malice in the case of a contemplated but unintended death, as it is in the case of an intended death. Accordingly, it was wrong to suggest that a death of which an accused had the necessary foresight could not be regarded as accidental or mistaken for the purpose of s 169(6).

The traditional requirement that provocation be given by the victim perhaps reflects the idea that one justification for the defence is that V was partly to blame, although there is no requirement that V intended to provoke anyone,[310] and at least in England the defence can now be based on conduct which could not be regarded as in any sense culpable.[311] The courts have also accepted that the defence may be available if D lost control because of a mistaken belief about the occurrence, nature, or circumstances of provocative conduct, or in the mistaken belief that the victim was a party to it. But in *R v White (Shane)*[312] a belief as to the circumstances was held not to support the defence unless it was one which an ordinary person might have held. This contrasts with self-defence, which may be based on an unreasonable mistake.[313]

The rule governing abnormal mistakes is qualified if D had a characteristic which may have affected his perception. An extreme example is *R v Campbell*.[314] D had killed the male victim with a number of blows with an axe and there was expert evidence supporting the claim that the lasting effects of childhood abuse may have had the result that when V placed his hand on D's thigh D lost control because he experienced a "flashback" in which he interpreted the act as a homosexual advance by his childhood abuser. This "flashback", or delusion, was to

---

309 *Timoti v R* [2005] NZSC 37, para 20.
310 For example *R v Campbell* [1997] 1 NZLR 16; (1996) 14 CRNZ 117 (CA); *R v Taaka* [1982] 2 NZLR 198 (CA); *R v Twine* [1967] Crim LR 710 (CCA); cf *R v McGregor* [1962] NZLR 1069 (CA), 1073.
311 *R v Doughty* (1986) 83 Cr App R 319; [1986] Crim LR 625 (CA) (crying of a baby).
312 *R v White (Shane)* [1988] 1 NZLR 122 (CA), 126-127; see also *R v Hansford* (1987) 33 CCC (3d) 74; 55 CR (3d) 347; contrast *R v Kenney* [1983] 2 VR 470.
313 See 15.1.3(1). The difference may cause difficulty if both defences have to be considered: *Adams*, CA169.15 (looseleaf); and if there is a mistaken belief that V was a party to provocation which had been offered the case would appear to be within s 169(6), with no requirement of reasonableness.
314 *R v Campbell* [1997] 1 NZLR 16; (1996) 14 CRNZ 117 (CA).

be attributed to the hypothetical person possessed of ordinary self-control. Similarly, in *R v Oakes*[315] it was recognised that, when a woman had killed her partner, the existence of battered woman's syndrome was a relevant characteristic in that it could lead to heightened awareness of or sensitivity to threatening behaviour, including an earlier and greater perception of danger than would be experienced in the absence of the syndrome.

(7) Self-induced provocation

In some cases, conduct which leads D to lose self-control may itself be a reaction to D's previous behaviour. In *Edwards v R*[316] D made a blackmail demand of V, but V responded by attacking D with a knife. D wrested the knife from V and stabbed him to death. The Privy Council held that as the attack by V with a knife was an extreme reaction to the blackmail, provocation should have been left to the jury. It was said, however, that "on principle" the defence would not have been available if V's reaction had been no more than a "predictable" response. In *R v Johnson*,[317] on the other hand, the English Court of Appeal appeared to reject this limitation in holding that the defence could not be withdrawn merely because D was led to loss of self-control by V's violent reaction to threatening conduct by D.

The possible reaction of an ordinary person is a question of opinion for the jury, and in principle the predictability of the provocative conduct should be no more than a factor for the jury to consider.[318] Exceptionally, s 169(5) excludes the defence in the extreme case when the supposed provocation consists of a person "doing anything which the offender incited him to do in order to provide the offender with an excuse for killing or doing bodily harm to any person".

16.5.2 Involuntary manslaughter

"Involuntary manslaughter" describes killings where D is guilty of culpable homicide, but not of murder, manslaughter under provocation, killing or in furtherance of a suicide pact, or of infanticide. Its scope is exceptionally wide and depends on the definition of culpable homicide in s 160(2), which was summarised in 16.3. More particularly, s 160(2) provides that:

"(2) Homicide is culpable when it consists in the killing of any person—

"(a) By an unlawful act; or

"(b) By an omission without lawful excuse to perform or observe any legal duty; or

"(c) By both combined; or

"(d) By causing that person by threats or fear of violence, or by deception, to do an act which causes his death; or

"(e) By wilfully frightening a child under the age of 16 years or a sick person.

---

315 *R v Oakes* [1995] 2 NZLR 673 (CA), 676.
316 *Edwards v R* [1973] AC 648; [1973] 1 All ER 152 (PC); cf *R v Allwood* (1975) 18 A Crim R 120, 132, 133; *R v Radford* (1985) 20 A Crim R 388, 401; Ashworth, "Self-induced provocation and the Homicide Act" [1973] Crim LR 483.
317 *R v Johnson* [1989] 2 All ER 839; [1989] 1 WLR 740 (CA).
318 Orchard, "Provoked provocation" (1974) 6 NZULR 63, 65; cf s 169(4), which seems to make it a jury question, untrammelled by rules as to how an ordinary person might react, as much as s 3 Homicide Act 1957 (UK).

It is convenient first to consider paras (a), (d), and (e) and then paras (b) and (c)."

(1) *Killing by an unlawful act: s 160(2)(a)*

This is manslaughter at common law and, insofar as it is consistent with the scheme of the Act, it is thought that "unlawful act" is to be given the same meaning as it has at common law.[319]

In the 19th century it was at one stage thought that it could be enough that the act was a tort,[320] but in *R v Franklin*[321] Field J ruled that a mere civil wrong was not sufficient. In *R v Lamb*[322] the Court regarded it as settled law that it is irrelevant whether D might be subject to civil liability, and that the act must be "unlawful in the criminal sense of that word". In *Lamb*, D had shot and killed a friend when he pointed a revolver at him in jest, and pulled the trigger in the mistaken belief that the gun would not fire. D's conduct did not constitute the offence of assault, for he had not intended V to suffer or anticipate the application of force, and on the basis that his act did not involve any other offence, it was held to follow that the killing was not manslaughter by an unlawful act.[323]

As *Lamb* shows, for an act to be unlawful because it is an offence it will be necessary that D acted with whatever mens rea was required for that act to be an offence,[324] and it must also be done without lawful justification or excuse.[325] Similarly, the act will not be unlawful if the actus reus is not itself a criminal act. In *R v Dias*,[326] the accused had self-administered heroin and then gave the syringe to an associate who did the same. The friend died soon after administering heroin to himself. On an appeal against conviction for aiding and abetting manslaughter, the conviction was quashed. The Court of Appeal held that because the act of self-injection of a prohibited drug was not an offence, it was not an unlawful act for the purposes of manslaughter; and because self-manslaughter was not an offence there was no principal offence to which the offender could be a secondary party. The Court rejected the possibility that the offence of possession of a prohibited drug could supply the element of unlawfulness

---

319 Cf *Murray v R* [1962] Tas SR 170, 173, 192; *R v McCallum* [1969] Tas SR 73, 84. This might require acceptance that the words are "not otherwise clear in their meaning": *R v Machirus* [1996] 3 NZLR 404; (1996) 14 CRNZ 172 (CA), 410; 179. But these provisions were not intended to change the law (Criminal Code Bill Commission, *Report of the Royal Commission Appointed to Consider the Law Relating to Indictable Offences: With an Appendix Containing a Draft Code Embodying the Suggestions of the Commissioners*, London, Eyre & Spottiswode for HMSO, 1879, 23), and this might justify recourse to developing common law interpretation of the same general terms.

320 For example *Fenton's Case* (1830) 1 Lew CC 179; 168 ER 1004 (trespass to property by throwing stones down a mine).

321 *R v Franklin* (1883) 15 Cox CC 163.

322 *R v Lamb* [1967] 2 QB 981; [1967] 2 All ER 1282 (CA), 988; 1284.

323 D might have been guilty of manslaughter by gross negligence, but there had not been adequate directions on this. In New Zealand, liability on the basis of failure to exercise care could arise under ss 156 and 160(2)(b), although this would now require a high degree of negligence: 16.5.2(5)(c).

324 See also *R v Jennings* [1990] Crim LR 588 (CA).

325 *R v Scarlett* (1994) 98 Cr App R 290; [1993] 4 All ER 629 (CA).

326 *R v Dias* [2002] 2 Cr App R 5. In some cases, however, D may be a joint principal in the act of injection, and that latter act may be unlawful: eg *R v Rogers* [2003] EWCA Crim 945; [2003] 1 WLR 1374. *R v Kennedy* [2005] EWCA Crim 685 also purports to find that D was a joint principal in administering heroin to V, although the latter decision is implausible on its facts, and difficult to distinguish from *Dias*. See above, 3.3.3(2)(f).

sufficient for manslaughter, on the basis that the causative act was essentially the injection of the heroin rather than its possession.[327]

It has also been suggested that in principle it must be an offence against the person and not, for example, merely an offence against property.[328] This is not a requirement in New Zealand,[329] where it seems that an act may be "unlawful" if it is an offence of any kind, even if it is an offence of strict or, perhaps, absolute liability. In R v Myatt[330] two people had died as a result of a collision between power boats, one of which had been driven by D. One basis on which manslaughter charges were put was that D had committed offences against bylaws and regulations governing power boat use, and the Court of Appeal expressed the view that "unlawful act" included any act in breach of one of the "many provision of Acts, regulations and bylaws which create offences".[331]

Moreover, in R v Grant[332] the Court of Appeal rejected a submission that there must be a causal connection between the death and a circumstance that is necessary for the act to be an offence (for example, absence of a licence or, as in Grant, the fact that D acts in a public place). Subsequently, in R v Hawkins[333] Goddard J held that the offence of driving without a licence could not support a charge of manslaughter even though D had also been subject to epileptic fits, and such a fit had caused the fatal collision, because the fatal collision would have occurred even if D had had a driver's licence. This appears to be the causal requirement rejected in Grant, and the decision may be doubted.

The wide interpretation of unlawful act in Myatt is, however, qualified by a further requirement: the act must have been dangerous. In Australia the courts have required the act to be "fraught with a risk of serious harm to some person",[334] but in England the test is wider: the act "must be such as all sober and reasonable people would inevitably recognise must subject the other person to, at least, the risk of some harm resulting therefrom, albeit not serious harm".[335]

In New Zealand, the requirement that the unlawful act be likely to harm another was recognised in R v Grant,[336] where it was thought to be the probable explanation of an earlier decision that a particular instance of causing death by driving without a licence was not manslaughter.[337] Some New Zealand first instance authority supports the need for a risk of serious harm,[338] but in confirming the requirement of dangerousness in R v Myatt[339] the Court of Appeal adopted the English rule that it suffices that there was a risk of some harm, and there need not be a

---

327 R v Dias [2002] 2 Cr App R 5, para 22.
328 Smith and Hogan, Criminal Law (9th ed), London, Butterworths, 1999, 370.
329 It is clear that certain property offences, in particular arson, will constitute unlawful acts for the purposes of manslaughter. See R v Goodfellow (1986) 83 Cr App R 23; R v Willoughby [2005] 1 Cr App R 29; R v Aramakutu [1991] 3 NZLR 429; (1991) 7 CRNZ 114 (CA).
330 R v Myatt [1991] 1 NZLR 674; (1990) 7 CRNZ 304 (CA), 678-680; 308-310.
331 Cf DPP v Newbury [1977] AC 500; [1976] 2 All ER 365 (HL); in New Zealand the problematic case of R v Cato [1976] 1 All ER 260; [1976] 1 WLR 110 (CA) would involve the offence of administering a controlled drug: s 6(1)(c) Misuse of Drugs Act 1975.
332 R v Grant [1966] NZLR 968 (CA).
333 R v Hawkins 21/2/01, Goddard J, HC Napier T18/00.
334 R v Phillips [1971] ALR 740; (1971) 45 ALJR 467 (HCA), 758; 479; Wilson v R (1992) 174 CLR 313; 66 ALJR 517 (HCA); R v McCallum [1969] Tas SR 73, 88.
335 R v Church [1966] 1 QB 59; [1965] 2 All ER 72 (CA), 70; 76, approved in DPP v Newbury [1977] AC 500; [1976] 2 All ER 365 (HL).
336 R v Grant [1966] NZLR 968 (CA).
337 R v Faigan 15/7/27 (CA).

risk of serious harm, although no doubt something more than "trivial or transitory" harm must have been foreseeable.[340] In many cases (including *Myatt*) when an offence has caused death, serious harm will have been foreseeable, but sometimes a conviction will be possible only if a risk of some harm is enough. An example may be *R v Renata*,[341] where D was found guilty of manslaughter when a relatively minor assault resulted in death because V had an unknown abnormal physical condition.

In *Myatt* the Court of Appeal also said that it was not essential that D be in breach of legislation which had public safety as its primary objective: "All that is necessary is that the particular unlawful act is likely to do harm to a particular person or to a class of persons of whom [the victim] is one, which does not mean the public at large in every case."[342] But even this test is too narrow, according to the House of Lords. In *A-G's Reference (No 3 of 1994)*,[343] it was held that a killing will be manslaughter if D intentionally injures a woman who is pregnant, and after birth her child dies as a result of D's assault on the mother. The House confirmed what is implicit in *Myatt*, that D's act need not be directed at the person who dies,[344] and further held that it is enough that the act is likely to harm somebody, even if harm to V, or a class including V, is not reasonably foreseeable. If D's dangerous unlawful act caused the death of the child after it was born, it was no defence that this might not have been reasonably foreseeable.

The act must be accompanied by whatever mens rea is needed to make it an offence, and it is also said that it must be done "intentionally",[345] but on the English authorities the test of dangerousness is objective: it is enough if a reasonable person would have known that the act was likely to harm somebody.[346] In *Renata*[347] the Court of Appeal did not go further than holding that an assault with intent to cause minor harm was an "unlawful act", but in *Myatt* it had accepted the objective nature of the test of dangerousness.[348] D will be liable if she was aware of the risk of harm to another, or of facts creating the risk, but it seems that ignorance or mistake will not excuse if a reasonable person would have recognised the true facts or risk.[349] In Canada a narrow exception applies when, without fault, D lacks the capacity to

---

338   *R v Fleeting (No 1)* [1977] 1 NZLR 343, 346; *R v T* 27/10/99, Hammond J, HC Hamilton T1866/99; *R v Hawkins* 21/2/01, Goddard J, HC Napier T18/00 (where this view arises from a misreading of *Myatt*).
339   *R v Myatt* [1991] 1 NZLR 674; (1990) 7 CRNZ 304 (CA), 679-681; 309-311.
340   *R v Creighton* (1993) 105 DLR (4th) 632; [1993] 3 SCR 3; (1993) 83 CCC (3d) 346 (SCC).
341   *R v Renata* [1992] 2 NZLR 346; (1991) 7 CRNZ 616 (CA).
342   *R v Myatt* [1991] 1 NZLR 674; (1990) 7 CRNZ 304 (CA), 680; 310.
343   *A-G's Reference (No 3 of 1994)* [1998] AC 245; [1997] 3 All ER 936 (HL), 263-264, 272-274; 950-951, 958-960.
344   Approving *R v Mitchell* [1983] QB 741; [1983] 2 All ER 427 (CA), where D was guilty of manslaughter when he hit A who fell against V, who died as a result of injuries caused by this; the contrary reasoning in *R v Dalby* [1982] 1 All ER 916; [1982] 1 WLR 425 (CA) is clearly incorrect.
345   *DPP v Newbury* [1977] AC 500; [1976] 2 All ER 365 (HL), 506; 366; *A-G's Reference (No 3 of 1994)* [1998] AC 245; [1997] 3 All ER 936 (HL), 274; 960.
346   *DPP v Newbury* [1977] AC 500; [1976] 2 All ER 365 (HL), 506; 366; *A-G's Reference (No 3 of 1994)* [1998] AC 245; [1997] 3 All ER 936 (HL), 274; 960; cf *Wilson v R* (1992) 174 CLR 313; 66 ALJR 517 (HCA).
347   *R v Renata* [1992] 2 NZLR 346; (1991) 7 CRNZ 616 (CA), 349; 619.
348   *R v Myatt* [1991] 1 NZLR 674; (1990) 7 CRNZ 304 (CA), 678-679; 308.
349   *R v Watson* [1989] 2 All ER 865; [1989] 1 WLR 684 (CA); *R v Dawson* (1985) 81 Cr App R 150; [1985] Crim LR 383 (CA); *R v Ball* [1989] Crim LR 730 (CA); *A-G's Reference (No 3 of 1994)* [1998] AC 245; [1997] 3 All ER 936 (HL), 270; 960; cf *R v Gedson* 4/12/97, Fisher J, HC Rotorua T51/97.

appreciate the risk,[350] and in New Zealand there is a further qualification when harm results from influence on the mind of the victim.[351]

Although since *R v Lamb*,[352] it has been generally assumed that an "unlawful act" must be an offence, some doubt remains whether this is necessarily the case. In particular, it has been suggested that it might be enough if D does something which is in itself not an offence, such as persuading V to undertake severe physical exertion or drink a dangerous quantity of alcohol, with intent to cause death and without justifications or excuse.[353] In *A-G's Reference (No 3 of 1994)*[354] there is also a dictum suggesting that this category of manslaughter comprises killings "where the defendant's act was both unlawful and dangerous because it was likely to cause harm to some person", but it seems that a comma must be inserted after unlawful, for otherwise an offence which is already excessively wide overflows sensible bounds.

Nonetheless, even if an offence is required, if death follows a series of acts by D the immediate cause of death need not necessarily be an offence which is likely to harm another. The killing will be manslaughter if the fatal act was part of the same transaction or series of events as an earlier unlawful and dangerous act committed by D, even if it is disputable whether it was a significant cause.[355] For example, D might form a mistaken but reasonable belief that his assault has killed V, whom he then kills by disposing of the supposed corpse,[356] or even without such belief he might accidentally cause death in trying to conceal his earlier offence.[357] However, the killing will not be culpable if the immediate cause was an act by D which was justified or excused, even if this was preceded by unlawful acts by D.[358]

Finally, a further restriction on manslaughter by an unlawful act has now been established. While it seems clear that s 160(2)(a) can apply only where a positive act is a significant cause of death, and a killing by a mere omission will be exclusively within the province of s 160(2)(b),[359] there are also cases where death results from a positive act which is unlawful only because it is accompanied by a failure to exercise care. At common law, even an offence committed by a positive act is not an "unlawful act" in this context if the act would have been lawful but for the fact that it was negligently performed: for example, careless operation or

---

350 *R v Creighton* (1993) 105 DLR (4th) 632; [1993] 3 SCR 3; (1993) 83 CCC (3d) 346 (SCC); it appears that the majority would also ignore D's special knowledge of the activity (for example drug taking) which would increase D's ability to appreciate the risk, but rather discounts the concession by imposing a duty to inform oneself of risks in some cases.
351 See 16.5.2(3).
352 *R v Lamb* [1967] 2 QB 981; [1967] 2 All ER 1282 (CA).
353 *Adams*, CA160.07 (looseleaf), citing *R v Packard* (1841) Car & M 236; 174 ER 487.
354 *A-G's Reference (No 3 of 1994)* [1998] AC 245; [1997] 3 All ER 936 (HL), 269; 955-956; cf Stephen, *A Digest of the Criminal Law (Indictable Offences)*, London, Macmillan & Co, 1877, 143 where an act "commonly known to be likely to cause harm" is regarded as sufficient, if neither justified nor excused; but by 1883 he had modified this class to acts "commonly known to be dangerous to life": Stephen, *A History of the Criminal Law of England*, London, Macmillan and Co, 1883, vol III, 16. But he also there included all crimes, torts, acts contrary to public policy or morality, or injurious to the public. There is no modern authority supporting such a sweeping rule.
355 Although often it will be a cause: *R v McKinnon* [1980] 2 NZLR 31 (CA); see 4.9, 16.4.6.
356 *R v Church* [1966] 1 QB 59; [1965] 2 All ER 72 (CA).
357 *R v Le Brun* [1992] 1 QB 61; [1991] 4 All ER 673 (CA); cf *R v Watson* [1989] 2 All ER 865; [1989] 1 WLR 684 (CA); *A-G's Reference (No 3 of 1994)* [1998] AC 245; [1997] 3 All ER 936 (HL), 270; 956.
358 *R v Grant* [1966] NZLR 968 (CA); cf *R v Wesley* (1859) 1 F & F 528; 175 ER 838; *R v Setrum* (1976) 32 CCC (2d) 109.
359 *R v Rau* [1972] Tas SR 59, 62; cf *R v Lowe* [1973] QB 702; [1973] 1 All ER 805 (CA).

dangerous driving of a motor vehicle.[360] In such a case the common law requires gross negligence for manslaughter, and the unlawful act rule does not apply.[361] However, as will be seen, before 1997 in New Zealand gross negligence was not required for manslaughter when death resulted from a failure to observe a duty of care in relation to dangerous activities, and in *Myatt*[362] it was assumed that an offence of "positive act" negligence was an "unlawful act" within s 160(2)(a). However, the law governing manslaughter by omission has been changed to require a high degree of negligence,[363] and in *R v Powell*[364] it was held that this applies when an unlawful act involving negligence is relied on to support a manslaughter charge.

In the result, this aspect of New Zealand law is now aligned with the common law. Should the alleged unlawful act be an offence of strict or absolute liability, it may be that for manslaughter gross negligence (as a minimum) will also have to be proved. It would be incongruous if the conclusion in *Powell* could be avoided merely because D committed an offence for which no fault need be proved.[365]

(2)   *Inducing victims to kill themselves: s 160(2)(d)*

It is provided by s 160(2)(d) that culpable homicide includes the killing of a person by "causing that person by threats or fear of violence, or by deception, to do an act which causes his death". This allows for a finding of both causation and culpability in certain cases where the immediate cause of death is an act of the victim in response to conduct of D. For example, V may leap into a river and drown,[366] jump from a window and die from the fall,[367] or die as a result of an accidental fall downstairs while attempting to escape.[368] In most cases V will have sought to escape after threats from D,[369] but the rule could apply if V committed suicide rather than suffer torture, and the extension of it to cases of deception might apply if, for example, V was deceived into consuming poison, or was led to walk into a concealed pit.[370]

Section 160(2)(d) was considered in *R v Tomars*,[371] where after intimidatory driving by D a motorcyclist had swerved in front of another car, and had been killed. It was held that the paragraph would apply if: (a) D had caused V to fear violence; (b) such fear was a "not insignificant" cause of V's driving as he did; (c) such driving by V was the kind of reaction that could reasonably have been foreseen by a reasonable person in D's position, given D's conduct immediately beforehand;[372] and (d) such driving by V contributed in a not insignificant

---

360   In New Zealand, these offences are now found in ss 35(1)(b) and 37(1) Land Transport Act 1998.
361   *Andrews v DPP* [1937] AC 576; [1937] 2 All ER 552 (HL).
362   *R v Myatt* [1991] 1 NZLR 674; (1990) 7 CRNZ 304 (CA); and in *R v Storey* [1931] NZLR 417 (CA) the offence was charged as manslaughter by the "unlawful act" of negligently driving a motorcar.
363   See 16.5.2(5)(c).
364   *R v Powell* 22/11/01, CA192/01; in this case the alleged unlawful act requiring negligence was careless operation or dangerous driving of a motor vehicle.
365   Cf the apparent attempt to avoid s 150A in *R v Hawkins* 21/2/01, Goddard J, HC Napier T18/00 (where the indictment specified unlicensed driving as a causative unlawful act but also specified the circumstance that D was subject to epileptic fits).
366   *R v Pitts* (1842) Car & M 284; 174 ER 509.
367   *R v Curley* (1909) 2 Cr App R 109 (CCA).
368   *R v Mackie* (1973) 57 Cr App R 453; [1973] Crim LR 438 (CA).
369   As a matter of construction, it seems that such threats must be of violence, although that need not involve threats of serious injury: Cf *R v Mackie* (1973) 57 Cr App R 453; [1973] Crim LR 438 (CA), 461; 439.
370   *Adams*, CA160.16 (looseleaf).
371   *R v Tomars* [1978] 2 NZLR 505 (CA); see also 3.3.3(2)(a).

way to his death. Under this test, negligence, or even recklessness, by V or the driver of the other car, would not necessarily exclude such causation.[373]

In some cases where V has acted in fear of D the courts have said that the fear must be "well grounded", and that there must be a "reasonable relationship" between D's conduct and V's reaction, but those requirements are now incorporated in the test of reasonable foreseeability.[374] Moreover, although it is sometimes assumed that V must believe that there is "immediate" danger,[375] the essential requirements that V must act as a result of D's conduct and in a reasonably foreseeable way may be satisfied even though V knows D is not able instantly to inflict harm (as when a threat is made through a locked door).[376]

There remains one doubtful question. At common law, a case where V dies as a result of trying to escape from D is treated as being governed by the law relating to manslaughter by an unlawful act, so that for liability D's conduct must be unlawful and such as any reasonable person would realise was likely to create the risk of some harm to a person.[377] In *Tomars* it was recognised that such cases could be within s 160(2)(a), although in the interests of simplicity it will generally be preferable that the prosecution rely solely on the more explicit s 160(2)(d). This paragraph, it was acknowledged, will not apply if D's conduct was legally justified (for example a threat of reasonable parental discipline), but the Court inclined to the view that apart from that any conduct capable of producing fear of violence could suffice.[378] The requirement that V's conduct be reasonably foreseeable may be justified as an aspect of causation, which para (d) requires, but it may be doubted whether the courts would be warranted in imposing a further gloss requiring D's conduct to be unlawful and likely to cause harm.[379]

(3) *Killing by frightening: s 160(2)(e)*

As previously mentioned (16.2.3(2)), under s 163 the general rule is that no one is criminally responsible for killing "by any influence on the mind alone", or for killing by any disorder or disease arising from such influence. The abolition of this special rule has been proposed,[380] and in view of modern medical knowledge it appears to be arbitrary. For example, if as a result of D's dangerous unlawful act V indulges in physical exertion which causes death from heart failure there appears to be nothing to preclude liability; but if the same act causes mere fright or emotional stress which produces in V a chemical or physiological process which causes

---

372 Moreover, personal characteristics of the accused, such as age and intellegence, are not relevant to the causation question. See R v *Marjoram* [2000] Crim LR 372 (CA).
373 R v *Tomars* [1978] 2 NZLR 505 (CA), 511; cf R v *Storey* [1931] NZLR 417 (CA), 442-443.
374 R v *Tomars* [1978] 2 NZLR 505 (CA), 510; the same will be true of requirements that V's response be "proportionate" to the threat, or "within the ambit of reasonableness": R v *Williams* [1992] 2 All ER 183; [1992] 1 WLR 380 (CA).
375 R v *Halliday* (1889) 61 LT 701, 702.
376 R v *Lewis* [1970] Crim LR 647 (CA); Elliott, "Frightening a person into injuring himself" [1974] Crim LR 15, 19.
377 For example R v *Mackie* (1973) 57 Cr App R 453; [1973] Crim LR 438 (CA); *DPP v Daley* [1980] AC 237; [1979] 2 WLR 239 (PC), 245-246; 245-246; R v *Williams* [1992] 2 All ER 183; [1992] 1 WLR 380 (CA).
378 R v *Tomars* [1978] 2 NZLR 505 (CA), 510.
379 On this view, s 160(2)(d) could well apply if V flees in fear of D, and the physical exertion causes V to die of heart failure: Cf R v *Hayward* (1908) 21 Cox CC 692; *Adams*, CA160.16 (looseleaf).
380 Crimes Bill Consultative Committee, *Crimes Bill 1989: Report of the Crimes Consultative Committee Presented to the Minister of Justice April 1991*, Wellington, Department of Justice, 1991, 104.

heart failure the rule in s 163 excludes liability.[381] However, ss 160(2)(e) and 163 provide for an exception: it is culpable homicide if D causes death by "wilfully frightening a child under 16 or a sick person", including cases where such conduct produces some fatal disorder or disease.[382] There is an absence of authority on this provision, but it may be that a person will be "sick" if she has a condition making her unusually susceptible to injury or death from fright. "Wilfully" will require that D intend to frighten, or is at least subjectively reckless as to the risk and, although it seems to have been otherwise at common law, the modern approach to mens rea requirements suggests that it should be interpreted as applying to all the elements in s 160(2)(e), so that D must at least be aware of a real risk that V is under 16 or sick.[383] But such "wilfulness" might well take the place of the elements of unlawfulness and dangerousness required when s 160(2)(a) applies.[384]

(4) *Killing by unlawful omission: s 160(2)(b)*

Under s 160(2)(b), it is culpable homicide if D kills by "an omission without lawful excuse to perform or observe any legal duty". The effect of this is that if death results from D's failure to fulfil a legal duty, D may be guilty of manslaughter, and indeed of murder if the requisite mens rea was present.[385] Sections 151-153 and 155-157 Crimes Act 1961 codify certain "duties tending to the preservation of life" which were recognised at common law, and provide for criminal responsibility where harm may have resulted from a mere omission or, in some instances, from positive conduct which was accompanied by an omission to comply with a legal duty. In practice, most cases of omissions which might involve culpable homicide will be within these statutory provisions. However, s 160(2)(b) refers to "any legal duty" and in R v Mwai[386] the Court of Appeal held that the same phrase in s 145 includes duties recognised by the common law as well as by statute, and even, remarkably, the common law version of a codified duty. Whether a person owes a duty on admitted or established facts is a question of law.[387]

It is convenient first to outline the scope of the codified duties, and then to consider the fault required for manslaughter, and the possibility of a defence of lawful excuse. The codified duties fall into two general categories: duties to provide the necessaries of life; and duties of persons who do dangerous acts, who are in charge of dangerous things, or who have undertaken to do things which may prevent danger to life.

---

381 This was the conclusion of the Alberta Court of Appeal in R v Powder (1981) 29 CR (3d) 183 (Alta CA).
382 For cases at common law allowing for a finding of manslaughter where the death of an infant or a person suffering from an abnormal condition had apparently resulted from fright caused by D, see R v Towers (1874) 12 Cox CC 530; R v Hayward (1908) 21 Cox CC 692.
383 Cf R v Hende [1996] 1 NZLR 153 (CA); contrast R v Hayward (1908) 21 Cox CC 692, 693 where Ridley J appears to have directed that even reasonable ignorance of V's illness would not excuse.
384 Cf *Adams*, CA160.17 (looseleaf); R v Tomars [1978] 2 NZLR 505 (CA).
385 For example R v Gibbins and Proctor (1918) 13 Cr App R 134 (CCA); R v MacDonald [1904] St R Qd 151 (Qld SC); such omissions may also support charges of offences of injuring under s 188, s 189, or s 190; or, if mere personal endangerment is proved, criminal nuisance (s 145); cf R v Mwai [1995] 3 NZLR 149; (1995) 13 CRNZ 273 (CA); R v Turner (1995) 13 CRNZ 142 (CA).
386 R v Mwai [1995] 3 NZLR 149; (1995) 13 CRNZ 273 (CA), 156-157; 281.
387 R v Singh [1999] Crim LR 582 (CA).

(a) Duties to provide necessaries

Under ss 151-153, there may be liability in certain cases where D omits, without lawful excuse, to provide another with the "necessaries of life" (s 151), or "necessaries" (s 152), or "necessary food, clothing or lodging" (s 153). In each case there is criminal responsibility if the result is that V's life is endangered[388] or his health is permanently injured,[389] and it is culpable homicide if death results.

Section 153 imposes the duty and liability on an employer who contracts to provide necessary food, clothing, or lodging for any servant or apprentice under 16. It is of little practical significance today.

Sections 151 and 152 are more important. These apply to those in charge of helpless people, and to parents and guardians of children. More particularly, D may be criminally responsible if one of the specified results is caused to V by an omission to supply or provide either "the necessaries of life" (s 151) or "necessaries" (s 152), provided that:

(i) D "has charge of" V, who is unable by reason of detention, age, sickness, insanity, or any other cause to withdraw from such charge, and is unable to provide himself with the necessaries of life;[390] or

(ii) D "as a parent or person in place of a parent is under a legal duty to provide necessaries" for V, who is a child under 16 and in D's actual custody, but who need not be helpless.[391]

In this context, "necessaries" in s 152 is synonymous with "necessaries of life" in s 151. These include any thing or service required to sustain life or health, such as medical treatment,[392] food and clothing,[393] lodging or shelter,[394] and, no doubt, heating. The refusal of a parent to consent to surgery on a child may be an omission to "supply" or "provide" a necessary,[395] but it seems that leaving V unconscious where she is asphyxiated by drowning will not.[396] However, while the expression "necessaries of life" is flexible and capable of adjusting to changing times and circumstances, it comprehends *provisions*, ie goods and services required to sustain life, and so does not extend to include the parental function of protecting a child from physical

---

388 Which occurs when there is a "reasonable possibility" that death will ensue if the duty is not performed: *R v Moore* [1954] NZLR 893 (CA).
389 Under ss 151 and 152 the maximum penalty is 7 years' imprisonment, and 5 years' under s 153.
390 Section 151(1); this "seeks to ensure that those who have the care of one who cannot care for him or herself supply that person with the necessaries of life": *Auckland Area Health Board v A-G* [1993] 1 NZLR 235; (1992) 8 CRNZ 634, 247; 647 (Thomas J).
391 Section 152(1); this imposes criminal responsibility but unlike the other provisions it does not create the duty. See also the offences of abandoning a child under 6 (s 154), and cruelty to a child (s 195).
392 For example *R v Moore* [1954] NZLR 893 (CA); *R v Burney* [1958] NZLR 745 (CA); but in *Auckland Area Health Board v A-G* [1993] 1 NZLR 235; (1992) 8 CRNZ 634, 249-250; 649, Thomas J excluded treatment (specifically, ventilation) when the patient was beyond recovery, and it provided no medial or therapeutic benefit, beyond deferring brain death.
393 For example *R v Foster* (1906) 26 NZLR 1254 (CA); *R v Gibbins and Proctor* (1918) 13 Cr App R 134 (CCA).
394 Cf *R v Plummer* (1844) 1 Car & K 600; 174 ER 954.
395 Cf *Oakey v Jackson* [1914] 1 KB 216.
396 *R v Phillips* [1971] ALR 740; (1971) 45 ALJR 467 (HCA); and omission to arrange medical attention was not a cause of death. However, if D created the danger, D would have a duty to rescue, and failure to try to do so might well bring the case within s 151: Cf *R v Miller* [1983] 2 AC 161; [1983] 1 All ER 978 (HL).

violence.[397] (In such a case, there might, instead, be failure to perform "a legal duty" for the purposes of homicide under s 160(2)(b).[398])

These sections overlap, in that D may have charge of a helpless person who is also a child covered by s 152; but the parental duty ceases when the child turns 16, whereas the s 151 duty may continue or revive if V is or becomes helpless while in D's charge.[399]

More than one person may owe the duties. In the earlier codes, the parental duty applied only to "the head of the family", but now parents who are living together may both be liable as parents,[400] or one person may have the duty as parent and, if V is helpless, another as a person having charge,[401] or several may jointly have charge,[402] including persons performing parental duties from time to time, for example, as caregivers of a child.[403] But guilt requires both duty and individual fault, so that even if necessaries are withheld by a number of persons, it may be that only one is guilty.[404]

Section 151 applies when D "has charge of" a helpless person, and it is expressly provided that it applies "whether such charge is undertaken by him *under* any contract or is imposed upon him by law or by reason of his unlawful act or otherwise howsoever". The obligation to provide necessaries to a person under the accused's charge is not lessened by the fact that the person lives in an apartment on the lower floors of the house occupied by the accused and is "fiercely" independent. Such a charge may be based on a number of factors, including the person's dependency; the accused's familial relationship with the person; the accused's awareness of the person's need; the accused's control over the person's living conditions and personal care; the accused's failure to make decisions that would have resulted in the person receiving the necessaries of life; and the person's incapacity to withdraw from the accused's charge owing to age and illness.[405]

In some cases "charge" of, and responsibility for, a helpless person may be imposed on D because of their relationship and the circumstances, regardless of whether D has *done* anything: for example, when the helpless person is D's spouse or child and is living with D.[406] Alternatively, it may arise from the fact that the helpless person lived with D, who had accepted the responsibility of care,[407] or from the fact that D took control of the helpless person, even

---

397 *R v Lunt* [2004] 1 NZLR 498; (2003) 20 CRNZ 681 (CA). Contrast the law in Canada: *R v Peterson* (2005) 201 CCC (3d) 220 (Ont CA), 231; *R v Popen* (1981) 60 CCC (2d) 232 (Ont CA). There may, however, be failure to perform "a legal duty", for the purposes of homicide under s 160(2)(b), where a parent has omitted to take reasonable steps to discharge the common law duty to protect his or her child from the foreseen or reasonably foreseeable illegal violence of another person: *R v Lunt* [2004] 1 NZLR 498; (2003) 20 CRNZ 681 (CA), paras 26, 28.
398 That is, where a parent has omitted to take reasonable steps to discharge the common law duty to protect his or her child from the foreseen or reasonably foreseeable illegal violence of another person: *R v Lunt* [2004] 1 NZLR 498; (2003) 20 CRNZ 681 (CA), paras 26, 28.
399 Cf *R v Chattaway* (1922) 17 Cr App R 7.
400 Cf *R v Watson and Watson* (1959) 43 Cr App R 111 (CCA).
401 For example *R v Bubb* (1850) 4 Cox CC 455; *R v Gibbins and Proctor* (1918) 13 Cr App R 134 (CCA); cf *R v Witika* [1993] 2 NZLR 424; (1992) 9 CRNZ 272 (CA).
402 For example *R v Stone and Dobinson* [1977] QB 354; [1977] 2 All ER 341 (CA).
403 *R v Lunt* [2004] 1 NZLR 498; (2003) 20 CRNZ 681 (CA), para 28.
404 For example *R v Bubb* (1850) 4 Cox CC 455; *R v Conde* (1867) 10 Cox CC 547.
405 *R v Paterson* (2005) 201 CCC (3d) 220 (Ont CA).
406 For example *R v Smith* [1979] Crim LR 251 (CA); *Bonnyman v R* (1942) 28 Cr App R 131 (CCA); *R v Chattaway* (1922) 17 Cr App R 7; *R v Bubb* (1850) 4 Cox CC 455.

temporarily, so that help from others was less likely.[408] The words "or otherwise howsoever" were added in 1961. However, it had already been held that the section applied when D had assumed the responsibility of caring for V voluntarily, and not under contract,[409] and the addition of these words suggests that it may be enough if D in fact has control of a helpless person, even if it is doubtful whether D has accepted responsibility.[410] In *R v Stone and Dobinson*,[411] S had allowed an elderly relative to live in his home, where she became helpless. It was held that a jury could find an assumption of duty by S from the fact that V was a relative occupying a room in his home, and an assumption of duty by S's mistress because she had made some attempt to wash and feed the unco-operative lodger. The case has been criticised,[412] and it is doubtful whether it should have been significant that S was a relative, or that the mistress had done something rather than nothing. Under s 151 S might perhaps be responsible simply because he had control as a result of his occupancy, and others might have "charge" if they share a residence with a helpless person, at least if no one else has assumed full responsibility. Generally, it will be enough if the accused voluntarily assumes responsibility for the care of a helpless stranger.[413]

There remain doubtful cases. In particular, it is not clear whether the duty to supply necessaries (which perhaps includes a duty to rescue) might arise simply because D caused V's helplessness (for example, through rendering V unconscious by an unlawful act),[414] and perhaps D never has "charge" of a helpless person unless she has a statutory or contractual obligation to provide care, or has assumed responsibility to do so, or at least controls or shares the place where V is.[415] But even if s 151(1) does not apply, there remains the possibility that an equivalent common law duty may be relied upon.[416]

(b) Duties of those doing dangerous acts and those in charge of dangerous things

These are provided for by ss 155 and 156:

"**155 Duty of persons doing dangerous acts**

"Every one who undertakes (except in case of necessity) to administer surgical or medical treatment, or to do any other lawful act the doing of which is or may be dangerous to life, is under a legal duty to have and to use reasonable knowledge, skill, and care in doing any such act, and is criminally responsible for the consequences of omitting without lawful excuse to discharge that duty.

---

407 For example *R v Foster* (1906) 26 NZLR 1254 (CA): grandmother who assumed sole charge of her inadequate daughter's infant; *R v Bubb* (1850) 4 Cox CC 455: cohabitee of an infant's father, who provided means of supporting the child; *R v Instan* [1893] 1 QB 450: niece living with helpless person, who had provided funds for the support of both of them.
408 *Taktak v R* (1988) 14 NSWLR 226; 34 A Crim R 334 (CA); and a kidnapper will clearly have "charge" as a result of unlawful assumption of control.
409 *R v Foster* (1906) 26 NZLR 1254 (CA).
410 Cf *R v Chattaway* (1922) 17 Cr App R 7, where what is required was described as "custody, charge, or care or control".
411 *R v Stone and Dobinson* [1977] QB 354; [1977] 2 All ER 341 (CA).
412 Williams, *TBCL*, 262-266.
413 See eg *Taktak v R* (1988) 14 NSWLR 226; 34 A Crim R 334 (CA).
414 A duty was recognised in *R v Lawford and Van Den Wiel* (1993) 69 A Crim R 115; there are conflicting dicta in *R v Phillips* [1971] ALR 740; (1971) 45 ALJR 467 (HCA), 745, 753, 756; 471, 476, 478.
415 Cf *R v Plummer* (1844) 1 Car & K 600; 174 ER 954 (husband refusing shelter to estranged wife).
416 Cf *R v Mwai* [1995] 3 NZLR 149; (1995) 13 CRNZ 273 (CA).

"**156 Duty of persons in charge of dangerous things**

"Every one who has in his charge or under his control anything whatever, whether animate or inanimate, or who erects, makes, operates, or maintains anything whatever, which, in the absence of precaution or care, may endanger human life is under a legal duty to take reasonable precautions against and to use reasonable care to avoid such danger, and is criminally responsible for the consequences of omitting without lawful excuse to discharge that duty."

These sections overlap, but neither applies unless there is a reasonable possibility that someone will die if reasonable care is not taken; a risk of injury, even serious injury, is insufficient.[417] In other respects they are of wide application.

Although s 155 specifically applies to the administration of surgical or medical treatment, it also expressly extends to "any other lawful act" which may be dangerous to life; for example, the organisation of a bungy jump.[418] At common law, in *R v Burdee*,[419] an unqualified person was held guilty of manslaughter after the death of an elderly and ill woman was accelerated because she followed D's advice not to eat for 3 days. It may be doubted whether D "administers" medical treatment by merely giving advice, although doing so might perhaps be "any other lawful act" within s 155. It is even possible that liability could still arise on the basis of breach of a duty at common law to refrain from incompetent medical advice.[420] Although s 155 applies only if D "undertakes" to do the relevant act, it is probable that this is satisfied if she chooses to do it, even if there was no antecedent promise or agreement to act, and again, any doubts might be resolved by applying the common law.[421]

Regarding s 156, it will be a question of fact whether D has charge or control of the dangerous thing, and there may be more than one person who shares it. Thus, in *R v Turner*,[422] there was sufficient evidence that a factory was under the charge or control of the factory's general manager and also of the managing director of the company which owned it; the latter not having delegated full control to another, and having continued to direct and guide operations.

In *Turner* the Court of Appeal also said that "anything whatever" had been "deliberately chosen as a phrase of wide import", and that it is to be construed, as in the past, as covering things that are dangerous when in operation as well as things which are inherently dangerous in their static condition.[423] The latter could include, for example, explosives, loaded firearms, toxic substances, exposed electric wiring, and things with hidden defects making them dangerous.[424] But many cases will involve things which are dangerous only when in operation,

---

417 *R v Myatt* [1991] 1 NZLR 674; (1990) 7 CRNZ 304 (CA), 681; 311.
418 *R v Collett* T122/90, cited in McMullin, *Report of Sir Duncan McMullin to Hon Douglas Graham, Minister of Justice, On Sections 155 and 156 of the Crimes Act 1961*, Wellington, Department of Justice, 1995, 6.
419 *R v Burdee* (1916) 86 LJKB 871 (CCA).
420 Cf *R v Mwai* [1995] 3 NZLR 149; (1995) 13 CRNZ 273 (CA); in *Auckland Area Health Board v A-G* [1993] 1 NZLR 235; (1992) 8 CRNZ 634, 255; 655, Thomas J did not doubt that the accused in *Burdee* would have accelerated death within s 164, but did not attempt to identify the basis for manslaughter under the Act. In such a case, if V is competent and aware of the risks there may be doubt on the question of causation.
421 Cf *R v Bateman* (1925) 19 Cr App R 8; [1925] All ER Rep 45 (CCA), 12, 13; 48, 49.
422 *R v Turner* (1995) 13 CRNZ 142 (CA).
423 *R v Turner* (1995) 13 CRNZ 142 (CA), 149.
424 This list is taken from the judgment of Wylie J in *Hilder v Police* (1989) 4 CRNZ 232, 235; in *Primrose v Police* (1985) 1 CRNZ 621 it was held that a can of petrol was within s 156 when it was thrown on a fire; perhaps it could be dangerous in its "static state".

for example, trams,[425] gigs,[426] cars,[427] and speedboats;[428] or things which are dangerous to some because of surrounding circumstances, for example, an unfenced swimming pool in which a child drowns.[429] It was further held in *Turner* that a thing may endanger human life because the thing itself provides the danger (such as a loaded firearm or an explosive), or because it is operated so as to produce something which may do so: for example, a factory producing food for human consumption (as in *Turner*, where contaminated food had been produced), or a factory or quarry producing fumes, smoke, or rocks.

Section 11 Summary Offences Act 1981 creates an offence of endangering safety, which applies to things which in the absence of care are "likely to cause injury", not just things which may endanger life. There have been decisions that hold s 11 does not apply when danger is created only because of the manner in which the thing is used.[430] These may be doubted, but in any event such a principle has no application to s 156.

However, it remains possible that "anything whatsoever" in s 156 could be confined to things which are "inherently dangerous" in the sense that there is a danger to life if care is not exercised when they are used for the purpose for which they were designed. This would justify the exclusion of things such as candles and pencils which in unusual cases may be used in such a way that death is an unintended consequence.[431] But the judgment in *Turner* does not encourage any gloss on the terms of s 156, and the better view seems to be that it includes absolutely anything provided that in the circumstances there is a real and reasonably foreseeable risk that it will endanger life if it is used carelessly. It is not even confined to physical or tangible things, and has been held to encompass to an organised cycling event.[432] Moreover, even if for some reason s 156 does not apply, there is a common law duty of the same kind which may. In *R v Mwai*[433] the Court of Appeal thought that bodily fluid containing HIV was a thing within s 156, imposing on D a duty to exercise care to avoid endangering life (at least without the informed consent of an endangered person), by using a condom if engaging in sexual intercourse. But the Court held that in any event a similar common law duty applied, citing, in particular, *R v Burnett*,[434] where D offended by taking a person infected with smallpox into a public place. Such a case is not within s 156, for while bodily fluid may be "anything", a person could not be.

---

425 *R v Dawe* (1911) 30 NZLR 673 (CA).
426 *R v Officer* [1922] GLR 175.
427 *R v Storey* [1931] NZLR 417 (CA).
428 *R v Myatt* [1991] 1 NZLR 674; (1990) 7 CRNZ 304 (CA).
429 *R v Turton (No 2)* (1989) 5 CRNZ 274.
430 *Hilder v Police* (1989) 4 CRNZ 232 (power boat and para-flying apparatus not included); *Morley v Police* [1996] 1 NZLR 551 (unicycle not included, but ultimately the reason may have been insufficient likelihood of injury).
431 See *R v McCallum* [1969] Tas SR 73; *R v Dabelstein* [1966] Qd R 411 (CCA), where insertion of such objects in a woman's vagina resulted in death. Cf *Timbu Kolian v R* (1968) 119 CLR 47; [1969] ALR 143 (HCA), 57; 150.
432 *R v Anderson* [2005] 1 NZLR 774; (2004) 20 CRNZ 1086 (CA). For a comprehensive list of the range of items identified as "anything whatever" for the purposes of s 156, see *Adams*, CA156.02 (looseleaf).
433 *R v Mwai* [1995] 3 NZLR 149; (1995) 13 CRNZ 273 (CA), 156, 157; 281, 282.
434 *R v Burnett* (1815) 4 M & S 271; 105 ER 835.

(c) Duty to avoid dangerous omissions

Section 157 provides that every one who "undertakes" to do any act, the omission of which is or may be dangerous to life, is criminally responsible for the consequence of omitting, without lawful excuse, to do it. No penalty is provided, but it will be culpable homicide if death results, or an offence under s 190 if injury is caused.

An obligation to do particular acts may arise from the undertaking of a general duty of care. For example, in R v Crump; R v Johnston[435] a number of boys had drowned in an accident which occurred in the course of activities at a bushcraft camp. D, a camp organiser, was charged with manslaughter, it being alleged that in terms of s 157 he had undertaken the duty of ensuring the safety of the boys, and had failed to do so by omitting to repair the handle of the door of the car in which the boys drowned. (The charge failed, however, because it could not be shown that any of the boys would have escaped had the handle been repaired.) No doubt the required undertaking may be express or implied and need not be contractual,[436] although s 157 is based on cases at common law where D was held criminally responsible when death was caused by his omitting to perform a contractual duty, as where a mine shaft was left unprotected or unventilated,[437] a railway signal was not turned on,[438] or a level crossing barrier was left up.[439] Some authority suggested that there was no liability if D owed no duty of care to V,[440] but s 157 does not preserve such a distinction. Holding D responsible to the world at large on the basis of a private contract or undertaking may be justified because, but for D's undertaking, the harm would probably have been prevented by someone else's doing the requisite act.

(d) Other duties

Even if none of these codified duties applies, liability under s 160(2)(b) may arise if death results from a breach of some other statutory duty,[441] or a duty recognised only at common law (16.5.2(4)). For example, although the law recognises no general duty to save life, there will be a duty to try to rescue V from immediate danger if V is a child under D's care, or is a helpless person for whom D has responsibility.[442] Similarly, D as V's parent, has a common law duty to take reasonable steps to protect her from the forseen or foreseeable illegal violence of another person.[443] The same might be true if V is endangered as a result of D's act, be it lawful or unlawful, as when D accidentally sets fire to a place where V is.[444] Even if none of the code duties applies, such cases might be within s 160(2)(b).

---

435 R v Crump; R v Johnston [1970] NZ Recent Law 191.
436 Adams, CA157.02 (looseleaf).
437 R v Hughes (1857) 7 Cox CC 301 (CCA); R v Haines (1847) 2 Car & K 368; 175 ER 152.
438 R v Pargeter (1848) 3 Cox CC 191.
439 R v Pittwood (1902) 19 TLR 37; cf R v Pocock (1851) 5 Cox CC 172 (undertaking to repair a road).
440 R v Smith (1869) 11 Cox CC 210.
441 R v Foster (1906) 26 NZLR 1254 (CA); cf the differently worded Tasmanian Code, under which only the Code duties apply to culpable homicide: R v Phillips [1971] ALR 740; (1971) 45 ALJR 467 (HCA).
442 Cf R v Middleship (1850) 5 Cox CC 275 (CA); R v Russell [1933] ALR 76; [1933] VLR 59, 83, 86; 75, 81; 3.2.1(2)(b).
443 R v Lunt [2004] 1 NZLR 498; (2003) 20 CRNZ 681 (CA).
444 Cf R v Miller [1983] 2 AC 161; [1983] 1 All ER 978 (HL); Green v Cross (1910) 103 LT 279; 3.2.1(2)(e).

(5) Fault required for manslaughter by omission

The mens rea requirement for involuntary manslaughter by omission has been the subject of important statutory modification by the Crimes Amendment Act 1997. For an understanding of this, it is necessary to say something of the history.

(a) History: liability for mere negligence

In relation to dangerous activities and dangerous things, the terms of ss 155 and 156 (and their predecessors) impose criminal responsibility for failure to have and to use "reasonable" knowledge, skill, care, and precautions. This was held to effect a major departure from the common law.

In civil law (subject to the accident compensation legislation), a person is liable to pay compensation for harm caused by her negligence, and for negligence it suffices that she was in breach of a duty of care and failed to exercise "reasonable" care — the degree of care which would be exercised by a reasonable person. At common law, however, if criminal liability for manslaughter by omission is alleged, such "ordinary" or "civil" negligence is not enough. Instead, there must be "a very high degree" of negligence, or "gross negligence". A leading statement of the rule is in *R v Bateman*,[445] where death had resulted from medical treatment:

> "In explaining to juries the test which they should apply to determine whether the negligence, in the particular case, amounted or did not amount to a crime, the judges have used many epithets, such as 'culpable', 'criminal', 'gross', 'wicked', 'clear', 'complete'. But whatever epithet be used, and whether an epithet be used or not, in order to establish criminal liability the facts must be such that, in the opinion of the jury, the negligence of the accused went beyond a mere matter of compensation between subjects and showed such disregard for the life and safety of others as to amount to a crime against the State and conduct deserving punishment."

This test is somewhat circular, and is exceptional in leaving it to the jury to decide what conduct should be criminal, but was reaffirmed by the House of Lords in *R v Adomako*.[446]

In New Zealand this approach did not in the past apply to s 155 or s 156. In *R v Storey*,[447] it was alleged that D was guilty of manslaughter because his negligent driving of a motorcar had caused death. The Court of Appeal held that the statutory requirement of "reasonable" care in what are now ss 155 and 156 meant that the same standard applied as governs civil liability, so that "gross" negligence was unnecessary:[448]

> "The standard should be neither too high nor too low: it should be a 'reasonable' standard, the standard of skill and care which would be observed by a reasonable man."

---

445 *R v Bateman* (1925) 19 Cr App R 8; [1925] All ER Rep 45 (CCA), 11-12; 48.
446 *R v Adomako* [1995] 1 AC 171; [1994] 3 All ER 79 (HL); the fault requirement may be described as "recklessness": *Andrews v DPP* [1937] AC 576; [1937] 2 All ER 552 (HL); but conscious awareness of the risk is not needed, nor need the definition of "reckless" in *R v Lawrence* [1982] AC 510; [1981] 1 All ER 974 (HL) be used: *Adomako*, disapproving *R v Seymour* [1983] 2 AC 493; [1983] 2 All ER 1058 (HL).
447 *R v Storey* [1931] NZLR 417 (CA), approving *R v Dawe* (1911) 30 NZLR 673 (CA).
448 *R v Storey* [1931] NZLR 417 (CA), 435 (Myers CJ); an anomalous result was that the fault sufficient for manslaughter was identical to that needed for more recently created offences of causing death by dangerous or negligent driving, although they carry much lesser penalties: see now ss 36 and 38 Land Transport Act 1998. The explanation was that these offences had been created because juries were reluctant to convict for manslaughter in motoring cases.

Of course, for conviction such negligence had to be proved beyond reasonable doubt, whereas proof on the balance of probability suffices to establish civil liability.

The principle in *Storey* imposed liability if D fell in any way below the standard of knowledge, skill, and care which would be exercised by a reasonable person engaging in the activity.[449] When the activity is dangerous to life, that is likely to be a demanding standard. The mere fact that D makes a mistake or error of judgment does not *necessarily* mean he was negligent[450] — in all the circumstances a reasonable person might have made it — but often it will suffice to show negligence. Expert witnesses on appropriate standards in dangerous activities will be unwilling to acknowledge mistakes and errors as acceptable, and "reasonable" is liable to be seen as much the same as "ideal".

A lower standard does not apply merely because D lacked appropriate qualifications for the activity, and indeed lack of qualifications may show that even embarking on the activity was negligent.[451] On the other hand, a higher standard does not apply merely because D has special skills or qualifications.[452]

What is "reasonable" will, of course, depend on the circumstances. If D has to make an instant decision in an emergency, this will be important on the question whether an appropriate standard was met, although that is its only significance. Section 155 does not apply "in case of necessity", but the exception does not mean that properly qualified people are not required to exercise reasonable skill and care in an emergency; rather, it may exempt from the duty unqualified or insufficiently qualified people who are required to act in emergencies.[453] Liability under these provisions is determined by an objective test, and, as to awareness, it will be enough that a reasonable person would have been aware of the risk in question, whether or not D was aware of it;[454] but if D knew of the risk because of "special knowledge" there might be liability even if a reasonable person might not have been aware of it.[455]

Storey gave effect to the ordinary meaning of the terms of ss 155 and 156, but the result was that a low degree of fault was enough for conviction of a major crime, making New Zealand law markedly more severe than in most similar jurisdictions where the "gross negligence" requirement applies. Similarly-worded statutes in Canada and Australia have been held not to override the common law standard.[456]

---

449 In the case of medical treatment it will normally suffice that D act "in accordance with a practice accepted at the time as proper by a responsible body of medical opinion, even though other doctors adopt a different practice": R v Yogasakaran [1990] 1 NZLR 399; (1989) 5 CRNZ 69 (CA), 404; 74.
450 Long v R [1995] 2 NZLR 691; (1995) 13 CRNZ 124, 694; 127-128.
451 R v Bateman (1925) 19 Cr App R 8; [1925] All ER Rep 45 (CCA), 13; 49; R v Creighton (1993) 105 DLR (4th) 632; [1993] 3 SCR 3; (1993) 83 CCC (3d) 346 (SCC), 678; 72; 392; cf R v Webb (1834) 1 M & Rob 405; 174 ER 140; R v Burdee (1916) 86 LJKB 871 (CCA); for dangerous acts, the possession of "reasonable" knowledge and skill is expressly required by s 155.
452 R v Myatt [1991] 1 NZLR 674; (1990) 7 CRNZ 304 (CA), 682; 312.
453 R v Yogasakaran [1990] 1 NZLR 399; (1989) 5 CRNZ 69 (CA), 405; 74.
454 Cf R v Burney [1958] NZLR 745 (CA); it is submitted that contrary dicta in R v Filimoehala 16/12/99, CA367/99 and in R v Edmonds (1991) 7 CRNZ 510, 513 cannot be right.
455 Cf R v Dant (1865) Le & Ca 567; 169 ER 1517; there is a difference of opinion as to the effect of a drug user's acquired knowledge of the effects of drugs in R v Creighton (1993) 105 DLR (4th) 632; [1993] 3 SCR 3; (1993) 83 CCC (3d) 346 (SCC), although the majority emphasise an unvarying standard of care: Cf R v Myatt [1991] 1 NZLR 674; (1990) 7 CRNZ 304 (CA).

Nevertheless, *Storey* was reaffirmed in *R v Yogasakaran*.[457] In that case, D was an anaesthetist who caused a patient's death when he injected the wrong drug during an emergency in an operating theatre. He had sought the appropriate drug from a drawer in a trolley where it should have been, but the drawer had been improperly stocked by someone who had put the wrong drug there. D was convicted of manslaughter (although no penalty was imposed) and, there being evidence that D had not complied with normal practice when he injected the drug without having checked the label on its container, the conviction was upheld on appeal. The jury had been directed in accordance with *Storey*, which was approved. The Court of Appeal acknowledged that New Zealand law was more severe than elsewhere, but *Storey* accorded with the natural meaning of the statute, which had been drafted at a time when the common law was at best unsettled on the issue. The Court doubted whether the rule produced "unjust results" in practice (and included the present case in this), noting that its severity was "mitigated" by the need to prove causative negligence beyond reasonable doubt,[458] by the caution to be expected of juries, and by the exceptionally wide discretion the judge has in sentencing.

(b) History: liability for gross negligence

The rule in *Storey* was held to apply where the applicable statutory provision expressly imposes criminal responsibility for a failure to have and to use "reasonable" knowledge, skill, and care. This is done by ss 155 and 156, but not by the other sections which codify duties, and when these were relied upon gross negligence was required.

In *R v Burney*,[459] D's infant had died from malnutrition and infection from a condition which developed a few days before death, and it was alleged that D had offended against s 151 by failing to obtain medical attention early enough. The Court of Appeal rejected an argument that D was guilty only if she knew of V's need. It was held that, whether the charge be manslaughter or endangering life, negligence was sufficient fault, and that ignorance resulting from negligence did not provide a "lawful excuse". The Court added, however, that this was so only if there was negligence "of a high degree"; for *Storey* (above) applied only when the statute defined the applicable standard of care.[460]

In *R v Walker*,[461] what would suffice under *Burney* was described as "negligence of a sufficiently high degree to incur criminal responsibility". There is no doubt that this is the gross negligence

---

456 *R v Baker* [1929] 1 DLR 785; (1929) 51 CCC 71, affirmed [1929] 2 DLR 282; [1929] SCR 354 (SCC); *Callaghan v R* (1952) 87 CLR 115; [1952] ALR 941 (HCA), where the High Court of Australia emphasised that the Court was engaged in interpreting "a criminal code dealing with major crimes involving grave moral guilt".
457 *R v Yogasakaran* [1990] 1 NZLR 399; (1989) 5 CRNZ 69 (CA), the Privy Council refused special leave to appeal.
458 When V was already gravely ill there may well be doubt whether error in treatment significantly accelerated death: see, for example, *Long v R* [1995] 2 NZLR 691; (1995) 13 CRNZ 124.
459 *R v Burney* [1958] NZLR 745 (CA).
460 *R v Burney* [1958] NZLR 745 (CA), 753-754, it was held that there had been sufficient evidence of such negligence, and that a direction that D's omission had to be "neglectful and inexcusable" had been adequate. In *R v Witika* [1993] 2 NZLR 424; (1992) 9 CRNZ 272 (CA), 436; 287-288, the Court of Appeal rejected a submission that under s 152 it was necessary that D knew V suffered a "life threatening" condition, and approved a direction that what was required was that D "should have known ... that there was a serious condition requiring treatment". *Burney* was applied to s 157 in *R v Crump; R v Johnston* [1970] NZ Recent Law 191.
461 *R v Walker* [1958] NZLR 810 (CA), 815, 816.

required for manslaughter at common law. In essence, this requires the jury to decide whether D's conduct fell below a reasonable standard to such an extent as to be deserving of punishment.[462] While no particular form of words has to be employed in every case when directing the jury, "reckless" has sometimes been thought to be the most appropriate description of the high degree of negligence required.[463]

When responsibility depends on mere negligence, the fact that D suffered from a disability which limited his capacity to meet a reasonable standard of care will be irrelevant to liability, and the public interest may even prevent it from mitigating penalty.[464] When gross negligence is required it is possible, but uncertain, that such a personal characteristic might have to be taken into account.[465]

Adams[466] was sharply critical of the dicta in *Burney* and *Walker*, going so far as to suggest that they were formulated per incuriam. However, his criticisms overlooked the fact that at common law the requirement of gross negligence has been applied to breach of a duty to act, as well as to other forms of manslaughter by negligence,[467] and while it may seem odd to say that negligence by D may provide a "lawful excuse", it makes sense to say that ignorance or incapacity on D's part provides such an excuse, so long as it does not result from gross negligence. The conclusion might also be rationalised on the basis that in this context, when the statute is silent on the issue, absence of gross negligence is an excuse recognised at common law which is not inconsistent with the statute, so that it is preserved by s 20. In any event, the principle supported in *Burney* has now been confirmed by statute.

(c) A general requirement of gross negligence

In *R v Yogasakaran*,[468] the Court of Appeal doubted whether in practice unjust results followed from the rule that in the context of dangerous activities mere negligence was sufficient fault for criminal liability. Nevertheless, in 1995 the Minister of Justice requested Sir Duncan McMullin, a retired judge of the Court of Appeal, to consider and report on whether the standard of care applicable under ss 155 and 156 should be changed. Sir Duncan's investigation led him to recommend that the law be brought into line with that of the United Kingdom, Australia, and Canada, by making gross negligence essential to criminal liability for breach of any of the duties codified in the Crimes Act. In his view, mere negligence is not a sufficient degree of fault to justify conviction of such a serious crime as manslaughter; and it was anomalous that simple negligence sufficed under ss 155 and 156, but a high degree of negligence was required when s 151, s 152, s 153, or s 157 were relied upon, especially as there may be cases falling under both groups of sections. Moreover, although the recommended changes would apply to all dangerous activities, there was some evidence that the severe rule in *Yogasakaran* caused particular problems in the medical context: it might lead to the avoidance

---

462 See 16.5.2(5).
463 *Andrews v DPP* [1937] AC 576; [1937] 2 All ER 552 (HL); *Bonnyman v R* (1942) 28 Cr App R 131 (CCA); the latter case was cited by the Court of Appeal in *R v Burney* [1958] NZLR 745 (CA), 754 (see 16.5.2(5)(b)); cf *R v Adomako* [1995] 1 AC 171; [1994] 3 All ER 79 (HL).
464 *R v Abraham* (1993) 10 CRNZ 446 (CA).
465 Orchard, "Culpable homicide: Part II" [1977] NZLJ 447, 450-453; cf the difference of opinion in *R v Creighton* (1993) 105 DLR (4th) 632; [1993] 3 SCR 3; (1993) 83 CCC (3d) 346 (SCC); in *R v Holness* [1970] Tas SR 74, age was regarded as relevant.
466 *Adams*, (2nd ed), para 1107.
467 For example *R v Nicholls* (1874) 13 Cox CC 75; *R v Lowe* [1973] QB 702; [1973] 1 All ER 805 (CA).
468 *R v Yogasakaran* [1990] 1 NZLR 399; (1989) 5 CRNZ 69 (CA); see 16.5.2(5)(a).

of justified but risky surgery ("defensive medicine"), the failure to report information and experience from which others could learn, and might even discourage some from practising medicine in New Zealand.

The recommendations in the McMullin Report were implemented by the Crimes Amendment Act 1997,[469] s 2 of which inserted s 150A into the Crimes Act:

"**150A Standard of care required of persons under legal duties**

"(1) This section applies in respect of the legal duties specified in any of sections 151, 152, 153, 155, 156, and 157.

"(2) For the purposes of this Part, a person is criminally responsible for—

"(a) Omitting to discharge or perform a legal duty to which this section applies; or

"(b) Neglecting a legal duty to which this section applies—

only if, in the circumstances of the particular case, the omission or neglect is a major departure from the standard of care expected of a reasonable person to whom that legal duty applies in those circumstances."

As is clear from the report and the explanatory note which accompanied the Bill, the purpose of s 150A(2) is to apply to each of the specified sections the requirement that gross negligence is needed for criminal responsibility. This applies for the purposes of Part VIII of the Act, so that gross negligence will be needed if a breach of any of these duties is relied on to support a charge of manslaughter, endangering under ss 151-153, or injuring contrary to s 190. The requirement will not, however, apply if a breach of one of these duties is the basis of some other charge. In particular, it was intended that the ordinary standard of negligence should apply if such a breach is alleged to result in an offence of criminal nuisance, which under s 145 is punishable by a maximum of one year's imprisonment.[470] Section 145 requires that D "knew" that the act or omission in question "would endanger" another's life, safety, or health, but even if this requires conscious advertence to the risk[471] it will remain the case that when either s 155 or s 156 applies it will suffice that, with such knowledge, D's conduct fell in any way below the standard of care of a reasonable person.

The formula, "major departure" from the standard of care expected of a reasonable person, was recommended by Sir Duncan McMullin, who suggested that while it would bring New Zealand law into line with other jurisdictions it would also "go a considerable way toward removing any circularity of expression or ambiguity arising out of the use of the term 'gross'

---

469 For a highly critical, but perhaps jaundiced, appraisal of this reform, see Dawkins, "Medical manslaughter" [1997] NZLJ 393.
470 Sir Duncan McMullin had recommended that the gross negligence requirement should also apply to s 145, but this was rejected on the basis that ordinary negligence was not an inappropriate fault requirement for this less serious offence.
471 Although it is doubtful whether this is essential: it may be that it will suffice if D "knew" of the risk in the sense that she knew it would arise *if* an appropriate level of care was not maintained, even if it is not shown that she was aware that this in fact occurred; cf *R v Turner* (1995) 13 CRNZ 142 (CA), where convictions under s 145 were upheld after danger to life had resulted from failure to exercise reasonable care in the operation of a mussel processing factory in breach of s 156. The Court held that it could be inferred that D "must have known" of the risk (*R v Turner*, 159) but the basis of this was also described as conduct which D "should have known" (153), or "ought to have" realised (160) would endanger life.

negligence".[472] This is puzzling. If the law is brought into line with that of other jurisdictions then, whatever the statutory formula, the test of liability is gross negligence. What that involves has been considered in 16.5.2(5)(a) and (b), and in *R v Adomako*[473] the House of Lords concluded that whatever descriptive words are employed, it requires the jury to determine whether the breach of a reasonable standard of care was so bad that it should be judged to be criminal and deserving of punishment. This is an inherently uncertain and somewhat circular question but, it was held, it cannot usefully be made more precise. If the requirement is to be expressed in a single word, "reckless" (in its "ordinary sense") is appropriate.[474]

Consistently with the purpose of s 150A, in directing juries on the requirement of a "major departure" from the standard of care of a reasonable person, judges employ the concept of gross negligence developed at common law. This was confirmed by Young J in *R v McKie*,[475] where a train driver faced a charge of manslaughter after a fatal collision between his train and a stationary train. It was said that D had failed to respond to a light warning of an obstruction on the line and had failed to verify an assumption that the line was clear by reference to a warrant left by a previous driver in accordance with standard procedure. While recognising that s 150A requires gross negligence, Young J nevertheless held that it does not require "gross misconduct", such as acting under the influence of alcohol, deliberately breaching regulations or protocols, or consciously taking a substantial risk of serious harm. It is not essential that D's state of mind be established, although it may be relevant to whether there was gross negligence, which may be more readily established if D knowingly ran a risk.[476] However, ignorance of the need to take particular steps to avoid danger to life will not excuse if it arises from gross negligence.[477]

Whether negligence is of such a high degree as to be "gross" and deserving of punishment is a matter of degree involving a value judgment on which there may be legitimate scope for disagreement. In *McKie* it was held that where there is evidence that D's negligence caused death, the issue should be left to the jury unless "it could not sensibly and reasonably be contended that the negligence involved a major departure from the required standard of care".

---

472 McMullin, *Report of Sir Duncan McMullin to Hon Douglas Graham, Minister of Justice, On Sections 155 and 156 of the Crimes Act 1961*, Wellington, Department of Justice, 1995, 26; the formula had been previously proposed by the Crimes Consultative Committee, in preference to "very serious deviation" which was used in defining criminal negligence in cl 24 of the Crimes Bill 1989, although the Consultative Committee did not recommend applying this to ss 155 and 156. On the other hand, Crimes Bill Consultative Committee, *Crimes Bill 1989: Report of the Crimes Consultative Committee Presented to the Minister of Justice April 1991*, Wellington, Department of Justice, 1991, 38, recommended that gross negligence should be required in cases within these sections.
473 *R v Adomako* [1995] 1 AC 171; [1994] 3 All ER 79 (HL), 187; 89.
474 *R v Adomako* [1995] 1 AC 171; [1994] 3 All ER 79 (HL), 187; 89; in this context "reckless" does not require actual awareness of the risk of killing, and in *Adomako* it was held not to be necessary to use the definition in *R v Lawrence* [1982] AC 510; [1981] 1 All ER 974 (HL), rejecting *R v Seymour* [1983] 2 AC 493; [1983] 2 All ER 1058 (HL). *Lawrence* would render D "reckless" if D gave no thought to an obvious and serious risk of injuring another. That would not necessarily involve gross negligence in relation to causing death, and the use of such a definition is likely to be a misdirection, and not merely unnecessary.
475 *R v McKie* 3/8/00, Young J, HC Dunedin T13/00.
476 *Re A-G's Reference (No 2 of 1999)* [2000] QB 796; [2000] 3 All ER 182 (CA).
477 *R v Burney* [1958] NZLR 745 (CA); cf *R v Hare* 15/11/99, CA332/99 (where the negligence included failure to read a notice explaining the operation of a jet ski, which D drove with fatal consequences); in *R v Filimoehala* 16/12/99, CA367/99 and *R v Edmonds* (1991) 7 CRNZ 510, there are dicta suggesting the need for actual awareness of the danger, but these appear to be wrong.

On the other hand, while the issue is essentially one for the jury, the jury will need to be given guidance in the summing up. This should be tailored to the particular circumstances and should include a reminder of any particular matter which D might rely on as indicating that any negligence there may have been was not gross.[478]

Where proof of gross negligence is required, it is not permissible for the Crown to prove ordinary negligence by reference to causative acts and omissions and then to seek to adduce evidence of further blameworthy conduct, not causative of the fatality, in order to show that there had been a major departure from the ordinary standard of care. In *R v Fenton*[479] the appellant had caused the death of a passenger in the utility vehicle he was driving when he failed to exercise reasonable care to avoid danger to human life. It was held that matters which were merely part of the background to the accident and went to prove acts or omissions not causative of the fatality (in this case, the vehicle's lack of a warrant of fitness and registration, the appellant's failure to wear a seatbelt, and the fact he had converted the vehicle without the owner's permission), were inadmissible to prove gross negligence causing death.

(6) Duties of care and unlawful acts

Section 150A applies only to the legal duties "specified" in ss 151-153 and 155-157 of the Act. As has been seen, however, breach of a common law duty may support a charge of culpable homicide.[480] It is implicit in *R v Burney* that in such a case gross negligence has always been required, and this will continue to be the case. Moreover, where death results from breach of a duty in one of the specified sections, and, it seems, whenever it results from negligent conduct, the need to prove gross negligence (and danger to life itself) cannot be evaded by alleging "killing by an unlawful act" where the unlawful act is one for which a lesser degree of negligence suffices.[481] In *R v Powell*,[482] where the accused was charged with manslaughter after he ran over a striking worker on a picket line, it was held that the "major depature test" in s 150A applies, not only to prosecutions for manslaughter by omission to observe a specified legal duty but also to manslaughter by an unlawful act involving negligence. The Court of Appeal held that where the unlawful act relied on as the basis for a manslaughter charge involves ordinary carelessness or negligence (in that case careless operation of a motor vehicle contrary to s 37(1) Land Transport Act 1998), it must nonetheless be proved that the act was grossly negligent, just is required as for breaches of the legal duties to which s 150A expressly applies.

What about a case where the unlawful activity is a joint adventure between the defendant and the victim? In tort law, such circumstances do not give rise to a duty of care, on the basis that ex turpi causa non oritur actio.[483] This point was considered in *R v Wacker*,[484] where it was held that, as a matter of public policy, there was no reason why the *criminal* law should decline to hold a person responsible for another's death simply because the two were engaged in some

---

478 *R v Spencer* 5/4/01, CA353/00 (where the particular fact was that a danger on a work site had not been recognised by others, including experts, who had visited the site).
479 *R v Fenton* [2003] 3 NZLR 439, (2003) 20 CRNZ 76 (CA), para 14.
480 See 16.5.2(4).
481 *R v Burney* [1989] 1 NZLR 732; (1989) 4 CRNZ 133.
482 *R v Powell* [2002] 1 NZLR 666 (CA).
483 The doctrine that an action may not be founded on an illegality. Per *Saunders v Edwards* [1987] 1 WLR 1116, 1134, the courts will not "promote or countenance a nefarious object or bargain which it was bound to condemn."
484 *R v Wacker* [2002] EWCA Crim 1944, [2003] QB 1207.

joint unlawful activity at the time. D was convicted of conspiracy to facilitate the entry into the United Kingdom of illegal immigrants and of 58 counts of manslaughter, after the dead bodies of 58 Chinese immigrants were found in the lorry he had driven to England from Europe. (They died of suffocation after D closed the air vent in order to avoid detection.) D appealed against the manslaughter convictions on the basis that the ex turpi causa doctrine meant no duty of care was owed to the immigrants, since they shared the same joint illegal purpose, and so there could be no liability for manslaughter.

Quite rightly, the Court of Appeal rejected his appeal. Instead, the Court ruled that the ex turpi causa principle is not part of the criminal law. The function of the criminal law is to protect its citizens and give effect to the State's duty to try those who have deprived citizens of their rights of life, limb and property. The withdrawal of a civil remedy has nothing to do with whether as a matter of public policy the criminal law applies.[485]

The key point is that criminal and civil laws serve different functions. In civil law, the dispute is between D and V. Where ex turpi causa applies, public policy may disentitle V from recovering against D; but it does not prevent the state from penalising D. That is quite a different matter, since transferring assets to V is no longer a consideration. V's failure to recover is for reasons that concern V. It is not because D has done no wrong. And so the criminal law may be applied to hold D responsible for the harm he does V, notwithstanding V's own participation. Presumably, the same reasoning holds for the tort doctrine of volenti non fit injuria which, for reasons personal to V, would also defeat any civil claim by V.

Notice that the ruling is a negative one: ex turpi causa does not cancel any criminal law duty of care. Its negation does not establish, positively, that any duty of care exists. Clearly, on the facts of *Wacker*, the relationship of dependence between immigrants and driver, and the fact that D himself had closed the vent, justified a finding that the driver owed a duty of care in the first place. Such findings may be unlikely to arise where two or more individuals, on a basis of equality rather than dependence, enter into a joint and dangerous criminal enterprise — say, a planned bank raid. The court may well find that the respective bank robbers owe no duty of care to each other. So, if robber E is injured in the course of the raid it does not follow that his partner in crime F will be criminally responsible for the death of E even if she could have saved him by driving to a hospital rather than fleeing.

(7) Lawful excuse

Each of the provisions in Part VIII of the Act which imposes criminal responsibility for omissions requires that D's conduct be "without lawful excuse". The courts have not attempted a comprehensive definition of this phrase,[486] although in *R v Burney*[487] it was said that "it is of the essence of a defence of lawful excuse that the exculpatory reason put forward must be shown to be lawful in its nature, and not to have an unlawful origin". On the other hand, what is required is an "excuse", not a "justification", and this might mean that D may be freed from responsibility even though his conduct was in some sense improper.[488] Indeed, the express terms of ss 155 and 156 allow the possibility of lawful excuse notwithstanding that

---

485 *R v Wacker* [2002] EWCA Crim 1944, [2003] QB 1207.
486 *Wong Pooh Yin v Public Prosecutor* [1955] AC 93; [1954] 3 All ER 31 (PC), 100; 34.
487 *R v Burney* [1958] NZLR 745 (CA), 753-754.
488 Cf *R v McFall* (1975) 26 CCC (2d) 181 (BC CA), 184, 202.

D has failed to exercise reasonable care, and s 150A(2) (above) imposes a requirement which is additional to those established by the terms of the ensuing sections.

It may be that "lawful excuse" will include any of the general defences (such as impossibility, insanity, automatism, self-defence, or defence of property). Their availability, however, is not dependent on such a provision, and the provision is not confined to such cases. It appears to allow a defence in at least two further types of case.

First, D may have been subject to one of the duties and may have failed to perform it in ignorance of the circumstances which required further care or action. When the fault expressly required for any criminal responsibility was an absence of reasonable knowledge and care, such ignorance could excuse if it was reasonable in the circumstances, but in *R v Burney*[489] it was accepted that in other cases it could also excuse provided it did not arise from a high degree of negligence. This result, however, is now achieved more directly by s 150A(2). Moreover, under s 150A(2) the burden of proof will lie on the prosecution, although it may be otherwise when "lawful excuse" is relied upon.[490]

Secondly, D may be aware of the relevant circumstances, and may fail to do what is required by the duty, perhaps deliberately, but there may be circumstances which the court accepts as exculpatory, having regard to the terms and objects of the legislation.

Such circumstances may sometimes rebut an allegation of absence of reasonable care,[491] and at common law they may mean there is no duty to act. They may also be regarded as providing a "lawful excuse". For example, in *R v Mwai*[492] D was held to be in breach of s 156 when, being infected with HIV, he had sexual intercourse without a condom and without revealing his condition. The Court of Appeal said that had he disclosed his condition, so that his partner consented to the risk, it was "certainly arguable" that there would be no further duty to avoid the danger. An alternative view would be that such informed consent would provide a "lawful excuse". That is perhaps a preferable analysis, in that the terms of s 156 do not recognise exceptions to the existence of the duty, and it avoids the need to decide whether "reasonable" precautions or care have been taken, and whether there was a "major departure" from the standard of a reasonable person.[493]

Further examples arise from cases concerning the withdrawal or non-provision of life-prolonging medical treatment. Subject to statutory exceptions, everyone has the right to refuse

---

489 *R v Burney* [1958] NZLR 745 (CA); 16.5.2(5)(b).
490 *R v Burney* [1958] NZLR 745 (CA), 753. If D does have the burden of proving "lawful excuse", proof on the balance of probabilities will be needed: for example *Sheehan v Police* [1994] 3 NZLR 592; (1994) 12 CRNZ 39. This question also increases the importance of the dubious assumption that general defences are incorporated in the formula: Cf *Summary Proceedings*, Wellington, Brooker's, 1994, SO29.07 (looseleaf). For general discussion of the burden of proof in relation to such an "exception" see Orchard, "The golden thread: Somewhat frayed" (1988) 6 Otago LR 615; and see *R v Rangi* [1992] 1 NZLR 385 (CA).
491 Cf *R v Yogasakaran* [1990] 1 NZLR 399; (1989) 5 CRNZ 69 (CA), 405; 74 where the Court held that the exception of cases of "necessity" in s 155 did not free a qualified person from the duty to exercise reasonable care when action in an emergency was required; it is implicit that the mere fact of an emergency would not provide a "lawful excuse" either, although the Court recognised that it would be a "major factor" to be considered in deciding whether the "appropriate professional standard" had been met.
492 *R v Mwai* [1995] 3 NZLR 149; (1995) 13 CRNZ 273 (CA) 156; 282.
493 The consent contemplated in *Mwai* would involve consenting to a risk of an infection which could cause death; it appears to be implicit that this would not be "consent to the infliction of death" within the meaning of s 63.

medical treatment,[494] if she has the mental capacity to make a true choice.[495] Such refusal will undoubtedly provide a "lawful excuse" for not providing treatment which is needed if death is to be avoided. In other cases, modern developments in medicine and technology have led to a recognition that duties to prolong life are not absolute. In some cases a patient may be alive but unable to choose or communicate a choice. Here, although death will quickly follow, it may sometimes be lawful to withdraw life supporting treatment. This will be so if the patient is in a persistent vegetative state and is non-sentient, or is in a closely analogous state, with no hope of recovery, so that there is no medical or therapeutic benefit from maintaining the treatment, and it does not advance the patient's best interests to do so.[496] Even if a fully sentient patient (or those lawfully acting for him) desires treatment, which is necessary if there is to be a chance of survival, it may nevertheless be lawful for health providers to decline to treat, if in conformity with standards and practices commanding general approval within the medical profession a clinical judgment is made in good faith that the treatment is not in the patient's best interests.[497] In assessing the patient's best interests the doctors may take into account pain that the treatment would involve, its prospects of success, and the likely quality of life that would result. Moreover, since resources are finite, it may be that the courts will be unable to avoid the conclusion that even if an individual's "best interests" might favour treatment, its withdrawal may be lawful if a bona fide clinical judgment is made in accordance with generally accepted medical standards and practice that it is not appropriate, having regard to the needs of others who depend on the provider's resources.[498]

(8)   *Killing by unlawful act and omission*

Section 160(2)(c) expressly provides that homicide is culpable if it consists of killing by a combination of an unlawful act and omission to comply with a legal duty. There is an absence of authority on this paragraph, which may be unnecessarily included, simply owing to an abundance of caution. It perhaps prevents an argument that, if D injures V by an unlawful act, the chain of causation is necessarily broken if V's death might have been avoided had T not failed without lawful excuse to discharge a duty to provide the necessaries of life to V.

---

494   Section 11 New Zealand Bill of Rights Act 1990.
495   Cf *B v Croydon Health Authority* [1995] 1 All ER 683; [1995] 2 WLR 294 (CA), 689; 299; parents may also lawfully refuse consent to life prolonging treatment of a child if it is not in the child's "best interests": *Re T (a minor) (wardship: medical treatment)* [1997] 1 All ER 906 (CA).
496   See, for example, *Auckland Area Health Board v A-G* [1993] 1 NZLR 235; (1992) 8 CRNZ 634; *Airedale NHS Trust v Bland* [1993] AC 789; [1993] 1 All ER 821 (HL); the High Court has jurisdiction to declare the withdrawal to be lawful if specified conditions are met (see *Auckland Area Health Board v A-G*); alternatively, in New Zealand it has jurisdiction to confirm the lawfulness of it by consenting on behalf of the patient: *Re G* 13/12/96, Fraser J, HC Dunedin M126/96.
497   *Shortland v Northland Health Ltd* [1998] 1 NZLR 433; (1997) 4 HRNZ 121 (CA). The Court said that in these circumstances Northland Health was not "in breach of its duty" under s 151, and that the "extent of the duty" to provide necessaries has to be assessed in the context of a particular case. This perhaps suggests that at least some instances of "lawful excuse" will have the effect that the duty ceases to exist.
498   Cf *R v Cambridge Health Authority, ex p B* [1995] 2 All ER 129; [1995] 1 WLR 898 (CA); in *Shortland v Northland Health Ltd* [1998] 1 NZLR 433; (1997) 4 HRNZ 121 (CA), no issue of resource allocation arose, although the Court did comment that the doctors must decide what is best for the patient "in clinical terms and within the resources available".

16.6 Infanticide

As has been mentioned,[499] in some other jurisdictions there is a partial defence of diminished responsibility, under which murder is reduced to manslaughter if D suffers such abnormality of mind as substantially impaired his mental responsibility. There is no such general defence in New Zealand, but a form of it applies in some cases where a mother who has not fully recovered from the effects of giving birth kills a child. Infanticide is provided for by s 178, and is both a substantive offence and a defence to charges of murder and manslaughter. It is derived from English legislation,[500] and allows for substantial leniency.

16.6.1 Scope of infanticide

Section 178(1) provides that:

> "Where a woman causes the death of any child of hers under the age of 10 years in a manner that amounts to culpable homicide, and where at the time of the offence the balance of her mind was disturbed, by reason of her not having fully recovered from the effect of giving birth to that or any other child, or by reason of the effect of lactation … to such an extent that she should not be held fully responsible, she is guilty of infanticide, and not of murder or manslaughter, and is liable to imprisonment for a term not exceeding 3 years."

The liability of other parties is not affected: s 178(8). The verdict may be returned on a charge of infanticide, or when murder or manslaughter is charged and the evidence supports a finding of infanticide: s 178(2). The dual role of infanticide as a hybrid offence and a defence[501] leads to an anomaly in relation to the burden of proof. If D is charged with murder or manslaughter, she will be entitled to a finding of infanticide if there is a sufficient evidential foundation for it, which leaves the jury in reasonable doubt, but if infanticide is charged the prosecution will have the burden of proving all its requirements beyond reasonable doubt.[502] This may be a difficult burden and, if a charge of infanticide is to be defended, consideration may have to be given to charging manslaughter, or even murder, in the alternative. However, the judge should always put infanticide to the jury, even where it is not relied on by the defence, if there is evidence to found the defence.[503]

Infanticide under s 178 is wider than the English equivalent in three significant respects. It extends to the killing of a child under the age of 10 years (rather than under 12 months), the child killed need not be the child whose birth caused mental disturbance, and the child killed need not be a natural child of the mother. Section 178 may apply when D kills "any child of hers", and in R v P[504] Heron J interpreted this as including any child "who can, in fact and law and common sense, be said to be hers", not just her natural child. Whether V was such a child will be "largely a question of fact", depending on the particular circumstances "and no doubt the family and social customs of the time". Heron J accepted that it would not suffice that D

---

499 See 16.5.
500 Infanticide Act 1938 (UK), which replaced the Infanticide Act 1922 (UK); for the history, see Seaborne Davies, "Child-killing in English law" (1937) 1 MLR 203; O'Donovan, "The medicalisation of infanticide" [1984] Crim LR 259.
501 See R v Gordon 16/12/04, CA276/04.
502 Adams, CA178.04 (looseleaf).
503 R v Gordon 16/12/04, CA276/04, para 20.
504 R v P [1991] 2 NZLR 116; (1991) 7 CRNZ 48 (CA).

had temporary care of the child, but *R v P* was a clear case for the application of s 178: V had been a 5-year-old whom D had cared for as a mother for some 2 1/2 years, and indeed D had been granted custody and appointed guardian of V by the Family Court.

For infanticide to be established, the child must have been alive when D did something which might have caused death.[505] Moreover, a mistaken belief that the child was dead might preclude a finding of infanticide, for it will mean that D did not have the mens rea needed for assault, or, in all probability, culpable homicide (and therefore infanticide) by an unlawful act.[506] In New Zealand, as in England, the legislation is expressed in terms confined to a case where a child has been killed. If the child survived, s 178 could have no application to a charge of assault or injury, but in England it has been held that there can be a conviction of attempted infanticide.[507] This would allow appropriate mitigation of what would otherwise be attempted murder, when infanticide was the offence which was in truth intended. However, it contrasts with the prevailing view that provocation is no defence to attempted murder.[508]

16.6.2 Insanity

The fact that the balance of D's mind was disturbed as a result of having given birth will not generally mean that D was insane. However, s 178(3) provides for acquittal "on account of insanity caused by childbirth" if the requirements of s 178(1) are met "to the extent that she was insane". The section goes on to make special provision for the effect of such a verdict, which is similar to the effect of other verdicts of insanity, although s 178(4)(b) requires that D be discharged from custody if two doctors certify that D is no longer insane and has no need for care and treatment in a hospital.

In *R v O'Callaghan*,[509] Quilliam J held that the defence available under s 178(3) is insanity as defined in s 23, although the subsection establishes that the effects of childbirth may be a disease of the mind within s 23. For a finding of insanity, the further requirements of s 23 will have to be satisfied, and D will have the burden of proof. Quilliam J further held that although s 178(3) is expressed to apply "upon the trial" of a woman for infanticide, murder, or manslaughter, it should be read as also applying to a charge of attempted murder, although not to alternative charges of assault or injury (to which s 23 alone could apply). This is a complex result, and the interpretation may be doubted.

Cases are more problematic where serious violence is induced by a mental disorder falling short of the legal defence of insanity. Often, an imperative of public protection may overshadow considerations of reduced responsibility. Yet a Court may be faced with balancing rightful condemnation of violent conduct, which has brought tragedy and grief to others, against D's reduced moral responsibility because of mental disorder, in circumstances where issues of risk to others have limited application. In *R v Harrison-Taylor*,[510] where the accused had been convicted of murdering her 8-month-old son by asphyxiation, the Court accepted

---

505 Cf s 181, which provides for the offence of concealing the dead body of a child; this requires proof that the child was dead when D acted.
506 *R v G* (1984) 1 CRNZ 275, where such a belief arose from dissociation consequent on childbirth; in appropriate cases there might perhaps be culpable homicide on the basis of negligent omission to fulfil a legal duty: *Adams*, CA171.10 (looseleaf).
507 *R v Smith* [1983] Crim LR 739; cf *R v O'Callaghan* (1984) 1 CRNZ 185, 186.
508 See 16.5.1, n 121.
509 *R v O'Callaghan* (1984) 1 CRNZ 185.
510 *R v Harrison-Taylor* 12/9/05, Ellen France J, HC Auckland CRI-2004-092-1510.

that evidence of personality characteristics, together with personal circumstances reducing the offender's ability to cope, justified reducing the 17-year minimum term to 12 years.[511] Nonetheless, the Court accepted, as a general principle, that intellectual capacity unrelated to the mental elements of criminal responsibility would seldom justify a departure from the statutory presumption of life imprisonment.[512]

Contrast *R v Wright*,[513] where a first time young mother, suffering from Munchausen's syndrome by proxy, had confessed to smothering her 8-month-old son with a blanket. The Court of Appeal reduced a 7-year sentence to 4 years, on the basis that the trial judge's allowance for the mitigating mental condition of the appellant was manifestly inadequate.

16.6.3 Conclusion

Depression after childbirth is common, and even psychoses or dissociation may occur,[514] but it is widely thought that the killing of a child is more likely to be the result of social and emotional pressures or personality disorder.[515] In theory, these latter factors will not suffice for s 178 to apply, although sympathy for the mother's plight may mean that the required mental disturbance will readily be found. Retention of the offence/defence (without any special insanity rule) was favoured by the Crimes Consultative Committee, who noted that abolition "would significantly increase the potential penalty for this class of offender, although it is plain enough that a degree of leniency would continue to be extended in practice".[516]

---

511 See Sentencing Act 2002, s 102.
512 *R v Harrison-Taylor* 12/9/05, Ellen France J, HC Auckland CRI-2004-092-1510, para 35; *R v Mayes* [2004] 1 NZLR 81, para 32.
513 *R v Wright* (2001) 18 CRNZ 527 (CA).
514 Cf *R v G* (1984) 1 CRNZ 275.
515 Williams, *TBCL*, 694, 695; O'Donovan, "The medicalisation of infanticide" [1984] Crim LR 259.
516 Crimes Bill Consultative Committee, *Crimes Bill 1989: Report of the Crimes Consultative Committee Presented to the Minister of Justice April 1991*, Wellington, Department of Justice, 1991, 54. Generally, a non-custodial sentence is appropriate for infanticide: *R v Wright* [2001] 3 NZLR 22; (2001) 18 CRNZ 527 (CA), 27; 532. This case also suggests that the fact that a mental disorder is "exacerbated" by recent parturition does not suffice to bring the case within s 178.

Chapter 17

NON-FATAL OFFENCES OF VIOLENCE

17.1	**Introduction**	562
17.2	**Assault**	562
17.2.1	Mens rea	564
(1)	*Transferred malice*	565
17.2.2	Force	566
(1)	*"Applying" force*	567
17.2.3	Assault by omission	568
(1)	*Directly or indirectly*	569
17.2.4	Consent	569
(1)	*Withdrawal of the consent defence*	571
(2)	*Consent to deviant sexual acts*	572
(3)	*Public policy*	575
(4)	*Consent and sport*	576
17.3	**Wounding with intent**	578
17.3.1	Grievous bodily harm	578
(1)	*Psychological and emotional harm*	579
17.3.2	"Wounds"	582
(1)	*"Indirect" wounding*	583
17.3.3	"Maims"	583
17.3.4	"Disfigures"	584
17.3.5	"Injure"	584
17.3.6	Mens rea	585
(1)	*"With intent"*	585
(2)	*"Reckless disregard"*	586
17.4	**Injuring with intent**	587
17.5	**Injuring by unlawful act**	587
17.6	**Aggravated wounding**	589
17.6.1	Mens rea	590
17.6.2	"Violent means"	591
17.6.3	Proof of offence	591

| 17.7 | Aggravated assault | 592 |

17.7.1 Assault with intent to obstruct..593
(1) *Mistake*..593
(2) *Honest belief that V is using excessive force*..594
(3) *Self-defence*..595
(4) *In the "execution of duty"*...595

17.8 Offences against children..596

17.8.1 Discipline of children..597
(1) *Proposed legislative change*..597
(2) *Scope of permitted discipline*...598
(3) *What is "reasonable" force?*..599

17.9 Assault by a male on a female..600

17.9.1 Mens rea..600

17.10 Cruelty to a child...601

17.10.1 "Wilfully neglects"..601

17.10.2 "Neglects"..602

17.10.3 "Custody, control, or charge"..602

17.10.4 "Ill-treats"...603

17.1 Introduction

In this chapter we consider those offences involving the infliction of a physical harm to the person, falling short of murder or manslaughter. Because assault is an included element in many of these offences, we commence our discussion with an analysis of assault, and will consider the other offences in ascending degrees of seriousness. Although "person" by definition includes corporate and unincorporated associations which could conceivably be guilty of committing some of these offences either as principals or parties,[1] in the present context "person" will be limited to human subjects. This limitation excludes unborn children; abortion and related offences will not be considered here.

17.2 Assault

Assault covers a broad range of human conduct. At one end of the scale it may include an unconsented-to kiss on the cheek,[2] while at the other end it may include a grievous physical attack, falling short of murder or manslaughter but nonetheless resulting in severe injury to the victim. However, while such injury is a common feature of many assaults, injury is by no means a *necessary* requirement for an assault at law. This is because under New Zealand law the separate common law concepts of "assault" and "battery" have been incorporated into the unitary concept of "assault". An assault in New Zealand *may* include a battery, which consists of the actual application of unlawful force to another. As to whether a battery *must* involve the

---

1   Section 2 Crimes Act 1961.
2   *Police v Bannin* [1991] 2 NZLR 237, also reported as *B v Police* (1991) 7 CRNZ 55, 244; 62; *Hughes v Callaghan* [1933] GLR 330.

direct application of unlawful force upon the victim, there appears, at present, to be a significant division of opinion amongst commentators. Some would argue that indirect measures, including the setting of a booby trap, may also lead to the infliction of a battery.[3] However, under New Zealand law an assault may involve the use of force applied indirectly to the person of another,[4] which necessarily implies a battery.

At the same time, an assault may also consist simply of a *threat* by one person to inflict unlawful force on another, regardless of whether the person threatening actually delivers on the threat by physically attacking the victim; provided the assault is accompanied by a relevant "act" or "gesture". In New Zealand, words alone cannot amount to an assault.[5] But a threat to strike a person, even at such a distance as to make contact impossible, has been held to constitute an assault if it instils a fear of immediate violence in the mind of the hearer.[6] Thus if A, walking down one side of the street, gesticulates in a threatening manner while calling out to B, on the other side of the road, and threatens to "punch your lights out", that will be a relevant assault if A has the ability to deliver on the threat or causes B to believe on reasonable grounds that he has that ability. In *Fogden v Wade*,[7] it was held that walking towards a woman at night and making indecent suggestions to her may constitute an assault. In that case the accused had not merely spoken to the woman but had moved towards her and she thought that she was about to be molested.

An assault on the basis of threats and gestures alone is possible because of the way in which assault is defined in the Crimes Act 1961. According to s 2:

> "Assault means the act of intentionally applying or attempting to apply force to the person of another, directly or indirectly, or threatening by any act or gesture to apply such force to the person of another, if the person making the threat has, or causes the other to believe on reasonable grounds that he has, present ability to effect his purpose."

The definition creates four varieties of assault:

(i)   An application of (direct or indirect) force to another;

(ii) An attempted application of (direct or indirect) force to another;

(iii) A threat (involving an act or gesture) to apply force to another, where D has the present ability to apply such force; and

(iv) A threat (involving an act or gesture) to apply force to another, which causes V to believe on reasonable grounds that D has the present ability to apply such force.

The effect of this definition is that, for assault, the threat in case (iii) need not be communicated to the victim. In *R v Kerr*,[8] where the accused was seen by a third person to approach within a few feet of the victim while holding an axe at waist level, it was held that it made no difference

---

3   For a contrary view, see Hirst, "Assault, battery and indirect violence" [1999] Crim LR 557. The distinction between "assault" and "battery" is considered in *R v Rolfe* (1952) 36 Cr App R 4.
4   See *R v McMasters* [1920] GLR 351.
5   But cf *R v Wilson* [1955] 1 All ER 744; [1955] 1 WLR 493; (1955) 39 Cr App R 12 (CCA) ("get out the knives").
6   *R v Mostyn* (2004) 145 A Crim R 304 (NSWCCA).
7   *Fogden v Wade* [1945] NZLR 724.
8   *R v Kerr* [1988] 1 NZLR 270; (1987) 2 CRNZ 407 (CA).

that the victim was unaware of the threatening display, because the state of mind of the recipient of the threatening act or gesture need not be a relevant consideration. Similarly, in the Canadian case of *R v Melaragni*,[9] it was held that where a bullet misses its intended victim and the victim is unaware of being shot at, the firing of the gun in the direction of the victim will constitute assault under s 265(1)(b) of the Criminal Code. This is in contrast to the position at common law, where there must be some threatening act sufficient to raise in the mind of the person threatened a fear of immediate violence.[10] However, it would seem that at both common law and in New Zealand there could be no assault if the threat is made, for example, to strike a person with a fist, at such a distance that it was impossible for the blow to strike the victim, or where a firearm is aimed at a range to which the bullet could not possibly carry.[11] In New Zealand, a conviction for assault in such circumstances would be impossible because the accused would lack the "present ability to effect his purpose" and there would be no objective basis for the putative victim to believe that the accused has that ability.

Where there have been threats accompanied by relevant acts or gestures, the threats need only cause the person threatened to believe on reasonable grounds that the threatener has the ability to effect his purpose — even if he does not in fact have that present ability. On this basis, pointing an unloaded gun at another person may constitute an assault if a reasonable person would have believed that it was loaded and the accused had the present capacity to use it to kill or injure.[12] By contrast, where an allegation of assault is based simply on D's conduct it is D's ability as the threatener to carry out her threats that will be determinative. In *Stephens v Myers*, Tindal CJ said:[13]

> "It is not every threat, where there is no actual personal violence, that constitutes an assault, there must, in all cases, be the means of carrying the threat into effect."

17.2.1 Mens rea

At common law, an assault may be committed intentionally or recklessly. In *R v Venna*,[14] it was held that a physical injury inflicted deliberately *or* recklessly on a constable attempting to arrest the accused constituted the offence of assault occasioning actual bodily harm. The accused had lashed out with his legs and injured the hand of a constable who was trying to pick him up after falling or being knocked to the ground. The English Court of Appeal held that there was no reason "in logic or in law" why a person who recklessly applies physical force to the person of another should be outside the criminal law of assault; although it is equally clear that where one who *accidentally* bumps into another lacks the mens rea for assault.

However, in New Zealand the definition of assault in s 2(1) operates to exclude the common law definitions of assault and battery and requires that the act of applying, attempting to apply, or threatening to apply force to the person of another must be done "intentionally".[15] Recklessness will not suffice. This would imply that if, assuming the facts in *Venna*, D had lashed out with his feet, knowing the arresting officer was close to him and knowing that by

---

9   *R v Melaragni* (1992) 75 CCC (3d) 546 (Ont Ct, Gen Div).
10 *Halsbury's Laws of England* vol 11(1) (4th ed reissue), London, Butterworths, 1990, para 488.
11 *Halsbury's Laws of England* vol 11(1) (4th ed reissue), London, Butterworths, 1990, para 488.
12 See *R v St George* (1840) 9 C & P 483; 173 ER 921.
13 *Stephens v Myers* (1830) 4 C & P 349, 349-350.
14 *R v Venna* [1976] QB 421; [1975] 3 All ER 788 (CA).
15 *R v Young* 9/7/92, CA86/92.

lashing out he would probably kick the officer, D could not in New Zealand be guilty of any offence requiring proof of an assault. An intentional application of force to the person of another (or an intentional attempt to do so) must be proved before an accused can be guilty of an assault within the definition of s 2(1).[16]

It follows that an accidental or fortuitous application of force will not suffice. Similarly, generalised threats unrelated to a particular victim will not amount to assault simply because they happen to cause alarm. Thus if D, while in a drunken state, begins to shout loudly and issue broad, non-specific threats ("I'm going to shoot you all") while walking down the street unarmed, he cannot be convicted of assaulting V, who is alarmed by the threats, because he lacks both the intention to apply force and the present ability to carry out the threats.

Neither could D be guilty of assault if, seeing V lying in the gutter, he were to kick her inert body while believing that she was dead. Even if V was conscious and affected emotionally by D's acts, there would be no assault because there must be an intention to apply force to, or to threaten, a living person. A belief that the victim is dead will negate the requisite intent.[17]

There is no assault where the threatening gesture is accompanied by words indicating that there is no intention to carry out the threat. In *Tuberville v Savage*[18] a man who had put his hand menacingly on his sword and said "If it were not assize-time, I would not take such language from you" was held not to have committed an assault. His words showed that he did not intend to assault the victim, despite his menacing gesture. On the other hand, a present *conditional* threat can be an assault: for example where an accused, holding a knife, threatens to stab the complainant if she comes a step closer.[19]

(1)   *Transferred malice*

Where a person, intending to apply force to one person, unintentionally strikes another, two offences of assault may have been committed. There could be an *attempted* assault on the intended victim and assault by the application of force on the second person, through the doctrine of transferred malice. In *R v Latimer*, Lord Coleridge CJ stated:[20]

> "It is common knowledge that a man who has an unlawful and malicious intent against another, and, in attempting to carry it out, injures a third person, is guilty of what the law deems malice against the person injured, because the offender is doing an unlawful act, and has that which the judges call general malice."

Where D does an act intending to cause injury to or at least to assault someone, but has no particular victim in mind (for example, if he simply fires a gun into a crowded supermarket), he may be charged with wounding with intent or injuring with intent. If D wounds V mistakenly believing him to be P, he may still be guilty of wounding V with intent.[21] He intended to wound a human being: the mistake is irrelevant.

---

16   Of course, reckless conduct may be an important evidential factor from which the relevant intention may be inferred: *R v Young* 9/7/92, CA86/92.
17   *R v G* (1984) 1 CRNZ 275, 280.
18   *Tuberville v Savage* (1669) 1 Mod Rep 3; 86 ER 684.
19   *Police v Greaves* [1964] NZLR 295 (CA).
20   *R v Latimer* (1886) 17 QBD 359; [1886-90] All ER Rep 386.
21   *R v Smith* (1855) 1 Dears 559; 169 ER 845; *R v Stopford* (1870) 11 Cox CC 643. See also *R v McMasters* [1920] GLR 351; *Chandler v R* 10/2/93, Greig J, HC Napier AP4/93. For further discussion of transferred mens rea, see 4.8.

However, the doctrine of transferred malice does not extend to the situation where D intends to commit one offence but commits a totally different offence; for example, when he throws a stone at a window for the purposes of criminal damage which misses and hits V by mistake.[22] The element of intent to assault or injure a human being, necessary for an assault, would be lacking and recklessness if established would, in any event, be insufficient mens rea for an assault in New Zealand.

The mere fact that the facts disclose a situation that might give rise to the application of the doctrine of transferred malice does not mean the doctrine must be applied. To avoid problems of proof to which the doctrine may give rise, it may be preferable simply to amend the charge, where that is possible, to one that does not require the proof of a particular intent.[23]

17.2.2 Force

The statutory expression "force to the person of another" has been given a wide interpretation both at common law and under the Crimes Act 1961. "Force" does not necessarily imply violence and it is not necessary for violence to be established under an assault charge.[24] Force, like violence, involves a gradation of physical conduct from one end of the spectrum to the other. While the use of force may include the exercise of physical power to inflict physical injury or damage to persons, that degree of force is not *necessary* for an assault. In *Police v Raponi* Wylie J said:[25]

> "A mere touching can amount to assault ... [A] pat on the bottom or a kiss can be an assault, the mere brushing of some part of a person's body can be an assault."

However, the reason why such conduct amounts to an assault is not simply because it involves an element of force, but also because the physical conduct is unlawful. Unlawfulness will turn on whether the physical contact was consented to, and whether the accused intended to act in a manner that is unlawful. Touching someone in order to attract their attention, or as a social greeting, or in the course of conversation, or while standing in a crowded bus or train, are all physical contacts that are normal aspects of daily living. They are not unlawful, either because there is an implied consent to such activity or because there is a general exception embracing all physical contact which is generally acceptable in the ordinary conduct of daily life.[26] So merely tapping a person on the shoulder to get their attention is "a trivial interference with a citizen's liberty" and not an assault.[27] Grasping a person's arm to get their attention would not normally amount to an assault, although the same action would be, if done in order to restrain that person.[28] For there to be an assault the prosecution must establish that the defendant's intention in applying force was such that the force was unlawful.[29]

---

22   See *R v Pembliton* (1874) LR 2 CCR 119; (1874) 12 Cox CC 607.
23   See *R v Irwin* (1998) 123 CCC (3d) 316 (Ont CA), 321 (Doherty JA), where, to avoid problems associated with the transferred intent doctrine, the Court amended a charge of assault causing bodily harm to a charge of unlawfully causing bodily harm.
24   *Police v Raponi* (1989) 5 CRNZ 291, 296. See also *R v Terewi* (1985) 1 CRNZ 623 (CA), where "force" was held to include a threat to use physical power, so that self-defence is available against threats as well as against actual force.
25   *Police v Raponi* (1989) 5 CRNZ 291, 296.
26   *Collins v Wilcock* [1984] 3 All ER 374; (1984) 79 Cr App R 229, 378; 234.
27   *Donnelly v Jackman* [1970] 1 All ER 987; [1970] 1 WLR 562.
28   See *Hughes v Callaghan* [1933] GLR 330; *Milne v Police* (1990) 6 CRNZ 636.
29   See *R v Kimber* [1983] 3 All ER 316; [1983] 1 WLR 1118 (CA), 319; 1122 (Lawton LJ).

However, where such an intent is present, the least touching of another person, whether or not in anger, will amount to an assault. The amount of force used is immaterial.[30] Thus a tap on the shoulder which is known to be unwanted would be an assault. The breadth of this principle is said to reflect the fundamental nature of the interest so protected.[31]

> "[T]he law cannot draw the line between different degrees of violence, and therefore totally prohibits the first and lowest stage of it; every man's person being sacred, and no other having a right to meddle with it, in any the slightest manner.[32]

The effect is that everybody is protected not only against physical injury but against any form of physical molestation.

At common law it was sometimes stated that a battery could only be committed where the action was "angry, or revengeful, or rude, or insolent",[33] effectively a requirement that the conduct be "hostile". However, this would no longer seem to be a formal requirement, the better view being, as already noted, that the accused's conduct must be intentional and without consent or other justification.[34] At this end of the spectrum the practical distinction between conduct which is lawful and unlawful may be between conduct which is broadly acceptable according to social convention and conduct which is unnecessarily intrusive and may properly be called "rude" or "insulting".[35] However, conduct which might otherwise be regarded as a "meddling" in the autonomy of another person may still be lawful if it is done bona fide for the purpose of offering consolation or comfort.[36] For this reason, it would not be an assault to use reasonable force to restrain a person who is emotionally distraught to prevent him from harming himself.

(1) *"Applying" force*

Because the definition of assault requires an act of intentionally "applying" force to another person, using force to pull away from another person falls outside the concept of applying force, and will not constitute an assault.[37] (However, if D, by pulling himself free from an unlawful arrest by P, causes P's death, his conduct may still constitute manslaughter.)[38] If the alleged assault goes no further than a "bracing and a leaning of a body to resist a push" that action may not of itself constitute the direct or indirect application of force necessary for an assault;[39] although if the facts show that the accused physically thrust his body forward, thereby forcing the victim back, that would constitute an assault.[40] Indeed, a deliberate forward thrusting of the body in the mere attempt to apply force to the complainant would be an

---

30 See *Cole v Turner* (1704) 6 Mod Rep 149; 90 ER 958 (Holt CJ): "The least touching of another in anger is a battery". See also *Police v Bannin* [1991] 2 NZLR 237, also reported as *B v Police* (1991) 7 CRNZ 55, 244; 62.
31 *Collins v Wilcock* [1984] 3 All ER 374; (1984) 79 Cr App R 229, 378; 234.
32 *"Blackstone's Commentaries on the Laws of England*, 17th ed (1830) vol 4, 120."
33 See Hawkins *A Treatise of the Pleas of the Crown* (8th ed 1795), London, Professional Books, 1973, vol 1, ch 62, s 2.
34 *T v T* [1988] Fam 52, 64-67; *R v Brown* [1994] 1 AC 212; [1993] 2 All ER 75 (HL), 244; 90. See also *Hughes v Callaghan* [1933] GLR 330 (kissing a 4-year-old girl on the cheek without her consent held to be an assault even though act was not "indecent, violent or hostile").
35 *Hughes v Callaghan* [1933] GLR 330, 331.
36 *Hughes v Callaghan* [1933] GLR 330, 331.
37 *R v Sherriff* [1969] Crim LR 260.
38 See *R v Porter* (1873) 12 Cox CC 444.
39 *Mitchell v Police* (1989) 5 CRNZ 190.
40 *Mitchell v Police* (1989) 5 CRNZ 190, 191.

assault, even if the actual application of force be prevented by a physical barrier, eg a gate or a car door.

17.2.3 Assault by omission

Because the definition of assault requires an "act" of the accused, the commonly-held view is that an assault cannot be committed by a simple omission.[41] We have already expressed doubt about this interpretation.[42] At common law there is some authority for the view that the word "assault" does not necessarily imply an assault, though it may be narrower than "cause" in requiring the causation of some physical impact upon the body of another. This could occur where, for example, the victim is caused to jump out of a window or run into some protruding object.[43] In *R v Wilson* the Court of Appeal held that "infliction" of grievous bodily harm may occur without an actual assault, for example, where the accused has done something intentionally which, though not a direct application of force to the body of the victim, does directly result in force being applied to the victim's body, so that she suffers harm.[44] There would seem to be no reason in principle why the statutory requirement for an "act" must be construed narrowly to exclude the possibility of assault by omission. Indeed, to insist on this requirement produces anomalies in the law. It has, for example, been held that if D digs a pit with the intention that P should fall into it, and he does, that is an assault.[45] Similarly, if D is sitting in a corridor and anticipating the arrival of P who is running towards him, puts out his leg with the intention that P should trip over it, and he does, that would clearly be an assault.[46] Smith asks:[47]

> "Should it not equally be an assault if D, having dug the pit with no criminal intention, decides to leave it uncovered so that P will fall into it — which he does? Or if D's legs are already extended and he decides not to draw them back, so that P will fall over them?"

By analogy with the reasoning in cases such as *Wilson* (above), if it were accepted that "act" in s 2 simply means "conduct" and includes both acts ("willed muscular movements") and omissions, the concept of "apply[ing]" force could also be given an extended meaning to include not only the physical application of force but also conduct which results in force being applied to the victim's body. Such an approach would avoid the necessity of adopting the legal fiction of a "continuing act" to transform a simple omission into a relevant "act" for the purposes of establishing liability for an assault.[48] The approach would also, it is submitted, make better sense of the concept of applying force "indirectly", which is particularly apt to describe the results that occur when someone omits to perform a particular duty.

---

41 See, for example, *Adams*, CA196.05 (looseleaf).
42 See 3.2.1(3).
43 See *R v Wilson* [1983] 1 All ER 993; *R v Jenkins* [1983] 1 All ER 1000; (1983) 76 Cr App R 313 (CA).
44 See *R v Salisbury* [1976] VR 452, cited with approval in *R v Wilson* [1983] 1 All ER 993, 998.
45 *R v Clarence* (1888) 22 QBD 23; [1886-90] All ER Rep 133 (Wills J).
46 Smith, "Liability for omissions in the criminal law", (1984) 4 LS 88, 98.
47 Smith, "Liability for omissions in the criminal law", (1984) 4 LS 88, 98. Of course, where the assault is by omission (as in this example), criminal liability would follow only if D is under a legal duty to prevent the assault from occurring (for example, if D is P's parent). For discussion, see 3.2.1ff.
48 See *Fagan v MPC* [1969] 1 QB 439; [1968] 3 All ER 442. See also 3.2.1(2)(d).

(1) Directly or indirectly

Many unlawful acts may be committed through the innocent agency of other persons or objects. This is especially true of assault, for which there is no requirement that the accused must actually touch the body of another. Whereas an assault by direct application of force implies that the person who intended the application of that force was the same person who actually applied it by the use of his body, an assault by the indirect application of force implies that the person who intended the application of force gave effect to his intention through some instrumentality *apart* from his person.[49] So where D wires a toaster in such a way as to cause an electric shock to the person who turns it on, that is an assault by the indirect application of force.[50]

The case law is littered with examples of indirectly caused assaults. They include causing a victim to suffer an impact by knocking away another supporting person or object,[51] striking a horse so that its rider is thrown,[52] causing people to be crushed by creating a crowd panic,[53] and pouring acid into a machine which squirts it on to the victim when the victim activates the machine.[54] Similarly, if D, while walking down the street, deliberately "shoulders" P causing her crash into V, who falls and is injured, D would be guilty of two assaults, one by "directly" applying force to P and the other by "indirectly" applying force to V (assuming he intended to apply force unlawfully to both). P would be both the innocent agent through whom the assault on V is committed as well as the object of a direct assault. In *R v S*[55] it was held to be an assault where S caused an 8-year-old boy to jab himself with a pencil. Liability was determined on the basis of an intentional application of force, indirectly via the medium of an innocent agent, against "the person of another" — who happened to be the innocent agent himself.[56]

17.2.4 Consent

At common law, assault and battery are defined so as to require only the threat or application of "unlawful" force. This means that wherever the act charged is in itself unlawful, it is unnecessary to prove absence of consent by the victim in order to convict the offender.[57] However, as we have already seen, there may be many acts which in themselves are harmless and lawful, and which become unlawful only if they are done without the consent of the person affected. Where D, an adult male, kissed a 3 ½ year old girl on the cheek in the street, this was held to be an assault because it was un-consented to.[58] It was held there was no need for the act to be indecent, violent or hostile, although there might have been a defence if the defendant had been providing needed comfort or consolation. Thus an innocent act of familiarity or

---

49 *R v S* [1994] DCR 76.
50 See *Kovalev v Police* 22/5/00, Randerson J, HC Auckland, A40/00.
51 *R v McMasters* [1920] GLR 351. The accused was charged with assaulting his wife and child after he knocked his wife down with his hand when she was carrying the baby. It was conceded that he had not intended to hit the child and since assault may not be committed recklessly, it is unclear what was the actual basis for liability.
52 *Dodwell v Burford* (1661) 1 Mod Rep 24; 86 ER 703.
53 *R v Martin* (1881) 8 QBD 54.
54 *DPP v K (a minor)* [1990] 1 All ER 331; (1990) 91 Cr App R 23.
55 *R v S* [1994] DCR 76.
56 *R v S* [1994] DCR 76, 84.
57 *R v Donovan* [1934] 2 KB 498 (CCA), 507.
58 *Hughes v Callaghan* [1933] GLR 330.

affection in one case may, in another, be an assault for the simple reason that consent was known to be absent. Where, in such a case, there is a reasonable possibility that V consented, the onus of negativing consent lies on the prosecution. Unless a jury is satisfied beyond reasonable doubt that the victim did not consent, the accused is entitled to an acquittal.[59]

Since the mens rea of assault is intention, the prosecution must also prove that the defendant *intended to apply force to the person of the victim without his consent*. If she did not intend the whole of this italicised phrase — and in particular, if she did not realise he had not consented — she is entitled to an acquittal, and the prosecution will have failed to prove the charge. In respect of ordinary assaults, it is the defendant's subjective belief, not the grounds on which it was based, which goes to negative the intent.[60] Similarly, where the offence alleged is indecent assault, a genuine belief in consent, even in the absence of reasonable grounds, will be a defence.[61]

At common law, consent would be vitiated where fraud deceives V as to the identity of the person or the nature of the act. Typically, this would occur where the defendant fraudulently misrepresented his identity as a means of securing consent or misrepresented the nature and quality of the act consented to by the victim.[62] However, there are limits to how far the concept of the "identity of the person" may extend. In *R v Richardson*,[63] the appellant, a dentist, had been suspended from practising. She had, nonetheless, continued to treat patients with their consent. Allowing her appeal against conviction, the Court of Appeal held that the concept of "identity of the person" cannot be extended to cover the qualifications or attributes of the defendant. In respect of all the charges brought against her, the complainants had been fully aware of the identity of the appellant and had consented to treatment from her, although their consent had been procured by her failure to inform them that she was no longer qualified to practice.[64] Otton LJ held that, while such behaviour was clearly reprehensible and might well found a civil claim for damages, it was not a basis for finding criminal liability in the field of offences against the person.

Of interest is the Court's observation that the concept of informed consent has no place in the criminal law. Otton LJ considered that it would be a mistake to introduce a duty to communicate to a patient information about the risk of an activity before the patient's consent can be treated as valid. In the context of criminal law this must be correct. The criminal law is not concerned to achieve therapeutic compliance between offender and victim, such as might be expected to exist between a doctor and her patient. Where consent is concerned, the issue is simply whether the victim agreed to the defendant's conduct, provided the victim has not been misled about who the defendant is or about the nature and quality of the act done.

However, where the victim is a patient, it is unlawful, so as to make it both the tort of battery and the crime of assault, to administer medical treatment without her consent to an adult who is conscious and of sound mind. Such a person is completely at liberty to decline treatment, even if this will result in her death.[65]

---

59 *R v Donovan* [1934] 2 KB 498 (CCA), 507. See also *R v May* [1912] 3 KB 572.
60 See *R v Kimber* [1983] 3 All ER 316; [1983] 1 WLR 1118 (CA), 319; 1121, 1122; also the discussion of intention and circumstances at 4.2.5, 4.5.
61 *R v Nazif* [1987] 2 NZLR 122 (CA).
62 See 18.2.1(3)(e), and cases there discussed.
63 *R v Richardson* (1998) 2 Cr App R 200.
64 In this context, see "R v Richardson" [1999] Crim LR 62 regarding the distinction between "attribute" and "identity".

17.2.4 Consent

(1) Withdrawal of the consent defence

We have noted that the statutory definition of assault in s 2(1) does not make any reference to consent. Nor is consent part of the definition of other assault crimes where consent might, conceivably, be a defence.[66] Rather, because consent is a common law justification, excuse, or defence, it is preserved by s 20 to the extent that it is not inconsistent with the offence charged. Appropriately, such inconsistency with the language of the statutory offence will not be readily found if the particular provision charged is one where consent has traditionally been available as a defence, and where to remove the issue of consent from the jury would be to remove the only real issue and amount to a direction to convict. In *R v B*,[67] the accused faced alternative charges of sexual violation and indecent assault of his 17-year-old intellectually impaired granddaughter. The trial judge withdrew the defence of belief in consent on the charges of indecent assault, not because the complainant was incapable of consenting, but on the grounds of public policy, maintaining that as one of "the most vulnerable of all members of society", the complainant was entitled to protection from sexual predation. However, the Court of Appeal considered that the trial judge had gone too far in this ruling and considered that effectively directing a jury to convict was a course that was rarely permissible.

It is arguable that, apart from those cases where the statute expressly excludes the defence of consent, the practical effect of modern case law developments is to maximise the availability of a consent defence rather than to reduce its ambit. In *R v B* the Court was clearly unwilling to extend the public policy rule to cases of diminished capacity, and was cautious in describing the scope of those authorities which do limit the availability of consent as a defence. Traditionally, the common law refused to allow consent to charges like assault and homicide arising from particularly violent encounters, such as duelling or fencing with naked swords.[68] The justification for disallowing consent in such cases, and in other activities like fist fights and prize fights, was the common incidence of terrible injuries being inflicted and the fact that the lives of the participants were endangered or sacrificed.[69] However, in the Canadian case of *R v Crosby*[70] the appellate Court held that the trial Judge had erred when instructing the jury that consent was vitiated if force was applied intentionally during a fist fight and serious harm resulted. The appellant, in the course of a confrontation outside a bar, had punched the victim in the head, causing a haemorrhage from which he died. On appeal against a conviction for manslaughter for having caused the victim's death by the unlawful act of assault, it was held that a consensual fight between adults who do not intend to cause each other serious bodily harm does not automatically become an assault if, despite their intention, serious bodily harm occurs. The jury ought to have been instructed that the Crown had to prove beyond a

---

65 See *Airedale NHS Trust v Bland* [1993] AC 789; [1993] 1 All ER 821 (HL), 891; 889 (Lord Mustill). See also *St George's Healthcare NHS Trust v S; R v Collins, ex p S* [1998] 3 All ER 673, where it was held that the right of a pregnant woman to autonomy and self-determination was not diminished merely because her decision to exercise it might appear morally repugnant.
66 See, for example, s 188 ("wounding with intent") and s 196 ("common assault").
67 *R v B* (1993) 11 CRNZ 64. See also Brookbanks, "Indecent assault: Withholding consent defence" [1994] NZLJ 317.
68 See *Re Barronet* (1852) 1 E & B 1; 118 ER 337; *R v Orton* (1878) 14 Cox CC 226.
69 *R v Coney* (1882) 8 QBD 534, 544 (Mathew J).
70 *R v Crosby* (2005) 192 CCC (3d) 23 (PEISC), distinguishing *R v Jobidon* [1991] 2 SC R 714; 66 CCC (3d) 454 on the ground that there the appellant intended to inflict more than non-trivial harm. Compare *A-G's Reference (No 6 of 1980)* [1981] 1 QB 715; [1981] 2 All ER 1057 (CA), 719; 1059: "most fights will be unlawful regardless of consent".

reasonable doubt either that the accused intended to cause more than trivial bodily harm or that the victim did not consent to the application of force.

Historically, the distinction between a prize fight and blows struck in the course of other legal sports was that in the former, the blow was said to be struck in anger and likely to do "corporal hurt", while in the latter the blow was struck "in sport" and not intended to cause bodily harm.[71] Generally, with sports that involve physical contact, players are deemed to consent, or at least consent is implied, to the use of the kind of force that can reasonably be expected to occur in the course of the game. However, this does not generate an unlimited licence to use force, and force used outside the normal course of play may constitute an assault.[72]

Similar reasoning may apply in other areas of lawful conduct where a requirement of consent to reasonable force may be implied. In *R v Donovan*,[73] where the appellant was charged with caning a 17-year-old girl for the purposes of sexual gratification, it was held that because the blows struck were likely or intended to do bodily harm, the act was per se unlawful and could not be rendered lawful simply because the person who was the subject of the beating consented to it.

At common law, until recently the general approach of the courts has been that it was not in the public interest that people should try to cause, or should cause, each other actual bodily harm "for no good reason".[74] The courts distinguished "minor struggles" which, by implication, could not be the subject of assault charges where the parties consented, from fights in which actual bodily harm was intended and/or caused, which were unlawful regardless of consent.[75] This limitation on consent did not, however, affect the legality of properly conducted games and sports, lawful discipline, reasonable surgical operations, or dangerous exhibitions.[76] In each such case, the exercise of a legal right, or (as the case may be) necessity in the public interest, was seen to be sufficient justification even where actual bodily harm occurred.

(2)   *Consent to deviant sexual acts*

However, in recent years a new testing-ground for the doctrine of consent has emerged in relation to sado-masochistic and other unusual consensual acts of a sexual nature; one which has caused the courts to radically rethink the parameters of proscribed consensual sexual activity. The result of these developments is that the courts appear to be increasingly willing to accommodate a defence of consent even in cases involving actual bodily harm, provided the alleged conduct is consensual, private, and does not involve significant intentional injury.

The challenge first emerged in *R v Brown*,[77] a case involving a group of sado-masochists, in which the House of Lords held that it was contrary to public policy to extend the exemptions concerning consensual violent acts to sado-masochistic conduct, particularly in light of the

---

71   *R v Coney* (1882) 8 QBD 534, 539 (Cave J).
72   *R v Billinghurst* [1978] Crim LR 553; *Police v O* (1980) DCR 151. See below, 17.2.4(4).
73   *R v Donovan* [1934] 2 KB 498 (CCA).
74   *A-G's Reference (No 6 of 1980)* [1981] 1 QB 715; [1981] 2 All ER 1057 (CA), 719; 1059.
75   *A-G's Reference (No 6 of 1980)* [1981] 1 QB 715; [1981] 2 All ER 1057 (CA), 719; 1059.
76   *A-G's Reference (No 6 of 1980)* [1981] 1 QB 715; [1981] 2 All ER 1057 (CA), 719; 1059. Other instances where consent may make the infliction of bodily harm lawful include ritual circumcision, tattooing, ear-piercing, and violent sports: *R v Brown* [1994] 1 AC 212; [1993] 2 All ER 75 (HL) (Lord Templeman), 231; 79.
77   *R v Brown* [1994] 1 AC 212; [1993] 2 All ER 75 (HL) (Lord Templeman), 231; 79.

risk of serious injury and possible corruption of others, notwithstanding that the case involved consensual sexual activity by adults in private.[78] In *Brown* the majority, following the decision in *R v Donovan*,[79] approved the proposition that it was immaterial that the victim had consented to the infliction of bodily harm. The Court's reasoning was that sado-masochistic libido does not provide the requisite "good reason" for allowing consent to excuse or justify the deliberate causing of non-trivial bodily harm.

However, in *R v Wilson*[80] the English Court of Appeal took a much broader approach to the issue of consensual infliction of bodily harm. There the accused, at his wife's instigation, had branded his initials on her buttocks with a hot knife. He was charged with assault occasioning actual bodily harm. The trial judge ruled that despite the wife's consent he was bound by the majority decision in *R v Brown*, and had no alternative but to convict. In allowing the appeal against conviction, the Court made the following observation:[81]

> "We are abundantly satisfied that there is no factual comparison to be made between the instant case and the facts of either *R v Donovan* ... or *R v Brown* ... Mrs Wilson not only consented to that which the appellant did, she instigated it. There was no aggressive intent on the part of the appellant. On the contrary, far from wishing to cause injury to his wife, the appellant's desire was to assist her in what she regarded as the acquisition of a desirable piece of personal adornment, perhaps in this day and age no less understandable than the piercing of nostrils or even tongues for the purposes of inserting decorative jewellery ... Does public policy or the public interest demand that the appellant's activity should be visited by the sanctions of the criminal law? The majority in *R v Brown* clearly took the view that such considerations were relevant. If that is so, then we are firmly of the opinion that it is not in the public interest that activities such as the appellant's in this appeal should amount to criminal behaviour. Consensual activity between husband and wife, in the privacy of the matrimonial home, is not, in our judgment, normally a proper matter for criminal investigation, let alone criminal prosecution."

Although the Court expressed its desire that the law should be allowed to develop on a case-by-case basis rather than upon "general propositions" to which exceptions can arise,[82] it is nevertheless possible to draw from the decision some guidelines regarding the circumstances in which consent may be a defence to the infliction of actual bodily harm. If *Wilson* is to be accepted as good law, it suggests that an exception will be made where:

(i) The "victim" not only consents to but instigates the accused's conduct;

(ii) There is no aggressive intent on the accused's part;

(iii) The appellant's desire is to assist his partner in acquiring a desirable piece of personal adornment;

---

78   See Dawkins, "Criminal law" [1997] NZ Law Review 20, 42ff.
79   *R v Donovan* [1934] 2 KB 498 (CCA).
80   *R v Wilson* [1996] 3 WLR 125 (CA).
81   *R v Wilson* [1996] 3 WLR 125 (CA), 127, 128.
82   *R v Wilson* [1996] 3 WLR 125 (CA), 128.

(iv) The conduct is consensual activity between "husband and wife" in the privacy of their own home. (Presumably, this limitation would extend generally to partners living in a domestic relationship.)

These concessions seem to create a surprisingly broad exception to the general rule that infliction of injury for no good reason cannot be consented to. For a start there would seem to now be no limitation on the nature of the consensual injury inflicted where the above conditions are met. For example, there appears to be no reason why W should not be permitted to carve his initials on his wife's buttocks or even to burn them on with acid,[83] provided the injury was of a similar degree of severity.

Other questions arise. Would consent have made the conduct lawful if, for example, W's intention was not to assist his wife in acquiring a personal adornment, but rather to make her an object of titillation for friends who were invited to their home for a private "viewing" of her adornment, or for the publication of her personal adornment in a magazine devoted to body marking? In other words, does the qualification that the act must occur in private limit the exposure of the results of the consensual activity after the event? There is also a troubling question concerning the Court's use of the notions of "intent" and "desire" in the passage quoted. Suppose that W had caused serious injury to his wife when he branded his initials on her buttocks. Would the injury have been any less "intended" because, as he claimed, his "desire" was to assist her to acquire a personal adornment? According to conventional theory, there could be little doubt that W intended to cause his wife actual bodily harm, regardless whether his intent was "aggressive". His claimed "desire", on this view, would have constituted his motive (not intent) for acting as he did; and, as such, was or should have been irrelevant in determining criminal responsibility.

However, it remains unclear whether *Wilson* is good law in New Zealand. The Courts, while approving *Brown*, have seemed unwilling to extend the ability to inflict consensual harm in the manner approved in *Wilson*. In *R v Cocker*,[84] for example, it was decided that the consensual administration of nitrous oxide in the course of a sexual encounter could nevertheless amount to the offence of stupefaction, contrary to s 197. The Court held that inhaling nitrous oxide to the point of stupefaction was a dangerous activity for which consent was no defence. The Court did not consider whether it made any difference that the behaviour took place in the context of a legitimate sexual encounter.

More recently, the English Court of Appeal has re-affirmed the policy of the law espoused in *R v Brown*: namely, that whether or not the violent activity takes place in private, and even if the victim agrees to it, serious violence is not lawful merely because it enables the perpetrator (or victim) to achieve sexual gratification.[85] In *Dica* the appellant had had unprotected consensual sexual intercourse with two complainants, knowing that he was suffering from HIV, and was reckless whether they might become infected. The Court concluded that

---

83 See *R v Emmett* [1999] EWCA Crim 1710, in which V allowed her sexual partner to cover her head with a plastic bag, tying it tightly at the neck so that she lost consciousness and was at risk of death; and pouring lighter fuel on victim's breasts and setting it alight, causing serious burns. The Court held that the woman's consent to these events did not provide a defence. See also *R v Boyea* [1992] 156 JPR 505 (CA), in which V allowed D to put his hand into her vagina and twist it, causing internal and external injuries to vagina and pubis. V's consent was held to be irrelevant.
84 *R v Cocker* 23/9/04, France J, HC Wellington CRI-2004-085-1865.
85 *R v Dica* [2004] EWCA Crim 1103, para 42, per Lord Justice Judge.

although the appellant was not guilty of rape, since the complainants had consented to sexual intercourse, the absence of consent to the risk of infection by HIV meant that there was no defence to a charge of causing grievous bodily harm under s 20 of the Offences Against the Person Act 1861 (UK).[86]

(3) *Public policy*

On the issues of public policy and public interest, the Court's arguments do raise a difficulty. Its refusal to visit the accused's actions with the sanctions of the criminal law is advanced on the basis that "consensual activity between husband and wife in the privacy of the matrimonial home"[87] is not the law's business. While admirably libertarian in spirit, this is not to say, however, that *all* activity between spouses in the privacy of the home is permissible, since such a broad extension would have to include conduct in the nature of domestic violence which is now regularly the subject of criminal prosecution. The problem with permitting any kind of bodily harm to be inflicted by one person upon another, within the cloak of "privacy", is the danger that the claimed consent is a mere phantom, the submissive party being either too terrified or so inured to the overbearing demands of his partner that complaint that he was not consenting is not considered to be a realistic option. The difficulty is exacerbated by the fact that the defence applies to "private" conduct — the very location where there is no way of independently testing whether the victim's "consent" was genuine. The rule now established by the court arguably leaves the victims of such abusive relationships exposed to even greater or more exquisite degrees of physical violence without effective protection from the criminal law.[88]

However, at least in the context of English law, some drawing back from the implicit liberality of *R v Wilson* regarding privacy issues may be discernible in the decision of the European Court of Human Rights in *Laskey, Jaggard and Brown v UK*.[89] The case involved an application made to that Court by three of the defendants in *R v Brown*. They argued that their convictions were the result of an unforeseeable application of a provision in the criminal law which amounted to an unlawful and unjustifiable interference with their right to respect for their private life guaranteed by art 8 European Convention for the Protection of Human Rights and Fundamental Freedoms. In determining that there was evidence of pressing social need, conceived in terms of protection of health (under art 8(2)), the Court held that the State is entitled to undertake the regulation, by way of the criminal law, of activities which involve the infliction of physical harm, whether those activities occur in the course of sexual conduct or otherwise. While the Court concluded that there was a need for balance between considerations of public health and criminal deterrence, on the one hand, and the personal autonomy of the individual, on the other, in determining the level of consensual harm the law should tolerate, the Court was in no doubt that the applicants' actions, involving as they did extreme violence (genital torture), could not be characterised as trifling or transient. It drew an analogy between the applicants' acts and acts of rape and sexual abuse. Indeed, one judge, in rejecting the view that human rights protection should extend to sado-masochistic activity, asserted that:[90]

---

86 *R v Dica* [2004] EWCA Crim 1103, para 39.
87 *R v Donovan* [1997] QB 47, 50.
88 For an alternative view of the decision, see Dawkins, "Criminal law" [1997] NZ Law Review 20, 45, 46.
89 *Laskey, Jaggard and Brown v UK* [1997] 24 EHRR 39.
90 *Laskey, Jaggard and Brown v UK* [1997] 24 EHRR 39, 61 (Judge Pettiti). For discussion, see Moran, "*Laskey v The United Kingdom*: Learning the limits of privacy" [1998] 61 MLR 77.

"The protection of private life means the protection of a person's intimacy and dignity, not the protection of his baseness or the promotion of criminal immoralism."

The Court's apparent unwillingness to endorse egregious forms of harmful sexual conduct (ie as sexual practices requiring the protection of the law) may signal the limits to the notion of privacy that courts are willing to recognise when circumscribing the application of criminal sanctions.

(4) *Consent and sport*

Apart from contexts where consent is no defence, we have seen that an assault will normally only occur where the act done is contrary to the will and without the consent of the victim. However, at common law it has long been recognised that a blow struck in sport and not intended to cause bodily harm does not constitute assault even though not expressly consented to. This exception may be explained either on the basis that some physical conduct is impliedly consented to during sport, or because, subject to the context provided by the agreed rules of a game, such physical contact falls within a general exception which embraces physical contact acceptable in the ordinary course of playing the particular sport.[91]

The reality of much modern sport appears to strain the application of these simple precepts. Many sports, including acknowledged contact sports like rugby, rugby league, ice-hockey, boxing, kick-boxing, and other new generation "gladiatorial" sports, may involve extreme violence resulting, not infrequently, in serious disabling injury and even the death of the participants. In such circumstances, where death is the result of an accident the person responsible for the injury would not normally be liable for manslaughter,[92] although it could rarely be said that violence sufficient to cause death was "permissible" within the rules of a particular sport.

A sport or a game will not necessarily be lawful (where consent may be a defence) simply because it is conducted according to the rules. However, it is not clear when such activity becomes unlawful. An earlier suggested limitation was that it may be unlawful if "the risk of death or serious injury" is normally associated with it, or if it is regarded as "essentially dangerous, and … it is more probable than not that serious injury may result".[93] The relevant association may be provided by the fact that exposure to serious risk is part of the purpose of the activity. In *R v McLeod*[94] M was giving an exhibition of his skills as a marksman at a "Wild West" show. He invited W to take a seat about 21 feet away from him with a view to shooting the ash from the cigarette he was smoking. However, W moved his head and the bullet passed through his cheek causing a serious but not dangerous injury. M was charged with a number of offences including assault, assault causing actual bodily harm, and actual bodily harm under such circumstances that if death had occurred he would have been guilty of manslaughter. Although it was accepted that the accused had fired with the full consent of W, it was held that because a lethal weapon was used in risky circumstances, if death had occurred M would have been guilty of manslaughter and he was duly convicted. The Court appeared to distinguish between death resulting from the "wilful and wanton act[s]" of impermissible "sports" (fighting without gloves, using weapons of an "improper and deadly" nature) and

---

91   *Collins v Wilcock* [1984] 3 All ER 374; (1984) 79 Cr App R 229, 378; 234 (Goff LJ).
92   *R v McLeod* (1915) 34 NZLR 430 (CA), 434.
93   *Adams* (2nd ed), paras 614, 615.
94   *R v McLeod* (1915) 34 NZLR 430 (CA).

accidental death resulting from permissible sports (football, wrestling, boxing with gloves). The injury to W could hardly be described as an accident, since the very purpose of the exhibition depended upon the fact that W was put in some danger of being injured.

However, such distinctions are increasingly difficult to draw given that dangerous sports and competitive endeavours are now commonplace and generally accepted. The notion of "extreme" sport has redefined the conventional physical limits of many sports, and many new non-contact competitor sports regularly involve activity which courts a risk of death. In these cases it is very difficult to draw a line between permissible conduct and conduct which may be outlawed for public policy reasons because of its inherent dangerousness. For many such sporting endeavours, it is the possibility of breaking the conventional boundaries of human endeavour to do the very thing that would, for an earlier generation, have been regarded as "impossible" and inherently perilous that provides the very justification for the sport. People, presumably, contract to engage in such activities and consent to the risk of death or serious injury because such risks are part of the attraction of the particular activity.

If society is prepared to lend its tacit, albeit uncomprehending, approval to consensual participation in "extreme" sports where, even without competitive contact, the risk of at least serious bodily injury is high, it seems difficult to deny the right to other sportsmen and women to participate in contact sports where the risk of dangerous and intentional injury is also present. This does not mean that it is impossible to regulate the illicit use of violence in particular sports through the rules of a game, but does suggest that it is becoming increasingly difficult to ban sporting activities simply because they are "essentially dangerous" and likely to cause serious injury. Boxing is the classic case. Boxers intend to injure and impliedly consent to injury, and it can no longer be claimed that the law gives protection in respect of unintended injuries or that no intentional injury is permissible.[95] The suggested prohibition against fighting "in a spirit of anger or a hostile spirit and with the predominant intention of inflicting substantial bodily harm so as to disable or otherwise physically subdue the opponent"[96] may well suggest the upper limits of permissible physical conduct in a boxing match, but it is an unhelpful limit. Determining when that "spirit of anger or hostile spirit" is present, or the point at which intervention is appropriate to prevent one opponent from "hurting" the other, can only be a fraught exercise when the object of the contest is to batter (therefore hurt) the opponent into submission.

It may be that, apart from the most aggressively violent behaviour (for example biting off part of an opponent's ear, a deliberate head high tackle, deliberately breaking an opponent's limb, etc), the regulation of what is permissible, and therefore may be consented to, is best left to be determined by the application of the rules of a particular sport or code. Because the range of conduct that may be consented to in the name of sport generally is so much broader than could ever have been contemplated at common law, there is a danger that the legal proscription of particular types of conduct will impact much more severely on one type of activity than on another where the relative degree of risk of harm is in each case identical. Arguably, the criminal law should only be involved in the regulation of sporting activity where the intentional activity is so obviously a breach of the rules of the game and contrary to notions of fair play that any reasonable person would recognise it as unacceptable, particularly where it involves the infliction of grave injury, and/or injury that could result in the death of the victim. Beyond

---

95 See *Adams*, CA63.14 (looseleaf).
96 *Pallante v Stadiums Pty Ltd (No 1)* [1976] VR 331.

this, the law may be better to defer to those actually involved in the playing of a particular sport to determine what, if any, should be the boundaries of lawful physical contest.[97]

17.3 Wounding with intent

A number of offences defined in the Crimes Act 1961 are defined in terms of wounding, causing grievous bodily harm (ie really serious harm) and injuring. These offences are defined in such a way as to achieve a range of combinations in the manner in which harm may be inflicted with differing mental states. The principal offences are wounding with intent (s 188) and injuring with intent (s 189). Both will be considered.

The offence of wounding with intent (s 188 Crimes Act 1961) is the most serious of these various offences. As we shall see, the offence defined in the section involves a number of discrete mens rea and actus reus elements, including (among the actus reus elements) some concepts which have become legal terms of art. In this discussion, we will examine the separate meanings given to the concepts of "grievous bodily harm", "wounding", "maiming", and "disfiguring", each of which expresses a different way in which the offence may be committed.

The terms of s 188 are as follows:

> "**188 Wounding with intent**
>
> "(1) Every one is liable to imprisonment for a term not exceeding 14 years who, with intent to cause grievous bodily harm to any one, wounds, maims, disfigures, or causes grievous bodily harm to any person.
>
> "(2) Every one is liable to imprisonment for a term not exceeding 7 years who, with intent to injure anyone, or with reckless disregard for the safety of others, wounds, maims, disfigures, or causes grievous bodily harm to any person."

The section defines five separate offences: wounding (or maiming, etc) with intent to cause grievous bodily harm (s 188(1)); causing grievous bodily harm with intent to cause grievous bodily harm; wounding with intent to injure (s 188(2)); wounding with reckless disregard for the safety of others (s 188(2)); and causing grievous bodily harm with intent to injure. While each of these offences has its principal application in relation to the deliberate infliction of serious harm by way of a criminal assault, on rare occasions the sections may be implicated where medical treatment, provided without consent, has caused serious bodily harm; a possibility that will also be considered below.

17.3.1 Grievous bodily harm

Section 188 does not define grievous bodily harm. Neither is the expression defined elsewhere in the Crimes Act 1961. However, the meaning of "grievous bodily harm" has been considered at common law, where it is said that the words are to be given their "ordinary and natural meaning".[98] In *R v Ashman*,[99] it was said of the expression that:

> "It is not necessary that such harm should ... be either permanent or dangerous, if it be such as seriously to interfere with comfort or health, it is sufficient."

---

97 For a discussion of when unlawful acts may occur within a lawful game, see *Adams*, CA63.14 (looseleaf).
98 *DPP v Smith* [1961] AC 290, also reported as *R v Smith* [1960] 3 All ER 161 (HL) , 334; 171.
99 *R v Ashman* (1858) 1 F & F 88; 175 ER 638, 88, 89; 639.

However, it will be a misdirection, when summing up to a jury on a charge of wounding with intent to cause grievous bodily harm, to invite the jury to convict if the only intent established is to interfere seriously with health or comfort.[100] It is now common for juries to be directed that "grievous bodily harm" means really serious bodily injury.[101] On this basis, a broken nose has been held to be grievous bodily harm;[102] although a nose injury causing bleeding need not necessarily result in a fracture for grievous bodily harm to be found, provided the injury could be said to have caused "really serious harm".[103] Injuries such as fractures, injuries to any organ, disfigurement, or physical incapacitation may all be included within the expression.[104] If, in a surgical operation, a kidney were to be removed from a healthy living person for transplanting into a recipient, but without a legally effective consent being given, the resulting injury would, in our view, amount to intentionally causing grievous bodily harm.[105] In *Ashman* it was held that a blow to the temple of the victim, caused by powder from a gun discharged by the defendant, which caused a weakness to the victim's eye for some months following the discharge, was sufficient to constitute grievous bodily harm. Grievous bodily harm also accommodates "prospective" harm, in the sense that it need not be limited to the immediate consequences of external assault or injury as might typically result from a blow. Although in the generality of cases the effect is instant (a blow causes a wound), the consequences may be delayed, for example where an offender infects another person with HIV through unprotected sexual intercourse.[106] In such cases the grievous bodily injury is established even before those prospective consequences eventually occur.

Whether an injury amounts to "bodily harm" will depend on the nature of the injury and its consequences whether short- or long-term. At the opposite end of the spectrum from prospective harms, the fact that the victim recovered completely from the injury, or was left with only a cosmetic disability, will be irrelevant if the immediate consequences of the injury interfered temporarily with his health in a relevant way. For example, a compound fracture of an arm or leg would constitute a "really serious bodily harm" even if the fracture healed completely and left no visible scarring or disability. The existence of pain, affecting a person's ability to function fully, will be relevant in determining whether "bodily harm" has occurred.[107] Similarly, in the medical example given above, although the victim may make a full recovery from the operation to remove a kidney, that does not in any way mitigate the temporary interference with health or the emotional pain associated with the un-consensual removal of a kidney.

(1) *Psychological and emotional harm*

The expression "bodily harm" is not defined in the Crimes Act 1961. An issue which therefore arises is whether the expression is apt to include psychological harm. In R v *McCraw*,[108] where the accused had written obscene and threatening letters to several women threatening to rape

---

100   R v *Metharam* [1961] 3 All ER 200; (1961) 45 Cr App R 304 (CCA).
101   See *DPP v Smith* [1961] AC 290, also reported as R v *Smith* [1960] 3 All ER 161 (HL), 334; 171 (Viscount Kilmuir).
102   R v *Saunders* [1985] Crim LR 230.
103   See R v *Waters* [1979] 1 NZLR 375 (CA), 380 (McMullin J).
104   Carter and Harrison, *Offences of Violence*, London, 1991, para 3.29.
105   See Skegg and Paterson (eds), Medical Law in New Zealand, Wellington, Brookers, 2006, ch 5, 150.
106   R v *Mwai* [1995] 3 NZLR 149; (1995) 13 CRNZ 273 (CA), 153; 278.
107   *Wayne v Boldiston* (1992) 85 NTR 8 (NT SC).
108   R v *McCraw* (1991) 7 CR (4th) 314.

them, the Supreme Court of Canada upheld a conviction for threatening to cause serious bodily harm. It did so on the basis that rape was likely to have serious psychological consequences for the victim, as well as possible serious physical effects. Since "bodily harm" was defined in the Canadian Criminal Code to mean "any hurt or injury", the Court could see no reason in principle why psychological harm should be excluded. Similarly, in *R v Miller*,[109] evidence that the victim had been in a "hysterical and nervous condition" was held to be sufficient evidence to leave the case to the jury on a charge of assault occasioning actual bodily harm. The judge ruled that "if a person is caused hurt or injury resulting, not in any physical injury, but in an injury to the state of his mind for the time being, that is within the definition of actual bodily harm". This decision received qualified approval by the English Court of Appeal in *R v Chan-Fook* where, delivering the judgment of the Court, Hobhouse LJ said:[110]

> "The body of the victim includes all parts of his body, including his organs, his nervous system and his brain. Bodily injury therefore may include injury to any of those parts of his body responsible for his mental and other faculties ... Accordingly the phrase 'actual bodily harm' is capable of including psychiatric injury. But it does not include mere emotions such as fear or distress nor panic nor does it include, as such, states of mind that are not themselves evidence of some identifiable clinical condition ... [J]uries should not be directed that an assault which causes an hysterical and nervous condition is an assault occasioning actual bodily harm. Where there is evidence that the assault has caused some psychiatric injury, the jury should be directed that the injury is *capable of amounting to actual bodily harm*; otherwise there should be no reference to the mental state of the victim following the assault unless it be relevant to some other aspect of the case."

Chan-Fook has been applied by the New Zealand Court of Appeal in *Owen v Residual Health Management Unit*.[111] The Court held that *Chan-Fook* "put beyond doubt" that the phrase "actual bodily harm" is capable of including psychiatric injury but does not include mere emotions such as fear, distress, panic, or a hysterical or nervous condition. The Court also applied *R v Mwai*,[112] where the Court of Appeal earlier had acknowledged the artificiality of separating the mind from the physical body, holding the two to be "inseparable". In *Mwai* the Court expressly applied the approach taken in *Chan-Fook* to a charge under s 188(2), holding that grievous bodily harm includes really serious psychiatric injury identified as such by appropriate specialist evidence.

It seems that relevant psychiatric injury, sufficient to justify a charge under s 188, may occur in circumstances in which the victim is unaware that an assault has taken place. In *R v Donaldson*,[113] V, an 18-year-old youth, completed some work for the defendant, after which they both began drinking. V became very drunk and fell into a state of unconsciousness. While he was in this vulnerable state, D took the opportunity to perform various indecent acts on V and videotaped the entire episode. V only became aware that he had been sexually violated

---

109 *R v Miller* [1954] 2 QB 282; [1954] 2 All ER 529, 292; 534.
110 *R v Chan-Fook* [1994] 2 All ER 552; [1994] 99 Cr App R 147 (CA), 558-559; 153-153 (emphasis added). See also *R v Ireland; R v Burstow* [1998] AC 147; [1997] 4 All ER 225 (HL). Both *Chan-Fook* and *Ireland and Burstow* are considered in *R v Dica* [2004] EWCA Crim 1103, paras 28 and 29.
111 *Owen v Residual Health Management Unit* [2000] 3 NZLR 475 (CA), 480.
112 *R v Mwai* [1995] 3 NZLR 149; (1995) 13 CRNZ 273 (CA), 155; 280. See also *R v Cuerrier* [1998] 127 CCC (3d) 1 (SCC).
113 *R v Donaldson* (1997) 14 CRNZ 537 (CA).

after he had been identified and interviewed by the police, who showed him the seized video. Although he had no recollection of the events, the whole incident had a profound psychological impact on him. Although D was convicted on a charge of sexual violation, which does not require proof that the victim suffered a psychiatric injury, it is implicit that relevant psychiatric injury may be caused to an unconscious defendant who subsequently becomes aware of the circumstances of a criminal assault on him.

Where psychiatric injury is relied upon as a basis for an allegation of bodily harm, but its occurrence has not been admitted by the defence, expert evidence should be called by the prosecution. The matter should not be left to be inferred by the jury from the general facts of the case, and in the absence of appropriate expert evidence a question whether the assault occasioned psychiatric injury should not be left to the jury.[114]

(a)   The "silent caller"

The harassment of women by repeated silent telephone calls, sometimes accompanied by heavy breathing, has become a significant social problem in many countries. One question which arises is whether the making of a series of silent telephone calls can amount to an assault even where no physical violence has been applied directly or indirectly to the person of the victim. This issue has been considered by the House of Lords in *R v Ireland; R v Burstow*,[115] in relation to the question whether the causing of psychiatric injury by such conduct could amount to "inflicting" grievous bodily harm. Concluding that it could, Lord Steyn said:[116]

> "The answer to [the] question [whether a silent caller may be guilty of an assault] seems to me to be 'Yes, depending on the facts'. It involves questions of fact within the province of the jury. After all, there is no reason why a telephone caller who says to a woman in a menacing way 'I will be at your door in a minute or two' may not be guilty of an assault if he causes his victim to apprehend immediate personal violence. Take now the case of the silent caller. He intends by his silence to cause fear and he is so understood. The victim is assailed by uncertainty about his intentions. Fear may dominate her emotions, and it may be the fear that the caller's arrival at her door may be imminent. She may fear the *possibility* of immediate personal violence. As a matter of law the caller may be guilty of an assault."

In New Zealand, the traditional view was that words alone cannot constitute an assault because of the requirement in s 2(1) for threats "by any act or gesture".[117] However, in *R v Ireland; R v Burstow*,[118] Lord Steyn observed that the premise that an assault can never be committed by words alone, and by implication that it cannot be committed by silence, depended on the "slenderest authority", namely the 19th-century observation by Holroyd J that "no words or singing are equivalent to an assault".[119] His Lordship held that the proposition that a gesture may amount to an assault, but that words can never suffice, is "unrealistic and indefensible":[120]

---

114   *R v Chan-Fook* [1994] 2 All ER 552; [1994] 99 Cr App R 147(CA), 559; 152.
115   *R v Ireland; R v Burstow* [1998] AC 147; [1997] 4 All ER 225 (HL).
116   *R v Ireland; R v Burstow* [1998] AC 147; [1997] 4 All ER 225 (HL), 162; 236.
117   See also *Adams*, CA2.03.06 (looseleaf).
118   *R v Ireland; R v Burstow* [1998] AC 147; [1997] 4 All ER 225 (HL), 162; 236.
119   *Meade's and Belt's Case* (1823) 1 Lew CC 184; 168 ER 1006, 185; 1007.
120   *R v Ireland; R v Burstow* [1998] AC 147; [1997] 4 All ER 225 (HL), 162; 236.

"A thing said is also a thing done. There is no reason why something said should be incapable of causing an apprehension of immediate personal violence, eg a man accosting a woman in a dark alley saying 'Come with me or I will stab you.' I would, therefore, reject the proposition that an assault can never be committed by words."

While this dictum has not yet been applied by a New Zealand court, it clearly suggests the direction in which the law should move. With the growing incidence worldwide of stalking-related offences[121] and the expanding use of electronic means to effect them, it seems almost unarguable that the law should reflect social realities by acknowledging that an assault can occur by words alone and, by extension, by means of silent phone calls. Indeed, repeated telephone calls are one of the most common methods stalkers employ to communicate with their victims.[122]

In any event, the specific requirements of the definition of assault in s 2(1) need not be determinative when considering the elements of an offence under s 188. There is no requirement that the conduct defined in s 188 be prefaced upon an assault. In *R v Mwai*, Hardie Boys J held that all that is required for the actus reus of an offence under s 188 is an act causing grievous bodily harm. To require an external assault or injury is an unnecessary limitation on the section.[123] Accordingly, psychological damage (other than transient fear, distress, or panic) caused by the actions of a caller will amount to bodily harm within s 188. The issue for the jury would then be whether the accused intended to cause injury in that sense by making the silent call.

17.3.2 "Wounds"

At common law, in order to constitute a wounding there must be an injury to the person by which the skin is broken; the continuity of the whole skin must be severed, not merely that of the cuticle or upper skin.[124] However, the skin severed need not be external, so that striking someone in the face causing the inside of his mouth to bleed will be a relevant wounding.[125] On the other hand, it will not be sufficient to prove that a flow of blood was caused, unless there is some evidence to show where the blood came from.[126] Although it is not necessary that the wounding should have been caused by an instrument (an injury caused by a kick may be a wounding),[127] an injury that merely causes internal bleeding would not constitute a wound because there is no breaking of the skin. Thus, if D throws a blunt object at V which strikes him above the eye, causing a black eye and redness in the eye due to the rupture of an internal blood vessel, that would not constitute a wounding because there is no severing of the skin.[128] However, provided there is a severing of the skin there will still be a wounding whether

---

121 See Mullen, Pathé, and Purcell, *Stalkers and Their Victims*, Cambridge, Cambridge University Press, 2000.
122 Mullen, Pathé, and Purcell, *Stalkers and Their Victims*, Cambridge, Cambridge University Press, 2000, 231.
123 *R v Mwai* [1995] 3 NZLR 149; (1995) 13 CRNZ 273 (CA), 153; 278. See also *R v Chan-Fook* [1994] 2 All ER 552; [1994] 99 Cr App R 147, 557; 151: "an injury can be caused to someone by injuring their health; an assault may have the consequence of infecting the victim with a disease or causing the victim to become ill. The injury may be internal and may not be accompanied by any external injury" (per Lord Hobhouse).
124 "Criminal law, evidence and procedure" in *Halsbury's Laws of England* vol 11(1), (4th ed reissue), London, Butterworths, 1990, para 470. See *R v Wood* (1830) 1 Mood CC 278; 168 ER 1271; *Moriarty v Brooks* (1834) 6 C & P 684; 172 ER 1419; *R v Beckett* (1836) 1 M & Rob 526; 174 ER 181.
125 *R v Smith* (1837) 8 C & P 173; 173 ER 448.
126 *R v Waltham* (1849) 3 Cox CC 442.
127 *R v Duffill* (1843) 1 Cox CC 49.
128 See *C v Eisenhower* [1984] QB 331; [1983] 3 All ER 230.

or not there is a flow of blood.[129] It is therefore important in a prosecution for wounding with intent to establish the nature of the injury by medical evidence.

The common law meaning attributed to "wound", namely a breaking of the continuity of the skin, has broadly been adopted by New Zealand courts. In *R v Waters*,[130] where the accused had, inter alia, attacked the complainant, banging her face against the floor and causing her nose to bleed heavily, McMullin J was not prepared to rule that internal bleeding which came from the nose could never amount to a wounding, since it was a question of fact for determination in each case. He said:[131]

> "A breaking of the skin would be commonly regarded as a characteristic of a wound. The breaking of the skin will be normally evidenced by a flow of blood and, in its occurrence at the site of a blow or impact, the wound will more often than not be external. But there are those cases where the bleeding which evidences the separation of tissues may be internal."

(1) *"Indirect" wounding*

Since there is no requirement that a wound must be caused by any particular instrument or object, it would seem to follow that a wound may be caused indirectly. This could occur where, for example, D deliberately pushes V on to a sharp object, like a broken bottle, which causes the wound, or where D throws the same object at V causing injury. There is no legal requirement that the assailant and victim must be in direct contact before there can be a wounding. A wounding could also occur where an object already attached to the person of the victim is used as an instrument to cause injury to the victim. For example, if V is holding a fork and D deliberately knocks her arm so that V is impaled on her own fork, that would be a relevant wounding by D. In *R v Sheard*[132] the victim, who was wearing a hard-rimmed hat, was struck on the head. The resulting injury caused by the effect of the impact of the hard rim was held to be a wounding.

A different type of case would be where D, intending to strike and injure A, by accident or mistake misses and wounds V. Here the wounding is direct; and the doctrine of transferred malice (above, 4.8) will supply the necessary conditions of culpability to make D's wounding of V unlawful.

17.3.3 "Maims"

At common law, "maim" means "depriving another of the use of such of his members as may render him the less able in fighting, either to defend himself, or to annoy his adversary".[133] In New Zealand it has been held to involve the cutting or taking away of some part of a person, and has a connotation of permanence;[134] or removal of a part that does not naturally regrow. It would, however, presumably make no difference to a charge of maiming that the part violently removed was successfully reattached by surgery. The essence of the offence is the non-consensual removal of a body part, regardless of its consequences.

---

129 *R v Devine* (1982) 8 A Crim R 45.
130 *R v Waters* [1979] 1 NZLR 375 (CA).
131 *R v Waters* [1979] 1 NZLR 375 (CA), 378.
132 *R v Sheard* (1837) 2 Mood 13; 169 ER 6.
133 *Blackstone's Commentaries on the Laws of England*, 17th ed (1830) vol 4, 205.
134 *R v Rapana and Murray* (1988) 3 CRNZ 256, 257 (Williamson J).

Because of its association with combat defence using hand weapons, the concept may have less relevance in present times than once it had.[135] Nonetheless, an interesting question may arise where, for example, V, an associate of a gang known to use extreme violence, agrees to the cutting of a finger, or part of a finger, as part of an initiation rite for entry into the gang. Given that the amputation is consensual, could a prosecution for maiming be sustained? The answer is probably "yes", given recent case law developments in relation to sado-masochistic activity of an extreme kind which causes grievous bodily harm (above, 17.2.4(2)). If the protection of public health now mandates making such infliction of grievous bodily harm unlawful, notwithstanding that its "victims" positively welcomed it,[136] it is difficult to see why a different rule would apply where the consensual maiming is of a non-sexual nature.

17.3.4 "Disfigures"

At common law, "disfiguring" consisted of some external injury which may detract from personal appearance.[137] The natural and ordinary meaning of "disfiguring" is "to deform or deface; to mar or alter the figure or appearance of a person".[138] In *R v Rapana and Murray*,[139] the victim alleged he had been disfigured when he was forced to submit to a tattooing down one side of his face using a broken pen and a needle. At the time of trial there were no longer any marks on his face as a result of the incident. The issue for the Court was whether disfiguring necessarily connotes some permanent disfigurement rather than merely temporary change. Noting that the natural meaning of the word "disfigure" does not involve permanent injury or damage, the Court held that the word should be accorded the same meaning in the context of s 188(2).[140] Provided the two essential elements are proved — namely, a disfiguring and an intent to injure — the concept is apt to cover situations like acid throwing and involuntary tattooing where there has been an initial injuring but no permanent damage or marking.[141]

17.3.5 "Injure"

Injury is relevant only to the lesser offence defined in s 188(2) and to the offences defined in s 189. The term is defined in s 2(1), and means "to cause actual bodily harm". It appears that the expression does not require proof of physical injury, and may include injury producing an hysterical or nervous condition. Thus, if D physically assaults V in a manner which causes only minor physical injury but which is highly intimidatory and as a result of which V suffers a psychological injury in the nature of shock or hysteria, the resulting mental injury would amount to "actual bodily harm"[142] provided it could be said to be more than trifling or transitory.[143] However, for the reasons discussed earlier in relation to psychological and

---

135 In ancient times, the punishment for mayhem was the loss of the like part: *Blackstone's Commentaries on the Laws of England*, 17th ed (1830) vol 4, 205, 206.
136 See *R v Dica* [2004] EWCA Crim 1103, para 42, (per Lord Justice Judge).
137 See Butler and Garsia, *Archbold: Criminal Pleading, Evidence and Practice* (36th ed), London, Sweet & Maxwell, 1966, para 2654. This definition does not appear in the most recent edition of *Archbold* (Richardson (ed), *Archbold Criminal Pleading, Evidence and Practice*, London, Sweet & Maxwell, 2005) because in 1967, s 18 Offences Against the Person Act 1861 (UK) was amended to delete reference to disfiguring. However, the term still appears in a number of English provisions, in particular those relating to explosives or corrosive substances: see ss 28 and 29 Offences Against the Person Act 1861 (UK).
138 *Shorter Oxford Dictionary* (1993 ed), Oxford, Claredon Press, 1993, vol 1, 691.
139 *R v Rapana and Murray* (1988) 3 CRNZ 256.
140 *R v Rapana and Murray* (1988) 3 CRNZ 256, 257.
141 See *R v James* (1980) 70 Cr App R 215 (CA); *Burrell v Harmer* [1967] Crim LR 169.
142 See *R v Miller* [1954] 2 QB 282; [1954] 2 All ER 529, 292; 534.

emotional harm,[144] although psychiatric injury may suffice, other cognitive or emotional reactions like fear, distress, or panic do not.[145]

17.3.6 Mens rea

The offences defined in s 188 involve two alternative mens rea states. The crime of wounding with intent to cause grievous bodily harm in subs (1) may only be committed intentionally. Recklessness on the part of the accused will not suffice. However, the crime defined in subs (2), of wounding with intent to injure, may be committed either intentionally, or "with reckless disregard for the safety of others".

(1) *"With intent"*

The Crown carries the legal burden of proving the specific intent to cause grievous bodily harm, or the intent to injure, as the case may be. It will not often be the case that the defendant makes a statement that she intended to cause really serious harm. Evidence of intent usually rests on circumstantial evidence (the nature of the assault and the physical environment in which it occurs), or is inferred from the acts and statements made by the accused before, at, or after the event. In *R v Taisalika*,[146] where the accused had struck the complainant on the side of the head with a glass causing a serious injury, it was held that the nature of the blow and the gash it produced to the complainant's head were factors which pointed strongly to the necessary intent. However, to establish intent under the section it will not be enough to prove that the accused had foreseen that such harm was likely to result from his acts, or that he had been reckless whether such harm would result.[147] This is because the intent required to be proved for a charge of aggravated wounding has traditionally been regarded as an intent to produce a "particular evil consequence",[148] the equivalent of "malice aforethought".[149] Of course, although the required intent cannot be proved by foresight that serious injury is likely to result from a deliberate act, foresight and recklessness are evidence from which that intent may be inferred. But they cannot be equated, either separately or in conjunction, with intent to do grievous bodily harm.[150]

It is worth noting that where an intention to cause grievous bodily harm is proved, and death results, the accused may be guilty of murder on the basis of the constructive intent provision in s 167(b) ("means to cause to the person killed any bodily injury that is known to the offender to be likely to cause death").[151] However, where death does not result, proof of an intent to

---

143 *R v McArthur* [1975] 1 NZLR 486; *R v Donovan* [1934] 2 KB 498.
144 See 17.2.1(1).
145 *R v Chan-Fook* [1994] 2 All ER 552; [1994] 99 Cr App R 147 (CA). See also *R v Burstow* [1996] Crim LR 331.
146 *R v Taisalika* 25/6/93, CA94/93.
147 *R v Belfon* [1976] 3 All ER 46; [1976] 1 WLR 741 (CA). See 4.2.3, 4.2.7. On the other hand, the mere fact that the accused does not recall whether he had the necessary intent at the relevant time would be insufficient to establish a lack of intent. Loss of memory of past events is not the same as lack of intent at the time: *R v Taisalika* 25/6/93, CA94/93.
148 *Hyam v DPP* [1975] AC 55; [1974] 2 All ER 41 (HL), 86; 62, 63 (Lord Diplock).
149 *Hyam v DPP* [1975] AC 55; [1974] 2 All ER 41 (HL), 86; 62, 63 (Lord Diplock).
150 *R v Belfon* [1976] 3 All ER 46; [1976] 1 WLR 741 (CA), 53; 749. For a critique of the decision in *R v Belfon*, see Buzzard, " 'Intent' " [1978] Crim LR 5 and Smith " 'Intent': A reply" [1978] Crim LR 14.
151 In such a case, for murder to be proved the prosecution would also need to prove the accused's subjective knowledge that the death of the victim was a real risk: *R v Gush* [1980] 2 NZLR 92 (CA), 96.

cause grievous bodily harm will not be sufficient to support a conviction for attempted murder; to prove an attempted murder nothing less than an intent to kill will do.[152]

What makes the offence in s 188(1) so serious, warranting a maximum sentence of 14 years' imprisonment, is not what D actually does, but rather the intent with which he does it. Consequently, the offence may be committed even though V suffered only minor harm. If D, intending to stab V violently in the abdomen, succeeds only in inflicting a superficial cut to a finger, he may still be guilty of wounding with intent to cause grievous bodily harm.[153]

(2)   "Reckless disregard"

The alternative offence defined in s 188(2) may be committed where the accused wounds, maims, disfigures, etc "with reckless disregard for the safety of others". Reckless disregard contemplates a wanton indifference to the interests of others, but within the hierarchy of offences created by the section implies a mental state less culpable than intending to cause grievous bodily harm. This is reflected in the penalty prescribed in the section (a term of imprisonment not exceeding 7 years). In New Zealand recklessness invariably requires subjective foresight, unless the statutory context clearly requires that a different meaning be given to the concept.[154] For the purposes of s 188, therefore, recklessness requires foresight of dangerous consequences that could well happen, together with an intention to continue with that course of conduct regardless of the risk.[155]

An intentional or reckless frightening, without more, is insufficient for s 188(2); the person charged must be proved to have been aware that the consequences of her voluntary act might be to cause some injury to the victim, though not necessarily grievous bodily harm.[156] An example of a reckless wounding would be where D, standing in the middle of a crowd, begins to swing a heavy chain, with the intention of intimidating those around him. If V, standing in the crowd, is then struck by the chain and injured, D will be guilty of wounding V with reckless disregard if — and only if — D foresaw that someone could well be injured by his actions and continued swinging the chain regardless of the risk. Notice that, as usual under the doctrine of transferred mens rea,[157] it is not necessary that D should have foreseen that V, in particular, might be struck by the chain.

The difference in penalties as between subss (1) and (2) is substantial. This fact evidently influenced the accused in *R v Kaho*[158] to apply for a direction under s 339 that a verdict under s 188(2) could be returned when he had been charged with an assault under s 188(1). The Court refused the application. It held that, as a matter of logic, it could not be said that proof of an intention to cause grievous bodily harm could lead to a conclusion that the accused had acted with "reckless disregard", since the offence in s 188(2) is not subsumed within the offence defined in s 188(1).

---

152   *R v Belfon* [1976] 3 All ER 46; [1976] 1 WLR 741 (CA), 52; 748.
153   See *R v Hunt* (1825) 1 Mood CC 93; 168 ER 1198, 96; 1200: "if there was an intent to do grievous bodily harm, it was immaterial whether grievous bodily harm was done."
154   *R v Harney* [1987] 2 NZLR 576 (CA), 579. See 4.3ff.
155   *R v Harney* [1987] 2 NZLR 576 (CA), 579.
156   Cf *R v Sullivan* [1981] Crim LR 46 (CA), 47.
157   See 4.8.
158   *R v Kaho* 31/5/01, Paterson J, HC Auckland T002621.

17.4 Injuring with intent

This crime is defined in s 189 Crimes Act 1961. The offence contains elements which are endemic to the crime of wounding with intent, discussed above, and which will not be separately considered. It is sufficient to note that, as with a prosecution under s 188, proof of an assault is not necessary. What must be proved is that the accused's direct or indirect acts caused "actual bodily harm".[159] Neither is it relevant that the injury actually caused with the requisite intent was not a serious bodily harm.[160]

17.5 Injuring by unlawful act

This offence is one of the few provisions of the Crimes Act 1961 that allows prosecution for negligent acts alone. As a matter of charging practice, where a charge has been laid under another section, but the case may fall within this section, it is considered prudent to include a separate count under the section in the indictment.[161] However, before this course is followed, there must be some evidence to support the charge.[162] If the principal charge alleged is attempted murder, an application under s 339 may be made requesting the court to direct the jury to return a lesser verdict. However, the indictment for attempted murder must first identify an actual bodily injury before an offence under s 190 can be offered in the alternative.[163]

The section provides:

> "**190 Injuring by unlawful act**
>
> "Every one is liable to imprisonment for a term not exceeding 3 years who injures any other person in such circumstances that if death had been caused he would have been guilty of manslaughter."

The offence has its origins not in English law but in the Draft Code of 1879, where it was entitled "Negligent Acts punishable with two years imprisonment".[164] The section aims to punish negligent conduct that results in injury such that the offender would have been liable for manslaughter if death had been caused. In a sense, the title "injuring by unlawful act" is a misnomer, since an omission without lawful excuse to perform a legal duty would clearly suffice, as would any of the forms of conduct specifically qualifying as culpable homicide by virtue of s 160(2). An unlawful act is a sufficient but not a necessary condition of liability under the section.

The ambit of s 190 is unclear. The section says nothing about the manner in which the injury must be caused. In particular, like s 188, there is no reference to assault or the use of violence. The fact that the offence occurs in a statutory context of serious offences against the person is not conclusive that proof of an assault or something akin to assault is required. Since grievous bodily harm may be caused otherwise than by wounding and may even result from an act

---

159 Per the definition of "injure" in s 2.
160 See *R v Hunt* (1825) 1 Mood CC 93; 168 ER 1198, 96; 1200: "if there was an intent to do grievous bodily harm, it was immaterial whether grievous bodily harm was done."
161 *R v Carr (No 2)* [1995] 2 NZLR 339; (1995) 13 CRNZ 1. See also *R v Kaho* 31/5/01, Paterson J, HC Auckland T002621.
162 *R v Panine* 25/6/02, HC, Ronald Young J, Wellington T841/01.
163 *R v Kaho* 31/5/01, Paterson J, HC Auckland T002621, para 11.
164 Criminal Code Bill Commission, *Report Relating to Indictable Offences*, London, Eyre & Spotiswoode for HMSO, 1879, s 201. See also s 186 Criminal Code Act 1893.

which is not an assault (where, for example, someone creates fear in another causing him to attempt to escape, suffering serious injury in the process),[165] the same must also be true of "injuring" under s 190. What is implicit in the section is that the accused caused the injury either by a direct act or by some culpable omission, whether or not the victim suffers permanent damage as a result. Because the present section omits the proviso whereby its predecessor under the Crimes Act 1908 was made inapplicable to the "duty" provisions in ss 151 to 154, it is arguable that an omission to perform a legal duty could now provide the basis of a prosecution under the section. Suppose the following example:

"D is the operator of a 'bungy-jumping' operation which uses a large crane suspended over an enclosed harbour area as a platform from which patrons jump. V, whom D has personally attended in attaching the bungy cord to her ankles, jumps after receiving assurances from D that the jump is 'perfectly safe'. However, at the end of the jump and after the jump cord has taken up the tension, the bindings around V's ankles slip and she plunges into the sea. V, who cannot swim, is saved from drowning by an assistant of the company who dives into the water and manages to pull V to safety. V suffers from water ingestion and is profoundly distressed by the experience but suffers no lasting consequences from her ordeal."

In such circumstances a prosecution under s 190 would be possible. V has suffered "injury" in that she experienced interference with her health or comfort, albeit not permanently. Furthermore there could be little doubt that had she died D would have been liable for manslaughter as a person in charge of a dangerous thing who failed to take "reasonable precautions against and to use reasonable care to avoid such danger".[166]

The question of liability under s 190 arose in a similar way in *Primrose v Police*.[167] In that case, the appellant encouraged another youth to throw a can of petrol belonging to the appellant into a bonfire, as a result of which the youth suffered serious injury. The Court accepted that the appellant had shouted at the boy to get away, but the warning was not heeded. Hillyer J held that, had death resulted, manslaughter would have been committed. Because there was an omission without lawful excuse to perform or observe a legal duty, as a result of which someone was injured, it was held that the conviction under s 190 was justified.[168]

By its nature, the section is concerned with seriously negligent acts that could have resulted in the victim's death. Typically, offences involving the use of firearms, where the accused has failed to take proper precautions, resulting in injuries suffered by V, could be brought within the ambit of the section.[169] Where it is not possible to establish such a high degree of negligent risk-taking, it may be appropriate to charge the lesser negligence offence in s 13 Summary Offences Act 1981.[170]

---

165 *R v McCready* [1978] 3 All ER 967; [1978] 1 WLR 1376 (CA), 970; 1381.
166 Section 156 Crimes Act 1961.
167 *Primrose v Police* (1985) 1 CRNZ 621.
168 Cf *R v McLeod* (1915) 34 NZLR 430 (CA), in which it was held that shooting the ash off a cigarette held in the mouth of a consenting victim, where the victim was wounded in the cheek, was a "risky" event such that it would have been manslaughter if death had ensued. Bodily injury inflicted in such circumstances would constitute careless use of a firearm under s 53 Arms Act 1983 (hence, an unlawful act) and would be manslaughter under s 53(4) in the event of death ensuing.
169 See *R v McLeod* (1915) 34 NZLR 430. See also s 53 Arms Act 1983.
170 As occurred in *Primrose v Police* (1985) 1 CRNZ 621.

17.6 Aggravated wounding

The crime of aggravated wounding or injury is defined in s 191 Crimes Act 1961:

"**191 Aggravated wounding or injury**

"(1) Every one is liable to imprisonment for a term not exceeding 14 years who with intent—

"(a) To commit or facilitate the commission of any crime; or

"(b) To avoid the detection of himself or of any other person in the commission of any crime; or

"(c) To avoid the arrest or facilitate the flight of himself or of any other person upon the commission or attempted commission of any crime—

"wounds, maims, disfigures, or causes grievous bodily harm to any person, or stupefies or renders unconscious any person, or by any violent means renders any person incapable of resistance.

"(2) Every one is liable to imprisonment for a term not exceeding 7 years who, with any such intent as aforesaid, injures any person."

In essence, an offence is committed when one person harms another with any of the intents set out in s 191(1). The element of aggravation in the title relates not to the nature of the harm inflicted (though this will determine whether the offence is under s 191(1) or s 191(2)), but rather to the reasons for the offending; being to facilitate the commission of a crime, or to avoid detection or arrest. The section bears some parallels to the further definition of murder in s 168, which allows a prosecution for murder where the accused causes the death of the victim for purposes similar to those specified in s 191(1)(a)-(c), although in that context the accused need not mean to cause death or know that it is likely to ensue.

So far as the actus reus is concerned, the meanings of wounding, maiming, disfiguring, grievous bodily harm, and injury are considered earlier (17.3.1-5) The meaning of "stupefies" in subs (1) is considered in *R v Sturm*,[171] a case in which the appellant had been indicted on six counts under s 191 of unlawfully stupefying four male complainants in order to facilitate the commission of sexual violations and other indecencies. An appeal by way of case stated asked:

"Where a person is charged with stupefying another with intent to facilitate the commission of a crime pursuant to s 191 of the Crimes Act 1961, is the Crown required to prove that the victim was placed in a 'stupor' in so far as that term is generally understood within medicine and medical science."

By way of answer, the Court of Appeal rejected a narrow meaning of "stupefies" as requiring a mental state approaching unconsciousness and held that it means to cause an effect on the mind or nervous system of a person which really seriously interferes with that person's mental or physical ability to act in a way which might hinder an intended crime.[172] Accordingly, "stupefies" is apt not just to describe a state where a person is rendered senseless or insentient but also to describe a state where the administration of drugs has engendered disinhibition and stimulated uncharacteristic behaviour.[173]

---

171 *R v Sturm* [2005] 3 NZLR 252; (2005) 21 CRNZ 627 (CA).
172 *R v Sturm* [2005] 3 NZLR 252; (2005) 21 CRNZ 627 (CA), para 113.

According to this approach, the expression "stupefies or renders unconscious" in s 191(1) signifies the Legislature's intention that both expressions should have different meanings.[174] However, whether an interference is sufficiently serious to amount to stupefaction is a matter of fact and degree for the jury or other trier of fact to determine, just as it is a jury matter whether, in a case of alleged grievous bodily harm, the bodily injury is really serious.[175]

17.6.1 Mens rea

To establish liability under the section, the prosecution must first prove that the accused intended to do one of the things specified in s 191(1)(a)-(c). Because the intent nominated is a further or "ulterior" intent,[176] recklessness will not suffice for this aspect of the mens rea. But once that "preliminary" intent is established, is it necessary for the prosecution to prove in every case that the accused had the particular *intent* to inflict the specific *type* of injury alleged (wounding maiming, stupefying, etc)? The statute is silent on this question, which was considered by the Court of Appeal in R v Tihi.[177]

In *Tihi*, the accused and his associates stole a taxi after evicting its driver, with a view to driving to another part of the country. In the course of evicting the driver a co-accused had put his arm around the driver's neck and held a small knife against it. The driver was unaware of the knife but received a small cut near his eye. The co-accused gave evidence that he had no intention of cutting the victim and was unaware he had done so until he saw him wiping his cheek with a handkerchief. The issue for the Court was whether, under s 191(2), it was necessary to prove intent or some other form of mens rea in respect of the injury itself, in addition to the intention to commit the crime of unlawful taking. The Court agreed that a purely accidental injury could not attract criminal liability since, if mens rea were irrelevant, the "curious" result would be that purely accidental harm inflicted in the circumstances mentioned in the section would attract a maximum prison term of 14 (or 7) years.[178] The Court was unwilling to find that the offence imposed strict liability in respect of the occurrence of injury, because that would run counter to the well established presumption in favour of mens rea in all criminal offences. In the words of Casey J:[179]

> "The introductory phrase 'with intent to' in subs (1) establishes a connection between the harm and the conduct described in (a), (b) and (c), in that it must have been inflicted as part of the offender's purpose of implementing that conduct, tending to the conclusion that he must at least have turned his mind to the risk of harm... . Accordingly, before he can be guilty, it must be shown that the accused either meant to cause the specified harm, or foresaw that his actions were likely to expose others to the risk of suffering it."

This means that either intention or recklessness will suffice as the mens rea required for wounding (etc), notwithstanding that recklessness will not suffice for the other mens rea element, required under paras (a)-(c). This approach is seen also in *Gillan v Police*.[180] In that

---

173 R v Sturm [2005] 3 NZLR 252; (2005) 21 CRNZ 627 (CA), para 109.
174 R v Sturm [2005] 3 NZLR 252; (2005) 21 CRNZ 627 (CA), para 102.
175 R v Sturm [2005] 3 NZLR 252; (2005) 21 CRNZ 627 (CA), para 113.
176 See 4.2.7.
177 R v Tihi [1989] 2 NZLR 29; (1989) 4 CRNZ 289 (CA).
178 R v Tihi [1989] 2 NZLR 29; (1989) 4 CRNZ 289 (CA), 31; 291.
179 R v Tihi [1989] 2 NZLR 29; (1989) 4 CRNZ 289 (CA), 31, 32; 291, 292.
180 Gillan v Police (2004) 149 A Crim R 354 (SCSA).

case, the accused was convicted of unlawful and malicious wounding, a similar offence to that nominated in s 191, following an altercation in a hotel. She had thrown a glass at the victim, striking him on the head and, after the glass had shattered, cutting him quite badly. Upholding the conviction, the appellate Court held that it was open to the Magistrate to find that the appellant intentionally threw the glass at the victim and therefore, by inference, foresaw the likelihood that the glass would break and cause lacerations to the face.

However, where the indictment alleges that the accused "stupefies" the victim with one of the intents nominated in (a)-(c), it may be difficult to escape the conclusion that only an intent to stupefy will suffice. This seems to follow from the fact that, unlike the other verbs listed in subs (1) ("wounds", "maims", "disfigures", "renders unconscious"), which may occur inadvertently or accidentally, stupefying requires the purposive act of "putting someone in a stupor". It cannot be done inadvertently or accidentally.[181]

17.6.2 "Violent means"

The offence under s 191 may be committed where an accused uses "violent means" to incapacitate another while intending to commit a crime, avoid detection, or escape. In *R v Crossan*[182] it was held that the words "by any violent means whatever" (used in the predecessor to s 191)[183] are unfettered by any context which might throw a gloss upon the words or limit their meaning. In *Crossan*, the accused, intending to have sexual intercourse with the victim against her will, had threatened to shoot her with a loaded revolver unless she submitted to sexual intercourse. The Court held that while a mere threat *simpliciter* would not amount to "violent means", a threat made with a loaded revolver in such a way as to lead the person to believe that it would be used, could have the effect of rendering a person "incapable of resistance" as effectively as if the person were physically incapable, and was properly described as a "violent means". By implication, the term "any violent means" now used in s 191(1) is not limited by the preceding words ("wounds" etc). It is clear from *Crossan* that conduct that involves no physical assault or injury may qualify as "violent means".

The analysis in *Crossan* was approved in *R v Claridge*[184] where the accused, while attempting to escape from prison, had struck a prison officer with an iron bar causing him to fall from a prison wall and sustain injuries. It was held that the purpose of the attack was obviously to render the officer incapable of resistance and that to so attack another with an iron bar was to employ violent means. It is worth noting that the Court in that case did not consider it necessary to decide the question raised in 17.6.1 whether the several acts (wounding, maiming, etc) required any intent; since once the "violent means" was established, and the causal link between such means and incapacity to resist is present, the necessary intent is "self-evident".[185]

17.6.3 Proof of offence

A person may only be found guilty of an offence under s 191(1)(c), or indeed under the corresponding s 192(1)(c) governing aggravated assault (below), if there is proof of the

---

181 See *R v Sturm* [2004] 1 NZLR 570; (2003) 20 CRNZ 513.
182 *R v Crossan* [1943] NZLR 454.
183 See s 195 Crimes Act 1908.
184 *R v Claridge* (1987) 3 CRNZ 337 (CA).
185 *R v Claridge* (1987) 3 CRNZ 337 (CA), 340.

commission or attempted commission of a crime by the person committing the assault or by the person whose arrest or flight he intends to avoid or facilitate.[186] This restriction derives from the original provision in the Draft Code of 1879 from which the present section evolved, which referred to the "flight of the *offender* upon the commission or attempted commission" of a crime.[187] That format required proof that the person whose flight is facilitated actually committed or attempted to commit the crime.[188] Thus if D is acquitted of robbery, he could not then be convicted on a count of wounding with intent to avoid arrest or to facilitate his flight upon the commission or attempted commission of robbery.

17.7 Aggravated assault

This offence, created by s 192, was substantially redrafted in 1961. It now provides:

"**192 Aggravated assault**

"(1) Every one is liable to imprisonment for a term not exceeding 3 years who assaults any other person with intent—

"(a) To commit or facilitate the commission of any crime; or

"(b) To avoid the detection of himself or of any other person in the commission of any crime; or

"(c) To avoid the arrest or facilitate the flight of himself or of any other person upon the commission or attempted commission of any crime.

"(2) Every one is liable for imprisonment for a term not exceeding 3 years who assaults any constable or any person acting in aid of any constable, or any person in the lawful execution of any process, with intent to obstruct the person so assaulted in the execution of his duty."

The provision defines two quite distinct offences, namely aggravated assault and assault with intent to obstruct a person in the execution of his duty. The offence defined in subs (1) requires that the accused intentionally assaults some other person, and the aggravating features are identical to those specified in s 191(1)(a)-(c). As with s 191(1)(c), the offence in s 192(1)(c) requires proof of the commission or attempted commission of a crime by the person committing the assault or by the person whose arrest or flight he intends to avoid or facilitate.[189]

The mens rea for assault with any of the intents nominated in s 192(1)(a)-(c) may be divided into two parts. First there is the intent to assault (above, 17.2.1). Secondly, there is the mens rea necessary to constitute the element of aggravation, namely, an intent to commit, facilitate, or to avoid detection in the commission of a crime, etc. Where the aggravated intent is the commission of a more serious crime of violence, the mens rea required is an intention to cause the result of the offence aimed at, or subjective foresight that the actions performed by him were likely to expose others to the risk of suffering it.[190]

---

186 *R v Wati* [1985] 2 NZLR 236; (1984) 1 CRNZ 380 (CA), 238; 382.
187 See Criminal Code Bill Commission, *Report Relating to Indictable Offences*, London, Eyre & Spotiswoode for HMSO, 1879, C-2345; s 188 (emphasis added).
188 *R v Wati* [1985] 2 NZLR 236; (1984) 1 CRNZ 380 (CA), 238; 382.
189 *R v Wati* [1985] 2 NZLR 236; (1984) 1 CRNZ 380 (CA), 238; 382.

17.7.1 Assault with intent to obstruct

This offence is defined in s 192(2). The offence first requires proof of an assault. For an aggravated assault then to be established, the subsection requires proof of two separate intents on the part of the person charged: the ordinary intent involved in the definition of assault in s 2, and the further intent that the assault was with intent to obstruct the person so assaulted in the execution of his duty. The "crucial" words, "with intent to obstruct the person so assaulted in the execution of his duty", must be read as a "composite description" of the further intent required by the subsection.[191] The Crown must prove (i) that the defendant assumed (in the sense of having a positive state of mind in relation to the matters) that the person she assaulted was a constable who was acting in the execution of his duty, and (ii) that she did intend to obstruct him in the performance of his duty.[192] Thus if D's evidence is that she did not give any thought to whether V was a constable in the execution of his duty, and assaulted him because she believed that, whoever he was, he was acting in a highhanded manner, she cannot be guilty of an assault under s 192(2) because knowledge or belief that the victim was a constable in the execution of his duty is the essence of the offence. On the other hand, evidence that the accused wilfully shut his eyes to the likelihood that the person assaulted was a constable, or was indifferent to that fact, may be evidence from which relevant knowledge could be inferred.[193]

The section does not expressly require that the person assaulted must be acting in the execution of his duty. It may be that the offence is committed if the offender believes the person assaulted to be acting in the execution of his duty and intends so to obstruct him, even if it should later transpire that for some technical reason the victim was not in fact acting in the execution of his duty.[194]

(1) *Mistake*

Evidence of the state of mind of a defendant, including evidence of any mistaken beliefs on his part, whether of fact or of law, may be relevant to the question of intent. For example, evidence that D was honestly mistaken about the facts and believed the person he struck to be a trespasser would be relevant to the existence of the intent required in the subsection. Faced with such evidence, the Crown may be unable to prove that the defendant had the requisite state of mind for an offence under s 192(2). However, it will be no defence to a prosecution under the section if it is proved that the accused knew that the person being assaulted was a constable who was acting in the execution of his or her duty, but made a mistake about the legal extent of the constable's powers in the circumstances.[195] Such a mistake would

---

190 *R v Tihi* [1989] 2 NZLR 29; (1989) 4 CRNZ 289 (CA). Although Tihi relates to a charge of aggravated wounding under s 191, the mens rea requirement for each offence is identical. Contrast this with the position in Canada, where the mens rea for aggravated assault requires objective foresight of the risk of bodily harm: *R v Foti* (2002) 169 CCC (3d) 57, 63; *R v Godin* [1994] 2 SCR 484, 485.
191 *R v Simpson* [1978] 2 NZLR 221 (CA), 223. See also *R v Reynhoudt* (1962) 107 CLR 381; [1962] ALR 483 (HCA).
192 *R v Simpson* [1978] 2 NZLR 221 (CA), 225.
193 *Waaka v Police* [1987] 1 NZLR 754; (1987) 2 CRNZ 370 (CA), 759; 375. See the discussion of wilful blindness, at 4.5.1.
194 *R v Simpson* [1978] 2 NZLR 221 (CA), 225.
195 *Waaka v Police* [1987] 1 NZLR 754; (1987) 2 CRNZ 370 (CA), 759; 375. Cf *R v Lee* (2001) 1 Cr App R 293: mistake will not provide a defence where the belief is not about facts relating to the identity or conduct of police but is about the legal consequences of believed antecedent facts.

be characterised as a "pure" mistake of law, ignorance of which is no excuse (at least, when the ignorance is in respect of the very offence committed by the offender).[196]

(2) Honest belief that V is using excessive force

What is the legal position when D sees police officers restraining another person and intervenes because she believes (mistakenly) that the police officers are using excessive force in effecting an arrest? This issue arose in R v Thomas,[197] in which the accused and her friends intervened when they saw police officers restraining another person. At the hearing, the accused said she knew the persons effecting the "arrest" were police officers and as such were entitled to use force in effecting an arrest. However, she intervened because she believed, as a matter of fact, that they were using excessive force and were, therefore, acting in excess of their duty; thus justifying her intervention "in the defence of ... another".[198] In the Court of Appeal (by way of case stated), it was held that the mens rea requirement that an accused must know the police officer is acting in the execution of his duty is not met by the prosecution's simply proving that the accused knew the police officer was exercising a "prima facie legitimate type of police power such as arrest". The Court held that an honest belief in a state of affairs (such as excessive use of force by the police officer) which, if true, would make the defendant's act innocent or justified, is a good defence to a charge of obstruction. To similar effect, it has been held in R v Christiansen[199] that the use of excessive force takes a constable outside the scope of her duty and, therefore, that an accused will lack the intent required by s 192(2) if he honestly believes the constable is using excessive force in effecting an arrest.

In Thomas, both the defences of mistake of fact and self-defence were available and were successfully pleaded. Significantly, the decisions in Thomas and Christiansen admit of the possibility that there may be some circumstances where a citizen may challenge the manner in which an enforcement officer is exercising a legitimate power without being guilty of obstruction. A person observing a police arrest will not necessarily become an "officious bystander"[200] by virtue simply of acting according to a genuine belief that the police are using excessive force. This makes good sense. Otherwise, if a member of the public were never able to challenge how a police officer exercised an admitted police power, in circumstances where there were indications that the officer was going beyond the legitimate bounds of her authority, it is arguable that the public's ability to protect itself against misuse of police power would be severely compromised.[201] In effect, such a limitation would amount to a substantial fettering of the ability of genuinely concerned citizens to intervene and prevent what they believe to be

---

196   Waaka v Police [1987] 1 NZLR 754; (1987) 2 CRNZ 370 (CA). See 14.3.
197   R v Thomas [1991] 3 NZLR 141; (1991) 7 CRNZ 123 (CA).
198   Section 48.
199   R v Christiansen 24/10/01, CA196/01.
200   The High Court Judge, on appeal from the District Court, had implied that the accused in R v Thomas had acted as an "officious bystander" when she sought to challenge the way in which the arrest was being effected, honestly believing that the police were acting in excess of their powers. It may be that the judge was over-influenced by the fact that the accused and her associates had been drinking to excess before the incident, and considered that for this reason they lacked the capacity to make a reasoned judgment in the matter. However, the defence of honest mistake of fact has never been prefaced by a requirement that the person making the mistake must be sober, although evidence of intoxication may be considered together with other matters in determining whether the accused actually held the belief claimed.
201   Compare R v Thomas [1991] 3 NZLR 141; (1991) 7 CRNZ 123 (CA), 143; 125 (Casey J): "One has only to ask what would be the position if a bystander saw an outraged constable continuing to beat an unconscious suspect over the head."

a real and unjustified risk of serious danger to a victim as a result of excessive police conduct.[202]

However, there are limits to the ability of a citizen to intervene in such a case. If, for example, there was evidence that the intervener wilfully shut her eyes to the question whether the person effecting the arrest was a police officer acting in the execution of her duties or was indifferent to these matters, this is likely to negate her claim of honest belief.[203] Moreover, as was noted above, if D was aware that the victim was a police constable but entertained an incorrect understanding of the law regarding the extent of the constable's powers, that would constitute a mistake of law and would be no defence.[204]

(3)   *Self-defence*

The above analysis is buttressed by the law regarding self-defence. The "fundamental right" of self-defence cannot be excluded by the general provisions of the Summary Offences Act 1981. In *R v Thomas*, the accused claimed self-defence under s 48 Crimes Act 1961 on the basis that she was entitled to use reasonable force in the defence of another person whom she believed was the victim of excessive force (being used by the police in making an arrest). It was her belief that the police were acting unlawfully and were not acting in the execution of their duty. In such circumstances, all that is required is a subjective honest belief on D's part. Provided the degree of force used is reasonable in the circumstances *as she perceives them*, there is no reason why self-defence or defence of another should not justify the use of force that would otherwise be an assault, given that the accused did not realise the officer was acting in the execution of his duty.[205]

(4)   *In the "execution of duty"*

Whether a constable is acting in the "execution of his duty" will depend upon an examination of the facts in each case. Generally, a police officer acts in the execution of her duty from the point at which she commences a lawful task connected with her functions as a police officer. She continues to act in the execution of that duty for as long as she is engaged in pursuing that task and until it is completed.[206] The concept of "execution of duty" is an important constitutional protection against excessive or inappropriate police intervention, and an implicit recognition of the fact that police powers of arrest or search are enormously wide and potentially intrusive into almost every area of human activity.[207] In New Zealand, a prosecution for obstruction or assault of a police officer requires knowledge on the part of the offender that the person assaulted was both a constable and acting in the execution of her duties. Because

---

202   *R v Thomas* [1991] 3 NZLR 141; (1991) 7 CRNZ 123 (CA), 143, 144; 125, 126.
203   See *Waaka v Police* [1987] 1 NZLR 754; (1987) 2 CRNZ 370 (CA), 759; 375; *R v Thomas* [1991] 3 NZLR 141; (1991) 7 CRNZ 123 (CA), 143; 125, 126.
204   See s 25 Crimes Act 1961; also *Waaka v Police* [1987] 1 NZLR 754; (1987) 2 CRNZ 370 (CA), 759; 375.
205   *R v Thomas* [1991] 3 NZLR 141; (1991) 7 CRNZ 123 (CA), 144; 125, 126; *R v Christiansen* 24/10/01, CA196/01. Where the circumstances involve a developing fact situation in which the potential for mistake, and possible over-reaction, exists, it may be prudent for the judge to leave to the jury the possibility that, in a state of heightened anxiety engendered by the events, the defendant may have perceived a greater threat from the complainant than had actually been offered. See *Corker v WA* (2004) 146 A Crim R 33, 38, per Wheeler J. For general discussion of this issue, see above, 15.1.3.
206   *DPP Reference No 1 of 1993; R v K* (1993) 118 ALR 596 (FCA) , 601.
207   Cameron and Young (eds), *Policing at the Crossroads*, Wellington, Allen & Unwin in association with Port Nicholson, 1986, 25.

of the enormously variable circumstances in which a police officer may be required to intervene in the course of her professional occupation, the question whether the officer is actually acting "in the execution of her duty," may often be unclear to an observer. In most cases, the question will be determined by the terms of the enactment under which she purports to act, and by whether her conduct conformed with any statutory duty imposed upon her.[208] In some cases, the "execution" of a duty may involve the right of entry to premises for the purposes of detecting breaches of a particular statute, and may be accompanied by a requirement of "reasonable grounds" for suspecting that a particular activity is taking place.[209] Although a wrongful trespass committed by a constable may take her outside the course of her duty, a trivial trespass, amounting to only a "trivial interference with a citizen's liberty", does not.[210]

The obligations of the police in the execution of their duties under statute are well expressed in the following passage from the judgment of Myers CJ in *Burton v Power*:[211]

> "The Police are charged with the preservation of order and peace within the country, and it is their duty to carry out that charge with moderation, fairness, and discretion, and within the law. So long as they do that, they are entitled to and should receive the support of the Courts and of every good citizen. If they carry out their duties unfairly and immoderately, the Court would not hesitate to express its condemnation of their action and would see that no person suffered by reason thereof. But, on the other hand, it is the duty of every citizen, especially in times when susceptibilities and passions are likely to be aroused, with the likelihood of resultant breaches of the peace, to refrain from conduct calculated to produce that kind of disruption within the country."

17.8 Offences against children

The Crimes Act 1961 defines a number of offences involving non-fatal assaults that specifically proscribe assaults on and mistreatment of children. Section 194(a), which defines the offence of assaulting a child under the age of 14 years, does not appear to have a common law equivalent and was unknown in earlier enactments of New Zealand's criminal legislation. It was first enacted in Police Offences legislation in 1952.[212] The general law relating to criminal assaults applies to assaults under this section. Prima facie, this would include the possibility of consent as a defence, since the section does not expressly exclude a defence of consent. However, since the offence is designed to protect children below the age of 14 years, it is submitted that the principles governing sexual offences against young persons apply also to s 194,[213] and that, for the purposes of this offence, child victims are legally incapable of consenting to an assault.

Where the evidence of an assault goes no further than an allegation that the accused was "hitting the child when [the child was] going berserk", where the hitting involved two smacks with an open hand on the child's bottom, there may be no justification for treating the incident as anything more than a "pat on the bottom". While evidence of a technical assault, it may not

---

208 See, for example, *Donaldson v Police* [1968] NZLR 32 (s 3(e) Police Offences Act 1927 held to imply a duty "to enforce the law" and to prevent the obstruction of the highway).
209 See, for example, *Neiman v Police* [1967] NZLR 304, interpreting ss 208 and 209 Sale of Liquor Act 1962.
210 *Donnelly v Jackman* [1970] 1 All ER 987; [1970] 1 WLR 562, 989; 565. See also *Pounder v Police* [1971] NZLR 1080, 1085.
211 *Burton v Power* [1940] NZLR 305; [1940] GLR 192, 307; 193.
212 See s 5 Police Offences Amendment Act (No 2) 1952.
213 Cf 18.7-18.9.

merit the stigma of a conviction and may justify a discharge without conviction.[214] However, the Court in *R v Hende* noted that unauthorised acts of discipline against children should never be treated lightly, and prosecution in such cases may be justified in the interests of the community.[215]

17.8.1 Discipline of children

The extent to which children may legitimately be disciplined by the use of corporal punishment is governed by s 59 Crimes Act 1961. Essentially, the section permits parents and persons "in the place of the parent" to use force to discipline a child. The expression "in the place of the parent" is exclusive of teachers from whom the right to use corporal punishment has now been removed by legislation.[216] The prohibition against the use of corporal punishment by teachers, private school managers, early childhood centre employees or owners, and others employed as supervisors or controllers of children enrolled in or attending a school, is absolute.[217] Such a person may only use force by way of correction or punishment if that person is also a guardian of the student or child.

The absence in the statute of any reference to "legal" guardian leaves open the question whether a teacher acting as a de facto guardian of a student or child would be authorised by the exception[218] to administer force by way of correction or punishment in an appropriate case. Since the intent of the section would appear to be to prohibit the use of force by way of discipline outside a domestic setting, it may be that a person who was caring for a student or child, effectively in loco parentis, who was also involved in teaching the child, would be protected provided the force used was reasonable in terms of s 59(1). The possibility awaits consideration by the courts.

(1) *Proposed legislative change*

The issue of whether parents ought to have the right to physically discipline their children has been a matter of public debate in New Zealand since at least 2001. In that year, a survey conducted by the Ministry of Justice to ascertain public attitudes towards the physical discipline of children revealed that 80 percent of the public agreed that a person parenting a child should be allowed by law to smack the child with an open hand if they are naughty. At the same time, the use of objects to smack a child and smacking them in the head and neck area drew an overwhelmingly negative response from the public.[219] Legislation currently before the Justice and Electoral Select Committee is aimed at abolishing child discipline as a justification for force.[220] The Bill would repeal s 59, with the effect that the statutory protection for the use of force by parents and guardians would be removed. It is intended that this reform would stop force, and associated violence and harm, from being inflicted on children under the guise of domestic discipline.[221]

---

214 *R v Hende* [1996] 1 NZLR 153 (CA), 158.
215 *R v Hende* [1996] 1 NZLR 153 (CA), 158.
216 Section 59(3) Crimes Act, as inserted by s 28(3) Education Amendment Act 1990.
217 Section 139A Education Act 1989.
218 Section 139A(1) and (2) Education Act 1989.
219 See Carswell, *Survey on Public Attitudes towards the Physical Discipline of Children*, Wellington, Ministry of Justice, 2001.
220 See Crimes (Abolition of Force as a Justification for Child Discipline) Amendment Bill (9 June 2005 No 271-1).

Predictably, the response to the proposed legislation has been varied, with a full spectrum of views represented. On the one hand the organisation Save the Children supports complete repeal of the protection provided by s 59, on the grounds that the provision is a breach of children's fundamental rights and is contrary to other established principles favouring children's best interests.[222] At the other end of the spectrum the organisation Family Integrity advocates smacking, which may be a 10-15 minute process aimed at "driving the foolishness, the sinful manifestations, out of the child's personality..."[223] However, while there is substantial official agreement about the need to repeal s 59, there is a division of opinion about what constitutes "violence" for the purposes of the conduct impugned. While the New Zealand Children's Commissioner considers all smacking as physical abuse and properly condemned as violence, the architect of the Bill, MP Sue Bradford, has suggested an amendment in the Bill to clarify that it is not her intention to ban physical discipline absolutely. She does not consider all smacking as physical abuse. This disagreement reflects the divisions in public opinion around this issue. Clearly, while a majority of adults are opposed to allowing the infliction of discipline using instruments or involving any assaults to the head and neck area, many would also favour allowing the use of minor physical force (the use of a smack to the hand or leg) as a legitimate form of correction. Should the law ultimately change, in order to reflect this widespread view, it may be necessary for the law to acknowledge the operation of a de minimis rule to the effect that there are some infractions that are sufficiently trivial and the harm so minimal that there would be no social purpose in pursuing the matter before the criminal courts.[224]

(2) *Scope of permitted discipline*

Under current law, where force by way of discipline is authorised, the force used must be reasonable in the circumstances.[225] In *R v Drake*,[226] a mother administered severe blows to her 8-year-old child, causing the child's death. It was held that the punishment and its result were so "monstrously disproportionate" to any offence committed by the child that it was evident that the punishment was actuated by malice and not by a desire to discipline. The Court held that, in determining whether it was solely correction that was administered, it is necessary to consider both the events at the time and the relationship between the parent and child prior to those events. In addition, factors like the gravity of the child's offence, the character of the child, and the likely effect on the character of the child may be relevant to the question whether force was applied by way of correction.[227] In the absence of any exemption grounded in the purpose of correction, the use of force upon a child becomes a non-consensual criminal assault.

---

221 Crimes (Abolition of Force as a Justification for Child Discipline) Amendment Bill (9 June 2005 No 271-1), Explanatory Note.
222 Submission by Save the Children New Zealand to the Justice and Electoral Select Committee on the Crimes (Abolition of Force as Justification for Child Discipline) Amendment Bill, paras 5-8.
223 See Chalmers and Torbit, "Row over Christian smacking manual", The Dominion Post, 19/7/06, 1.
224 See the discussion in Brookbanks, "The Physical Discipline of Children: Proposals for Reform?" in Robertson (ed), *Essays on Criminal Law: A Tribute to Professor Gerald Orchard* Wellington, Brookers, 2004 163, 177.
225 Cf *R v Hopley* (1860) 2 F & F 2023; 175 ER 1024: the common law allowed the infliction of "moderate and reasonable" corporate punishment to correct what was "evil" in a child. See Brookbanks, previous note, 166.
226 *R v Drake* (1902) 22 NZLR 478 (CA), 486, per Denniston J.
227 *R v Halcro* [1995] 1 SCR 440 (SCC), affirming (1993) 80 CCC (3d) 320.

(3) What is "reasonable" force?

Force used for the purpose of correction must be "reasonable in the circumstances". Severe beatings will never be reasonable.[228] The word "reasonable" in the Canadian equivalent to s 59 has been held to mean "moderate" or "not excessive", and it has been suggested that whether force is excessive should depend primarily on the age and physical condition of the child.[229] However, it is surely the case that determining whether the force used has exceeded what is reasonable in the circumstances requires the court to consider such matters as the nature of the offence calling for correction, the age and character of the child, the likely effect of the punishment on the particular child, the degree and gravity of the punishment, the circumstances under which it was inflicted, and the injuries (if any) suffered.[230] The use of an implement is certainly a relevant factor: in R v W, the Court of Appeal observed that there was "ample evidence" entitling the jury to conclude that the force used was unreasonable and to convict D of assault, where D had struck his 6-year-old stepson twice across the bare buttocks with a leather belt.[231]

In *Sharma v Police*,[232] the High Court held that the slapping of a 9-year-old child three times — once on the head and twice on the legs — was not reasonable and the defence of child discipline failed. However, although the appeal against conviction was dismissed, the Court held that the existence of a protection order under the Domestic Violence Act 1995, nominating the child as a "protected person", did not preclude the appellant from raising s 59 as a justification for the use of force.

(a) Cultural characteristics

It would now appear to be a requirement of New Zealand law that in determining what constitutes reasonable force in s 59 Crimes Act 1961, a court may not exclude from its consideration a defendant's cultural background where relevant. This issue was considered in *Erick v Police*,[233] in which a father had struck his 6-year-old son numerous times about the back and face with a belt when the child had been persistently disobedient. "[E]xtensive injuries" were inflicted, although there was no permanent damage. On appeal, the High Court upheld the conviction and agreed that the force used by way of correction was unreasonable. It expressed the view that in determining the reasonableness of domestic discipline, a court may consider the "cultural characteristics" of the family or group concerned. It appeared to accept that what might be judged by the broader "New Zealand standard" as excessive force, may well by a more robust Niue yardstick represent correction that was not unreasonable in the particular cultural circumstances, and that such discipline might be administered by a variety of instruments, including sticks, belts, and "anything that is handy".

To fail to consider relevant cultural circumstances may well result in the application of an unduly rigid objectivism when determining the defendant's criminal responsibility.[234] Moreover, "reasonable in *all* the circumstances", if given a broad interpretation, is apt to include characteristics pertaining to defendants' families as well as to defendants themselves.

---

228 Robertson (ed), *Adams*, CA59.02.
229 R v Halcrow (1993) 80 CCC (3d) 320 (Southin JA).
230 R v Dupperon (1984) 16 CCC (3d) 453; 43 CR (3d) 70.
231 R v W 31/10/01, CA216/01. Cf *A v UK* [1998] Crim LR 892.
232 *Sharma v Police* [2003] 2 NZLR 473.
233 *Erick v Police* 26/2/85, Heron J, HC Auckland M1734/84, noted [1985] NZ Recent Law 227.

There is merit in the view that since legal provision is made for defendants' ethnic and other characteristics in the context of the provocation defence, it would be appropriate to allow recourse to similar personal characteristics where domestic correction is the issue under s 59.[235] However, by the same token subjective personal characteristics should not be allowed to overwhelm the objective character of the standard. In the final analysis, the criminal law exists to *stipulate* standards of conduct, not to permit citizens to act by their own mores, however ingrained or respectable those personal standards may be. Defendants ought to be held to a general standard that is applicable to all New Zealanders.[236] The "reasonable" New Zealander is a person not of exclusively British blood or background but an ordinary person in terms of a population of markedly mixed racial origins with a substantial Polynesian minority.[237]

17.9 Assault by a male on a female

Section 194(b) defines the separate offence of assault by a male on a female. On such a charge it is necessary for the prosecution to establish both an assault and the respective sexes of the two persons involved.[238] Absence of consent is not included as an express ingredient of the offence but is implicitly available because of the requirement for proof of an assault.

17.9.1 Mens rea

The mental elements of a charge under s 194(b) require the prosecution to prove that the accused intended to apply force to the complainant (the assault requirement), and that he knew she was a female. Normally, it will be assumed that the accused knew the victim was a female, but if the question is raised the prosecution must prove such knowledge.[239] There is normally no need for the prosecution explicitly to show that there was no consent, or no belief in consent, unless there was something to which the accused could point to raise a reasonable doubt on that issue.[240] The fact that an accused suffers from an impaired mental state will not necessarily exclude the requisite intent in a charge under the section. In *Police v Bannin*, the circumstances in which the accused held the victim while she struggled to escape, were held to be sufficient to have created within him the realisation that he was holding her against her will, notwithstanding his impaired mental state, and were, impliedly, sufficient evidence of an intention to assault.[241] However, intent is a factual question to be determined in every case

---

234 See comment, *Erick v Police* [1985] NZ Recent Law 227, 228. It has been suggested that a reference to "reasonable under the circumstances" in s 43 Criminal Code (Can) (the equivalent of s 59), although imposing an objective standard, permits some element of subjectivity to be considered: Greenspan (ed), *Martin's Annual Criminal Code 1997*, Aurora, Ontario, Canada Law Book Inc, 1996, CC/88.
235 Comment, *Erick v Police* [1985] NZ Recent Law 227, 228.
236 See *R v Baptiste and Baptiste* (1980) 61 CCC (2d) 438, where it was held that in determining whether the force used was reasonable under the circumstances, the court must consider the customs of contemporary Canadian community, not the customs of the accused's former country where corporal punishment may have had greater acceptance.
237 *R v Tai* [1976] 1 NZLR 102 (CA).
238 *Police v Bannin* [1991] 2 NZLR 237, also reported as *B v Police* (1991) 7 CRNZ 55, 244; 62; but see *R v Bernier* (1998) 124 CCC (3d) 383, where it was held that the guilt of the accused on a charge of indecent assault did not depend on evidence which could prove the hostile nature of an assault. The accused had used force within the meaning of the relevant statutory provisions by voluntarily touching the complainants without their consent.
239 *Chandler v R* 10/2/93, Greig J, HC Napier AP4/93.
240 *Police v Bannin* [1991] 2 NZLR 237, also reported as *B v Police* (1991) 7 CRNZ 55, 245; 62, 63.

where mental state may be in issue, and should not be assumed simply because the offender is capable of apparently purposive actions. In such a case, expert psychiatric testimony will normally be required to assess the offender's state of mind at the time of the offence and to guide the court on the broader issue of the offender's criminal responsibility.

17.10 Cruelty to a child

Although the same wrongdoing may fall within a range of other offences, cruelty to a child is also a substantive offence created by s 195 Crimes Act 1961. In *R v Mead* the applellant was charged with several counts of wilfully ill-treating a child under his care or control in a manner likely to cause unnecessary suffering contrary to s 195. The ill-treatment alleged included excessive and menial domestic chores, deprivation of food, cold baths, verbal abuse, force-feeding of cold and rotten food, and hitting. The Court held that for a charge of wilfully neglecting a child, five elements must be proved:[242]

(i) The parents must have custody, control or charge of a child;

(ii) The child must be under 16 years;

(iii) The accused must ill-treat or neglect the child;

(iv) The ill-treatment or neglect must be wilful; and

(v) The ill-treatment or neglect of the child must be in a manner to cause the child unnecessary suffering.

In dismissing the appeal, a majority of the Court of Appeal noted that the particular form that the ill-treatment took was not an ingredient in the offence. The key question for the jury is whether the alleged "course of conduct" amounts to ill-treatment or neglect.[243]

In *Police v L*,[244] there was agreement that wilful neglect is not proved simply by proving negligence on the part of the parents.[245] Indeed, the meaning of "wilfully neglects" has been considered at length by the House of Lords in *R v Sheppard*.[246]

17.10.1 "Wilfully neglects"

In *R v Sheppard*,[247] parents had been charged with wilfully neglecting their infant child. The majority held that the offence of wilful neglect was not one of strict liability to be judged by the objective test of what a reasonable person would have done. Rather, the prosecution is required to prove not only that the child needed adequate medical care, but also that the defendant had deliberately or recklessly failed to provide such care. A genuine lack of appreciation that the child needed medical care, or a failure through stupidity, ignorance, or personal inadequacy to provide that care, are good defences. The word "wilful", which

---

241 *Police v Bannin* [1991] 2 NZLR 237, also reported as *B v Police* (1991) 7 CRNZ 55, 255; 74.
242 *R v Mead* [2002] 1 NZLR 594 (CA) para 69 (per Thomas J). These are essentially the same elements as identified in earlier decisions, but broken down in greater specificity. See, eg, *Police v L* [1993] DCR 617, 620 (Judge Erber).
243 *R v Mead* [2002] 1 NZLR 594, para 84, per Thomas J. See also *R v Ryder* [1995] 2 NZLR 271; (1995) 13 CRNZ 81 (CA), 272; 83.
244 *Police v L* [1993] DCR 617, 620 (Judge Erber).
245 See *MacKenzie v Hawkins* [1975] 1 NZLR 165.
246 *R v Sheppard* [1981] AC 394; [1980] 3 All ER 899 (HL).
247 *R v Sheppard* [1981] AC 394; [1980] 3 All ER 899 (HL).

describes the state of mind of the actual doer of the act, was held to imply more than merely a "voluntary" act, and extends not only to the doing of the act itself but to the consequences to which the positive acts give rise.[248] In R v Hende,[249] the New Zealand Court of Appeal approved Lord Diplock's construction of the meaning of "wilfully". Eichelbaum CJ, delivering the judgment of the Court, said:[250]

> "In our view, the appropriate constructional approach is to regard the words 'ill-treats ... the child ... in manner likely to cause him unnecessary suffering ...' as a composite expression, which 'wilfully' qualifies as a whole."

In *Police v L*,[251] Judge Erber held that wilful neglect is proved if the parents were reckless whether harm was the consequence of their failure to provide care. Such recklessness will be established when it is proved that the parents, *being aware* both that care was required for the child and that a failure to provide or obtain it could well result in harm to the child, refrained from providing or obtaining such care despite that risk of consequential harm.[252] Normally for a prosecution to be brought under the section there would need to be some evidence of gross and habitual abuse or neglect sufficient to justify a claim that the child had been cruelly treated. Mere inadequate parenting should not qualify as wilful neglect where the parent(s) have done their best to make adequate provision for their children but have been prevented from doing so by insufficiency of financial means or lack of domestic support.

17.10.2 "Neglects"

In *Sheppard* Lord Diplock held that to "neglect" a child is to omit to act, to fail to provide adequately for her needs; meaning, in the context of the statute, her physical rather than her spiritual, educational, moral, or emotional needs.[253] The actus reus in a case of wilful neglect is simply a failure, for whatever reason, to provide a child, whenever she in fact needs something, with the thing she needs. Because the crime of cruelty to a child is a generic offence, a relevant failure need not be limited to medical aid, and could include a range of necessities including food, clothing, and accommodation. It is arguable that the New Zealand provision also extends to a failure to provide adequate emotional support to a child, if a consequence of such failure has been to cause "any mental disorder or disability". In *Police v L*,[254] a consequence of the alleged neglect was that the three children (ages 5, 3, and 2) were developmentally delayed and severely understimulated, were not toilet-trained, and in the case of one child appeared to be intellectually handicapped and autistic. However, in the absence of cogent evidence in relation to "mental disorder or disability" this question was not pursued at the hearing.

17.10.3 "Custody, control, or charge"

A condition precedent to criminal responsibility under the section is that the accused has "custody, control, or charge" of the child.[255] Although the question of whether a person is in

---

248 R v *Sheppard* [1981] AC 394; [1980] 3 All ER 899 (HL), 404 and 405; 904 (Lord Diplock).
249 R v *Hende* [1996] 1 NZLR 153 (CA).
250 R v *Hende* [1996] 1 NZLR 153 (CA), 156.
251 *Police v L* [1993] DCR 617.
252 *Police v L* [1993] DCR 617. See also 4.7.
253 R v *Sheppard* [1981] AC 394; [1980] 3 All ER 899 (HL).
254 *Police v L* [1993] DCR 617.
255 See also s 10A(b) Summary Offences Act 1981 ("a person to whom the care or custody" of a child has "been lawfully entrusted").

"custody, control, or charge" of a child has been held to be one of fact,[256] it is suggested that the legal meaning of the words, insofar as they may be ambiguous, must necessarily be a matter of law.[257] In the comparable Canadian provision, "guardian" is defined to include a person who has *in law or in fact* the "custody or control" of a child.[258] In *Thompson v Grey* the claim that there must be some legal relationship, such as parent and child or guardian and ward, was rejected. The view of the Court was that the word "care" was apt to include those having the temporary care of children and that the words of the statute extended to "persons with whom they (the children) live and who have in fact charge of them and who in fact control them".[259] This interpretive approach, which places the protective responsibility for children with those who have the *actual* custody and care of them, is consistent with modern legislation aimed at the protection of children. It emphasises the practical status of a child as a "member of [a] family" requiring protection, rather than the formal legal status of the carer.[260]

17.10.4 "Ill-treats"

Where a charge alleges the ill-treatment (rather than wilful neglect) of a child, the actus reus is the action of ill-treating (that is, badly treating) the child in a way that is likely, in an objective sense, to cause the child unnecessary suffering.[261] The word "likely" in the section means "that could well happen", and connotes a real or substantial risk rather than an assessment or balancing of the probabilities.[262] It follows that the *actual* production of "unnecessary suffering", etc is not a necessary consequence of ill-treatment, and does not have to be proved by the prosecution. It is only necessary for the prosecution to prove that there was a *real risk* that those consequences could well result from the conduct alleged. In the majority of cases, of course, it will be the consequential suffering, actual bodily harm, or injury that will have alerted the authorities to the case and provide the impetus for a criminal prosecution.[263]

---

256 See *Thompson v Grey* (1904) 24 NZLR 457.
257 *Adams* CA195.05 (looseleaf).
258 Section 214 Criminal Code (Can).
259 *Thompson v Grey* (1904) 24 NZLR 457, 474.
260 See, for example, s 2 Domestic Violence Act 1995, in which "child of the applicant's family" is defined to mean "a child who ordinarily or periodically resides with the applicant (whether or not the child is a child of the applicant and the respondent or either of them)". Compare also s 178 Crimes Act 1961 ("any child of hers" held to include not only natural children, but also any children who could, in fact, law, and common sense be said to be hers: *R v P* [1991] 2 NZLR 116; (1991) 7 CRNZ 48 (HC)).
261 *R v Hende* [1996] 1 NZLR 153 (CA), 156.
262 See *R v Gush* [1980] 2 NZLR 92 (CA), 96; *R v Fatu* [1989] 3 NZLR 419; (1989) 4 CRNZ 638 (CA), 430; 648.
263 Regarding whether "ill-treats" is limited to physical ill-treatment, see the discussion in *Adams*, CA195.07 (looseleaf).

Chapter 18

SEXUAL OFFENCES

18.1	Introduction	606
18.2	Sexual violation	607
18.2.1	Elements of sexual violation	609
(1)	*Meaning of "genitalia"*	609
(2)	*"Continuation" of sexual connection*	610
(3)	*Consent*	612
(4)	*Marital rape*	621
(5)	*Sentencing*	622
18.2.2	Mens rea of sexual violation	622
(1)	*Without believing that V consents*	623
(2)	*Without believing "on reasonable grounds" that V consents*	623
18.3	Inducing sexual connection by coercion	628
18.3.1	Threats to commit an imprisonable offence: s 129A(5)(a)	629
18.3.2	Threats of accusation or disclosure: s 129A(5)(b)	630
18.3.3	Threatened actions involving "detriment" to the victim: s 129A(5)(c)	630
18.4	Attempt to commit sexual violation	631
18.4.1	Mens rea	631
18.5	Evidentiary matters	632
18.5.1	Address and occupation of complainant	633
18.5.2	Delay in making complaint	633
18.5.3	Character of the complainant	634
18.5.4	Corroboration	636
18.6	Incest	636
18.6.1	Definition	637
18.6.2	Elements of the offence	637
(1)	*Knowledge*	637
(2)	*Proving the relationship*	638
(3)	*Mode of proof*	638
18.7	Sexual conduct with dependent family member	639
18.7.1	Mens rea	640
18.7.2	Actus reus	640

18.8	**Meeting young person under 16 following sexual grooming**	641
18.8.1	Mens rea	643
18.9	**Sexual conduct with a child under 12: s 132**	644
18.9.1	Sexual connection and attempts	645
18.10	**Sexual conduct with a young person under 16: s 134**	645
18.10.1	Consent	646
18.10.2	Proving consent-based defences	646
18.10.3	Marriage	647
18.10.4	Parties	648
18.10.5	Proof of age	648
18.11	**Indecent assault: s 135**	648
18.11.1	Indecent act	649
18.11.2	Elements of assault	649
18.11.3	Indecently	650
18.11.4	Consent	651
18.11.5	Mens rea	652
18.11.6	A lesser included offence?	653
18.12	**Sexual exploitation of person with significant impairment**	654
18.12.1	Significant impairment	656
18.12.2	Mens Rea	656
18.12.3	Consent	657
18.12.4	Acquiescence, submission, participation, or undertaking	658
18.13	**Other sexual offences**	659

18.1 Introduction

Sexual offences in New Zealand are contained in Part 7 of the Crimes Act 1961, which also provides the definitions of offences against religion, morality, and public welfare, including blasphemous libel[1] and various forms of offensive behaviour. This chapter will consider crimes of a sexual nature, including sexual violation, sexual intercourse within prohibitions of age and status, and offences of indecency. The chapter will not separately consider offences of bestiality or the "social sanitation" offences associated with prostitution and procuring sexual intercourse. Neither will the innovations in sexual offences committed outside New Zealand be considered.

It should be observed at the outset of the chapter that over the last 20 years New Zealand law on sexual offences has undergone a radical revision and is still undergoing change at the hands

---

1   Section 123 Crimes Act 1961.

of both the courts and legislators. Some of these changes, which will be considered shortly, have been driven by changing social values, and in particular by changing perceptions of the roles and status of women in society. In addition, with an increasing media profile being given to sexual abuse in all its forms there has come a greater awareness of the needs of the victims of sexual offending, which has led to changes in the way in which criminal litigation, especially that involving women and children as victims, is conducted. Not only have there been major changes to the definitions of substantive sexual crimes, but in addition there have been a number of significant changes in the law of evidence and criminal procedure which are principally geared towards making the trial process less distressing for those who are required to give evidence in such cases.

Most recently, the Crimes Amendment Act 2005 has effected a major overhaul. The Act seeks to modernise the law relating to sexual offences by placing them in a contemporary context, one that reflects changes in social attitudes toward sexual matters.[2] This is achieved by two changes of general application in the Act. First, all sexual offences, including rape, now apply on a gender-neutral basis. Secondly, sexual connection — rather than sexual intercourse — has been made the basis of most sexual offences. It is intended that these and other changes will streamline the law, making it easier to understand and apply, while improving coverage for vulnerable groups. The legislation also seeks to ensure that penalties for sexual offences are set at appropriate levels.

Key recommendations of the Law and Order Committee that have been carried into the legislation to deal with the following issues: sexual conduct with a young person under 16; sexual violation, particularly the offence of rape, and definitions of specific terms; sexual conduct with a dependent family member; sexual exploitation of a person under 18; and sexual exploitation of a person with a significant impairment. Each of these matters will be considered in detail below.

However, the discussion commences by looking first at the most serious of the redefined sexual offences: sexual violation, which includes the traditional offence of rape.

18.2 Sexual violation

Traditionally, the crime of rape was regarded as the most serious sexual offence. However, the punishment of rape has varied at different times, reflecting changing attitudes towards its seriousness. Before the Norman Conquest the offence was punishable with death. However, during William the Conqueror's reign the offence was punished by mutilation involving castration and the loss of the eyes.[3] During Edward I's reign the offence was reduced to a trespass with a punishment of only 2 years' imprisonment and a fine. However, this remarkable leniency was short-lived, and in 1285 rape became a capital felony, remaining so until the 19th century.[4] In England the maximum punishment for rape is life imprisonment, while in New Zealand the offence is punishable by up to 20 years' imprisonment.[5]

---

2   Crimes Amendment Bill (No 2) as Reported from the Law and Order Committee, Commentary, 22 October 2004, 2.
3   *Ancient Laws and Institutes of England 1840: The Laws of King William the Conqueror*, London, Great Britain Public Records Office, 1840, XII, XVIII cited in *Rook and Ward on Sexual Offences*, London, 1990, 23.
4   *Ancient Laws and Institutes of England 1840: The Laws of King William the Conqueror*, London, Great Britain Public Records Office, 1840, XII, XVIII cited in Rook and Ward on Sexual Offences, London, 1990, 23.
5   Section 128B Crimes Act 1961, as substituted by s 2 Crimes Amendment Act (No 3) 1993.

The key concepts in the modern law are "sexual violation" and "sexual connection", and their definitions have been modified by the Crimes Amendment Act 2005. Rape itself, which is specifically defined as a type of sexual violation, previously could be committed only by a man against a woman, but has now been redefined as a gender non-specific offence. (This development is contrary to the recommendation of the majority of the Law and Order Committee, which supported its being retained as a gender-based form of sexual violation.) New definition of "genitalia" and "penis" in s 2 of the Crimes Act 1961 now extend the offence of rape to include persons who have undergone surgical construction or reconstruction of their genitalia. The previous definition of rape, requiring "the act of a male who rapes a female", has been repealed. Consistent with these changes, the notion of "sexual intercourse" has been removed from the legislation and replaced by a generic and newly-defined concept of "sexual connection". The drafting of this expression reflects the previous definition, except that the earlier expression "occasioned by the penetration" has been replaced by the words "introduction into the genitalia or anus".

The new s 128 reads:

"**128 Sexual violation defined**

"(1) Sexual violation is the act of a person who—

"(a) rapes another person; or

"(b) has unlawful sexual connection with another person.

"(2) Person A rapes person B if person A has sexual connection with person B, effected by the penetration of person B's genitalia by person A's penis—

"(a) without person B's consent to the connection; and

"(b) without believing on reasonable grounds that person B consents to the connection.

"(3) Person A has unlawful sexual connection with person B if person A has sexual connection with the person B—

"(a) without the person B's consent to the connection; and

"(b) without believing on reasonable grounds that person B consents to the connection.

"(4) One person may be convicted of sexual violation of another person at a time when they were married to each other."

The new definition of "sexual connection" in s 2 provides:

"**Sexual connection** means—

"(a) Connection effected by the introduction into the genitalia or anus of one person, otherwise than for genuine medical purposes, of—

"(i) a part of the body of another person; or

"(ii) an object held or manipulated by another person; or—

"(b) connection between the mouth or tongue of one person and a part of another person's genitalia or anus; or "(c) the continuation of connection of a kind described in paragraph (a) or (b)."

18.2.1 Elements of sexual violation

From these new definitions a number of specific points in the crime of sexual violation can be identified. It is useful to summarise them before discussing the law in more detail.

First, the section defines a *generic* offence of sexual violation which is not gender specific; ie the offence is not limited to unlawful conduct by a male against a female but may embrace any combination of genders on the part both of the assailant and of the victim of a relevant sexual assault.

Secondly, the crime of rape, previously a gender- and anatomically-specific offence, has been re-defined to accommodate invasive sexual assaults on persons who have undergone gender reassignment surgery, but otherwise remains as a particular subspecies within the generic definition of sexual violation. Where rape is alleged, that offence will still typically be committed by a male against a female, although a female was always able to be a secondary party to such an offence.[6] But the use of the new descriptors "Person A" and "Person B" signifies that more than simply a man and a woman engaging in an act of (non-consensual) intercourse is intended to be caught by the section. Since the conduct defined includes "penetration" of the genitalia by a person's penis, anal "rape" is evidently excluded, because the anus is not included within the definition of "genitalia", and penetration in any other sense would appear to be foreclosed. Anal rape would, nonetheless, be included within the offence of unlawful sexual connection defined in s 128(3). The descriptors are apt, however, and are evidently intended to include invasive assaults on persons with surgically reconstructed genital organs, regardless of the person's original sexual identity.

Thirdly, the defence of believed consent will only be available where the accused is able to adduce *reasonable grounds* for his or her belief in consent.

Fourthly, the offence of sexual violation by unlawful sexual connection is not anatomically specific but may involve any non-consensual "connection" involving penetration of any part of the genitalia or anus, otherwise than for genuine medical reasons, or oral contact with any part of the genitalia or the anus of either the offender or the victim, whether male or female.[7]

Fifthly, sexual connection by "introduction" is not anatomically specific, and may be effected by non-human objects. The "slightest degree" of "introduction" is sufficient to achieve sexual connection.[8]

Sixthly, the offence may be committed by a husband against his wife or vice versa notwithstanding that they are married.

(1) Meaning of "genitalia"

In earlier legislation, the crime of rape was defined as the act of a male person having sexual intercourse with a female without her consent. Under current law, sexual connection is complete upon relevant "introduction" of the slightest degree.[9] This is generally taken to mean

---

6   See *R v Ram* (1893) 17 Cox CC 609.
7   For an examination of the law of rape from a male perspective see Morgan-Taylor and Rumney, "A male perspective on rape" (1994) 144 NLJ 1490.
8   See s 2(1A).

that there does not have to be a full act of intercourse issuing in ejaculation. Any penetration, however slight or of short duration, will suffice. Where rape is alleged, the common law definition may still apply, according to which penetration will be complete if any part of the man's penis is "within the labia or the pudendum ... no matter how little".[10] The replacement in 1994 of "vagina" by "genitalia" in s 128[11] meant that any penetration of the vulva would suffice for the crimes of female rape and sexual violation by unlawful sexual connection. The further re-definition of "sexual connection" in terms of "introduction into..." appears not to alter this position.

The consequences of these changes in the law may be seen by considering the decision of the Court of Appeal in *R v Karotu*,[12] a case involving an appeal under the earlier law against conviction on counts of sexual violation by unlawful sexual connection. The appellant practised a form of traditional island therapy known as "riring", which involved massage. The conduct alleged included massaging the clitoris of one complainant, and massaging and having oral contact with the genitalia of the other. On appeal to the Court of Appeal on a question of law, the question for the Court was whether sexual connection under the previous definition could be proved where there had been no penetration of the vagina but only penetration of the vulva. The Court held that the word "vagina" in the former s 128(5) should be interpreted according to its clearly understood medical meaning — that is, "the membranous canal leading from the vulva to the uterus" — and that the word should not be given a more liberal interpretation so as to embrace the whole of the genital area within the labia.

However, by substituting "genitalia" for "vagina", the effect of the 1994 amendment and its further refinement in the 2005 amendment has been to supersede *Karotu*; such that, wherever sexual violation by unlawful sexual connection is alleged, the merest invasion of the genitalia, whether or not this involves penetration of the vagina, will suffice.[13] Obviously, the 1994 and 2005 amendments have changed the law significantly, and future offenders should not suppose that leniency will be extended to them on the purported basis that the alleged violation involved only "slight", non-vaginal, penetration that might previously have been treated simply as an indecent assault. Whatever may have been the legislative intent regarding non-vaginal penetration prior to 1994, it is now clear that *any* non-consensual invasion of the genitalia, including of the vagina, the vulva, or of re-constituted genitalia, will constitute unlawful sexual connection. Thus the previously vital distinction between vaginal and non-vaginal penetration is no longer valid and will not support a defence to a charge of sexual violation.[14]

(2) *"Continuation" of sexual connection*

The provision for continuation in the s 2 definition of "sexual connection" at subs (c) requires a brief comment. We have noted above that, as a matter of legal definition, sexual connection is complete upon the slightest degree of invasion. This means that if D decides to have sexual intercourse with P without her consent the act of rape is complete once D has perpetrated

---

9   See s 2(1A).
10 *R v Lines* (1844) 1 Car & Kir 393; 174 ER 861; approved in *R v Karotu* (1994) 11 CRNZ 691 (CA), 694 (Casey J). For a further discussion of the meaning of "penetration" in this context see *Adams*, CA128.01-02 (looseleaf).
11 As amended by s 2 Crimes Amendment Act 1994.
12 *R v Karotu* (1994) 11 CRNZ 691 (CA), 694.
13 See s 2(1A).
14 See also *R v Randall* (1991) 55 SASR 447; 53 A Crim R 380; *R v Manuel* 11/3/94, T180/93.

even the slightest degree of penetration. But what happens if, after D has penetrated P in an act of consensual sexual intercourse, P withdraws her consent? If the act of sexual connection is "complete" upon penetration and up to that point P consents to the conduct, can one say that D has raped P because at the point P withdraws her consent D continues with the act of intercourse? Apparently so, according to their Lordships in the Privy Council decision in *R v Kaitamaki*.[15]

In *Kaitamaki*, D had been charged with one count of rape. He had broken into a house and allegedly twice raped the young woman occupier. There was no dispute that intercourse had taken place twice, but D's defence was that the woman consented or that the appellant honestly believed she was consenting. At the trial D gave evidence that after he had penetrated the woman for the second time he became aware that she was not consenting but that he did not desist from intercourse. The jury was directed that if the appellant continued the act of intercourse having realised that the woman was not consenting, it then became rape. On an appeal against conviction, the appellant argued that for the purposes of the Crimes Act 1961 a man who penetrated a woman with her consent could not become guilty of rape by continuing the intercourse after a time when he realised the woman was no longer consenting. Rape, it was contended, was penetration without consent and once penetration was complete the act of rape was concluded.

The Court of Appeal rejected this argument and dismissed the appeal. In the Privy Council, the appeal turned on the meaning of "complete" in the former s 127[16]. Their Lordships, agreeing with the majority decision of the Court of Appeal, held that "complete" is used in the statutory definition in the sense of *having come into existence*, but not in the sense of having come to an end. Sexual intercourse is a continuing act[17] which only ends with withdrawal, because the offence of rape was defined by s 128(1) as "having" intercourse without consent. It followed that the appellant had been rightly convicted and the appeal was dismissed.

The reference within the s 2 definition of "sexual connection" to "the continuation of connection" is clearly intended to incorporate the principle laid down in *Kaitamaki*, so that by implication any offence involving "sexual connection" will continue until the accused desists from the activity which constitutes the actus reus of the offence. It will not be a defence to say that the victim consented to the initial act of sexual connection if consent is withdrawn while the connection persists.[18] It may be thought that this ruling might create hardship, particularly in situations involving sexually inexperienced persons who, in situations of sexual connection falling short of actual intercourse, do not desist immediately when consent to continuing intimacy is withdrawn. While the courts are mindful of the difficulties created by such cases, they will nonetheless be concerned to uphold the intent of the legislation, which is to protect people from sexual exploitation when they have either not consented to sexual activity or withdrawn consent that earlier was perhaps given. The purpose of the law is to

---

15 *R v Kaitamaki* [1984] 1 NZLR 385, also reported as *Kaitamaki v R* (1984) 1 CRNZ 211; [1985] AC 147 (PC).
16 The notion of sexual connection being "complete" is not expressly carried over in the amended legislation. However, it is surely implicit in the idea that the "slightest degree" of "introduction" of any object, anatomical or inanimate, into the genitalia of another person without their consent is "enough to effect a connection", whether or not the "introduction" proceeds to invasive penetration. See s 2(1A).
17 See 3.2.1(2)(d), 3.2.1(3).
18 See also *R v Everson* 9/11/95, CA194/95.

uphold the right to personal autonomy in matters of sexual intimacy, and to punish those who fail to respect that right in others.

(3) Consent

Before looking at the ways in which the statute deals with the issue of consent, it might be useful to make some general observations about consent. The requirements of consent have been usefully summarised in the following passage:[19]

> "Consent must be a free and voluntary consent. It is not necessary for the victim to struggle or scream. Mere submission in consequence of force or threats is not consent. The relevant time for consent is the time when sexual intercourse occurs. Consent, previously given, may be withdrawn, thereby rendering the act non-consensual. A previous refusal may be reversed thereby rendering the act consensual. That may occur as a consequence of persuasion, but, if it does, the consequent consent must, of course, be free and voluntary and not mere submission to improper persuasion by means of force or threats."

The essence of true consent is that it is freely given by a rational and sober person so situated as to be able to form a rational opinion upon the matter to which he consents.[20] However, as with so many other concepts within the criminal law, the existence or non-existence of consent is often a matter of perception and it is never possible to determine in advance whether a particular transaction will be consensual or non-consensual. It has been observed that cases in which there is an apparent consent are always attended by circumstances which will enable a jury to determine whether there was or was not consent. The issue is essentially one of fact for the jury.[21] Each case must be considered in the light of its own facts.

The problems associated with the meaning of consent in this context are well illustrated in *R v Brewer*.[22] The complainant attended a job interview, during which the accused asked her what she would do to ensure she got the job over another applicant. After indicating that she was desperate for the job, the accused said "[w]ell, if you take off your top I can practically offer you a job". The complainant said she became frightened that the accused would attack her physically if she did not cooperate, whereupon the accused took off the complainant's shirt and fondled and kissed her breasts. The accused then said she would "definitely get the job" if she performed oral sex upon him. The complainant reluctantly complied and shortly afterwards left the room. The accused was charged under s 129A(1)(c) with inducing sexual connection by coercion.

In the High Court, on a pretrial application, Robertson J approved the view that to consent is "consciously to apply one's mind and agree to what another has proposed or desired" and appeared to agree with the proposition that submission arising from a lack of practical choices open to a victim is not consent: "It is yielding out of an inexorable instinct for human preservation."[23]

---

19 *Case Stated by DPP (No 1 of 1993)* (1993) 66 A Crim R 259, 265 (King CJ).
20 *R v M* [1993] DCR 1144, 1146 (Judge Inglis QC).
21 *R v Cook* [1986] 2 NZLR 93 (CA), 98.
22 *R v Brewer* 26/5/94, CA516/93.
23 *Brewer v R* [1994] 2 NZLR 229, also reported as *B v R (T216/93)* (1993) 11 CRNZ 419, 236; 425; Waye, "Rape and the unconscionable bargain" (1992) 16 Crim LJ 94, 94, 95. See *R v D (C)* (2000) 145 CCC (3d) 290.

On appeal against a conviction for sexual violation by unlawful sexual connection, the Court of Appeal accepted that consent would not be vitiated merely because it was induced by promises. Nor, it held, could "desperation for work" be regarded as inducing and negating consent, since the complainant would still have a choice whether to consent or not. One can still consent "with reluctance" even though some degree of coercion is present. On the other hand, a consent would not be genuine if the degree of coercion was so great that the complainant was not in a position to make a decision of her own free will. In this sense could it be said that an "inexorable instinct for human preservation" negates consent, although consent may also be negated in lesser circumstances.

So if, for example, D says to P "have sex with me and I will give you the job", the mere proposition will not of itself amount to coercion sufficient to negate consent. The reason for this is that P's choice is not foreclosed, and she still has the capacity to make an autonomous decision whether to have intercourse with D. If, however, D were to say: "You will only get the job if you have sex with me now, before X returns" knowing that X was due back very shortly, it would be arguable that the degree of coercion would be sufficiently great to submerge P's free choice and negate consent.

The present law governing the validity of consent was substituted by the Crimes Amendment Act 2005. The new s 128A involves a complete redrafting of the former section and aims to provide greater clarity about the circumstances that do not amount to consent in sexual matters. It has added a number of new instances where consent to sexual activity is negated. While these provisions do not appear to change the law as regards unconsensual sexual activity, they clarify the legal position and make it explicit. The terms of s 128A are as follows:

> "**128A Allowing sexual activity does not amount to consent in some circumstances**
>
> "(1) A person does not consent to sexual activity just because he or she does not protest or offer physical resistance to the activity.
>
> "(2) A person does not consent to sexual activity if he or she allows the activity because of—
>
> "(a) force applied to him or her or some other person; or—
>
> "(b) the threat (express or implied) of the application of force to him or her or some other person; or
>
> "(c) the fear of the application of force to him or her or some other person.
>
> "(3) A person does not consent to sexual activity if the activity occurs while he or she is asleep or unconscious.
>
> "(4) A person does not consent to sexual activity if the activity occurs while he or she is so affected by alcohol or some other drug that he or she cannot consent or refuse to consent to the activity.
>
> "(5) A person does not consent to sexual activity if the activity occurs while he or she is affected by an intellectual, mental, or physical condition or impairment of such a nature and degree that he or she cannot consent or refuse to consent to the activity.

"(6) One person does not consent to sexual activity with another person if he or she allows the sexual activity because he or she is mistaken about who the other person is.

"(7) A person does not consent to an act of sexual activity if he or she allows the act because he or she is mistaken about its nature and quality.

"(8) This section does not limit the circumstances in which a person does not consent to sexual activity.

"(9) For the purposes of this section—

"**allows** includes acquiesces in, submits to, participates in, and undertakes

"**sexual activity**, in relation to a person, means,—

"(a) sexual connection with the person; or

"(b) the doing on the person of an indecent act that, without the person's consent, would be an indecent assault of the person."

Subsection (8) may be taken as an indication that all matters bearing on the existence of consent will be relevant, and may include any coercion of the complainant such that he could be said not to be in a position to make a decision of his own free will.[24] Similarly, evidence that the complainant suffered from post-traumatic stress disorder, whether or not that condition falls within the scope of s 128A(5), may be admitted to support a claim that true consent had been lacking.[25] The matters specified in subss (3) to (7) may be important parts of the surrounding circumstances from which consent, or the lack of it, may be inferred. However, they are not determinative in themselves.[26] The relevance of such matters is that they assist a tribunal of fact to determine whether the complainant understood her situation and was capable of making up her mind when agreeing to sexual acts; which is of the essence to a valid consent.[27]

(a) Failure to "protest or offer physical resistance": s 128A(1)

The absence of consent, which is an essential element in the actus reus of sexual violation, is not to be equated simply with the use of force. The issue is: did the complainant consent? There may be an absence of consent even though no force is used at all and even though the complainant offers no protest or resistance. The critical issue is not whether the act was against the victim's will, but whether it was without her consent. For this reason, it is wrong to assume that the complainant must show signs of injury or that she must always physically resist before there can be a conviction for sexual violation. In R v Hallett,[28] several people were charged with the rape of a prostitute outside a brothel. Coleridge J instructed the jury that if there was no resistance on the complainant's part, but the non-resistance proceeded merely from being overpowered by actual force, or from her not being able because of lack of strength to resist any longer, or because she considered that the number of the assailants meant that resistance was useless, then consent was absent and the actus reus was proved.[29]

---

24 R v Brewer 26/5/94, CA516/93.
25 Cf R v Pauga [1992] 3 NZLR 241; (1992) 8 CRNZ 169.
26 See R v Isherwood 14/3/05, CA182/04.
27 R v Isherwood 14/3/05, CA182/04.
28 R v Hallett (1841) 9 C & P 748; 173 ER 1036.
29 R v Hallett (1841) 9 C & P 748; 173 ER 1036.

18.2.1 ELEMENTS OF SEXUAL VIOLATION

The Crown is not required to prove a positive dissent by the complainant. In *R v Murphy*[30] the accused was convicted of rape after he had swapped places with another man he found in his bed and had sex with a woman who had been sleeping there. M had returned to his house to find a couple asleep in his bed. He asked them to leave but only the man did so. He claimed she had rolled over and said she "just wanted to sleep". Soon afterwards, M had sex with the woman from behind. No words were spoken, and she did not look at him. In convicting the accused, the jury evidently disbelieved his claim that the woman made the sexual advances and was a willing participant throughout, and preferred the Crown's view that a reasonable person would not get into bed with a woman he had never met before. If that did happen, a reasonable person would then ensure the woman knew it was not the same man she had been in bed with earlier, before any sexual activity took place.

The case illustrates the principle that the fact that a person does not protest or offer resistance to sexual connection does not by itself constitute consent.[31] There was no suggestion that M had used force. However, the Judge directed that if a person consented to sex by reason of a mistaken identity, it was not a valid consent.[32] It has also been held that submission to the inevitable, or out of despair when trapped, is not real consent, even if the submission involves a degree of physical assistance given by the victim to the offender.[33] In *R v Daniels*, the victim assisted one of the offenders by helping him to place his penis in her vagina, an act which in the circumstances of the case was held to be "not truly voluntary".[34]

But where the appellant's own evidence was throughout consistent with a belief in consent and there is nothing in the complainant's evidence or the surrounding circumstances which objectively indicates that the complainant is not consenting, the evidence may be insufficient to support a charge of sexual violation.[35] In *R v Tawera* the complainant did not request the appellant to stop during 10 minutes in which he performed oral sex on her and had full sexual intercourse, nor was she threatened in any way. She had not attempted to push his head away during oral sex and made no reply when he requested sexual intercourse. Nor did she make any attempt to get off the appellant before the act was completed, or give any overt indication that the appellant should desist. The Court concluded that there was nothing said, done, or exhibited by the complainant from the time the sexual advances commenced to the conclusion of the incident which would outwardly demonstrate she was not consenting. In these circumstances it was unwilling to allow the convictions for sexual violation by unlawful sexual connection and rape to stand, since the evidence was such that the jury was left in a reasonable doubt on the issue of consent.[36] Normally, it will not be enough for a complainant to say, "I was afraid of serious bodily harm and therefore consented". In practice, in order to prove lack

---

30 *R v Murphy* 26/9/96, CA310/96.
31 Section 128A(1).
32 Section 128A(6).
33 *R v Daniels* [1986] 2 NZLR 106, also reported as *R v Daniels and Tihi* (1986) 2 CRNZ 164 (CA).
34 *R v Daniels* [1986] 2 NZLR 106, 110.
35 *R v Tawera* (1996) 14 CRNZ 290 (CA).
36 See also *R v Bursey* (1957) 118 CCC 219; 26 CR 167 (Ont CA). It is curious that the defendant in *Tawera* was not also charged with having sexual intercourse with a girl under care or protection under the former s 131, since the complainant was only 16 and was, at the time of the offence, as far as can be judged, "living with him as a member of his family" (cf s 131(1)(a). The new s 131(1) refers to having sexual connection with "a dependent family member"). She evidently regarded him as a guardian. Had he been charged under the former s 131, the fact that the complainant had consented, or that he believed she had, would have been no defence.

of consent beyond reasonable doubt, the prosecution will normally have to lead evidence that the victim had a genuine reason to be afraid and (where possible) made some attempt to avoid the outrage.[37]

Tawera may be contrasted with the Canadian case of *R v Ewanchuk*,[38] which adopts a subjective approach to the question of the complainant's non-consent, focusing purely on her actual state of mind rather than on how (if at all) she manifested that state of mind. The Court in *Ewanchuk* rejected the notion that a complainant's failure to communicate her fear, including any steps she might take to project a relaxed and unafraid appearance to her attacker, necessarily renders her subjective feelings irrelevant. It held that if the trier of fact accepts the complainant's testimony that she did not consent, regardless of how strongly her outward conduct may contradict that claim, the absence of consent is established. This approach is surely correct. It exposes as specious any notion of implied consent resting on the assumption that, unless a woman protests or resists, she should be deemed to consent.[39] At first glance, however, it is difficult to reconcile this approach with that in *Tawera*, which seems to concentrate on the objective indicia of consent. It is submitted that the decision in *Tawera* should be understood as turning only on a point of evidence and not as laying down any substantive rule or presumption of law regarding the actus reus element of non-consent. The prosecution must prove that V did not consent; it does not have to prove that she manifested that lack of consent (although evidence of the latter will help with the former). The strictness of this view is offset by the fact that outward behaviour will also be relevant to proof of D's mens rea: ie to whether D's belief that V was consenting was a reasonable one for him to have had.[40] However, the fact that there has been no communication of the complainant's lack of consent is of marginal relevance to the actus reus issue, which is simply whether consent was present, considered from the standpoint of the complainant.[41]

(b)   Force, threat or fear: s 128A(2)

Under s 128A(2), consent may be negatived where force, threat of force, or fear of force to the complainant or some other person is the reason sexual activity has been allowed. Consent may be absent even though there is no conduct and no misrepresentation by the offender that is intended to extort consent. The essence of consent, as has already been noted, is that it:[42]

> "should be freely given ... Although the victim of duress may intentionally submit to another, this submission arises from the lack of practical choice open to the victim. Submission is not consent. It is yielding out of an inexorable instinct for human preservation."

So if P submits or acquiesces to sexual connection because of the actual, threatened, or feared application of "force" to P or to another, consent will be negated. An honestly held fear of

---

37   *R v Jones* [1935] 2 WWR 270; (1934) 63 CCC 341.
38   *R v Ewanchuk* (1999) 131 CCC (3d) 481 (SCC), 494. But see Brett, "Sexual offenses and consent" (1998)11 Can J Law & Juris 69.
39   *R v Ewanchuk* (1999) 131 CCC (3d) 481 (SCC), 518 (L'Heureux-Dubé J).
40   Note that this approach to the issue of honest belief in consent is also advocated by L'Heureux-Dubé and McLachlin JJ, in their dissenting judgments in *R v Esau* (1997) 116 CCC (3d) 289, 300, 308.
41   *R v Moungakiholoto* HC, Auckland, T001435, 13/11/00, Baragwanath J.
42   Waye, "Rape and the unconscionable bargain" (1992) 16 Crim LJ 94, 95. Cited in *Brewer v R* [1994] 2 NZLR 229, also reported as *B v R (T216/93)* (1993) 11 CRNZ 419, 235; 424-425.

force will negate consent, whether or not the fear was reasonable, and there is no requirement that the application of force be immediately at hand.

A useful illustration of the difference between genuine consent and mere submission is *R v Olugboja*.[43] In that case, the 16-year-old complainant, having previously been raped by one defendant, was pushed on to a settee whereupon a second defendant had intercourse with her. She did not struggle or resist, and did not cry out for help. The English Court of Appeal held that the events leading up to the intercourse, together with the complainant's reaction to those events, justified the jury's finding that she did not consent, even though she submitted to intercourse without being subjected to violence or threats of violence.

On the other hand, force certainly includes the use of physical coercion or direct physical violence to bring about submission. One exception was said to arise in *Case Stated by DPP*,[44] where it was held that "rougher than usual handling" in the nature of "boisterous playfulness" as a means of attempting to persuade a wife to consent to sexual intercourse will not of itself negate consent, provided that the conduct is actually acceptable to the wife. However, it is difficult to imagine the concept of "rougher than usual handling" having any wider application than within the context of marriage or of a relationship in the nature of marriage. Indeed, the mere touching of a stranger may negate consent.[45] Because of these possible variations, the parameters of (im)permissible force are not clear. In *Olugboja*, the Court assumed that fear may vitiate consent in rape even though it is not a fear of violence, but did not specify the sort of fear that might have that effect. However, the degree of force, the relative strengths, ages, and sexes of the complainant and of the third party, and the relationship between the complainant and the assaulted third party may all be relevant factors in determining whether an application of force will vitiate consent.[46]

Whether psychological pressure alone will vitiate consent is not yet clear. It is possible to imagine a situation in which a person is told that unless she agrees to sexual activity with the offender, whose mana or charisma she admires, something malevolent of a "spiritual" nature might occur. The implied threat is not of force per se, but to invoke "forces" which the complainant fears because of her belief in their power adversely to affect her life. Such a case may turn on whether the threat involves the "fear of the application *of force* to that person or some other person". Mere fear or apprehension that something untoward might happen to the complainant in the event that consent is not forthcoming would not seem to satisfy the requirement that force be "actual" or "threatened". Nor would it seem to satisfy the requirement under s 128A(2)(c) of "fear of the *application* of force". What is required, it appears, is a fear that the complainant will suffer some bodily harm, albeit not grave harm, if she does not consent.

The Canadian case of *R v F (DS)*[47] supplies a useful illustration of this type of implied threat. After engaging in unwanted sexual advances to the complainant, D had then said that "if you leave now I'll kick both you and your brother out". The Court held that, while the words were not of themselves sufficient to constitute a threat to apply force, in the context of the complainant's fears and a history of ongoing physical abuse, it was open to the jury to find

---

43 *R v Olugboja* [1981] 3 All ER 443 (CA).
44 *Case Stated by DPP (No 1 of 1993)* (1993) 66 A Crim R 259, 266.
45 Bryant, "The issue of consent in the crime of sexual assault" (1989) 68 Can Bar Rev 94, 112.
46 Bryant, "The issue of consent in the crime of sexual assault" (1989) 68 Can Bar Rev 94, 113.
47 *R v F (DS)* (1999) 132 CCC (3d) 97, 117 (Ont CA).

that the words did constitute a threat to apply force and that the complainant submitted to the act of intercourse by reason of that threat. The wording of the New Zealand provision permits the same approach to be taken in a similar fact situation.

(c)   Sexual activity while complainant asleep or unconscious: s 128A(3)

The new s 128A(3) introduces sexual activity occurring while the complainant is asleep or unconscious as a further case of non-consent. The subsection is expressed in absolute terms; suggesting that, provided the complainant is unconscious at the time of the activity, prior consent to, or acceptance of, unconscious sexual activity will not constitute consent.[48] Neither will a consensual continuance of activity that commenced while the complainant was asleep or unconscious render the prior conduct consensual.[49] This has very significant implications for sexual activity occurring within intimate relationships in the nature of marriage or civil union. It implies that any "unconsented–to" sexual connection *of any degree*, occurring while the complainant is asleep or unconscious, will necessarily amount to unlawful sexual connection, regardless of the pre-agreed preferences or agreements of the parties. At this stage, the parameters of this remarkable rule have not been tested by the courts. However, its practical absurdity ought to be the subject of early law reform.

(d)   Sexual activity while complainant affected by alcohol or some other drug: s 128A(4)

Subsection (4) deals with incapacity induced by alcohol or some other drug. Like subs (3), the subsection is new and deals with the problem of drug-induced unconsciousness and sedative incapacitation rendering a person unable to resist or object.

(e)   Sexual activity while complainant affected by impairment: s 128A(5)

The relationship between subs (5) and the offence of sexual exploitation of a person with significant impairment, contrary to s 138 (below, 18.12), will involve difficult judgements of degree. Where the accused has sexual activity with someone who is "affected by an intellectual, mental, or physical condition or impairment", the court will need to determine whether the impairment was sufficiently severe as to deprive the complainant of the capacity to give or withhold consent. If that is the case then, subject to the other elements of the offence being present, a conviction for sexual violation is appropriate. If not, then consideration should be given to s 138, at least where the accused has taken advantage of the complainant's vulnerability.

When will the complainant's capacity to consent be negated? Broadly speaking, the capacity to consent focuses attention on V's mental capacity at the time of the sexual act, in particular on V's ability to understand the meaning and implications of his decision. Those questions involve matters of psychological rather than palpable fact, and may require determination on a case-by-case basis.

To some extent, the common law is already familiar with such difficulties. In *Fletcher*,[50] for example, V was 13 years old and of weak intellect. It was ruled that she was incapable of giving consent if so deficient mentally as to be unable to make any judgment about what she should do. But the codification effected by s 128A(5) also signals the opportunity to reject some early authority to the effect that arousal of what was termed "animal instinct" would preclude a

---

48   *Adams*, CA128A.05(1).
49   *Adams*, CA128A.05(1).
50   *Fletcher* (1859) Bell 63, 169 ER 1168, 70; 1171.

finding of rape.[51] Those cases should be disregarded. It is clearly unacceptable that D should be able to defend a charge of sexual violation, in cases where V is, say, a learning-disabled person, by raising the possibility of sexual arousal on the part of V prior to connection.[52] A rational understanding of the nature of the act should be required.

(f)   Mistake as to identity: s 128A(6)

Consent may also be negated where the complainant makes a mistake about the identity of the person with whom the sexual connection occurs. The reason for this is that consent is not effective if the complainant has not been given an opportunity to make an informed choice as to who she will share sexual intimacies with. Under earlier law, the mistake was limited to a mistaken belief that the offender was the complainant's spouse. This limitation no longer applies. However, s 128A(6) will continue to apply to situations where consent is obtained as a result of a man impersonating a woman's husband or partner. In such cases, for personation to occur there must be an intentional passing off by assuming the character of another person, something that can only be established by considering what was in the mind of the accused person (usually as evidenced by his overt acts).[53] Because the Act now imposes an objective standard for belief in consent, it is arguable that there is now an evidential onus on the "imposter" to show reasonable grounds for believing that the woman was not mistaken as to identity.

(g)   Other mistakes

Even if a mistake by the complainant is of a kind not covered by s 128A(6), the existence of the provision does not limit the circumstances in which consent is vitiated,[54] and earlier decisions where consent was found to be either valid or vitiated presumably retain their authority unless inconsistent with the new provision.[55] In *Papadimitropoulos v R*,[56] the complainant was a Greek woman whom the accused had fraudulently induced into believing that she and the accused had gone through a ceremony of marriage. She could not speak English. The marriage "proceeding" was only the lodging of the notice of their intention to marry. Following the false marriage, sexual intercourse took place on a number of occasions, although it was clear that the complainant would not have consented to the acts of intercourse if she had not believed she was married. The High Court of Australia affirmed that mistakes about the identity of the alleged rapist and the character of the physical act done would negate any apparent consent of the victim, but that since, here, the victim was neither mistaken whether she was taking part in an act of sexual intercourse nor mistaken about the identity of the defendant, her mistake did not negate her consent. In *R v Murphy*,[57] on the other hand, consent was negated because it was unreasonable for the accused to have intercourse with a stranger before ascertaining that she knew his true identity. However, where the mistake is

---

51   *Fletcher* (1866) LR 1 CCR 39; *Barratt* (1873) LR 2 CCR 81.
52   Speaking of this possibility, Palles CB remarked that it would be "abhorrent to our best feelings and ... discreditable to any jurisprudence in which it might succeed in obtaining a place": *Dee* (1884) 15 Cox CC 579, 594.
53   *R v Kake* [1960] NZLR 595 (CA).
54   See s 128A(3).
55   Orchard, "Sexual violation: The rape law reform legislation" (1986) 12 NZULR 97, 100.
56   *Papadimitropoulos v R* (1958) 98 CLR 249; [1958] ALR 21 (HCA).
57   See 18.2.1(3)(a).

directed to the nature of the relationship with the accused person and not the defendant's identity, it will not negate consent.

Similarly, consent will not necessarily be negated simply because the complainant was mistaken as to the accused's purpose. In R v Mobilio,[58] the accused was charged with eight counts of rape relating to his activities when employed as a radiographer. It was alleged that on eight separate occasions he had introduced an ultrasound transducer or probe into the vaginas of a number of young women without their consent. Although this procedure was normally practised by passing the probe over the patient's abdomen, it was sometimes performed as an internal examination. Upon referral by their own doctors to the clinic in which the defendant worked, the victims had each consented to the procedure. The Victorian Supreme Court had to decide whether the consent was negated on the basis that the transducer was not being used for medical diagnostic purposes but rather to satisfy the defendant's prurient sexual needs. The Court held that the consent in each case was not negated by a mistake as to the defendant's purpose, but was real even though given for a purpose with an entirely different moral complexion. The fact that the accused acted in a most improper way does not, of itself, negate consent.[59] It must be proved that the mistake was such as to actually negate consent at the time of the act of unlawful sexual connection. It is likely, therefore, that a mistaken belief that a voyeur present at a medical examination is a doctor present in that capacity,[60] or ignorance that a partner is infected[61] with a disease, will continue to fall within the sorts of mistaken beliefs that do not negate consent to sexual connection.

(h)   Mistake about the "nature and quality of the act": s 128A(7)

In the criminal law there is no general rule that fraud vitiates consent. Under earlier law, s 128 provided expressly for only two forms of fraud — impersonation of the husband, and fraud in respect of the nature and quality of the act. It was thought that no other form of fraud could negative an actual consent to the act of intercourse.[62] The comparable provisions in the present statute refer only to "mistake" about identity and about the nature and quality of the act, which leaves the question: does "mistake" now include consent induced by fraud more generally? The issue does not appear to have arisen directly in the case law, but it seems generally to be assumed that the law on this point is unchanged, and that consent given as a result of fraud is a valid consent, unless the induced mistake is about identity or the nature and quality of the act.

This may sometimes lead to difficulties. The fraud is likely to be a significant factor in inducing a consent, but it is not clear that there will be a consequent "mistake" about identity or the nature and quality of the act. For example, it is arguably inapt to suggest that when the complainant in R v Flattery[63] submitted to intercourse in the belief that the defendant was

---

58   R v Mobilio [1991] 1 VR 339; (1990) 50 A Crim R 170. See discussion of this case in Waye, "Rape and the unconscionable bargain" (1992) 16 Crim LJ 94, 99.
59   See Brewer v R [1994] 2 NZLR 229, also reported as B v R (T216/93) (1993) 11 CRNZ 419, 235; 425.
60   See Bolduc v R (1967) 63 DLR (2d) 82; [1967] SCR 677 (SCC); also Roberts, "Dr Bolduc's speculum and the Victorian rape provisions" (1984) 8 Crim LJ 296.
61   R v Clarence (1888) 22 QBD 23; [1886-90] All ER Rep 133, 44; 145: "The woman's consent here was as full and conscious as consent could be. It was not obtained by any fraud, either as to the nature of the act or as to the identity of the agent. The injury done was done by a suppression of the truth."
62   Adams (2nd ed), para 977.
63   R v Flattery (1877) 2 QBD 410.

treating her medically, consent was vitiated because she was "mistaken" as to the nature and quality of the act. Rather, it appears that she was induced to consent by a fraudulent representation about the beneficial consequences of the act. Similarly, in *R v Williams*,[64] where the appellant, a choirmaster, had intercourse with the 16-year-old complainant under the pretence that her breathing was not quite right, and that he had to perform an "operation" to make an air passage to enable her to produce her voice properly, the language of mistake seems inappropriate to describe an affirmative belief *induced by fraud* that she was being medically and surgically treated. What if, on the same facts, the complainant made no mistake as to the nature of the act of intercourse but accepted the choirmaster's assurances that it would, in any event, improve her breathing, and agreed to intercourse on that basis? Clearly, in those circumstances, the fraudulent representation would be an important factor in the girl's consent but it could hardly be said she was "mistaken" as to the nature of the act itself. Yet we would want to ensure that the deceitful choirmaster was unable to benefit from his outrageous misrepresentation and would regard him as a fit object for punishment.

What seems critical in cases of rape where consent is induced under the pretext of "medical treatment" is the element of *fraudulent persuasion*, often involving complainants who are either young and inexperienced or persons who are sexually naive. If a purpose of rape legislation is to protect the sexual autonomy of women then the law should target that conduct which impugns the ability of a woman to make a free and autonomous decision to have sexual intercourse, even in circumstances where there is some understanding of the nature of the act of sexual connection.[65] In essence, consent may be vitiated by other factors, in addition to a mistake.

For these reasons we would suggest that the wording of s 128A(7) might be improved were it amended to refer to "a mistake, or a belief induced by fraud, as to the nature, quality, or consequences of the act". This range of application would better reflect the diversity of circumstances where consent may be vitiated by fraud than is possible through the limited concept of mistake.

(4) *Marital rape*

At common law the traditional rule, until quite recently, was that a man could not rape his wife, save in certain exceptional cases. The common law position was largely based on the view of Lord Hale, who stated that a husband "cannot be guilty of a rape committed by himself upon his lawful wife, for by their mutual matrimonial consent and contract the wife hath given up herself in this kind unto her husband, which she cannot retract".[66] It is only in recent decades that the basis of this rule has begun to be questioned in the common law.

In New Zealand, the common law in this regard is no longer applicable and the issue of spousal immunity is now covered exclusively by statute. Under the former s 128(3) Crimes Act 1961,

---

64   *R v Williams* [1923] 1 KB 340; [1922] All ER Rep 433 (CCA).
65   See *R v Harms* [1944] 2 DLR 61, where the victim consented to an act of sexual intercourse after being fraudulently persuaded that it was a necessary part of her medical treatment. The case was held to be rape. But cf *Boro v Superior Court* 163 Cal App 3d 1224; 210 Cal Rptr 122 (1985), where the Californian Court of Appeal held that it was not rape when a quack doctor persuaded a woman that she had a fatal disease which could be treated by sexual intercourse with a donor injected with a vaccinating serum, and had intercourse under the pretence that he was the anonymous donor. It was held the woman understood the nature and quality of the act.
66   1 Hale PC 629. See *Rook and Ward on Sexual Offences*, London, 1990, para 2.19.

as amended in 1980, a man could not be convicted of the rape of his wife unless at the time of the intercourse they were living apart in separate residences.[67] This exception was abolished in 1985 when the present s 128 was enacted. Subsection (4) now provides that a person can be convicted of sexual violation in respect of sexual connection with another person notwithstanding that they were married at the time the sexual connection occurred. As well as being no defence to a charge of sexual violation, the fact that the parties are married or have been in a continuing relationship will not warrant a reduction in sentence. There is now, therefore, no distinction in principle to be drawn between sexual violation in marriage and outside of marriage.[68] Furthermore, as *R v D*[69] makes clear, even if D's alleged act of sexual connection is no more than digital penetration of his wife's vagina, there will be no lessening in the seriousness of the charge where the act is itself one of "forceful aggression" and calculated to belittle the wife and degrade her.[70]

(5) *Sentencing*

Once an offence of sexual violation has been proved the court is bound, in sentencing, to consider the terms of s 128B(2) and (3),[71] which mandates the imposition of a sentence of imprisonment unless having regard to "(a) the particular circumstances of the person convicted; and (b) the particular circumstances of the offence, including the nature of the conduct constituting it", the Court thinks that the offender should not be sentenced to imprisonment. This provision applies whether or not the offender is married to the victim.[72] In *R v D* there was held to be no mitigation in viewing the incident as an act of aggression rather than as an expression of sexual interest, but leniency could be extended in fixing the term of imprisonment required by s 128B(2) because of factors peculiar to the particular case. In *R v D* these included the fact that the offender was unlikely to reoffend in this way, that he had no proclivity for perversion or sexual violation of victims, and the good reputation of the offender in his local area.[73]

18.2.2 Mens rea of sexual violation

The statutory definition of sexual violation is silent on the required mental element. Sexual violation requires an "act" (s 128(1)), and it is implicit that this must be conscious and voluntary.[74] Apart from this the only specified fault element is that the offender acted "without believing on reasonable grounds" that the other person consented to the sexual connection in question.[75] However, being a "true" crime, it is clear that the offence requires mens rea as to the remaining ingredients of the actus reus, and so cannot be committed accidentally. In

---

67 See s 189(1) and Schedule 1 Family Proceedings Act 1980.
68 *R v D* [1987] 2 NZLR 272 (CA). For an analysis of the case and its implications for marital rape, see Brookbanks, "Case and comment: Sexual violation within marriage" [1989] NZLJ 3.
69 *R v D* [1987] 2 NZLR 272 (CA).
70 *R v D* [1987] 2 NZLR 272 (CA), 276.
71 Inserted by s 2 Crimes Amendment Act (No 3) 1985.
72 See *R v N (an accused)* [1987] 2 NZLR 268; (1987) 2 CRNZ 513 (CA), 270; 515 (Casey J), where a sentence of 3 years' imprisonment imposed on the applicant for the sexual violation of his wife was upheld on appeal: "Parliament has made no distinction in the penalties between spousal and other kinds of rape, and the sense of outrage and violation experienced by a woman in that position can be equally as severe."
73 *R v D* [1987] 2 NZLR 272 (CA), 275.
74 Orchard, "Sexual violation: The rape law reform legislation" (1986) 12 NZULR 97, 102. See generally 3.4.
75 Section 128(2)(b) and (3)(b).

effect, since it is usually meaningless to talk of a person *recklessly* having intercourse, the offence requires that D intend to have intercourse with the victim.

Of course, intercourse or sexual connection per se is not a crime, unless it occurs without the consent of the victim. It follows, therefore, that there are two different mental elements in the crime of sexual violation. The first is the *intention* to have sexual intercourse. The second is the *absence of belief, based on reasonable grounds*, in consent. Accordingly, we may say that the offence of unlawful sexual connection (including rape) will be committed where a sane person:

(i) Intentionally has sexual connection;

(ii) In circumstances where the victim does not consent;

(iii) Either without believing that the victim consents, or without having a reasonable belief that the victim consents.

(1) *Without believing that V consents*

It follows from this that there are alternative grounds for establishing mens rea on the part of the defendant. Irrespective of whether there are reasonable grounds for believing that V has consented, D will have the mens rea of sexual violation if he in fact does not believe V has consented. But what does "believe" actually mean in this context? As a subjective standard, belief requires an assessment of the actual state of mind of the accused. However, argument may arise as to what states of mind qualify as "believing". Would it suffice, for example, on a charge of rape that the accused assumed the victim was consenting but made no inquiry to that effect. Would indifference to whether or not the victim was consenting negate a belief in consent? It would seem that if a person has thought about the matter and has concluded, without doubt, that the other person is consenting, that will constitute a belief in consent.[76] However, where the accused admits to having doubts about whether the victim was consenting, or asserts that he believed she was *probably* consenting, that would seem to raise a serious question whether the accused possessed the requisite belief in consent. Certainly, it would raise a doubt that he "cared" whether or not she consented.

The indifference criterion appears not to be decisive, since it has been held that in "rare cases" a person may not be guilty of rape if, intending to have intercourse with a woman whether or not she is consenting, he mistakenly believes on reasonable grounds that in fact she is consenting.[77] Rather, the standard of belief appears to be that of subjective recklessness.[78] If D recognises that there is a genuine (and not merely "fantastic" or "remote"[79]) possibility that V is not consenting, then he has the mens rea for sexual violation. This is, in essence, the definition of recklessness approved in *DPP v Morgan*,[80] namely, an "intention of having intercourse willy-nilly not caring whether the victim consents or no".[81]

(2) *Without believing "on reasonable grounds" that V consents*

The mens rea test discussed in 18.2.2(1) used to be the *only* applicable test. Before its amendment in 1985,[82] and as a result of the decision in *DPP v Morgan*,[83] the law was that if, at

---

76 Orchard, "Sexual violation: The rape law reform legislation" (1986) 12 NZULR 97, 103.
77 *R v Brown* (1975) 10 SASR 139 (Bray CJ). See also the comments in *R v Wozniak* (1977) 16 SASR 67, 71.
78 For further discussion, see 4.3, 4.3.2.
79 *R v Wozniak* (1977) 16 SASR 67, 74.
80 *DPP v Morgan* [1976] AC 182; [1975] 2 All ER 347 (HL), 215; 362.

the time of intercourse, the defendant had a mistaken belief that the woman was consenting, he could not be convicted of rape, even if he had no reasonable grounds for such a belief.[84] While this approach reflects the standard of recklessness now applied by New Zealand courts in respect of the majority of statutory offences,[85] it is no longer the sole basis of liability for sexual violation.

In R v Clarke,[86] the New Zealand Court of Appeal affirmed that the introduction of an objective standard into s 128 was intended to displace the subjective approach enunciated in *Morgan* — namely that honest belief in consent was sufficient to deny mens rea and exculpate the defendant. The statutory test now effectively gives rise to a mixed subjective and objective standard of mens rea.[87] In *Millar v MOT*,[88] Somers J described s 128 as making rape an offence of negligence. Accordingly, sexual violation is now established *either* when the accused was *aware* of the possibility that the victim might not be consenting but persisted regardless, *or* when he was indifferent and gave no thought to the possibility that the victim might not be consenting in circumstances in which a reasonable person would have thought about that possibility, *or* even when he positively assumed that the victim had consented in circumstances in which a reasonable person would have recognised the truth.

The impact of these changes should not be underestimated. In effect, they have converted rape in New Zealand into a negligence-based offence insofar as "fault" in sexual violation offences now lies exclusively in the fact that D's belief falls short of an objective standard. This approach is contrary to developments in English law where, in relation to sexual offences generally, the House of Lords has concluded that, as a matter of principle, the "honest belief" (ie subjective) approach to mistakes is preferable.[89] On the other hand, in jurisdictions where recklessness remains the mens rea requirement for rape, it has often been argued that recklessness should, in that context, bear the objective meaning proposed in *MPC v Caldwell*.[90] In *R v Kitchener* Kirby P stated:[91]

> "To criminalise conscious advertence to the possibility of non-consent, but to excuse the reckless failure of the accused to give a moment's thought to that possibility, is self-evidently unacceptable. In the hierarchy of wrongdoing such total indifference to the

---

81 See *R v Satnam; R v Kewal* (1984) 78 Cr App R 149; [1985] Crim LR 236 (CA), 154; 237. The Court approved the expression "couldn't care less" adopted in *R v Kimber* [1983] 3 All ER 316; [1983] 1 WLR 1118 (CA), 320; 1123, to describe a reckless state of mind. See also *R v Taylor* (1985) 80 Cr App R 327 (CA), 332. These decisions represent a retreat by the English Court of Appeal from its earlier view, expressed in *R v Pigg* [1982] 2 All ER 591; [1982] 1 WLR 762 (CA), that reckless rape could be committed where the accused "gave no thought to the possibility that the woman might not be consenting" (599; 772).
82 Section 2 Crimes Amendment Act (No 3) 1985.
83 *DPP v Morgan* [1976] AC 182; [1975] 2 All ER 347 (HL).
84 See, for example, *R v Kaitamaki* [1980] 1 NZLR 59 (CA), 63, 64.
85 Cf *Adams*, CA20.29 (looseleaf).
86 *R v Clarke* [1992] 1 NZLR 147 (CA), 149.
87 *R v Clarke* [1992] 1 NZLR 147 (CA), 149.
88 *Millar v MOT* [1986] 1 NZLR 660; (1986) 2 CRNZ 216 (CA), 677; 234.
89 See *B (a minor) v DPP* [2000] 2 AC 428; [2000] 1 All ER 833 (HL), 462; 837 (Lord Nicholls). Indeed, in Lord Nicholls' view, the persistence of the "traditional formulation" that a mistaken belief must be based on reasonable grounds is no more than a relic from the days when the defendant in a criminal case could not give evidence in his own defence.
90 *MPC v Caldwell* [1982] AC 341, also reported as *R v Caldwell* [1981] 1 All ER 961 (HL). See 4.3.1.
91 *R v Kitchener* (1993) 29 NSWLR 696, 697, approved in *R v Tolmie* (1995) 84 A Crim R 293, 303.

consent of a person to have sexual intercourse is plainly reckless, at least in our society today. Every individual has a right to the human dignity of his or her own person. Having sexual intercourse with another, without the consent of that other, amounts to an affront to that other's human dignity and an invasion of the privacy of that person's body and personality. It would be unacceptable to construe a provision ... so as to put outside the ambit of what is 'reckless' a complete failure to advert to whether or not the subject of the proposed sexual intercourse consented to it or declined consent. Such a law would simply reaffirm the view that our criminal law, at crucial moments, fails to provide principled protection to the victims of unwanted sexual intercourse, most of whom are women."

As academics have recognised, the justification for importing an objective standard attaching to the accused's belief, contrary to normal principles of criminal liability,[92] in respect of one of the most serious crimes, is based on sexual violation's being a special case:[93]

"In the absence of consent the conduct involved is a very serious intrusion on the person of another, and the crime is unusual in that the attitude and conduct of the complainant is of central importance. Moreover, there will often be a clear risk of absence of consent, and it will usually be easy for the other person to ascertain the true position. In these circumstances a 'casual assumption' that a partner is willing, in the absence of struggles and screams, is said to be unacceptable, and there is sufficient culpability if a belief in consent is not supported by reasonable grounds. Full recognition of personal autonomy in sexual relations is widely thought to require this conclusion."

In s 128, the New Zealand Legislature has given statutory endorsement to these arguments. This means that where an accused has not considered the question of consent, and a risk that the complainant was not consenting to the sexual intercourse would have been obvious to someone with the accused's mental capacity if they had turned their mind to it, the accused is to be taken to have satisfied the requisite mens rea for s 128. The same standard would also apply to situations where consent has been withdrawn during sexual connection, such that the accused was not continuing with the reasonable belief that the victim was in fact consenting.[94]

(a) "Reasonable grounds"

As we have said, the requirement in s 128(2) and (3) that there be "reasonable grounds" for a belief in consent signals a rejection of the rule in *Morgan* and establishes reasonableness as a substantive requirement of mens rea. However, it is likely that in practice this change will have limited impact on verdicts, because the reasonableness or otherwise of an alleged mistake has always been relevant when assessing an offender's credibility. When actual absence of consent is proved there will seldom be a real possibility of mistake, whether reasonable or unreasonable.[95] In addition, the requirement for a "reasonable" belief in consent implies a "hard" objective standard.[96] There is no warrant for reading it down to "reasonable in the

---

92 Cf Hall, *General Principles of Criminal Law* (2nd ed), Indianapolis, Bobbs-Merrill, 1960, 363: "moral obligation is determined not by the actual facts but by the actor's opinion regarding them."
93 Orchard, "Sexual violation: The rape law reform legislation" (1986) 12 NZULR 97, 103.
94 *R v Tolmie* (1995) 84 A Crim R 293, 305.
95 Orchard, "Sexual violation: The rape law reform legislation" (1986) 12 NZULR 97, 105.

circumstances as he believed them to be" or in some other way bringing in a subjective approach to justify the accused's belief.[97] This means that there is no room for intoxication as a factor in determining whether reasonable grounds existed for the accused's subjective belief that the victim was consenting.[98] So if D, while drunk, has sexual connection with P, and mistakenly interprets her non-resistance as consent, the fact that he was drunk is not an issue that the jury may make allowance for when determining whether his belief that P consented was reasonable. The test is, therefore, whether a reasonable *sober* person would have believed that the victim was consenting — not whether the drunken defendant reasonably believed she was consenting.

Note that, on this question, the prosecution bears the burden of proving that the accused did not believe on reasonable grounds that the complainant consented.[99]

(b) Relevance of personal "characteristics"

The insistence on a strict objective standard in this context does not necessarily mean that subjective characteristics are never relevant in evaluating the accused's belief. However, the extent to which they may be relevant is, at this stage, a matter of some uncertainty. References in present case law to factors that might be considered to be relevant "characteristics" to be taken into account in applying the objective test are oblique at best, and do not provide a conclusive basis in precedent for departing from a purely objective test. It is in any event clear, on the authority of *R v P (T129/92)*,[100] that intellectual impairment and blind lust are, together with intoxication, factors that are irrelevant to the question of reasonable grounds. The defendant in *R v P (T129/92)* was a 30-year-old moderately intellectually disabled man who was convicted of sexual violation by rape of a 30-year-old intellectually disabled woman. He had an IQ in the range of 48-50 points. Although the Court held that the defendant's intellectual disability was irrelevant in determining the objective element within belief in consent, it was a relevant "special circumstance" in determining whether he should be sentenced to imprisonment.[101] However, given that objective liability is generally prefaced upon the normative response of a sane, sober *adult* in the situation of the accused, we might expect that some concession could be made to an offender who suffered from a severe intellectual impairment, or to one whose very youth and inexperience in sexual matters and in interpreting such subtle indicia as consent, might mean that he is more likely to make a mistake that would not be made by a mature adult. An argument of reciprocity might suggest that since the statute

---

96 As opposed to a "soft" objective standard, which would allow the tribunal of fact to consider the issue of reasonableness in the light of the accused's actual beliefs and other external conditions that might modify his beliefs.
97 *R v Clarke* [1992] 1 NZLR 147 (CA), 149. It is, nevertheless, true to say that the test for belief in consent imposes a "mixed subjective and objective mens rea formula" which the courts generally avoid when legislation does not expressly provide for it. See *Millar v MOT* [1986] 1 NZLR 660; (1986) 2 CRNZ 216 (CA), 668; 225.
98 *R v Clarke* [1992] 1 NZLR 147 (CA), 149.
99 In 2004, the Law and Order Committee considered and rejected a proposed amendment to s 128 that would have required the accused to prove that she had reasonable grounds for believing the victim consented, by providing evidence of the steps taken to ascertain consent at the time of the offending. The Committee considered that such an amendment would effectively revise New Zealand's consent laws and be a major departure from the general rule that the Crown bears the burden of proof. See Crimes Amendment Bill (No 2) as Reported from the Law and Order Committee, Commentary, 22 October 2004, at p 12.
100 *R v P (T129/92)* (1993) 10 CRNZ 250; 1 HRNZ 417, 253; 420.
101 *R v P (T129/92)* (1993) 10 CRNZ 250; 1 HRNZ 417, 253; 420. See s 128B(2).

now expressly makes provision in s 128A(5) for the greater protection of vulnerable victims who, because of a particular intellectual, mental or physical condition, are incapable of consent, similar protection should be available to defendants with identical vulnerabilities.

In *R v Cox*,[102] where the defendant was over 60 years of age, the Court suggested that the relevant question was whether a "mature male" or a "reasonable adult" might have grounds for believing in consent. This may be taken to imply that the *age* of the offender is a relevant characteristic in assessing reasonableness. Clearly sex could not be a relevant characteristic in this context, given the now gender-neutral character of the offence of sexual violation. But beyond these two examples little is clear. Some commentators have favoured an "individualised" approach to whether a mistake is reasonable, rather than a purely objective test, which would allow consideration to be given to the "attitudes and capabilities of the defendant which he cannot be expected to control", perhaps even including intoxication.[103] Others would allow consideration of "physical or mental disabilities" of the accused, but exclude intoxication.[104] It would seem that the Minister of Justice at the time anticipated that some personal factors, such as mental deficiency, would be taken into account.[105]

The categories of what might qualify as relevant personal characteristics are not closed. It is open to the courts to determine whether a particular factor is relevant to the assessment of reasonableness. Some assistance in this regard might be gained from the decision of the English Court of Appeal in *R v Bowen*,[106] where, in the context of duress, their Honours ruled on the characteristics that may be relevant in determining whether a person of *reasonable firmness, sharing the characteristics of the accused* would have committed an offence.[107] The Court accepted that mere pliability, vulnerability, and timidity are not relevant characteristics that may be vested in the reasonable person; but listed age, sex, pregnancy, serious physical disability, recognised mental illness or psychiatric condition, and *mental impairment* as factors that might be taken into account as affecting the person's ability to resist pressure.[108] By the same token, characteristics due to self-induced abuse, such as alcohol, drugs, or glue-sniffing, were held not to be relevant.

While there are obvious differences in the social policy objectives undergirding the defences of duress and consent, the purpose of the objective standard is the same in each case; namely, to hold people to a standard of conduct that applies universally and generally supports the Rule of Law. This purpose is not compromised where limited exceptions to a general rule of liability are drawn which recognise the special susceptibility to error of particular classes of persons. Apart from the possible exception of sex, for the reason already mentioned, there would seem to be no reason in principle why the other relevant listed characteristics — including age, recognised mental illness or psychiatric condition, and mental impairment —

---

102 *R v Cox* 7/11/96, CA213/96.
103 See, for example, Pickard, "Culpable Mistakes and Rape: Relating Mens Rea to the Crime" (1980) 30 U Toronto LJ 75, 79.
104 Temkin, "The limits of reckless rape" [1983] Crim LR 5, 16.
105 (1985) 465 NZPD 6435. For further discussion of the merits of allowing for individual peculiarities within a negligence test, see 4.6.2.
106 *R v Bowen* [1996] 4 All ER 837; (1996) 2 Cr App R 157 (CA).
107 Under the common law defence of duress a jury is required to consider, amongst other things, whether a sober person of reasonable firmness, sharing the characteristics of the accused, would have responded to the situation of emergency by acting as the accused acted: *R v Graham* [1982] 1 All ER 801; [1982] 1 WLR 294 (CA), 806; 300; *R v Martin* [1989] 1 All ER 652; (1989) 88 Cr App R 343 (CA).
108 *R v Bowen* [1996] 4 All ER 837; (1996) 2 Cr App R 157 (CA), 844; 166.

should not be accepted as characteristics modifying the reasonableness test in the context of s 128. Since the Minister has already foreshadowed a political intention that some personal characteristics should be taken into account, the suggested list would properly recognise the special limitations of those classes of people who might be expected to make mistakes in this area, without seriously undermining any value the objective requirement might have.[109]

If this is accepted as a legitimate approach to the issue of belief in consent, some modification to the present law may be necessary. In particular, notwithstanding *R v P (T129/92)* (above), on the basis of the comments in *Bowen*[110] there appears little justification for holding that *intellectual impairment* can never be relevant when determining reasonable grounds. While courts may legitimately exclude merely below-average intelligence *per se* as a relevant factor on the basis that other mental characteristics such as inherent weakness, vulnerability, and susceptibility to threats are inconsistent with the requirements of an objective test,[111] genuine intellectual disability is a substantial disability, and people with mental retardation have a reduced ability to cope with and function in the everyday world;[112] an inability that involves no ascription of fault on their part.

18.3 Inducing sexual connection by coercion

Supplementing the crime of sexual violation, s 129A defines the separate offence of inducing sexual connection by certain threats. The section defines a generic offence of inducing sexual connection by threat and then particularises the types of threats that will trigger the offence. In addition, s 129A creates an offence of inducing an indecent act by any such threat.[113] These crimes may be committed by any person who has sexual connection with or who does an indecent act on another person (as defined in s 129A(3) and (4)), knowing that the other has been induced to consent by one of certain specified kinds of express or implied threats. These include threats to:

(i) Commit an imprisonable offence "not involv[ing] the actual or threatened application of force to any person" (subs (5)(a));

(ii) Make an "accusation or disclosure" (whether true or untrue) about misconduct by any person (whether living or dead) likely to seriously damage the reputation of another (subs (5)(b)); or

(iii) Make improper use of any "power or authority" arising out of an occupational or vocational position or a "commercial relationship" existing between the person making the threat and the person consenting to the "detriment" of another (subs (5)(c)).

The threat need not have been made by the offender. Neither must the circumstances indicate that the threat was the reason why the complainant consented.[114] This may be a justification for the offence's being one of subjective mens rea, in that the defendant must *know* that the threat induced the complainant's consent. "Knowledge" here carries its usual meaning, requiring more than mere recognition of a possibility: the defendant will have the requisite

---

109 See Orchard, "Sexual violation: The rape law reform legislation" (1986) 12 NZULR 97, 105.
110 *R v Bowen* [1996] 4 All ER 837; (1996) 2 Cr App R 157 (CA).
111 *R v Bowen* [1996] 4 All ER 837; (1996) 2 Cr App R 157 (CA), 843; 165.
112 *R v P (T129/92)* (1993) 10 CRNZ 250; 1 HRNZ 417, 252; 419.
113 See s 129A(2).
114 Orchard, "Sexual violation: The rape law reform legislation" (1986) 12 NZULR 97, 105.

knowledge only if she is sure of the reason for consent, or "knew what the answer was going to be" if inquiry was made.[115]

Section 129A describes an acquiescence to sexual connection induced by a specified relevant threat as "consent". Provided no other factors are present, such as violence, it appears that sexual violation is not committed because that offence can only be committed where consent is absent. It is clear, therefore, that there are important differences between the two offences. Although the offence is purely indictable,[116] it is punishable by a maximum term of imprisonment of 14 years in contrast to the maximum penalty of 20 years for sexual violation.[117] Furthermore, the offence defined in s 129A is not subject to the statutory presumption in favour of imprisonment for sexual violation,[118] and has not been made subject to a separate provision regarding attempts.[119] Its separation from sexual violation suggests that the two crimes are to be regarded as significantly different.[120]

18.3.1 Threats to commit an imprisonable offence: s 129A(5)(a)

One implication to be drawn from s 129A(5)(a) is that, if the specified threats in that section do not vitiate a consent, nor do threats to commit some lesser wrong — which, if successful in inducing consent to sexual connection, would therefore fall outside the scope of either s 128 or s 129A. Suppose, for example, that A threatens B that unless she has intercourse with him he will commit a non-imprisonable summary offence (say, offensive behaviour, or fighting in a public place),[121] knowing that it would cause B great shame or embarrassment.

The offences defined in s 129A give particular expression to the offence of blackmail in ss 237 and 238. In the context of s 129A, as with s 237, to "threaten" carries its ordinary meaning of to "make clear an [unwelcome] intention".[122] The relevant threat may be either express or implied, and it will be a question for the jury whether on the whole of the evidence the conduct of the accused (or another) included a relevant threat.[123] Evidence at the trial that the accused intended no threat may be inadmissible, the question for the jury being whether his conduct, including his language at the time the alleged threat was expressed, induced the victim to consent to intercourse taking place.[124] However, because the essence of the offence is "inducing" consent to sexual connection it will be necessary for the prosecution to prove a clear causal nexus between the alleged threat and the consent. A relevant threat in the absence of evidence of induced consent will be insufficient under s 129A to establish liability.

---

115 Orchard, "Sexual violation: The rape law reform legislation" (1986) 12 NZULR 97, 105. See *R v Crooks* [1981] 2 NZLR 53 (CA), 56-59; 4.5.
116 See the Schedule 1 Summary Proceedings Act 1957.
117 Section 128B(1).
118 See s 128B(2) and (3)
119 Under s 129, the attempt to commit sexual violation is punishable by 10 years' imprisonment. The absence of a similar provision for attempting to induce sexual connection by coercion means that the maximum penalty for an attempt is 7 years: s 311(1).
120 Orchard, "Sexual violation: The rape law reform legislation" (1986) 12 NZULR 97, 101.
121 Sections 4 and 7 Summary Offences Act 1981. Both offences are punishable by a fine not exceeding $1000.
122 *R v Wyatt* (1921) 16 Cr App R 57 (CCA), 60.
123 See *R v Collister* (1955) 39 Cr App R 100 (CCA).
124 *R v Plaisted* (1909) 22 Cox CC 5.

18.3.2 Threats of accusation or disclosure: s 129A(5)(b)

Section 129A(5)(b) covers situations where consent is coerced by a threat to report or recount the commission of an offence or sexual misconduct by another. It criminalises, in effect, a species of blackmail where the demand is satisfied by an act of sexual connection. The subsection covers situations where sexual connection occurs as a result of a threat by the offender to make a disclosure that creates a real risk that the victim's reputation will be seriously damaged. It may include a disclosure of criminal offending by the victim, but could also include such mundane matters as a threat to inform the victim's parents of her previous immorality,[125] or to make a false allegation that he is a thief, thereby affecting his future employment prospects. However, moral or economic pressure alone will not be enough in the absence of a threat of disclosure which induces consent to sexual connection.

18.3.3 Threatened actions involving "detriment" to the victim: s 129A(5)(c)

The elements of the offence under s 129A(5)(c) are:

(i)   There has been sexual connection or an indecent act ;

(ii) The alleged offender knew that the victim had been induced to consent by;

(iii) An express or implied threat;

(iv) To make improper use to the detriment of the other person;

(v)   Of a power or authority, arising either out of an occupational or vocational position held by the alleged offender, or out of a commercial relationship existing between them.

The subsection is aimed at certain cases of sexual harassment, and covers cases where V is induced to consent by threats — for example of dismissal, educational failure, or eviction — which involve a misuse of D's "power or authority".

A critical element in the subsection is that the threatened action must involve "detriment" to the victim. The meaning of "detriment" was considered in *Brewer v R*[126] where a young woman, "desperate" for employment, complained that she had complied with the sexual demands of her prospective employer because he had promised employment upon compliance. In a pretrial ruling Robertson J held that the allegations did not constitute an offence against s 129A(1)(c). The requirements of "threat" and "detriment" meant there had to be some "pressing, urging, forcing, or inducing action by improper use of the accused's vocational or occupational position to cause loss or damage to the position of the other".[127] Thus "detriment" cannot be interpreted to mean a "failure to grant a right or hypothetical benefit"; and on the facts in *Brewer* it was held that the mere abuse, for sexual advantage, by the accused of his position as interviewer of a potential employee did not amount to threatening the victim with any immediate loss or damage, and so no detriment could be said to have arisen.

This may be so, but the insistence that "threat" necessarily implies a "pressing, urging [or] forcing" seems to go somewhat further than "making clear an intention" to do something

---

125 See Smith and Hogan, *Criminal Law* (9th ed), London, Butterworths, 1999, 463.
126 *Brewer v R* [1994] 2 NZLR 229, also reported as B v R *(T216/93)* (1993) 11 CRNZ 419. See also *R v Brewer* 26/5/94, CA516/93.
127 *Brewer v R* [1994] 2 NZLR 229, also reported as B v R *(T216/93)* (1993) 11 CRNZ 419, 235; 424-425.

unwelcome, a test suggested by the earlier authorities.[128] Apparently, however, it reflects the Legislature's intention regarding s 129A.[129]

A question may arise over the meaning of "improper" in this subsection. Does it mean, for example, that liability under s 129A is excluded if the threatened action was not only legitimate but proper, even though the accused intended the threat to induce sexual favours?[130] The best approach, it is submitted, would be to recognise that in such cases the legitimate power or authority may still be used improperly. This could occur where, for example, a lecturer says to a student "I would normally insist that your essay be handed in on the due date (a true statement and legitimate exercise of authority), but I'll make an exception if you will come home with me tonight" (an inducement to consent and an improper use of authority).[131] The focus in such cases should not be upon whether there might be a legitimate basis for the threatened action, but rather whether the accused has used her "authority and control" over the victim to induce consent.[132] In our example, the lecturer's threat is to exercise her authority to further a purpose for which the authority was not intended. Hence the use is improper.

18.4 Attempt to commit sexual violation

Attempt to commit sexual violation is defined as a separate offence in s 129 Crimes Act 1961. It specifies a penalty of up to 10 years' imprisonment for anyone who attempts to commit sexual violation or assaults anyone with intent to commit sexual violation. The section defines two separate offences. However, there is no special definition of the elements of an attempt under s 129, so that the general definition of an attempt in s 72 applies. Accordingly, for an attempt, the act of the accused must be sufficiently proximate to the offence of sexual violation. Proof of an attempted physical penetration is not required if the actions of the accused can properly be regarded as more than mere preparation and show that the accused has embarked on committing the crime.[133] Thus the act of the accused in "jabbing" his erect penis against the complainant's vaginal area will constitute the actus reus of attempted sexual violation.[134] It is no defence that he was incapable of carrying out the final act of penetration.[135]

18.4.1 Mens rea

The mens rea of attempted rape has been a matter of some controversy, because of the difficulty raised by the more general question whether recklessness is consistent with the concept of attempt.[136] The English Court of Appeal has concluded, at least for the purposes of the crime of rape, that recklessness is sufficient in respect of the "circumstance" that the woman did not consent, but that the "result" — the act of sexual intercourse — must be intended in the full sense.[137] In *R v Khan*,[138] Russell LJ held that the mens rea for attempted

---

128 See *R v Wyatt* (1921) 16 Cr App R 57 (CCA), 60.
129 *Brewer v R* [1994] 2 NZLR 229, also reported as *B v R (T216/93)* (1993) 11 CRNZ 419, 234; 424 (Robertson J).
130 Orchard, "Sexual violation: The rape law reform legislation" (1986) 12 NZULR 97, 102.
131 See *R v Nichol* (1807) Russ & Ry, 130; 168 ER 720 (CCR).
132 See Bryant, "The issue of consent in the crime of sexual assault" (1989) 68 Can Bar Rev 94, 128, fn 171.
133 *A-G's Reference (No 1 of 1992)* [1993] 2 All ER 190; [1993] 1 WLR 274 (CA).
134 *R v Khan* [1990] 2 All ER 783; [1990] 1 WLR 813 (CA), 785; 816.
135 *R v Khan* [1990] 2 All ER 783; [1990] 1 WLR 813 (CA), 785; 816.
136 For arguments favouring the inclusion of recklessness in attempts, see Williams, "The problem of reckless attempts" [1983] Crim LR 365. See also Smith and Hogan, *Criminal Law* (7th ed), London, Butterworths, 1992, 306. Contrary views have been expressed by other distinguished commentators, regarding which see *R v Khan* [1990] 2 All ER 783; [1990] 1 WLR 813 (CA), 786; 817 (Russell LJ).

rape is precisely the same as for the substantive offence at common law, namely an intention to have intercourse plus a knowledge of, or recklessness about, the woman's absence of consent. The only difference between the two offences is that, in rape, sexual intercourse takes place while in attempted rape it does not. According to Russell LJ:[139]

> "No question of attempting to achieve a reckless state of mind arises; the attempt relates to the physical activity; the mental state of the defendant is the same. A man does not recklessly have sexual intercourse, nor does he recklessly attempt it. Recklessness in rape and attempted rape arises not in relation to the physical act of the accused but only in his state of mind when engaged in the activity of having or attempting to have sexual intercourse."

So an attempt at sexual violation may occur where an accused intends to commit sexual violation and is recklessly indifferent whether there is an absence of consent,[140] provided he goes beyond the stage of preparation. Unlike the crime of attempted murder, which cannot be committed recklessly[141] and has a *unitary* mens rea element (namely an intention to kill), the crime of attempted rape and, in the New Zealand context, sexual violation, has a *bifurcated* mens rea. Thus an intention to have intercourse without consent, which goes to the actus reus of the offence, is not inconsistent with reckless indifference to the views of the victim. This second element, the absence of consent, may be characterised as an additional circumstance of the offence for which recklessness will suffice:[142]

> "If a man sets out to perform an act of intercourse on a woman with reckless indifference to her wishes but fails to achieve penetration his effort to do so has in every sense been an attempt to do something which is prohibited by law. He has attempted rape."

A proper jury direction on a charge of attempted sexual violation should therefore include words to the effect that, when he made the attempt to penetrate the victim or otherwise to have sexual connection with her, the accused was either aware that the victim was not consenting, or realised that she might not be consenting and was determined to have sexual connection whether or not the victim was consenting.[143] It follows that there will be no offence if, at the time of the act of attempted sexual intercourse, the accused honestly believed that the complainant was consenting, or had considered the risk that she may not be consenting but had affirmatively concluded that the risk was negligible — whether or not he had reasonable grounds for so concluding.

18.5 Evidentiary matters

There are four provisions in the Evidence Amendment Act (No 2) 1985, relating to evidential questions in the prosecution of sexual offences, which we will now briefly consider.

---

137 See *R v Millard and Vernon* [1987] Crim LR 393 (CA) (Mustill LJ), approved in *R v Khan* [1990] 2 All ER 783; [1990] 1 WLR 813 (CA), 787, 788; 818, 819.
138 *R v Khan* [1990] 2 All ER 783; [1990] 1 WLR 813 (CA), 788; 819.
139 *R v Khan* [1990] 2 All ER 783; [1990] 1 WLR 813 (CA), 788; 819.
140 See *R v Evans* (1987) 30 A Crim R 262. Cf *R v Zorad* [1979] 2 NSWLR 764, 773; also *A-G's Reference (No 3 of 1992)* [1994] 1 WLR 409; (1994) 98 Cr App R 383 (CA).
141 See *R v Mohan* [1976] QB 1; [1975] 2 All ER 193 (CA); *R v Whybrow* (1951) 35 Cr App R 141 (CCA).
142 *R v Evans* (1987) 30 A Crim R 262, 273 (Bollen J).
143 See *R v Zorad* [1979] 2 NSWLR 764.

18.5.1 Address and occupation of complainant

Section 139 Criminal Justice Act 1985 prohibits the publication of the name of the complainant in the case of certain specified sexual offences, and of any name or particulars likely to lead to the complainant's identification. This provision is itself reinforced by the terms of s 23AA Evidence Act 1908. The effect of the section is that, except with the leave of the judge, the complainant shall not be required to state her address or occupation in court; that no one involved in the proceedings, including lawyers and court staff, is to disclose the information in court; and that no evidence is to be given or sought relating to such matters. The judge is prevented from giving leave unless the information is of "such direct relevance"[144] to facts in issue that to exclude it would be contrary to the interests of justice. The purpose of the provisions is to minimise the risk or fear that the complainant might be subject to harassment or attack.[145]

The amendment in 1986 deleted reference to the complainant's name from s 23AA(2)(c). The reference to "name" in the section heading is now redundant. The change reflects the fact that it would not be practicable to give the accused fair notice of the allegations against him if it were not possible to disclose the complainant's identity.

18.5.2 Delay in making complaint

At common law, in cases of rape and other sexual offences against females, the fact that the victim made a complaint (to a person to whom the complaint would naturally be made) shortly after the alleged occurrence and the particulars of the complaint, to the extent that they relate to the charge against the accused, could be given in evidence on the part of the prosecution. The purpose of such evidence was to establish the credibility of the complainant's testimony to the facts alleged, in that it showed consistency on her part.[146] It was also considered to be evidence negativing consent, where consent was in issue.[147]

Under the previous law, if there was no complaint at the first reasonable opportunity, it was likely that the defence would suggest that the failure to complain diminished the credibility of the complainant's evidence. However, in practical terms it was often likely that the failure was simply the result of trauma suffered by the victim rather than evidence of consent. The fact that there may be a reason for not complaining in such circumstances is now recognised by legislation. Section 3 Evidence Amendment Act 1985 has enacted s 23AC Evidence Act 1908, which, although it does not alter the existing law on recent complaint, provides that should the issue be raised, the judge is authorised to tell the jury that there may be "good reasons" why the victim of a sexual offence refrained from or delayed in making a complaint. This means that a judge has a discretion to make a comment where appropriate in a particular case, without being required to make a formal direction. An amendment to the section in 1995 extended the protection to complaints alleging an offence under s 144A Crimes Act (sexual conduct with children outside New Zealand); see s 2 Crimes Amendment Act 1995.

---

144 Section 23AA(3) Evidence Act 1908. See s 88 Evidence Act 2006.
145 Orchard, "Sexual violation: The rape law reform legislation" (1986) 12 NZULR 97, 109.
146 McGechan, *Garrow and McGechan's Principles of the Law of Evidence* (7th ed), Wellington, Butterworths, 1984, 57.
147 See *R v Lillyman* [1896] 2 QB 167; [1895-9] All ER Rep 586; *R v Osborne* [1905] 1 KB 551; [1904-7] All ER Rep 54.

More generally, the courts now recognise that delays in making complaints may not be unusual, particularly in cases of sexual abuse involving young children in a family setting and extending over a period of years.[148] It is acknowledged that for victims of sexual abuse to complain often takes considerable courage and emotional strength. Furthermore, courts are reluctant to authorise the staying of proceedings, based solely on the passage of time between the abuse and the charge, where to do so would force victims to report incidents before they were psychologically prepared for the consequences of that reporting. Otherwise, sexual abusers would be able to take advantage of the failure to report that they themselves caused — something the courts consider should not be encouraged. In *W v R (T2/98)*,[149] Randerson J observed that it is common in such cases to find complainants who lack confidence, have low self-esteem, and are unwilling to come forward unless they feel that they have the support of others in making their complaints known publicly. However, his Honour conceded that the courts will be more ready to find some form of prejudice to the defence where there is a very long delay.[150]

18.5.3 Character of the complainant

In the past, where consent was the central defence in a rape trial, it was a common tactic and permissible for defence counsel to endeavour to elicit information regarding the past sexual experience and reputation of the complainant.[151] Obviously, where the defence was able to impugn the character of the complainant by showing her generally to be a person of "loose" morals, it might thereby raise a doubt in the mind of the jury whether her claimed refusal to consent on the present charge was believable.

However, since 1977 the common law right to cross-examine a complainant in a rape trial regarding her sexual experience with anyone other than the accused, or about her sexual reputation, has been severely restricted. These restrictions were first introduced by the Evidence Amendment Act 1977, which created s 23A Evidence Act 1908, applying specifically to the crimes of rape, attempted rape, and assault with intent to commit rape, as well as being a party to and conspiring to commit any such offence. In 1985, a new s 23A was substituted by s 2 Evidence Amendment Act (No 2) 1985, and further amended by s 2 Evidence Amendment Act 1989 and s 8 Crimes Amendment Act 1995. The present s 23A, which now applies to any offence "of a sexual nature", prohibits any question or evidence relating to the complainant's sexual experience or reputation, except by leave of the judge. Leave may be granted only if the information is of such direct relevance to facts in issue that to exclude it would be contrary to the interests of justice.[152] For this purpose, it will be insufficient that the information raises an inference as to the "general disposition or propensity" of the complainant in sexual matters. Leave is not required under the section if the purpose of the evidence is to rebut evidence of the proscribed kind which has been given, or if the accused is alleged to have been a party to another's offence and the evidence concerns the complainant's sexual experience with that other.[153]

---

148 *T (CA175/97) v A-G* 27/8/97, CA175/97; see *R v L (W K)* (1991) 64 CCC (3d) 321 (SCC), 328.
149 *W v R (T2/98)* (1998) 16 CRNZ 33, 45.
150 *W v R (T2/98)* (1998) 16 CRNZ 33, 42.
151 McGechan, *Garrow and McGechan's Principles of the Law of Evidence* (7th ed), Wellington, Butterworths, 1984, 170. See also *R v Bills* [1981] 1 NZLR 760 (CA).
152 Section 23A(3) Evidence Act 1908. See s 88 Evidence Act 2006.
153 Section 23A(4) Evidence Act 1908.

Although these provisions would appear to have been effective in excluding evidence of the complainant's sexual experience in the majority of trials,[154] the criteria of "direct relevance" and "the interests of justice" in s 23A(3) may create uncertainty over their application in a particular case. Cross-examination is now permissible only if the judge is satisfied that the conditions referred to in s 23A(3) are met.

These criteria, which are said to constitute a "strong test",[155] were considered in *R v Duncan*.[156] In that case, defence counsel sought to put to the complainant that she had written letters making allegations against a boarder in her home similar to those made against the accused, and further that she had previously told her mother that she had been interfered with when much younger. The Court acknowledged that, given the severe limitations on cross-examination imposed by s 23A, such questioning can be relevant, particularly in child abuse cases, where it may be necessary "to explore the possibility of fabrication to gain attention or through malice, or transferred attribution from actual offender to present accused ... There can be occasions when questioning along these lines far from being a character-blackening exercise of little relevance, is well justified in the overall interests of justice."[157] Leave for such examinations may be granted where the examinations are more than "mere fishing expeditions".[158]

In *R v Accused (CA92/92)*,[159] the Court of Appeal held that the existence of a second complaint of an indecent assault allegedly made on the complainant by a person other than the accused some months earlier than the offence alleged, and bearing a "remarkable" similarity to the present complaint, prevented the examination sought from amounting solely to a "fishing expedition", and justified the application for leave to cross-examine. The Court observed that while the legislation set out to protect complainants, "it was not intended to avoid exposing the prosecution case to legitimate scrutiny".[160]

The position is different for child complainants. Where the issue of character goes to the question of whether a witness under oath can be believed, it is established that evidence may be called to discredit the witness.[161] However, that does not pertain to evidence from child witnesses, for whom special evidential considerations apply. It is now well accepted, for example, that children may tell lies yet remain essentially honest. And even expert witnesses testifying under s 23G Evidence Act 1908 are not permitted to express opinions as to a particular child complainant's truthfulness. For these reasons, in *R v E*[162] the Court refused to permit evidence to be given by the child complainant's grandfather that he knew her general character and that, on the strength of that knowledge, he would not believe her testimony under oath.

---

154 Orchard, "Sexual violation: The rape law reform legislation" (1986) 12 NZULR 97, 110.
155 *R v McClintock* [1986] 2 NZLR 99; (1986) 2 CRNZ 158 (CA).
156 *R v Duncan* [1992] 1 NZLR 528, also reported as *R v D* (1991) 7 CRNZ 446 (CA).
157 *R v Duncan* [1992] 1 NZLR 528, also reported as *R v D* (1991) 7 CRNZ 446 (CA), 535; 454.
158 *R v Duncan* [1992] 1 NZLR 528, also reported as *R v D* (1991) 7 CRNZ 446 (CA), 535; 454.
159 *R v Accused (CA92/92)* [1993] 1 NZLR 553 (CA), 557.
160 *R v Accused (CA92/92)* [1993] 1 NZLR 553 (CA), 557. For a more detailed examination of the relevant case law and principles applicable to this area of the law see *Adams*, CA128.05 (looseleaf).
161 See *R v Brosnan* [1951] NZLR 1030 (CA); *R v Gunewardene* [1951] 2 KB 600 (CCA); *R v Richardson; R v Longman* [1969] 1 QB 299 (CA).
162 *R v E* (1998) 16 CRNZ 506.

18.5.4 Corroboration

At common law, the established practice was that when a sexual offence was charged the judge was required to warn the jury to the effect that it was "unsafe" or "dangerous" to convict on the uncorroborated evidence of the complainant. However, the judge could add that the jury may convict in the absence of corroboration if it were convinced of the essential truth of the complainant's evidence. "Corroboration", in this context, came simply to mean independent testimony which supported or strengthened evidence from which the accused's guilt could be inferred.[163]

Nonetheless, in respect of sexual offending, the rules regarding corroboration have been severely criticised,[164] particularly insofar as they supported a presumption that the evidence given by a complainant was inherently unreliable. Consequently, the requirement for corroboration was eventually abolished by s 3 Evidence Amendment Act (No 2) 1985, which enacted s 23AB Evidence Act 1908. The section provides that where a person is charged with an offence of a sexual nature, corroboration is unnecessary before that person may be convicted; and the judge is not required to give a warning to the jury relating to the absence of corroboration.

The section reflects Parliament's recognition that there is no special danger in sexual cases calling for special caution before acting on the word of the complainant alone. The judge remains free to comment on the absence of supporting evidence, if she thinks that the particular case calls for such comment.[165]

It should be noted, however, that s 23AB was largely a superfluous creation. In *Daniels*, the Court of Appeal observed that s 23AB appeared to have been drafted on the mistaken assumption that, prior to the amendment, corroboration of the complainant's evidence was necessary for the accused to be convicted. In rejecting this proposition, the Court noted that what was necessary was merely a warning to the jury of the danger of convicting on uncorroborated evidence. Trial judges were nonetheless free to go on to tell juries that they were fully entitled to convict without corroboration if, having borne the warning in mind, they were convinced of the essential truth of the complainant's account. While no formal warning is now "required", the section clearly preserves a discretion to warn in an appropriate case; although, where the judge does decide to comment on the absence of supporting evidence, no particular form of words is now required.[166]

18.6 Incest

The crime of incest is defined in s 130 as follows:

"(1) Sexual connection is incest if —

"(a) it is between 2 people whose relationship is that of parent and child, siblings, half-siblings, or grandparent and grandchild; and

"(b) the person charged knows of the relationship

---

163 As to the meaning of corroboration, see *DPP v Kilbourne* [1973] AC 729; [1973] 1 All ER 440 (HL), 750; 751; 456; also *R v Poa* [1979] 2 NZLR 378 (CA), 383.
164 Orchard, "Sexual violation: The rape law reform legislation" (1986) 12 NZULR 97, 112.
165 *R v Daniels* [1986] 2 NZLR 106, also reported as *R v Daniels and Tihi* (1986) 2 CRNZ 164 (CA), 111; 166.
166 Section 23AB(2) Evidence Act 1908, as inserted by s 3 Evidence Amendment Act 1985.

"(2) Every one of or over the age of 16 years who commits incest is liable to imprisonment for a term not exceeding 10 years."

The offence is almost identical in substance to the corresponding offence prior to its 2005 amendment, although the structure of the provision has been changed. However, an important substantive change lies in the removal of the concept of "sexual intercourse" and its substitution with "sexual connection", which exposes the crime of incest to a much broader range of sexual activity. The section applies to both natural and adoptive parents, but does not apply to step-relationships.[167]

18.6.1 Definition

At one time punishable as a capital offence, the offence of incest is now punishable by up to 10 years' imprisonment in respect of offenders over the age of 16 years.[168] The offence is gender non-specific within the degrees prohibited by s 130(1)(a) and, with the new requirement for "sexual connection", would appear to allow for an incestuous relationship between same-sex partners,[169] and for a sexual relationship involving conduct other than penile/vaginal intercourse.

18.6.2 Elements of the offence

For the offence of incest there must be:

(i) Sexual connection;

(ii) Within a prohibited relationship; and

(iii) Knowledge of the relationship between the parties.

Since incest no longer requires proof of sexual intercourse, it may be committed both by penetrative intercourse and any other conduct covered by the definition of sexual connection. As discussed above (18.2.1), sexual connection is sufficiently proved by the slightest degree of introduction into the genitalia or anus of one person by a part of the body of another or by an object held or manipulated by another person.[170]

The offence may also be prosecuted as an attempt where the prosecution is able to prove conduct going beyond mere preparation which shows that the accused had embarked on committing the crime[171] (for example, where the victim's father had climbed into his or her bed and had begun to position his body with a view to having sexual connection).

(1) *Knowledge*

The section requires that the accused "knows" of the relationship between the parties. This suggests that the mens rea of the offence involves two elements: the accused must (i) *intend* to have unlawful sexual connection (ii) *knowing* that he or she is related to the other. Accordingly, the offence is not one that can be committed while the accused is unconscious or is otherwise unaware of what he is doing. The section does not require that the accused must know that

---

167 *R v Geddeson* (1906) 25 NZLR 323.
168 Section 130(2).
169 Thus an earlier suggestion that incest can only be committed between a male and a female no longer applies: see *R v N* (1992) 9 CRNZ 471.
170 Section 2(1) Crimes Act 1961, definition of "sexual connection" and s 2(1A).
171 See *A-G's Reference (No 1 of 1992)* [1993] 2 All ER 190; [1993] 1 WLR 274 (CA).

the other party is within a *prohibited* relationship as such, only that they are related in a particular way (parent/child, brother/sister, etc). To require the prosecution to prove as part of its case that the offender knew the relationship was one prohibited by law would contradict s 25 Crimes Act 1961, which specifies that the fact that an offender is ignorant of the law is no excuse. However, lack of knowledge of the *existence* of the relationship would be a good defence, amounting to a lack of mens rea.[172] In R v *Carmichael*,[173] the English Court of Criminal Appeal held that in order to rebut evidence of knowledge that a child born to his wife during wedlock is his daughter, the accused may not only testify denying paternity, but also prove that his wife had told him he was not the father. The Court also allowed that, as evidence of the sincerity of his belief, the accused could testify that he had told his second wife he was not the father, even though this evidence would tend to illegitimise the child, whom he had previously acknowledged as his daughter.

(2) Proving the relationship

Generally, an admission by the defendant will be sufficient evidence of the relationship.[174] However, an admission may be insufficient in the absence of evidence that the accused had intercourse with the victim's mother at the time of conception. So, in R v *Hemmings*,[175] where the defendant's partner was the daughter of a woman who was married to another man at the time of her conception, it was held that there must be sufficient evidence, regardless of any admission, to rebut the presumption of legitimacy which arises when there is evidence that the child was born or conceived during marriage. The Court held there was not "a particle of evidence" that the mother had committed adultery with the accused.

(3) Mode of proof

Proof of the relationship and age of the parties is normally achieved by certificates of marriage and birth. The nomination of the age of 16 as the cut-off point of liability for incest is evidently intended to protect both boys and girls under that age, with the result that where a person under the age of 16 permits a man or a woman to have incestuous connection she commits no offence. In effect, the nomination of the age of 16 establishes an irrebuttable presumption that a child or young person below that age is incapable of committing incest regardless of how active the child might have been in promoting the activity. Sexual connection may be inferred from the circumstances, and proof that the parties were together in bed may be supplemented by evidence of earlier incidents of sexual passion.[176]

There is no separate statutory offence in New Zealand of inciting a person under the age of 16 to have incestuous sexual connection. It would, nevertheless, be possible to prosecute such an offence where there was evidence, in terms of s 66(1)(d), that the accused had been a party by inciting, counselling, or procuring the commission of the crime of incest (to be committed by the older party), regardless of whether the full offence is actually committed.

---

172 See R v *Baillie-Smith* (1977) 64 Cr App R 76; [1977] Crim LR 676 (CA). There a conviction of incest was quashed because the judge failed to leave to the jury the critical question, namely whether the defendant at the material time realised it was his daughter and not his wife with whom he was having intercourse.
173 R v *Carmichael* (1940) 27 Cr App R 183 (CCA).
174 R v *Jones* (1933) 24 Cr App R 55 (CA); R v *Seaton* [1933] NZLR 548 (CA), 557 (Myers CJ).
175 R v *Hemmings* [1939] 1 All ER 417 (CCA).
176 R v *Ball* [1911] AC 47 (HL), 71; R v *Bloodworth* (1913) 9 Cr App R 80 (CCA). See also R v *Stone* (1910) 6 Cr App R 89 (CCA).

18.7 Sexual conduct with dependent family member

Although named as one, in fact three offences are created in s 131 Crimes Act 1961, as follows:

"**131 Sexual conduct with dependent family member**

"(1) Every one is liable to imprisonment for a term not exceeding 7 years who has sexual connection with a dependent family member under the age of 18 years.

"(2) Every one is liable to imprisonment for a term not exceeding 7 years who attempts to have sexual connection with a dependent family member under the age of 18 years.

"(3) Every one is liable to imprisonment for a term not exceeding 3 years who does an indecent act on a dependent family member under the age of 18 years.

"(4) The dependent family member cannot be charged as a party to the offence.

"(5) It is not a defence to a charge under this section that the dependent family member consented."

Prior to 2005, the offence was defined as "sexual intercourse with a girl under care or protection". The reformulated provision establishes a gender-neutral offence, perpetrated where the offender has sexual connection with a "dependent family member" under the age of 18 years. "Dependent family member" is defined in s 131A to include the traditional constellations of quasi-parental relationships (parent, step-parent, foster parent, guardian, uncle or aunt or parent, step-parent, or foster parent of such person) together with siblings and half-siblings, spouses or de facto partners of parents, etc, and family or whanau members with a significant role in the child or young person's care or upbringing.[177] The offence only requires that sexual activity takes place with a dependent family member, consent being irrelevant. Moreover, it is not a requirement of the offence that the complainant was living under the same roof as the accused when the sexual conduct occurred. The expanded definition of "dependent family member" presupposes that sexual connection may occur outside the victim's home, albeit within the context of a family dependency situation. The essence of the offence is not the geographical context in which it occurs but the nature of the relationship with the person upon whom the child or young person is dependent.

As with other sexual offences, the ambit of the offence has been widened to comprehend victims and offenders on a gender-neutral basis and extend to all sexual conduct, and not just sexual intercourse. The offence, like its predecessor,[178] is intended to protect young persons vulnerable in a family situation from sexual exploitation by older family members who have a direct or quasi-parental role involving some degree of power or authority over them.[179] Earlier authority, suggesting that the provision targets offending that involves "the negation of parental responsibilities",[180] still applies, although the focus is clearly on active sexual exploitation within family relationships.

In alleging an offence against s 131, the prosecution is required to prove that:

---

177 See s 131A(1).
178 *X v Police* (1993) 10 CRNZ 385, 388.
179 Crimes Amendment Bill (No 2) as Reported from the Law and Order Committee, Commentary, 22 October, 2004, 14.
180 *S v Police* (1990) 7 CRNZ 173, 174.

(i) The accused intentionally has or attempts to have sexual connection, or performs an indecent act, with any dependent family member under the age of 18 years;

(ii) The accused has "power or authority" over the dependent family member; and

(iii) The accused was a dependent family member, which is defined in s 131A to include:

   (a) Parent, step-parent, foster parent, guardian, uncle, or aunt; or

   (b) The parent, step-parent, or foster parent of a person in (a); or

   (c) A child of his or her parent or step-parent; or

   (d) The spouse or de facto partner of a person described in (a) or (b); or

   (e) A member of the same family, whanau or other culturally recognised family group other than a person in (a)-(d) above, but having responsibility for, or a significant role in, the child or young person's care or upbringing; or

   (f) He or she lives as a member of the other person's family, not being a person nominated in (a)-(d) above, but having power or authority over him or her; and responsibility for, or a significant role in, his or her care or upbringing.

18.7.1 Mens rea

It is not clear from either s 131 or s 131A whether the accused must be aware of the existence of the relationship (for example, that the complainant is the nephew of the other person's de facto partner within s 131A(1)(a)). Neither is it clear whether the accused must know of the attributes of the relationship, in particular whether she has "a responsibility for" or a "significant role" in the complainant's care in terms of s 131A(1)(c)(ii). By contrast, for incest, proof of knowledge of the relationship is an express element of the offence.[181] Under ordinary principles of interpretation (above, 5.2.3), this is surely a mens rea offence. As such, ignorance on the part of the accused, of either the relationship and/or factors bringing the relationship within the definition of dependency in s 131A, ought to support an acquittal for lack of mens rea. Of course, ignorance that a known relationship falls within s 131A would be a matter of ignorance of law and so would not excuse.

Section 131 is confined to sexual conduct with dependent family members under the age of 18 years. By contrast with the offences defined in ss 132 and 134A, which concern conduct with complainants under the age of 16, there is no express provision concerning any mistaken belief that the complainant is over the prescribed age.[182] Again, however, on ordinary principles of interpretation this should be a matter of mens rea; as such, an honest belief that the complainant was of or over the age of 18 will provide a defence.[183]

18.7.2 Actus reus

In effect, there are three separate offences defined in the section, which are distinguished by virtue of the nature of the relationship between the offender and the victim. In the first subcategory, the victim must be in a relationship as stepchild, foster child, or ward of the

---

181 See s 130(1)(b).
182 See ss 132(4) and 134A.
183 Cf B *(a Minor) v DPP* [2000] 2 WLR 452 (HL); *R v K* [2001] UKHL 41; [2002] 1 AC 462 (HL); *R v Kumar* [2004] EWCA Crim 3207; above, 4.3.2.

accused, and be living with him or her as a member of his or her family. These are all relationships one generation above the dependent family member. In the second subcategory, a family member is someone belonging to the same family, whanau, or culturally recognised group as the dependent family member. In the third subcategory, the accused is a person twice removed from the immediate family and essentially a non-family member but having a significant role in the dependent family member's care or upbringing. In the first and second it is the *protected relationship* which constitutes the essence of the offence; in the third, it is the *protected status*, although all subcategories are indicative of a dominating influence and dependence.[184]

There is no longer a requirement that the victim be living with the offender "as a member of his family"; but if she is, this may bring the offender within the third subcategory by virtue of s 131A(1)(c). This is an acknowledgement of the particular vulnerability recognised by s 131 which arises from the closeness of the living circumstances and the constraints upon complaining and escaping. The phrase "living with him as a member of his family" suggests a reasonable length of time and degree of continuity,[185] and has been held to mean "as if she were a member of the family of which he is a part"[186] or as referring to the relationship in which the persons concerned are living in the same domestic situation. In relation to the accused, a family is "his" if he is a member of the group of people who comprise it.[187] Although short periods of time (for example, periods of one, 2, and 4 days) may not be sufficiently long to constitute "living with" another "as part of his family", periods of 7 weeks, 10 days, and 14 days have been held to qualify, even where the accused came to where the victim was living so that the victim became part of one family.[188]

By virtue of s 131(4), a dependent family member cannot be charged as a party to an offence under s 131.

18.8 Meeting young person under 16 following sexual grooming

Section 131B defines a new offence punishable by imprisonment of up to 7 years where a person intentionally meets or communicates with a person under the age of 16 with the intention of dealing with the young person for the purposes of sexual exploitation:

> "**131B Meeting young person under 16 following sexual grooming, etc**
>
> "(1) Every person is liable to imprisonment for a term not exceeding 7 years if,—
>
> "(a) having met or communicated with a person under the age of 16 years (the young person) on an earlier occasion, he or she takes one of the following actions:
>
> "(i) intentionally meets the young person:
>
> "(ii) travels with the intention of meeting the young person:
>
> "(iii) arranges for or persuades the young person to travel with the intention of meeting him or her; and

---

184 *R v H* [1993] 1 NZLR 129, 131.
185 *R v H* [1993] 1 NZLR 129, 131.
186 *R v H* [1993] 1 NZLR 129, 131 (Hardie Boys J).
187 *R v H* [1993] 1 NZLR 129, 134 (McKay J).

"(b) at the time of taking the action, he or she intends—

"(i) to take in respect of the young person an action that, if taken in New Zealand, would be an offence against this Part, or against any of paragraphs (a)(i), (d)(i), (e)(i), (f)(i), of section 98AA(1); or

"(ii) that the young person should do on him or her an act the doing of which would, if he or she permitted it to be done in New Zealand, be an offence against this Part on his or her part.

"(2) It is a defence to a charge under subs (1) if the person charged proves that,—

"(a) before the time he or she took the action concerned, he or she had taken reasonable steps to find out whether the young person was of or over the age of 16 years: and

"(b) at the time he or she took the action concerned, he or she believed on reasonable grounds that the young person was of or over the age of 16 years."

The provision was inserted in the Crimes Amendment Act 2005 during its second reading and did not benefit from the Select Committee's consideration. The provision is based on s 15 Sexual Offences Act 2003 (UK) and is directed principally at internet "grooming". The section applies in any situation where either the accused or the complainant is a New Zealand citizen or ordinarily resident in New Zealand, regardless whether the offence occurred in New Zealand.

The offence defined is a substantive-inchoate offence which allows the Police to intervene at an early stage and before any specific grooming has actually taken place. It is, therefore, analogous to conspiracy or attempts liability. However, the provision permits intervention in circumstances in which a prosecution for attempted sexual connection under either s 132(2) or 134(2) may not have been possible because of difficulties around proof of the proximity requirement.[189]

The elements of the offence are:

(a) The offender met or communicated with a young person on an earlier occasion.

(b) The young person was under the age of 16.

(c) The offender then either

(i) intentionally met the young person again; or

(ii) travelled with the intention of meeting the young person; or

(iii) arranged for or persuaded the young person to travel with the intention of meeting him or her; and

(d) At the time of the action taken, the offender intended

---

188 R v H [1993] 1 NZLR 129, 131.
189 Adams, CA131B.01.

(i) to commit an offence against Part 7 of the Act with that young person or an offence against paras (a)(i), (d)(i), (e)(i), (f)(i) of section 98AA(1); or

(ii) that the young person do an act against him or her that would be an offence against Part 7 if done in New Zealand.

The Act provides a defence if the person charged proves he had taken reasonable steps to find out whether the young person was of or over 16 years of age and, at the time of the actions taken, he believed on reasonable grounds that the young person was of or over the age of 16 years.

The Act only requires a single prior meeting or communication with the young person which, although labelled as "sexual grooming" in the section heading, need not amount to actual grooming activity. The first meeting or communication may, in fact, have been quite innocent. The actus reus of the offence is thus the original meeting (innocent or otherwise) together with a further meeting, or travelling, or arranging for or persuading the young person to travel for the purpose of meeting the offender. The statute is unclear whether the accused must have personally communicated with the complainant.

Where, under s 131B(1)(a)(iii), arranging for travel is alleged, the offence is complete where the arrangements are made to meet the complainant with the relevant intent. In such a case, since the offence is already committed, there is no need for the arranged travel actually to occur. Similarly, under s 131B(1)(a)(ii), where travelling to meet is alleged, there is no need for the meeting actually to occur. The offence is complete on proof of the travel. On the other hand, merely trying to persuade the complainant to meet may be insufficient for an offence under s 131B; although no doubt it may amount to an attempt.

18.8.1 Mens rea

The mens rea element of the offence is complex. It will be satisfied where:

(a) There is a voluntary initial meeting or communication; and

(b) The accused intentionally:

(i) meets; or

(ii) travels with the intention of meeting the young person; or

(iii) arranges or persuades the young person to travel with the intention of meeting him or her; and

(c) The accused intends to commit on the young person an offence against:

(i) Part 7 of the Act; or

(ii) against the nominated paragraphs in s 98AA(1); or

(iii) an act done on the offender which would be an offence against Part 7 of the Act;

(d) The accused does not believe, on reasonable grounds, that the young person was aged 16 years or over, having also taken reasonable steps to find out whether the young person was of or over 16 years of age. (The burden of proof in this matter rests on the accused.)

It is unclear whether the accused must intend to engage in the proscribed sexual activity at the particular meeting, or whether it will suffice that she had an intention to do so at some future time. However, in the absence of an actual meeting or documented explicit communication, proving mens rea could be extremely difficult, at least without evidence of a pattern of grooming activity or previous similar predatory sexual behaviour.

18.9 Sexual conduct with a child under 12: s 132

Section 132, previously "sexual intercourse with a girl under 12", has been re-defined as a gender-neutral offence. It also incorporates the previous offence of indecency with a girl under 12 in the new offence of doing an indecent act on a child.[190] The section provides as follows:

> "**132 Sexual conduct with child under 12**
>
> "(1) Every one who has sexual connection with a child is liable to imprisonment for a term not exceeding 14 years.
>
> "(2) Every one who attempts to have sexual connection with a child is liable to imprisonment for a term not exceeding 10 years.
>
> "(3) Every one who does an indecent act on a child is liable to imprisonment for a term not exceeding 10 years.
>
> "(4) It is not a defence to a charge under this section that the person charged, believed that the child was of or over the age of 12 years.
>
> "(5) It is not a defence to a charge under this section that the child consented.
>
> "(6) In this section,—
>
> "(a) child means a person under the age of 12 years; and
>
> "(b) doing an indecent act on a child includes indecently assaulting the child."

It is a measure of the seriousness with which the Legislature regards the offence of having sexual conduct with a child[191] that it is purely indictable and punishable by up to 14 years' imprisonment. By contrast, the alternative offence of attempting to have sexual connection with a child in s 132(2) has a right of election and carries a maximum penalty of 10 years.[192]

The aim of the section is to protect young complainants who are especially vulnerable to sexual exploitation by reason of their age. Where a child does not consent, a charge of sexual violation will also lie under s 128.[193] However, under s 128 the offender would be able to defend on the grounds of a reasonable belief in the victim's consent.[194] By contrast, it is no defence under s 132 that the child consented, or that the accused believed the child was over the age of 12 years.[195]

Proof of the age of the victim is, of course, crucial in this offence, since it is the age of the victim that underlies the wrongful nature of the defendant's conduct. It will generally be

---

190 Section 132(3).
191 By definition, a person under the age of 12 years is a child: s 132(6)(a).
192 First Schedule to the Summary Proceedings Act 1957.
193 Neither can a defendant charged under s 132 escape conviction merely because the evidence at trial shows that a charge of sexual violation would have been justified. Cf *R v Neale* (1844) 1 Car & K 591; 174 ER 951.
194 See s 128(3).

necessary to adduce some evidence in addition to the child's verbal statement of her age to prove that she is in fact under 12.[196] Where there is doubt whether the child was under the age of 12 when sexual conduct occurred, the difficulty may sometimes be resolved by charging the lesser offence created by s 134, of having sexual conduct with a young person under 16 (see 18.10). However, the latter offence has a lesser maximum sentence.

18.9.1 Sexual connection and attempts

As with other offences under Part 7, where "sexual connection" is required, it will be sufficiently proved by any degree of "introduction" into the genitalia of the victim. There is no need to prove actual penetration of the vagina where traditional sexual intercourse is contemplated.[197] Neither are rupture of the hymen or ejaculation necessary elements of the offence.[198] This being the case, since the full offence may be committed by any degree of penetration of the victim's genitalia, the offence of attempting to have sexual connection with a child under the age of 12 years, contrary to s 132(2), will be complete where there is conduct, being more than mere preparation but falling short of actual penetration of the victim, that shows that the accused had embarked on committing the crime with intent to have unlawful sexual connection.[199]

18.10 Sexual conduct with a young person under 16: s 134

Section 134 defines the new offence of sexual conduct with a young person under 16, as follows:

> "**134 Sexual conduct with young person under 16**
>
> "(1)   Every one who has sexual connection with a young person is liable to imprisonment for a term not exceeding 10 years.
>
> "(2)   Every one who attempts to have sexual connection with a young person is liable to imprisonment for a term not exceeding 10 years.
>
> "(3)   Every one who does an indecent act on a young person is liable to imprisonment for a term not exceeding 7 years.
>
> "(4)   No person can be convicted of a charge under this section if he or she was married to the young person concerned at the time of the sexual connection or indecent act concerned.
>
> "(5)   The young person in respect of whom an offence against this section was committed cannot be charged as a party to the offence if the person who committed the offence was of or over the age of 16 years when the offence was committed.
>
> "(6)   In this section,—

---

195 Section 132(4). Note that s 132 is silent on the question of the accused's *belief* in consent. Thus it does not expressly eliminate the possibility of a defence of honest belief in consent. However, such a defence appears to be impliedly excluded by the fact that, if such consent existed *in fact*, it would constitute no defence.
196 *Inglis v Police* (1986) 2 CRNZ 463, 465.
197 *R v N* (1992) 9 CRNZ 471, 473.
198 See *R v Hughes* (1841) 9 C & P 752; 173 ER 1038; *R v Lines* (1844) 1 Car & Kir 393; 174 ER 861.
199 *A-G's Reference (No 1 of 1992)* [1993] 2 All ER 190; [1993] 1 WLR 274 (CA).

"(a) young person means a person under the age of 16 years; and

"(b) doing an indecent act on a young person includes indecently assaulting the young person."

The section covers the identical forms of sexual activity with young people (people under the age of 16) that s 132 covers for children.

18.10.1 Consent

Whereas consent is no defence in relation to children (persons under the age of 12 years), a limited consent defence is provided in s 134A. The section no longer restricts the defence of belief in consent to a person who is under the age of 21 years, a limitation that was considered unjust and arbitrary because it was enacted at a time when 21 was the age of majority.[200] The extended defence will now apply to any person, regardless of age, provided the conditions of s 134A(1) are met. Essentially, this means the accused must now prove that she took reasonable steps to determine the age of the young person, and believed on reasonable grounds that the young person was 16 or older.[201] But where there is a wide age and maturity gap between the accused and a young person, it is anticipated that it will be more difficult for an older defendant to establish the defence. This is because what will be considered reasonable steps for an older person to take, and consequently their reasonable belief, is likely to be more stringent than for a person closer in age to the complainant charged with the same offence.[202] This is consistent with the aim of the provision to protect vulnerable young people from exploitative and predatory sexual and or indecent behaviour[203].

18.10.2 Proving consent-based defences

The defence provided in s 134(1) requires that the person charged must "prove" that before the time of the act, he or she took reasonable steps to ascertain the young person's age (whether of or over 16) and that he or she believed the young person was of or over the age of 16, and that the young person consented. These are, on any view, onerous requirements and suggest that the onus on the accused in this regard is a legal (persuasive) onus and not merely an evidentiary onus, requiring the accused to establish these facts on the balance of probabilities. Parliament has made the conduct a crime and expects citizens engaging in sexual activity with young persons to make a reasonable effort to ascertain the age of prospective partners and to reasonably establish their belief in that regard. These are rather more than casual requirements.[204] However, in order to establish the defence of consent the accused is bound to seriously address the issue of the young person's age, since mere proof that the young person consented and that the person believed he or she was over 16 years of age is not per se a defence.[205]

---

200 See Crimes Amendment Bill (No 2) as Reported from the Law and Order Committee, Commentary, 22 October 2004, 6.
201 Section 134A(1)(a) and (b).
202 Crimes Amendment Bill (No 2) as Reported from the Law and Order Committee, Commentary, 22 October 2004, 6.
203 Crimes Amendment Bill (No 2) as Reported from the Law and Order Committee, Commentary, 22 October 2004, 6.
204 *R v Osborne* (1992) 17 CR (4th) 350. See also the discussion in *Adams*, CA134A.02 (looseleaf).
205 See s 134A(2).

Whether an accused did take reasonable steps to ascertain the complainant's age will depend on the circumstances. In *R v Osborne*[206] it was held that there must be an "earnest" inquiry or some other compelling factor that obviates the need for an inquiry. An accused may only discharge that requirement by showing what steps he took and that these steps were all that could reasonably be required of him in the circumstances. It will not be sufficient to state that further inquiries were not made because they would open the accused to ridicule, embarrassment, or rejection.[207] On the other hand, in order to rely on the defence, the accused need not necessarily directly ask the victim his or her age or ask collateral questions that would disclose her age. It would, however, be open to a jury to conclude that the offenders' belief that the victim was of or over the age of 16 was unreasonable if it was clearly open to him or her to so enquire and he or she deliberately chose not to. The age differential between the accused and the victim may be considered in determining whether the steps taken were reasonable; the greater the disparity in ages, the more inquiry will be required.[208]

In proving the defence under s 134A(1) the accused must prove that he had taken "reasonable steps" to "find out" whether the young person was of the requisite age and that he or she believed "on reasonable grounds" that the young person was 16 or over. Belief may be inferred from the circumstances, including the conduct of the accused and the young person, and need not be sworn to by the accused. Both the belief of the accused and reasonable grounds for the belief must be established by some evidence, so that the accused makes it appear to the jury that he or she did believe on reasonable grounds that the young person was of or over the age mentioned.[209] In such a case, the personal appearance of the young person will be a material piece of evidence, though not necessarily proof, to establish the grounds and belief. The jury must be satisfied on the balance of probabilities that the young person's appearance, taken together with any other available evidence including the accused's testimony (whether sworn or unsworn), establishes both the accused's belief and reasonable grounds for that belief. However, belief may be negatived where there is evidence that the accused never directed his mind to the question of age.[210]

18.10.3 Marriage

Under the Marriage Act 1955, the marriage of persons under the age of 16 years is prohibited.[211] However, the proviso in s 17(2) of that Act, states that "No marriage shall be void by reason only of an infringement of the provisions of this section." By implication, a person under the age of 16 may be "married" because they have undergone a marriage in New Zealand and are thus exempt from prosecution under s 134(4). However, the exemption does not apply to civil unions, which cannot be contracted by persons under the age of 16.[212] Neither does it eliminate the risk of a "married" young person being prosecuted for indecent assault, under s 135 (below, 18.11), in appropriate circumstances.

---

206 *R v Osborne* (1992) 17 CR (4th) 350, 363 (Goodridge CJN).
207 *R v Osborne* (1992) 17 CR (4th) 350, 363 (Goodridge CJN).
208 *R v K (R A)* (1996) 106 CCC (3d) 93, cited in Greenspan (ed), *Martin's Annual Criminal Code 1997*, Aurora, Ontario, Canada Law Book Co, 1996, cc/248.
209 *R v Perry and Pledger* [1920] NZLR 21, 23 (CA).
210 *DPP v Cole* (1994) 100 NTR 1.
211 See s 17 Marriage Act 1955.
212 Section 7 Civil Union Act 2004.

18.10.4 Parties

Section 134(5) preserves the protection against party liability attaching to the complainant where the offender is over the age of 16. However, where the accused is under 16 the complainant can also be prosecuted. The logic of this is that where the accused is under 16 the complainant is likely to be a willing partner, and may be equally culpable.

18.10.5 Proof of age

In any prosecution under ss 131, 131B, 132, and 134, proof of age is an essential element. The fact of a child's age may be proved by any lawful evidence.[213] The question of how age should be proved in such cases was considered in *R v Forrest & Forrest*,[214] where the appellants had been charged under the previous s 134 with having sexual intercourse with a girl under 16. There was no dispute that intercourse had taken place; the principal issue for the Court was whether the Crown had established that the girl was under 16. The only evidence led by the Crown regarding the girl's age came from the girl herself, who produced what she claimed to be her own birth certificate. The Court held that in such a case the issue of proof of age is a matter to which the prosecution "should seriously address itself", adducing the best evidence possible. Since this was not done the appeal was allowed and the convictions quashed. North P said:[215]

> "In a case where exactitude is important, in which it is sought to prove a person's age by his own production of his own birth certificate, it should surely be possible for the deponent to testify ... as to the day on which he has habitually celebrated his birthday, to the age at which he first went to school, and in what year, and similar details as to leaving school, or other matters supporting, though from the mouth of the deponent himself, his identification of himself with the person named in the certificate."

At common law, evidence must be given identifying the person concerned with the person to whom the certified copy of a birth certificate relates.[216] Age may also be proved by direct evidence from someone who was present at the birth[217] or from witnesses who have seen the child and are able to testify as to what they believe his age to be.[218] Since the Crimes Act does not specify how the age of the complainant must be proved, it seems that all of these methods may be legitimate evidence of age in a particular case.

18.11 Indecent assault: s 135

The offence of indecent assault is an electable offence, defined in a straightforward manner:

> **"135 Indecent assault**
>
> "Every one is liable to imprisonment for a term not exceeding 7 years who indecently assaults another person."

---

213 *R v Cox* [1898] 1 QB 179; [1895-99] All ER Rep 1285, 180; 1287.
214 *R v Forrest & Forrest* [1970] NZLR 545 (CA) (North P).
215 *R v Forrest & Forrest* [1970] NZLR 545 (CA), 547 (North P).
216 *R v Bellis* (1911) 6 Cr App R 283 (CCA).
217 See, for example, *R v Nicholls* (1867) 10 Cox CC 476 (CCA).
218 *R v Cox* [1898] 1 QB 179; [1895-99] All ER Rep 1285.

The essence of the offence is indecency,[219] which may occur in the context of an assault or as an ostensibly consensual act. It is the element of indecency which distinguishes the offence from common assault and makes it a rather more serious crime. The offence, like all the offences in Part 7, is gender-neutral. Force is not required for the offence, and the absence of force which often generally distinguish an offence under this section from sexual violation.

18.11.1 Indecent act

The requirement of indecency is subject to an expanded definition of "indecent act" in s 2(1B). The definition provides:

"(1B) For the purposes of this Act, one person does an indecent act on another person whether he or she —

"(a)   does an indecent act with or on the other person; or

"(b)   induces or permits the other person to do an indecent act with or on him or her."

While the words in paragraph (b) expand the definition of an indecent act, and are apt for dealing with incidents involving children, case law will continue to determine the elements of assault and indecency (below, 18.11.2-3). However, earlier case law suggesting that an indecent assault must be directed "at" the complainant is no longer prescriptive, since under the expanded definition an indecent act may occur where an accused "induces" or "permits" an indecent act to be done with or upon him.

18.11.2 Elements of assault

Indecent assault is a species of assault more generally. The essential requirements of an assault are that the accused must have:

(i)   Intentionally applied or attempted to apply force to the person of another, directly or indirectly; or

(ii)   Threatened by an act or gesture to apply force to the person of another; and

(iii) Has, or causes the person being threatened to believe on reasonable grounds that he has, the ability to effect his purpose.[220]

For the purpose of assault, even the slightest touching may constitute force, and at common law the least touching of another in anger was a battery.[221] However, to be an assault the touching must be intentional, and the offence cannot be committed accidentally.[222] It follows that, in the present context, because a typical case of indecency involves some form of physical contact there will usually be force sufficient for an assault. However, even where there is no physical contact between the accused and the victim, the threatened application of force, which causes the victim to believe in the accused's ability to carry out such an assault, may in an appropriate case amount to an indecent assault. This could occur where, for example, a man

---

219   *R v Court* [1989] AC 28; [1988] 2 All ER 221 (HL), 33; 222 (Lord Griffiths).
220   See s 2 Crimes Act 1961.
221   See *Blackstone's Commentaries on the Laws of England*, 17th ed (1830) vol 3, 120; *Cole v Turner* (1704) 6 Mod Rep 149; 90 ER 958.
222   *R v Court* [1989] AC 28; [1988] 2 All ER 221 (HL), 34; 223 (Lord Griffiths). His Lordship cites the example of accidentally ripping a woman's clothing while attempting to force an exit from a train.

indecently exposes himself to a young girl while walking towards her and making indecent suggestions.[223]

18.11.3 Indecently

It is a question of fact for the jury whether an assault committed by the defendant was indecent. In *R v Dunn*, the Court of Appeal approved a jury direction on the meaning of "indecent" in the following terms:

> "It is the modern and popular use and acceptance of that term today. We are talking in this case of 'now', the present day application of that word. It is used in a criminal statute so it must be something which will warrant the sanction of the law, not some trifling or unimportant episode, something sufficient to invoke the law that must appeal to you as a matter of common sense ... The criminal law deals with matters of substance and that is what you have to deal with here. Now 'indecent' is a word which very largely speaks for itself. It is a word ... which the statute uses and it is not qualified in the statute in any way at all."[224]

Whether ordinary people would consider an act indecent will sometimes depend on the purpose with which the action is carried out. In *R v Court*,[225] the House of Lords held that smacking a girl a number of times outside her shorts on her buttocks for no apparent reason is an equivocal action. However, because there was evidence that the accused's purpose was to satisfy a "buttock fetish", it was held to be an indecent assault. The Court held that on a charge of indecent assault it was necessary for the prosecution to prove not only that the accused intentionally assaulted the victim but that in doing so he intended to commit an assault which right-minded persons would think was indecent. Note, however, if the outward nature of the assault is *incapable* of being regarded as indecent, the undisclosed intention of the accused cannot make the assault an indecent one.[226]

An assault that is not inherently indecent may be rendered indecent by its surrounding circumstances. In *Inglis v Police* it was held that a kiss on the lips of a 7-year-old girl alone in a bedroom with a 20-year-old youth, was indecent. Hillyer J said:

> "This was not the sort of innocent peck on the cheek frequently given to children, nor does it appear that the appellant was in the position of an aged uncle or aunt who commonly demonstrate affection in that way."[227]

Similarly, in *Police v B*,[228] a 22-year-old man who kissed a 14-year-old girl on the stomach, thigh, and knee while she lay on her bed under a duvet, was held to have committed an indecent assault having regard to the "time and place and circumstances".

---

223 See *R v Rolfe* (1952) 36 Cr App R 4 (CCA). See also *DPP v Rogers* [1953] 2 All ER 644; [1953] 1 WLR 1017.
224 "*R v Dunn* [1973] 2 NZLR 481 (CA), 482, 483."
225 *R v Court* [1989] AC 28; [1988] 2 All ER 221 (HL). See also 4.4.
226 *R v Court* [1989] AC 28; [1988] 2 All ER 221 (HL), 33; 222 (Lord Keith).
227 "*Inglis v Police* (1986) 2 CRNZ 463, 466. Cf *R v Leeson* (1968) 52 Cr App R 185; [1968] Crim LR 283 (CA), where it was held that an assault by kissing a girl against her will was rendered indecent by accompanying suggestions that she should submit to sexual intercourse."
228 *Police v B* [1994] DCR 581.

In *Beal v Kelley*,[229] an indecent assault was held to have occurred where the appellant pulled a boy towards himself, having just asked the boy to handle his exposed penis. The assault itself was not indecent, but the element of indecency was sufficiently established by proof of the circumstances surrounding the assault. Touching naked young boys on the hands, arms, and torso,[230] and a grown woman's embracing and cuddling a young girl,[231] are both situations where the courts have determined that the accompanying circumstances may render the conduct indecent.[232]

In the UK, the courts have recognised the existence of a category of indecent assault where, rather than being inherently indecent or rendered indecent by its accompanying circumstances, the assault is, at most, *capable* of being considered indecent.[233] Where, as in *R v Court*, an equivocal act could have either an innocent explanation — for example horseplay or physical discipline — or an indecent one, the spanking administered by the accused was said to be *capable* of being considered indecent. Whether it would be considered indecent by right-minded persons would depend on a variety of factors, including the relationship between the parties, and importantly, the reason why the appellant acted as he did.[234]

The effect of the decision in *R v Court* is that evidence of motive may be admissible on the issue of indecency only if right-minded persons *may* consider the assault indecent, and would want to know why the defendant acted as he did before reaching a conclusion.[235] However, such evidence would be irrelevant and inadmissible if right-minded persons would not consider the assault indecent.

It needs to be remembered, however, that consideration of motive is only relevant in circumstances where the act on the face of it does not clearly manifest an intention to, in some way, affront the sexual modesty or integrity of the victim. It will not apply where the act of the accused unequivocally shows such an intention, as where there is a deliberate indecent touching or where the circumstances surrounding the act manifest such an intent. In such cases the indecency of the assault may be inferred from the nature of the act itself; as where a woman induces an underage boy to have intercourse with her[236] or a man inserts his finger into a 15-year-old girl's vagina.[237]

18.11.4 Consent

Consent is a defence to a charge under s 135. However, unlike sexual violation, which requires proof of a "belief on reasonable grounds"(s 128(2)(b) and (3)(b)) before the defence will be available, for indecent assault an "honest" belief as to consent is sufficient. The essence of a charge of indecent assault is that the prosecution must prove that the defendant intended to touch the victim without her consent. If he did not intend to do this, or if he did not so intend because he believed (albeit wrongly) that the victim was consenting, the prosecution will have

---

229 *Beal v Kelley* [1951] 2 All ER 763; (1951) 35 Cr App R 128.
230 *R v Sutton* [1977] 3 All ER 476; [1977] 1 WLR 1086 (CA).
231 *R v Goss and Goss* (1990) 90 Cr App R 400 (CA).
232 See *Rook and Ward on Sexual Offences*, London, Waterlow, 1990, 4ff, and cases discussed there.
233 *R v Court* [1989] AC 28; [1988] 2 All ER 221 (HL), 35; 224 (Lord Griffiths).
234 *Rook and Ward on Sexual Offences*, London, Waterlow, 1990, 6.
235 *Rook and Ward on Sexual Offences*, London, Waterlow, 1990, 6.
236 *R v Hare* [1934] 1 KB 354; [1933] All ER Rep 550 (CCA).
237 *R v McCormack* [1969] 2 QB 442; [1969] 3 All ER 371 (CA), 445; 373 (Fenton Atkinson LJ).

failed to prove the charge. It is the defendant's belief, not the grounds on which it was based, which goes to negative the intent.[238]

This principle was applied in *R v Nazif*,[239] where the 61-year-old offender had allegedly indecently assaulted a 16-year-old girl with whom he was acquainted. As she left his shop the accused grabbed her hand and, holding her with one hand, started kissing her neck while putting his other hand first on her breast then on her genitals. On appeal against his conviction, the appellant argued that the trial judge had misdirected the jury when he said that "if you believe a person is consenting to an assault that consent must be based on reasonable grounds". The Court of Appeal disagreed and held that, except in cases where it is otherwise provided by statute or where there are "other dominant public interest features", it would be contrary to principle that a person who believes the victim of an assault consented to it should be found guilty of an assault. As Somers J said:[240]

> "Where there is evidence of such belief it will be for the Crown to negative it. The reasonableness or otherwise of the grounds of such belief will be material to the question of whether the accused in fact held it."

The fact that indecent assault offences do not involve a "dominant public interest feature" would seem to be the principal reason why the Legislature has chosen not to redefine them as offences that may be committed negligently, by requiring proof of a belief based on objectively reasonable grounds. At present, an honest belief in consent will be a good defence to any sexual assault charge other than sexual violation, unless the defence of consent has itself been excluded expressly by statute.

Recklessness whether the victim consented will also be sufficient mens rea for indecent assault.[241] Although the issue has not been definitively settled, it is probable that only subjective, or *R v Cunningham*[242] recklessness will suffice. In *R v Kimber*, the English Court of Appeal indicated that a defendant is reckless about consent if he "couldn't care less" whether or not the victim is consenting.[243] The implication of this is that *Caldwell* recklessness[244] is not enough: the defendant *must have realised* that the victim might not be consenting but decided to go ahead anyway.[245]

18.11.5 Mens rea

The mens rea of an indecent assault by its nature implies some extra mental element beyond what is required for common assault. In *R v Court*,[246] Lord Griffiths held that the "extra" mental element necessary for an indecent assault should be that which constitutes the essence of the offence. In the case of an offence of indecent assault, the mens rea was said to be an intention to do something "indecent" to the woman, in the sense of an affront to her sexual modesty;

---

238 *R v Kimber* [1983] 3 All ER 316; [1983] 1 WLR 1118 (CA), 319; 1121, 1122.
239 *R v Nazif* [1987] 2 NZLR 122 (CA).
240 *R v Nazif* [1987] 2 NZLR 122 (CA), 128.
241 *R v Kimber* [1983] 3 All ER 316; [1983] 1 WLR 1118 (CA), 320; 1123.
242 *R v Cunningham* [1957] 2 QB 396; [1957] 2 All ER 412 (CCA); see 4.3.1.
243 *R v Kimber* [1983] 3 All ER 316; [1983] 1 WLR 1118 (CA), 320; 1123.
244 *MPC v Caldwell* [1982] AC 341, also reported as *R v Caldwell* [1981] 1 All ER 961 (HL); see 4.3.1.
245 Rook and Ward on Sexual Offences, London, Waterlow, 1990, 19; *R v Bonora* (1994) 35 NSWLR 74. However, for a contrary approach see *DPP v K (a minor)* [1990] 1 All ER 331; (1990) 91 Cr App R 23; also *Fitzgerald v Kennard* (1995) 38 NSWLR 184; (1995) 84 A Crim R 333 (CA).
246 *R v Court* [1989] AC 28; [1988] 2 All ER 221 (HL), 34; 223.

or an intent to do that which the jury would find indecent.[247] In the case of an offence under s 133 (now repealed), the same mens rea would apply, with the rider that the intention to do anything indecent which affronts the girl's sexual integrity should suffice, particularly given that the offence may be committed without the victim's being aware of the indecency having occurred.

An indecent assault may occur under the section in circumstances where, as in *R v Kerr*,[248] the victim was unaware of the threat. In that case the accused was seen to lower his trousers and approach the sleeping victim with an axe held at waist height. He was held to be guilty of assault with a weapon even though the victim was unaware of his approach and there was no physical contact. All that seems to be required in such cases is that the accused, by a threatening act or gesture, displays hostility towards another.[249] There is no requirement for evidence that the accused's conduct created a fear of violence in the mind of the victim; where the alleged assault is based upon a "threatening by any act or gesture" by the accused to apply force, the state of mind of the recipient of the threatening act or gesture is irrelevant.[250] In the example given in 18.9.1, it would equally have been an indecent assault if the victim had had her back to the accused and had been completely unaware of his indecent words and conduct.

18.11.6 A lesser included offence?

One issue which the courts have had to consider is whether indecent assault is a lesser included offence within the definition of sexual violation. Important consequences turn on this where, for example, on a charge of sexual violation there is doubt whether a relevant "introduction" has occurred. Can the court substitute a charge of indecent assault on the grounds that the physical elements of indecent assault are necessarily included in the offence of sexual violation?

It would seem not. The issue arose in *R v Norris*.[251] At the close of the prosecution case on a charge of sexual violation, there was doubt whether penetration had been established. Section 339 Crimes Act 1961 permits a conviction of any crime "included" in the crime charged, where the evidence does not prove the crime actually charged but does prove the included, lesser, offence. Tipping J held that while at first glance it would seem that indecent assault must necessarily be included within a charge of sexual violation, on analysis it is clear that the mental element of sexual violation is different from that of indecent assault. For the former, the Crown must show that the complainant did not consent and that the accused did not believe on reasonable grounds that the complainant was consenting. However, in the case of an indecent assault, while lack of consent must also be proved, an honest belief in consent alone is sufficient to exculpate. Accordingly, it could not be said that the commission of sexual violation necessarily includes the commission of indecent assault. A person may be convicted of sexual violation but on the same facts be acquitted of indecent assault.

The decision in *Norris* may be compared to *R v Leonard*.[252] In that case, the accused, having pleaded guilty to one charge of sexual violation and five charges of indecent assault, applied for leave to appeal out of time against the conviction for sexual violation, on the ground that

---

247   *R v Court* [1989] AC 28; [1988] 2 All ER 221 (HL), 34; 223.
248   *R v Kerr* [1988] 1 NZLR 270; (1987) 2 CRNZ 407 (CA).
249   *R v Kerr* [1988] 1 NZLR 270; (1987) 2 CRNZ 407 (CA).
250   *R v Kerr* [1988] 1 NZLR 270; (1987) 2 CRNZ 407 (CA), 274; 411.
251   *R v Norris* (1988) 3 CRNZ 527.
252   *R v Leonard* 6/6/91, CA179/90.

he should not have pleaded guilty to that charge because the victim had clearly consented. The accused, a 63-year-old man, had kissed the 11-year-old complainant on the vagina but over her underpants in circumstances where there could not have been sexual connection. The Court accepted that since consent had been freely given, and in the absence of any other evidence to support the charge of sexual violation, this was an exceptional case in which the accused upon the admitted facts could not in law have been convicted of sexual violation. But Sir Gordon Bisson, delivering the judgment of the Court, then ruled:[253]

> "However, there is no doubt that the particular conduct the basis of the charge of sexual violation on the admitted fact amounted to an indecent assault. We substitute a conviction of indecent assault for that of sexual violation."

The Court cited no authority for this ruling. In light of the ruling in *Norris*, it is arguable that the Court misled itself in assuming that the fact that the "particular conduct" founding the sexual violation charge "included", or in the Court's words "amounted to", an indecent assault; and that the Court failed to distinguish between the common physical elements of both crimes and the differing mental elements. On the authority of *Norris*, it cannot be said that indecent assault is a lesser included offence within the crime of sexual violation. Although the outcome would seem to be correct, it is arguable that the proper procedure would have been for the Court to amend the count of sexual violation to one of indecent assault, per s 335(1), "so as to make it conformable with the proof".

18.12 Sexual exploitation of person with significant impairment

Section 138 creates three offences of having exploitative sexual activity with a person with a significant impairment, as follows:

> "**138 Sexual exploitation of person with significant impairment**
>
> "(1) Every one is liable to imprisonment for a term not exceeding 10 years who has exploitative sexual connection with a person with a significant impairment.
>
> "(2) Every one is liable to imprisonment for a term not exceeding 10 years who attempts to have exploitative sexual connection with a person with a significant impairment.
>
> "(3) For the purposes of subsections (1) and (2), a person has exploitative sexual connection with a person with a significant impairment (the 'impaired person') if he or she—
>
> "(a) has sexual connection with the impaired person knowing that the impaired person is a person with a significant impairment; and
>
> "(b) has obtained the impaired person's acquiescence in, submission to, participation in, or undertaking of the connection by taking advantage of the impairment.
>
> "(4) Every one is liable to imprisonment for a term not exceeding 5 years who exploitatively does an indecent act on a person with a significant impairment.

---

253 R v Leonard 6/6/91, CA179/90, 3, 4.

"(5) For the purposes of subsection (4), a person exploitatively does an indecent act on a person with a significant impairment (the 'impaired person') if he or she—

"(a) does an indecent act on the impaired person knowing that the impaired person is a person with a significant impairment; and

"(b) has obtained the impaired person's acquiescence in, submission to, participation in, or undertaking of the doing of the act by taking advantage of the impairment.

"(6) For the purposes of this section, a significant impairment is an intellectual, mental, or physical condition or impairment (or a combination of 2 or more intellectual, mental, or physical conditions or impairments) that affects a person to such an extent that it significantly impairs the person's capacity—

"(a) to understand the nature of sexual conduct; or

"(b) to understand the nature of decisions about sexual conduct; or

"(c) to foresee the consequences of decisions about sexual conduct; or

"(d) to communicate decisions about sexual conduct."

The essence of the new offences is exploitative activity undertaken with knowledge of the relevant impairment and evidence of acquiescence obtained by taking advantage of the impairment. This provision replaces the former offence of having sexual intercourse with a severely subnormal woman or girl and is intended to cover acts prohibited by the now repealed former s 142. Section 138 is now the only provision specifically proscribing sexual conduct with a significantly impaired person,[254] and it brings any relevant mental, intellectual or physical impairment within its ambit.

The current legislation does not proscribe any form of sexual contact with psychiatric patients. This is consistent with the view that the 2005 amendments are not intended to criminalise the situation where a person with a psychiatric condition or an intellectual disability is capable of, and wishes to, pursue a genuinely consensual sexual relationship with another person.[255] An earlier requirement that the Crown prove that the complainant lacked the capacity to give consent was removed on the recommendation of the Law and Order Committee, giving effect to the policy objective of protecting persons with significant impairments, without placing additional proof requirements on the Crown.[256] Thus the Crown is only required to prove that the accused had sexual connection with, or did an indecent act with a person with an impairment by taking advantage of their impairment.

The rationale for s 138 is, principally, to protect vulnerable people from exploitation. It is doubtful now whether the earlier suggested rationale, namely, to guard against all the problems

---

254 Contrast the position in English law, where both the Mental Health Act 1959 and the Sexual Offences Acts of 1956 and 1967 define a range of offences that may be committed against those who are mentally handicapped or psychiatrically unwell.
255 See Ministry of Justice, Review of Sexual Crimes under the Crimes Act 1961 (Paper 3), undated, para 31, discussed in *Adams*, CA138.01.
256 Crimes Amendment Bill (No 2) as Reported from the Law and Order Committee, Commentary, 22 October 2004, 18.

that can arise when a severely subnormal woman becomes pregnant[257] still applies, since the essence of the new offence is exploitative sexual conduct.[258]

18.12.1 Significant impairment

Proof of a "significant impairment" experienced by the victim is axiomatic to successful prosecution under s 138. The concept has no previous legislative history in New Zealand, although some assistance in the interpretation of the expression is provided in the extended definition in subs (6). However, that subsection only defines the relevantly impaired capacities associated with significant impairment. It says nothing about the types of intellectual, mental, or physical conditions that might qualify as relevant impairments. These are left to be determined by the courts on a case-by-case basis. There is no suggestion that a relevant impairment must be permanent or enduring. It could be argued that any condition could qualify, whether permanent or transient, or of long or short duration, which has the effect of diminishing the complainant's cognitive and communicative capacities for the duration of the exploitative sexual conduct in question. This leaves open the question of whether conditions like alcoholism and drug addiction, which may significantly impair cognitive and communicative capacities, are relevant impairments for the purposes of the section. In addition, whether someone has an intellectual or mental condition that significantly impairs their capacity to understand the "nature" of decisions about sexual conduct may depend on what the "nature" of such decisions is thought to be.[259] In some circumstances, such decisions are culturally determined and may not be self-evident to a lay juror.

The degree of actual intellectual or mental impairment may also be critical in some cases. In *R v B*[260] the complainant, who had been the victim of a sexual assault by a family member, was described as being in the "twilight zone" of mental impairment; being in the borderline range between normal intellect and people who have an intellectual disability. She had a diminished capacity to look after herself and impaired cognitive abilities, though was not suffering from a diagnosable intellectual disability. Her mental condition was related to problems associated with hydrocephalus (water on the brain) and epilepsy. In disallowing the defence of consent to a charge of indecent assault, the Court concluded that it is in a twilight zone such as the complainant occupied — "the world of the adult who is really still a child" — that protection is most needed.

This analysis suggests some useful parameters for "significant impairment" under s 138: namely, whether the complainant's capacity for self-protection is so reduced by a relevant disability or impairment that he effectively occupies a child-like state, a vulnerability which exposes him to sexual exploitation.

18.12.2 Mens Rea

To be guilty of an offence under the section, the accused must "know" that the complainant has a significant impairment. "Know" implies subjective mens rea: that the accused believes

---

257 *R v Whittaker* 27/8/97, CA23/97.
258 The re-wording of the offence as a gender-neutral crime aimed at prohibiting exploitative sexual conduct against significantly impaired person generally, avoids the difficult interpretative issues that arose in relation to "severe submormality" in the previous provision. A brief history of this issue can be found in the second edition of this work, at 665-666.
259 *Adams*, CA138.02.
260 *R v B* (1993) 11 CRNZ 64.

the other person has a significant impairment, and has no serious doubt about the matter (above, 4.5). Such knowledge may be inferred from surrounding facts, for example the accused's acknowledgement in a diary that the complainant was simple-minded and intellectually disabled, and his knowledge of her circumstances through close contact with her family.[261]

However, knowledge will involve more than simply an appreciation that the complainant was seriously intellectually, mentally, or physically impaired. The extended definition of "significant impairment" in subs (6) means that it must be proved that the accused knew that the impairment was of such a degree as to significantly impair the complainant's capacity to understand the nature of sexual conduct, or the nature of decisions about sexual conduct, or to foresee the consequences of such decisions, or to communicate such decisions. Thus an accused would be prevented from denying mens rea if it was proved that she knew that the complainant's capacity to understand the nature of sexual conduct was significantly impaired, even if he claimed he did not know she was incapable of communicating decisions about sexual conduct; but mens rea would be lacking if he honestly believed that the complainant did have the capacity to do the things specified in subs (6)(a)-(d).

Prima facie, the requirements for knowledge of impairment and obtaining of acquiescence, etc, in s 138(3)(b) are to be read conjunctively, so that an accused may be guilty only if he possessed the relevant knowledge and then obtained acquiescence by taking advantage of the known impairment. The identical mens rea requirement applies whether sexual connection under subs (3) or doing an indecent act under subs (5) is alleged.

However, mens rea is not defeated by the accused's attributing to the alleged sexual conduct a legally innocent purpose, if the requisite elements of knowledge and conduct have been established. The mere fact that the accused had no hostility towards the complainant will not negate mens rea. In R v McNally[262], the accused sought to defend a charge under the previous section involving an 18-year-old complainant with a mental age of 12 years, on the basis that he regarded his involvement with her as an extramarital affair with a young woman whom he thought was an ordinary person, possibly slow, but definitely not subnormal. The explanation was clearly rejected by the jury. On appeal, McKay J said:[263]

> "It is quite unreal to describe these offences as if they were instances of extra marital consensual sex. This was not a single isolated offence, but one which was repeated. It is difficult to see how McNally could have been other than well aware of her subnormality, and the issue of his knowledge has been settled by the jury's verdict. He took advantage of her in circumstances involving a gross breach of trust."

18.12.3 Consent

Section 138 is silent on the question of consent. Ostensibly, the protective nature of the offence would seem to imply that consent is no defence. However, the new offence is not as restrictive as the offence provision it replaces and, as noted above, seeks to preserve the right of people with mental or physical impairments to pursue genuinely consensual sexual relationships with others when they choose. This suggests that, even where a person suffers from a significant

---

261 R v Whittaker 27/8/97, CA23/97.
262 R v McNally 6/4/93, CA441/92.
263 R v McNally 6/4/93, CA441/92, 5.

impairment, he may nonetheless retain a capacity to make meaningful personal decisions, including whether to consent to sexual activity. Unlike a "severely subnormal woman or girl", the subject of the former section, who was presumptively incapable of consent, a person with a "significant impairment" may, or may not, be capable of consenting to sexual conduct. The way in which the section now operates is to stipulate that, where such a person does consent, their consent is to be honoured unless it has been obtained by the accused's taking advantage of their impairment with the necessary mens rea.

18.12.4 Acquiescence, submission, participation, or undertaking

Before leaving the issue of consent, it is necessary to consider the significance of the expressions in s 138(3)(b) and (5)(b). Under those subsections, exploitative sexual conduct is established where, with relevant mens rea, the accused obtains "acquiescence in, submission to, participation in, or undertaking of the [sexual act] by taking advantage of the impairment". Arguably, if the complainant actually consents then the words "acquiescence", etc are superfluous, even where the impairment has been exploited.

However, the emphasis in the offence is on the element of "taking advantage" of the impairment. Thus the words "acquiescence in ..." etc, might be understood as including situations where actual consent has been obtained by taking advantage of the impairment.[264] Once the Crown has proved that the relevant sexual activity has taken place, the issue is simply whether the accused has brought about the activity by exploiting the complainant's impairment. This analysis penalises the wrongfulness of the accused's exploitative conduct, while nonetheless allowing the complainant to consent to sexual activity where that exploitative element is absent.[265]

While this is a possible approach, in our view it is not the correct one. In particular, the definition of the offence is expressed not simply in terms of sexual exploitation, but in terms of exploitation where the capacity for consent is significantly impaired. "Taking advantage" of an impairment is not a mere feature of the complainant's consent but, rather, an additional circumstance of the actus reus. If consent capacity is intact and a valid consent is given, the offence is not established simply upon proof that the accused took advantage of the impairment. We suggest, therefore, that there are four elements to the offence:

(a)   sexual conduct (connection or indecent act);

(b)   knowledge of the relevant impairment;

(c)   taking advantage of the impairment; and

(d)   absence of a capacitated and free consent.

The Crown must prove the first three elements beyond a reasonable doubt. The accused may avoid conviction if he or she can discharge an evidentiary onus to suggest there was a genuine consent (or, presumably, an honest belief in consent). The Crown must then disprove consent beyond a reasonable doubt.

---

264   *Adams*, CA138.04.
265   *Adams*, CA138.04.

18.13 Other sexual offences

The reforms of 2005 have had a significant impact on the structure and content of sexual offences in New Zealand. In particular, all sexual offences are now gender-neutral and many former gender-specific offences have been repealed. As the foregoing discussion shows, the Legislature has opted for a range of generic sexual offences, many of which are geared toward protecting those with special needs on account of age or disability. The offence of "anal intercourse" previously contained in s 142 and first introduced by the s 5 Homosexual Law Reform Act 1986, has been repealed and not replace. Proscribed acts of anal intercourse are now included in the statutory definition of "sexual connection" which informs the conduct element in a range of newly defined offences, including sexual conduct with a dependent family member (s 131), sexual conduct with a child under 12 (s 132), sexual conduct with a young person under 16 (s 134), and sexual exploitation of a person with significant impairment (s 138).

A small band of offences involving bestiality and indecent acts with animals has been preserved,[266] although prosecutions in this area are rare. Other unusual offences, like conspiracy to induce sexual intercourse (s 136), inducing sexual intercourse under pretence of marriage (s 137), which were rarely, if ever, prosecuted, have also been repealed, while wholly new offences, like meeting a young person under 16 following sexual grooming (s 131B), have been created. Such "new generation" sexual offences supplement other sexual offences created in response to international trends in the sexual exploitation of children.[267]

---

266 See ss 142A (compelling indecent act with animal), 143 (bestiality) and 144 (indecency with animal) Crimes Act 1961.
267 See ss 144A-144C Crimes Act 1961. These offences concern sexual conduct with children and young people outside New Zealand and involve such other activities as organising or promoting child sex tours.

Chapter 19

THEFT AND RECEIVING

19.1	Property, rights, and justice	662
19.2	Theft	664
19.3	Actus reus	665
19.3.1	Property	665
(1)	*What counts as property?*	665
(2)	*Things in action and other intangible property*	666
(3)	*Bank accounts*	666
(4)	*Documents*	667
(5)	*Information*	667
(6)	*Services*	668
(7)	*Gas, water, and electricity*	668
(8)	*Body parts*	668
(9)	*Wild creatures*	670
19.3.2	Owned by another	671
(1)	*What proprietary interests are protected by s 218(1)?*	671
(2)	*Theft by an owner from others with proprietary interests*	672
(3)	*Theft by an absolute owner? When D's interest is better than V's*	673
(4)	*Has D become an absolute owner?*	674
(5)	*Abandoning, losing, and finding things*	679
19.3.3	Taking, using, or dealing with	681
(1)	*Taking*	682
(2)	*Usage or dealing*	683
19.4	Mens rea	686
19.4.1	Dishonestly	686
19.4.2	Without claim of right	688
19.4.3	Intent to deprive permanently	689
(1)	*Dishonest borrowing and conditional intentions*	689
(2)	*Dishonest borrowing v replacement*	690
(3)	*Supplementary theftuous intents*	691
19.5	Receiving	692
19.5.1	The actus reus	693
(1)	*Receiving something*	693
(2)	*Property*	694
(3)	*Stolen or obtained by any crime*	694
19.5.2	Mens rea	696

19.5.3 Evidence of criminality: the doctrine of recent possession..697

19.1 Property, rights, and justice

According to Hume,[1]

> "A man's property is something related to him: This relation is not natural, but moral and founded upon justice. 'Tis very preposterous, therefore, to imagine, that we can have any idea of property, without fully comprehending the nature of justice .... The origin of justice explains that of property."

The recognition and protection of property rights in our society raise deep questions of political philosophy. In part, this is because the concept of "property" is itself amorphous. There is a tendency to associate property with "things" — to think of property in terms of objects endowed with spatial dimensions, that can be touched and seen. The association is often appropriate, but can be misleading. Property, understood in the context of a legal system, is a legal phenomenon — and rights of property are not physical things but legal constructs. Indeed, in an important sense proprietary rights are a species of personal right. They are rights between persons, which are held by one person against another person or persons.[2] That I own something means, in law, that I have certain rights to deal with that thing which others do not have and that others owe me certain duties not to deal with it.

These rights and duties are not absolute. D is not free to torture her cat. Ownership of land does not mean the police have no right, under any circumstances, to enter; neither does it make one free to build upon the land without permission. Property may be subject to taxation and even expropriation by the State.

Moreover, the rights associated with ownership of property vary across different types of property. As we shall see, the human body is not susceptible of ownership in the same way as is a kettle. Similarly, the legal nature of property has varied across different periods of social and legal development. In the early common law, ownership was conceived of in terms of the right to possession:[3] this explains, for instance, why the tort of conversion could only be committed against a plaintiff in possession or with an immediate proprietary right to possession.[4]

The extent to which property is a pre-legal concept (rather than a creation of law) is a matter of controversy. Property rights are distinguished from other interpersonal rights by the fact that they exist in respect of some thing; yet that thing may be tangible or intangible and, independent of the law, property seems to lack any clear-cut definition.[5] Despite this, much of our law and society takes property to be a foundational concept. In both civil and criminal law, sanctions for wrongs such as conversion, theft, and the like, normally require proof of a

---

1 Hume, *A Treatise of Human Nature*, 2nd ed, Selby-Bigge and Nidditch, eds, New York, Oxford Press, 1978, 491.
2 Hume, *A Treatise of Human Nature*, 2nd ed, Selby-Bigge and Nidditch, eds, New York, Oxford Press, 1978, 491.
3 Cf Hohfeld, *Fundamental Legal Conceptions as Applied in Judicial Reasoning* (1919) 71ff; Harris, *Property and Justice*, New York, Clarendon Press, 1996, 120ff.
4 Pollock and Maitland, *The History of English Law* (2nd ed, 1911) Vol. I, 57, Vol. II, 153ff; Tigar, "The Right of Property and the Law of Theft" (1984) 62 Texas LR 1443.
5 Gray, "Property in Thin Air" [1991] CLJ 252.

harm. Implicitly, these sanctions take it for granted that there is some right of property that can be harmed, such that corrective justice is called for; or even, in Locke's work, so that the government of a society is warranted.[6] This sort of proposition — that property may be prior to tort and criminal law, and even prior to law — informs much political theory, especially by libertarian philosophers.[7] Property rights are defended by liberal political philosophers, too, on the ground that autonomy is augmented when individuals are able to choose for themselves how they deal with their property, spend their money, etc.[8] If my well-being is increased by breaking crockery from time to time, without risking harm to others, that should be my affair — provided the crockery is mine.

At the same time, the reasons for law to recognise property are not only individualistic. Donne's admonition that no man is an island also has communitarian implications for the law of property. In a social context, property rights help to co-ordinate the activities of society members, by limiting the freedom of citizens to conduct themselves without trespassing unduly upon the private lives of others. Property rights can enhance liberty, yet their free use by one may restrict the capacity for well-being of another. Even in societies which endorse a free-market economic philosophy, the law typically contains a panoply of constraints on monopolistic, exploitative, or otherwise unfair action. Similarly, taxation derogates from absolute notions of property, but may be justified by redistributive arguments — including the need to foster minimum standards of living in others. In economic terms, a selective recognition of property rights offers chances both to foster economic prosperity and to provide for non-economic externalities like basic needs and human rights.

Legal institutions of property, therefore, must accommodate both the principles and privileges of ownership, with its implications for corrective justice, and the need to allocate social wealth, driven by concerns of distributive justice. However, by contrast with corrective justice, which presupposes a notion of property, distributive justice may operate prior to the law's conception of property.[9] An absolutist legal conception of property would generate a system in which autonomy, consent, and individual fault are determinative. These concepts are certainly important to the common law. But they are not the only considerations. For example, in many jurisdictions constructive trusts are now imposed for reasons of fairness, say upon the break-up of a domestic relationship where no formal arrangements existed regarding distribution of property. The recognition of property in commercial contexts may be determined by the need to allocate risk in unforeseen circumstances, or by considerations of priority in insolvency. Indeed, the Canadian Supreme Court has even suggested that proprietary remedies can be created, or even refused, on a discretionary basis according to whether "there is reason to grant to the plaintiff the additional rights that flow from recognition of a right of property."[10]

---

6   Locke, *Two Treatises of Government*, Book II, § 123. Cf *Entick v Carrington* (1765) 19 St Tr 1029, 1060: "[t]he great end for which men entered into society was to secure their property".
7   See, eg, Nozick, *Anarchy, State and Utopia*, Oxford, Blackwell, 1974.
8   See Waldron, *The Right to Private Property*, New York, Oxford University Press, 1988; Simmonds, "The Possibility of Private Law" in Tasioulas (ed), *Law, Values and Social Practices*, Dartmouth, Aldershot, 1997, 75.
9   According to Grey, "The Disintegration of Property" in *Property: NOMOS xxii,*: (1980) 69, 81: "The substitution of a bundle-of-rights for a thing-ownership conception of property has the ultimate consequence that property ceases to be an important category in legal and political theory".
10 *Lac Minerals Ltd v Corona Resources Ltd* (1989) 61 DLR 14, 51.

By and large, these distributive factors are not the concern of the criminal law, since it is not for the criminal law to decide when property rights exist. Rather, property offences exist primarily to reinforce and protect those rights once recognised by the civil law. Indirectly, therefore, property offences are not merely a means to protect individuals' autonomous rights over property, but also a tool for reinforcing political decisions about the distribution of scarce resources in society. Prima facie rules of property arise in the civil law for a variety of underlying reasons. Yet the criminal law does not look behind the prima facie rules. It takes ownership, and its facets, as an axiom.

Inevitably so. Both civil and criminal law share a conception of ownership. Notwithstanding what has been said here about when ownership should be recognised, its recognition necessarily involves certain legal consequences, at least in a liberal society.[11] Ownership of property confers upon the owner a set of powers, in particular to use and to alienate (transfer) the property, and to exclude others from doing the same. Without these powers there is no ownership. In the context of property offences, the function of the criminal law is to protect those rights of ownership. This means that the criminal law must take its lead from the civil law: the creature it protects is a creation of the civil law.

In the criminal law, that protection is achieved by a variety of offences which impose obligations on non-owners not to usurp the powers of an owner. First among them, and the primary subject of this chapter, is the prohibition of theft.

19.2 Theft

The crimes against rights of property are contained in Part 10 of the Crimes Act 1961. That Part was fundamentally reformed in 2003, when the previous Part was repealed in its entirety and replaced by a new set of provisions that redefine many of the key concepts in property offences, including dishonesty, property, and colour of right. Consequently, the previous case law is of limited relevance to the current legislation.

Theft is now defined in s 219(1) Crimes Act 1961:

"Theft or stealing is the act of,—

"(a)   dishonestly and without claim of right, taking any property with intent to deprive any owner permanently of that property or of any interest in that property; or

"(b)   dishonestly and without claim of right, using or dealing with any property with intent to deprive any owner permanently of that property or of any interest in that property after obtaining possession of, or control over, the property in whatever manner."

Section 219 is concerned solely with the definition of theft, and does not as such create an offence. That task is left to s 223, which enacts a graduated series of offences according to the value of the property stolen.[12]

---

11   Cf Honoré, "Ownership" in Guest (ed), *Oxford Essays in Jurisprudence*, London, Oxford University Press, 1961, 107.
12   According to s 223, every one who commits a theft as defined under s 219 is liable to be sentenced to imprisonment, for up to 7 years if the value of the property stolen is greater than $1,000; for up to one year if the value exceeds $500 but not $1,000; or for up to 3 months if the value is not greater than $500.

Under s 219, one may commit theft in two ways: by taking another's property; and by using or dealing with another's property that is within one's possession or control. Both manners of theft contain six elements, each of which must be proved by the prosecution. The first three elements comprise the actus reus:

(i) There must be property;

(ii) The property must be owned by another (ie someone other than D); and

(iii) Either:

    (a) D must *take* the property; or

    (b) D must *use* or *deal* with the property, after obtaining possession or control over it.

The other three elements comprise the mens rea:

(iv) D must intend permanently to deprive any owner of either the property or any interest in the property; and

(v) D must act dishonestly; and

(vi) D must act without claim of right.

Each of these elements will be considered below.

19.3 Actus reus

As we noted above, there are three elements to the actus reus of theft. The defendant must (i) take, use, or deal with any (ii) property, which is (iii) at least in part owned by another.

19.3.1 Property

Section 219 specifies that the thing stolen must be "any property". What counts as property is elucidated by s 2(1), which now reads:

> "Property includes real and personal property, and any estate or interest in any real or personal property, money, electricity, and any debt, and any thing in action, and any other right or interest"

By this definition, the traditional restrictions on what property can be the subject of theft have been abandoned. Anything that is property within the meaning set out in s 2(1) can be stolen, whether tangible or intangible. Unlike the old common law rule, there is no further requirement that the thing stolen have any economic value, although value will be relevant to sentencing decisions.[13]

(1) *What counts as property?*

By virtue of s 2(1), most things can be stolen. The section specifically includes real as well as personal property, as well as any rights and interests therein. The scope of the section is sufficient to include both equitable and legal proprietary interests.

At the same time, s 2(1) is an *inclusive* provision rather than a definition. It remains necessary to show that the thing stolen is, in law, an item of "property"; and the definition of that term

---

13 See s 223.

is a matter for the civil law. Most instances of theft are straightforward: D absconds with a television set or some other chattel — a piece of tangible personal property. Other cases, however, may be less obvious. Suppose D usurps V's right of way, or takes a train ride without first buying a ticket. Are these cases of theft? Although most things are capable of being owned, even in the civil law it is sometimes unclear whether particular rights constitute a form of legal or equitable property (ie rights in rem) or merely give rise to entitlements to sue others in contract, tort, or equity (rights in personam). In what follows, we survey some of the main areas of difficulty.

(2)   *Things in action and other intangible property*

Prior to the 2003 revamp of property offences, the offence of theft pertained only to tangible property. This limitation, that the item stolen must have a physical existence, meant that theft did not extend to a number of things regarded as "property" in civil law. Hence, in *R v Wilkinson*,[14] the Court of Appeal held that a fraudulently obtained electronic transfer of funds fell outside the ambit of theft because the assets involved were intangible. The restriction was a by-product of an age when value resided primarily in tangible property. In the modern world, the increasingly electronic nature of our wealth has made the protection of intangible assets an inevitable extension.

The most common forms of intangible asset comprise *things in action*. A thing in action, also called a "chose in action", is something in which the law acknowledges property rights but which has no physical existence. Such rights cannot be asserted physically and can be vindicated only by legal action (hence a thing "in action"). Examples of choses in action are a debt, shares in a company, and a trade mark or copyright. Under s 2(1), all these things are now capable of being stolen.

(3)   *Bank accounts*

The relationship between banker and customer is one of debtor and creditor[15] or, if the account is in overdraft, vice versa. Since debts are a type of chose in action, it follows that the customer's right to draw on a credit balance is property within the scope of s 2(1), and can be stolen. Additionally, an agreed overdraft facility, which has not been fully drawn down, gives the customer a legal right against the bank and so also constitutes a chose in action.[16]

Suppose, for example, that D is a director of company C, with signing authority over C's account with bank B. If D dishonestly draws cheques on that account for personal purposes, thereby causing C's account with B to be debited, D now commits theft. He steals C's right of action, against B, for the amount by which C's account is debited.[17]

That is the standard case. Suppose instead, however, that D dishonestly draws a cheque on C's account when the account is in overdraft beyond the authorised limit. In this situation, it seems there is no theft. When an account is overdrawn beyond its agreed limit, the bank has no legal obligation to meet the cheque. Hence, C has no chose in action against B, and there is nothing for D to steal.[18]

---

14   *R v Wilkinson* [1999] 1 NZLR 403; (1998) 16 CRNZ 179 (CA).
15   *Foley v Hill* (1848) 2 HLC 28, 9 ER 1002.
16   *Kohn* (1979) 69 Cr App R 395.
17   *Kohn* (1979) 69 Cr App R 395; cf *Williams (Roy)* [2001] 1 Cr App R 362.

(4) Documents

Even before the revamped definition of theft, it was possible to steal the documentary manifestation of intangible assets. Hence, although one could not steal a chose of action, there could be theft of the piece of paper which represented that chose of action; so, for example, theft of a cheque was theft of the piece of paper rather than theft of the proceeds.[19] This remains a possible option for prosecutors, although will only be necessary where the document relates to something that is not itself property — for example, information.

(5) Information

It seems that mere information does not qualify for protection as intangible property.[20] In the English case of *Oxford v Moss*,[21] a university student took an examination paper before the examination and copied it before returning the paper to its original location. He was held not to have committed theft. Even though the information on the examination paper was no longer confidential, in the eyes of the law the university had not been deprived of any property. It would have been different if the student had not returned the examination paper itself, since he could then have been convicted of stealing the paper on which the examination was typed.

Moreover, even where the right being interfered with *is* property for the purposes of the Act, the interference may not always count as theft. Breach of copyright, for instance, *violates* a chose in action. But photocopying a textbook *deprives* the copyright owner neither of the book nor of copyright in that book.[22] To breach a right is not to steal it.

Where information amounts to a trade secret, it is separately protected by the offence of taking, obtaining, or copying trade secrets, contrary to s 230. It is at least arguable, however, that broader protection should be available through the law of theft. Information can be worth an enormous amount of money. It may be the subject of contract, and its acquisition often involves the expenditure of considerable human and financial resources. We take it for granted that the recipe for Coca Cola is secret, both from us and from the manufacturer's competitors. Certainly it receives protection under the civil law, albeit not from the law of property.[23] Why not from the law of theft? In modern times, a nation's economic activity depends upon owners being able to protect the intangible rewards of their labours just as much as the tangible chattels they produce. The knowledge generated by research and development activities is vital to economic growth, and the case for criminalising theft of that knowledge is at least arguable.[24] The requirement under New Zealand law that the thing stolen be property (at civil

---

18 Cf *Navvabi* [1986] 3 All ER 102. D might, however, be guilty of obtaining the proceeds of the cheque by deception, contrary to s 240.
19 *R v Bennitt* [1961] NZLR 452. Cf *Bishop v NZ Law Soc* [1932] NZLR 452 (theft of documents of title to land).
20 Cf *Federal Commissioner of Taxation v United Aircraft Corp* (1943) 68 CLR 525 (HCA), 534-5 (Latham CJ); *Boardman v Phipps* [1967] 2 AC 46, 102-3 (Lord Cohen), 127-8 (Lord Upjohn), though for more equivocal views see at 89-91 (Viscount Dilhorne), 107 (Lord Hodson), 115 (Lord Guest).
21 *Oxford v Moss* (1979) 68 Cr App R 183. See [1979] Crim LR 119.
22 Cf *Lloyd* [1985] QB 829; *Rank Film Distributors Ltd v Video Information Centre* [1982] AC 380, 445; *Storrow and Poole* [1983] Crim LR 332.
23 *Fraser v Thames Television* [1984] QB 44; *A-G v Observer Ltd* [1990] 1 AC 107, Stuckey, "The Equitable Action for Breach of Confidence: Is Information Ever Property?" (1981) 9 Sydney LR 402.
24 See Cross, "Protecting Confidential Information under the Criminal Law of Theft and Fraud" (1991) 11 OJLS 264.

law) bears instructive contrast with the United States, where the Model Penal Code defines a specialist, criminal-law concept of property: "'Property' means anything of value".[25]

On the other hand, extending the law of theft to include the theft of information raises difficult questions concerning the proper scope of protection. Should all confidential information be protected, or just trade secrets? When is information sufficiently confidential? What if the information is a matter of public interest?[26] The area may be better regulated by specialist provisions such as s 230, and not by theft.

(6) Services

A service is not by itself property.[27] So, for example, a ride on a train cannot be stolen,[28] though D's activity may comprise some other offence such as obtaining by deception;[29] and one might steal the piece of paper on which the ticket is printed.

(7) Gas, water, and electricity

At common law, gas and water — having a corporeal existence — are considered to be tangible property and, as such, could be stolen.[30] However electricity, like other forms of energy such as heat, is not property.[31] Nonetheless, by express stipulation in s 2(1), electricity is deemed to be property for the purposes of the Crimes Act 1961.[32] Heat and other forms of energy remain outside the scope of theft.

(8) Body parts

Some things, though corporeal, cannot be owned at all. At common law this included wild animals (ferae naturae) when at large, and the human body, even when deceased;[33] so a human corpse cannot be stolen, although the corpse of a farm animal can.[34] The position with regard to wild animals is now covered specifically by s 218 (see 19.3.1(9)). However, the question of the human body or body parts is not addressed in the Crimes Act, and remains uncertain.

There is an interim right to possession (not ownership) of a corpse which vests in those charged with its burial.[35] Apart from this, the courts have sometimes recognised a limited possessory right in a corpse or body part if being used as a medical specimen or exhibit as in a museum, at least where the item has acquired different attributes by undergoing a lawful application of skill (for example dissection or embalming);[36] and the Human Tissue Act 1964 allows certain persons a right of possession to a body in particular circumstances.

---

25 Model Penal Code, § 223.0(6).
26 Cf. Cripps, "The Public Interest Defence to the Action for Breach of Confidence and the Law Commission's Proposals on Disclosure in the Public Interest" (1984) 4 OJLS 361.
27 *Bagley* (1923) 17 Cr App R 162.
28 Cf *Boulton* (1849) 1 Den 508, 169 ER 349; *Beecham* (1851) 5 Cox 181.
29 Contrary to s 240. See ch 20 below.
30 *White* (1853) Dears 203, 169 ER 696; *Firth* (1869) LR 1 CCR 172 (gas); *Ferens v O'Brien* (1883) 11 QBD 21 (water, once severed from land). Note that water in a lake or pond counts as a severable part of the land on which it stands, so is a form of real property.
31 Cf *Low v Blease* [1975] Crim LR 513.
32 Cf *R v Koura* [1996] 2 NZLR 9; (1996) 13 CRNZ 463 (CA).
33 *Williams v Williams* (1882) 20 Ch D 659; [1881-1885] All ER Rep 840, 662f; 843f. (Extending to a corpse the logic of the proposition that a live human body cannot be subject to ownership.)
34 *R v Edwards* (1877) 13 Cox CC 384.
35 *Calma v Sesar* (1992) 106 FLR 446; *Dobson v North Tyneside HA* [1996] 4 All ER 474, 478.

At the level of principle, there are difficult issues here. The fact that there may be certain limited rights to a corpse or parts thereof does not resolve the question of whether that corpse or its parts can be stolen. The problem is that for something to be property, it must at least be *susceptible* of being owned. Even though there may be possessory rights in some circumstances, it appears that body parts are incapable at civil law of being owned.[37] In turn, if they cannot be owned, it would seem that, like the corpse itself, they are not property and cannot be stolen.

One way of responding to this difficulty would be for the courts to become more willing to recognise that body parts can be the "property" of someone, as s 219 requires, especially where legitimate work has been done on the item (for example by preparation of a kidney for transplantation); although the rights to such items might vest only in certain eligible persons and be accompanied by stringent duties.[38] By virtue of s 218(1), someone with possessory rights is deemed to be the "owner" for the purposes of Part 10 of the Crimes Act; correspondingly, where there is a deemed owner, the body parts may be regarded as property within Part 10. If so, a second problem for the law would be to identify *when* such possessory rights can arise. For example, it remains unclear under present law whether anyone has a property right to a body part designated for transplant surgery; and thus whether such items can be stolen.

It is certainly arguable that body parts deserve the protection of the criminal law.[39] Indeed, perhaps it is time that the old rule that there can be no property in a body or its parts — a rule of dubious ancestry[40] — was itself abandoned. However, there is also something to be said for the view that interference with such things as body parts, in which there are no ordinary rights of ownership, is not the sort of wrongdoing for which property offences are the suitable means of control, and warrants criminalisation by means of separate, more specific, legislation.[41]

---

36   *R v Kelly* [1998] 3 All ER 741 (CA), applying *Doodeward v Spence* (1908) 6 CLR 406; [1909] 15 ALR 105. In the latter case, Griffith CJ was careful not to say that a corpse could be owned, but rather that it could be in the lawful possession of someone, and that the law would protect that lawful possession. Note that preserving a brain in paraffin before a post-mortem examination does not turn it into an item in which others could have a right of possession or property: *Dobson v North Tyneside HA* [1996] 4 All ER 474. See MacLean, "Resurrection of the body snatchers" (2000) 150 NLJ 174.

37   Quaere human hair manufactured into wigs, or sperm in a sperm bank. It appears that there may be property rights in the by-products of the living body: in *R v Welsh* [1974] RTR 478, a man was convicted of theft of a urine sample. Cf *R v Rothery* [1976] RTR 550; [1976] Crim LR 691; also *Herbert*, The Times, 22 December 1960, (1960) 25 JCL 163 (cutting off hair — though surely an offence against the person rather than property?). A T H Smith opines that body parts even if originally res nullius should, as in the case of wild animals, be able to become property by occupatio: Smith, "Stealing the body and its parts" [1976] Crim LR 622. This seems to be consistent with the reasoning of Griffith CJ in *Doodeward v Spence* (1908) 6 CLR 406; [1909] 15 ALR 105. See also Matthews, "Whose body? People as property" (1983) 36 CLP 193.

38   Arguably, if ownership is regarded as having the largest bundle of rights available in respect of something, the extent of those available rights will naturally vary for different items — thus the fact that the bundle will be a small one in the case of body parts may still be consistent with the ascription of ownership. Contra, however, if the maximum bundle available lacks rights which are fundamental to any concept of ownership: cf Honoré, "Ownership" in Guest (ed), *Oxford Essays in Jurisprudence*, London, Oxford University Press, 1961, 107, 108-110.

39   See Lavoie, "Ownership of human tissue: Life after *Moore v Regents of the University of California*" [1989] 75 Va LR 1363; *Adams*, CA218.03 (looseleaf).

40   Compare Smith, "Stealing the body and its parts" [1976] Crim LR 622, 623-624.

41   Cf s 150.

(9) Wild creatures

At common law, a wild creature is property, in that it is susceptible of ownership, but it is res nullius — owned by nobody — and so cannot be stolen.[42] In New Zealand, wild animals belong to the Crown but, if such an animal is lawfully captured or killed, the person making the capture or killing thereupon acquires ownership of the creature.[43] Consequently, any subsequent taking of the animal or its carcase can be theft.

Section 218 modifies this position. For the purposes of the Crimes Act 1961, s 218 provides:

"(3) All living creatures wild by nature, such as are not commonly found in a condition of natural liberty in New Zealand, are, if kept in a state of confinement, capable of being stolen, not only while so confined, but after they have escaped from confinement.

"(4) All other living creatures wild by nature are, if kept in a state of confinement, capable of being stolen so long as they remain in confinement, or are being pursued upon escaping from confinement.

"(5) A wild living creature is in a state of confinement so long as it is in an enclosure designed to prevent escape, or otherwise secured, and to allow its owner to take possession of it when he or she pleases.

"(6) Shellfish of all types are capable of being stolen when in oyster beds, marine farms, layings, and fisheries that are the property of any person and that are sufficiently marked out or shown as such property."

It follows that a wild creature may be stolen only if (i) it is kept in captivity (eg in a zoo); or (ii) it has escaped from captivity and is being pursued; or it has escaped from captivity and is not commonly found in a condition of natural liberty in New Zealand. A number of creatures will fall outwith this provision. For example, bees that return to a hive seemingly cannot be stolen, since they are not confined.[44] Neither does a poacher steal the rabbit she captures.

Quite apart from the inadequate definition of "confinement" in subs (5), these provisions need reconsideration as a whole. Too much is left as an unarticulated implication, so that it is unclear how far s 218 displaces the default common law rules in situations not explicitly determined by that section. The difficulty is compounded by the fact that the section rests on a foundational common law distinction between animals that are "wild by nature" and those that are "tame by nature".[45] The application of this distinction is unclear in cases of animals, such as deer, that exist both in the wild and in farm or domestic environments.

Moreover, even if the categorisation of a species is settled, particular animals may be wild (feral) without being "wild by nature" — for example, cats or horses that are living in a wild state. On a plain reading of s 218, it seems that any such creature, being merely a wild instance

---

42 Even the landowner does not own or possess the wild animals on his land: Cf *R v Howlett and Howlett* [1968] Crim LR 222.
43 Section 9 Wild Animal Control Act 1977.
44 This seems to be an implication of s 218(4). However, an alternative reading of the subsection might be that it has no application to unconfined wild creatures, which fall to be decided on common law rules. On that view, bees returning to a hive have been reduced into possession and, as such, are the subject of proprietary rights.
45 See *Hamps v Darby* [1948] 2 KB 311; [1948] 2 All ER 474 (CA), 320-1; 477.

of a species that is classified as "tame by nature", is not covered by s 218 and is instead property that may be stolen under any circumstances, provided it has an owner — generally, but not always, the Crown.[46]

19.3.2 Owned by another

In addition to being property, the thing stolen must also in fact be owned by someone. Moreover, although the Act does not say so explicitly, that person — ie the victim — must be someone other than D. This requirement is implicit in s 219, which requires that D have "an intent to deprive any owner". But it is also an implication of general principle. One cannot steal property from oneself. Some other person must have an interest in the subject matter of the theft before that item can be stolen.

This is not to deny that D can steal something she owns. D's ownership may not be absolute: V, say, may have a lien, or some other interest in the property. In such a case the property can be stolen by D (or by anyone else). But if D is absolute owner of the property, she cannot steal it. There is no "owner" for the purposes of s 219.

The scope and range of "ownership" is elaborated in s 218(1) and (2):

"(1) For the purposes of this Part, a person is to be regarded as the owner of any property that is stolen if, at the time of the theft, that person has—

"(a) possession or control of the property; or

"(b) any interest in the property; or

"(c) the right to take possession or control of the property.

"(2) An owner of any property may be guilty of theft against another owner of that property."

The key provision is s 218(1), the effect of which is that property can be stolen whenever someone other than D has any proprietary or possessory right or interest in that property. Put most generally, for the purposes of theft an item is deemed to be "owned" by everyone with any form of proprietary interest in the item, whatever the nature of that interest — ie whether it be a right of ownership or possession or a proprietary interest existing only at equity. D commits the actus reus of a theft whenever she takes, uses, or deals with property in which someone else has such a proprietary interest. By virtue of s 218(2), this is true even if D herself has a proprietary interest in the property; indeed, even if D is the owner.

The rule stated here gives rise to a number of special cases, which benefit by further discussion.

(1) *What proprietary interests are protected by s 218(1)?*

Section 218(1) protects practically any form of proprietary interest, whether of ownership or possession, and whether at common law or equity. Although s 218(1)(a) mentions "possession or control", it is not clear that the latter term adds anything much. Physical control would in any event also constitute a possessory interest, and any other right of control would presumably only qualify if it were enforceable in rem, ie if it were a *proprietary* interest, falling within s 218(1)(b) ("any interest in the property").

---

46 Section 57(3), sched 5 Wildlife Act 1953.

On the other hand, equitable proprietary interests should be distinguished from contingent and future interests, such as the "mere equity" that may arise when D enters into an agreement to sell goods to V on some future date (by contrast with contracts of sale that transfer ownership immediately). Thus if, before the agreed date of the future transfer, D were to resell the goods to T, D would not commit theft from V. The reference in s 218(1)(c) to "the right to take possession or control of the property" suggests that any such right falling short of a proprietary interest should be a present, vested right to delivery or possession.

So construed, para (c) itself will rarely be needed. It extends the criminal law to include cases where there is a purely contractual or other right to immediate delivery, which otherwise is insufficient to give a proprietary right in the goods.[47]

(2)   *Theft by an owner from others with proprietary interests*

As has been mentioned, one upshot of s 218 is that even an owner may commit theft, provided the victim of the theft has an interest recognised under that section. This might occur, for example, in a case where someone else has a lien over the owner's goods. (A lien is a right to possession enforceable against anyone, including the owner, until some condition is satisfied.) In the old case of *Cox*,[48] a garage repairing a car had a lien over it. D dishonestly retrieved the car and was convicted of theft, as the lien had conferred a possessory interest. Similarly, in *Larkin v Brown*[49] P retook a horse which was arguably subject to an auctioneer's lien. D arrested him for theft of the horse, whereupon P sued D alleging false imprisonment and assault. The Court held that the lien, if established, would give the auctioneers a proprietary interest in the horse, and thus that D would be justified in arresting P.

A bailee of goods also has a possessory title therein, and so may be the victim of theft. The theft may be committed by a third party,[50] or even by the owner, at least if the owner has no right to terminate the bailment and reclaim the goods at will. In tort law, such an act would be a conversion.[51] Under s 218, it can also be a theft.

The standard case in which an owner may commit theft is if there is more than one owner. This case is addressed explicitly by s 218(2). If D and V are co-owners of a chattel and D dishonestly sells the chattel, D is guilty of theft. Such a scenario might arise in respect to family property, or property belonging to members of a club. Similarly, a partner may be convicted of theft of property belonging to the partnership.[52]

---

47   Such a right will therefore not support an action in conversion: *Jarvis v Williams* [1955] 1 All ER 108; [1955] 1 WLR 71; Watts; "The tort of conversion and equity's rules against merger" [1994] NZ Recent LR 336, 337, 338, criticising *Campbell v Dominion Breweries Ltd* [1994] 3 NZLR 559 (CA).

48   *R v Cox* [1923] NZLR 596 (CA). A repairer of goods has a lien over the improved goods until the repair is paid for. Cf the famous case of *Slowly* (1873) 12 Cox 269: V sold onions to D, for which he had not yet been paid. Until paid, V (being a seller in possession) was entitled to assert a lien over the goods. D nonetheless took the goods, and was held guilty of theft.

49   *Larkin v Brown* (1906) 8 GLR 654.

50   Cf *R v Brown* [1948] NZLR 928 (CA), where D, a search officer employed by the New Zealand Railways Board, was convicted of theft of a quantity of cutlery consigned to the railway for transportation.

51   *City Motors (1993) Pty Ltd v Southern Aerial Super Service Pty Ltd* (1961) 106 CLR 477; [1962] ALR 184; *Roberts v Wyatt* (1810) 2 Taunt 268; 127 ER 1080; *Howe v Teefy* (1927) 27 SR (NSW) 301.

52   Cf *Bonner* [1970] 2 All ER 97n.

(3) Theft by an absolute owner? When D's interest is better than V's

In principle, there should be one important exception to the general proposition that property may be stolen from anyone having a proprietary interest therein. Consider the following, fairly straightforward, case:

> Suppose that V is a thief who has stolen a television set from D. D remains absolute owner of the television, but while in possession V has a lesser proprietary (possessory) interest in the television, which he may maintain against anyone save D. V's interest is sufficient for s 218(1). Consequently, if T dishonestly removes the television from V's house, T is himself guilty of stealing from V.

Now the exception. In a case of this sort, D — the owner — surely cannot steal the television by retaking it from V. This is not just because D is unlikely to be dishonest in doing so but because V has no property right in the television maintainable against D. Vis-à-vis D, the television belongs to no-one else. By contrast, vis-à-vis T, the television belongs to both D and V; hence T can steal it from V and from D.

Similarly, it is submitted that an owner who reclaims his goods from a bailee at will commits no theft. If the owner has a better right to possession, the mere assertion of that right over a lesser property interest should not be theft. In such a case, the fact that D has an absolute title to the goods should be a full answer to the claim that he has stolen them. D merely exercises her property rights.[53]

A useful illustration of this exception is the English Crown Court decision in *Meredith*.[54] D's car had been impounded by the police and removed to a police station. Without consent, D then recovered his car from the police station. D was acquitted of theft, after the trial Judge ruled that the police had no right to retain possession of the car against the owner.[55]

The importance of this point cannot be overstated. Consistency of criminal law and civil law concepts is essential in theft, which after all is concerned with the protection of property rights.[56] It would be more than odd if D could be convicted of theft when she had not in fact interfered with V's property rights. As Williams writes, "the object of the law of theft is to attach a penal sanction to certain violations of property rights; so (it may be urged) if there is no violation of property rights under the general (civil) law, there should be no theft".[57] It was said in this text, as far back as chapter 1, that there ought to be no criminalisation without

---

53 Compare the Model Penal Code, § 223.0(7): "'property of another' includes property in which any person other than the actor has an interest *which the actor is not privileged to infringe* ..." (emphasis added).
54 *R v Meredith* [1973] Crim LR 253.
55 Contrast, in England, *R v Turner (No 2)* (1971) 55 Cr App R 336 (CA), an unsatisfactory decision rightly criticised by, among others, Smith, *The Law of Theft* (7th ed), London, Butterworths, 1993, para 2-54, and Smith, *Property Offences: The Protection of Property Through the Criminal Law*, London, Sweet & Maxwell, 1994, para 4-43; the decision can be distinguished if necessary on the basis of the language of the Theft Act 1968 (UK).
56 Cf Smith, "Civil law concepts in the criminal law" [1972] 31 CLJ 197. Though see *Rao v Police* (1988) 3 CRNZ 697, 699, 700; also *R v Morris* [1984] AC 320; [1983] 3 All ER 288 (HL), 334; 294, for the dubious (and unnecessary) claim that the criminal law should not be concerned with the niceties of the civil law. The approach taken in *R v Walker* [1984] Crim LR 112 (CA) and in *R v Tillings & Tillings* [1985] Crim LR 393 is to be preferred. Compare too *Dobson v General Accident Fire and Life Assurance Corp plc* [1990] 1 QB 274; [1989] 3 All ER 927, 289; 937: whether property belongs to another "is a question to which the criminal law offers no answer and which can only be answered by reference to civil law principles".

harm.[58] In theft, the relevant harm is infringement of another's property rights. Protection against that harm *is the very purpose* of criminalising theft. The proprietary rights which being protected are creatures of civil law. Therefore, unless those civil law rights are in fact infringed, the harm does not occur and theft should not lie.

(4)   Has D become an absolute owner?

Assuming, therefore, that an absolute owner cannot steal her own goods, cases will often arise when D acquires property innocently enough but subsequently, and dishonestly, decides to keep it from the person from whom the property was acquired. Such cases will usually involve "using or dealing with" the property, under s 219(1)(b),[59] rather than "taking" it under s 219(1)(a). For example:

> D enters into a hire-purchase contract with V Ltd. to acquire a television set. She takes the television set home, intending to honour the agreement. However, a few months later, she finds herself in financial difficulties. She stops paying V Ltd, sells the television, and pockets the proceeds.

In this case, D steals the television set when she offers it for sale (ie deals with it). In a hire-purchase agreement, possession passes but the property in the goods remains with the seller until all instalments have been paid. Thus an on-sale by the possessor is theft. Likewise, borrowing something, and then selling it on, may amount to theft — on the basis of the selling rather than the borrowing — since the borrower legitimately acquires possession but does not acquire ownership.

However, other cases may be more difficult:

> D purchases a table from V on one month's credit. When he takes delivery of the table, D intends to honour his obligation to V. Later, however, D decides not to pay. He sells the table to T, an innocent third party, and absconds with the cash.

Does D steal the table? The general rule is that if V — the person from whom the property is acquired — retains ownership or some other interest in the property, D will be guilty of theft by his later dishonest dealing with the goods. Otherwise, if V delivers the goods and transfers property in them to D, who subsequently forms the intent not to pay for them, D does not commit theft. It is therefore crucial to determine whether, and at what point in time, D has become the owner of property that formerly belonged to V. The criminal law provides no answer to this question, which must be decided by reference to civil law rules.

In deciding whether ownership has passed already to D for the purposes of theft, there are two principal issues. The first is to ascertain whether title has prima facie passed or whether D merely has possession. Here one needs to look at the terms of the agreement between V and D, in particular whether V has reserved some property right in the goods.

The second issue is that, even where a prima facie transfer of title has been identified, the transferor's intention may be vitiated. In general, there are three ways in which this may occur.

---

57   Williams, "Theft, consent and illegality" [1977] Crim LR 127, 138. Per Smith, *Property Offences: The Protection of Property Through the Criminal Law*, London, Sweet & Maxwell, 1994, para 5-49, "if the civil law sees no reason to permit the owner to complain of an interference with his property why should the criminal law do so?"
58   See 1.3.1; also ch 21.
59   Below, 19.3.3(2).

First, the transaction may be induced by D's wrongful duress, fraud, false pretences, undue influence, etc. In such cases any title acquired by D will be at least voidable[60] and, upon avoidance of the transaction, subsequent dealings with the goods can constitute theft.[61] Secondly, the transaction may be vitiated by V's fundamental mistake. Whether or not D induced the mistake, provided that mistake is "fundamental" it negates V's consent to the transfer — and therefore the passing of title — altogether. In that case, the transaction is void.[62] V retains title to the goods and they can be stolen by D. Finally, V, acting on behalf of the true owner, may not have authority to pass title. In that case, again, the transaction is void and D cannot become owner of the property.

In the following sections, we discuss aspects of these problems in more detail.

(a)   Has ownership passed, prima facie?

The general rule, which is subject to various statutory and common law provisos, is that title passes if and when the transferor so intends it to pass.[63] It is not possible here to give a comprehensive account of the civil law regarding transfer of property. Rather, we propose briefly to mention some well-known situations and to illustrate the relationship between the relevant civil law rules and the criminal law of theft.

(i) *Contracts for sale of goods:* Where ascertained goods are sold, the rules on passing of title are to be found in the Sale of Goods Act 1908. The basic rule, stated in s 19, is that where there is a contract for the sale of specific or ascertained goods, property in them passes when the buyer and seller so intend. In the case of sale of unascertained goods, s 18 provides that no property in them is to be transferred to the buyer unless and until the goods are ascertained.[64] Section 20 provides that if there is no agreement then property passes at the time the contract is made.[65]

One consequence of s 19 is that a seller may pass possession but reserve ownership. Indeed, s 21(1) provides explicitly that the seller may reserve the right of disposal of the goods until certain conditions are fulfilled. This is standard, for example, in hire-purchase contracts, where property remains in the seller until the buyer has paid for the goods. Although the buyer has possession, unauthorised dealing with the property may be theft under s 219(2): for example, where D usurps P's rights of ownership over the goods by granting a security over them before they have been paid for[66] or by selling them without authority.[67]

---

60   Indeed, in cases of grave physical duress or fundamental misrepresentation the transfer may even be void: Lanham, "Duress and Void Contracts" (1966) 29 MLR 615. Obtaining by such means may also directly constitute theft by taking, since V's consent to the transfer is likely to be negated.
61   Note that, where the transfer is induced by D's fraud or false pretences, the appropriate offence is likely to be that of obtaining by deception. See ch 20.
62   Voidability is not an option in the case of a unilateral mistake. A transaction can be voidable, as opposed to void, only when D has acted in some way wrongfully. If P's mistake is fundamental, the transaction is void; if not, the transaction is entirely valid and unimpeachable.
63   Cf *Fawcett v Star Car Sales Ltd* [1960] NZLR 406 (CA).
64   The provision was held in *Jansz v GMB Imports Pty Ltd* [1979] VR 581 to be absolute, and so to prevail over any contrary expressed intentions of the parties. For a modern case see *Re Goldcorp Exchange (in receivership)* [1994] 3 NZLR 385; [1995] 1 AC 74 (PC): buyers had no legal or equitable interest in an undifferentiated bulk of gold bullion.
65   Provided the goods are specific and deliverable, and the contract is unconditional. Other rules in s 20 apply where these criteria are not met.
66   *R v Nottingham* [1992] 1 NZLR 395 (CA).

(ii) *Rescission:* In *R v Walker*,[68] D had sold V a defective videorecorder, which V returned for repair. After some time, V then issued a summons claiming the price of the video as the "return of money paid for defective goods". D thereafter sold the video. His conviction for theft was quashed. Arguably, the summons had the effect of rescinding the original contract of sale; revesting ownership of the machine in D.

(iii) *Receptacles:* The owner of a vending or similar machine, such as a coin-operated telephone, becomes the owner of any money as soon as it is inserted.[69] This is explicable on the general rule: the depositor intends to pass ownership when he inserts a coin in prepayment. Even if the machine malfunctions and he does not get what he pays for, his remedy is a refund, not a retrieval of the particular coin inserted. It is thus the actus reus of theft to retake money from such a machine, except by authorised means (for example pressing the refund button).

Similarly, when petrol is sold at a service station, ownership passes when the petrol is pumped into the tank of the vehicle. Thus a motorist who fills his tank intending to pay for the petrol, but then decides not to pay for it and drives off, commits no theft.[70] He already owns (and has possession of) the petrol before he forms the mens rea of theft, and is simply a dishonest debtor.

(iv) *Contents:* If a person puts a valuable ring in a desk drawer, and after death her executor sells the desk, the buyer may not keep the ring on finding it since it was not included in the sale,[71] and a dishonest usage or dealing with it would constitute theft. Ownership of the ring remains in the executor since he does not intend to pass title thereto when he sells the desk.

(b)   Is the passing of title negated by mistake?

V's consent to the transfer of title may be negated by a "fundamental" mistake, whether or not induced by fraud or misrepresentation. A mistake is fundamental if and only if its existence makes it reasonable to say that there is no intention on V's part to transfer *this* property to *this* person.[72] As the High Court of Australia put it, what this means is that a mistake is sufficiently fundamental if it is "as to the identity of the transferee or as to the identity of the thing delivered or as to the quantity of the thing delivered".[73] However, applying this test is not always clear-cut.

(i) *Mistakes regarding property:* Mistake as to the identity of the property will always defeat consent. In *R v Davies*[74] the proprietor of a nursing home induced two old ladies to endorse cheques made out to them by signing on the back, and then paid the cheques into his own account. The victims had not known that they were endorsing cheques, but merely thought that they

---

67 Cf *Hendy Lennox (Industrial Engines) Ltd v Grahame Puttick Ltd* [1984] 2 All ER 152; [1984] 1 WLR 485 (D's credit period had expired and S had demanded delivery up).
68 *R v Walker* [1984] Crim LR 112 (CA).
69 *Martin v Marsh* [1955] Crim LR 781; *Hollings* (1940) 4 J Cr L 370; cf *R v Jean* [1968] 2 CCC 204.
70 *R v Greenberg* [1972] Crim LR 331; *Edwards v Ddin* [1976] 3 All ER 705; [1976] 1 WLR 942.
71 *Thomas v Greenslade* [1954] CLY 3421; *Moffatt v Kazana* [1969] 2 QB 152; [1968] 3 All ER 271.
72 Williams, "Mistake in the law of theft" (1977) 36 CLJ 62, 64.
73 *Ilich v R* (1987) 162 CLR 110, 126. In other cases, a person who knows his receipt is pursuant to another's mistake may have an affected conscience, such that the receipt is held on trust for the mistaken transferor: for example *Chase Manhattan Bank NA v Israel-British Bank (London) Ltd* [1981] Ch 105; [1979] 3 All ER 1025. Misappropriation of the receipt would then be theft, since the transferor retains an equitable interest in the property.
74 *R v Davies* [1982] 4 Cr App R (S) 302.

were signing pieces of paper. For this reason property in the cheques never passed to D, who was thus rightly convicted of theft. Here the mistake was obviously fundamental: in each case V believed the property to be a valueless piece of paper, whereas in reality it was a bill of exchange — a different type of thing altogether.

(ii) *Mistakes regarding quantity:* If the owner intends to deal only with a specific number of goods handed over, there is no consent as to the excess. But if V's intention is to hand over a group of things, mistake as to the number of items in the group does *not* negative the intention to hand them all over.

An example of the former variety is *Russell v Smith*:[75]

> D was a driver for a haulage company. He was instructed to collect a one-ton load of pig meal from P. P, when loading the meal, inadvertently loaded an additional eight sacks. When D discovered the error, he appropriated the eight sacks and sold them.

P intended to give D the number of sacks corresponding to one ton of meal; there was no intention to put the additional sacks on the lorry. Thus P remained owner of the eight sacks, which are then stolen when D sells them. Contrast this case with an example where P offers to sell D all the pig meal then stored at his warehouse; which P mistakenly thinks amounts to one ton's worth, when in fact it is eight sacks more than that weight. In the latter case, D acquires ownership of the entirety. The excess is his.

The distinction at work here is between a mistake that simply motivates or underlies P's intention to pass title to certain goods, and one that negates P's very intention to pass title in those goods which were in fact delivered. It is, in short, the difference between a mistake as to *what* P is passing to D, and a mistake as to *why* he is doing so.[76]

Suppose that C is a wages clerk. When making up the pay packets one week, he accidentally puts a $100 note, which has stuck to another note, into D's packet, which now contains $250 instead of $150. Upon discovering the error, D resolves to say nothing and spends the money. He is guilty of stealing the $100 note by dealing. (C's mistake was a fundamental one of quantity, and the $100 note still belongs to the employer.) Compare, on the other hand, *Moynes v Coopper*,[77] where a wages clerk miscalculated the amount due to D. Although the employee was thus overpaid, the clerk intended to pay the amount of money actually paid. Hence title in the whole amount paid passed to D, and D could not be convicted of theft.

(iii) *Mistakes regarding the transferee:* Mistake as to the identity of the other party may vitiate consent, but only if the identity was crucial to V's decision to give consent.[78] In *R v Hudson*, D received and paid into his bank account a cheque which was inadvertently made out to him, but obviously intended for someone else with the same surname. He was convicted of stealing the cheque.[79]

---

75 *Russell v Smith* [1958] 1 QB 27; [1957] 2 All ER 796.
76 Analogous to the distinction in contract law between a mistake "in the motive or reason for making an offer", and a mistake in the terms of the offer itself: *Imperial Glass Ltd v Consolidated Supplies Ltd* (1960) 22 DLR (2d) 759.
77 *Moynes v Coopper* [1956] 1 QB 439; [1956] 1 All ER 450. See also *Ilich v R* (1987) 162 CLR 110.
78 Thus *Cundy v Lindsay* (1878) 3 App Cas 459; [1874-1880] All ER Rep 1149 may be distinguished from *King's Norton Metal Co Ltd v Edridge Merrett & Co Ltd* (1897) 14 TLR 98, where the rogue's assumed name was of no particular significance.

It seems that a mistake about the transferee's identity supplies the best explanation of another well-known case, R v Middleton.[80] In that case, D went to withdraw 10 shillings from his Post Office savings account, which had at that time a balance of 11s. The Post Office practice was to pay out withdrawals pursuant to a warrant obtained by D and a letter of advice from the Postmaster General sent direct to the relevant branch. Unfortunately the clerk consulted the wrong letter of advice, which related to a different account-holder, and paid out £8 16s 10d. The Court of Criminal Appeal held that D was properly convicted of larceny, as the clerk's intention to pass title to the money was vitiated by his mistake. Since the clerk clearly did intend to give D £8 16s 10d, and not 10s, he made no mistake about the nature or quantity of the property transferred.[81] Rather, his mistake is best seen as being about D's identity, which he had mistaken for that of the person named in the letter of advice.[82]

In 1972, the English Court of Appeal purported to follow Middleton in R v Gilks.[83] G placed various bets at a betting shop, including one on "Fighting Taffy", which was unplaced in a race won by "Fighting Scot". When he went to collect his winnings on the various bets he had placed, the bookmaker mistakenly thought G had backed the winner, and calculated and paid out an amount well in excess of G's true winnings. G, realising the mistake, decided to pocket the entirety. He was convicted of theft, on the footing that Middleton had established, in such cases, that property in money paid by mistake does not pass. It is submitted, however, that this reasoning is flawed. The bookmaker's error was an antecedent one of calculation, of the type that occurred in Moynes v Coopper, and not of the sort found in Middleton. He paid G (the right person) exactly the amount he intended. Therefore ownership of the money had passed to G, and he should not have been convicted of theft.

(c)   Was the transferor authorised to pass title?

Property will not pass if the transferor does not have the owner's authority to pass title. In R v Bhachu, a dishonest cashier acted in collusion with D by "selling" the goods to her at a price below the authorised price.[84] In such a case, the cashier does not have the authority to

---

79   R v Hudson [1943] KB 458; [1943] 1 All ER 642. But this is not an absolute rule, at least where the parties deal face to face. In Ingram v Little [1961] 1 QB 31; [1960] 3 All ER 332 a contract for sale of a car to a rogue under a false name (whose cheque bounced) was held void, but in Lewis v Averay [1972] 1 QB 198; [1971] 3 All ER 907 a similar sale to a rogue believing him to be a certain television actor was held valid. Possibly the only explanation for this anomaly is that in the latter case there was no actual misrepresentation by the buyer. Even before these cases, the considerable difficulties in this area of law had been pointed out by Williams, "Mistake as to party in the law of contract" (1945) 23 Can Bar Rev 271; cf Sutton, "Reform of the law of mistake in contract" (1976) 7 NZULR 40.
80   R v Middleton (1873) 12 Cox CC 417.
81   R v Middleton (1873) 12 Cox CC 417, 428 (Bramwell B (dissenting)): "No doubt the clerk did not intend to do an act of the sort described, and give to Middleton what did not belong to him. Yet he intended to do the act he did. What he did he did not do involuntarily, nor accidentally, but on purpose."
82   R v Middleton (1873) 12 Cox CC 417, 419: the clerk "certainly meant that the prisoner should take up that money, though he only meant this because of a mistake he made as to the identity of the prisoner with the person really entitled to that money". Cf Orchard, "The borderland of theft revisited" [1973] NZLJ 110, 112; Smith and Hogan, Criminal Law, London, Butterworths, 1965, 354. On whether the facts really support such a finding, contra the dissent by Cleasby B (1873) 12 Cox CC 417, 441, 442. See Turner, "Two cases of larceny" in Turner and Radzinowicz (eds), The Modern Approach to Criminal Law, London, Macmillan and Co, 1948, 356, 359.
83   R v Gilks [1972] 3 All ER 280; [1972] 1 WLR 1341. See the criticism by Smith in [1972] Crim LR 586; Orchard, "The borderland of theft revisited" [1973] NZLJ 110, 111ff. Compare R v Prince (1868) LR 1 CCR 150.

pass title on V's behalf, and the goods are stolen by D when she takes them out of the shop.[85] By contrast, an unintentional error on the part of an agent does not mean that the agent's conduct is unauthorised, even if the recipient is dishonest.[86]

(5) *Abandoning, losing, and finding things*

It is also possible for ownership to be relinquished through abandonment. Intentionally abandoned goods are ownerless and cannot be stolen.[87] However, an item may be lost rather than abandoned. Consider the following example:

> David finds a wallet in a busy street, and picks it up. He looks in the wallet for evidence of the owner's identity and finds none, but does find some money. He puts the wallet in his pocket. Does David commit the actus reus of a theft?

Typically, in "finding" cases, it is important to resolve whether the thing found belongs to another: whether, in this scenario, there is another person with a right of property in the wallet and its contents. In turn, this is likely to depend on whether the wallet is abandoned or merely lost. If lost, then the person who originally lost the wallet remains its owner. By contrast, if abandoned, the wallet is unowned until David picks it up and puts it in his pocket.

Generally speaking, the courts are reluctant to find that goods have been "abandoned" rather than merely lost.[88] Abandonment is a technical status, and it will not suffice, for example, merely to put rubbish out for collection,[89] or to bury a dead animal.[90] Normally, as in these examples, some right in the subject-matter will be preserved. Abandonment of ownership requires a giving up of the owner's physical control of an item, accompanied by the cessation of any intention to possess that item or to exclude other persons from its possession — ie a deliberate relinquishing of all rights over the item.[91]

Let us assume, since it contains money, that in David's case the wallet was not abandoned. It is worth noting that if David had formed an honest belief that the goods were abandoned rather than lost, he would not commit theft.[92] However, this is because of the lack of mens rea (dishonesty), rather than the absence of an actus reus.

(a) When does a finder acquire ownership?

Once abandoned, ownership of items vests in the first person to take possession of them. Possession, in turn, is normally taken by intentionally exercising control over the items. This may be done physically (as David does with the wallet, in the example above). Where chattels

---

84 *R v Bhachu* (1977) 65 Cr App R 261. Cf *R v Tideswell* [1905] 2 KB 273.
85 In such circumstances, the cashier herself steals the goods by dealing with them when she offers to sell them at an undervalue.
86 *R v Jackson* (1826) 1 Mod 119; 168 ER 1208; *R v Prince* (1868) LR 1 CCR 150.
87 *Ellerman's Wilson Line Ltd v Webster* [1952] 1 Lloyd's Rep 179, 180.
88 Cf. Hudson, "Is Divesting Abandonment Possible at Common Law?" (1984) 100 LQR 110.
89 *Williams v Phillips* (1957) 41 Cr App R 5. As long as the rubbish remained on the owner's premises it was not abandoned; property in it passed when collected by the local authority.
90 *R v Edwards* (1877) 13 Cox CC 384.
91 Cf Hudson, "Abandonment" in Palmer and McKendrick (eds), *Interests in Goods*, London, Lloyd's of London Press, 1993 ch 15; *Arrow Shipping Co v Tyne Improvement Commissioners (The Crystal)* [1894] AC 508; *Keene v Carter* (1994) 12 WAR 20.
92 *R v White* (1912) 7 Cr App R 266; *Rowlands v Police* 28/7/04, MacKenzie J, HC Napier CRI-2003-441-29.

are abandoned on occupied land, however, the occupier will often acquire possession even before the chattel is found. In such cases, the finder may commit theft.

In general, there are three types of cases in which the occupier acquires a better title than the finder.[93] First, if the thing found is embedded in,[94] under,[95] or otherwise attached[96] to the land, it belongs to the occupier or owner (as the case may be) of the land regardless of who finds it.

Secondly, if something is found loose by an employee on the employer's property, the employer has a superior right to possession of that thing, in priority to the employee-finder.[97]

Finally, where the item is found lying loose on the land, the occupier can acquire a prior title either by (a) restricting public access to the land upon which the items lie,[98] or (where the land is open to public access) by (b) manifesting an intention to exercise control over the land and the things thereon.[99] Obviously if the item is found by a visitor inside D's private home, D has a superior title since the public does not have general access to the home. A more interesting illustrations of possibility (a) is *Woodman*,[100] in which D took scrap metal from a factory site. E, the occupier of the site, had no knowledge of the existence of the scrap, as it had sold all the scrap on the site to B for removal. In fact, B had removed the bulk of the scrap but left some pieces behind, which B deemed too inaccessible to be worth the cost of removing. The site had been wound down and was now disused, although a barbed-wire fence had been erected around the site to exclude trespassers. Nonetheless, D's conviction was upheld by the English Court of Appeal. Even if ownership of the remaining scrap had been abandoned by B, ownership would have reverted to D as the occupier of the land, since D had manifested an intention to exclude trespassers by fencing off the site.

On the other hand, where the premises are open to the public, the occupier's position is weaker, and she gains prior title only if she has (b) manifested an intention to exercise control over the things that are or might be on the premises. In *Parker v British Airways Board*,[101] Parker found a gold bracelet in an executive lounge at Heathrow airport. He handed the bracelet in to British Airways (who, as lessees, occupied the lounge), asking that the bracelet be returned to him if unclaimed. British Airways sold the bracelet. Parker succeeded in an action for conversion of the bracelet. The English Court of Appeal held that Parker's rights as finder could be displaced only if British Airways could show as occupiers an obvious intention to exercise such control

---

93   See Riesman, "Possession and the Law of Finders" (1939) 52 Harv LR 1105; Tay, "Problems in the Law of Finding" (1964) 37 ALJ 350; Harris, "The Concept of Possession in English Law" in Guest (ed.), *Oxford Essays in Jurisprudence*, London, Oxford Unversity Press, 1961, 69, 80ff.
94   *Elwes v Brigg Gas Company* (1886) 33 Ch D 562.
95   *Rowe* (1859) Bell 93, 169 ER 1180; *South Staffordshire Water Co v Sharman* [1896] 2 QB 44 (items lying under water; though in the latter case the defendant was also an employee — contrast *R v Ellerm* [1997] 1 NZLR 200 (CA), discussed below in this section).
96   Eg sealed inside a fixture: *City of London Corporation v Appleyard* [1963] 2 All ER 834; *Moffatt v Kazana* [1969] 2 QB 152; [1968] 3 All ER 271.
97   *The Title of the Finder* (1899) 33 ILT 225; *Willey v Synan* (1937) 57 CLR 200; *Grafstein v Holme* [1958] 12 DLR (2d) 727.
98   *Parker v British Airways Board* [1982] QB 1004, 1013, 1019 (Donaldson LJ), 1020 (Eveleigh LJ), 1021 (Sir David Cairns).
99   *Parker v British Airways Board* [1982] QB 1004, 1013, 1018; *Tamworth Industries v A-G* [1991] 3 NZLR 616, 620.
100 *R v Woodman* [1974] QB 754.
101 *Parker v British Airways Board* [1982] QB 1004.

over the lounge and things in it that the bracelet was in their possession before the plaintiff found it.[102] On the evidence, there was no manifestation of such an intention as would give the defendants a right superior to that of the plaintiff; the airline's instructions to staff for dealing with lost articles were not published to users of the lounge, and it did not carry out searches for lost articles.

An interesting, but less convincing, analysis of abandonment is found in *R v Ellerm*.[103] In that case, D had dishonestly recovered rimu logs from the bed of a lake. The logs had apparently been abandoned by their original owner some decades ago, after sinking during storms that arose while the logs were being towed across the lake. The lake itself was the property of the Crown, which exercised an active management of the lake and lakebed.

On these facts, the Court of Appeal upheld D's conviction. However, although the decision seems to be correct, its reasoning may be doubted. On the footing that the original owner's interest in the logs had been abandoned in law,[104] the Court held that the Crown's role as owner and manager of the land upon which the logs lay "falls short of any ownership in the logs in the lake, but arguably gives a right to their possession",[105] on the basis that "the owner or occupier of land who has manifested a sufficient intention to exercise control over the land and the things which might be on the land has rights over chattels on that land (even if they are not attached to or imbedded in the land)".[106]

It is submitted that the Court was right to ascribe proprietary rights to the Crown on the basis of its control over the land and contents thereon. However, the Court erred in concluding that the rights fell short of ownership. Ownership of items which are abandoned or otherwise res nullius vests in the first person to come into possession of them. There is no middle ground: once one possesses abandoned goods, one owns them. Where the items are not embedded, possession itself is taken by intentionally exercising control over them. As we have seen, the occupier of land may do this either by restricting public access to the land upon which the items lie, or by manifesting an intention to exercise control over the land and the things thereon. Certainly the Crown had done sufficient to satisfy the latter test.[107] It was therefore in possession of the rimu logs, and thus their owner.

19.3.3 Taking, using, or dealing with

So far, we have considered what can be stolen: what sort of *property* is susceptible of theft. The other major issue for the actus reus of theft is what sort of *action*, in connection with that property, is prohibited? Under s 219(1), D must either (a) *take* or, in a case where D already has it, (b) use or deal with the stolen property.

---

102 It was also suggested that D's rights might be displaced had he acted dishonestly. However, unless D's dishonesty were such as to make him a trespasser ab initio, it is hard to see how this qualification can be justified. See Smith, *Property Offences: The Protection of Property Through the Criminal Law*, London, Sweet & Maxwell, 1994, § 4-20, 4-21.
103 *R v Ellerm* [1997] 1 NZLR 200 (CA).
104 *R v Ellerm* [1997] 1 NZLR 200 (CA), 204.
105 *R v Ellerm* [1997] 1 NZLR 200 (CA), 205.
106 *R v Ellerm* [1997] 1 NZLR 200 (CA), 208.
107 *R v Ellerm* [1997] 1 NZLR 200 (CA), 204, 205.

(1) Taking

The actus reus of theft under s 219(1) is "taking" property owned by another, something that is partially defined in s 219(4):

> "For tangible property, theft is committed by a taking when the offender moves the property or causes it to be moved."

In respect of tangible property, therefore, this element of theft is satisfied by showing that there is a physical "taking", causing the item to be moved. Consequently, a failure to return goods acquired in circumstances not amounting to theft does not constitute a taking, although it may amount to theft by using or dealing.[108] The thing stolen need not be removed or carried off: it is enough for theft under s 219 if it is moved only slightly.[109]

The statute is, by contrast, silent about the taking of intangible property. Clearly, one does not "take" such property by physical displacement. However, it is enough for a taking that one acquires ownership or control of the item.[110] Especially in the context of intangible assets, therefore, one might obtain, accept, or assert ownership or control over the asset, and this action would constitute a taking of the thing. Thus if, for example, without authorisation D transfers V's shares into her name, she commits the actus reus of theft.

(a)   Answer to charge: D's taking was by consent

It will be a complete answer to the charge of theft by taking that D took the property with consent. This is stated explicitly in s 219(3):

> "In this section, taking does not include obtaining ownership or possession of, or control over, any property with the consent of the person from whom it is obtained, whether or not consent is obtained by deception."

This reflects the property law rule that rights of possession give title only against a wrongdoer.[111] If D acquires possession of goods with the consent of the person from whom they are obtained then there is no taking, even if the consent is obtained by a fraudulent misrepresentation. (In such cases, there may be a subsequent theft by usage or dealing,[112] and the charge of obtaining by deception may also lie.[113]) However, consent must be distinguished from submission: a "consent" obtained by threats is not, in law, an effective consent; and things obtained by such means can be stolen by a taking.[114]

---

108   Below, 19.3.3(2)(d).
109   Cf R v Coslet (1782) 1 Leach 236; 168 ER 220, where it was held sufficient that D moved a parcel from one end of a wagon to the other; also R v Taylor [1911] 1 KB 674, where D pulled a pocket-book partly out of another person's pocket.
110   This is an implication of s 219(3), which excludes from the "taking" any obtaining of ownership, possession, or control with consent. See below, 19.3.3(1)(a).
111   Cf Jeffries v Great Western Ry Co (1856) 5 El & Bl 802; 119 ER 680, 805; 681.
112   Thus a receiver, who does not commit theft by taking, may deal with the goods. See 19.5.
113   Section 240. See ch 20.
114   R v Parker [1919] NZLR 365 (CA). This is implicit in offences such as robbery (s 234), which presuppose that D commits a theft. Cf R v Mitchell [1988] 2 NZLR 208; (1988) 3 CRNZ 515 (CA); Lanham, "Duress and Void Contracts" (1966) 29 MLR 615.

One interesting case is that of a supermarket. The House of Lords has held in *R v Morris*[115] that a shopper acts with the implied authority of the supermarket owner when he takes goods from the shelf, puts them on his trolley, and takes them to the checkout counter to pay the correct price. The shopper obtains an authorised possession, although property does not pass until the price is paid and a contract is concluded between the customer and cashier.[116] It follows from this that, in effect, the prospective shoplifter has a period of grace while still in the supermarket. Since her possession is authorised,[117] she can only be convicted of theft when she later *converts* the goods by smuggling them beyond the point of sale without permission.

(2) *Usage or dealing*

Formerly in the common law, where a person legitimately in possession of goods later decided to appropriate them to his own use there could be no larceny, because the common law offence required a "taking and carrying away" contrary to the will of the owner. This problem was resolved in the New Zealand Criminal Code of 1893, and until recently in the Crimes Act 1961, by extending the basic offence of theft to include *conversion* of property. It is usually said that there is a conversion whenever a person (however innocently she obtained possession) acts inconsistently with the rights of the owner[118] and without authorisation to do so.[119] Examples include deliberate destruction of or damage to something, the sale or attempted sale of it,[120] granting a chattel security over something that was not yours,[121] and obliterating the identifying marks on something.[122] If D has possession of a thing for particular, limited purposes, then using it for other purposes will amount to conversion.[123]

Since 2003, however, the language of conversion has been abandoned. In its place, s 219(1)(b) provides that D commits the actus reus of theft when she does an act of "using or

---

115 *R v Morris* [1984] AC 320; [1983] 3 All ER 288 (HL). Cf *Dronjak v Police* [1990] 3 NZLR 75; (1988) 3 CRNZ 141, 77; 143.
116 Cf *Davies v Leighton* (1979) 68 Cr App R 4; [1978] Crim LR 575. The decision in *Morris* has since been overruled by the House of Lords in *DPP v Gomez* [1993] AC 442; [1993] 1 All ER 1 (HL), which decided that a person who takes possession, even with consent, commits theft if he does so with the intent permanently to deprive. However, these decisions turn on the meaning of "appropriation" in s 1 Theft Act 1968 (UK), and would appear to be irrelevant in the New Zealand context.
117 In *Dobson v General Accident Fire and Life Assurance Corp plc* [1990] 1 QB 274; [1989] 3 All ER 927, 289; 937, Bingham LJ suggests that "it might be said that a supermarket consents to customers taking goods from its shelves only when they honestly intend to pay and not otherwise". That view, however, should be doubted, for two reasons. First, it would largely obliterate the distinction between theft and obtaining by deception. Ex hypothesi, V would never authorise dishonest conduct or consent to a dishonest transaction if she knew the full facts. Secondly, the analysis would extend the scope of theft too far into the realm of preparatory activity, rendering theft primarily a "thought" crime. (These very criticisms may be levelled at English law following *Gomez* [1993] AC 442; [1993] 1 All ER 1 (HL).)
118 *R v Maihi* [1993] 2 NZLR 139; (1992) 9 CRNZ 304 (CA), 141; 306; *R v Ilich* (1987) 162 CLR 110; (1987) 69 ALR 231, 115-117, 124; 235, 236; *Adams*, CA219.03 (looseleaf); Turner, *Kenny's Outlines of Criminal Law* (17th ed), Cambridge, Cambridge University Press, 1958, para 245.
119 *McNicholl v Police* (1990) 6 CRNZ 603, 605.
120 *Clouston v Bragg* [1949] NZLR 1073.
121 *R v Dunbar* [1963] NZLR 253 (CA) (D had the loan of a boat, which he pledged as security for a financial transaction); cf *R v Nottingham* [1992] 1 NZLR 395 (CA).
122 *R v Russell* [1977] 2 NZLR 20 (CA).
123 Cf *Clouston v Bragg* [1949] NZLR 1073, where a car dealer sold a car having been given possession only by the owner.

dealing with any property … after obtaining possession of, or control over, the property in whatever manner".

Prima facie, the scope of this language is very wide. Virtually any conduct in connection with property could be described as using or dealing with the property, including the examples given above: destroying it, pledging it as a security, selling it or even offering it for sale, etc. It may be that even touching or handling an item will count as dealing with it, since doing so would exercise a right of ownership. Certainly, s 219(1)(b) appears to encompass *at least* all those activities that under the previous law, or in the law of torts, would be a conversion.

(a)   Answer to charge: D's usage or dealing was by consent?

Indeed, s 219(1)(b) may be even wider. By contrast with "conversion", which requires a *usurpation* of the owner's rights, there is nothing in s 219(1) to suggest that D's using or dealing must be unauthorised or otherwise inconsistent with the owner's rights. Indeed, the fact that there is no provision corresponding to s 219(3), which excludes from the scope of theft consensual *takings*, suggests the opposite conclusion with respect to consensual usage or dealing. Prima facie, *any* usage or dealing will suffice, however innocent.

The broader interpretation contemplated here is also lent weight by the fact that it would give some effect to the legislative move from "conversion" to "usage or dealing"; since, as was said in *R v Maihi*, conversion "requires a use or dealing with the property or conduct in relation to it inconsistent with the rights of the owner."[124] If a requirement of inconsistency were implied back into s 219(1)(b), the new legislative terminology would effectively revert to the old.

Be that as it may, the narrower reading is to be preferred. It would better reflect the core idea that theft involves some form of harmful interference with another person's property rights, and that any dealing with another person's property lacks the character of theft unless it conflicts with the victim's rights.[125]

A moment's reflection reveals the scope of the difficulty. Suppose that D borrows a book, legitimately, from V. On the broader interpretation, anything and everything D subsequently does with the book would constitute the actus reus of a theft, regardless whether there is anything wrongful about D's conduct. This unfortunate result would cut the law of theft adrift from its mooring, in acts that infringe property rights. In effect, it would expose D to conviction for theft on the basis of his mental state,[126] even though may have a proprietary right to act as he does.

It is to be hoped that s 219(1)(b) will be interpreted so as to limit this possibility. The courts might do so by one of two means. First, they could read into the section an implicit qualification that the usage or dealing must be unauthorised.[127] Alternatively, the courts could qualify the mens rea element by reading in a requirement that D must intend to deprive the owner

---

124   *R v Maihi* [1993] 2 NZLR 139; (1992) 9 CRNZ 304 (CA), 141; 306.
125   Cf Model Penal Code, § 223.2 (the interference must be "unlawful").
126   Usually, where D's dealing with the property is authorised, D will lack mens rea because he will believe that it is authorised and therefore will not be dishonest (see 19.4.1). However, if, for any reason, D does not realise he has authority to deal with the property, his dealing may be theft.
127   Compare, in England, *R v Morris* [1984] AC 320; [1983] 3 All ER 288 (HL); an approach that was later rejected in *DPP v Gomez* [1993] AC 442; [1993] 1 All ER 1 (HL).

permanently of the property *by that act of using or dealing*.[128] Future litigation on this point seems assured.

(b)   The requirement of prior "obtaining"

In any event, the usage or dealing must occur *after* D has first obtained possession or control of the property (in whatever manner). It seems, therefore, that the conman who offers the Auckland harbour bridge for sale to an unsuspecting tourist will not commit theft: although he is "dealing with" the property, he has not beforehand acquired possession or control of it.

A more serious example arises from the pre-2003 case of *R v Wilkinson*.[129] In *Wilkinson*, the Court of Appeal held that a fraudulently obtained electronic transfer of funds was not theft because its effect was to extinguish a chose in action owned by V and create another (owned by D), and a chose in action was not capable of being stolen under the pre-2003 law. By contrast, V's chose in action is now "property" capable of being stolen, and under s 219 it is "dealt with" when extinguished by the electronic transfer. But, in order to steal the chose in action by dealing with it, D must first have obtained possession or control of it; and, depending on the facts, this may not occur. Without ever having control of the asset, he might simply cause it to be extinguished. In such a case, it seems there is no theft.

(c)   Answer to charge: D's usage or dealing was subsequent to her becoming the absolute owner

For the reasons given in 19.3.2(3), it will be a complete answer to a charge of theft that, at the time of the alleged using or dealing, D had already become the absolute owner of the property. Where this possibility is raised, the civil law rules regarding passing of ownership will need first to be applied in order to determine whether, by the time D dealt with the property dishonestly, title had already passed to her. These rules are outlined above, at 19.3.2(4). By way of example, suppose that V sells a valuable necklace on credit to D. V delivers the necklace and transfers title in it to D who, subsequently, decides to abscond, taking the necklace without paying for it. D does not commit theft.

(d)   Theft by keeping or omission

The mere decision to steal is not sufficient for theft. There must be conduct as well,[130] amounting to a usage or dealing. However, the conduct may be a continuing act or omission, as distinct from a fresh positive act,[131] and, unlike a taking, need not involve moving the goods. It seems, therefore, that the dealing may be by omission, as distinct from a fresh positive act, and it is sufficient for theft that D keeps property lawfully obtained. In the pre-2003 case of *Subritzky*,[132] failing to return a toy taken innocently by D's child was held to be theft by conversion and, it is submitted, would be theft by usage or dealing also. Similarly, in *R v Oram*,[133] a finder of lost goods who decided to keep them, when it was reasonably easy to trace the owner, was held guilty of theft by conversion. Likewise borrowing a thing, and then

---

128   Contrast *R v Morris* [1984] AC 320; [1983] 3 All ER 288 (HL).
129   *R v Wilkinson* [1999] 1 NZLR 403; (1998) 16 CRNZ 179 (CA).
130   Cf *R v Maihi* [1993] 2 NZLR 139; (1992) 9 CRNZ 304 (CA); *Broom v Police* [1994] 1 NZLR 680; (1993) 11 CRNZ 20.
131   See 3.2.1(2)(d), and more generally, 3.2.1ff.
132   *R v Subritzky* [1990] 2 NZLR 717.
133   *R v Oram* (1908) 27 NZLR 955.

keeping it having decided not to return it, may amount to theft — on the basis of the keeping rather than the borrowing.

Under the pre-2003 law, however, the act of keeping had to amount to a *conversion*, being in some way inconsistent with V's rights. Very often, this depended upon the intention with which D acted: thus, in *Police v Moodley*,[134] merely putting the item in a drawer for safekeeping, as opposed to keeping the thing for oneself, was held not to be a theft.

The decision seems right and, notwithstanding the new statutory language, it is submitted that a similar restriction is needed in the application of s 219(1)(b) to the possibility of theft by keeping. The essence of keepings is that they are a form of omission. As we saw in chapter 3, the law is rightly reluctant to impose criminal liability for mere omissions, unless the circumstances give rise to a specific duty obligating D to act. It is submitted that this general principle of the common law applies also to theft. In other words, an omission cannot be a "dealing" unless it is in contravention of D's duty to return the goods to V. Suppose the following three cases:

(1) D1 has hired a car from V. The period of hire has not expired. D1 decides to keep the car, which he leaves sitting on the driveway.

(2) D2 has hired a car from V. The period of hire has not expired. D1 decides to sell the car, which he then ships to Australia, intending to trade it in there for a new vehicle.

(3) D3 has hired a car from V. The period of hire has since expired. D1 decides to keep the car, which he leaves parked on his driveway.

Depending on the issue of authorisation (above, 19.3.3(2)), case (2) can be theft: D deals with the car by his positive act of shipping it to Australia. Equally, however, it is submitted that case (1) cannot be not theft. Since the bailment has not expired, D is under no duty to do return the car, and his omission to do so should not be regarded as an actus reus of theft.

Case (3) is more complex. D's omission to return the car is in breach of the duty he owes to V, so prima facie is a conversion.[135] In our view, it is a case of theft.

19.4 Mens rea

There are three elements to the mens rea of theft.[136] The defendant's actions must be (i) dishonest; (ii) without claim of right; and done (iii) with intent permanently to deprive. We consider these elements in turn.

19.4.1 Dishonestly

The element of dishonesty has a statutory definition, set out in s 217:

> "dishonestly, in relation to an act or omission, means done or omitted without a belief that there was express or implied consent to, or authority for, the act or omission from a person entitled to give such consent or authority."

---

134 *Police v Moodley* [1974] 1 NZLR 644.
135 Cf R *v Maihi* [1993] 2 NZLR 139; (1992) 9 CRNZ 304 (CA).
136 For discussion of the doctrine of recent possession and its evidential role in the proof of mens rea, see 19.5.3.

Under this definition, dishonesty will be established if D acts without believing that he has received *legal* authorisation or consent, from an appropriate person, to take, use, or deal with the property. Note that D need not believe he has express permission. A belief that he has *implied* authority (such as a supermarket grants customers to take goods from shelves and put them in trolleys) would also prevent a finding of dishonesty.[137]

Three key points emerge from the definition. First, D need not think that his acts are *un*authorised and without consent: it is enough that he does not positively believe that he has authority or consent to behave as he does. Thus one who gives no thought to the matter, or is unsure of his authority to deal with the goods, would seem to be dishonest.

Secondly, test of dishonesty is subjective. It is a defence that D had an *honest belief* that she was entitled so to act. Therefore, the necessary dishonesty is negatived if D believes, even mistakenly, that her actions were authorised or consensual. Moreover, D's belief does not have to be reasonable. A jury may be less likely to credit her with honesty if the facts did not warrant her belief,[138] but if there is a reasonable possibility that D did so believe then she must be acquitted.

Thirdly, and perhaps most importantly, the definition differs significantly from the pre-2003 requirement that a thief act "fraudulently". The former requirement of fraudulence was understood to require *moral* dishonesty, so that D could not be liable for theft if he believed it was morally right to depart from his legal obligations.[139] By contrast, the new definition of theft no longer contains a mens rea requirement of moral obloquy — of "dishonesty" in its true sense. What counts now is simply D's belief about the facts, not his moral evaluation of those facts: ie, whether D believed his conduct had received *technical* authorisation (by consent or otherwise).

The two can diverge. Suppose, for instance, that without authorisation a farmer borrows a bale of his neighbour's hay, expecting to replace it with a bale of his own. He has an intention permanently to deprive his neighbour of the particular bale he "borrowed" and knows that he has no legal right to borrow the bale. This was not larceny, because the farmer was not accounted dishonest.[140] However, under the new definition, it is theft. Even though the farmer doubtless believes that his neighbour, upon finding out, *would* consent to his borrowing the bale, this is not the same as a belief that he has authority to take the bale.[141] (Indeed, he does *not* have such authority: the borrowing is clearly a tort even if the neighbour would so consent.)

---

137 See, in the context of burglary, *Police v Barwell* 6/7/06, John Hansen J, HC Christchurch CRI-2006-409-000077. (One who enters retail premises which are open to the public, intending while there to commit a crime, has an implied authority to enter and does not do so "without authority".)
138 Cf *Cheape v NZ Law Soc* [1955] NZLR 63, 68, where the *conduct* was said of itself to be "altogether inconsistent with honesty and fair dealing".
139 As in, eg, *R v Coombridge* [1976] 2 NZLR 381 (CA), 387: "if an accused person sets up a claim that in all the circumstances he honestly believed that he was justified in departing from his strict obligation, albeit for some purpose of his own, then his defence should be left to the jury for consideration provided at least that there is evidence on which it would be open to a jury to conclude that in all the circumstances his conduct, although legally wrong, might nevertheless be regarded as honest. In other words the jury should be told that the accused cannot be convicted unless he has been shown to have acted dishonestly". See further 19.4.1 in the second edition of this work.
140 [1956] Crim LR 360.
141 For this reason, the presumption in *Murphy v Gregory* [1959] NZLR 868, 872, that a belief the owner would consent gives rise to colour (or "claim") of right, should be doubted. It only does so if it leads D to believe his act was legally justified.

Under ss 217 and 219, it no longer matters that ordinary persons would regard D's act as acceptable practice. What counts is merely whether D believes his acts are consensual or authorised.

Consider, too, the facts of *Police v Minhinnick*:[142]

> D, a Maori, covertly removed a New Zealand Cross, then worth $10,000, from the Rotorua Museum. He was aware when he did so that his actions were contrary to law, but was inspired by cultural and spiritual beliefs that, he felt, obliged him to take the medal and return it to his ancestral burial ground.

This case would now be a theft. Similarly, suppose that D finds a $5 note on the street and picks it up. He sees nobody in the vicinity, and there is no obvious way of tracing the owner of the note, so he pockets it and later spends it. Assuming D knows that, legally speaking, "finders" does not mean "keepers", this seems also now to be theft.

The definition of dishonesty in s 217 threatens to convert most intentional usurpations of property rights into theft. But remedying interferences with property rights is the job of the civil law. Criminal law requires something more: a moral wrong, sufficient to mark that interference out as deserving the attention of the criminal law — ie as more than a mere tort or breach of trust. It is submitted that someone who is not *morally* dishonest lacks the guilty mind that makes her actions a criminal rather than civil wrong. Abolishing this requirement from theft is an error.

19.4.2 Without claim of right

"Claim of right" is defined in s 2 in the following terms:

> "**claim of right**, in relation to any act, means a belief that the act is lawful, although that belief may be based on ignorance or mistake of fact or of any matter of law other than the enactment against which the offence is alleged to have been committed."

While this definition replaces the former element of "colour of right" in theft, there is little practical difference between the two.[143] In essence, D acts with a claim of right when he acts with an honest belief that the taking or dealing with the thing is *legally* justified, ie permissible in both civil and criminal law;[144] notwithstanding that the belief may be based on ignorance, mistake of fact, or even a mistake of law (apart from a mistake about the law of theft itself).

The essence of the defence of claim of right is lawfulness of purpose, and it is for the prosecution to prove the absence thereof.[145] Examples of claim of right defences may be seen in the old case of *R v Bernhard*,[146] where a woman who blackmailed her former lover thought

---

142 *Police v Minhinnick* [1978] NZLJ 199.
143 Compare *Singh v Police* [2003] NZAR 596. The new definition nonetheless helps to clarify the law, by making it explicit that claim of right, like colour of right, depends on D's believing that he has a *legal*, not moral, right to act as he does.
144 Cf the definition of "justified", also in s 2: "not guilty of an offence and not liable to any civil proceeding."
145 Cf *Murphy v Gregory* [1959] NZLR 868, 872: "Where an accused person really believes he has the right asserted, it is a good defence even if he is mistaken in both fact and in law."
146 [1938] 2 KB 264; [1938] 2 All ER 140 (CCA). V agreed to pay his mistress (D) a sum of money, which he did not; she then threatened to expose him to his wife and the public unless he paid up. D was acquitted of demanding money with menaces with intent to steal, as she — mistakenly — thought she had a valid claim to the money.

she had a right to the money claimed; and in *R v Skivington*,[147] where D held up a wages clerk and demanded his wife's wages. Though this was an assault, it was held that there was no theft and therefore no robbery, since he believed he had a lawful claim.

Skivington illustrates that since colour of right is a defence to theft, it is also a defence to any other crime, such as robbery, in which the intent to steal is a necessary element.[148] In such cases, if D believes he is entitled to the money, the charge fails for lack of theftuous intent; it is irrelevant whether D believed he had a right to use force or menaces.

Conversely, although D's belief need not extend to justification of the action taken to obtain the thing, the "claim of right" must relate to the thing stolen. If D believes that she has a right to X, this is a defence to any charge alleging intent to *steal* X, as the requisite intent is simply not there. But that belief does not entitle her to steal Y in order to obtain X; and a belief of right to take X does not per se prove or imply an additional belief of right to take Y. In *Wicks v Police*,[149] D received by mistake and kept a barrister's file, and attempted to use it to force the barrister to settle a tort claim. He was convicted of theft: although he believed that his tort claim was justified, he admitted that he had no right to the file.

The distinction, however, is a narrow one. In *Wicks*, D was guilty of theft, whereas the defendant in *Bernhard* was not. Yet both are essentially cases of blackmail, the legal difference being that D's conduct in *Bernhard* did not constitute any crime apart from blackmail.[150] But where (unlike *Skivington*) D's independent crime is merely another theft — and that by way of set-off, as it were — it is more difficult to see a substantial moral difference between the two.

19.4.3 Intent to deprive permanently

The standard intent required for theft is the intent *permanently to deprive* an owner of the property or any interest therein. The intention need not be for D to keep the thing for himself: it is sufficient that D intends the victim to be (or is morally certain the victim will be)[151] permanently deprived of the thing. Therefore D will be guilty of theft where he steals to give to another, he himself receiving no benefit.[152]

(1) *Dishonest borrowing and conditional intentions*

But even if dishonesty and the absence of claim of right are proven, there is no theft where D intends to deprive only temporarily. Dishonest borrowing is not theft, no matter how much inconvenience it causes the owner. If D, a law student, dishonestly takes a book from the law library by concealing it in his bag, he commits theft if he intends not to return the book, but not if he means to keep the book only until the end of term. To fulfil the requirements of theft, D must have the intention to deprive V of her property *permanently*.

---

147 *R v Skivington* [1968] 1 QB 166; [1967] 1 All ER 483 (CA).
148 *R v Bhaskaran* 19/8/98, CA185/98; *R v Heard* (1985) 1 CRNZ 474.
149 *Wicks v Police* (1984) 1 CRNZ 328. By way of comparison, had D been charged with demanding with intent to steal (s 239), he would have had a colour of right defence.
150 On the particular facts of the case, in New Zealand D would have committed an offence under s 237, for which claim of right is not a defence: *R v Cargill* [1995] 3 NZLR 263; (1995) 13 CRNZ 291 (CA).
151 See 4.2.4, 4.2.7.
152 Cf *Leakey v Quirke* [1918] NZLR 550.

Thus, where a joyrider intends to take only temporarily, even for a period of several days, he is not guilty of theft of the car although there may be theft of the petrol consumed during the joyride.[153] The joyrider commits a separate offence of vehicle conversion under s 226.[154]

In other cases, where s 226 does not apply, this can lead to quite a fine distinction between the intent to deprive only temporarily and the conditional intent to deprive permanently.[155] As we saw in 4.2.8, a conditional intent is treated in law as sufficient for intention. To illustrate the implications of this, consider the facts of two cases. In *R v Hare*,[156] D found a letter containing important business information. He wrote to the sender demanding money for its return, and threatening to send copies to interested persons if money was not paid. D was convicted of theft. By contrast, in *Broom v Police*,[157] D recovered a stolen bicycle, and negotiated its return in response to an advertisement by the owner, in which a reward was offered. D's conviction for theft was set aside on appeal, on the footing (inter alia) that he had no intent to deprive the owner permanently.

The difference between these cases is that in *R v Hare* the defendant meant not to return the letter unless a ransom was paid. By contrast, Broom apparently had no thought of not returning the bicycle — he was merely temporarily withholding it in the hope of negotiating a reward.

(2)   *Dishonest borrowing v replacement*

One case where the lack of intent to deprive permanently was decisive is *R v Morunga*.[158] D was a bar manager and supervised the gaming machines located in the bar. He developed the habit of removing coins from the machines and reinserting them in order to gamble. The Court of Appeal held that this was not theft. Even though he was, without authorisation, taking and dealing with the coins, this is not sufficient for theft. D did not intend to deprive the owner permanently of the coins; rather, when inserting them into the machines, D was returning the coins to the owner, his employer.

Contrast the English case of *Velumyl*,[159] in which D dishonestly borrowed £1,050 from his employer's safe, without authority and in breach of company rules. D apparently intended to repay the amount borrowed. He was nonetheless convicted of theft. Although D intended to return an equivalent sum of money, it would not be the identical notes and coins that he had taken; merely substitute money to the same value. Hence, the Court concluded, D intended to deprive his employer permanently of the particular notes and coins that he appropriated.

Similarly, if D were to take a bag of sugar from V's kitchen, intending to buy another bag and replace it, D would still intend to deprive V permanently of the particular bag taken. *A fortiori*, a case where D intends to give V some money to pay for the sugar. In light of the current statutory definition of dishonesty (above, 19.4.1), it seems that these cases are theft.

---

153   *R v Bailey* [1924] QWN 38; cf *Neal v Gribble* [1978] RTR 409; (1978) 68 Cr App R 9.
154   Cf *Murphy v Gregory* [1959] NZLR 868.
155   Cf *R v Morunga* (2000) 17 CRNZ 396 (CA), 400.
156   *R v Hare* (1910) 29 NZLR 641 (CA). Cf *Thomas v A-G* 14/8/97, CA139/96, 7; *Wicks v Police* (1984) 1 CRNZ 328.
157   *Broom v Police* [1994] 1 NZLR 680; (1993) 11 CRNZ 20. Cf *R v Gardner* (1862) 9 Cox CC 253.
158   *R v Morunga* (2000) 17 CRNZ 396 (CA).
159   *R v Velumyl* [1989] Crim LR 299.

(3) Supplementary theftuous intents

As an alternative to the standard theftuous intent, ie permanently to deprive, D may be guilty of theft where she acts with one of the supplementary intents specified in s 219(2):

"An intent to deprive any owner permanently of property includes an intent to deal with property in such a manner that—

"(a) the property cannot be returned to any owner in the same condition; or

"(b) any owner is likely to be permanently deprived of the property or of any interest in the property."

We consider these alternatives in turn.

(a) Cannot be returned in the same condition

Paragraph (a) applies to cases where D's intended dealing with the property will damage or change it in a manner that cannot be rectified. The paragraph does not appear to apply to treatment that merely *risks* altering the property; the intended dealing must be such that the item "cannot", rather than may not, be returned in its original condition.

While "same" suggests "identical", it is submitted that the alteration must be significant rather than trivial. Uncontroversial examples falling within s 219(2)(a) would occur where D steals V's oats by wrongfully feeding them to V's animals,[160] or takes V's horse intending to kill it and return the carcase.[161] No doubt it would also be theft to take V's battery, intending to return it only after using it and thereby depleting its power.

In these examples, the property is tangibly altered. More difficult problems arise in respect of intangible property and property with intangible value. In the English case of *Beecham*,[162] D took railway tickets, intending to return them only after they had been used to complete a journey. Although the tickets were to be returned in their original condition, they would then be valueless and were ruled to be stolen. This seems right, but the same result in New Zealand would create questions about the extent to which a thing's value is a part of its "condition". A useful illustration is *Lloyd*,[163] in which a film projectionist borrowed films and passed them to E, who made and sold pirate copies of the films. Notwithstanding that the commercial value of the original films was thereby diminished, it is submitted that they should not be accounted stolen. Compare, too, the following example:

O, a law student, owns a textbook on criminal law. D dishonestly takes the book, intending to keep it until the criminal law exam has been sat by both D and O.

It is submitted that this is not theft, even though the case has many similarities with that of the railway ticket. If that is right, two options are available. Either "value" will have to be treated as irrelevant to a things "condition", or it may be that the value must be *entirely* exhausted before paragraph (a) will apply.

---

160 R v *Morfit* (1816) Russ & Ry 307; 168 ER 817.
161 R v *Cabbage* (1815) Russ & Ry 292; 168 ER 809. For other examples, see R v *Richards* (1844) 1 Car & Kir 532; 174 ER 925; R v *Duru* [1973] 3 All ER 715; (1973) 58 Cr App R 151; R v *Smails* (1957) 74 WN (NSW) 150.
162 R v *Beecham* (1851) 5 Cox CC 181. See also Smith, "Stealing Tickets" [1998] Crim LR 723.
163 R v *Lloyd* [1985] QB 829 (CA).

(b) Likely to be permanently deprived

The second of the alternatives in s 219(2) substantially extends the scope of theft beyond the paradigm of intentional deprivation, to criminalise unauthorised risk-taking. Thus it would be apt to cover situations where D, in a bout of anti-social behaviour, takes V's property and throws it away; ie where D does not act in order to deprive V permanently, but simply does not care whether the property is ever retrieved.

The risk of permanent deprivation must, at least, be "likely". In *R v Gush*, the Court of Appeal (in a different context) regarded an outcome as being likely when it is "such as could well happen";[164] it was not thought necessary that the outcome be more likely than not, or likely to occur on the balance of probabilities.

Additionally, the risk must be inherent in the course of dealing that D intends. Consider, once again, the case of D, a law student, who dishonestly takes a book from the law library by concealing it in his bag, meaning to keep the book only until the end of term. Suppose, this time, that D realises there is a chance he will be unable to return the book (eg because he has a habit of losing books in his possession). On the standard requirements of theft under s 219(1), he does not commit theft. In order to fulfil the standard definition of theft under s 219(1), D must have the *intention* to deprive V of her property permanently.[165]

It is submitted that s 219(2)(b) does not change this result. When D dishonestly takes the book, the risk of his losing it is incidental rather than bound up with his dishonest intention (which is, rather, to keep it). Given that D intends to *return* the book, it would be an odd result indeed if s 219(2)(b) were construed so as to deem the opposite. Such a wide construction would effectively expand the mens rea of theft to include recklessness. As such, it would extend the offence considerably beyond what, in ordinary language, most people would think of as "theft". Where D intends to deal with the property in a manner that, *necessarily*, means the property (or an interest therein) is likely to be lost, s 219(2)(b) clearly applies. But the paragraph should not be extended to criminalise incidental and unintended risk-taking.

19.5 Receiving

"[T]here would not be so many thieves if there were no receivers."[166] The crime of receiving is in many ways a special case of being an accessory to theft,[167] one which deserves independent criminalisation because of the important role that fences — and indeed end-purchasers — of stolen goods play in the economics of the offence. It should be noted, however, that although receiving is normally (and historically) associated with theft, the modern offence can be committed in respect of *anything* obtained by crime. Thus one who launders the proceeds of an illegal drug deal may be guilty of receiving under s 246.[168] Section 246(1), which is drafted in remarkably wide terms, provides that:

---

164 *R v Gush* [1980] 2 NZLR 92 (CA), 94.
165 Cf *Crump* (1825) 1 C & P 658, 171 ER 1357. This would be a case of recklessness whether the owner is deprived, rather than of intention: above, 4.1, 4.2.
166 *R v Battams* (1979) 1 Cr App R (S) 15, 16. See generally Smith, *Property Offences: The Protection of Property Through the Criminal Law*, London, Sweet & Maxwell, 1994, ch 30.
167 Indeed, this was how it was first criminalised, in 1692, 3 & 4 W & M c 13 (receivers deemed to be accessories). Earlier law disclosed an offence only if D actually received or abetted the thief himself: *Dawson's Case* (1602) 2 Bracton 337, 339. The old position is now reversed, and receiving the thief does not constitute receiving the goods stolen: *R v Wiley* (1850) 4 Cox CC 412; 169 ER 408.

"Every one is guilty of receiving who receives any property stolen or obtained by any other crime, knowing that property to have been stolen or so obtained, or being reckless as to whether or not the property had been stolen or so obtained."

The penalties, which are set down in s 247, are the same as for theft of something of equivalent value, reflecting the perception that receiving is a form of participation in theft. In this respect the statute has obvious limitations: its association with theft makes it a somewhat inflexible tool for prosecuting those who deal in the proceeds of crime more generally. Neither does the Act draw any distinction between the lay receiver who might once in her lifetime buy stolen goods for her own consumption, and the professional criminal receiver who maintains an organisation and thus supports the theft industry.[169]

Under s 246, there are four main elements of receiving. The three actus reus elements are that: the defendant (a) receives (b) something that counts as property, and (c) the property received was stolen or obtained by crime. The fourth component relates to mens rea: (d) when he receives it, D *knows* or *is reckless whether* the thing was stolen or obtained by crime.

19.5.1 The actus reus

(1) *Receiving something*

The property in question must be received from another person.[170] However, D need not take personal physical custody of the goods. According to s 246(3), the requirement of "receiving" is satisfied as soon as D acquires (joint or sole) possession *or* control over the property, *or* aids in concealing or disposing of it. On this point, subs (3) essentially reproduces the rule formerly laid down by s 260 (now repealed). As such, the previous law concerning what counts as receiving appears still to be relevant.

Regarding the first of the alternatives specified in s 246(3), therefore, "possession" may be established by showing (i) that the goods are either in D's immediate physical custody, or located at a place over which D has control (for example in D's house).[171] In either case, proof of possession also requires that the prosecution show a mental element, (ii) an intent by D to possess the goods.[172] Thus D cannot be in possession of property that he does not know exists. Suppose, for instance, that T, having stolen a wallet, disposes of it by slipping the wallet into D's bag without D's knowledge. In such a case, for the purposes of receiving D does not take

---

168 Cf *Stevens v Police* (1988) 4 CRNZ 69. Enactment of the offence considered in Howarth, "Handling stolen goods and handling salmon" [1987] Crim LR 460 would therefore be unnecessary in New Zealand.
169 Cf Hall, *Theft, Law and Society* (2nd ed), Indianapolis, Bobbs-Merrill, 1952, ch 5; Klockars, *The Professional Fence*, New York, Free Press, 1974; Chappell and Walsh, "Receiving stolen property: The need for a systematic inquiry into the fencing process" (1974) 11 Criminology 484; Blakey and Goldsmith, "Criminal Redistribution of Stolen Property: The Need for Reform" (1976) 74 Mich LR 1512. The difference would, however, normally be reflected in sentencing.
170 *R v Seymour* [1954] 1 All ER 1006; [1954] 1 WLR 678, 1007; 679. This decision represented an attempt by the Court of Criminal Appeal to correct the tendency to find someone guilty of receiving, rather than theft, whenever they were found in "recent possession" of stolen goods. (See 19.5.3) Lord Goddard CJ emphasised that to find someone guilty of receiving, the jury must be satisfied that D received from someone else: "If he is the thief, he cannot be found guilty of receiving because a man cannot receive from himself, but must receive the property from somebody else." Thus where the evidence is as consistent with theft as it is with receiving, the indictment ought to contain a count for theft and a count for receiving.
171 *Police v Emirali* [1976] 2 NZLR 476 (CA).
172 *R v Kennedy* [2001] 1 NZLR 314; (2000) 18 CRNZ 501 (CA), esp para 14; *Dong Wai v Audley* [1937] NZLR 290.

possession of the wallet, at least until she knows she has it. Similarly, if goods stolen by another are found in D's house, it must be shown either that D had arranged for them to be delivered there[173] or, alternatively, that D had realised the goods were present and intentionally exercised control over them.[174]

If D lacks actual custody of the stolen goods, he may nonetheless be found to have "control" over them. This occurs when custody is in the hands of an agent or servant acting under D's direction; through whom D exercises control over the goods.[175] Again, the exercise of such control must be intentional.[176]

It is not necessary for a finding of possession that D should know the thing was stolen — such knowledge goes rather to the mens rea of receiving.[177]

(2) *Property*

To fall within s 246, the thing received must constitute "property". Property itself is defined in s 2(1); the scope of that definition, which includes both tangible and intangible property, is considered above, 19.3.1.

(3) *Stolen or obtained by any crime*

The thing received must be something that was itself unlawfully obtained, not its proceeds or a substitute.[178] However, D need not receive the whole of the thing stolen. It is sufficient, for example, that D receives parts of a car which has been stolen (for example the wheels or radio), or parts of a stolen stereo system, such as the tape deck or amplifier. Furthermore, the property need not be in the same state or condition as it was when stolen. A stolen car can be received even though substantially damaged in an accident before it arrives in D's hands. Similarly, s 246 would apply to the receipt of mutton from a sheep which was alive when stolen.[179]

Exceptionally, the proceeds can sometimes be received when they themselves have been obtained by a criminal act. This might occur, for example, when D receives money that was obtained from an illegal drug deal,[180] or from an act of money laundering.[181]

It is not necessary to prove the identity of either the person who actually committed the crime, or the owner of the property.[182] Provided the evidence discloses that the property was obtained by theft or another crime, even the acquittal of the particular person charged with committing that theft is irrelevant to the charge of receiving.[183]

---

173 *R v Lloyd* [1992] Crim LR 361.
174 Cf *R v Cavendish* [1961] 2 All ER 856; [1961] 1 WLR 1083.
175 Cf *R v Smith* (1855) 1 Dears 494; 169 ER 818; *R v Miller* (1854) 6 Cox 353.
176 *R v Kennedy* [2001] 1 NZLR 314; (2000) 18 CRNZ 501 (CA), para 14.
177 *R v Kennedy* [2001] 1 NZLR 314; (2000) 18 CRNZ 501 (CA), para 14.
178 Cf *R v Lucinsky* [1935] NZLR 575; [1935] GLR 515 (CA); *R v Walkley* (1829) 4 C & P 132; 172 ER 640.
179 *Cowell and Green* (1796) 2 East PC 617.
180 *Stevens v Police* (1988) 4 CRNZ 69.
181 Contrary to s 243, which s 246 thus supplements.
182 *R v Carr & Wilson* (1882) 10 QBD 76 (bonds stolen from an English ship moored in Holland, thief and circumstances of the theft unknown). In *R v Fuschillo* [1940] 2 All ER 489; (1940) 27 Cr App R 193, D was charged with receiving a large quantity of sugar, although it was not proven who had stolen it or from whom it was stolen. The Court of Criminal Appeal applied dicta in *R v Sbarra* [1918-19] 2 All ER Rep Ext 1453; (1918) 13 Cr App R 118, to the effect that: "The circumstances in which a defendant receives goods may of themselves prove that the goods were stolen, and, further, may prove that he knew it at the time when he received them. It is not a rule of law that there must be other evidence of the theft."

However, it *is* essential to prove that the property was stolen,[184] or obtained by some other *crime*. So, for example, where the person charged with originally stealing a thing is acquitted (or cannot be charged at all) on the ground of legal incapacity such as minority or insanity, the receivers cannot be convicted in the absence of other evidence showing the property to have been obtained by a crime.[185] An illustration of this is the case of *R v Farrell*,[186] in which the person from whom D received a stolen cheque was acquitted of theft on the ground of insanity. Consequently, the Court held that the evidence against D lacked an essential ingredient of the receiving charge, namely that the cheque was "obtained by any crime". In such a case D's subsequent handling of the cheque might, of course, be a dealing sufficient for D himself to be charged with theft under s 219.

(a) Goods which are no longer stolen

Goods are no longer stolen, and cannot be received, once they re-enter into the possession of a legal owner. By s 246(4), this may occur in two ways:

"If—

"(a) any property stolen or obtained by any other crime has been returned to the owner; or

"(b) legal title to any such property has been acquired by any person—

"a subsequent receiving of it is not an offence, even though the receiver may know that the property had previously been stolen or obtained by any other crime."

The first way in which goods become not stolen, then, is if they are restored to the original owner. Suppose, for example, that the owner recovers stolen goods but then returns them to the location where they were discovered in order to trap a would-be receiver. In that case, the subsequent purchaser cannot be guilty of receiving. Additionally, property counts as having been returned to its legal owner when it is restored to an authorised possessor in such a way that it is now under the owner's control. Hence if, alternatively, the police recover the stolen goods but then, with the consent of the owner, return them to the location where they were discovered in order to entrap a would-be receiver, the subsequent purchaser cannot be convicted of receiving.[187] However, if the owner does not know of the recovery and no agency exists between the owner and the police, the goods remain stolen as they have not in those circumstances been restored to the owner.[188]

---

183 *R v Dee & Hennessy* (1875) 3 NZCA 58. Neither is a conviction admissible against the receiver.
184 "Stolen or" was inserted in 1985 into the predecessor of s 246, in order to cover cases where the property was first obtained legitimately before then being stolen (by conversion or, now under s 219, by usage or dealing); in which case it would not have been "obtained" by crime. Cf *Anderson v Police* [1983] NZLR 509 (CA).
185 *Walters v Lunt* [1951] 2 All ER 645; (1951) 35 Cr App R 94 (property received from a child aged 7: no conviction for receiving since the child, being under 8 years old, could not be guilty of larceny). See Brown, "Receiving goods stolen by children or the insane" [1979] NZLJ 506.
186 *R v Farrell* [1975] 2 NZLR 753; following the rule in *Walters v Lunt* [1951] 2 All ER 645; (1951) 35 Cr App R 94.
187 *R v Dolan* (1855) Dears 436; 169 ER 794; *R v Schmidt* (1866) LR 1 CCR 15; *R v Hancock* (1878) 14 Cox CC 119.
188 *Fry v Police* [1975] NZ Recent Law 295.

Secondly, goods may cease to be stolen if a third party acquires legal ownership of them, usually by purchasing them in good faith. Normally in such cases the rule nemo dat quod non habet will prevent third parties from acquiring ownership, since at law a person cannot transfer to another any better title to goods than she has herself.[189] However, there are some exceptions to this, most of which are contained in the Sale of Goods Act 1908.[190]

19.5.2 Mens rea

Under s 246(1), D must either *know*, or be *reckless* whether, the property was stolen or obtained by a crime. It is not necessary that D should be aware of the particular manner in which the thing was obtained,[191] so long as he is aware that it was, or may have been, obtained by a crime.

D must have the requisite knowledge or recklessness at the time the thing was received.[192] If D receives property innocently, he is not guilty of an offence under s 246. However, retaining property after discovering that it was obtained by crime may amount to theft by subsequent dealing.[193]

The meaning of "knowledge" was considered in 4.5, where it was said that knowing means "knowing, or correctly believing". In essence, this requirement is satisfied when D accepts, or assumes, and has no serious doubt, that the goods he receives were obtained by crime;[194] or, exceptionally, in some cases when D is wilfully blind about that prospect.[195]

Since 2003, however, the precise definition of knowledge has become less important in the context of receiving, because recklessness now also suffices. The meaning of recklessness is considered in 4.3: in the context of s 246, it requires that D be *aware of a risk* that the goods were stolen or obtained by crime, and the risk is an unreasonable one to disregard. D need not believe them to be stolen: it is enough that he suspects that to be the case, at least where he thinks the chances are more than negligible.

When is the risk unreasonable, or more than negligible? In *Dean v Police*,[196] it was suggested that recklessness requires "foresight of dangerous consequences that could well happen together with an intention to continue the course of conduct regardless of rsk"; ie conscious awareness that the property *could well be* stolen. While the matter was obiter on the facts of the case (since D was found to be unaware of the risk), this standard offers a pointer to how, in practice, the test of recklessness will be applied.

It is unfortunate that s 246 now widens the offence in this manner, to the point that even a mere (albeit genuine) suspicion will be enough. Admittedly, it is difficult to prove the mens rea of handling, hence the perceived need for a recent possession doctrine (19.5.3 below);

---

189   Sections 23 and 26(1) Sale of Goods Act 1908.
190   For example, if the rogue has obtained a voidable title to the goods that has not been avoided at time of on-sale (ss 25 and 26(2) Sale of Goods Act 1908), or is a fraudulent buyer in possession (ss 26(2), 27(2)), or is a mercantile agent with authorised possession (s 3 Mercantile Law Act 1908).
191   *Stevens v Police* (1988) 4 CRNZ 69; cf *DPP v Nieser* [1959] 1 QB 254; [1958] 3 All ER 662.
192   *R v Kennedy* [2001] 1 NZLR 314; (2000) 18 CRNZ 501 (CA); *R v Johnson* (1911) 6 Cr App R 218; *R v Smith* (1935) 25 Cr App R 119; *R v Tennet* [1939] 1 All ER 86.
193   *R v Stone* [1920] NZLR 462; [1920] GLR 357 (CA). See above, 19.3.3(2)(d).
194   Cf *R v Crooks* [1981] 2 NZLR 53 (CA), 56, a leading authority on the requirement of knowledge in the pre-2003 offence of receiving. See also *R v White* (1859) 1 F & F 665; 175 ER 898; *R v Nosworthy* (1907) 26 NZLR 536; 9 GLR 434 (CA); *R v Simpson* [1978] 2 NZLR 221 (CA), 225.
195   Above, 4.5.1. Cf *R v Crooks* [1981] 2 NZLR 53 (CA), 57-9; *R v Griffiths* (1974) 60 Cr App R 14 (CA), 18.
196   *Dean v Police* 13/7/06, John Hansen J, HC Rotorua CRI-2006-463-57.

fewer dishonest handlers would escape conviction if recklessness were sufficient. But in meeting that concern, it would have been better to require, at least, that D believes the goods are *probably* stolen or obtained by crime.[197] Overextending the offence of receiving is undesirable. It is improbable that the reform will much affect the position of professional receivers, who are likely to know rather than suspect the provenance of the goods. Thus its greatest value will be against the casual or occasional receiver: the purchaser at a flea market, or the pawnbroker, who recognises a risk that (ie is uncertain whether) the goods are stolen and has no way of establishing whether they are, but who would not buy or accept the goods if she knew the truth. Such forms of legitimate commercial activity may be stifled if the otherwise honest purchaser or broker is required to risk criminal conviction by her activity.[198]

19.5.3 Evidence of criminality: the doctrine of recent possession

Proof of the mens rea elements in receiving can be difficult. The prosecution may be able to establish that D had possession of stolen goods, but unless it can give some account of how those goods were acquired, or of what D intended to do with the goods, it may be very difficult to prove that D knew or believed the goods were stolen. To meet this challenge, judges have evolved a common law device of prima facie inference from which proof of possession can, under certain circumstances, support an inference of criminality. This is known as the doctrine of recent possession.

The "doctrine" of recent possession is a commonsense rule that, where D acquired possession willingly,[199] the proof of possession by D of recently stolen property is sufficient evidence to justify a finding that D is either the thief or a dishonest receiver, in the absence of a credible explanation of how D came by the property.[200] It has been described as:[201]

> "a convenient way of referring compendiously to the inferences of fact which, in the absence of any satisfactory explanation by the accused, may be drawn as a matter of common sense from other facts, including, in particular, the fact that the accused has in his possession property which it is proved had been unlawfully obtained shortly before he was found to be in possession of it."

Although in some jurisdictions it has been held that the rule is limited to theft, its application to receiving may be justified on the pragmatic ground that criminal receivers can rarely be detected in the act of receiving, so that direct evidence is rarely available.[202]

---

197 As Spencer proposes: "Handling, Theft and the Mala Fide Purchaser" [1985] Crim LR 92, 95-6. Blakey and Goldsmith, "Criminal Redistribution of Stolen Property: The Need for Reform" (1976) 74 Mich LR 1512, 1560 advocate a standard of awareness of "a substantial risk" that the property was stolen.
198 See Williams, "Handling, theft and the purchaser who takes a chance" [1985] Crim LR 432, 435-436.
199 A proviso stated in *R v York* (2005) 193 CCC (3d) 331 (BC CA).
200 For more detailed discussion, see Adams, "Recent possession" [1967] NZLJ 399, 495, 511; *Adams*, CA219.09 (looseleaf).
201 *DPP v Nieser* [1959] 1 QB 254; [1958] 3 All ER 662, 266; 668-669. See also *R v Raviraj* (1987) 85 Cr App R 93 (CA): the doctrine is only an extension of a general proposition that guilt may be inferred from unreasonable behaviour by the accused in response to his being confronted with facts which prima facie suggest his guilt.
202 Hall, *Theft, Law and Society* (2nd ed), Indianapolis, Bobbs-Merrill, 1952, 175. However, where the actus reus of receiving is constituted only by concealment or disposal (see 19.5.1(1)), actual knowledge must be proved and the doctrine of recent possession does not apply: *R v Hyde-Harris* [1968] NZLR 315.

Before the inference from recent possession can be invoked, the prosecution must prove the relevant property was stolen, and that it was stolen recently. How recent is "recent"? It depends on the facts and, in particular, on the nature of the property.[203] Possession of a stolen £20 note would be unlikely to support any inference of theft or handling after more than a few days. Eleven months was too long for stereo equipment in one English case,[204] but the doctrine was applicable after 4 months in the case of a corporate bond.[205]

The classic direction is found in R v Aves:[206]

> "Where the only evidence is that an accused person is in possession of property recently stolen, a jury may infer guilty knowledge (a) if he offers no explanation to account for his possession, or (b) if the jury are satisfied that the explanation he does offer is untrue. If, however, the explanation offered is one which leaves the jury in doubt whether he knew the property was stolen, they should be told that the case has not been proved, and therefore the verdict should be Not Guilty."

Thus stated, it is clear that recent possession is simply a matter of ordinary evidential inference from circumstances. The onus of proving both actus reus and mens rea remains on the prosecution. Its dependence on the fact of possession makes the evidential inference of limited value against sophisticated professional fences, who are unlikely to take actual possession of the goods for themselves, or who, if they do take possession, are likely to take the precaution of ensuring they can offer a plausible explanation, for example by integrating possession of stolen goods with their other, legitimate, business activities.[207]

The doctrine of recent possession has been held compatible with s 23(4)(b) New Zealand Bill of Rights Act 1990, which gives persons arrested or detained the right to refrain from making any statement, and with s 25(c) and (d), which refers to the right to be presumed innocent until proven guilty according to law, and the right not to be compelled to be a witness or to confess guilt.[208]

---

203 *Richardson v Police* 15/11/88, McGechan J, HC Palmerston North AP258/88; *R v Mahoney* (2000) 114 A Crim R 130 (NSW CCA).
204 *R v Simmons* [1986] Crim LR 397 (CA).
205 *R v Livock* (1914) 10 Cr App R 264.
206 *R v Aves* [1950] 2 All ER 330; (1950) 34 Cr App R 159, 160. See also *R v Ketteringham* (1926) 19 Cr App R 159; *R v Hepworth* [1955] 2 QB 600; [1955] 2 All ER 918; *R v Cash* [1985] QB 801; [1985] 2 All ER 128 (CA).
207 Cf Hall, *Theft, Law and Society* (2nd ed), Indianapolis, Bobbs-Merrill, 1952, 189-190; Klockars, *The Professional Fence*, New York, Free Press, 1974, 80-93.
208 *R v Clarke* 16/12/93, CA417/93.

Chapter 20

DECEPTION

20.1	Introduction	700
20.2	Obtaining by deception or causing loss by deception	701
20.3	Deception	702
20.3.1	False representation	702
(1)	*A representation*	702
(2)	*False*	706
(3)	*Known to be false*	706
(4)	*Reckless whether it is false*	706
(5)	*In a material particular*	707
20.3.2	Omission to disclose	707
20.3.3	A fraudulent device, trick, or stratagem	708
(1)	*Deceitful*	709
(2)	*Fraudulent*	709
(3)	*Fraud: a new offence*	710
20.4	Causation	711
20.4.1	Remoteness	712
20.4.2	Machines	712
20.5	The object of the deception	713
20.5.1	Obtaining any property, etc: s 240(1)(a)	713
(1)	*The subject matter obtained*	713
(2)	*The act of "obtaining"*	714
20.5.2	Obtaining credit: s 240(1)(b)	714
(1)	*Debt or liability*	714
(2)	*Obtains credit*	714
20.5.3	Inducing another to deal with a document, etc: s 240(1)(c)	715
20.5.4	Causing loss to any other person: s 240(1)(d)	716
20.6	Without claim of right	717
20.7	Intent to deceive	717
20.8	Intent to obtain, etc, by the deception	717

20.1 Introduction

Theft is not the only way of usurping another's property rights. Sometimes, the wrongfulness of the defendant's behaviour may be more subtle. It may, for example, lie in the fact that D duped V into transferring ownership consensually or into performing services for D, or in the fact that she fraudulently gained from the use of V's assets even though V suffered no loss. In common with theftuous offences, wrongdoing of this sort involves dishonest behaviour by D regarding the property of another. However, its prevention often requires the enactment of offences which differ substantially from traditional forms of theft.

The extent to which such offences are necessary has sometimes been questioned.[1] For example, although acquisition by deception may not give rise to tortious claims in trespass or conversion,[2] other civil law remedies, such as deceit, are usually available to the aggrieved party. In addition, much commercial wrongdoing is controlled by administrative regulation of the marketplace, buttressed by the civil sanctions available to professional bodies. Given such existing sanctions, and the commitment in New Zealand to a broadly liberal economic philosophy, is it really essential to fence in the marketplace with criminal law?

The answer is yes. Our rights to private property are part of the very fabric of modern New Zealand.[3] Property relations are shared elements which help to structure our interpersonal relations within the community. As such, they are integral to our membership of society, and to the understanding we have of our own lives. In particular, one feature of our participation in a broadly liberal society is the autonomy we have in respect of our property — the freedom to use, control, and dispose of that property as we wish.

Of course, there are limitations to our autonomy as proprietors. Even the freedoms of contract and testament are substantially constrained by law. Neither may we use our assets to fund criminal activities, and we are compelled by the State to contribute through taxation to certain communal goals which may not be of direct personal benefit to us. Nonetheless, the importance of individualism to the New Zealand polity means that personal property rights have attracted better protection from the criminal law than many more abstract social or community values, such as an unpolluted environment or a well-educated populace. By contrast with these examples, the occurrence of harms is more readily criminalised and prosecuted when there is an identifiable victim whose concrete individual rights have been transgressed.

This imbalance may be reason for complaint, but not on the basis that property rights deserve reduced protection. Indeed, the harms involved in property offences shade into those addressed by offences against the person, and any suggestion that offences against property are concerned solely with material loss would be misleading. The violation of our homes by a burglary, for example, may cause psychological injury and distress quite independent of the quantum of loss. Offences such as theft, obtaining by deception, and blackmail are generally

---

1 See, for example, *R v Jones* (1703) 2 Ld Raymond 1013; 92 ER 174; *R v Goodhall* (1821) Russ & Ry 461; 168 ER 898.
2 Since possession and/or title will normally have passed, at least prima facie.
3 Cf Waldron, *The Right to Private Property*, Oxford, Clarendon Press, 1988; Ryan, *Property and Political Theory*, Oxford, Blackwell, 1984; Nozick, *Anarchy, State and Utopia*, Oxford, Blackwell, 1974; Epstein, "Property as a fundamental civil right" (1992) 29 Cal West LR 187; Harris, *Property and Justice*, New York, Clarendon Press, 1996.

categorised as property offences, and understandably so, for they involve wrongful acquisition of property. But they are also, in a very real sense, offences against the person. In each case, the conduct prohibited can be seen as an attack upon the victim's entitlement to dispose of his property by his own full and informed choice. Thus, the conduct represents an attack upon the victim's rights of free will and autonomy, and upon his freedom to exercise control over his own situation. Blackmail, for instance, involves D infringing V's legitimate control over his own affairs by imposing her free will in place of his. This subjugation of V resembles an assault as much as it does a "property" wrong. Obtaining by deception, understood in this sense, is a crime partly because it entails the manipulation or exploitation of another. Unlike the corresponding civil law remedies, property offences, in differing ways, protect the individual's entitlement to respect as an autonomous member of our society.

20.2 Obtaining by deception or causing loss by deception

With the revamp of the property offences in 2003, the various former offences regulating dishonest obtaining and defrauding were repealed and consolidated into a new offence of obtaining or causing loss by deception. The offence under s 240 reads as follows:

"(1) Every one is guilty of obtaining by deception or causing loss by deception who, by any deception and without claim of right,—

"(a) obtains ownership or possession of, or control over, any property, or any privilege, service, pecuniary advantage, benefit, or valuable consideration, directly or indirectly; or

"(b) in incurring any debt or liability, obtains credit; or

"(c) induces or causes any other person to deliver over, execute, make, accept, endorse, destroy, or alter any document or thing capable of being used to derive a pecuniary advantage; or

"(d) causes loss to any other person.

"(2) In this section, **deception** means—

"(a) a false representation, whether oral, documentary, or by conduct, where the person making the representation intends to deceive any other person and—

"(i) knows that it is false in a material particular; or

"(ii) is reckless as to whether it is false in a material particular; or

"(b) an omission to disclose a material particular, with intent to deceive any person, in circumstances where there is a duty to disclose it; or

"(c) a fraudulent device, trick, or stratagem used with intent to deceive any person."

There are six elements of this new offence:

(i)   A deception;

(ii) Causation;

(iii) An obtaining, inducement, or loss of the sorts specified in s 240(1)(a)-(d);

(iv) No claim of right;

(v) Intent to deceive; and, it is submitted,

(vi) An intent to obtain, induce, or cause loss by the deception.

We consider these elements below.

20.3 Deception

What counts as a deception is defined in s 240(2), and may take three forms. It consists of (a) a false representation, where the representor either knows or is reckless whether it is false; or (b) a failure to disclose some material fact, in circumstances where there is a duty to do so; or (c) a fraudulent device, trick, or stratagem. In all three cases, the deceptive conduct must be perpetrated with intent to deceive; for convenience, this element will be treated separately in 20.7.

20.3.1 False representation

The most common form of deception is by a false representation, falling within s 240(2)(a). Apart from the element of intent to deceive, in order to satisfy paragraph (a) the prosecution must show that there was (i) a representation by D; (ii) that the representation was false; and that D either (iii) knew it to be false in a material particular, or was reckless whether that was the case.

(1) *A representation*

What counts as a representation is not further defined and there is no reason to limit the variety of matters that may fall within the scope of s 240(2)(a). Typical examples of a representation may be about a past or present fact, about a future event, or about an existing intention, opinion, belief, knowledge, or other state or mind. There is, however, one limitation to the scope of the paragraph, in that the representation must be *capable* of being false. This means that it must contain, expressly or impliedly, a proposition of fact.

For example, if D states to V, "the owner has authorised me to sell this car", he asserts a fact which may be true or false. That is a plain case of a representation. But other statements are less clear-cut. Suppose that D says to V, "it is a good car for its age". This seems to express an opinion, rather than state a fact. Even though one may make true or false statements about one's opinion, the opinion itself is not capable of being false.[4] It is similar if D's statement is about a future event: the assurance that "New Zealand will win the next rugby World Cup" is prima facie no more than a prediction. Such a proposition may *become* false, but is usually not false when made.[5]

In cases such as these, it will be necessary for the prosecution to establish a further, *implied* representation by D in order to satisfy the actus reus. There are two standard implied representations in this situation. The first is *that D herself genuinely holds that opinion or believes that prediction*. This is a representation about D's existing mental state, and as such is capable of being false:[6]

---

4   Cf *Bisset v Wilkinson* [1927] AC 177 (PC); *McAlpine Snowline Ltd v Wethey* (1986) 2 NZCPR 388.
5   See the note by White, "Trade descriptions about the future" (1974) 90 LQR 15; also Pearce, "Theft by false promises" (1953) 101 U Pa LR 967.
6   *Edgington v Fitzmaurice* (1885) 29 Ch D 459, 483.

"it is very difficult to prove what the state of a man's mind at a particular time is, but if it can be ascertained it is as much a fact as anything else. A misrepresentation as to the state of a man's mind is therefore, a misstatement of fact."

In *R v King*,[7] for example, a second-hand car dealer stated that the mileage reading on a particular car "may not be correct". Impliedly, he also represented that he was not certain the reading was wrong. The latter representation is one of present fact, about the dealer's mental state, and capable of being a deception.

The second representation is normally inferred only if D is in a better position to express the opinion or prediction than V. In such cases, there is generally an implicit representation that D's view is a reasonable one given the information available to him. A useful statement of this rule may be found in the words of Bowen LJ in *Smith v Land and House Property Corp*:[8]

"if the facts are not equally known to both sides, then a statement of opinion by the one who knows the facts best involves very often a statement of a material fact, for he impliedly states that he knows facts which justify his opinion."

Assistance may also be gleaned from *NZ Motor Bodies Ltd v Emslie*.[9] In that case, D prepared (for the purpose of a takeover by P) a budget forecasting turnover and profit. The budget contained gross inaccuracies. Although the prediction may have been believed by D,[10] the Court held that it involved a false representation, since the making of the forecast implied that present facts existed which justified its conclusions.

In the civil law, and presumably under s 240(2), an exaggeration of quality is not a false pretence unless carried to such an extent as to amount to a misrepresentation of fact. The question here is whether the statement goes beyond praise which does not appear to be serious or more than a mere opinion. A description of land as "fertile and improveable" has been held to be mere sales talk.[11] However, a statement that use of a carbolic smoke ball will prevent influenza is a more specific claim and may amount to a representation.[12]

(a)   Implications from conduct

Implicit in the foregoing section is that the law does not restrict its analysis of representations merely to the literal meaning of express words used by D. Rather, the test is "what meaning was actually conveyed to the party complaining".[13] This rule is buttressed by s 240(2)(a), which states that the representation may be "oral, documentary, or by conduct"[14] and thus need not be express.

---

7   *R v King* [1979] Crim LR 122.
8   *Smith v Land and House Property Corp* (1884) 28 Ch D 7, 15. Cf *Brown v Raphael* [1958] Ch 636; [1958] 2 All ER 79.
9   *NZ Motor Bodies Ltd v Emslie* [1985] 2 NZLR 569.
10   And as such would not have been a deception within s 240(1)(a). The case involved a claim for damages for negligent misrepresentation; on these facts, it would appear not to disclose a criminal offence, since D (who did not prepare the forecast personally) did not realise the forecast was ungrounded.
11   *Dimmock v Hallett* (1866) LR 2 Ch App 21. See also *R v Bryan* (1857) Dears & B 265; 169 ER 1002.
12   *Carlill v Carbolic Smoke Ball Co* [1893] 1 QB 256; [1891-94] All ER Rep 127.
13   *Bisset v Wilkinson* [1927] AC 177 (PC), 183. See *R v Taylor* [1991] 1 NZLR 413 (CA), 417; *R v Cooper* (1877) 2 QBD 510, 513.
14   Cf *R v Giles* (1865) Le & Ca 502; 169 ER 1490, 508; 1493. For comprehensive discussion of representations implied from conduct, see Smith, *Property Offences: The Protection of Property Through the Criminal Law*, London, Sweet & Maxwell, 1994, para 17.5.

An example of representation by conduct may be found in *R v Barnard*,[15] where D, by wearing a university cap and gown, was held to have falsely represented that he was a member of Oxford University in order to obtain credit from a tradesman; whether or not he had made such a claim by words, his actions alone constituted a false representation.[16]

According to Lord Reid, writing a cheque implies a representation that it will be honoured when presented for payment.[17] Since this is a prediction of future events, a further representation must be implied from it that the drawer of the cheque presently intends and expects that it will be honoured when presented. Another common situation is the use of a credit card or bank card, which involves a representation that the person using it has authority to do so.[18] Similarly, countersigning a traveller's cheque amounts to a representation that D is the person authorised to sign and use it.[19]

Where D purports to sell goods to V, there is usually an implied representation that D has the capacity to pass ownership of the goods,[20] and that the goods are genuine.[21] Conversely, where D buys or orders goods, she impliedly represents her intention to pay for them; and where payment on the spot is expected (for example at a restaurant or service station), she impliedly represents also that she has the ability to pay. So, for instance, where D takes a taxi, she implies by her conduct that she has money for the fare.[22]

(b)   Positive representations arising from silence

As in contract law, silence or non-disclosure will generally not be regarded as representation.[23] This point is addressed in part by s 240(2)(b), which deems omissions to disclose to be representations where there is a duty to make disclosure (below, 20.3.2). By

---

15 *R v Barnard* (1837) 7 C & P 784; 173 ER 342.
16 See *R v Parker and Bulteel* (1916) 25 Cox CC 145: a banker who keeps his doors open and continues to trade may thereby represent that he is solvent.
17 *DPP v Turner* [1974] AC 357; [1973] 3 All ER 124, 367; 128. (Note that this representation encompasses the implied representations stated in the old case of *R v Hazelton* (1874) LR 2 CCR 134. It is submitted that the earlier case may now be disregarded.) Cf *R v Gilmartin* [1983] QB 953; [1983] 1 All ER 829, 962; 835 (Goff LJ) (in the context of ss 15 and 16 Theft Act 1968 (UK)): "by the simple giving of a cheque, whether post-dated or not, the drawer impliedly represents that the state of facts existing at the date of handing over the cheque is such that in the ordinary course the cheque will, on presentation for payment on or after the date specified in the cheque, be met." Thus the test is "not the known state of the appellant's account at the moment the cheque was issued, but whether it had been proved that he did not honestly believe that the cheque would, in the ordinary course, be met": *R v Miller* [1955] NZLR 1038 (CA), 1049. See also Smith, *Property Offences: The Protection of Property Through the Criminal Law*, London, Sweet & Maxwell, 1994, para 17.52.
18 *MPC v Charles* [1977] AC 177; [1976] 3 All ER 112; *R v Lambie* [1982] AC 449; [1981] 2 All ER 776. These decisions, however, fail to address the causation point (20.4), that the vendor accepting the card may rely only upon the minimum representation required to validate the charge transaction — ie that the customer is the person named on the face of the card (itself an implied representation: *R v Abdullah* [1982] Crim LR 122). See Smith; "The idea of criminal deception" [1982] Crim LR 721.
19 *R v Griffiths* [1960] NZLR 850 (CA).
20 *R v Sampson* (1885) 52 LT (NS) 772. Cf *Eichholz v Bannister* (1864) 17 CB (NS) 708; 144 ER 284, 723; 290, "in almost all the transactions of sale in common life the seller by the very act of selling holds out to the buyer that he is the owner of the article he offers for sale".
21 *R v Williams* [1980] Crim LR 589.
22 *R v Waterfall* [1970] 1 QB 148; [1969] 3 All ER 1048, 150; 1049 (Lord Parker).
23 Cf *Smith v Hughes* (1871) LR 6 QB 597; [1861-73] All ER Rep 632.

implication, a failure to disclose some material information, when there is no duty so to do, is ordinarily not a deception.

However, the general rule is qualified in some circumstances, so that — quite apart from s 240(2)(b) — silence will sometimes generate a positive representation falling within the scope of s 240(2)(a). One such exception occurs where D's conduct gives rise to an implied representation that is false, and which D silently fails to refute.[24] A controversial example of this is the case of *Dronjak v Police*,[25] in which D allowed a supermarket cashier to charge an incorrect price, by not pointing out the presence of another, higher price tag on the goods. This decision is questionable, as it effectively creates a higher duty of disclosure in the criminal law context than is imposed in the context of civil obligations.[26] Consistency with the civil law is essential in s 240, since it would be wrong to find D guilty of obtaining by deception something for which he is entitled to sue under a valid contract. Nonetheless, the controversy over *Dronjak* is restricted to whether D's presentation of the goods to the cashier amounts to a representation that the price tag showing is the only or correct tag. Once this proposition is conceded (as, with respect, it should not be), the second principle — that D may be convicted for deliberately failing to correct a misapprehension he creates — would appear unobjectionable.

A second exception to the general rule is the case of half-truths, where D's silence has the effect of distorting the meaning of some positive representation that she makes. It seems clear that an incomplete representation accompanied by silence as to material facts can be a false representation, if there is an implication from the circumstances that all material information has been disclosed. Thus it is a misrepresentation for a vendor to state that the properties are let, and omit the further truth that the tenants have been given notice to quit.[27]

Thirdly, the failure to negate an understanding that is implied from a course of dealing may also result in a false representation. In *R v Silverman*,[28] D had been convicted of obtaining property by deception under s 15 Theft Act 1968 (UK) by grossly overcharging for rewiring and redecoration of a house. Although the conviction was quashed on other grounds, the English Court of Appeal held that in the situation of mutual trust, which had built up over a number of years, D had impliedly represented that his firm was going to get no more than a modest profit from the work. Watkins LJ referred to dicta of Lord Reid in *DPP v Ray* that "a man intending to deceive can build up a situation in which his silence is as eloquent as an express statement".[29] At first glance, to penalise such conduct may seem unduly severe, but this severity is tempered in practice by the need also to establish the intent to defraud.

Fourthly, the failure to disclose a change of circumstances or of intention may amount to a distinct deception where the original representation is repeated, or may be regarded as continuing. An example of the latter is *DPP v Ray*,[30] where D ordered food in a restaurant, ate

---

24   It is clear that D can expressly negative the usual implications of his conduct: cf *R v Douglas* (1972) 8 CCC (2d) 275.
25   *Dronjak v Police* [1990] 3 NZLR 75; (1988) 3 CRNZ 141.
26   Of course, it would be otherwise if D had himself actively interfered with the price labelling, as occurred in *Rao v Police* (1988) 3 CRNZ 697.
27   *Dimmock v Hallett* (1866) LR 2 Ch App 21. Cf *R v Kylsant* [1932] 1 KB 442; [1931] All ER Rep 179; *R v Bishirgian* [1936] 1 All ER 586; also *The Siboen & the Sibotre* [1976] 1 Lloyds Rep 293.
28   *R v Silverman* (1988) 86 Cr App R 213; [1987] Crim LR 574; also *R v Stevens* (1844) 1 Cox CC 83.
29   *DPP v Ray* [1974] AC 370; [1973] 3 All ER 131, 380; 133.

the meal, then decided to leave without paying. The majority of the House of Lords held that by entering and ordering the meal D had represented that he intended to pay for it. This representation was analysed as an ongoing one, sustained by D's subsequent behaviour: "By continuing in the same role and behaving just as before he was representing that his previous intention continued."[31] The representation became false at the moment that D decided not to pay; thereafter, D may rightly be convicted of obtaining by deception anything that he *subsequently* ordered.

(2) False

The representation must in fact be false.[32] There can be no deception where the representor makes a statement believing it to be false, when it is in fact true.[33] Since this is an element of the actus reus, the onus lies on the prosecution to prove the falsity of the representation.[34]

(3) Known to be false

Additionally, the prosecution must establish either that D *knows or believes* his representation is false in a material particular, or is reckless whether it be false. So far as knowledge or belief is concerned, as was stated earlier (in 4.5), absolute certainty is not required.[35] Wilful blindness regarding the falsity of the statement will also be enough.[36]

(4) Reckless whether it is false

Alternatively, under s 240 it is sufficient that the person making the false representation is *reckless* whether the statement is false in a material particular. The element of recklessness is new and significantly expands the scope of the offence.

Recklessness with respect to circumstances (ie with respect to the falsity of D's representation) is considered in detail in 4.3.2. No doubt D will be reckless where he positively believes that his statement may be false. However, as we saw in 4.3.2, it now appears that, in the light of *B (a minor) v DPP*[37] and *R v Nazif*,[38] the scope of recklessness is even wider. Prima facie, under current law, recklessness with respect to circumstances is established unless D has a positive belief that the circumstance is lacking; in the context of s 240, *unless D positively believes that his statement is true.*

---

30 *DPP v Ray* [1974] AC 370; [1973] 3 All ER 131, 380; 133 (criticised in [1974] Crim LR 181-183: in fact, D ordered nothing subsequent to his deciding not to pay); cf *R v Rai* [2000] 1 Cr App R 242. Cf *Fagan v MPC* [1969] 1 QB 439; [1968] 3 All ER 442; see 3.2.1(2)(d); White, "Continuing representations in criminal law" (1986) 37 NILQ 255.
31 *DPP v Ray* [1974] AC 370; [1973] 3 All ER 131, 386; 139 (Lord Morris).
32 *R v Spencer* (1828) 3 C & P 420; 172 ER 483.
33 *R v Deller* (1952) 36 Cr App R 184 (CCA). D sold a car purportedly free of encumbrances, believing that in fact he had only the use and possession of the car under a hire purchase agreement. Though made dishonestly, D's representation might indeed have been true; the purported sale and hiring back to D was arguably a sham concealing the true transaction of a loan on the security of the car, which would have been void for non-registration.
34 However, proof may be either by direct evidence or by inference from the circumstances: cf *R v Mandry and Wooster* [1973] 3 All ER 996; [1973] 1 WLR 1232; *R v Kingston* (1905) 24 NZLR 431.
35 *R v Crooks* [1981] 2 NZLR 53 (CA).
36 See 4.5.1.
37 *B (a minor) v DPP* [2000] 2 AC 428; [2000] 1 All ER 833 (HL).
38 *R v Nazif* [1987] 2 NZLR 122 (CA).

Given that s 240 abolishes the traditional requirement of moral dishonesty, the scope of this new mens rea rule potentially is very broad indeed. However, it may be that this breadth will in practice be tempered by the requirement, discussed below (20.7-8), that D must intend V to act on that deception. Indeed, where D does make a representation intending it to be acted on, arguably it is no hardship to hold D to the higher standard of sincerity that s 240 imposes.

In accordance with general principles, the test of D's recklessness is purely subjective. Thus, notwithstanding the broadened terms of s 240(2)(a), it remains the case that a belief, however unreasonable, that the representation is true will prevent the defendant's conduct from constituting a deception.[39]

(5) *In a material particular*

The knowledge or recklessness must concern the falsity of a "material particular". The qualification appears to allow for trivial or *de minimis* falsehoods; it excludes falsehoods that are "immaterial", ie unimportant or inconsequential.[40] Given the requirement that the deception be made with intent to deceive (20.7), and that it cause the obtaining or loss (20.4), it may well be unnecessary; any deception satisfying those further criteria will almost certainly be "material".[41]

20.3.2 Omission to disclose

By virtue of s 240(2)(b), it is also a deception not to disclose a material particular[42] in circumstances where there is a duty to disclose it. At common law, such instances would have been regarded as equivalent to a positive representation,[43] and this principle is essentially codified by s 240.

When is D under a duty of disclosure? The relevant principles here are those governing liability for omissions, considered earlier (at 3.2.1(2)). In the context of s 240, many such duties will originate in the civil law, especially in the law of contract and equity.

It may be, however, that not all civil law duties will be carried across into s 240. Under contract law, a misrepresentation may be inferred from a failure to disclose a change in circumstances which makes false a representation that originally was true.[44] Yet in Australia, it has been held that this rule does not apply in the criminal law. In *Nelson v R*,[45] D made an insurance claim for theft of her car, truthfully stating that she did not know who had taken it. Before the claim was settled, she discovered that a friend had arranged for the removal and burning of the car; but she did not tell the insurer this. The Court of Criminal Appeal held that her conduct was

---

39 *R v Conrad* [1974] 2 NZLR 626 (CA). Of course, whether there were reasonable grounds for D's belief may be considered by the jury when deciding whether D in fact had that belief.
40 Cf *R v Mallett* [1978] 1 WLR 820; [1978] 3 All ER 10 (CA), 822-823; 12-13.
41 Notwithstanding the suggestion in *R v Maslen and Shaw* (1995) 79 A Crim R 199 (NSW CCA), 202-203 that the test of materiality is objective. It may be that something can be material notwithstanding that it was not, subjectively, a crucial matter for the victim (and this was the context of the observation in *Maslen and Shaw*); but that does not preclude the obverse rule, that a deception becomes material, inter alia, if it is crucial to the victim.
42 See above, 20.3.1(5).
43 Cf *R v Firth* (1990) 91 Cr App R 217; [1990] Crim LR 326.
44 *With v O'Flanagan* [1936] Ch 575; [1936] 1 All ER 727 (CA).
45 *Nelson v R* [1987] WAR 57. The original conviction was under s 409(1) Criminal Code (WA), which is essentially the same as s 240.

not an offence. The rule of equity, that a person has a duty to disclose in a pre-contractual situation where a statement inducing a contract becomes false prior to conclusion of the contract, "is not a rule which has anything to do with the criminal offence of obtaining something by a false pretence".[46]

On the other hand, where D subsequently realises that her original representation was false, the doctrine in *R v Miller* may well place her under a duty to counteract the effects of that initial, innocent deception.[47] At present, this possibility remains moot: there is no case in which it has been held that the rule in *Miller* carries over into deception.

In the absence of a duty to disclose, a failure to do so will fall outwith s 240. Suppose that D and E, who are bystanders, see V about to make an expensive mistake of some sort (ie to incur a loss within the meaning of s 240(1)(d)). They could warn V but agree not to, perhaps because they do not like V. That would be a case of an omission made with intent to cause loss, but it would rightly lie outside the scope of s 240. In order to constitute an offence, the omission must be made in circumstances either where it gives rise by silence to an implied representation (s 240(2)(a); above, 20.3.1(1)(b)), or where D is under a pre-existing duty of disclosure (s 240(2)(b)). Deception, while not depending on a representation, at least requires some conduct or scheme going beyond merely taking advantage, sub silentio, of another's spontaneous mistake.

20.3.3 A fraudulent device, trick, or stratagem

The third mode of deception is by a fraudulent device, trick, or stratagem. This modus operandi is expressed in very broad terms. In essence, it comprises any form of fraudulent conduct.

Obviously, such conduct would include the use of deceit or falsehood. In *R v Lewis*,[48] for example, it was held that an arrangement made for mock bidding at an auction could be fraudulent, since the scheme was intended, through a deception, to induce innocent buyers to bid more than necessary. Similarly, in *A-G's Reference (No 1 of 1982)*,[49] manufacturing fake whisky was held to be a common-law conspiracy to defraud unknowing purchasers. Such behaviour would now fall within the scope of s 240.

However, especially given the supplementary provisions in s 240(2)(a)-(b), it is clear that fraudulent devices are not restricted to schemes involving a false representation or non-disclosure. The formula encompasses *any* dishonest conduct or scheme.[50] In *Scott v Metropolitan Police Commissioner*,[51] for example, the defendants bribed cinema employees to let them borrow films, which were then copied in breach of copyright. Their behaviour was certainly a fraudulent stratagem, even though it involved no falsehood.[52]

---

46 *Nelson v R* [1987] WAR 57, 60 (Burt CJ). The application of the equitable law rule was also rejected by Lord Hodson in *DPP v Ray* [1974] AC 370; [1973] 3 All ER 131, 389; 142; although his Lordship was in the minority, this specific point does not seem to have been disputed by the majority. However, see *R v Rai* [2000] 1 Cr App R 242, a decision arguably inconsistent with *Nelson*.
47 *R v Miller* [1983] 2 AC 161; [1983] 1 All ER 978 (HL); discussed at 3.2.1(2)(e).
48 *R v Lewis* (1869) 11 Cox CC 404.
49 *A-G's Reference (No 1 of 1982)* [1983] QB 751.
50 *R v Olan, Hudson & Hartnett* (1978) 41 CCC (2d) 145; 86 DLR (3d) 212; *R v Sebe* (1987) 35 CCC (3d) 97.
51 *Scott v Metropolitan Police Commissioner* [1975] AC 819; [1974] 3 All ER 1032 (HL). See also *R v Walsh and Harney* [1984] VR 474; (1983) 9 A Crim R 307; *R v Horsington and Bortolus* [1983] 2 NSWLR 72; *R v Sinclair* [1968] 1 WLR 1246 (CA); *R v Hollinshead* [1985] AC 975; [1985] 2 All ER 769.

(1) Deceitful

That having been said, the fraudulent device, etc, must nonetheless — like the two other modes of deception in s 240(2) — be accompanied by an intent to deceive another person. Hence a fraudulent trick that does not seek to induce, in someone else, a state of mind comprising a misperception or false belief will be insufficient.[53] As such, the conspiracy to defraud in *Scott v MPC* (above) may well fall outwith the scope of s 240.

The point of s 240(2)(c) is that deceptions can sometimes be perpetrated without making a false statement or duty-bound non-disclosure. Sometimes, the scrupulous wrongdoer may induce a victim into error by conduct that is misleading, or even merely ambiguous, and involves no outright falsity. When she does so intentionally and fraudulently, her conduct becomes the stuff of s 240.

(2) Fraudulent

The final paragraph of s 240(2) may seem anomalous, in that it retains the old-fashioned element of fraudulence, ie moral dishonesty. The requirement of fraudulence is, however, essential, since the paragraph does not otherwise identify any wrongful conduct by the defendant. There is nothing wrong with having a scheme to make money. It becomes problematic when it, for example, involves making false statements — or when it is fraudulent.

To illustrate the importance of this requirement, suppose that a solicitor acting in her professional capacity agrees to perform certain services for her client which will cause loss to another party. These facts disclose no conspiracy to defraud unless the services go beyond her ordinary duties as a solicitor.[54] Similarly, many business decisions do — and are meant to — prejudice the economic interests of rivals, yet one is entitled to neglect those rival interests provided the decision involves a legitimate course of action. Thus in *R v Zemmel*,[55] the defendants' agreement to delay paying a creditor was held not to be a conspiracy to defraud at common law; and would not be a fraudulent stratagem for the purposes of s 240.

The term "fraudulent" predates the enactment of s 240, and means dishonestly in the traditional *moral* sense — and not in the technical sense now ascribed to "dishonesty" by s 217 (above, 19.4.1). Section 217 is irrelevant to s 240, which effectively preserves the earlier case law on fraudulence. The leading case is *R v Coombridge*, where the Court of Appeal stated:[56]

> "We think that in order to act fraudulently an accused person must certainly, as the judge pointed out in the present case, act deliberately and with knowledge that he is acting in breach of his legal obligation. But we are of opinion that if an accused person sets up a claim that in all the circumstances he honestly believed that he was justified

---

52 At common law, such conduct constitutes the crime of conspiracy to defraud. In *R v Weaver* (1931) 45 CLR 321; [1931] ALR 249 (HCA), 334; 251, the High Court of Australia said that conspiracy to defraud embraces "every kind and description of fraudulent statement, conduct, trick, or device", including "false accounts, fabricated shares, false representations or conduct". Section 240 appears to have similar scope; subject, however, to what is said in 20.3.3(1) following.

53 Cf *Re London and Globe Finance Corp* [1903] 1 Ch 728, 733 (Buckley J): "to deceive is by falsehood to induce a state of mind."

54 *R v Tighe* (1926) 26 SR (NSW) 94.

55 *R v Zemmel* (1985) 81 Cr App R 279; [1985] Crim LR 213.

56 *R v Coombridge* [1976] 2 NZLR 381 (CA), 387.

in departing from his strict obligations, albeit for some purpose of his own, then his defence should be left to the jury for consideration provided at least that there is evidence on which it would be open to a jury to conclude that in all the circumstances his conduct, although legally wrong, might nevertheless be regarded as honest. In other words the jury should be told that the accused cannot be convicted unless he has been shown to have acted dishonestly."

In *R v Williams*, the Court of Appeal declared the above to be "how the test has been applied in this country for many years".[57] This test is subjective. It is a defence that D had an *honest belief* that she was entitled so to act. Therefore, the necessary fraudulence is negatived if D believes, even mistakenly, that her actions were *morally* justified notwithstanding her legal obligations:[58]

"if the defendant sets up a claim of honest belief that he was justified in departing from his strict obligations, his defence must be left to the jury if there is some evidence from which the jury might conclude that his conduct, although legally wrong, might nevertheless be regarded as honest. It is for the prosecution to prove the defendant did not have such a belief."

D's belief does not have to be reasonable. A jury may be less likely to credit her with honesty if the facts did not warrant her belief,[59] but if there is a reasonable possibility that D did so believe then she must be acquitted.

(3) *Fraud: a new offence*

With the inclusion of s 240(2)(c) in the new s 240, New Zealand has, for the first time, a general criminal offence of fraud. The common law knew no such offence, so that the defrauding of one individual by another did not *per se* constitute a crime.[60] For the most part, fraud was criminalised through more specific offences, which addressed particular forms of economic activity when done with a dishonest intent, and through a traditional offence of *conspiracy* to defraud, operative where the fraud involved two or more persons acting together.[61]

Like conspiracy to defraud, the scope of the new crime is extremely wide, because of the broad definition of fraudulent "device, trick or stratagem"; conduct that need not otherwise be a criminal wrong. The gist of the wrong is the fraudulence, and not (just) the conduct itself. For

---

57 *R v Williams* [1985] 1 NZLR 294 (CA), 308. In particular, the Court of Appeal in *Williams* declined to adopt the mixed objective-subjective test of dishonesty established by the English Court of Appeal in *R v Ghosh* [1982] QB 1053; [1982] 2 All ER 689 (CA), according to which dishonesty is determined according to the ordinary standards of reasonable people, qualified by the proviso that the defendant must have been aware that his behaviour would be regarded as dishonest according to those standards. But is there any such thing as a common standard of (dis)honesty shared by all? In a multicultural society with wide internal socio-economic variation, that is surely unlikely. For discussion, see Halpin, "The test for dishonesty" [1996] Crim LR 283, and references there cited; also Smith, *Property Offences: The Protection of Property Through the Criminal Law*, London, Sweet & Maxwell, 1994, 7-47ff.
58 *R v Firth* [1998] 1 NZLR 513; (1997) 15 CRNZ 406 (CA), 519; 413.
59 Cf *Cheape v NZ Law Soc* [1955] NZLR 63, 68, where the conduct was said of itself to be "altogether inconsistent with honesty and fair dealing", and therefore fraudulent.
60 *R v Wheatly* (1761) 2 Burr 1125; 97 ER 746. An exception was the old offence of Cheat, which was confined to fraud "in a subject concerning the public, which, as between subject and subject, would only be actionable by a civil action": *R v Bembridge* (1783) 22 St Tr 1; 99 ER 679 (Lord Mansfield).
61 *R v Hevey* (1782) 1 Leach 232; 168 ER 218. See Hadden, "Conspiracy to defraud" [1966] 24 CLJ 248; Gillies, "The offence of conspiracy to defraud" (1977) 51 ALJ 247.

these reasons, the offence might be thought prima facie objectionable and one to be used sparingly. Its broad drafting offers little guidance to prospective offenders — by contrast, a series of offences each of which specifies an actus reus more narrowly offers better guidance to citizens, by warning clearly that proposed conduct falls within the reach of the criminal law.[62]

With this in mind, it is arguable that s 240(2)(c) should be restrictively interpreted so as to require that the "device" or "stratagem" be, at least, a civil wrong. The underlying problem here is the difficulty of drawing a boundary between mere sharp practice in the commercial sphere and criminal dishonesty. The two shade into each other, and in practice it may be no more than the element of "fraudulence" that redesignates a transaction from unscrupulous to illegal.

20.4 Causation

Section 240(1) provides that the obtaining or causing of loss must be *by* any deception. It follows that the obtaining or loss must occur as a consequence of the deception itself, and not merely coincidentally. Characteristically, this will occur where there is *inducement* of or *reliance* by the victim of the deception. By contrast, there will be no offence under s 240 where the representee is aware of the falsity of the representation, but hands over the property anyway, although in this situation there may be an attempt to obtain.[63]

It will be sufficient if the deceptive representation was *one* of the reasons for which the representee acted as she did, even if not the *only* reason.[64] Conversely, there is no reliance where she is unaffected by the representation, even if she believes it.[65] In *R v Roebuck*,[66] for example, V "confirmed" the truth of D's representation by her own inquiries, without relying on D's say-so. D was acquitted. His representation did not cause the obtaining, since it was not a reason why V handed over the property.

Note that the requirement of inducement does not mean that the false pretence must be a credible one. If V did in fact believe the representation, it does not matter that a reasonable person would not have believed it.[67]

Where there is an obtaining within the terms of s 240(1)(a), the paragraph specifies that the deception may beget the obtaining "directly or indirectly". Thus, for example, the offence can

---

62 See the discussion of fair warning at 2.1.3.
63 Cf *R v Hensler* (1870) 11 Cox CC 570. D wrote a begging letter claiming (falsely) to be a shipwrecked and destitute widow. The recipient of the letter sent 5 shillings despite knowing the falsehood of D's claims. D could not be guilty of obtaining by false pretences but was convicted of attempting to obtain.
64 Cf *R v Hamilton* (1991) 92 Cr App R 54; [1990] Crim LR 806; *R v Gauci* (1995) 79 A Crim R 506, 509; *R v English* (1872) 12 Cox CC 171; also the discussion of multiple causes at 3.3.2(3). In *R v Anderson* [2000] 2 Qd R 393, the Queensland Court of Appeal suggested that the representation need only be a minor factor. This analysis is consistent with the language of s 240, provided the representation is still one of the reasons (albeit not the most important reason) why the transfer was made.
65 *R v Laverty* [1970] 3 All ER 432; (1970) 54 Cr App R 495; *R v Dale* (1836) 7 C & P 352; 173 ER 157; *R v Strickland* (1850) 14 JP 784. This traditional view of the causation requirement no longer represents the law in England, following the decisions in *MPC v Charles* [1977] AC 177; [1976] 3 All ER 112 and *R v Lambie* [1982] AC 449; [1981] 2 All ER 776. These more recent cases effectively dilute the requirement to find a deception by D which causes the obtaining. As such, it is submitted that they are mistaken.
66 *R v Roebuck* (1856) D & B 24; 169 ER 900; cf *R v Winning* (1973) 12 CCC (2d) 449.
67 *R v Piri Hira Hoani* (1915) 34 NZLR 902; *R v Giles* (1865) Le & Ca 502; 169 ER 1490; *R v Jessop* (1858) Dear & B 442; 169 ER 1074. Cf *R v Madden* 29/5/03, CA433/02.

be committed where the deception causes the representee to initiate a process whereby something is delivered, even where the thing is actually obtained from someone other than the representee.[68] In *R v Bennitt*,[69] D falsified timesheets, thus obtaining an overpayment of wages. The Supreme Court held that the original false representation operated through each stage of the transaction; there was a nexus in the chain of events from D's representation to the eventual receipt of the cheque.

The proviso, "directly or indirectly", is omitted from s 240(1)(b)-(d); but it is submitted that the conclusion would have been the same even had it been omitted from s 240(1)(a). Causation may be indirect as well as direct, and the proviso will very often be a precaution rather than a necessity.[70]

20.4.1 Remoteness

Sometimes, however, the final transaction by which something is obtained may be too remote from the original representation for causation to be established on ordinary principles. In the unreported English case of *R v Lewis*,[71] D obtained a teaching post through a forged teacher's certificate; but it was held that her salary was obtained as a result of performing the obligations of her post, and not by the deception. Such a case would now fall within the scope of s 240(1)(a), since the salary was at least obtained "indirectly" by the deception. On the other hand, since there is no such proviso in the other paragraphs, any loss caused (s 240(1)(d)), or other consequence within s 240(1)(b)-(c), will fall outside the scope of s 240 if its occurrence is too remote and indirect to be "caused" by the deception.

20.4.2 Machines

In principle, the need for deception and reliance excludes from s 240 the unauthorised obtaining of money from an automatic teller machine, or of soft drinks from a vending machine, since a machine cannot be induced to believe propositions. A useful illustration is the Australian case of *Kennison v Daire*.[72] After D's bank account had been closed, D withdrew money from an automatic teller machine with his bank card. The Court denied that this was an obtaining by false pretences and instead convicted D of larceny, ruling that a machine cannot be deceived and does not "rely" on representations but simply delivers money or goods in response to a certain input. According to King CJ:[73]

---

68 Cf *R v Kovacs* [1974] 1 All ER 1236; [1974] 1 WLR 370; *R v Charles* [1977] AC 177; (1976) 68 Cr App R 334; *R v Clarkson* [1987] VR 962; (1987) 25 A Crim R 277, 980; 296.

69 *R v Bennitt* [1961] NZLR 452.

70 Cf *R v Button* [1900] 2 QB 597, where D's representation that he had never before won a race enabled him to gain a handicap advantage and thereby win two races. Notwithstanding that the prize was directly obtained only by winning the race, the causal connection here is clear, since the representation made it more likely that D would win the race itself. Cf *R v Lambassi* [1927] ALR 295; [1927] VLR 349; contrast *R v Clucas* [1949] 2 KB 226; [1949] 2 All ER 40 which, it is submitted, was wrongly decided.

71 Cited in *Russell on Crime* (12th ed), London, Stevens & Sons, 1964, vol 2, 1186, n 66, discussed in *R v King* [1987] QB 547; [1987] 1 All ER 547. See too the criticism of *R v Miller* (1992) 95 CR App R 421; [1992] Crim LR 744 by Smith, *Property Offences: The Protection of Property Through the Criminal Law*, London, Sweet & Maxwell, 1994, para 17.125.

72 *Kennison v Daire* (1985) 38 SASR 404.

73 *Kennison v Daire* (1985) 38 SASR 404, 406; cf dicta in *Davies v Flackett* [1973] RTR 8; [1972] Crim LR 708.

"The crime of obtaining money by false pretences requires, in my opinion, the intervention of a human being who is induced by the false pretence to part with money. A machine cannot be deceived by a false pretence or other fraud."

In New Zealand, the proper offence in this case would be under s 228 (dishonestly using a document) or, if a computer is involved, under s 249 (accessing computer system for dishonest purpose).

20.5 The object of the deception

By virtue of s 240(1), the object of the offence encompasses almost any conceivable advantage to the defendant as well as any loss to the victim.

20.5.1 Obtaining any property, etc: s 240(1)(a)

The core paragraph is (a), which includes the obtaining of any type of property, privilege, service, pecuniary advantage, benefit or valuable consideration. The section is apt, for example, to cover deceptive actions in the hiring of property, even though (because of a lack of intent to deprive permanently) such conduct could not be theft.

(1) The subject matter obtained

"Property" is defined in s 2, and its scope is discussed in 19.3.1: it includes any tangible or intangible property (or interest therein), real or personal. Hence there may now be an obtaining of such things as a bank account,[74] which would no doubt also count as a benefit and, indeed, as a pecuniary advantage.

The inclusion of "services" is an important expansion of the scope of the paragraph. Just as private law has been reluctant to give restitution for services unless they generate an end-product,[75] the tendency to understand economic wealth in tangible terms has meant that criminal law has been slow to protect services. To deceive another person into doing work has never been an offence of obtaining property, even though intangible economic value may be involved in the transaction. Partly, this is because the performance of services does not necessarily transfer wealth, since services are not themselves a form of wealth but rather its source or product.[76] In a sense, therefore, the protection of services by criminal law is needed to protect the victim of a deception from wasting economically valuable activity — from loss — as much as it is to prevent the defendant's gain therefrom.

What counts as a service is not defined in the Act, and will no doubt give rise to interpretive difficulties. In *R v Cara*,[77] a decision concerning s 228 of the Act (dishonestly taking or using a document), the scope of "services" was thought, obiter, to be restricted to activities having an element of financial or economic value. In part, the preferred interpretation depended on the specific legislative history of s 228, and s 240(1)(a) is expressed in more expansive terms.

---

74 Something impossible under the predecessor s 246: *R v Wilkinson* [1999] 1 NZLR 403; (1998) 16 CRNZ 179 (CA).
75 Cf *BP Exploration Co (Libya) Ltd v Hunt (No 2)* [1979] 1 WLR 783, 799 (Robert Goff J): "the identity and value of the resulting benefit to the recipient may be debatable".
76 Marshall regarded this as obvious: "services and other goods, which pass out of existence in the same instant that they come into it, are of course, not part of the stock of wealth": *Principles of Economics* (8th ed, 1947) 56. Contrast, perhaps, the *right* to a service: "some have suggested that [an employee] may now be said to acquire something akin to a property in his employment": *Hill v Parsons* [1972] Ch 305, 321 (Sachs LJ).
77 *R v Cara* [2005] 1 NZLR 823; (2004) 21 CRNZ 283, paras 138-142.

Moreover, given that services are not themselves a form of wealth, there seems no reason to require that under s 240 the defendant receive anything of marketable value. Suppose, for example, that D pretends to be an enrolled student at a private university and has her stock of knowledge increased by receiving a tutorial on criminal law. The criminal wrong here is not that D obtains something of marketable value, but that she deceives the tutor into providing the tutorial. Thus the law is justified in convicting her for obtaining services even though no realisable wealth has been transferred.

(2) The act of "obtaining"

Under s 240(1)(a), D must obtain "ownership or possession of, or control over" the thing. There is no requirement that the obtaining be by *transfer*, so that D may obtain something that did not previously exist.[78] But, for the offence to be constituted, there must actually *be* an obtaining. By way of example, in the English case of *Bogdal v Hall*,[79] D made a fraudulent application for an unemployment benefit. It was not proved that he actually received any payments. Although D had attempted to obtain property by deception, he could not be convicted of the full offence.

It seems that there is no need for D to obtain the thing personally. By virtue of s 217, "Obtain, in relation to any person, means obtain or retain for himself or herself or for any other person".[80] As s 217 also makes clear, the offence includes situations where the deception enables D or another to *retain* something that she already possesses.

20.5.2 Obtaining credit: s 240(1)(b)

There are two ingredients of this paragraph. D must incur a debt or liability, and she must obtain credit in respect of that liability. These were also elements of the predecessor offence under the former s 247 (obtaining credit fraudulently), and it is submitted that the law governing those terms in the former section continues to apply.

(1) Debt or liability

The debt or liability must be legally enforceable against D (or whomever the credit is obtained); there is therefore no offence where the credit is obtained under a contract which is void[81] or illegal.[82]

It is implicit in the section that the credit is obtained by deception, and the offence is committed, even if D has an intention to repay.[83]

(2) Obtains credit

Traditionally, the credit obtained must be in respect of a monetary obligation.[84] Thus if D receives a benefit in return for an obligation to perform services or deliver goods in the future,

---

78 This is typically the case with "transfers" of choses in action, such as bank accounts — such transactions have the effect of extinguishing the previous chose in action and creating a new one in the hands of the recipient: R v Wilkinson [1999] 1 NZLR 403; (1998) 16 CRNZ 179 (CA).
79 Bogdal v Hall [1987] Crim LR 500.
80 Cf DPP v Stonehouse [1978] AC 55; [1977] 2 All ER 909 (HL).
81 R v Leon [1945] KB 136; [1945] 1 All ER 14 (CCA).
82 R v Garlick (1958) 42 Cr App R 141.
83 Cf R v Carpenter (1911) 76 JP 158; 22 Cox CC 618, 160; 624, approved in R v Kritz [1950] 1 KB 82; [1949] 2 All ER 406. Cf R v Greenstein [1976] 1 All ER 1; [1975] 1 WLR 1353.

he does not obtain credit within the terms of s 240(1)(b) — the proper allegation would be under s 240(1)(a), in respect of the initial benefit obtained. The credit obtained need not be pursuant to a specific contract,[85] or for any minimum length of time. Thus filling one's tank at a self-service petrol station constitutes an obtaining of credit at least until the filling is completed and one is due to pay.[86]

There is no "obtaining" where D merely gets an extension of time to pay an existing debt. However, there is a sufficient "obtaining" where D incurs a fresh liability even where this is simply a substitute for an old debt, for example executing a bill of sale to pay off an overdraft,[87] or making use of a bank overdraft facility to draw a cheque paying a credit card bill. On the other hand, where D pays for goods by drawing a cheque which he knows will bounce, strictly speaking the obtaining is of property (s 240(1)(a)), rather than credit, by deception.[88]

20.5.3 Inducing another to deal with a document, etc: s 240(1)(c)

It is difficult to see an independent role for this category. There will be very few occasions when resort to s 240(1)(c) is required, since most if not all cases falling potentially within the paragraph will also involve a benefit or a loss to someone. For example, someone who deceives a club secretary into issuing a membership card[89] will obtain an item of property and/or a benefit. Paragraph (c) might be appropriate in the case of one who deceitfully persuades a testatrix to change her will[90] (at least before the testatrix dies, when any benefits and losses will crystallise).

The scope of the induced conduct, which we have loosely termed dealing, is very wide: another person (who need not be the immediate victim of the deception) must be induced or caused to do any of "deliver over, execute, make, accept, endorse, destroy, or alter" the document or thing.

The definition of a "document" is found in s 217, and is also expressed in very wide terms — as well as paper or other material used for writing or printing, it includes film, storage devices such as tapes and computer discs, and any other medium for recording, storing, or supplying information. In addition, "document" has been held also to refer to the information there recorded, so that the copy of an original document is, for the purposes of Part 10 of the Act, the same as the original.[91]

Section 240(1)(c) goes even further, by supplementing "document" with any "thing capable of being used to derive a pecuniary advantage" — a clear effort to let no wrongdoer pass. The "thing" must, it seems, be tangible. It will be capable use to derive a pecuniary advantage if it can generate some benefit to which D is not already entitled,[92] such as to modify the terms of

---

84 *Fisher v Raven* [1964] AC 210; [1963] 2 All ER 389, 231; 394 (Lord Dilhorne LC), followed in *R v Kinsman* [1969] NZLR 678 (CA). In England the decision in *Fisher v Raven* has been overturned by s 360(2)(b) Insolvency Act 1986 (UK).
85 *R v Kinsman* [1969] NZLR 678 (CA); *R v Peters* (1886) 16 QBD 636.
86 Cf *R v Jones* [1898] 1 QB 119.
87 *R v Thornton* [1964] 2 QB 176; [1963] 1 All ER 170 (CCA).
88 Cf *R v Cosnett* (1901) 20 Cox CC 6; 65 JP 472.
89 Cf *R v Bassey* (1931) 22 Cr App R 160.
90 Cf *Tillings and Tillings* [1985] Crim LR 393.
91 *R v Walsh* 26/6/06, CA208/05.

an existing obligation.[93] There is no requirement, once the dealing is induced, that any such advantage must subsequently be realised.

20.5.4 Causing loss to any other person: s 240(1)(d)

This element of the new offence differs significantly from its predecessor offence, conspiracy to defraud, in that the object of the deception must be to cause *loss* to *a person* and does not appear to include a fraud on the public.[94] Hence it appears no longer to be sufficient that the deception causes an official to act contrary to his public duty,[95] unless some benefit (etc) is thereby obtained within the ambit of s 240(1)(a); or, perhaps, the official's contravention is by dealing with a valuable document, potentially falling within s 240(1)(c).

There is no requirement under this paragraph that the deception should cause, or be designed to, benefit anyone. The essence of paragraph (d) is conduct that harms the victim's interests; the law looks at the effect of the wrong on the victim, irrespective of whether the defendant sought to make a gain. Suppose, for instance, that D tricks V into believing that V's lottery ticket has the wrong numbers and is valueless, with the consequence that V destroys the ticket. D commits an offence against s 240.

What qualifies as the subject matter of a "loss"? Presumably any item of property or other valuable thing, at least provided the value is quantifiable. But it may not be sufficient if, for example, D tricks V into disclosing confidential information, unless D then uses that information to cause a further, identifiable loss to V. (Even so, the disclosure may count as a benefit to D and thereby fall within s 240(1)(a).) Another difficult question is whether there can be loss of a chance. If D deceives V into not pursuing a contested legal claim against V, V loses only the possibility of winning; had the claim been pursued, perhaps the claim would have been unsuccessful. It is uncertain whether s 240(1)(d) extends to such cases. Arguably, the test should be whether D's right to pursue the chance has value; if it does, s 240 should apply.[96]

In one respect, the scope of s 240(1)(d) is narrower than the former offence of conspiracy to defraud. It is no longer sufficient that the conspiracy merely puts V's economic interests potentially *at risk*. Formerly, a conspiracy to defraud could be committed where V's interests or rights were (deliberately and dishonestly) risked.[97] This sort of economic prejudice, which involves potential but not actual loss, falls outside the scope of s 240(1)(d). The effective narrowing is a limited one, however, since most such cases will simultaneously fulfil one of the other paragraphs of s 240(1).

There is no requirement in s 240(1)(d) that the person who suffers the loss be the very person who is deceived. Thus D may contravene s 240 by deceiving T into acting to the detriment of a third party, V.

---

92   R v *Firth* [1998] 1 NZLR 513; (1997) 15 CRNZ 406 (CA), 516-517; 410: there is no pecuniary "advantage" in receiving that to which one already has a right.
93   R v *Cattermole* 15/9/05, CA94/05.
94   Or to affect the market price of something: see former s 257, prior to its substitution in 2003.
95   Cf *Scott v MPC* [1975] AC 819; [1974] 3 All ER 1032 (HL), 841; 1040.
96   Cf *Wills v Petroulias* (2003) 58 NSWLR 598 (NSW CA).
97   R v *Allsop* (1976) 64 Cr App R 29 (CA); *Adams v R* (1994) 12 CRNZ 379; [1995] 1 WLR 52 (PC), 390; 65.

20.6 Without claim of right

D must act without claim of right. The meaning of this requirement is detailed above, at 19.4.2. In summary, D acts with a claim of right when she acts with an honest belief that the taking or dealing with the thing is consonant with her civil and criminal law duties and obligations, notwithstanding that her belief may be based on a mistake. Conversely, if she does not positively believe that her actions are lawful, she acts without claim of right.

Suppose, for example, that D uses a ruse to borrow a sum of money from V to which he believes he is otherwise entitled (perhaps as a result of a disputed earlier debt). Although he commits the actus reus of an offence against s 240, he lacks the mens rea, since he acts with claim of right.

20.7 Intent to deceive

Strictly speaking, this element is part of the definition of "deception" (above, 20.3). However, since it is common to all forms of deception, it is convenient to deal with the element separately.

The meaning of intent is considered in 4.2. In essence, this requirement means that no offence is committed unless the false statement, non-disclosure, trick, etc, is to be made or used by D *in order* to deceive V, or in the knowledge that V is *virtually certain* to be deceived. It is insufficient that the deception is done in the mere awareness, without so intending, that V *may* be deceived. That would be a case of recklessness rather than intent, and falls outside the scope of s 240(2).

Note that the intent to deceive must exist at the time when the deception is perpetrated: so, for example, where credit is obtained, a *later* decision not to repay is insufficient.[98]

20.8 Intent to obtain, etc, by the deception

Apart from specifying that it must be done without claim of right, the statute is silent about the mens rea pertaining to the key actus reus element of obtaining, inducing, or causing loss under s 240(1). This suggests three possible interpretations: that it is a matter of strict liability, that it is an implied mens rea element (ie recklessness, on normal interpretive principles; above, 5.2.3); or that D must intend the obtaining, etc. On balance, we incline toward the last of these.

Strict liability can surely be ruled out. Suppose that D and E play a trick on their friend V, by pretending that V has, say, won a prize in a lottery. Unexpectedly, V goes out and buys a car with her "winnings". D and E are horrified: yet, while the disaster may be their fault, because the trick was not played in order to bring such consequences about, their conduct lacks the character of criminality.

Between the two mens rea alternatives, the better view, that s 240 requires an *intent* to obtain (etc), is buttressed by the requirements that any deceptive representation or non-disclosure be in respect of a material particular (s 240(2)(a)-(b); above, 2.3.2), and be causally linked to the obtaining or loss (above, 20.3). Additionally, under s 217, D must obtain the benefit, etc, "for" himself or another. Taken together, these elements suggest that the obtaining or loss must itself be purposeful, and in particular that it must be *by means of* the deception. This would rule out recklessness: thus s 240 would not apply to any untruths that D utters only incidentally to a transaction and which are not intended to induce reliance by the representee. D must not

---

98 Cf *R v McKay* [1961] NZLR 256 (CA).

simply intend to deceive; he must intend to obtain, and he must intend to obtain *by* the deception.

Suppose, this time, that D falsely tells V that E Ltd is selling a certain type of car more cheaply than its rival, F Ltd. By itself, this would not be sufficient to establish an offence against s 240 even if V then purchases such a car from E Ltd. D must *intend* that V should act on that deception. If, for example, D had made the statement thinking that V had already bought the car from F Ltd, he would lack the requisite intention.

Neither, on this view, will it be sufficient if D merely suspects or foresees that V *may* rely on a false statement made by D. In such a case, there is an insufficient nexus between the intent to receive and the obtaining or loss. The gist of the offence is obtaining, etc, *by* deliberate deception. Therefore, the requirement of intent in s 240 should, it is submitted, encompass the whole of that transaction.[99]

The example above raises a further point, concerning the relationship between the deception and the obtaining. The person who commits the offence is the person who deceives, within the scope of s 240(2). By virtue of s 217, it seems that the benefit may accrue to someone else (since it may be obtained "for any other person"). Hence, in the example, it can only be D that commits the offence and not E Ltd.

---

[99] Cf *R v Wakeling* (1823) Russ & R 504; 168 ER 920 (D's false representation that he had no boots, made in order to avoid having to work, did not make him guilty of obtaining the boots then supplied to him).

Chapter 21

THE MORAL LIMITS OF CRIMINALISATION

21.1   The Harm Principle 720
21.1.1   What counts as a harm? 722
21.1.2   Seriousness 723
21.1.3   Harms as wrongs 724
21.1.4   Balancing requirements 724
21.1.5   Remote harms 726
21.2   The Offence Principle 727
21.2.1   Offensive conduct as a wrong 728
21.2.2   A communicative and conventional wrong 729
21.3   Legal moralism 729
21.4   Paternalism 731
21.5   Negative grounds for intervention: regulatory alternatives 733
21.5.1   Tax 733
21.5.2   Tort law 734
21.5.3   Other mechanisms 734
21.5.4   Contra: some advantages of using the criminal law 735
21.6   Negative grounds for intervention: the rule of law 735
21.6.1   Rule of Law constraints on criminalisation 735
21.6.2   The individuation of offences 736
21.7   Negative grounds for intervention: practical constraints 737
21.7.1   What side-effects will criminalisation have? 737
21.7.2   Pragmatics of the criminal justice system 738

Over the past few chapters we have investigated some of the better-known common law and statutory offences. There are, of course, many other offences known to New Zealand law, both minor and serious. Beyond that, however, there are many forms of wrongdoing that are not offences at all — and rightly so. The criminal law is not a tool to be deployed wherever someone may do wrong. As a regulatory device, it is a bluntly coercive, morally loaded sledgehammer, something to be used sparingly and with care. This is the problem of *criminalisation*: although it may frequently be appropriate, indeed necessary, to have criminal prohibitions, we should always be careful of overextending the reach of the criminal law, and of infringing too far upon citizens' rights of free choice and individual liberty. We *should* use the criminal law to prohibit conduct — but we should not over-prohibit.

The question becomes, therefore, *when* should we extend the criminal law to regulate conduct? Suppose that a responsible Legislature seeks to enact a decent, morally justifiable range of criminal prohibitions. What criteria should it apply when deciding whether to proscribe something? The decision whether a particular action or state of affairs is sufficiently serious to warrant criminalisation always involves difficult judgments, and will be affected by the political values and social structure of a society. There is no sphere of industrial, commercial, or administrative activity untouched by the criminal law. As criminal lawyers, however, we may still enquire whether conduct is ever made criminal which does not merit that designation.

A useful starting point is that there should be parsimony in criminalisation: offences "should be created only when absolutely necessary".[1] The criminal sanction is the most drastic of the State's standard tools for regulating the conduct of individuals. It represents the most severe infringement of a person's liberty, and, as such, should be available only where there is a clear social justification.

Broadly speaking, we can identify two types of criteria that must be met if the creation of an offence is to be morally legitimate. There must, first, be a prima facie *positive* case for State regulation, in that the activity at issue must be "sufficiently serious". Secondly, certain *negative* constraints must also be met. In particular, it must be shown that the *criminal* law offers the best method of regulation, being preferable to alternative methods of legal control that are available to the State; and the practicalities must be considered of drawing up an offence in terms that are effective, enforceable, and meet Rule of Law and other concerns. It may be, if these negative constraints cannot be met, that the State ought not to criminalise certain types of conduct notwithstanding the positive case for doing so.

In this chapter, we will focus mainly on the competing *positive* grounds for state intervention: the main types of reasons why the state might validly choose to intervene and criminalise some action. Later in the chapter, we will briefly discuss some of the constraints that might nonetheless make the criminal law an inappropriate response.

When is behaviour, prima facie, sufficiently serious to warrant criminalisation? This question is highly controversial, because it raises squarely the issue of the limits of the state's moral authority over individuals. Joel Feinberg's classic discussion of the problem identifies four possible grounds of justifiable intervention: harm to others, offence to others, immorality, and harm to self.[2] As we shall see, liberal philosophers (including Feinberg himself) tend to endorse only the first two of those grounds, rejecting the case for criminalising conduct on purely moralistic or paternalistic grounds. In what follows, we offer a short introduction to these four grounds of state intervention.

21.1 The Harm Principle

At the core of liberalism is the proposition that the State is justified in intervening to regulate conduct only when that conduct causes *harm to others*. Conduct that merely harms oneself, or

---

1   Cf Lord Williams of Mostyn, (18/6/99) HL Deb, vol 602, col WA58.
2   Feinberg, *The Moral Limits of the Criminal Law* (4 volumes), New York, Oxford University Press, 1984-1988: vol 1, *Harm to Others* 1984; vol 2, *Offense to Others* 1985; vol 3, *Harm to Self* 1986; vol 4, *Harmless Wrongdoing* 1988.

which is thought to be immoral but otherwise harmless, is on this account ineligible for prohibition. Famously, the Harm Principle was first articulated by John Stuart Mill:[3]

"The principle is, that the sole end for which mankind are warranted, individually or collectively, in interfering with the liberty of action of any of their number is self-protection. That the only purpose for which power can rightfully be exercised over any member of a civilised community against his will is to prevent harm to others. His own good, either physical or moral, is not a sufficient warrant."

Expressed in this way, the Harm Principle is a negative constraint: in the absence of harm, the State is not morally entitled to intervene. It does not follow that, conversely, the State *is* justified in intervening whenever D's conduct causes harm to others. That conclusion can only be reached after further factors are considered, such as those to be discussed below. Perhaps more importantly, Mill offers no definition of what counts as a *harm*; without which, the application of the Harm Principle remains hopelessly indeterminate.

Liberal philosophers have built on Mill's analysis in an attempt to eradicate these problems. The most detailed exposition is now offered by Feinberg, who summarises the principle as follows:[4]

"It is always a good reason in support of penal legislation that it would be effective in preventing (eliminating, reducing) harm to persons other than the actor (the one prohibited from acting) and there is no other means that is equally effective at no greater cost to other values."

Notice that this is formulated as a positive claim. On Feinberg's account, if creating a criminal offence would prevent harm to others, there is a positive reason in favour of criminalisation. This leaves it possible for Feinberg, and us, to accept the legitimacy of other, supplementary, grounds for criminalisation (such as offence).

In principle, one might subscribe to Feinberg's version of the Harm Principle and at the same time consistently accept that the State is also justified in criminalising some conduct on the grounds that it is immoral. That would, however, be inconsistent with the principle espoused by Mill. Especially for liberals, part of the point of the Harm Principle is that it forces an inquiry into the consequences of conduct — does it hurt anyone? Proponents of a particular criminal offence cannot simply allege that the relevant conduct is immoral but must identify precisely what are the particular effects of that conduct:[5] the particular way in which it damages the lives of other persons. That claim can then be subjected to public debate. Empirical evidence of a link to the alleged harm can be demanded and scrutinised.

Consider, for example, the decision by the English courts in *Brown*[6] that, in the context of sado-masochistic sexual activity, it is an offence to inflict actual bodily harm on another person notwithstanding that the "victim" consents. One justification offered for this act of judicial criminalisation was that the legalisation of such activities might encourage the seduction and "corruption of young men".[7] But would it? It is a cheap claim to make when no supporting

---

3 Mill, *On Liberty*, London, Longman, Roberts & Green, 1869, ch 1, para 9.
4 Feinberg, *The Moral Limits of the Criminal Law* vol 1: *Harm to Others*, New York, Oxford University Press, 1984, 26.
5 Packer, *The Limits of the Criminal Sanction*, California, Stanford University Press, 1968, 262.
6 *R v Brown* [1994] 1 AC 212; [1993] 2 All ER 75 (HL). See also 17.2.4(2).
7 *R v Brown* [1994] 1 AC 212; [1993] 2 All ER 75 (HL), 246; 92 (Lord Jauncey).

evidence is offered. Given the presumption against criminalisation, the onus is on its proponents to bring clear evidence that creating a new offence *will* prevent harm from occurring.

In the following paragraphs we consider aspects of the Harm Principle in more detail.

21.1.1 What counts as a harm?

A harm, on Feinberg's account, is a "thwarting, setting back, or defeating of an interest".[8] When we are harmed, one or more of our interests is left in a worse state than it was beforehand. In turn, a person's *interests* comprise the things that make his life go well;[9] thus we are harmed when our lives are changed for the worse. In particular, harm involves the impairment of a person's opportunities to engage in worthwhile activities and relationships, and to pursue valuable, self-chosen, goals. In this sense, harm is prospective rather than backward-looking: it involves a diminution of one's opportunities to enjoy or pursue a good life.

Characteristically, harm is brought about though the impairment of V's personal or proprietary resources. However, as Feinberg observes, what makes such impairment harmful is not the impairment *per se* but its implication for V's well-being:[10]

> "A broken arm is an impaired arm, one which has (temporarily) lost its capacity to serve a person's needs effectively, and in virtue of that impairment, its possessor's welfare interest is harmed."

Similarly, of interference with another's proprietary resources, Joseph Raz observes that "[a]ny harm to a person by denying him the use or the value of his property is a harm to him precisely because it diminishes his opportunities".[11]

Clearly, people have interests in their property and in their personal integrity. But we also have other interests that are capable of being harmed. Hyman Gross suggests that before it can be said that a person has an interest in something, the thing (or X) must "be of sufficient value to [the person] that the assertion of a claim by or on behalf of [that person] based on the loss

---

8   Feinberg, *The Moral Limits of the Criminal Law* vol 1: *Harm to Others*, New York, Oxford University Press, 1984, 33.
9   In Feinberg's account, "One's interests ... consist of all those things in which one has a stake .... These interests, or perhaps more accurately, the things these interests are *in*, are distinguishable components of a person's well-being: he flourishes or languishes as they flourish or languish. What promotes them is to his advantage or *in his interest*; what thwarts them is to his detriment or *against his interest*." Feinberg, *The Moral Limits of the Criminal Law* vol 1: *Harm to Others*, New York, Oxford University Press, 1984, 34 (emphasis in original). See, too, his "Harm to Others: a Rejoinder" in [1986] *Criminal Justice Ethics* 16, 26, where Feinberg recapitulates: "I argued that to harm a person was to set back his interest and violate his right. To have an interest, in turn, is to have a stake in some outcome, just as if one had 'invested' some of one's own good in it, thus assuming the risk of personal harm or setback."
10 Feinberg, *The Moral Limits of the Criminal Law* vol 1: *Harm to Others*, New York, Oxford University Press, 1984, 53. Cf Kleinig's claim that, in the case of a temporary hurt or an abduction that has no lasting effects upon its victim, there may be interference with a welfare interest but no harm: Kleinig, "Crime and the Concept of Harm" (1978) 15 Am Phil Q 27, 32; Feinberg, *The Moral Limits of the Criminal Law* vol 1: *Harm to Others*, New York, Oxford University Press, 1984, 52-53.
11 Raz, "Autonomy, Toleration, and the Harm Principle" in Gavison (ed), *Issues in Contemporary Legal Philosophy*, Oxford, Clarendon Press, 1987, 313, 327. Cf Perry, "Corrective v. Distributive Justice" in Horder (ed), *Oxford Essays in Jurisprudence* (4th series), Oxford, Clarendon Press, 2000, 237, 256: "The main reason that personal injury constitutes harm is that it interferes with personal autonomy. It interferes, that is to say, with the set of opportunities and options from which one is able to choose what to do in one's life."

or significant impairment of X is not unreasonable".[12] He offers a four-part categorisation of the types of cases where one's interests are harmed: (i) "violations of interest in retaining or maintaining what one is entitled to have" (eg theft); (ii) "offenses to sensibility" (eg obscenity); (iii) "impairment of collective welfare" (eg counterfeiting, which undermines the economy); and (iv) "violations of governmental interests" (eg contempt of court).[13]

We consider offences to sensibility in 21.2 below, under the rubric of the Offence Principle. But categories (iii) and (iv) show that we can be harmed without directly being the victim; and, indeed, when there is no victim at all. Hence, on occasion, it may be appropriate to enact "victimless" crimes. Tax evasion is rightly a crime notwithstanding that there is no particular victim who is deprived of assets directly. Perhaps it is not the same sort of wrong as is theft. But if T illegitimately reduces his tax burden, T effectively takes from, and wrongs, his fellow taxpayers. The money must come from somewhere: if not from T, then from others. The obligation to pay tax is a collective duty, one that each person owes to his fellow citizens and not merely to the State.

Similarly, attacks on the integrity of the currency (eg counterfeiting) or on the operation of the judicial systems (eg contempt of court) matter because they undermine State-implemented regimes that exist for the benefit of us all. State intervention is warranted because the community as a whole would also suffer harm were these general regimes to be undermined. Undermining the currency, for example, would tend to destabilise the systems that co-ordinate a nation's economic activity;[14] which, in turn, would deprive people of many opportunities for personal and social advancement. Minimising or preventing that sort of indirect, prospective harm to our interests is rightly the business of the State.

21.1.2 Seriousness

Indeed, once the nature of the harm is identified, we can see why some apparently victimless crimes, such as counterfeiting, are regarded as very serious indeed. This is one of the payoffs of the Harm Principle: in forcing us to consider more precisely why we are concerned about the activity that is to be criminalised, it gives us tools with which to rank the seriousness of offences and thus decide what level of punishment, if any, is appropriate.

Andrew von Hirsch and Nils Jareborg have developed this point in the context of victim-oriented crimes.[15] In their seminal paper, the authors identify four generic interests that we all have directly: (i) physical integrity (health, safety, avoidance of physical pain); (ii) material support and amenity (nutrition, shelter, basic amenities); (iii) freedom from humiliation or degrading treatment; and (iv) privacy and autonomy. The justification of any existing or prospective crime can then be assessed in two steps, as follows.

First, one should identify which category of interest the crime is designed to protect. Secondly, it is necessary to assess the degree to which standard instances of that crime will adversely affect the living standard — the opportunities for V to live a good life — of a typical victim. Von Hirsch and Jareborg divide the severity of these effects into four bands: (a) subsistence (simple survival with only basic human functions); (b) minimal well-being (maintaining

---

12 Gross, *A Theory of Criminal Justice*, New York, Oxford University Press, 1979, 116.
13 Gross, *A Theory of Criminal Justice*, New York, Oxford University Press, 1979, 119-121.
14 Cf *R v St Margaret's Trust Ltd* [1958] 2 All ER 289, 293.
15 von Hirsch and Jareborg, "Gauging Criminal Harm: A Living-Standard Analysis" (1991) 11 OJLS 1.

minimal levels of comfort and dignity); (c) adequate well-being (maintaining adequate levels of comfort and dignity); and (d) significant enhancement (above-adequate quality of life).

On this approach, we can see that homicide attacks physical integrity in such a way as to undermine even subsistence; it is, thus, more serious than a typical robbery and much more serious than petty theft or a minor assault. On the other hand, motorway traffic regulations become extremely important, since they too are concerned with saving lives and thus protect our fundamental interests. It may be that, because less culpable, dangerous driving should be punished less severely than murder. But, like murder, the existence of an offence of dangerous driving is justified within the Harm Principle by the desirability of saving lives.

21.1.3 Harms as wrongs

In Feinberg's words,[16]

> "One person *wrongs* another when his indefensible (unjustifiable and inexcusable) conduct violates the other's right, and in all but certain very special cases such conduct will also invade the other's interest and thus be harmful in the sense [of a setback to interests]."

In order to fall within the scope of the Harm Principle and be a prima facie candidate for criminalisation, the harm must also be a wrong.[17] Suppose, for example, that a judge sentences P to imprisonment for life following P's conviction of murder. One may expect that P's interests will be set back by such a sentence. He will lose his freedom and, no doubt, many opportunities to advance his life and prospects. None the less, the judge does no wrong in depriving P of his freedom in this way. Her act of sentencing falls outside the Harm Principle because, although P's situation is worsened when he is deprived of his liberty, P has lost nothing to which he had a right.

The example illustrates that our interests can be set back without our being wronged. Indeed, this is something that often occurs in economic transactions. In a broadly free market, individuals are left alone to pursue their own interests. In so doing, they wrong no-one even if their self-advancing conduct has deleterious side-effects for others. Side-effects are a natural feature of competitive interaction: if D tenders successfully for a contract, D may know that in so doing she will deprive others of that contract and, in turn, weaken their commercial viability, cause employees to be laid off, and so forth. Yet D does no wrong and the case falls outside the scope of the Harm Principle.

21.1.4 Balancing requirements

Even if the harm *is* wrongful, it should not necessarily be criminalised. The Harm Principle provides for a balancing of interests, one that considers the extent and likelihood of the harm involved and weighs that against the implications of criminalisation. Feinberg's account presents a number of factors to be taken into account at this stage:[18]

---

16 Feinberg, *The Moral Limits of the Criminal Law* vol 1: *Harm to Others*, New York, Oxford University Press, 1984, 34.
17 Cf Raz, "Autonomy, Toleration, and the Harm Principle" in Gavison (ed), *Issues in Contemporary Legal Philosophy*, Oxford, Clarendon Press, 1987, 313, 328: "Since 'causing harm' by its very meaning demands that the action is prima facie wrong it is a normative concept acquiring its specific meaning from the moral theory within which it is embedded."

"(a) the greater the *gravity* of a possible harm, the less probable its occurrence need be to justify prohibition of the conduct that threatens to produce it;

"(b) the greater the *probability* of harm, the less grave the harm need be to justify coercion;

"(c) the greater the *magnitude of the risk* of harm, itself compounded out of gravity and probability, the less reasonable it is to accept the risk;

"(d) the more *valuable* (useful) the dangerous conduct, both to the actor and to others, the more reasonable it is to take the risk of harmful consequences, and for extremely valuable conduct it is reasonable to run risks up to the point of clear and present danger;

"(e) the more *reasonable* a risk of harm (the danger), the weaker is the case for prohibiting the conduct that creates it."

A responsible legislator should, therefore, consider the gravity and likelihood of the wrongful harm and weigh that against the social value of the conduct to be prohibited and the degree of intrusion upon citizens' lives that criminalisation would involve. The greater the gravity and likelihood of the harm, the stronger the case for criminalisation; conversely, the more valuable the conduct is, or the more the prohibition would limit liberty, the stronger the case against criminalisation. In addition, other rights that a citizen may have, eg to free speech or privacy, should be respected.[19] These rights may militate against creating certain types of crimes, especially (as we shall see below) in the context of offensive behaviour.

It is a calculation of this sort that justifies the setting of speed limits. In New Zealand, for example, it is prohibited to drive on the highway at speeds in excess of 100 kilometres per hour. Is this a legitimate criminal law? The answer is, yes. Driving at 105 kilometres per hour may not be inherently immoral or wrong. But the faster one drives, the higher the probability that if something goes wrong, serious injury and property damage will result. Hence the case falls within the scope of the Harm Principle, and is amenable to criminal regulation. On the other hand, even though setting the speed limit at (say) 20 kilometres per hour would save more lives, the social costs, in terms of inefficient transportation systems, would be too great. Decisions of this sort require a balancing of factors, such as the effect on public mobility of setting the limit too low, against the costs, in terms of scale and likelihood of injuries, of setting the limit too high.

Resolution of that balancing process will depend on reference to standard cases. The Harm Principle is in play here because speeding *standardly* causes or creates a risk of harm, even if not in every instance. Inevitably, the criminal law is a blunt instrument, regulating in terms of average cases and incapable of reflecting the myriad variations upon those cases that real life delivers.

To a large extent, this constraint is a matter of resources, and of their efficient use — it is simply uneconomic to frame and administer laws that take into account the idiosyncracies of

---

18 Feinberg, *The Moral Limits of the Criminal Law* vol 1: *Harm to Others*, New York, Oxford University Press, 1984, 216.
19 Von Hirsch characterises this as the "standard harms analysis": "Extending the Harm Principle: 'Remote' Harms and Fair Imputation" in Simester and Smith (eds), *Harm and Culpability*, Oxford, Clarendon Press, 1996, 259, 261.

every person's situation. Hence, criminal law tends to prohibit actions on the basis of their typical risks and consequences, leaving further refinement, if any, to the realm of exceptions. It is an offence, we have said, to drive faster than 100 kilometres per hour. This is so notwithstanding that there is no intrinsic significance to that speed. Depending on the circumstances (perhaps the road is empty) and on the particular driver (perhaps he is Michael Schumacher), there may on occasion be no significant risk when a driver travels at a faster clip than 100. Nonetheless, specifying a precise limit is a convenient and enforceable means by which to regulate dangerous driving; and the limit itself is determined by reference to risks in standard cases.

21.1.5 Remote harms

Andrew von Hirsch has observed that many actions are not immediately harmful but may lead to harm *remotely*.[20] My selling you a hand gun, for example, does not in itself harm you but rather puts you in a position where subsequently you may harm another person. This possibility is an implicit feature of inchoate offenses, such as incitement to murder; and of what are sometimes called "substantive inchoate" offenses, such as the offense of being in possession of an instrument for burglary. It is a crime to carry an article, such as a crowbar, for use in connection with a burglary.[21] The justification for this offense is not that I have the crowbar, but rather that I may use it.

Remote harms present a particular challenge for the Harm Principle. While it may sometimes be appropriate, very often there are difficulties about basing criminalisation on remote harms, especially those predicated on the eventual criminal choices of third persons. Consider the following hypothetical. Suppose that, as Charles Murray has argued, there is evidence that unregulated premarital sex yields higher rates of illegitimate births, leading to more children growing up in impoverished households with weakened parental control; and that, in turn, this generates higher crime rates by offspring.[22] If we concede the empirical links, we can conclude that unregulated premarital sex leads to harm. But, as von Hirsch argues, it does not follow that there is even a prima facie case for criminalising premarital sex. The harm is produced not by D's own conduct but by the subsequent choices of third parties (in this case, offspring) whom D does not control. That being so, it is not clear why the harm should be D's lookout: why should D be accountable, through the criminal law, for the freely-chosen subsequent actions of others?[23]

> "to hold him liable merely because another person chooses to follow his example, or otherwise permits herself to be influenced, infringes basic notions of the separateness of persons as choosing agents. It is that other person who has made the culpable choice of doing harm, not the original actor."

---

20   Von Hirsch, "Extending the Harm Principle: 'Remote' Harms and Fair Imputation" in Simester and Smith (eds), *Harm and Culpability*, Oxford, Clarendon Press, 1996, 259, 261.
21   Section 233 Crimes Act 1961.
22   See Murray, *The Emerging British Underclass*, Choice in Welfare series no 2, London, IEA Health and Welfare Unit, 1990; also Murray, *Underclass: The Crisis Deepens*, Choice in Welfare series no 33, London, IEA Health and Welfare Unit, 1994. Cf von Hirsch, "Extending the Harm Principle: 'Remote' Harms and Fair Imputation" in Simester and Smith (eds), *Harm and Culpability*, Oxford, Clarendon Press, 1996, 259, 266.
23   Von Hirsch, "Extending the Harm Principle: 'Remote' Harms and Fair Imputation" in Simester and Smith (eds), *Harm and Culpability*, Oxford, Clarendon Press, 1996, 259, 267.

Why, in other words, should D lose an otherwise harmless option just because of the subsequent independent choices that others may make?

On occasion it is apt to prohibit an activity because of a remote harm. This may occur where D's act in some way underwrites the later wrongdoing by others. For example, it may be appropriate to prohibit D from publishing a book detailing various ways of killing one's enemies, because the link between D's activity and murders by others is sufficiently close that the remote harm can fairly be imputed back to D. But in the absence of special reasons for imputing remote harms to D, the mere existence of such harms supplies no reason for criminalising D's otherwise innocent conduct.

To invoke the Harm Principle, we have noted, an action must not only be conducive to harm; it must also be a wrong. This constraint is particularly apposite to remote harm. The criminal law, as we have mentioned, embodies by its nature an element of blame or censure. But in remote harm cases, it is not clear why D should be condemned for her non-harmful action, just because that action happens to be linked, through chains of complex social interaction, to the subsequent injurious behavior of some separate and autonomous person, E. It seems unjust to impose penal censure on D, at least where D has no power to control the harmful choices of E, and where D has not sought to assist or encourage those choices.

21.2 The Offence Principle

Suppose that, one day, D and E catch a bus into town. While riding on the bus, they decide to have sexual intercourse, oblivious of the other passengers. Their conduct may not harm anyone else, and seems to fall outside the scope of the Harm Principle. Yet it will cause great offence, no doubt, to many others on the bus who are forced to experience their activity, and there seems to be widespread agreement that conduct of this sort may legitimately be criminalised.

Feinberg certainly thinks so. In his view,[24]

> "It is *always a good reason in support of a proposed criminal prohibition that it would probably be an effective way of preventing serious offense (as opposed to injury or harm) to persons other than the actor, and that it is probably a necessary means to that end* ...."

Many, probably most, liberals agree that actions may sometimes be prohibited on the grounds of their offensiveness, and there is widespread acceptance of the Offence Principle as a secondary principle of criminalisation, one that supplements the Harm Principle.

When is the Offence Principle in play? Merely showing that D's conduct is evil or unpleasant will not invoke the Offence Principle. For Feinberg, conduct is offensive when it affronts other people's sensibilities; i.e. when it causes them to undergo an unpleasant and disliked psychological experience, by way of reaction to the conduct. Causing any such affront, in his view, constitutes prima facie grounds for invoking the criminal law, provided that enough people are sufficiently affronted.

There must, however, be *serious* offence to others. Moreover, on Feinberg's account, the case for criminalisation must satisfy a sophisticated balancing test that is designed to criminalise offence more sparingly. First, a responsible legislator should consider the impact of the

---

[24] Feinberg, *The Moral Limits of the Criminal Law* vol 2: *Offense to Others*, New York, Oxford University Press, 1985, 1 (emphasis original).

conduct on its audience, by examining the magnitude of the affront to see how pervasively and intensely it is felt. As part of that examination, a standard of "reasonable avoidability" is imposed: the easier it is for members of the public to avoid settings where the conduct occurs, the less serious the offence is. Pornography may cause affront to many when viewed, but the seriousness of that affront is diminished if one must specifically visit an adult cinema to see it.

Secondly, the importance of the offending conduct should be examined from the actor's perspective. The more central the conduct is to an actor's way of life, the greater is the claim not to have the conduct prohibited. As part of this examination, a standard of "alternative opportunities" is applied: restrictions on the conduct become more acceptable if there are satisfactory alternative times and places at which the actor could perform the conduct with less offense (say by showing pornography only at home or in adult cinemas and not more generally).

The broader social impact of the conduct needs also to be considered. The more independent general usefulness the supposedly offending conduct has, the less the claim to prohibition. For this purpose, free expression of opinion is, following Mill, deemed to have its own social value, "in virtue of the great social utility of free expression and discussion generally, as well as the vital personal interest most people have in being able to speak their minds fearlessly".[25] I may cause considerable and widespread offence when I advocate the legalisation of, say, necrophilia; but the importance of preserving free political debate is such as to outweigh any case for criminalisation that the offence may generate.

21.2.1 Offensive conduct as a wrong

The application of these considerations means that, on Feinberg's account, some conduct that widely offends should still be legally permissible, for example when committed in settings readily avoidable by others. Thus, although acts of indecent exposure may legitimately be criminalised when done on city streets, similar conduct might nonetheless be permitted at designated beaches, at which those not so inclined need not bathe.

Even so, however, Feinberg underplays a further consideration: the need for the affront to be wrongful. It is not affront *per se* to the sensibilities of others — even widespread affront — that should justify possible state intervention, but affront *plus* valid reasons for objecting to the conduct.[26] Suppose, for example, that the sight of an interracial couple holding hands causes enormous affront in a particular community. It seems to us that, regardless of the scale of the reaction, there is no case for invoking the Offence Principle here, because there is nothing wrong with that couple's behaviour.

This point is particularly important in the criminal law, which *punishes*, and censures, the offender for having done wrong. That being the case, the criminalisation of conduct should require a plausible claim of wrongdoing. With conduct that supposedly is offensive, one must therefore ask: why does the actor deserve censure? If the essence of offence is merely that the conduct displeases many people, then it is not clear that wrongdoing has occurred at all. "I don't like it" should never suffice as a basis for criminalisation, regardless of the numbers who

---

25   Feinberg, *The Moral Limits of the Criminal Law* vol 2: *Offense to Others*, New York, Oxford University Press, 1985, 44.
26   Simester and von Hirsch, "Rethinking the Offense Principle" (2002) 8 *Legal Theory* 269.

say it. Better reasons need to be provided why there is something reprehensible about the behaviour that deserves a censuring response.

What makes offensive conduct wrong, in general, is that it treats other persons with a gross lack of consideration or respect. Racial insults are a paradigm of this class of case: they tend both to cause affront in the audience and to do so by communicating contempt for that audience. Another variety of offence is exhibitionism. Suppose that D is sitting peaceably in the park, but cannot concentrate on his newspaper because E and F are copulating noisily on the grass nearby. D may rightly complain. He has a legitimate claim not to have the intimate facts of E and F's relationship forced upon him. This may be singularly in point in locations like parks, which we value, *inter alia*, as places to interact with other persons who are not intimates, and where, consequently, such offensive activities are likely to cause much greater discomfort than they would in more private contexts.

21.2.2 A communicative and conventional wrong

In so far as offensive conduct is something that communicates to V, the person experiencing the conduct, a lack of respect and consideration, it is characteristically a form of expressive action. As such, even if one accepts the Offence Principle as a legitimate ground of criminalisation, such cases should be criminalised sparingly because of the importance of allowing free expression in a society. The need to accommodate diverse and sometimes inconsistent styles of life, which may depend for their success on being publicly manifested, militates in favor of a "thick skin" approach to the regulation of expressive acts, even when those acts are offensive to others. Friction is a characteristic of social interaction, at least in a pluralistic society. Such societies require of their members a certain robustness of sensibility, so that incivility may be tolerated for the sake of personal and cultural diversity.

A second reason for caution with the Offence Principle is how close its application can resemble that of the next principle we shall discuss, legal moralism. Some of the most uncontroversial examples of offence involve sexual activity in public places. The examples are uncontroversial because there remains a strong moral consensus disapproving of such conduct, a consensus which underpins the convention that it should not be done. What counts for the Offence Principle may be the convention, but what generates the convention is the widespread moral view.

At the same time, the convention is not *merely* the articulation of a moral view. Legal moralism is concerned with regulating actions that are morally wrong: the Offence Principle, by contrast, is concerned with how we treat each other. Conventions such as those governing acceptable conduct in public places thus serve an important instrumental purpose, by helping to delineate the boundaries between personal and public, and setting the terms of our interaction with strangers. D's respect for V implies respect for the terms under which they (usually, by convention) interact. This holds independently of the particular terms of the convention. When D exposes himself, uninvited, to V, he both violates the applicable social convention and, further, wrongs V by failing to respect the socially-agreed terms under which she interacts with others.

21.3 Legal moralism

According to the legal moralist, it is legitimate to use the criminal law to prohibit immorality *per se*. As Feinberg encapsulates it, the legal moralist holds that it "can be morally legitimate to prohibit conduct on the ground that it is inherently immoral, even though it causes neither harm nor offense to the actor or to others".[27] Legal moralism finds it justifiable to criminalise acts that are free-floating evils and which neither infringe the rights of, nor harm, any other person. Most obviously, such acts might include the violation of religious norms, together with private immorality.[28] A good example of this possibility is *Brown*, mentioned earlier,[29] in which the House of Lords held that, in the context of sado-masochistic sexual activity, the infliction of actual bodily harm upon a consenting adult "victim" was an offence. From the perspective of the Harm Principle, there is no wrong to V since the activity occurs with V's consent. But from the perspective of legal moralism, D's conduct may be regarded as inherently wrong — and therefore legitimately criminalisable. Indeed, V's consent simply makes V, too, a participant in the offence.

Lord Devlin famously argued for legal moralism on the ground that a society's moral values are an indispensable part of its structural framework.[30] In turn, if *per se* harmless immorality were permitted, this would tend to undermine the social fabric, dissolving the moral consensus underpinning society and leading, ultimately, to social disintegration and anarchy. Strictly speaking, Devlin's argument is not an argument in favour of pure legal moralism. Rather, it invokes the Harm Principle. Social disintegration, if it occurred, would certainly be a bad thing for the lives and interests of citizens. Further, if permitting some immoral act would lead to social disintegration then, subject to the problem of remote harms noted in 21.1.5, the state has prima facie reason to criminalise the act. To do so would not violate the liberal precepts of the Harm Principle.

The main problem with Devlin's argument is the need to establish an empirical link between mere immorality and social disintegration. Adultery happens frequently and legally, but there is no sign of a causal link from it to chaos. It may be that certain, specific, immoral acts will tend to threaten the continuance of the social structure, but that possibility needs to be investigated for *each* specific act, and cannot simply be asserted as a general truth for *all* immoral acts, however minor.

More generally, pure legal moralism shares with Lord Devlin's defence the characteristic of entrenching the *status quo ante*. By its nature, legal moralism is conservative, in that immorality is measured against the prevailing social mores of the time: difference is, by that standard, immoral and may therefore be suppressed. One objection to this approach, therefore, is that change need not be bad. The abolition of slavery was a good thing; so, too, it is desirable that mixed-race couples may now publicise their association, even in communities where segregation formerly was enforced. Especially in a heterogeneous society containing a wide variety of subcultures, moral stagnation seems unattractive. Difference, even conflict, between the lives and values of citizens can be a dynamic force for the evolution of a vigorous, thriving, and valuable culture.

A related difficulty with legal moralism is the problem of identifying a stable classification of immoral acts. Is homosexuality immoral (wherefore it may be prohibited)? It depends who,

---

27 Feinberg, *The Moral Limits of the Criminal Law* vol 1: *Harm to Others*, New York, Oxford University Press, 1984, 27.
28 See eg Feinberg, *The Moral Limits of the Criminal Law* vol 4: *Harmless Wrongdoing*, New York, Oxford University Press, 1988, 20-25.
29 *R v Brown* [1994] 1 AC 212; [1993] 2 All ER 75 (HL); see 21.1 above.
30 Devlin, *The Enforcement of Morals*, London, Oxford University Press, 1965, 8-14.

when, and where one asks. As Peter Alldridge has pointed out, some activities that once were regarded as *malum in se* are now entirely permissible, whereas some commercial activities that formerly were permitted are now regarded as very serious wrongs.[31] Prohibition on grounds of immorality exposes even legislators to the charge that, in truth, they are simply imposing their own moral prejudices upon the nation.

But the best-known criticisms of legal moralism concern its clash with the liberal ideal of autonomy. Criminalisation takes options away from people. It is an intrusive and condemnatory form of coercion. Accepting the general case for criminalising mere immorality will, inevitably, lead to restrictions of individuals' autonomy, especially because the criminal law is very coarse-grained, so that its prohibitions are typically framed in broad rather than narrow terms. Given the diversity of human needs and preferences, criminal prohibitions will inevitably deprive some individuals of options that are valuable to them: such persons will, in effect, be harmed by the prohibitions.

The strongest cases for depriving people of opportunities in this way arise where D's activity is likely to diminish the opportunities for others to live good lives. In these cases, a condition of D's well-being (her autonomy) is weighed against a condition of V's well-being: like is compared with like. But in these very cases, D's conduct is by definition harmful. Where, by contrast, the conduct is merely immoral, the interests of persons (such as D) are being weighed only against abstract judgements of morality. There is no well-being or autonomy-based reason *for* criminalisation, only against: like is not being compared with like. In a liberal society, the interests of persons should take priority at this point. Thus it is arguable that mere immorality is, by itself, insufficient for criminalisation.

21.4 Paternalism

Feinberg summarises the paternalistic justification of criminalisation as follows:[32]

"It is always a good reason in support of a prohibition that it is probably necessary to prevent harm (physical, psychological, or economic) to the actor himself and there is probably no other means that is equally effective at no greater cost to other values."

Like the Harm Principle, paternalism demands harm. But it goes beyond the Harm Principle in that it warrants the criminalisation of self-harm: D may be prohibited, *for her own sake*, from performing certain acts. A standard legal example of such prohibitions is the criminal law duty to wear seat belts when driving a car.[33] The duty is imposed for D's own benefit, on the grounds that persons who fail to wear a seat belt are likely to suffer much more severe injuries in an accident than are those who wear one.[34]

---

31 Alldridge, "Making Criminal Law Known" in Shute and Simester (ed), *Criminal Law Theory: Essays on the General Part*, Oxford, Oxford University Press, 2002, 103, 107ff.
32 Feinberg, *The Moral Limits of the Criminal Law* vol 1: *Harm to Others*, New York, Oxford University Press, 1984, 26-27.
33 We concentrate here on the driver on the ground that back-seat passengers who fail to wear seat belts may harm not only themselves but also those seated in front of them.
34 It is sometimes argued that there is harm to others in such cases, since the State is likely to incur greater costs in providing health care to drivers who are more seriously injured after failing to wear a seat belt. This argument is not straightforward, however, since the State's intervention is voluntary; it is open to the State to refuse to treat such persons, or to require them to take out private insurance.

Prima facie, there seems little that is objectionable about a law requiring persons to wear seat belts when in a car. But this is one of the strongest cases for paternalistic intervention. The obligation is a minor one, falling only on those who choose to drive and not significantly hindering the performance of that activity. It is a burden easily discharged, while the harm at risk is substantial. At the same time, failure to wear a seat belt is rarely a matter of conscious choice by D, still less of a choice that is integral to her style of life. Thus the case is one where the disvalue attached to the infringement of D's autonomy is minor, and arguably outweighed by the interest in D's welfare that is advanced.

Relatedly, paternalistic intervention may be appropriate more generally in cases where D's choice to harm herself cannot be said to be considered or responsible. Children and the mentally defective have extensive restrictions imposed upon their ability to engage in sexual intercourse, on the grounds that their choice to do so may not be fully understood.

But even if this argument be accepted in respect of seat belts and irresponsible actors, it cannot be generalised very far. In *Harm to Self*, Feinberg considers the theory of paternalism in detail — and rejects it:[35]

> "The cases for and against legal paternalism then can be summed up as follows. In favor of the principle is the fact that there are many laws now on the books that *seem* to have had paternalism as an essential part of their implicit rationales, and that some of these at least, seem to most of us to be sensible and legitimate restrictions. It is also a consideration in favor of paternalism that preventable personal harm (set-back interest) is universally thought to be a great evil, and that such harm is no less harmful when self-caused than when caused by others. If society can substantially diminish the net amount of harm to interests caused from *all* sources, that would be a great social gain. If that prospect provides the moral basis underlying the harm to others principle, why should it not have application as well to self-caused harm and thus support equally the principle of legal paternalism?
>
> "On the other side, it is argued that a consistent application of legal paternalism would lead to the creation of new crimes that would be odious and offensive to common sense, leading to the general punishment of risk-takers, the enforcement of prudence, and the interference with saints and heroes. Moreover, hard paternalistic justification of any restriction of personal liberty is especially offensive morally, because it invades the realm of personal autonomy where each competent, responsible, adult human being should reign supreme."

The obligation is on the legal paternalist to show why it is justified to coerce D and promote her welfare at the expense of her autonomy.

One way of approaching that challenge is by arguing that autonomy is only of instrumental value: having options is valuable, that is to say, only in so far as the options themselves are valuable. On this view, there is no value in permitting self-maiming, say by cutting one's arm off, because there is no value in the activity that is being permitted. However, this argument establishes only that there is no obligation on the State positively to foster or support such activities. It does not follow that the State has the right to *prohibit* valueless activities. Justified

---

35   Feinberg, *The Moral Limits of the Criminal Law* vol 3: *Harm to Self*, New York, Oxford University Press, 1986, 25.

proscription through the criminal law requires something stronger: positive reasons why we should coerce, threaten, and impose sanctions upon a wrongdoer. The paternalistic legislative assertion, "We are sending you to jail for your own good," makes very little sense when addressed to responsible, autonomous, citizens in a mature liberal democracy. It amounts to saying, "we shall harm you lest you harm yourself".

A moment's reflection, moreover, reveals that the potential for invasive paternalism is enormous. So many features of modern life are not especially good for us — getting drunk, playing dangerous sports, smoking, eating fatty foods, failing to partake of regular exercise. A consistent paternalist should seek to eliminate them all. But freedom includes the freedom to go wrong. Respect for persons as autonomous agents involves respect for individuals as deliberating agents who have the capacity independently to pursue goals and values which they have themselves adopted. If we are not allowed to choose badly then, in effect, our choices are no longer determined by our own goals and values. A paternalistic legal system which made people's choices for them may well end up alienating people from their own conduct:[36]

> "Why not interfere with someone else's shaping of his own life? ... I conjecture that the answer is connected with that elusive and difficult notion: the meaning of life. A person's shaping his life in accordance with some overall plan is his way of giving meaning to his life; only a being with the capacity to so shape his life can have or strive for a meaningful life."

Our well-being does not just require the successful pursuit of valuable goals; it requires also that we identify and engage with those goals — that they be *our* goals. Paternalism, by contrast, imposes the state's goals and values upon us. In the criminal law, moreover, it does so coercively. When a person's choices are pre-empted by the law, she does not shape her own life.[37] And to live a meaningful life, one must shape it oneself.

21.5 Negative grounds for intervention: regulatory alternatives

Perhaps we can establish a positive case for regulating some candidate activity through the criminal law. But we need also to consider whether, none the less, there are reasons *not* to criminalise. The next stage of the inquiry involves considering whether the criminal law is the most appropriate tool for regulating the activity. In particular, the advantages and disadvantages of using the criminal law should be measured against those accruing to alternative regulatory mechanisms. As a general rule, if some other form of State intervention falling short of criminalisation would be effective to regulate the conduct at issue, that alternative should be preferred. The criminal prohibition should be deployed only as a last resort.

21.5.1 Tax

On occasions in the past, western Governments have attempted to regulate alcohol by criminal prohibition. The results were disastrous; sales and consumption simply went underground, creating a black market ripe for extortion and racketeering. Nowadays, control is exercised via licensing arrangements and tax. One of the standard modern functions of the tax system is to regulate behaviour by manipulating the cost of products in order to reduce (or sometimes,

---

36   Nozick, *Anarchy, State and Utopia*, Oxford, Blackwell, 1974, 50.
37   Raz, *The Morality of Freedom*, Oxford, Clarendon Press, 1986, 382.

increase[38]) demand. The mechanism of tax is one means by which the State can influence, without prohibiting outright, the behaviour of citizens. Part of the overt rationale for tobacco and alcohol duties is to deter consumers from smoking and drinking and to correct mispricing of cigarettes and alcohol, whereby the market price does not reflect the true cost to society (including health care costs) of the product.

Consumption taxes of this sort do, of course, affect options. If the price of his cigarettes is increased, D will have less money left for other activities. In the absence of offsetting income tax rebates, such measures tend to have a disproportionate effect on the poor. As such, tax measures are both an improvement on criminalisation in so far as they are less coercive and preserve more options for citizens and, at the same time, less equitable than criminalisation in so far as they are likely to affect different socio-economic classes differentially.

21.5.2 Tort law

A second option is for the State to regulate an activity by means of a statutory or common-law tort. Intervention through the civil law involves a substantial intrusion of the legal process, but remains less coercive than the criminal justice process: there is no arrest, no imprisonment, and no record of a criminal conviction. In some situations, therefore, the creation of a statutory tort may be an excellent alternative to criminal sanctions. This is especially so when considering compliance incentives for large corporations. An industrial accident costing many lives may lead to a company being fined some tens of thousands of pounds: that same company will be far more concerned by the millions of pounds it might incur in tort damages.

It is not a complete alternative. Tort law effectively prices rather than prohibits; thus it lacks the mandatory character of the criminal law. Moreover, in many instances tortfeasors may be able to defray the costs of liability by means of insurance.

21.5.3 Other mechanisms

There is a variety of other methods for addressing harmful or odious behaviour, including advertising and licensing. The classic example of the former is the series of drink-driving advertising campaigns, which has been instrumental in bringing about a sea-change in public attitudes toward the wrongfulness of driving while drunk. Although not appropriate to all varieties of wrong (for example, there is normally no need to polemicise against performing acts that are already widely perceived as *mala in se*), education and advertising can in some instances raise awareness of the potential harmfulness of an activity, in circumstances where that harmfulness had previously gone unremarked.

Licensing is also a familiar form of modern regulation. The performance of many activities requires a licence: eg, running a public house, possessing a firearm, and even driving. All of these activities import risks of harm, either direct or remote. But each is valuable, and it may be inappropriate, because of the social costs, to criminalise the activity altogether. So the activities are permitted, but only under conditions that are regulated by means of licensing systems. The criminal law, in turn, sits in the background to prohibit persons from carrying out each activity without, or in breach of, the licence. Licensing systems represent a significant limitation of individual liberty, but fall a long way short of outright prohibition. Moreover,

---

38   For example, in the case of children. One reason for providing benefits and/or tax credits to parents is that children are, *inter alia*, public goods; hence the State has reason to subsidise part of the cost of their upbringing

they offer a more flexible tool than do generalised criminal laws, since the terms of each licence can be adapted to specific cases by the magistrates or authority responsible for administering that licence.

21.5.4 Contra: some advantages of using the criminal law

Even though alternative methods of regulation, if practical, should normally be preferred to the criminal law, it is worth noting that there are sometimes advantages in resorting to criminalisation. Unlike any other area of law, the criminal law systematically stigmatises activities (through prohibition) and persons (though conviction and punishment). But sometimes that stigmatisation is appropriate. The symbolic significance of enacting that some activity is a criminal offence can be a reason *in favour* of criminalisation, at least where stigmatisation of the activity is desirable. If used selectively, the creation of a criminal law can be a tool for communicating to the public that the prohibited activity is a serious wrong that *must* not be done.

There are also some practical considerations. Given that the State pays the costs of investigating, prosecuting, and punishing criminal conduct, it may be better placed to regulate wrongs than are, say, private individuals through the law of tort. Suppose that my next-door neighbour throws a stone through one of the panes in my greenhouse, which it will cost some $50 to replace. It is likely to be impractical for me to pursue her through the law of tort. But a criminal prosecution will cost me only my time. In this respect, criminal regulation by the State may augment the Rule of Law, through increasing the consistency with which legal rights are enforced in like cases, rather than leaving the matter to irregular administration by individual claimants.

21.6 Negative grounds for intervention: the rule of law

If the criminal law *is* to be used, its deployment should comply with a variety of constraints, both principled and pragmatic. We cannot explore all these constraints in detail here, but will endeavour to give at least a flavour of their variety and character.

21.6.1 Rule of Law constraints on criminalisation

First, it is desirable that the form of the criminal law proposed meets Rule of Law constraints, which were discussed in chapter 2 (see 2.1.1-4). In particular, the law should be prospective not retrospective (2.1.2). Secondly, the law should give fair warning, by defining the prohibited activity with sufficient certainty (2.1.3). It needs to be understandable, predictable, and not vague. The more clearly defined the offence, the less potential there is for injustice with respect to those whose conduct falls close to its limits. Further, the more certainty there is in the drafting, the more confident society can be that an individual convicted under that offence is fairly labelled (2.1.4). The law must make clear what sort of criminal each offender is — what the conviction is for. The criminal law speaks to society as well as wrongdoers when it convicts them, and it should communicate its judgment with precision, by accurately naming and describing the crime of which they are convicted.

Specificity of drafting has an additional dimension, in that more narrowly-defined crimes are less likely to lead to discretionary enforcement. If an offence is too broadly drafted, so that it requires selective prosecution, the liability of defendants is, in effect, remaindered to the decisions of officials — creating the risk of unfair, inappropriate, or potentially even discriminatory prosecutions.[39] It is not unknown for defendants to be found guilty of offences even though, in the view of the court, a prosecution should not have been brought.[40] This possibility should be minimised.

21.6.2 The individuation of offences

How many offences do we need? Do we really need to distinguish theft from deception, rape from other forms of sexual violation, and injuring from wounding with intent? Or would it be enough just to have just a few generic crimes including, say, violation of another's property right; violation of another's person; damaging the environment; and so on? The answer to the last question is, No. While the law may sometimes draw unnecessary distinctions, broad category-offences would be inappropriate. Enacting only generic crimes would tend to suppress the fact that, within each field of harmful wrongdoing, each of our existing offences may involve a different wrong, a different harm, or both. It is for this reason that they are rightly separate offences.

In looking to explain and justify the existence of any offence, it is necessary to identify what harm, and what wrong, is addressed by that crime. Obtaining by deception may, for example, lead to much the same immediate harm as does theft — a straightforward diminution of V's resources — but the wrong is different. Moreover, it does not undermine the proprietary regime in the same way as does theft. As such, the two are rightly distinguished by criminal law.[41]

This claim, about the importance of drawing distinctions, is an extension of the principles of fair warning (2.1.3) and fair labelling (2.1.4). *Ex ante*, citizens need to know where they stand. They need advance warning concerning their actions; in particular, about whether what they are going to do is a crime and, if so, what sort of crime it is. *Ex post*, offenders ought to be labelled with an adequate degree of precision, in order that the criminal record identifies the gist of D's criminal wrongdoing. Both principles require that each offence is labelled and defined in such a way that it conveys to citizens an accurate moral picture of the prohibited conduct, one that is neither misleading nor unduly vague or over-generalised. Offences should, so far as is practical, reflect meaningful distinctions in the public mind between different types of culpable wrongdoing. This requires that they are drawn up in such a way that they capture, and differentiate, significant differences in the harmfulness, wrongfulness, and/or culpability of various types of action.

By way of illustration, the differences between murder, maiming, and criminal damage are significant because the harms (and indeed the wrongs) at stake are quite different. Their differences are clearly sufficient to warrant enacting separate offences, since the meaning and moral significance of each action is clearly distinguished in the public mind. Attempted murder, too, is rightly distinguished from murder because of the difference in resulting harm. Likewise, although the harms of theft and of criminal damage are similar, the manners in which they are

---

39 Cf the use, not intended by the United Kingdom legislature, of anti-social behaviour orders in that country against prostitutes and beggars: Burney, " 'No Spitting': Regulation of Offensive Behaviour in England and Wales" in von Hirsch and Simester (eds), *Incivilities: Regulating Offensive Behaviour*, Oxford, Hart Publishing, 2006, 195, 206; also Simester and von Hirsch, "Regulating Offensive Conduct through Two-Step Prohibitions" in von Hirsch and Simester (eds), *Incivilities: Regulating Offensive Behaviour*, Oxford, Hart Publishing, 2006, 173, 191.
40 Cf *Smedleys Ltd v Breed* [1974] AC 839; *Hart v Bex* [1957] Crim LR 622.
41 Sections 219 and 223 Crimes Act 1961; see 19.2.

inflicted involve two different forms of wrongdoing; forms that are sufficiently distinct in the public mind to warrant independent recognition by the criminal law.

Occasionally, too, there may be a case for distinguishing between two harmful activities on the grounds of culpability. An assault being negligent with regard to any consequential risks to life would typically lack the same culpability as an assault being reckless about those same risks — and, if ever worthy of being criminalised as form of a homicide (which we doubt), ought surely to be a separate offence and not lumped in with murder or reckless manslaughter.

Not every difference is worthy of capture. Even though New Zealand now distinguishes three tiers of theft by value of the property stolen,[42] nobody would suggest that there should be a much more refined series of theft offences, graded in minute detail (say, theft of less than $50 value; theft of less than $100 value; theft of less than $200 value; and so on). Excessively specific offences risk clogging the trial process with unmeritorious technical argument, and obfuscating the moral clarity of the law's communications. At least in the context of non-specialist activities such as property offences, people (both ex ante and ex post) need to know the law's requirements in gist and not precisely. As such, meaning is better conveyed through publicly-shared moral distinctions that are broadly rather than narrowly significant, provided those broader distinctions communicate an adequately nuanced statement of the prohibited wrongdoing. The degree of specificity that the law should adopt when distinguishing various harms and wrongs is, therefore, a trade-off that depends in part on the range of moral differentiations informing the public imagination. The fragmentation of the particular must be balanced against the vagueness of the general.

21.7 Negative grounds for intervention: practical constraints

Finally, in addition to Rule of Law constraints, a variety of other considerations must be taken into account before concluding that criminalisation through the proposed offence is the right response.

21.7.1 What side-effects will criminalisation have?

Suppose that a clearly drafted law is proposed that criminalises the failure to disclose one's HIV-positive status to a sexual partner. One thing to consider before enacting such a law is whether it will have the effect of deterring those persons who are most at risk of contracting HIV from being tested. By not knowing their status, they keep themselves outside the scope of the offence — but without advancing the underlying aim of the offence, which is to protect their partners. In these sorts of cases, the legislator should consider whether, in effect, enacting the proposed law will do more harm than good.

It has not escaped judicial notice that one of the concerns about the use of drugs is consequential criminality: the prospect that drug users will steal, deal in drugs, enter into prostitution, or commit other crimes in order to finance their habit.[43] But a responsible legislator might also think that these considerations argue for *de*criminalisation. The price of illegal drugs is high because the drugs are illegal — if not illegal, no doubt users will need less

---

42   Cf Simester and Sullivan, "On the Nature and Rationale of Property Offences" in Duff and Green (eds), *Defining Crimes: Essays on the Special Part of the Criminal Law*, Oxford, Oxford University Press, 2005, 168, 188-190.

43   Cf R v Aramah (1982) 4 Crim App R (S) 407, 408-409 (Lord Lane CJ). See more generally Alldridge, "Dealing with Drug Dealing" in Simester and Smith (eds), *Harm and Culpability*, Oxford, Clarendon Press, 1996, 239.

money to pay for their habits, leading (it may be thought) to a significant reduction in consequential crime. Compare, too, the eras of alcohol prohibition, which led to an upsurge in violent conflict between gangs involved in the black market that arose to replace the licit trade. If criminalisation of an activity is likely to produce such undesirable consequences as these, that is a powerful reason not to prohibit.

21.7.2 Pragmatics of the criminal justice system

A proposed offence might also be rejected for pragmatic reasons. In particular, the offence needs to be capable of being administered, by enforcement authorities and prosecutors. Ideally, it will be specified in clear and unambiguous terms, so that (as well as giving fair warning to citizens) those responsible for its administration will be confident of their ability to use the new law with predictable outcomes. Further, the terms it uses will cohere with and not reinvent existing legal concepts, facilitating understanding by professionals within the criminal justice system and avoiding the need for costly retraining exercises.

Another consideration is policing. The detection of some proposed crimes may be too difficult: this is one reason not to criminalise, say, unmarried sexual intercourse in private. Alternatively, crimes may be detectable only by invasive methods of surveillance; it needs to be considered to what extent the power to use such methods is desirable. There is also the question of cost: how expensive are the means of investigation? Will enforcement agencies be able to afford to monitor the new offence? Will effective policing of the offence require additional resources and legal powers?

There are many other issues that must be resolved when a new offence is created (mode of trial, evidential requirements, sentencing options, etc.). We cannot do justice to them all here. The key point is that, even though a prima facie case can be made in favour of criminalising an activity, eg because it is harmful to others, it does not follow that criminal legislation is the best response. Other forms of intervention need to be considered; indeed, it may sometimes be best not to legislate at all. The criminal law is a powerful, expensive, and invasive tool. It should not be used lightly.

TABLE OF STATUTES AND REGULATIONS

Abbreviations

1	Criminal Law: Definition and Application: ch 1	12	Compulsion: ch 12
2	Interpretation, Proof, and the Rule of Law: ch 2	13	Duress of Circumstances, Necessity, and Impossibility: ch 13
3	The Actus Reus: ch 3		
4	Mens Rea: ch 4	14	Mistake: ch 14
5	Strict and Absolute Liability: ch 5	15	Self-Defence and Defence of Property: ch 15
6	Secondary Participation: ch 6	16	Culpable Homicide: ch 16
7	Vicarious and Corporate Liability: ch 7	17	Non-fatal Offences of Violence: ch 17
8	The Inchoate Offences: ch 8	19	Theft and Receiving: ch 19
9	Infancy: ch 9	20	Deception: ch 20
10	Insanity: ch 10	21	The Moral Limits of Criminalisation: ch 21
11	Intoxication: ch 11		

A

Acts Interpretation Act 1924
s 5	2.2.1
s 5(j)	2.2.1

Arms Act 1983   14.3.1, 14.4.1(1)
s 50	3.2.2(2)
s 50(1)(b)	14.3.1
s 53	16.1, 17.5
s 53(4)	17.5

Aviation Security Act 1982 (UK)   13.2.3(2)

C

Canadian Charter of Rights and Freedoms (Canada)
s 1	10.3.1
s 11(d)	10.3.1

Children, Young Persons, and Their Families Act 1989   9.2.1, 9.3, 9.3.1, 9.4
Part 2	9.2.1
s 13	9.2.1
s 14(1)	9.3.1
s 14(1)(d)	9.2.1
s 14(1)(e)	9.3.1
s 14(1)(f)	9.2.1
Part 3	
s 198	9.3.1
s 198(2)	9.3.1
Part 4, s 272(1)	9.3, 9.4.1

Civil Aviation Regulations 1953
Part 7, reg 173(2)	5.2.3(2)

Civil Union Act 2004
Part 2, s 7	18.10.3

Companies Act 1948 (UK)   13.6.1

Crime and Disorder Act 1998 (UK)
s 34	9.4

Crimes Act 1900 (ACT)
s 428N	10.3

Crimes Act 1900 (New South Wales)
s 393	8.3.4(3)
s 428G	11.1
s 428H	11.1

Crimes Act 1908   15.1.1, 17.5
Part 3	
s 43(2)	10.3
s 44	12.1
s 73	15.1.1
s 76	15.1.1
Part 8	
s 184	16.5.1
s 193	16.2.3(6)
s 195	17.6.2

Crimes Act 1958 (Vic)   8.4.1(1)
s 321G	8.4.1(1)

Crimes Act 1961   2.3.1(2), 3.1, 3.2.1(2), 8.2, 8.2.3(1),(2), 8.3.1,7, 8.4, 10.3.4,8, 13.3.4(1),(2), 15.2, 15.2.2(4), 17.2, 17.2.2, 17.3, 17.3.1,1(1), 17.5,8, 18.2.1(2), 19.3.1 (7),3(2)
s 2	4.2, 4.3.2, 7.2.1, 17.1,2, 17.2.3, 17.4, 17.7.1, 18.2
s 2(1)	3.2.1(3), 17.2.1,4(1), 17.3.1(1),5, 19.3.1,1(1), (2),(3),(7)
s 2(1A)	18.2.1,1(1),(2), 18.6.2
s 2(1B)	18.11.1
s 2(1B)(b)	18.11.1
Part 1	
s 6	8.3.9
s 7	8.3.2,9
s 9	2.1.1,2, 8.3.1
s 10A	2.1.2
Part 3	
s 20	1.4.1, 6.4.4(4), 11.1, 13.1, 13.2.2,3(3), 13.3.4,4(2), 13.6.4, 14.2.5, 16.5.2(5), 17.2.4(1)
s 20(1)	13.2.3(2)
s 21	6.4.4(4), 6.6.2, 9.2, 9.2.1

739

s 21(2)	6.3.1, 6.6.2, 9.2.1
s 22	6.6.2, 9.3, 9.3.2
s 22(1)	9.3
s 22(2)	6.3.1, 6.6.2
s 23	6.6.2, 10.3, 10.3.1,4(1), 10.4.2, 16.5, 16.6.2
s 23(1)	2.3.1(2), 10.3.1, 15.1.3(1)
s 23(2)	10.3, 10.3.3(3)
s 23(2)(a)	10.3.4
s 23(2)(b)	10.3, 10.3.4,4(2),5
s 23(3)	10.3.7
s 23(4)	6.6.2
s 24	1.3.2(4), 6.4.4(1), 11.2.4, 12.1,2,3,4,6, 12.6.1,2, 12.8,9, 12.10.1,2,2(1),3,4, 12.14, 12.14.1, 13.2, 13.2.1,3(2),(3),4, 13.3.4 (1), 13.5.2, 13.6.4, 14.2.2
s 24(1)	6.6.2(1), 12.7, 12.10.1, 13.2.3(2),(3)
s 24(2)	12.4,5,7, 12.10.4,4(1)
s 24(2)(e)	12.2
s 24(2)(k)	12.10.4
s 24(2)(ka)	12.10.4
s 24(3)	12.4,13
s 25	4.1, 14.3, 14.3.1, 14.4.1 (1), 15.2.2(4), 17.7.1(2), 18.6.2(1)
s 41	13.3.4(2)
s 44	13.3.4(2)
s 46	13.3.4(2)
s 48	11.2.4, 12.4, 13.3.4(1),(2), 14.2.5, 15.1.1,2,3,3(1),(2), (3),(5),4,4(1),(6),5, 15.2.2 (1),3, 17.7.1(2),(3)
s 49	15.1.1
s 50	15.1.1
s 52	13.3.4(1), 15.2, 15.2.1,2,2 (1),(2),(3)
s 53	15.2, 15.2.2,2(2),(4)
s 54	15.2.2(4)
s 55	14.2.2, 15.2, 15.2.3,4
s 56	13.3.4(1), 15.2, 15.2.1,2,2 (1),(3),3
s 57	15.2.1
s 58	15.2.1
s 59	17.8.1,1(1),(3)
s 59(1)	17.8.1
s 59(3)	17.8.1
s 61	13.3.4(1),(3)
s 61A	13.3.4(1),(3)
s 62	2.1.3(1), 15.1, 15.1.5, 15.2.3
s 63	16.2.3(3),(6), 16.5.2(7)
Part 4	
s 66	6.2,3,4, 6.4.2,4(1), 6.6.4,4 (2),5,6, 7.2, 8.4
s 66(1)	3.3.3(2), 6.3, 6.4.1,1(2), (4),4(1),(4), 6.5, 6.5.2,4, 6.6.2(2),3, 8.4.2,3, 16.4.5
s 66(1)(a)	6.2,3, 6.3.1
s 66(1)(b)	6.2,4, 6.4.4,4(1), 6.6, 6.6.6 (2)
s 66(1)(c)	6.4
s 66(1)(d)	6.2,4, 6.4.4, 6.6, 6.6.2(2),6 (2), 8.4, 18.6.2(3)
s 66(2)	3.3.3(2), 6.2,3, 6.4.4(4), 6.5, 6.5.1,2,3,4, 6.6, 6.6.3, 5,6(1), 8.3.8, 11.2.1(1), 16.4.5
s 68	6.2
s 68(2)	8.4
s 69	6.2, 8.4
s 70(1)	6.4.4(4)
s 71	6.2
s 72	4.2, 8.2, 8.2.1,2,2(1),5(1), 18.4
s 72(1)	8.2.1,2,2(2),3(4),5,5(1), (2), 16.5.1
s 72(2)	8.2.2,3(1),(4)
s 72(3)	8.2.2,3(1)
Part 5	
s 73	16.4.5
s 78	16.4.5
s 79	16.4.5
s 90	4.3.1(2)
s 92	16.4.5
s 93	16.4.5
s 95	8.2
s 98AA(1)	18.8.1
s 98AA(1)(a)(i)	18.8
s 98AA(1)(d)(i)	18.8
s 98AA(1)(e)(i)	18.8
s 98AA(1)(f)(i)	18.8
Part 6	
s 105	4.1
s 116	8.3.1
s 119	16.4.5
s 122	16.4.5
Part 7	18.1,8, 18.8.1, 18.9.1, 18.11
s 123	18.1
s 124	2.1.3(1)
s 127	18.2.1(2)
s 128	3.2.1(3), 4.3.2, 6.3.1, 6.6.4 (2), 14.2.1, 16.4.5, 18.2, 18.2.1(1),(3),(4),2(2), 18.3.1, 18.9
s 128(1)	18.2.1(2),2
s 128(1)(a)	6.6.4(2), 12.10.4
s 128(2)	6.3.1, 18.2.2(2)
s 128(2)(b)	4.6.2, 8.2.1, 18.2.2, 18.11.4
s 128(3)	18.2.1,1(4),2(2), 18.9
s 128(3)(b)	18.2.2, 18.11.4
s 128(4)	18.2.1(4)
s 128A	18.2.1(3)
s 128A(1)	18.2.1(3)
s 128A(2)	18.2.1(3)
s 128A(2)(c)	18.2.1(3)
s 128A(3)	18.2.1(3)
s 128A(4)	18.2.1(3)
s 128A(5)	18.2.1(3),2(2)
s 128A(6)	18.2.1(3)
s 128A(7)	18.2.1(3)
s 128A(8)	18.2.1(3)
s 128B	18.2
s 128B(1)	18.3
s 128B(2)	18.2.1(5),2(2), 18.3
s 128B(3)	18.2.1(5), 18.3
s 129	8.2, 18.3,4
s 129A	18.3, 18.3.1,3
s 129A(1)	18.2.1(3), 18.3.3

s 129A(2)	18.3	s 151(1)	16.5.2(4)
s 129A(3)	18.3	s 152	3.2.1(2), 16.5.2(4),(5)
s 129A(4)	18.3	s 152(1)	16.5.2(4)
s 129A(5)(a)	18.3, 18.3.1	s 153	16.5.2(4),(5),(6)
s 129A(5)(b)	18.3, 18.3.2	s 154	3.2.1(2), 16.5.2(4), 17.5
s 129A(5)(c)	18.3, 18.3.3	s 155	3.2.1(2), 13.3.4(3), 16.5.2
s 130	18.6		(4),(5),(6),(7)
s 130(1)(a)	18.6.1	s 156	6.4.3, 16.5.2(1),(4),(5),(7),
s 130(1)(b)	18.7.1		17.5
s 130(2)	18.6.1	s 157	3.2.1(2), 16.5.2(4),(5),(6)
s 131	18.2.1(3), 18.7, 18.7.1,2,	s 158	1.3.2(1), 3.2, 3.2.1(3),
	18.10.5, 18.13		8.2.5(1), 16.2, 16.2.1,3(6),
s 131(1)	18.2.1(3)		16.4.3
s 131(4)	6.6.4, 18.7.2	s 159	16.2.2
s 131A	18.7, 18.7.1	s 159(1)	16.2.2
s 131A(1)	18.7	s 159(2)	16.2.2
s 131A(1)(a)	18.7.1	s 160	1.4, 7.2
s 131A(1)(c)	18.7.2	s 160(2)	16.3, 16.5.2, 17.5
s 131A(1)(c)(ii)	18.7.1	s 160(2)(a)	11.2.8(1), 16.4.4, 16.5.2
s 131B	18.8, 18.10.5, 18.13		(1),(2),(3)
s 131B(1)(a)(ii)	18.8	s 160(2)(b)	3.2.1(3), 16.5.2(1),(4)
s 131B(1)(a)(iii)	18.8	s 160(2)(c)	16.2.3(4), 16.5.2(5)
s 132	18.7.1, 18.9,10, 18.10.5,	s 160(2)(d)	3.3.3(3), 16.2.3(6), 16.5.2
	18.13		(2)
s 132(2)	18.8,9, 18.9.1	s 160(2)(e)	16.2.3(2), 16.5.2(3)
s 132(3)	18.9	s 160(3)	16.3
s 132(4)	18.7.1, 18.9	s 160(4)	16.1
s 132(6)(a)	18.9	s 162	12.10.4(1), 16.2.3(1)
s 133	18.11.5	s 163	16.2.3(2), 16.5.2(3)
s 134	2.3.1(1), 18.9,10, 18.10.5,	s 164	16.2.3(3), 16.5.2(4)
	18.13	s 165	3.3.4(2), 16.2.3(4)
s 134(1)	18.10.2	s 166	3.3.3(2), 16.2.3(5)
s 134(2)	18.8	s 167	6.2, 16.4, 16.4.1,5
s 134(4)	18.10.3	s 167(a)	11.2.1, 16.4.1,2,3,6
s 134(5)	18.10.4	s 167(b)	11.2.1,1(1),3, 16.4.2,3,4,6,
s 134A	2.3.1(1), 18.7.1, 18.10.1		17.3.6(1)
s 134A(1)	18.10.1,2	s 167(c)	4.8, 8.3.6, 16.2.2, 16.4.3
s 134A(1)(a)	18.10.1	s 167(d)	3.4.3, 16.4.3,4,5,6, 16.5.1
s 134A(1)(b)	18.10.1		(6)
s 134A(2)	18.10.2	s 168	16.4, 16.4.4,5, 17.6
s 135	4.3.2, 18.10.3, 18.11,	s 168(1)	16.4.5
	18.11.4	s 168(1)(a)	6.5.2, 16.4.5
s 136	18.13	s 168(2)	16.4.5
s 137	18.13	s 168(2)(k)	16.4.5
s 138	18.2.1(3), 18.12, 18.12.1,	s 169	13.2.3(1), 16.5, 16.5.1,1
	3, 18.13		(2),(4),(5)
s 138(3)	18.12.2	s 169(1)	16.5.1,1(4)
s 138(3)(b)	18.12.2,4	s 169(2)	16.5.1,1(1),(2)
s 138(5)	18.12.2	s 169(2)(a)	10.3.8, 11.2.7(1), 16.5.1,1
s 138(5)(b)	18.12.4		(3),(5)
s 138(6)	18.12.1,2	s 169(2)(b)	11.2.7(1), 16.5.1,1(4),(5)
s 138(6)(a)	18.12.2	s 169(3)	16.5.1(1)
s 138(6)(d)	18.12.2	s 169(4)	16.5.1(1),(2)
s 142	18.12,13	s 169(5)	16.5.1(2),(7)
s 142A	18.13	s 169(6)	16.4.3,4, 16.5.1(6)
s 143	18.13	s 169(7)	6.6.3
s 144	18.13	s 170	16.5.1(2)
s 144A	18.5.2, 18.13	s 172(1)	16.1
s 144C	18.13	s 173	8.2, 8.4.3
s 145	16.5.2(4),(5)	s 174	8.4, 8.4.3,3(1),(2)
s 147	6.6.4(2)	s 177	16.1
s 150	19.3.1(8)	s 178	10.3.9, 16.1,6, 16.6.1,3,
Part 8	16.1, 16.5.2(5),(7)		17.10.3
s 150A	4.6.1(1), 16.5.2(1),(5),(6)	s 178(1)	16.6.1,2
s 150A(2)	16.5.2(5),(7)	s 178(2)	16.6.1
s 151	3.2.1(2), 8.3.3, 16.5.2(4),	s 178(3)	16.6.2
	(5),(6),(7), 17.5	s 178(4)(b)	16.6.2

741

s 178(8)	6.6.3, 16.6.1	s 219(1)(b)	19.3.2(4),3(2)
s 179	16.2.3(6)	s 219(2)	19.3.2(4), 19.4.3(3)
s 179(a)	8.4	s 219(2)(a)	19.4.3(3)
s 179(b)	6.6.5	s 219(2)(b)	19.4.3(3)
s 180	16.5	s 219(3)	19.3.3(1),(2)
s 180(2)	16.2.3(6)	s 219(4)	19.3.3(1)
s 180(5)	6.6.3	s 223	19.2, 19.3.1, 21.6.2
s 181	16.6.1	s 226	19.4.3(1)
s 182	16.2.2	s 228	20.4.2, 20.5.1(1)
s 183	13.3.4(1), 16.2.2	s 230	19.3.1(5)
s 183(1)	13.3.4(1)	s 231	4.2.7
s 187A	13.3.4(1)	s 233	3.4.2(2), 21.1.5
s 187A(3)	13.3.4(1)	s 233(1)(a)	3.2.2(2), 4.2.7
s 188	3.2.1(3), 12.10.4, 16.2.2, 16.5.2(4), 17.2.4(1), 17.3, 17.3.1,1(1),6,6(2), 17.4,5, 17.6.3	s 234	16.4.5, 19.3.3(1)
		s 235	12.10.4
		s 237	12.7, 12.10.4, 18.3.1, 19.4.2
s 188(1)	17.3, 17.3.6,6(1),(2)	s 238	18.3.1
s 188(2)	17.3, 17.3.1(1),4,5,6,6(2)	s 239	19.4.2
s 189	16.5.2(4), 17.3, 17.3.5, 17.4	s 240	2.2.1,4, 19.3.1(3),(6),3(1), 20.2, 20.3.1(1),(4),2,3,3 (1),(2),(3), 20.4, 20.4.1,2, 20.5.1(1),4, 20.6,8
s 189(1)	12.10.4		
s 189(2)	12.10.4		
s 190	16.5.2(4),(5), 17.5	s 240(1)	20.4,5, 20.5.4, 20.8
s 191	12.10.4, 17.6, 17.6.1,2, 17.7	s 240(1)(a)	20.2, 20.3.1(1), 20.4, 20.4.1, 20.5.1,1(1),(2),2 (2),4
s 191(1)	17.6, 17.6.1,2, 17.7		
s 191(1)(a)	17.6, 17.6.1, 17.7	s 240(1)(b)	20.4, 20.4.1, 20.5.2,2(2)
s 191(1)(c)	17.6, 17.6.1,3, 17.7	s 240(1)(c)	20.4.1, 20.5.3,4
s 191(2)	4.3.1(2), 17.6, 17.6.1	s 240(1)(d)	20.2, 20.3.2, 20.4, 20.4.1, 20.5.4
s 192	17.7		
s 192(1)(a)	17.7	s 240(2)	20.3, 20.3.1(1),3(1),(2), 20.7,8
s 192(1)(c)	17.6.3, 17.7		
s 192(2)	17.7.1,1(1),(2)	s 240(2)(a)	20.3.1,1(1),(4),2,3, 20.8
s 194	17.8	s 240(2)(b)	20.3.1(1),2,3, 20.8
s 194(a)	17.8	s 240(2)(c)	20.3.3(1),(3)
s 194(b)	17.9, 17.9.1	s 240A	6.4.4(4), 6.5.2
s 195	16.5.2(4), 17.10	s 241	16.4.5
s 196	17.2.4(1)	s 242	6.5.2
s 197	5.2, 17.2.4(2)	s 243	19.5.1(3)
s 199	3.2.1(3)	s 246	19.5, 19.5.1(2),(3),2, 20.5.1(1)
s 201	4.7		
s 202A(4)(b)	15.1.3(3)	s 246(1)	19.5, 19.5.2
s 205(1)	4.1	s 246(3)	19.5.1(1)
s 205(1)(b)	1.4, 1.4.1, 4.1,5, 5.2.3(1)	s 246(4)	19.5.1(3)
s 208	16.4.5	s 247	19.5, 20.5.2
s 209	16.4.5	s 249	20.4.2
s 210	8.3.5	s 257	8.3.1, 20.5.4
s 210(2)	8.3.5	s 258(1)	8.2.1
s 210(3)	8.3.5	s 260	19.5.1(1)
Part 10	19.2, 19.3.1(8), 20.5.3	s 261	8.2.5(1)
s 217	19.4.1, 20.3.3(2), 20.5.1 (2),3, 20.8	s 269(1)	4.1
		s 269(2)(a)	4.8
s 218	19.3.1(8),(9),2(1)	s 293	14.2.1(2)
s 218(1)	19.3.1(8),2,2(1),(3)	s 294	3.2.1(3), 16.4.5
s 218(1)(a)	19.3.2(1)	s 295	8.2
s 218(1)(b)	19.3.2(1)	s 302	8.2
s 218(1)(c)	19.3.2(1)	Part 11	
s 218(2)	19.3.2,2(2)	s 306	5.2.3(2)
s 218(4)	19.3.1(9)	s 310	8.3.1,3
s 218(5)	19.3.1(9)	s 310(1)	8.3.1
s 219	19.2, 19.3.1,1(8),2,3(1), (2), 19.4.1, 19.5.1(3), 21.6.2	s 310(3)	8.3.9
		s 311	8.2, 8.4.4
		s 311(1)	18.3
s 219(1)	19.2, 19.3.3,3(1),(2), 19.4.3(3)	s 311(2)	6.4.2, 8.4, 8.4.1
		s 312	6.2
s 219(1)(a)	19.3.2(4)	Part 12	

s 335(1)	18.11.6
s 339	16.1, 17.3.6(2), 17.5, 18.11.6
s 343	6.2
s 361	7.2
Part 13	
s 385(1)(a)	10.3.10
s 386(4)	10.3.10
Crimes Amendment Act 1973	
s 2	12.10.4
Crimes Amendment Act 1980	15.1.2
Crimes Amendment Act (No 3) 1985	
s 2	12.10.4, 18.2.1(5),2(2)
s 7	12.10.4
Crimes Amendment Act (No 3) 1993	
s 2	18.2
Crimes Amendment Act 1994	
s 2	18.2.1(1)
Crimes Amendment Act 1995	
s 2	18.5.2
s 8	18.5.3
Crimes Amendment Act 1997	16.5.2(5)
s 2	4.6.1(1), 16.5.2(5)
Crimes Amendment Act 2005	18.1,2, 18.2.1(3), 18.8
Criminal Attempts Act 1981 (UK)	8.2.3(1), 8.3.5
s 1	8.2.1
s 1(1)	8.2.3(1),5(1)
s 1(2)	8.2.5
Criminal Code 2002 (ACT)	
s 28	10.3
Criminal Code Act 1893	10.3, 15.1.1, 15.2
s 23	10.3
s 23(3)	10.3
s 24	12.1
s 165	16.5.1
s 173	16.2.3(6)
s 186	17.5
Criminal Code (Canada)	
s 2	10.3.2
s 16(3)	10.3.7
s 16(4)	10.3.1
s 17	12.2, 12.10.4,4(1)
s 24(1)	8.2.5,5(2)
s 38(2)	15.2.2(1)
s 43	17.8.1(3)
s 214	17.10.3
s 228	16.2.3(2)
s 265(1)(b)	17.2
s 273.2	8.2.1, 14.2
s 465(1)(c)	8.2.6
Criminal Code (Cth)	
s 7.3	10.3
Criminal Code (NT)	
s 43C	10.3
Criminal Code (Qld)	
s 4	8.2.3(1)
s 27	10.3, 10.3.3
s 31	12.2, 12.10.4(1)
Criminal Code (Tas)	
s 16	10.3, 10.3.3
s 20	12.10.4(1)
Criminal Code (Western Australia)	
s 4	8.2.3(1)
s 27	10.3

s 31	12.2, 12.10.4(1)
s 409(1)	20.3.2
Criminal Damage Act 1971 (UK)	11.1.1(2)
s 1(1)	4.3.1(1)
Criminal Justice Act 1954	10.5
s 44(3)	16.2.1
Criminal Justice Act 1985	1.3.3(1)
s 115(1)(b)	10.5.2
s 115(2)	10.5.2
Part 1, s 4	2.1.2
Part 2, s 19	14.4.1(1)
Part 7	10.1.1
s 113	10.3.3(2), 10.4.1
s 115	10.5
Part 9, s 139	18.5.1
Criminal Justice Amendment Act 1969	
s 2	10.5
s 39G	10.5
Criminal Law Act 1967 (UK)	
s 3	15.1.3(3)
Criminal Law Act 1977 (UK)	8.3.10
s 1(1)	8.3.5
s 5(7)	8.3.7
s 5(8)	8.3.10
s 5(9)	8.3.10
Criminal Law Consolidation Act 1935 (SA)	
s 269C	10.3
Criminal Procedure (Insanity) Act 1964 (UK)	
s 1	10.3.3(2)
s 4(5)	10.1.1
Criminal Procedure (Mentally Impaired Persons) Act 2003	1.3.3(1), 10.1.1
Part 1, s 2	10.1.1
Part 2	
s 7	10.1.2
s 7(1)	10.1.2
s 9	10.1.1
s 14	10.1.1
s 20	10.3, 10.4.3
s 20(1)	10.3.3(4), 10.4.2
s 20(2)	10.4.2
s 20(2)(c)	10.4.2
s 20(4)	10.4, 10.4.1
s 24	10.1.1, 10.5.1,2
s 24(1)	10.5.1
s 24(2)(b)	10.5
s 25	10.1.1, 10.5.1,2
s 25(1)(a)	10.5.3
s 25(1)(b)	10.5, 10.5.3
s 25(1)(d)	10.1.1, 10.5.4
s 26	10.5.3
s 26(1)	10.5.3
s 33	10.5.3
s 33(3)	10.5.2
s 34	10.1.2
s 34(1)(a)	10.1.2
s 34(1)(b)	10.1.2,3
Customs Act 1901 (Aust)	
s 223B(1)(b)	5.2.1

D

Dog Control Act 1996

s 57(2) — 3.2.2(1), 5.2.3(1)

D

Dog Control and Hydatids Act 1982
Part 4, s 56(4) .... 5.2.3(1)
Domestic Violence Act 1995 .... 17.8.1(3)
Part 1, s 2 .... 17.10.3

E

Education Act 1989
Part 11
s 139A 17.8.1
s 139A(1) 17.8.1
s 139A(2) 17.8.1
Education Amendment Act 1990
Part 1, s 28 .... 17.8.1
European Convention of Human Rights and Fundamental Freedoms
art 5(1) 10.3.3
Evidence Act 1908
s 23A 18.5.3
s 23A(3) 18.5.3
s 23A(4) 18.5.3
s 23AA 18.5.1
s 23AA(2)(c) 18.5.1
s 23AA(3) 18.5.1
s 23AB 18.5.4
s 23AB(2) 18.5.4
s 23AC 18.5.2
s 23G 18.5.3
Evidence Act 2006
Part 3, s 88 .... 18.5.1,3
Evidence Amendment Act 1977 .... 18.5.3
Evidence Amendment Act 1985
s 3 .... 18.5.2,4
Evidence Amendment Act (No 2) 1985 .... 18.5
s 2 .... 18.5.3
s 3 .... 18.5.4
Evidence Amendment Act 1989
s 2 .... 18.5.3

F

Fair Trading Act 1986 .... 7.2.5
Part 1, s 13(a) .... 6.4.4(4)
Family Proceedings Act 1980
Part 11, s 189(1) .... 18.2.1(4)
Schedule 1 .... 18.2.1(4)
Films, Videos, and Publications Classification Act 1993 .... 2.1.3(1)
Firearms Act 1968 (UK) 13.2.1
s 5(1) 13.2.1

G

Gaming and Lotteries Act 1977
Part 1, s 7(1) 14.3

H

Health and Safety in Employment Act 1992
Part 2, s 6 .... 2.1.3, 7.2.4
Homicide Act 1957 (UK)
s 1 .... 16.4, 16.4.5
s 2 .... 10.3.8, 15.1.4(5), 16.5
s 3 .... 16.5.1(1),(5),(7)

Homosexual Law Reform Act 1986
s 5 .... 18.13
Human Tissue Act 1964 .... 19.3.1(8)

I

Immigration Act 1964 .... 3.2.2(1)
s 14 .... 13.6.1
s 14(5) 5.1.2, 13.6.4
Indian Penal Code
s 94 .... 12.2, 12.10.4(1)
Infanticide Act 1922 (UK) 16.6
Infanticide Act 1938 (UK) 16.6
Insolvency Act 1986 (UK)
s 360(2)(b) .... 20.5.2(2)
Intellectual Disability (Compulsory Care and Rehabilitation) Act 2003 .... 1.3.3(1), 10.1.1, 10.5.1,3
Part 1, s 9 .... 10.5.3
International Covenant on Civil and Political Rights
art 9(1) 10.3.3
Interpretation Act 1889 (UK)
s 2 .... 7.2
Interpretation Act 1999
Part 2
s 5 .... 2.2.1,3
s 7 .... 2.1.2
Part 5
s 29 .... 7.2.1,4
s 30 .... 7.2.1,4

L

Land Transport Act 1998
Part 2, s 8 .... 4.6.1(1)
Part 3, s 22 .... 8.2.2(1)
Part 5
s 35(1)(b) .... 16.5.2(1)
s 36 .... 16.1, 16.5.2(5)
s 37(1) .... 16.5.2(1),(6)
s 38 .... 5.1, 16.1, 16.5.2(5)
s 39 .... 16.1
Part 6, s 60 .... 8.2.2(1)
Law Reform (Year and a Day Rule) Act 1996 (UK) .... 16.2.3(1)
Local Elections and Polls Act 1976
Part 2, s 55 .... 5.2.3(1),(2), 8.3.5

M

Machinery Act 1950
s 17 .... 5.2.3(2)
s 17(1) 5.1.2
s 27 .... 5.2.3(2)
Marriage Act 1955 .... 18.10.3
Part 3
s 17 .... 18.10.3
s 17(2) 18.10.3
Mental Health Act 1911
s 31 .... 10.5
Mental Health Act 1959 (UK) 18.12
Mental Health (Compulsory Assessment and Treatment) Act 1992 .... 10.1.3, 10.5.1,2,3
s 2 .... 10.1.3

Part 2, s 28(2)	10.5.3	s 1(2)	4.2.2
Part 4			
s 45	10.1.3	**R**	
s 45(3)	10.1.3	Resource Management Act 1991	1.3.2(3)
s 46	10.1.3	Part 3, s 15	1.3.2(3), 14.2.5
s 47(1)	10.1.3	Part 12	
s 47A	10.1.3	s 340	7.2.5
s 48(3)	10.1.3	s 341	14.2.5
s 54(1)	10.4	s 341(2)	14.2.5
Mercantile Law Act 1908		**Restrictive Trade Practices Act**	
Part 1, s 3	19.5.1(3)	**1976 (UK)**	7.2.4
Misuse of Drugs Act 1975	6.4.4(4), 7.2.1, 8.2.2(1),	**Road User Charges Act 1977**	
	14.2.1(1)	Part 1, s 23(2)(a)	5.2.3(2)
s 2	7.2.1		
s 2(2)	3.4.2(2)	**S**	
s 6(1)(c)	8.3.4(1),(6), 16.5.2(1)		
s 6(2A)	8.3.4(1)	Sale of Goods Act 1908	19.3.2(4), 19.5.1(3)
s 7	3.2.2(2), 3.4.2(2)	Part 2	
s 7(1)(a)	3.3.3(2)	s 18	19.3.2(4)
		s 19	19.3.2(4)
N		s 20	19.3.2(4)
Narcotics Act 1965	14.2.1	s 21(1)	19.3.2(4)
New Zealand Bill of Rights Act		s 23	19.5.1(3)
1990	2.1.2,3	s 25	19.5.1(3)
Part 1, s 5	5.1.1(3)	s 26(1)	19.5.1(3)
Part 2		s 26(2)	19.5.1(3)
s 11	16.2.3(4), 16.5.2(7)	s 27(2)	19.5.1(3)
s 23(4)(b)	19.5.3	**Sale of Liquor Act 1962**	
s 25(c)	2.3, 2.3.1(1), 5.1.1(3),	s 208	17.7.1(4)
	5.2.3(2), 19.5.3	s 209	17.7.1(4)
s 25(d)	19.5.3	**Securities Act 1978**	
s 25(i)	9.4	Part 2	
s 26(1)	2.1.2,3	s 58	6.6.2(2)
s 27	14.4.2	s 58(2)	6.6.2(2)
s 27(1)	5.2.3(2)	**Securities Markets Act 1988**	7.2.4
		Sentencing Act 2002	1.3.3(1), 10.1.2
O		Part 1	
Offences Against the Person Act		s 6	2.1.2
1861 (UK)		s 7	1.3.3(1)
s 4	8.4.1,3(2)	s 8	1.3.3(1)
s 18	17.3.4	s 9	1.3.3(1)
s 20	17.2.4(2)	s 10	1.3.3(1)
s 23	3.3.3(2), 4.3.1	s 11	1.3.3(1)
s 28	17.3.4	s 17	1.3.3(1)
s 29	17.3.4	s 24	10.1.2
Offensive Publications Act 1892	5.2.1	s 25	1.3.3(1)
Official Secrets Act 1989 (UK)	13.3.5	s 26	1.3.3(1)
		Part 2	
P		s 39	7.2, 7.2.1, 16.2.1
Parole Act 2002	1.3.3(1), 16.1	s 39(1)	16.2.1
Part 1, s 7	1.3.3(1)	s 102	16.6.2
Penal Code of the Federated		s 102(1)	16.1
Malay States		s 102(2)	16.1
s 94	12.7	s 103	16.1
Penal Institutions Act 1954		s 104	16.1
s 32	5.2.3(2)	s 106	1.2.3, 14.4.1(1)
s 32(1)	5.2.3(2)	s 108	1.2.3
s 32(1)(g)	5.1.2(1), 5.2.3(2)	s 111	1.3.3(1)
Police Offences Act 1927		**Sexual Offences Act 2003**	
s 3(e)	17.7.1(4)	s 15	18.8
Police Offences Amendment Act		**Shop Trading Hours Act 1977**	14.3.1
(No 2) 1952		**Social Security Act 1964**	
s 5	17.8	Part 3, s 127	2.1
Public Bodies Corrupt Practices		**Summary Offences Act 1981**	17.7.1(3)
Act 1889 (UK)		s 2	4.3.2
		s 4	18.3.1

745

s 7	18.3.1
s 10	4.3.2, 14.2.1(1)
s 10A(b)	17.10.3
s 11	14.2, 16.5.2(4)
s 13	17.5
s 23(a)	14.2.1
s 29	2.3.1(1), 14.2.5
s 36	8.3.1
Summary Proceedings Act 1957	9.3, 9.3.1, 9.4.1
Part 1, s 6(2)	8.2,4
Part 2	
s 67(8)	2.3.1(1), 12.11
s 76	6.2
Schedule 1	18.3,9
Summary Proceedings Amendment Act 1961	
s 3	8.4
s 3(1)	8.2
Summary Proceedings Amendment Act 1973	
s 4(2)	8.2

T

Theft Act 1968 (UK)	19.3.2(3)
s 1	19.3.3(1)
s 15	20.3.1(1)
s 16	20.3.1(1)
Trade Descriptions Act 1968 (UK)	7.2.4
Traffic Regulations 1976	

Part 6, reg 52	5.1.2
Transport Act 1962	
Part 4, s 36	14.3.1
Part 5	
s 56	7.2.1
s 63	15.2.2(4)
Trespass Act 1980	14.2.5
s 3	13.3.4(2), 14.2.5
s 3(1)	13.3.4(2), 14.2.5
s 3(2)	13.3.4(2), 13.6.4, 14.2.5
Trial of Lunatics Act 1883 (UK)	
s 2	10.3.3(2)

V

Victims' Rights Act 2002	1.3.3(1)

W

Water and Soil Conservation Act 1967	
s 34(1)(b)	1.3.2(3)
Water Resources Act 1991 (UK)	
s 85(1)	3.3.3(2)
Wild Animal Control Act 1977	
Part 1, s 9	19.3.1(9)
Wildlife Act 1953	
Part 5, s 57(3)	19.3.1(9)
Schedule 5	19.3.1(9)
Wireless Telegraphy Act 1949 (UK)	8.4.1

TABLE OF CASES

Abbreviations

1 Criminal Law: Definition and Application: ch 1
2 Interpretation, Proof, and the Rule of Law: ch 2
3 The Actus Reus: ch 3
4 Mens Rea: ch 4
5 Strict and Absolute Liability: ch 5
6 Secondary Participation: ch 6
7 Vicarious and Corporate Liability: ch 7
8 The Inchoate Offences: ch 8
9 Infancy: ch 9
10 Insanity: ch 10
11 Intoxication: ch 11
12 Compulsion: ch 12
13 Duress of Circumstances, Necessity, and Impossibility: ch 13
14 Mistake: ch 14
15 Self-Defence and Defence of Property: ch 15
16 Culpable Homicide: ch 16
17 Non-fatal Offences of Violence: ch 17
19 Theft and Receiving: ch 19
20 Deception: ch 20
21 The Moral Limits of Criminalisation: ch 21

A

(Children) (Conjoined Twins: Surgical Separation), Re A [2001] Fam 147 (CA) 4.2.4, 13.3.2,5,5(1),(3), 13.5.1,2

A-G v Able [1984] QB 795; [1984] 1 All ER 277 6.4.2,4(1)
A-G v Observer Ltd [1990] 1 AC 107 19.3.1(5)
A-G v Whelan [1934] IR 518 (CCA) 12.3.1, 12.10.1, 13.2
A-G for Ceylon v Perera [1953] AC 200; [1953] 2 WLR 238 (PC) 16 5 1(4)
A-G for Jersey v Holley [2005] UKPC 23; [2005] 3 WLR 29 (PC) 16.5.1(5)
A-G for Northern Ireland v Gallagher [1963] AC 349; [1961] 3 All ER 299 (HL) 3.4.3, 4.9.1(4), 11.2.2
A-G for Northern Ireland's Reference (No 1 of 1975) [1977] AC 105; [1976] 3 WLR 235 (HL) 15.1.4
A-G for the State of South Australia v Brown [1960] AC 432; [1960] 1 All ER 734 (PC) 3.4.1(3), 10.3.9
A-G of Canada v Balliram (2003) 173 CCC (3d) 547 (Ont SC) 10.1.2
A-G of Hong Kong v Tse Hung-Lit [1986] AC 876 3.3.3(2)
A-G's Reference (No 1 of 1975) [1975] QB 773; [1975] 2 All ER 684 (CA) 6.3.1, 6.4.1(5),4(2)
A-G's Reference (No 1 of 1982) [1983] QB 751 20.3.3
A-G's Reference (No 1 of 1992) [1993] 2 All ER 190; [1993] 1 WLR 274 (CA) 18.4, 18.6.2, 18.9.1
A-G's Reference (No 2 of 1992), Re [1994] QB 91; [1993] 4 All ER 683 (CA) 3.4.1(2)
A-G's Reference (No 2 of 1999), Re [2000] QB 796; [2000] 3 All ER 182 (CA) 7.2, 7.2.6(1), 16.5.2(5)

A-G's Reference (No 3 of 1992) [1994] 1 WLR 409; (1994) 98 Cr App R 383 (CA) 18.4.1
A-G's Reference (No 3 of 1994) [1998] AC 245; [1997] 3 All ER 936 (HL) 4.8, 16.2.2, 16.4, 16.4.3,5, 16.5.2(1)
A-G's Reference (No 3 of 1994), Re [1996] QB 581; [1996] 2 All ER 10 4.8
A-G's Reference (No 4 of 1980) [1981] 2 All ER 617; [1981] 1 WLR 705 (CA) 3.3.2(3), 4.9.1(2)
A-G's Reference (No 6 of 1980) [1981] 1 QB 715; [1981] 2 All ER 1057 (CA) 17.2.4(1)
A-G's References (Nos 1 and 2 of 1979) [1980] QB 180; [1979] 3 All ER 143 (CA) 4.2.8
Abbott v R [1977] AC 755; [1976] 3 All ER 140 (PC) 6.2, 12.10.4(1)
Adair v Leigh Hotel Ltd (1984) 6 NZTC 61,853 6.3.1
Adams v Camfoni [1929] 1 KB 95 7.1.2
Adams v R (1994) 12 CRNZ 379; [1995] 1 WLR 52 (PC) 20.5.4
Agnes Gore's Case (1611) 9 Co Rep 81; 77 ER 853 4.8
Ahern v R (1988) 165 CLR 87 8.3.12
AHI Operations Ltd v Dept of Labour [1986] 1 NZLR 645 5.1.2, 5.2.3(2)
Airedale NHS Trust v Bland [1993] AC 789; [1993] 1 All ER 821 (HL) 3.2.1(2),(5), 16.2.2,3(3),(4), 16.5.2(7), 17.2.4
Albert v Lavin [1982] AC 546; [1981] 3 All ER 878 (HL) 14.2.2
Allen v Whitehead [1930] 1 KB 211; [1929] All ER Rep 13 7.1.1
Allied Marine Transport Ltd v Vale do Rio Doce Navegacao SA, The Leonidas [1985] 2 All ER 796 (CA) 3.2.1
Alphacell Ltd v Woodward [1972] AC 824 (HL) 3.3.3(2)
Anderson v Police [1983] NZLR 509 (CA) 19.5.1(3)

747

Table of Cases

Anderton v Ryan [1985] AC 560; [1985] 2 All ER 355	8.2.5,5(3)
Andrews v DPP [1937] AC 576; [1937] 2 All ER 552 (HL)	16.5.2(1),(5)
Angland v Hosken [1935] NZLR 271	6.6.4(1)
Anon (1634) Kel 53; 84 ER 1079	3.3.3(2), 6.3.1
Anon (1871) 7 Mad 35	14.3
Anon ("The Harlot's Case") (1560) Crompton's Justice 24	3.3.3(1)
Arkwright v Newbold (1881) 17 Ch D 301	3.2.1
Arnold v Wood (1996) 89 A Crim R 264	14.2.1
Arrow Shipping Co v Tyne Improvement Commissioners (The Crystal) [1894] AC 508	19.3.2(5)
Arthur (1981) 12 BMLR 1	3.2.1(2)
Arthur v Police 13/12/93, Tipping J, HC Christchurch AP369/93	10.1.2
Arthur Guinness, Son, and Co (Dublin) Ltd v Owners of the Motor Vessel Freshfield (The Lady Gwendolen) [1965] P 294; [1965] 2 All ER 283 (CA)	7.2.4(2)
Ashton v Police [1964] NZLR 429	6.1, 6.4.3
Askey v Golden Wine Co Ltd [1948] 2 All ER 35; (1948) 64 TLR 379	1.2.2
Auckland Area Health Board v A-G [1993] 1 NZLR 235; (1992) 8 CRNZ 634	3.2.1(2), 16.2.2,3(3), 16.5.2(4),(7)
A v UK [1998] Crim LR 892	17.8.1(3)

B

B (1981), Re [1990] 3 All ER 927	3.2.1(2)
B (a minor) v DPP [2000] 2 AC 428; [2000] 1 All ER 833 (HL)	2.1, 4.3.2, 5.1.2(1), 5.2.3 (2), 11.2.3, 18.2.2(2), 20.3.1(4)
B (a Minor) v DPP [2000] 2 WLR 452 (HL)	18.7.1
Bagley (1923) 17 Cr App R 162	19.3.1(6)
Balcom v City of Independence 160 NW 305 (1916)	4.6.2
Banditt v R [2005] HCA 80	4.3.2
Barker v Levinson [1951] 1 KB 342; [1950] 2 All ER 825	7.1.2
Barker v R (1983) 153 CLR 338 (HCA)	2.2.3
Barnett v Chelsea & Kensington Hospital Mgmt Cttee [1969] 1 QB 428; [1968] 1 All ER 1068	3.3.4(1)
Barnfather v London Borough of Islington Education Authority [2003] EWHC (Admin) 418; [2003] 1 WLR 2318	5.2.3(2)
Barratt (1873) LR 2 CCR 81	18.2.1(3)
Barronet, Re (1852) 1 E & B 1; 118 ER 337	17.2.4(1)
Barronet's Case (1852) 22 LJ MC 25	14.4.2
Barton v Armstrong [1976] AC 104	6.4.1(5)
Bay of Plenty Regional Council v Bay Milk Products [1996] 3 NZLR 120	2.3
Bayer v Police [1994] 2 NZLR 48 (CA)	13.3.4(2), 13.6.4, 14.2.5
Beal v Kelley [1951] 2 All ER 763; (1951) 35 Cr App R 128	18.11.3
Beckford v R [1988] AC 130; [1987] 3 All ER 425 (PC)	14.2.2, 15.1, 15.1.3(2),4(4)

Bedder v DPP [1954] 2 All ER 801; [1954] 1 WLR 1119 (HL)	16.5.1(5)
Beecham (1851) 5 Cox 181	19.3.1(6)
Bell v Lever Bros Ltd [1932] AC 161; [1931] All ER Rep 1	3.2.1
Bernard v Russell 164 A 2d 577 (1960)	4.6.2
Berry v Sugar Notch Borough 43 Atl 240 (1899) (Pa)	3.3.2(2)
Beverley's Case (1603) Co Rep 123b; 76 ER 1118	11.1
Bird v Jones (1845) 7 QB 742; 115 ER 668	3.2.1(1)
Bishop v NZ Law Soc [1932] NZLR 452	19.3.1(4)
Bisset v Wilkinson [1927] AC 177 (PC)	20.3.1(1)
Blackburn v Bowering [1994] 3 All ER 380 (CA)	12.12
Blake v DPP [1993] Crim LR 586	15.1.3(3)
Blakey v DPP [1991] RTR 405; [1991] Crim LR 763	6.4.1(5)
Boardman v Phipps [1967] 2 AC 46	19.3.1(5)
Bogdal v Hall [1987] Crim LR 500	20.5.1(1)
Bolduc v R (1967) 63 DLR (2d) 82; [1967] SCR 677 (SCC)	18.2.1(3)
Bolton (Engineering) Co, H L, Ltd v T J Graham & Sons Ltd [1957] 1 QB 159; [1956] 3 All ER 624 (CA)	7.2.4,4(2)
Bonner [1970] 2 All ER 97n	19.3.2(2)
Bonnyman v R (1942) 28 Cr App R 131 (CCA)	16.5.2(4),(5)
Booth v MOT [1988] 2 NZLR 217	14.3.1
Boro v Superior Court 163 Cal App 3d 1224; 210 Cal Rptr 122 (1985)	18.2.1(3)
Boulton (1849) 1 Den 508; 169 ER 349	19.3.1(6)
BP Exploration Co (Libya) Ltd v Hunt (No 2) [1979] 1 WLR 783	20.5.1(1)
Bradshaw v Ewart-James [1983] QB 671; [1983] 1 All ER 12	7.1.1,2
Brambles Holdings Ltd v Carey (1976) 15 SASR 270	7.2.4(3)
Bratty v A-G for Northern Ireland [1963] AC 386; [1961] 3 All ER 523 (HL)	2.3, 3.4.1(1),(2),(3),4, 10.3.1,2,3(2),(4), 11.2.6
Brewer v R [1994] 2 NZLR 229, also reported as *B v R (T216/93)* (1993) 11 CRNZ 419	18.2.1(3), 18.3.3
Britten v Alpogut [1987] VR 929; (1986) 23 A Crim R 254	8.2.5(3)
Broadhurst v R [1964] AC 441; [1964] 1 All ER 111 (PC)	11.2.2
Broom v Police [1994] 1 NZLR 680; (1993) 11 CRNZ 20	19.3.3(2), 19.4.3(1)
Broome v Perkins (1987) 85 Cr App R 321; [1987] Crim LR 271	3.4.1(2)
Brown v Raphael [1958] Ch 636; [1958] 2 All ER 79	20.3.1(1)
Brown v US 256 US 335	4.6.1(2)
Brown and Edney v Police (1984) 1 CRNZ 576	15.2.2(4)
Brown and R, Re (1983) 4 CCC (3d) 571	16.4.3
Buchanans Foundry Ltd v Dept of Labour [1996] 3 NZLR 112	5.1.1(2)
Buckoke v GLC [1971] 1 Ch 655 (CA)	13.3.2
Burnard v Police [1996] 1 NZLR 566	6.4.1(3)

Burns v Bidder [1967] 2 QB 227; [1966] 3 All ER 29   3.4.1(2), 4.9.1(4), 5.1.2, 13.6.2
Burns v HM Advocate (1996) The Juridical Review 416   15.1.3(4)
Burns v Nowell (1880) 5 QBD 444 (CA)   2.1.3, 3.4.2(1), 5.1.2, 14.4.2
Burrell v Harmer [1967] Crim LR 169   17.3.4
Burton v Power [1940] NZLR 305; [1940] GLR 192   17.7.1(4)
Bush v Commonwealth (1880) 78 Ky 268   3.3.3(1)
B v Croydon Health Authority [1995] 1 All ER 683; [1995] 2 WLR 294 (CA)   16.5.2(7)
B v Police (1990) 7 CRNZ 607 (CA), also reported as *Police v B* [1990] 2 NZLR 504; (1990) 5 CRNZ 575; [1991] 2 NZLR 527   6.3.1
B v Police (1991) 7 CRNZ 55, also reported as *Police v Bannin* [1991] 2 NZLR 237   2.3, 3.4.1(2),(3), 4.2.7, 4.3.2, 4.6.2, 5.2.2(2), 17.2, 17.2.2, 17.9, 17.9.1
B v R (T216/93) (1993) 11 CRNZ 419, also reported as *Brewer v R* [1994] 2 NZLR 229   18.2.1(3), 18.3.3

C

C (a minor) v DPP [1996] 1 AC 1; [1995] 2 WLR 383 (HL)   9.3, 9.3.2
Callaghan v R (1952) 87 CLR 115; [1952] ALR 941 (HCA)   16.5.2(5)
Callow v Tillstone (1900) 83 LT 411; 19 Cox 576   6.4.4(4)
Calma v Sesar (1992) 106 FLR 446   19.3.1(8)
Cameron (1983) 7 Crim LJ 168   16.2.3(5)
Campbell v Dominion Breweries Ltd [1994] 3 NZLR 559 (CA)   19.3.2(1)
Campbell v Ward [1955] NZLR 471   8.2.3(1)
Canterbury Central Co-op Dairy Co Ltd v McKenzie [1923] NZLR 426   5.1.1(2)
Cardin Laurant Ltd v Commerce Commission [1990] 3 NZLR 563; (1989) 3 TCLR 470   6.4.1(5),4(4), 7.2.5
Carlill v Carbolic Smoke Ball Co [1893] 1 QB 256; [1891-94] All ER Rep 127   20.3.1(1)
Carver v Pierce (1648) Sty 66; 82 ER 534   1.2.3
Case Stated by DPP (No 1 of 1993) (1993) 66 A Crim R 259   18.2.1(3)
Cassady v Reg Morris Transport Ltd [1975] RTR 470; [1975] Crim LR 398   6.4.3
Chan Wing-Siu v R [1985] AC 168; [1984] 3 All ER 877 (PC)   6.5.4
Chandler v DPP [1964] AC 763   4.2.3
Chandler v R 10/2/93, Greig J, HC Napier AP4/93   17.2.1(1), 17.9.1
Charbonneau v MacRury 153 A 257 (1931)   4.6.2
Chase Manhattan Bank NA v Israel-British Bank (London) Ltd [1981] Ch 105; [1979] 3 All ER 1025   19.3.2(4)
Chaulk v R (1991) 62 CCC (3d) 193; (1990) 2 CR (4th) 1 (SCC)   10.3.7
Cheape v NZ Law Soc [1955] NZLR 63   19.4.1, 20.3.3(2)
Chief Constable of Avon and Somerset Constabulary v Shimmen (1987) 84 Cr App R 7; [1986] Crim LR 800   4.3

Churchill v Walton [1967] 2 AC 224; [1967] 1 All ER 497 (HL)   8.3.5
City Motors (1993) Pty Ltd v Southern Aerial Super Service Pty Ltd (1961) 106 CLR 477; [1962] ALR 184   19.3.2(2)
City of London Corporation v Appleyard [1963] 2 All ER 834   19.3.2(5)
Civil Aviation Dept v MacKenzie [1983] NZLR 78, also reported as *MacKenzie v Civil Aviation Dept* (1983) 1 CRNZ 38 (CA)   5.1, 5.1.1,1(2),(3),2, 5.2.2 (1),(3),3(2), 13.4, 14.2.4
Clarke v Police 18/11/03, William Young J, HC Wellington CRI-2003-485-28   14.2.1
Clouston v Bragg [1949] NZLR 1073   19.3.3(2)
Clunis v Camden and Islington Health Authority [1998] QB 978; [1998] 3 All ER 180 (CA)   1.2.2
Clyne v Bowman (1987) 33 A Crim R 280   8.4
Cole v Turner (1704) 6 Mod Rep 149; 90 ER 958   17.2.2, 18.11.2
Coles, G F, & Co Ltd v Goldsworthy [1958] WAR 183   7.2.4(3)
Collector of Customs v Kozanic (1983) 1 CRNZ 135   8.2.5(2)
Collins v Wilcock [1984] 3 All ER 374; (1984) 79 Cr App R 229   17.2.2,4(4)
Commonwealth v Peaslee (1901) 177 Mass 267; 59 NE 55 (1900)   8.2.3(1)
Commonwealth v Root 403 Pa 571; 170 A 2d 310 (1961)   3.3.3(2)
Connally v General Construction Co (1926) 269 US 385   2.1.3(1)
Cook v Atchison [1968] Crim LR 266   3.4.4
Cooke v Police 7/11/02, HC Christchurch AP118/02   13.2.2,4
Cooper v McKenna, ex p Cooper [1960] Qd R 406   3.4.4
Cooper v MOT [1991] 2 NZLR 693   6.4.3,4(3)
Cope v Sharpe [1912] 1 KB 496   13.3.2
Coppen v Moore (No 2) [1898] 2 QB 306   7.1.2,2(1), 7.2.3
Cordas v Peerless Transportation Co 27 NYS 2d 198   4.6.2
Corker v WA (2004) 146 A Crim R 33   17.7.1(3)
Cowell and Green (1796) 2 East PC 617   19.5.1(3)
Crawford v Haughton Ltd [1972] 1 All ER 535   7.1
Crump (1825) 1 C & P 658; 171 ER 1357   19.4.3(2)
Crutchley (1831) 5 C & P 133   13.2
Cundy v Lindsay (1878) 3 App Cas 459; [1874-1880] All ER Rep 1149   19.3.2(4)
Cunliffe v Goodman [1950] 2 KB 237   4.2.1
Curran v Northern Ireland Co-ownership Housing Assn Ltd [1987] AC 718; [1987] 2 All ER 13   3.2.1
C v Eisenhower [1984] QB 331; [1983] 3 All ER 230   17.3.2

D

Davey v Lee [1967] 2 All ER 423; [1967] 3 WLR 105   8.2.3(1)

Davies v Flackett [1973] RTR 8;
[1972] Crim LR 708 .... 20.4.2
Davies v Leighton (1979) 68 Cr App
R 4; [1978] Crim LR 575 .... 19.3.3(1)
Dawson's Case (1602) 2 Bracton 337 .... 19.5
De Lambert v Ongley [1924] NZLR 430 .... 15.2.2(2)
De Malmanche v McKenzie
[1989] DCR 567 .... 14.3
Dean v Police 13/7/06, John
Hansen J, HC Rotorua
CRI-2006-463-57 .... 19.5.2
Deans v Police 5/3/87,
Holland J, HC Christchurch AP7/87 ...... 15.1.3(5),4, 15.2.2(1)
Dee (1884) 15 Cox CC 579 .... 18.2.1(3)
*Dept of Health v Multichem Laboratories
Ltd* [1987] 1 NZLR 334 .... 4.3, 5.1.1(1)
Dept of Labour v Latailakepa [1982]
1 NZLR 632 (CA) 2.1.2
Dimmock v Hallett (1866) LR 2 Ch
App 21 .... 20.3.1(1)
*Director General of Fair Trading v Pioneer
Concrete (UK)* [1995] 1 AC 456; [1994]
3 WLR 1249 (HL) .... 7.1.2(1), 7.2.4
Diriye v Police 20/07/06,
Baragwanath J, HC Auckland
CRI-2006-404-7 .... 14.4.1(1)
Dixon v Police 13/2/86,
Jeffries J, HC Palmerston North
AP5/86; [1986] NZ Recent Law 233 .... 15.1.4,4(3)
*Dobson v General Accident Fire and Life
Assurance Corp plc* [1990] 1 QB 274;
[1989] 3 All ER 927 .... 19.3.2(3),3(1)
Dobson v North Tyneside HA [1996]
4 All ER 474 .... 19.3.1(8)
Dodwell v Burford (1661) 1 Mod Rep
24; 86 ER 703 .... 17.2.3(1)
Don Jayasena v R [1970] AC 618 .... 2.3
Donaldson v Police [1968] NZLR 32 .... 17.7.1(4)
Dong Wai v Audley [1937] NZLR 290 .... 3.4.2(2), 19.5.1(1)
Donnelly v CIR [1960] NZLR 469 .... 4.7
Donnelly v Jackman [1970] 1 All
ER 987; [1970] 1 WLR 562 .... 17.2.2, 17.7.1(4)
Doodeward v Spence (1908) 6 CLR 406;
[1909] 15 ALR 105 .... 19.3.1(8)
Downey v R [1971] NZLR 97 (CA) 16.4.4,5
DPP v Beard [1920] AC 479;
[1920] All ER Rep 21 (HL) .... 11.1.1(1), 11.2, 11.2.2,7
DPP v Bell [1992] RTR 335;
[1992] Crim LR 176 .... 12.3.1
DPP v Camplin [1978] AC 705; [1978]
2 All ER 168 (HL) .... 4.6.2, 16.5.1(1),(5)
DPP v Cole (1994) 100 NTR 1 .... 18.10.2
DPP v Daley [1980] AC 237; [1979]
2 WLR 239 (PC) .... 3.3.3(3), 16.5.2(2)
DPP v Doot [1973] AC 807; [1973]
1 All ER 940 (HL) 8.3.2
DPP v Gomez [1993] AC 442; [1993]
1 All ER 1 (HL) .... 19.3.3(1),(2)
DPP v H [1997] 1 WLR 1406 .... 10.3.6
DPP v K (a minor) [1990] 1 All ER 331;
(1990) 91 Cr App R 23 .... 17.2.3(1), 18.11.4
DPP v K and B (1997) 1 Cr App R 36 .... 6.6.2
DPP v Kent and Sussex Contractors Ltd
[1944] 1 KB 146; [1944] 1 All ER 119 .... 7.2
DPP v Kilbourne [1973] AC 729;
[1973] 1 All ER 440 (HL) 18.5.4

DPP v Majewski [1977] AC 443; 3.4.3, 11.1, 11.1.1(2),
[1976] 2 All ER 142 (HL) .... 15.1.3(5)
DPP v Morgan [1976] AC 182; [1975] 4.3.2, 5.2.2(3), 14.2, 18.2.2
2 All ER 347 (HL) .... (1),(2)
DPP v Newbury [1977] AC 500; [1976]
2 All ER 365 (HL) .... 16.5.2(1)
DPP v Nieser [1959] 1 QB 254; [1958]
3 All ER 662 .... 19.5.2,3
DPP v Nock [1978] AC 979; [1978]
2 All ER 654 (HL) .... 8.1, 8.3.5,11(2)
DPP v Ottewell [1970] AC 642; [1968]
3 All ER 153 (HL) 2.2.3
DPP v Ray [1974] AC 370; [1973]
3 All ER 131 .... 20.3.1(1),2
DPP v Rogers [1953] 2 All ER 644;
[1953] 1 WLR 1017 .... 18.11.2
DPP v Shannon [1975] AC 717; [1974]
3 WLR 546 .... 8.3.10
DPP v Smith [1961] AC 290, also
reported as *R v Smith* [1960] 3 All 2.3.2, 4.2.1,3, 12.6,
ER 161 (HL) 16.4.2,4,5, 17.3.1
DPP v Stonehouse [1978] AC 55; [1977]
2 All ER 909 (HL) .... 8.2.3(1), 20.5.1(2)
DPP v Turner [1974] AC 357; [1973]
3 All ER 124 .... 20.3.1(1)
DPP v Withers [1975] AC 842; [1974]
3 All ER 984 .... 8.3.1
DPP for Northern Ireland v Lynch
[1975] AC 653; [1975] 1 All ER 913
(HL) 13.3.1,4
DPP for Northern Ireland v Maxwell
[1978] 3 All ER 1140; [1978]
1 WLR 1350 (HL) .... 6.2, 6.4.4(3),(4)
DPP Reference No 1 of 1993; R v K
(1993) 118 ALR 596 (FCA) .... 17.7.1(4)
Drewery v Police (1988) 3 CRNZ 499 ... 6.6.5, 8.2.3(1),(3),(4)
Dronjak v Police [1990] 3 NZLR 75;
(1988) 3 CRNZ 141 .... 19.3.3(1), 20.3.1(1)
Du Cros v Lambourne [1907] 1 KB 40 .... 1.3.2(5), 6.1, 6.4.3
Dugdale v R (1853) 1 E & B 435;
118 ER 499 .... 3.2.2(2)
Durey v Police (1984) 1 CRNZ 392 .... 4.7

E

*East Suffolk Rivers Catchment Board v
Kent* [1941] AC 74; [1940] 4 All
ER 527 .... 3.2.1
Edgington v Fitzmaurice (1885) 29 Ch
D 459 .... 20.3.1(1)
Edwards v Ddin [1976] 3 All ER 705;
[1976] 1 WLR 942 .... 19.3.2(4)
Edwards v R [1973] AC 648; [1973]
1 All ER 152 (PC) .... 16.5.1(7)
Eichholz v Bannister (1864) 17 CB (NS)
708; 144 ER 284 .... 20.3.1(1)
Ellerman's Wilson Line Ltd v Webster
[1952] 1 Lloyd's Rep 179 .... 19.3.2(5)
Elliott v C (a minor) [1983] 2 All
ER 1005; [1983] 1 WLR 939 (DC) .... 4.3.1(2), 4.6.2
Elwes v Brigg Gas Company (1886)
33 Ch D 562 .... 19.3.2(5)
Entick v Carrington (1765) 19 St Tr
1029 .... 19.1
*Environment Agency v Empress Car Co
(Abertillery) Ltd* [1999] 2 AC 22 (HL) .... 3.3.3(1),(2)

Erick v Police 26/2/85,
Heron J, HC Auckland M1734/84;
[1985] NZ Recent Law 227 — 17.8.1(3)

F

F (Mental Patient: Sterilisation), Re
[1990] 2 AC 1 (HL) — 3.2.1(2), 13.3.5(2)
F (Mental Patient: Sterilisation), Re
[1990] 2 AC 1; [1989] 2 WLR 1025
(HL) — 13.3.2,5(2), 13.5.2
Fagan v MPC [1969] 1 QB 439; [1968] — 3.2.1(2), 4.9.1(1), 17.2.3,
3 All ER 442 — 20.3.1(1)
Fain v Commonwealth (1879) 39 Am
Rep 213 — 3.4.1(2)
Fawcett v Star Car Sales Ltd
[1960] NZLR 406 (CA) — 19.3.2(4)
*Federal Commissioner of Taxation v
United Aircraft Corp* (1943)
68 CLR 525 (HCA) — 19.3.1(5)
Felthouse v Bindley (1862) 11 CB (NS)
869; 142 ER 1037 — 3.2.1
Fenton's Case (1830) 1 Lew CC 179;
168 ER 1004 — 16.5.2(1)
Ferens v O'Brien (1883) 11 QBD 21 — 19.3.1(7)
Ferguson v Weaving [1951] 1 KB 814;
[1951] 1 All ER 412 — 6.2
Finau v Dept of Labour [1984] — 3.2.1(2),2(1), 3.4.2(1),
2 NZLR 396 (CA) — 5.1.1(1),2, 13.6.3,4
Firth (1869) LR 1 CCR 172 — 19.3.1(7)
Fisher v Raven [1964] AC 210; [1963]
2 All ER 389 — 20.5.2(2)
Fitzgerald v Kennard (1995)
38 NSWLR 184; (1995) 84 A Crim R
333 (CA) — 18.11.4
Flack v Hunt (1980) 70 Cr App R 51;
[1980] Crim LR 44 — 4.3.1
Fletcher (1859) Bell 63; 169 ER 1168 — 18.2.1(3)
Fletcher (1866) LR 1 CCR 39 — 18.2.1(3)
Flyger v Auckland CC [1979]
1 NZLR 161 — 11.2.8(1)
Fogden v Wade [1945] NZLR 724 — 17.2
Foley v Hill (1848) 2 HLC 28;
9 ER 1002 — 19.3.1(5)
Foster v Warblington Urban Council
[1906] 1 KB 648; [1904-07] All
ER Rep 366 (HL) — 15.2.2(3)
Fowler v Padget (1798) 7 TR 509;
101 ER 1103 — 4.9, 5.1
Fox v Mackreth (1788) 2 Cox Eq Cas
320 — 3.2.1
Francis v Police 1/5/03,
Heath J, HC Auckland AP194/02 — 2.3.1(1)
Frankland and Moore v R
[1987] AC 576; [1987] 2 WLR 1251
(PC) — 2.3.2, 4.2.3
Fraser v Thames Television
[1984] QB 44 — 19.3.1(5)
Frost v Police (1988) 4 CRNZ 539 — 4.3.2

G

G, Re 13/12/96,
Fraser J, HC Dunedin M126/96 — 16.5.2(7)
G F Coles & Co Ltd v Goldsworthy
[1958] WAR 183 — 7.2.4(3)

Galvin v Police 22/4/86,
Bisson J, HC Rotorua M44/85 — 15.2.2(1)
*Gammon (Hong Kong) Ltd v A-G of
Hong Kong* [1985] AC 1; [1984] 2 All
ER 503 (PC) — 5.1.1, 5.2.3(2)
Gautret v Egerton (1867) LR 2 CP 371 — 3.2.1
Generous, The (1818) 2 Dods 322;
165 ER 1501 — 13.3.1, 13.6.2
George v Police (1989) 5 CRNZ 411 — 6.4.3
Gerakiteys v R (1984) 153 CLR 317;
51 ALR 417 — 8.3.4(3),(5)
Gifford v Police [1965] NZLR 484 (CA) — 7.1.1,2
Gillan v Police (2004) 149 A Crim R
354 (SCSA) — 17.6.1
Giorgianni v R (1985) 156 CLR 473;
58 ALR 641 (HCA) — 6.4.4(3),(4)
Gladstone v R (1996) 109 CCC (3d)
193 (SC) — 8.2.3(1)
Goddard v Osborne (1978)
18 SASR 481 — 12.8, 12.10.1
Goldcorp Exchange (in receivership), Re
[1994] 3 NZLR 385; [1995] 1 AC 74
(PC) — 19.3.2(2)
Golden-Brown v Hunt (1972) 19 Fed
LR 438 — 2.1.3
Goldsbro v Walker [1993]
1 NZLR 394; (1992) 5 TCLR 46 (CA) — 6.3.1
Gollins v Gollins [1964] AC 644; [1963]
2 All ER 966 (HL) — 4.2.1
Gomez [1993] AC 442; [1993] 1 All
ER 1 (HL) — 19.3.3(1)
Gordon v Schubert [1956] NZLR 431 — 1.3.2(1), 4.1
Gorris v Scott (1874) LR 9 Ex 125 — 3.3.2(2)
Goundan v Police 28/5/99,
Durie J, HC Wellington AP97/99 — 15.2.2(1)
Grafstein v Holme [1958] 12 DLR (2d)
727 — 19.3.2(5)
Graham [1982] 1 All ER 801; [1982]
1 WLR 294; (1982) 74 Cr App R 235
(CA) — 13.1
Grant v Borg [1982] 2 All ER 257;
[1982] 1 WLR 638 (HL) — 2.1.3
Green v Cross (1910) 103 LT 279 — 16.5.2(4)
Grey v Police 31/10/01, HC Hamilton
AP65/01 — 2.3.1(1)
G v Federal Republic of Germany (1989)
60 DR 256 — 2.1.3

H

*H L Bolton (Engineering) Co Ltd v T J
Graham & Sons Ltd* [1957] 1 QB 159;
[1956] 3 All ER 624 (CA) — 7.2.4,4(2)
Hadba v The Queen (2004) 146 A Crim
R 291 — 11.1
Halaunga v Police 17/12/04,
Winkelman J, HC Auckland
CRI-2003-404-232 — 6.4.4(3)
Halsey v Esso Petroleum Co Ltd [1961]
2 All ER 145; [1961] 1 WLR 683 — 1.2.1
Hamilton v Whitehead (1988)
166 CLR 121; 82 ALR 626 (HCA) — 7.2.5
Hamilton CC v Fairweather
[2002] NZAR 477 (HC) — 5.2.3(2)
Hamps v Darby [1948] 2 KB 311;
[1948] 2 All ER 474 (CA) — 19.3.1(9)
Hardcastle v Bielby [1892] 1 QB 709 — 7.1

751

Harding v Price [1948] 1 KB 695; [1948] 1 All ER 283	3.4.2(3), 5.2.1, 13.6.1(1)
Hardy v Motor Insurers' Bureau [1964] 2 QB 745; [1964] 2 All ER 742 (CA)	4.2.3
Harrild v Director of Proceedings [2003] 3 NZLR 289	16.2.2
Harris v Harrison [1963] Crim LR 497 (PC)	15.2.2(4)
Hart v Bex [1957] Crim LR 622	13.3.3, 21.6.1
Hastings v Police 19/7/01, Priestley J, HC Whangarei AP24/01	15.2.2(2)
Hastings CC v Simons [1984] 2 NZLR 502 (CA)	1.3.2(3), 5.2.3(2)
Haughton v Smith [1975] AC 476; [1973] 3 All ER 1109 (HL)	8.2.3(1),(3)
He Kaw Teh v R (1985) 157 CLR 523; 59 ALJR 620	5.2.1
Hedges v Waitakere CC 21/5/92, Barker J, HC Auckland AP114/92	2.1.2
Heigho, Re 18 Idaho 566; 100 P 1029 (1910)	4.8
Helleman v Collector of Customs [1966] NZLR 705	5.2.3(2)
Henderson v R [1949] 2 DLR 121; (1948) 91 CCC 97 (SCC)	6.6.6(1), 8.2.2,3(1)
Hendy Lennox (Industrial Engines) Ltd v Grahame Puttick Ltd [1984] 2 All ER 152; [1984] 1 WLR 485	19.3.2(4)
Higgins v Police (1984) 1 CRNZ 187	8.2.5(2)
Hilder v Police (1989) 4 CRNZ 232	4.3, 16.5.2(4)
Hill v Baxter [1958] 1 QB 277; [1958] 1 All ER 193	3.4.1(2),3(1),4
Hill v Chief Constable of West Yorkshire [1989] AC 53; [1987] 1 All ER 1173	3.2.1
Hill v Parsons [1972] Ch 305	20.5.1(1)
Hilton's Case (1838) 2 Lew CC 214; 168 ER 1132	3.3.3(2)
HM Advocate v Kidd 1960 SLT 82	3.4.1(3)
Hobart v R (1982) 25 CR (3d) 214 (Ont CA)	6.4.1(1)
Hollings (1940) 4 J Cr L 370	19.3.2(4)
Holmes v DPP [1946] AC 588; [1946] 2 All ER 124 (HL)	16.5.1,1(4)
Hope v Brown [1954] 1 All ER 330; [1954] 1 WLR 250	8.2.3(1)
Horsley v MacLaren (1971) 22 DLR (3d) 545; [1972] SCR 441	3.2.1
Howe [1987] AC 417	13.1
Howe v Teefy (1927) 27 SR (NSW) 301	19.3.2(2)
Hughes v Callaghan [1933] GLR 330	17.2, 17.2.2,4
Hyam v DPP [1975] AC 55; [1974] 2 All ER 41 (HL)	4.2.1,2,3,4, 17.3.6(1)

I

I P H v Chief Constable of South Wales [1987] Crim LR 42	9.3.2
Iannella v French (1968) 119 CLR 84; [1968] ALR 385	5.2.3(2)
Ilich v R (1987) 162 CLR 110	19.3.2(4)
Imperial Glass Ltd v Consolidated Supplies Ltd (1960) 22 DLR (2d) 759	19.3.2(4)
Impress (Worcester) Ltd v Rees [1971] 2 All ER 357	3.3.3(2)
Inglis v Police (1986) 2 CRNZ 463	18.9, 18.11.3
Ingram v Little [1961] 1 QB 31; [1960] 3 All ER 332	19.3.2(4)

Innes v Police 24/4/91 Williamson J, HC Invercargill AP 17/91	6.4.1(2)
Inspector of Factories v Tarbert St Food Centre (1985) Ltd [1989] DCR 471	14.3.1, 14.4.1(1)
Invicta Plastics Ltd v Clare [1976] RTR 251; [1976] Crim LR 131	8.4.1
IRD v Thomas (1989) 13 TRNZ 697	5.2.3(2)
ITW v Police 11/09/03, William Young J, HC Christchurch CRI-2003-409-35	14.2.1

J

J B H and J H (Minors) v O'Connell [1981] Crim LR 632	9.3.2
J M (a minor) v Runeckles (1984) 79 Cr App R 255	9.3
Jackson v A-G [2006] 2 NZLR 534 (HC)	5.1.2(1), 5.2.3(2)
Jaggard v Dickinson [1981] QB 527; [1980] 3 All ER 716	11.1.1(2), 11.2.4
James & Son Ltd v Smee [1955] 1 QB 78; [1954] 3 All ER 273	7.1.2
Jansz v GMB Imports Pty Ltd [1979] VR 581	19.3.2(4)
Jarvis v Williams [1955] 1 All ER 108; [1955] 1 WLR 71	19.3.2(1)
Jefferson v Ministry of Agriculture and Fisheries 12/8/86, Barker J, HC Rotorua M286/85	14.2.1(2)
Jeffries v Great Western Ry Co (1856) 5 El & Bl 802; 119 ER 680	19.3.3(1)
Jemielita v R (1995) 81 A Crim R 409 (WA CCA)	3.3.3(2)
Jenkins v Police (1986) 2 CRNZ 196	15.1.4,4(3)
Jensen v Police 2/5/03, Nicholson J, HC Auckland A39/03	1.3.3(1)
Joe v Police 21/12/95, Goddard J, HC Wellington AP230/95	3.4.3(1), 5.1.1(1),(3)
John Henshell (Quarries) Ltd v Harvey [1965] 2 QB 233; [1965] 1 All ER 725	7.2.4
Johnson v Phillips [1975] 3 All ER 682; [1976] 1 WLR 65; [1975] Crim LR 580	13.3.2
Johnson v R (1976) 136 CLR 619; 11 ALR 23 (HCA)	16.5.1(4),(5)
Johnson v Rea Ltd [1962] 1 QB 373; [1961] 1 WLR 1400	3.2.1
Johnson v Youden [1950] 1 KB 544; [1950] 1 All ER 300	6.4.4(3), 7.2.5, 14.3
Jones v Commonwealth (1955) 281 SW 2d 920	3.3.2(3)
Jones v State 220 Ind 384; 43 NE 2d 1017 (1942)	3.3.3(3)
Jull v Treanor (1896) 14 NZLR 513	7.1.2

K

Kaitamaki v R (1984) 1 CRNZ 211; [1985] AC 147 (PC), also reported as *R v Kaitamaki* [1984] 1 NZLR 385	3.2.1(2),(3), 4.9.1(1), 6.2, 8.3.2, 18.2.1(2)
Kamara v DPP [1974] AC 104; [1973] 2 All ER 1242 (HL)	8.3, 8.3.1,2,5
Kannangara Aratchige Dharmasena v R [1951] AC 1	8.3.10

Kapi v MOT (1991) 8 CRNZ 49 (CA)	12.3, 12.10.4, 13.2.2,3(2), (3), 13.3.4(2), 13.6.4, 14.2.3,5
Kapi v MOT [1992] 1 NZLR 227; (1991) 7 CRNZ 481	11.2.4, 13.2.2
Kay v Butterworth (1945) 61 TLR 452	3.4.1(2), 4.9.1(4)
Keates v Earl of Cadogan (1851) 10 CB 591; 138 ER 234	3.2.1
Keech v Pratt [1994] 1 NZLR 65, also reported as *Police v Pratt* (1993) 10 CRNZ 659	3.4.3(1), 5.1.1(1)
Keene v Carter (1994) 12 WAR 20	19.3.2(5)
Keith v Worcester St RR 82 NE 680 (1907)	4.6.2
Kelly v R [1923] VLR 704 (SC Vic)	3.2.1(2)
Kelt v Police 21/2/03, Durie J, HC Napier, AP57/2002	13.2.4
Kennedy v R [2005] EWCA Crim 685	3.3.3(2)
Kennison v Daire (1985) 38 SASR 404	20.4.2
Kidd v Reeves [1972] VR 563	5.2.1
Kilbride v Lake [1962] NZLR 590	3.4.2(1), 5.1.2
King v Police 5/8/87, Quilliam J, HC Dunedin AP11/87	15.1.3(5),4
King's Norton Metal Co Ltd v Edridge Merrett & Co Ltd (1897) 14 TLR 98	19.3.2(4)
Knuller (Publishing, Printing and Promotions) Ltd v DPP [1973] AC 435; [1972] 3 WLR 143 (HL)	2.1.2
Kohn (1979) 69 Cr App R 395	19.3.1(3)
Kokkinakis v Greece (1994) 17 EHRR 397	2.1.3, 2.2
Koury v The Queen (1964) 43 DLR (2d) 637; [1964] SCR 212	8.3.8
Kovalev v Police 22/5/00, Randerson J, HC Auckland, A40/00	17.2.3(1)
Kumar v Immigration Dept [1978] 2 NZLR 553 (CA)	14.3

L

Lac Minerals Ltd v Corona Resources Ltd (1989) 61 DLR 14	19.1
Laing v Police 28/3/00, Gendall J, HC Wellington AP19/00	10.1.2
Lang v Lang [1955] AC 402; [1954] 3 All ER 571	4.2.2
Larkin v Brown (1906) 8 GLR 654	19.3.2(2)
Larkins v Police [1987] 2 NZLR 282; (1987) 3 CRNZ 49	6.2, 6.4.1(1)
Laskey, Jaggard and Brown v UK [1997] 24 EHRR 39	17.2.4(3)
Le Lievre v Gould [1893] 1 QB 491 (CA)	1.3.2(5)
Leakey v Quirke [1918] NZLR 550	19.4.3
Lee Chun-Chuen v R [1963] AC 220; [1963] 1 All ER 73 (PC)	16.5.1(1),(4)
Lennard's Carrying Co Ltd v Asiatic Petroleum Co Ltd [1915] AC 705; [1914-15] All ER Rep 280 (HL)	7.2, 7.2.4(1)
Levis (City) v Tetreault; Levis (City) v 2629-4470 Quebec Inc (2006) 207 CCC (3d) 1	14.3.1, 14.4.1
Lewin v Bland [1985] RTR 171	7.2.4(2)
Lewis v Averay [1972] 1 QB 198; [1971] 3 All ER 907	19.3.2(4)
Lietzke (Installations) Pty Ltd v EMJ Morgan Pty Ltd (1973) 5 SASR 88	3.2.1

Lim Chin Aik v R [1963] AC 160; [1963] 1 All ER 223 (PC)	2.1.3, 3.4.2(3), 5.2.1, 14.4.2
Linework Ltd v Department of Labour [2001] 2 NZLR 639 (CA)	7.2.4,5
Linnet v CMP [1946] KB 290; [1946] 1 All ER 380	7.1.1
Lloyd [1985] QB 829	19.3.1(5)
London and Globe Finance Corp, Re [1903] 1 Ch 728	20.3.3(1)
Long v R [1995] 2 NZLR 691; (1995) 13 CRNZ 124	16.5.2(5)
Low v Blease [1975] Crim LR 513	19.3.1(7)
Luc Thiet Thuan v R [1997] AC 131; [1996] 2 All ER 1033 (PC)	16.5.1(5)
Lynch v DPP for Northern Ireland [1975] AC 653; [1975] 1 All ER 913 (HL)	6.4.4(1), 12.1, 12.3.1, 12.6.1, 12.10.1,4(1)

M

McAlpine Snowline Ltd v Wethey (1986) 2 NZCPR 388	20.3.1(1)
McComiskey v McDermott [1974] IR 75	4.6.2
McCone v Police [1971] NZLR 105 (CA)	3.4.1(2), 5.1.2
McCrone v Riding [1938] 1 All ER 157	4.6.3
McGhee v R (1995) 183 CLR 82; 69 ALJR 650 (HCA)	16.5.1
McHale v Watson (1966) 115 CLR 199; [1966] ALR 513	4.6.2
Machinery Movers Ltd v Auckland Regional Council [1994] 1 NZLR 492; (1993) 2 NZRMA 661	7.2.5
McKay v Police [1997] 3 NZLR 199	15.1.3(2)
MacKenzie v Civil Aviation Dept (1983) 1 CRNZ 38 (CA), also reported as *Civil Aviation Dept v MacKenzie* [1983] NZLR 78	5.1, 5.1.1,1(2),(3),2, 5.2.2 (1),(3),3(2), 13.4, 14.2.4
MacKenzie v Hawkins [1975] 1 NZLR 165	5.2.2(2),3(2), 17.10
Mackley v Police (1994) 11 CRNZ 497	14.2.1
McKnight v NZ Biogas Industries Ltd [1994] 2 NZLR 664 (CA)	5.2.3(2), 14.2.5
McLaren Transport Ltd v MOT [1986] 2 NZLR 81	5.2.3(2)
McLorie v Oxford [1982] QB 1290; [1982] 3 WLR 423	15.2
McNicholl v Police (1990) 6 CRNZ 603	19.3.3(2)
MaCrae v Buller District Council 12/12/05, Chisholm J, HC Greymouth CRI-2005-418-1	14.4.1(1)
Maddy's Case 1 Vent 158; 2 Keb 829; 86 ER 108	16.5.1
Madison v State 234 Ind 517; 130 NE 2d 35 (1955)	3.3.3(2)
Maitland Valley Conservation Authority v Cranbrook Swine Inc (2003), 225 DLR (4th) 255 (Ont CA)	14.4.1
Makoare v R 20/10/99, CA469/99	11.2.7(1)
Mancini v DPP [1942] AC 1; [1941] 3 All ER 272 (HL)	5.1.1(3), 16.5.1(5)
Marac Life Assurance Ltd v CIR [1986] 1 NZLR 694 (CA)	2.2.2
Margate Pier Co v Hannam (1819) 3 B & Ald 266; 106 ER 661	5.1

Marguson v Grant (1921) 57 DLR 710 (CA)	15.2.2(2)
Marshall v Curry [1933] 3 DLR 260; (1933) 60 CCC 136	13.3.5(2)
Martin v Marsh [1955] Crim LR 781	19.3.2(4)
Martin v State of Alabama (1944) 17 So (2d) 427	3.2.2(1)
Martin (Anthony) [2002] 2 WLR 1; [2002] 1 CAR 27; [2002] Crim LR 136	12.6.2
Martyn v Police [1967] NZLR 396	6.4.1(4)
Masciantonio v R (1995) 183 CLR 58; 129 ALR 575 (HCA)	16.5.1(4),(5)
Maxwell v HM Advocate 1980 SLT 241	8.3.11(2)
Mayer v Marchant (1973) 5 SASR 567	5.2.1
Meade's and Belt's Case (1823) 1 Lew CC 184; 168 ER 1006	17.3.1(1)
Megavitamin Laboratories (NZ) Ltd v Commerce Commission (1995) 6 TCLR 231; 5 NZBLC 103,834	6.4.4(4)
Melrose v R 26/3/03, HC Auckland, T022282	15.1.4
Meridian Global Funds Management Asia Ltd v Securities Commission [1994] 2 NZLR 291 (CA)	7.2.4(1)
Meridian Global Funds Management Asia Ltd v Securities Commission [1995] 3 NZLR 7; [1995] 2 AC 500 (PC)	7.2.4,4(1)
Meyers v R (1997) 71 ALJR 1488	16.4.2,6
Millar v MOT [1986] 1 NZLR 660; (1986) 2 CRNZ 216 (CA)	2.2.3, 2.3, 4.3.2, 4.5.1, 5.1.1,1(2),2(1), 5.2.1,2(1), (2),(3),(4),(5),3(1),(2), 6.4.4(3), 14.2.1,1(1),4, 14.3.1, 18.2.2(2)
Milne v Police (1990) 6 CRNZ 636	17.2.2
Mitchell v Police (1989) 5 CRNZ 190	17.2.2(1)
Moffatt v Kazana [1969] 2 QB 152; [1968] 3 All ER 271	19.3.2(4),(5)
Moriarty v Brooks (1834) 6 C & P 684; 172 ER 1419	17.3.2
Morley v Police [1996] 1 NZLR 551	16.5.2(4)
Morris v Beardmore [1981] AC 446; [1980] 2 All ER 753 (HL)	15.2
Morris v Wellington City Corp [1969] NZLR 1038	7.2.4
Moses v Winder [1980] Crim LR 232	4.9.1(4)
MOT v Barnett (1986) 3 DCR 382	6.4.1(5)
MOT v Beregi [1992] DCR 261	4.9.1(4)
MOT v Coastal Carriers Ltd [1990] DCR 529	5.2.3(1)
MOT v Crawford [1988] 1 NZLR 762; (1988) 3 CRNZ 163	11.2.5
MOT v Strong [1987] 2 NZLR 295	3.4.3(1), 10.3.6, 11.2.5
MOT v Wilke [1992] DCR 104	14.3.1
Mousell Brothers v London and North-Western Railway Co [1917] 2 KB 836	7.1
Moynes v Coopper [1956] 1 QB 439; [1956] 1 All ER 450	19.3.2(4)
MPC v Caldwell [1982] AC 341, also reported as R v Caldwell [1981] 1 All ER 961 (HL)	1.3.2(2), 2.2.2, 4.3.1(1), 18.2.2(2), 18.11.4
MPC v Charles [1977] AC 177; [1976] 3 All ER 112	20.3.1(1), 20.4
Mulcahy v R (1868) LR 3 HL 306	8.3.3,5(1)
Murdoch v British Israel World Federation (NZ) Inc [1942] NZLR 600 (CA)	10.3.5,7
Murphy v Gregory [1959] NZLR 868	15.2.2(4), 19.4.1,2,3(1)

Murphy v Weir [1968] NZLR 657	7.1.1
Murray v McMurchy [1949] 2 DLR 442	13.3.5(2)
Murray v Ongoongo [1985] BCL 1843	5.1.2
Murray v R (1962) Tas SR 170	16.5.2(1)
MV Yorke Motors v Edwards [1982] 1 All ER 1024; [1982] 1 WLR 444 (HL)	13.6.3
M'Growther's Case (1746) Fost 13	12.6.1, 12.10.4
M'Naghten's Case (1843) 10 Cl & Fin 200; 8 ER 718; [1843-60] All ER Rep 229 (HL)	2.3.1(2), 10.2.2, 10.3.7

N

National Coal Board v Gamble [1959] 1 QB 11; [1958] 3 All ER 203	6.1, 6.4.4(1)
Navvabi [1986] 3 All ER 102	19.3.1(3)
Neal v Gribble [1978] RTR 409; (1978) 68 Cr App R 9	19.4.3(1)
Neiman v Police [1967] NZLR 304	17.7.1(4)
Nelson v R [1987] WAR 57	20.3.2
Nichols v Hall (1873) LR 8 CP 322	13.6.1(1)
Nicholson v Dept of Social Welfare [1999] 3 NZLR 50 (CA)	2.1, 3.2.1(2)
Niven v MOT (1988) 4 CRNZ 16 (HC)	2.3.1(1)
Nordik Industries Ltd v Regional Controller of Inland Revenue [1976] 1 NZLR 194	7.2.4,4(3)
Northern Ireland v Lynch [1975] AC 653; [1975] 1 All ER 913 (HL)	1.4.1
NZ Maori Council v A-G [1987] 1 NZLR 641 (CA)	2.2.2
NZ Motor Bodies Ltd v Emslie [1985] 2 NZLR 569	20.3.1(1)

O

Oakey v Jackson [1914] 1 KB 216	16.5.2(4)
Oakley-Moore v Robinson [1982] RTR 74	13.6.1
Oldcastle's case (1491) 1 Hale PC 50; 1 East PC 70	13.2
Osland v R (1998) 197 CLR 316; 159 ALR 170 (HCA)	6.3, 15.1.4(5)
Overseas Tankship (UK) Ltd v Miller Steamship Co Pty [1967] 1 AC 617; [1966] 2 All ER 709 (PC)	1.2.1
Overseas Tankship (UK) Ltd v Morts Dock & Engineering Co Ltd (The Wagon Mound) [1961] AC 388; [1961] 1 All ER 404 (PC)	1.2.1
Owen v Residual Health Management Unit [2000] 3 NZLR 475 (CA)	17.3.1(1)
Oxford v Moss (1979) 68 Cr App R 183	19.3.1(5)
O'Connor v Killian (1985) 15 A Crim R 353	8.2.3(1)
O'Neill v MOT [1985] 2 NZLR 513	5.1.1(1), 11.2.8(1)
O'Neill v Police 22/11/93, CA392/93	13.3.4(2), 14.2.5
O'Sullivan v Fisher [1954] SASR 33	3.2.2(1), 3.4.1(1),2(1)

P

Packett v R (1937) 58 CLR 190	16.5.1(4)
Pallante v Stadiums Pty Ltd (No 1) [1976] VR 331	17.2.4(4)

Palmer v R [1971] AC 814; [1971] 1 All ER 1077 (PC)	15.1.4(1),5
Palmer-Brown v Hohaia (1984) 1 CRNZ 306 (CA), also reported as *Palmer-Brown v Police* [1985] 1 NZLR 365	3.2.2(1)
Palmer-Brown v Police [1985] 1 NZLR 365, also reported as *Palmer-Brown v Hohaia* (1984) 1 CRNZ 306 (CA)	3.2.2(1)
Papachristou v City of Jacksonville (1972) 405 US 156; 31 L Ed 2d 110	2.1.3, 3.2.2(1)
Papadimitropoulos v R (1958) 98 CLR 249; [1958] ALR 21 (HCA)	18.2.1(3)
Park v Lawton & another [1911] 1 KB 588	5.1.2
Parker v British Airways Board [1982] QB 1004	19.3.2(5)
Parker v R [1964] AC 1369; [1964] 2 All ER 641 (PC)	16.5.1(4)
Paxhaven Holdings Ltd v A-G [1974] 2 NZLR 185	15.2.2(3)
Pearson's Case (1835) 2 Lew CC 144; 168 ER 1108	11.1, 11.2.8
Peek v Gurney (1873) LR 6 HL 377; [1861-73] All ER Rep 116	3.2.1
People v Beardsley 113 NW 1128 (1907)	3.2.1(2)
People v Campbell 124 Mich App 333; 335 NW 2d 27 (1983)	3.3.3(2)
People v Decina 2 NY 2d 133 (1956)	4.9.1(4)
People v Elder 100 Mich 515; 59 NW 237 (1894)	3.3.3(2)
People v Lewis 124 Cal 551; 57 P 470 (1899)	3.3.3(2)
Pepper (Inspector of Taxes) v Hart [1993] AC 593; [1993] 1 All ER 42 (HL)	2.2.2
Perka v R (1984) 14 CCC (3d) 385 (SCC), also reported as *R v Perka* [1984] 2 SCR 232	12.3.1, 13.2.2, 13.3.3
Pharmaceutical Soc v London Provincial Supply Assn Ltd (1880) 5 App Cas 857	7.2
Phillips v R [1969] 2 AC 130; [1969] 2 WLR 581 (PC)	16.5.1(4),(5)
Pickering v Ministry of Agriculture 4/3/98, Hammond J, HC Hamilton AP5/97	5.2.3(2)
Pilgram v Dean [1974] 2 All ER 751; [1974] 1 WLR 601	3.4.2(1)
Police v Anthoni [1997] DCR 1034	13.2.2
Police v B [1990] 2 NZLR 504; (1990) 5 CRNZ 575; [1991] 2 NZLR 527, also reported as *B v Police* (1990) 7 CRNZ 607 (CA)	6.3.1
Police v B [1994] DCR 581	18.11.3
Police v Bannin [1991] 2 NZLR 237, also reported as *B v Police* (1991) 7 CRNZ 55	2.3, 3.4.1(2),(3), 4.2.7, 4.3.2, 4.6.2, 5.2.2(2), 17.2, 17.2.2, 17.9, 17.9.1
Police v Barwell 6/7/06, John Hansen J, HC Christchurch CRI-2006-409-000077	19.4.1
Police v Chappell [1974] 1 NZLR 225	4.6.1(3),3
Police v Creedon [1976] 1 NZLR 571 (CA)	5.1.1(2), 5.2.2(2),(3),3(2)
Police v Cunard [1975] 1 NZLR 511	4.7
Police v Emirali [1976] 2 NZLR 476 (CA)	3.2.2(2), 3.4.2(2), 19.5.1(1)
Police v Greaves [1964] NZLR 295 (CA)	17.2.1
Police v Jay [1974] 2 NZLR 204	8.2.5(2)
Police v Kawiti [2000] 1 NZLR 117; (1999) 17 CRNZ 88	13.2.3(1),(3),4
Police v L [1993] DCR 617	17.10, 17.10.1,2
Police v L 11/12/01, Doogue J, HC Masterton M21/2001	10.5.1
Police v L (a young person) [1990] DCR 172	4.3.1
Police v Matsubara [2004] DCR 385	12.3,6
Police v Minhinnick [1978] NZLJ 199	19.4.1
Police v Moodley [1974] 1 NZLR 644	19.3.3(2)
Police v O (1980) DCR 151	17.2.4(1)
Police v O'Neill [1993] 3 NZLR 712	13.3.4(2), 14.2.5
Police v Pratt (1993) 10 CRNZ 659, also reported as *Keech v Pratt* [1994] 1 NZLR 65	3.4.3(1), 5.1.1(1)
Police v Purser Asphalts & Contractors Ltd [1990] 1 NZLR 693, also reported as *Purser Asphalts and Contractors Ltd v Police* (1988) 3 CRNZ 540	7.2, 7.2.1
Police v R [1997] DCR 431	10.1.1
Police v Raponi (1989) 5 CRNZ 291	17.2.2
Police v Shadbolt [1976] 2 NZLR 409	4.7
Police v Starkey [1989] 2 NZLR 373; (1989) 4 CRNZ 400	5.1.1(2), 5.2.2(2),3(1),(2), 8.3.5
Police v Sutherland 26/6/06, Clifford J, HC Wellington CRI-2006-435-1	4.3.1(2)
Police v T [2004] DCR 311	10.5.4
Police v Taggart [1973] 1 NZLR 732	14.3
Police v Travers [1996] DCR 671	10.1.2
Police v Wylie [1976] 2 NZLR 167 (CA)	4.2.8, 8.2.3(3),(4)
Police v XYZ [1994] DCR 401	10.5.4
Porter v Honey [1988] 3 All ER 1045; [1988] 1 WLR 1420 (HL)	3.2.2(1)
Postermobile plc v Brent London Borough Council 8/12/97 (QBD)	14.4.1
Pou v Police 6/7/00, Laurenson J, HC Whangarei AP22/000	6.4.1(1)
Poulterer's Case (1610) 9 Co Rep 55b; 77 ER 813	8.3.2
Pounder v Police [1971] NZLR 1080	17.7.1(4)
Primrose v Police (1985) 1 CRNZ 621	16.5.2(4), 17.5
Proctor v Police 5/4/84, Vautier J, HC Auckland M1333/83	10.3.1
Proudman v Dayman (1941) 67 CLR 536; [1944] ALR 64	5.1.1
Purdie v Maxwell [1960] NZLR 599	3.4.1(1)
Purdy (1946) 10 JCL 182	13.2
Purdy v Collector of Customs 25/10/78, White J, SC Wellington M459/78	8.3.9
Purser Asphalts and Contractors Ltd v Police (1988) 3 CRNZ 540, also reported as *Police v Purser Asphalts & Contractors Ltd* [1990] 1 NZLR 693	7.2, 7.2.1
P v Police 14/9/06, Baragwanath J, HC Auckland CRI-2006-404-203.	10.1.2

Q

Quinn v Hill [1957] ALR 1127;
[1957] VR 439 .... 3.2.1

R

R (TP) v West London Youth Court
[2006] Mental Health LR 40 .... 10.3.2
Rabey v R (1980) 15 CR (3d) 225;
[1980] 2 SCR 513 (SCC) .... 10.3.3(3)
Race Relations Board v Applin [1973]
1 QB 815; [1973] 2 All ER 1190 .... 8.4.1
Racine v CNR [1923] 2 DLR 572 .... 3.2.1
Rank Film Distributors Ltd v Video
Information Centre [1982] AC 380 .... 19.3.1(5)
Rao v Police (1988) 3 CRNZ 697 .... 19.3.2(3), 20.3.1(1)
Regina v Dalaney and Budge (1982)
69 CCC (2d) 276 (Al QB) .... 8.2.5(1)
Remillard v R (1921) 59 DLR 340;
62 SCR 21 (SCC) 6.6.3
Reniger v Fogassa (1550) 1 Plowd 1;
75 ER 1 .... 13.3.2,3
Rhone (The) v Peter AB Widener (The)
(1993) 101 DLR (4th) 188; [1993]
1 SCR 497 (SCC) .... 7.2.4(3)
Richardson v Police 15/11/88,
McGechan J, HC Palmerston North
AP258/88 .... 19.5.3
Rini v Police 12/11/98,
Fisher J, HC Whangarei T981696 .... 10.5.2,4
Roberts v Wyatt (1810) 2 Taunt 268;
127 ER 1080 .... 19.3.2(2)
Robinson v California 370 US 660; 8 L
Ed 2d 758 (1962) .... 3.2.2(1)
Rooke v Auckland CC [1980]
1 NZLR 680 .... 11.2.8(1)
Rose v Loo Kee [1927] GLR 403 .... 3.2.2(2), 3.4.2(2)
Rowe (1859) Bell 93; 169 ER 1180 .... 19.3.2(5)
Rowlands v Police 28/7/04,
MacKenzie J, HC Napier
CRI-2003-441-29 .... 19.3.2(5)
Rubie v Faulkner [1940] 1 KB 571;
[1940] 1 All ER 285 .... 6.4.3
Russell v Smith [1958] 1 QB 27; [1957]
2 All ER 796 .... 19.3.2(4)
Ryan v R (1967) 121 CLR 205; [1967]
ALR 577 .... 3.4.3, 8.2.3(2)
R v Abdul-Hussain [1999] Crim
LR 570 (CA) .... 12.7, 13.2.1,3(2)
R v Abdullah [1982] Crim LR 122 .... 20.3.1(1)
R v Abebe [2000] 1 VR 429 .... 16.5.1(5)
R v Abraham (1993) 10 CRNZ 446
(CA) .... 16.5.2(5)
R v Abramovitch (1912) 7 Cr App
R 145 .... 10.4
R v AC Hatrick Chemical Pty Ltd
(1995) 152 A Crim R 384 .... 16.2.1
R v Accused (CA92/92) [1993]
1 NZLR 553 (CA) 18.5.3
R v Acott [1997] 1 All ER 706; [1997]
1 WLR 306 (HL) .... 16.5.1(1)
R v Adams [1957] Crim LR 365 .... 16.2.3(3)
R v Adomako [1995] 1 AC 171; [1994]
3 All ER 79 (HL) .... 4.6.2, 16.5.2(5)
R v Ahearne (1852) 6 Cox CC 6 .... 8.3.10

R v Ahluwalia [1992] 4 All ER 889;
(1993) 96 Cr App R 133 (CA) .... 16.5.1(3)
R v Alexander (1913) 9 Cr App R 139
(CCA) .... 16.5.1(5)
R v Allan [1965] 1 QB 130; [1963]
2 All ER 897 (CCA) .... 6.4.1(2),3
R v Allsop (1976) 64 Cr App R 29
(CA) 20.5.4
R v Allwood (1975) 18 A Crim R 120 .... 16.5.1(7)
R v Ancio [1984] 1 SCR 225; (1984)
10 CCC (3d) 385 (SCC) 8.2.1
R v Anderson [1965] NZLR 29 (CA) .... 16.5.1(1),(2),(3),(5)
R v Anderson (1984) 80 Cr App R 64;
[1984] Crim LR 550 (CA) 6.6.5
R v Anderson [1986] AC 27; [1985]
2 All ER 961 (HL) .... 8.3.5(1),(2)
R v Anderson [2000] 2 Qd R 393 .... 20.4
R v Anderson [2005] 1 NZLR 774;
(2004) 20 CRNZ 1086 (CA) .... 16.5.2(4)
R v Anthony [1965] 2 QB 189 .... 8.3.4(3)
R v Antonelli and Barberi (1905) 70 JP
4 .... 8.4.3
R v Aramah (1982) 4 Crim App R (S)
407 .... 21.7.1
R v Aramakutu [1991] 3 NZLR 429;
(1991) 7 CRNZ 114 (CA) .... 16.4.1,4, 16.5.2(1)
R v Ardalan [1972] 2 All ER 257;
[1972] 1 WLR 463 .... 8.3.4(4)
R v Arnold (1724) 16 St Tr 695 .... 10.2
R v Arrowsmith [1975] QB 678; [1975]
1 All ER 463 (CA) 14.4.2
R v Ashman (1858) 1 F & F 88;
175 ER 638 .... 17.3.1
R v Aston [1989] 2 NZLR 166; (1989)
4 CRNZ 241 (CA) .... 10.3.8, 16.5.1(5)
R v Atkinson (1869) 11 Cox CC 330 .... 6.4.1(2)
R v Atofia [1997] DCR 1053 .... 12.8,9, 13.2.4
R v Atofia 15/12/97, CA453/97;
CA455/97 .... 12.8
R v Austin (1905) 24 NZLR 983 (CA) .... 8.2.5(2)
R v Aves [1950] 2 All ER 330; (1950)
34 Cr App R 159 .... 19.5.3
R v B (1993) 11 CRNZ 64 .... 17.2.4(1), 18.12.1
R v B 21/4/05, CA4/05 .... 10.4.2, 10.5.1
R v B (No 5) 7/9/01, William
Young J, HC Christchurch, T19/01 .... 8.2.3(1)
R v Bailey [1924] QWN 38 .... 19.4.3(1)
R v Bailey [1983] 2 All ER 503; [1983]
1 WLR 760 (CA) .... 3.4.3,4, 11.1.1(2)
R v Baillie-Smith (1977) 64 Cr App
R 76; [1977] Crim LR 676 (CA) .... 18.6.2(1)
R v Bainbridge [1960] 1 QB 129; [1959]
3 All ER 200 (CCA) .... 6.4.4(4)
R v Baird (1985) 3 NSWLR 331;
32 A Crim R 67 .... 4.5
R v Baker (1909) 28 NZLR 536 (CA) .... 6.4.1(4),4(4), 6.6.5
R v Baker [1929] 1 DLR 785; (1929)
51 CCC 71; [1929] 2 DLR 282;
[1929] SCR 354 (SCC) .... 16.5.2(5)
R v Baker [1994] Crim LR 444 (CA) .... 6.6.6(2)
R v Baker & Ward (1999) 2 Cr App
R 335 (CA) .... 12.6, 12.10.3(1)
R v Ball [1911] AC 47 (HL) .... 18.6.2(3)
R v Ball [1989] Crim LR 730 (CA) .... 16.5.2(1)
R v Bamber (1843) 5 QB 279;
114 ER 1254 .... 3.4.2, 5.1.2, 13.6.1
R v Banks (1873) 12 Cox CC 393 .... 8.4.1(1)

R v Baptiste and Baptiste (1980)
61 CCC (2d) 438 17.8.1(3)
R v Barbouttis (1995) 37 NSWLR 256;
82 A Crim R 432 (NSW CA) 8.3.11(3)
R v Barker [1924] NZLR 865 (CA) 8.2.2(1),3(1)
R v Barnard (1837) 7 C & P 784;
173 ER 342 20.3.1(1)
R v Barnes 16/6/05, CA69/05 10.4.2
R v Barrett & Barrett (1981) 72 Cr App
R 212; [1980] Crim LR 641 (CA) 14.3.1
R v Barton [1977] 1 NZLR 295 (CA) 11.2.7(1), 16.5.1(4),(5)
R v Bassey (1931) 22 Cr App R 160 20.5.3
R v Bateman (1925) 19 Cr App R 8;
[1925] All ER Rep 45 (CCA) 4.6.1(1),4, 16.5.2(4),(5)
R v Batt [1987] 1 NZLR 760 (CA) 10.1.2
R v Battams (1979) 1 Cr App R (S) 15 19.5
R v Baxter (1975) 27 CCC (2d) 96
(Ont CA) 15.2.2(1)
R v Bayford 9/12/04, Ronald
Young J, HC Palmerston North
CRI-2004-254-97 10.5.1,2
R v Becerra (1975) 62 Cr App R 212
(CA) 6.6.6(1),(2)
R v Beckett (1836) 1 M & Rob 526;
174 ER 181 17.3.2
R v Beecham (1851) 5 Cox CC 181 19.4.3(3)
R v Belfon [1976] 3 All ER 46; [1976]
1 WLR 741 (CA) 4.2, 4.2.3, 17.3.6(1)
R v Bell [1984] 3 All ER 842;
[1984] Crim LR 685 3.4.1(2)
R v Bellingham Coll Lun 636 10.2.1
R v Bellis (1911) 6 Cr App R 283
(CCA) 18.10.5
R v Bembridge (1783) 22 St Tr 1;
99 ER 679 20.3.3(3)
R v Benge (1865) 4 F & F 504;
176 ER 665 3.3.2(3),3(2)
R v Bennett (1978) 68 Cr App R 168;
[1979] Crim LR 454 (CA) 8.3.5,11(2)
R v Bennett [1995] Crim LR 877 11.2.1
R v Bennitt [1961] NZLR 452 19.3.1(4), 20.4
R v Bernhard [1938] 2 KB 264; [1938]
2 All ER 140 (CA) 15.2.2(4)
R v Bernier (1998) 124 CCC (3d) 383 17.9
R v Berry (1876) 1 QBD 447 10.1.2
R v Beuth [1937] NZLR 282 (CA) 6.2
R v Bhachu (1977) 65 Cr App R 261 19.3.2(4)
R v Bhaskaran 19/8/98, CA185/98 19.4.2
R v Billinghurst [1978] Crim LR 553 17.2.4(1)
R v Bills [1981] 1 NZLR 760 (CA) 18.5.3
R v Bingley (1821) Russ & Ry 446;
168 ER 890 6.3
R v Bird [1985] 2 All ER 513; [1985]
1 WLR 816 (CA) 15.1.4(3)
R v Bishirgian [1936] 1 All ER 586 20.3.1(1)
R v Blaue [1975] 3 All ER 446; [1975] 3.3.2(3),3(3),4(2), 16.2.3,3
1 WLR 1411 (CA) (4)
R v Bloodworth (1913) 9 Cr App R 80
(CCA) 18.6.2(3)
R v Boardman 29/10/03, CA173/03 11.2.1(1), 15.1.6
R v Bone [1968] 2 All ER 644; [1968]
1 WLR 983 (CA) 12.11
R v Bonora (1994) 35 NSWLR 74
(CCA) 4.3.2, 18.11.4
R v Boreman [2000] 1 All ER 307 (CA) 16.4.6
R v Born with a Tooth (1992)
76 CCC (3d) 169 (CA) 14.2.5, 15.2.2,2(3)

R v Bourne (1952) 36 Cr App R 125
(CCA) 6.6.2(1),(2)
R v Bournewood Community and Mental
Health NHS Trust [1998] 3 All
ER 289 (HL) 13.3.2
R v Bournewood Mental Health Trust, ex
p L [1999] 1 AC 485 (HL) 13.5.2
R v Bowen [1996] 4 All ER 837; (1996)
2 Cr App R 157 (CA) 13.2.3(1), 18.2.2(2)
R v Bowern (1915) 34 NZLR 696 (CA) 6.3.1, 6.6.1
R v Boyd 24/6/03, CA89/03 1.3.3(1)
R v Boyea [1992] 156 JPR 505 (CA) 17.2.4(2)
R v Bradish [1990] 1 QB 981; (1990)
90 Cr App R 271 (CA) 13.2.1
R v Brain (1834) 6 C & P 349;
172 ER 1272 16.2.2
R v Bransgrove [1954] NZLR 1076
(CA) 10.3.10
R v Breau (1959) 125 CCC 84;
32 CR 13 5.1.2
R v Brewer 26/5/94, CA516/93 18.2.1(3), 18.3.3
R v Bridger [2003] 1 NZLR 636;
(2002) 19 CRNZ 676 (CA) 15.1.2,3(1)
R v Briggs [1977] 1 All ER 475 (CA) 4.3.1
R v Briggs 29/11/01, CA244/01 6.4.1(2)
R v Bristow [1960] SASR 210 16.2.3(4)
R v Broad [1997] Crim LR 666 (CA) 8.3.6
R v Brooks [1945] NZLR 584 (CA) 9.2,3, 10.4
R v Brosnan [1951] NZLR 1030 (CA) 18.5.3
R v Brough 27/2/97, CA507/96 3.2.1(2), 6.4.3
R v Brown (1776) 1 Leach 148;
168 ER 177 16.5.1(6)
R v Brown (1841) Car & M 314;
174 ER 522 3.4.2
R v Brown [1948] NZLR 928 (CA) 19.3.2(2)
R v Brown [1968] SASR 467 10.3.5
R v Brown (1975) 10 SASR 139 18.2.2(1)
R v Brown 20/5/87,
Smellie J, HC Auckland, T51/87 15.1.4(1)
R v Brown [1994] 1 AC 212; [1993] 6.6.4(1), 17.2.2,4(1),(2),
2 All ER 75 (HL) 21.1.3
R v Brown and Stratton [1998] Crim
LR 485 (CA) 11.2.1
R v Bruzas [1972] Crim LR 367 16.5.1,1(4)
R v Bryan (1857) Dears & B 265;
169 ER 1002 20.3.1(1)
R v Bryce [2004] EWCA Crim 1231;
[2004] 2 Cr App R 35 6.4.1(5),4(3)
R v Bubb (1850) 4 Cox CC 455 3.2.1(2), 16.5.2(4)
R v Budd [1962] Crim LR 49 3.4.4
R v Burdee (1916) 86 LJKB 871 (CCA) 16.5.2(4),(5)
R v Burgess [1991] 2 QB 92; [1991]
2 All ER 769 (CA) 10.3.3(2),(4)
R v Burke [1987] Crim LR 480, also 3.4.3, 6.6.2(1),3, 12.9,
reported as R v Howe [1987] AC 417; 12.10.4(1), 13.2.1,3(1),
[1987] 1 All ER 771 14.2.3
R v Burke [1991] 1 AC 135; [1990]
2 WLR 1313 (HL) 4.2.1
R v Burley [2000] Crim LR 843 12.12
R v Burnett (1815) 4 M & S 271;
105 ER 835 16.5.2(4)
R v Burney [1958] NZLR 745 (CA) 4.6.1(1),4, 16.5.2(4),(5),
(7)
R v Burney [1989] 1 NZLR 732; (1989)
4 CRNZ 133 16.5.2(6)
R v Burr [1969] NZLR 736 (CA) 2.3, 3.4.1(2),(3), 10.3.1,
16.5

R v Bursey (1957) 118 CCC 219; 26 CR 167 (Ont CA)	18.2.1(3)
R v Burstow [1996] Crim LR 331	17.3.5
R v Busby 26/9/01, CA211/01	15.1.3(3)
R v Butt (1884) 15 Cox CC 564	6.3.1
R v Button [1900] 2 QB 597	20.4
R v Byrne [1960] 2 QB 396; [1960] 3 All ER 1 (CA)	10.3.8
R v Cabbage (1815) Russ & Ry 292; 168 ER 809	19.4.3(3)
R v Cairns (1999) 2 Cr App R 137 (CA)	13.2.1
R v Caldwell [1981] 1 All ER 961 (HL), also reported as MPC v Caldwell [1982] AC 341	1.3.2(2), 2.2.2, 4.3.1(1), 18.2.2(2), 18.11.4
R v Calhaem [1985] QB 808; [1985] 2 All ER 266 (CA)	6.4.2
R v Cambridge Health Authority, ex p B [1995] 2 All ER 129; [1995] 1 WLR 898 (CA)	16.5.2(7)
R v Campbell (1977) 38 CCC (2d) 6 (Ont CA)	16.5.1
R v Campbell (1991) 93 Cr App R 350 (CA)	8.2.2(2),3(1),(4)
R v Campbell (1997) 15 CRNZ 138 (CA)	16.5.1(4)
R v Campbell [1997] 1 NZLR 16; (1996) 14 CRNZ 117 (CA)	16.5.1(2),(4),(5),(6)
R v Campbell (2000) Ont Sup CJ LEXIS 1180 16	10.3.3(4)
R v Camtais Barbeau (1996) 110 CCC (3d) 69 (Que CA)	4.5.1
R v Cancoil Thermal Corp & Parkinson (1986) 27 CCC (3d) 295; 52 CR (3d) 188	5.1.2, 14.4.1
R v Cara [2005] 1 NZLR 823; (2004) 21 CRNZ 283	20.5.1(1)
R v Cargill [1995] 3 NZLR 263; (1995) 13 CRNZ 291 (CA)	19.4.2
R v Carker (No 2) [1967] SCR 114; (1968) 2 CRNS 16 (SCC)	12.7
R v Carmichael (1940) 27 Cr App R 183 (CCA)	18.6.2(1)
R v Carpenter (1911) 76 JP 158; 22 Cox CC 618	20.5.1(1)
R v Carr (No 2) [1995] 2 NZLR 339; (1995) 13 CRNZ 1	17.5
R v Carr & Wilson (1882) 10 QBD 76	19.5.1(3)
R v Carroll (1835) 7 C & P 145; 173 ER 64	11.1
R v Carter [1959] ALR 335; [1959] VR 105	3.4.1(2)
R v Cash [1985] QB 801; [1985] 2 All ER 128 (CA)	19.5.3
R v Castles [1969] QWN 36	16.2.2
R v Catholique (1980) 104 DLR (3d) 161	2.1.3
R v Cato [1976] 1 All ER 260; [1976] 1 WLR 110 (CA)	3.3.2(1), 16.5.2(1)
R v Cattermole 15/9/05, CA94/05	20.5.3
R v Cave 1/08/05, CA393/04	14.3.1
R v Cavendish [1961] 2 All ER 856; [1961] 1 WLR 1083	19.5.1(1)
R v Chan-Fook [1994] 2 All ER 552; [1994] 99 Cr App R 147 (CA)	17.3.1(1),5
R v Chandra (2005) 198 CCC (3d) 80	11.2.1(2)

R v Charles [1977] AC 177; (1976) 68 Cr App R 334	20.4
R v Charles (2005) 197 CCC (3d) 42 (Sas CA)	14.4.1
R v Charlson [1955] 1 All ER 859; [1955] 1 WLR 317	3.4.1(2), 10.3.3(2)
R v Chartrand (1994) 116 DLR (4th) 207 (SCC)	4.2.4,7
R v Chattaway (1922) 17 Cr App R 7	3.2.1(2), 16.5.2(4)
R v Chaulk [1990] 3 SCR 1303; (1991) 62 CCC (3d) 193 (SCC)	10.3.1,7
R v Cheatham [2000] NSWCCA 282	10.3.4(1)
R v Cheshire [1991] 3 All ER 670; [1991] 1 WLR 844 (CA)	3.3.2(1),3(2),4(3), 16.2.3 (5)
R v Chignell [1991] 2 NZLR 257, also reported as R v Chignell and Walker (1990) 6 CRNZ 103 (CA)	4.9.1(1),(2), 6.4.4(4), 16.4.6
R v Chignell and Walker (1990) 6 CRNZ 103 (CA), also reported as R v Chignell [1991] 2 NZLR 257	4.9.1(1),(2), 6.4.4(4), 16.4.6
R v Chow (1987) 11 NSWLR 561; 30 A Crim R 103 (CA)	8.3.4(1)
R v Christiansen 24/10/01, CA196/01	14.2.1(1), 17.7.1(2),(3)
R v Church [1966] 1 QB 59; [1965] 2 All ER 72 (CCA)	4.9.1(2), 16.5.2(1)
R v Church of Scientology of Toronto (1997) 116 CCC (3d) 1; 33 OR (3d) 65 (Ont CA)	7.2, 7.2.4(1)
R v Churchill [1967] 2 AC 224 (HL)	6.4.4(3)
R v Cinous (2002) 162 CCC (3d) 129 (SCC)	12.11
R v Cinous [2002] 2 SCR 3	11.2.1(2)
R v City of Sault Ste Marie (1978) 85 DLR (3d) 161; [1978] 2 SCR 1299 (SCC)	5.1.1,1(3),2, 5.2.3(2), 7.1.2 (1)
R v Clarence (1888) 22 QBD 23; [1886-90] All ER Rep 133	17.2.3, 18.2.1(3)
R v Claridge (1987) 3 CRNZ 337 (CA)	17.6.2
R v Clark [1951] OR 791; (1951) 101 CCC 166	8.3.8
R v Clark (1983) 1 CRNZ 132 (CA)	10.3.10, 10.4, 10.4.2
R v Clark and Bagg (1842) 6 JP 508	16.2.3(5)
R v Clarke (1985) 80 Cr App R 344; [1985] Crim LR 209	4.1
R v Clarke [1992] 1 NZLR 147 (CA)	11.2.4, 18.2.2(2)
R v Clarke 16/12/93, CA417/93	19.5.3
R v Clarkson [1971] 3 All ER 344; [1971] 1 WLR 1402 (Can CMAC)	1.3.2(5), 6.4.1(2),2,3
R v Clarkson [1987] VR 962; (1987) 25 A Crim R 277	20.4
R v Clucas [1949] 2 KB 226; [1949] 2 All ER 40	20.4
R v Cocker 23/9/04, France J, HC Wellington CRI-2004-085-1865	17.2.4(2)
R v Codd 5/5/06, Simon France J, HC Auckland CRI-2005-004-12997	10.1.2
R v Codere (1916) 12 Cr App R 21	10.3.4(2)
R v Codina (1999) 132 CCC (3d) 338 (Ont CA)	8.2.2(1)
R v Cogan; R v Leak [1976] QB 217; [1975] 2 All ER 1059 (CA)	6.3.1, 6.6.2(2)
R v Colburne (1991) 66 CCC (3d) 235 (Que CA)	8.2.1
R v Cole [1994] Crim LR 582	13.2.1
R v Collett T122/90	16.5.2(4)

R v Collins (1864) 9 Cox CC 497	8.2.5,5(3)	R v Cugullere [1961] 2 All ER 343;	
R v Collister (1955) 39 Cr App R 100 (CCA)	18.3.1	[1961] 1 WLR 858 (CCA)	3.2.2(2)
R v Conde (1867) 10 Cox CC 547	3.2.1(2), 16.5.2(4)	R v Cunningham [1957] 2 QB 396; [1957] 2 All ER 412 (CCA)	4.3.1, 18.11.4
R v Coney (1882) 8 QBD 534	1.3.2(5), 6.4.1(2),3, 17.2.4 (1)	R v Cunningham [1982] AC 566; [1981] 2 All ER 863 (HL)	16.4, 16.4.2
R v Conrad [1974] 2 NZLR 626 (CA)	20.3.1(4)	R v Curley (1909) 2 Cr App R 109 (CCA)	16.5.2(2)
R v Conway [1988] 3 All ER 1025; [1988] 3 WLR 1238 (CA)	13.2.1,2, 13.5.1	R v Curr [1968] 2 QB 944; [1967] 1 All ER 478 (CA)	8.4.2
R v Conway [1989] QB 290 (CA)	12.10.2	R v Currie [1969] NZLR 193 (CA)	6.5.4
R v Cook [1986] 2 NZLR 93 (CA)	18.2.1(3)	R v Curtis (1885) 15 Cox CC 746	3.2.1(2)
R v Coombridge [1976] 2 NZLR 381 (CA)	19.4.1, 20.3.3(2)	R v Curtis [1988] 1 NZLR 734 (CA)	6.5, 6.5.4
R v Cooper (1877) 2 QBD 510	20.3.1(1)	R v Custance (2005) 194 CCC (3d) 225	14.3.1
R v Cooper (1978) 40 CCC (2d) 145	10.3.2	R v Cuthbertson [1980] 2 All ER 401	8.3.3
R v Cooper 29/6/88, Williamson J, HC Christchurch T16/88	6.3.1	R v D [1987] 2 NZLR 272 (CA)	18.2.1(4),(5)
		R v D (1991) 7 CRNZ 446 (CA), also reported as R v Duncan [1992] 1 NZLR 528	18.5.3
R v Cooper [1993] 1 SCR 146; (1993) 18 CR (4th) 1 (SCC)	16.4.2,6	R v D [2004] EWCA Crim 1391; [2004] All ER (D) 11	4.2.4
R v Cooper [1994] Crim LR 531	4.9.1(1)	R v D (C) (2000) 145 CCC (3d) 290	18.2.1(2)
R v Cooper (2005) 190 CCC (3d) 342 (BCCA)	11.2.1(2)	R v Dabelstein [1966] Qd R 411 (CCA)	16.5.2(4)
R v Cooper and Schaub [1994] Crim LR 531	3.2.1(2)	R v Dadson (1850) 3 Car & Kir 148; 4 Cox CC 358	4.4
R v Cope (1921) 16 Cr App R 77	8.4.1,1(1)	R v Dalby [1982] 1 All ER 916; [1982] 1 WLR 425 (CA)	3.3.3(2), 16.5.2(1)
R v Corbett [1996] Crim LR 594 (CA)	3.3.3(3)	R v Dale (1836) 7 C & P 352; 173 ER 157	20.4
R v Cornejo (2003) 181 CCC (3d) 206	14.2, 14.2.1(3)	R v Dalloway (1847) 2 Cox CC 273	3.3.1,4(1)
R v Cornwall (1730) 2 Str 881; 93 ER 914	6.3	R v Daly (2005) 198 CCC (3d) 185 (BCCA)	14.3
R v Coslet (1782) 1 Leach 236; 168 ER 220	19.3.3(1)	R v Daniels [1986] 2 NZLR 106, also reported as R v Daniels and Tihi (1986) 2 CRNZ 164 (CA)	18.2.1(3), 18.5.4
R v Cosnett (1901) 20 Cox CC 6; 65 JP 472	20.5.2(2)		
R v Cottle [1958] NZLR 999 (CA)	2.3.1(2), 3.4.3,4, 10.3.1,3, 3(2), 11.2.4	R v Daniels and Tihi (1986) 2 CRNZ 164 (CA), also reported as R v Daniels [1986] 2 NZLR 106	18.2.1(3), 18.5.4
R v Court [1989] AC 28, [1988] 2 All ER 221 (HL)	4.4, 18.11, 18.11.2,3,5	R v Dant (1865) Le & Ca 567; 169 ER 1517	16.5.2(5)
R v Cox [1898] 1 QB 179; [1895-99] All ER Rep 1285	18.10.5	R v Darwish [2006] 1 NZLR 688	8.3.9
R v Cox [1923] NZLR 596 (CA)	19.3.2(2)	R v Davies [1975] QB 691; [1975] 1 All ER 890 (CA)	16.5.1(6)
R v Cox [1990] 2 NZLR 275; (1990) 5 CRNZ 653 (CA)	3.2.2(2), 3.4.2(2), 5.2.3(2)	R v Davies [1982] 4 Cr App R (S) 302	19.3.2(4)
R v Cox (1995) 2 Cr App R 513; [1995] Crim LR 741 (CA)	16.5.1(1)	R v Davis (1881) 14 Cox CC 563	10.3.3(2)
R v Cox 7/11/96, CA213/96	4.6.2, 18.2.2(2)	R v Davis [1980] 1 NZLR 257 (CA)	15.1.9
R v Crabbe (1985) 156 CLR 464; (1985) 16 A Crim R 19	4.3.2	R v Davis and Wagstaffe (1883) 15 Cox CC 174; 6 C & P 177; 172 ER 1196	16.2.3(5)
R v Creamer [1966] 1 QB 72	4.4.4(4)	R v Dawe (1911) 30 NZLR 673 (CA)	16.5.2(4),(5)
R v Creighton (1993) 105 DLR (4th) 632; [1993] 3 SCR 3; (1993) 83 CCC (3d) 346 (SCC)	4.6.2, 16.5.2(1),(5)	R v Dawson [1978] VR 536	12.6
		R v Dawson (1985) 81 Cr App R 150; [1985] Crim LR 383 (CA)	15.2.2(2), 16.2.3(3), 16.5.2 (1)
R v Croft [1944] 1 KB 295; [1944] 2 All ER 483 (CCA)	6.6.6(2), 16.2.3(6)	R v Dawson and Wenlock [1960] 1 All ER 558; [1960] 1 WLR 163	8.3.2
R v Crooks [1981] 2 NZLR 53 (CA)	4.5, 4.5.1, 6.4.4(3), 18.3, 19.5.2, 20.3.1(1)	R v De Mey 17/12/04, CA169/04	15.1.3(2)
		R v Deana (1909) 2 Cr App R 75	15.1.3(2)
R v Crosby (2005) 192 CCC (3d) 23 (PEISC)	17.2.4(1)	R v Dear [1996] Crim LR 595 (CA)	3.3.3(2),(3)
R v Crossan [1943] NZLR 454	17.6.2	R v Dee & Hennessy (1875) 3 NZCA 58	19.5.1(3)
R v Crossan 7/7/98, Chisholm J, HC Invercargill T980970	6.4.3	R v Deighton (1900) 18 NZLR 891	10.2.2, 10.3.1,9
		R v Deller (1952) 36 Cr App R 184 (CCA)	1.4, 2.1.1, 20.3.1(2)
R v Cruse (1838) 8 C & P 541; 173 ER 610	11.1.1(1)	R v Delon (1992) 29 NSWLR 29	3.4.2(2)
R v Cuerrier [1998] 127 CCC (3d) 1 (SCC)	17.3.1(1)	R v Demirian [1989] VR 97; (1988) 33 A Crim R 441	3.3.3(1), 6.3, 6.6.1
		R v Dery (2005) 197 CCC (3d) 534 (QCA)	8.2.6

R v DeSousa [1992] 2 SCR 944; (1992) 76 CCC (3d) 124 (SCC)	12.3.1
R v Deutsch (1986) 30 DLR (4th) 435; [1986] 2 SCR 2 (SCC)	8.2.3(1)
R v Devine (1982) 8 A Crim R 45	17.3.2
R v Dhaliwal [2006] EWCA Crim 1139; [2006] All ER (D) 236	16.2.3(6)
R v Diamond (1920) 84 JP 211	8.4.1(1),3
R v Dias [2002] 2 Cr App R 5	3.3.3(2), 16.5.2(1)
R v Dica [2004] EWCA Crim 1103	17.2.4(2), 17.3.1(1),3
R v Dickie [1984] 1 WLR 1031; 3 All ER 173 (CA)	10.4.1
R v Dimozantos (1992) 56 A Crim R 345	8.4.1(1),3
R v Dionne (1987) 38 CCC (3d) 171 (CA)	8.4.1
R v Dixon [1961] 3 All ER 460	10.4
R v Dixon [1979] 1 NZLR 641 (CA)	4.9.1(2), 16.4.2
R v Doherty (1887) 16 Cox CC 306	11.1, 11.1.1, 11.2.1(2)
R v Doherty (2000) 146 CCC (3d) 336	15.1.3(2)
R v Dolan (1855) Dears 436; 169 ER 794	19.5.1(3)
R v Donaldson (1997) 14 CRNZ 537 (CA)	17.3.1(1)
R v Donnelly [1970] NZLR 980 (CA)	8.2.5(1), 8.3.11(2)
R v Donovan [1934] 2 KB 498 (CCA)	15.2.2(2), 17.2.4,4(1),(2), 17.3.5
R v Donovan [1997] QB 47	17.2.4(3)
R v Dougherty [1966] NZLR 890 (CA)	16.5.1(5)
R v Doughty (1986) 83 Cr App R 319; [1986] Crim LR 625 (CA)	16.5.1(6)
R v Douglas (1972) 8 CCC (2d) 275	20.3.1(1)
R v DPP ex p Kibelene [1999] 3 WLR 972 (HL)	2.3.1(2)
R v Drake (1902) 22 NZLR 478 (CA)	17.8.1(2)
R v Droste (1984) 6 DLR (4th) 607; [1984] 1 SCR 208 (SCC)	16.4.3
R v Drummond (1993) 9 CRNZ 228	8.2.3(1), 8.3.4(3)
R v Dubeau (1993) 80 CCC (3d) 54	14.4.1
R v Dubois (1959) 32 CR 187	3.3.3(2)
R v Dudley and Stephens (1884) 14 QBD 273; [1881-85] All ER Rep 61	13.3.2,5(3)
R v Duffill (1843) 1 Cox CC 49	17.3.2
R v Duffy [1949] 1 All ER 932 (CCA)	16.5.1(2),(3),(5),(6)
R v Dunbar [1963] NZLR 253 (CA)	19.3.3(2)
R v Duncan [1992] 1 NZLR 528, also reported as R v D (1991) 7 CRNZ 446 (CA)	18.5.3
R v Dunn [1973] 2 NZLR 481 (CA)	18.11.3
R v Dupperon (1984) 16 CCC (3d) 453; 43 CR (3d) 70	17.8.1(3)
R v Dupuis [1974] RL 379 (Que Prov Ct)	15.2.2(2)
R v Duru [1973] 3 All ER 715; (1973) 58 Cr App R 151	19.4.3(3)
R v Duval [1995] 3 NZLR 202; (1995) 13 CRNZ 215	10.1.1
R v Duvivier (1981) 5 A Crim R 89	16.5.1
R v Dyson (1823) Russ & Ry 523; 168 ER 930	16.2.3(6)
R v Dyson [1908] 2 KB 454; [1908-10] All ER Rep 736 (CA)	16.2.3(1),(3)
R v E (1998) 16 CRNZ 506	18.5.3
R v Eagleton (1855) Dears CC 515; [1843-60] All ER Rep 363	8.2.3(1)
R v Edgar (2000) 142 CCC (3d) 401	15.1.5
R v Edmonds (1991) 7 CRNZ 510	16.5.2(5)

R v Edwards (1877) 13 Cox CC 384	19.3.1(8),2(5)
R v Edwards [1975] QB 27; [1974] 3 WLR 285 (CA)	12.11
R v Egan (1897) 23 VLR 159; [1897] ALR 37	3.4.3
R v Ellerm [1997] 1 NZLR 200 (CA)	19.3.2(5)
R v Elliot [1981] 1 NZLR 295 (CA)	10.1.2
R v Ellis (1986) 84 Cr App R 235; [1987] Crim LR 44 (CA)	4.8, 14.1
R v Emery (1993) 14 Cr App R (S) 394	3.2.1(2)
R v Emery [1996] DCR 374	6.5.2
R v Emmett [1999] EWCA Crim 1710	17.2.4(2)
R v English (1872) 12 Cox CC 171	20.4
R v English (1993) 68 A Crim R 96	8.2.5(2)
R v Enright [1961] VR 663	16.5.1(5)
R v Erutoe [1990] 2 NZLR 28; (1990) 5 CRNZ 538 (CA)	16.5.1(3)
R v Esau (1997) 116 CCC (3d) 289	14.2, 18.2.1(3)
R v Evans (1987) 30 A Crim R 262	8.2.1, 18.4.1
R v Evans and Gardiner (No 2) [1976] VR 523	3.3.3(2), 16.2.3(4),(5)
R v Everson 9/11/95, CA194/95	18.2.1(2)
R v Ewanchuk (1999) 131 CCC (3d) 481 (SCC)	14.3, 18.2.1(3)
R v Ewart (1905) 25 NZLR 709 (CA)	5.2.1
R v F (DS) (1999) 132 CCC (3d) 97, 117 (Ont CA)	18.2.1(3)
R v Faigan 15/7/27 (CA)	16.5.2(1)
R v Falconer (1990) 171 CLR 30; 65 ALJR 20 (HCA)	10.3.1,3
R v Farduto (1912) 10 DLR 669; 21 CCC 144	3.4.1(1)
R v Farquhar 20/3/06, CA4/06	15.1.6
R v Farrell [1964] NSWR 1143	11.2.1(1)
R v Farrell [1975] 2 NZLR 753	19.5.1(3)
R v Fatu [1989] 3 NZLR 419; (1989) 4 CRNZ 638 (CA)	17.10.4
R v Fenton [2003] 3 NZLR 439; (2003) 20 CRNZ 76 (CA)	3.3.2(2),4(1), 11.2.8(1), 16.5.2(5)
R v Ferrers (1760) 19 St Tr 886	10.2.1
R v Figueira (1982) 63 CCC (2d) 409 (Ont CA)	15.2.2(1)
R v Filimoehala 16/12/99, CA367/99	16.5.2(5)
R v Finlay [2003] EWCA Crim 3868 (CA)	3.3.3(2)
R v Firth (1990) 91 Cr App R 217; [1990] Crim LR 326	3.2.1(3), 20.3.2
R v Firth [1998] 1 NZLR 513; (1997) 15 CRNZ 406 (CA)	20.3.3(2), 20.5.3
R v Fisher (1837) 8 C & P 182; 173 ER 452	16.5.1(2)
R v Fisher [2004] Crim LR 938	12.3
R v Fitzmaurice [1983] 1 QB 1083; [1983] 1 All ER 189 (CA)	8.4.4
R v Flattery (1877) 2 QBD 410	18.2.1(3)
R v Fleeting (No 1) [1977] 1 NZLR 343	3.3.2(2),(3), 16.2.3, 16.5.2(1)
R v Flynn (1867) 16 WR 319 (Ir)	3.3.3(3), 16.2.3(5)
R v Fontaine (2004) 183 CCC (3d) 1 (SCC)	10.3.1
R v Foox [2000] 1 NZLR 641; (1999) 17 CRNZ 216 (CA)	14.3.1
R v Forges du Lac Inc (1997) 117 CCC (3d) 71	7.2.4
R v Forrest (1886) 20 SALR 78	3.3.3(1)
R v Forrest & Forrest [1970] NZLR 545 (CA)	18.10.9

R v Foster (1906) 26 NZLR 1254 (CA)	3.2.1(2), 16.5.2(4)	R v Goodhall (1821) Russ & Ry 461;	
R v Fotheringham (1989) 88 Cr App		168 ER 898	20.1
R 206; [1988] Crim LR 846 (CA)	11.1.1(2)	R v Goodspeed (1911) 6 Cr App R 133	6.6.6(1)
R v Foti (2002) 169 CCC (3d) 57	17.7	R v Gordon [1963] SR (NSW) 631	11.2.1(1)
R v Fox (1870) 19 WR 109 (CCR)	8.4.3	R v Gordon (1993) 10 CRNZ 430 (CA)	4.1, 10.3.8,10, 15.1.4(5)
R v Franklin (1883) 15 Cox CC 163	6.5.1, 16.5.2(1)	R v Gordon 16/12/04, CA276/04	16.6.1
R v Franklin (2001) 119 A Crim R 223		R v Gorrie (1918) 83 JP 136	9.3, 9.3.2
(Vic CA)	6.3.1	R v Gosney [1971] 2 QB 674; [1971]	
R v Frew [1993] 2 NZLR 731; (1992)		3 All ER 220 (CA)	4.6.3, 5.1.1(2)
9 CRNZ 445	15.2.2(4),3,4	R v Gosney [1977] 2 NZLR 130 (CA)	6.2
R v Frickleton [1984] 2 NZLR 670	12.6.1, 12.9,11,13, 13.3.4	R v Goss and Goss (1990) 90 Cr App	
(CA)	(2)	R 400 (CA)	18.11.3
R v Fryer [1981] 1 NZLR 748 (CA)	11.2.7(1), 16.4.4, 16.5.1	R v Gosset (1993) 105 DLR (4th) 681	4.6.2
	(2),(5)	R v Gotts [1992] 2 AC 412; [1992]	
R v Fuschillo [1940] 2 All ER 489;		1 All ER 832 (HL)	12.10.4
(1940) 27 Cr App R 193	19.5.1(3)	R v Gough [1993] AC 646; [1993] 2 All	
R v G (1984) 1 CRNZ 275	3.4.1(2), 16.6.1,3, 17.2.1	ER 724 (HL)	13.3.4(2)
R v G [2003] UKHL 50; [2004]		R v Gould and Barnes [1960] Qd R 283	16.4.4
1 AC 1034	4.3.1(2),2	R v Graham [1982] 1 All ER 801;	12.6.2, 12.9, 13.2.1, 14.2,
R v G [2006] EWCA Crim 821	5.2.3(2)	[1982] 1 WLR 294 (CA)	14.2.3, 18.2.2(2)
R v G and another [2003] UKHL 50;		R v Grant (1966) NZLR 968 (CA)	3.3.3(2), 16.2.3, 16.5.2(1)
[2004] 1 AC 1034	1.3.2(2)	R v Grant [1975] 2 NZLR 165	8.2.2(1)
R v Galey [1985] 1 NZLR 230 (CA)	6.4.1(2)	R v Grayson 4/7/05, CA436/04	15.1.6
R v Gamble [1989] NI 268	6.5.3	R v Greatrex [1999] 1 Cr App R 126	
R v Gardiner [1982] 2 SCR 368; [1982]		(CA)	6.5.3
68 CCC (2d) 477 (SCC)	10.1.2	R v Green [1993] 2 NZLR 513; (1993)	
R v Gardner (1862) 9 Cox CC 253	19.4.3(1)	9 CRNZ 523 (CA)	10.3.7, 10.4, 10.4.1
R v Garlick (1958) 42 Cr App R 141	20.5.2(1)	R v Greenberg [1972] Crim LR 331	19.3.2(4)
R v Gauci (1995) 79 A Crim R 506	20.4	R v Greenfield 5/2/02, CA322/01	8.3.2,3
R v Geddeson (1906) 25 NZLR 323	18.6	R v Greenstein [1976] 1 All ER 1;	
R v Gedson 4/12/97,		[1975] 1 WLR 1353	20.5.2(1)
Fisher J, HC Rotorua T51/97	5.2.3(2), 16.5.2(1)	R v Grice [1975] 1 NZLR 760 (CA)	11.2.7, 13.4
R v Gemmell [1985] 2 NZLR 740;	6.6.5, 8.2.6, 8.3.1,2,3,4,5,5	R v Griffiths [1960] NZLR 850 (CA)	20.3.1(1)
(1985) 1 CRNZ 496 (CA)	(1),6,8	R v Griffiths [1966] 1 QB 589; [1965]	
R v Genser (1986) 27 CCC (3d) 264	8.3.5	2 All ER 448	8.3.4(4),12
R v George 16/5/96, CA550/95	6.4.1(1)	R v Griffiths (1974) 60 Cr App R 14	
R v Georgiadis (2002) 133 A Crim R		(CA)	4.5, 19.5.2
152	8.3.4(3)	R v Gross (1913) 23 Cox CC 455;	
R v GH [1977] 1 NZLR 50	10.5.1,2	(1913) 77 JP 352	4.8, 16.5.1(6)
R v Ghosh [1982] QB 1053; [1982]		R v Grundy [1977] Crim LR 534 (CA)	6.6.6,6(2)
2 All ER 689 (CA)	20.3.3(2)	R v Gullefer [1990] 3 All ER 882;	
R v Giannetto [1997] 1 Cr App R 1		[1990] 1 WLR 1063	8.2.3(1)
(CA)	6.4.1(1)	R v Gunewardene [1951] 2 KB 600	
R v Gibbins and Proctor (1918) 13 Cr		(CCA)	18.5.3
App R 134 (CCA)	3.2.1(2),(3), 16.5.2(4)	R v Gunning [2005] SCJ No 25 (QL);	
R v Gilbert-Smith (1912) 8 Cr App		196 CCC (3d) 123	12.11
R 72	10.4	R v Gunthorp [2003] 2 NZLR 433, CA	6.3.1
R v Giles (1865) Le & Ca 502;		R v Gush [1980] 2 NZLR 92 (CA)	4.3, 6.5.2,4, 16.4.2, 17.3.6
169 ER 1490	20.3.1(1), 20.4		(1), 17.10.4, 19.4.3(3)
R v Gilks [1972] 3 All ER 280; [1972]		R v H [1993] 1 NZLR 129	18.7.2
1 WLR 1341	19.3.2(4)	R v Hackell 10/10/02, CA131/02	15.1.2,4,4(4)
R v Gill [1963] 2 All ER 688; [1963]		R v Hadfield (1800) 27 St Tr 1281	10.2.1
1 WLR 841 (CCA)	12.11	R v Hagen 4/12/02, CA195/02	11.2.1(1),3
R v Gill (1999) 19 NZTC 15,526	4.6.1	R v Haines (1847) 2 Car & K 368;	
R v Gilmartin [1983] QB 953; [1983]		175 ER 152	16.5.2(4)
1 All ER 829	20.3.1(1)	R v Hakaraia [1989] 1 NZLR 745	
R v Gilmour [2000] 2 Cr App R 407;		(CA)	16.4.4
[2000] Crim LR 763 (NI CA)	6.5.3, 6.6.3	R v Halcro [1995] 1 SCR 440 (SCC)	17.8.1(2)
R v Godbaz (1909) 28 NZLR 577		R v Halcrow (1993) 80 CCC (3d) 320	17.8.1(3)
(CA)	15.1.5	R v Hall (1928) 21 Cr App R 48	
R v Godin [1994] 2 SCR 484	17.7	(CCA)	16.5.1(6)
R v Goldstone 17/06/97,		R v Hall (1985) 81 Cr App R 260;	
Williams J, HC Auckland T74/97	14.4.1(1)	[1985] Crim LR 377 (CA)	4.5
R v Gonder (1981) 62 CCC (2d) 326	13.4	R v Hallett (1841) 9 C & P 748;	
R v Gonzague (1983) 4 CCC (3d) 505	8.4.1(2)	173 ER 1036	18.2.1(3)
R v Goodall (1974-1975) 11 SASR 94	7.2.5	R v Hallett [1969] SASR 141	3.3.3(3)
R v Goodfellow (1986) 83 Cr App R 23	16.5.2(1)	R v Halliday (1889) 61 LT 701	3.3.3(3), 16.5.2(2)

R v Hamblyn (1997) 15 CRNZ 58 (CA)	10.3.4(1)	R v Hennessy [1989] 2 All ER 9; [1989] 1 WLR 287 (CA)	10.3.3(4)
R v Hamilton [1985] 2 NZLR 245 (CA)	6.4.4(4), 6.5, 6.5.2,3(1),4, 6.6.3, 16.4.4	R v Hennigan [1971] 3 All ER 133 (CA)	3.3.2(1),3(2)
R v Hamilton (1991) 92 Cr App R 54; [1990] Crim LR 806	20.4	R v Hensler (1870) 11 Cox CC 570	3.3.1, 20.4
R v Hamilton (2005) 255 DLR (4th) 283 (SCC)	6.4.1(4)	R v Hepworth [1955] 2 QB 600; [1955] 2 All ER 918	19.5.3
R v Hancock (1878) 14 Cox CC 119	19.5.1(3)	R v Hevey (1782) 1 Leach 232; 168 ER 218	20.3.3(3)
R v Hancock [1986] 1 AC 455; [1986] 1 All ER 641 (HL)	4.2.3,4,4(2)	R v Hewitt (1996) 84 A Crim R 440 (Vic SC)	6.3.1
R v Handley (1874) 13 Cox CC 79	16.2.2	R v Hibbert (1995) 99 CCC (3d) 193	12.3
R v Hansen (2005) 22 CRNZ 83 (CA)	2.3.1(1)	R v Hicklin (1868) 3 QB 360	4.1
R v Hansford (1987) 33 CCC (3d) 74; 55 CR (3d) 347	16.5.1(6)	R v Higgins (1801) 2 East 5; 102 ER 269	8.2
R v Hapgood (1870) LR 1 CCR 221; 11 Cox CC 471	6.6.5	R v Hill [1953] NZLR 688	3.3.3(1)
R v Harawira [1989] 2 NZLR 714; (1989) 4 CRNZ 348 (CA)	6.3	R v Hill (1986) 25 CCC (3d) 322 (SCC)	16.5.1(5)
R v Harbour [1995] 1 NZLR 440; (1995) 12 CRNZ 317 (CA)	2.3	R v Hill [2004] 2 NZLR 145 (CA)	6.4.4(4)
R v Hardie [1984] 3 All ER 848; [1985] 1 WLR 64 (CA)	4.6.2, 11.1.1(2)	R v Hinchcliffe (1906) 8 GLR 652	16.2.3(6)
R v Hardiman [1995] 2 NZLR 650; (1995) 13 CRNZ 68 (CA)	16.4.5	R v HM Coroner for East Kent, ex parte Spooner and others (1989) 88 Cr App R 10	7.2.6(1)
R v Hare (1910) 29 NZLR 641 (CA)	4.2.8, 19.4.3(1)	R v Ho 12/4/05, Winkelmann J, HC Auckland CRI-2005-092-567	1.3.3(1)
R v Hare [1934] 1 KB 354; [1933] All ER Rep 550 (CCA)	18.11.3	R v Hobbs [2002] 2 Cr App R 324 (CA)	8.3.2
R v Hare 15/11/99, CA332/99	16.5.2(5)	R v Hogan (1851) 2 Den 277; 169 ER 504	3.4.2
R v Harms [1944] 2 DLR 61	18.2.1(3)	R v Holland (1841) 2 Mood & R 351; 174 ER 313	16.2.3(4)
R v Harney [1987] 2 NZLR 576 (CA)	4.3.1(2), 4.6.2, 5.2.1, 16.4.2, 17.3.6(2)	R v Hollinshead [1985] AC 975; [1985] 2 All ER 769	20.3.3
R v Harrington (1866) 10 Cox CC 370	16.5.1(4)	R v Holness [1970] Tas SR 74	16.5.2(5)
R v Harris (1836) 7 C & P 446; 173 ER 198	2.2.3	R v Hopley (1860) 2 F & F 2023; 175 ER 1024	17.8.1(2)
R v Harris (1979) 69 Cr App R 122	8.3.11(2)	R v Hopwood (1913) 8 Cr App R 143	4.8
R v Harrison [1941] NZLR 354 (CA)	6.3.1, 6.6.1	R v Horne [1994] Crim LR 584 (CA)	13.2.3(1)
R v Harrison-Taylor 12/9/05, Ellen France J, HC Auckland CRI-2004-092-1510	16.6.2	R v Horsey (1862) 3 F & F 287; 176 ER 129	3.3.3(2)
R v Hart [1986] 2 NZLR 408; (1986) 3 CRNZ 474 (CA)	3.3.3(1), 3.4.3	R v Horsington and Bortolus [1983] 2 NSWLR 72	20.3.3
R v Hartley [1978] 2 NZLR 199 (CA)	6.6.3	R v Howard (2003) 20 CRNZ 319 (CA)	15.1.2,2(1),3(2),4
R v Hasan [2005] 2 WLR 709; [2005] 2 AC 467; [2005] UKHL 22	12.3,7,9, 12.10.1,2,3(1),4, 12.13, 13.2.3(2)	R v Howe [1982] 1 NZLR 618 (CA)	4.3.1(2), 5.2.1
R v Hawkins 21/2/01, Goddard J, HC Napier T18/00	3.3.2(2),4(1), 16.2.3, 16.5.2(1)	R v Howe [1986] QB 626; [1986] 1 All ER 833 (CA)	6.6.3
R v Hay (1987) 3 CRNZ 419	14.2.1(2)	R v Howe [1987] AC 417; [1987] 1 All ER 771, also reported as R v Burke [1987] Crim LR 480	3.4.3, 6.6.2(1),3, 12.9, 12.10.4(1), 13.2.1,3(1), 14.2.3
R v Hayes (Dennis Francis) [2002] EWCA Crim 1945	11.2.1(2)	R v Howell [1974] 2 All ER 806	11.2.7
R v Hayward (1908) 21 Cox CC 692	16.2.3(2), 16.5.2(2),(3)	R v Howes (1971) 2 SASR 293	8.3.4(3)
R v Hazelton (1874) LR 2 CCR 134	20.3.1(1)	R v Howlett and Howlett [1968] Crim LR 222	19.3.1(9)
R v Heard [1985] 1 CRNZ 474	19.4.2	R v Hubbard (1990) 6 CRNZ 80	6.5.3
R v Heath (1810) Russ & Ry 184; 168 ER 750	3.2.2(2)	R v Hudson [1943] KB 458; [1943] 1 All ER 642	19.3.2(4)
R v Heesom (1878) 14 Cox CC 40	4.2.2	R v Hudson (1966) 1 QB 448; [1965] 1 All ER 721 (CCA)	4.6.2
R v Hegarty [1994] Crim LR 353	13.2.3(1)	R v Hudson; R v Taylor [1971] 2 QB 202; [1971] 2 All ER 244 (CA)	12.6.1, 12.7, 12.10.1, 12.14.2, 13.2.3(2)
R v Hemmerly (1976) 30 CCC (2d) 141 (Ont CA)	15.2.2(4)	R v Huggins (1730) 2 Stra 883; 93 ER 915	7.1, 7.2.3
R v Hemmings [1939] 1 All ER 417 (CCA)	18.6.2(2)	R v Hughes (1841) 9 C & P 752; 173 ER 1038	18.9.1
R v Hende [1996] 1 NZLR 153 (CA)	16.5.2(3), 17.8, 17.10.1,4		
R v Henderson [1990] 3 NZLR 174; (1990) 6 CRNZ 137 (CA)	16.2.2		
R v Hendrickson [1977] Crim LR 356 (CA)	6.4.1(4)		

R v Hughes (1857) 7 Cox CC 301
(CCA) 16.5.2(4)
R v Hughes (1857) Dears & B 248;
169 ER 996 3.2.1(2)
R v Humphries [1982] 1 NZLR 353
(CA) 8.3.12
R v Hunt (1825) 1 Mood CC 93;
168 ER 1198 17.3.6(1), 17.4
R v Hunt [1987] AC 352; [1987] 1 All
ER 1 (HL) 2.3
R v Hurley and Murray [1967] VR 526
(Vic SC) 12.10.2,2(1),3
R v Hurst (1995) 1 Cr App R 82 13.2.3(1)
R v Husseyn (1978) 67 Cr App R 131n;
[1978] Crim LR 219 (CA) 4.2.8
R v Hutchinson 7/7/03, CA92/03 13.1, 13.2.2,3(2)
R v Hyam [1975] AC 55; [1974] 2 All
ER 41 (HL) 16.4
R v Hyde-Harris [1968] NZLR 315 19.5.3
R v Iby (2005) 154 A Crim R 55 (NSW
CCA) 16.2.2
R v ICR Haulage Ltd [1944] 1 KB 551;
[1944] 1 All ER 691 (CA) 7.2
R v Ilich (1987) 162 CLR 110; (1987)
69 ALR 231 19.3.3(2)
R v Ilyas (1984) 78 Cr App R 17 8.2.3(1)
R v Instan [1893] 1 QB 450 3.2.1(2), 16.5.2(4)
R v Iona 27/3/03, CA416/02 1.3.3(1)
R v Ireland; R v Burstow [1998] AC 147;
[1997] 4 All ER 225 (HL) 16.2.3(2), 17.3.1(1)
R v Irwin (1998) 123 CCC (3d) 316
(Ont CA) 17.2.1(1)
R v Isherwood 14/3/05, CA182/04 18.2.1(3)
R v Isitt (1978) 67 Cr App R 44 (CA) 3.4.1(2),(3)
R v Izod (1904) 20 Cox CC 690 16.2.2
R v Jackson (1826) 1 Mod 119;
168 ER 1208 19.3.2(4)
R v Jackson [1918] NZLR 363 16.5.1(5)
R v Jackson (1987) 11 NSWLR 318 8.3.12
R v Jakac [1961] VR 367 4.2.3
R v Jakeman (1983) 76 Cr App R 223;
[1983] Crim LR 104 (CA) 4.9, 8.3.5(2)
R v James (1980) 70 Cr App R 215
(CA) 17.3.4
R v James (1985) 82 Cr App R 226;
[1986] Crim LR 118 8.4.1
R v James [2006] 2 WLR 887; [2006]
1 All ER 759 (CA) 16.5.1(5)
R v Janis 28/5/92,
Heron J, HC Wellington T91-95/91 8.3.4(1),(2)
R v Jean [1968] 2 CCC 204 19.3.2(4)
R v Jenkins [1983] 1 All ER 1000;
(1983) 76 Cr App R 313 (CA) 17.2.3
R v Jennings [1990] Crim LR 588 (CA) 16.5.2(1)
R v Jensen [1980] VR 194 6.6.6(1)
R v Jessop (1858) Dear & B 442;
169 ER 1074 20.4
R v Jobidon [1991] 2 SC R 714;
66 CCC (3d) 454 17.2.4(1)
R v Johnson (1841) Car & M 218;
174 ER 479 6.6.6(2)
R v Johnson (1911) 6 Cr App R 218 19.5.2
R v Johnson [1989] 2 All ER 839;
[1989] 1 WLR 740 (CA) 16.5.1(7)
R v Johnston (1986) 2 CRNZ 289 (CA) 8.3.2,4(1),9
R v Jones (1703) 2 Ld Raymond 1013;
92 ER 174 20.1

R v Jones [1898] 1 QB 119 20.5.2(2)
R v Jones (1933) 24 Cr App R 55 (CA) 18.6.2(2)
R v Jones [1935] 2 WWR 270; (1934)
63 CCC 341 18.2.1(3)
R v Jones (1974) 59 Cr App R 120;
[1974] Crim LR 663 8.3.12
R v Jones (1990) 3 All ER 886; [1990]
1 WLR 1057 (CA) 8.2.3(1),(4)
R v Jones (1991) 8 CR (4th) 137 (SCC) 14.3.1
R v Jordan (1956) 40 Cr App R 152
(CCA) 3.3.3(2), 16.2.3,3(5)
R v Jorgensen [1995] 4 SCR 55; (1996)
102 CCC (3d) 97 (SCC) 14.4.1,1(1)
R v Joyce [1968] NZLR 1070 (CA) 6.4.4(1), 12.7,8, 12.10.3,4,
13.4
R v Joyce 24/2/98, CA364/97 15.1.3
R v Juanetty (2005) 200 CCC (3d) 116 16.4.1
R v Julien [1969] 2 All ER 856; [1969]
1 WLR 839 (CA) 15.1.4(3)
R v K [2001] 3 All ER 897; [2001]
3 WLR 471 (HL) 4.3.2, 5.2.1,3(2), 11.2.3
R v K [2001] UKHL 41; [2002]
1 AC 462 (HL) 18.7.1
R v K (R A) (1996) 106 CCC (3d) 93 18.10.2
R v Kaho 31/5/01,
Paterson J, HC Auckland T002621 17.3.6(2), 17.5
R v Kahu [1947] NZLR 368 (CA) 2.3, 16.5.1(1)
R v Kaitamaki [1980] 1 NZLR 59
(CA) 18.2.2(2)
R v Kaitamaki [1984] 1 NZLR 385,
also reported as Kaitamaki v R (1984) 3.2.1(2),(3), 4.9.1(1), 6.2,
1 CRNZ 211; [1985] AC 147 (PC) 8.3.2, 18.2.1(2)
R v Kake [1960] NZLR 595 (CA) 18.2.1(3)
R v Kamipeli [1975] 2 NZLR 610 (CA) 2.3.2, 3.4.3, 5.2.2(1), 9.1,
11.2, 11.2.1,1(1),(2),2,3,6,
7, 15.1.3(5)
R v Karotu (1994) 11 CRNZ 691 (CA) 18.2.1(1)
R v Keane [1921] NZLR 581 (CA) 5.2.2(2)
R v Keating (1992) 76 CCC (3d) 570 12.4
R v Kelly [1992] Crim LR 181 8.2.2(2)
R v Kelly [1998] 3 All ER 741 (CA) 19.3.1(8)
R v Kemp [1957] 1 QB 399; [1956]
3 All ER 249 (CA) 10.3.3(2)
R v Kennedy (1972) 7 CCC (2d) 42 5.1.2
R v Kennedy [2001] 1 NZLR 314;
(2000) 18 CRNZ 501 (CA) 19.5.1(1),2
R v Kennedy [2005] EWCA Crim 685 16.5.2(1)
R v Kenney [1983] 2 VR 470 16.5.1(6)
R v Kerr [1976] 1 NZLR 335 (CA) 2.3, 15.1.1
R v Kerr [1988] 1 NZLR 270; (1987)
2 CRNZ 407 (CA) 17.2, 18.11.5
R v Kerr [2004] SCC 44 15.1.3(3)
R v Kerster (2003) 175 CCC (3d) 28
(BCCA) 8.2.5
R v Ketteringham (1926) 19 Cr App
R 159 19.5.3
R v Khan [1990] 2 All ER 783; [1990]
1 WLR 813 (CA) 4.3.2, 8.2.1, 18.4, 18.4.1
R v Kimber [1983] 3 All ER 316; [1983] 4.3.2, 17.2.2,4, 18.2.2(1),
1 WLR 1118 (CA) 18.11.4
R v Kimura (1992) 9 CRNZ 115 (CA) 6.4.4(4), 6.6.2(3)
R v Kina 23/5/96 (NSW SC) 10.3.3(2)
R v King (1962) 35 DLR (2d) 386;
[1962] SCR 746 (SCC) 10.3.3(4)
R v King [1979] Crim LR 122 20.3.1(1)
R v King (1987) 7 CRNZ 591 (CA) 16.5.1(1),(3)

R v King [1987] QB 547; [1987] 1 All ER 547	20.4.1	R v Lawrence [1982] AC 510; [1981] 1 All ER 974 (HL)	4.3.1(1), 16.5.2(5)
R v King [1995] 3 NZLR 409; (1995) 13 CRNZ 289	2.1.2	R v Le Brun [1992] 1 QB 61; [1991] 4 All ER 673 (CA)	4.9.1(2),(3), 16.5.2(1)
R v King (2004) 150 A Crim R 409	16.2.2	R v Leaaetoa 30/6/94, CA520/93	16.4.2
R v Kingi 10/8/05, CA122/05	15.1, 15.1.4	R v Leahy [1985] Crim LR 99	6.4.4(4)
R v Kingston (1905) 24 NZLR 431	20.3.1(2)	R v Leak [1976] QB 217; [1975] 2 All ER 1059 (CA)	6.6.2(2)
R v Kingston [1994] QB 81; [1993] 4 All ER 373 (CA)	11.2.8	R v Leblanc (1985) 22 CCC (3d) 126 (Ont CA)	16.5.1
R v Kingston [1995] 2 AC 355; [1994] 3 All ER 353 (HL)	1.3.2(1), 3.4.1(3), 4.1, 11.1, 11.2.8	R v Lee [2000] NLJ 1491	15.1.3
R v Kinsman [1969] NZLR 678 (CA)	20.5.2(2)	R v Lee (2001) 1 Cr App R 293	17.7.1(1)
R v Kirikiri [1982] 2 NZLR 648	3.3.3(2), 16.2.3,3(5)	R v Leeson (1968) 52 Cr App R 185; [1968] Crim LR 283 (CA)	18.11.3
R v Kissling 4/5/05, CA403/04	15.1.4	R v Leilua 20/9/85, CA19/84	16.5.1(5)
R v Kitchener (1993) 29 NSWLR 696	4.3.2, 18.2.2(2)	R v Leilua [1986] NZ Recent Law 118	16.5.1(5)
R v Kitson (1955) 39 Cr App R 66 (CCA)	13.3.2	R v Lemon; R v Gay News Ltd [1979] AC 617; [1979] 1 All ER 898	
R v Kneale [1998] 2 NZLR 169; (1997) 15 CRNZ 392 (CA)	15.1.3(2)	(HL)	4.2.3, 5.1, 5.2.3(2)
R v Knutsen [1963] Qd R 157	3.3.3(2)	R v Leolahi [2001] 1 NZLR 562; (2001) 18 CRNZ 505 (CA)	14.3.1
R v Kopelani 23/11/05, CA79/05	6.6.3	R v Leon [1945] KB 136; [1945] 1 All ER 14 (CCA)	20.5.2(1)
R v Koura [1996] 2 NZLR 9; (1996) 13 CRNZ 463 (CA)	19.3.1(7)	R v Leonard 6/6/91, CA179/90	18.11.6
R v Kovacs [1974] 1 All ER 1236; [1974] 1 WLR 370	20.4	R v Lesbini [1914] 3 KB 1116 (CCA)	16.5.1(5)
R v Krause (1902) 66 JP 121	8.4.1(1),3	R v Lester (1955) 39 Cr App R 157	3.4.2(2)
R v Kritz [1950] 1 KB 82; [1949] 2 All ER 406	20.5.2(1)	R v Leuta [2002] 1 NZLR 215	15.1.4(4)
R v Kumar [2004] EWCA Crim 3207	18.7.1	R v Lewis (1869) 11 Cox CC 404	20.3.3
R v Kwok Chak Ming (No 1) [1963] HKLR 226	16.4.3	R v Lewis [1970] Crim LR 647 (CA)	3.3.3(3), 16.5.2(2)
R v Kylsant [1932] 1 KB 442; [1931] All ER Rep 179	20.3.1(1)	R v Lewis [1975] 1 NZLR 222 (CA)	3.3.2(3),3(2), 6.2,3, 6.6.2 (2),3
R v L (W K) (1991) 64 CCC (3d) 321 (SCC)	18.5.2	R v Li 28/6/00, CA140/00; CA141/00	15.1.2
R v Lafaele (1987) 2 CRNZ 677 (CA)	16.5.1(5)	R v Lillyman [1896] 2 QB 167; [1895-9] All ER Rep 586	18.5.2
R v Laga [1969] NZLR 417	16.5.1	R v Lines (1844) 1 Car & Kir 393; 174 ER 861	18.2.1(1), 18.9.1
R v Lalonde (1995) 37 CR (4th) 97	13.3.1	R v Linneker [1906] 2 KB 99	8.2.3(1)
R v Lamb [1967] 2 QB 981; [1967] 2 All ER 1282 (CA)	4.6.2, 16.5.2(1)	R v Lipman [1970] 1 QB 152; [1969] 3 All ER 410 (CA)	3.4.3, 11.2.7
R v Lambassi [1927] ALR 295; [1927] VLR 349	20.4	R v Little 12/6/01, William Young J, HC Christchurch T17/01	3.3.4(1)
R v Lambie [1982] AC 449; [1981] 2 All ER 776	20.3.1(2), 20.4	R v Livermore (1995) 43 CR (4th) 1; 102 CCC (3d) 212; [1995] 4 SCR 123	
R v Lamont 27/4/92, CA442/91	12.6, 13.2.2,3,4	(SCC)	14.2
R v Lang (1998) 16 CRNZ 68 (CA)	8.3.4(6)	R v Livock (1914) 10 Cr App R 264	19.5.3
R v Langlois (1993) 80 CCC (3d) 28	12.3.1, 12.10.4	R v Lloyd [1985] QB 829 (CA)	19.4.3(3)
R v Langlois (2005) 195 CCC (3d) 152 (BCCA)	10.3.10	R v Lloyd [1992] Crim LR 361	19.5.1(1)
R v Laniel Canada Ltd (1991) 63 CCC (3d) 574	14.4.1	R v Longman (1981) 72 Cr App R 121; [1982] Crim LR 38	8.3.10
R v Larsonneur (1933) 24 Cr App R 74; 149 LT 542 (CCA)	1.3.2(5), 3.2.2(1), 13.6.2	R v Loo Manson (1925) 43 CCC 30 (Alta CA)	15.1.3(2)
R v Latif [1996] 1 WLR 104; [1996] 2 Cr App R 92 (HL)	3.3.3(2)	R v Loper 22/5/00, CA502/99	6.4.1(2)
R v Latimer (1886) 17 QBD 359; [1886-90] All ER Rep 386	4.8, 17.2.1(1)	R v Loukes [1996] Crim LR 341	6.6.1,2(2)
R v Latimer (2001) 193 DLR (4th) 577	13.2.2, 13.5.1	R v Lowe (1850) 3 Car & Kir 123; 175 ER 489	3.3.3(2)
R v Latouche (2000) 147 CCC (3d) 420 (Can CMAC)	14.3	R v Lowe [1973] QB 702; [1973] 1 All ER 805 (CA)	16.5.2(1),(5)
R v Lavallee [1990] 1 SCR 852; (1990) 76 CR (3d) 329 (SCC)	10.3.10, 15.1.4(5)	R v Lucinsky [1935] NZLR 575; [1935] GLR 515 (CA)	19.5.1(3)
R v Lavender [2005] HCA 237	4.6.2	R v Lunt [2004] 1 NZLR 498; (2003) 20 CRNZ 681 (CA)	3.2.1(2), 16.5.2(4)
R v Laverty [1970] 3 All ER 432; (1970) 54 Cr App R 495	20.4	R v M [1993] DCR 1144	18.2.1(3)
R v Lawford and Van Den Wiel (1993) 69 A Crim R 115	16.5.2(1)	R v M (ML) [1994] 2 SCR 3; (1994) 89 CCC (3d) 96	14.3
		R v McArthur [1975] 1 NZLR 486	15.2.2(2), 17.3.5
		R v McCallum [1969] Tas SR 73	16.5.2(1),(4)

R v McCarthy [1954] 2 QB 105; [1954] 2 All ER 262 (CCA)	16.5.1(5)
R v McCarthy [1962] NZLR 1069 (CA)	16.5.1(6)
R v McCarthy [1992] 2 NZLR 550; (1992) 8 CRNZ 58 (CA)	10.3.8, 13.2.3(1), 16.5.1 (4),(5)
R v McClintock [1986] 2 NZLR 99; (1986) 2 CRNZ 158 (CA)	18.5.3
R v McCormack [1969] 2 QB 442; [1969] 3 All ER 371 (CA)	18.11.3
R v McCraw (1991) 7 CR (4th) 314	17.3.1(1)
R v McCready [1978] 3 All ER 967; [1978] 1 WLR 1376 (CA)	17.5
R v McCullough (1982) 6 A Crim R 274 (Tas CCA)	11.2.4
R v McCullum (1973) 57 Cr App R 645; [1973] Crim LR 582 (CA)	4.8, 14.1
R v MacDonald [1904] St R Qd 151	3.2.1(2), 16.5.2(4)
R v MacDonald (1990) 54 CCC (3d) 97; 75 CR (3d) 238	6.5.4
R v McDonnell [1966] 1 QB 233; [1966] 1 All ER 193 (CCA)	7.2.5
R v McDonough (1962) 47 Cr App R 37 (CCA)	8.4.4
R v McFall (1975) 26 CCC (2d) 181 (BC CA)	16.5.2(7)
R v McGregor [1962] NZLR 1069 (CA)	13.2.3(1), 16.5.1(2),(3), (5),(6)
R v Machirus [1996] 3 NZLR 404; (1996) 14 CRNZ 172 (CA)	16.5.2(1)
R v McInnes [1971] 3 All ER 295; [1971] 1 WLR 1600 (CA)	15.1.4(3)
R v McIntyre (1847) 2 Cox CC 379	16.2.5(5)
R v McKay [1961] NZLR 256 (CA)	20.7
R v McKechnie (1991) 94 Cr App R 51	3.3.3(2),4(3)
R v McKeown [1984] 1 NZLR 630 (CA)	16.4.2,4,6
R v Mackie [1957] NZLR 669 (CA)	6.6.5, 8.2.3(1)
R v Mackie (1973) 57 Cr App R 453; [1973] Crim LR 438 (CA)	16.5.2(2)
R v McKie 3/8/00, Young J, HC Dunedin T13/00	16.5.2(5)
R v McKinnon [1980] 2 NZLR 31 (CA)	3.3.2(3), 4.9.1(3), 16.2.3, 16.4.6, 16.5.2(1)
R v McLeod (1915) 34 NZLR 430 (CA)	17.2.4(4), 17.5
R v McMasters [1920] GLR 351	17.2, 17.2.1(1),3(1)
R v Macmillan [1966] NZLR 616 (CA)	10.3.5
R v McNally 6/4/93, CA441/92	18.12.2
R v McNamara (No 1) (1981) 56 CCC (2d) 193	6.6.5, 7.2.4
R v McRae (1993) 10 CRNZ 61 (CA)	3.2.2(2), 3.4.2(2)
R v McShane (1978) 66 Cr App R 97; [1977] Crim LR 737 (CA)	6.6.5, 8.4
R v Madden 29/5/03, CA433/02	20.4
R v Mahoney (2000) 114 A Crim R 130 (NSW CCA)	19.5.3
R v Maihi [1993] 2 NZLR 139; (1992) 9 CRNZ 304 (CA)	19.3.2(3)
R v Mailloux (1985) 25 CCC (3d) 171 (Ont CA)	10.3.10
R v Makoare 18/4/00, CA469/99	16.5.1(4)
R v Makoare [2001] 1 NZLR 318; (2000) 18 CRNZ 511 (CA)	16.4.2, 16.5.1(1),(4),(5)
R v Malcherek [1981] 2 All ER 422; [1981] 1 WLR 690 (CA)	16.2.3,3(4)
R v Malcolm [1951] NZLR 470 (CA)	6.6.3,6(1)
R v Mallett [1978] 1 WLR 820; [1978] 3 All ER 10 (CA)	20.3.1(5)
R v Malott (1998) 155 DLR (4th) 513	15.1.4(5)
R v Manchuk [1937] 4 DLR 737; [1938] SCR 18 (SCC)	16.5.1(6)
R v Mandry and Wooster [1973] 3 All ER 996; [1973] 1 WLR 1232	20.3.1(2)
R v Manley (1844) 1 Cox CC 104	6.3.1
R v Manning (1672) T Raym 212; 83 ER 112	16.5.1,1(2)
R v Manuel 11/3/94, T180/93	18.2.1(1)
R v Marjoram [2000] Crim LR 372 (CA)	16.5.2(2)
R v Marriott (1838) 8 C & P 425; 173 ER 559	3.2.1(2)
R v Martin (1827) 3 C & P 211; 172 ER 390	3.3.3(2)
R v Martin (1881) 8 QBD 54	3.3.3(2), 17.2.3(1)
R v Martin (1983) 32 SASR 419; 9 A Crim R 376	3.4.1(2)
R v Martin (1984) 51 ALR 540; 16 A Crim R 87 (HCA)	3.4.3, 11.2.7
R v Martin [1989] 1 All ER 652; (1989) 88 Cr App R 343 (CA)	13.2.1, 18.2.2(2)
R v Martin (1995) 13 WAR 472	16.2.2, 16.4.3
R v Martin (2000) 2 Cr App R 42 (CA)	13.2.1
R v Martin 24/3/04, Wild J, HC Wanganui, CRI-2003-083-432B	13.3.4(4)
R v Martin (Anthony) [2002] 2 WLR 1; [2002] 1 Cr App R 27; [2002] Crim LR 136	15.1.3(1)
R v Martineau [1990] 2 SCR 633; (1990) 79 CR (3d) 129 (SCC)	1.2.2
R v Maslen and Shaw (1995) 79 A Crim R 199 (NSW CCA)	20.3.1(5)
R v Mason [1987] 2 NZLR 249; (1987) 3 CRNZ 7 (CA)	10.1.2
R v Matoka [1987] 1 NZLR 340 (CA)	2.3, 16.5.1(1),(5),(6)
R v Matthews [2003] EWCA Crim 192; [2003] 2 Cr App R 30	4.2.4
R v Matthews and Alleyne [2003] Crim LR 553 (CA)	16.4.1
R v May [1912] 3 KB 572	17.2.4
R v Mayberry [1973] Qd R 211	6.2
R v Mayes [2004] 1 NZLR 81	16.6.2
R v Mazeau (1840) 9 C & P 676; 173 ER 1006	6.3.1
R v Mead [2002] 1 NZLR 594 (CA)	17.10
R v Meads and Smith 20/4/00, CA514/99	16.4.2
R v Meek [1981] 1 NZLR 499 (CA)	5.2.3(2)
R v Melaragni (1992) 75 CCC (3d) 546 (Ont Ct, Gen Div)	17.2
R v Menniti [1985] 1 Qd R 520; (1984) 13 A Crim R 417	6.6.6(2)
R v Menzies 16/10/97, CA222/97	16.4.6
R v Meredith [1973] Crim LR 253	19.3.2(3)
R v Metharam [1961] 3 All ER 200; (1961) 45 Cr App R 304 (CA)	12.6, 17.3.1
R v Metuariki [1986] 1 NZLR 488; (1986) 2 CRNZ 116 (CA)	5.2.1,2(2),(3), 14.2.1(1)
R v Meynell [2004] 1 NZLR 507; (2003) 20 CRNZ 526 (CA)	16.4.2
R v Meyrick (1929) 21 Cr App R 94	8.3.4,4(5)
R v Michael (1840) 9 C & P 356; 173 ER 867	3.3.3(1),(2), 6.3.1

R v Mickle [1978] 1 NZLR 720 (SC)	6.6.4(2)
R v Middleship (1850) 5 Cox CC 275 (CA)	16.5.2(4)
R v Middleton (1873) 12 Cox CC 417	19.3.2(4)
R v Millard and Vernon [1987] Crim LR 393 (CA)	4.3.2, 18.4.1
R v Miller (1854) 6 Cox 353	19.5.1(1)
R v Miller [1954] 2 QB 282; [1954] 2 All ER 529	15.2.2(2), 17.3.1(1),5
R v Miller [1955] NZLR 1038 (CA)	20.3.1(1)
R v Miller [1983] 2 AC 161; [1983] 1 All ER 978 (HL)	3.2.1(2), 4.3.1(1), 4.9.1(1), 16.5.2(4), 20.3.2
R v Miller (1992) 95 CR App R 421; [1992] Crim LR 744	20.4.1
R v Miller 16/6/06, CA26/06	15.1.6
R v Milloy [1993] 1 Qd R 298; (1991) 54 A Crim R 340	3.4, 3.4.1(2)
R v Mills (1857) 7 Cox CC 263; 1 Dears & B 205; 169 ER 978	3.3.1
R v Mills [1963] 1 QB 522; (1962) 47 Cr App R 49 (CCA)	8.3.4
R v Millward [1994] Crim LR 527 (CA)	6.6.2(2)
R v Mita [1996] 1 NZLR 95	16.5.1(1),(3),(4)
R v Mitchell [1983] QB 741; [1983] 2 All ER 427 (CA)	16.4.3, 16.5.2(1)
R v Mitchell [1988] 2 NZLR 208; (1988) 3 CRNZ 515 (CA)	19.3.3(2)
R v Mobilio [1991] 1 VR 339; (1990) 50 A Crim R 170	18.2.1(3)
R v Mohan [1976] QB 1; [1975] 2 All ER 193 (CA)	4.2.2, 18.4.1
R v Mokaraka [2002] 1 NZLR 793; (2001) 19 CRNZ 316 (CA)	6.4.4(4), 6.5.2
R v Molis [1980] 2 SCR 356; (1980) 55 CCC (2d) 558	14.4.2
R v Molodowic (2000) 143 CCC (3d) 31 (SCC)	10.3.10
R v Moloney [1985] AC 905; [1985] 1 All ER 1025 (HL)	4.2, 4.2.1,2,3,4
R v Monkhouse [1923] GLR 13	10.2.2, 10.3
R v Monkhouse (1850-1851) 4 Cox CC 55	11.1.1(1)
R v Moore [1954] NZLR 893 (CA)	16.5.2(4)
R v Moore and Dorn [1975] Crim LR 229 (CA)	4.9.1(2)
R v Morby (1881-1882) LR 8 QBD 571	3.3.4(1)
R v Morfit (1816) Russ & Ry 307; 168 ER 817	19.4.3(3)
R v Morhall [1996] AC 90; [1995] 3 All ER 659 (HL)	13.2.3(1), 16.5.1(5)
R v Morris [1984] AC 320; [1983] 3 All ER 288 (HL)	19.3.2(3),3(1),(2)
R v Morris (Lee) [2001] 3 NZLR 759	8.3.5,12
R v Morunga (2000) 17 CRNZ 396 (CA)	19.4.3(1),(2)
R v Most (1881) 7 QBD 244	8.4.1,3
R v Mostyn (2004) 145 A Crim R 304 (NSWCCA)	17.2
R v Moungakiholoto HC, Auckland, T001435, 13/11/00, Baragwanath J	18.2.1(3)
R v Mrzljak (2004) 152 A Crim R 315	10.3.2
R v Mubila [1956] 1 SA 31	3.3.3(3)
R v Mullins [1980] Crim LR 37 (CA)	4.3.1
R v Murphy 26/9/96, CA310/96	18.2.1(3)

R v Murray 22/10/87, Eichelbaum J, HC Wellington T26/87	15.1.4,4(1)
R v Murray Wright Ltd [1970] NZLR 476 (CA)	7.2, 16.2.1
R v Murtagh [1955] Crim LR 315	6.6.3
R v Muy Ky Chhay (1994) 72 A Crim R 1 (NSW CCA)	16.5.1(1),(3),(4)
R v Mwai [1995] 3 NZLR 149; (1995) 13 CRNZ 273 (CA)	4.7, 12.6, 16.2.3(2), 16.4.5, 16.5.2(4),(7), 17.3.1,1(1)
R v Myatt [1991] 1 NZLR 674; (1990) 7 CRNZ 304 (CA)	3.3.2(1),4(1), 16.5.2(1), (4),(5)
R v N (1992) 9 CRNZ 471	18.6.1, 18.9.1
R v N (an accused) [1987] 2 NZLR 268; (1987) 2 CRNZ 513 (CA)	18.2.1(5)
R v Nathan [1981] 2 NZLR 473	6.5.4, 6.6.1
R v Nazif [1987] 2 NZLR 122 (CA)	4.3.2, 14.2.1(1), 17.2.4, 18.11.4, 20.3.1(4)
R v Neale (1844) 1 Car & K 591; 174 ER 951	18.9
R v Nedrick [1986] 3 All ER 1; [1986] 1 WLR 1025 (CA)	4.2, 4.2.3,4
R v Nelson (1992) 71 CCC (3d) 449; 13 CR (4th) 359	15.1.3
R v Nepia [1983] NZLR 754 (CA)	2.3, 16.5.1(1),(2),(5)
R v Newland [1954] 1 QB 158; [1953] 2 All ER 1067	8.3.1
R v Ngamoki 7/11/97, Heron J, HC Palmerston North T5/97	6.6.4(1)
R v Ngatai 9/4/01 Williams J, HC Auckland T001864	6.3.1
R v Ngawaka 6/10/04, CA111/04; CA146/04; CA174/04	6.6.6,6(1)
R v Nichol (1807) Russ & Ry, 130; 168 ER 720 (CCR)	18.3.3
R v Nicholls (1867) 10 Cox CC 476 (CCA)	18.10.5
R v Nicholls (1874) 13 Cox CC 75	3.2.1(2), 16.5.2(5)
R v Nichols [1998] 1 NZLR 608; (1997) 15 CRNZ 350	8.3.12
R v Noel [1960] NZLR 212 (CA)	2.3.2, 16.5.1(5)
R v Norris (1988) 3 CRNZ 527	18.11.6
R v Nosworthy (1907) 26 NZLR 536; 9 GLR 434 (CA)	19.5.2
R v Nottingham [1992] 1 NZLR 395 (CA)	19.3.2(4),3(2)
R v Oakes [1995] 2 NZLR 673 (CA)	15.1.4(5), 16.5.1(4),(5),(6)
R v Officer [1922] GLR 175	16.5.2(4)
R v Olan, Hudson & Hartnett (1978) 41 CCC (2d) 145; 86 DLR (3d) 212	20.3.3
R v Olugboja [1981] 3 All ER 443 (CA)	18.2.1(3)
R v Oommen (1993) 21 CR (4th) 117 (CA)	10.3.7
R v Oommen [1994] 2 SCR 507; (1994) 91 CCC (3d) 8 (SCC)	10.3.7
R v Oram (1908) 27 NZLR 955	19.3.3(2)
R v Ortiz (1986) 83 Cr App R 173 (CA)	12.10.2
R v Orton (1878) 14 Cox CC 226	17.2.4(1)
R v Osborne [1905] 1 KB 551; [1904-7] All ER Rep 54	18.5.2
R v Osborne (1992) 17 CR (4th) 350	18.10.5
R v Oxford (1840) 4 State Tr (NS) 498	10.2.1
R v O'Brien [1954] SCR 666; (1954) 110 CCC 1 (SCC)	8.3.5(2)

R v O'Brien (2003) 20 CRNZ 572 (CA)	4.9.1(3)
R v O'Callaghan (1984) 1 CRNZ 185	16.6.1,2
R v O'Connor (1980) 146 CLR 64 (HCA)	11.2, 11.2.7
R v O'Connor (1980) 146 CLR 64; 29 ALR 449 (HCA)	3.4.3,3(1)
R v O'Connor [1991] Crim LR 135	11.1.1(2), 11.2.4
R v O'Flaherty [2004] 2 Cr App R 314	6.6.6(1)
R v O'Flaherty [2004] EWCA Crim 526; [2004] 2 Cr App R 20	6.5.1
R v O'Grady [1987] QB 995; [1987] 3 All ER 420 (CA)	11.1.1(2), 11.2.4, 15.1.3(5)
R v P [1991] 2 NZLR 116; (1991) 7 CRNZ 48 (CA)	16.6.1, 17.10.3
R v P & O European Ferries (Dover) Ltd (1990) 93 Cr App R 72; [1991] Crim LR 695	16.2.1
R v P (T129/92) (1993) 10 CRNZ 250; 1 HRNZ 417	4.6.2,4, 18.2.2(1)
R v Packard (1841) Car & M 236; 174 ER 487	16.5.2(1)
R v Padlie 28/11/95, CA209/95; CA232/95; CA237/95	6.4.2
R v Paenga (No 4) 22/2/06 Heath J, HC Tauranga, CRI-2004-070-2905	11.2.8(1)
R v Page [1933] ALR 374; [1933] VLR 351	8.2.3(1),4
R v Pagett (1983) 76 Cr App R 279; [1983] Crim LR 393 (CA)	3.3.3(2), 16.2.3, 16.4.3
R v Paniani [2000] 1 NZLR 234; (1999) 17 CRNZ 519 (CA)	16.5.1(6)
R v Panine 25/6/02, HC, Ronald Young J, Wellington T841/01	17.5
R v Pargeter (1848) 3 Cox CC 191	16.5.2(4)
R v Park [1995] 2 SCR 836, (1995) 99 CCC (3d) 1 (SCC)	14.2
R v Parker [1919] NZLR 365 (CA)	19.3.1(1)
R v Parker [1977] 2 All ER 37	4.3.1
R v Parker [1997] Crim LR 760	16.5.1(5)
R v Parker and Bulteel (1916) 25 Cox CC 145	20.3.1(1)
R v Parks (1990) 56 CCC (3d) 449 (Ont CA)	10.3.3(4)
R v Parks (1992) 95 DLR (4th) 27; [1992] 2 SCR 871 (SCC)	10.3.3(2),(4)
R v Parnell (1881) 14 Cox CC 508	8.3.4
R v Paterson [1976] 2 NZLR 394 (CA)	3.3.3(2), 6.3.1, 6.6.1, 8.3.5(2)
R v Paterson (2005) 201 CCC (3d) 220 (Ont CA)	16.5.2(4)
R v Pauga [1992] 3 NZLR 241; (1992) 8 CRNZ 169	18.2.1(3)
R v Pearson [1992] Crim LR 193 (CA)	16.5.1(2)
R v Pembliton (1874) LR 2 CCR 119; (1874) 12 Cox CC 607	4.8, 17.2.1(1)
R v Pene 1/7/80, CA63/80	6.4.1(2),(4)(1)
R v Peneha (1993) 11 CRNZ 183	8.2.3(3),(4)
R v Perka [1984] 2 SCR 232, also reported as Perka v R (1984) 14 CCC (3d) 385 (SCC)	12.3.1, 13.2.2, 13.3.3
R v Perman [1996] 1 Cr App R 24 (CA)	6.6.6(1)
R v Perry and Pledger [1920] NZLR 21, 23 (CA)	18.10.2
R v Petel [1994] 1 SCR 3	15.1.3
R v Peters (1886) 16 QBD 636	20.5.2(2)

R v Peterson (2005) 201 CCC (3d) 220 (Ont CA)	16.5.2(4)
R v Petro-Canada (2003) 171 CCC (3d) 354 (Ont CA)	5.1.1(1)
R v Petters and Parfitt [1995] Crim LR 501 (CA)	6.5.1
R v Pham 6/7/98, Williams J, HC Auckland T98/98	6.5.3
R v Phillips [1971] ALR 740; (1971) 45 ALJR 467 (HCA)	3.3.3(1), 16.5.2(1),(4)
R v Phillips [1991] 3 NZLR 175 (CA)	2.3, 2.3.1(1)
R v Phillips [2004] EWCA Crim 112	4.2.4
R v Pigg [1982] 2 All ER 591; [1982] 1 WLR 762 (CA)	4.3.2, 18.2.2(1)
R v Pink [2001] 2 NZLR 860	6.6.6,6(2)
R v Pira (1991) 7 CRNZ 650	16.4.2
R v Piri [1987] 1 NZLR 66 (CA)	6.5.2, 16.4, 16.4.1,2,4,5
R v Piri Hira Hoani (1915) 34 NZLR 902	20.4
R v Pita (1989) 4 CRNZ 660 (CA)	16.5.1(4),(5)
R v Pitts (1842) Car & M 284; 174 ER 509	3.3.3(3), 16.5.2(4)
R v Pittwood (1902) 19 TLR 37	3.2.1(2), 3.3.2,2(3),4(1), 16.5.2(4)
R v Plaisted (1909) 22 Cox CC 5	18.3.1
R v Plummer (1844) 1 Car & K 600; 174 ER 954	3.2.1(2), 16.5.2(4)
R v Poa [1979] 2 NZLR 378 (CA)	18.5.4
R v Pocock (1851) 5 Cox CC 172	16.5.2(4)
R v Pollock [1973] 2 NZLR 491 (CA)	6.4.4(1)
R v Pommell (1995) 2 Cr App R 607	13.2.1
R v Pope 31/5/88, CA305/87	6.5.2
R v Popen (1981) 60 CCC (2d) 232 (Ont CA)	16.5.2(4)
R v Porritt [1961] 3 All ER 463; [1961] 1 WLR 1372 (CA)	16.5.1(6)
R v Portelli (2004) 148 A Crim R 282	15.1.3(2)
R v Porter (1873) 12 Cox CC 444	17.2.2(1)
R v Porter (1933) 55 CLR 182; [1936] ALR 438 (HCA)	10.3.3
R v Porter (2003) 138 A Crim R 581	11.2.1(2)
R v Poulton (1832) 5 C & P 329; 172 ER 997	16.2.2
R v Powder (1981) 29 CR (3d) 183 (Alta CA)	16.2.3(2), 16.5.2(3)
R v Powell 22/11/01, CA192/01	16.5.2(1)
R v Powell [2002] 1 NZLR 666 (CA)	16.5.2(6)
R v Powell; R v English [1999] 1 AC 1; [1997] 4 All ER 545 (HL)	6.5.3,4
R v Prince (1868) LR 1 CCR 150	19.3.2(4)
R v Prince (1875) LR 2 CCR 154; [1874-80] All ER Rep 881	5.2.1,3(2)
R v Prince (1988) 44 CCC (2d) 510 (Man CA)	16.2.2
R v Purcell 20/6/05, CA42/05	11.2.1(1)
R v Purdy (1946) 10 J Cr L 182	12.10.4
R v Qiu Jiang 3/5/06, CA495/05	8.3.12
R v Quick [1973] 1 QB 910; [1973] 3 All ER 347 (CA)	3.4.1(2),3, 10.3.3(4)
R v R (1981) 28 SASR 321; 4 A Crim R 127	16.5.1(5)
R v R [1992] 1 AC 599; [1991] 4 All ER 481 (HL)	2.1.2
R v Rabey (1977) 79 DLR (3d) 414; 37 CCC (2d) 461	10.3.3(3)
R v Rabey [1980] 2 SCR 513; (1980) 15 CR (3d) 225	3.4.1(2)

767

R v Radford (1985) 20 A Crim R 388	16.5.1(7)	R v Roebuck (1856) D & B 24;	
R v Radford (1985) 42 SASR 266	10.3.3	169 ER 900	20.4
R v Rai [2000] 1 Cr App R 242	20.3.1(1),2	R v Rogers [2003] EWCA Crim 945;	
R v Ram (1893) 17 Cox CC 609	6.6.4(2), 18.2.1	[2003] 1 WLR 1374	3.3.3(2), 16.5.2(1)
R v Ramsay [1967] NZLR 1005 (CA)	4.9.1(2), 16.4.6	R v Rolander [1989] 1 NZLR 366;	
R v Randall (1991) 55 SASR 447;		(1988) 3 CRNZ 603 (CA)	10.1.2
53 A Crim R 380	18.2.1(1)	R v Rolfe (1952) 36 Cr App R 4	17.2, 18.11.2
R v Raney (1942) 29 Cr App R 14	16.5.1(5)	R v Rollo [1956] NZLR 522 (CA)	3.4.2(2)
R v Ranger (1988) 4 CRNZ 6 (CA)	15.1.2,2(1),3(5),4(4),(5),	R v Rolph [1962] Qd R 262	10.3.2
	15.2.2(1)	R v Ronaki 13/5/04, CA451/03	15.1.6
R v Rangi [1992] 1 NZLR 385 (CA)	2.3, 16.5.2(7)	R v Rongonui [2000] 2 NZLR 385;	
R v Ransford (1874) 13 Cox CC 9;		(2000) 17 CRNZ 310 (CA)	16.5.1(1),(4),(5)
31 LT 488	8.2.2(1), 8.4.1(1)	R v Rongonui 9/5/01, CA321/00	16.5.1(5)
R v Rapana and Murray (1988)		R v Rook [1993] 2 All ER 955; [1993]	
3 CRNZ 256	17.3.3,4	1 WLR 1005 (CA)	6.6.6(1),(2)
R v Rapira [2003] 3 NZLR 794;	6.4.4(4), 6.5.2,3(1), 6.6.3,	R v Rose [1961] AC 496	10.3.8
(2003) 20 CRNZ 396 (CA)	9.3.2, 16.4.5	R v Rotana (1995) 12 CRNZ 650 (CA)	10.3.3,10
R v Raroa [1987] 2 NZLR 486; (1987)	12.6, 12.6.1,2, 12.8,9,	R v Rothery [1976] RTR 550;	
2 CRNZ 596 (CA)	12.10.1	[1976] Crim LR 691	19.3.1(8)
R v Ratti [1991] 1 SCR 68 (SCC)	10.3.10	R v Roulston [1976] 2 NZLR 644 (CA)	2.3.1(2), 10.3.1
R v Rau [1972] Tas SR 59	16.5.2(1)	R v Rowe [1951] 4 DLR 238;	
R v Raven [1982] Crim LR 51	16.5.1(5)	[1951] SCR 713 (SCC)	16.4.5
R v Raviraj (1987) 85 Cr App R 93		R v Rowley [1991] 4 All ER 649; [1991]	
(CA)	19.5.3	1 WLR 1020 (CA)	8.2.2(1), 8.4.1(3)
R v Raw (1984) 12 A Crim R 299 (WA		R v Royce 1/7/82, CA203/81	10.1.2
CA)	6.5.3	R v Russell (1832) 1 Mood & R 356;	
R v Rawiri 9/8/02,		168 ER 1302	16.2.3(6)
Fisher J, HC Auckland T014047	9.3.2	R v Russell [1933] ALR 76;	
R v Redmile [1987] 1 NZLR 157 (CA)	10.1.2	[1933] VLR 59	3.2.1(2), 16.5.2(4)
R v Rees [1990] 1 NZLR 555; (1990)		R v Russell [1977] 2 NZLR 20 (CA)	19.3.3(2)
5 CRNZ 487 (CA)	6.4.4(3)	R v Ruzic (2001) 197 DLR (4th) 577	12.13
R v Reid [1992] 3 All ER 673; [1992]		R v Ryder [1995] 2 NZLR 271; (1995)	
1 WLR 793 (HL)	4.3.1(1),(2), 4.6.2	13 CRNZ 81 (CA)	16.4.2,6, 17.10
R v Renata [1992] 2 NZLR 346;	6.4.4(4), 6.5.3(1), 16.2.3	R v S 20/12/91, CA273/91	2.3
(1991) 7 CRNZ 616 (CA)	(3), 16.5.2(1)	R v S [1994] DCR 76	6.3.1, 17.2.3(1)
R v Reyland 13/7/04, CA439/03	15.1.2	R v S (No 2) (1991) 7 CRNZ 576	10.5.4
R v Reynhoudt (1962) 107 CLR 381;		R v Sadler (1911) 14 GLR 117	8.3.4(3)
[1962] ALR 483 (HCA)	17.7.1	R v Saengsai-Or [2004] NSWCCA 108;	
R v Richards (1844) 1 Car & Kir 532;		147 A Crim R 172	5.2.1
174 ER 925	19.4.3(3)	R v Safety-Kleen Canada (1997)	
R v Richards [1974] QB 776; [1973]		145 DLR (4th) 276; 114 CCC (3d)	
3 All ER 1088 (CA)	6.6.3	214	7.2.4(1)
R v Richards [2002] EWCA Crim 3175	3.3.2(2)	R v Salisbury [1976] VR 452	17.2.3
R v Richards [aiding and abetting] (1992)		R v Sampson (1885) 52 LT (NS) 772	20.3.1(1)
9 CRNZ 355, also reported as		R v Samuels [1985] 1 NZLR 350 (CA)	6.2, 6.4.4(1),(4)
R v Wentworth [1993] 2 NZLR 450	4.2.4, 6.4.4(1), 7.2.1	R v Sanders [1984] 1 NZLR 636;	
R v Richards [conspiracy] (1992)		(1984) 1 CRNZ 194 (CA)	8.3.4(1),9
9 CRNZ 403	8.3.4(1),(2),(6),5(1),8	R v Sarah (1990) 5 CRNZ 663 (CA)	16.5.1(1)
R v Richardson (1998) 2 Cr App R 200	17.2.4	R v Sarich 16/5/05, CA407/04	15.1.2
R v Richardson (1999) 1 Cr App R 392		R v Satnam; R v Kewal (1984) 78 Cr	
(CA)	11.1.1(2)	App R 149; [1985] Crim LR 236 (CA)	4.3.2, 18.2.2(1)
R v Richardson; R v Longman [1969]		R v Saunders [1985] Crim LR 230	17.3.1
1 QB 299 (CA)	18.5.3	R v Saunders and Archer (1573) 2	
R v Ridley (1811) 2 Camp 650	3.2.1(2)	Plowd 473; 75 ER 706	6.4.4(4), 6.6.6(2)
R v Ring (1892) 17 Cox CC 491	8.2.5	R v Savage [1991] 3 NZLR 155 (CA)	15.1.4,4(3),(6), 16.5.1(5)
R v Robert Millar (Contractors) Ltd		R v Savage 21/7/06,	
[1970] 2 QB 54; [1970] 1 All ER 577		Lang J, HC Whangarei	
(CA)	7.2	CRI-2005-029-1267	8.3.4(3)
R v Roberts [1942] 1 All ER 187 (CCA)	3.2.1(2)	R v Savoury (2005) 200 CCC (3d) 94	
R v Roberts (1972) 56 Cr App R 95;		(Ont CA)	12.11
[1972] Crim LR 27	3.3.3(3),4(2)	R v Sbarra [1918-19] 2 All ER Rep	
R v Robinson (1915) 2 KB 342;		Ext 1453; (1918) 13 Cr App R 118	19.5.1(3)
[1914-15] All ER Rep Ext 1299		R v Scarlett [1993] 4 All ER 629;	
(CCA)	8.2.3(1)	(1994) 98 Cr App R 290 (CA)	15.1.4, 16.5.2(1)
R v Robinson (1987) 2 CRNZ 632		R v Schmidt (1866) LR 1 CCR 15	19.5.1(3)
(CA)	15.1.4	R v Schriek [1997] 2 NZLR 139;	
R v Rodley (1913) 9 Cr App R 69	4.2.7	(1996) 14 CRNZ 449 (CA)	6.4.1(2),2

R

R v Scott [1967] VR 276	4.9	R v Smith [1960] 2 QB 423; [1960]	
R v Scott (1979) 68 Cr App R 164 (CA)	6.4.4(4)	1 All ER 256 (CCA)	4.1, 4.3.2
R v Scriva (No 2) [1951] ALR 733;		R v Smith [1960] 3 All ER 161 (HL),	
[1951] VLR 298	16.5.1(6)	also reported as DPP v Smith	2.3.2, 4.2.1,3, 12.6,
R v Scully (1824) 1 C & P 320;		[1961] AC 290	16.4.2,4,5, 17.3.1
171 ER 1213	3.3.3(3)	R v Smith [1964] NZLR 834	16.5.1
R v Seaton [1933] NZLR 548 (CA)	18.6.2(2)	R v Smith [1979] Crim LR 251 (CA)	3.2.1(2), 16.5.2(4)
R v Sebe (1987) 35 CCC (3d) 97	20.3.3	R v Smith (1982) 7 A Crim R 437	4.3.1(2)
R v Seiffert (1999) 104 A Crim R 238	6.5.1,3	R v Smith [1983] Crim LR 739	16.6.1
R v Setrum (1976) 32 CCC (2d) 109	16.5.2(1)	R v Smith (1995) 12 CRNZ 616 (CA)	10.3.10
R v Seu 8/12/05, CA81/05	15.1.2(1)	R v Smith 5/4/95, CA271/94	10.4.2
R v Sew Hoy [1994] 1 NZLR 257;		R v Smith (Morgan) [2001] 1 AC 146;	
(1993) 10 CRNZ 581 (CA)	8.2.5(3), 8.3.11(2)	[2000] 3 WLR 654 (HL)	16.5.1(1),(5)
R v Seymour [1954] 1 All ER 1006;		R v Sockett (1908) 72 JP 428	6.6.4(2)
[1954] 1 WLR 678	19.5.1(1)	R v Speck [1977] 2 All ER 859; (1977)	
R v Seymour [1983] 2 AC 493; [1983]		65 Cr App R 161 (CA)	3.2.1(2)
2 All ER 1058 (HL)	16.5.2(5)	R v Spencer (1828) 3 C & P 420;	
R v Shama [1990] 2 All ER 602; [1990]		172 ER 483	20.3.1(2)
1 WLR 661	3.2.1(3)	R v Spencer 5/4/01, CA353/00	16.5.2(5)
R v Sharp [1987] QB 853; [1987] 3 All		R v Spurge [1961] 2 QB 205; [1961]	
ER 103 (CA)	12.10.3	2 All ER 688	3.4.1(2), 4.9.1(6)
R v Sharples [1990] Crim LR 198	2.1.2	R v St George (1840) 9 C & P 483;	
R v Shayler [2001] 1 WLR 2206	13.3.5	173 ER 921	17.2
R v Sheard (1837) 2 Mood 13;		R v St Margaret's Trust Ltd [1958] 2 All	
169 ER 6	17.3.2(1)	ER 289	21.1.1
R v Sheehan [1975] 2 All ER 960;		R v Stack [1986] 1 NZLR 257; (1986)	
[1975] 1 WLR 739 (CA)	11.1.1, 11.2.1(2),8	2 CRNZ 238 (CA)	6.6.5
R v Shephard [1919] 2 KB 125 (CA)	8.4.3(2)	R v Stanley (1977) 36 CCC (2d) 216	15.2
R v Shepherd (1862) 9 Cox CC 123	3.2.1(2)	R v Steane [1947] KB 997; [1947] 1 All	
R v Sheppard [1981] AC 394; [1980]		ER 813 (CCA)	4.2.7
3 All ER 899 (HL)	4.7, 17.10, 17.10.1,2	R v Steele (1976) 65 Cr App R 22	2.1.2
R v Sherriff [1969] Crim LR 260	17.2.2(1)	R v Stephen (1984) 79 Cr App R 334	4.6.2
R v Shivpuri [1987] AC 1; [1986] 2 All		R v Stephenson [1979] QB 695; [1979]	
ER 334 (HL)	8.2.5	2 All ER 1198 (CA)	4.3.1, 14.2.1(2)
R v Silverman (1988) 86 Cr App R 213;		R v Stevens (1844) 1 Cox CC 83	20.3.1(1)
[1987] Crim LR 574	20.3.1(1)	R v Stone (1910) 6 Cr App R 89 (CCA)	18.6.2(3)
R v Simmons [1986] Crim LR 397 (CA)	19.5.3	R v Stone [1920] NZLR 462;	
R v Simpson (1915) 84 LJKB 1893		[1920] GLR 357 (CA)	19.5.2
(CCA)	16.5.1(6)	R v Stone [1999] 2 SCR 290; (1999)	
R v Simpson [1978] 2 NZLR 221 (CA)	4.5, 17.7.1, 19.5.2	134 CCC (3d) 353 (SCC)	10.3.3(4)
R v Simpson (1988) 46 DLR (4th) 466;		R v Stone and Dobinson [1977] QB 354;	3.2.1(2), 3.3.4(1), 4.6.2,
[1988] 1 SCR 3 (SCC)	6.5.4	[1977] 2 All ER 341 (CA)	16.5.2(4)
R v Sinclair [1968] 1 WLR 1246 (CA)	20.3.3	R v Stopford (1870) 11 Cox CC 643	17.2.1(1)
R v Singh [1999] Crim LR 582 (CA)	16.5.2(4)	R v Storer 2/5/06, CA368/05	1.1.2.1(1)
R v Singh 10/12/03, CA53/03;		R v Storey [1931] NZLR 417 (CA)	3.3.2(3), 4.6.4, 16.2.3,
CA67/03	6.4.4(1)		16.5.2(1),(2),(4),(5)
R v Siracusa (1990) 90 Cr App R 340		R v Strawbridge [1970] NZLR 909	2.3.1(4), 5.2.1,2(1),(2),(3),
(CA)	8.3.5(1)	(CA)	3(2), 14.2.1
R v Skivington [1968] 1 QB 166; [1967]		R v Strickland (1850) 14 JP 784	20.4
1 All ER 483 (CA)	19.4.2	R v Stripp (1979) 69 Cr App R 318	3.4.1(2),4
R v Skokolic [1929] NZLR 521	10.1.2	R v Sturm [2004] 1 NZLR 570; (2003)	
R v Slovack [1980] 1 WWR 268	13.4	20 CRNZ 513	17.6.1
R v Smails [1957] 74 WN (NSW) 150	19.4.3(5)	R v Sturm [2005] 3 NZLR 252; (2005)	
R v Smith (1826) 2 C & P 449;		21 CRNZ 627 (CA)	17.6
172 ER 203	3.2.1(2)	R v Styles 6/11/03, CA 297/03	15.1.2(1)
R v Smith (1837) 8 C & P 173;		R v Subritzky [1990] 2 NZLR 717	19.3.3(2)
173 ER 448	17.3.2	R v Sullivan [1981] Crim LR 46 (CA)	17.3.6(2)
R v Smith (1855) 1 Dears 494;		R v Sullivan [1984] 1 AC 156; [1983]	
169 ER 818	19.5.1(1)	2 All ER 673 (HL)	10.3.3(1),(2)
R v Smith (1855) 1 Dears 559;		R v Susak [1978] AC 55; [1977] 2 All	
169 ER 845	17.2.1(1)	ER 909 (HL)	8.2.3(1)
R v Smith (1869) 11 Cox CC 210	3.2.1(2), 16.5.2(4)	R v Susak (1999) 105 A Crim R 592	
R v Smith (1914) 11 Cr App R 36		(NTSC)	8.2.3(1),(4)
(CCA)	16.5.1(5)	R v Sutton [1977] 3 All ER 476; [1977]	
R v Smith (1935) 25 Cr App R 119	19.5.2	1 WLR 1086 (CA)	18.11.3
R v Smith [1959] 2 QB 35; [1959] 2 All	3.3.2(3),3(2),4(2), 16.2.3	R v Swindall and Osborne (1846) 2 Car	
ER 193	(5)	& Kir 230; 2 Cox CC 141; 175 ER 95	3.3.3(3), 6.4.4(4)

769

R v T [1990] Crim LR 256	3.4.1(2)	
R v T [1997] 1 Qd R 623 (CA)	4.7	
R v T 27/10/99, Hammond J, HC Hamilton T1866/99	16.5.2(1)	
R v Taaffe [1984] AC 539; [1984] 1 All ER 747 (HL)	4.8, 8.3.11(1)	
R v Taaka [1982] 2 NZLR 198 (CA)	16.5.1(1),(2),(3),(4),(5),(6)	
R v Tai [1976] 1 NZLR 102 (CA)	16.5.1(1),(2),(3),(5), 17.8.1(3)	
R v Taisalika 25/6/93, CA94/93	17.3.6(1)	
R v Taktak (1988) 14 NSWLR 226; 34 A Crim R 334	3.2.1(2)	
R v Tamatea (2003) 20 CRNZ 363 (HC)	6.4.1(3)	
R v Tarei 5/8/05, Heath J, HC Tauranga CRI-2004-087-1673	3.2.1(5), 16.2.3(1)	
R v Tarei (No 3) 5/8/05, Heath J, HC Tauranga CRI-2004-087-1673	16.2.3(3),(4),(5)	
R v Tavete [1988] 1 NZLR 428; (1987) 2 CRNZ 579 (CA)	2.3, 10.4.1, 11.2.1,1(2), 15.1.2,6	
R v Tawera (1996) 14 CRNZ 290 (CA)	18.2.1(3)	
R v Taylor (1859) 1 F & F 511; 175 ER 831	8.2.4	
R v Taylor [1911] 1 KB 674	19.3.3(1)	
R v Taylor (1985) 80 Cr App R 327 (CA)	18.2.2(1)	
R v Taylor [1991] 1 NZLR 413 (CA)	20.3.1(1)	
R v Te Moni [1998] 1 NZLR 641; (1997) 15 CRNZ 439 (CA)	6.5.3, 6.6.3	
R v Teichelman [1981] 2 NZLR 64 (CA)	12.4,5,6, 12.6.2, 12.7,8,9, 12.10.4, 12.11,13, 13.3.4(2)	
R v Tennet [1939] 1 All ER 86	19.5.2	
R v Terewi (1985) 1 CRNZ 623 (CA)	12.4, 15.1.3,3(3),(5),4(3),(4), 17.2.2	
R v Terry [1964] VR 248	16.5.1(2)	
R v Terry 9/9/96, CA50/96	4.9	
R v Thain [1985] NI 457	4.4	
R v Thomas (1981) 6 A Crim R 66	3.2.2(2)	
R v Thomas [1991] 3 NZLR 141; (1991) 7 CRNZ 123 (CA)	11.2.4, 14.2.1(1),2, 15.1.3, 3(5), 17.7.1(2),(3)	
R v Thomson 14/6/05, CA1/05	6.4.1(2)	
R v Thomson 2/3/06, CA406/05	12.13	
R v Thornton [1964] 2 QB 176; [1963] 1 All ER 170 (CCA)	20.5.2(2)	
R v Thornton (No 2) [1996] 2 All ER 1023; [1996] 1 WLR 1174 (CA)	16.5.1(3),(4),(5)	
R v Tideswell [1905] 2 KB 273	19.3.2(4)	
R v Tighe (1926) 26 SR (NSW) 94	20.3.3(2)	
R v Tihi [1989] 2 NZLR 29; (1989) 4 CRNZ 289 (CA)	4.3, 4.3.1(2), 5.2.3(2), 17.6.1, 17.7	
R v Tihi [1990] 1 NZLR 540; (1990) 5 CRNZ 472 (CA)	11.2.1,1(1),(2)	
R v Tillings & Tillings [1985] Crim LR 393	19.3.2(3)	
R v Timoti [2005] 1 NZLR 466; (2004) 21 CRNZ 90 (CA)	16.5.1(3),(5)	
R v Tipple 22/12/05, CA217/05	4.3, 4.3.1(2)	
R v Tolmie (1995) 37 NSWLR 660	4.3.2	
R v Tolmie (1995) 84 A Crim R 293	18.2.2(2)	
R v Tolson (1889) 23 QBD 168; [1886-90] All ER Rep 26	5.1, 5.2.1, 10.3.3(4), 14.2	
R v Tomars [1978] 2 NZLR 505 (CA)	3.3.3(2),(3), 16.2.3, 16.5.2(2),(3)	

R v Tomkins [1985] 2 NZLR 253; (1985) 1 CRNZ 627 (CA)	6.5.2,3(1), 6.6.3	
R v Toner (1991) 93 Cr App R 382; [1991] Crim LR 627	3.4.1(2)	
R v Tooley (1709) 2 Ld Raym 1296; 92 ER 349	16.5.1(2)	
R v Topia 8/6/06, Potter J, HC Whangarei S05-029-1272	1.3.3(1)	
R v Tosti [1997] Crim LR 746 (CA)	8.2.3(4)	
R v Towers (1874) 12 Cox CC 530	16.2.3(2), 16.5.2(3)	
R v Trilloe (1842) 2 Mood CC 260; 169 ER 103	16.2.2	
R v Trounson [1991] 3 NZLR 690; (1991) 8 CRNZ 491 (CA)	16.2.3(1),(4),(5), 16.5.1(5)	
R v Trudgeon (1988) 39 A Crim R 252	8.3.5	
R v Tucker (1984) 36 SASR 135; 13 A Crim R 447	3.4.1(2)	
R v Tuhoro [1998] 3 NZLR 568; (1998) 15 CRNZ 568 (CA)	6.5.2, 16.4.5	
R v Tukaki 14/6/06, CA360/05	11.2.1,3	
R v Tumanako (1992) 64 A Crim R 149	16.5.1(6)	
R v Turaki 23/6/05, CA405/04	16.5.1(6)	
R v Turanga [1993] 1 NZLR 685	6.4.1(1)	
R v Turner [1975] QB 834; [1975] 1 All ER 70 (CA)	16.5.1(5)	
R v Turner (1995) 13 CRNZ 142 (CA)	16.5.2(4),(5)	
R v Turner (No 2) (1971) 55 Cr App R 336 (CA)	19.3.2(3)	
R v Turton (No 2) (1989) 5 CRNZ 274	16.5.2(4)	
R v Twine [1967] Crim LR 710 (CA)	16.5.1(2),(6)	
R v Tyler (1838) 8 C & P 616; 173 ER 643	6.3.1, 12.6.1	
R v Tyrrell [1894] 1 QB 710; [1891-94] All ER Rep 1215	6.6.4(1), 8.3.4(6)	
R v Uddin [1999] QB 431; [1998] 2 All ER 744 (CA)	6.5.3	
R v Valderrama-Vega [1985] Crim LR 220	12.3.1	
R v van der Hulst 18/5/06, CA469/05	15.1.6	
R v Vang (1999) 132 CCC (3d) 32; 21 CR (5th) 260 (Ont CA)	6.5.1	
R v Vantandillo (1815) 4 M & S 73; 105 ER 762	13.3.2	
R v Vasil [1981] 1 SCR 469; (1981) 58 CCC (2d) 97 (SCC)	16.4.4	
R v Velumyl [1989] Crim LR 299	19.4.3(2)	
R v Venna [1976] QB 421; [1975] 3 All ER 788 (CA)	17.2.1	
R v Vickers [1957] 2 QB 664; [1957] 2 All ER 741 (CCA)	16.4	
R v W 31/10/01, CA216/01	17.8.1(3)	
R v Waaka 9/7/01, Hammond J, HC Hamilton T010076	6.6.2(3)	
R v Wacker [2002] EWCA Crim 1944; [2003] QB 1207	16.5.2(6)	
R v Wahrlich [1976] 2 NZLR 9 (CA)	6.6.2(3)	
R v Wakeling (1823) Russ & R 504; 168 ER 920	20.8	
R v Walker [1958] NZLR 810 (CA)	5.2.1,3(2), 16.5.2(5)	
R v Walker [1962] Crim LR 458 (CA)	8.3.4	
R v Walker (1980) 48 CCC (2d) 126	5.1.2	
R v Walker [1984] Crim LR 112 (CA)	19.3.2(3),(4)	
R v Walker (1990) 90 Cr App R 226	4.2.1	
R v Walkley (1829) 4 C & P 132; 172 ER 640	19.5.1(3)	

R v *Wall* (1802) 28 St Tr 51   3.3.3(3), 16.2.3(5)
R v *Waller* [1991] Crim LR 381 (CA)   13.2.1
R v *Walsh* 26/6/06, CA208/05   20.5.3
R v *Walsh and Harney* [1984] VR 474;
(1983) 9 A Crim R 307   20.3.3
R v *Waltham* (1849) 3 Cox CC 442   17.3.2
R v *Wang* [1990] 2 NZLR 529; (1989)   15.1.4,4(4),(5),(6), 15.2.2
4 CRNZ 674 (CA)   (1)
R v *Ward* [1956] 1 QB 351; [1956]
1 All ER 565 (CA)   4.2.3, 4.6.2
R v *Warren* 20/11/00, CA315/00   16.5.1(5)
R v *Waterfall* [1970] 1 QB 148; [1969]
3 All ER 1048   20.3.1(1)
R v *Waters* [1979] 1 NZLR 375 (CA)   17.3.1,2
R v *Wati* [1985] 2 NZLR 236; (1984)
1 CRNZ 380 (CA)   17.6.3, 17.7
R v *Watson* [1989] 2 All ER 865;
[1989] 1 WLR 684 (CA)   16.5.2(1)
R v *Watson* (1999) 137 CCC (3d) 422   14.3
R v *Watson and Watson* (1959) 43 Cr
App R 111 (CCA)   16.5.2(4)
R v *Weaver* (1931) 45 CLR 321; [1931]
ALR 249 (HCA)   20.3.3
R v *Webb* (1834) 1 M & Rob 405;
174 ER 140   16.5.2(5)
R v *Welsh* (1869) 11 Cox CC 336   16.5.1
R v *Welsh* [1974] RTR 478   19.3.1(8)
R v *Wentworth* [1993] 2 NZLR 450,
also reported as R v *Richards [aiding
and abetting]* (1992) 9 CRNZ 355   4.2.4, 6.4.4(1), 7.2.1
R v *Wentworth* 26/5/93, CA10/93   6.4.4(4)
R v *Weshaver* (1993) 17 CR (4th) 401
(SCC)   15.1.4(3)
R v *Wesley* (1859) 1 F & F 528;
175 ER 838   16.5.2(1)
R v *West* (1848) 2 Car & K 784; 2 Cox
CC 500   16.2.2, 16.4.3
R v *West London Coroner, ex p Gray*
[1988] QB 467; [1987] 2 All ER 129   3.2.1(2)
R v *Wheatly* (1761) 2 Burr 1125;
97 ER 746   20.3.3(3)
R v *Wheelhouse* [1994] Crim LR 756
(CA)   6.6.2(2)
R v *White* (1859) 1 F & F 665;
175 ER 898   19.5.2
R v *White* [1910] 2 KB 124;
[1908-10] All ER Rep 340 (CCA)   3.1, 3.3.1,2(1)
R v *White* (1912) 7 Cr App R 266   19.3.2(5)
R v *White* [1945] GLR 108   8.3.4(3)
R v *White (Shane)* [1988] 1 NZLR 122
(CA)   16.5.1(2),(4),(5),(6)
R v *Whitehouse* [1941] 1 DLR 683;
(1940) 75 CCC 65 (BC CA)   6.6.4(1)
R v *Whitehouse* [1977] QB 868   6.6.4(1)
R v *Whitehouse* [2000] Crim LR 172
(CA)   4.3
R v *Whittaker* 27/8/97, CA23/97   18.12, 18.12.2
R v *Wholesale Travel Group Inc* (1991)
84 DLR (4th) 161; [1991] 3 SCR 154
(SCC)   5.1.1(3)
R v *Whybrow* (1951) 35 Cr App R 141
(CA)   8.2.1, 18.4.1
R v *Whyte* [1987] 3 All ER 416; [1987]
85 Cr App R 283 (CA)   15.1.4(3)
R v *Wickliffe* [1987] 1 NZLR 55;
(1986) 2 CRNZ 310 (CA)   3.4.3, 16.1, 16.4.5,6
R v *Wilcox* [1982] 1 NZLR 191 (CA)   6.6.1(1), 8.2.2,3(1),(4)

R v *Wiley* (1850) 4 Cox CC 412;
169 ER 408   19.5
R v *Wilkinson* [1999] 1 NZLR 403;   19.3.1(2),3(2), 20.5.1(1),
(1998) 16 CRNZ 179 (CA)   (2)
R v *Willer* (1986) 83 Cr App R 225
(CA)   13.2
R v *Williams* [1923] 1 KB 340;
[1922] All ER Rep 433 (CCA)   18.2.1(3)
R v *Williams* [1980] Crim LR 589   20.3.1(1)
R v *Williams* [1985] 1 NZLR 294 (CA)   20.3.3(2)
R v *Williams* [1987] 3 All ER 411;
(1983) 78 Cr App R 276   12.6.2
R v *Williams* [1992] 2 All ER 183;
[1992] 1 WLR 380 (CA)   3.3.3(2),(3), 16.5.2(5)
R v *Williams* (2002) 176 CCC (3d) 449
(SCC)   8.1
R v *Williams* (2003) 168 CCC (3d) 67   12.10.1
R v *Williamson* (1972) 2 NSWLR 281   12.8
R v *Willoughby* [1980] 1 NZLR 66   6.6.4(1), 8.2.2(1)
R v *Willoughby* [2005] 1 Cr App R 29   16.5.2(1)
R v *Wilson* [1955] 1 All ER 744; [1955]
1 WLR 493; (1955) 39 Cr App R 12
(CCA)   17.2
R v *Wilson* [1983] 1 All ER 993   17.2.3
R v *Wilson* [1996] 3 WLR 125 (CA)   17.2.4(2)
R v *Wilton* (1993) 64 A Crim R 359   6.6.6(2)
R v *Windle* [1952] 2 QB 826; [1952]
2 All ER 1 (CA)   10.3.5
R v *Winning* (1973) 12 CCC (2d) 449   20.4
R v *Winterburn* 8/10/98, CA30/98   15.1.6
R v *Witika* (1991) 7 CRNZ 621 (CA)   6.4.3
R v *Witika* [1993] 2 NZLR 424;   3.2.1(2), 6.4.3,4(4), 6.6.6
(1992) 9 CRNZ 272 (CA)   (1), 13.6.4, 16.5.2(4),(5)
R v *Wood* (1830) 1 Mood CC 278;
168 ER 1271   17.3.2
R v *Wood* [1982] 2 NZLR 233 (CA)   5.2.1,2(2),(3), 14.2.1
R v *Woodman* [1974] QB 754   19.3.2(5)
R v *Woods* [1969] 1 QB 447; [1968]
3 All ER 709 (CA)   4.5
R v *Woods* (1981) 74 Cr App R 312;
[1982] Crim LR 42 (CA)   11.1.1(2), 11.2.4
R v *Woollin* [1999] 1 AC 82; [1998]
4 All ER 103 (HL)   4.2.3,4, 16.4.1,4
R v *Woolnough* [1977] 2 NZLR 508
(CA)   13.3.4,4(1)
R v *Wozniak* (1977) 16 SASR 67   18.2.2(1)
R v *Wrenn, Ross and Thomas* (1989)
4 CRNZ 165 (CA)   8.3.4(6)
R v *Wright* (2001) 18 CRNZ 527 (CA)   16.6.2
R v *Wright* [2001] 3 NZLR 22; (2001)
18 CRNZ 527 (CA)   16.6.3
R v *Wrigley* [1957] Crim LR 57   4.8
R v *Wyatt* (1921) 16 Cr App R 57
(CCA)   18.3.1,3
R v *Wyles* [1977] Qd R 169 (CA)   6.3
R v *Yelds* [1928] NZLR 18 (CA)   8.2.2(1),3(1)
R v *Yogasakaran* [1990] 1 NZLR 399;   4.6.1,1(1),(2),2,4, 13.3.4
(1989) 5 CRNZ 69 (CA)   (3), 16.1, 16.5.2(5),(7)
R v *York* (2005) 193 CCC (3d) 331
(BC CA)   19.5.3
R v *Young* 9/7/92, CA86/92   4.2, 4.3.2, 17.2.1
R v *Young* 8/3/06, CA266/05   15.1.3(2)
R v *Young and Webber* (1838) 8 C
& P 644; 173 ER 655   6.4.1(2)
R v *Zemmel* (1985) 81 Cr App R 279;
[1985] Crim LR 213   20.3.3(2)

TABLE OF CASES

R v Zhou 11/9/06,
Potter J, HC Auckland,
CRI-2005-092-10395 16.5.1(5)
R v Zigov 12/11/03,
Williams J, HC Auckland T031264 6.4.1(1),3
R v Zorad [1979] 2 NSWLR 764
(CCA) 8.2.1, 18.4.1

S

S M Savill Ltd v MOT [1986]
1 NZLR 653 5.2.3(1),(2), 6.1, 7.1.2
SA Ambulance Transport Inc v
Wahlheim (1948) 77 CLR 215; [1949]
ALR 1 4.6.2
Salaca v R [1967] NZLR 421 (CA) 12.6,7,11
Sansregret v R [1985] 1 SCR 570 4.3.1(2), 4.5.1
Saunders v Edwards [1987]
1 WLR 1116 16.5.2(6)
Savill, S M, Ltd v MOT [1986]
1 NZLR 653 5.2.3(1),(2), 6.1, 7.1.2
Schultz v Pettit (1980) 25 SASR 427 6.6.2
Scott v Killian (1985) 40 SASR 37;
19 A Crim R 187 6.6.4(1)
Scott v Metropolitan Police Commissioner
[1975] AC 819; [1974] 3 All ER 1032
(HL) 20.3.3
Scott v MPC [1975] AC 819; [1974]
3 All ER 1032 (HL) 20.5.4
Semayne's Case (1604) 5 Co Rep 91a;
77 ER 194 15.2
Severinsen v DSW 31/5/94,
Penlington J, HC Hamilton AP1/94 4.5.1
Sharma v Police [2003] 2 NZLR 473 17.8.1(3)
Shaw v DPP [1962] AC 220; [1961]
2 All ER 446 (HL) 2.1.2
Shaw v R [2001] 1 WLR 1519; [2002]
1 Cr App R 10; [2002] Crim LR 140 15.1.3(1)
Sheehan v Police [1994] 3 NZLR 592;
(1994) 12 CRNZ 39 16.5.2(7)
Sheldrake v DPP [2004] UKHL 43;
[2004] 3 WLR 976 2.3.1(1)
Sherras v de Rutzen [1895] 1 QB 918;
[1895-99] All ER Rep 1167 5.1, 5.2.1,2(2),3(2)
Shortland v Northland Health Ltd
[1998] 1 NZLR 433; (1997) 4 HRNZ
121 (CA) 16.5.2(7)
Shortland v Police 23/4/96,
Tipping J, HC Invercargill AP74/95 15.1.2
Shoukatallie v R [1962] AC 81; [1961]
3 All ER 966 4.9.1(2)
Siboen & the Sibotre, The [1976] 1
Lloyds Rep 293 20.3.1(1)
Simpson v Peat [1952] 2 QB 24; [1952]
1 All ER 447 4.6.1(1),(2)
Singh v Police 22/2/00,
Williams J, HC Auckland A185/99 15.2.2(4)
Singh v Police [2003] NZAR 596 19.4.2
Sione v Labour Dept [1972] NZLR 278 3.4.1(2),3, 5.1.2
Sivyer v Taylor [1916] NZLR 586 7.1.2
Slowly (1873) 12 Cox 269 19.3.2(2)
Smedleys Ltd v Breed [1974] AC 839 13.3.3, 21.6.1
Smith [1960] 2 QB 423; [1960] 1 All
ER 256 (CA) 4.2.2
Smith v Hughes (1871) LR 6 QB 597;
[1861-73] All ER Rep 632 20.3.1(1)

Smith v Land and House Property Corp
(1884) 28 Ch D 7 20.3.1(1)
Smith v Police (1988) 3 CRNZ 262 4.3.1
Smyth v Police [1973] 1 NZLR 56 3.3.3(2)
Snyder v Massachusetts 291 US 97
(1934) 1.3.1
Sodeman v R (1936) 55 CLR 192;
[1936] ALR 156 (HCA) 10.3.1,5
Somerset v Hart (1884) 12 QBD 360 7.1.1
Sopp v Long [1970] 1 QB 518; [1969]
1 All ER 855 (CA) 7.1.2,2(1)
South Staffordshire Water Co v Sharman
[1896] 2 QB 44 19.3.2(5)
Southwark London Borough Council v
Williams [1971] Ch 734; [1971] 2 All
ER 175 (CA) 13.3.2,3(1)
St George's Healthcare NHS Trust v S;
R v Collins, exp S [1998] 3 All ER 673 17.2.4
Stansbie v Troman [1948] 2 KB 48;
[1948] All ER 599 3.3.3(2)
Stapleton v R (1952) 86 CLR 358;
[1952] ALR 929 (HCA) 10.3.5
Starri v SA Police (1995) 80 A Crim R
197 3.4.2
State v Angelina 73 WVa 146; 80 SE
141 (1913) 3.3.3(3)
State v O'Neil (1910) 126 NW 454 2.1.3
State v Talley 102 Ala 25 (1894) 6.4.1(1)
State v Wood (1881) 53 Vt 560 3.3.3(2)
Steinberg v Police (1983) 1 CRNZ 129 3.4.3
Stephens v Myers (1830) 4 C & P 349 17.2
Stephenson v State 205 Ind 141; 179 NE
633 (1932) 3.3.3(3)
Stevens v Police (1988) 4 CRNZ 69 19.5, 19.5.1(3),2
Stingel v R (1990) 171 CLR 312; 97
ALR 1 (HCA) 16.5.1(2),(5)
Stockdale v Coulson [1974] 3 All
ER 154; [1974] 1 WLR 1192 3.4.2, 5.1.2, 13.6.1
Storrow and Poole [1983] Crim LR 332 19.3.1(5)
Strowger v John [1974] RTR 124;
[1974] Crim LR 123 3.4.2(1)
Strutt v Clift [1911] 1 KB 1 7.1.2
Stuart v R (1974) 134 CLR 426; 4 ALR
545 (HCA) 6.4.1(4), 16.4.4
Subramaniam v Public Prosecutor [1956]
1 WLR 965 (PC) 12.7
Summers v SPCA [1991] 2 NZLR 469;
(1990) 6 CRNZ 201 4.3,7, 5.2.2(2)
Surujpaul v R [1958] 3 All ER 300;
(1958) 42 Cr App R 266 (PC) 6.6.2(3)
SW v UK (1996) 21 EHRR 363 2.1.2
Sweet v Parsley [1970] AC 132; [1969] 2.2.3, 5.1.1, 5.2.2(2),3(2),
1 All ER 347 (HL) 14.2.1
Sweetman v Industries and Commerce
Dept [1970] NZLR 139 6.3.1, 6.6.2(3),4(2)
S v Kennedy (1951) 4 SA 431 (A) 10.3.1
S v Masilela 1968 (2) SA 558 4.9.1(3)
S v Nkosiyana [1966] (4) SA 655 8.4.1
S v Police (1990) 7 CRNZ 173 18.7
S v Robinson 1968 (1) SA 666 6.4.4(4)
S v Thomo [1969] (1) SA 385 (AD) 6.2

T

T (a minor) (wardship: medical treatment),
Re [1997] 1 All ER 906 (CA) 16.5.2(7)

W

T *(CA175/97) v A-G* 27/8/97,
CA175/97 18.5.2
Taktak v R (1988) 14 NSWLR 226;
34 A Crim R 334 (CA) 16.5.2(4)
Tamworth Industries v A-G [1991]
3 NZLR 616 19.3.2(5)
Taylor v NZ Poultry Board [1984]
1 NZLR 394 1.3.1
Taylor v Police (1990) 6 CRNZ 470 4.3, 4.3.1
Tesco Supermarkets Ltd v Nattrass
[1972] AC 153; [1971] 2 All ER 127
(HL) 1.3.2(5), 7.2.4,4(1),(3)
Tessymond's Case (1828) 1 Lew CC
169; 168 ER 1000 3.3.3(2), 6.3.1
Thabo Meli v R [1954] 1 All ER 373;
[1954] 1 WLR 228 (PC) 4.9.1(2), 16.4.6
Theeman v Police [1966] NZLR 605 6.4.3
Thomas v A-G 14/8/97, CA139/96,
7 19.4.3(1)
Thomas v Greenslade [1954] CLY 3421 19.3.2(4)
Thompson v Grey (1904) 24 NZLR 457 17.10.3
Thompson v Police 6/5/96,
Tipping J, HC Invercargill AP35/96 15.1.3(3)
Thornton v Mitchell [1940] 1 All ER 339 6.3.1, 6.6.1
Tifaga v Dept of Labour [1980] 3.2.2(1), 3.4.2(1), 5.1.1(1),
2 NZLR 235 (CA) 2, 13.1.1, 13.3.1,4, 13.4,
13.6.1,2,3
Tillings and Tillings [1985] Crim
LR 393 20.5.3
Timbu Kolian v R (1968) 119 CLR 47;
[1969] ALR 143 (HCA) 16.5.2(4)
Timoti v R [2005] NZSC 37 16.4.3, 16.5.1(4),(5),(6)
Timoti v R [2006] 1 NZLR 323; (2005)
21 CRNZ 804 (CA) 16.4.4
Tipple v Police [1994] 2 NZLR 362;
(1993) 11 CRNZ 132 14.4.1(1)
Title of the Finder, The (1899) 33 ILT
225 19.3.2(5)
Tolson (1889) 23 QBD 168 13.3.2
Trow v Police 4/4/05,
Nicholson J, HC Auckland
CRI-2004-404-208 10.5.1
Tuberville v Savage (1669) 1 Mod Rep
3; 86 ER 684 17.2.1
Tuck v Robson [1970] 1 All ER 1171 6.4.3
Tuck & Sons v Priester (1887) 19 QBD
629 (CA) 2.2.3
Tuialli v Police 19/3/87,
Greig J, HC Auckland AP310/86 15.1.3(5),4
Tuli v Police (1987) 2 CRNZ 638 15.1.3(3)
T v T [1988] Fam 52 17.2.2
T v UK; V v UK [1999] Crim LR 579 9.3,4

U

US v Dynar (1997) 147 DLR (4th) 4.5, 8.2.5,5(1),(2),(3),
399; 115 CCC (3d) 481 (SCC) 8.3.11(3)
US v Freed 401 US 601; 28 L Ed
2d 356 (1971) 5.1.1(3)
US v Kozminski 108 SCT 2751 2.2.3

V

Van Den Hoek v R (1986)
161 CLR 158; 69 ALR 1 (HCA) 16.5.1(4)
Van Gaalen v Police [1979]
2 NZLR 204 (CA) 15.2.2(4)

van Niewkoop v Registrar of Companies
[2005] 1 NZLR 796 (HC) 6.6.2(2),4(2)
Vane v Yiannopoullos [1965] AC 486;
[1964] 3 All ER 820 (HL) 7.1.1
Verrier v DPP [1967] 2 AC 195; [1966]
3 All ER 568 (HL) 8.3.12
Vincent v Lake Erie Transportation Co
(1910)124 NW 221 13.3.5(1)

W

Waaka v Police [1987] 1 NZLR 754; 4.3.2, 5.2.3(2), 14.2.1(1),
(1987) 2 CRNZ 370 (CA) 14.3.1, 14.4.1(1), 17.7.1,1
(1),(2)
Wairarapa Election Petition, Re [1988]
2 NZLR 74 5.2.3(2)
Walden v Hensler (1987) 163 CLR 561;
75 ALR 173 (HCA) 15.2.2(4)
Walsh v Sainsbury (1925) 36 CLR 464;
[1925] ALR 343 8.4.1
Walters v Lunt [1951] 2 All ER 645;
(1951) 35 Cr App R 94 19.5.1(3)
Warner v MPC [1969] 2 AC 256;
[1968] 2 All ER 356 (HL) 5.1, 5.2.1
Warren v R [1987] WAR 314; (1985)
15 A Crim R 317 6.6.3
Watmore v Jenkins [1962] 2 QB 572;
[1962] 2 All ER 868 3.4.1(2)
Wayne v Boldiston (1992) 85 NTR 8
(NT SC) 17.3.1
Western Australia v Oates (2004)
148 A Crim R 202; [2004] WASC 170 8.3.12
Westminster CC v Croyalgrange Ltd
[1986] 2 All ER 353; [1986]
1 WLR 674 (HL) 4.5.1
White (1853) Dears 203; 169 ER 696 19.3.1(7)
White v Ridley (1978) 140 CLR 342;
52 ALJR 724 (HCA) 3.3.3(2), 6.3.1, 6.6.6(1)
Wicks v Police (1984) 1 CRNZ 328 4.2.8, 15.2.2(4), 19.4.2,3
(1)
Wihongi v Police 10/5/99,
Fisher J, HC Auckland T990080 10.1, 10.5.2
Wilcox v Jefferey [1951] 1 All ER 464 6.4.1(2)
Wilcox v Police [1994] 1 NZLR 243;
(1993) 10 CRNZ 704 13.3.4(2)
Wilcox v Police [1995] 2 NZLR 160;
(1995) 12 CRNZ 468 (CA) 13.3.4(2)
Willey v Synan (1937) 57 CLR 200 19.3.2(5)
Willgoss v R (1960) 105 CLR 295
(HCA) 10.3.5
Williams v Phillips (1957) 41 Cr App
R 5 19.3.2(5)
Williams v Police [1981] 1 NZLR 108 15.1.3
Williams v Williams (1882) 20 Ch
D 659; [1881-1885] All ER Rep 840 19.3.1(8)
Williams (Roy) [2001] 1 Cr App R 362 19.3.1(3)
Wills v Petroulias (2003)
58 NSWLR 598 (NSW CA) 20.5.4
Wilson v R (1992) 174 CLR 313;
66 ALJR 517 (HCA) 16.5.2(1)
Wings Ltd v Ellis [1984] 1 All ER 1046 7.2.4(3)
Winship, Re 397 US 358; 25 L Ed
2d 368 (1970) (USSC) 2.3
Winterwerp v The Netherlands (1979) 2
EHRR 387 10.3.3
Winzar v Chief Constable of Kent The
Times, 28 March 1983 3.2.2(1)

773

With v O'Flanagan [1936] Ch 575;
[1936] 1 All ER 727 (CA)   3.2.1(2), 20.3.2
Wong Pooh Yin v Public Prosecutor
[1955] AC 93; [1954] 3 All ER 31
(PC)   16.5.2(7)
Wood v Richards (1977) 65 Cr App
R 300; [1977] Crim LR 295   4.6.1(2), 13.3.2
Woodgate v Knatchbull (1787) 2 Term
Rep 148; 100 ER 80   7.1
Woods v Brown (1907) 26 NZLR 1312;
10 GLR 70   4.2.2
Woollin [1999] 1 AC 82; [1998] 4 All
ER 103 (HL)   4.2.4
Woolmington v DPP [1935] AC 462;   2.3, 2.3.1(2), 5.1.1(3),2,
[1935] All ER 1 (HL)   10.3.1
W v R (T2/98) (1998) 16 CRNZ 33   18.5.2

X

X v Police (1993) 10 CRNZ 385   18.7

Y

Yip Chiu-Cheung v R [1995] 1 AC 111;
[1994] 2 All ER 924 (PC)   1.3.2(1), 4.1, 8.3.5,5(2)
Yorke v Lucas (1985) 158 CLR 661
(HCA)   6.4.4(4)
*Yorkton Agricultural & Industrial
Exhibition Assn v Morley* (1967)
66 DLR (2d) 37   4.6.2
Young v Cassels (1914) 16 GLR 391   8.4.1
Yuen Kun Yeu v A-G of Hong Kong
[1988] AC 175   3.2.1

Z

Zamora No 2, The [1921] 1 AC 801
(PC)   4.5.1

SUBJECT INDEX

Abbreviations

1	Criminal Law: Definition and Application: ch 1	12	Compulsion: ch 12
2	Interpretation, Proof, and the Rule of Law: ch 2	13	Duress of Circumstances, Necessity, and
3	The Actus Reus: ch 3		Impossibility: ch 13
4	Mens Rea: ch 4	14	Mistake: ch 14
5	Strict and Absolute Liability: ch 5	15	Self-Defence and Defence of Property: ch 15
6	Secondary Participation: ch 6	16	Culpable Homicide: ch 16
7	Vicarious and Corporate Liability: ch 7	17	Non-fatal Offences of Violence: ch 17
8	The Inchoate Offences: ch 8	19	Theft and Receiving: ch 19
9	Infancy: ch 9	20	Deception: ch 20
10	Insanity: ch 10	21	The Moral Limits of Criminalisation: ch 21
11	Intoxication: ch 11		

A

abandoned goods	19.3.2(5)
abetting *see also* secondary participation	6.4.1(2), 6.4.4(1)
abortion, procuring	13.3.4(1), 16.2.2
absence of fault *see* strict liability	
absolute liability *see also* regulatory offences; strict liability	
availability of defence	5.1.2
burden of proof	5.1, 5.1.2
determining fault standard	5.2.3(2)(d)
justification of	5.1.2(1)
mistake	14.2.4
vicarious liability and	7.1, 7.1.2
accessories after the fact	6.2
accountability for conduct	1.3.2(5)
acts distinguished from omissions	3.2.1(5)
acts mala in se	1.2.1
acts mala prohibita	1.2.1
actus non facit reum maxim	1.3.2(2), 1.3.2(3), 14.2
actus reus	
accountability for	1.3.2(5), 3.4
behavioural element	3.2, 3.2.1
burden of proof	2.3
concurrence requirement *see* mens rea	
consequences of behaviour *see* causation; intervening causes	
defined	1.4, 3.1
inchoate offences *see* attempts; conspiracy; incitement	
involuntary behaviour *see* automatism; involuntariness	
mens rea where actus reus involves circumstances *see* mens rea	
omissions *see* omissions	
possessory offences	3.2.2(2)
situational offences	3.2.2, 3.2.2(1)
administration of offences, criminalisation and	21.7.2

advertence *see also* intention; recklessness	1.3.2(2)
advertising campaigns	21.5.2
age of criminal responsibility *see* infancy	
agency, innocent *see* innocent agency	
aggravated assault	
elements of offence	17.7
with intent to obstruct	17.7.1
"execution of duty"	17.7.1(4)
honest belief that force excessive	17.7.1(2)
mistake	17.7.1(1)
self-defence	17.7.1(3)
aggravated wounding	
elements of offence	17.6
mens rea	17.6.1
proof	17.6.3
stupefaction	
intent	17.6.1
"renders unconscious"	17.6
"stupefies"	17.6
"violent means"	17.6.2
aggression and substance use	11.1
aiding *see also* secondary participation	6.4.1(1), 6.4.4(1)
alcohol use *see also* intoxication	
aggression and substance use	11.1
alcoholism	10.3.3(2)
alibi	1.4.1
amnesia	11.1.1
anal intercourse	18.13
animals	
sexual offences involving	18.13
theft of wild creatures	19.3.1(9)
anxiety disorders	10.3.3(1)
arteriosclerosis	10.3.3, 10.3.3(1)
assault *see also* aggravated assault; aggravated wounding	
battery	17.2
children	17.8

775

Subject Index

consent	
availability as defence	17.2.4(1)
burden of proof	17.2.4
consensual sexual activity	17.2.4(2), 17.2.4(3)
sport	17.2.4(4)
defined	17.2
force	17.2.2
``applying'' force	17.2.2(1)
direct/indirect application	17.2.3(1)
indecent *see* **indecent assault**	
injuring by unlawful act	17.5
injuring with intent	17.4
innocent agents	17.2.3(1)
male upon female	17.9, 17.9.1
mens rea	17.2.1, 17.2.1(1)
omissions	17.2.3
threats and	17.2
transferred malice	17.2.1(1)
wounding with intent *see* **wounding with intent**	
ATM machines, deception involving	20.4.2
attempts	
actus reus	8.2.2
acts done ``for the purpose of accomplishing his object''	8.2.2(2)
behavioural element	3.2
omissions	8.2.2(1)(c)
possessory offences	8.2.2(1)(b)
words constitutive of an attempt	8.2.2(1)(a)
conspiracy	8.2.6, 8.3.7
defined	8.2
impossibility	8.2.5
factual	8.2.5(2)
imaginary crimes	8.2.5(3)
legal	8.2.5(1)
incest	18.6.2
incitement	8.4.1(3)
mens rea	8.2.1
murder, duress of circumstances and	13.2.1, 13.2.4
penalties	8.2
preparation and proximity tests	8.2.2, 8.2.3(1)
``commencement of execution''	8.2.3(1)(d)
``common sense'' approach	8.2.3(3)
``dangerous proximity'' theory	8.2.3(4)
Eagleton	8.2.3(1)(a)
``equivocality'' rule	8.2.3(1)(f)
inadequacy of	8.2.3(2)
``last act''	8.2.3(1)(e)
Rubicon	8.2.3(1)(c)
``series of acts''	8.2.3(1)(b)
sexual conduct with child under 12	18.9.1
sexual violation	18.4, 18.4.1
successful	8.1
withdrawal	8.2.4
attribution, rules of	7.2.4
autism	10.3.2
automatism *see also* **involuntariness**	1.4.1
antecedent fault	3.4.3
strict liability offences	3.4.3(1)
behaviour, responsibility for	3.4.1(2)
burden of proof	3.4.4, 10.3.1
concussion	3.4.1(2), 3.4.1(4)
defined	3.4.1(2)

dissociation	3.4.1(2)
epilepsy	3.4.1(4)
hyperglycaemia	10.3.3, 10.3.3(4), 10.3.3(4)(a)
hypnotism	3.4.1(2)
hypoglycaemia	3.4.1(2), 10.3.3(3), 10.3.3(4), 10.3.3(4)(a)
imperfect deliberative capacity	3.4.1(3)
insanity and	10.3.3(4)
intoxication	11.1, 11.2.6
mens rea	3.4.1(2), 4.9.1(4)
sane/insane distinction	3.4.1(4)
self-induced	3.4.3
sleepwalking	3.4.1(2), 10.3.3, 10.3.3(4)(b)
autonomy	
causation and	3.3.3(2), 3.3.3(2)(b), 3.3.3(2)(e)
criminalisation, effect of	1.3.1
liability for acts or omissions and	1.3.2(5)
omissions and	3.2.1(1)
property rights and	20.1
secondary liability and	1.3.2(5)

B

bailment, theft in relation to	19.3.2(2), 19.3.2(3)
bank accounts, theft in relation to	19.3.1(3)
battered women	
compulsion	12.13, 12.14
diminished responsibility	10.3.8
provocation	16.5.1(3), 16.5.1(6)
self-defence	15.1.4(5)
imminence of threat	15.1.4(6)
self-preservation	15.1.4(5)(a)
battery	17.2
behaviour *see* **actus reus; causation; involuntariness; omissions**	
belief *see also* **intention; knowledge; mistake; recklessness**	
aggravated assault	17.7.1(2)
compulsion	12.9
duress of circumstances	13.2.2, 13.2.3
property, defence of	15.2.2(4)
self-defence	15.1.2, 15.1.3
sexual violation	18.2.2(1)
bestiality	18.3
``beyond reasonable doubt''	2.3
bigamy	1.4.1
blackmail	20.1
blameworthiness *see* **culpability**	
body parts, rights in	19.3.1(8)
``born alive''	16.2.2
``brain death''	16.2.2
brain tumours	10.3.3(2)
breath-alcohol offences	11.2.8(1)
duress of circumstances	13.3.2(3)
burden and standard of proof	
absolute liability	5.1, 5.1.2
assault	17.2.4
automatism	3.4.4
``beyond reasonable doubt''	2.3
compulsion	12.11
infancy	9.3.2
infanticide	16.6.1
insanity	2.3.1(2), 10.3.1

intoxication	11.2
mens rea	2.3, 2.3.2, 4.1
virtually certain consequences	4.2.4(2)
mistake of fact	14.2.1(1)
provocation	16.5.1(1)
self-defence	15.1.6
sexual conduct with young person under 16	18.10.2, 18.10.5
statute silent as to mens rea	2.3.1(4)
statutory modification: reverse-burden provisions	2.3.1(1)
strict liability offences	2.3.1(3), 5.1, 5.1.1, 5.1.1(3)(b)
Woolmington, approach in	2.3
wounding with intent	17.3.6(1)
"but for" test	3.3.1

C

Caldwell	4.3.1(1), 4.3.1(2)
care and protection proceedings	9.3.1
sexual intercourse with girl under	18.7
care recipient, detention as	10.1.1, 10.1.2, 10.1.3
causation	3.3
accountability and	1.3.2(5)
"but for" test	3.3.1
homicide *see* **homicide**	
intervening causes *see* **intervening causes**	
legal causation	3.3.2
multiple causes	3.3.2(3)
salience	3.3.2(2)
significant cause	3.3.2(1)
moral element	3.3.2
obtaining by deception or causing loss by deception	20.4, 20.4.1, 20.4.2
omissions	3.2.1(4), 3.3.4
censure *see* **conviction/censure**	
cerebral arteriosclerosis	10.3.3, 10.3.3(1)
"chain" conspiracy	8.3.4(5)
children and young persons	
assaults on	17.8
crimes committed by *see* **infancy**	
cruelty to	17.10
"custody, control, or charge"	17.10.3
ill-treatment	17.10.4
"neglect"	17.10.2
"wilfully neglects"	17.10.1
discipline of	17.8.1
killing of a child	16.2.2
sexual offences against *see* **sexual offences**	
chose in action, theft of	19.3.1(2), 19.3.1(3)
civil law	
criminal law distinguished	
acts intrinsically morally wrong	1.2.1
convictions	1.2.3
harmful nature of prohibited event	1.2.1
public interest in criminalisation of behaviour	1.2.1
punishment	1.2.2
relevance of distinction	1.2
duty to intervene	3.2.1
liability in tort	1.2.1

regulation of activity by means of tort law	21.5.2
remedies in tort	1.2.2
civil union and person under 16 years	18.10.3
claim of right	
defence of property and	15.2.2(4)
obtaining or causing loss by deception without	20.6
theft without	19.4.2
coercion *see also* **compulsion**	
common law	12.3.1
inducing sexual connection by *see* **sexual offences**	
colour of right	19.4.2
common law offences	2.1.2
companies *see* **corporate liability**	
company shares, theft in relation to	19.3.1(2)
compulsion	1.4.1
background to statutory defence	12.2
battered women	12.13, 12.14
burden of proof	12.11
coercion of wife	12.3.1
concept of	12.1
defined	12.4
duress by threats: English common law	12.1, 12.3
duress of circumstances distinguished	12.3, 12.3.2
elements of	12.5, 12.6
excluded offences	12.10.4
honest belief that threat will be carried out	12.9
"immediately following a refusal to commit an offence"	12.7
involuntariness	13.1.1
involuntariness and	12.3.1
M'Growther's Case	12.2
murder	12.10.4(1)
nature of defence	12.3
opportunity to escape or seek protection	12.10.1
reform proposals	12.14
immediacy or inevitability	12.14.2
non-specific threats	12.14.1
reasonableness test	12.14.3
secondary liability	6.6.1(1)
self-defence and	12.12
terminology	12.1
theoretical bases	12.3
threat to kill or cause grievous bodily harm	12.6
implied threat	12.6.1
mistake	12.6.2
threatener to be present during commission of offence	12.8
threats to others apart from accused	12.10.2
volunteers: parties to conspiracies or associations	12.10.3
concussion	3.4.1(2), 3.4.1(4), 10.3.3(2), 10.3.3(3)
conduct crimes	3.2
conjoined twins	13.3.2, 13.3.5(3)
consent	
assault *see* **assault**	
indecent assault	18.11.4

777

Subject Index

nature of	18.2.1(3)
proof of consent-based defences	18.10.2
sexual conduct with child under 12	18.9
sexual conduct with young person under 16	18.10.1, 18.10.2
sexual exploitation of person with significant impairment	18.12.3
sexual violation *see* **sexual violation**	
theft and	
taking property	19.3.3(1)(a)
using or dealing with property	19.3.3(2)(a)
consequentialism	1.3.3
conspiracy	
actus reus	8.3.4
acts subsequent to formation	8.3.4(1)
``chain'' conspiracy	8.3.4(5)
conspiring with ``persons unknown''	8.3.4(3)
proof of agreement	8.3.4(2)
purely internal conspiracies	8.3.4(6)
``wheel'' conspiracy	8.3.4(4)
attempted	8.2.6, 8.3.7
compulsion and	12.10.3
conspiracy to defraud	20.3.3, 20.3.3(1), 20.3.3(3)
convictions where acquittal of co-conspirators	8.3.10
criminalisation	8.3, 8.3.4(6), 8.3.11(3)
defences	8.3.5
defined	8.3, 8.3.3
extraterritorial	8.3.2, 8.3.9
impossibility	8.3.11
culpability and	8.3.11(3)
desired end impossible	8.3.11(2)
imaginary crimes	8.3.11(1), 8.3.11(3)
joinder with substantive offence	8.3.12
mens rea	8.3.5
agreements and acquiescence	8.3.5(1)
partial conspiracy	8.3.5(2)
penalties	8.3.1
scope	8.3.1
secondary liability	6.6.5, 8.3.8
variation over content of agreement	8.3.6
when ``complete''	8.3.2
consumption taxes	21.5.1
continuing act	
assault	17.2.3
concurrence of actus reus and mens rea	4.9.1(1)
murder	16.4.6
omissions-based liability and	3.2.1(2)(d)
conviction/censure	
criminal-civil distinction	1.2.3
fair labelling, principle of	2.1.4
legitimacy of	1.3, 1.3.2
accountability	1.3.2(5)
advertence, relevance of	1.3.2(2)
justificatory/excusatory defences	1.3.2(4)
limits	1.3.2(5)
mens rea requirement	1.3.2(1)
regulatory offences	1.3.2(3)
secondary liability	1.3.2(5)
social significance	1.2.3
copyright, theft in relation to	19.3.1(2), 19.3.1(5)
corporal punishment	17.8.1

corporate liability	
attribution of direct liability	7.2.4
alter ego vs identification doctrine	7.2.4(1)
mens rea offences	7.2.4(3)
negligence	7.2.4(2)
direct/vicarious distinction	7.2.2
homicide	7.2, 16.2.1
law reform proposals	
aggregative approach	7.2.6(1)
``reactive fault''	7.2.6(3)
safety cultures	7.2.6(2)
personal liability and	7.2.5
presumption of liability	7.2.1
regulatory offences	5.1.1(3)(a), 7.1.2, 7.1.2(1)
scope	7.2, 7.2.1
secondary liability	7.2
vicarious	7.2.2, 7.2.3
corpses, rights in	19.3.1(8)
corroboration	18.5.4
counselling *see also* **secondary participation**	6.4.1(4), 6.4.4(1)
credit obtained by deception	20.5.2
criminal law	
age of criminal responsibility *see* **infancy**	
burden and standard of proof *see* **burden and standard of proof**	
civil law distinguished	
acts intrinsically morally wrong	1.2.1
convictions	1.2.3
harmful nature of prohibited event	1.2.1
public interest in criminalisation of behaviour	1.2.1
punishment	1.2.2
relevance of distinction	1.2
common law offences	2.1.2
consent and	17.2.4, 18.2.1(3)
conviction *see* **conviction/censure**	
defining features	1.2
legitimacy of	1.3, 1.3.2
accountability	1.3.2(5)
advertence, relevance of	1.3.2(2)
culpability	1.3.2(2)
justificatory/excusatory defences	1.3.2(4)
mens rea requirement	1.3.2(1)
regulatory offences	1.3.2(3)
secondary liability	1.3.2(5)
presumption of innocence	2.3
prohibitory nature of *see* **criminalisation**	
punishment *see* **punishment/sanctions**	
purpose	1.2
rational capacity and	9.1
Rule of Law and	2.1
statutory interpretation *see* **statutory interpretation**	
criminal offences	
actus reus *see* **actus reus**	
crime, defined	1.2
elements of	1.4, 1.4.1
mens rea *see* **mens rea**	

parties to *see* **secondary participation**	
Criminal Procedure (Mentally Impaired Persons) Act 2003	10.1.1, 10.5
criminal proceedings	
defences *see* **defences**	
evidence *see* **burden and standard of proof; evidence**	
unfitness to stand trial	10.1.1, 10.1.2
criminalisation	
accountability, requirement for	1.3.2(5)
autonomy, restriction of	1.3.1
clarity in statement of the law	2.1.3, 2.1.4
conspiracy	8.3, 8.3.4(6), 8.3.11(3)
defined	1.3
derivative liability and	6.1
fair labelling	2.1.4
fair warning	2.1.3
evaluative concepts, use of	2.1.3(1)
fraud	20.3.3(3)
harm principle	1.2.1, 21.1
balancing requirements	21.1.4
harm as wrongs	21.1.3
meaning of harm	21.1.1
remote harms	21.1.5
seriousness of harm	21.1.2
inchoate offences	8.1
legal moralism	21.3
legitimacy of	1.3
negligence and	4.6.4
culpability	1.3.2(2)
nullum crimen sine lege (principle of legality)	2.1.1
offence principle	21.2
opposition to overuse	1.3.1
paternalism	21.4
practical advantages	21.5.4
practical constraints	21.7
administration of offences	21.7.2
consequential criminality associated with certain activities	21.7.1
negative side-effects	21.7.1
policing of offences	21.7.2
property offences	19.1, 20.1
public interest in prosecution of offences	1.2.1
regulatory alternatives	21.5
advertising campaigns	21.5.3
licensing	21.5.3
tax	21.5.1
tort law	21.5.2
retrospective crimes	2.1.2
Rule of Law constraints	21.6
individuation of offences	21.6.2
specificity of drafting of offences	21.6.1
sport and	17.2.4(4)
stigmatisation appropriate	21.5.4
strict liability and	5.1.1(3)(a)
cruelty to children *see* **children and young persons**	
culpability	
advertence, relevance of	1.3.2(2)
objective vs subjective	1.3.2(2)
rational capacity and	9.1
regulatory offences and	1.3.2(3)

requirement for	1.3, 1.3.2(1)
culpable homicide *see also* **homicide; infanticide; manslaughter; murder; provocation**	
penalties	16.1
scope	16.3, 16.5.2

D

dangerous activities, duties re *see* **legal duties**	
dangerousness, use of standards of	2.1.3(1)
dead bodies, rights in	19.3.1(8)
deception *see* **obtaining or causing loss by deception**	
defences	
absolute liability	5.1.2
automatism *see* **automatism**	
compulsion *see* **compulsion**	
conspiracy	8.3.5
defence of property *see* **property, defence of**	
excusatory	1.3.2(4)
compulsion	12.3
duress of circumstances	13.1
mistake and	14.2.3
impossibility *see* **impossibility of compliance**	
infancy *see* **infancy**	
infanticide	16.6.1
insanity *see* **insanity**	
intoxication *see* **intoxication**	
justificatory	1.3.2(4)
mistake and	14.2.2
necessity	13.1
mistake *see* **mistake**	
necessity *see* **necessity**	
operation of	1.4.1
provocation *see* **provocation**	
rational capacity and	9.1
self-defence *see* **self-defence**	
strict liability *see* **strict liability**	
``delegation'' principle *see* **vicarious liability**	
delusions	10.3.7
derivative liability *see* **secondary participation; vicarious liability**	
desert	1.3.3
detection of offences, criminalisation and	21.7.2
deterrence	
criminal vs civil sanctions	1.2.2
criminalisation, function of	1.3
inchoate offences and	8.1
strict liability and	5.1.1(3)(a)
diabetic states	3.4.1(2), 10.3.3, 10.3.3(3), 10.3.3(4), 10.3.3(4)(a)
diminished responsibility	
battered women	10.3.8
infanticide	16.1
insanity	10.3.8
voluntary manslaughter	16.5
discipline of children	17.8.1
disease of the mind *see* **insanity**	
disfiguring	17.3.4
dissociation	3.4.1(2), 10.3.3(3)

779

SUBJECT INDEX

doli incapax presumption | 9.2, 9.3, 9.3.2
domestic violence *see also* battered women | 17.2.4(3)
driving offences
   breath-alcohol offences
      duress of circumstances | 13.3.2(3)
      involuntariness | 11.2.8(1)
   duress of circumstances | 13.3.2(3)
drug use *see also* intoxication
   aggression and substance use | 11.1
   consequential criminality and intervening causes in overdose cases | 21.7.1
    | 3.3.3(2)(f)
drunkenness *see* intoxication
duress by threats *see also* compulsion
   English common law | 12.1, 12.3
duress of circumstances *see also* impossibility of compliance; necessity
   availability and scope of defence | 13.1, 13.2
   characteristics of accused | 13.2.3(1)
   compulsion distinguished | 12.3, 12.3.2
   English common law | 13.2.1
   excusatory defence | 13.1
   honest belief of imminent peril | 13.2.2, 13.2.3
   imminence/immediacy of threat | 13.2.3(2)
   impossibility distinguished | 13.1.1
   involuntariness | 13.1.1
   law reform proposals | 13.5, 13.5.1, 13.5.2
   murder/attempted murder and | 13.2.1, 13.2.4
   necessity distinguished | 12.3, 13.1
   New Zealand formulation | 13.2.2, 13.2.3, 13.2.4
   terminology | 13.1
   "Dutch Courage" | 3.4.3
duties *see* legal duties
dwellinghouse, defence of | 15.2.3, 15.2.4

E

Eagleton, test in | 8.2.3(1)(a)
education campaigns | 21.5.3
electricity, theft of | 19.3.1(7)
electronic communications, assault and | 17.3.1(1)(a)
emergencies *see* medical treatment
Empress | 3.3.3(2)(e)
endangering safety | 16.5.2(4)(b)
epilepsy | 3.4.1(4), 10.3.3, 10.3.3(2)
equitable interests, theft in relation to | 19.3.2(2)
evidence
   burden of proof *see* burden and standard of proof
   diseases of the mind and insanity | 10.3, 10.3.3, 10.3.10
      burden of proof | 2.3.1(2), 10.3.1
      determination of insanity by consensus | 10.4.2
      raising insanity ``where it appears from the evidence'' | 10.4
   intoxication
      burden of proof | 11.2
      fact of intent vs capacity to form intent | 11.2.1, 11.2.1(1)
      sufficiency of evidence to raise defence and justify acquittal | 11.2.1(2)

provocation | 16.5.1(1)
self-defence | 15.1.6
sexual offences | 18.5
   address and occupation of complainant | 18.5.1
   character of complainant | 18.5.3
   corroboration | 18.5.4
   delay in making complaint | 18.5.2
ex turpi causa principle | 16.5.2(6)
excusatory defences *see* defences
extraterritorial conspiracies | 8.3.2, 8.3.9

F

fair labelling, principle of | 2.1.3, 2.1.4
fair warning
   principle of | 2.1.3
   evaluative concepts, use of | 2.1.3(1)
   regulatory offences | 5.1.2(1), 5.2.3(2)(b)
false representation *see* obtaining or causing loss by deception
fault *see also* culpability | 1.3, 1.3.2, 1.4
felony murder rule | 16.4.4, 16.4.5
fitness to plead | 10.1.1, 10.1.2
foetus, killing of | 16.2.2
force
   assault | 17.2.2, 17.2.2(1), 17.2.3(1)
   defence of property | 15.2.2(1)
   discipline of children | 17.8.2
   self-defence | 15.1.4, 15.1.5
foresight *see also* intention; recklessness | 1.3.2(2)
found articles, theft in relation to | 19.3.2(5)
fraud *see also* obtaining or causing loss by deception
   criminalisation | 20.3.3(3)
   fair warning and use of evaluative concepts | 2.1.3(1)

G

gang associations
   compulsion and | 12.10.3
gas, theft of | 19.3.1(7)
grievous bodily harm | 17.3.1, 17.3.1(1), 17.3.1(1)(a)
   threat of, as element of compulsion defence | 12.6
gross negligence *see* negligence

H

Hadfield's Case | 10.2.1
harm
   as element of crime | 1.4
   criminalisation of | 1.2.1, 21.1
   balancing requirements | 21.1.4
   harm as wrongs | 21.1.3
   meaning of harm | 21.1.1
   remote harms | 21.1.5
   seriousness of harm | 21.1.2
   inadvertence to *see* negligence
   self-defence and | 15.1
HIV infection
   consensual sexual activity involving risk of | 17.2.4(2)

I

grievous bodily harm	17.3.1
homicide *see also* **infanticide; manslaughter; murder; provocation**	
causation	16.2.3
acceleration of death	16.2.3(3)
causing preventable death	16.2.3(4)
death resulting from treatment	16.2.3(5)
killing by influence on the mind	16.2.3(2)
life support, withdrawal of	16.2.3(1), 16.2.3(3), 16.2.3(5), 16.5.2(7)
year and a day rule	16.2.3(1)
corporate liability	7.2, 16.2.1
``culpable homicide''	16.3
defined	16.2
finding of death	16.2.2
killing of a child	16.2.2
necessity	13.3.5(3)
offender	16.2.1
suicide induced by secondary party	16.2.3(6)
victim	16.2.2
hospital orders	10.1.2
human body, rights in	19.3.1(8)
human rights	
retrospective criminalisation	2.1.2
husband and wife	
coercion	12.3.1
hyperglycaemia	10.3.3, 10.3.3(4), 10.3.3(4)(a)
hypnotism	3.4.1(2), 10.3.3(3)
hypoglycaemia	3.4.1(2), 10.3.3(3), 10.3.3(4), 10.3.3(4)(a)
hysteria	10.3.3(1)

I

ignorance of law	
assault with intent to obstruct	17.7.1(1)
exceptions	14.4
non-published law	14.4.2
``officially induced'' error	14.4.1
mens rea	14.3.1
principle of	14.1, 14.3
property, defence of	15.2.2(4)
ill-treatment of children *see* **children and young persons**	
impossibility	
attempts	8.2.5
factual impossibility	8.2.5(2)
imaginary crimes	8.2.5(3)
incitement	8.4.4
legal impossibility	8.2.5(1)
conspiracy	
culpability and	8.3.11(3)
desired end impossible	8.3.11(2)
imaginary crimes	8.3.11(1), 8.3.11(3)
impossibility of compliance	13.6
absolute impossibility	13.6.1
absolute liability and	5.1.2
antecedent fault	13.6.2
freedom from fault	13.6.2
necessity and duress distinguished	13.1.1
omissions and	3.4.2
ignorance of duty distinguished	3.4.2(3), 13.6.1(1)
public policy	13.6.3

statutory inconsistency with common law defence	13.6.4
impulses, irresistible	3.4.1(3), 10.3.9
incest	
attempts	18.6.2
defined	18.6, 18.6.1
elements of offence	18.6.2
mens rea	18.6.2(1)
penalties	18.6.1
proof of the relationship	18.6.2(2), 18.6.2(3)
secondary liability	18.6.2(3)
``sexual connection''	18.6
inchoate offences	
attempts *see* **attempts**	
behavioural element	3.2
conspiracy *see* **conspiracy**	
criminalisation	8.1
incitement *see* **incitement**	
meeting young person under 16 following sexual grooming	18.8, 18.8.1
nature of	8.1
secondary liability	6.6.5
incitement	
actus reus	8.4.1
attempt to incite	8.4.1(3)
behavioural element	3.2
communication of incitement	8.4.1(1)
renunciation of incitement	8.4.1(2)
defined	8.4
impossibility	8.4.4
mens rea	8.4.2
murder	8.4.3, 8.4.3(1), 8.4.3(2)
penalties	8.4
secondary liability	6.4.1(3), 6.4.4(1)
suicide	8.4
indecency, use of standards of	2.1.3(1)
indecent act on child under 12	18.9
indecent act on young person under 16	18.10
indecent acts with animals	18.13
indecent assault	18.11
actus reus	18.11.2
consent	18.11.4
``indecently''	18.11.3
lesser included offence within definition of sexual violation	18.11.6
mens rea	18.11.5
inducing sexual connection by coercion *see* **sexual offences**	
infancy	
age of criminal responsibility	9.2, 9.2.1
care and protection proceedings	9.3.1
children between 10 and 14	9.2.1, 9.3
children under 10	9.2, 9.2.1, 9.2.2
doli incapax presumption	9.2, 9.3
rebuttal	9.3.2
innocent agency, doctrine of	9.2.1
law reform	9.4
overseas jurisdictions	9.4
Young Offenders (Serious Crime) Bill	9.4.1
nature of defence	9.1
New Zealand Bill of Rights Act 1990	9.4
relevance of defence	9.4
young person over 14	9.2.1
infanticide	

781

Subject Index

availability of defence	16.6, 16.6.3
burden of proof	16.6.1
insanity and	16.6.2
murder induced by mental disorder falling short of insanity	16.6.2
scope	16.6.1
information, theft in relation to	19.3.1(5)
"injure"	17.3.5
injuring by unlawful act	17.5
injuring with intent	17.4
injury, sports	17.2.4(4)
innocent agency	
assault	17.2.3(1)
child offender and	9.2.1
incitement to murder	8.4.3(1)
intervening causes and	3.3.3(2)(d)
scope	6.3.1
innocent until proven guilty	2.3
insanity	
alcoholism and	10.3.3(2)
automatism and	10.3.3(4)
diabetic states	10.3.3(4)(a)
sleepwalking	10.3.3(4)(b)
defined	10.3
delusions	10.3.7
diminished responsibility	10.3.8
disease of the mind	
effects of disease relevant not origins	10.3.3(1)
internal/external cause test	10.3.3(3)
legal meaning	10.3.3
medical evidence	10.3, 10.3.3
disposition options	10.5
immediate release	10.5.4
"patient", detention as	10.5.3
range of orders available	10.5.1
restricted patient order	10.4
special care recipient	10.1.1, 10.1.2, 10.5.1, 10.5.3
special patient	10.1.1, 10.1.2, 10.5.1, 10.5.2
evidence	
burden of proof	2.3.1(2), 10.3.1
determination of insanity by consensus	10.4.2
raising insanity "where it appears from the evidence"	10.4, 10.4.1
weighing medical evidence	10.3.10
Hadfield's Case	10.2.1
history of defence	10.2, 10.2.1, 10.2.2
infanticide and	16.6.2
International Covenant on Civil and Political Rights	10.3.3
irresistible impulses	10.3.9
knowledge of wrongfulness of act	10.3.5
legal conception of	10.1
"mental abnormality"	10.1.1
M'Naghten Rules	
automatic states	10.3.3(4), 10.3.3(4)(a), 10.3.3(4)(b)
delusions	10.3.7
development	10.2.2
New Zealand formulation	10.3
wrong, test of	10.3.5
natural imbecility	10.3.2
"nature and quality" of act or omission	10.3.4, 10.3.4(1), 10.3.4(2)

nature of defence	10.1
person "under disability"	10.1.1
personality disorders	10.3.3(1), 10.3.3(3)
presumption of sanity	10.3.1
sentencing and mental disorder	10.1.2
strict liability and	10.3.6
"subnormality"	10.3.2
terminology	10.1.1
unfitness to stand trial	10.1.1, 10.1.2
verdict	10.5
volitional disorders and	10.3
wrong, meaning of	10.3.5
intellectual property rights, theft in relation to	19.3.1(2), 19.3.1(5)
intellectually disabled persons	
duress of circumstances	13.2.3(1)
insanity and	10.3.2
negligence and	4.6.2
sentencing	10.1.2, 10.5
sexual exploitation of person with significant impairment	18.12
sexual offences against	
sexual violation and consent	18.2.1(3)(e), 18.2.2(2)(b)
transfer of offender to care facility	10.1.3
intention	
actus reus involving circumstances	4.2.5
attempts and	8.2.1
belief	4.2.2, 4.2.5
categories of	4.2
conditional intent	4.2.8
culpability	1.3.2(1)
defined	4.2
foresight and	4.2.3
intoxication and	11.2.2
motive or desire	4.2.2
multiple intentions	4.2.6
paradigm category	4.2.1, 4.2.2, 4.2.3
proof of mens rea	2.3.2
recklessness distinguished	4.4
ulterior intent	4.2.7
virtually certain consequences	4.2.4
evidence	4.2.4(2)
objective and subjective elements	4.2.4(1)
International Covenant on Civil and Political Rights	
insanity defence and	10.3.3
intervening causes	
effect of	3.3.3
natural events	3.3.3(1)
novus actus interveniens	3.3.3
omissions and	3.3.4(2), 3.3.4(3)
summary of approach	3.3.3(4)
third party intervention	3.3.3(2)
act done in concert with victim	3.3.3(2)(f)
Empress	3.3.3(2)(e)
foreseeable and culpable	3.3.3(2)(c)
foreseeable and innocent	3.3.3(2)(a)
foreseeable and intentional	3.3.3(2)(b), 3.3.3(2)(e), 3.3.3(2)(f)
innocent agency	3.3.3(2)(d)
victim, intervention of	3.3.3(3)
intoxication	
aggression and substance use	11.1
amnesia and	11.1.1
availability of defence	11.2
capacity and intent	11.2.2

English law	11.1.1
basic/specific intent distinction	11.1.1(1), 11.1.1(2)
evidence	
burden of proof	11.2
fact of intent vs capacity to form intent	11.2.1, 11.2.1(1)
sufficiency of evidence to raise defence and justify acquittal	11.2.1(2)
history of defence	11.1
involuntariness	11.1, 11.2.8
automatism	11.2.6
breath-alcohol offences	11.2.8(1)
Kamipeli	11.2.1
manslaughter	11.2.7
provocation	11.2.7(1), 16.5.1(5)(c)
mistake	11.2.4
negligence	11.2.5
pure methamphetamine	10.3.3(1)
recklessness	11.2.3
self-defence and	15.1.3(5)
self-induced	3.4.3, 11.1, 11.2
sexual connection and consent	18.2.2(2)(a)
strict liability offences	11.2.5, 11.2.6
involuntariness	
absolute liability and	5.1.2
acts, responsibility for	3.4
antecedent fault	3.4.3, 4.9.1(4)
strict liability offences	3.4.3(1)
burden of proof	3.4.4, 10.3.1
compulsion	12.3.1, 13.1.1
concussion	3.4.1(4)
disease of the mind and	10.3.3(3), 10.3.3(4)
duress of circumstances	13.1.1
epilepsy	3.4.1(4)
impaired consciousness *see* **automatism**	
imperfect deliberative capacity	3.4.1(3)
impulsive actions	3.4.1(3)
intoxication	11.1, 11.2.8
automatism	11.2.6
breath-alcohol offences	11.2.8(1)
loss of physical control	3.4.1(1)
nature of	3.4.1
necessity	13.1.1
omissions	3.4.2
ignorance of duty	3.4.2(3), 13.6.1(1)
possessory offences	3.4.2(2)
situational offences	3.4.2(1)
situational offences and	1.3.2(5)
volitional disorders and insanity defence	10.3
irresistible impulses	3.4.1(3), 10.3.9

J

joint unlawful act, standard of care	16.5.2(6)
judicial activism	2.1.3
justificatory defences *see* **defences**	

K

Kamipeli	11.2.1
killing by frightening	16.5.2(3)
killing by influence on the mind	16.2.3(2)
killing by unlawful act	16.5.2(1)

standard of care	16.5.2(6)
killing by unlawful act and omission	16.5.2(8)
killing by unlawful omission	16.5.2(4)
duties involving dangerous acts and things	16.5.2(4)(b)
duties to provide necessaries	16.5.2(4)(a)
duty to avoid dangerous omissions	16.5.2(4)(c)
fault standard	16.5.2(5)
gross negligence	16.5.2(5)(b), 16.5.2(5)(c)
historical standards	16.5.2(5)(a), 16.5.2(5)(b)
``major departure'' test	16.5.2(5)(c)
other duties	16.5.2(4)(d)
killing of a child	16.2.2
kleptomania	10.3.3(2)
knowledge	
actus reus involving circumstances	4.5
defined	4.5
intention and	4.2.5
obtaining or causing loss by deception	
false representations	20.3.1(3), 20.3.1(5)
receiving property	19.5.2
wilful blindness	4.5.1

L

land, theft of	19.3.1, 19.3.1(1)
Law Commission	
battered defendants	12.14, 13.5.2
legal duties	
duties involving dangerous activities or things	16.5.2(4)(b)
standard of care	16.5.2(5), 16.5.2(5)(a), 16.5.2(5)(b), 16.5.2(5)(c)
duties to provide necessaries	3.2.1(2)(b), 16.5.2(4)(a)
duty to avoid omissions dangerous to life	16.5.2(4)(c)
duty to intervene	
persons with particular responsibilities	3.2.1(2)(c)
persons with special relationship to the harm	3.2.1(2)(e)
persons with special relationship to victim	3.2.1(2)(b)
secondary liability and	6.4.3
ignorance of	
impossibility distinguished	13.6.1(1)
non-codified duties	16.5.2(4)(d)
legal moralism	21.3
legal responsibility for conduct	1.3.2(5)
legality, principle of	2.1.1, 2.1.2
licensees, liability of	7.1, 7.1.1, 7.1.2
licensing systems	21.5.3
lien, theft in relation to	19.3.2(2)
life imprisonment	16.1
life support, withdrawal of	16.2.3(1), 16.2.3(3), 16.2.3(5), 16.5.2(7)
lost articles, theft in relation to	19.3.2(5)

M

maiming	17.3.3
mala in se	1.2.1
mala prohibita	1.2.1
``malice aforethought''	16.4, 17.3.6(1)

Subject Index

manslaughter
inducing victims to kill themselves	16.5.2(2)
infancy, defence of	9.4
intoxication and	11.2.7, 11.2.7(1)
involuntary	16.5.2
involuntary/voluntary distinction	16.5
joint unlawful act, standard of care	16.5.2(6)
killing by frightening	16.5.2(3)
killing by unlawful act	16.5.2(1)
killing by unlawful act, standard of care	16.5.2(6)
killing by unlawful act and omission	16.5.2(8)
killing by unlawful omission	16.5.2(4)
duties involving dangerous acts and things	16.5.2(4)(b)
duties to provide necessaries	16.5.2(4)(a)
duty to avoid dangerous omissions	16.5.2(4)(c)
lawful excuse	16.5.2(7)
mens rea	16.5.2(5), 16.5.2(5)(a), 16.5.2(5)(b), 16.5.2(5)(c)
non-codified duties	16.5.2(4)(d)
life imprisonment	16.1
under provocation *see* **provocation**	

marital rape 18.2.1(4)
marriage of person under 16 years 18.10.3
medical treatment
body parts, rights in	19.3.1(8)
causation and homicide	16.2.3(1), 16.2.3(3), 16.2.3(4), 16.2.3(5)
life support, withdrawal of	16.2.3(1), 16.2.3(3), 16.2.3(5), 16.5.2(7)
necessity	
emergencies	13.3.2, 13.3.4(1), 13.3.4(3), 13.3.5(3)
sterilisation	13.3.2, 13.3.5(2)
negligence in case of emergency	4.6.2

meeting young person under 16 following sexual grooming 18.8, 18.8.1
mens rea
actus reus involving behavioural element	
negligence	4.6.3
actus reus involving circumstances	
intention	4.2.5
recklessness	4.3.2
aggravated assault	17.7.1, 17.7.1(1), 17.7.1(2), 17.7.1(3)
aggravated wounding	17.6.1
assault	17.2.1, 17.2.1(1)
assault by male upon female	17.9.1
attempt to commit sexual violation	18.4.1
attempts	8.2.1
automatism	3.4.1(2), 4.9.1(4)
burden of proof	2.3, 2.3.2, 4.1
virtually certain consequences	4.2.4(2)
concurrence with actus reus	4.9
automatism	4.9.1(4)
causation approach	4.9.1(3)
complex single transaction	4.9.1(2)
fresh acts, continuing acts, or subsequent omissions	4.9.1(1)
conspiracy	8.3.5, 8.3.5(1), 8.3.5(2)
cruelty to children	17.10.1
defined	1.4, 4.1

determining fault standard	5.2.3
absolute/strict liability	5.2.3(2)(d)
basic presumption of mens rea	5.2.3(2)(a)
inferred from statutory language	5.2.3(2)(c)
overriding presumption of mens rea	5.2.3(2)(b)
statute explicit or judicial precedent	5.2.3(1)
fault standards	4.1
good motives	4.1
incest	18.6.2(1)
incitement	8.4.2
indecent assault	18.11.5
intention *see* **intention**	
intoxication and *see* **intoxication**	
killing by unlawful act	16.5.2(6)
killing by unlawful omission	16.5.2(5), 16.5.2(5)(a), 16.5.2(5)(b), 16.5.2(5)(c)
knowledge	4.5, 4.5.1
meeting young person under 16 following sexual grooming	18.8.1
mistake of fact *see* **mistake**	
mistake of law	14.3.1
murder *see* **murder**	
negligence *see* **negligence**	
obtaining or causing loss by deception	20.8
receiving	19.5.2
recklessness *see* **recklessness**	
requirement for	1.3.2(1)
secondary participation *see* **secondary participation**	
sexual conduct with dependent family member	18.7.1
sexual connection induced by coercion	18.3
sexual exploitation of person with significant impairment	18.12.2
sexual violation *see* **sexual violation**	
statute silent as to	5.2
absolute liability	5.2.2(5)
burden of proof	2.3.1(4)
implied mens rea	2.3.1(4), 5.1, 5.2.2(2)
options pre-*Millar*	5.2.1
options today	5.2.2
statute explicit	5.2.2(1)
Strawbridge category	5.2.2(3)
strict liability	5.2.2(4)
theft	19.4
"dishonestly"	19.4.1
intent to deprive permanently	19.4.3
transferred malice	4.8
vicarious liability and	7.1
where actus reus involves circumstances	
knowledge	4.5
wilfulness	4.7
wounding with intent	17.3.6, 17.3.6(1), 17.3.6(2)

mental illness/disorder/impairment *see also* **insanity; intellectually disabled persons**
during incarceration	10.1.3
"mental disorder", Canadian definition	10.3.2

N

mother's murder of child induced by disorder falling short of insanity	16.6.2
provocation and	16.5.1(5)(e)
restricted patient order	10.4
sentencing, effect on	10.1.2, 10.5
sexual exploitation of person with significant impairment	18.12
sexual violation and consent	18.2.1(3)(e), 18.2.2(2)(b)
unfitness to stand trial	10.1.1
mercy killing	13.3.4(4)
methamphetamine	10.3.3(1)
M'Growther's Case	12.2
miscarriage, procuring	13.3.4(1)
mistake *see also* **ignorance of law**	
assault with intent to obstruct	17.7.1(1)
compulsion	12.6.2
exculpatory nature of	14.1
excusatory claims	14.2.3
intoxication	11.2.4
justificatory claims	14.2.2
mens rea	14.2
burden of proof	14.2.1(1)
mistakes negativing mens rea	14.2.1
negligence and	14.2.1(3)
recklessness and	14.2.1(2)
necessity	13.3.3
necessity and	13.3.3, 14.2.5
offences of resisting and	14.2.1
property, transfer of	19.3.2(4)(b)
provocation and	16.5.1(6)
regulatory offences and	14.2.4
self-defence *see* **self-defence**	
sexual violation *see* **sexual violation**	
statutory defences and	14.2.5
M'Naghten Rules *see* **insanity**	
money machines, deception involving	20.4.2
mood (affective) disorders	10.3.3(1)
morality	
acts mala in se	1.2.1
causation and	3.3.2
desert and function of punishment	1.3.2
insanity and knowledge of wrong	10.3.5
limits of criminalisation	
harm principle	1.2.1, 1.3.1, 21.1
legal moralism	21.3
offence principle	21.2
paternalism	21.4
practical constraints	21.7
regulatory alternatives	21.5
Rule of Law constraints	21.6
necessity and	13.3.4(4)
"morally certain" consequences	4.2.4
Munchausen's syndrome by proxy	16.6.2
murder *see also* **provocation**	
compulsion	12.10.4(1)
duress of circumstances and	13.2.1, 13.2.4
incitement to	8.4.3, 8.4.3(1), 8.4.3(2)
infancy, defence of	9.4
life imprisonment	16.1
mens rea	16.4
concurrence with actus reus	16.4.6
felony murder rule	16.4.4, 16.4.5
intentional killing	16.4.1
killing in furthering an unlawful object	16.4.4

reckless killing	16.4.2
transferred	16.4.3
necessity	13.3.2
muteness	10.1.1

N

natural events, causation and	3.3.3(1)
natural imbecility *see also* **insanity**	10.3.2
necessaries, duty to provide	3.2.1(2)(b), 16.5.2(4)(a)
necessity *see also* **duress of circumstances; impossibility of compliance**	
abortion	13.3.4(1)
availability and scope of defence	13.1, 13.3.1, 13.3.2, 13.3.5
specific statutory defences	13.3.4(1)
duress of circumstances distinguished	12.3, 13.1
emergency operations	13.3.2, 13.3.4(1), 13.3.5(3)
impossibility distinguished	13.1.1
involuntariness	13.1.1
justificatory defence	13.1
law reform proposals	13.5, 13.5.1, 13.5.2
mercy killing	13.3.4(4)
mistake	13.3.3
moral imperatives	13.3.4(4)
murder	13.3.2
New Zealand formulation	13.3.4
procuring miscarriage	13.3.4(1)
rationale of defence	13.3.5
"best interests" medical treatment	13.3.5(2)
homicide and lesser-evils approach	13.3.5(3)
lesser-evil justification	13.1, 13.3.5(1)
Rule of Law and	13.3.3(1)
self-defence and	15.1.4(1)
sterilisation	13.3.2, 13.3.5(2)
strict liability and	13.4
teleological	12.1
terminology	13.1
traditional vs modern doctrine	13.3.3
trespass	13.3.4(1)
negligence	
actus reus involving behavioural element	4.6.3
characteristics of defendant	4.6.2
corporate liability	7.2.4(2)
criminalisation and	4.6.4
culpability	1.3.2(2)
emergencies	4.6.1(2)
fair warning and use of evaluative concepts	2.1.3(1)
injuring by unlawful act	17.5
intoxication	11.2.5
joint unlawful act, standard of care	16.5.2(6)
killing by unlawful act, standard of care	16.5.2(6)
killing by unlawful omission	16.5.2(5)
gross negligence	16.5.2(5)(b), 16.5.2(5)(c)
historical fault standards	16.5.2(5)(a), 16.5.2(5)(b)
"major departure" test	16.5.2(5)(c)
mistake	14.2.1(3)
nature of	4.6
ordinary/gross distinction	4.6.1(1)
reasonable risk	4.6.1

785

test for	4.6.1	terms of offence	3.2.1(3)
neurotic disorders	10.3.3(1)	imposing liability for	
New Zealand Bill of Rights Act 1990		continuing act doctrine	3.2.1(2)(d)
		persons with particular responsibilities	3.2.1(2)(c)
child defendants	9.4	persons with special	
fair warning and	2.1.3	relationship to the harm	3.2.1(2)(e)
non-published laws	14.4.2	persons with special	
presumption of innocence	2.3	relationship to victim	3.2.1(2)(b)
retrospective criminalisation	2.1.2, 2.1.3	secondary liability	6.4.3
reverse-burden provisions	2.3.1(1)	statutory offences	3.2.1(2)(a)
strict liability and burden of proof	5.1.1(3)(b)	involuntariness and	3.4.2
novus actus interveniens *see* **intervening causes**		ignorance of duty	3.4.2(3), 13.6.1(1)
		possessory offences	3.4.2(2)
nullum crimen sine lege (principle of legality)	2.1.1	situational offences	3.4.2(2)
		self-interest and	3.2.1(1)
		ownership of property	19.1, 19.3.2

O

P

obscenity, use of standards of	2.1.3(1)		
obsessional states	10.3.3(1)		
obtaining or causing loss by deception		**"P" (pure methamphetamine)**	10.3.3(1)
		parole laws	1.3.3(1)
attempts	20.2.4	**parties to offences** *see* **secondary participation**	
causation	20.4		
machines	20.4.2	**paternalism**	21.4
remoteness	20.4.1	**"patient", detention as**	10.1.1, 10.1.2, 10.5.3
credit obtained	20.5.2	**persistent vegetative state**	16.2.2
criminalisation of fraud	20.3.3(3)	**personality disorders**	10.3.3(1), 10.3.3(3)
"deception", defined	20.3	**physical impairment**	
elements of offence	20.2	sexual exploitation of person with significant impairment	18.12
false representations			
change in circumstances	20.2.1(1)(b)	sexual violation and consent	18.2.1(3)(e), 18.2.2(2)(b)
falsity	20.3.1(2)	**plead, fitness to**	10.1.1, 10.1.2
falsity of a "material particular"	20.3.1(5)	**policing of offences, criminalisation and**	21.7.2
implications from conduct	20.3.1(1)(a)	**possession**	
knowledge of falsity	20.3.1(3)	attempts and	8.2.2(1)(b)
recklessness as to falsity	20.3.1(4)	behavioural element	3.2.2(2), 3.4.2(2)
"representation", meaning of	20.3.1(1)	self-defence and	15.1.3(3)
silence	20.3.1(1)(b)	**post-traumatic stress disorder**	10.3.8
fraudulent device, trick, or stratagem	20.3.3	**predictability in criminal law** *see* **fair warning**	
conspiracy to defraud and	20.3.3, 20.3.3(1), 20.3.3(3)	**presumption of innocence**	2.3
"fraudulent"	20.3.3(2)	**privacy, sexual conduct and**	17.2.4(3)
intent to deceive	20.3.3(1)	**prize fights, consent in**	17.2.4(1)
intent to deceive	20.7	**procuring** *see also* **secondary participation**	6.4.1(5), 6.4.4(2)
loss caused to any other person	20.5.4		
mens rea	20.8	**procuring miscarriage**	13.3.4(1)
object of offence	20.5	**proof** *see* **burden and standard of proof; evidence**	
"obtaining any property"	20.5.1		
act of	20.5.1(2)	**property, concept of**	19.1
"property", defined	19.3.1, 20.5.1(1)	**property, defence of**	
services, inclusion of	20.5.1(1)	dwellinghouse	15.2.3
omission to disclose	20.3.2	land, buildings or movable property	15.2.2
without "claim or right"	20.6	"claim of right" requirement	15.2.2(4)
offence principle, criminalisation and	21.2	"peaceable possession"	15.2.2(3)
omissions		"striking" or doing "bodily harm"	15.2.2(2)
acts distinguished	3.2.1(5)	use of "reasonable force"	15.2.2(1)
assault and	17.2.3	law reform	15.2.4
attempts and	8.2.2(1)(c)	nature of right	15.2
autonomy, restriction of	1.3.2(5), 3.2.1(1)	statutory provisions	15.2.1
causation	3.3.4	**property offences** *see also* **obtaining or causing loss by deception; receiving; theft**	
causation and	3.2.1(4), 3.3.4		
excluding liability for	3.2.1		
rationale	3.2.1(1)		

criminalisation	19.1, 20.1
property ownership	19.1, 19.3.2
prospectivity	2.1.2
provocation	
actual loss of self-control	16.5.1(4)
``anything done or said''	16.5.1(2)
burden of proof	16.5.1(1)
cooling time	16.5.1(3)
evidence	16.5.1(1)
history of defence	16.5.1
intoxication and	11.2.7(1), 16.5.1(5)(c)
mistake or accident	16.5.1(6)
objective test	16.5.1(5)
age, gender, and race	16.5.1(5)(f)
characteristics of offender	16.5.1(5)(c)
characteristic's relevance to gravity of provocation	16.5.1(5)(d)
circumstances of case	16.5.1(5)(b)
mental abnormality	16.5.1(5)(e)
``ordinary person'' standard	16.5.1(5)
proportionality	16.5.1(5)(a)
self-induced	16.5.1(7)
tests for	16.5.1
public interest in criminalisation of behaviour	1.2.1
public welfare regulatory offences *see* **absolute liability; regulatory offences; strict liability**	
punishment/sanctions *see also* **deterrence**	
criminal-civil distinction	1.2.2
desert	1.3.3
legitimacy of	1.3, 1.3.2
accountability	1.3.2(5)
advertence, relevance of	1.3.2(2)
justificatory/excusatory defences	1.3.2(4)
limits	1.3.2(5)
mens rea requirement	1.3.2(1)
regulatory offences	1.3.2(3)
secondary liability	1.3.2(5)
punitive nature of criminal law	1.2.2
reparation	1.3.3(1)
restorative justice	1.3.3(1)
retributivist vs consequentialist theories	1.3.3
pure methamphetamine (``P'')	10.3.3(1)
pyromania	10.3.3(2)

R

rape *see* **sexual violation**	
real property, theft of	19.3.1, 19.3.1(1)
reasonable person test	4.6.2
reasonableness, use of standards of	2.1.3(1)
receiving	
actus reus	
possession or control of something	19.5.1(1)
``property'', defined	19.3.1, 19.5.1(1)
things stolen or obtained by crime	19.5.1(3)
mens rea	19.5.2
recent possession	19.5.3
recklessness	
actus reus involving circumstances	4.3.2
attempts and	8.2.1
Caldwell, definition in	4.3.1(1), 4.3.1(2)
culpability	1.3.2(1)
foresight and	4.3, 4.3.1
inadvertence to risk	4.3.1
indifference to risk	4.3.2
intention distinguished	4.4
intoxication	11.2.3
mistake	14.2.1(2)
obtaining or causing loss by deception	
false representations	20.3.1(4), 20.3.1(5)
reasonable risk	4.3
receiving property	19.5.2
reckless knowledge	4.3.2, 4.5.1
regulatory offences *see also* **absolute liability; strict liability**	
categories of	5.1
corporate liability	5.1.1(3)(a), 7.1.2, 7.1.2(1)
culpability and	1.3.2(3)
determining fault standard	5.2.3(2)(b), 5.2.3(2)(d)
mistake	14.2.4, 14.2.5
social significance	5.1.1(3)(a), 5.1.2(1)
reparation	1.3.3(1)
resisting, offences of	14.2.1
restorative justice	1.3.3(1)
restricted patient order	10.4
result crimes	
behavioural element	3.2
defined	3.1
retributivism	1.3.3
retrospective crimes	2.1.2
Rubicon test	8.2.3(1)(c)
Rule of Law	
clarity in statement of the law	2.1.3, 2.1.4
criminal law and	2.1
fair labelling	2.1.4
fair warning	2.1.3
evaluative concepts, use of	2.1.3(1)
ignorance of law	14.1, 14.3
necessity and	13.3.3(1)
nullum crimen sine lege (principle of legality)	2.1.1
retrospective crimes	2.1.2
statutory interpretation and	2.1.3, 2.2

S

sado-masochism	17.2.4(2)
sanctions *see* **punishment/sanctions; sentencing**	
``scope of employment'' principle *see* **vicarious liability**	
secondary participation	
abetting	6.4.1(2), 6.4.4(1)
aiding	6.4.1(1), 6.4.4(1)
autonomy, restriction of	1.3.2(5)
conduct constituting	6.4, 6.4.1
connection to commission of offence	6.4.2
conspiracy	6.6.5
conspiracy and	8.3.8
conviction for different offences with same actus reus	6.6.3
corporate liability	7.2
counselling	6.4.1(4), 6.4.4(1)

787

criminalisation and	6.1
derivative nature	6.1
exceptions: liability without the primary offence	6.6.2
no requirement that principal be charged and convicted	6.6.2(3)
principal coerced	6.6.2(1)
principal procured to act without mens rea	6.6.2(2)
general principles	6.6
inchoate offences	6.6.5
inciting	6.4.1(3), 6.4.4(1)
innocent agents	6.3.1
``joint enterprise'' liability	6.5
collateral offence ``known to be a probable consequence''	6.5.2
``common intention''	6.5.1
conviction for lesser offence	6.5.3(1)
``in the prosecution of the common purpose''	6.5.3
offence committed was object of common purpose	6.5.4
legal responsibility and	1.3.2(5), 6.1
liability normally dependent on commission of offence	6.6.1
mens rea	6.4.4
intention to aid, abet, incite, or counsel	6.4.4(1)
intention to procure	6.4.4(2)
knowledge of essential matters	6.4.4(3), 6.4.4(4)
principal's	6.4.4(4)(b)
modes of	6.2
omissions where legal duty or power to prevent crime	6.4.3
parties to offences	6.2
principal offenders	6.3, 6.3.1
procuring	6.4.1(5), 6.4.4(2)
sexual conduct with young person under 16	18.10.4
sexual offences *see* **sexual offences**	
statutory exclusion of liability	6.6.4
statute defines class of participants	6.6.4(2)
victim excepted from participation	6.6.4, 6.6.4(1)
strict liability for circumstantial elements of actus reus	6.4.4(4)(d)
strict liability for consequences of principal's conduct	6.4.4(4)(c)
variations within a type of offence	6.4.4(4)(a)
withdrawal, effect of	6.6.6
self-defence	1.4.1
assault with intent to obstruct	17.7.1(3)
availability	15.1
battered women	15.1.4(5)
imminence of threat	15.1.4(6)
pre-emptive strikes	15.1.4(5)
self-preservation	15.1.4(5)(a)
belief in circumstances justifying force	15.1.3
intoxication	15.1.3(5)
psychological abnormalities	15.1.3(1)
unreasonable mistakes	15.1.3(4)
variety of circumstances	15.1.3(2)
compulsion and	12.12
evidence	15.1.6

excessive force	15.1.5
imminence of threat	15.1.4(6)
intention to kill	15.1.2(1)
lawful/unlawful force	15.1
legislative history	15.1.1
offences not involving use of force	15.1.3(3)
possession of an offensive weapon	15.1.3(3)
reasonable force	15.1.4
pre-emptive strikes	15.1.4(4)
proportionality	15.1.4(1)
retreat	15.1.4(3)
unjust threat requirement	15.1.4(2)
statutory test	15.1.2, 15.1.2(1)
self-incrimination	2.3
sentencing *see also* **punishment/ sanctions**	
laws governing	1.3.3(1)
life imprisonment	16.1
mental disorder and	10.1.2
reparation	1.3.3(1)
restorative justice	1.3.3(1)
retrospective increase in penalty	2.1.2
sexual violation	18.2.1(5)
services	
obtaining or causing loss by deception	20.5.1(1)
theft and	19.3.1(6)
sexual conduct, consent in	17.2.4(2), 17.2.4(3)
sexual offences	
anal intercourse	18.13
bestiality	18.3
evidence	18.5
address and occupation of complainant	18.5.1
character of complainant	18.5.3
corroboration	18.5.4
delay in making complaint	18.5.2
gender-neutral application	18.1, 18.2, 18.13
incest *see* **incest**	
indecent act on child under 12	18.9
indecent act on young person under 16	18.10
indecent acts with animals	18.13
indecent assault	18.11
actus reus	18.11.2
consent	18.11.4
``indecently''	18.11.3
lesser included offence within definition of sexual violation	18.11.6
mens rea	18.11.5
law reform	18.1
meeting young person under 16 following sexual grooming	18.8, 18.8.1
sexual conduct with child under 12	18.9
attempts	18.9.1
consent	18.9
indecent act	18.9
sexual conduct with dependent family member	18.7
actus reus	18.7.2
``dependent family member''	18.7
former offence of ``sexual intercourse with a girl under care and protection''	18.7
gender-neutral offence	18.7
mens rea	18.7.1

S

sexual conduct with young person under 16	18.10
consent	18.10.1
marriage or civil union	18.10.3
party liability	18.10.4
proof of age	18.10.5
proof of consent-based defence	18.10.2
sexual connection as basis of	18.1
``sexual connection'', defined	18.2
sexual connection induced by coercion	
elements of offence	18.3
mens rea	18.3
penalties	18.3
threat to commit imprisonable offence	18.3.1
threats involving ``detriment''	18.3.3
threats of accusation or disclosure	18.3.2
sexual exploitation of person with significant impairment	18.12
acquiescence, submission, participation, or undertaking	18.12.4
consent	18.12.3
mens rea	18.12.2
`significant impairment''	18.12.1
sexual violation *see* **sexual violation**	
sexual violation	
attempts	18.4, 18.4.1
consent	18.2.1(3)
complainant affected by alcohol or drug	18.2.1(3)(d)
complainant asleep or unconscious	18.2.1(3)(c)
complainant impaired	18.2.1(3)(d)
failure to protest or offer physical resistance	18.2.1(3)(a)
matters not amounting to	18.2.1(3)
mistake about nature and quality of act	18.2.1(3)(h)
mistakes as to identity	18.2.1(3)(f)
mistakes not limited	18.2.1(3)(g)
nature of	18.2.1(3)
submission by force, threat or fear of force	18.2.1(3)(b)
withdrawal of	18.2.1(2)
defined	18.2
elements of offence	18.2.1
genitalia, meaning of	18.2.1(1)
indecent assault as lesser included offence	18.11.6
marital rape	18.2.1(4)
mens rea	18.2.2
belief in consent	18.2.2(1)
believing on ``reasonable grounds''	18.2.2(2), 18.2.2(2)(a), 18.2.2(2)(b)
characteristics of offender	18.2.2(2)(b)
rape	
gender-neutral offence	18.2
history of offence	18.2
sentencing	18.2.1(5)
sexual connection	
``continuation'' of, following withdrawal of consent	18.2.1(2)
defined	18.2

shares, theft in relation to	19.3.1(2)
silent callers	17.3.1(1)(a)
sine qua non test	3.3.1
situational offences	
accountability in	1.3.2(5)
behavioural element	3.2.2, 3.2.2(1), 3.4.2(1)
sleepwalking	3.4.1(2), 10.3.3, 10.3.3(4)(b)
Some Criminal Defences with Particular Reference to Battered Defendants (Law Commission)	12.14, 13.5.2
special care recipient, detention as	10.1.1, 10.1.2, 10.5.1, 10.5.3
special patient, detention as	10.1.1, 10.1.2, 10.5.1, 10.5.2
sport, consent in	17.2.4(4)
spouses	
coercion of wife	12.3.1
stalking offences	17.3.1(1)(a)
standard of proof *see* burden and standard of proof	
status offences *see* situational offences	
statutory interpretation	
ascertaining meaning of an offence	
legislative background	2.2.2
ordinary meaning	2.2.1
strict construction	2.2.3
summary of approach	2.2.4
evaluative concepts, use of	2.1.3(1)
implied mens rea	5.1
judicial activism	2.1.3
judicial restraint	2.2
retrospective crimes	2.1.2
Rule of Law considerations	2.1.3, 2.2
stealing *see* theft	
sterilisation, necessity and	13.3.2, 13.3.5(2)
Strawbridge	5.2.1, 5.2.2(2), 5.2.2(3)
strict liability *see also* **absolute liability; regulatory offences**	
absence of fault defence	
availability	5.1.1
nature of	5.1.1(1)
standard of care	5.1.1(2)
burden of proof	2.3.1(3), 5.1, 5.1.1, 5.1.1(3)(b)
culpability and	1.3.2(3)
determining fault standard	5.2.3(2)(d)
duress of circumstances	13.3.2(4)
insanity and	10.3.6
intoxication	11.2.5, 11.2.6
breath-alcohol offences	11.2.8(1)
involuntariness and antecedent fault	3.4.3(1)
justification of	5.1.1(3)(a), 5.1.1(3)(b)
mistake and	14.2.4, 14.2.5
necessity and	13.4
New Zealand Bill of Rights Act 1990	5.1.1(3)(b)
vicarious liability and	5.1.1(3)(a), 7.1, 7.1.2
stupefaction	
aggravated wounding	
intent to stupefy	17.6.1
``renders unconscious''	17.6
``stupefies''	17.6
consensual sexual activity amounting to	17.2.4(2)

789

suicide
incitement	8.4
inducement	16.2.3(6)
killing pursuant to pact	16.5

Summary Proceedings Act 1957
reverse-burden provision	2.3.1(1)

T

tax system	21.5.1
theft	
abandoned goods	19.3.2(5)
actus reus	19.3
bailment and	19.3.2(2), 19.3.2(3)
body parts	19.3.1(8)
co-owner, in relation to	19.3.2(2)
corpses	19.3.1(8)
defined	19.2
elements of offence	19.2
equitable interests	19.3.2(2)
future or contingent interests	19.3.2(2)
gas, water, and electricity	19.3.1(7)
intangible property	19.3.1(2)
bank accounts	19.3.1(3)
chose in action	19.3.1(2), 19.3.1(3)
documents evidencing	19.3.1(4)
information	19.3.1(5)
trade secrets	19.3.1(5)
lien, in relation to	19.3.2(2)
lost articles	19.3.2(5)
mens rea	19.4
``dishonestly''	19.4.1
intent to deprive permanently	19.4.3
without ``claim of right''	19.4.2
``property'', defined	19.3.1
property to be ``owned by another''	19.3.2
interests protected	19.3.2(1)
theft by absolute owner	19.3.2(3)
theft by owner from others with interest	19.3.2(2)
time that title to goods passes	19.3.2(4)
real property	19.3.1, 19.3.1(1)
services and	19.3.1(6)
``taking'' any property	19.3.3(1)
consent	19.3.3(1)(a)
``using or dealing with'' any property	19.3.3(2)
conduct required: keeping or omission	19.3.3(2)(d)
consent	19.3.3(2)(a)
prior ``obtaining'' required	19.3.3(2)(b)
title already passed	19.3.3(2)(c)
wild creatures	19.3.1(9)

third parties, causation and *see* **intervening causes**

tort law *see* **civil law**
trade mark, theft in relation to	19.3.1(2)
trade secrets	19.3.1(5)
transferred malice	4.8
assault	17.2.1(1)
conspiracy	8.3.6
killing of a child	16.2.2
murder	16.4.3
trespass, necessity and	13.3.4(1)

U

``ulterior intent'' crimes	4.2.7
unborn child	
incitement to murder and	8.4.3(2)
killing of	16.2.2
``under disability'' *see also* **insanity**	10.1.1
unfitness to stand trial	10.1.1, 10.1.2
unreasonableness, use of standards of	2.1.3(1)
utilitarian theory of punishment	1.3.3

V

vending machines, deception involving	20.4.2
vicarious liability	
corporate bodies	7.2.2, 7.2.3
criminalisation and	6.1
delegation principle	7.1, 7.1.1
nature of	1.3.2(5), 7.1
scope of employment principle	7.1, 7.1.2
due diligence defence	7.1.2(1)
victims	
intervening causes	3.3.3(3)
act done in concert with third party	3.3.3(2)(f)
secondary participation, exemption from liability	6.6.4, 6.6.4(1)
volenti non fit injuria	16.5.2(6)
voluntariness *see* **automatism; involuntariness**	

W

water, theft of	19.3.1(7)
``wheel'' conspiracy	8.3.4(4)
wild creatures, theft of	19.3.1(9)
wilful blindness	
knowledge and	4.5.1
recklessness and	4.3.2
wilfulness	4.7
``with intent'' crimes	4.2.7
Woolmington	2.3, 5.1.1(3)(b)
wounding with intent	
burden of proof	17.3.6(1)
defined	17.3
``disfigures''	17.3.4
grievous bodily harm	17.3.1, 17.3.1(1), 17.3.1(1)(a)
indirect wounding	17.3.2(1)
``injure''	17.3.5
``maims''	17.3.3
mens rea	17.3.6
``reckless disregard''	17.3.6(2)
``with intent''	17.3.6(1)
penalties	17.3
psychological harm	17.3.1(1), 17.3.1(1)(a)
silent callers	17.3.1(1)(a)
``wounds''	17.3.2, 17.3.2(1)

Y

year and a day rule	16.2.3(1)

Y

Young Offenders (Serious Crime) Bill 9.4.1

young persons *see* children and young persons; infancy

Youth Court 9.3, 9.3.3